lonely planet

England

**Ryan Ver Berkmoes
Neal Bedford
Lou Callan
Fionn Davenport
Nick Ray**

LONELY PLANET PUBLICATIONS
Melbourne • Oakland • London • Paris

ENGLAND

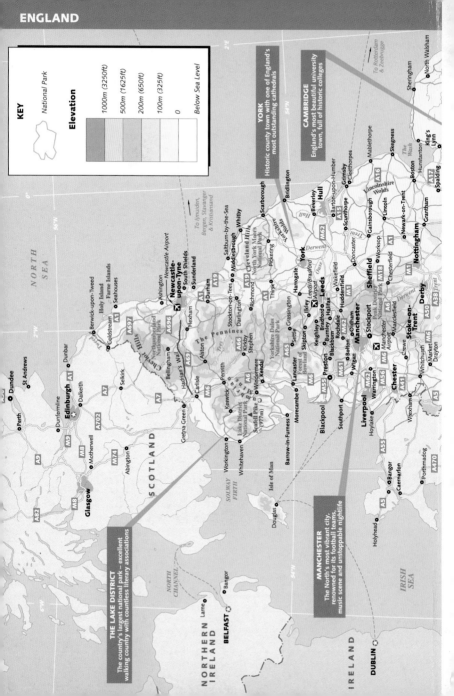

KEY

National Park

Elevation

1000m (3250ft)
500m (1625ft)
200m (650ft)
100m (325ft)
0
Below Sea Level

THE LAKE DISTRICT
The country's largest national park – excellent walking country with countless literary associations

MANCHESTER
The North's most vibrant city, renowned for its football teams, music scene and unstoppable nightlife

YORK
Historic county town with one of England's most outstanding cathedrals

CAMBRIDGE
England's most beautiful university town, full of historic colleges

ntents – Text

...DON

y 158	**158**
...ation 159	
...mation 160	
...l London 184	
...London 207	

East London 208	Places to Eat 222
South London 209	Entertainment 232
West London 211	Shopping 240
Organised Tours 213	Getting There & Away ..242
Places to Stay 214	Getting Around 244

...TH-EASTERN ENGLAND   **250**

...hire 251	Ightham Mote 286	Portsmouth & Southsea ..315
...or or Eton 254	Leeds Castle 286	Southampton 320
...Park 259	**East Sussex** **287**	New Forest 321
...................................**259**	Rye 287	**Isle Of Wight** **324**
...ord 259	Hastings 289	Cowes 325
...am 263	Battle 290	Ryde 325
...ley Abbey 264	Pevensey Castle 291	Ventnor 326
...ill 265	Bodiam Castle 291	South Coast 326
...................................**265**	Eastbourne 292	West Wight 326
...bury 267	Beachy Head 294	**Essex** **327**
...ate 276	Charleston Farmhouse ..294	Southend-on-Sea 327
...stairs 276	Long Man of Wilmington 295	Colchester 331
...ich 277	Lewes 295	Harwich 332
...................................279	Glyndebourne 297	Dedham Vale 332
...ey Marsh & Around ...283	Brighton 298	Saffron Walden 333
...ghurst Castle Gardens 283	**West Sussex** **304**	Audley End House 334
...oaks 283	Arundel 304	**Hertfordshire** **334**
... House 284	Bignor Roman Villa 305	St Albans 334
...well 285	Chichester 305	Hatfield House 338
...r Castle 285	**Hampshire** **309**	**Buckinghamshire** **338**
...hurst Place & Gardens 285	Winchester 309	Aylesbury 339

...SSEX   **340**

...l & Bath **343**	**Exmoor National Park** ...**373**	Lyme Regis 394
...l 343	Dulverton 376	Sherborne 396
...................................352	Dunste 376	Shaftesbury 397
...rset **362**	Minehead 377	**Wiltshire** **398**
...................................362	Exford 378	Salisbury 398
...ey Hole 365	Porlock 378	Stonehenge 405
...dar Gorge 365	Lynton & Lynmouth 379	Stourhead 408
...dge 366	**Dorset** **380**	Longleat 408
...lip Hills 366	Bournemouth 380	Bradford-on-Avon 409
...e 367	Poole 382	Chippenham & Around ..411
...ton Mallet 367	Christchurch 382	Lacock 412
...onbury 367	Wimborne 383	Devizes 412
...tock Hill 371	South-East Dorset 383	Avebury 413
...ton 372	Dorchester 387	Marlborough 417
...cacute House 372	Weymouth 389	Malmesbury 417
...es Motor Museum 373	Weymouth to Lyme Regis .393	Swindon 418

...ON & CORNWALL   **419**

| ...n ....**421** | Exeter ....422 | South Devon Coast ......428 |

ENGLAND

LONDON — Pulsating capital city and the centre of the country's cultural life

STONEHENGE — England's most famous – and most mysterious – prehistoric site

BATH — Beautiful spa town with some of England's finest Georgian architecture

THE COTSWOLDS — Picturesque region of picture-postcard villages and honey-coloured stone cottages

WARWICK CASTLE — England's most impressive medieval castle, romantically located next to the River Avon

England
1st edition – June 2001

Published by
Lonely Planet Publications Pty Ltd ABN 36 005 607 983
90 Maribyrnong St, Footscray, Victoria 3011, Australia

Lonely Planet Offices
Australia Locked Bag 1, Footscray, Victoria 3011
USA 150 Linden St, Oakland, CA 94607
UK 10a Spring Place, London NW5 3BH
France 1 rue du Dahomey, 75011 Paris

Photographs
Most of the images in this guide are available for licensing from
Lonely Planet Images.
email: lpi@lonelyplanet.com.au

Front cover photograph
Longleat House maze, Warminster (John Chard, Tony Stone Images)

ISBN 1 86450 194 4

text & maps © Lonely Planet 2001
photos © photographers as indicated 2001

Printed by The Bookmaker International Ltd
Printed in China

Although the authors
and Lonely Planet try
to make the informa-
tion as accurate as
possible, we accept
no responsibility for
any loss, injury or
inconvenience sus-
tained by anyone
using this book.

Contents – Text

THE AUTHORS

THIS BOOK

FOREWORD

INTRODUCTION

FACTS ABOUT ENGLAND

History 21	Government & Politics 38	Architecture ......
Geography 33	Economy 39	Society & Conduc
Climate 33	Population & People 39	Religion
Ecology & Environment 34	Education 40	Language
Flora & Fauna 35	Arts 40	

FACTS FOR THE VISITOR

Highlights 58	Video Systems 80	Emergencies ......
Suggested Itineraries 61	Photography & Video 80	Legal Matters
Planning 62	Time 80	Business Hours ..
Responsible Tourism 63	Electricity 81	Public Holidays &
Tourist Offices 63	Weights & Measures 81	Events
Visas & Documents 64	Laundry 81	Courses ....
Embassies & Consulates 67	Toilets 81	Work ....
Customs 68	Health 81	Accommodation
Money 69	Women Travellers 85	Food ....
Post & Communications 73	Gay & Lesbian Travellers 85	Drinks ....
Internet Resources 75	Disabled Travellers 85	Entertainment ....
Books 76	Senior Travellers 86	Spectator Sports
Films 77	Travel with Children 86	Shopping ....
Newspapers & Magazines 78	Useful Organisations 87	
Radio & TV 79	Dangers & Annoyances 88	

ACTIVITIES

Walking 102	Fishing 114	Steam Railways ..
Cycling 109	Horse Riding & Pony	
Golf 113	Trekking 115	
Surfing & Swimming 113	Canal & Waterway Travel 115	

PUBS

GETTING THERE & AWAY

Air 131	Land 138	Sea ....

GETTING AROUND

Air 143	Bicycle 155	Local Transport ..
Bus 143	Hitching 155	Organised Tours
Train 146	Walking 156	
Car & Motorcycle 152	Boat 156	

Plymouth 432
North Devon 436
Dartmoor National Park 439
Princetown 443
Postbridge 444
Buckfastleigh 444
Widecombe-in-the-Moor ..445
Moretonhampstead 445
Chagford 447

Castle Drogo 447
Okehampton 447
Lydford 448
Tavistock 449
Cornwall 449
South-East Cornwall 450
Truro 453
Roseland Peninsula 454
South-West Cornwall 454

Penzance 456
West Cornwall 458
St Ives 461
Newquay 464
North Cornwall 466
Isles of Scilly 469

FROM THE THAMES TO THE WYE   **472**

Oxfordshire 472
Oxford 474
Woodstock 484
Oxfordshire Cotswolds 485
South of Oxford 485
Henley-on-Thames 486
The Cotswolds & Around 488
Northern Cotswolds 490
Southern Cotswolds 498

Cirencester 500
Gloucester 502
Berkeley 507
Cheltenham 507
Tewkesbury 512
Forest of Dean 513
Newent 515
Herefordshire 515
Hereford 516

Hay-on-Wye 519
Ross-on-Wye 522
Ledbury 523
Worcestershire 524
Worcester 524
Great Malvern 529
Vale Of Evesham 531

THE MIDLANDS   **533**

Birmingham 534
Warwickshire 543
Coventry 543
Kenilworth 547
Warwick 548
Leamington Spa 551
Stratford-upon-Avon 552
Northamptonshire 558
Northampton 559
Bedfordshire 561
Bedford 561
Woburn Abbey & Safari
  Park 563
Whipsnade 563
Leicestershire & Rutland 564
Leicester 564
Rutland 569

Shropshire 570
Shrewsbury 570
Ironbridge Gorge 576
Wenlock Edge 579
Much Wenlock 580
Bridgnorth 580
The Long Mynd & Church
  Stretton 581
Bishop's Castle 582
Clun 582
Ludlow 583
Staffordshire 586
Lichfield 586
Stafford 587
Stoke-on-Trent 588
Leek 591
Derbyshire 591

Derby 591
Chesterfield 593
Peak District 594
Bakewell 598
Tideswell 600
Eyam 601
Castleton 601
Edale 604
Hayfield 604
Buxton 604
Dovedale 607
Matlock Bath & Matlock 607
Nottinghamshire 608
Nottingham 609

EASTERN ENGLAND   **616**

Suffolk 619
Ipswich 619
Stour Valley 620
Lavenham 623
Kersey 624
Hadleigh 624
Bury St Edmunds 624
Suffolk Coast 627

Norfolk 629
Norwich 630
Norfolk Broads 635
Norfolk Coast 636
King's Lynn 637
Cambridgeshire 641
Cambridge 642
Ely 658

Peterborough 660
Lincolnshire 661
Lincoln 662
Grantham 667
Stamford 668
Boston 669
Skegness 670

NORTH-WESTERN ENGLAND 671

Manchester **671**
Cheshire **684**
Chester 685
Liverpool **693**
Isle of Man 703
Douglas 704
Castletown to Port Erin 705
Peel 705
Ramsey to Douglas 706
Lancashire **707**
Lancaster 707
The Ribble Valley 709
Blackpool 711

YORKSHIRE 714

West Yorkshire **715**
Leeds 717
Bradford 723
Haworth 724
Ilkley 727
Pennine Yorkshire 728
South Yorkshire **730**
Sheffield 730
East Riding of Yorkshire **735**
Hull (Kingston-upon-Hull) ..735
Humber Bridge 738
Wolds Way 739
Beverley 739
East Riding of Yorkshire
  Coast 741
North Yorkshire **742**
York 743
Nunnington Hall 757
Scarborough 757
Filey 762
Harrogate 762
Thirsk 765
**North York Moors National
  Park** **766**
Sutton Bank 769
Coxwald & Kilburn 770
Helmsley 770
Hutton-le-Hole 772
Pickering 773
North Yorkshire Moors
  Railway 774
Danby 775
Staithes 775
Whitby 776
Cook Country Walk 782
Robin Hood's Bay 782
Ravenscar 783
**Yorkshire Dales National
  Park** **783**
Leeds-Settle-Carlisle Line   786
Skipton 786
Wharfedale 787
Malhamdale 788
Ribblesdale 789
Wensleydale 790
Richmond 790
Fountains Abbey & Studley
  Royal Water Garden 793

CUMBRIA 795

Carlisle 796
Cockermouth 801
Kendal 802
Lake District National Park 804
Windermere & Bowness 807
Ambleside 811
Grasmere & Wordsworth
  Country 812
Langdale 813
Coniston 815
Hawkshead 817
Keswick 818
Borrowdale & Buttermere ..822
Ullswater & Around 824
East Cumbria **825**
Penrith 825
Alston & Around 827
Kirkby Lonsdale 828
Kirkby Stephen 828
Cumbrian Coast **828**
Grange-over-Sands 829
Cartmel 829
Ulverston 830
Barrow-in-Furness &
  Around 831
Ravenglass to Whitehaven 832

NORTH-EASTERN ENGLAND 835

County Durham **837**
Durham 837
Bishop Auckland 842
Beamish Open-Air
  Museum 843
Barnard Castle 843
The Durham Dales 844
North to Hadrian's Wall 846
The Tees Valley **847**
Darlington 847
Hartlepool 849
Saltburn-by-the-Sea 849
Newcastle-upon-Tyne **850**
Northumberland Coast **857**
Warkworth 858
Alnwick 858
Dunstanburgh Castle 859
Farne Islands 859
Bamburgh 860
Holy Island (Lindisfarne) ...860
Berwick-upon-Tweed 861
Hadrian's Wall **864**
Corbridge 865
Hexham 866
Hexham to Haltwhistle 867
Haltwhistle 868
Haltwhistle to Brampton 869
Brampton 869
**Northumberland National
  Park** **870**
Bellingham 870
Rothbury 872
Kielder Water 872
Wooler & Around 874

GLOSSARY 876

GLOSSARY OF RELIGIOUS ARCHITECTURE 879

INDEX 888

MAP LEGEND back page

METRIC CONVERSION inside back cover

Contents – Maps

FACTS FOR THE VISITOR

Chapter Breakdown 58

GETTING AROUND

English Railways..................148

LONDON

Colour Maps 161–80

SOUTH-EASTERN ENGLAND

South-Eastern England 252–3	Eastbourne..........................293	New Forest 323
Windsor & Eton 255	Lewes 296	Isle of Wight 324
Guildford 260	Brighton..............................299	Southend-on-Sea 328
Canterbury..........................269	Chichester 306	St Albans 335
Canterbury Cathedral..........270	Winchester..........................310	St Albans Cathedral 336
Dover..................................279	Winchester Cathedral..........311	
Rye 287	Portsmouth & Southsea 316	

WESSEX

Wessex 341	Glastonbury 368	Salisbury 399
Bristol 344	Exmoor National Park 374	Stonehenge 406
Bath....................................353	Weymouth..........................390	Bradford-on-Avon 409
Wells 363	Lyme Regis 394	Avebury 414

DEVON & CORNWALL

Devon & Cornwall 420	Dartmoor National Park 440	St Ives 462
Exeter 423	Penzance 456	Newquay 465
Plymouth 433	West Cornwall 459	Isles of Scilly......................469

FROM THE THAMES TO THE WYE

From the Thames to the	The Cotswolds 489	Hereford 516
Wye.....................................473	Gloucester 503	Hay-on-Wye 520
Oxford.................................475	Cheltenham 509	Worcester 525

THE MIDLANDS

The Midlands 534–5	Leicester..............................565	Bakewell 599
Birmingham 536	Shrewsbury 571	Castleton & Edale 603
Coventry 544	Ironbridge Gorge 577	Nottingham 610
Warwick 549	Ludlow.................................583	
Stratford-upon-Avon 552	Peak District........................595	

EASTERN ENGLAND

Eastern England 617	King's Lynn 639	Ely 659
Norwich 631	Cambridge 644	Lincoln................................663

NORTH-WESTERN ENGLAND

North-Western England 672
Manchester 674–5

Chester 686
Liverpool 694

Isle of Man 703
Lancaster...........................708

YORKSHIRE

Yorkshire 716–17
Leeds....................................718
Haworth 725
Sheffield.............................731
Hull 736
Beverley 740

York......................................744
York Minster 747
Scarborough 758
Harrogate 764
North York Moors National
   Park..................................767

Helmsley 771
Pickering 773
Whitby................................778
Yorkshire Dales National
   Park..................................784
Richmond 792

CUMBRIA

Cumbria...............................796
Carlisle................................797
Cockermouth 801

Kendal 803
Lake District National
   Park..................................805

Windermere & Bowness......808
Keswick 819

NORTH-EASTERN ENGLAND

North-Eastern
England 836
Durham 838

Durham Cathedral 838
Newcastle-upon-Tyne 851
Berwick-upon-Tweed 861

Hadrian's Wall &
   Northumberland National
   Park..................................871

MAP LEGEND – SEE BACK PAGE

MAP INDEX

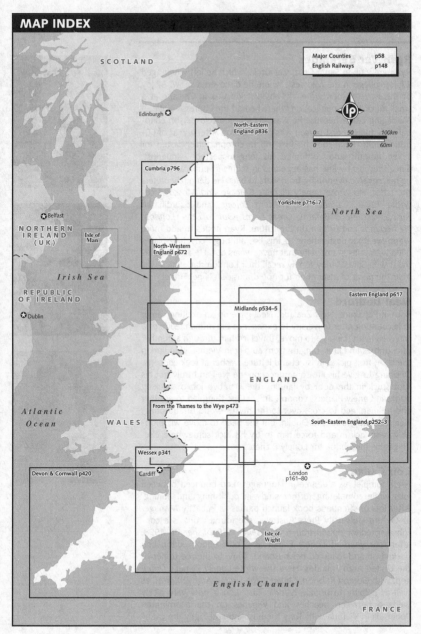

SCOTLAND

Edinburgh ✪

| Major Counties | p58 |
| English Railways | p148 |

0   50   100km
0   30   60mi

Cumbria p796

North-Eastern England p836

Yorkshire p716–7

North Sea

✪ Belfast

NORTHERN IRELAND (UK)

Isle of Man

Irish Sea

North-Western England p672

REPUBLIC OF IRELAND

✪ Dublin

Eastern England p617

Midlands p534–5

ENGLAND

Atlantic Ocean

WALES

From the Thames to the Wye p473

South-Eastern England p252–3

Wessex p341

Devon & Cornwall p420

Cardiff ✪

London p161–80

Isle of Wight

English Channel

FRANCE

The Authors

Ryan Ver Berkmoes

Ryan grew up in Santa Cruz, California, which he left when aged 17 for college in the Midwest, where he discovered snow. All joy of this novelty soon wore off. His first job was in Chicago at a small muckraking publication where he had the impressive title of Managing Editor because he was second on a two-person editorial staff and the first person was called Editor. After a year of 60-hour weeks, Ryan took his first trip to Europe, which lasted for seven months and confirmed his long-suspected wanderlust. Since then his by-line has appeared in scores of publications and he has covered everything from wars to bars. He definitely prefers the latter. He wrote Lonely Planet's *Chicago* and *Moscow*, co-wrote *Texas*, *Canada* and *Western Europe*, and coordinated *Russia, Ukraine & Belarus*, *Great Lakes*, *Out to Eat – London*, *Netherlands* and *Britain*. In the future, Ryan hopes to add more warm-weather destinations to this list, although covering places filled with pubs is a novelty that never wears out. He and his journalist wife Sara Marley fondly recall their London flat, which was near the point of inspiration for noted musician Nigel Tufnel.

Neal Bedford

Born in Papakura, New Zealand, Neal gave up an exciting career in accounting after university to experience the mundane life of a traveller. With the urge to move, travel led him through a number of countries and jobs, ranging from au pair in Vienna, lifeguard in the USA, fruit picker in Israel and lettuce washer at rock concerts. Deciding to give his life some direction, he well and truly got his foot stuck in the door by landing the lucrative job of packing books in Lonely Planets' London office. One thing led to another and he managed to cross over to the mystic world of authoring. Neal currently resides in Dublin, but the need to move will probably soon kick in and force him to try his luck somewhere else. This is his third book for Lonely Planet.

Lou Callan

After completing a degree in languages, Lou bounced between jobs while completing further study in publishing and editing. After lots of strenuous book launch parties as Publicity Manager at Oxford University Press Australia, she found work as a contributing editor on *Australian Bookseller & Publisher*. In 1998, after four years at Lonely Planet as a phrasebook editor, Lou packed up and followed her husband, Tony, to the red dunes of the United Arab Emirates. Here she wrote Lonely Planet's *Dubai* and, with Gordon Robison, *Oman & the United Arab Emirates*, as well as helping to update *Middle East*. Lou is now very nicely wedged between beaches and wineries on the Mornington Peninsula in Victoria with Tony the husband and Ziggy the cat.

Fionn Davenport

Fionn was born in and spent most of his youth in Dublin – that is, when his family wasn't moving him to Buenos Aires, Geneva or New York (all thanks to his dad, whose job took him far and wide). Infected with the travel disease, he became a nomad in his own right after graduating from Trinity College, moving first to Paris and then to New York, where he spent five years as a travel editor and sometime writer. The call of home was too much to resist, however, so armed with his portable computer, his record collection and an empty wallet he returned to Dublin where he decided to continue where he left off in New York. Only it was quieter, wetter and a hell of a lot smaller. When he's not deejaying in pubs and clubs throughout the city he's writing and updating travel guides. He has written about many destinations throughout the world. He has previously worked on Lonely Planet's *Spain*, *Dublin*, *Ireland*, *Sicily* and *Britain*.

Nick Ray

A Londoner of sorts, Nick hails from Watford, England, the sort of town that makes you want to travel. He studied history and politics at Warwick University and stumbled out clutching a piece of paper that said he knew stuff about things. Usually farther from home, contributing to this book sent him darting about the green fields of England, not to mention a few pubs along the way. More often than not he is to be found writing books in the more obscure parts of Africa or Asia, and Cambodia in particular, a country he thinks of as a second home.

FROM THE AUTHORS

Ryan Ver Berkmoes Thanks to the many tourism authorities in Yorkshire, London and the rest of the country.

I owe a huge debt to Steve Fallon for writing LP's *London*, which formed the basis for my own London research. I'm also indebted to Steve for being a good friend. Also in London the following chums made my stay in England a delight and helped immeasurably in giving me enthusiasm for the book: Mike Rothschild, Andrew Humphreys, Gadi Farfour, Damien Simonis, Jane Brockhouse, James Lownie, David & Jane Ellis, Sam, Jennie & Kate Harvey, Laura Board, Kate Norton, Jim Burcke & Barbie Hadley and many others.

It was a delight to work with the other authors, Neal Bedford (who has odd taste in underwear), Lou Callan (who never saw a south-eastern town she didn't like – almost), Fionn Davenport (who has no taste for beer) and Nick Ray (who will taste all beer).

Lonely Planet's London office finally proved their value in matters beyond warm beer on occasional Fridays. Kath Leck tossed the project to me in the first place. Tim Ryder, Ed Pickard, Tim Fitzpatrick, Amanda Canning and the rest were so efficient that my drool cup never had a chance to get full. And thanks to all my other friends in the London LP office (Jennifer Cox, Michelle Hawkins, Lorna Gallagher et al), not just for their fine professionalism, but for their willingness to join me for those warm beers.

Finally, cheers and a snog to my favourite partner in my favourite flat, Sara Marley.

Neal Bedford Thanks firstly goes to Ryan for all the guidance I received during the research and writing. Hearty thanks to John Richards for his wisdom on Manchester and Dawn Hedley and Nick Rowley for their northern England travel tips. Big thanks to everyone in the London LP office, in particular for their extra special effort (which they had no choice in giving!): Paul Bloomfield, Katrina Browning, Imogen Franks, Tom Hall, Howard Ralley, Tim Ryder, Sam Trafford, Angie Watts and Dave Wenk. And also to the ex-LPers – Tom Bevan, Nicky Robinson and Anna Sutton. As always, special thanks to the tourist offices throughout the country that made my life easier. My gratitude and sympathy goes out to those who had to put up with me on the road, the Bevans and friends for their wonderful hospitality (the best B&B in England), Robert Box and Claire Delamey for doing my head in (!), and Nik Pickard and Rachel Parker for being great friends. Thanks to Tony Ludlam, part of the Dublin contingent that kept me on track. And a big *bussi* to Christina Tlustos for all the support and guidance.

Lou Callan Special thanks to Tony Cleaver, my darling husband and travel companion; to Sarah and Nigel Biggs in the UK, who are always so generous and helpful; and to Danny Foster in the UK for the phone calls and the beers.

Fionn Davenport Thanks to everybody at the tourist information centres, who were extremely friendly, courteous and helpful. A big thanks to all the folks in Cambridge; you made my stay a very pleasant one. Cheers to all the staff at The Dôme, who gave me plenty of great tips and steered me in the right direction. Lastly, thanks to Ryan and Sara for putting me up: your hospitality is greatly appreciated and I look forward to seeing you both again.

Nick Ray Many thanks to many people, most importantly my loving girlfriend Kulikar for enriching my life, to my wonderful parents for their enduring support and to my fantastic friends, the finest around. A big thank you also to my relatives in Worcestershire for pointers in that part of the country, particularly Nick George and Sarah Barr. In Nottingham, a big hello to the Johnson brothers, Chris and Andrew, who gave me a full-on introduction to that fine city. Thanks to Brigham Whitney for hospitality in Bristol. Cheers also to the many good folk of England who helped me out in many ways and proved that, but for a few idiots, the English are generally a pretty decent bunch. In particular, thanks to the staff of numerous tourist information centres for their insights and to many of the staff at LP's London office and my fellow authors for suggestions, advice and patience.

This Book

This is the 1st edition of Lonely Planet's *England*. Ryan Ver Berkmoes was coordinating author and wrote the London, Yorkshire and introductory chapters; Neal Bedford wrote the North-Eastern England, North-Western England and Cumbria chapters; Lou Callan wrote the South-Eastern England chapter; Fionn Davenport wrote the Eastern England chapter; and Nick Ray wrote the Devon & Cornwall, Wessex, From the Thames to the Wye and The Midlands chapters.

From the Publisher

This 1st edition of *England* was produced in Lonely Planet's London office and coordinated by Tim Ryder (editing) and Ed Pickard (mapping and design). Tim was assisted with editing and proofing by Imogen Franks, Abigail Hole, Claire Hornshaw, Anna Jacomb-Hood, Evan Jones, Sally Schafer, Arabella Shepherd and Sam Trafford. Ed was helped with the mapping by James Ellis, Jolyon Philcox, Ian Stokes, Angie Watts and David Wenk. The index was produced by Tim, with Ed's invaluable assistance. Paul' Bloomfield and Michala Green stepped in to help with last-minute layout checks. Adam McCrow designed the front cover, Lachlan Ross drew the back-cover map and Jane Smith drew the illustrations. Special thanks to Sam for coordinating the editing while Tim was away, and to Michala and Finola Collins for additional research.

Foreword

ABOUT LONELY PLANET GUIDEBOOKS

The story begins with a classic travel adventure: Tony and Maureen Wheeler's 1972 journey across Europe and Asia to Australia. Useful information about the overland trail did not exist at that time, so Tony and Maureen published the first Lonely Planet guidebook to meet a growing need.

From a kitchen table, then from a tiny office in Melbourne (Australia), Lonely Planet has become the largest independent travel publisher in the world, an international company with offices in Melbourne, Oakland (USA), London (UK) and Paris (France).

Today Lonely Planet guidebooks cover the globe. There is an ever-growing list of books and there's information in a variety of forms and media. Some things haven't changed. The main aim is still to help make it possible for adventurous travellers to get out there – to explore and better understand the world.

At Lonely Planet we believe travellers can make a positive contribution to the countries they visit – if they respect their host communities and spend their money wisely. Since 1986 a percentage of the income from each book has been donated to aid projects and human rights campaigns.

Updates Lonely Planet thoroughly updates each guidebook as often as possible. This usually means there are around two years between editions, although for more unusual or more stable destinations the gap can be longer. Check the imprint page (following the colour map at the beginning of the book) for publication dates.

Between editions up-to-date information is available in two free newsletters – the paper *Planet Talk* and email *Comet* (to subscribe, contact any Lonely Planet office) – and on our Web site at www.lonelyplanet.com. The *Upgrades* section of the Web site covers a number of important and volatile destinations and is regularly updated by Lonely Planet authors. *Scoop* covers news and current affairs relevant to travellers. And, lastly, the *Thorn Tree* bulletin board and *Postcards* section of the site carry unverified, but fascinating, reports from travellers.

Correspondence The process of creating new editions begins with the letters, postcards and emails received from travellers. This correspondence often includes suggestions, criticisms and comments about the current editions. Interesting excerpts are immediately passed on via newsletters and the Web site, and everything goes to our authors to be verified when they're researching on the road. We're keen to get more feedback from organisations or individuals who represent communities visited by travellers.

Lonely Planet gathers information for everyone who's curious about the planet – and especially for those who explore it first-hand. Through guidebooks, phrasebooks, activity guides, maps, literature, newsletters, image library, TV series and Web site we act as an information exchange for a worldwide community of travellers.

Research Authors aim to gather sufficient practical information to enable travellers to make informed choices and to make the mechanics of a journey run smoothly. They also research historical and cultural background to help enrich the travel experience and allow travellers to understand and respond appropriately to cultural and environmental issues.

Authors don't stay in every hotel because that would mean spending a couple of months in each medium-sized city and, no, they don't eat at every restaurant because that would mean stretching belts beyond capacity. They do visit hotels and restaurants to check standards and prices, but feedback based on readers' direct experiences can be very helpful.

Many of our authors work undercover, others aren't so secretive. None of them accept freebies in exchange for positive write-ups. And none of our guidebooks contain any advertising.

Production Authors submit their raw manuscripts and maps to offices in Australia, USA, UK or France. Editors and cartographers – all experienced travellers themselves – then begin the process of assembling the pieces. When the book finally hits the shops, some things are already out of date, we start getting feedback from readers and the process begins again …

WARNING & REQUEST

Things change – prices go up, schedules change, good places go bad and bad places go bankrupt – nothing stays the same. So, if you find things better or worse, recently opened or long since closed, please tell us and help make the next edition even more accurate and useful. We genuinely value all the feedback we receive. A well-travelled team reads and acknowledges every letter, postcard and email and ensures that every morsel of information finds its way to the appropriate authors, editors and cartographers for verification.

Everyone who writes to us will find their name in the next edition of the appropriate guidebook. They will also receive the latest issue of *Planet Talk*, our quarterly printed newsletter, or *Comet*, our monthly email newsletter. Subscriptions to both newsletters are free. The very best contributions will be rewarded with a free guidebook.

Excerpts from your correspondence may appear in new editions of Lonely Planet guidebooks, the Lonely Planet Web site, *Planet Talk* or *Comet*, so please let us know if you *don't* want your letter published or your name acknowledged.

Send all correspondence to the Lonely Planet office closest to you:

Australia: Locked Bag 1, Footscray, Victoria 3011
USA: 150 Linden St, Oakland, CA 94607
UK: 10a Spring Place, London NW5 3BH
France: 1 rue du Dahomey, 75011 Paris

Or email us at: talk2us@lonelyplanet.com.au

For news, views and updates see our Web site: www.lonelyplanet.com

HOW TO USE A LONELY PLANET GUIDEBOOK

The best way to use a Lonely Planet guidebook is any way you choose. At Lonely Planet we believe the most memorable travel experiences are often those that are unexpected, and the finest discoveries are those you make yourself. Guidebooks are not intended to be used as if they provide a detailed set of infallible instructions!

Contents All Lonely Planet guidebooks follow roughly the same format. The Facts about the Destination chapters or sections give background information ranging from history to weather. Facts for the Visitor gives practical information on issues like visas and health. Getting There & Away gives a brief starting point for researching travel to and from the destination. Getting Around gives an overview of the transport options when you arrive.

The peculiar demands of each destination determine how subsequent chapters are broken up, but some things remain constant. We always start with background, then proceed to sights, places to stay, places to eat, entertainment, getting there and away, and getting around information – in that order.

Heading Hierarchy Lonely Planet headings are used in a strict hierarchical structure that can be visualised as a set of Russian dolls. Each heading (and its following text) is encompassed by any preceding heading that is higher on the hierarchical ladder.

Entry Points We do not assume guidebooks will be read from beginning to end, but that people will dip into them. The traditional entry points are the list of contents and the index. In addition, however, some books have a complete list of maps and an index map illustrating map coverage.

There may also be a colour map that shows highlights. These highlights are dealt with in greater detail in the Facts for the Visitor chapter, along with planning questions and suggested itineraries. Each chapter covering a geographical region usually begins with a locator map and another list of highlights. Once you find something of interest in a list of highlights, turn to the index.

Maps Maps play a crucial role in Lonely Planet guidebooks and include a huge amount of information. A legend is printed on the back page. We seek to have complete consistency between maps and text, and to have every important place in the text captured on a map. Map key numbers usually start in the top left corner.

Although inclusion in a guidebook usually implies a recommendation we cannot list every good place. Exclusion does not necessarily imply criticism. In fact there are a number of reasons why we might exclude a place – sometimes it is simply inappropriate to encourage an influx of travellers.

Introduction

As a visitor to England today you can enjoy the rich history and panoply of English life past and present. Can there be any place where the past has been better documented? And the range of cultures, classes and diversity that comprise English life today will astound those who picture England as some tweedy place where all people do is sip warm beer in country pubs.

For such a small country – England's size places it between Greece and Eritrea – its influence on the world has been outsize. Shakespeare, the Industrial Revolution, common law, basic human rights, the Beatles and much more have all come from England.

But before you contemplate England and the English, it's important to know a few facts about just what England is. It's not Wales and it's not Scotland. In fact England comprises 50,085 sq miles (129,721 sq km) out of the island of Great Britain's 88,795 sq miles (229,978 sq km). England's population of about 50 million is far greater than

that of Scotland and Wales combined (barely 10 million). The population density of England is one of the highest in the world with about 1000 people per sq mile (about 400 per sq km). This concentration of people is a boon for visitors as there's great vibrancy and always something going on. It also means that even in areas of great natural beauty, such as the Lake District or the Yorkshire Dales, the presence and evidence of humans is always palpable. Certainly, despite what the Welsh and Scots would argue, much of what people think of as British is really English. Ironically, this fact is lost on many of the English.

Perhaps it's because the English have always looked outwards that most still think of themselves as British ahead of English. In contrast, their Welsh and Scottish cohabitants of their wet island think of themselves as Welsh and Scottish first and British second (make the common tourist mistake and call them English only at your peril).

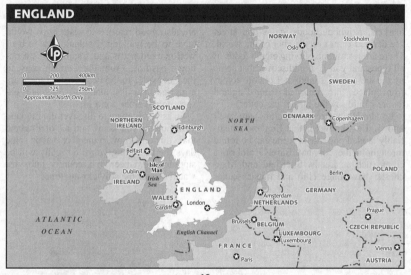

But this looking outwards is best done through a one-way mirror. The haughtiness that has inspired the English to resist invasion – Churchill's 'their finest hour' and 'we'll fight them on the beaches' are not regarded as mere bluster but rather as statements of fact – extends to life today. For many English, being part of the European Union (EU) is something best done with one's nose held shut. Apocryphal stories abound of the havoc being wrought in traditional English life by those 'bureaucrats in Brussels'. Usually the tales involve some sort of twee activity or odd farm foodstuff that few English actually enjoy but which suddenly take on national significance when seemingly threatened. And tales of EU meddling are quite selective given that efforts by the EU to force England to clean up its many polluted beaches are all but ignored by commentators.

Visitors to London who stick to the West End, Knightsbridge and Kensington won't realise that they are in one of the most diverse cities on the planet and they should be forgiven if they think London is nothing but tourists, ex-pats and the occasional English person. But scratch the surface of this fascinating capital city and you'll find a place where over 125 languages are spoken by its primary school students. There are markets, neighbourhoods, cafes and street life derived from every corner of the world. There are restaurants serving ethnic foods of all types and you'll soon discover that some of the best food found in London comes from places far removed from England (some would say the farther the better).

London's theatres and clubs are well known. Less known is that England's justifiably lauded pop music scene can be found throughout the country. Barely salubrious cities such as Leeds, Sheffield and Manchester have huge club and music scenes that draw mobs at the weekend.

Although today's England offers plenty for visitors, it's the past that will fill the days. You can ponder the Druids and their remarkable ability to move rocks at Stonehenge. Give the Romans their due at Bath, where the essential ablution got its name, and up north at Hadrian's Wall, where the unbathed Scots were kept at bay.

Religious life before and after Henry VIII sent the Catholics packing has left its monumental mark everywhere – from simply elegant country Gothic churches to the massive cathedrals of Durham and Winchester. Fountains Abbey in Yorkshire recalls the time when monks were all that stood between knowledge and the Dark Ages.

Britain's royalty continues to soldier on, some would say more as marketing icons than inspirational leaders. Buckingham Palace may underwhelm anyone who's already been to a convention hotel, but another of the Queen's homes at Windsor Castle reeks of history.

Shakespeare's haunts at Stratford-upon-Avon are just a bit of England's literary heritage. Follow in Wordsworth's footsteps in the Lake District or feel the moods of the ill-fated Brontë sisters in the hills above Haworth in Yorkshire. The plethora of at-times eccentric avocations of the English are also good reasons to visit. Tops would have to be walking. England is a web of well-marked paths and 'rambling' is a national pastime. From the Cornish coast to the Cotswolds to the Peak District there are a myriad of walks, many of which are reason enough alone for a trip.

So as you prepare to discover the England you thought you knew and all of England that you don't know, remember that on some days the best thing you'll do really will be sipping warm beer in a country pub; just watch out for the silly closing times.

Facts about England

England dominates both the political entity that is the United Kingdom and the geographical entity that is the island of Great Britain. Although the Scots and the Welsh made an enormous contribution to the British Empire it was, and in some ways remains, an English empire.

England's position on the edge of continental Europe, removed but in many ways an integral part, has always created unique opportunities and problems. The pendulum has swung from isolation to integration and back again a number of times. In this era of the European Union (EU) and the Channel Tunnel, England is probably more European than it has been for 700 years, even if the mere thought of this would cause many a Conservative politician to shudder with horror.

Despite this, travellers will find a country where the institutions and symbols that had such an enormous role in shaping the modern world remain cherished and intact – from the monarchy to the parliament, the British Museum to York Cathedral, Fountains Abbey to Ironbridge Gorge, Eton College to Oxford University, Old Trafford to Lord's Cricket Ground. The list goes on and on.

Perhaps its most significant contribution, however, is the English language – anyone who uses the language has England at the foundation of their consciousness. This can make England seem strangely familiar, but beyond this first impression lies a foreign country that still has the ability to bewilder.

It's an overpopulated, crowded country so day-to-day life can be difficult and intense. The country's fertility has meant that it has supported a (relatively) large population for thousands of years. Every square inch of land has, in some way, been modified or altered by human activities. The result of this collaboration between humanity and nature is often breathtakingly beautiful, although 19th- and 20th-century capitalism has also produced some pretty grim industrial and urban developments.

A remarkable proportion of the country, however, remains unspoiled. There are few more seductive sights than the English countryside on a sunny day – the vivid greens, the silky air, the wildflowers, the ballooning trees, the villages, the grand houses and the soaring church spires.

HISTORY
The Celts

England had long been settled by small bands of hunters when, around 4000 BC, a new group of immigrants arrived from Europe. Using stone tools, these Neolithic tribes were the first to leave enduring marks on the island as they farmed the chalk hills radiating from Salisbury Plain. They also began the construction of stone tombs and, around 3000 BC, the great ceremonial complexes at Avebury and Stonehenge.

The next great influx involved the Celts, a people from central Europe who had mastered the smelting of bronze and (later) iron. They started arriving around 800 BC and brought two forms of the Celtic language: the Gaelic, which is still spoken in Ireland and Scotland, and the Brythonic, which was spoken in England and is still spoken in Wales.

The Romans

Julius Caesar made investigative forays into England in 55 and 54 BC, but the real Roman invasion didn't take place until nearly 100 years later in AD 43. Quite why the Romans decided to extend their power across the English Channel is unclear. It may have been that Emperor Claudius felt the need to display his military prowess, it may have been fear of the Celts in Britain joining forces with the Gauls in France, or it may simply have been the feeling that there was money to be made in England. The latter certainly turned out to be true, but the expense of obtaining it was great; the Romans' British holdings never had the desired impact on the Empire's profit and loss account.

Claudius' forces crossed the channel to Kent and controlled England all the way to the Welsh border before AD 50. The 'wretched British', as a Roman note discovered near Hadrian's Wall referred to them, did not give in easily. The centurions had their hands full quelling the warlike Welsh and, between AD 60 and 61, the warrior queen Boudicca, also know as Boadicea, who fought her way as far as Londinium, the Roman port on the present site of London. Nevertheless, opposition was essentially random and sporadic and posed no real threat to the well-organised Roman forces. In reality the stability and wealth the Romans brought was probably welcomed by the general population, and by around AD 80 Wales and the north of England were under Roman control.

Scotland proved more tricky, and in 122 the Emperor Hadrian decided that the barbarians to the north were a lost cause – rather than conquer them, he'd settle for simply keeping them at bay. Accordingly, he ordered a wall (Hadrian's Wall) to be built right across the country – to the south would be civilisation and the Roman Empire, to the north would be the savages. Only 20 years later, the Romans made another attempt at bringing the unruly northerners into line and constructed the Antonine Wall, farther north. This was soon abandoned and for nearly 300 years Hadrian's Wall marked the furthermost limit of the Roman Empire. Paved roads radiated from London to important regional centres – Ermine St ran north to Lincoln, York and Hadrian's Wall, and Watling St ran north-west to Chester.

The Romans brought stability and considerable economic advancement to England for nearly four centuries. After it was recognised by Emperor Constantine in 313, they also brought Christianity. By this time the Empire was already in decline but the Romans were not driven out by the English, nor did they withdraw to fight fires closer to home. England was simply abandoned. Money stopped coming from Rome and,

although the outposts stumbled on for some time, eventually they crumbled and were deserted. The end of Roman power in England is generally dated at around 410.

The Anglo-Saxon & Viking Invasions

As Roman power faded, England went downhill. The use of money, once supplied by Rome, dwindled. As a result, trade declined, rural areas lost their population, travel became unsafe and local fiefdoms developed. Heathen Angles, Jutes and Saxons – Teutonic tribes originating from north of the Rhine – began to move into the vacuum created by the Roman departure. During the 5th century, these tribes advanced across what had been Roman England, absorbing the Celts so thoroughly that today most place names in England have Anglo-Saxon origins.

By the end of the 6th century, England had split into a number of Anglo-Saxon kingdoms, and by the 7th century these kingdoms had come to think of themselves collectively as English. The Celts, particularly in Ireland, kept Latin and Roman-Christian culture alive. Christianity, a fragile late-Roman-period import, may have declined at first but the arrival of St Augustine in 597 was followed by the swift spread of Augustinian missions.

As memories of Rome faded and the Celts merged with the Anglo-Saxons, England was divided into three strong kingdoms. In the 7th century, Northumbria was the dominant kingdom, extending its power far across the border into Scotland. In the 8th century, Mercia became stronger and King Offa marked a clear border between England and Wales, delineated by Offa's Dyke. Mercia's power eventually withered, to be replaced by that of King Egbert of Wessex, who was the first to rule all England. At the same time, the fierce northern Vikings inflicted a new round of attacks on the country.

In 865 a Viking army moved in to conquer the Anglo-Saxon kingdoms. The Norwegian Vikings took northern Scotland, Cumbria and Lancashire, while the Danes conquered eastern England, making York their capital. They spread across England until, in 871, they were confronted by Alfred the Great of Wessex.

England was divided between the northern Danelaw and southern Wessex, the old Roman Watling St approximating the border. Alfred's successor, Edward the Elder, ended up controlling both Wessex and the Danelaw, but in subsequent generations control of England seesawed from Saxon (Edgar, king of Mercia and Northumberland) to Dane (Canute and his hopeless sons) and back to Saxon (Edward the Confessor).

Edward the Confessor had been brought up in Normandy – a Viking duchy in France – alongside his cousin Duke William, the future Conqueror. Edward's death left two contenders for the crown: Harold Godwineson, his English brother-in-law, and William, his Norman cousin. Harold eventually gained the throne but ruled for less than a year, during which time he marched north to defeat one Viking invasion, then turned south to meet another.

The Normans & the Plantagenets

The year 1066 is of enormous importance in English history because the Norman invasion in that year capped a millennium of invasions and since then there have been no more. In that year William, soon to be dubbed 'the Conqueror', landed with 12,000 men and defeated Harold at the Battle of Hastings. The Norman conquest of England was completed rapidly – English aristocrats were replaced by French-speaking Normans, dominating castles were built and the feudal system was imposed.

The Normans were efficient administrators. By 1085–86 the Domesday Book had provided a census of the country, its owners, its inhabitants and its potential. William I was followed in 1087 by William II and, when he was killed by a mysterious arrow while hunting in the New Forest, he was succeeded by Henry I. Intermarriage between Normans and Saxons was already becoming common, Henry himself marrying a Saxon princess.

A bitter struggle for the throne followed Henry I's death, and was not finally determined until Henry II (count of Anjou and grandson of Henry I) took the throne as the first of the Plantagenet Norman kings in 1154. Henry II also inherited more than half of modern France and his power actually surpassed that of the French king.

Not only was the enduring English habit of squabbling between royalty becoming established, but an almost equally enduring habit of squabbling between royalty and the Church was also under way. Henry II blotted his copybook by having Thomas à Becket, that 'turbulent priest', murdered in Canterbury Cathedral in 1170.

Richard I (the Lion-Heart) was too busy crusading around the Holy Land to bother much about governing England; and by the end of his brother John's reign much of the Norman land in France had been lost, disputes with the Church in Rome were neverending and the powerful barons were so fed up they forced John to sign the Magna Carta in 1215.

This first real bill of human rights may have been intended purely as an agreement between lords and their king, but its influence was to spread further afield as its concepts of human rights served as a guiding force for both governments and the Church.

The Magna Carta did not end the power struggle between the king and his barons. In 1265 the barons held both Henry III and Prince Edward, but Edward escaped, defeated the barons and followed Henry III as Edward I in 1272. During his reign English control was extended across the Welsh and Scottish borders.

Edward II ascended the throne in 1307, but his lack of military success (he led his army to a horrendous defeat at the hands of Robert the Bruce of Scotland), his favouring of personal friends over his barons and, it's said, his homosexuality brought his reign to a grisly end when his wife, Isabella, and her lover, Roger Mortimer, had him murdered in Berkeley Castle, Gloucestershire.

Things were scarcely better during Edward III's 50-year reign. His long rule

Wars – a Hundred Years' & the Roses

Wars are rarely what they seem. In recent times, WWI was the 'Great War' until WWII came along to give it a number. The Hundred Years' War was an on-again, off-again affair that effectively lasted for 116 years, from the first English success at Crécy in 1346 to the final English realisation that they could not hold France as well as England in 1453. It's been suggested that the war was as much a French civil war as an Anglo-French conflict, but the struggle really resulted from the entangled English and French royal family lines and their conflicting spheres of control. The Black Death, shortage of funds and other 14th-century catastrophes such as the death of the Black Prince and a Peasants' Revolt combined to provide plentiful interruptions.

The Wars of the Roses (1455–85) were a similarly stop-and-start dispute, which only got their name nearly 400 years later, courtesy of romantic novelist Sir Walter Scott. It's been estimated that over the 30 years from 1455 until Henry VII grabbed the throne, actual 'war' only occupied 60 weeks. Medieval warfare was nothing like later blood-and-death struggles; damaging a rival economically by destroying villages and crops was as likely to be the policy as full-on fighting.

saw the start of the Hundred Years' War with France in 1337 and the arrival of the Black Death in 1349. After a series of return bouts, the plague eventually carried off one and a half million people, more than a third of the country's population. The young Richard II had barely taken the throne before he was confronted with the Peasants' Revolt in 1381. Its brutal suppression led to unrest across an already deeply unsettled country.

As well as this clash between the peasantry and the ruling class, the 14th century saw considerable changes in society, exemplified by the rise of English in place of French, the language of the nobility.

In 1380, John Wycliffe made the first English translation of the Bible, but this threatened the position of the Church and royalty (who interpreted its Latin contents for the people) and when William Tyndale dared to print the Bible in English 150 years later, he was burned at the stake.

Geoffrey Chaucer's *Canterbury Tales*, first published around 1387, was not only one of the first books to be written in English, it was also one of the first printed books.

The struggle to retain English control over territory in France was a prime cause of the Hundred Years' War, and to finance these adventures the Plantagenet kings had to concede a considerable amount of power to parliament, which jealously protected its traditional right to control taxation.

The Houses of Lancaster & York

Richard II was an ineffectual king and in 1399 Henry IV seized the throne as the first king of the House of Lancaster. His father, John of Gaunt, one of the younger sons of Edward III, was not only the power behind the throne during Edward III's last years but had also been the major influence on Richard II.

Henry IV was followed by Henry V, who decided it was time to stir up the dormant Hundred Years' War. He defeated the French at Agincourt and Shakespeare later ensured his position as one of the most popular English kings.

Henry VI ascended the throne as an infant and devoted himself to building (King's College Chapel in Cambridge and Eton Chapel near Windsor) interspersed with bouts of insanity. When the Hundred Years' War finally ground to a halt in 1453, the English forces returned from France and threw their energies into the Wars of the Roses (the battle for control of the crown between the houses of Lancaster and York).

Once again it was a question of succession, with Henry VI represented by the red rose of Lancaster and Richard, Duke of York, by the white rose of York. Henry VI may have been helpless but his wife, Margaret of Anjou, was made of different mettle and in 1460 her forces defeated and killed Richard, only for Richard's son Edward to take revenge on her and her king a year later.

As Edward IV, he was the first Yorkist king but he now had to contend with Richard Neville, the scheming earl of Warwick. Labelled 'the kingmaker', the earl teamed up with Margaret of Anjou to bring Henry VI back to the throne and shuttle Edward IV into exile in 1470. Then in 1471 Edward IV came bouncing back to kill the earl and capture Margaret and Henry. Soon after, Henry was murdered in the Tower of London.

Edward IV was a larger-than-life king, but his 12-year-old son Edward V reigned for only two months in 1483 before being murdered, with his younger brother, in the Tower of London. Whether Richard III, their uncle and the next king, was their killer has been the subject of much conjecture, but few tears were shed when he was tumbled from the throne by Henry Tudor, first king of the Tudor dynasty, in 1485.

The Tudors

Henry VII, a Lancastrian descended on his mother's side from John of Gaunt, patched things up with the House of York by marrying the daughter of Edward IV and arranging strategic marriages for his own children.

Matrimony may have been a more useful tool than warfare for Henry VII, but the multiple marriages of his successor, Henry VIII, were a very different story. Fathering an heir was Henry VIII's immediate problem and the Church's unwillingness to cooperate with this quest led to a split with the Catholic Church. Parliament made Henry the head of the Church of England and the Bible was translated into English. In 1536 Henry VIII 'dissolved' the smaller monasteries in Britain and Ireland, as much a blatant takeover of their land and wealth as another stage in the struggle between Church and State. The general populace felt little sympathy for the wealthy and often corrupt monasteries, and in 1539–40 another monastic land grab swallowed the larger ones as well. The property was sold or granted to members of the nobility, raising money for the king's military campaigns and ensuring the loyalty of his followers.

Nine-year-old Edward VI followed Henry VIII in 1547 but only ruled for six years. During his reign Catholicism declined and Protestantism grew stronger. His devoutly Catholic sister Mary I reversed that pattern, but she too had a short reign (just five years).

Elizabeth I, the third child of Henry VIII, seemed to have inherited a nasty mess of religious strife and divided loyalties, but her 45-year reign (1558–1603) saw a period of boundless English optimism epitomised by the defeat of the Spanish Armada, the global explorations of English seafarers, the expansion of trade, the literary endeavours of William Shakespeare and the scientific pursuits of Francis Bacon.

The Stuarts & the Commonwealth Interlude

The one thing the Virgin Queen failed to provide was an heir, so she was succeeded by James I, first king of the inflexible Stuart dynasty. Since he was already James VI of Scotland, he effectively united England, Scotland and Wales into one country. His attempts to smooth relations with the Catholics were set back by the anti-Catholic outcry that followed Guy Fawkes' Gunpowder Plot, a Catholic attempt to blow up parliament and king in 1605 (which is still celebrated on 5 November – Guy Fawkes' Night). The power struggle between monarchy and parliament became even more bitter during Charles I's reign, eventually degenerating into the Civil War, which pitched the king's royalists (Cavaliers) against the parliamentarians (Roundheads). Catholics, traditionalist members of the Church of England and the old gentry supported Charles I, whose power base was the north and west. The Protestant Puritans and the new rising merchant class, based in

London and the towns of the South-East, supported parliament.

The 1644–9 struggle resulted in victory for the parliamentary forces, the execution of Charles I and the establishment of the Commonwealth, ruled by Oliver Cromwell, the brilliant parliamentary military leader. A devastating and cruel rampage around Ireland starting in 1649 failed to exhaust his appetite for mayhem.

By 1653 he had also become fed up with parliament and as the 'Protector' assumed near dictatorial powers. Oliver Cromwell laid the foundation for the British Empire by modernising the army and navy. He was followed half-heartedly by his son, but in 1660 parliament decided to re-establish the monarchy as the alternatives were proving far worse.

Charles II (the exiled son of Charles I) proved to be an able, though often utterly ruthless, king who brought order out of chaos, and the Restoration foreshadowed a new burst of scientific and cultural activity after the strait-laced Puritan ethics of the Commonwealth. Colonies soon stretched down the American coast and the East India Company established its headquarters in Bombay.

Unfortunately, James II (1685–8) was not so far-sighted and his attempts to ease restrictive laws on Catholics ended with his defeat at the hands of William III, better known as William of Orange (the Dutch husband of Mary II, the Protestant daughter of James II). To take their joint throne, however, William and Mary had to agree to a Bill of Rights, and with the later Act of Settlement Britain was established as a constitutional monarchy with clear limits on the powers of the monarchy and a ban on any Catholic (or anyone married to a Catholic) ascending the throne.

Although William and Mary's Glorious Revolution of 1688 was relatively painless in Britain, the impact on Ireland, where the Protestant ascendancy dates from William's victory over James II at the Battle of the Boyne, laid the seeds for the troubles that have continued until now.

Mary died before William, who was fol-

lowed by Anne (the second daughter of James II), but the Stuart line died with her in 1714. The throne was then passed to distant (but safely Protestant) German relatives.

Empire & Industry

In the 18th century the Hanoverian kings increasingly relied on parliament to govern and from 1721 to 1742 Sir Robert Walpole became Britain's first prime minister in all but name. Bonnie Prince Charlie shattered this period of tranquillity in 1745 by attempting to seize the throne, but this Jacobite Rebellion ended in disaster for Scotland at the Battle of Culloden.

Stronger English control over the British Isles was mirrored by even greater expansion overseas as the British Empire absorbed more and more of America, Canada and India, and the first claims were made to Australia after Captain James Cook's epic voyage in 1768.

The Empire's first major reverse came when the American colonies won their independence in 1782. This setback led to a period of isolation. During this time, Napoleon rose to power in France before naval hero Nelson and military hero Wellington curtailed, then ended, his expansion in 1815.

Meanwhile, at home, Britain was becoming the crucible of the Industrial Revolution. Canals (following the Bridgewater Canal in 1765), steam power (patented by James Watt in 1781), steam trains (launched by George Stephenson in 1830), the development of coal mines and water power transformed the means of production and transport, and the rapidly growing towns of the Midlands became the first industrial cities.

Medical advances led to a dramatic increase in the population but the rapid change from an agricultural to an industrial society caused great dislocation. Nevertheless, by the time Queen Victoria took the throne in 1837 Britain was the greatest power in the world. Britain's fleets dominated the seas, linking an enormous empire, and its factories dominated world trade.

Under prime ministers Disraeli and Gladstone, the worst excesses of the Industrial Revolution were addressed – education became universal, trade unions were legalised and the right to vote was extended to most men. Women didn't get the vote until after WWI.

The Edwardian Era to WWII

Queen Victoria died in 1901 and the ever-expanding Britain of her era died with her. It wasn't immediately evident that a century of relative decline was about to commence when Edward VII, so long the king in waiting, ushered in the relaxed new Edwardian era. In 1914 Britain – along with the rest of Europe – bumbled into the Great War (WWI), a war of stalemate and horrendous slaughter. It not only added trench warfare to the dictionary but also dug a huge trench between the ruling and working classes as thousands of ordinary men lost their lives at the behest of their commanding officers.

The old order was shattered, and by the war's weary end in 1918 one million Britons had died and 15% of the country's accumulated capital had been spent. The euphoria of victory brought with it an extension of the right to vote to all men aged 21 and women aged 30 and over. It wasn't until 1928 that women were granted the same rights as men.

Political changes also saw the eclipse of the Liberal Party. It was replaced by the Labour Party, which won power, albeit in coalition with the Liberals, for the first time in the 1923 election. James Ramsay MacDonald was the first Labour prime minister. A year later the Conservatives were back in power, but the rankling 'us and them' mistrust that had developed during the war, fertilised by soaring unemployment, led to the 1926 General Strike. When over half a million workers hit the streets, the heavy-handed government response included sending in the army, which set the stage for the labour unrest that was to plague Britain for the next 50 years.

However, in the mid-1920s, it did look as if Britain had finally solved one centuries-

That'll Be Two Bob

Until 1971 Britain used a system of money some would call quaint, others would just call weird. The British monetary system defied logic – although its many colourful denominations were put to delightful use by generations of English writers.

For the record, here's what is meant when you hear reference to the old system:

Farthing – a quarter-penny coin that was discontinued in 1956
Half penny – just that
Penny – or pence, a basic part of English currency dating back to AD 75
Three pence – a coin worth just that
Sixpence – another eponymous coin
Shilling – 12 pence, also called one 'bob'
Florin – two shillings
Halfcrown – two shillings and six pence
Crown – five shillings
Pound – 20 shillings, usually a note
Sovereign – a pound coin made from gold

Just to keep things interesting, a 'guinea' was a term for 21 shillings; however, there was no coin or note known by that name.

The changeover in 1971 was predictably traumatic for the traditionalist English. There were all manner of predictions of doom and gloom over going to a decimal-based system; in fact many of the arguments don't sound all that different from those of the anti-euro crowd today.

old problem. The war had no sooner ended than Britain was involved in another struggle, the bitter Anglo-Irish War, which commenced in 1919 and ground to a halt in mid-1921 with Ireland finally achieving independence. Unhappily, the decision to divide the island in two was to have long-term repercussions.

The unrest of the 1920s worsened in the 1930s as the world economy slumped,

Say You Want a Revolution

Far from being the mere result of a few inventions such as the steam engine, the railway, iron smelting and the like, the Industrial Revolution is now thought to be more the result of social rather than technical change.

At the start of the 18th century, England already had long experience with trading. Much wealth was produced by taking raw materials and turning them into products that could be sold for greatly increased value. The many ports and the nation's maritime traditions meant that trade with other nations was part of the culture.

Thus, when Britain had unprecedented population growth beginning later in the 18th century – the 1770 population of 8.3 million almost doubled in 50 years – people weren't just left wanly poking at the land hoping something would grow but, rather, the nation's industrial production and employment grew symbiotically with the population.

A heritage of technological innovation meant that new methods were found to feed more people. It also meant that there was little shortage of work for the expanding population. The British government relentlessly scoured the planet for resource-rich lands to colonise. The raw materials of these lands – cotton from India and America being a good example – supported an increasingly larger workforce. Advances in mill technology, especially in Yorkshire and Lancashire, brought the price of goods made from cotton down to the level where they found wide acceptance. The value of annual English cotton production increased 7000% from 1760 to 1800.

One theory on the Industrial Revolution credits the mass production of cotton clothes with aiding the British population explosion: wool clothes were hard to wash and spread disease while easily washed cotton was more hygienic.

Certainly the lower incidence of infectious diseases from the mid-18th century onwards helped the population grow. An increasing sense of cleanliness spurred on the long task of cleaning up the cities, many of which were little more than medieval cesspools well into the 19th century. New foods brought from other lands, such as corn and new types of grain, helped feed the population. In

ushering in a decade of misery and political upheaval. Even the royal family took a knock when Edward VIII chose to abdicate in 1936 in order to marry a woman who was not only twice divorced but also American.

The less-than-charismatic George VI followed his brother Edward, but the scandal hinted at the prolonged 'trial by media' that the royal family would undergo 50 years later.

Britain dithered through the 1920s and 1930s with mediocre and visionless government failing to confront the country's problems. Meanwhile on the Continent, the 1930s saw the rise of imperial Germany under Adolf Hitler. By the time Prime Minister Neville Chamberlain returned from Munich in 1938 with a promise of 'peace in our time', the roller coaster was already rattling downhill to disaster. On 1 September

1939, Hitler invaded Poland and two days later Britain declared war.

WWII
German forces swept through France and pushed a British expeditionary force back to the beaches of Dunkirk in May/June 1940. Only an extraordinary flotilla of rescue vessels turned a disaster into a brave defeat. By mid-1940, the other countries of Europe were either ruled by or under the direct influence of Nazi Germany. Stalin had negotiated a peace agreement, the USA was neutral, and Britain, under Winston Churchill's stirring leadership, was virtually isolated. Neville Chamberlain, reviled for his policy of appeasement, had stood aside to let Churchill lead a wartime national coalition government.

From July to October 1940, the Royal

Say You Want a Revolution

contrast, neighbouring Ireland, which had almost no industrial development, suffered a series of horrific famines during the 19th century.

Although the Industrial Revolution touched all of Britain, England was at the centre. Abundant supplies of iron ore and coal in Yorkshire, Lancashire, Northumberland and Staffordshire fed local factories and South Yorkshire in particular became a centre of iron and later steel production. Railways were built, first to haul ore and later to haul people. An early line linked Manchester and Liverpool in 1830. The English proved adept at digging up the fairly level landscape for canals. Over 4000 miles of canals were built in a little under 100 years beginning in the 1720s. The Grand Union Canal linked London to Bristol and its important port.

The Industrial Revolution fed upon itself like a firestorm. England in 1750 was largely rural and society was farm-based; 100 years later 50% of the population lived in cities. Manchester and Birmingham in the Midlands had an inexhaustible hunger for labour. Regular wages, no matter how meagre, lured many people away from the uncertainty of living off the land. Others were forced into the cities when they were thrown off their farms by the creation of large industrial estates.

Urban life led to wholesale change in English culture, especially in the 19th century. In the anonymous cities, people shed inhibitions that predominated in close-knit communities. The first police forces were created in the 1820s, primarily to deal with anti-social behaviour. Illegitimate births soared and women began taking jobs outside of the home. However for most people life was simply work: a 14-hour day was the norm and anyone over the age of six was likely to be employed. However, the huge, grim and impersonal factories and mills associated with the Industrial Revolution didn't appear until the Victorian era. By this time labour laws began to regulate working conditions.

Perhaps the greatest social change that can be traced to the Industrial Revolution is the creation of the middle class. For the first time in England a large class of working people was created in the late 19th century – people who had disposable income that could be used not just to buy goods (that would fuel commerce and industry) but also for leisure pursuits such as tourism.

Air Force withstood the Luftwaffe's bombing raids to win the Battle of Britain. Churchill's extraordinary exhortations inspired the country to resist and Hitler's invasion plans were blocked. Sixty thousand civilian Britons were killed during the war and these were primarily English as the industrial cities of the Midlands and London were pummelled.

As in WWI a stalemate ensued, although this time the English Channel was the trench between the opposing forces. But, as in WWI, the entry of the USA into the conflict (although only after Japanese forces bombed the US fleet in Pearl Harbor in December 1941) tipped the balance.

The British colony of Hong Kong fell within days and Singapore fell by February, but in Europe the arrival of American forces and the bitter fighting in the USSR, which Hitler had invaded in June 1941, began to change things round. In late 1942, German forces were defeated in North Africa and the 1940–41 raids on England were answered with Allied raids on Germany in 1942–3. Tragically, the Allied forces mirrored the German decision to bomb cities rather than military targets, resulting in huge civilian losses that failed to cripple Hitler's war machine.

By 1944 Germany was in retreat, the Allies had complete command of the skies and the long-awaited D-Day invasion took place on the Normandy beaches in June 1944. Meanwhile, the Red Army was pushing back the German forces from the east. In May 1945 it was all over for Germany. Hitler was dead, Germany was a smoking ruin and Europe was to suffer new divisions that would last for nearly 50

Kings & Queens

Nobody glancing at England's tempestuous story could ever claim that the country's history was dull. The position of king or queen of England (or, perhaps worse, potential king or queen) would probably rank with being a drug dealer in a present-day American ghetto as one of history's least safe occupations. They've died in battle (an arrow through the eye for Harold II), been beheaded (Charles I), murdered by a wicked uncle (Edward V at the age of 12) or been knocked off by their queen and her lover (Edward II, for whom a particularly horrible death was concocted as 'punishment' for his homosexuality).

The English monarchs have often been larger-than-life characters: wife abusers of the very worst kind (Henry VIII), sufferers from insanity (George III), even stutterers (George VI). And as for scandal, the current royal family's antics during the 1990s were only a fleeting shadow of what their predecessors got up to. Nor has it been left solely to the men. England has been led by some powerful women, from the day Queen Boudicca charged her chariot through the Romans, right down to Maggie Thatcher, who projected herself as a queen even if she wasn't one. The two most successful monarchs in English history were probably Elizabeth I and Victoria, and the hapless Henry VI was lucky to be married to Margaret of Anjou, who seemed to have a private army which she led with much greater aplomb than her husband.

Debate continues over the suitability of Charles to take over from his long-lived handbag-carrying mother Elizabeth II. Her rule since 1952 has seen some of the sharpest challenges to the monarchy that have occurred in centuries. Given that many of the wounds have been self-inflicted, the Queen's stoic rule has not always been in tune with her subjects. The mass orgy of grief after the death of Diana Princess of Wales stood in stark contrast to the stiff-upper-lipped Windsors (a name incidentally the Royal family cooked up for itself during WWI to hide their deep German roots).

Still, the Queen has started paying income tax and has booted quite a few of the minor relatives off the list of those benefiting from the largess of the tax-payers. Charles is known for his philanthropic activities and his populist (and usually astute) views on the worst atrocities of modern architecture. His relationship with his old flame Camilla Parker-Bowles is gaining grudging approval from a public that is still mystified why he'd choose the horse-minded Camilla over the clothes-minded Diana. However, Charles looks to remain a king in waiting for the foreseeable future as his mother shows no sign of abdicating in his favour. She also shows no sign of dying and comes from long-lived stock: her mother Queen Elizabeth the Queen Mother – or Queen Mum – turned a spry 100 in 2000, an age that hasn't dampened her enthusiasm for gin.

Much less controversial is Charles' and Diana's son William. Having inherited his mother's looks,

years. Three months later, two US atomic bombs forced the surrender of Japan and ended WWII.

Postwar Reconstruction

Fortunately there was greater postwar wisdom in 1945 than in 1918. The Marshall Plan, which helped rebuild an economically strong Europe, stood in stark contrast to the post-WWI demands for reparations. An electorate hungry for change tumbled Churchill from power and ushered in the Labour Party's Clement Attlee.

In the 1930s the brilliant economist John Maynard Keynes had suggested a new theory (known as Keynesian Economics) that government could and should influence the economy. His ideas were also a factor in the much lower levels of unemployment that followed the war. Nationalisation of key industries, government manipulation of the economy and the institution of the National Health Service (NHS) were all part of the creation of the postwar welfare state, but rebuilding after the damage of the war was to be a slow process.

Kings & Queens

William is already a staple of the tabloids even as he ponders his university education and there are calls by some to skip Charles and make Wills the next king. Certainly his popularity is strong: at the public ceremony for the 100th birthday of the Queen Mum the crowd's loudest cheers were saved for the appearance of the handsome prince.

Following are all the kings and queens of England, from the mighty Alfred to the enduring Liz:

Saxons & Danes
Alfred the Great 871–99
Edward the Martyr 975–9
Ethelred II (the Unready)
  979–1016
Canute 1016–35
Edward the Confessor 1042–66
Harold I 1035–66
Harold II 1066

Normans
William I (the Conqueror)
  1066–87
William II (Rufus) 1087–1100
Henry I 1100–35
Stephen 1135–54

Plantagenet (Angevin)
Henry II 1154–89
Richard I (the Lion-Heart)
  1189–99
John 1199–1216
Henry III 1216–72
Edward I 1272–1307
Edward II 1307–27
Edward III 1327–77
Richard II 1377–99

Lancaster
Henry IV (Bolingbroke)
  1399–1413
Henry V 1413–22
Henry VI 1422–61 & 1470–71

York
Edward IV 1461–70 &
  1471–83
Edward V 1483
Richard III 1483–5

Tudor
Henry VII (Tudor) 1485–1509
Henry VIII 1509–47
Edward VI 1547–53
Mary I 1553–8
Elizabeth I 1558–1603

Stuart
James I 1603–25
Charles I 1625–49

Commonwealth & Protectorate
Oliver Cromwell 1649–58
Richard Cromwell 1658–9

Restoration
Charles II 1660–85
James II 1685–8
William III (of Orange)
  1689–1702
Mary II 1689–94
Anne 1702–14

Hanover
George I 1714–27
George II 1727–60
George III 1760–1820
George IV 1820–30
William IV 1830–37
Victoria 1837–1901

Saxe-Coburg-Gotha
Edward VII 1901–10

Windsor
George V 1910–36
Edward VIII 1936
George VI 1936–52
Elizabeth II 1952–

The postwar generation experienced rationing and belt-tightening for many years after hostilities ceased. Britain's depleted reserves also had to cope with the retreat from Empire as one by one the colonies became independent: India in 1947, Malaya in 1957 and Kenya in 1963. In 1953 Elizabeth II became queen; she is now the world's second-longest reigning monarch behind Prince Rainier of Monaco.

Postwar Britain was a less powerful nation but the recovery was still sufficiently strong for Prime Minister Harold Macmillan to boast in 1957 that most people in Britain had 'never had it so good'.

The Swinging Sixties to the Thatcher Years

By the 1960s the wartime recovery was really complete, the last vestiges of the Empire had been sloughed off and the Beatles era suddenly made grey old England a livelier place. On the surface the economy also looked stronger and more resilient, but even though Harold Wilson's Labour Party seemed to be doing the right things it was building on shaky foundations. The 1970s brought the oil crisis, inflation and increased international competition – a combination that quickly revealed the British economy's inherent weaknesses and antagonised already poor industrial relations.

Neither Labour, under Wilson and Jim Callaghan, nor the Conservatives, under Ted Heath, proved capable of controlling the industrial strife of 1974 and its repercussions later in the decade finally brought drastic change. In the 1979 election the 'Iron Lady', Margaret Thatcher, led the Conservatives to power and ushered in the tough new era of Thatcherism.

Her solutions were brutal and their consequences are still being debated. British workers and their unions were obstructive and Luddite? She broke them. British companies were inefficient and unimaginative? She drove them to the wall. The postwar nationalised companies were a mistake? She sold them off. To the horror of those who thought a female leader would be more pacific than a man, she led Britain into battle after Argentina invaded the Falkland Islands in 1982.

The new harder-working, more competitive Britain was also a polarised Britain, with a new trench dug between the people who prospered from the Thatcher years and the many others who found themselves not only jobless but jobless in a harsher environment.

Despite her lack of popularity with the majority of the population, by 1988 Thatcher was the longest-serving British prime minister of the 20th century. Her repeated electoral victories were aided by the Labour Party's dark days of destructive internal struggles.

England into the 21st Century

The unpopular flat-rate poll tax reached even her own party's limits of tolerance, and in 1990 Thatcher was dumped by her party in favour of the bland John Major. Unfortunately for the Labour Party, the immense reserves of suspicion they had managed to bank up were enough to see Major

win the 1992 election. But the end came with a vengeance in 1997 when New Labour, under leader Tony Blair, rocketed to power with a record parliamentary majority of more than 170 seats.

In its early days the government disappointed many old Labour stalwarts by keeping a tight reign on public spending. Voters, hoping for immediate improvements in the creaking health and transportation sectors, which the Tories had allowed to run down, were disappointed by a lack of progress. The Blair government also had a series of damaging miscues of which the most comic and embarrassing was their attempt to stage manage the election for London's mayor, which backfired horribly. It also faced continuing widespread hostility to all things European, especially the euro, the much derided single currency of the EU. The government was also rocked by spontaneous public action against high fuel prices, which almost brought the country to a halt in the autumn of 2000. Earlier, the Blair government opened up the taps on public expenditure, with billions promised for health, transportation and education. At the time of writing, talk is turning to the next election in 2001. It remains to be seen if voters think the promised improvements are too little too late.

However, Tony Blair can take some comfort from the fact that the leader of the Conservative opposition is William Hague, a little-loved leader who attempts to soften his staid image by wearing an American-style baseball cap. It doesn't work.

One major accomplishment of the Blair government has long-term and yet uncertain ramifications for the role of England in Britain. Constitutional reform and devolution have given much greater autonomy to Scotland and Wales. This, more than anything, again brought out the question of whether the English think of themselves as British or English first. With Scotland and Wales enjoying their own elected assemblies, some English are beginning to ask why England's interests should still be only represented within the greater British government. For his part, Hague has further

Camping it up for the Notting Hill Carnival

National Birds of Prey Centre, Gloucestershire

Re-enacting the Civil War in Oxford

Seeing and being seen at Royal Ascot

OLIVIER CIRENDINI

Plentiful provisions in Rye, Kent

JON DAVISON

Effigy to St Michael, Oxford

ANDREW LUBRAN

Seaside merry-go-round on Brighton beach

DENNIS JOHNSON

Picture this: souvenirs of elegant Bath

muddied the English versus British debate by championing an image of Britain that is most in tune with the most traditionally minded English.

After a good showing by the British Olympic team at the Sydney 2000 games, the majority of English people still seem happiest displaying the Union Jack rather than the Cross of St George, the traditional flag of England showing a red cross on a white background. What's certain is that questions of England's role in Britain and what makes one British or English are likely to become more prominent in the coming years.

GEOGRAPHY

Covering 50,085 sq miles, England is the largest of the three political divisions within the island of Great Britain. Bound by Scotland to the north and Wales to the west, England is no more than 20 miles (32km) from France across the narrowest part of the English Channel and now that the Channel Tunnel has been completed, it's no longer completely cut off from mainland Europe.

Much of England is flat or low-lying. The highest point (Scafell Pike in Cumbria) is only 978m above sea level; Scotland and Wales have more mountains and higher peaks.

England can be divided into a number of distinct geographical areas. In the north of the country a ridge of limestone hills and valleys, known as the Pennines, stretches from Derbyshire to the border with Scotland 250 miles (403km) north. To the west are the Cumbrian Mountains and the Lake District, probably the best known of England's national parks.

South of the Pennines is the heavily populated central area known as the Midlands, the industrial heartland since the 19th century. At its centre is Birmingham, Britain's second-largest city after London. The Black Country stretches from north of Birmingham through Staffordshire to Wolverhampton.

The south-west peninsula, known as the West Country and including Cornwall, Devon, Dorset and parts of Somerset, is a plateau with granite outcrops and a rugged coastline. High rainfall and rich pastures provide good dairy farming – Devon cream is world-famous. The numerous sheltered coves and beaches, and the mild climate, make the West Country a favourite holiday destination for the British. The wild grass-covered moors of Dartmoor and Exmoor are popular with walkers.

The rest of the country is lowlands; a mixture of farmland, low hills, an industrial belt and densely populated cities, including the capital. The eastern part of this region, including Lincolnshire and East Anglia (Norfolk, Suffolk and Cambridgeshire), is almost entirely flat and at sea level. The Fens are the rich agricultural lands, once underwater but drained in the 18th century, that extend from Lincoln to Cambridge.

London is in the south-east of the country, on the River Thames. Farther south are hills of chalk known as downs. The North Downs stretch from south of London to Dover where the chalk is exposed as the famous white cliffs. The South Downs run across Sussex, parallel to the south coast.

CLIMATE

Climatologists classify England's climate as temperate maritime – read mild and damp.

Despite the country being fairly far north, temperatures in England are moderated by light winds that blow in from seas warmed by the Gulf Stream. In winter, when the sea is warmer than the land, this stops temperatures inland falling very far below 0°C. In summer, when the sea is cooler than the land, it keeps summer temperatures from rising much above 30°C. The average high in London from June to August is 21°C; the average low is 12°C.

Variations in the weather across England are not as great as across Britain. It tends to be colder in the North but not as cold as in Scotland. London, the South-East and the West Country are the warmest regions.

Rainfall is greatest in hilly areas (the Lake District and the Pennines) and in the West Country. Some of these areas can get

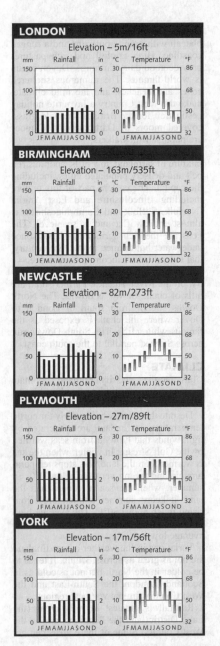

up to 4500mm of rain per year. The eastern side of England gets the lowest amount of rain in the whole of the UK. Some parts of Essex and Kent have recorded an annual rainfall of less than 600mm.

You can, however, expect some cloudy weather and rain anywhere in England at any time. An umbrella or raincoat is recommended. Once you've seen the blue skies suddenly cloud over and a gloomy day-long downpour begin, you'll understand why London, Manchester and other English cities have so many charter flights to Ibiza, Tenerife and other hot spots.

ECOLOGY & ENVIRONMENT

In a place as small as England, with its long history of human occupation, it's hardly surprising that the way the countryside looks today is largely the result of human interaction with the environment. As the population has grown, so too have the demands made upon the land to yield more food, firewood and building materials. This has led to the extinction of unknown numbers of plant and animal species.

Since WWII the pattern of land use in England has changed dramatically, which has had a similarly dramatic effect on wildlife. Modern farming methods have changed the lie of the land in some places from a cosy patchwork of small fields separated by thick hedgerows to vast open cultivated areas. As well as protecting fields from erosion, hedgerows provide habitat for wildlife and shelter for other plant species. Tens of thousands of miles of hedgerows have been destroyed and their destruction continues – since 1984 over 25% of hedgerows have disappeared.

The general reduction in England's biodiversity over the last 50 years has numerous other causes, including the increased use of pesticides, blanket planting of conifers in areas such as the North York Moors National Park (see Flora later in the chapter) and huge road-building schemes. For many years government policy favoured road over rail, allocating billions of pounds a year to new roads and encouraging private car ownership. Vehicle numbers have nearly quadrupled over the last 30 years. The problem is so bad that pressure groups have been established, dedicated to preventing new road construction and to stopping cars using existing roads.

Tourism is also taking a terrible toll on the environment. Eight million day-trippers per year flock to the New Forest in Hampshire, eroding the soil, churning up meadows and generally disturbing the wildlife. Most come by car. It's a similar story in parts of the Lake District and the Peak District, England's most visited national park. Slowly the authorities are realising that better public transport will have to be provided if these problems are to be resolved.

Despite all this bad news, large tracts of the country are also protected as nature reserves, national parks and Sites of Special Scientific Interest (SSSIs) where development is restricted.

England also has hundreds of wildlife and environmental groups. For more information try Greenpeace (☎ 020-7865 8100, fax 7865 8200, e info@uk.greenpeace .org), Canonbury Villas, London N1 2PN, or visit their Web site at www.greenpeace .org.uk.

Friends of the Earth (☎ 020-7490 1555, fax 7490 0881), 26–28 Underwood St, London N1 7JQ, is another good source for information and contacts. Its Web site is at www.foe.co.uk.

To find out more about the problems posed by tourism, contact Tourism Concern (☎ 020-7753 3330, fax 7753 3331), Stapleton House, 277–281 Holloway Rd, London N7 8HN, or visit online at www .tourismconcern.org.uk.

Pollution

The UK has been a perennial loser on the EU's list of countries with polluted beaches (finishing 13th out of the 15 EU nations in the annual survey released in 2000). Most of the UK's polluted beaches are in England – the EU singled out 15 in Cornwall and Devon for failing to meet minimum standards. The popular beach resort of Blackpool was on the list as well. Many of England's

problems stem from the long practice of dumping raw sewage into the ocean. This practice – more commonly associated with the developing world – has been widespread in England. Only in recent years have major efforts been made to stop it.

More sinister than sewage (if you can imagine that!) is the waste water discharged into the Irish Sea from the nuclear fuel plant at Sellafield, on the Cumbrian coast near the Lake District. Run by British Nuclear Fuels Ltd (BNFL), a government-owned company, the complex takes nuclear fuel used by other nuclear power plants in Britain and elsewhere and reprocesses it into new fuel that can be used again. As part of the process it uses over a million gallons of water each day. This water, which becomes slightly radioactive, is then dumped back into the Irish Sea. Needless to say, the Irish aren't happy about this and have called for the plant's immediate closure. However, the British government, mindful of the huge fortune of public money that has been invested at Sellafield, will only commit to reducing the radioactivity of the discharged water to 'near to zero' by 2020.

Other problems have involved radioactive discharges into the air, and in one incident it was found that pigeons roosting in abandoned but still radioactive buildings had spread radioactive contamination throughout village playgrounds where people fed them.

Elsewhere in England there are many concerns over the large number of ageing nuclear power plants, some of which have been operating for 10 or more years past their original design life.

FLORA & FAUNA
Flora
England was once almost entirely covered with woodland, but gradually tree coverage fell until it was the lowest for any European country except Ireland. As long ago as 1919 the Forestry Commission drew up a long-term plan to plant two million hectares of trees by the year 2000, a target already achieved by the early 1980s as a result of substantial grants to landowners. The trees

JANE SMITH

A prickly customer: hedgehogs are among England's most popular wildlife.

planted, unfortunately, were mainly fast-growing conifers instead of indigenous broadleaves. Very little can grow beneath conifers and large areas of ancient peatland were destroyed to create the plantations. These problems have now been recognised and more broadleaf woods are being planted. An ambitious program to create forests on the perimeter of big cities is also well under way.

Apart from the vast stands of conifers (mainly in the north of England), other trees common in England include the oak, chestnut, lime (not the citrus variety), ash and beech.

Despite the continued destruction of plant habitat, there's still a wide variety of wildflowers, particularly in spring. Small white snowdrops are the first to flower, sometimes as early as February. Around Easter (late March or early April), parks around the country are bright with daffodils. In woodlands there are purple carpets of bluebells, and yellow primroses, buttercups and cowslips are common in meadows. Tall purple foxgloves flower from June to September. In summer, cultivated fields may be edged with red poppies.

Gorse bushes, with small yellow flowers and a mass of sharp spines instead of leaves, flourish on heaths and other rough sandy places. Found in the same habitat, broom is similar but lacks the prickles. Fern-like bracken is also common.

The moors nurture several varieties of flowering heathers, bracken and whortleberries (aka bilberries) growing on small shrubs. These tiny blue-black berries are good to eat when they ripen in the summer.

A classic plant identification book is *The Concise British Flora in Colour*, with 1486 beautifully accurate paintings of different species by artist-vicar William Keble Martin.

Fauna

There are over 100 protected animal species in Britain but the once common beaver, wolf and reindeer are now extinct.

The red deer is England's largest mammal, with herds found on Exmoor and Dartmoor and in the Lake District. Fallow deer, introduced long ago by the Romans, live in small herds of 20 or so and can still be seen in the New Forest and Epping Forest. Roe deer are smaller, about the size of a large goat, and are quite common in forest areas where they do considerable damage to young trees. Other species that have been introduced include the Asian muntjac and the Chinese water deer. As England's forest cover is spreading the number of deer is increasing.

There are large numbers of foxes, especially in urban areas – they can even be found prowling in the alleys of London. Although nocturnal, the fox can often be seen before dark scavenging around rubbish bins. Badgers are much more shy and they only come out at night, although their setts (burrows) may be seen in woods. Another animal that you're more likely to see as a roadside casualty is the equally nocturnal hedgehog.

The grey squirrel, introduced from North America, is very common and has almost entirely replaced the smaller red squirrel. Having escaped – or been released by animal rights protesters – from fur farms, the foreign mink is also prospering. Otter numbers are rising as England's rivers are cleaned up and recently they have been spotted on the outskirts of several big cities. Once very rare, the pine marten is again being seen in some forested regions. Stoats and weasels are rarely encountered.

Rabbits are extremely common but the brown hare, with longer legs and ears, is less so. Small species of rodent include the brown rat (originally from Asia), the tiny shrew and harvest mouse (once common in hedgerows) and the water vole (water rat). At dusk, bats sometimes put in an appearance in rural areas.

Two species of seal – the grey seal and the common seal (which is actually less common than the grey) – frequent the English coast.

England's only venomous snake is the adder (aka the viper), which inhabits dry and ferny places on heaths and moors; numbers had fallen from hundreds of thousands to less than 20,000 before it was added to the list of protected species. Other reptiles include the harmless grass snake, the slow-worm, the common lizard and amphibians such as frogs, toads and newts.

Among England's various fish species, the salmon and brown trout are best known.

Birds

Bird-watching is a popular pastime in England – the mild climate and varied landscape support a wide variety of species.

While coastal bird species seem to be doing well, the same can't be said for inland species. Several species that were quite common only 30 years ago are rapidly dwindling as their habitats are destroyed. Endangered species now include the corn bunting, grey partridge, yellow wagtail, turtle dove, bullfinch, song thrush and lapwing. Some, such as the tree sparrow, are down 87% since 1970. Although the reason for the decline of traditional English species is still heavily debated, it is generally thought that pesticides, herbicides and a loss of crop diversity have all played a roll. On the other hand, goldfinches, swallows, nuthatches and greater spotted woodpeckers are making a comeback.

England's back gardens harbour the sparrow, thrush, blackbird, blue tit and the easily recognisable red-breasted robin. Pigeons are so abundant that they're now considered a pest, particularly in cities (London has embarked on a campaign to rid Trafalgar Square of these 'rats with wings'). Crows are very common, as is the black and white magpie, a member of the crow family.

Skylarks are becoming less common each year but you can still hear them twittering high above open ground. The once-common tawny owl recently joined them on the list of endangered birds.

Lakes and inland waterways support all sorts of bird life. The mute swan is England's biggest bird. All swans, except for two groups on the River Thames, are said to belong to the monarch. A fair number of the birds have died from lead poisoning after swallowing discarded fishing weights.

The aggressive Canada goose, introduced 300 years ago, has bred so successfully that it's now seen as a menace: large numbers of them can strip fields of crops, and that's not to mention their droppings.

Of the several species of duck, the mallard is most common. The male, with its green head and narrow white collar, is easily recognisable.

The pheasant was introduced from Russia over 900 years ago and, while originally reared on large estates for shooting, it now also breeds in the wild. Other game birds include the partridge and grouse.

Raptors are now rare. There are a few heavily protected golden eagles in the Lake District. Kestrels and sparrowhawks are sometimes seen hunting near motorways.

Around the coast are large populations of seagulls, terns, cormorants, gannets, shags, razorbills and guillemots. The tiny, comical puffin, with its clumsy red-and-yellow bill, is a member of the auk family. It comes to land only to breed, which it does in numerous colonies across the length of the British Isles from the Isle of Wight to the Shetland Islands.

Twitchers (or bird-watchers) should contact the Royal Society for the Protection of Birds (RSPB; ☎ 01767-680551), The Lodge, Sandy, Bedfordshire SG19 2BR, which runs over 100 reserves. It has a Web site at www.rspb.org.uk.

Membership of the Wildfowl and Wetlands Trust (☎ 01453-891900, e membership@wwt.org.uk), Slimbridge, Gloucestershire GL2 7BT, gives free entry to its reserves. Its Web site is at www.wwt.org.uk.

Bird-watching is so popular in England that bookshop shelves groan under the load of ornithological reference books.

National Parks

England's national parks – Dartmoor, Exmoor, the Lake District, the Peak District, the Yorkshire Dales, the North York Moors, Northumberland and the Broads – together with the New Forest, cover about 7% of the country.

But, unlike national parks in some other countries, England's are not wilderness areas where humans have been excluded. Nor are they owned by the nation; most of the land within the national parks is privately owned or belongs to charitable trusts such as the National Trust (NT; see Useful Organisations in the Facts for the Visitor chapter). However, they do include places of outstanding natural beauty that have been given special protection through a 1949 act of parliament.

National park status doesn't guarantee visitors any special rights of access. It means that development is controlled through planning committees and that information centres and recreational facilities are provided for visitors.

For more details, contact the Association of National Park Authorities (☎ 01647-440245, fax 440187), Ponsford House, Moretonhampstead, Devon TQ13 8NL, or visit its Web site at www.anpa.gov.uk.

GOVERNMENT & POLITICS

At present the United Kingdom doesn't have a written constitution but operates under a mixture of parliamentary statutes, common law (a body of legal principles based on precedents dating back to Anglo-Saxon customs) and convention.

The monarch is the titular head of State, but the current Queen is purely a figurehead who acts almost entirely on the advice of 'her' ministers and parliament.

Parliament is made up of three separate elements – the Queen, the House of Lords and the House of Commons. In practice, the supreme body is the House of Commons, which is the only one to be directly elected

every five years. An earlier election can be called at the request of the party in power or if the party in power loses a vote of confidence.

Voting is not compulsory and candidates are elected if they win a simple majority in their constituencies (a committee is currently considering whether Britain should change to some form of proportional representation). There are 659 constituencies (seats) – 529 for England, 40 for Wales, 72 for Scotland and 18 for Northern Ireland.

The House of Lords consists of the 25 senior archbishops and bishops of the Church of England; 573 life peers (whose peerages cannot be passed on to the next generation); and 92 hereditary peers (whose titles are passed on from one generation to the next). The 12 law lords act as the highest court in the country. In 1999 over 1000 hereditary peers were tossed out of the House of Lords in the first stage of reform; as a compromise move, 92 were allowed to remain, having been selected by the entire House of Lords before most members left for good.

Exactly what form the next stage of reform will take is unclear. There is general support to make the House of Lords some sort of directly elected body. At present it remains a deeply undemocratic body with few powers beyond the ability to hold up and amend legislation.

The prime minister is the leader of the majority party in the House of Commons and is technically appointed by the Queen. All other ministers are appointed on the recommendation of the prime minister, most of them coming from the House of Commons. Ministers are responsible for government departments. The senior 20 or so ministers make up the Cabinet, which, although answerable to parliament, meets confidentially and in effect manages the government and its policies.

For the last 150 years a predominantly two-party system has operated. Since 1945 either the Conservative Party (also known as the Tory party) or the Labour Party has held power. The Conservatives draw support mainly from the countryside and suburbia, Labour from urban industrialised areas, Scotland and Wales.

Traditionally, the Conservatives were regarded as right-wing, free-enterprise supporters, while Labour was left-wing in the social-democratic tradition. However, in the 1990s Labour shed much of its socialist credo and accepted many of the arguments of the free-marketers. The New Labour government that was elected in 1997 has proven to be quite centrist. It's adopted many of the market reforms long favoured by moderate conservatives.

Since 1972 Britain has been a member of the EU, albeit rather grudgingly. The result is that some British legislation now originates in Brussels rather than London. In general British governments have resisted moves towards closer integration with Europe. The current Labour government has promised a referendum before Britain will start using the single European currency (the euro). However, this is emerging as the most contentious issue in modern British politics, with the Tories engaging in all sorts of euro-scare tactics in the hope of saving the pound and winning votes. Industry and business is solidly for the euro as sticking with the strong pound makes British products uneconomic to customers in euro-priced Europe. Not working in the euro's favour, however, has been its poor showing on the world exchange markets.

ECONOMY

Britain dominated 19th-century world trade, but when the 20th century dawned decline was already under way. It had been the pioneering influence in many of the 19th century's leading engineering fields, from railways to ocean liners, but it didn't enjoy the same dominant role when it came to 20th-century developments such as automobiles and aircraft. Following WWII, much of industry was nationalised as initially railways, gas and electricity services, coal mines, steel manufacturing and shipbuilding, and later even cars, came under government control. But, if anything, public ownership only accelerated the decline until the worldwide upheavals in manufacturing

in the 1970s and 1980s turned gradual fall into a precipitous drop.

Meanwhile, many traditional industries, such as mining and engineering, simply disappeared and only North Sea oil shielded Britain from a disastrous economic crash.

For better or worse Margaret Thatcher waged a relentless assault on the power of the trade unions and the old-school-tie brigade with their ossified work and business practices. The result was huge change and social upheaval and by 1992 Britain's economy was in such poor shape that the government was forced to withdraw from the European Exchange Rate Mechanism. Politically this was a disaster, but economically it marked a turning point; exchange rates fell and exporters found business looking up again as a result of a devalued pound.

The Labour government had the good fortune to come to power at a time when the British economy was gaining strength and showing solid, long-term growth. Early in 2000 it was announced that the number of unemployed had fallen below one million for the first time since the boom years of 1975. Although the figure is debatable and many jobs are part-time, it still points to what in many places has become a job-seeker's market. Along the M4 motorway west from London, there are towns with less than 1% unemployment. High-tech and service jobs account for much of the growth.

In the Midlands and north of England there are still pockets of economic depression, especially in places that never recovered from the collapse of heavy industry in the 1980s. Many fear that the North will continue to stagnate while the South-East continues to grow.

POPULATION & PEOPLE

Britain has a population of around 60 million, or around 625 inhabitants per sq mile, making the island one of the most crowded on the planet. Most of the population is concentrated in England (which has a population of 51 million), in and around London, and in the central part of the country around Birmingham, Manchester, Liverpool, Leeds,

Sheffield and Nottingham. To these figures you can factor in an annual influx of over 25 million tourists.

The English (or Anglo-Saxons as they are sometimes called) are a diverse bunch, as one would expect given the variety of peoples who have made this island their home. But in general they are predominantly Germanic in origin.

Particularly since the Industrial Revolution, England has attracted large numbers of people from Scotland, Wales and Ireland. Since WWII there has also been significant immigration from many ex-colonies, especially the Caribbean, Pakistan and India.

In the 18th, 19th and 20th centuries there were also significant influxes of refugees, most recently from troubled corners of the globe such as the Balkans and Africa.

Outside London and the big Midlands cities, however, the population is overwhelmingly Anglo-Saxon, although the immigrant influence can be felt in the Chinese and Indian restaurants that can be found in even the smallest of towns. Recently population growth has been virtually static, even negative, and emigrants have often outnumbered immigrants.

EDUCATION

Schooling is compulsory for those aged between 5 and 16, and an increasing number of young people stay on at school (or further education college) until they're 18. Education for those aged up to 18 is free. The number of people going on to university (and the number of universities) has also been growing, putting such pressure on funding that the government now expects students to pay their own tuition fees and living expenses by taking out loans.

Despite what should sound a fairly rosy scenario, there's a widely held perception that education standards have been falling, with hotly disputed figures suggesting a rise in the number of people leaving 11 years of compulsory schooling unable to read or write properly. Along with the euro, the National Health Service and transport, education remains at the top of the English political agenda.

ARTS

The greatest artistic contributions of the English have been in literature, theatre, popular music and architecture. Although there are notable exceptions, there's not an equivalent tradition of great painters, sculptors or classical composers.

Perhaps the most distinctive phenomenon is the huge number of extraordinary country houses. The elite of a mighty empire, the aristocrats of the 18th and 19th centuries surrounded themselves with treasures in the most beautiful houses and gardens of Europe.

Fortunately, although their successors have often inherited their arrogance, inheritance taxes have forced many to open their houses and priceless art collections to the public. England is a treasure trove of masterpieces from every age and continent. The architectural heritage is superb but, with a few exceptions, the 20th century failed to add anything more inspiring than motorways, high-rise housing estates and tawdry suburban development.

English publishers churn out close to 100,000 new titles a year, and the range and quality of theatre, music, dance and art is outstanding.

Literature

Anyone who has studied English literature will find that the landscapes and people they have read about can still be found to some extent. Travelling in the footsteps of the great English writers, and their characters, can be one of the highlights of visiting England. A wealth of books capture a moment in time, a landscape or a group of people. This guide can only make a few suggestions as to where to start.

Literature classes usually begin with *Beowulf*, the epic Anglo-Saxon poem written between the 7th and 8th centuries. A new verse translation, by Seamus Heaney, the Irish Nobel Prize winner, of the struggle between the heroic Scandinavian king and the monster Grendel was published in 2000.

After the Normans took over in 1066, English prose was usually in French. Although English was again the language of choice by the 14th century, the cross-channel influence remained. As a language English became much more flexible and words from other languages, such as French and Latin, were freely used and adapted.

Geoffrey Chaucer's *Canterbury Tales* (modern translation by Neville Coghill), written in the 14th century, is an early classic and the forerunner of travel tales ever since. This book may have launched a thousand boring lectures but in its natural environment it gives a vivid insight into medieval society, in particular into the lives of pilgrims on their way to Canterbury.

The mythical exploits of King Arthur have been the basis for stories and prose for centuries. In 1469 Thomas Malory tied them together with *The Death of Arthur*, which featured not only Arthur but those other stalwarts of medieval drama: Galahad, Lancelot, Guinevere and the Holy Grail. The stories are highly moralistic and promote self-sacrifice for the greater good and religious salvation.

The 16th century marked the beginning of a good period for English literature. Thomas More did his best to thumb his nose at the follies of monarchs with his writings. His *Utopia* (1516) is a satirical look at a mythological place where the kings and queens wisely listened to the sound advice of philosophers such as himself. More's humanism certainly helped him get his name plastered on the side of scores of secondary schools in recent centuries.

Mention English literature and no figure stands taller than William Shakespeare. Many visitors will be tempted to retrace his steps – to Stratford-upon-Avon where he lived and to the re-created Globe Theatre in London near the site where his works were originally dramatised. Unlike some of the other writers of the era, whose works have been buried under a million tedious lectures, Shakespeare's brilliant plots and sharp prose have turned him into an icon. Most of his works were written from 1600 to 1615 and include *Hamlet*, *Macbeth* and *King Lear*. His popular touch – he was trying to make a living from this stuff after all – survives and many a writer regularly dips

into a Shakespeare plot for his or her work today.

Very different to Shakespeare, John Milton is another victim of dull-witted lectures. His situation is not helped by his moralistic humanism, which was drawn directly from Christian and biblical teachings. *Paradise Lost* (1667) is his epic poem tracing the role of Satan in the downfall of Adam and Eve. Milton's works are studied as much for their splendid use of language and brilliant thought as they are for their insights into the era of Puritan thinking.

Society was satirised by John Dryden, who set the standard with works that include *Mac Flecknoe* (1682). Alexander Pope continued the tradition with the *Rape of the Lock* (1712), which took the accidental snipping of a lady's hair as the basis for a skewering of contemporary society. A Renaissance-man in his own right, Pope made a fortune from his translation of the *Iliad* and his annotations of Shakespeare's works.

Jonathan Swift's *Gulliver's Travels* (1726) is often mistaken for a children's work with its early chapters devoted to the diminutive yet plucky Lilliputians. But the real heart of the book lies in the later sections when Gulliver finds himself among the Yahoos. Helped along by a fair dose of bestiality, Swift leaves few societal notions unscathed.

The most vivid insight into 17th-century London life comes courtesy of Samuel Pepys' diary, which contains a complete account of the plague and the Great Fire of London. It was but one of the earliest examples of what has become the brilliant English tradition of historical works. Edward Gibbon's six-volume *History of the Rise and Fall of the Roman Empire* (1776–88) is renowned for its scholarship and was a staple of the hand-luggage of generations of travellers facing a long sea voyage.

The popular English novel, as we know it, only appeared in the 18th century with the growth of a literate middle class. Samuel Richardson and Henry Fielding popularised the form with respective works

Clarissa and *Tom Jones*.

If you plan to spend time in the Midlands, read Elizabeth Gaskell's *Mary Barton*, which paints a sympathetic picture of the plight of workers during the Industrial Revolution. This was also the milieu about which Charles Dickens wrote most powerfully. *Hard Times*, set in fictional Coketown, paints a brutal picture of the capitalists who prospered in it. His realism was much in demand at a time when English society was undergoing radical change as part of the Industrial Revolution. Such issues were also the subjects for poets, including Alfred, Lord Tennyson.

In the early 19th century Jane Austen wrote about the prosperous, provincial middle class. The intrigues and passions boiling away under the stilted constraints of 'propriety' are beautifully portrayed in *Emma* and *Pride and Prejudice*. The Brontë sisters – Charlotte, *Jane Eyre*; Emily, *Wuthering Heights;* and Anne, *Tenant of Wildfell Hall* – set their moving and moody dramas in the Yorkshire Dales.

If you visit the Lake District, you'll find constant references to William Wordsworth, the romantic poet who lived there for the first half of the 19th century. Modern readers may find him difficult, but at his best he has an exhilarating appreciation of the natural world.

More than most writers, Thomas Hardy relied on a sense of place and on the relationship between place and people. His best work provides an evocative picture of Wessex, the region of England centred on Dorchester (Dorset), where he lived. *Tess of the d'Urbervilles* is one of his greatest novels.

Moving into the 20th century, the pace of English writing only increased. DH Lawrence chronicled life in the Nottinghamshire coal-mining towns in the brilliant *Sons and Lovers*. Other writers looked to exotic places abroad for their inspiration. Rudyard Kipling set *The Jungle Book* in the vast reaches of the Empire and EM Forster made a case for the hopeless future of British rule in India with *A Passage to India*.

Written during the 1930s Depression,

George Orwell's *Down and Out in Paris and London* describes the author's destitute existence as a temporary vagrant. Some travellers today may find they can still identify with him. At about the same time, Graham Greene wrote of the seedy side of Brighton in *Brighton Rock* and found no end of inspiration among the exploits of the English in their worldwide ventures.

The English tradition of satire was notably added to in the mid-20th century by Evelyn Waugh with his hilarious *Scoop* and withering *Brideshead Revisited*, among other works. Orwell took on fascism and communism with *Animal Farm* and *1984*.

Doris Lessing painted a picture of 1960s London in *The Four-Gated City*, part of her 'Children of Violence' series. Iris Murdoch combined English eccentrics with sly commentary on modern life in *An Accidental Man*. Julian Barnes deconstructed English suburbia in *Metroland*.

One of the funniest and most vicious portrayals of Britain in the 1990s was by Martin Amis in *London Observed*, a collection of stories set in the capital. In other interesting perspectives, Hanif Kureishi writes about the lives of young Pakistanis in London in *The Black Album*, and Caryl Phillips describes the Caribbean immigrants' experience in *The Final Passage.*

High Fidelity, by Nick Hornby, the story of a record-shop owner in Holloway, North London, has made many a reader's top ten list. Ted Hughes, poet laureate until his death in 1999, had one of the best-selling books of poetry ever with *Birthday Letters*, the first time he had written about his wife Sylvia Plath, who committed suicide in 1963.

Japanese-born Kazuo Ishiguro came to England aged five. His acclaimed *The Remains of the Day* follows the reminiscences of an elderly English butler. Mathew Kneale continues the proud tradition of following the English abroad with *English Passengers*.

Topping one bestseller list after another, JK Rowling's Harry Potter series of books about the exploits of a young wizard are popular with readers of all ages. She's a worthy successor to the English tradition of children's writers that includes AA Milne, whose *Winnie the Pooh* prowls Ashdown Forest in Sussex, and Beatrix Potter, whose *Peter Rabbit* hops about the Lake District. Another classic author was Roald Dahl, whose *Charlie and the Chocolate Factory* gripped many a child's imagination.

Theatre

London is still one of the world's theatre capitals, with a historical legacy stretching back to Shakespeare and medieval times.

It is the best city in the world for live theatre, bar none. For too many tourists, a night at the theatre will involve such pap as Agatha Christie's *Mousetrap*, now in its fifth decade and the longest running play in history, or Andrew Lloyd Webber's *Cats*, now into a second decade. The average issue of *Time Out* (London's listings magazine) has more than 100 different shows being staged. Some are the mass-audience musicals and feel-good fare of Lord Lloyd Webber and others; others will simply be great West End drama such as the long-running *An Inspector Calls;* but many more will be innovative and interesting performances in smaller theatres all over the capital. There are many good regional theatres as well; see the listings for details.

There is no 'Golden Age' of English theatre. Rather, the art of English drama has been one of development and evolution. Although it's easy – and usually correct – to deride the undemanding crowd-pleasers found in many West End theatres, it's also easy to forget that before the age of TV many of these theatres staged nothing but the lightest of comedies, which would appeal to the masses. The coming of TV took away the mass audience and forced the theatres to look for more interesting work that could be differentiated from both TV and the movies. These forms of mass entertainment also had another unexpected benefit for London's theatre: they worked as a form of welfare for many veteran stage performers. One role in a Hollywood movie or TV show could bring in more money than a year's worth of performances on the stage.

But in the early days of English theatre, a good performance usually meant that the actors might actually have something to eat or somewhere to sleep. Wandering troupes of actors were the norm of medieval theatre. And although the plots of the simple plays presented had their roots in the Bible or Greek classics, it was common for liberties to be taken in the interest of amusing the audiences in market towns, who weren't known for their high-brow tastes. A common ploy was to joke up the birth of Christ by filling the shepherd ranks with rogues.

The growth of cities led to the emergence of an urban class – people who weren't tied to labour in the fields had more leisure time. It also ensured a mass of people from which to draw an audience. London's first permanent theatre was built by James Burbage in 1576, and his son Richard gained fame as a leading actor in Shakespeare's plays. Shakespeare himself worked in a milieu not far removed from that of the theatre today. He juggled the demands of a fickle public with the commercial demands of theatre owners whose venues included the Globe and the Rose.

During this, the Elizabethan Age, actors were exclusively men who worked under the sponsorship of a noble patron. Men without masters were officially designated 'Rogues and Vagabonds'. All parts – male and female – were played by males.

After Charles II returned to England in 1660, he encouraged the adoption of theatrical practices he had seen on the Continent. Most significant was the use of women to play women. This innovation took London audiences by storm and was matched by contemporary material by the likes of Congreve and Vanbrugh. The former's *Way of the World* was a gossipy intrigue that was a huge hit.

Theatres were built throughout the larger cities of England through the 18th century. The technical innovation of gas-lighting at London's Drury Lane and Covent Garden theatres in 1820 had a huge impact. Until then drama had either been performed in naturally lit theatres during the day or by the wavering dim light of candles at night.

Although gas didn't stop theatres from regularly burning down, its intensity could be controlled, which meant that for the first time the lighting of a play assumed a dramatic role in the staging of the production.

The Development of Modern Theatre

The latter part of the 19th century saw the rise in England of actor-managers, who became leading lights in their own theatres. George Alexander and Charles Wyndham were powerful examples of this breed. They had their own followings and could demand the best co-stars, writers, musicians and other support staff. Works ranged from crowd-pleasing musicals to serious works such as Oscar Wilde's *The Importance of Being Earnest*.

Serious drama was marked in the early part of the 20th century by new stagings of Shakespeare that eschewed elaborate staging for a purity of the words. London audiences were treated to works from abroad by the likes of Anton Chekhov and Eugene O'Neill. Most popular, however, were comedies about contemporary society by writers such as Somerset Maugham and Noel Coward.

In the 1950s Sir Laurence Olivier, Sir John Gielgud, Dame Peggy Ashcroft and others were at their professional peak in the West End. They brought force and energy to classic productions of Shakespeare's works, among others. A wave of young actors in the 1960s, such as Peter O'Toole and Albert Finney, brought a gritty realism to productions that addressed the issues of the day.

During the 1970s, scores of theatres began operating away from the West End and while they tended to come and go with great rapidity, these small theatres often produced compelling work and served as a breeding ground for new talent. Cut-backs in government funding in the late 1970s caused many marginal operations to close while others had to scramble about for corporate sponsorship.

Fuelling the English interest in theatre has been the phenomenal popularity of amateur theatre groups – some 17,000 are thought to exist. While some embody the very meaning of the word amateur, others

stage productions that rival the best of the pros. Professional regional theatre has a long and proud tradition but, after the lean years of funding during the 1980s and 1990s, many excellent theatres are on life support. If the government delivers on the promises for greatly increased cultural funding that were announced in 2000, it won't be a moment too soon.

In London, the National Theatre is the nation's flagship theatre and offers a cocktail of revived classics, contemporary plays and appearances by radical young companies. The Barbican in London and three theatres in Stratford-upon-Avon are home to the excellent Royal Shakespeare Company (RSC). Most regional cities have at least one world-class company and the facilities to stage major touring productions.

London's many fringe theatre productions offer an invigorating selection of the amazing, the boring, the life-changing and the downright ridiculous. On any night of the year you should be able to watch performances of plays by great British dramatists such as Harold Pinter, John Osborne, Alan Ayckbourn, Alan Bennett, David Hare and Simon Gray. Careful perusal of the schedules in *Time Out* may also turn up opportunities to see actors of the calibre of Dame Judi Dench, Daniel Day-Lewis or Vanessa Redgrave strut their stuff.

American movie and TV stars are also treading the West End boards, from Kevin Spacey in *The Iceman Cometh* to George Wendt, Patrick Duffy and Richard Thomas in *Art* and Kathleen Turner and Jerry Hall playing a stripped-down Mrs Robinson in *The Graduate*. Perhaps they were inspired by a naked Nicole Kidman's 'theatrical viagra' in *The Blue Room*.

London stage-performers to strike it big in Hollywood include Kenneth Branagh and ex-wife Emma Thompson. Sam Mendes segued from success in the intimate Donmar Warehouse to the Oscar for best director for *American Beauty*.

Cinema

Film-makers are constantly whingeing that if only there was sufficient funding and support at home, then British directors and actors (such as Alan Rickman, Tim Roth, Emma Thompson and Mike Figgis) wouldn't have to move to Hollywood for work. Even film-makers who mostly work in the country aren't always assured of support. Mike Leigh, who won the 1996 Palme d'Or at the Cannes Film Festival for the outstanding *Secrets and Lies*, has made a number of compelling films about life in contemporary England that never found large audiences.

It's a pity because there is a wealth of talent and tradition associated with film in England. Hollywood has always known this and saw the British film industry as an important resource long before it lured Alfred Hitchcock across in the 1940s.

Hollywood became a symbiotic part of English cinema after WWII. Even such artistic triumphs as Carol Reed's *The Third Man* were made with a large amount of Hollywood cash. But this shouldn't be used to diminish the English contribution to the movies. Just consider those of David Niven, Richard Attenborough, David Lean, Elizabeth Taylor, Michael Caine and Alec Guinness to name but a very few. Furthermore the technical wizardry of English studios was essential for the production of science-fiction epics such as George Lucas' *Star Wars*.

The 1990s saw something of a renaissance for the commercial fortunes of English cinema, which was often dismissed as being able to churn out little more in the way of hits than the biannual Bond movie. With the help of TV cash from the likes of Channel Four and the BBC, films such as *Four Weddings and a Funeral* found audiences worldwide and brought in much-needed revenue. The hits that followed – *The Full Monty, Notting Hill, Lock, Stock and Two Smoking Barrels* and *Billy Elliot* – continued to win the English film industry wide respect. Even a primarily Hollywood movie such as *Shakespeare in Love* boasted a cast and crew who were largely English.

See Films in the Facts for the Visitor chapter for more details of films made in or about England.

Classical Music & Opera

London is arguably Europe's classical music capital, and most of the major companies undertake country-wide tours. There are five symphony orchestras, various smaller outfits, a wonderful array of venues, reasonable prices and high standards of performance. The biggest dilemma facing concert-goers is the enviable one of picking from the embarrassment of riches on offer.

Despite this, finding home-grown classical music to listen to can be a struggle. Before the 20th century, virtually the only truly major English composer was Henry Purcell (1659–95). But you should be able to track down concerts of music by local big names such as Edward Elgar, Ralph Vaughan Williams, Benjamin Britten or William Walton. John Tavener found a wider following after his music was played to a worldwide audience at the funeral of Diana, Princess of Wales.

London's flagship opera company, the Royal Opera, based in Covent Garden, seemed poised to leave its troubled past behind when its grand home reopened after a long and costly renovation. But all was not to be as backstage sniping and resignations again brought unwanted drama to the house. The Royal Opera House is also home to the Royal Ballet, foremost of the many acclaimed dance troupes in England.

Popular Music

For nearly 50 years English acts have been at the vanguard of innovation in music, proudly pushing back boundaries. And England remains a world leader – the music charts are an institution and being number one in the singles charts is still a big deal. The records that have been produced are remarkable as much for their diversity as their quality, and the record-buying public has eagerly embraced movements from all over the musical spectrum.

In the early 1960s, rhythm and blues, skiffle, folk and soul converged to form a new pop sound that pushed an obscure band called The Beatles into the spotlight. What followed owed much to their inventiveness and experimentation. Hot on their heels were a string of classic English acts such as The Kinks, The Rolling Stones and The Who. The unique Englishness of their music belied the international appeal that these acts had, which explains their continued popularity at home and abroad when many of their original fans are collecting their pensions.

Drink and drugs took their toll on the bands of the 1960s, but these excesses spawned the movements that followed them. Psychedelia and Progressive rock ruled the roost during the early 1970s with Genesis, Pink Floyd and Led Zeppelin taking the whole record-buying world on a trip that had begun with the Beatles' *Sergeant Pepper*. Their long guitar solos and ambling basslines gave the mid-1970s a bloated feel only broken by the dynamic David Bowie. Before long, the short sharp shock of punk rattled the cages of a complacent musical aristocracy.

Led by the Clash, the Buzzcocks and most of all the Sex Pistols, a whole new sound emerged that helped a new generation of teenagers to scare their parents. Growing into their shoes were New Wave acts, which merged punk's intensity with other influences including soul, dance and blues. The Stranglers, The Jam and Joy Division ushered out the cruder extremes of punk, and led the way for the early 1980s pop renaissance.

Spandau Ballet, Depeche Mode and Duran Duran provided a dandy dress sense, a camp sense of fun and a thumping electronic sound that was briefly the perfect soundtrack for England's moody industrial decline. As the decade wore on, bands seeking to convey a deeper message came to the fore. The Smiths' melancholy bedsit music launched a thousand quiffs, before their owners flattened them dancing to the bouncing, innovative beats of New Order and the Pet Shop Boys.

Somewhere down the line, however, someone took an acid tablet and everything went mad for a while. In the late 1980s and early 1990s the new Manchester scene produced fabulous albums by the Stone Roses, The La's and Happy Mondays. Elsewhere

acid house parties and illegal raves were fast becoming the order of the day. This anonymous, pumping dance music gave rise to both the house scene that spread from clubs in England to Ibiza and to more well known dance acts such as the Prodigy.

English music, forever reinventing itself, then turned the whole thing back on its head during the 1990s. After a period of looking forward, Oasis and Blur harked back to both the 1960s and the early 1980s with a sound that became known as Britpop – textbook guitar music that caught the public's imagination. Britpop merged with more commercial pop into the hybrid sound that ruled the roost at the end of the decade. Take That, the Spice Girls and their offspring, and numerous imitators such as Steps and Five were the stuff of popular legend. At the time of writing, a unique blend of dance, drum'n'bass and soulful rhythms known as UK Garage was setting the popular pace.

Visual Arts

William Hogarth (1697–1764) emancipated English art from European influences with a series of paintings and engravings satirising social abuses. The most famous of these is probably *A Rake's Progress*. The founding president of the Royal Academy of Arts, Joshua Reynolds (1723–92), and his rival Thomas Gainsborough (1727–88) raised the artist to a new level of dignity in England. The former did so through his prodigious output and influence on men of letters such as Dr Samuel Johnson and James Boswell, the latter through his individual genius and the patronage of the royal family.

The tradition of landscape painting, which started with Gainsborough, was continued by John Constable (1776–1837) and was the inspiration for a whole generation of French impressionists. Constable's contemporary romantics, JMW Turner (1775–1851) and William Blake (1757–1827), could not have been more different. Blake used personal symbolism to express a mystical philosophy in drawings, prints and poetry – he disliked oils and canvas. Turner, on the other hand, was equally at home with oils as he was with watercolours and he increasingly subordinated detail to the effects of light and colour. By the 1830s, with paintings such as *Snow Storm: Steamboat off a Harbour's Mouth*, his compositions seemed entirely abstract and were widely vilified.

John Everett Millais (*Christ in the House of His Parents*, 1850) and William Holman Hunt (*The Scapegoat*, 1854) attempted to recapture the simplicity of early Italian art. This gave way to the pseudo-medievalism of Dante Gabriel Rossetti (*Beata Beatrix*, 1864) and his followers William Morris (1834–96) and Edward Burne-Jones (*King Cophetua and the Beggar Maid*, 1862). Morris has had a lasting influence on the design of English furniture, stained-glass, tapestry and fabrics, and his emphasis on good workmanship has been the inspiration for generations of small, craft-based workshops in England.

In the 20th century the monumental sculptures of Henry Moore (1898–1986), the contorted, almost surreal, painting of Francis Bacon (1909–92), and David Hockney's stylish, highly representational paintings of friends, swimmers and dachshunds ensured the place of English art in the international arena.

Both Paul Nash (1889–1949), who was an official war artist in WWI and WWII, and Graham Sutherland (1903-80), an official artist in WWII, followed in the romantic and visionary tradition of Blake, Samuel Palmer and Turner. Nash introduced surrealism to English painting and incidentally wrote *The Shell Guide to Dorset* (1936). Sutherland is renowned for his paintings of ruined buildings. Another official war artist, Moore's drawings of people sheltering from air-raids in London's underground consolidated his reputation as one of the most influential English artists of all time.

Richard Hamilton's photomontage *Just what is it that makes today's homes so different, so appealing?* (1956) launched the pop art movement in England. Peter Blake designed the psychedelic cover of The Beatles' *Sergeant Pepper's Lonely Hearts Club Band* (1967) and heralded an explosion of British popular culture.

In the 1970s and 1980s conceptual and land artists, such as Richard Long, competed with performance artists, such as Gilbert and George. Through the Thatcher era the commercial galleries held sway until the 1990s when a number of prolific young artists working in a variety of media burst upon the scene: Rachel Whiteread's resin casts of commonplace objects, including an entire East End house, has earned her international acclaim; Damien Hirst's use of animals, both alive and dead, in his work has provoked much debate; Tracey Emin sewed the names of everyone she'd ever slept with inside a tent and then went on to and displayed her filth-covered bed; and the Chapman brothers' gross figures with misplaced genitals have attracted the attention of censors. Chris Ofili won the 1999 Turner prize with a painting of the Virgin Mary that included elephant dung among its components.

ARCHITECTURE

England's architectural heritage reaches back more than 5000 years to remarkable Stonehenge. Although the record is sometimes sparse, there are survivors from every period since.

Roman and Saxon work is rare, which is not so surprising considering the Roman heyday is nearly 2000 years old. Complete Norman buildings are also rare, but there are still many examples of 900-year-old craftsmanship in the many churches and cathedrals.

Buildings from the 16th and 17th centuries are more common, and more ordinary domestic architecture survives alongside the grand houses. Rural England is still home to a number of thatched cob cottages, many of which date from the 17th century.

Some of the styles that can be seen in churches also appeared in the castles. While church design focused more on decorative or imaginative elements, the design of castles was based largely around their military function. The benefits of living in a large utilitarian pile of stones, however, gradually vanished as times grew more peaceful.

From the 16th century, most of the great architectural innovations were made in houses. Often the English nobility adopted and adapted various European styles. Sometimes castles were completely abandoned or swallowed up by new, improved versions.

One of the most distinctive features of the English countryside and of English culture is the ongoing love affair between the rich and their enormous, and beautiful, country residences. No other country has a comparable number. Like churches, many have evolved over time and incorporate all sorts of architectural styles.

Monumental English architecture has always been outstanding and domestic vernacular architecture was certainly visually appealing up until the Industrial Revolution. Since then the guiding principle for new buildings has often been to spend as little money as possible – aesthetic considerations were for the wealthy few – and, post-WWII, much building has shown a lack of regard for the overall fabric of the cities. Prince Charles has been an outspoken advocate of a more humanistic and aesthetically sensitive architectural approach.

It's not all bad news though and some fine new buildings do make it past the drawing board, especially in London where the Lloyd's Building is a particularly stunning example.

Fortunately, there's also a strong campaign to protect the island's architectural heritage (thanks in particular to the National Trust and English Heritage). This nostalgic obsession is, however, sometimes carried to extremes and can encourage conservatism in modern architecture and design.

While distinct architectural styles and periods in England are certainly identifiable, the categories were not always rigid – different styles often influenced each other, and certain periods partially overlapped.

The standard works of reference on British architecture are the wonderfully detailed *Buildings of Britain* books by Nikolaus Pevsner. See also the Glossary of Religious Architecture later in the book.

Church Architecture

As buildings surviving from the Middle Ages, England's many fine medieval churches provide numerous examples of interesting and unique architecture, and attract a large number of curious visitors.

While this rich collection of churches is of great interest to history and architecture buffs, the terminology can be confusing to outsiders. You're invited to inspect ceilings in chancels, inscriptions in naves, misericords in choirs, monuments in chapels and tombs in transepts. Furthermore, the church might be Saxon or Norman, Early English or perpendicular, or more likely a combination of two or more of these styles. It may not even be a church after all, but an abbey, chapel, minster or cathedral. What does it all mean?

Basically no matter what the name, they're all places of Christian worship. Technically, a cathedral is the principal church of a diocese and contains the bishop's throne (a diocese is the district for which a bishop is responsible). In practice a cathedral is usually larger and grander than a church, although there are some large churches and some small cathedrals. In contrast, a church is usually a more local affair; the term 'parish church' indicates its local nature. Chapels are even smaller than churches, and are often the 'churches' of nonconformist groups such as Methodists or Baptists.

An abbey is where a group of monks or nuns live (or lived). The abbey church was a church intended principally for use by the monks or nuns, rather than the general population.

When Henry VIII dissolved the monasteries in the 1530s, many of the abbeys in England and Ireland were destroyed or converted into private homes, although some survived as churches. Thus there are abbey churches that were taken over by the general populace (such as Malmesbury Abbey in Wiltshire) and also stately homes that are known as abbeys (such as Beaulieu Abbey in Hampshire). A minster (such as Wimborne Minster in Dorset) refers to a church at one time connected to a monastery.

English churches are fascinating to wander around, especially once you've learned something about the various periods, styles and design elements. Very few of them are uniformly of one style. Usually a window from one period has cut into a wall from another. When decay, subsidence or an accident brought part of a church down, the reconstruction was carried out in whatever was the current style; growing congregations or increased wealth often inspired extensions or more magnificent towers or spires, inevitably in the latest style.

Political changes also affected churches and their design. For example, during the Reformation of the 16th and 17th centuries many church statues and images were destroyed as they were thought to distract the congregation from worship.

Although the great churches were often built using the cutting edge of building technology for their particular time, it wasn't unusual for catastrophic collapses to occur even during construction.

Architectural Styles & Periods
Neolithic & Bronze Ages The communal burial mounds of the agriculturally based Neolithic people comprise some of the oldest surviving examples of construction in Britain. Dating from around 3500 BC, these 'barrows' are concentrated around the chalky regions of Dorset and Wiltshire.

Stonehenge, arguably England's most famous historical landmark, is thought to have been built by a Bronze Age race. Construction of this mysterious monolithic circle began around 3000 BC.

Celtic & Roman The Celtic invaders began to arrive in 700 BC, ushering in the Iron Age and building a number of fortified villages and hilltop forts of which Maiden Castle in Dorset is one impressive example.

The Celts were followed about 700 years later by the Roman invaders. The Roman occupation lasted 350 years and left behind an impressive architectural legacy, including the grand Fishbourne Palace in West Sussex (built around AD 75) and several Roman baths (one of which gave the town of Bath its name).

Anglo-Saxon Following the withdrawal of the Romans, the Vikings were the next invaders to set foot on English soil. England's first churches were built during this Anglo-Saxon era (from around AD 700 to 1050). Saxon churches were generally small, squat, solid and unembellished; and were characterised by round arches and square towers.

Most Anglo-Saxon churches were built of wood so few survive. Stone churches have fared better; a notable example is St Laurence in Bradford-on-Avon, Wiltshire. All Saints at Brixworth and All Saints at Earls Barton, both near Northampton, have very clear Anglo-Saxon origins.

Norman After the Norman invasion of 1066, Saxon architecture gave way to Norman. As in Saxon churches, the architectural style was characterised by rounded arches and squat, square towers. The difference in appearance largely comes down to questions of detail and decoration.

Surviving Norman churches are generally larger than their Saxon predecessors. 'Massive', 'thick' and 'bulky' are all adjectives applied to the Norman style.

The Norman style only lasted about a century and there are no purely Norman churches left in England. However, Norwich, Peterborough and Durham cathedrals are all predominantly Norman.

Gothic The Gothic style developed primarily to serve the needs of the Church. The period spanned almost four centuries and is classified into three distinct but related styles. Gothic churches look much lighter and more delicate than their heavier predecessors.

Early English The Early English style was popular from around 1150 to 1280. This period was the first distinct phase of Gothic design, although the Gothic tag itself was not dreamt up until the 17th century. Early English churches are characterised by pointed arches, ribbed vaults and lancet windows (narrow, pointed windows used singly or in groups).

Salisbury Cathedral is the finest example of Early English; Lichfield Cathedral and Rievaulx Abbey (in Yorkshire) are also mostly Early English.

Decorated The mid-Gothic or Decorated period followed Early English from 1280 to 1380. As the name indicates, the Decorated period was marked by ornate window tracery and other elaborate design elements.

Examples of the style include the chapter houses of Salisbury Cathedral, Southwell Minster and York Minster, the naves of Lichfield Cathedral and Exeter Cathedral and the Angel Choir at Lincoln Cathedral.

Perpendicular The third Gothic phase thrived between 1380 and 1550, characterised by more rectilinear designs with an emphasis on strong vertical lines. The nave of Canterbury Cathedral is a good example.

Engineering developments meant that arches could span further and windows could be much larger and closer together, so many of the perpendicular churches are fantastically light and spacious. Stained glass and elaborate fan vaults were also widely featured, notably at King's College Chapel in Cambridge and Henry VII's Chapel in Westminster Abbey.

Many half-timbered houses survive from this time, their great oak beam frames infilled with brick and other materials; examples can be found in Kent, Cheshire, Hereford and Worcestershire.

Elizabethan & Jacobean During the Gothic period most domestic architecture was either very modest or primarily defensive. The terms Early English, Decorated and perpendicular are not very relevant to ruggedly constructed castles. However, by

Norman Capital   Early English window   Early English Arch

Geometric Window   Perpendicular Arch   15th-Century Capital the mid-16th century domestic architecture was much more important.

After the Reformation, church architecture came to a virtual standstill for a century and, in more peaceful times, impressing the neighbours was more important than physically fighting them off.

Houses such as Hardwick Hall and Knole combine the perpendicular's large areas of glass with the beginnings of an understanding of classical architecture, both in terms of overall proportions and symmetry and in details such as columns and cornices.

Renaissance In the first half of the 16th century, Henry VIII brought in French, Flemish and Italian craftsmen to work on the royal palaces. This imported talent was largely responsible for the introduction of what's sometimes called the Renaissance architectural style. Although Renaissance architecture began in Italy in about 1420, pure classical architecture in Britain had to wait much longer.

Palladianism The course of English architecture was fundamentally altered not once but twice by the work of the Italian architect Andrea Palladio. His famous *Four Books of Architecture* showing his own austere buildings and his imagined reconstructions of Roman ruins was published in 1570 and the illustrations were closely followed by Inigo Jones who built his masterpieces – the Banqueting Hall (London) and Queen's House (Greenwich, London) – around 1620.

English Baroque Like the Renaissance style, the Baroque originated in Italy. In England it came later (late 17th century to the 1720s) and was less well defined, but it includes the work of some of the most famous and flamboyant architects. It uses classical features such as columns, arches and pediments in an exuberant way with dramatic juxtapositions of forms and amazingly elaborate silhouettes.

The greatest and most influential of the Baroque architects was Sir Christopher Wren who, in the aftermath of the Great Fire of 1666, radically changed the appearance of the City of London. His masterpiece was St Paul's Cathedral but he was responsible for no fewer than 53 churches. The secular style is most famous in the work of Nicholas Hawksmoor and Sir John Vanbrugh, who collaborated on Castle Howard (Yorkshire) and Blenheim Palace (Oxfordshire). This was the era when some of the greatest country houses in England were built. See the boxed text '406 rms w/vu' on the following page.

Neo-Palladianism Lord Burlington, an aesthetically minded aristocrat, was responsible for a return to simpler classical forms after the excesses of the Baroque period. In the design of his own house in Chiswick (London) he led the way with strict adherence to rules of proportion and symmetry. Soon the accepted form for country houses was a central block with a columned portico and flanking wings. Holkham Hall in Norfolk (William Kent, 1734) and Prior Park in Bath (John Wood the Elder, 1735) are good examples.

The terraced houses of John Wood the Elder and John Wood the Younger in Bath, and Robert Adam in Edinburgh, show the same ideals put to different use in a city context.

Neoclassicism The neoclassical style, which flourished between 1760 and 1830, was the result of a more accurate study of classical ruins, not only in Italy but in Greece and Asia Minor. A new generation of architects had a bigger vocabulary of classical motifs and felt free to assemble them as they wished.

Architect Robert Adam was a key proponent of the style, and was known for his decorative interiors; the house at No 20 Portman Square in London is one famous example of his work.

There was little religious building during the 17th century apart from Sir Christopher Wren's magnificent St Paul's Cathedral (and other London churches), which adopted neoclassical designs copied from the Continent.

406 rms w/vu

If the term 'English Country House' makes you think of some charming cottage set among pansies in the countryside, think again. English country houses had little cottages, but they were far from the main house and were probably home to some third-string worker such as the official mucker.

Instead, when you think English country house, think: mansion, palace, vast estate, huge pile and so on. From the 16th century onwards these enormous homes soon replaced castles as the primary homes of the nobility, gentry, ruling class and anyone else at the top of the English social heap. They easily had 100 rooms or more and were run by a huge staff. Every effort was made to one-up the neighbours, who might be, oh, say about 5000 acres to the west.

The fashion for these fabulous digs reached its zenith in the 18th century when dozens were built throughout much of England. The houses were designed by top architects and were filled with all manner of collected treasure. The grounds, which at times were even more impressive than the houses themselves, were the work of designers such as Capability Brown. These were no small collection of roses either, but vast landscapes that spread over hundreds of acres. It was no big deal to re-route a river, move a hill, dig a lake or otherwise radically alter the landscape in pursuit of a 'natural ideal'. Also critical was the fact that the lords of these estates had hundreds of tenant farmers and other employees who lived little better than serfs.

Examples of houses with stunning landscapes include Stourhead in Wiltshire and Blenheim Palace in Oxfordshire, the birthplace of Winston Churchill. The latter is itself Baroque.

Many of the houses built in the early 18th century were designed according to the principles of Andrea Palladio and included all of his required Palladian touches, including fake Roman ruins. Holkham Hall in Norfolk is a fine example of this and features enough carved marble to make a Roman senator feel right at home.

Late in the 18th century, neoclassicism was all the rage. It was a methodical and formal style that led to estates whose symmetry of house and property couldn't be fully appreciated until the advent of the aeroplane afforded a bird's eye view. Syon House, west of London, exemplifies this form. Harewood House in Yorkshire is another example.

Country houses continued to be built through the 19th century using a variety of architectural styles from mock Tudor to Gothic Revival to classic Victorian.

Grand as they were, the houses were always doomed. Even the fortunes that built them couldn't keep up with the soaring maintenance bills – just heating the notoriously draughty piles cost virtually a small fortune. And in the 20th century taxes signalled the end for many of the houses.

Some houses – works of art really – were abandoned by their owners and fell into ruin. Others were taken over for a variety of uses that could take advantage of their many rooms. Boarding schools, sanatoriums, hotels, jails and secret government installations (the WWII code-breaking centre was at Bletchley Park) were just some of the uses found for the properties. Others were given to the National Trust and English Heritage, who were left with the bills for upkeep. Many homes, especially in the south-east, have been sold to the nouveau rich such as sports heroes and rock stars.

But some remain in the hands of their private owners, who maintain them as labours of love or even obsession. When a new roof costs over £1 million, it takes a lot of effort to keep things afloat. Some owners are lucky to have fortunes so huge that they can hang on, others open the homes to guests (and tempt their purses with everything from embossed fudge to tea towels) while others barely hang on by slowly liquidating the art-works that were such an integral part of the homes in the first place.

Gothic & Greek Revivals The Greek Revival served to counter the more eclectic approach of neoclassicism with an emphasis on accurate recreations of Greek forms and aimed to replicate the heavy massing of Greek prototypes.

The British Museum, designed by Sir Robert Smirke and built between 1823 and 1846, is one notable example of this style, which started at the end of the 18th century and carried on until the 1840s.

The first phase of the Gothic Revival (1840s) was based on earnest historic research. This was combined with a passionate belief that a return to Gothic architecture could achieve social reform and that classicism was linked to the urban depravations of industrialism.

Decorated and occasionally Early English Gothic were design sources for churches, schools and vicarages with asymmetric, irregular plans. High Victorian Gothic used a wider range of sources, including perpendicular, northern Italian and French Gothic forms for all types of building. The Houses of Parliament (1834), by Augustus Pugin and Sir Charles Barry, are an early example of Gothic Revival architecture, while Alfred Waterhouse's Manchester Town Hall (1868) provides an example of how the style had moved on.

Arts & Crafts Heavy-handed Victorian church 'restorations' (often a complete rebuilding) inspired William Morris to found the Society for the Protection of Ancient Buildings in 1877. Morris' ideas, together with the writings of John Ruskin, led to an increased appreciation of craft skills in new building as well as restorations. Many very original buildings as well as new ideas about the planning and layout of towns meant that England was very influential during this period. Foreign visitors were especially interested in the Garden City Movement of which Letchworth is the first example.

The 20th Century The rise of the Nazis meant that many European modern movement architects (for example, Bauhaus) fled to England in the 1920s and 1930s and had a profound effect. One of the most famous and fun examples of their work is the Penguin Pool at London Zoo by Lubetkin.

Swedish modernism was also influential, evident in the huge number of postwar housing estates and public buildings that were built to replace bomb damage and

Listed Buildings

You'll soon hear about 'listed buildings' when you are in England. In a fine example of a good literal English name, listed buildings are just that: buildings on a list.

In this case the lists are maintained by the Department for Culture, Media & Sport, which decides what buildings to list in consultation with English Heritage, the government's conservation agency. There are different classes of list:

Grade I – the absolute finest buildings in the land; think Westminster Abbey and you have an idea of the quality of the 6000 buildings with this designation. These buildings are sacrosanct and often receive government grants for maintenance.

Grade II* – buildings not up to the standards of Grade I buildings but still deemed worthy of protection from alteration or destruction; 18,000 buildings qualify for this category.

Grade II – a cool 500,000 buildings that have been noted for one reason or another but are not granted much (if any) protection.

All buildings that were built before 1700 and are still reasonably authentic are automatically listed. The same goes for most of those dating from 1700 to 1840. Standards get increasingly stringent from there. Only buildings dating from after 1939 of the absolutely highest calibre can be listed and even then they have to be at least 30 years old. Those familiar with much of the postwar construction around England will know that this part of the list isn't exactly bulging.

slum clearance. The tough, sculptural concrete buildings in 1960s brutalist style, such as the National Theatre by Sir Denys Lasdun, are just beginning to be appreciated again (but by a few – a very, very few).

During the late 1970s and early 1980s, two distinct responses to modernism developed. Postmodern architects returned once more to traditional architectural vocabularies, assembling motifs from many different styles in an ironic way.

In the 1980s the redevelopment of the Docklands area of London gave the greatest scope for postmodern architecture, often by American architects such as Cesar Pelli,

who designed the main 500m tower at Canary Wharf and has been severely criticised. Terry Farrell's buildings on the Thames at Charing Cross and Vauxhall are more popular.

In contrast, high-tech architecture in the 1980s and early 1990s celebrated the potential of technology, usually with complex lightweight structural skeletons such as Stansted Airport by Norman Foster, the Waterloo International train terminal by Nicholas Grimshaw and the Lloyd's Building in London (by Richard Rogers) with brilliantly coloured service pipes on the outside.

The Norman & Richard Show

Dominating modern architecture in England are Norman Foster and Richard Rogers. These two men, who were partners in the 1960s, have won the bulk of major architectural commissions around London and the south-east for the past 30 years.

Although both have firms that have won contracts and designed projects world-wide, London is where you will find their best (as well as most controversial) work.

Foster favours clean designs with flowing lines. This is reflected in his new glass roof for the Great Court of the British Museum, where the lines are sinuous and definitely sensuous. The same can be said for his wobbly Millennium Bridge across the Thames, and his Canary Wharf station for the Jubilee Line extension is almost organic in its flow of form.

Farther afield, Foster created the Stansted Airport terminal as a bold and bright exclamation point to a journey. He walks a real tightrope with his redevelopment plan for Wembley Stadium, which does away with the iconic twin towers.

In contrast, the work of Rogers is anything but sinuous. Rather, it is technical and intricate, and often looks like the work of a mad child with a collection of building blocks.

With its spindly yellow towers and vast expanse of curving white, the Millennium Dome always provokes a reaction among those seeing it for the first time. But the strongest reactions are often reserved for his 1980s Lloyd's Building in the City of London. The guts of the building are all there to see on the outside whether you want to or not. It was a natural progression from the work that put Rogers on the map, the inside-out Centre Pompidou in Paris that he designed with Renzo Piano.

But if much of the work of Foster and Rogers wins plaudits or at least sparks strong opinions, some of it has a harder time. Rogers is the designer of a massive complex called Paddington Basin to be built near the station of the same name. It is so huge it has actually provoked fear among some residents. The components are awash with the kind of obsessive and revealing details that make the Lloyd's Building just that, the Lloyd's Building.

Meanwhile, Foster has won the competition to design the new headquarters for the London mayor and council, which will be built near Tower Bridge. It's a dramatic glass tube topped with an ovoid 'eye'. The new London mayor and probable future tenant, Ken Livingston, dismissed any question that Foster's sensual eye had scored here when he called it 'a glass testicle'.

Today the boundaries are harder to define, although many young architects are using restaurants and bars to make a very minimal style fashionable.

Diverse, recent additions to the cityscape include the controversial Millennium Dome by Richard Rogers and the Millennium Bridge by Foster. See the boxed text 'The Norman and Richard Show'.

SOCIETY & CONDUCT
Traditional Culture

It's difficult to generalise about the English and their culture but there's no doubt they're a creative, energetic and aggressive people who've had an impact on the world that's entirely out of proportion to their numbers.

Many visitors arrive with strong preconceptions about English characteristics, the most common being that the English are reserved, inhibited and stiflingly polite. The reaction to the death of Princess Diana showed just how outdated this stereotype is. Remember, however, that England is one of the planet's most tourist-inundated and crowded countries, and that some of the famed reserve is a protective veneer developed to help deal with a constant crush of people. Remember also, that although regional and class differences have shrunk, accents and behaviour still vary widely depending on where you are and who you're mixing with.

Terms such as 'stiff-upper-lip', 'cold' and 'conservative' might apply to some sections of the middle and upper classes, but in general they don't apply to the working class or to northerners. Visit a nightclub, a football match, a good local pub, or a country B&B and other terms such as uninhibited, tolerant, exhibitionist, passionate, aggressive, sentimental, hospitable and friendly might spring to mind more readily.

No country in the world has more obsessive hobbyists, some of whom teeter on the edge of complete madness. Train and bus spotters, twitchers, sports fanatics, fashion victims, royalists, model-makers, egg collectors, ramblers, pet owners, gardeners, they all find a home here.

England is a country of sceptical individualists who deeply resent any intrusion on their privacy or freedom, so it's hardly surprising that their flirtation with state socialism was brief. Change happens slowly and only after endless consultations, committee meetings, departmental get-togethers and government referrals.

Dos & Don'ts

The English are reasonably tolerant and it's not particularly easy to cause offence (without meaning to). That said, it's as well to be aware that most locals would no sooner speak to a stranger in the street than fly to the moon. If you're obviously a tourist battling with directions, there's no problem – but try starting a general conversation at the bus stop and you'll find people staring at you as if you're mad.

Queuing

The English are notoriously addicted to queuing, and many comedy sketches depend on the audience accepting that people might actually join a queue without knowing what it's for. The order of the queue is sacrosanct – few things are more calculated to spark an outburst of tutting than an attempt to 'push in'. And make certain you stand on the right on escalators.

Clothes

In some countries what you wear or don't wear in churches can get you into trouble. In general, England is as free and easy about this as it is about how you dress in the street. Bear in mind, however, that if you go into mosques or temples you may be expected to take off your shoes and cover your arms, legs and/or head.

Some classy restaurants and many clubs operate strict dress codes. In restaurants that usually means a jacket and tie for men and no trainers for anyone; in clubs it means whatever the management and their bouncers choose it to mean and can vary from night to night.

Treatment of Animals

The English are widely believed to love their animals more than their children: the

Royal Society for the Prevention of Cruelty to Animals (RSPCA) was established before the National Society for the Prevention of Cruelty to Children (NSPCC) and still rakes in equal donations.

Not surprisingly, fox-hunting, the ancient sport derided by Oscar Wilde as 'the unspeakable in pursuit of the inedible', has become highly controversial.

England's 200-odd hunts are estimated to kill about 20,000 foxes a year (another 40,000 are killed by vehicles and over 100,000 are trapped or shot). Pro-hunt campaigners argue that many foxes actually owe their existence to the hunters since fox-hunting farmers are less likely to dig up the hedgerows and small woods that provide living quarters for their prey.

Nevertheless, most people see hunting as a cruel sport, inappropriate to a 'civilised' society. Anti-hunting sentiment in England runs strong and polls suggest that the majority of the population would support a ban, figures mirrored in a recent free vote on the subject in parliament. The pro-hunters, though, are a well-organised and powerful bunch; they've managed to stave off efforts to ban the hunt despite several efforts by the government.

As often in England, hunting is tied up with class. Hunting is mainly a sport of the upper class or at least the wealthy. The famous attire, starting with a 'pink' (which in fox-hunting parlance means red!) jacket, can cost thousands from a London tailor and that's without the fees to join a specific hunt and the cost of the horses.

Recent years have seen high-profile lobbies against factory farming and the export of live animals. Perhaps 10% of the population are vegetarians, or near-vegetarians. Most supermarkets stock free-range eggs and meat supposedly from animals who have been allowed to roam free.

RELIGION

The Church of England, a Christian church that became independent of Rome in the 16th century (see The Tudors under History earlier in the chapter), is the largest, wealthiest and most influential in the land. Like the Church of Scotland, it's an 'established' church. This means that it's officially the national church, with a close relationship with the State (the queen or king appoints archbishops and bishops on the advice of the prime minister).

Although 70% of the population still claim to be Christian, the latest survey suggests that only 8.2% regularly attend church, a fall of a million people in the last two decades. It's difficult to generalise about the form of worship – it varies from the pomp and ceremony of High church to the less traditional Low church, which has been more influenced by Protestantism and more recently by the evangelical movement. Evangelical (and other charismatic churches) are the only ones attracting growing congregations.

Traditionally, the Church of England has been aligned with the ruling classes, but some sectors became very critical of the Conservatives in their declining years. In 1994, after many years of agonising, the first women were ordained as priests. The debate has now moved on to the rights and wrongs of gay priests.

Other significant Protestant churches with no connection to the State include Methodists, Baptists, the United Reformed Church and the Salvation Army.

At times since the 16th century, Roman Catholics have been terribly persecuted; one modern legacy is the ongoing problem of Northern Ireland. Today about one in 12 English people considers themselves a Catholic, but over the last 20 years the number attending Mass has also slumped.

Recent estimates suggest there are now well over one million Muslims in England, together with significant numbers of Sikhs and Hindus. Nowadays more English non-Christians visit their places of worship than do Christians.

LANGUAGE

English is probably England's most significant contribution to the modern world. The English, of every class and background, take enormous pleasure in using their language and idiom inventively (nowhere, for instance, are there more crossword fanatics). The language continues to evolve and to be used and exploited to the full. See the Glossary later in the book for examples.

English English can be incomprehensible to overseas visitors – even to those who assume they've spoken English all their lives. Regional dialects may be disappearing but significant variations, especially in accent, still flourish and some can be virtually impenetrable to outsiders. It's OK to ask someone to repeat what they've said, but remember that they probably can't quite get your oddball accent either.

Facts for the Visitor

HIGHLIGHTS

Planning a trip around England can be bewildering for the first-timer and is no more straightforward if you live here. The country may be small, but its long history as an influential world power has left it with a rich heritage of medieval castles and cathedrals, historic cities and towns, stately homes and elegant gardens. Added to this are the natural attractions: the national parks and beautiful coastal regions. England's highlights are so numerous that to make life easier we've broken them down into categories.

Historic Cities & Towns

Bath

Blessed with superb Georgian architecture, but unfortunately inundated with tourists (South-Western England).

CHAPTER BREAKDOWN

WESSEX ....Chapter

SCOTLAND

Northumberland

NORTH-EASTERN ENGLAND

Newcastle-upon-Tyne

NORTHERN IRELAND

CUMBRIA

Lake District

Durham

Isle of Man

North Yorkshire

YORKSHIRE

NORTH-WESTERN ENGLAND

York

East Riding of Yorkshire

Lancashire

Leeds

IRISH SEA

NORTH SEA

Manchester

Peak District

IRELAND

Liverpool

Cheshire

Derby-shire

Notting-hamshire

Lincolnshire

Staffordshire

THE MIDLANDS

Rutland

Norfolk

Shropshire

Leicestershire

EASTERN ENGLAND

Birmingham

Coventry

Northamp-tonshire

Cambridgeshire

WALES

Hereford & Worcester

Warwick-shire

Suffolk

FROM THE THAMES TO THE WYE

Cotswolds

Buck-ingham-shire

Bedford-shire

Hertford-shire

St George's Channel

Gloucester-shire

Oxford-shire

Essex

Bristol

LONDON

ATLANTIC OCEAN

Bristol Channel

Bath

Wiltshire

Berkshire

Surrey

Kent

Somerset

WESSEX

Hampshire

SOUTH-EASTERN ENGLAND

West Sussex

East Sussex

Devon

Dorset

Strait of Dover

DEVON & CORNWALL

Cornwall

Isle of Wight

FRANCE

ENGLISH CHANNEL

0   100   200km
0   50   100mi

Beverley
Unspoilt, little-visited market town with two superb medieval churches (East Riding of Yorkshire).

Cambridge
Famous university town with a compact centre. King's College Chapel is one of Europe's most impressive buildings (Cambridgeshire).

Liverpool
Once a great port and industrial city, boasts a superb legacy of Victorian and Edwardian architecture, a strong cultural identity and vibrant nightlife (North-Western England).

Oxford
Gorgeous university town with evocative architecture, marred only by the huge crowds in summer (Oxfordshire).

Richmond
On the edge of the Yorkshire Dales, overlooking the River Swale, with a cobbled marketplace at the foot of a ruined castle (North Yorkshire).

Shrewsbury
Interesting town with half-timbered architecture and curious medieval streets (Shropshire).

Whitby
Atmospheric fishing port on magnificent coastline (North Yorkshire).

Winchester
Ancient English capital, rich in history, with a great cathedral (Hampshire).

York
Proud city with a spectacular cathedral and medieval walls, and many excellent museums (North Yorkshire).

Cathedrals & Churches

Canterbury Cathedral
The Church of England's most important cathedral, crowded with ghosts of the past (Kent).

Durham Cathedral
Monolithic Norman cathedral, overwhelming in scale, on a spectacular site overlooking Durham (County Durham).

Ely Cathedral
Huge building looming over the fens (Cambridgeshire).

King's College Chapel
Perpendicular masterpiece with outstanding acoustics and one of Britain's best boys' choirs (Cambridge).

Lincoln Cathedral
Unusual cathedral with a site surpassed only by Durham (Lincolnshire).

Rievaulx Abbey
Romantic abbey ruins on a beautiful site (North Yorkshire).

What's in a Name?

England dominates the rest of the UK in all things to such an extent that not only the English but most of the world tend to say 'England' when referring to the UK as a whole. The island of Britain (England, Scotland and Wales) together with Northern Ireland make up the country whose official name is the United Kingdom of Great Britain and Northern Ireland.

It may seem an obvious point but it's important to get the name of the country right. While you won't have any problems during your England travels, beware if you cross the borders: the Scots, the Welsh and the people of Northern Ireland find it deeply insulting if you tell them how much you like being 'here in England' when you're in their part of the UK.

St Paul's Cathedral
Sir Christopher Wren's masterpiece, with a great view from the dome (London).

Salisbury Cathedral
Stylistically coherent, with Britain's tallest spire; a soaring elegance (Wiltshire).

Wells Cathedral
Centrepiece of the best medieval cathedral precinct in Britain, with brilliant western front sculpture (Somerset).

Westminster Abbey
Rich in history – since King Harold, almost every monarch has been crowned here – and with an excellent boys' choir (London).

Winchester Cathedral
Architectural styles from Norman to perpendicular in perfect harmony (Hampshire).

York Minster
Largest medieval church in Britain, incorporating Roman ruins and superb stained glass (North Yorkshire).

Museums & Galleries

British Museum
Outstanding museum with comprehensive coverage of archaeology of ancient civilisations (London).

HMS *Victory* and HMS *Mary Rose*
The world's oldest commissioned warship and Nelson's flagship at the Battle of Trafalgar; and Henry VIII's flagship rescued from the mud beneath Portsmouth Harbour (Portsmouth).

Ironbridge Gorge
Historic birthplace of the Industrial Revolution, restored and recreated over a number of sites, including the world's first iron bridge (Shropshire).

National Gallery
National collection of European art from the 15th to the early 20th century (London).

Tate Modern
Huge museum on the River Thames covering modern art since 1900 (London).

Victoria and Albert Museum
Bewildering array of applied and decorative arts, including furniture, paintings, woodwork, jewellery, textiles and clothing (London).

York Castle Museum
Intriguing museum of everyday life, including reconstructed streets and authentically furnished rooms from the 17th to the 20th century (York).

Medieval Castles

Alnwick
Dramatic castle begun in the 12th century and converted to a great house without losing its medieval character (Northumberland).

Bodiam Castle
A perfectly symmetrical 14th-century castle (Sussex).

Dover
Massive fortress begun shortly after the Norman Conquest, but encompassing a Roman lighthouse, Saxon church and tunnels last used in WWII (Kent).

Leeds
Extraordinarily beautiful castle in the middle of a lake; marred by crowds (Kent).

Tower of London
Begun in 1078, a fortress, royal residence and state prison, now home to the British crown jewels (London).

Windsor
Royal residence with restored state rooms and the beautiful St George's Chapel (Berkshire).

Historic Houses

Blenheim Palace
Enormous baroque-style private house built by Sir John Vanbrugh in 1704, set in parkland (Oxfordshire).

Castle Howard
Another Vanbrugh masterpiece with a dramatic setting in superb landscaped gardens (North Yorkshire).

Charleston Farmhouse
Home to Vanessa Bell, Duncan Grant and David Garnett (of the Bloomsbury Group), decorated with frescoes and postimpressionist art, and with a charming garden (East Sussex).

Haddon Hall
Dating from the 12th century and added to for 500 years, one of the most complete, surviving medieval manor houses (Derbyshire).

Hampton Court Palace
Begun in 1514 and a royal residence until the 18th century, an enormous, fascinating complex surrounded by beautiful gardens (London).

Ightham Mote
Small moated manor house that has scarcely changed for 500 years (Kent).

Knole House
Enormous house dating from the 15th century and virtually untouched since the 17th century, set in parkland (Kent).

Royal Pavilion
Exotic fantasy, combining Indian, Chinese and Gothic elements, built by George IV in 1815 (Brighton, Sussex).

The Queen's House
Inigo Jones masterpiece, built in 1635 (Greenwich).

Coast

Beachy Head
Spectacular chalk cliffs backed by rolling downland rich in wild flowers (East Sussex).

Brighton
Tacky but vibrant resort town (East Sussex).

Ilfracombe to Lynton/Lynmouth
Humpbacked cliffs overlooking the Bristol Channel and backed by the beautiful Exmoor National Park (Devon).

Land's End to St Ives
Beautiful coast and a landscape littered with historical reminders and relics (Cornwall).

St Ives
Picturesque village and artists' haunt with two excellent sandy beaches (Cornwall).

Scarborough
Classic English seaside resort with a superb location (North Yorkshire).

Scarborough to Saltburn
Unspoiled coastline with beautiful fishing villages (particularly Staithes and Robin Hood's Bay) and major cliffs, backed by the North York Moors National Park (North Yorkshire).

Tintagel
Surf-battered headland, topped by a ruined castle, believed to be King Arthur's birthplace (Cornwall).

Gardens

Forde Abbey
Former Cistercian abbey with wide lawns,

ponds, huge trees and colourful borders (Dorset).

Great Dixter
Series of gardens begun by Sir Edwin Lutyens featuring wild flowers and brilliant spring bulbs (Kent).

Hidcote Manor Gardens
One of Britain's most famous modern gardens (Gloucestershire).

Regent's Park
Vast lawns, spectacular Queen Mary's Rose Garden with 60,000 roses, ornamental ponds and a zoo (London).

Royal Botanic Gardens
Three hundred acres of formal gardens, woods, rock gardens, conservatories and the magnificent Palm House; arguably the world's greatest botanical collection (Kew, London).

Sissinghurst
Magical garden created by Vita Sackville-West and Harold Nicholson of the Bloomsbury Group (Kent).

Stourhead and Stourton
Two very different neighbouring gardens. Stourhead comprises superb landscaped parkland designed in the 1740s around a lake. The flower garden of Stourton House is in perfect contrast (Wiltshire).

Stowe Landscape Garden
Enormously influential garden started in the 17th century, now being restored by the National Trust (Buckinghamshire).

Studley Royal & Fountains Abbey
Superb water garden on a grand scale, framing extraordinary monastic ruins (North Yorkshire).

Trelissick Garden
Rhododendrons, magnolias, hydrangeas and subtropical plants thrive in this area's mild climate (Cornwall).

Prehistoric Remains

Avebury & Around
Some suggest that this is more impressive than Stonehenge; extensive remains, including a stone circle and avenue, and nearby Silbury Hill and West Kennet Long Barrow (Wiltshire).

Castlerigg Stone Circle
Stone circle with a beautiful location near Keswick in the Lake District (Cumbria).

Stonehenge
Extraordinary monument, unfortunately marred by crowds and the nearby road (Wiltshire).

Roman Sites

Chedworth Villa
Well-preserved mosaic floors at this remote rural villa (Gloucestershire).

Fishbourne Palace
Britain's only Roman palace, with beautiful mosaics (near Chichester, West Sussex).

Hadrian's Wall
Evocative ruins of the Romans' monumental attempt to divide two countries (Northumberland/Cumbria).

Train Journeys

Esk Valley Line
Through the evocative North York Moors National Park from Middlesborough to Whitby (North Yorkshire).

Leeds-Settle-Carlisle Line
Spectacular engineering feat running through the beautiful scenery of the Yorkshire Dales (North Yorkshire).

Sheffield-New Mills Line
Some of the most dramatic scenery of the Peak District National Park is on display on this line, which runs to Manchester (Midlands).

Tarka Line
From Exeter to Barnstaple through classic Devon countryside (Devon).

SUGGESTED ITINERARIES

With so much to choose from, it would be pointless to suggest a 'definitive' itinerary – how you plan your trip will depend on your particular interests and on the amount of time at your disposal. But to make sure you take in at least some of the highlights, you might want to consider the following:

One week
Visit London, Oxford, the Cotswolds, Bath and Wells.

Two weeks
Visit London, Salisbury, Avebury, Bath, Wells, Oxford or Cambridge, York and the Lake District.

One month
Visit London, Cambridge, York, the Yorkshire Dales or the North York Moors, the Lake District, Chester, the Cotswolds, Wells, Bath, Avebury, Salisbury, Oxford and Stratford-upon-Avon. You could also think about heading right on out to the westernmost tip of Cornwall.

Two months
As for the one-month itinerary, but stay put for a week or so in one place. Give serious thought to doing one of the long-distance walks described in the Activities chapter later in the book.

PLANNING
When to Go

Anyone who spends any extended period of time in England will soon sympathise with the locals' conversational obsession with the weather – although in relative terms the climate is mild and the rainfall not spectacular (see Climate in the Facts about England chapter).

Settled periods of weather – sunny or otherwise – are rare and rain is likely at any time. Even in midsummer you can go for days without seeing the sun, and showers (or worse) should be expected. To enjoy England it helps to convince yourself that you like the rain – after all, that's what makes it so incredibly green!

The least hospitable months for visitors are November, December, January and February – it's cold, and the days are short (less than eight hours of daylight in December). March is marginal – although there are 12 hours of daylight and daffodils appear in the south, it can still be very cold. October is also marginal – there are nearly 11 hours of daylight, temperatures are reasonable, and weather patterns seem to be unusually stable, which means you can get good spells of sun, or rain.

Temperatures vary but, as you would expect, it's generally true that the farther north you go, the colder it gets. There's also quite a difference in the number of daylight hours. In early spring or late autumn, it's probably best to concentrate a visit in the south, especially the mild South-West.

April to September are undoubtedly the best months for all of England, and this is when most sights and Tourist Information Centres (TICs) are open, and when most people visit. July and August are the busiest months, and best avoided if possible. The crowds on the coast, in the national parks, in London and in popular towns such as Oxford, Bath and York have to be seen to be believed. You're just as likely to get good weather in April, May, June, September and October.

There is so much to see and do in London that doesn't depend on the weather that the tourist season really extends year round.

What Kind of Trip

Although many people restrict their trip to England to a visit to London and a quick whip round the 'milk-run' towns of Oxford, Cambridge, Stratford-upon-Avon, Bath, York and Chester, you'll get more out of a stay if you take the time to explore some of the less touristy towns (Bristol, Manchester and Leeds for example) and the wonderful countryside. The remoter parts of northern England, in particular, are best appreciated on a longer stay. London is a great city, but it's also very expensive and unrepresentative of Britain as a whole – don't let it absorb all your time.

It's easy enough to get around the country by train or bus, although it's usually much cheaper to travel by bus than by train. Alternatively, there are plenty of coach tours, either around the whole country from London or around specific areas. There are several hop-on hop-off coach tours specifically designed for backpackers (see the Getting Around chapter).

Travellers who are planning to find work and long-term places to live should bear in mind that the peak tourist season generates casual jobs, which are often advertised in May and June. June can be a good time to look for housing as the universities and colleges close for summer and many students move back home; in addition, travellers pack up and move on to the Mediterranean. Everything tightens up in October and November when people return to rebuild their finances and hibernate through winter.

Maps

The best introductory map to England is published by the British Tourist Authority (BTA; 020-8846 9000) and is widely available in TICs (better yet, request a copy from the nearest BTA office before you leave home). TICs usually have excellent regional maps covering its area.

If you plan to use the trains, the bad news is that you have to buy the whole hefty timetable (£9) just to get the 'free' map that goes with it. You can try asking at train stations for maps, but you're likely to get lots of little pamphlets from the Train Operating

Companies (TOCs; see the Getting Around chapter), each showing just their services.

There's not much to distinguish the range of excellent road atlases in terms of accuracy or price (£7 to £10), but the graphics differ – pick the one you find easiest to read. If you plan to go off the beaten track, you'll need one that shows at least 3 miles to the inch.

The Ordnance Survey (OS) caters for walkers with a wide variety of maps at different scales. The OS Landranger maps at 1:50,000 or about 1¼ inches to the mile are ideal (£4.95). Its Explorer and Outdoor Leisure maps have even more detail – 1:25,000 – and should satisfy the most demanding hiker or walker. These maps are for sale in book shops and TICs.

What to Bring

Since anything you think of can be bought in English cities (including Vegemite and bad peanut butter), pack light and pick up extras as you go along, although you'll frequently find that prices are higher than they would be at home.

A travelpack – a combination of a backpack and shoulder bag – is the most popular item for carrying gear, especially if you plan to do any walking – a suitcase will probably force you to use expensive taxis. A travelpack's straps zip away inside the pack when not needed, making it easy to handle in airports and on crowded public transport. Most travelpacks have sophisticated shoulder-strap adjustment systems and can be used comfortably, even for long hikes.

If you don't plan to take your luggage with you on walks, then the always-popular bag with built-in handle and wheels will get you through airports and train stations – although buses will be a bit tougher.

Whether you bring a tent probably depends on how enthusiastic a camper you are; the weather hardly encourages camping and long-distance walks are well served by hostels, camping barns and bed and breakfasts (B&Bs). A sleeping bag is useful in hostels and when visiting friends.

A padlock is handy for locking your bag to a train or a bus luggage rack, and may also be needed to secure your hostel locker. A Swiss Army knife (or any pocketknife that includes a bottle opener and strong corkscrew) is useful for all sorts of things. For city sightseeing, a small daypack is harder for snatch thieves to grab than a shoulder bag.

Other possibilities include a compass, an alarm clock, a torch (flashlight), an adapter plug for electrical appliances, sunglasses and an elastic clothesline.

Rain gear is essential. Whether it's waterproof outdoor clothing or an umbrella or both, bring whatever you need because you can expect rain at anytime anywhere in England.

Toiletries are easily purchased. However, if you're heading to rural areas in the summer, bring something to repel the mosquitoes.

Use plastic carrier bags to keep things organised and dry inside your bag or backpack in case it's left sitting in the rain. Airlines lose bags from time to time, but there's a much better chance of getting them back if they're tagged with your name and address inside as well as on the outside.

RESPONSIBLE TOURISM

Except for its remoter and more mountainous reaches, England is a very crowded place even before the peak tourist season brings yet more millions to the streets. Congestion on the roads is a major problem and visitors will do residents – as well as themselves! – a favour if they forgo driving in favour of using public transport.

Mountain bikers should stick to roads or designated bike tracks as considerable damage has been done to mountain paths (for example, in the Yorkshire Dales) by cyclists. If you're rough camping make sure you ask permission of the landowner first and take care not to damage crops or leave any litter.

TOURIST OFFICES

The BTA stocks masses of information on England, and much of it is free. Its UK headquarters are at Thames Tower, Black's

Rd, Hammersmith, London W6 9EL. Contact the BTA before you leave home because some discounts are only available to people who book before arriving in Britain. Travellers with special needs (disability, diet and so on) should also contact the nearest BTA office for information. Its Web site is at www.bta.org.uk.

In London the British Travel Centre at 1 Regent St (see the London chapter) is a good starting point for information.

The English Tourism Board does not deal with the public, but rather is a group representing the interests of the regional and local tourist boards, which deal with the public. Useful regional bodies are listed at the start of the relevant chapters.

Local Tourist Offices

Every English town (and many villages) has its own TIC where a wide range of information is available, particularly about places within a 50-mile radius. Most also operate a local bed-booking system and a Book-A-Bed-Ahead (BABA) scheme. In addition there are National Park Visitor Information Centres. Local libraries are also good sources of information.

Most TICs open 9 am to 5 pm Monday to Friday, although in popular tourist areas they may also open on Saturday and stay open later in the evening. In real honey pots such as Stratford and Bath they'll be open seven days a week throughout the year. From October to March smaller TICs are often closed.

Many TICs have 24-hour computer databases that can be accessed even when the office is closed. Others put posters with basic information about accommodation and a town plan in the window.

Tourist Offices Abroad

Overseas, the BTA represents the tourist boards of England (as well as Scotland and Wales). Addresses of some overseas offices are as follows:

Australia
(☎ 02-9377 4400, fax 9377 4499, e visitbri tainaus@bta.org.uk) Level 16, The Gateway, 1 Macquarie Place, Circular Quay, Sydney, NSW 2000

Canada
(☎ 905-405 1840, fax 405 1835) 5915 Airport Rd, Suite 120, Mississauga, Ontario L4V 1T1

France
(☎ 01 44 51 56 20, fax 01 44 51 56 21) Maison de la Grande Bretagne, 19 rue des Mathurins, 75009 Paris (entrance in les Rues Tronchet et Auber)

Germany
(☎ 069-971123, fax 9711 2444, e gb-info@ bta.org.uk) Westendstrasse 16–22, 60325 Frankfurt

Ireland
(☎ 01-670 8000, fax 670 8244) 18–19 College Green, Dublin 2

Netherlands
(☎ 020-689 0002, fax 689 0003 e britinfo.nl@ bta.org.uk) Stadhouderskade 2, 1054 ES Amsterdam

New Zealand
(☎ 09-303 1446, fax 377 6965, e bta.nz@ bt.org.uk) 17th Floor, NZI House, 151 Queen St, Auckland 1

USA
Chicago: (☎ 800 462 2748, e travelinfo@ bta.org.uk) 625 North Michigan Ave, Suite 1001, Chicago IL 60611 (personal callers only)
New York: (☎ 212-986 2200, e travelinfo@ bta.org.uk) 551 Fifth Avenue, Suite 701, New York, NY 10176

There are more than 40 BTA offices worldwide; their addresses are listed on its Web site (www.bta.org.uk).

VISAS & DOCUMENTS

Unlike many other European countries, people in the UK are not required by law to carry identification, but it's always a good idea to have your passport or some other sort of photo ID on your person. Also, with very few exceptions, London is an excellent place to gather information about visas for other countries worldwide.

Jokes by Scots aside, there are virtually no border checks of any kind between England and Scotland or Wales.

Passport

Your most important travel document is a passport, which should remain valid until well after your trip; if it's just about to expire, renew it before you go. This may

Staying on track in Lincolnshire

Stunning views over the Vale of York, Kirkby Bank, Cleveland Way

An abundance of hot air, Bristol

Messing about on the canal, Bradford-on-Avon, Wiltshire

Bedruthen Steps, Cornwall

MARK DAFFEY

Exmoor National Park, Devon

CHRIS MELLOR

Fishermen try their luck on a frosty Staffordshire morning.

GRANT DIXON

View from Sutton Bank, North York Moors National Park

DOUG McKINLAY

Out for a gallop in Hyde Park, London

IAN CONNELLAN

Cycle Trail, New Forest

not be easy to do overseas, and some countries insist that your passport remains valid for a specified minimum period (usually three months) after your visit.

Applying for or renewing a passport can be an involved process taking from a few days to several months, so don't leave it till the last minute. Bureaucracy usually grinds faster if you do everything in person rather than relying on the mail or agents. First check what is required: passport photos, birth certificate, population register extract, signed statements, exact payment in cash, whatever.

Australian citizens can apply at post offices, or the passport office in their state capital; Canadians can apply at regional passport offices; New Zealanders can apply at any district office of the Department of Internal Affairs; and US citizens must apply in person (but may usually renew by mail) at a US Passport Agency office or some courthouses and post offices.

Citizens of European countries may not need a passport to travel to Britain. A national identity card can be sufficient, and usually involves less paperwork and processing time. Check with your travel agent or the British embassy.

Visas

At present, citizens of Australia, Canada, New Zealand, South Africa and the USA are given 'leave to enter' the UK at their point of arrival for up to six months, but are prohibited from working. If you're a citizen of the European Union (EU), you don't need a visa to enter the country and may live and work here freely.

Visa regulations are always subject to change, so it's essential to check with your local British embassy, high commission or consulate before leaving home.

The immigration authorities in the UK are tough; dress neatly and be able to prove that you have sufficient funds to support yourself. A credit card and/or an onward ticket will help.

Visa Extensions Tourist visas can only be extended in clear emergencies (such as an accident). Otherwise you'll have to leave the UK (perhaps going to Ireland or France) and apply for a fresh one, although this tactic will arouse suspicion after the second or third visa. To extend (or attempt to extend) your stay in the UK, contact the Home Office's Immigration & Nationality Department (☎ 020-8686 0688), Lunar House, 40 Wellesley Rd, Croydon CR2 2BY, before your existing visa expires. It opens 10 am to noon and 2 to 4 pm Monday to Friday. You can also ring the Visa & Passport Information Line on ☎ 0870 606 7766.

Student Visas Nationals of EU countries can enter the country to study without formalities. Otherwise, you need to be enrolled on a full-time course of at least 15 hours a week of weekday, daytime study at a single educational institution to be allowed to remain as a student. For more details, consult the British embassy, high commission or consulate in your own country.

Work Permits EU nationals don't need a work permit to work in Britain, but everyone else does. If the main purpose of your visit is to work, you have to be sponsored by a British company.

However, if you're a citizen of a Commonwealth country aged between 17 and 27 inclusive, you may apply for a Working Holiday Entry Certificate, which allows you to spend up to two years in the UK and take work that is 'incidental' to a holiday. You're not allowed to engage in business, pursue a career (evidently working as a bartender is not considered a career pursuit) or provide services as a professional sportsperson or entertainer.

You must apply to the nearest UK mission overseas – Working Holiday Entry Certificates are not granted on arrival in Britain. It's not possible to switch from being a visitor to a working holiday-maker, nor is it possible to claim back any time spent out of the UK during the two-year period. When you apply, you must satisfy the authorities that you have the means to pay for a return or onward journey and that you will be able to maintain yourself without recourse to public funds.

If you're a Commonwealth citizen and have a parent born in the UK, you may be eligible for a Certificate of Entitlement to the Right of Abode, which means you can live and work in Britain free of immigration control.

If you're a Commonwealth citizen with a grandparent born in the UK, or if the grandparent was born before 31 March 1922 in what is now the Republic of Ireland, you may qualify for a UK Ancestry Employment Certificate, which means you can work full time for up to four years in the UK.

Visiting students from the USA who are at least 18 years old and studying full time at a college or university can get a permit allowing them to work for six months. It costs US$200 and is available through the Council on International Educational Exchange (☎ 212-661 1414), 205 East 42nd St, New York, NY 10017; its Web site is at www.ciee.org. The British Universities North America Club (BUNAC; ☎ 020-7251 3472, fax 7251 0215, e enquiries@bunac .org.uk), 16 Bowling Green Lane, London EC1R 0QH, can also help you organise a permit and find employment. Its Web site is at www.bunac.org.

If you have any queries once you're in the UK, contact the Home Office's Immigration & Nationality Department (see the earlier Visa Extensions section).

Onward Tickets
Although you don't need an onward ticket to be granted 'leave to enter' on arrival (see Visas), this could help if there's any doubt over whether you have sufficient funds to support yourself and purchase an onward ticket in Britain.

Travel Insurance
Whichever way you're travelling, make sure you take out a comprehensive travel insurance policy that covers you for medical expenses and luggage theft or loss, and for cancellation of or delays in your travel arrangements. Ticket loss should also be included, but make sure you have a separate record of all the details – or better still, a photocopy of the ticket. There are all sorts of policies, but the international student travel policies handled by STA Travel and other student travel organisations are usually good value. Some policies offer lower and higher medical expense options – unless you're eligible for free treatment by the National Health Service (NHS; see the Health section later in the chapter), go for as much as you can afford. Other policies are cheaper if you forgo cover for lost baggage.

Buy insurance as early as possible. Otherwise you may find that you're not covered for delays to your flight caused by strikes or other industrial action. Always read the small print carefully for loopholes.

Paying for your ticket with a credit card often provides limited travel accident insurance, and you may be able to reclaim the payment if the operator doesn't deliver. In the UK, credit card providers are required by law to reimburse consumers if a company goes into liquidation and the amount in contention is more than £100.

Driving Licence & Permits
Your normal driving licence is legal for 12 months from the date you last entered the UK; you can then apply for a British licence at post offices. The International Driving Permit (IDP) is not needed in the UK.

Camping Card International
Your local automobile association also issues a Camping Card International, which is basically a camp site ID. They're also issued by local camping federations, and sometimes on the spot at camp sites. They incorporate third party insurance for damage you may cause, and many camp sites offer a small discount if you sign in with one. Some hostels and hotels also accept carnets for signing-in purposes, but won't give discounts.

Hostel Card
If you're travelling on a budget, membership of the Youth Hostel Association (YHA)

or Hostelling International (HI) is a must (£12 adult, £6 under-18). There are over 200 hostels in England and members are also eligible for all sorts of discounts. See the Accommodation section later in the chapter for more information about hostelling in England.

Student & Youth Cards

Most useful of these is the International Student Identity Card (ISIC), a plastic ID-style card with your photograph that costs £5 in the UK and provides cheap or free admission to museums and sights, inexpensive meals in some student restaurants and discounts on many forms of transport.

There's a worldwide industry in fake student cards, and many places now stipulate a maximum age for student discounts, or simply substitute a 'youth discount' for a 'student' one. If you're aged under 26 but not a student, you can apply for a GO25 card issued by the Federation of International Youth Travel Organisations (FIYTO), or a Euro 26 Card, which give much the same discounts for the same fee as the ISIC.

All these cards are issued by student unions, hostelling organisations and student travel agencies.

Seniors Cards

Many attractions reduce their admission price for people aged over 60 or 65 (sometimes as low as 55 for women); it's always worth asking even if you can't see a discount listed. Discount cards for people aged over 60 are available for rail and bus travel. See the Bus Passes & Discounts, and Railcards sections in the Getting Around chapter.

Other Documents

If you're visiting England on a Working Holiday Entry Certificate don't forget to bring any course certificates or letters of reference that might help you find a job.

Copies

All important documents (passport data page and visa page, credit cards, travel insurance policy, air/bus/train tickets, driving licence, and so on) should be photocopied before you leave home. Leave one copy with someone at home and keep another with you, separate from the originals.

It's also a good idea to store details of your vital travel documents in Lonely Planet's free online Travel Vault in case you lose the photocopies or can't be bothered with them. Your password-protected Travel Vault is accessible online anywhere in the world – create it at www.ekno.lonelyplanet .com.

EMBASSIES & CONSULATES
British Embassies, High Commissions & Consulates

British missions overseas include those listed below. If you need the details of others, consult the Foreign & Commonwealth Office Web site at www.fco.gov.uk.

Australia
High Commission: (☎ 02-6270 6666, fax 6270 6606) Commonwealth Ave, Yarralumla, Canberra, ACT 2600
Consulate: (☎ 02-9247 7521, fax 9251 6201) Level 16, The Gateway, 1 Macquarie Place, Sydney, NSW 2000
Web site: www.uk.emb.gov.au

Canada
High Commission: (☎ 613-237 1530, fax 232 2533) 80 Elgin St, Ottawa, Ontario K1P 5K7
Web site: www.britain-in-canada.org
Consulate: (☎ 416-593 1290, fax 593 1229) Suite 2800, 777 Bay St, College Park, Toronto, Ontario M5G 2G2
Web site: www.uk-canada-trade.org

France
Embassy: (☎ 01 44 51 31 00, fax 01 44 51 31 28) 35 rue du Faubourg Saint Honoré, 75383 Paris
Web site: www.amb-grandebretagne.fr

Germany
Embassy: (☎ 030-204 57562) Wilhelmstrasse 70–71, 10117 Berlin
Web site: www.britischebotschaft.de

Ireland
Embassy: (☎ 01-205 3822, fax 205 3890) 29 Merrion Rd, Ballsbridge, Dublin 4
Web site: www.britishembassy.ie

Netherlands
Embassy: (☎ 070-427 0427, fax 427 0345) Lange Voorhout 10, 2514 ED, The Hague
Consulate: (☎ 020-676 43 43, fax 676 10 69)

Koningslaan 44, 1075 AE Amsterdam
Web site: www.britain.nl

New Zealand
High Commission: (☎ 04-472 6049, fax 471 1974) 44 Hill St, Wellington 1
Consulate: (☎ 09-303 2973, fax 303 1836) 17th Floor, NZI House, 151 Queen St, Auckland 1
Web site: www.britain.org.nz

South Africa
High Commission: (☎ 021-461 7220, fax 461 0017) 91 Parliament St, Cape Town 8001
Consulate: (☎ 011-325 2133, fax 325 2132) Dunkeld Corner, 275 Jan Smuts Ave, Dunkeld West, Johannesburg 2196
Web site: www.britain.org.za

USA
Embassy: (☎ 202-588 6500, fax 588 7850) 3100 Massachusetts Ave, NW, Washington, DC 20008
Consulate: (☎ 212-745 0200, fax 745 3062) 845 Third Ave, New York, NY 10012
Web site: www.britainusa.com/ny.stm

Embassies & Consulates in England

It's important to realise what your own embassy – the embassy of the country of which you are a citizen – can and can't do to help you if you get into trouble. Generally speaking, it won't be much help in emergencies if the trouble you're in is remotely your own fault. Remember that you are bound by the laws of the country you are in. Your embassy will not be sympathetic if you end up in jail after committing a crime locally, even if such actions are legal in your own country.

In genuine emergencies you might get some assistance, but only if other channels have been exhausted. For example, if you need to get home urgently, a free ticket home is exceedingly unlikely – the embassy would expect you to have insurance. If you have all your money and documents stolen, it might assist with getting a new passport, but a loan for onward travel is out of the question.

Some foreign missions in London include:

Australia
High Commission: (☎ 020-7379 4334, fax 7240 5333) Australia House, Strand WC2

Canada
High Commission: (☎ 020-7258 6600, fax 7258 6333) 1 Grosvenor Square W1

France
Embassy: (☎ 020-7838 2050, fax 7838 2046) 58 Knightsbridge SW1

Germany
Embassy: (☎ 020-7824 1300, fax 7824 1435) 23 Belgrave Square SW1

Ireland
Embassy: (☎ 020-7235 2171, fax 7245 6961) 17 Grosvenor Place SW1

Netherlands
Embassy: (☎ 020-7590 3200, fax 7590 3458) 38 Hyde Park Gate SW7

New Zealand
High Commission: (☎ 020-7930 8422, fax 7839 4580) New Zealand House, 80 Haymarket SW1

South Africa
High Commission: (☎ 020-7451 7299, fax 7451 7284) South Africa House, Trafalgar Square WC2

USA
Embassy: (☎ 020-7499 9000, fax 7495 5012) 24 Grosvenor Square W1

CUSTOMS

Entering Britain, if you have nothing to declare go through the green channel; if you may have something to declare go through the red channel. If you are arriving from an EU country, go through a third, blue, channel.

Like other EU nations, the UK has a two-tier customs system: one for goods bought duty-free and one for goods bought in another EU country where taxes and duties have already been paid.

Duty Free

Duty-free sales to those travelling from one EU country to another were abolished in 1999. For goods purchased at airports or on ferries outside the EU, you are allowed to import 200 cigarettes or 250g of tobacco, 2L of still wine plus 1L of spirits over 22% or another 2L of wine (sparkling or otherwise), 50g of perfume, 250cc of toilet water, and other duty-free goods (including cider and beer) to the value of £136.

Tax & Duty Paid

Although you can no longer bring in duty-free goods from another EU country, you can bring in goods from another EU country, where certain goods might be cheaper, if taxes have been paid on them. The items are supposed to be for individual consumption but a thriving business has developed, with many English making day trips to France to load up their cars with cheap alcohol and cigarettes, which they often sell back in the UK. The savings can more than pay for the trip.

If you purchase from a normal retail outlet, customs uses the following maximum quantities as a guideline to distinguish personal imports from those on a commercial scale: 800 cigarettes, 200 cigars, 1kg of tobacco, 10L of spirits, 20L of fortified wine, 90L of wine (of which not more than 60L are sparkling) and 110L of beer.

Pets

To protect its rabies-free status, England has long had draconian pet quarantine policies that required any animal brought into the country to be quarantined for six months.

The rules thawed slightly in 2000, when a pilot scheme was introduced for dogs and cats only. And it's not just any pooches and pussies, but only those from certain countries: Andorra, Austria, Belgium, Denmark, Finland, France, Germany, Gibraltar, Greece, Italy, Liechtenstein, Luxembourg, Monaco, the Netherlands, Norway, Portugal, San Marino, Spain, Sweden and Switzerland.

In addition there are numerous further regulations: the pet must not have been outside the qualifying countries in the six months prior to travel to Britain; it must have an identity microchip implanted; and it must have various vaccinations, tests and certifications. The process is complex, but at least it is more relaxed than the previous 'no exceptions' policy.

If you are contemplating bringing your pet to England, you should contact your nearest UK mission to find out the latest details on the pet quarantine situation.

MONEY
Currency

The British currency is the pound sterling (£), which is divided into 100 pence (p).

Coins of 1p and 2p are copper; 5p, 10p, 20p and 50p coins are silver; and the bulky £1 coin is gold-coloured. The £2 coin, introduced into circulation in 1997, is gold-coloured on the edge with a silver centre.

Notes come in £5, £10, £20 and £50 denominations and vary in colour and size. The £50 notes can be difficult to change – avoid them.

Near the Scottish border you may also come across notes issued by three Scottish banks – Clydesdale Bank, Royal Bank of Scotland and Bank of Scotland – including a £1 note, which are legal tender on both sides of the border. If you have any problems getting them accepted in England, ask a bank to swap them for you.

Exchange Rates

Exchange rates at the time of going to print were:

country	unit		pounds
Australia	A$1	=	£0.39
Canada	C$1	=	£0.45
EU	€1	=	£0.59
France	1FF	=	£0.09
Germany	DM1	=	£0.31
Ireland	IR£1	=	£0.76
Japan	¥100	=	£0.62
New Zealand	NZ$1	=	£0.30
USA	US$1	=	£0.67

Exchanging Money

By 2002, most of the EU will have a single currency called the euro. Until then francs, Deutschmarks, pesetas and so on will remain in place or share equal status with the euro. The pound will continue to be the unit of currency in the UK as the British government has decided not to adopt the euro for the time being. You're likely to see some of the acrimonious debate on the issue in the press during your visit.

Cash Nothing beats cash for convenience – or risk. It's still a good idea, however, to travel with some cash in pounds sterling, if only to tide you over until you get to an exchange facility. There's no problem if you arrive sterling-less at any of England's airports; they usually have good-value exchange counters open for incoming flights.

Travellers Cheques & Eurocheques

Travellers cheques offer protection from theft. Ideally, your cheques should be in pounds and preferably issued by American Express (AmEx) or Thomas Cook, which are widely recognised, well represented and don't charge for cashing their own cheques.

Bring most cheques in large denominations. It's only towards the end of a stay that you may want to change a small cheque to make sure you don't get left with too much local currency. Travellers cheques are rarely accepted outside banks or used for everyday transactions in England so you need to cash them in advance.

Eurocheques, available if you have a European bank account, are guaranteed up to a certain amount. When cashing them, you will be asked to show your Eurocheque card bearing your signature and registration number as well as your passport or ID card. Eurocheques are not as commonly used in England as they are in continental Europe, and many places refuse to accept them. Some people may have never even seen them before.

Buying Travellers Cheques

The cost of buying travellers cheques varies considerably, depending on the seller. AmEx is often the cheapest, charging 1% commission with no minimum charge. Main post offices also offer very competitive rates. The English banks are usually more expensive and often want advance warning: NatWest charges 1% commission for sterling travellers cheques, with a £4 minimum charge; Lloyds TSB, HSBC and Barclays all charge 1.5% commission, with a minimum charge of £3.

Lost or Stolen Travellers Cheques

Keep a record of the numbers of your cheques and which cheques you have cashed, then if they're lost or stolen you will be able to tell the issuing agency exactly which cheques have gone. Keep this list separate from the cheques themselves.

As soon as you realise any cheques are missing, you should contact the issuing office or the nearest branch of the issuing agency. AmEx (☎ 029-2066 6111) and Thomas Cook (☎ 01733-318950), both of which operate 24 hours, seven days a week, can often arrange replacement cheques within 24 hours.

ATMs

Plastic cards make the perfect travelling companions – they're ideal for major purchases and let you withdraw cash from selected banks and automatic telling machines (ATMs), God's greatest gift to the travelling world since the backpack was invented. ATMs are usually linked up to international money systems such as Cirrus, Maestro or Plus, so you can enter your card, punch in your personal identification number (PIN) and get instant cash. But ATMs aren't fail-safe, especially if the card was issued outside Europe, and it's safer to go to a human teller. It can be a major headache if an ATM swallows your card.

Debit cards, which you use to withdraw money directly from your bank or savings account, are widely linked internationally – ask your bank at home for advice. Credit cards, on the other hand, may not be hooked up to ATM networks unless you specifically ask your bank to do this for you and request a PIN. However, once you've done this, you'll find most ATMs are linked to the Visa and/or MasterCard networks. AmEx cards are accepted in many ATMs as well. You might also ask which UK banks' ATMs will accept your particular card, and whether you pay a fee to use them.

Credit Cards

Visa, MasterCard, AmEx and Diners Club cards are widely accepted in England, although small businesses such as B&Bs prefer cash. Businesses sometimes make a charge for accepting payment by credit card so this isn't always the cheapest way to go. You can get cash advances using your Visa and MasterCard at many banks. If you have an AmEx card, you can cash up to £500 worth of personal cheques at AmEx offices in any seven-day period.

If you plan to use a credit card, make sure your credit limit is high enough to cover major expenses such as car hire or airline tickets.

If you're going to rely on plastic, go for two different cards. Better still, combine cards and travellers cheques so you have something to fall back on if an ATM swallows your card or the bank won't accept it.

Lost or Stolen Cards If a card is lost or stolen you must inform the police and the issuing company as soon as possible – otherwise you may have to pay for the purchases that the unspeakable thief has made using your card. Here are some numbers for cancelling your cards:

AmEx	☎ 01273-689955
Diners Club	☎ 01252-516261
MasterCard	☎ 01702-362988
Visa	☎ 0800 895082

International Transfers If you instruct your bank back home to send you a draft, be sure you specify the bank and the branch to which you want your money directed, or ask your home bank to tell you where a suitable one is. The whole procedure will be easier if you've authorised someone back home to access your account.

Money sent to you by telegraphic transfer should reach you within a week; by mail, allow at least two weeks. When it arrives, it will most likely be converted into local currency – you can then take it as is, or buy travellers cheques. The charge for this service is usually around £20.

You can also transfer money using AmEx or Thomas Cook or by post office Money-Gram. Americans can also use Western Union (☎ 0800 833833), although it has fewer offices in England from which to collect and charges 10% plus commission.

Moneychangers Changing your money is never a problem in London, with banks, bureaux de change and travel agencies all competing for your business. Just make sure you're getting the best deal possible. Be particularly careful using bureaux de change; they may seem to offer good exchange rates but frequently levy outrageous

commissions (branches of Chequepoint charge up to 8% to cash a sterling travellers cheque) and fees. Check the exchange rate, the percentage commission and any minimum charge very carefully.

Elsewhere in England, look for branches of the major banks for exchange services.

The exchange desks at the international airports charge less than most high-street banks and cash sterling travellers cheques for free; for other currencies they charge about 1.5% with a £3 minimum. They can also sell you up to £500 worth of most major currencies on the spot.

Other Methods Personal cheques are still widely used in England – a group of diners will often write separate cheques to pay for their share of a meal – and are validated by a cheque guarantee card. Increasingly, retail outlets are linked to the Switch and Delta networks, which allow customers to use a debit card (deductions are made directly from your English current account).

If you plan to stay a while in England, you may want to open a bank account, but it's no simple matter. Building societies tend to be more welcoming than banks and often have better interest rates. You'll need a permanent address in England, and it will smooth the way if you have a reference or introductory letter from your bank manager at home, plus bank statements for the previous year. Owning credit/charge cards also helps.

Make sure you look for a current account that pays interest (however tiny), gives you a cheque book and a cheque guarantee/debit card, and gives access to ATMs.

Security

Whichever way you decide to carry your funds, it makes sense to keep most of it out of easy reach of thieves in a money belt or something similar. It always makes sense to keep something like £50 apart from the rest of your cash for use in an emergency.

Take particular care in crowded places such as the London Underground and never leave wallets sticking out of trouser pockets or daypacks and never leave bags hanging over the back of chairs in pubs and restaurants. Also watch out on buses and around popular tourist attractions such as the Tower of London and Stonehenge.

Costs

England is expensive and London is horrific. While in London you will need to budget £30 to £35 a day for bare survival. Dormitory accommodation alone will cost a minimum of £10 to £20 a night, a one-day Travelcard is £3.90 (Zones 1 and 2), and drinks and the most basic sustenance will cost you at least £10, with any sightseeing or nightlife on top. There's not much point visiting if you can't enjoy some of the city's life, so if possible add another £15 a day.

Costs will obviously be even higher if you choose to stay in a central hotel and eat restaurant meals. Hotel rates start at around £30 per person and a restaurant meal will be at least £10. Add a couple of pints of beer (£2 each) and admission fees to a tourist attraction or nightclub and you could easily spend £55 per day – without being extravagant.

Once you start moving around the country, particularly if you have a transport pass, the costs will drop. Away from London, life is cheaper. Fresh food costs roughly the same as in Australia and the USA. However, without including long-distance transport, and assuming you stay in hostels and an occasional cheap B&B, you'll still need at least £25 per day. A country youth hostel will cost from £8; add £8 for food, £7 for admission charges and/or local buses, and £4 for miscellaneous items such as films, shampoo, books and telephone calls.

If you hire a car or use a transport pass, stay in B&Bs, eat one sit-down meal a day and don't stint on admission fees, you'll need £50 to £60 per day (still not including long-distance transport costs). Most basic B&Bs will cost from £15 to £25 per person and dinner will be from £8 to £15 (depending on whether you're eating in a restaurant or a pub and how much you drink); then add £5 for snacks and drinks, £4 for miscellaneous items and at least £7 for admission fees. If you're travelling by car you'll probably average a further £8 to £15 per day on petrol

Admission Prices

Throughout this book admission costs are given as adult/child. Child admission charges usually have a cut-off of 12 years of age, with some going as high as 16 or as low as 10.

At the time of writing, there were proposals to scrap entrance fees to all national galleries and museums in England. A final decision depends on agreement between the government departments concerned, but in the meantime it may be worth phoning ahead if you plan to visit one of the fee-charging national museums.

and parking (not including hire charges); if you travel using some sort of pass you'll probably average a couple of pounds a day on local transport or hiring a bike.

Train fares usually rise by around 5% in January. Bus fares usually increase by a few pence every April and October. Admission fees seem to rise by 50p or £1 a year.

Tipping & Bargaining

Many restaurants now add a 'discretionary' service charge to your bill, but in places that don't you are expected to leave a 10 to 15% tip unless the service was unsatisfactory. Waiting staff are often paid derisory wages on the assumption that the money will be supplemented by tips. It's legal for restaurants to include a service charge in the bill, but this should be clearly advertised. You needn't add a further tip. And you never tip to have your pint pulled in a pub.

Taxi drivers also expect to be tipped (about 10%), especially in London. It's less usual to tip minicab drivers.

Bargaining is virtually unheard of, even at markets, although it's fine to ask if there are discounts for students, young people or youth hostel members. Some 'negotiation' is also OK if you're buying an expensive item such as a car or motorcycle.

Taxes & Refunds

Value-added tax (VAT) is a 17.5% sales tax levied on most goods and services except food and books. Restaurants must by law include VAT in their menu prices.

It's sometimes possible for visitors to claim a refund of VAT paid on goods – a considerable saving. You're eligible if you've spent fewer than 365 days out of the two years prior to making the purchase living in the UK, and if you're leaving the EU within three months of making the purchase.

Not all shops participate in the VAT refund scheme, called the Retail Export Scheme or Tax-Free Shopping, and different shops will have different minimum purchase conditions (normally around £75 in one shop). On request, participating shops will give you a special form (VAT 407). This form must be presented with the goods and receipts to customs when you depart (VAT-free goods can't be posted or shipped home). After customs has certified the form, it should be returned to the shop for a refund (minus an administration/handling fee), which takes eight to 10 weeks to come through.

Several companies offer a centralised refunding service to shops and participating shops carry a sign in their window (for example, Tax-Free Shopping). You can avoid bank charges for cashing a sterling cheque by using a credit card for purchases and asking that the VAT refund be credited to your account. Cash refunds are sometimes available at major airports.

POST & COMMUNICATIONS
Post
Although the queues in post offices can be long, the Royal Mail (☎ 0845 600 0606) delivers quite good service. Post office hours can vary, but most open 9 am to 5 pm, Monday to Friday, and 9 am to noon on Saturday. First class mail is quicker and more expensive (27p per letter) than 2nd class mail (19p).

Air-mail letters to other European countries cost 36p, to the Americas and Australasia 45/65p (up to 10/20g).

If you don't have a permanent address, mail can be sent to poste restante in the town or city where you are staying. AmEx

Travel offices will also hold card-holders' mail free of charge.

An air-mail letter generally takes less than a week to get to the USA or Canada; around a week to Australia or New Zealand.

Telephone
To call England from abroad, dial your country's international access code, then 44 (the UK's country code), then the area code (dropping the initial 0) followed by the phone number.

British Telecom's (BT's) famous red phone-boxes survive only in conservation areas. More common these days are the glass cubicles with phones that accept coins, prepaid phonecards and/or credit cards.

All phones come with reasonably clear instructions. BT offers phonecards for £2, £5, £10 and £20 that are widely available from all sorts of retailers, including post offices and newsagents. A digital display on the telephone indicates how much credit is left on the card.

Some special phone codes worth knowing are:

☎ 0500	toll free
☎ 0800	toll free
☎ 0845	local call rate applies
☎ 0870	national call rate applies
☎ 0891	premium rate (49p per minute)
☎ 09064	premium rate (49p per minute)

Beware of other codes (such as six digits) that may indicate you're calling a mobile phone. This is usually considerably more expensive than calling a land line.

Local & National Calls & Rates Local calls are charged by time alone; national calls are charged by both time and distance. Daytime rates apply 8 am to 6 pm, Monday to Friday; the cheap rate applies 6 pm to 8 am, Monday to Friday; and the cheap weekend rate applies midnight Friday to midnight Sunday. The latter two rates offer substantial savings.

For directory enquiries/information call

☎ 192. These calls are free from public phones but cost 25p if you call from a private one. To get the operator call ☎ 100.

International Calls & Rates To call someone outside the UK dial 00, then the country code, the area code (you usually drop the initial zero if there is one) and the number. International direct dialling (IDD) calls to almost anywhere in the world can be made from almost all public telephones.

To make a reverse-charge (collect) call, dial ☎ 155 for the international operator. Direct dialling is cheaper. For international directory enquiries dial ☎ 153 (50p from private phones).

For most countries (including Europe, the USA and Canada) it's cheaper to phone overseas between 8 pm and 8 am Monday to Friday and at weekends; for Australia and New Zealand, however, it's cheapest 2.30 to 7.30 pm and midnight to 7 am every day. The savings are considerable.

There's a wide range of local and international phonecards. Lonely Planet's eKno Communication Card is aimed specifically at independent travellers and provides budget international calls, a range of messaging services, free email and travel information – for local calls, you're usually better off with a local card. You can join online at www.ekno.lonelyplanet.com, or by phone from England by dialling ☎ 0800 376 1704. Once you have joined, to use eKno from England, dial ☎ 0800 169 8646 (or ☎ 0800 376 2366 from a payphone).

Check the eKno Web site for joining and access numbers from other countries and updates on local access numbers and new features.

It's also possible to undercut BT international call rates by buying a special card (usually denominated £5, £10 or £20) with a Personal Identification Number (PIN) that you use from any phone, even a home phone, by dialling a special access number. There are dozens of cards available – with sci-fi names such as Alpha, Omega, Phone Com, Climax, Swiftlink and America First – available from newsagents and grocers. To decide which is best you really have to compare the rate each offers for the particular country you want – posters with the rates of the various companies are often displayed in shop doors or windows.

Mobile Phones England uses GSM 900/1800, which is compatible with the rest of Europe and Australia but not with the North American GSM 1900 or the totally different system in Japan (though some North Americans have GSM 1900/900 phones that do work here). If you have a GSM phone, check with your service provider about using it in England, and beware of calls being routed internationally (very expensive for a 'local' call).

If you want the convenience of a mobile in England, the simplest solution may be simply to buy one of the pay-as-you-talk phones sold not only from a plethora of high-street shops, but also from supermarkets, Woolworth's and just about anywhere else.

For under £70 you get a phone with a decent amount of air time and your own telephone number. As you use up your airtime, you simply buy more. There are no contracts or billing hassles. All four main mobile phone companies in England – Orange, Vodaphone, One 2 One and BT Cellnet – have variations on this scheme.

Fax

Many newsagents and tobacco shops offer a fax service. Ask at a TIC or just look for the signs.

Email & Internet Access

Travelling with a portable computer is a great way to stay in touch with life back home, but unless you know what you're doing it's fraught with potential problems. If you plan to carry your notebook or palmtop computer with you, remember that the power supply voltage in the countries you visit may vary from that at home, risking damage to your equipment. The best investment is a universal AC adapter for your appliance, which will enable you to plug it in anywhere without frying the innards. You'll also need a plug adapter for each country you visit – often it's easiest to buy these before you leave home. See the Electricity section later in the chapter for details about English power and plugs.

Also, your PC-card modem may or may not work once you leave your home country – and you won't know for sure until you try. The safest option is to buy a reputable 'global' modem before you leave home, or buy a local PC-card modem if you're spending an extended time in any one country. Keep in mind that the telephone socket in each country you visit will probably be different from the one at home, so ensure that you have at least a US RJ-11 telephone adapter that works with your modem.

England uses a unique phone connector; however, it's not too hard to procure an adapter that bridges the gap between English and RJ-11 modems. Hotels aimed at business travellers usually have sockets for RJ-11 plugs, while in others you can reroute the in-room telephone cord – which typically connects to the phone with an RJ-11 plug – into your modem. However at cheaper places and B&Bs, the phone may be hard-wired or there may not be a socket of any kind and when you ask the host for help you'll be met with a wide-eyed and bewildered stare.

For more information on travelling with a portable computer, see www.teleadapt.com or www.warrior.com.

Major Internet service providers (ISPs) such as AOL (www.aol.com), CompuServe (www.compuserve.com) and Earthlink (www.earthlink.net) have dial-in nodes in England. It's best to download a list of the dial-in numbers before you leave home. If you access your Internet email account at home through a smaller ISP or your office or school network, your best option is either to open an account with a global ISP, such as those mentioned above, or to rely on cybercafes and other public access points to collect your mail.

If you do intend to rely on cybercafes the best thing you can do is use a Web-based email service such as Hotmail (www.hotmail.com) or Yahoo (www.yahoo.com). This lets you log on to your email from any computer with Web access. There is a free eKno email option as well (www.ekno.lonelyplanet.com).

Otherwise, if you want to use your email service from home you'll need to carry three pieces of information with you to enable you to access your Internet mail account: your incoming (POP or IMAP) mail server name, your account name and your password. Your ISP or network supervisor will be able to give you these. Armed with this information, you should be able to access your Internet mail account from any net-connected machine in the world, provided it runs some kind of email software (remember that Netscape and Internet Explorer both have mail modules). It pays to become familiar with the process for doing this before you leave home.

Places with Internet access are common in England. Try libraries, hostels, cybercafes and the like; many are listed in this book. Otherwise, TICs usually know right where to send you.

INTERNET RESOURCES

England has no shortage of sites of interest to travellers. Towns, tourist boards, attractions, B&Bs, hotels and transportation companies all have Web sites. You will find many listed throughout this book. A good place to begin is the BTA Web site at www.bta.org.uk; another good site is at www.information-britain.co.uk.

The Web is also a rich resource for travellers in general. You can research your trip, hunt down bargain air fares, book hotels, check on weather conditions or chat with locals and other travellers about the best places to visit (or avoid!).

There's no better place to start your Web explorations than the Lonely Planet Web site (www.lonelyplanet.com). Here you'll find succinct summaries on travelling to most places on earth, postcards from other travellers and the Thorn Tree bulletin board, where you can ask questions before you go or dispense advice when you get back. You can also find travel news and updates to many of our most popular guidebooks, and the subWWWay section links you to the most useful travel resources elsewhere on the Web.

BOOKS

Countless guidebooks explore England's every nook and cranny. The book shops listed in this book as well as most TICs are literally groaning with scores of guidebooks. The latter are good for unusual local and specialist titles.

Most books are published in different editions by different publishers in different countries. As a result, a book might be a hardcover rarity in one country while it's readily available in paperback in another. Fortunately, bookshops and libraries search by title or author, so your local bookshop or library is best placed to advise you on the availability of the recommendations in this section.

Lonely Planet

Lonely Planet also publishes *Walking in Britain* and *Cycling Britain*, which make excellent companions to this book. *Britain* covers the entire island while *Scotland, Edinburgh* and *Wales* give detailed regional and local information of the neighbouring areas. *London* is a comprehensive guide to the capital while *London Condensed* provides essential information in a handy format. *Out to Eat – London* describes an enormous selection of London's best eateries, while the *London City Guide* video provides a visual complement. Lonely Planet's *Ireland* guide covers Northern Ireland as well as the Irish Republic. Those who want to get to grips with British English – Cockney in particular – should get hold of the Lonely Planet *British phrasebook*.

Guidebooks

Numerous books list B&Bs, restaurants, hotels, country houses, camping and caravan parks, and self-catering cottages, but often their objectivity is questionable as the places they cover pay for the privilege of being included. Those published by the tourist authorities are reliable (if not comprehensive) and widely available in TICs. The *Which?* books, produced by the Consumers' Association, are good and accurate: no money changes hands for recommendations.

People of a literary bent might like to look at the *Oxford Literary Guide to Great Britain and Ireland*, which details the many writers who have immortalised the towns and villages.

There are scores more specialist guidebooks you can spend hours looking them over in larger book shops. One favourite is the annual *Good Beer Guide*, which can steer you to the best English beers and ales and the pubs that serve them.

The Church Explorer's Guide, by Frank Bottomley, is a detailed look at what sorts of treasures can be found in England's scores of churches. This is a fine example of the dozens of special interest guidebooks available on a myriad of subjects.

Little of England remains in a truly natural state and the *National Trust Coast & Country Handbook* is a detailed examination of the industrial and agricultural uses that have claimed the countryside. It also has excellent sections showing the adaptability and diversity of English flora and fauna.

Travel

Bill Bryson's entertaining and perceptive *Notes from a Small Island* is a continuous bestseller that covers Britain. It's also a favourite with locals, who find his comfortable humour not overly scathing. *The Kingdom by the Sea*, by Paul Theroux, was written in 1982 and so is now a little dated, but nonetheless very readable. Theroux's eye is as keen and his mood just as irritable as in his other books.

Iain Sinclair walked throughout the grittier parts of the South-East in the 1990s and his reflections on where England is going form a powerful book in *Lights Out for the Territory*.

Dervla Murphy's *Tale of Two Cities*, written in 1987, offers a veteran travel writer's view of life among England's ethnic minorities in Manningham (in Bradford) and Handsworth (in Birmingham).

A seven-year quest around the alleys of

Spitalfield's Market in London is the basis for William Taylor's *This Bright Field*. He may cover few miles but he traverses a fascinating range of characters in this small corner of London.

No Voice from the Hall, by John Harris, recounts a fascinating search among once-grand country houses in the years after WWII. Their owners were chased away by taxes, leaving only memories and ghosts behind.

History & Politics

The Year 1000, by Robert Lacey and Danny Danzinger, was an unexpected bestseller and examines what life was like in England in 1000 (it was cold and damp then too).

The Isles: A History, by Norman Davies, is a much-acclaimed history of the British Isles and their diverse and restive peoples.

The Course of My Life, by Edward Heath, is the autobiography of one of Britain's most important politicians and prime ministers. *Windrush – The Irresistible Rise of Multicultural Britain*, by Mike and Trevor Phillips, traces the history of black Britain and the impact of immigrants on British society. Much of the book is focused on England.

A Traveller's History of England, by Christopher Daniell, is both a concise guide to English history and a good survey of English culture that is all geared to the traveller.

For a deeper look at England's long and well-documented past, *The English Experience*, by John Bowle, manages to be both scholarly and readable.

Hadrian's Wall, by David J Breeze and Brian Dobson, ponders the history of the Roman Wall that was designed to protect what is today's England from the savage Scottish tribes. The authors argue that the wall was a good deal for both sides.

The Day the World Took Off – the Roots of the Industrial Revolution is the companion book to a TV series of the same name produced by Channel 4. Authors Sally & David Dugan provide a lively commentary on events in England and their effects worldwide.

General

The English, by BBC television presenter Jeremy Paxman, is as literate as one would expect from possibly the toughest interviewer on British airwaves. It's all about just what the title suggests.

The Queen and Di, by Ingrid Seward, is just one of literally hundreds of books pertaining to the royal family. One of the most readable books on the monarchy is *The Royals*, by Kitty Kelley. Filled with juicy titbits and gossip, the book is impossible to buy in England because publishers are afraid of angering the royal family. Such lack of resolve is a disgrace.

That Was Satire, That Was, by Humphrey Carpenter, is a great look at the explosion – so to speak – of British satire beginning in the 1960s.

You can almost hear the posh accents spoken in *The English Country House Party*, by Phyllida Barstow. These institutions of those not yet taxed out of their country homes were long on protocol and short on impromptu fun.

The Knight in Medieval England and its companion *The Lady in Medieval England* (both by Peter Coss) provide a far more accurate portrayal of medieval life than any costume drama.

The Other Side of the Dale, by Gervase Phinn, aims to be a repeat of James Herriot's vet adventures. Only this time the little animals are school children (is there a difference?) and the protagonist is a school inspector.

FILMS

The English film industry has been having its best years in, well, years of late. A steady stream of commercial successes has injected life and energy into the industry. *Lock Stock and Two Smoking Barrels*, a comedy of some hapless London hoods and a sort of a British *Pulp Fiction*, was wildly popular.

Notting Hill managed to bring hordes of tourists to the already trendy neighbourhood. Previously, the 1990s were marked by several other hits. *Shakespeare in Love* used locations throughout England and nabbed the Oscar for Best Picture for 1998. *The Full Monty*, a tale of unemployed Sheffield steelworkers turned male strippers, became the most popular British film ever. *Four Weddings and a Funeral* remains popular, especially whenever TV programmers need a 'light, romantic comedy'.

Brassed Off is the sad story of a colliery band attempting to keep going while the South Yorkshire pit on which the members depend for work is closed by the Conservative government.

A world away from such gritty social realism are the spate of adaptations of Jane Austen novels that have hit the screens. *Pride and Prejudice* was made for television but *Emma* and *Sense and Sensibility* were feature-length films. Filming took place all round England; see if you can recognise Montacute in Somerset, Lacock in Wiltshire and Lyme Park in Cheshire.

The French Lieutenant's Woman, based on the John Fowles' novel of the same name, made great play with the landscape around Lyme Regis in Dorset. *Howard's End*, the Merchant-Ivory adaptation of the EM Foster novel, looked as if it was set in the Home Counties but actually strayed as far afield as Ludlow in Shropshire.

Among the scores of classics, *Chariots of Fire* looks at the competitive lives of Cambridge Olympic runners Harold Abrahams and Eric Liddell. *A Hard Day's Night* looks at 36 hours in the life of The Beatles and has many excellent London locations. *Monty Python and the Holy Grail* examines the legend of King Arthur with minimal regard for historical accuracy, but with high regard for the carrying capacity of swallows – whether African or European.

NEWSPAPERS & MAGAZINES
Newspapers

Breakfast need never be boring in England – there's a very wide range of dailies available that are sold nationally.

The bottom end of the English newspaper market is occupied by the *Sun*, the *Mirror*,

---

Ten English Films

Here are 10 famous films set in England and their locations:

Brief Encounter (1945) – A classic wartime weepy directed by David Lean. Carnworth station in Lancashire still has the look it did for the classic goodbye between Trevor Howard and Celia Johnson. The station however is closed.

Chariots of Fire (1981) – All that slow motion running to pop classical music mostly took place in and around Cambridge, although the quadrangle run was at Eton College.

The French Lieutenant's Woman (1981) – Meryl Streep walks with the waves in the same setting as in the novel: The Cobb at Lyme Regis in Dorset.

The Full Monty (1997) – Shot almost entirely in real locations in and around industrial Sheffield.

Howard's End (1992) – Peppard Cottage near Henley-on-Thames was the house while the local village was Dorchester-on-Thames in Oxfordshire.

Little Voice (1998) – The delightful story of the odd but talented singer, played by Jane Horrocks, was shot on location in Scarborough in Yorkshire.

A Man for All Seasons (1966) – It was mostly and authentically shot at Hampton Court.

Monty Python and the Holy Grail (1975) – Although it deals with the English legends of King Arthur and company, the film was mostly shot in Scotland, so never mind.

My Fair Lady (1964) – This musical version of George Bernard Shaw's *Pygmalion* was shot on location at London's pre-tourist-era Covent Garden. (This was also the setting for much of Alfred Hitchcock's 1972 *Frenzy*.)

The Railway Children (1970) – The story of the children and their pal the porter was shot around the Keighley and Worth Valley Railway near Haworth in Yorkshire.

Daily Star and the *Sport*. The *Sun* is a national institution with witty headlines and nasty, mean-spirited contents. After a long period in the doldrums, the *Mirror*, once a decent paper with left-wing sympathies, has started to reposition itself slightly (very slightly) more upmarket. The *Sport* takes bad taste to the ultimate, with a steady diet of semi-naked women of improbable proportions and stories of space invaders.

The middle-market tabloids – the *Daily Mail* and, to a lesser extent, the *Daily Express* – are Tory strongholds, thunderously supporting the Conservatives and playing to Middle England's fears with a steady diet of crime reports. The *Daily Mail* in particular makes no efforts to hide its allegiance. During the 2000 fuel crisis, it lambasted the French when their blockades of fuel terminals inconvenienced English tourists. Yet when English farmers and lorry drivers did the same, the *Mail* called the protestors heroes for giving the Labour government a hard time. In late 2000 the *Express* was purchased by one of the UK's leading publishers of pornographic magazines – its editorial fate under its new management remains to be seen.

The broadsheets can be stuffy and self-important, but are generally stimulating and well written, although they frequently show little regard for multiple sources and other voices in their stories. The *Daily Telegraph*, or 'Torygraph', outsells its rivals and its readership remains old fogeyish despite efforts to attract a new clientele (check out the frequent spectaculars on topics such as Lady Somebody and her horse or the latest in garden party fashion, for instance). *The Times*, once Britain's finest paper, has lost ground under Murdoch's ownership but remains conservative and influential. It has good travel pages as well. The *Independent* tries hard to live up to its title and seems to have been thrown a lifeline by the strong economy. The lively and innovative, if mildly left-wing, *Guardian* is read by the chattering classes.

The Sunday papers are essential to the English way of life. On their day of rest, the English still settle in comfy armchairs and plough their way through endless supplements; the *Sunday Times* must destroy at least one rainforest per issue. Most of the daily papers have a Sunday stablemate that shares their political views. The oldest of the Sundays, the *Observer*, is the seventh day version of the Guardian but usually not as good. What these virtual logs have in common is a lack of much news; the news sections of the Sunday papers are filled with the aimless musings of overseas correspondents and news features that seem sparked by press releases.

You can also buy the Paris-based *International Herald Tribune*, arguably the best brief source of international news available, and many foreign-language papers in major train stations and throughout London.

There are local and regional papers throughout England.

Magazines

Walk into any high-street newsagent and you'll realise that England boasts a magazine for almost any interest, with whole shelves of computer magazines, trainspotting magazines, heritage magazines, even magazines devoted to such esoteric interests as feng shui and naturism.

Most big towns have a listings magazine broadly along the lines of London's *Time Out*. Some are free, although the best cost about £2 and are mentioned in the relevant chapters of this book.

The biweekly satirical *Private Eye* is an institution that retains its sharp edge even at the risk of regular run-ins with the law.

Time and *Newsweek* are readily available, but the London-based *Economist* remains the best news weekly here or anywhere.

RADIO & TV
Radio

BBC radio caters for most tastes. Radio 1 (1089kHz and 1053kHz MW; 98.8MHz FM), its main pop music station, has undergone a revival after some years in the doldrums. At the same time, Radio 2 (88–90.2MHz FM) has broadened its outlook and now plays gooey 1960s, 1970s and 1980s stuff alongside even older tracks.

Radio 3 (1215kHz MW; 91.3MHz FM) sticks with classical music and plays, while the august Radio 4 (198kHz LW; 720kHz MW; 93.5MHz FM) offers a mixture of drama, news, current affairs and talk; its Today program (6 to 9 am Monday to Friday, from 7 am on Saturday) is particularly popular. Radio 5 Live (693kHz and 909kHz MW) provides a mix of sport, current affairs and talk.

The BBC World Service (648kHz MW) offers brilliant news coverage and quirky bits and pieces from around the globe.

The BBC also has numerous local services scattered about the country, although their coverage of local issues often seems to rely unduly on the exploits of heroic police dogs and the like.

You'll also find a range of commercial stations playing everything from pop music to classical.

TV

It's probably true to say that England still turns out some of the world's best TV, although the increasing competition as channels proliferate is resulting in slipping standards. Recent years have seen a spate of fly-on-the-wall documentaries that simply point a camera at the run-of-the-mill (hotels, driving schools, even Lonely Planet) and leave the viewer amused but none the wiser.

There are currently five regular TV channels – BBC1 and BBC2 are publicly funded by a TV licence and don't carry advertising; ITV and Channels 4 and 5 are commercial stations and do. Of these, Channel 4 has the most interesting programming, ITV has lots of soaps and mass-entertainment.

These stations are up against competition from Rupert Murdoch's satellite TV, BSkyB, and assorted cable channels. Cable churns out mostly missable rubbish, but Sky is slowly monopolising sports coverage and has pioneered pay-per-view screenings of the most popular events.

There are regional TV variations, but like regional radio they can be pretty lacking in stimulating fare.

VIDEO SYSTEMS

With many tourist attractions now selling videos as souvenirs it's worth bearing in mind that British videos are VHS PAL format and not compatible with NTSC or SECAM.

PHOTOGRAPHY & VIDEO
Film & Equipment

Although print film is widely available, slide film can be more elusive; if there's no specialist photographic shop around, Boots, the high-street chemist chain, is the likeliest stockist. Print film (36-exposure) costs from £3.50 for ISO 100 to £5 for ISO 400.

Technical Tips

With dull, overcast conditions common, high-speed film (ISO 200 or ISO 400) is useful. In summer, the best times of day for photography are usually early in the morning and late in the afternoon when the glare of the sun has passed.

Lonely Planet's full-colour *Travel Photography: A Guide to Taking Better Pictures*, written by internationally renowned travel photographer Richard I'Anson, is designed to take on the road.

Restrictions

Many tourist attractions either charge for taking photos or prohibit it altogether. Use of flash is frequently forbidden to protect delicate pictures and fabrics. Video cameras are often disallowed because of the inconvenience they can cause to other visitors.

Airport Security

You will have to put your camera and film through the x-ray machine at all English airports. The machines are supposed to be film-safe, but you may feel happier if you ask for exposed films to be examined by hand.

TIME

Wherever you are in the world, the time on your watch is measured in relation to the time at Greenwich – Greenwich Mean Time (GMT) – although strictly speaking, GMT is used only in air and sea navigation, and is otherwise referred to as Universal Time Coordinated (UTC).

British Summer Time (BST) muddies the water so that even Britain itself is ahead of GMT from late March to late October. But to give you an idea, San Francisco is eight hours and New York five hours behind GMT, while Sydney is 10 hours ahead of GMT. Phone the international operator on ☎ 155 to find out the exact difference.

Most public transport timetables use the 24-hour clock.

ELECTRICITY

The standard voltage throughout England (and Britain) is 240V AC, 50Hz. Plugs have three square pins and adapters are widely available.

WEIGHTS & MEASURES

In theory England has now moved to metric weights and measures although non-metric equivalents are still used by much of the population. Distances continue to be given in miles.

Most liquids other than milk and beer are sold in litres. For conversion tables, see the inside back cover.

LAUNDRY

Every high street has its laundrette. The average cost for a single load is about £3 to wash and dry. Bring soap powder with you; it can be expensive if bought in a laundrette. TICs should be able to direct you to one of these fun-filled social centres from wherever you are staying.

TOILETS

Although many public conveniences are still pretty grim (graffitied or rendered vandal-proof in solid stainless steel), those at train stations, bus terminals and motorway service stations are generally good, usually with facilities for disabled people and those with young children. At the London rail and coach terminals you usually have to pay 20p to use the facilities, but at least they're clean.

Elsewhere, you can try your charms on publicans or lose yourself in the anonymity of large department stores. McDonald's, a not necessarily welcome addition to every high street, almost always has clean toilets you can breeze in and use.

Many disabled toilets can only be opened with a special key that can be obtained from some tourist offices or by sending a cheque or postal order for £2.50 to RADAR (see the Disabled Travellers section later in the chapter), together with a brief description of your disability.

HEALTH

Travel health largely depends on predeparture preparations, day-to-day health care while travelling and how you handle any medical problem or emergency that does develop.

England is a healthy place to travel. Hygiene standards are high (despite what your nose tells you on a hot and crowded tube

---

No Kilos Please, We're English

One of the horrors of the year 2000 for the English was supposed to be the nightmare of another EU directive, this one mandating metrification. Suddenly your pound of carrots would become 0.45kg of carrots.

However, the expected outrage didn't occur. That's in large part because people ignored the new standard. One of the largest supermarkets – Tesco – announced that it would simply add the metric measurements to its existing imperial labels. Where the new standards were adopted, it was often with a bit of cynicism. One supermarket displayed two kinds of tomatoes: the loose ones were priced with imperial measurements, while the pre-packaged tomatoes were priced metrically. It was almost impossible to determine that the more convenient pre-packaged tomatoes did indeed cost much more.

Car salespeople – not known for candour – needn't change their spiel at all; the EU has ceded a permanent exemption for speed and distance. Pubs will be able to continue pulling pints, and milkmen can go on popping a morning pint on doorsteps.

train) and there are no unusual diseases to worry about. Your biggest risks will be from overdoing it on any activities you engage in, whether they be physical, chemical or other.

Predeparture Planning

Immunisations No immunisations are necessary.

Health Insurance Make sure you have adequate health insurance. See Travel Insurance earlier in the chapter for details.

Other Preparations Make sure you're healthy before you start travelling. If you are going on a long trip make sure your teeth are OK. If you wear glasses take your prescription.

If you require medication take an adequate supply, as it may not be available locally. Take packaging showing the generic name, rather than the brand, which will make getting replacements easier. To avoid any problems it's a good idea to have a legible prescription or letter from your doctor to show that you legally use the medication.

Basic Rules

Care in what you eat and drink is the most important health rule; stomach upsets are the most likely travel health problem (between 30% and 50% of travellers in a two-week stay experience this), but the majority of these upsets will be relatively minor. Even in England it doesn't pay to be complacent. Beware of dodgy street vendors selling even dodgier food, for instance.

Water

Tap water is always safe unless there's a sign to the contrary (for example, on trains). Don't drink straight from a stream – you can never be certain there are no people or cattle upstream.

Environmental Hazards

Sunburn Even in England, and even when there's cloud cover, it's possible to get sunburned surprisingly quickly – especially if you're on water, snow or ice. Use 15+ sunscreen, wear a hat and cover up with a long-sleeved shirt and trousers.

Heat Exhaustion Again, England may not seem like a place to worry about heat exhaustion, but that very complacency can lead to problems. Dehydration or salt deficiency can cause heat exhaustion. In hot conditions and if you're exerting yourself make sure you get sufficient nonalcoholic liquids. Salt deficiency is characterised by fatigue, lethargy, headaches, giddiness and muscle cramps. Vomiting or diarrhoea can rapidly deplete your liquid and salt levels.

Hypothermia Too much cold can be just as dangerous as too much heat. If you are walking or trekking at high altitudes, be prepared. In much of England you should always be prepared for cold, wet or windy conditions, even if you're just out walking. Every year people set out for walks on mild days – especially in the northern parks – and end up in trouble after the weather suddenly changes.

Hypothermia occurs when the body loses heat faster than it can produce it and the core temperature of the body falls. It is surprisingly easy to progress from very cold to dangerously cold due to a combination of wind, wet clothing, fatigue and hunger, even if the air temperature is above freezing. It is best to dress in layers; silk, wool and some of the new artificial fibres are all good insulating materials. A hat is important as a lot of heat is lost through the head. A strong, waterproof outer layer (and a 'space' blanket for emergencies) is essential. Carry basic supplies, including food containing simple sugars to generate heat quickly and fluid to drink.

Symptoms of hypothermia are exhaustion, numb skin (particularly toes and fingers), shivering, slurred speech, irrational or violent behaviour, lethargy, stumbling, dizzy spells, muscle cramps and violent bursts of energy. Irrationality may take the form of sufferers claiming they are warm and trying to take off their clothes.

To treat mild hypothermia, first get the

person out of the wind and/or rain, remove their clothing if it's wet and replace it with dry, warm clothing. Give them hot liquids – not alcohol – and some high-kilojoule, easily digestible food. Do not rub victims: instead, allow them to slowly warm themselves. This should be enough to treat the early stages of hypothermia. The early recognition and treatment of mild hypothermia is the only way to prevent severe hypothermia, which is a critical condition.

Jet Lag Probably the worst health hazard you'll face in England, jet lag is experienced when a person travels by air across more than three time zones (each time zone usually represents a one-hour time difference). It occurs because many of the functions of the human body (such as temperature control, pulse rate and emptying of the bladder and bowels) are regulated by internal 24-hour cycles. When we travel long distances rapidly, our bodies take time to adjust to the 'new time' of our destination, and we may experience fatigue, disorientation, insomnia, anxiety, impaired concentration and loss of appetite. These effects will usually be gone within three days of arrival, but to minimise the impact of jet lag:

- Rest for a couple of days prior to departure.
- Try to select flight schedules that minimise sleep deprivation; arriving late in the day means you can go to sleep soon after you arrive. For very long flights, try to organise a stopover.
- Avoid excessive eating (which bloats the stomach) and alcohol (which causes dehydration) during the flight. Instead, drink plenty of noncarbonated, nonalcoholic drinks such as fruit juice or water.
- Avoid smoking.
- Make yourself comfortable by wearing loose-fitting clothes and perhaps bringing an eye mask and ear plugs to help you sleep.
- Try to sleep at the appropriate time for the time zone you are travelling to.

Motion Sickness Eating lightly before and during a trip will reduce the chances of motion sickness. If you are prone to motion sickness try to find a place that minimises

movement – near the wing on aircraft, close to midships on boats, near the centre on buses. Fresh air usually helps; reading and cigarette smoke don't.

Commercial motion-sickness preparations, which can cause drowsiness, have to be taken before the trip commences. Ginger (available in capsule form) and peppermint (including mint-flavoured sweets) are natural preventatives. These precautions will be especially appreciated if you plan any ferry trips during stormy conditions.

Infectious Diseases
Fungal Infections To prevent fungal infections, wear loose, comfortable clothes, wash frequently and dry carefully. Always wear flip-flops (thongs) in shared bathrooms. If you get an infection, consult a chemist. Try to expose the infected area to air or sunlight as much as possible and wash all towels and underwear in hot water as well as changing them often.

Diarrhoea Simple things like a change of water, food or climate can all cause a mild bout of diarrhoea, but a few rushed toilet trips with no other symptoms is not indicative of a major problem.

Dehydration is the main danger with any diarrhoea, particularly in children or the elderly as dehydration can occur quickly. Under all circumstances fluid replacement (at least equal to the volume being lost) is the most important thing to remember. Weak black tea with a little sugar, soda water, or soft drinks allowed to go flat and diluted 50% with clean water are all good. With severe diarrhoea a rehydrating solution is preferable to replace minerals and salts lost. Keep drinking small amounts often. Stick to a bland diet as you recover.

HIV & AIDS Infection with the human immuno-deficiency virus (HIV) may lead to acquired immune deficiency syndrome (AIDS), which is a fatal disease. Any exposure to blood, blood products or body fluids may put the individual at risk. The disease is often transmitted through sexual contact or dirty needles – vaccinations, acupuncture, tattooing and body piercing can be potentially as dangerous as intravenous drug use. HIV/AIDS can also be spread through infected blood transfusions; but in England these are screened and safe.

Sexually Transmitted Diseases HIV/AIDS and hepatitis B can be transmitted through sexual contact. Other STDs include gonorrhoea, herpes and syphilis; sores, blisters or rashes around the genitals and discharges or pain when urinating are common symptoms. In some STDs, such as wart virus or chlamydia, symptoms may be less marked or not observed at all, especially in women. Chlamydia infection can cause infertility in men and women before any symptoms have been noticed. Syphilis symptoms eventually disappear completely but the disease continues and can cause severe problems in later years. While abstinence from sexual contact is the only 100% effective prevention, using condoms is also effective. The treatment of gonorrhoea and syphilis is with antibiotics. The different STDs each require specific antibiotics.

Insect Bites & Stings Bee and wasp stings are usually painful rather than dangerous. However, in people who are allergic to them severe breathing difficulties may occur and require urgent medical care. Anti-itch creams and lotions such as Calamine will provide relief and ice packs will reduce the pain and swelling.

If you're going to be in the parks during summer bring mosquito repellent and some antihistamine if you suffer from allergies; it can help limit your body's reaction to bites.

Women's Health

Gynaecological Problems Antibiotic use, synthetic underwear, sweating and contraceptive pills can lead to fungal vaginal infections, especially when travelling in hot climates. Fungal infections are characterised by a rash, itch and discharge and can be treated with a vinegar or lemon-juice douche, or with yoghurt. Nystatin, miconazole or clotrimazole pessaries or vaginal cream are the usual treatment. Maintaining

good personal hygiene and wearing loose-fitting clothes and cotton underwear may help prevent these infections.

STDs are a major cause of vaginal problems. Symptoms include a smelly discharge, painful intercourse and sometimes a burning sensation when urinating. Medical attention should be sought and male sexual partners must also be treated. For more details see the section on Sexually Transmitted Diseases earlier. Besides abstinence, the best thing is to practise safer sex using condoms.

Medical Services

Reciprocal arrangements with the UK allow residents of Australia, New Zealand and several other countries to receive free emergency medical treatment and subsidised dental care through the NHS; they can use hospital emergency departments, GPs and dentists (check the Yellow Pages phone directory). Long-term visitors with the proper documentation will receive care under the NHS by registering with a specific practice near where they live. Again check the phone book for one close to you. EU nationals can obtain free emergency treatment on presentation of an E111 form, validated in their home country.

Travel insurance, however, is advisable as it offers greater flexibility over where and how you're treated and covers expenses for an ambulance and repatriation that won't be picked up by the NHS (see the Travel Insurance section under Documents earlier in the chapter). Regardless of nationality, anyone will receive free emergency treatment if it's a simple matter like bandaging a cut.

Chemists (Pharmacies)

Chemists can advise on minor ailments such as sore throats, coughs and earache. There's always one local chemist that's open 24 hours; other chemists should display details in their windows or doorways, or look in a local newspaper. Since all medication is readily available either over the counter or on prescription there's no need to stock up.

WOMEN TRAVELLERS
Attitudes Towards Women

The occasional wolf-whistle and groper on the London Underground aside, women will find England reasonably enlightened. There's nothing to stop women going into pubs alone, although not everyone likes doing this; pairs or groups of women blend more naturally into the wallpaper. Some restaurants still persist in assigning the table by the toilet to lone female diners, but fortunately such places become fewer by the year.

Safety Precautions

Solo travellers should have few problems, although common-sense caution should be observed in big cities, especially at night. Hitching is always unwise.

While it's certainly not essential, it can help to go on a women's self-defence course before setting out on your travels, if only for the increased feeling of confidence it's likely to give you.

Condoms are now often sold in women's toilets as well as men's. Otherwise, all chemists and many service stations stock them. The contraceptive pill is only available on prescription in England, as is the 'morning-after' pill (actually effective for up to 72 hours after unprotected sex).

Organisations

Most big towns have a Well Woman Clinic or Centre that can advise on general health issues. Find its address in the local phone book or ask in the library. Should the worst come to the worst, Rape Crisis Centres can offer support after an attack.

If you'd like to stay with women while you're travelling it's worth joining Women Welcome Women (☎/fax 01494-465441), an organisation that exists to put women travellers in touch with potential hostesses. It's at 88 Easton St, High Wycombe, Bucks HP11 1LT.

GAY & LESBIAN TRAVELLERS

In general, England is tolerant of homosexuality. Certainly it's possible for people to acknowledge their homosexuality in a way that would have been unthinkable 20 years ago; there are several openly gay MPs in the present parliament.

In a bid to attract more 'pink pound' tourists, the BTA recently launched a massive advertising campaign overseas under the slogan 'You don't know the half of it'.

That said, there remain pockets of out-and-out hostility (you only need read the *Sun*, *Daily Mail* or *Telegraph* to realise the limits of toleration). The battle by the Labour government to lower the homosexual age of consent from 18 to 16, in line with that for heterosexuals, is also telling. It passed the House of Commons but needs to pass the House of Lords. Yet the usually docile Lords have repeatedly vetoed the measure. If it finally passes, it will automatically go to the Queen for her assent.

London has a flourishing gay and lesbian scene. Manchester and Brighton also have large gay scenes and in other cities of any size you'll find a community not entirely in the closet. However, overt displays of affection are not necessarily sensible away from acknowledged 'gay' districts and venues.

Organisations

The Gay Men's Press has two useful pocket guides: *London Scene* and *Northern Scene*. To find out what's going on pick up a free listings magazine such as the *Pink Paper* or *Boyz*, or *the Gay Times* (£2.50), which also has listings. *Diva* (£2) is for lesbians. They're all available at Gay's The Word bookshop (☎ 020-7278 7654), 66 Marchmont St, London WC1, and the freebies at most gay bars, clubs and saunas.

Another useful source of information is the 24-hour Lesbian & Gay Switchboard (☎ 020-7837 7324), which can help with most enquiries, general and specific. London Lesbian Line (☎ 020-7251 6911) offers similar help, but only from 2 to 10 pm Monday and Friday and 7 to 10 pm Tuesday to Thursday.

DISABLED TRAVELLERS

Many disabled travellers will find that England is an odd mix of user-friendliness and unfriendliness. These days few buildings go up that are not accessible to wheelchair users; large, new hotels and modern tourist attractions are therefore usually fine. However, most B&Bs and guesthouses are in hard-to-adapt older buildings, and this means that travellers with mobility problems may end up having to pay more for accommodation than their more able-bodied fellows.

It's a similar story with public transport. Newer buses sometimes have steps that lower for easier access, as do trains, but it's always wise to check before setting out. Tourist attractions sometimes reserve parking spaces near the entrance for disabled drivers.

The 1995 Disability Discrimination Act makes it illegal to discriminate against people with disabilities in employment or the provision of services. Under Part 3 of the Act, barriers to access have to be removed by 2004. This includes introducing physical features such as ramps and automatic doors, so the situation for wheelchair users should slowly improve.

Many ticket offices, banks and so on are fitted with hearing loops to assist the hearing impaired; look for the symbol of a large ear. Some tourist attractions, such as cathedrals, have Braille guides or scented gardens for the visually impaired.

Organisations

If you have a physical disability, get in touch with your national support organisation and ask for information about England. They often have complete libraries devoted to travel, and can put you in touch with travel agents who specialise in tours for the disabled.

The Royal Association for Disability and Rehabilitation (RADAR) stocks several useful titles, including *Holidays in the British Isles: A Guide for Disabled People* (£7.50). Contact RADAR (☎ 020-7250 3222) at Unit 12, City Forum, 250 City Rd, London EC1V 8AF.

The Holiday Care Service (☎ 01293-774535), 2nd Floor, Imperial Buildings, Victoria Rd, Horley, Surrey RH6 7PZ, pub-

lishes *A Guide to Accessible Accommodation and Travel for Britain* (£5.95) and can offer general advice.

Many TICs have leaflets with accessibility details for their particular area.

See the Trains section of the Getting Around chapter for details on obtaining the Disabled Persons Railcard, which gives discounts on fares.

SENIOR TRAVELLERS

Senior citizens are entitled to discounts on things such as public transport, museum admission fees and so on, provided they show proof of their age. Sometimes they need a special pass. The minimum qualifying age is generally 60 to 65 for men, 55 to 65 for women. See the Trains section of the Getting Around chapter for details on obtaining the Senior Railcard, which gives discounts on fares.

In your home country, there may be a lower age entitling you to special travel packages and discounts (on car hire, for instance) through organisations and travel agents that cater for senior travellers. Start hunting at your local senior citizens advice bureau.

TRAVEL WITH CHILDREN

England is notorious as a country whose residents prefer animals to children. Even though having babies is a trendy topic with the media, anyone travelling with children needs to be prepared for hotels that won't accept their offspring and for frosty stares if they bring them into restaurants.

That said, there are some child-friendly oases. Branches of TGI Friday lay on crayons and balloons for younger visitors (and, of course, McDonald's tries hard to cultivate future burger-buyers). Many pubs have given up the battle to exclude children and now lay on playgrounds and children's meals.

It never hurts to ask when making accommodation reservations if children are welcome. Modern, purpose-built hotels will almost certainly be able to rustle up a cot.

These days most supermarkets, big train

and bus stations, motorway service stations and major attractions will have toilets with baby-changing facilities. Some rail companies have also launched separate 'family carriages' – they're not all that special but it's a step in the right direction.

Breast feeding in public remains controversial. Women are fighting hard – a brave female MP even tried it in the House of Commons – but it'll be some time before the English feel relaxed about breasts displayed for any purpose other than titillation.

See Lonely Planet's *Travel with Children*, by Maureen Wheeler, for more information and advice.

USEFUL ORGANISATIONS

Membership of National Trust (NT; ☎ 020-8315 1111) and English Heritage (EH; ☎ 01793-414910) are worth considering if you plan to travel a lot around England and are interested in stately homes, castles, ruined abbeys and other historical buildings. They are nonprofit organisations dedicated to the preservation of the environment, and both care for hundreds of spectacular sites.

National Trust

Most NT properties cost nonmembers up to £5.50 to enter. Membership for those aged over/under 26 costs £30/15; membership for a couple is £51 and for a family is £57. It provides free admission to all the NT's English properties (as well as all its Welsh and Northern Irish ones) as well as an excellent guidebook and map. You can join at most major sites. There are reciprocal arrangements with the NT's partner organisations in Scotland, Australia, New Zealand and Canada, and the Royal Oak Foundation in the USA. In this book, National Trust properties are designated by NT after the phone number.

Web site: www.nationaltrust.org.uk

English Heritage

EH properties cost nonmembers between £1.50 and £6 to visit. Adult membership costs £28, a couple pays £46 and family membership costs £49.50. Membership gives free admission to all EH properties and an excellent guidebook and map. In this book, English Heritage properties are designated by EH after the phone number.

Web site: www.english-heritage.org.uk

Great British Heritage Pass

This pass gives you access to almost 600 NT, EH and expensive private properties. A seven-day pass costs £32, 15 days is £45, one month is £60. It's available overseas from the BTA or

Tracing Your Ancestors

Many visitors to England have ancestors who once lived in this country. Your trip would be a good chance to find out more about them and their lives; you may even discover relatives you never knew about. Records for England are kept in London.

Start your search with the Family Records Centre (☎ 020-8392 5300, fax 8392 5307), 1 Myddelton St, London EC1R 1UW (☻ Angel). This office is part of the Public Records Office and is used to dealing with people tracing their past. They have several publications they can send you outlining what you'll have to do. Their Web site is at www.pro.gov.uk/about/frc.

The office itself is very helpful and open 9 am to 5 pm weekdays (until 7 pm Tuesday and Thursday) and 9.30 am to 5 pm Saturday. Take your passport or another form of identification if you want to see original records. Remember that documents referring to individuals are closed for 100 years to safeguard personal confidentiality. It is also not possible to see documents or records until the PRO has preserved them, even though they may have been officially released.

If you'd like someone to complete the search for you (for a fee), the Association of Genealogists & Record Agents (no telephone number), 29 Badgers Close, Horsham, West Sussex RH12 5RU, can send you a list of professional record agents and researchers. The association can also supply the name of an agent who will search for living relatives. Their Web site is at www.agra.org.uk.

Never Been Here Before, by Jane Cox and Stella Colwell, (£6.99) is a useful guide to the Family Records Centre.

from larger TICs throughout England. It can only be purchased by non-Brits (show your passport).

DANGERS & ANNOYANCES

Crime

England is a remarkably safe country considering its size and the disparities in wealth. However, city crime is certainly not unknown, so taking caution, especially at night, is necessary. Pickpockets and bag snatchers operate in crowded public places such as the London Underground and popular museums.

Take particular care at night. When travelling by tube in London, choose a carriage containing lots of other people and avoid some of the deserted suburban tube stations; a bus or cab can be a safer choice. Watch out too when you are on lonely streets at night.

The most important things to guard are your passport, papers, tickets and money. It's always best to carry these items next to your skin, or in a sturdy leather pouch on your belt. Carry your own padlock for hostel lockers.

Be careful even in hotels; don't leave valuables lying around in your room. Never leave valuables in a car and remove all luggage overnight. This is especially true in seemingly safe rural locations. While you're out walking in the countryside, someone may well be walking off with your belongings. Look for secure parking areas near TICs and national park visitors centres.

Report thefts to the police and ask for a statement, or your travel insurance company may not pay out.

Drunkenness

The sight of a bleary-eyed lad of 20 ordering four pints of beer 15 minutes before closing time is but a precursor of trouble to come. The splattered evidence all over the pavements of English cities is a Sunday morning tradition. Worse, drunken brawls are not uncommon as liquored-up lager louts are tossed out onto the streets at the same time when the pubs close. The best you can do is give these yobs a wide berth – and watch where you step.

Touts & Scams

Hotel/hostel touts descend on backpackers at underground and main-line stations such as Earl's Court, Liverpool Street and Victoria. Treat their claims with scepticism and don't accept an offer of a free lift unless you know precisely where you are going (you could end up miles away).

Never accept the offer of a ride from an unlicensed taxi driver either – they'll drive you round and round in circles, then demand an enormous sum of money. Use a metered black cab, or phone a reputable minicab company for a quote.

Cardsharping – where tourists are lured into playing a game that seems to be going all one way until they join in whereupon the luck changes sides – seems to be on the wane, but in its place have come the mock auctions that operate primarily out of London's Oxford St. You may be handed a flyer advertising an auction of electrical and other goods at unbelievably cheap prices. But watch that word 'unbelievable' because that's just what they are. At the advertised venue you'll see attractive goods on display. However, you'll be asked to bid for goods in black plastic bags that you can't remove until the show's over. When you do remove it, you'll find your wonderful bargain has turned into fool's gold.

Beggars

The big cities, particularly London, have many beggars; if you must give, don't wave a full wallet around – carry some change in a separate pocket. All the arguments against giving to beggars in developing countries apply; it's probably better to donate something to a recognised charity than give directly. Shelter (☎ 020-7505 2000), 88 Old St, London EC1, is a charity that helps the homeless and gratefully accepts donations. Also consider buying the *Big Issue* (£1), a weekly magazine available from homeless street sellers who benefit directly from sales.

Racism

England is not without racial problems, particularly in some of the deprived inner cities, but in general tolerance prevails. Visitors are unlikely to have problems associated with their skin colour, but please let us know if you find otherwise.

Weather

Expect rain at any time and never assume that just because it's the middle of summer it will be warm and you'll do fine. That said, it's also wise to take more serious precautions if you will be out in rural areas.

When walking in the northern parks and countryside be properly equipped and cautious: the weather can become vicious at any time of the year. After rain peaty soil can become boggy; always wear stout shoes and carry a change of clothing.

Mists can come down with a startling suddenness, and you shouldn't venture to the heights without checking weather forecasts first. What's more, you should certainly make sure you're sensibly and warmly clad and shod, and that you have food, water and a compass for emergencies.

Wherever you are in England, ideally make sure someone knows where you're heading if it's off the beaten track or in dubious climatic conditions.

EMERGENCIES

The national emergency services number in England is ☎ 999. It is good for all police, fire and medical emergencies; ☎ 112, the emergency number for much of Europe, can also be used.

LEGAL MATTERS
Drugs

Illegal drugs of every type are widely available, especially in clubs. Nonetheless, all the usual dangers associated with drugs apply and there have been several high-profile deaths associated with ecstasy, the purity of which is often dubious. Possession of small quantities of cannabis usually attracts a small fine (still a criminal conviction) or a warning; other drugs are treated more seriously.

Driving Offences

The laws against drink-driving have got tougher and are treated more seriously than they used to be. Currently you're allowed to have a blood-alcohol level of 80mg/100mL but there's talk of reducing the limit. The safest approach is not to drink anything at all if you're planning to drive. For information about current speed limits and parking violations, see Car & Motorcycle in the Getting Around chapter.

Fines

In general you rarely have to cough up on the spot for an offence. The two main exceptions are trains (including those on the London Underground) and buses where people who can't produce a valid ticket for the journey when asked to by an inspector can be fined there and then; £5 on the buses, £10 on the trains, no excuses accepted.

BUSINESS HOURS

Offices are generally open 9 am to 5 pm, Monday to Friday. Shops may be open longer hours, and most are open 9 am to 5 pm Saturday. An increasing number of shops also open on Sunday, perhaps from 11 am to 4 pm. In rural country towns shops may have an early-closing day – usually Tuesday, Wednesday or Thursday afternoon. Late-night shopping is usually on Thursday or Friday.

In London and some of the other large cities there are a growing number of 24-hour stores of all kinds.

PUBLIC HOLIDAYS & SPECIAL EVENTS
Public Holidays

Most banks, businesses and some attractions and other places of interest are closed on public holidays: New Year's Day, Good Friday, Easter Monday, May Day Bank Holiday (first Monday in May), Spring Bank Holiday (last Monday in May), Summer Bank Holiday (last Monday in August), Christmas Day and Boxing Day (the day after Christmas).

English museums and other attractions may well observe the Christmas Day and Boxing Day holidays but generally stay open for the other holidays. Exceptions are those that normally close on Sunday; they're quite likely to close on bank holidays too. Some smaller museums close on Monday and/or Tuesday, and many places, such as the British Museum, close on Sunday morning.

Special Events

Countless events are held around the country all year. Many still re-enact traditional customs and ceremonies, some dating back hundreds of years; and even small villages have weekly markets. Useful BTA publications include Forthcoming Events and Arts Festivals, that list a selection of the year's events and festivals with their dates.

New Year
Celebrations throughout England with London leading the way
Mid-March
Crufts Dog Show – premier dog show; Birmingham
Cheltenham Gold Cup – horse race meeting; Cheltenham
Last week in March
Oxford/Cambridge University Boat Race – traditional rowing race; River Thames, Putney to Mortlake, London
First Saturday in April
Grand National – famous horse race meeting; Aintree, Liverpool
Early May
FA Cup Final – deciding match in England's premier football knock-out tournament; Wembley, London (when it reopens)
Brighton Festival – arts festival; runs for three weeks
Last week in May
Chelsea Flower Show – premier flower show; Royal Hospital, London
Bath International Festival – arts festival; runs for two weeks
First week in June
Beating Retreat – military bands and marching; Whitehall, London
Derby Week – horse racing and people watching; Epsom, Surrey
Mid-June
Trooping the Colour – the Queen's birthday parade with spectacular pageantry; Whitehall, London
Royal Ascot – more horses and hats; Ascot, Berkshire
Late June
Lawn Tennis Championships – runs for two weeks; Wimbledon, London
Henley Royal Regatta – premier rowing and

social event; Henley-on-Thames, Oxfordshire
Glastonbury Festival – huge open-air festival and hippy happening; Pilton, Somerset
Mardi Gras – one of Europe's biggest gay and lesbian parades and festivals; London
Early July
Hampton Court Palace International Flower Show; London
Late July
Cowes Week – yachting extravaganza; Isle of Wight
Farnborough International Aerospace Exhibition and Flying Display – world's largest aerospace exhibition; Farnborough, Surrey
Mid-August
Edinburgh International and Fringe Festivals – premier international arts festivals; runs for three weeks
Late August (August Bank Holiday)
Notting Hill Carnival – enormous Caribbean carnival; London
Reading Festival – outdoor rock and roll for three days; Reading, Berkshire
October
Horse of the Year Show – best-known showjumping event in Britain; Wembley, London
5 November
Guy Fawkes Day – commemorating an attempted Catholic coup; bonfires and fireworks around England

COURSES

No matter whether you want to study sculpture or Sanskrit, circus skills or computing, somewhere in England there's going to be a course. Local libraries are often a good starting point for finding information.

Language

Every year thousands of people come to England to study English and there are centres offering tuition all round the country. The problem is to identify the reputable ones, which is where the British Council (☎ 020-7930 8466), 10 Spring Gardens, London SW1, comes in. It produces a free list of accredited colleges that meet minimum standards for facilities, qualified staff and pastoral backup. It offers general advice to overseas students on educational opportunities in the UK since many normal colleges and universities now offer courses aimed at students from abroad.

The British Council has 243 offices in 110 countries around the world that can provide the same beginners information, so you don't have to wait until you get to England to ask for help in choosing a college. Their Web site is at www.britishcouncil.org.

The BTA also produces a useful brochure for people wanting to study in England.

WORK

If you're prepared to work at menial jobs and long hours for relatively low pay, you'll almost certainly find work in England. The trouble is that without skills, it's difficult to find a job that pays well enough to save money. You should be able to break even, but will probably be better off saving in your home country. Like millions before you, you'll probably want to start your search in London.

Traditionally, unskilled visitors have worked in pubs and restaurants and as nannies. Both jobs often provide live-in accommodation, but the hours are long, the work exhausting and the pay not so good (and then, with the former, there are all those pissheads to deal with). If you live in, you'll be lucky to get £130 per week; if you have to find your own accommodation you'll be lucky to get £180. Before you accept a job, make sure you're clear about the terms and conditions, especially how many hours (and what hours) you will be expected to work. A minimum wage of £3.60 per hour (£3 for those aged 18 to 21) was introduced in 1999, but if you're working under the table no one's obliged to pay you even that.

Accountants, health professionals, journalists, computer programmers, lawyers, teachers and clerical workers with computer experience stand a better chance of finding well paid work. Even so, you'll need some money to tide you over while you search. Don't forget copies of your qualifications, references (which will probably be checked) and a CV (résumé).

Teachers stand a good chance in London, where turnover can be high. You should contact the individual borough councils, which have separate education departments, although some schools recruit directly. To work as a trained nurse you have to register with the United Kingdom Central Council for Nursing which can take up to three months. The initial application fee is £70 (for overseas-trained nurses) and once the application has been accepted, a fee of £56 is required to be admitted to the register. The registration is then renewable every three years thereafter for a fee of £36. Contact the Overseas Registration Department (☎ 020-7333 9333, fax 7636 6935, e update@ukcc.org.uk), UKCCN, 23 Portland Place, London W1N 4JT. If you aren't registered you can still work as an auxiliary nurse. Its Web site is at www.ukcc.org.uk.

The free *TNT Magazine* is a good starting point for jobs and agencies aimed at travellers. For au pair and nanny work buy the quaintly titled *The Lady*. Also check the London *Evening Standard*, national newspapers and the government-operated Jobcentres, which are found in towns and cities throughout the country. They're listed under Employment Services in the Yellow Pages. Whatever your skills, it's worth registering with several temporary-employment agencies.

For details on all aspects of short-term work consult the excellent *Work Your Way Around the World*, by Susan Griffith (updated every two years). Another good source is *Working Holidays*, published by the London-based Central Bureau for Education Visits & Exchanges.

If you play a musical instrument or have other artistic talents, you could try working the streets. As every Peruvian pipe-player (and his fifth cousin once removed) knows, busking is fairly common in London. It has traditionally been banned in the Underground (£20 fine), though that has hardly stopped many musicians and there is now talk of LRT licensing buskers to play in certain stations after they have auditioned. The borough councils are also moving to license buskers at top tourist attractions and popular areas such as Covent Garden and Leicester Square. You will still be able to play elsewhere, but those areas will be off-limits to anyone without a permit.

Tax

As an official employee, you'll find income tax and National Insurance automatically deducted from your weekly pay-packet. However, the deductions will be calculated on the assumption that you're working for the entire financial year (which runs from 6 April to 5 April). If you don't work as long as that, you may be eligible for a refund. Contact the Inland Revenue or use one of the agencies that advertise in *TNT Magazine* (but check their fee or percentage charge first). Check a local telephone directory to find the closest Inland Revenue office.

ACCOMMODATION

This will almost certainly be your single greatest expense. Even camping can be expensive at official sites.

For travel on the cheap, there are two main options: youth hostels and B&Bs, although over the past few years several independent backpackers' hostels have opened and the number is growing, particularly in popular hiking regions.

In the middle range, superior B&Bs are often in beautiful old buildings and some rooms will have private bathrooms with showers or baths. Guesthouses and small hotels are more likely to have private bathrooms, but they also tend to be less personal. If money's not a concern, there are also some superb hotels, the most interesting in converted castles and mansions.

The various tourist boards operate a classification and grading system; participating hotels, guesthouses and B&Bs have a plaque at the front door. If you want to be confident that your accommodation reaches basic standards of safety and cleanliness, the first classification is 'listed', which denotes clean and comfortable accommodation. One crown means each room will have a washbasin and its own key. Two crowns means washbasins, bedside lights and a TV in a lounge or in bedrooms. Three crowns means at least half the rooms have private bathrooms and that hot evening meals are available. And so on up to five crowns.

In addition there are also various grades ('approved', 'commended', 'highly commended' and 'deluxe'), which may actually be more significant as they reflect a judgement on quality.

In practice there's a wide range within each classification and some of the best B&Bs don't participate at all because they have to pay to do so. A high-quality 'listed' B&B can be 20 times nicer than a low-quality 'three crown' hotel. In the end actually seeing the place, even from the outside, will give the best clue as to what to expect. Always ask to look at your room before deciding.

As ever, single rooms are in short supply. The worst value accommodation tends to be in big towns where you often pay more for inferior quality (abrupt service, chaotic decor, ropey fittings). There are rarely any really cheap B&Bs in the city centres which means those without cars are also stuck with bus services that tail off just when they're getting ready to go out in the evening.

TIC Reservations

Most TICs will book accommodation. In England and Wales the charge is a 10% fee, which is subtracted from the nightly price. A few TICs also charge an extra fee in these cases you should complain bitterly and point out that the 10% deposit (which they usually keep) should be sufficient.

Most TICs also participate in the Book-A-Bed-Ahead (BABA) scheme that allows you to book accommodation for the next two nights anywhere in England. Most charge around £3 and take a 10% deposit. Outside opening hours, most TICs put a notice and map in their window showing which local places have unoccupied beds. These services are particularly handy for big cities and over weekends and the peak summer season.

Camping

Free camping is rarely possible. Camp sites vary widely in quality; most have reasonable facilities, but they're usually tricky to get to without your own transport. The RAC's *Camping & Caravanning in Britain* has extensive lists; local TICs also have details.

Those planning to camp extensively, or tour with a van, should join the Camping & Caravanning Club (☎ 02476-694995), Greenfields House, Westwood Way, Coventry CV4 8JH. The world's oldest camping and caravanning club runs many English sites including club-owned sites, certificated sites with minimal facilities taking only five vans, and commercial sites, which range from enormous holiday parks to quiet overnight stops for backpackers. The annual dues are £27.50 and are good for one camp site and all who use it. You also receive a guide to several thousand camp sites in Britain and Europe and other useful services. You can visit the club's Web site at www.campingandcaravanningclub.co.uk.

Camping is possible at some NT properties; see the earlier listing under Useful Organisations for contact details. You can also camp at Forestry Commission (☎ 0131-334 0066, ℮ fe.holidays@forestry.gsi.gov.uk) facilities throughout Britain. Its Web site is at www.forestry.gov.uk/recreation/holidays.

The tourist boards rate caravan and camp sites with one to five ticks; the more ticks, the higher the standard.

YHA Hostels

Membership of a YHA gives you access to a network of hostels throughout England – and you don't have to be young or single to use them.

The local YHA association for England (☎ 0870 870 8808, ℮ customerservices@ yha.org.uk) is at 8 St Stephen's Hill, St Albans, Herts AL1 2DY. Membership prices are £12 for adults, £6 for youths under 18 and £24 for a family. Expect to pay anywhere from £7 in the country to £23 in London for adults and £6 to £20 for youths. Its Web site is at www.yha.org.uk.

Facilities All hostels have facilities for self-catering and some provide cheap meals. Advance booking is advisable, especially at weekends, bank holidays and at any time over the summer months. Booking policies vary: most hostels accept phone bookings and payment with Visa or MasterCard; some will accept same-day book-

ings, although they will usually only hold a bed until 6 pm; some participate in the BABA scheme; some work on a first come, first served basis.

The advantages of hostels are primarily price (although the difference between a cheap B&B and an expensive hostel isn't huge) and the chance to meet other travellers. The disadvantages are that some are still run dictatorially, you're usually locked out between 10 am and 5 pm, the front door is locked at 11 pm, you usually sleep in bunks in a single-sex dormitory, and many are closed during winter. Official youth hostels are rarely in town centres; fine if you're walking the countryside or have your own transport, a pain if you're not.

Throughout this book, higher hostel prices for adults are given first, followed by the reduced price for children. At YHA hostels, child means 'under 18' which is also the norm at independent hostels.

Independent Hostels

The growing network of independent hostels offers the opportunity to escape curfews and lockouts for a price of around £9 to £18 per night. Like YHA hostels, these are great places to meet other travellers, and they tend to be in town centres rather than out in the sticks, which will suit the non-walking fraternity. New places are opening fast so it's worth double-checking with the TIC.

Camping Barns & Bunkhouses

A camping barn – usually a converted farm building – is where walkers can stay for around £5 per night. Bunkhouses are a grade or two up from camping barns, have stoves for heating and cooking and may supply utensils. They may have mattresses, but you'll still need a sleeping bag. Most charge from £7.50. These can be found through the north of England.

University Accommodation

Many English universities offer their student accommodation to visitors during the holidays: usually for three weeks over Easter and Christmas and from late June to late September. Most such rooms are comfortable, functional single bedrooms but without single supplements. Increasingly, however, there are rooms with private bathroom, twin and family units, self-contained flats and shared houses.

University catering is usually reasonable; full- and half-board, B&B and self-catering options are available. Bed and breakfast normally costs from £18 to £25 per person. Several possibilities are listed in the London chapter. In other places, TICs invariably have details.

For more information contact British Universities Accommodation Consortium (BUAC; ☎ 0115-846 6444, fax 846 6333, 📧 buac@nottingham.ac.uk), Box No 1928, University Park, Nottingham NG7 2RD. Its Web site is at www.buac.co.uk.

B&Bs & Guesthouses

B&Bs are a great English institution and the cheapest private accommodation around. At the bottom end (£14 to £20 per person) you get a bedroom in a private house, a shared bathroom and an enormous cooked breakfast (juice, cereal, bacon, eggs, sausage, baked beans and toast). Small B&Bs may only have one room to let, and you can really feel like a guest of the family – they may not even have a sign outside.

More upmarket B&Bs have private bathrooms and TVs in each room. Traditionally the English have preferred baths to showers. In many B&Bs and private houses you may find just a bath or a highly complicated contraption that produces a thin trickle of scalding hot or freezing cold water. Get the home-owner to explain how it works if you want a half-decent shower.

Double rooms will often have two single beds (twin beds) rather than a double bed so you don't have to be lovers to share. Many B&Bs have conservative owners so it pays to be a little careful in what you say and how you act.

Guesthouses, which are often just large converted houses with half a dozen rooms, are an extension of the B&B concept. They range from £12 to £50 a night, depending on the quality of the food and accommoda-

English Interior Design

Visitors will gain a vivid insight into modern English interior design if they stay at B&Bs. Most feature do-it-yourself (DIY) renovation and strive for a popular style that has been described as 'cosy, with a country house, cottagey look'!

A classic example of a B&B will have embossed and flowery wallpaper, hung crookedly, and swirly-patterned synthetic carpets, laid badly. The light fittings will be mock candelabras and fussy lamps. The furniture will be covered in orange vinyl, purple velour and lace doilies. There will be a display of porcelain figures and ashtrays, and a collection of souvenirs – including at least one miniature wooden clog and a plastic sombrero. There'll be electric or gas heating and a fake fireplace with plastic logs and orange lights. Finally, there will be at least one print of a kitten in a gilt frame.

Bryn Thomas

tion. In general, they're less personal than B&Bs, and more like small budget hotels.

More expensive B&Bs can be truly luxurious and offer a range of services and amenities for their guests. At the highest end, you may even have the chance to enjoy fresh fruit instead of baked beans with your breakfast.

Hotels

The term hotel covers everything from local pubs to grand properties.

Pubs usually have a bar or two and a lounge where cheap meals are served; sometimes they'll also have a more upmarket restaurant. Increasingly in the countryside they also offer comfortable mid-range accommodation, but they can vary widely in quality. Staying in a pub can be good fun since it places you in the hub of the community, but they can be noisy and aren't always ideal for lone women travellers.

On the coast, and in other areas popular with tourists, there are often big, old-style, residential hotels. The cheapest have sometimes been taken over by long-term homeless families who are being 'temporarily' housed by local authorities. They're not places for foreign visitors at all, which is one reason why it's wise to stick with tourist board-approved places except in rural areas. Many others are just fine, although stay in enough old English hotels and you'll soon realise that the TV series *Fawlty Towers* was really a documentary.

More and more purpose-built chain hotels are appearing along motorways and in city centres. Most depend on business trade and offer competitive weekend rates to attract tourists; they also often have a flat rate per room (with twin or double beds and private bathroom), making them relative bargains for couples or small families.

The very best hotels are magnificent places, often with restaurants to match. Many boast fascinating histories and often have extensive grounds and other luxuries. In rural areas you'll find country-house hotels in superb settings, and castles complete with crenellated battlements, grand staircases and the obligatory rows of stags' heads. For these you can pay from around £60 to well over £100 per person.

Rental Accommodation

There has been an upsurge in the number of houses and cottages available for short-term rent. Staying in one place gives you an opportunity to get a real feel for a region and a community. Cottages for four can cost as little as £125 per week; some are even let for three days.

Outside weekends and July/August, it's not essential to book a long way ahead. You may be able to book through TICs, but there are also excellent agencies who supply glossy brochures to help the decision-making, but these typically cost more, as you have to help pay for those brochures.

Hoseasons Country Cottages (☎ 01502-501515, fax 584962), Sunway House, Lowestoft NR32 2LW, handles a huge range of cottages in all price categories. You can pay under £200 in the far-off-season but in these cases you'll want to confirm that the fireplace works. In the summer, the average weekly rate is closer to £500. But these cottages come very completely equipped. Its Web site is at www.hoseasons.co.uk.

The Landmark Trust (☎ 01628-825925, fax 825417, e bookings@landmarktrust.co.uk), Shottesbrooke, Maidenhead SL6 3SW, offers many of the most spectacular possibilities. This architectural charity was established to rescue historic buildings and is partly funded by renting the properties after they've been restored. The trust owns 164 unusual buildings, including medieval houses, castles and Napoleonic forts. For more details visit its Web site at www.landmarktrust.co.uk.

FOOD

England is the nation that brought us fatty sausages, mushy peas and margarine sandwiches, a cuisine so undesirable that there's no English equivalent for the French phrase *bon appétit*.

It's an image that has proved hard to shake off but, fortunately, things are improving fast, especially in the south. The use of fresh fruit and vegetables has increased immeasurably. In the main towns and cities a decent range of cuisines is available. Particularly if you like pizza, pasta and curry (and consider those a decent range of cuisines), you should be able to get a reasonable meal pretty well anywhere. Indeed, the one thing that may be hard to find (except in pubs) is traditional English cuisine – dishes like roast beef and Yorkshire pudding or steak and kidney pie.

These days you'll come across lots of restaurants serving what is called modern British cuisine, originally a term used to cover the mix-and-match use of all sorts of fresh ingredients served into continental-style dishes but now extended to include all manner of creatively prepared foods. Even the humble bangers and mash can rise to new heights when you take handmade thyme sausages and pair them with, say, a fennel mash. Generally, modern British really just means: 'Pretty good food that's not bad like the old British'.

Vegetarianism has taken off in a big way. Most restaurants will have at least a token vegetarian dish, although menus at better places often offer several choices. As anywhere, vegans will find the going tough.

Takeaways

Curries have overtaken fish and chips as England's most popular takeaways. Certainly they are the preferred choice of the mobs pouring out of the pubs at 11 pm.

Every high street has its complement of takeaway restaurants, from McDonald's and Pizza Hut to the ubiquitous local curry house and – especially in the north – fish and chip shops. Although there are some notable 'chippies' about, the best you can say about these places is that they provide piles of stodge for reasonable prices.

One of the best developments in high-street cuisine has been the emergence of takeaways specialising in fresh food. Chains such as Pret a Manger sell delicious sandwiches and salads made from fresh ingredients in innovative combinations. They have good juice too (see the boxed text 'The Chain Gangs' later).

Cafes

In the bigger towns, you will find cafes, usually referred to as caffs or greasy spoons. Although they often look pretty seedy, they're usually warm, friendly, very English places and invariably serve cheap breakfasts (eggs, bacon and baked beans) and English tea (strong, sweet and milky). They also have plain but filling lunches, usually a roast with three veg, or bangers and mash (sausages and mashed potato). Amid all the merry camaraderie, the food is often as grim as the furnishings.

There's another form of cafe you're likely to find in tourist areas. These specialise in teas and scones amid twee decor. You can usually buy various gift items (meaning cutesy crap, such as little spoons adorned with the Queen Mum and plates featuring images of the Union Jack) by the exit.

Pubs

These days most pubs also do food, although Sunday can be tricky. At the cheaper end pub meals are not very different from those in cafes, but at the expensive end they're closer to restaurants. For a detailed discussion of these English institutions, see the special section 'Pubs'.

Restaurants

There are many good and excellent restaurants in England. Seafood, various meats, roasts and many other dishes are often very well prepared. London has scores of restaurants that could hold their own in major cities worldwide.

That said, the entire dining experience in England still has major short-comings. The prices are too high and the service is not good enough. Worse, many places – often those with only adequate food but loads of customers – cheerfully expect those paying the inflated prices to suffer numerous indignities of which the worst is timed eating. You call to make a booking (almost mandatory at many places) and are given a window for your meal, usually something like 8 to 10 pm. Not finished with your coffee? Still nibbling on your dessert? Just want to sit, digest and stare into your partner's eyes? Tough. You must leave your table as the next suckers have been booked in. Oh, and that will be £100. Try this in Paris or New York and the restaurant owner would rapidly be moving back to England where he/she can get away with it.

When it's time to pay for your meal – good or bad – remember to ask for the 'bill'.

Self-Catering

The cheapest way to eat in England is to cook for yourself. Even if you lack great culinary skills, you can buy good-quality pre-cooked meals from the supermarkets (Marks & Spencer's are the most highly regarded).

Breakfast

If your accommodation includes breakfast, it's liable to be some combination of eggs, fatty bacon, sausages, fried mushrooms, baked beans, fried bread, toast, cereal and on and on. What you will rarely receive is any combination of the words 'fresh' and

The Chain Gangs

On many of England's high streets, it may seem as if the only places to eat are chain cafes and restaurants. It's a sorry development, driven by the costs of developing new restaurants in places where expenses are high. It's much easier for a corporation endlessly to replicate a concept with food and drink that can be easily prepared by semi-skilled staff than it is to run high-quality, unique restaurants with individual chefs, menus and concepts.

With the proliferation of chains in England, there may be times when you feel that you've no choice but to try one. Here's a run-down of some of the better options.

Pret a Manger is a massive chain of sandwich outlets that provide wonderfully fresh sandwiches in innovative variations: the chicken Caesar exudes parmesan, the 'more than mozzarella' comes with basil and pine nuts. The coffees are made to order. Pret deserves credit for lifting the standards of the English takeaway lunch.

Soup Opera has a range of freshly made soups that changes daily and can include interesting items such as Tuscan bean and smoked haddock chowder.

Café Flo, *Café Rouge* and *Dôme* all try to replicate casual French brasseries. The menus are heavy with salads, omelettes, steaks and frites, frites and more frites. All three are usually bright and airy, but something else they share is pokey service, possibly because the owners sit in corporate offices far away. (In fact, Café Flo and Dôme are both owned by the huge Whitbread group.) Expect to pay between £15 and £20 each, including drinks.

Pizza Express is a quirky chain that individualises its outlets with smart but eclectic decor. Individual pizzas (about £6) come in a panoply of flavours and are usually quite good. Some locations even have regular live jazz.

Café Pasta and *Spaghetti House* are considered the pick of the formula Italian joints. Both have items on the menu that go a few steps beyond spaghetti Bolognese. Expect to pay around £15 each with drinks.

Coffee

The days of a grim cup of weak and tasteless coffee in England are gone. Scores of outlets sell steaming cups of coffee in a myriad of permutations and sizes. Many of the purveyors are chains, and competition is fierce for prime high-traffic locations. Other quality coffee bars can be found in bookstores such as Waterstones, Books Etc and Borders, allowing you to ponder your pages over a frothy brew. Even train stations and other places once known for poor coffee have decent outlets.

Here are the major players in Britain's coffee wars. At all of them you have the choice of taking your beverage with you or remaining on the premises while you sip and possibly dip into a newspaper.

Aroma has stylish locations that belie its corporate ownership by McDonald's. The coffee comes in big, primary-coloured cups and you get a little chocolate on the side.

Coffee Republic has huge easy chairs at many of its outlets as well as baked goods and cold sandwiches.

Costa adds a menu of fresh soups, bakery items and hot and cold sandwiches at many of its locations. This is the choice for people who want more sustenance than just a hot drink.

Starbuck's continues its global assault and England is a major front for the ubiquitous US chain. Stores tend to be large with a variety of seating that makes them good for a longer-than-average stay.

For the latest on the onslaught of chain pubs, see the special section 'Pubs' after the Activities chapter.

'fruit'. Tourists tend to enjoy the traditional English breakfasts because they don't eat such things often at home. If they did they would die.

DRINKS

Takeaway alcoholic drinks are sold from neighbourhood off-licences rather than pubs. Opening hours vary, but although some stay open to 9 or 10 pm, seven days a week, many keep ordinary shop hours. Alcohol can also be bought at supermarkets and the diminishing collection of corner shops.

Most restaurants are licensed and their alcoholic drinks, particularly good wines, are always expensive. There are few BYO restaurants (where you can Bring Your Own bottles). Most charge an extortionate sum for 'corkage' – opening your own bottle for you.

Pubs

Pubs are allowed to open for any 12 hours a day Monday to Saturday. Most maintain the traditional 11 am to 11 pm hours; the bell for last orders rings out at about 10.45 pm. On Sunday most open from noon to 3 pm and from 7 to 10.30 pm, though many stay open all day. There are moves afoot to finally – and we mean finally – get rid of these silly laws, but unlike a lad intent on getting his last pint before the bell, the process is moving very slowly.

For many visitors, getting thrown out of a pub just when you are starting to relax after a gruelling day of touring is the worst aspect of an English holiday.

For much more on this English institution see the special section 'Pubs'.

Nonalcoholic Drinks

The English national drink is undoubtedly tea, although coffee is now just as popular and it's perfectly easy to get a cappuccino or espresso in southern towns. You can almost measure your geographical position by the strength of the tea in cafes. From a point somewhere around Birmingham the tea gets progressively stronger (and more orange), the sort of brew you can stand your teaspoon up in, or so idiom would have it.

Farther south you're as likely to be offered Earl Grey or a herbal tea as a traditional Indian or Sri Lankan brew.

Alcoholic Drinks

Beer English pubs generally serve an impressive range of beers – lagers, bitters, ales and stouts. What New Worlders know as beer is actually lager and, much to the distress of people who like good beer, lagers (including Fosters and Budweiser) now constitute a huge chunk of the market. Fortunately, the traditional English bitter is fighting back, thanks to the Campaign for Real Ale (CAMRA) organisation – look for its endorsement sticker on pub windows.

The wonderfully wide choice of beers ranges from very light (almost like lager) to extremely strong and treacly. They're usually served at room temperature, which may come as a shock if you've been raised on lager. But if you think of these 'beers' as something completely new, you'll discover subtle flavours that a cold, chemical lager can't match. Ales and bitters are similar; it's more a regional name difference than anything else. The best are actually handpumped from the cask, not carbonated and drawn under pressure. Stout is a dark, rich, foamy drink; Guinness is the most famous brand.

Beers are usually served in pints (from £1.60 to £2.50), but you can also ask for a 'half' (a half pint). The stronger 'special' or 'extra' brews vary in potency from around 2 to 8%. Seemingly nearly identical beers will have slightly different prices as they are taxed on their alcohol level. Thus a pint that's 4.3% alcohol (a typical amount) will cost a bit less than one that is 5.2% alcohol.

For recommendations on pints you should quaff as well as lots of information on where to quaff them, see the special section 'Pubs'.

Wine Good wine is widely available. Wine bars became popular in the 1980s and, while the concept is a bit old hat now, it did force many pubs to improve their selection of wines by the glass. Restaurants tend to have decent wine lists as well, and if you're looking for something for a picnic, big supermarkets have large and impressive selections, at very good prices.

Whisky First distilled in Scotland in the 15th century, whisky (spelt with an 'e' if it's Irish) is widely consumed in England. It is however Scotland's best-known product and biggest export; over 2000 brands are now produced.

There are two kinds of whisky: single malt, made from malted barley, and blended whisky, distilled from unmalted grain (maize) and blended with selected malts. Single malts are rarer (there are only about 100 brands) and more expensive than blended whiskies.

ENTERTAINMENT

Depending on where you're staying, you'll find a wonderful choice of concert halls, theatres, cinemas and nightclubs to fill your evenings. The world-class venues are mainly in London (see Entertainment in the London chapter) but most of the big towns have at least one good theatre and perhaps an art cinema to supplement the multiplexes. Choice is much more restricted if you're staying in the countryside.

However you budget both your time and money, make certain that you see some English theatre. It easily lives up to its reputation as the best in the world. And it's not all on in the theatres of London's West End – although there can be some fine shows here. Small yet impressive theatre companies can be found elsewhere in London and elsewhere in England. During the summer, some of the best troupes go on the road and perform in towns throughout England.

For nightlife, the major cities have many choices. Perhaps it's because the pubs close so early, but England has an excellent range of clubs. Many have DJs and theme nights that draw patrons from an entire region. Manchester, Sheffield, Leeds, Liverpool, Cardiff and many more places besides London all have very active clubbing scenes.

England invented rock music and bands continue to emerge from all over the country, like so many mushrooms after the rain. Most

hope to end up in some late-night dingy club in London as a prelude to a big recording contract. But you can hear some great music in most of the same towns that have good clubbing scenes. The best way to find out who and what is hot is to ask around.

The major cities throughout England have a good range of classical music. London's major orchestras are world-renowned.

SPECTATOR SPORTS

The English love their games and play and watch them with fierce, competitive dedication. They've been responsible for inventing or codifying many of the world's most popular spectator sports: cricket, tennis, football (soccer) and rugby. To this list add billiards and snooker, lawn bowls, boxing, darts, hockey, squash and table tennis.

The country also hosts premier events for a number of sports: Wimbledon (tennis), the FA Cup Final (football), Test Cricket, Badminton Horse Trials (equestrianism), the British Grand Prix (motor racing), the Isle of Man TT (motorcycle racing), the Derby and the Grand National (horse racing), the Henley Regatta (rowing), the Super League Final (rugby league) and the Admirals Cup (yachting).

All year round, London hosts major sporting events. If you want to see live action, consult *Time Out* for fixtures, times, venues and ticket prices. Also see Spectator Sports in the London chapter. Elsewhere, catching a football match at a top local club is a sure way to see the locals at their most boisterous.

Football

England's largest spectator sport and one of the most popular participation sports is football, occasionally known as 'soccer'.

Since the introduction of the Premier League in 1992, football has become very big business in England. This elite league, for the top 20 clubs in the country, has had huge cash injections, making the league and its players much better off than before (most players now earn about £15,000 a week). The extra money is mainly generated from television deals signed with Sky, one of the world's largest and richest satellite channels. Unfortunately, few of the smaller and less successful clubs have benefited from these changes. It's a case of the big clubs getting richer and the smaller ones struggling to survive.

This reconstruction has transformed the image of the game. In the 1980s British football was associated with hooliganism and violence. The 1990s saw clubs trying hard to appeal to a wider range of fans, realising the importance of making football more socially acceptable. On the whole, they have succeeded. Britain even has a Minister for Sport who is a keen Arsenal fan. Being broadcast on Sky has made the games more accessible not only to people in England but around the globe. Most football grounds are now suitable places for a family day out. (Of course, all these good feelings haven't stopped English – and they are English, not British as they will scream in your face – hooligans from shaming the entire nation with their antics, such as those at Euro 2000.)

England boasts some of the best and most expensive footballers in the world. Many of the bigger clubs have recently been floated on the stock markets and are being run as serious, money-making businesses. It has become so commercial that most clubs make as much money from selling their merchandise as from entry into the games.

The domestic football season lasts from August to May. Most matches are played on Saturday afternoons at 3 pm. Tickets cost from £12 to £40 and are usually very difficult to purchase so try to book them well in advance.

Some of the bigger clubs are Manchester United, Arsenal, Liverpool and Newcastle United. Wembley is where the English national team plays its home internationals each season, and also the place where the FA Cup final takes place in May. However, it's due to undergo a controversial reconstruction that's set to last through 2003.

Cricket

Sometimes called the English national game, cricket is still a popular participation sport. Every summer weekend, hundreds of teams play on idyllic village greens (and city sports fields) and display all the finest English characteristics – fair play, team spirit and individual excellence (plus maiming the opposing team and abusing the umpire).

Those not familiar with the game will need someone to explain the rules, and may find it slow. But at its best, cricket is exciting, aesthetically pleasing, psychologically involving and quintessentially English.

Several clubs founded in the 18th century still survive. The most famous and important is Marylebone Cricket Club (MCC), based at Lord's cricket ground in north London.

Every summer, the national side of at least one of the main cricket-playing countries (Australia, India, New Zealand, Pakistan, South Africa, Sri Lanka, West Indies, Zimbabwe) will tour and play a series of five-day test matches as well as crowd-pulling one-day matches. Tickets cost from £20 to £40 and tend to go fast. Those for county championship matches are a much more manageable £7 to £15.

Rugby

It was once said that the difference between football and rugby was that football was a gentlemen's game played by hooligans while rugby was a hooligan's game played by gentlemen. Class distinctions may have fallen away, but the hooligan element still lives on. A recent report listed rugby as Britain's most dangerous sport, with four times as many serious injuries per player as football.

Rugby (aka rugby football or rugger) takes its name from Rugby school in Warwickshire where the game is supposed to have originated when William Ellis picked up the ball and ran off with it during a football match in 1823.

The professional form of the game, rugby league, is played in the north of England, and differs from the traditionally amateur game of rugby union in that the team has only 13, rather than 15, players. Rules and tactics differ slightly, most notably in that possession changes from one team to the other after five tackles. Rugby league is primarily a summer game and the Super League final is held at Old Trafford in September. Teams to watch include St Helen's, Wigan and Warrington.

Rugby union is the preferred variation in Scotland and Wales although there are English teams, with Bath and Leicester among the better teams. Union fans will find London the place to be, with a host of good-quality teams (including the Harlequins, Richmond and Wasps).

Golf

Although games that involve hitting a ball with a stick have been played in Europe since Roman times, it was the Scottish version that caught on. Apparently dating from the 15th century, golf was popularised by the Scottish monarchy and gained popularity in London after James VI of Scotland also became James I of England.

London can boast the world's oldest golf club. James VI played on Blackheath in 1608 and London's Royal Blackheath takes the date of its founding from this royal teeing off.

See the Activities chapter for information about playing golf in England.

Horse Racing

Even the Queen turns up for Royal Ascot, which takes place for a week in late June. The cheapest tickets cost £5 but to be invited into the enclosure you must be well dressed and expect to cough up around £30. Booking is essential (☎ 01344-622211).

The Derby is run at Epsom (☎ 01372-726311) on the first Saturday in June. This is traditionally popular with the masses and you won't see a top hat and tails in the place – unlike Ascot.

The Grand National steeplechase at Aintree in Liverpool is probably the best known of all England's famous horse races. It's run in early April.

SHOPPING

Napoleon once dismissed the English as a nation of shopkeepers but today, as standardised chain stores sweep the high streets,

it would be truer to say they're a nation of shoppers. Shopping is the country's most popular recreational activity.

Multinational capitalism being what it is, there are very few things you can buy that would comprise a specifically English souvenir. On the other hand, if you can't find it for sale in London it probably doesn't exist. The capital has some of the world's greatest department stores as well as oodles of speciality shops. See Shopping in the London chapter for details.

Don't bother buying anything you can also purchase at home – it's probably cheaper there. Instead, concentrate on items unique to England.

What to Buy

Books of all sorts, especially unusual out-of-print books, are some of the best purchases that can be made in England. The specialist book shops of London, such as those along Charing Cross Rd, have a range of books and titles that are unmatched anywhere else in the world.

Albums, whether vinyl or CD, are another sought-after item. Unusual and hard-to-find recordings can be found in the quirky specialist music stores of London and most other towns of any size.

Antiques – from all those centuries of history – are sold everywhere. The range and prices span the gamut and for connoisseurs, entire holidays can be planned around antique shopping. The popularity of the BBC television series *Antiques Roadshow* is testament to the English love of all things old and collectible.

Classic clothing such as trench coats – literally derived from the garments of hapless millions of WWI troops – and suits are much sought after. In London the custom tailors of Savile Row and the shirt-makers of Jermyn St are popular with clients worldwide.

English design has always been excellent – even if some of the cars and office blocks don't do it credit – and there's a whole range of items from the whimsical to the practical that may catch your eye.

Activities

Pursuing a favourite activity or interest is one of the best ways of escaping the beaten track, especially in England where there is such a wealth of activities on offer. Becoming part of a country's life, and preferably an active participant, is much more rewarding than remaining an isolated spectator viewing the world through a camera lens or a train window.

In England, many activities not only open up some of the most beautiful and fascinating corners of the country, they are also well within the reach of those on the tightest budget. In fact, those travelling on a shoestring budget may find themselves walking or cycling out of necessity. Fortunately, a walk or ride through the countryside will almost certainly be a highlight – as well as the cheapest part – of an English holiday.

At the other end of the scale, those with big budgets may want to try one of the traditional English sports, which are still played with enthusiasm. These activities have many variations – often involving horses, hunting, shooting or fishing – and the sky is really the limit for how much you want to spend.

Most activities are well organised and have clubs and associations that can give visitors invaluable information and, sometimes, substantial discounts. Many of these organisations have national or international affiliations, so check with clubs in your own country before leaving home. The British Tourist Authority (BTA; see Tourist Offices in the Facts for the Visitor chapter) has brochures on most activities, and these are worth checking out as they can provide a useful starting point for further research.

Almost every sport, activity and hobby known to humankind has obsessive English devotees. Most are pleased to meet someone who shares their interest, and their response is often generous and hospitable to a fault.

Walking

Every weekend, millions of people take to the parks and countryside. Perhaps because England is such a crowded place, a high premium is placed on open space and the chance to find some fresh air. In English cities, ritual weekend expeditions to the shops and markets are very often combined with a stroll in a park, ending somewhere that sells tea or beer. And the countryside is invaded every weekend by people (and dogs) taking short walks – and ending up somewhere that sells tea or beer.

Although modern developments have had a negative impact, a surprising amount of the countryside appears frozen in time, conforming to a picture of rural England that every movie-goer, TV-watcher and book-reader is accustomed to.

The infrastructure for walkers is excellent. Every Tourist Information Centre (TIC) has details (free or for a nominal charge) of suggested walks that take in local points of interest. Hundreds of books are available that describe walks ranging from half-hour strolls to week-long expeditions, and these are widely available in TICs, newsagents, bookshops and outdoor-equipment shops.

Every village and town is surrounded by footpaths, so keen walkers should consider a week based in one interesting spot (perhaps in a self-catering cottage, a youth hostel or a camp site) with a view to exploring the surrounding countryside. Numerous short walks are detailed in this book.

ACCESS

Again, perhaps because England is so crowded, the rights of people to gain access to land, even privately owned land, are jealously protected. The countryside is crisscrossed by a network of countless 'rights of way', most of them over private land, that can be used by any member of the public.

They may traverse fields, moors, woodlands and even farmhouse yards.

These public footpaths and bridleways (the latter can be used by horse riders and mountain bikers) have existed for centuries, sometimes millennia. They are marked on maps and are often signposted where they intersect with roads. Some also have special markers at strategic points along their length (yellow arrows for footpaths, blue for bridleways, or other special markers if they are part of a particular walk). Some, however, are completely unmarked, so a good map, and the ability to use it, can be essential. If a path is overgrown or obstructed in some way, walkers are permitted to remove enough of the obstruction to pass, and to walk carefully through a crop. Discretion is advised – no farmer will appreciate damage to property.

Some rights of way cross land that is owned by the Ministry of Defence (MOD) and used occasionally by the army. When troop manoeuvres or firing are in progress, access is denied and red flags are put up to warn walkers.

There are some areas where walkers can move freely beyond the rights of way, and these are clearly advertised. For instance, the National Trust (NT) is now one of the largest landowners in Britain and some of its properties are open to the public. However, land within national parks does not necessarily fit into this category. National parks were set up in England by the Countryside Commission to protect the finest landscapes and to provide opportunities for visitors to enjoy them, but the land remains largely privately owned and farmed so access is restricted. It is almost always necessary to get permission from a landowner before pitching a tent. Areas of Outstanding Natural Beauty and Heritage Coasts are also legally protected, but again that doesn't guarantee unlimited access.

LONG-DISTANCE WALKS

The energetic, and the impecunious, should definitely consider some long-distance multi-day walks. Civilisation is never far away so it's easy to put together walks that connect with public transport and link hostels and villages. In most cases, a tent and cooking equipment is not necessary. Warm and waterproof clothing (including a hat and gloves), sturdy footwear, lunch and some high-energy food (for emergencies), a water bottle (with purification tablets), a first-aid kit, a whistle, a torch (flashlight), and a map and compass are all you need.

The best areas for long-distance walks include the Cotswolds, Exmoor National Park, Dartmoor National Park, North York Moors National Park, Yorkshire Dales National Park and the Lake District.

In England there are now nine long-distance paths (LDPs) called National Trails that have been developed by the Countryside Agency, a body created in 1999 by the merger of the Countryside Commission and the Rural Development Commission. Many of these are amalgamations of walks that had been developed by the Countryside Commission over the past 40 years. The National Trails offer walkers access to outstanding countryside and a number of them traverse the national parks. They follow routes that travellers have journeyed for thousands of years.

In addition, there are over 150 LDPs that are regional routes created by county councils and unofficial long-distance routes devised by individuals or groups such as the Ramblers' Association. Some are excellent, well organised and have good information available. On the other hand, all you need is a good map and you can plan your own!

Walkers may choose to walk the entire length of a long-distance trail (or way, as they are often called), which could be from 30 to 600 miles (48km to 966km) long, but many just choose a section that meets constraints of time and transport. City-dwelling walkers often manage to walk an entire trail over a series of weekends.

Some of the English long-distance walks, particularly along the coast and in the Yorkshire Dales and Lake District, can be crowded at the weekend and in July/August – advance bookings for accommodation are worthwhile at these times (contact the appropriate TICs for details).

The countryside can look deceptively gentle but, especially in the hills or on the open moors, the weather can turn very nasty very quickly at any time of the year. If you're walking in upland areas, it is vital to be well equipped and to carry (and know how to use) good maps and a compass. Always leave details of your route with someone trustworthy.

Maps, Guides & Information

Lonely Planet's *Walking in Britain* covers not only the main long-distance walks but also has a good selection of day hikes.

The Countryside Agency, in conjunction with Aurum Press and the Ordnance Survey (OS), publishes excellent guides for many trails. They include detailed track notes and incorporate the relevant sections from the OS 1:25,000 Explorer maps. There are hundreds of other specialist walking guides.

The Ordnance Survey (OS) organisation publishes a wide variety of maps covering the country which are widely available. For walkers, the Landranger maps at 1:50,000 – about 1¼ inches to the mile, covering about 25 x 25 miles (40km x 40km) – are usually sufficiently detailed. In some instances, where paths are unclear, the Explorer series (which is replacing the Pathfinder series) at 1:25,000 – about 2½ inches to the mile, covering around 12½ x 12½ miles – (20km x 20km) is useful. There are Pathfinder Walking Guides (covering short walks in popular areas) and Outdoor Leisure maps (covering most national parks), both at 1:25,000. The OS Web site, www.ordsvy.gov.uk, is very useful.

Those intent on a serious walking holiday should contact the Ramblers' Association (☎ 020-7339 8500), Camelford House, 87–90 Albert Embankment, London SE1 7TW. Its Web site, www.ramblers.org.uk, has numerous links and information on many walks. Its yearbook (£4.99) is widely available and itemises the information available for each walk and the appropriate maps; it also gives a list of nearby accommodation (hostels, B&Bs and bunkhouses).

Other good sources of local information are the many outdoor-gear shops that can be found in even the smallest of towns along popular walking routes. Many are listed in this book.

Luggage Services

In recent years there has been a welcome addition to the English walking scene in the form of luggage services that allow travellers to send their luggage on ahead each day to their next step, leaving them unencumbered and free to enjoy their walks. While purists may scoff, the services are especially good for travellers combining a long-distance walk as part of a larger walk. Rates are widely variable depending upon the services desired.

Two firms are:

Sherpa Van Project (☎ 020-8569 4101, fax 8572 9788, ℮ info@sherpavan.com) This operation offers luggage and bicycle carriage on a number of routes including The Pennine Way, the Dales Way, the Cleveland Way and the Sea To Sea (C2C) Cycle Way.
Web site: www.sherpavan.com

Coast to Coast Pack Horse (☎/fax 017683-71680, ℮ packhorse@cumbria.com) This firm exclusively serves the Coast to Coast Walk from St Bees in Cumbria to Robin Hoods Bay in Yorkshire. Besides transporting luggage and gear, they will transport faltering spouses and other companions who would rather take a lift to the next stop than walk.

South West Coast Path

At slightly over 610 miles (982km) long, this is the longest long-distance walk in England. It follows the coast through four counties from Minehead in Somerset, around Devon and Cornwall, to Poole in Dorset. The path is also known as the South West Way and the South West Peninsula Coastal Path.

The South West Coast Path is based on the trails used by coastguards to patrol the area in search of smugglers so it mostly sticks to the edge of the coast and a considerable amount of walking up and down hills is involved.

Few people walk the whole path in one go because this takes about six to seven weeks. The most scenic and popular part is the route that runs from Padstow to Falmouth around Land's End, a distance of 163 miles (262km) entirely within Cornwall. This section is a medium to basic walk and it can easily be done in two weeks. There's plenty to see – secret coves, wrecks, the remains of cliff castles, barrows (a heap of earth placed over prehistoric tombs), settlements, disused mines and quarries, a wide range of bird life, and seals – so a pair of binoculars is a good idea.

Accommodation is not a problem; there are many hostels, camp sites, B&Bs and pubs on or very near the path.

The South West Coast Path Association (☎ 01752-892237) publishes a single-volume guidebook and accommodation list for the whole route. The Aurum Press guides cover Minehead to Padstow, Padstow to Falmouth, Falmouth to Exmouth and Exmouth to Poole.

The path's Web site is at www.swcp .org.uk.

Cotswold Way

The Cotswold Way follows the western edge of the Cotswold Hills from Chipping Campden, just south of Stratford-upon-Avon, to Bath. The countryside and Cotswold villages are a delight and the way is also a walk through England's history, with numerous prehistoric hillforts and ancient burial barrows. There are Saxon and Civil War battle sites, reminders of the Romans, some fine stately homes, the ruins of a magnificent medieval monastery and many other historical markers and monuments. The path itself winds through fields and woods and over hills, and through a patch of England that is at its most affluent. The pretty-as-a-picture-postcard villages exude a heady aroma of solid bank accounts and expensive public schools.

The Cotswold Way is about 100 miles (161km) long and can be done in five days, although a week is better. It was approved for National Trail status in 1998, although the official designation has yet to occur while trails and signage are upgraded.

For all information on the trail, contact the Cotswold Way National Trail Office (☎ 01452-425637, [e] jronald@gloscc.gov

.uk), Environment Dept, Shire Hall, Gloucester GL1 2TH.

The Cotswold Way is well suited for walkers on a medium budget as pubs with rooms abound along its route. However, those on a tighter budget will find few hostels.

Cleveland Way

The 109-mile-long (175km) Cleveland Way is the second-oldest National Trail and unquestionably one of the greatest walks in England, showing a cross section of the best scenery in Yorkshire and a region rich in history, geology and wildlife.

It loops around the North York Moors National Park, passing through small Yorkshire villages and farmland, past the ruins of Rievaulx Abbey and over heather-covered moors. It then follows a spectacular coastline through fishing villages and seaside resorts. There is a rich assortment of relics that include Bronze-Age burial sites, Iron-Age forts, Roman signal stations, medieval abbeys and castles, and industrial relics from the 17th and 18th centuries. The region is also closely associated with Captain James Cook and there are monuments and museums commemorating his life.

The full walk is undeniably challenging and takes about a week. However, the way is never more than a couple of miles from a sealed road so there are numerous potential cut-out points and many options for tackling shorter sections, especially along the coast. For a longer hike, you can add on the Wolds Way, which begins at the Cleveland Way's endpoint in Filey (see the next section).

There are scores of Cleveland Way publications. The official *Cleveland Way – Accommodation & Information Guide* (50p) is available from visitor centres and local TICs, or free if you write to National Trails Officer (☎ 01439-770657), North York Moors National Park, The Old Vicarage, Bondgate, Helmsley, York YO6 5BP.

On the Web, you can find out more about the trail at www.clevelandway.gov.uk.

Wolds Way

One of the least used of the National Trails, the Wolds Way is a delight, not just for its scenery, but for its solitude. It starts at Hessle, near Hull, on the Humber estuary and winds its way over the Yorkshire Wolds for 80 miles (129km) to Filey on the coast. Here the trail meets up with the Cleveland Way (see the previous section).

The Wolds Way is a good introduction to long-distance walking as it has few serious climbs and the path conditions are usually good through the year. The *Wolds Way National Trail Guide*, by Roger Ratcliffe, (£9.99) covers the entire trail. Contact details are the same as the Cleveland Way.

The trail's Web site is at www. woldsway .gov.uk.

Cumbria Way

The Cumbria Way is a 68-mile (109km) walk that traverses the county of Cumbria and the incomparable landscape of the Lake District, first popularised for walkers by William Wordsworth and Samuel Taylor Coleridge. Most of the way lies within the Lake District National Park, and most of it follows valleys at relatively low altitudes, so bad weather is not a major issue. However, it also traverses several high passes and gives a dramatic taste of the mountains. A number of peaks are within easy reach.

If the weather does remain good (a day or so of rain is virtually inevitable and cannot be considered bad weather!), it's impossible to imagine a more beautiful walk. It takes in a full cross-section of the best of the Lake District – from the little-visited southern valleys to the shores of Coniston Water, the great peaks of the Langdale Pikes, Derwent Water, the flanks of Skiddaw, and another forgotten backwater between Keswick and Carlisle. As an introduction to the Lake District it's definitely unsurpassed.

This is not a National Trail but its popularity ensures that there are many publications available. A good Aurum Press book covering the walk is *The Cumbria Way* (£12.99), by Anthony Burton. And when the rain does hit, you might appreciate *Harvey's Cumbria Way Waterproof Map* (£7.95).

Hadrian's Wall

Hadrian's Wall runs for over 70 miles (113km) across the north of England from Bowness-on-Solway, west of Carlisle, to Newcastle-upon-Tyne. Much of the wall has disappeared completely or is in ruins but, in theory, the route would make an excellent long-distance trail, and an extra five miles (8km) would make it a coast-to-coast walk. Currently, however, this involves quite a bit of walking along roads and through towns – the best way to experience the wall is on a series of day hikes, totalling 27 miles (43km). A National Trail is being developed and is due for completion in 2002.

To walk the most interesting sections of the wall you could base yourself in or around Haltwhistle or at Once Brewed and make use of the good local public transport system. Alternatively, there are places to stay along the route at Greenhead, Gilsland and Brampton. As well as the wall itself, this route takes in several Roman forts, including Housesteads and Vindolanda, various turrets and temples, and also passes through Northumberland National Park, where the scenery is at its finest.

Hadrian's Wall, by Mark Richards, is an excellent two-volume guide (£7.99 each), one volume describing a walk that follows the route of the wall, the other giving detours into the countryside. There are many more maps and books available. For more information, contact the National Trail Officer (☎ 0191-232 8252, ⓔ david.mcglade@ countryside.gov.uk), Countryside Agency North East Region, Warwick House, Grantham Rd, Newcastle-upon-Tyne NE2 1QF.

Peddars Way & Norfolk Coast Path

This is an undemanding 88-mile (142km) trail that follows a Roman road across the middle of Norfolk from Knettishall Heath to the beautiful north Norfolk coast at Holme-next-the-Sea. It follows this coastline through a number of attractive, untouched villages such as Wells-next-the-Sea and Cromer.

Although the trail ends at Cromer, it's

possible to continue for another 40 miles (64km) to Great Yarmouth. The start of the trail (Knettishall Heath) is also the end of another path, the Icknield Way, which runs for 105 miles (169km) across England from Ivinghoe Beacon. Ivinghoe Beacon also happens to be the end of the Ridgeway (see the following section) so these three paths could be linked together into a long march of 284 miles (457km) from Avebury to Cromer.

There are several guidebooks, including *National Trail Guide: Peddars Way & Norfolk Coast Path*, by Bruce Robinson (£10.99). For more information, contact Peddars Way and Norfolk Coast Path National Trail Office (☎ 01328-711533, ℮ peddars.way@dial.pipex.com), 6 Station Rd, Wells-next-the-Sea, Norfolk NR23 1AE.

JANE SMITH

Pennine Way

The 256-mile (412km) Pennine Way can claim to be the granddaddy of English long-distance walks: it was first conceived back in 1935, although it was not 'officially' recognised until the 1960s. It can be one of the toughest walks in Britain if the weather is uncooperative as it follows the mountainous spine of northern England, ending just over the border in Scotland. It crosses long stretches of unprotected high country. Careful planning, good equipment and caution are all essential requisites for walking the Pennine Way. Completing the whole walk in two weeks is a real endurance test; allowing three weeks is far more realistic.

The walk starts at Edale, in the north of the Peak District, and immediately makes the tough climb up to the 600m-high Kinder Scout plateau. This 'in-the-deep-end' approach on the first day is followed by a long spell of 'bog hopping' across the exposed moors of the Dark Peak. Continuing north through Brontë country, the route goes right through the Yorkshire Dales National Park then joins Hadrian's Wall for a pleasant jaunt along the most interesting section of this ancient barrier. The final stretch of the walk crosses the full length of the Northumberland National Park before bringing weary walkers to a well-earned rest at Kirk Yetholm, just over the border in Scotland.

There are numerous books on the Pennine Way, including the two-volume *Pennine Way*, by Tony Hopkins (£10.99 each). For more information, contact the Countryside Agency (☎ 0113-246 9222), Yorkshire and the Humber Region, Victoria Wharf, Embankment IV, Sovereign St, Leeds LS1 4BA.

On the Web, you can find out more about the trail at www.pennineway.demon.co.uk.

The Ridgeway

The remains of a prehistoric track that is Britain's oldest road, the Ridgeway is now a National Trail beginning near Avebury (Wiltshire) and running north-east for 85 miles (137km) to Ivinghoe Beacon near Aylesbury (Buckinghamshire). It follows the high open ridge of the chalk downs and then descends to the Thames Valley before finally winding through the Chiltern Hills. Unfortunately the western section is popular with suburbanites trying out their 4WD Range Rovers.

The best guide is *The Ridgeway*, by Neil Curtis (£10.99). For more information, contact the Ridgeway National Trail Office (☎ 01865-810224), Cultural Services, Holton, Oxford OX33 1QQ.

On the Web, visit www.nationaltrails .gov.uk/ridgeway/rwayinto.htm.

Thames Path

This 173-mile (278km) path that runs the length of the River Thames, from the river's source in Gloucestershire to the Thames Barrier in London, was designated in 1996. This famous waterway rises at Thames Head, south of Cirencester, and flows through a varied landscape that includes quintessentially English villages, peaceful meadow-land and ugly suburban sprawl around the capital.

The Thames Path – National Trail Guide, by David Sharp, (£12.99) is a good all-round source. For more information, contact the Thames Path National Trail Office (☎ 01865-810224), Cultural Services, Holton, Oxford OX33 1QQ.

On the Web, you can visit www .nationaltrails.gov.uk/thames/thpainto.htm.

South Downs Way

The South Downs Way National Trail is a bridleway. It covers 100 miles (161km) between the coastal resort of Eastbourne and Winchester, a cathedral city and the ancient capital of England.

It's an easy walk, readily accessible from London so parts can be busy, especially at weekends. It covers a beautiful cross-section of classic English landscapes, beginning with spectacular chalk cliffs at Beachy Head, then traversing an open chalk ridge (the Downs) with great views, before entering rolling, wooded country as you approach Winchester.

The chalk downs are among the longest continuously inhabited parts of the island and the way itself follows an ancient ridgeway track that dates back 4000 years. It passes numerous prehistoric remains and some charming medieval villages. You are never far from a comfortable B&B and a good pub; there are also six youth hostels on or near the way, although they are all in the section between Eastbourne and Arundel.

The way can be walked in a week. For more information, contact South Downs Way National Trail Officer (☎ 01705-597618), Queen Elizabeth Country Park, Gravel Hill, Horndean, Hampshire PO8 0QE.

On the Web, visit www.nationaltrails .gov.uk/sdowns/sdowninto.htm.

Dales Way

The Dales Way links two of England's greatest national parks – the Yorkshire Dales and the Lake District – and, although it's not an official National Trail, it is a popular and well organised route. Some parts aren't signposted, however, so you need good maps.

Officially it begins at Ilkley, accessible from Leeds by regular trains, in a densely populated corner of West Yorkshire famous for its mill towns. Alternatively, you could start at Bolton Priory or Grassington (see the Yorkshire Dales National Park in the North-Eastern England chapter), both of which are on the way. Much of the walk follows river banks through the Yorkshire Dales so the walking is easy, although there are some open expanses of moorland between one dale (valley) and the next. The walk ends with a spectacular descent to Bowness on the shores of Lake Windermere, the main town in the Lake District National Park.

There are numerous guidebooks, including *The Dales Way Route Guide*, by Arthur Gemmell and Colin Speakman (£4). The TICs at Leeds, Grassington and Windermere are all good sources of information, as is the Ramblers' Association (see Maps, Guides & Information earlier in the chapter), which produces a useful accommodation brochure, the *Dales Way Handbook* (£1.50).

Coast-to-Coast Walk

The walk was devised by the creator of superb illustrated walking guides and near-legendary walker, Alfred Wainwright. It's an unofficial trail covering 190 miles (306km) from St Bees Head on the west coast to Robin Hood's Bay on the east. It traverses three national parks – the Lake District, Yorkshire Dales and North York Moors – and covers a range of England's most spectacular scenery, from sea cliffs to mountains, dales and moors.

The walk is serviced by the innovative Coast to Coast Packhorse (see the earlier Luggage Services section).

The classic guidebook is *A Coast to*

Coast Walk, by Alfred Wainwright and Michael Joseph (£10.99). The Ramblers' Association publishes the *Coast to Coast Walk Accommodation List* (£2.95).

Walking Tours

There are scores of companies offering walking tours of England. A few include:

Ramblers Holidays (☎ 01707-331133, ℮ ramhols@dial.pipex.com) Box 43, Welwyn Garden City, Herts AL8 6PQ. This company concentrates on the Lake District.

English Wanderer (☎ 01740-650900) 1 High St, Windermere, Cumbria LA23 1AF. This company arranges unescorted walks by setting up accommodation, providing maps and so on.

Cycling

Travelling by bicycle is an excellent way to explore England. Away from the motorways and busy main roads there's a vast network of quiet country lanes leading through peaceful villages. Bring your own bike or hire one when you arrive. Cycle routes have been suggested throughout this book.

INFORMATION

Lonely Planet's *Cycling Britain* has details of the best bike routes, information on places to stay and eat and a handy section on bicycle maintenance. Much of the book is devoted to English rides.

The BTA publishes a free booklet, *Cycling*, with some suggested routes, lists of cycle holiday companies and other helpful information. Many regional TICs have information on local cycling routes and places where you can hire bikes. They also stock cycling guides and books – look out for the range of OS route map/guides.

The Cyclists' Touring Club (CTC; ☎ 01483-417217, fax 426994, ℮ cycling@ ctc.org.uk), 69 Meadrow, Godalming, Surrey GU7 3HS, is a membership organisation providing comprehensive information (available free to members) about cycling in England and elsewhere. It can provide suggested routes (on- and off-road), lists of local cycling contacts and clubs, recommended accommodation, organised cycling holidays, a cycle-hire directory, and a mail-order service for OS maps and books for cyclists. Annual membership costs £25 (under-26s and seniors £15). Some cycling organisations outside England have

Sustrans & the National Cycle Network

Sustrans is a nonprofit group working towards the creation of a 6500-mile (10,461km) network of cycle paths that will pass through the middle of most major towns and cities in Britain. In 2000, the first 5000 miles (8047km) of routes were officially opened and the goal is to have the network pass within two miles of the homes of half the British population.

When Sustrans announced this objective in 1978 the charity was barely taken seriously, but the growth in popularity of bicycles, coupled with possibly terminal road congestion, has brought lots of attention to the idea of cycle paths. There's been official support for the network – including £43.5 million from the Millennium Commission. Sustrans has also benefited from some high-profile support from the government as well as big names like Neil Kinnock (politician), Jeremy Paxman (broadcast journalist) and Richard Rogers (famous architect).

Half the network is to be on traffic-free paths (including disused railways and canalside towpaths), the rest of the system along quiet minor roads. Cyclists will share the traffic-free paths with walkers, although it will be interesting to see how this combination mixes.

The Sustrans *Official Guide to the National Network* (£9.99) details 29 one-day rides throughout the network. Maps are available for all the routes (free for the shorter paths, £3.99 to £5.99 for map-guides for the national routes). For more information contact Sustrans (☎ 0117-929 0888, ℮ info@nationalcyclenetwork.org.uk), 35 King St, Bristol BS1 4DZ. Its Web site is at www .sustrans.org.uk.

reciprocal membership arrangements with the CTC.

See the earlier boxed text 'Sustrans & the National Cycle Network' for information on the group responsible for creating a national network of cycle paths, including several National Cycle Routes.

Tours

As for walking, there are many specialist tour companies catering to cyclists in England. Two possibilities include:

Country Lanes (☎ 01425-655022, fax 655177, e bicycling@countrylanes.co.uk) 9 Shaftesbury St, Fordingbridge, Hampshire SP6 1JF. This is a small company that runs a range of cycling trips in the Lake District, Cotswolds and the New Forest.

Acorn Activities (☎ 01432-830083, fax 830110) PO Box 120, Hereford HR4 8YB. This company organises trips in England that last from two to 14 days and include luggage-carrying services.

Orchard Cycle Tours (☎ 01865-863773, fax 865783) 1 The Orchard, Appleton, Oxfordshire, OX13 5LF. This operation plans a variety of trips in the Cotswolds, Oxfordshire and along the Thames.

Transporting Your Bicycle

Air Most airlines will carry a bike free of charge as long as the bike and panniers don't exceed the per-passenger weight allowance (usually 20kg). Hefty excess-baggage charges may be incurred if you do and this applies to internal and international flights. Note that some charter-flight companies do make a charge for the carriage of bikes.

Inform the airline that you will be bringing your bike when you book your ticket. Arrive at the airport in good time to remove panniers and pedals, deflate tyres and turn handlebars around – the minimum dismantling usually required by airlines.

Train Bikes can be taken on most train journeys in England. However, the privatisation of rail services in England means that each of the train companies can decide their own policy about bikes on trains.

Generally, bikes can be taken on local services free of charge on a first-come-first-served basis, though some train operating companies do not carry bikes on certain routes or during peak hours. On most long-distance routes it is necessary to make a reservation for your bike. Reservations will almost always incur a charge – usually around £3 for a single journey.

To be sure that you can take your bike you should make your reservation (and get your ticket) and check bike carriage details at least 24 hours before travelling – this is because some trains only carry one or two bikes. You should also check if there are going to be engineering works on the line because bikes cannot be carried on replacement bus services. A good place to start with this chore is the National Rail Enquiry Service (☎ 0845 748 4950) but you should also check with the train operator.

Roads, Lanes & Tracks

Bikes are not allowed on motorways, but you can cycle on all other roads (on the left!) unless the road is marked 'private'. A-roads tend to be busy and are best avoided. B-roads are usually quieter and many are pleasant for cycling.

The best roads for the cyclist are the unclassified roads, or 'lanes' as they are called. Linking small villages together, they are not numbered: you simply follow the signposts from village to village. There is a whole network of lanes throughout lowland England, meandering through quiet countryside via picturesque villages. Lanes are clearly shown on OS maps.

Cycles can be ridden on any unmade road (track) that is identified as a public right of way on OS maps. The right to cycle does not, however, usually exist on a footpath. The surface condition of tracks varies considerably: some are very poor and slow going.

WHERE TO CYCLE
South-Eastern England

The South-Eastern corner of England has more traffic than other parts of the country, but with careful route planning you can find quiet roads and tracks and forget how close you are to the busy city of London. North-west of London, the Chiltern Hills offer scenic cycling. The area to the south and east of London is characterised by the North and South Downs, two ridges of higher land running east-west, and the Weald in between – undulating, often wooded terrain. The landscape is beautiful in places and offers plenty of opportunities for good cycling. The south coast is heavily populated so the main roads here are busy and best avoided by cyclists.

You should also avoid cycling in London if possible; traffic is heavy and road surfaces can be poor. If you must cycle in the city, contact the London Cycling Campaign (☎ 020-7928 7220, fax 7928 2318) for maps and information. Its Web site is at www.lcc.org.uk.

South-Western England

The counties of Somerset, Dorset and Wiltshire have a varied landscape, with a combination of easy valley routes and steeper climbs in the hill ranges. Many parts of this region are popular with cyclists. The ancient woodland and open heath of the New Forest offer easy cycling.

Cornwall and Devon, with their steep country lanes, can be challenging. In the north, the coastline is rugged and sometimes inaccessible. Small roads drop steeply to pretty fishing villages nestling in the coves along the coast. The bleak, upland landscapes of Dartmoor, Bodmin Moor and Exmoor contrast starkly with the seaside towns on the south coast of Devon. The coast enjoys the best of the British climate but suffers its share of tourist traffic during the summer months.

Midlands

The Cotswolds area of Gloucestershire and Oxfordshire is a particularly attractive place to cycle, but there's a shortage of budget accommodation here. The dense network of motorways and heavily trafficked roads serving the industrial centres farther north mean that any extensive tour of the region would require careful planning in order to avoid these busy arteries. There are pockets of quiet roads with pretty villages and some forests, lakes and canals worth exploring – Charnwood Forest, for example, and parts of Hereford and Worcester, and Northamptonshire. The land is relatively low-lying and the cycling is gentler than in the north of England.

The Peak District (in Derbyshire) is one of the most popular cycling areas and marks the southern tip of the Pennines. There's challenging terrain, steep hills, rewarding scenery and a fairly good network of quieter roads, plus some excellent cycling/walking tracks along disused railway routes.

Eastern England

This is an excellent area for a first cycling tour and for those seeking an easy-going cycling holiday. East Anglia is generally low-lying and flat, with small areas of gently undulating country and woodland, particularly in Suffolk. Much of the area is characterised by arable farmland dissected by rivers, lakes (broads), marshes (such as the Fens) and many small, picturesque settlements.

Norfolk and Suffolk have a good network of quiet country roads. There are, however, two things to watch out for. First, breezes off the North Sea can sometimes be strong, especially in the Fens. Second, although the area is well served with bridges, roads sometimes run parallel to a river or canal and you may have to travel a little farther than expected to find a bridge. It pays to have a good map and to plan your route in advance.

Northern England

This region offers superb cycling, much of it strenuous – especially high up in the Pennines where you're exposed to the elements.

There are some exhilarating rides in the wild North York Moors. Take plenty of warm clothes and food for these exposed areas. To the west, the Yorkshire Dales offer tough cycling over the tops of the moors and gentler riding in the valleys. The scenery is superb, there's plenty of interest and some excellent pubs.

The Lake District of Cumbria is best explored by cyclists outside the months of July and August when its limited network of roads is crammed with tourist traffic. Use the smaller roads where possible and be prepared for some steep, long climbs in this magnificent region of mountains and lakes.

The area around Manchester and Liverpool, built-up and criss-crossed with motorways and other busy roads, is far less attractive to cyclists.

In the far north of England, Northumberland has quiet roads and plenty of historical interest. There are some very attractive sections of coastline in this area. Inland, the Cheviot Hills and Kielder Forest offer many rough tracks – great for the off-road rider to explore, but it's easy to get lost. Take good maps and a compass.

SOME SUGGESTED CYCLING ROUTES

The CTC provides useful touring sheets (available to members only; free) for every cycling region in England with accommodation suggestions. It can also help you plan a long-distance cycling trip, including ones spanning not just England, but also Scotland and Wales.

Wye Valley

The River Wye meanders some 130 miles (209km) from the Cambrian Mountains in Wales to the Severn estuary. It is usually possible to follow quiet roads near the river. A week to 10 days could easily be spent exploring the area.

The southern part of the Wye Valley is densely wooded and forms the border between the south-eastern corner of Wales and Gloucestershire in England. Chepstow, situated on the northern reaches of the Severn estuary, is an ideal and accessible starting point. The main road (A466) follows an attractive course alongside the river, but this road can be busy during the tourist season. Climb the steep valley sides onto quieter country roads and enjoy the expansive views out over the Severn estuary. It's undulating terrain with some steep hills.

A detour east into the Forest of Dean provides opportunities for family cycle rides and day excursions, many of the forest tracks being open to cyclists. Back by the River Wye, Monmouth and Ross-on-Wye are pleasant towns worth visiting.

Yorkshire Dales

A week-long cycle tour through this magnificent national park is an exhilarating experience and Skipton is a convenient starting point. Cycle northwards to Linton (in Wharfedale) and Hubbersholme. Climb north-west over Fleatmoss to Hawes; the roads are steep but the scenery is breathtaking. Take quiet roads eastwards along Wensleydale to Askrigg and Aysgarth, then north to Reeth.

For the intrepid, a detour over Tan Hill and back to Keld may be attempted. Alternatively, follow Swaledale westwards, then head north-west to Kirkby Stephen. From here, cycle south to Sedbergh and then through beautiful Dentdale. Head south to Horton-in-Ribblesdale, Stainforth and then east, passing Malham Tarn to Malham and back to Skipton.

This route covers about 130 miles (209km), but there are plenty of opportunities for scenic detours.

Cumbria Cycleway

This 260-mile (416km) circular route follows the borders of Cumbria. It's a mixture of lightly travelled roads and well groomed trails and covers a variety of terrain that includes moors in the east to rugged cliffs and coast in the west with long stretches of forest in between. Carlisle, with its transport links, is a good place to begin and/or end the trip.

Further information on the well marked route can be gathered from the Department of Planning (☎ 01539-773407), Cumbria County Council, County Offices, Kendal LA9 4RQ.

Bristol to Padstow

A week-long journey starts in Bristol and then proceeds south-west to Padstow on the Cornish coast. The scenery includes Glastonbury, Wells Cathedral, Somerset Levels, Exmoor National Park and long stretches of coast. The route includes two traffic-free stretches, the Tarka and Camel Trails.

The route is 230 miles (368km) long and includes a myriad of opportunities for detours, especially in the national park. This is a National Cycle Route and is well marked.

Hull to Harwich

This long route links two of England's great ports and features long stretches of gentle countryside and rocky coast in Eastern England and the cities of Norwich and Lincoln, and passes through the Norfolk Broads forest.

Another National Cycle Route, the journey is popular with Europeans who can take a ferry to one of the ports and depart from the other. It is 370 miles (592km) long.

JANE SMITH

Golf

Britain, and in particular Scotland, is the home of golf. There are, in fact, more courses per capita in Scotland than in any other country in the world. England is hardly lacking in courses either and has over 1300. London can boast the world's oldest golf club. James VI played on Blackheath in 1608 and London's Royal Blackheath Golf Club (☎ 020-8850 1042), Court Rd, London SE9 5AF takes the date of its founding from this royal teeing off.

All golf courses are tested for their level of difficulty and most are playable year round. Some of the private clubs only admit members, friends of members and golfers who have a handicap certificate or a letter of introduction from their club, but the majority welcome visitors.

Note that most clubs give members priority in booking tee-off times; it's always advisable to book in advance. It should be easier to book a tee-off time on a public course, but weekends on all courses are usually busy (like anywhere in the world). You should also check whether there's a dress code, and whether the course has golf

clubs for hire (not all do) if you don't have your own.

INFORMATION

The BTA has information on playing golf in England. Another good source is the English Golf Union (☎ 01526-354500, fax 354020, e info@englishgolfunion.org), National Golf Centre, Woodhall Spa, Lincolnshire LN10 6PU.

COSTS

A round of golf on a public course will cost as much as £20 to £25. Private courses are more expensive with green fees ranging from £20 right on up to £70 or more for championship courses (but averaging more like £35 to £40). Many clubs offer a daily or weekly ticket. It's always worth asking about passes. In addition, many hotels have arrangements for reduced fees or guaranteed tee-off times.

A set of golf clubs costs £5 to £10 (per round) to hire.

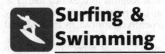

Surfing & Swimming

Most overseas visitors do not think of England as a place to go for a beach holiday – and there are good reasons for this, not least the climate and the water temperature. You definitely have to be hardy or equipped with a wetsuit to do anything more than take a quick dip. On the other side of the equation,

England has some truly magnificent coastline and some wonderful sandy beaches. And the English have been taking holidays by the seaside since the 18th century so there is a fascinating, sometimes bizarre, tradition to explore.

Visiting an English seaside resort should be high on the list of priorities for anyone wishing to gain an insight into English society. The resorts vary from staid retirement enclaves such as Eastbourne to vibrant cultural centres such as Brighton and cheerful family resorts such as Hastings. And then there's Blackpool, which pretty much defies categorisation. One thing remains common to them all, however, and that is that the fun happens on shore and it's done fully clothed!

English water temperatures in summer are roughly equivalent to winter temperatures in southern Australia (approximately 13°C). Winter temperatures are about 5 or 6°C colder, giving a temperature range not dissimilar to that in northern California. So getting in the water, at least in summer, is definitely feasible if you have a wetsuit. A 3mm fullsuit (steamer) plus boots will be sufficient in summer, while winter requires a 5mm suit plus boots, hood and gloves.

The best beaches, with the best chance of sun and surf and the genuine possibility of luring you into the water, are in Cornwall and Devon. Newquay, on the west Cornish coast (five or six hours by road from London), is the capital of the English surf scene. It has a plethora of surf shops and all the appropriate paraphernalia and trappings, from Kombis to bleached hair. The boards and wetsuits sold are good quality and competitively priced in international terms.

The most unusual aspect of surfing in England is the impact of the tides. The tidal range is huge, which means that there are often completely different sets of breaks at low and high tides. As is usually the case, the waves tend to be biggest and best on an incoming tide. Sadly, the waves in spring, autumn and winter tend to be bigger and more consistent than in summer. The conditions in summer are pretty unreliable.

The entire western coast of Cornwall and Devon is exposed to the Atlantic and there is a string of surf spots between Land's End and Ilfracombe. The shallow continental shelf, however, means the waves rarely get over 1.5m. Spring and autumn are the best times. There are a number of good breaks around Newquay including Fistral, England's premier surfing beach and home to the main surfing contests.

There is an excellent surfing Web site, www.britsurf.org, that has comprehensive links and surf reports from all around England, accommodation information, lively chat rooms, classified ads and a great deal more.

Far less salubrious is the Web site maintained by Surfers Against Sewage (☎ 0845 458 3001) at www.sas.org.uk. It gives full details of this group's campaign to stop just what its name implies. Although the situation is improving, many English municipalities still discharge a far amount of crap – literally – into their nearby sea.

Fishing

Angling, as a sport and pastime, was obviously well established in England by medieval times. *A Treatyse of Fysshnge With an Angle*, published in 1496, described fishing flies that are still in use today. The 17th century saw great improvements in equipment and also brought Izaak Walton's classic book on fishing, *The Compleat Angler*.

Fishing is divided into several distinct categories, topped by dry-fly fishing, considered by its proponents to be the highest form of the sport. An artificial lure, made to imitate a small insect, must be gently dropped on the surface in order to deceive and catch the fish. Fly fishing is used for that most cautious of game fish, the trout. Fish are described as coarse fish or game fish, the latter because they vigorously struggle against capture. Curiously, fishing is an activity with widely differing vocabularies between British and other forms of English.

RULES & REGULATIONS

Fishing is enormously popular in England, but also highly regulated. Many prime stretches of river are privately owned, and fishing there can be amazingly expensive. The Environment Agency (☎ 0870 166 2662) administers licences for rod fishing. A one-year licence (valid from 1 April to 31 March) for nonmigratory trout and coarse fishing costs £19/9.50 adult/youth and senior. The price for eight days costs £6.50 (no concessions) and one day is £2.50. Prices for salmon and sea trout are roughly triple. The Environment Agency has a useful Web site at www.environment-agency .gov.uk that is amply supplied with all sorts of fishy details.

Rod licences are available from every post office, bankside agents and Environment Agency Regional Offices. Tackle shops are good places to make fishing enquiries. Before fishing anywhere you must obtain the correct licence and the permission of the owner or tenants of the fishing rights.

There is a statutory close season (15 March to 15 June) when coarse fishing is banned on all rivers and streams – different rules apply on canals, lakes, ponds and reservoirs. The actual dates for close seasons vary according to the region and you'll need to check these in advance – the Environment Agency is the place to go for this information.

novice riders so most rides are at walking speed with the occasional trot. If you're an experienced rider there are numerous riding schools with horses to hire – TICs have details.

For more information you can contact the British Horse Society (☎ 01926-707700, e enquiry@bhs.org.uk), Stoneleigh Deer Park, Kenilworth, Warks CV8 2XZ. It publishes *Where to Ride*, listing places throughout the UK, and can also send you lists specific to a particular area (eg, the Cotswolds). Its Web site is at www.bhs.org.uk.

Horse Riding & Pony Trekking

Seeing the country from the saddle is highly recommended, even if you're not an experienced rider. There are riding schools catering to all levels of proficiency, many of them in national park areas.

Pony trekking is a popular holiday activity; a half-day should cost around £10 (hard hats are included). Many pony trekkers are

Canal & Waterway Travel

England's surprisingly extensive network of canals and waterways spread rapidly across the country at the same time as the Industrial Revolution transformed the nation. As a method of transporting freight (passengers were always secondary) they were a short-lived wonder, trimmed back by railways and killed off by modern roads. By WWII, much of the waterway system was in terminal decline; the once-bustling canals

The Key to the Locks

A lock enables boats to go up or down a hill. It's a bathtub-shaped chamber with either a single or a double door at the top end and a double door at the bottom. Sluices in the doors let water flow into or out of the lock when the paddles over the sluices are opened. A winding handle or key is used to open or close the paddles and this is one of the essential pieces of equipment for narrow-boat travel. The process of going through a lock is known as working the lock.

On narrow canals the locks are usually wide enough and long enough for just one boat at a time. On rivers or wider canals they may be large enough for two or more boats. In a wider lock it's essential to keep your boat roped to the side to prevent it yawing around as the water flows in or out of the lock. But don't tie it up tightly – the ropes will need to be shortened or lengthened as the water level changes. In fact it's best just to loop the lines around the bollards and hold them tight.

Another overriding consideration when travelling the canals is conserving water. Every time you use a lock, several thousand litres of water are released to flow downhill. As supplies are not always assured, limiting the water you release is an important part of canal use.

Operating the locks is not as daunting as it may look, and after a couple of locks, you'll be navigating them like a pro:

Descending Through an Empty Lock

1. If the lock is empty any boats waiting to ascend have priority.
2. Close the bottom gates and make sure that all the paddles are closed.
3. Raise the paddles at the top and wait for the lock to fill.

4. Wait for the water levels to be exactly equal inside and outside the lock before you try to open the gates. Even a few centimetres of difference will result in enough water pressure to keep the lock doors closed.
5. Open the gates and bring the boat into the lock.
6. Close the top gates and paddles.

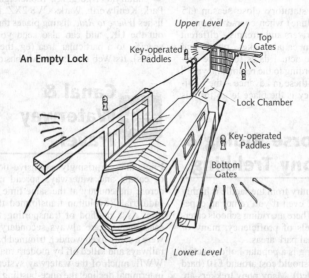

Upper Level

Top Gates

Key-operated Paddles

An Empty Lock

Lock Chamber

Key-operated Paddles

Bottom Gates

Lower Level

The Key to the Locks

7. Make certain the boat is far enough away from the sill at the base of the gates. Otherwise the boat may get hung up as the water goes down.
8. Open the bottom paddles to release the water from the lock.
9. When the lock has drained, open the gates and close all the paddles.
10. Leave the lock.

Descending Through a Full Lock

1. Bring the boat into the lock, opening the gates if necessary.
2. Continue with steps 6 to 10 above.

Ascending Through a Full Lock

1. If the lock is full any boats waiting to descend have priority.
2. Close the top gates and make sure that all the paddles are closed.

3. Raise the paddles at the bottom and wait for the lock to empty.
4. Wait for the water levels to be exactly equal inside and outside the lock before you try to open the gates. Even a few centimetres of difference will result in enough water pressure to keep the lock doors closed.
5. Open the gates and bring the boat into the lock.
6. Close the bottom gates and paddles.
7. Open the top paddles to release the water into the lock.
8. When the lock has filled, open the gates and close all the paddles.
9. Leave the lock.

Ascending Through an Empty Lock

1. Bring the boat into the lock, opening the gates if necessary.
2. Continue with steps 6 to 9 above.

Finally, *don't drop your key in the water*! Every year, scores of amateur boaters do just this, which more than anything marks them as amateurs. It's good to travel with a spare and should you lose one, you can usually procure another cheaply from a boat yard or canal-side shop.

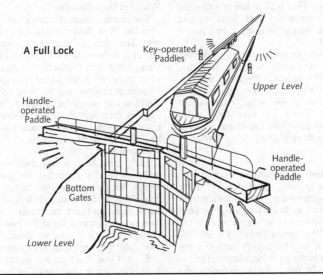

A Full Lock

Key-operated Paddles

Upper Level

Handle-operated Paddle

Handle-operated Paddle

Bottom Gates

Lower Level

had become stagnant channels of no economic significance. Today, however, the canals are booming once again as part of the leisure industry.

Exploring England by canal can be immensely rewarding. Narrow boats (narrow canal boats) can be rented from numerous operators around England and, for a family or a group, they can provide surprisingly economical transport and accommodation. They also allow you to explore a hidden side of England. While travelling the waterways, it's easy to forget that the England of motorways and ring roads even exists. Canals lead you to an England of idyllic villages, pretty countryside and convenient and colourful waterside pubs. More surprisingly, they can show you a very different side of some otherwise unremarkable cities. Birmingham from its canals is quite different to Birmingham from the ring road.

The canal system is also a wonderful example of the power and vision of the Industrial Revolution's great engineers. No obstacle stood in the way of these visionaries, who threw flights of locks up steep hillsides or flung amazing aqueducts across wide valleys. They built to last as well – the lock equipment which you 'work' as you travel along the canals is often well over a century old.

The canals are not restricted to narrow boat users. The canal towpaths have become popular routes for walkers and cyclists who can enjoy the same hidden perspective as people actually out on the waterways. There are over 2500 miles (4000km) of navigable canals and rivers in England, so there is plenty to explore.

HISTORY

As the Industrial Revolution swept across England, a growing need developed for means of transporting goods, ranging from coal and iron to fine Wedgwood pottery. The first serious canals appeared in the 1760s, led by James Brindley's Bridgewater Canal, used for conveying coal to the burgeoning factories in Manchester. The development of canal locks, enabling the

canal boats to go up and down hills, facilitated the spread of canals. Thomas Telford pioneered more modern canals, which took the shortest route from A to B, even when it involved multiple locks, tunnels, embankments and other complex engineering work. The Birmingham & Liverpool Junction was an example of this more advanced type of canal.

Some of the most interesting examples of canal engineering include the nearly two-mile-long (3km) Blisworth Tunnel near Stoke Bruerne (just south of Northampton). For particularly long inclines, locks were sometimes arranged in flights, where the top gate of one lock was also the bottom gate of the next. Ingenious attempts were made to design alternatives to canal locks. The inclined plane at Foxton, near Market Harborough (Leicestershire), dating from 1900, vertically moved boats 23m (75 feet) – the equivalent of a flight of 10 locks. The 1875 Anderton Lift near Northwich (Cheshire), simply floated the boats into a tank that was then lifted 15m (50 feet). When a valley or river intervened, some canal engineers carried their canals right across in aqueducts. A good example of this can be seen at Hebden Bridge in West Yorkshire.

For an interesting offshoot of the canals, visit the High Peak Trail in the Peak District. This early railway line has now been recycled to become a walking and bicycle track, but it was originally constructed by canal engineers still thinking in canal terms. Instead of engineering the long gentle inclines so they would be suitable for railway engines, they built the line with short steep rises up which the trains would have to be hauled, a dry-land equivalent of a canal's lock system.

Early canal boats were pulled by horses, walking on the towpaths alongside the canals, but by the mid-19th century steam power was starting to supersede horsepower. Later, diesel power replaced steam. Modern narrow boats for cruising still follow the traditional style, but come equipped with all mod cons, from refrigerators to televisions.

Even if you don't get out on the canals, it's fascinating to visit one of the canal museums around Britain. They can be found at Stoke Bruerne near Northampton, at Devizes in Wiltshire, at Ellesmere Port near Chester and right in the centres of Nottingham and Gloucester.

THE WATERWAYS

England's boating waterways consist of natural rivers and lakes plus artificial canals. About half of the navigable waterways are canals and half of those are 'narrow' canals, where the locks are just over 2m (7 feet) wide.

A narrow-boat trip can vary from lazy relaxation to surprisingly hard work. When you're chugging down a wide river with only the occasional lock to be worked, it's the easiest means of transport imaginable. On the other hand, on a steep section of canal where one lock is followed immediately by another, narrow-boat travel can be a combination of aerobics (keys to be wound, paddles to be raised and lowered), weight lifting (heavy lock gates to be pushed open and closed) and jogging (the lock crew runs on ahead to prepare the lock before the boat gets there). Canal travel is great if you have children and they're often exhausted by the end of the day!

Information

Information on the canal system is available from the Inland Waterways Association (☎ 01923-711114), PO Box 114, Rickmansworth, Herts WD3 1ZY. It publishes *The Inland Waterways Guide* (£3.25), a guide to hire with route descriptions. Its Web site is at www.waterways.org.uk.

Most of the waterways in England are operated by the British Waterways Board (☎ 01923-226422), Willow Grange, Church Rd, Watford, Hertfordshire WD17 4QA. It publishes *The Waterways Code for Boaters*, a free, handy booklet packed with useful information and advice. Also available is a complete list of boat-hire and hotel-boat companies.

Travelling the Waterways

No particular expertise or training is needed, nor is a licence required to operate a narrow boat. You're normally given a quick once-over of the boat and an explanation of how things work, a list of rules and regulations of the waterways and a brief foray out onto the river or canal and then you're on your way. Proceed with caution at first, although you'll soon find yourself working the locks like a veteran.

Narrow Boats

There are over 200 firms renting out narrow boats in England. Typically, a narrow boat will be 12m to 21m (39 feet to 69 feet) in length and no more than 2m (7 feet) or so wide. Narrow boats are usually surprisingly comfortable and well equipped with bunks and double beds, kitchen and dining areas, a fridge, cooker, flush toilet, shower and other mod cons. Usually they are rented out by the week although shorter periods are sometimes available.

Narrow boats usually come so well equipped for everyday living that food supplies are all you need to worry about and there are plenty of shopping opportunities along the waterways. Alternatively, careful planning can see you moored at a riverside pub or restaurant for most meals.

Boats can accommodate from two or three people up to a party of 10 or 12. Costs vary with the size of boat, the standard of equipment and the time of year. At the height of the summer season, a boat for four can vary from around £500 to £1000 per week. Larger boats work out cheaper per person; a boat for eight might cost £1000 per week. This means canal travel can cost not much over £100 per person for a week's transport and accommodation, a terrific travel bargain.

Although there are independent boat operators scattered all over the country, there are also centralised booking agencies who handle bookings for many of the individual companies. One of the biggest is Hoseasons (☎ 01502-501010, fax 514298), Lowestoft, Suffolk NR32 2LW. Its Web site is at www.hoseasons.co.uk.

If you only want a brief introduction to the canal system, there are over 50 firms operating day trips from various centres. A number of operators offer hotel-boat trips where you simply come along for the ride.

Steam Railways

The invention of the steam engine and the subsequent rapid spread of the railway to almost every corner of England transformed life in the 19th century. In 1963 the Beeching Report led to the closure of many rural lines and stations, and in 1968 British Rail stopped using steam trains. For many people these two events brought the first century of rail travel in England to a sad end. It wasn't long, however, before rail enthusiasts reopened some of the lines and stations and restored many of the steam locomotives and rolling stock used in the proverbial 'golden age of rail'.

There are now over 300 private railways in England, many of them narrow gauge, using steam or diesel locomotives from all

over the world. The main lines – and how you can get to go on them – are detailed in the appropriate sections of this book.

A useful guide to private steam railways is *Railways Restored* (£12.99), by Ian Allan Publishing (for orders ☎ 0711-027099). You can also order a copy via the Web by visiting www.ianallan.com.

CHRISTINE OSBORNE

RICHARD I'ANSON

TONY WHEELER

SIMON BRACKEN

Title page: Choose your beer (photograph by Simon Bracken)
Top: A victorious pub in St Mawes, Cornwall
Middle Left: Relaxing over a pint in Kentish Town, north London
Middle Right: The Greyhound, in the shadow of Corfe Castle, Dorset
Bottom: On the pull in the Westminster Arms, London

For many visitors, pubs epitomise England. There are more than 40,000 scattered from city centres to rural cross-roads. But, despite their central place in English life, pubs as an institution are under threat, primarily from the huge changes sweeping the industry. For much of the 20th century most pubs were owned by breweries, who insured that they had an outlet for their product. Most were run by publicans who leased the pub from the brewery and were then left alone to run the pub as they saw fit. Freehouses – pubs not tied to any brewery – were always in the minority, although they enjoyed a good reputation.

RICHARD I'ANSON

Now the industry is in turmoil. The breweries have largely sold their pubs or have themselves been bought by other conglomerates. Increasingly pubs are becoming part of branded chains. For more on this see Caught in Chains later.

This doesn't mean bleak news for pub-goers, however. There are scores of superlative pubs in every corner of England. Many, even those owned by conglomerates, are managed by publicans committed to running a fine establishment. That pubs come in a myriad of forms is a given. From ornate Victorian drinking houses to country inns surrounded by gardens and outdoor tables, pubs should play an important part in your English experience. And your consumption needn't be just liquid as many pubs serve excellent food; see Pub Grub later for details.

The Pre-Pub Era

Calling these places pubs only dates from the Victorian era when they were first known as 'Public Houses'. Before that public places to drink had a variety of names. In Roman times, tabernas (later taverns) were scattered throughout England and were places where the Romans could relax with some crude wine after a hard day contending with the local savages.

By the Middle Ages, there were three distinct forms of places to drink in English: taverns where you could get ale and food; inns which were scattered at least every 20 miles along major roads and offered drink, food, a place to sleep (with or without accompanying vermin) and various other pleasures; and ale houses, which were crude and notorious places where people simply went to get drunk.

Many of the inns, or coaching inns as they were sometimes called, survive along historic routes throughout England, although the vermin and other pleasures have a much lower profile. The main drink in all of these places was ale, which was in many cases the only safe form of

Choosing a Good Beer

If you need a little guidance, try reading the *Good Beer Guide* by Roger Protz, a must-read for the best pubs and beers England (and Britain) have to offer. Alternatively, contact the Campaign for Real Ale (CAMRA; ☎ 01727-867201) – the English beer drinkers' best friend. It lobbies for pub independence, liberalisation of opening hours and does much to promote the best English beers. Its annual Great British Beer Festival in London in early August is hugely popular with beer connoisseurs.

Our Quaffable Picks

Here's a highly subjective list of our favourite beers, some of which are harder to find than others. Please undertake your own extensive research to make your own amendments.

Adnams Bitter (Suffolk)
Barnsley Mayflower (Yorkshire)
Becketts Golden Grale (Hampshire)
Black Sheep Special Ale (Yorkshire)
Border Farne Island (Northumberland)
Burton Bridge Porter (Staffordshire)
Coniston Bluebird Bitter (Cumbria)
Fuller's London Pride (London)
Hop Back Summer Lightning (Wiltshire)
Jennings Cocker Hoop (Cumbria)
Marston Moor Golden Ale (Yorkshire)
Riverhead Black Moss Stout (Yorkshire)
St Austell XXXX Mild (Cornwall)
Taylor Landlord (Yorkshire)
Theakstons Old Peculiar (Yorkshire)
Young's Winter Warmer (London)

Note: When ordering a beer in a pub, first look for the hand-pumps, then select one of those and order it by name. Just asking for a 'beer' could well produce the nightmare result of being handed a pint of watery lager whose name includes the letters B, U and D.

liquid that could be drunk as basic water often contained enough foul elements to make it deadly. Almost every household brewed ale and those who were especially skilled at doing so soon found their product in demand by others, which led to the development of ale houses.

After William of Orange became king in 1688, he introduced his new subjects to the favourite drink of his native Holland: gin. Unfortunately gin proved to be the heroin of its day, prized by those addicted for its quick intoxication (ale was often quite weak). By the start of the 18th century, England was dotted with 'gin palaces', which

Top right: William Hogarth's *Gin Lane*, a salutary warning against the perils of the potent brew (reproduced by permission of the Founders' Library, University of Wales, Lampeter)

truly were dens of iniquity. Bales of hay were scattered about the shadowy corners so patrons could pass out on the premises and start drinking again upon coming to.

Much more respectable were the porterhouses that began appearing in the cities. As London urbanised from a collection of villages, the residents began looking for places to escape their cramped and usually grim homes. Porter, the robust form of ale popular with labourers and named after porters (because they drank so much of it!), was served in what were rudimentary pubs. It was thought to be fairly nutritious and many literally drank their supper. Stout was an especially heavy version of porter. (Contrary to popular thought, stout was originally an English drink. When rationing during WWI meant that English brewers couldn't get the fuel to dark roast their mash, the industry switched to much lighter ales. Ireland, without such restrictions, continued to brew stout and Guinness cleverly exploited this gap in the market.)

In the early 1800s, the British government passed an act against gin, which was having a debilitating effect on large segments of society. It increased gin taxes and encouraged farmers to stop growing maize (corn; used for gin) and switch to barley (for beer). The Industrial Revolution meant that the scores of workers engaged in hard, hot labour in mills and mines emerged from work with tremendous thirsts. Breweries began capitalising on this demand by selling beer to the public from originally private houses, hence the name 'public house'. Many defined the phrase bare bones. It was not uncommon for bars to have a trough along their front so that male patrons could drink and urinate without moving.

Obviously such efficiencies were not to everybody's taste and the breweries responded with grander pubs. Typically these were divided into two sections, the public bar was for standing and drinking while the saloon bar was more intimate with an open fire, seating, carpet and higher prices.

The Industrial Revolution also affected the drink itself. Before coal and gas were widespread, beer was brewed over wood fires, which rarely yielded consistent temperatures. One day's batch of beer would be dark brown while another day's batch would be pale and the beer generally had a smoky almost bacon-like taste. Industrialisation meant that beers could be produced on a vast scale to standardised qualities. The Industrial Revolution also led to a change in the temperature of beer. Although it was typically served at a tepid 65°F (18°C) until well into the 20th century, advances in refrigeration coupled with popular demand meant that the average temperature has fallen and continues to fall.

After WWI, pubs faced their first major threat – the emergence of cinemas and music halls, and later the advent of TV and radio. People now had other options for their free time. Pubs responded in numerous ways. Fruit machines (gambling devices), piped music, bad lagers such as those from the US and even aberrations such as karaoke proliferated as pubs competed for patrons' leisure time.

The 1960s and 1970s were especially grim for the traditional pub. The demand for all things 'modern' meant that scores of Victorian and earlier pubs around England had their beautiful interiors torn out to make way for dropped ceilings and soon-to-be-sticky carpets. A more positive development was the introduction in many pubs of food that went beyond white-bread sandwiches and packets of crisps.

Today's pubs are a polyglot. Some have tried to compete with clubs

What's in a Pub Name?

Wandering around English villages you'll come across hundreds of ancient pubs with workaday names such as The Red Lion, The King's Arms and The Fighting Cocks, with attractive signboards to illustrate them.

But what's this in Big Town high street? Yet another pub that manages to mix together some combination of 'rat', 'carrot', 'newt', 'slug', and 'firkin' in its name. Look closely at the signs and you'll find no trace of the individuality that marked out their predecessors. Instead come cartoon characters that look to have been designed with a kindergarten rather than an adult audience in mind.

Perhaps there's no point in mourning the passing of The Queen Victoria and The Bunch of Grapes. But many old pub names are as much a part of local history as England's medieval churches.

Take Nottingham's wonderful Ye Olde Trip to Jerusalem, a name that commemorates the Crusaders as they assembled for their long journey to the Holy Land. Or The Nobody Inn in Doddiscombsleigh, near Exeter, said to recall a mix-up over a coffin. Look harder at that Royal Oak sign and you'll see the head of Charles II peeping through the oak leaves – harping back to the story that the king had to hide in an oak tree at Boscobel after his defeat at the Battle of Worcester. Signs for The Five Alls regularly show the king who rules over all, the parson who prays for all, the lawyer who pleads for all, the soldier who fights for all, and John Bull who pays for all.

Finally, there's the astonishing I Am The Only Running Footman at 5 Charles St, London W1, a reminder of the 18th-century running footmen employed by wealthy men to run in front of their carriages lighting the way and shifting any obstacles.

The trend of chain pubs with stupid names has even brought comment from the government. In 2000, Culture Minister Chris Smith openly decried the loss of traditional pub names. Perhaps he was able to seek solace at the nearby Adam & Eve (81 Petty France, London SW1).

with loud music and beer-drinking contests, others are content to keep their sticky carpet and dwindling array of regulars, others mirror whatever their conglomerate owners deem the flavour of the moment. The best follow a simple formula: they welcome people of all ages, are comfortable, serve good beers and food, and are just simply pleasant places to pass a few congenial hours. Happy hunting as you find your own favourites around England.

Those Stupid Hours...

Prior to WWI English pubs were free to open whenever they wished. It was Lloyd George, who was then minister for armaments, who decreed

BRYN THOMAS

that drink was causing more damage to the British war effort than German submarines. Highly restrictive closing hours were introduced and the alcohol content of beer was weakened from an average of 6% to 8% down to about 4%.

For the next six decades English pubs closed in the afternoons as well as at 11 pm. Margaret Thatcher liberalised the pub hours so that they could remain open from 11 am to 11 pm. However, the evening closing time is still an aberration for those who find that just as they are enjoying their evening the last order bell is rung and they are chased out into the street. See the Dangers and Annoyances section of the Facts for the Visitor chapter for the unseemly behaviour common at closing time.

At the time of writing, the Labour government is trying to rectify this absurd situation by giving local governments and pubs the authority to decide their own hours. However, despite support from most pubgoers, the beer industry and, most importantly, the police and medical profession (who are tired of having their workload skyrocket at 11 pm every weekend), there are plenty of hand-wringers who are against this common-sense approach to drinking. Possibly fearing a return to the gin houses of the 18th century, they make dire predictions of streets filled with habitual drunks. This is despite the experience in Scotland where a relaxation of drinking hours is now seen as a positive move. There has been a noticeable reduction in the hordes of drunks roaming the streets after closing time – they trickle out through the night instead, causing less mayhem – and less binge ordering.

In the meantime, be prepared to see bars swarmed with drinkers ordering armloads of pints and other alcoholic drinks at about 10.20 pm every night.

Caught in Chains

In a country with so many good pubs, there is no reason to ever (ever!) submit to the bland pleasures of a chain pub. Sadly, these places are multiplying to such an extent that at least one of the chains should be named 'Rabbit on Heat'. Instead there's a motley assortment of faux twee names and other cutesy monikers intended to lure in the unsuspecting or undiscerning.

Most of these chains are owned by the huge multinational conglomerates. Bass operates thousands of pubs under such names as All Bar One (yuppie), Firkin (loud and heaving) and O'Neills (fake Irish). These McDonald's of publand have atmospheres created by corporate dictate and are as ephemeral as last year's fashion.

Of course, the majority of pubs have always been owned by large companies. But when the breweries were the owners they were mostly concerned with making certain that their beer was sold and individual pubs were free to find their own patrons and personality. Now that the owners of pubs are 'leisure' corporations, pubs are much more likely to be part of corporate leisure 'concepts'. That's not to say that all company-owned pubs are bad, far from it. Some of the best pubs in England are still owned by companies who have the sense to let the publicans get on with it.

Besides homogenising concepts, the pub chains have also opened pubs in places where pints were never poured previously. The consolidation of English banks and their exodus from high streets has left plenty of grand old bank buildings ripe for colonisation. Big and impressive, these spaces are also often draughty and noisy. One good ad – ironically for a bank – on British TV showed an elderly lady going to her bank branch to find that it had become a 'trendy wine bar'.

What follows is a partial list of some of the major pub chains you are likely to encounter in your travels around England. In almost every case you should be able to find a locally run pub oozing individuality nearby.

All Bar One apes the best modern local pubs. The pubs are light and airy, have big tables with comfortable chairs and serve decent beers and large plates of vaguely modern European food. Of course, these places lack the charm of the individual locals.

Choosing a Good Pub

Here are a few things to look for as you search out a good pub:

- Ownership by a good regional brewer such as Fuller's (London), Marston's (Staffordshire), John Smith's (Yorkshire), Taylor (Yorkshire) and Young's (London) usually means there will be good beer on tap.
- Hand-pulled pumps mean that the manager or landlord takes the trouble to stock real ale which requires far more care than keg lager. A willingness to put extra effort into serving real ale often translates into extra effort spent on food, atmosphere, cleanliness and so on.
- Avoid chains; see Caught in Chains for more details.
- Newspapers on tables means that patrons are encouraged to sit around and relax.
- A good menu.

A sticky carpet, fruit machines, piped music, signs for wet T-shirt contests, loud TVs, toxic air, comatose patrons, filth and the like are all BAD signs.

BEER STREET.

Beer, happy Produce of our Isle
Can sinewy Strength impart
And wearied with Fatigue and Toil
Can chear each manly Heart

Labour and Art upheld by Thee
Successfully advance
We quaff thy balmy Juice with Glee
And Water leave to France.

Genius of Health, thy grateful Taste
Rivals the Cup of Jove
And warms each English generous Breast
With Liberty and Love

Firkins are the successors to what was once the trend-setting Firkin chain. Ten years ago having Firkin in a pub name meant that the beer was brewed on the premises and that the manager was free to innovate as he or she saw fit. Now the pubs (which have Firkin as the second part of the name, eg Donkey & Firkin) have live sports and lots of imported lager.

Hogshead was once notable solely for its excellent range of hard-to-find beers from some of England's best and smallest breweries. Somewhere along the way that emphasis has been lost and these pubs are now chasing the same brand-conscious feel as All Bar One.

Moon under Water is an ironic name given that it comes from an article George Orwell once wrote for London's *Evening Standard*, fantasising about his one perfect pub, the Moon over Water. No doubt George would be saddened to see his idea capitalised upon and exploited a few decades later in a particularly uncharming chain.

O'Neill's is the previously mentioned fake Irish chain. In many ways this and the similar Scruffy Murphy's are Disney versions of the real

Top left: Hogarth's *Beer Street*, celebrating the benefits of beer for one and all (reproduced by permission of the Founders' Library, University of Wales, Lampeter)

thing and the ersatz memorabilia and unnaturally distressed surfaces are an insult to real Irish pubs in England that have been happily pouring pints for decades. There are several other fake Irish chains; a good way to spot one is to look for the huge old picture of James Joyce occupying much too prominent a spot.

SIMON BRACKEN

Rat & Parrot makes one wonder who exactly came up with the name. Owned by Scottish Courage – the one UK-based major brewer – these pubs seem to pop up wherever there are tourists. The blackboard 'specials' look as though they are produced by a computer.

Slug & Lettuce is another big and airy chain of pubs with acceptable food and OK beer. They are the haunt of modern folk, some of whom don't think anything can be good if it doesn't have a label (although who would want a slug – or a rat for that matter – on their label escapes us).

Tap & Spile deserves credit for trying to make a chain out of charming local pubs with lots of regional beers. Sadly, in some cases, this chain may actually cause the death of an authentic charming local.

Pub Grub

Most pubs serve some sort of food, a trend that developed in the 1960s. Some only serve lunch, which can often be a good deal, while others offer meals through the day. Many, especially in the country, serve roast lunches on Sunday. At the cheaper end pub meals are not very different from those in cafes, but at the expensive end they're closer to restaurants. Many pubs embrace both extremes with a cheap bar menu and a more formal adjoining restaurant.

The range of food offered is enormous, not just quality wise (from great to execrable) but also by type of cuisine (from Thai to trendy to airline). The most common menus have a range of nonthreatening items such as chilli con carne or lasagne which are easily microwaved by the untrained staff. Another ubiquitous item is the 'jacket potato', which can be nothing more than a baked potato slathered with some sort of topping. Yum. Other dishes such as cutlets and steaks usually come with the ubiquitous chips and watery peas and carrots. For some reason the current trend is to give everything a dusting of alfalfa spouts.

Just because a menu is simple, however, doesn't mean it's bad. Some of the best fish and chips in England can be found in pubs throughout the north. One sign that a pub's food might be a cut above the norm is if it has a menu that is written daily on a chalkboard. This reflects the kitchen's effort to work with what's fresh. Conversely the unchanging polychromatic chalkboards that are the hallmark of corporate pubs should be seen as red flags.

Many pubs have Thai restaurants attached and the food can be fresh and good – albeit a bit odd in a pub setting. However, treat with caution those pub menus that mix a couple of Thai dishes, a couple of curries and a few shop-worn standards such as spaghetti Bolognese. You can bet the kitchen has a warning for those wearing pace-makers: microwaves in use. You can always suss out a place by having a drink and looking at what other patrons are eating.

The best bets in pub eating are the growing number of 'gastro-pubs', which is short for gastronomy pubs. Here the food is often the vaguely defined as modern British, but it is also often inventive, good and reasonably priced. These can not only be good value but also memorable for their food quality, with chefs who've had years of training. The wines on offer – even by the glass – are often excellent. Some of these places rival top-notch restaurants in their presentation and preparation.

Whatever sort of pub you end up in, expect to place your orders for food either at the bar or at a food area nearby. A server will bring it to your table when it's ready.

Thanks

Kind appreciation to Roger Protz of the Campaign for Real Ale (CAMRA) for his generous assistance in preparing this section.

Getting There & Away

London is a transport hub for the world and competition between airlines means that you should be able to find tickets at good prices from just about anywhere. The emergence of several discount carriers has increased competition on flights from Europe and Ireland – routes that were once characterised by their ridiculously high fares.

Bus travel from Europe and Ireland is usually the cheapest option; but it can be bone-crunching and exhausting, and the savings are not huge compared with the cheap airfares you should be able to find.

Trains running through the Channel Tunnel have provided stiff competition for the multitude of ferries from Europe and fare wars for passengers, with and without their own transport, are frequent. The passenger train through the tunnel, the Eurostar, links London with Paris and Brussels and has numerous special offers throughout the year.

Ferries have lowered their prices and speeded up their services between Britain and Europe, and on the Irish routes as well.

Getting to England from Scotland and Wales is easy. The bus and train systems are fully integrated and in most cases you'll have no ides when you've crossed the border. See the Getting Around chapter for details.

AIR
Airports & Airlines
Airports London has the two main airports for transcontinental flights (Heathrow and Gatwick), but a few flights from North America and Asia do also go to Manchester Airport.

Flights from Europe and Ireland fly to London's five airports and scores of other airports throughout England, such as Manchester and Birmingham.

There are many flights between Glasgow and Edinburgh in Scotland and London; however, the train is often a cheaper and more convenient option.

Airlines Most of the world's major airlines serve London and some also serve regional cities. The following are reservations numbers you can use throughout Britain. Note that most are cheap-rate numbers.

Aer Lingus	☎ 0845 973 7747
Aeroflot	☎ 020-7355 2233
Air Canada	☎ 0870 524 7226
Air France	☎ 0845 084 5111
Air New Zealand	☎ 020-8741 2299
Alitalia	☎ 0870 544 8259
American Airlines	☎ 0845 778 9789
British Airways	☎ 0845 722 2111
British Midland	☎ 0870 607 0555
Cathay Pacific Airways	☎ 0845 758 1581
Continental Airlines	☎ 01293-776464
Delta Air Lines	☎ 0800 414767
El Al Israel Airlines	☎ 020-7957 4100
Emirates Airlines	☎ 0870 243 2222
Iberia	☎ 0870 606 2032

Warning

The information in this chapter is particularly vulnerable to change. Prices for international travel are volatile, routes are introduced and cancelled, schedules change, special deals come and go, and rules and visa requirements are amended. Airlines and governments seem to take a perverse pleasure in making price structures and regulations as complicated as possible. You should check directly with the airline or a travel agent to make sure you understand how a fare (and ticket you may buy) works. In addition, the travel industry is highly competitive and there are many lurks and perks.

The upshot of this is that you should get opinions, quotes and advice from as many airlines and travel agents as possible before you part with your hard-earned cash. The details given in this chapter should be regarded as pointers and are not a substitute for your own careful, up-to-date research.

KLM-Royal Dutch Airlines	☎ 0870 507 4074
Lufthansa Airlines	☎ 0845 773 7747
Olympic Airways	☎ 0870 606 0460
Qantas Airways	☎ 0845 774 7767
Sabena	☎ 0845 601 0933
Scandinavian Airlines (SAS)	☎ 0845 607 2772
Singapore Airlines	☎ 0870 608 8886
South African Airways	☎ 0870 747 1111
TAP Air Portugal	☎ 0845 601 0932
Thai Airways International	☎ 0870 606 0911
Turkish Airlines	☎ 020-7766 9300
United Airlines	☎ 0845 844 4777
Virgin Atlantic	☎ 01293-616161

In addition there are now several discount, no-frills airlines. They are not usually on computerised reservations systems such as those used by travel agents or those on travel Web sites such as www.travelocity .com and www.expedia.com. To check their fares you'll have to visit their Web sites or call their reservation numbers. There are often extra discounts for tickets bought on the Web site.

Buzz (☎ 0870 240 7070) An off-shoot of KLM, Buzz flies from London Stansted to several European destinations.
Web site: www.buzzaway.com

easyJet (☎ 0870 600 0000) A feisty carrier with bright orange jets, easyJet flies to several European destinations from London Luton and Liverpool.
Web site: www.easyjet.com

Go (☎ 0845 605 4321) An off-shoot of British Airways, Go flies from London Stansted to a variety of European destinations.
Web site: www.go-fly.com

Ryanair (☎ 0870 156 9569) An Irish-based airline, Ryanair flies from numerous British airports to various airports in Ireland, and from London Stansted to several European destinations. However, note that some of the European airports it flies to are secondary fields far from the cities Ryanair claims to serve. Always check where they really fly to.
Web site: www.ryanair.com

Virgin Express (☎ 020-7744 0004) Flying to a growing number of European cities (via Brussels), Virgin Express offers flights from London Stansted, Gatwick and Heathrow airports.
Web site: www.virgin-express.com

Buying Tickets

World aviation has never been so competitive, making air travel better value than ever. But you have to research the options carefully to make sure you get the best deal. The Internet is an increasingly useful resource for checking air fares.

Full-time students and those aged under 26 years (under 30 in some countries) have access to better deals than other travellers. You have to show a document proving your date of birth or a valid International Student Identity Card (ISIC) when buying your ticket and boarding the plane.

Generally, there is nothing to be gained by buying a ticket direct from the airline. Discounted tickets are released to selected travel agents and specialist discount agencies, and these are usually the cheapest deals going.

One exception to this rule is the expanding number of no-frills carriers, which mostly only sell direct to travellers. Unlike the 'full-service' airlines, no-frills carriers often make one-way tickets available at around half the return fare, meaning that it is easy to put together an open-jaw ticket when you fly to one place but leave from another.

The other exception is booking on the Internet. Many airlines, full-service and no-frills, offer some excellent fares to Web surfers. They may sell seats by auction or simply cut prices to reflect the reduced cost of electronic selling.

Many travel agencies around the world have Web sites, which can make the Internet a quick and easy way to compare prices. There are also an increasing number of on-line agents – such as www.travelocity.co.uk and www.deckchair.com – that operate only on the Internet. Online ticket sales work well if you are doing a simple one-way or return trip on specified dates. However, online super-fast fare generators are no substitute for a travel agent who knows all about special deals, has strategies for avoiding layovers and can offer advice on everything from which airline has the best vegetarian food to the best travel insurance to bundle with your ticket.

Air Travel Glossary

Alliances Many of the world's leading airlines are now intimately involved with each other, sharing everything from reservations systems and check-in to aircraft and frequent flyer schemes. Opponents say that alliances restrict competition. Whatever the arguments, there is no doubt that big alliances are the way of the future.

Cancelling or Changing Tickets If you have to cancel or change a ticket, you need to contact the original travel agent who sold you the ticket. Airlines only issue refunds to the purchaser of a ticket – usually the travel agent who bought the ticket on your behalf. There are often heavy penalties involved; insurance can sometimes be taken out against these penalties.

Courier Fares Businesses often need to send urgent documents or freight securely and quickly. Courier companies hire people to accompany the package through customs and, in return, offer a discount ticket which is sometimes a bargain. However, you may have to surrender all your baggage allowance and take only carry-on luggage.

Fares Airlines traditionally offer 1st class (coded F), business class (coded J) and economy class (coded Y) tickets. These days there are so many promotional and discounted fares available that few passengers pay full fare.

Lost Tickets If you lose your airline ticket an airline will usually treat it like a travellers cheque and, after enquiries, issue you with another one. Legally, however, an airline is entitled to treat it like cash and if you lose it then it's gone forever. Take good care of your tickets.

Onward Tickets An entry requirement for many countries is that you have a ticket out of the country. If you're unsure of your next move, the easiest solution is to buy the cheapest onward ticket to a neighbouring country or a ticket from a reliable airline which can later be refunded if you do not use it.

Open-Jaw Tickets These are return tickets where you fly out to one place but return from another. If available, this can save you backtracking to your arrival point.

Overbooking Since every flight has some passengers who fail to show up, airlines often book more passengers than they have seats. Usually excess passengers make up for the no-shows, but occasionally somebody gets 'bumped' onto the next available flight. Guess who it is most likely to be? The passengers who check in late. If you do get 'bumped' you are normally offered some form of compensation.

Reconfirmation Some airlines require you to reconfirm your flight at least 72 hours prior to departure. Check your travel documents to see if this is the case.

Restrictions Discounted tickets often have various restrictions on them – such as needing to be paid for in advance and incurring a penalty to be altered or cancelled. Others are restrictions on the minimum and maximum period you must be away.

Round-the-World Tickets RTW tickets give you a limited period (usually a year) in which to circumnavigate the globe. You can go anywhere the carrying airlines go, as long as you don't backtrack. The number of stopovers or total number of separate flights is decided before you set off and they usually cost a bit more than a basic return flight.

Ticketless Travel Airlines are gradually waking up to the realisation that paper tickets are unnecessary encumbrances. On simple one-way or return trips, reservations details can be held on computer, and the passenger merely shows ID to claim his or her seat.

Transferred Tickets Airline tickets cannot be transferred from one person to another. Travellers sometimes try to sell the return half of their ticket, but officials can ask you to prove that you are the person named on the ticket. On an international flight tickets are always compared with passports.

You may find the cheapest flights are advertised by obscure agencies. Most such firms are honest and solvent, but there are some rogue fly-by-night outfits around. Paying by credit card generally offers protection, as most card issuers provide refunds if you can prove you didn't get what you paid for. Similar protection can be obtained by buying a ticket from a bonded agent, such as one covered by the Air Travel Organiser's Licence (ATOL) scheme in the UK. Agents who only accept cash should hand over the tickets straight away and not tell you to 'come back tomorrow'. After you've made a booking or paid your deposit, call the airline and confirm that the booking was made. It's generally not advisable to send money (even cheques) through the post unless the agent is very well established – some travellers have reported being ripped off by fly-by-night mail-order ticket agents.

Many travellers change their routes halfway through their trips, so think carefully before you buy a ticket that is not easily refunded.

Travellers with Specific Needs

If they're warned early enough, airlines can often make special arrangements for travellers, such as wheelchair assistance at airports or vegetarian meals on the flight. Children under two years of age travel for 10% of the standard fare (or free on some airlines) as long as they don't occupy a seat. They don't get a baggage allowance. 'Skycots', baby food and nappies should be provided by the airline if requested in advance. Children aged between two and 12 can often occupy a seat for half to two-thirds of the full fare, and do get a baggage allowance.

The disability-friendly Web site, www .everybody.co.uk, has an airline directory that provides information on the facilities offered by various airlines.

Courier Flights

Courier flights are occasionally advertised in the newspapers, or you could contact air-freight companies listed in the phone book.

You may even have to go to the air-freight company to get an answer – the companies aren't always keen to give out information over the phone. *Travel Unlimited* (PO Box 1058, Allston, MA 02134, USA) is a monthly travel newsletter that publishes many courier flight deals from destinations worldwide. A 12-month subscription to the newsletter costs US$25, or US$35 for readers outside the USA. Another possibility (at least for US residents) is to join the International Association of Air Travel Couriers (IAATC). The membership fee of US$45 gets members a bimonthly update of air-courier offerings, access to a fax-on-demand service with daily updates of last-minute specials and the bimonthly newsletter the *Shoestring Traveler*. For more information, contact IAATC (☎ 561-582 8320) or visit the Web site at www.courier.org. However, be aware that joining this organisation does not guarantee that you'll get a courier flight.

In the UK, courier flights can sometimes be obtained from British Airways (☎ 0870 606 1133) and ACP Express (☎ 020-8897 5133).

Departure Tax

All domestic flights and those to destinations within the EU from Britain carry a £10 departure tax. For all other flights you pay £20. This is usually built into the price of your ticket.

Scotland

British Airways, British Midland, easyJet and Go all link London's airports with Glasgow and Edinburgh. Flights are frequent and take a bit over an hour. While special deals may bring return fares as low as £50, it's more common to pay £100 or more. By the time you add in transport to the airport and check-in, the savings in time aren't that much over the train, which is also usually cheaper.

Reaching London from smaller Scottish cities such as Aberdeen, or flying into one of the regional English cities from Glasgow or Edinburgh is really the domain of business travellers due to the expense.

Ireland

Competition on the many air routes between England and Ireland means that you can usually get a discount ticket for as little as £50 on any of the airlines serving the routes. Five carriers that offer frequent flights are British Airways, British Midland, Aer Lingus, Ryanair and British European. Besides the main Dublin to London route, there are lots of regional services linking smaller airports in both countries.

Continental Europe

There is not much variation in air fare prices for departures from the main European cities. All the major airlines usually offer some sort of deal, and travel agents generally have a number of deals on offer so shop around.

Expect to pay the equivalent of about £50 to £200 on major airlines for discounted return tickets to England. The low-cost carriers charge about £50 to £150 to the places they fly to, which coincidentally are usually the most competitive markets.

Across Europe many travel agencies have ties with STA Travel, where cheap tickets can be purchased and STA-issued tickets can be altered (usually for a US$25 fee). Outlets in major cities include: Voyages Wasteels in Paris (☎ 0 803 88 70 04 – within France only – fax 01 43 25 46 25), 11 rue Dupuytren, 75006 Paris; STA Travel in Berlin (☎ 030-311 0950, fax 313 0948), Goethestrasse 73, 10625 Berlin; Passaggi in Rome (☎ 06-474 0923, fax 482 7436), Stazione Termini FS, Galleria Di Tesla, Rome; and ISYTS in Athens (☎ 01-322 1267, fax 323 3767), 11 Nikis St, Upper Floor, Syntagma Square.

France has a network of student travel agencies that can supply discount tickets to travellers of all ages. OTU Voyages (☎ 01 44 41 38 50) has a central office in Paris at 39 Ave Georges Bernanos (5e) and another 42 offices around the country. Its Web site is at www.otu.fr.

Acceuil des Jeunes en France (☎ 01 42 77 87 80), 119 rue Saint Martin (4e), is another popular discount travel agency.

General travel agencies in Paris that offer some of the best services and deals include Nouvelles Frontières (☎ 0 803 33 33 33), 5 Ave de l'Opéra (1er), and Voyageurs du Monde (☎ 01 42 86 16 00) at 55 rue Sainte Anne (2e). Nouvelles Frontières' Web site is at www.nouvelles-frontieres.com.

Belgium, Switzerland, the Netherlands and Greece also have good agencies that sell discount air tickets. In Belgium, Acotra Student Travel Agency (☎ 02-512 86 07), rue de la Madeline, Brussels, and WATS Reizen (☎ 03-226 16 26), de Keyserlei 44, Antwerp, are both well-known agencies. In Switzerland, SSR Voyages (☎ 01-297 11 11) specialises in student, youth and budget fares. There is a branch in Zurich at Leonhardstrasse 10 and others in most major Swiss cities. Its Web site is at www.ssr.ch.

NBBS Reizen (☎ 020-624 09 89), Rokin 66, Amsterdam, is the official student travel agency in the Netherlands. There are several other agencies around the city. Another recommended agent in Amsterdam is Malibu Travel (☎ 020-626 32 30), Prinsengracht 230.

In Athens, check the many travel agencies in the backstreets between Syntagma and Omonia Squares. For student and non-concessionary fares, try Magic Bus (☎ 01-323 7471, fax 322 0219).

The USA

Since the late 1990s there has been a permanent price war between the USA and London, the busiest transcontinental route in the world.

Fares on all major airlines flying from the East Coast to London have fallen as low as US$300 in winter, US$400 in spring and autumn, and US$600 in summer. From the West Coast fares are about US$100 higher.

Given how low the advertised fares are, you may not need a travel agent and instead can contact the airlines directly or check their Web sites.

However, should you need an agent, Council Travel (☎ 800 226 8624), America's largest student travel organisation, has around 60 offices in the USA; its head office is at 205 E 42 St, New York, NY 10017. Call for details of your local office, or visit its Web site at www.ciee.org. STA Travel (☎ 800 777 0112) has offices in Boston, Chicago, Miami, New York, Philadelphia, San Francisco and other major cities. Call the toll-free 800 number for office locations, or visit its Web site at www.statravel .com.

The major American newspapers all produce weekly travel sections in which you will find a number of ads from ticket consolidators. Ticket Planet (www.ticketplanet .com) is a leading ticket consolidator in the USA and is recommended. However, given the state of regular fares, you may not save much.

Canada

Canada enjoys the same kind of discount fares to Britain as the USA (see previous section).

Canadian discount air-ticket sellers are known as consolidators, and their air fares tend to be about 10% higher than those sold in the USA. The *Globe & Mail*, the *Toronto Star*, the *Montreal Gazette* and the *Vancouver Sun* carry travel agents, advertisements and are a good place to look for cheap fares.

Travel CUTS (☎ 800 667 2887) is the national student travel agency in Canada and has offices in all major cities. Its Web site is at www.travelcuts.com.

Australia

There are many competing airlines and a wide variety of air fares for flights between Europe and Australia. Round-the-world (RTW) tickets are often real bargains and, since Australia is pretty much on the other side of the world from England, it can sometimes work out cheaper to keep going on a RTW ticket than do a U-turn on a return ticket.

Expect to pay anywhere from A$1800 in the low season to A$3000 in the high season for return tickets from Australia to England.

Flights from Australia to England generally go via South-East Asia with stopovers in Kuala Lumpur, Bangkok or Singapore. If a long stopover between connections is necessary, transit accommodation is sometimes

included in the price of the ticket. If it's at your own expense, it may be worth considering a more expensive ticket. The very cheapest may entail two or more stops on the way to England.

Quite a few travel offices specialise in discount air tickets. Some travel agents, particularly smaller ones, advertise cheap air fares in the travel sections of weekend newspapers, such as the *Age* in Melbourne and the *Sydney Morning Herald*.

Two well-known agents for cheap fares are STA Travel and Flight Centre. STA Travel (☎ 03-9349 2411) has its main office at 224 Faraday St, Carlton, Vic 3053, and offices in all major cities as well as on many university campuses. Call ☎ 131 776 Australia-wide for the location of your nearest branch, or visit its Web site at www .statravel.com.au. Flight Centre (☎ 131 600 Australia-wide) has a central office in Sydney at 82 Elizabeth St, and dozens of offices throughout Australia. Its Web site is at www.flightcentre.com.au.

New Zealand

The best value fares for travel from New Zealand are usually RTW fares, often cheaper than a return ticket. Depending on which airline you choose, you may fly across Asia, with possible stopovers in India, Bangkok or Singapore, or across the USA, with possible stopovers in Los Angeles, Honolulu or one of the Pacific Islands.

Prices are similar to those from Australia (see previous section) but the trip is even longer; about two 12-hour flights minimum.

The *New Zealand Herald* has a travel section in which travel agents advertise fares. Flight Centre (☎ 09-309 6171) has a large central office in Auckland at National Bank Towers (on the corner of Queen St and Darby St) and many branches throughout the country. STA Travel (☎ 09-309 0458) has its main office in Auckland at 10 High St and other offices in Auckland as well as in Hamilton, Palmerston North, Wellington, Christchurch and Dunedin. Check their Web site at www.statravel .com.au.

Going underground: the best way of getting around in London

Oxo Tower, London

One of the Victorians' greatest engineering feats: Tower Bridge by night

Something to reflect upon: traditional red phone-boxes are still dotted around London.

Rooms with a view: the BA London Eye

London life passes you by if you go by taxi.

Changing of the Guard, Buckingham Palace

A magnificent lion atop Westminster Bridge

Asia

Although most Asian countries now offer fairly competitive deals, Bangkok, Singapore and Hong Kong are still the best places to shop around for discount tickets.

Khao San Rd in Bangkok is the budget travellers' headquarters. Bangkok has a number of excellent travel agents, but there are also some suspect ones; ask the advice of other travellers before handing over your cash. STA Travel (☎ 02-236 0262), 33 Surawong Rd, is a good and reliable place to start.

In Singapore, STA Travel (☎ 737 7188) in the Orchard Parade Hotel, 1 Tanglin Rd, offers competitive discount fares to Britain. Singapore has hundreds of travel agents, so you can compare prices on flights before you buy. Chinatown Point shopping centre, on New Bridge Rd, has a good selection of travel agents.

Hong Kong has a number of excellent, reliable travel agencies and some not-so-reliable ones. A good way to check on a travel agent is to look it up in the phone book: fly-by-night operators don't usually stay around long enough to get listed. Many travellers use the Hong Kong Student Travel Bureau (☎ 2730 3269), 8th floor, Star House, Tsimshatsui. You could also try Phoenix Services (☎ 2722 7378), 7th floor, Milton Mansion, 96 Nathan Rd, Tsimshatsui. Hong Kong's travel market can be unpredictable but some excellent bargains are available if you are lucky.

India

Although you can get cheap tickets in Mumbai (formerly Bombay) and Calcutta, Delhi is the real wheeling and dealing centre.

In Delhi there are a number of discount travel agencies around Connaught Place but, as always, be careful before handing over your cash. If you use one of these discount agents, double-check with the airline to make sure that the booking has been made. STIC Travels (☎ 011-332 5559), an agent for STA Travel, has an office in Delhi in Room 6 at the Hotel Imperial in Janpath.

In Mumbai, STIC Travels (☎ 022-218 1431) is located at 6 Maker Arcade, Cuffe Parade. Another travel agent in Mumbai that comes highly recommended is Transway International (☎ 022-262 6066), 2nd floor, Pantaky House, 8 Maruti Cross Lane, Fort. Most of the international airline offices in Mumbai are in or around Nariman Point.

Africa

Nairobi and Johannesburg are probably the best places in eastern and South Africa to buy tickets. Some major airlines have offices in Nairobi, which is a good place to determine the standard fare before you make the rounds of the travel agencies. Getting several quotes is a good idea as prices are always changing. Flight Centres (☎ 02-210024) in Lakhamshi House, Biashara St, has been in business for many years.

In Johannesburg, the South African Student's Travel Services (☎ 011-716 3045) has an office at the University of the Witwatersrand. STA Travel (☎ 011-447 5551) has an office in Johannesburg on Tyrwhitt Ave in Rosebank.

The main international airports in West Africa are Abidjan, Accra, Bamako, Dakar and Lagos. There are also some regular charter flights from some European countries to Banjul (Gambia). It is usually better to buy tickets in West Africa through a travel agency rather than from the airline. Travel agents' fares are generally the same as those offered by the airlines, but agents may be more helpful if anything goes wrong.

In Abidjan, Saga Voyages (☎ 32 98 70) is located opposite Air Afrique in Le Plateau. Haury Tours (☎ 22 16 54, fax 22 17 68, e haury@africaonline.co.ci), 2nd floor, Chardy Bldg in Le Plateau. It's an affiliate of the French travel group Nouvelles Frontières.

In Accra, try Expert Travel & Tours (☎ 021-775498) on Ring Rd East near the US embassy.

There are several agencies dealing in international and regional flights in Bamako. Two of the best are TAM (☎ 23 92 00, e tvoyage@sotelma.net) on Square Lumumba and ATS Voyages (☎ 22 44 35) on Ave Kassa Keita.

Agencies in Dakar include Senegal Tours (☎ 823 31 81), 5 Place de l'Indépendance, and SDV Voyages (☎ 839 00 81), 51 Ave Albert Sarraut.

In Lagos there are many travel agencies in the Race Course Rd complex on the southern side of Tafawa Balewa Square on Lagos Island. Most of the airline offices are in this area too. Try L'Aristocrate Travels & Tours (☎ 01-266 7322), on the corner of Davies and Broad Sts, or Mandilas Travel (☎ 01-266 3339) on Broad St.

South America

Venezuela has the cheapest air links with England, and is the most convenient northern gateway to Europe. TAP Air Portugal and Iberia often have the cheapest tickets to Europe.

In Caracas, IVI Tours (☎ 02-993 60 82), Residencia La Hacienda, Piso Bajo, Local 1-4-T, Final Avenida Principal de las Mercedes, is the agent for STA Travel in Venezuela and often has a range of good deals.

Rio de Janeiro is Brazil's main international gateway and there are plenty of travel agents. The Student Travel Bureau (☎ 021-259 0023), an affiliate of STA Travel, is at Rua Visconde de Piraja 550, Ipanema.

Buenos Aires Aeropuerto Internacional Ministro Pistarini has excellent air connections to the UK. ASATEJ (☎ 011-4315 14570), Argentina's nonprofit student travel agency and the agent for STA Travel, is located on the 3rd floor, Oficina 319-B, at Florida 835, Buenos Aires.

LAND
Bus

You can get to England from Europe by bus with a short ferry/hovercraft ride across the Channel, or the train underneath, as part of the deal. Buses are slower and less comfortable than trains, but they are cheaper, especially if you qualify for the 10% to 20% discount available to people aged 13 to 25 or over 60, or take advantage of the discount fares on offer from time to time.

Eurolines (☎ 0870 514 3219), 52 Grosvenor Gardens, London SW1, is a consortium of European coach companies that operates Europe's largest international bus network. Its Web site, www.eurolines.com, has links to the sites of all the national operators.

You can book Eurolines tickets through any National Express (☎ 0870 580 8080, www.gobycoach.com) office, including Victoria Coach Station (London's international bus terminal), and at many travel agencies. Eurolines offices and affiliated companies can be found across Europe, including Amsterdam (☎ 020-560 87 87), Barcelona (☎ 93 490 4000), Berlin (☎ 030-86 0960), Brussels (☎ 02-203 0707) and Madrid (☎ 91 528 1105).

The following are example single/return adult fares and journey times: Amsterdam f118/165 (nine hours); Barcelona 21,900/30,800 ptas (22–24 hours); Berlin DM127/212 (22½ hours); Brussels BF2150/3030 (seven hours); Dublin IR£32/58 (11 hours).

At peak times in summer (when you should add between 5% and 10% to the above fares), you should make reservations a few days in advance. Also note that on trips from places such as Barcelona, you'll pay the same fare and save about 20 hours and your sanity by getting a discount fare with an airline such as easyJet.

See the Getting Around chapter for details of the National Express bus network that spans England, Wales and Scotland.

Train

See the Getting Around chapter for details of the integrated rail network between England, Scotland and Wales.

Eurostar The Eurostar passenger train service travels between London and Paris and London and Brussels, via the Channel Tunnel, with stops in Lille and Calais (France) and Ashford (England).

The London terminal is at Waterloo station. There are around 16 trains per day to/from Paris' Gare du Nord and around 11 per day to/from Brussels' Gare du Midi. The Paris-London journey takes three hours, Brussels-London takes two hours and 40 minutes. Both these journey times will be reduced by 30 minutes when the high-speed track through Kent is finally completed. Immigration formalities are usually completed on the train, but British customs is at Waterloo.

You can buy tickets from travel agencies, major train stations or by phoning Eurostar directly (☎ 0870 518 6186 in the UK, or 0 836 35 35 39 in France). The Eurostar Web site (www.eurostar.com) often has special deals. The normal single/return fare from Paris and Brussels is an eye-opening £250, but there are numerous special deals and it's not uncommon to pay £79 for a return fare. Children and those aged 12 to 25 or over 60 are eligible for discounts.

Bicycles are only allowed on the Eurostar if they're collapsible; otherwise you can use the Esprit Parcel Service (☎ 01 55 31 58 31) in France, which will take your bike for around 200FF.

There are numerous good possibilities for train connections to the Eurostar in Brussels, Lille and Paris. For enquiries about European trains contact Rail Europe on ☎ 0870 584 8848, or visit the Web site (www.raileurope.com). Another good rail Web site is the international Deutsche Bahn site (www.bahn.de).

Eurotunnel These trains carry vehicles and freight through the Channel Tunnel. Immigration formalities and customs are carried out before you drive onto the train.

Eurotunnel terminals are clearly signposted and connected to motorway networks. Travel time from motorway to motorway, including loading and unloading, is one hour; the shuttle itself takes 35 minutes. This sounds impressive, but the total time by hovercraft is under two hours, and ferries only take 2½ hours.

Specially designed shuttle trains run all day, departing up to four times an hour from 6 am to 10 pm and every hour between 10 pm and 6 am. A car and its passengers costs from £270. You can make an advance reservation (☎ 0870 535 3535) or pay by cash or credit card at a toll booth. There are also

day-trip fares that cost £69 or less. Eurotunnel's Web site is at www.eurotunnel.com.

Train & Ferry Connections Another option is the rail/ferry link, which involves trains at either end and a ferry across the Channel. Trains arrive in London at Victoria, Liverpool Street and Charing Cross train stations, depending which ferry terminal you arrive at. There are information centres at all the main stations.

Fares to London depend on where you are coming from in Europe. Think £100 to £200. Rail/ferry links run from Oostende (Belgium) and Calais (France) to Dover and Charing Cross, from Hoek van Holland (the Netherlands) to Harwich and Liverpool Street, and Boulogne (France) to Folkestone and Charing Cross.

See the Sea section later in the chapter for details of ferry sailings.

Car & Motorcycle

Drivers of vehicles registered in other EU countries will find bringing a car into England a fairly straight-forward process. The car must have registration papers and a nationality plate and the driver must have insurance. Although the International Insurance Certificate (Green Card) is no longer required, it remains excellent proof that you are covered. Check at your nearest British embassy for details for non-EU countries.

There are motorways from all the main ferry ports and the Channel Tunnel that converge on the M25 motorway around London. You can use this often clogged artery to skirt (maybe slog) past the city and on to other destinations.

SEA

There's a bewildering array of alternatives between Britain and mainland Europe. This chapter outlines the main ones, but doesn't give a complete listing. Many ferry links from Ireland to both Scotland and Wales are the best means of reaching England.

Competition from the Channel Tunnel and low-fare airlines has led to mergers of once competing ferry companies and now the entire market is so competitive that there are constant special deals.

Services are comprehensive but fares are complicated. The same ferry company often has a host of different prices for the same route, depending upon the time of day or year, the validity of the ticket or the size of a vehicle. Return tickets may be much cheaper than two one-way fares; on some routes a standard five-day return costs the same as a one-way ticket; and vehicle tickets may also cover a driver and passenger. There are cheap day-return tickets, but they're strictly policed. Also on longer ferry rides there will be options for more deluxe accommodation including cabins.

The listings below are limited to high-season return fares for a single foot passenger/one car and a driver. Remember that you will often be able to beat these fares through special offers at all but the busiest times. You definitely have to plan ahead to get the best deals. Contact details for the companies mentioned is in the boxed text 'Ferry Companies'.

France

On a clear day, you can see across the Channel from England to France. A true budget traveller would obviously swim – it's only seven hours and 40 minutes if you match the record.

Dover/Folkestone/Newhaven From the Continent the shortest ferry link is to Dover and Folkestone from Calais and Boulogne (France).

Dover is the most convenient port for those who plan onward travel by bus or train. P&O Stena Line ferries (£48/321, 1¼ hours) and Hoverspeed catamarans (£48/330, 45 minutes) operate between Calais and Dover every one to two hours.

Hoverspeed also runs its catamarans, Seacats, between Folkestone and Boulogne (£48/298, 55 minutes) and between Newhaven and Dieppe (£56/360, two hours) from late April to early September.

Portsmouth P&O European Ferries operates three to four ferries per day between Cherbourg and Le Havre to Portsmouth (£60/190, five to six hours during the day, a couple of hours longer at night).

Brittany Ferries has at least one sailing per day between St Malo and Portsmouth (£75/292, nine hours). There are other ferries run by other operators that travel via the Channel Islands to Portsmouth. See The Channel Islands chapter for details.

Spain

From Plymouth, Brittany Ferries operates at least one ferry per week to Santander on Spain's north coast (£154/460, 24 hours).

P&O European Ferries operates a twice-weekly service between Bilbao and Portsmouth (£100/440, 35 hours).

Ferry Companies

Europe to Britain
Brittany Ferries (☎ 0870 901 2400)
  Web site: www.brittany-ferries.co.uk
DFDS Seaways (☎ 0870 533 3000)
  Web site: www.dfdsseaways.co.uk
Fjord Line (☎ 0191-296 1313)
  Web site: www.fjordline.no
Hoverspeed (☎ 0870 240 8070)
  Web site: www.hoverspeed.co.uk
P&O European Ferries (☎ 0870 242 4999)
  Web site: www.poef.com
P&O North Sea Ferries (☎ 01482-377177)
  Web site: www.ponsf.com
P&O Scottish Ferries (☎ 01224-572615)
  Web site: www.poscottishferries.co.uk
P&O Stena Line (☎ 0870 600 0600)
  Web site: www.posl.com
Smyril Line (UK agent; ☎ 01224-572615)
  Web site: www.smyril-line.fo
Stena Line (☎ 0870 570 7070)
  Web site: www.stenaline.com

Ireland to Britain
Irish Ferries (☎ 0870 517 1717)
  Web site: www.irishferries.ie
P&O Irish Sea (☎ 0870 242 4777)
  Web site: www.poirishsea.com
Sea Containers Ferries (☎ 0870 552 3523)
  Web site: www.steam-packet.com
Stena Line (☎ 0870 570 7070)
  Web site: www.stenaline.com
Swansea Cork Ferries (☎ 01792-456116)
  Web site: www.swansea-cork.ie

Scandinavia

Until you see the ferry possibilities, it's easy to forget how close Scandinavia and Britain are, and why the Vikings found British villages so convenient for their pillaging expeditions.

Newcastle Norway's Fjord Line operates ferries all year from Stavanger (20 hours), Haugesund (22½ hours) and Bergen (27 hours) in Norway to Newcastle. The boats sail three times a week in summer and twice-weekly at other times. Fares cost £200/690 (for a foot passenger/car and four people sharing one cabin) between either Norwegian city and Newcastle.

DFDS Seaways operates ferries from Kristiansand in Norway. They depart twice weekly (£198/336, 18 hours). Fares include a berth in an economy cabin.

Harwich Harwich is the major port linking southern England to Denmark and northern Germany. DFDS Seaways has two or three ferries per week to Esbjerg (£168/276, 20 hours). Fares include a berth in an economy cabin.

Belgium, the Netherlands & Germany

There are two direct links with Germany but many people prefer to drive from the Dutch ferry ports.

Dover Hoverspeed operates Seacat catamarans between Oostende (Belgium) and Dover. There are at least three trips per day (£28/215, two hours).

Harwich DFDS Seaways has three ferries per week between Hamburg and Harwich. The fare (£168/276, 19½ hours) includes a berth in an economy cabin.

Stena Line has two fast ferries per day from Hoek van Holland, in the Netherlands (£44/260, four hours).

Hull P&O North Sea Ferries has daily ferries between Rotterdam (13 hours) and Zeebrugge (13½ hours) and Hull. The fares on both routes cost £81/136.

Newcastle DFDS Seaways has a daily service from Ijmuiden in the Netherlands (£118/256, 15 hours), near Amsterdam. The fare includes a berth in an economy cabin.

Ireland

There's a great variety of ferry services between Britain and Ireland using modern car ferries. There are often special deals worth investigating and the off-season fares are significantly lower. On some routes the cost for a car includes up to four or five passengers at no additional cost. If you can hitch a ride in a less than full car, it costs the driver nothing extra.

From south to north, ferry possibilities include:

Cork to Swansea, Wales Swansea Cork Ferries has a 10-hour crossing that costs £68/378 (for up to five people and one car). It operates several times per week from mid-March to early November.

Rosslare to Fishguard and Pembroke, Wales From Pembroke, Irish Ferries has two daily crossings that take just under four hours. The fares cost £20/179. From Fishguard, Stena Line has two daily regular ferries that take 3½ hours and cost £40/179. The frequent catamaran service takes under two hours and costs £50/209.

Dublin and Dun Laoghaire to Holyhead, Wales Irish Ferries has two slow ferries daily from Dublin (£40/189, three hours). Fast ferries travel four times daily (£50/239, two hours). Stena Line has several slow ferries per day from Dublin (£184, 3¼ hours), foot passengers are not accepted. Stena fast ferries go from Dun Laoghaire (£50/229, two hours).

Dublin to Liverpool, England Sea Containers has daily catamarans (£50/249, 3¾ hours, one or two daily).

Belfast to Troon, Scotland Sea Containers Ferries operates a number of daily catamaran services (£50/249, 2½ hours).

Belfast to Stranraer, Scotland Stena Line operates several daily slow ferries (£40/189, three hours). The frequent fast ferry service (1¾ hours) is slightly more expensive.

Larne to Cairnryan, Scotland P&O Irish Sea operates at least two daily slow ferries (£42/238, 2¼ hours). Frequent fast ferries are more expensive (£50/290) and take one hour.

Getting Around

Public transport in England is generally good but it can be expensive. During most of the 1980s and 1990s government policy was openly hostile to public transportation. Car ownership was favoured, and local rail and bus services suffered. The chaos-filled privatisation of British Rail is but one dismal illustration of this. The Labour government has made great promises to reverse this decline, but it will take years for the results to be felt. This is bad news for visitors without their own wheels, as transport to many national parks and small villages is poor.

It's certainly worth considering car rental for at least part of your trip. However, if you're not driving, with a mix of local buses, the odd taxi, walking and occasionally hiring a bike, and plenty of time, you can get almost anywhere.

Buses are nearly always the cheapest way to get around. Unfortunately they're also the slowest (sometimes by a considerable margin). With discount passes and tickets bought in advance, trains can be competitive on price; they're quicker and often take you through beautiful countryside relatively unspoiled by the modern age.

Ticket types and prices vary considerably. Travelling by bus and train can be as complicated as finding a cheap airline ticket. For many the convenience of a train or bus pass will outweigh any potential savings from endlessly looking for the best deal.

See the bus and train fare tables in this chapter to get an idea of the way the different tickets stack up. If you know how far you're travelling (even if your planned journey is not specifically covered) you can get a rough idea of costs by working from the mileage columns.

The transport systems of England, Wales and Scotland are integrated and much of the following information will apply for travel between the three countries.

AIR

Most regional centres are linked to London by regular flights. However, unless you're travelling from the outer reaches of Britain, in particular northern Scotland, planes are only marginally quicker than trains if you include the time it takes to get to airports. And the journeys aren't anywhere near as scenic.

Domestic Air Services

The main operators are British Airways (BA), British Midland, KLM uk, easyJet, Go and Ryanair. See the Getting There & Away chapter for contact information.

There are all the usual advance purchase and discount fares available. There are also youth fares (for under-26s), but Apex and special-offer fares are usually cheaper. Depending on how flexible you are you may be able to find a ticket that compares favourably with the cheaper train fares.

Air Passes

If you're flying into the UK on BA you may be eligible for a One World Visit Europe Air Pass. This allows you to buy tickets on all UK domestic flights for an additional £59 each. This can be an excellent deal if you want to get from London to far northern Scotland and the islands, but isn't useful for a trip just in England. However, the same scheme allows you to buy tickets for flights to other parts of Europe; if you are combining England with, say, Italy, it might be good value. These air pass tickets must be arranged at least seven days prior to arrival in the UK.

British Midland offers a similar scheme called the Discover Europe Airpass, which is only available to visitors from outside Europe.

BUS

Road transport in England is almost entirely privately owned and run. National Express (☎ 0870 580 8080) runs the largest national network and completely dominates the market, but there are often smaller competitors on the main routes. You can visit the National Express Web site at www.gobycoach.com. National Express is part of Eurolines, the European bus network (see Bus in the Getting There & Away chapter for details).

In Britain, long-distance express buses are usually referred to as coaches, and in many towns there are separate bus and coach stations. Over short distances coaches are more expensive (though quicker) than buses. There is a network of bus companies serving England and the most important ones are highlighted in the relevant chapters of this book.

Unless otherwise stated, prices quoted in this book are for economy single tickets. See the Bus Fares table for a rough idea of long-distance bus fares.

To convert miles to kilometres, multiply by 1.61.

Local Buses & Information

Although local and regional buses seem to cover the length of England, they often do not do so in a way useful to the visitor. Away from cities, buses may run at times designed to serve schools and industry. This means that there may be few midday services and even fewer weekend services. You might plan a spectacular hike in one of the national parks only to find that there is no bus service at all on the day you finish.

A number of counties operate telephone enquiry lines that try to explain the fast-changing and often chaotic timetables; wherever possible, these numbers have been provided. Before commencing a journey off the main routes it is wise to phone for the latest information.

An even better alternative for bus information is the National Bus Enquiry Service (☎ 0870 608 2608). A government initiative, it is meant to provide all timetable and fare in-

ROAD DISTANCES (MILES)

1 mile = 1.61km

	Birmingham	Bristol	Cambridge	Cardiff, Wales	Carlisle	Dover	Edinburgh, Scotland	Exeter	Glasgow, Scotland	Lincoln	Liverpool	London	Oxford	Penzance	Sheffield	York
Birmingham	---															
Bristol	85	---														
Cambridge	95	146	---													
Cardiff, Wales	100	45	190	---												
Carlisle	199	282	257	300	---											
Dover	178	187	130	240	400	---										
Edinburgh, Scotland	295	375	338	390	98	450	---									
Exeter	164	84	251	111	355	244	454	---								
Glasgow, Scotland	295	375	370	390	97	470	44	453	---							
Lincoln	85	170	90	200	182	200	260	260	280	---						
Liverpool	95	165	170	170	126	278	219	258	220	120	---					
London	110	115	54	155	313	71	375	200	397	131	193	---				
Oxford	66	75	83	110	271	130	360	154	360	127	160	57	---			
Penzance	270	190	360	230	465	350	560	110	560	365	363	280	263	---		
Sheffield	76	183	122	201	159	247	236	256	256	47	79	168	141	366	---	
York	135	215	150	245	117	266	195	299	220	75	100	188	185	405	58	---

formation, similar to the National Rail Enquiry Service (see Trains later in this chapter). However, at the time of writing, it was in its early stages and information was only available for several northern counties. You should definitely try it; it should have been extended to cover the area you seek information about.

Bus Passes & Discounts

Besides the national passes mentioned below, there are literally scores of regional and local bus passes. Most can be bought from the driver as you board the bus. If you are going to spend any amount of time in one area, it is always worth asking what sorts of Rover (good for unlimited use on

Bus Fares from London

The sample fares below are for unrestricted single and return travel from London by National Express coach. Within each category, the first fare is available to anyone and the second fare requires one of the National Express discount cards (see Bus in this chapter for details).

If you can avoid travelling on Fridays, you can save a few pounds off these fares. National Express has advance purchase fares on many routes that also save a few pounds, so it's worth checking if your trip qualifies for such a fare. For destinations close to London there are day return fares that cost just a bit more than the regular single fare.

On some of the routes below you will have to change coaches/buses one or more times.

destination	best time (hours)	single (£)	return (£)
Brighton	1¾	7.50/6	12.50/10
Cambridge	2	8/6.50	12.50/10
Canterbury	2	8/6.50	12.50/10
Oxford*	1¾	7	7.50
Dover	2½	9.50/7.50	15/12
Salisbury	2¾	12/9.50	18/14
Stratford	2¾	11/10	16/13
Bath	3	11.50/9.50	22/17
Birmingham	2½	10/9	15/12
Bristol	2¼	11/11	18/18
Lincoln	4¾	19.25/13.75	28.25/20.75
Shrewsbury	4½	12.50/10.50	18/15
Exeter	3¾	16.50/13.50	30/24
Manchester	4	15/13	25/19.50
York	4	18/15	28/23
Liverpool	4½	15/13	25/19.50
Scarborough	5¾	22/18	34/26
Durham	4¾	20/16	32/25
Carlisle	5½	22/18	33/27
Wales			
Cardiff	3¼	14/11.50	24/19.50
Scotland			
Edinburgh	8	22/18	33/27
Glasgow	7	22/18	33/27

* Operated by Oxford Tube (☎ 01865-772250); fares given are for an unrestricted single and a one-day return ticket; an open return costs £9.50.

specified types of transport in a specified area) or other regional passes are available. In addition, some rail passes include certain bus services.

Discount Card National Express sells discount coach cards that give you 20% to 30% off standard adult fares. These cards are available to full-time students, and those aged between 16 and 25, and 50 or over. They can be purchased from all National Express agents and cost £9. A passport photo is required – ISIC cards are accepted as proof of student status and passports for date of birth.

Travel Pass The National Express Travel Pass allows unlimited coach travel within a specified period. It's available to all overseas visitors, but it must be bought outside Britain, usually from a Eurolines agent.

The costs (adults/under-26s) of the various passes are:

5 days	£65/50
7 days	£95/75
14 days	£135/105
30 days	£185/145

Tourist Trail Pass Over 2000 National Express ticket agents sell this family of passes, which can be bought by anyone in the UK. The passes allow for a certain number of days of unlimited bus travel within a larger but limited period. The passes are sold at a discount to those aged under 16 and to holders of any of the National Express discount cards described above. The costs (adult/discount) of the various passes are:

2 days in 3	£49/39
5 days in 10	£85/69
7 days in 21	£120/94
14 days in 30	£187/143

Backpackers Buses

The Stray Travel Network is an excellent bus service (☎ 020-7373 7737, fax 7373 7739) designed especially for those staying in hostels, which is useful for all budget travellers. Buses run on a regular circuit between London, Windsor, Bath, Manchester, Haworth, the Lake District, Glasgow, Stirling, Edinburgh, York, Nottingham, Cambridge and back to London, and call in on hostels. You can get on and off the bus where you like and catch another one as it comes along, which is usually daily in the peak season.

There are four ticket options:

1 day	£24
3 days in 2 months	£79
4 days in 2 months	£99
6 days in 4 months	£129

Tickets are available from branches of STA Travel; call ☎ 020-7361 6150 for information and details of the nearest branch. You can also visit the Stray Travel Web site at www.straytravel.com.

Postbus

Royal Mail postbuses provide a stable, reliable service to remoter areas and can be useful for walkers. For information and timetables contact the Postbus Helpline (☎ 01246-546329) or Customer Services (☎ 0845 774 0740). Postbuses take four to 10 people, but most don't carry bicycles.

Tour Buses

Several companies operate bus tours in towns around England. They have regular buses circulating on a fixed route and your one-day ticket lets you get on and off the bus as many times as you like. Useful local tour companies are mentioned throughout this book.

TRAIN

Despite the damage wrought by privatisation, Britain still has a useful rail service. There are several recommended trips on beautiful lines through sparsely populated country. See the Highlights section in the Facts for the Visitor chapter for some ideas.

The main routes are served by fast trains that travel at speeds of up to 140 mph – for example, you can travel from London to York in just over two hours.

Privatisation

Following the privatisation of the railways, which was instigated by the Conservatives, the rail system appears to be becoming less reliable than it was in the days when it was the single nationalised company known as British Rail. Services are provided by 25 train operating companies. A separate company, Railtrack, owns and maintains the track and the stations. For the sake of convenience, the British Rail logo and name are still used on directional signs.

What all this diversification means is that Britain's railways have become a Tower of Babel, with the different companies and Railtrack often not working together for the common (read: passengers') good. The number of rail-users plummeted after the Paddington and Hatfield rail disasters of 1999 and 2000 respectively. Railtrack has since carried out a major overhaul of the tracks in Britain but still customers have kept away. At the time of writing many rail companies were offering cheap tickets to entice passengers back onto the trains but after a further tragedy at Selby, it seems unlikely that confidence in the indusry will return for a while yet.

The main railcards (see Railcards later) are accepted by all the companies and travellers are still able to buy a ticket to any destination from most train stations and travel agents. Note that travel agents are not able to sell the full range of tickets.

Passengers can travel only on services provided by the company that issued their ticket and each company is able to set whatever fare it chooses. Thus, on routes served by more than one operator, passengers can choose to buy a cheaper ticket with a company offering a less direct service or pay more for a faster service. The era of competition also means that companies often have special offers such as 'two for the price of one', or special reductions for tickets bought in advance.

Information

National Rail Enquiries (☎ 0845 748 4950 in the UK, ☎ 44 1332-387601 outside the UK) is an excellent service that can provide all timetable and fare information. It's also worth visiting Railtrack's Web site (www .railtrack.co.uk) and www.thetrainline.com for their useful timetable features.

The individual train companies publish free timetables, but collecting these is probably best left to the train spotters. The Thomas Cook *European Timetable* (£9.50) and the *OAG Rail Guide* (£7.50) list all the most important services yet manage to be reasonably svelte. Both publications can be found at larger newsstands in train stations.

See Buying Tickets later in this chapter for details of the complex procedure for buying train tickets in England.

Classes

There are two classes of rail travel: 1st and standard. First class costs 30% to 50% more than standard and, except on very crowded trains, is not really worth the extra money. However, it can be a bargain at the weekend when you can upgrade many standard-class tickets for £6 to £12.

On overnight trains (between London and Plymouth and Penzance, and on the routes to Scotland) there are sleeping compartments with one berth in 1st class and two in standard. There's a variety of fares for these services, and at times they can work out to be better value than a night in a hotel. It's essential to reserve berths in advance.

Unless stated otherwise, the prices quoted in this book are for standard-class adult single tickets.

Tickets

Since privatisation the complexity of the ticketing system has significantly increased with each company operating different discount schemes that change throughout the year. Finding the best ticket for your journey isn't easy. The thing to do is to tell the ticket seller exactly what you want to do and let them find the best option for you.

Children under five travel free; those aged between five and 15 pay half-price for most tickets (except for certain heavily discounted tickets). However, when travelling with children it is almost always worth

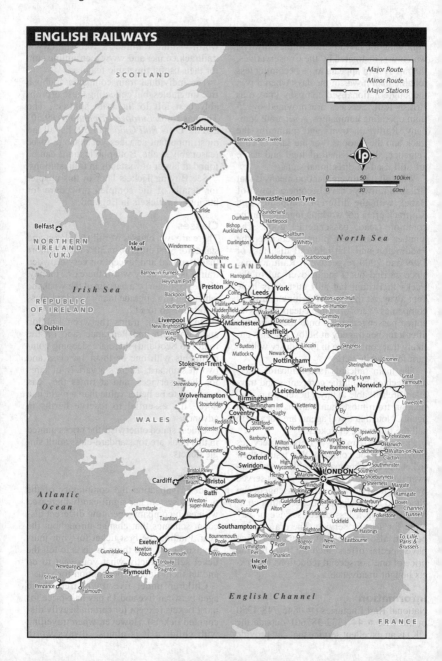

ENGLISH RAILWAYS

Major Route
Minor Route
Major Stations

buying a Family Railcard (see the following section).

For longer journeys, the price you pay for a ticket depends on the degree of flexibility you require, the availability of cheap tickets and any railcards that you hold. For the cheapest fares, you have to book well in advance and commit yourself to travelling on specified trains. Note that failure to travel on the specified train will usually mean having to pay a penalty fine and that these tickets may not be refundable. Always check what restrictions and conditions apply. You can purchase unrestricted tickets for longer journeys on the day of travel, although these are usually

Rail Fares from London

The following are sample standard fares that were in effect between London and selected destinations in England as well as Wales and Scotland at the time of research. Where there is more than one route between London and a destination, the faster route is given, although the slower one is likely to be cheaper. Also, note that the journey times are the best times possible and may involve one or more connections.

The single fares given are for unrestricted tickets. Day return tickets are a cheap option but require you to return on the same day. These are only listed for destinations under two hours away from London. The fares given under cheap return are the cheapest tickets available. These tickets are for travel on specific trains and are subject to availability, and must always be booked in advance.

destination	best time (hours)	single (£)	day return (£)	cheap return (£)
Brighton	¾	13.70	14.60	18.80
Cambridge	1	14.50	14.60	18.80
Canterbury	1½	15.90	15.40	17.10
Oxford	¾	15.10	14.80	18.90
Dover	1¼	19.80	18.30	20.60
Salisbury	1¼	22.50	21.90	26.70
Stratford	1¾	20	19.50	22.50
Bath	1½	34	31	25.50
Birmingham	1½	43.50	27	15
Bristol	1½	36	32	18.50
Lincoln	1¾	37	39	21
Shrewsbury	2½	55	–	18
Exeter	2	39	–	28
Manchester	2½	85	–	20
York	2	58	–	23
Liverpool	2½	79	–	20
Scarborough	2¾	60	–	29
Durham	2¾	74	–	23
Carlisle	3½	91	–	27
Wales				
Cardiff	2	43.50	–	23
Scotland				
Edinburgh	4	86	–	30
Glasgow	5	91	–	53

significantly more expensive than those purchased in advance.

Advance purchase of tickets is not normally necessary for shorter journeys – just buy them at the station before you embark on the train. If you are returning the same day, ask about cheap day returns (often about the same price as a single), which are usually available after 9.30 am. Some stations do not have ticket offices or machines, in which case you must purchase the ticket on the train.

See the train fare table for examples of ticket prices.

Buying Tickets First phone National Rail Enquiries (☎ 0845 748 4950) for timetable and fare information (and the phone number of the train company, if necessary). You can then purchase the ticket from a train station or over the phone from the train company directly (using a credit card). With the latter option, make sure you specify that you will pick the ticket up at the originating station on the day of travel. Get there early as queues can be long and don't forget your reference number (in case your tickets aren't there).

Alternatively, you can book tickets on the Internet at www.thetrainline.com, but normally your tickets are mailed to you (and to UK addresses only), a nonstarter if you're travelling, or live outside of the UK. However, using this site can be useful to find out if there is a fare deal enticing enough to make the cost of the calls worthwhile.

Railcards

You can get discounts of up to 33% on most fares (except certain heavily discounted tickets) if you're aged between 16 and 25, over 60, studying full time, or disabled – but you must first buy the appropriate railcard. There is also a railcard for families. A couple of journeys usually pays for the cost of the card.

The cards are valid for one year and most are available from major stations.

Young Person's Railcard
This costs £18 and gives you 33% off most tickets and some ferry services. You must be aged between 16 and 25, or a student of any age studying full time in the UK; you need proof of age, proof of student status (if necessary) and a passport-size photo.

Senior Railcard
This costs £18 and gives a 33% discount to anyone aged over 60. You need to have proof of age.

Family Railcard
This costs £20 and gives discounts of 33% (20% for some tickets) for up to four adults travelling together, providing a card-holder is a member of the party. Up to four accompanying children pay a flat fare of £2 each.

Disabled Person's Railcard
This costs £14 and gives a 33% discount to a disabled person and one person accompanying them. Pick up an application form from a station and then send it to the Disabled Person's Railcard Office, PO Box 1YT, Newcastle-upon-Tyne NE99 1YT. It can take up to three weeks to process this card so you should apply early.

Network Card
This is valid for London and the entire southeast of England, from Dover to Weymouth, Cambridge to Oxford, and is worth considering if you plan to do a lot of rail travel in this area. It costs £20. Discounts of 34% apply to up to four adults travelling together providing a card-holder is a member of the party. Children pay a flat fare of £1. Travel is permitted only after 10 am Monday to Friday and at any time at the weekend.

Train Passes

As with the bus, there are oodles of local and regional passes for rail travel. Many are mentioned throughout this book. If you will be spending any amount of time in one place, it is always worth checking to see if there is a local rail pass, many of which are valid on buses as well.

Eurail passes are not recognised in England, but visitors to Britain should consider a BritRail pass, which must be bought before you arrive in the country. Most large travel agencies will have details, as does Rail Europe's Web site (www.raileurope .com). See the next sections for details of the different passes. Children's passes are usually half (or less) the cost of an adult pass. Youth passes are good for those aged between 15 and 25, and are available for

A Suggested Rail Itinerary

The following 14-day itinerary includes tourist highlights as well as some of the most scenic rail trips. Journey times are approximate. Most of the suggested stops are on main lines so services are fairly frequent. The National Rail Enquiry Service (☎ 0845 748 4950 in the UK, ☎ 44 1332-387601 outside the UK), the Railtrack Web site (www.railtrack.co.uk) or one of the timetable publications mentioned in the text will be very useful in planning your schedule.

origin	destination	journey time (hours)
London	York	2
York	Durham	50 minutes
Durham	Newcastle	20 minutes
Newcastle	Carlisle	1¼
Carlisle	Windermere (via Oxenholme)	1¼
Windermere	Chester (via Oxenholme and Crewe)	3½
Chester	Cheltenham (via Crewe and Birmingham)	2
Cheltenham	Bath (via Bristol)	50 minutes
Bath	Oxford (via Didcot)	1¼
Oxford	London	1

Route

From London's King's Cross station, it's only two hours to York. With Roman walls, medieval streets and the largest Gothic cathedral in England, York is high on every visitor's list. Under an hour to the north is Durham, tiny in comparison with York, but with another magnificent cathedral, rising high above the River Wear.

From Durham, continue north to Newcastle, which is worth a brief stop, and then follow Hadrian's Wall west to Carlisle. The scenery in this part of northern England is stunning.

To reach the Lake District from Carlisle, you need to change trains in Oxenholme. Stay two nights in Windermere so that you can spend at least one full day taking in the superb scenery that inspired Wordsworth and many other poets and artists. To get to the walled city of Chester, with its black and white Tudor buildings, you need to change trains in Oxenholme and Crewe.

From Chester, change at Birmingham New Street station for Cheltenham, the grand Regency town on the edge of the Cotswolds. From Cheltenham, move on to the beautiful city of Bath, a 12-minute train journey beyond Bristol (which itself is easily worth a stop for its restored waterfront).

Bath to Oxford requires a change at Didcot. Spend two nights in England's famous university town, allowing time for an excursion to nearby Blenheim Palace. The trip back to London takes only one hour.

Options

Among the detours you might want to consider are an initial leg from London to Scarborough via Lincoln and Hull. This allows time in these two historic towns and some time in Scarborough, a classic seaside resort. This option will take at least two extra days, but add three or more if you can. From Scarborough, you can head directly to York (one hour).

From Bristol you can head south-west to explore Cornwall before swinging back up, possibly via the fine cathedral city of Salisbury, to Bath. This detour can also easily add three or more days to your schedule.

Finally, there are a myriad of options for returning to London through the south-east. From Oxford you can head south to Southampton via Winchester, another historic cathedral town. From Southampton, head east visiting the score of seaside towns and cities such as Portsmouth, Brighton, Hastings, Rye and Canterbury. Train services on these lines in the south-east are relatively fast and frequent. This detour can consume two or many more days.

standard class only. Senior passes are open to those aged 60 and over, and are for 1st class travel only.

BritRail passes are good throughout Britain. There is no England-only rail pass although there are regional passes, such as the BritRail SouthEast Pass. Holders of BritRail, Eurail and Euro passes are entitled to discounted fares on Eurostar trains (for example, London to Paris or Brussels for £79). There is also a variant of the BritRail pass that includes Ireland for not much more. BritRail passes also cover the Heathrow Express trains, a useful arrangement that is 'under review' at the time of writing.

BritRail Classic There are several flavours of BritRail Classic passes, all of which are for consecutive days of travel. Prices are youth fares/adult standard class/adult 1st class/senior 1st class:

8 days	US$215/265/400/340
15 days	US$280/400/600/510
22 days	US$355/505/760/645
30 days	US$420/600/900/765

Anyone getting their money's worth out of the 30-day pass should qualify for some sort of award for heroism from Railtrack.

BritRail Flexipass These passes are usually a better option for travellers as you don't have to get on a train every day and ride for hours to get full value. They are good for a certain number of days within a 60-day period. Prices are youth fares/adult standard class/adult 1st class/senior 1st class:

4 days	US$185/235/350/300
8 days	US$240/340/510/435
15 days	US$360/515/770/655

BritRail Pass'n'Drive BritRail Pass'n' Drive combines a BritRail Flexipass with the use of a Hertz rental car for side trips. The package is available in various combinations: a three-day Flexipass plus two days' car rental in one month costs US$279

for one person or US$219 each for two people in one car. There are options that allow you to customise this pass in almost any way.

BritRail SouthEast Pass The regional SouthEast Pass covers the dense network of railways in the south-east of England, including all the rail lines in and around London.

The passes combine a set number of days over a period of validity. The prices given below are for standard/1st class.

3 days in 8	US$74/105
4 days in 8	US$105/142
7 days in 15	US$142/189

CAR & MOTORCYCLE

Travelling by private car or motorcycle enables you to get to remote places, and to travel quickly, independently and flexibly. Unfortunately, the independence you enjoy does tend to isolate you and cars are nearly always inconvenient in city centres.

Despite the traffic density, England has the safest roads in the EU. There are five grades of road. Motorways (triple carriageways) and main A-roads (dual carriageways) deliver you quickly from one end of the country to another, but you miss the most interesting countryside. Be careful in foggy or wet conditions. Minor A-roads are single carriageways and are likely to be clogged with slow-moving lorries. Life on the road is more relaxed and interesting on the B-roads and minor roads. Fenced by hedgerows, these roads wind through the countryside from village to village. You can't travel fast, but it's unlikely that you'll want to.

If you can, avoid bringing a car into London. Traffic moves slowly and parking is expensive. Traffic wardens and wheel clampers operate with extreme efficiency and if your vehicle is towed away it'll cost you over £100 to get it back.

At around 99p per litre, petrol is expensive and diesel is only a few pence cheaper. However, the distances you travel aren't great.

Road Rules

Anyone using the roads should read the Highway Code (often available in Tourist Information Centres, TICs). A foreign driving licence is valid in Britain for up to 12 months from the time of your entry into the country. If you're bringing a car from Europe make sure you're adequately insured.

Briefly, vehicles drive on the left-hand side of the road; front seat belts are compulsory and if belts are fitted in the back they must be worn; the speed limit is 30 mph (48 kph) in built-up areas, 60 mph (96 kph) on single carriageways and 70 mph (112 kph) on dual or triple carriageways; you give way to your right at roundabouts (traffic already on the roundabout has the right of way); and motorcyclists must wear helmets.

See Legal Matters in the Facts for the Visitor chapter for information on drink-driving rules.

Parking

Many places in England, big and small, could easily be overrun by cars. As a result, there are often blanket bans on, or at least active discrimination against, bringing cars into the centre of towns. It's a good idea to go along with it even if sometimes you'll have to walk farther. The parking will be easier and you'll enjoy a place more if it's not cluttered up with cars. This particularly applies in small villages – park in the car parks, not on the street.

In bigger cities there will often be 'short-stay' and 'long-stay' car parks. Prices are usually the same for stays of up to two or three hours, but the short-stay car parks rapidly become much more expensive if you stay for longer. The long-stay car parks may be slightly less convenient but they're much cheaper.

A yellow line painted along the edge of the road indicates that there are parking restrictions. The only way to establish the exact restrictions is to find the nearby sign that spells them out. Double yellow lines means no parking at any time, a single line means no parking for at least an eight-hour period between 7 am and 7 pm, and a bro-ken line means there are some restrictions. In some cities there are also red lines, which mean no stopping or parking.

Rental

Rates are expensive in England; often you will be best off making arrangements in your home country for some sort of package deal. The big international rental companies charge from around £120 per week for a small car such as a Ford Fiesta or Fiat Punto.

The main companies include:

Avis	☎ 0870 606 0100
Budget	☎ 0541-565656
Europcar	☎ 0870 607 5000
Hertz	☎ 0870 844 8844
National Car Rental	☎ 0870 400 4502
Thrifty Car Rental	☎ 01494-751600

Purchase

If you're planning to tour around England (or Britain or even Europe) you may want to buy a vehicle. It's possible to get something reasonable for around £1000. Pick up a copy of *Loot* (five times weekly in London, less often elsewhere) or *Autotrader* (every Thursday) for adverts. The monthly *Motorists' Guide* lists models and their average prices.

All cars require a Ministry of Transport (MOT) safety certificate valid for one year and issued by a licensed garage, full third-party insurance (shop around but expect to pay at least £300), a registration form signed by both the buyer and seller (with a section to be sent to the MOT), and a licence disc proving you've paid your Vehicle Excise Duty (VED) – a tax of £82.25/155 for six months/one year (£55/100 for a vehicle with an engine of 1100cc or less). These discs are sold at post offices on presentation of a valid MOT certificate, registration document and proof of insurance.

You're strongly advised to buy a vehicle with a valid MOT certificate and a VED disc; both remain with the car through a change of ownership. Third-party insurance goes with the driver rather than the car, so you'll have to arrange this (and beware of letting others drive the car unless they are

A Suggested Driving Itinerary

If you're only visiting England for a short holiday, you can pack in a lot more if you have your own set of wheels and plan your itinerary carefully.

On the following 12-day route, you could travel from the airport to London and from London to Cambridge by train or bus, pick up your rental car there, tour around the country and return the car to the airport as you leave, without going back to London.

origin	destination	road distances (miles)
London	Cambridge	61
Cambridge	Lincoln	94
Lincoln	York	81
York	Durham	75
Durham	Windermere	115
Windermere	Chester	113
Chester	Stratford-upon-Avon	65
Stratford-upon-Avon	Bath	99
Bath	Salisbury (via Avebury)	59
Salisbury	Windsor	75
Windsor	London	23

Route

Leave London on the M11 that leads directly to Cambridge. Spend the day in this ancient university town and take a punt out on the river. From Cambridge, take the A604 to Huntingdon to join the A1, stopping at Stamford for a quick look at this unspoiled old town. Continue along the A1, turning off onto the A46 for Lincoln. This Roman city has a superb Norman cathedral and castle.

Leave Lincoln on the A15, the Roman road known as Ermine Street, heading north. Join the M180 for 7 miles, then take the A15 over the Humber Bridge. Immediately after crossing the bridge, take the A63 for 7 miles, then the A1034 to Market Weighton, following signs for York via the A1079. York Minster is the largest Gothic cathedral in England, and York is a fascinating place to explore.

Head west out of York on the A59 to join the A1. Leave the A1(M) and get on the A690 to

listed on the policy). For further information contact a post office or a Vehicle Registration Office and ask for leaflet V100.

Camper Van

Camper vans are popular for touring around England and the rest of Europe, particularly with shoestring travellers. Often three or four people will band together to buy or rent a van. Look for adverts in *TNT* magazine if you wish to form or join a group.

Both *Autotrader* and *Loot* carry adverts for vans. The Van Market in Market Rd (off Caledonian Rd) in London is a long-running institution where private sellers congregate on a daily basis (closed at the

time of writing). Some second-hand dealers offer a 'buy-back' scheme for when you return, but buying and reselling privately is better (if you have the time) in order to avoid giving money to a dealer.

Vans usually feature a fixed high-top or elevating roof and two to five bunks. Apart from the essential camping gas cooker, professional conversions may include a sink, a fridge and built-in cupboards. You will need to spend a minimum of £1000 to £2000 for something reliable enough to get you around.

Motorcycle Touring

England is made for motorcycle touring, with good quality winding roads and stun-

A Suggested Driving Itinerary

Durham. Durham is a World Heritage Site with one of the finest cathedrals in the country.

From Durham, take the A691 to Consett, and then the A692 4 miles south-west to join the A68 going north, which meets the A69. Follow the A69 west through Haydon Bridge to Bardon Mill, where signposts direct you for the 3-mile journey to Housesteads Fort, part of Hadrian's Wall. After stopping to see the fort, continue west along the B6318 to rejoin the A69, following signposts for Carlisle. Two miles east of Carlisle, take the M6 south to the A66, which you follow west for a mile. Turn left onto the scenic A592, which leads into the heart of the Lake District, past Ullswater to Windermere. Stay two nights in Windermere to give yourself time for a long walk in this beautiful area.

From Windermere take the A591 south-east to join the M6 south-bound, eventually taking the M56 to Chester. Spend the night in Chester before taking the A41 and A442 south to join the M54 near Telford. You may wish to stop at nearby Ironbridge Gorge to see this cradle of the Industrial Revolution and its interesting museums, or at Warwick, south of Birmingham, to see its impressive castle.

Bypass Birmingham on the M6 and join the M40 (watch the signs as this is an easy exit to miss). Take the A3400 to Stratford-upon-Avon for a quick look at Shakespeare's birthplace and to see a play performed by the Royal Shakespeare Company in the evening.

The following day, visit Blenheim Palace, one of the most impressive stately homes in the country. The A3400 and the A44 lead you to Woodstock, and Blenheim stands on the edge of the town.

From Blenheim drive through the Cotswold villages to the beautiful town of Bath. Take the A4095 to Witney, the A40 to the village of Burford, the B4425 through Bibury to Cirencester, and the A433, then the A46, to Bath.

From Bath, follow the A4 to the prehistoric complex of Avebury, less well known than Stonehenge but more atmospheric. Continue east along the A4 to join the A346 and A338 south to Salisbury, well known for its cathedral.

Leave Salisbury on the A360 north to join the A303 near Stonehenge, continuing east onto the M3. At Basingstoke, take the A33 to join the M4, stopping at Windsor to see the castle. Heathrow airport is only about 10 miles from Windsor, so you could stay the night in the Windsor area and drop off your rental car at the airport as you leave. Gatwick is just a bit farther via the M25 and M23, so you can do the same thing if you are using London's second airport.

ning scenery to stimulate the senses. Just make sure your wet-weather gear is up to scratch. Crash helmets are compulsory.

The Auto-Cycle Union (☎ 01788-566400, fax 573585), ACU House, Wood St, Rugby CV21 2YX, publishes a very useful booklet about motorcycle touring throughout all of Britain.

Motoring Organisations

The two largest motoring organisations in the UK, both of which offer 24-hour breakdown assistance, are the Automobile Association (AA; ☎ 0800 444999) and the Royal Automobile Club (RAC; ☎ 0800 550550). One year's membership starts at £44 for the AA and £39 for the RAC, and both will extend your cover to include continental Europe. Your motoring organisation at home may have a reciprocal arrangement with the AA or RAC.

BICYCLE

See Cycling in the Activities chapter.

HITCHING

Hitching is never entirely safe in any country in the world, and we don't recommend it. Travellers who decide to hitch should understand that they are taking a small but potentially serious risk. People who do choose to hitch will be safer if they travel in pairs and let someone know where they are planning to go.

Hitching is becoming less common in England. The same mutual suspicions between hitchers and drivers that exist elsewhere are becoming the norm. You may travel for weeks and not see anyone hitching.

It's against the law to hitch on motorways or the immediate slip roads. Make a sign and use approach roads near roundabouts or service stations.

WALKING

See Walking in the Activities chapter.

BOAT

See the various regional chapters for local ferry services, such as those to the Isle of Wight. If you fancy exploring the inland waterways, see Canal & Waterway Travel in the Activities chapter.

LOCAL TRANSPORT

English cities usually have good public transport. The biggest problem you'll have is sorting through it: in another one of those anti-public transport initiatives by the former Conservative government, local buses throughout Britain were privatised with often shambolic results. Local governing bodies were disbanded and companies allowed to compete willy-nilly. In many towns, no one is quite sure who's running buses where but the TICs can usually provide timetable and fare information for local transport. Fortunately London managed to retain overall control over its partially privatised system. It's actually easier to find your way around London by bus than Leeds!

Taxis

See the London chapter for information on the famous London taxis and their minicab competitors. Outside London and other big cities, taxis are usually reasonably priced. In rural areas you can expect to pay around £1.40 per mile, which means they are definitely worth considering as a means of reaching an out-of-the-way hostel or attraction or the beginning of a walk. A taxi over a short distance will often be very competitive with a local bus, especially if there are three or four people to share the cost. More importantly, when it's Sunday and you find that the next bus due to visit the charming town you've hiked to is on Monday, a taxi can get you to a transport hub for a reasonable cost.

ORGANISED TOURS
General Tours

Since travel is so easy to organise in England, there is very little need to consider a tour. Still, if your time is limited and/or you prefer to travel in a group, there are some interesting possibilities. The British Tourist Authority (BTA) has information on this. See also Backpackers Buses in the Bus section earlier in the chapter.

Drifters (☎ 020-7262 1292, fax 7706 2673), 22 Craven Terrace, London W2 3QH, runs day trips from London starting from £17, and longer trips lasting up to two weeks around Britain. The trips are aimed at people in their 20s. You can visit the Web site at www.driftersclub.com.

Contiki (☎ 020-7637 0802, fax 7637 2121), Royal National Hotel, Bedford Way, London WC1H 0DG, has trips aimed at young people that last from seven to 16 days. Further details can be obtained from the Web site at www.contiki.com.

Tracks (☎ 020-7937 3028, fax 01797 344164), The Flots, Brookland, Romney Marsh, Kent TN29 9TG, specialises in budget trips. Its English tours range from day trips to three-day breaks. Check out the Web site at www.tracks-travel.com.

Shearings Holidays (☎ 01942-824824, fax 230949), Miry Lane, Wigan WN3 4AG, has a very wide range of four- to eight-day coach tours covering the whole country, mostly aimed at mature travellers.

For those aged over 60, Saga Holidays (☎ 0800 300500, fax 01303-776647), Saga Building, Middleburg Square, Folkestone, Kent CT20 1AZ, offers holidays ranging from cheap coach tours and resort holidays to luxury cruises around England. Saga's Web site is at www.saga.co.uk.

Nature Tours

In national parks you can often join nature walks led by park wardens, sometimes free of charge; ask at information centres for details of what's available. Seashore rambles can also be an enlightening experience if led by an expert.

Several companies offer wildlife holidays, ranging from weekend breaks to longer residential courses, which include activities ranging from nature rambles to bird-, fox- and badger-watching from special hide-outs.

The following are just a few possibilities. Enquire locally at TICs for more.

Wildlife Breaks (☎/fax 01926-842413, ℮ oaktreefarm@btinternet.com), Oaktree Farm, Buttermilk Lane, Yarningale Common, Claverdon, Warwickshire CV35 8HP, has tours that seek out badgers, birds, butterflies and other winsome creatures.

In the Peak District, Peak National Park Centre (☎ 01433-620373, fax 620346), Losehill Hall, Castleton, Derbyshire S30 2WB, has tours from one to three days aimed at wildlife enthusiasts as well as nature painters and walkers. You can visit the Web site at www.peakdistrict.org.

If you want to volunteer to work on an environmental project, contact the British Trust for Conservation Volunteers (BTCV; ☎ 01491-821600, fax 821603), 36 St Mary's St, Wallingford OX10 0EU, or visit its Web site at www.btcv.org.

London

☎ 020

What can be said about London that hasn't been said so many times before? That the weighty resonance of its very name suggests history and might? That it is the premier city in Europe in terms of size, population and per-capita wealth? That its opportunities for entertainment by day and by night go on and on and on?

London is all these things and much, much more. Not only is it home to such familiar landmarks as Big Ben and Tower Bridge, it also boasts some of the greatest museums and art galleries in the world and more lush parkland than any other capital city. It is also an amazingly tolerant place for its size, its people pretty much unshockable.

Visitors are often surprised to find how multicultural the British capital is, with a quarter of all Londoners belonging to one of almost three dozen ethnic minorities, most of whom get along fairly well together.

It's a cosmopolitan mixture of the developed and developing worlds, of chauffeurs and beggars, of the establishment and the avant-garde, with seven to 12 million inhabitants (depending on where you stop counting) and almost 30 million visitors a year. London has been a major recipient of the vast sums of money raised by the National Lottery – for projects such as the huge new Tate Modern art gallery opened in 2000 – and the number of visitors to the city seems likely to grow even more.

HISTORY

Although a Celtic community established itself around a ford across the River Thames, it was the Romans who first developed the square mile now known as the City of London. They built a bridge and an impressive city wall, and made the city an important port and the hub of their road system.

The Romans left, but trade went on. Few traces of Dark Age London can now be found, but the city survived the incursions of

Highlights

- Walking the banks of the Thames
- Going for a spin on the London Eye
- Knocking back good ales in an old pub
- Enjoying the world's best array of live theatre
- Being perplexed by Tate Modern's art
- Losing yourself in the Hampton Court Palace maze

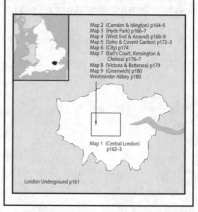

Map 2 (Camden & Islington) p164–5
Map 3 (Hyde Park) p166–7
Map 4 (West End & Around) p168–9
Map 5 (Soho & Covent Garden) p172–3
Map 6 (City) p174
Map 7 (Earl's Court, Kensington & Chelsea) p176–7
Map 8 (Victoria & Battersea) p179
Map 9 (Greenwich) p180
Westminster Abbey p180

Map 1 (Central London) p162–3

London Underground p161

the Saxons and Vikings. Fifty years before the Normans arrived, Edward the Confessor built his abbey and palace at Westminster.

William the Conqueror found a city that was, without doubt, the richest and largest in the kingdom. He raised the White Tower (part of the Tower of London) and confirmed the city's independence and right to self-government.

During the reign of Elizabeth I the capital began to expand rapidly. Unfortunately, virtually all traces of medieval, Tudor and Jacobean London were destroyed by the Great Fire of 1666. The fire gave Sir Christopher Wren the opportunity to build his famous churches, and did nothing to halt or discipline the city's growth.

By 1720 there were 750,000 people in London and the city, as the seat of parliament and focal point of a growing empire, was becoming ever richer and increasingly important. Georgian architects replaced the last of medieval London with their imposing symmetrical architecture and residential squares.

As a result of the Industrial Revolution and rapidly expanding commerce, the population jumped from 2.7 million in 1851 to 6.6 million in 1901 and a vast expanse of suburbs developed to accommodate them.

Georgian and Victorian London was devastated by the Luftwaffe in WWII – huge swathes of the centre and the East End were totally flattened. After the war, ugly housing and low-cost developments were thrown up on the bomb sites. The city's docks never recovered – shipping moved east to Tilbury, and the Docklands declined to the point of dereliction until rediscovery by developers in the 1980s.

Not-So-Dirty Old Man River

The cleanliness of the River Thames has improved greatly in recent years – things could hardly be worse than in 1858, when during the 'Great Stink' the stench was so bad that the windows of the House of Commons had to be covered in sheets soaked in lime chloride. As species after species of fish died out during Victorian times, the banks of the river became a purple-pink mass of writhing, uneaten tube worms; by 1962 the combined impact of untreated sewage and industrial pollution had killed off virtually every sign of life in the river. But since 1974 a cleanup has brought back almost 120 species of fish, including salmon – last seen in the Thames in 1833 – for which special ladders over the weirs have been built. With them have come the herons and cormorants who feed on them; even otters have been spotted on the river's upper reaches. Much of the murkiness of the river in London is because it is the brackish centre of two tidal zones: a freshwater one and a marine one.

Riding on a wave of Thatcherite confidence and deregulation, London boomed in the 1980s. The new wave of property developers proved to be only marginally more discriminating than the Luftwaffe, and most think their buildings only slightly better than the eyesores of the 1950s. What the projects planned for the first years of the new millennium will bring remains to be seen.

London got its first true mayor in 2000. Feisty Ken Livingstone was elected by a large majority – not necessarily because of his liberal politics, but because he has promised to act in the interests of Londoners, rather than submit to the whims of Tony Blair's government.

ORIENTATION

The city's main geographical feature is the Thames, a sufficiently deep (for anchorage) and narrow (for bridging) tidal river that enabled the Romans to build a port that was easily defended from the dangers of the North Sea. Running from west to east, it divides the city into its northern and southern halves. But because it flows in wide bends, creating peninsulas in its wake, it is not always clear on what side of the river you are – especially in the far west and east.

Despite London's great size, the Underground system (the 'tube') makes most of it easily accessible, and the official and ubiquitous – though geographically misleading – Underground map is easy to use. Most important sights, theatres, restaurants and even affordable places to stay lie within a reasonably compact rectangle formed by the tube's Circle Line (colour-coded yellow), which encircles central London just north of the river.

In this chapter, the nearest tube or train station has been given for each address; Map 1 shows the location of tube stations and the areas covered by the detailed district maps.

It's common for people to refer to areas by their postcode – see the boxed text 'London's Bewildering Postcodes'.

Borough names and postcodes are often given on street signs, which is obviously

London's Bewildering Postcodes

London's postcodes can be a useful way of getting your geographical bearings when you're dealing with locations in London. For instance, addresses in W1 are somewhere around Soho and the West End. While not quite as far-reaching socio-economic statements as Paris' 20 *arrondissements*, the codes are good for making general assumptions – SW3 (Chelsea) is definitely a higher rent neighbourhood than E3 (Bow) – and are included in the listings for this book. But like so many English institutions, there are eccentricities, lots of eccentricities. How on earth can SE28 be closer to London's centre than SE2? Or N16 border N1? If there's a north (N), a west (W) and an east (E) why isn't there a south (S)? And what happened to the north-east (NE)?

When they were introduced in 1858, the postcodes were fairly clear, with all the compass points represented as well as an east and west central (EC and WC). But not long afterwards NE and S were merged with E, SE and SW and the problems began. The real convolution came during WWI when a numbering system was introduced for inexperienced sorters (regular employees were off fighting in 'the war to end all wars'). No 1 was the centre of each zone, but other numbers related to the alphabetical order of the postal districts' names. Thus anything starting with a letter near the beginning of the alphabet, like Chingford, would get a low number (E4), even though it was miles from the centre at Whitechapel, while Poplar, which borders Whitechapel, is E14.

vital when names are duplicated (there are 47 Station Rds) or cross through a number of districts. To further confuse visitors, many streets change name – Holland Park Ave becomes Notting Hill Gate, which becomes Bayswater Rd, which becomes Oxford St... Sometimes they duck and weave like the country lanes they once were. Street numbering can also bewilder: on big streets the numbers on opposite sides can be way out of kilter (315 might be opposite 520) or, for variation, they can go up one side and down the other.

Most of London's airports lie some distance from the centre, but transport is easy (if not cheap). See the Getting Around section later in the chapter for details.

Maps

A decent map is vital. Ideally, get a single-sheet map so you can see all of central London at a glance; the Lonely Planet *London City Map* (£3.99) has three separate maps at different scales, as well as an inset map of Theatreland and an index. The bound *Mini London A-Z Street Atlas & Index* (£3.75) provides comprehensive coverage of London in a discreet size. Both of these publications will help you avoid standing bewildered on a corner holding some immense fold-out

map that's about to be blown away by the latest rain squall.

INFORMATION

Lonely Planet produces several publications with more detailed coverage of London – see Books in the Facts for the Visitor chapter.

Time Out magazine (issued every Tuesday; £1.95) is a thorough listings guide recommended for every visitor. Another good read is the only daily newspaper that is well and truly a Londoner, the *Evening Standard* (35p). This widely read afternoon tabloid can vacillate from right to left (usually when matters directly affecting London are being discussed). Its Thursday entertainment supplement *Hot Tickets* can often be a better and more eclectic source of information than *Time Out*.

Free magazines are available from pavement bins, especially in Earl's Court, Notting Hill and Bayswater. *TNT Magazine*, *Southern Cross* and *SA Times* cover Australian, New Zealand and South African news and sports results, but are mostly invaluable for their entertainment listings, excellent travel sections and useful classifieds;

[continued on page 181]

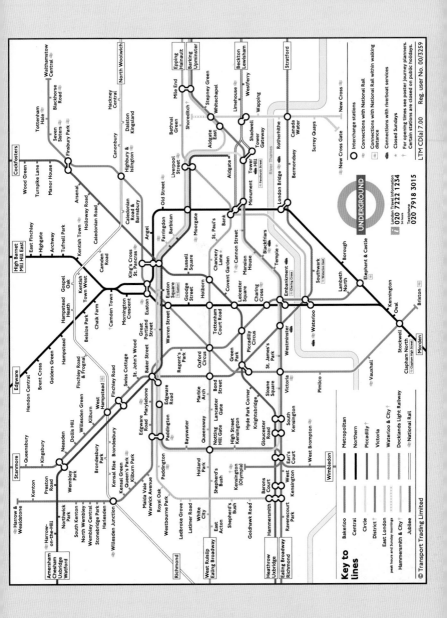

MAP 1 – CENTRAL LONDON

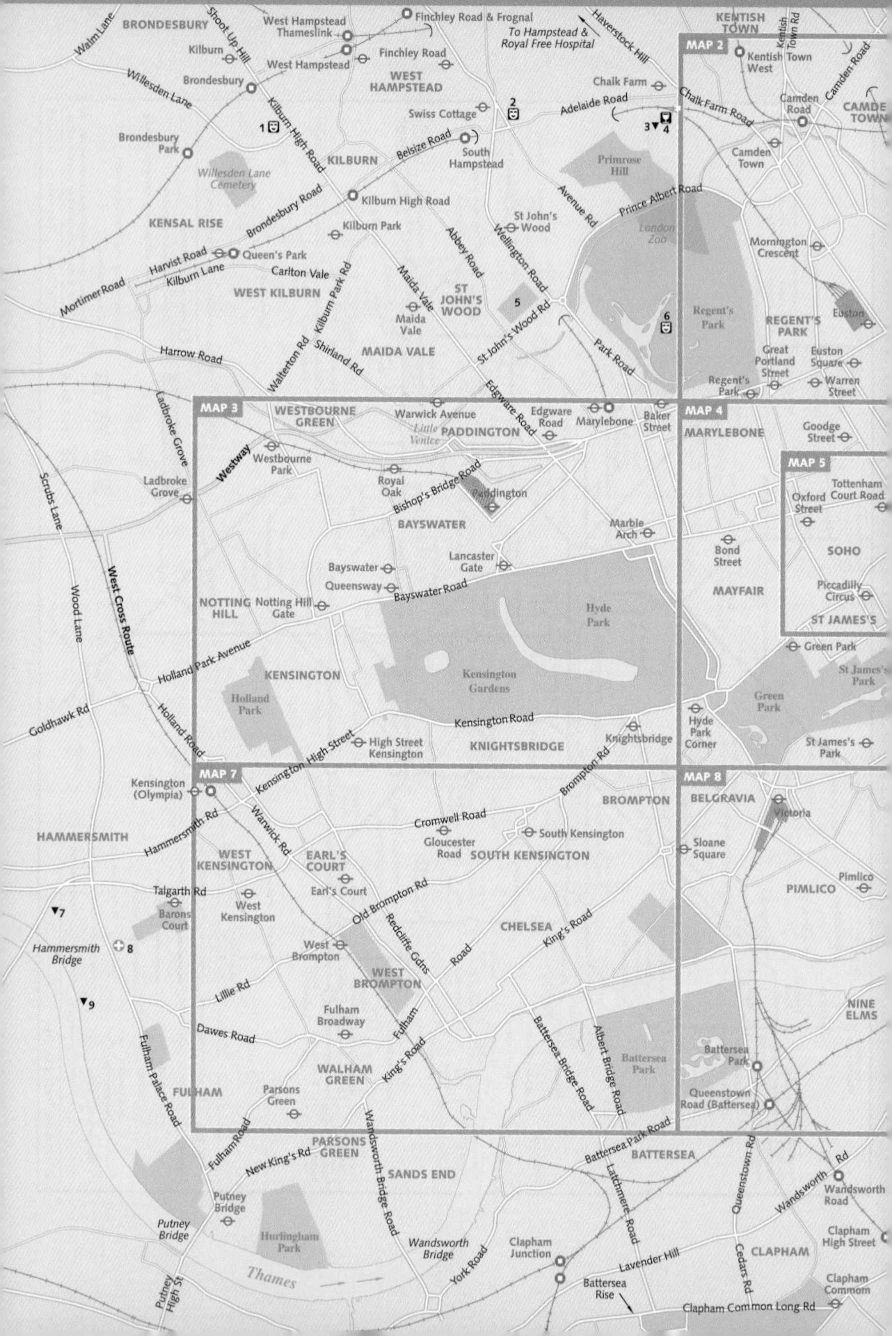

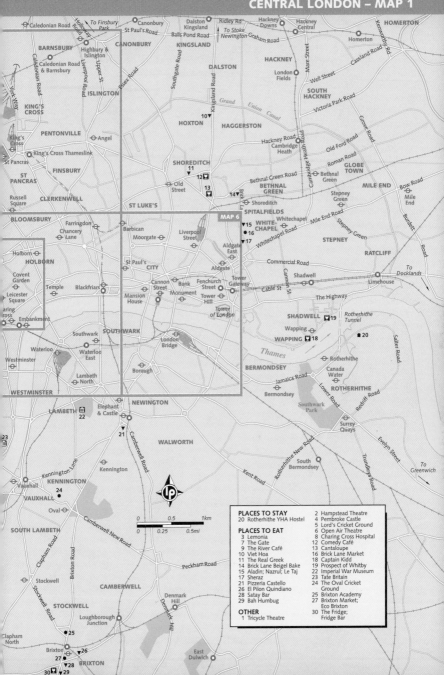

MAP 6

PLACES TO STAY
20 Rotherhithe YHA Hostel

PLACES TO EAT
3 Lemonia
7 The Gate
9 The River Café
10 Viet Hoa
11 The Real Greek
14 Brick Lane Beigel Bake
15 Aladin; Nazrul; Le Taj
17 Sheraz
21 Pizzeria Castello
26 El Pilon Quindiano
28 Satay Bar
29 Bah Humbug

OTHER
1 Tricycle Theatre

2 Hampstead Theatre
4 Pembroke Castle
5 Lord's Cricket Ground
6 Open Air Theatre
8 Charing Cross Hospital
12 Comedy Café
13 Cantaloupe
16 Brick Lane Market
18 Captain Kidd
19 Prospect of Whitby
22 Imperial War Museum
23 Tate Britain
24 The Oval Cricket
   Ground
25 Brixton Academy
27 Brixton Market;
   Eco Brixton
30 The Fridge;
   Fridge Bar

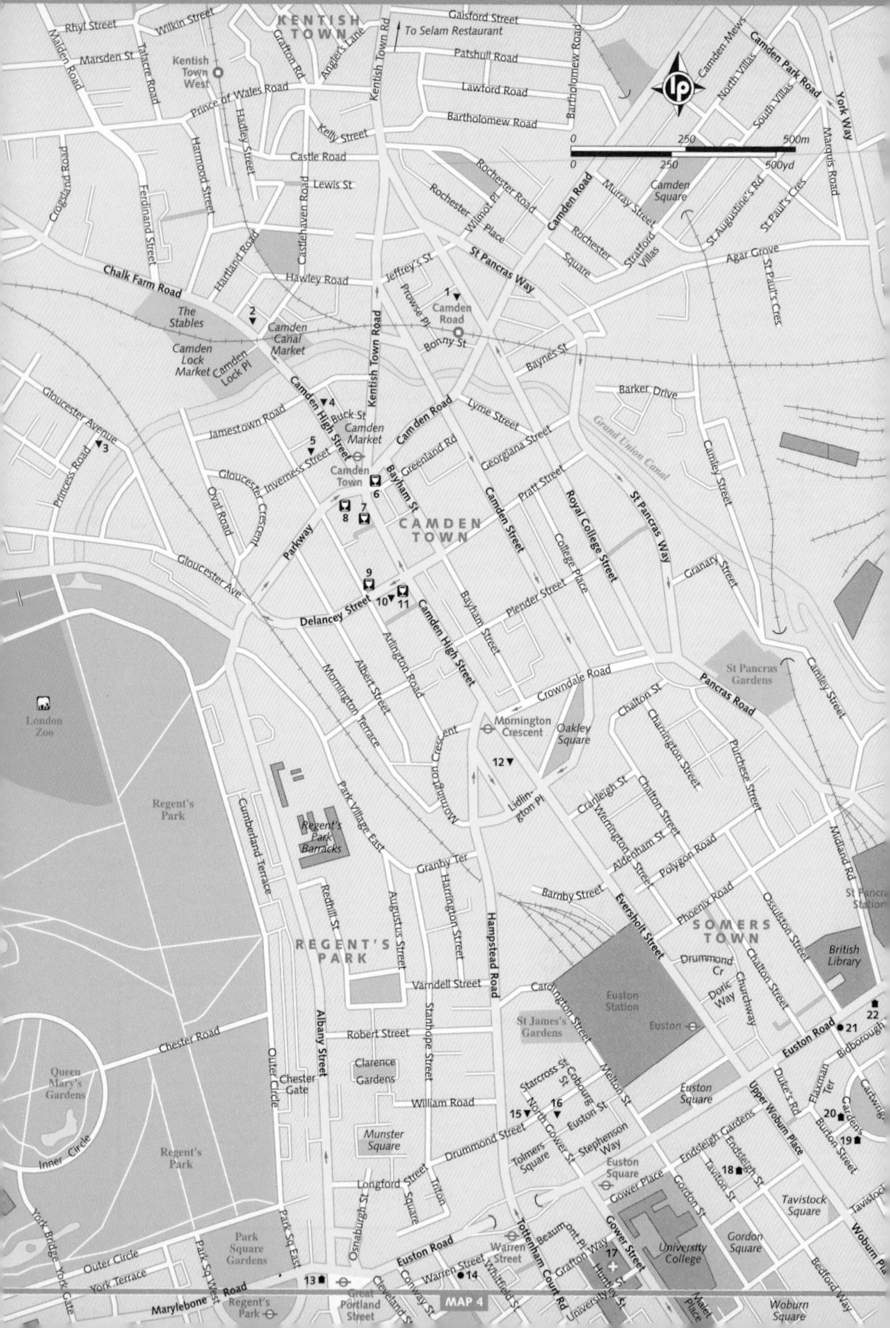

MAP 2

Rhyl Street
Wilkin Street
Marsden St
Terrace Road
Maiden Road
Prince of Wales Road
KENTISH TOWN
Kentish Town West
Crafton Rd
Anglers Lane
Kentish Town Rd
Galsford Street
To Selam Restaurant
Patshull Road
Lawford Road
Bartholomew Road
Bartholomew Road

Crossfield Road
Ferdinand Street
Harmood Street
Hadley Street
Kelly Street
Castle Road
Lewis St
Chalk Farm Road
Hartland Road
Hawley Road
Jeffrey's St
Prowse Pl
Camden Road
Rochester Rd
Wilmot Pl
St Pancras Way
Rochester Road
Camden Road
Murray Street
Camden Square
Rochester Square
Stratford Villas
St Augustine's St
St Paul's Cres
Agar Grove
St Paul's Cres
York Way
Marquis Road

The Stables
2 ▼
Camden Canal Market
1 ▼ Camden Road
Bonny St
Baynes St
Barker Drive
Grand Union Canal
Camley Street

Camden Lock Market
Camden Lock Pl
Gloucester Avenue
3 ▼
Jamestown Road
Camden High Street
Buck St
Camden Market
4 ▼
5
Gloucester Crescent
Inverness Street
Oval Road
Camden Town
6
7 ▼
8
Parkway
Bayham St
CAMDEN TOWN
Camden Road
Lyme Street
Greenland Rd
Georgiana Street
Pratt Street
Camden Street
Royal College Street
St Pancras Way
College Place
Granary Street
St Pancras Gardens
Camley Street

Gloucester Ave
9 ▼
10 ▼ 11
Delancey Street
Camden High Street
Bayham Street
Plender Street
Pancras Road
St Pancras Station

Mornington Terrace
Albert Street
Arlington Road
Crowndale Road
Chalton St
Charrington Street
Purchese Street
Midland Rd

London Zoo
Mornington Crescent
Oakley Square
12 ▼
Lidlin- gton Pl
Cranleigh St
Werrington Street
Aldenham Street
Polygon Road
Phoenix Road
SOMERS TOWN
Oakley Street
British Library

Regent's Park
Regent's Park Barracks
Park Village East
Granby Ter
Harrington Street
Hampstead Road
Barnby Street
Eversholt Street
Drummond Cr
Doric Way
Churchway

Cumberland Terrace
Redhill St
Augustus Street
Varndell Street
Cardington Street
Euston Station
Euston
Euston Square
Euston Road
22
21

Chester Road
Albany Street
Robert Street
Stanhope Street
Clarence Gardens
William Road
St James's Gardens
North Gower Street
Melton St
Euston St
Duke's Rd
Upper Woburn Place
Flaxman Ter
Euston St
20
19

Queen Mary's Gardens
REGENT'S PARK
Chester Gate
Outer Circle
Munster Square
Drummond Street
Starcross St
Cobourg St
Euston St
Stephenson Way
Euston Square
Gordon St
Endsleigh Gardens
18
Tavistock Square

Inner Circle
Regent's Park
Longford Street
Tilton St
Tolmers Square
Gower Place
University College
Gordon Square
Bedford Way

15 ▼
16 ▼
Drummond Street

York Bridge
York Terrace
Outer Circle
Park Square Gardens
Park Sq East
Park St East
Osnaburgh Street
Cleveland St
Euston Road
Warren Street
Conway St
Beaumont
Warren Street
Gosfield St
Tottenham Court Road
Grafton Way
Gower Street
University St
Gower St
Huntley St
Maple Place
Woburn Square

13 ▼
14 ●
MAP 4
Marylebone Road
Regent's Park
Great Portland Street

MAP 2

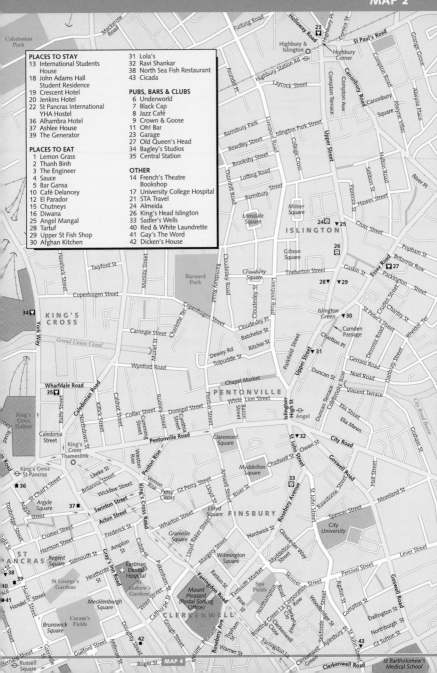

PLACES TO STAY
13 International Students House
18 John Adams Hall Student Residence
19 Crescent Hotel
20 Jenkins Hotel
22 St Pancras International YHA Hostel
36 Alhambra Hotel
37 Ashlee House
39 The Generator

PLACES TO EAT
1 Lemon Grass
2 Thanh Binh
3 The Engineer
4 Sauce
5 Bar Gansa
6 Café Delancey
12 El Parador
15 Chutneys
16 Diwana
26 Angel Mangal
28 Tartuf
29 Upper St Fish Shop
30 Afghan Kitchen
31 Lola's
32 Ravi Shankar
38 North Sea Fish Restaurant
43 Cicada

PUBS, BARS & CLUBS
6 Underworld
7 Black Cap
8 Jazz Café
9 Crown & Goose
11 Oh! Bar
23 Garage
27 Old Queen's Head
34 Bagley's Studios
35 Central Station

OTHER
14 French's Theatre Bookshop
17 University College Hospital
21 STA Travel
24 Almeida
26 King's Head Islington
33 Sadler's Wells
40 Red & White Laundrette
41 Gay's The Word
42 Dicken's House

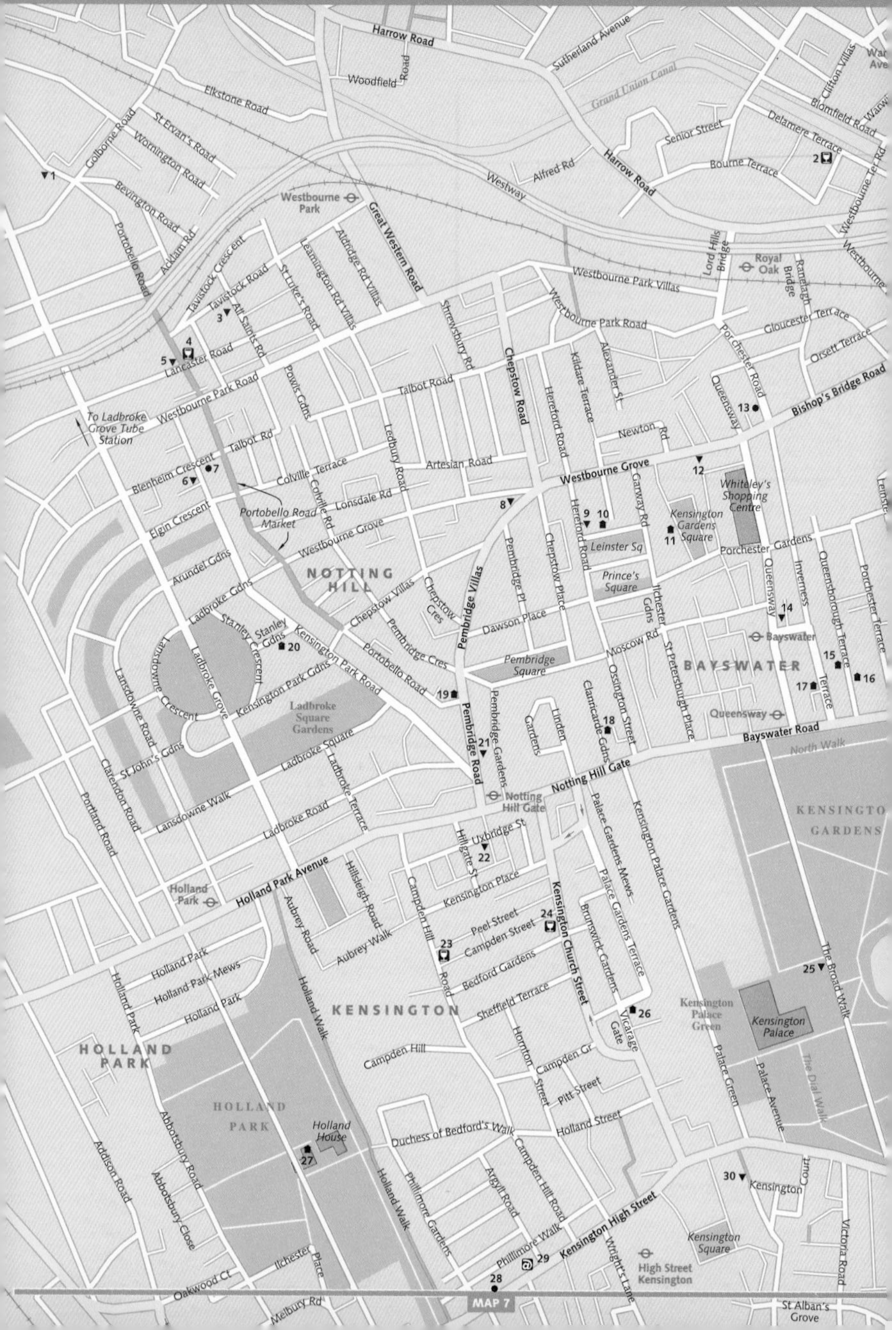

MAP 3

Harrow Road
Woodfield
Sutherland Avenue
Grand Union Canal
War Avenue

Elkstone Road
Colborne Road
St Evan's Road
Wornington Road
Bevington Road
Senior Street
Blomfield Road
Delamere Terrace
Bourne Terrace

▼1
Alfred Rd
Harrow Road
2●

Westway
Royal Oak
Lord Hills Bridge
Ranelagh Bridge

Portobello Road
Adam Rd
Tavistock Crescent
Westbourne Park
Great Western Road
Westbourne Park Villas
Westbourne Park Road
Gloucester Terrace
Orsett Terrace

Tavistock Road
3▼
St Luke's Road
Ledbury Road
Ledbury Rd Villas
Shrewsbury Rd
Kildare Terrace
Alexander St
Porchester Road
Queensway
13●
Bishop's Bridge Road

5▼
4■
Lancaster Road
Talbot Road
Hereford Road
Newton Rd

To Ladbroke
Grove Tube
Station
Westbourne Park Road
Talbot Rd
Artesian Road
Westbourne Grove
12▼
Whiteley's
Shopping
Centre

Blenheim Crescent
6▼ ▼7
Colville Terrace
Lonsdale Rd
8▼
9■ 10
Hereford Rd
Kensington
Gardens
Square
11●
Porchester Gardens

Elgin Crescent
Portobello Road
Market
Westbourne Grove
Leinster Sq
Inverness Terrace

Arundel Gdns
NOTTING
HILL
Chepstow Villas
Prince's
Square
Queensway
14▼
Bayswater

Ladbroke Gdns
Stanley Cres
Stanley
Gdns
Chepstow Cres
Pembridge Villas
Pembridge Cres
Dawson Place
Moscow Rd
Chester Gdns
Ossington Street
Palace Court
BAYSWATER
15▼
17▼ 16■

20
19■
Portobello Road
Pembridge Square
Pembridge Road
Moscow Rd
Queensway
Bayswater Road

Ladbroke Grove
Kensington Park Gdns
Ladbroke Square
Gardens
18▼
Linden Gardens
Clanricarde Gdns
Queensway
North Walk

Lansdowne Crescent
St John's Gdns
Ladbroke Square
Ladbroke Road
21▼
Pembridge Gardens
Notting
Hill Gate
Notting Hill Gate
Palace Gardens Terrace
Kensington Palace Gdns
KENSINGTON
GARDENS

Portland Road
Claremont Rd
Lansdowne Walk
Holland Park Avenue
Holland
Park
Uxbridge St
22▼
Hillgate St
Kensington Place
24■
Kensington Church Street
Brunswick Gardens
Palace Gardens Mews

Holland Park
Holland Park Mews
Aubrey Road
Aubrey Walk
Campden St
Peel Street
23■
Campden Street
Bedford Gardens
25▼
The Broad Walk

HOLLAND
PARK
HOLLAND
PARK
Holland
House
27■
KENSINGTON
Sheffield Terrace
Campden Hill
Hornton Street
Campden Gr
Bedford Gardens
26●
Kensington
Palace Green
Kensington
Palace
The Flower Walk
Palace Avenue

Addison Road
Abbotsbury Road
Abbotsbury Close
Holland Walk
Duchess of Bedford's Walk
Phillimore Gardens
Holland Street
30▼ Kensington

Oakwood Ct
Ilchester Place
Melbury Rd
Phillimore Walk
Campden Hill Road
Argyll Road
28■
29●
Kensington High Street
Wright's Lane
High Street
Kensington
Kensington Square
St Alban's Grove

MAP 7

MAP 3

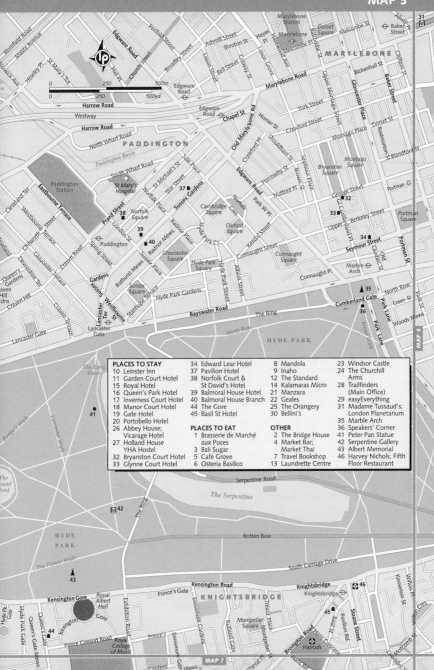

PLACES TO STAY
10 Leinster Inn
11 Garden Court Hotel
15 Royal Hotel
16 Queen's Park Hotel
17 Inverness Court Hotel
18 Manor Court Hotel
19 Gate Hotel
20 Portobello Hotel
26 Abbey House;
   Vicarage Hotel
27 Holland House
   YHA Hostel
32 Bryanston Court Hotel
33 Glynne Court Hotel
34 Edward Lear Hotel
37 Pavilion Hotel
38 Norfolk Court &
   St David's Hotel
39 Balmoral House Hotel
40 Balmoral House Branch
44 The Gore
45 Basil St Hotel

PLACES TO EAT
1 Brasserie de Marché
   aux Puces
3 Bali Sugar
5 Café Grove
6 Osteria Basilico

8 Mandola
9 Inaho
12 The Standard
14 Kalamaras Micro
21 Manzara
22 Geales
25 The Orangery
30 Bellini's

OTHER
2 The Bridge House
4 Market Bar;
   Market Thai
7 Travel Bookshop
13 Laundrette Centre

23 Windsor Castle
24 The Churchill
   Arms
28 Trailfinders
   (Main Office)
29 easyEverything
31 Madame Tussaud's;
   London Planetarium
35 Marble Arch
36 Speakers' Corner
41 Peter Pan Statue
42 Serpentine Gallery
43 Albert Memorial
46 Harvey Nichols; Fifth
   Floor Restaurant

MAP 4

York

Marylebone Road

Park Crescent

MAP 2

Maple St

Capper

Torrington Place

BLOOMSBURY

Oldbury Pl

Devonshire Mews West

Devonshire Street

Carburton St

Henry St

10

11

Gower Street

12

13

Senate House (University of London)

Nottingham Pl

Beaumont Street

Devonshire Mews

Devon-shire Ct.

Great Portland Street

Hallam Street

Clipstone St

Howland Street

Whitfield St

Tottenham Court Road

Clarence St

Tottenham St

Chenies Street

Alfred St

Store Street

Montague St

Nottingham St

Harley Street

Weymouth Street

Portland Place

FITZROVIA

Cleveland Street

Goodge Court

Street

Goodge Street

British Museum

Paddington Street

1

Marylebone High Street

MARYLEBONE

New Cavendish Street

Foley St

Ogle St

Middlesex Hospital

Windmill

Percy St

Bedford Square

Bloomsbury Street

Moxon St

Aybrook St

Duchess Street

Cavendish Square

Langham Street

9

Langham Pl

Chandos Pl

Riding House Street

Wells Street

Berners Mews

Rathbone Pl

Greese St

Bedford Avenue

Blandford St

George Street

2

Thayer St

Mandeville Pl

8

Queen Anne Street

Mortimer Street

Margaret Street

Market Place

Eastcastle Street

Winsley

Rathbone St

Newman St

Bernes St

Tottenham Court Road

New Oxford St

Chiltern St

Welbeck Street

St Christopher Pl

Wigmore Street

Henrietta Pl

Vere St

Old Cavendish St

Hollies St

Oxford Circus

Oxford Street

Poland Street

Chapel St

Soho

Soho Square

St Giles Hig

Charing Cross Road

Edwards Mews

5

Bond St

Blen-heim St

Dering St

Princes St

Hanover Square

Noel St

Wardour Street

Berwick Street

Dean Street

Frith Street

Greek St

SOHO

Old Compton Street

Romilly St

3

Oxford Street

Gilbert Street

Davies Street

South Molton St

New Brook St

Maddox St

Gt Marlborough St

Carnaby Street

Broadwick St

Brewer Street

Peter St

North Row

4

Binney Street

Brook Street

6

Brook's Mews

Avery Row

St George St

Conduit St

Kingly St

Beak St

Golden Square

Bridle Lane

Gt Windmill St

Shaftesbury Avenue

Gerrard Street

Lisle St

Cranbourn St

Leicester Square

Upper Brook St

Lees Pl

US Embassy

Grosvenor Square

Grosvenor Street

Grosvenor Hill

Bruton Pl

Clifford Street

Savile Row

Warwick St

Brewer Street

Glasshouse St

Pepsi Trocadero

Piccadilly Circus

Coventry St

Leicester Square

Irving St

National Gallery

Upper Grosvenor St

Park St

Adam's Row

Carlos St

Mount Row

Bourdon St

Bruton La

Grafton St

Bruton St

Albemarle St

Dover St

Stafford St

Vigo St

Sackville St

Piccadilly

Jermyn Street

St James's Square

Haymarket

Panton St

Orange St

St Martin's St

Whitcomb St

Trafa Squ

MAYFAIR

Mount Street

Aldford St

South Street

Hay's Mews

Hill Street

Charles Street

Berkeley Square

Royal Academy of Arts

Duke St

St James's St

ST JAMES'S

Charles II Street

Cockspur St

Park La

Park Lane

Deanery St

Curzon St

Bolton St

Stratton St

70

Queen's Walk

The Ritz

68

King St

Pall Mall

Carlton House Terrace

54

Admiralty Arch

Old Admiralty Offices

Hors Guar Parad

Market Mews

71 69

72

Curzon Mews

Shepherd St

Hertford Street

Old Park La

Brick St

Down St

Piccadilly

Hamilton Pl

Green Park

Spencer House

St James's Place

Marlborough House

The Mall

HYDE PARK

Serpentine Road

Rotten Row

Hyde Park Corner

73

Hyde Park Corner

Duke of Wellington Pl

Constitution Hill

GREEN PARK

Lancaster House

Clarence House

Cleveland Row

St James's Palace

ST JAMES'S

St James's

PARK

Park Lake

Foreign & Commonwealth Office

King Charl

62

Knightsbridge

Wilton Row

Grosvenor Cres

Halkin Street

67

65

64

BUCKINGHAM PALACE GARDENS

Buckingham Palace

Spur Rd

Birdcage Walk

Anne's Gate

Old Queen St

Gt Georg St

63

Belgrave Square

Chapel Street

Groom Pl

Chester Street

Wilton Cres

66

Royal Mews

Buckingham Gate

Catherine Pl

Wilfred St

Buckingham Gate

Wellington Barracks

Petty France

Home Office

St James's Park

Caxton St

Tothill Street

Victoria Street

Dean Yard

Gt

New Scotland Yard

MAP 8

MAP 3

MAP 5

MAP 4

MAP 2

Russell Square

Queen Sq

15

16

14

Bloomsbury Square

Bloomsbury Way

High Holborn

HOLBORN

High Holborn

Holborn

COVENT GARDEN

Royal Opera House

Covent Garden

Covent Garden

Aldwych

Bush House

India House

Australia House

Strand

Somerset House

32

33

34 35

Temple

Strand

Charing Cross

Charing Cross Station

Embankment

Victoria Embankment Gardens

Cleopatra's Needle

Embankment Pier

Northumberland Avenue

Old War Office

Banqueting House

Horse Guards Ave

Ministry of Defence

Richmond Ter

56

Whitehall Pl

Ct Scotland Yard

Gray's Inn Road

Clerkenwell Road

CLERKENWELL

Farringdon Station

17

19

18

20

24

23

25

Smithfield Market

21

22

St Bartholomew's Hospital

Newgate Street

Central Criminal Court

St Paul's Cathedral

Holborn Circus

Holborn Viaduct

City Thameslink Station

Fleet Street

Ludgate Circus

Ludgate Hill

28

27

26

Queen Victoria Street

30

31

Inner Temple

Inner Temple Gardens

Victoria Embankment

Blackfriars

Blackfriars Station

White Lion Hill

MAP 6

Blackfriars Bridge

T H A M E S

HQS Wellington

HMS President

Barge House St

36

Tate Modern

SOUTHWARK

37

38

Southwark Street

Waterloo Bridge

National Film Theatre

Royal National Theatre

47

Queen Elizabeth Hall

48 46

49

Royal Festival Hall

SOUTH BANK

Stamford Street

Upper Ground

Theed St

45

Waterloo East Station

Union Street

Festival Pier

Hungerford Bridge

New Pedestrian Access

Jubilee Gardens

50

Waterloo International Terminal

Waterloo Station

Mepham St

41

42

39

40

The Cut

43

44

Nelson Sq

BOROUGH

Westminster Pier

53

52

51

County Hall

York Road

Addington St

Westminster Bridge Road

Westminster

57

Bridge St

Westminster Bridge

61

Parliament Square

58

Houses of Parliament

60

59

Florence Nightingale Museum

LAMBETH

Victoria Tower Gardens

Archbishop's Park

Lambeth North

0   250   500m

0   250   500yd

To Elephant & Castle & Pizzeria Castello

MAP 4

PLACES TO STAY
4 Goldsmid House
6 Claridges
10 Indian Student YMCA
11 Carr Saunders Hall
12 Hotel Cavendish; Arran House Hotel
13 Jesmond Hotel; Ridgemount Hotel
14 Haddon Hall
19 The Rookery
27 City of London YHA Hostel
38 Holiday Inn Express Southwark
52 Travel Inn Capital

PLACES TO EAT
7 Rasa W1
16 Mille Pini
17 Gaudí
18 St John
20 The Greenery
21 Club Gascon
26 Dim Sum
28 Da Vinci
30 Ye Olde Cheshire Cheese
33 The Admiralty
36 Oxo Tower Restaurant & Brasserie
37 The Tall House

39 Tas
40 Konditor & Cook
41 Mesón Don Felipe
51 Fish!
68 The Little Square
71 Shepherd Café Bar
72 Hard Rock Café
73 Pizza on the Park

PUBS, BARS & CLUBS
15 The Queen's Larder
23 Cock Tavern
24 Ye Olde Mitre
44 The Fire Station
63 Westminster Arms
69 Ye Grapes

OTHER
1 Daunt Books
2 Wallace Collection
3 Selfridges
5 easyEverything
8 Wigmore Hall
9 Broadcasting House; BBC Experience
22 St Bartholomew-the-Great
29 Bridewell Theatre
31 Temple Church
32 Courtauld Gallery

34 Gilbert Collection
35 Hrmitage Rooms
42 Young Vic Theatre
43 Old Vic Theatre
45 BFI London IMAX Cinema
46 Museum of the Moving Image
47 Book Market
48 Purcell Room
49 Hayward Gallery
50 British Airways London Eye
53 London Aquarium
54 Institute for Contemporary Arts; ICA Café
55 10 Downing Street
56 Cenotaph
57 Portcullis House
58 Big Ben
59 St Stephen's Entrance
60 Jewel Tower
61 Winston Churchill Statue
62 Cabinet War Rooms
64 Queen Victoria Memorial
65 Buckingham Palace Ticket Office
66 Queen's Gallery
67 Memorial to Canadian War Dead
68 Thomas Cook (Main Office)

RICK GERHARTER

London's West End is a magnet for jugglers...

RICHARD I'ANSON

... and the ubiquitous South American buskers.

MAP 5

PLACES TO STAY
19 Fielding Hotel
49 Hazlitt's Hotel
51 Oxford St YHA Hostel
91 Strand Palace

PLACES TO EAT
1 Rasa Samudra
3 Soba
11 Ruskins Café
12 Coffee Gallery
13 Mandeer
20 Café des Amis du Vin
21 Café Pacifico
22 Belgo Centraal
25 Food for Thought
26 Neal's Yard Salad Bar
27 World Food Café
28 Rock & Sole Plaice
29 Franx Snack Bar
39 Maison Bertaux
40 Pollo
42 Old Compton Café
43 Pâtisserie Valerie
44 Bar Italia
45 Garlic & Shots
46 Gopal's of Soho
48 Mildred's
53 YO! Sushi
55 Spiga
59 Melati
64 Wong Kei
65 Chuen Cheng Ku
66 Gerrard's Corner
67 Mr Kong
68 Fung Shing
69 Cam Phat
70 Tokyo Diner
75 Gaby's
80 Calabash
88 Orso
90 Simpson's-in-the-Strand
109 L'Odéon

PUBS, BARS & CLUBS
5 100 Club
10 Museum Tavern
15 The End
30 First Out
31 Astoria
32 Velvet Room
34 Borderline
56 Balans
57 O Bar
58 Rupert St
74 Cork & Bottle Wine Bar
79 Lamb & Flag
94 Retro Bar
104 Comedy Store
106 Scruffy Murphy's
123 Sherlock Holmes

THEATRES
9 Dominion
16 Shaftesbury
18 New London; Talk of London
23 Cambridge
24 Donmar Warehouse
36 Phoenix
38 Palace
41 Prince Edward
52 London Palladium
60 Lyric
61 Apollo
62 Gielgud
63 Queen's
71 Ambassadors
72 St Martin's
73 Wyndham's
77 Albery
83 Drury Lane
84 Fortune
85 Aldwych
86 Strand
87 Duchess
89 Lyceum
93 Savoy
95 Vaudeville

96 Adelphi
99 Duke of York's
100 Garrick
102 Comedy
103 Prince of Wales
107 Piccadilly
114 Criterion
116 Her Majesty's
117 Haymarket

OTHER
2 HMV
4 Council Travel
6 On the Beat
7 Division One
8 Virgin Megastore
14 Sir John Soane's Museum
17 Bikepark
33 Waterstone's
35 Foyle's
37 Blackwell's
47 Trax
50 Black Market Records
54 Hamley's
76 Motor Books
78 Stanford's
81 London Transport Museum
82 Theatre Museum
92 YHA Adventure Shop
97 Trafalgar Square Post Office
98 Coliseum;
101 Half-Price Ticket Booth
105 Rock Circus
108 The European Bookshop
110 St James's Piccadilly
111 Waterstone's
112 Tower Records
113 Eros Statue
115 Britain Visitor Centre
118 American Express
119 Nelson's Column
120 St Martin-in-the-Fields; Café in the Crypt
121 easyEverything
122 Charles I Statue

Gateway to the world's most extensive underground railway

MAP 5

Riding House Street

Mortimer Street

Charlotte St

Percy Street

Maxwell Street

Bedford Avenue

Mortimer Street

Wells Street

Wells Mews

Berners Mews

Berners Street

Newman Street

Rathbone Street

Gresse Street

Tottenham Court Road

Little Portland Street

Margaret Street

Eastcastle Street

Windmill Street

Great Portland Street

Great Titchfield Street

Rathbone Place

Street

7

Tottenham Court Road

9

Hanway

6

8

Market

Oxford Street

Soho Street

Place

Oxford Street

2

Charing Cross Road

Sutton Row

31

Regent Street

3 ▼ ● 4

Noel Street

Hollen St

Great Chapel Street

Carlisle Street

Soho Square

32

34 ▢ 33

Oxford Circus

Oxford Circus

Argyll Street

Wardour Street

Manette Street

48 ▼

49

47 ●

Princes St

51

D'Arblay Street

Dean Street

Creek Street

Hanover Street

▢ 52

Great Marlborough Street

Poland Street

50 ●

Bateman Street

53 ▼

Berwick Street

Frith Street

▼ 45

40

▼ 46

44

42

41

39

Liberty

Newburgh St

Broadwick Street

Inestre Place

SOHO

43

Old Compton Street

Romilly Street

69

Maddox Street

Carnaby Street

Kingly Street

Marshall Street

Berwick Street Market

55 ▼

56

Peter Street

57 ▢

58 ▢

Shaftesbury Avenue

Conduit Street

New Burlington Pl

Beak Street

Great Pulteney Street

Bridle Lane

Lexington Street

63

62

CHINA-TOWN

Gerrard Street

67 ▢ 68

Regent Street

Kingly Street

Ganton Street

Golden Square

Brewer Street

59 ▼

61 ▢

60 ▼

Rupert Street

64 ▼

66

Wardour Street

Lisle Street

New Burlington St

Warwick Street

Sherwood Street

Great Windmill Street

65 ▼

Boyle Street

Savile Row

Heddon St

108 ●

106 ▢

107

Denman Street

London Trocadero

Leicester

Clifford Street

Old Burlington Street

Piccadilly Circus

105 ●

Coventry Street

103 ▢

104 ▢

New Bond Street

Cork Street

Vigo Street

Glasshouse Street

Piccadilly Circus

113 ▲

Oxendon St

Whitcomb Street

Albemarle Street

Burlington Gardens

▼ 109

112 ●

114 ▢

Panton Street

102

Brown's Hotel

Royal Arcade

Old Bond Street

Burlington Arcade

Royal Academy of Arts

Sackville Street

Swallow Street

Piccadilly

111 ●

St Alban's Street

Haymarket

Orange Street

Suffolk Street

Stafford Street

Dover Street

110 ▢

Jermyn Street

Duke of York Street

Regent Street

117 ▢

116 ▢

118 ⚥

Fortnum & Mason

115 ⚥

Charles II Street

ST JAMES'S

St James's Square

Bury St

Duke Street

King St

St James's Street

Piccadilly

Berkeley Street

Pall Mall

MAP 5

BLOOMSBURY

British Museum

Bloomsbury Street

Great Russell Street

Bloomsbury Way

Little Russell St.

Museum Street

Bury Place

Barter Street

Southampton Place

Southampton Row

Procter St.

High Holborn

Holborn

Whetstone Park

Gate Street

Lincoln's Inn Fields

HOLBORN

Lincoln's Inn Fields

New Oxford Street

West Central Street

High Holborn

Stukeley Street

Macklin Street

Newton Street

Kingsway

Sardinia St.

Portsmouth Street

Bucknall Street

Shaftesbury Avenue

Grape Street

St Giles High Street

Drury Lane

Parker Street

Great Queen Street

Wild Court

Wild Street

Portugal Street

Lincoln's Inn Fields

Bush House

India House

Denmark Street

New Compton Street

Charing Cross Road

Shaftesbury Avenue

Shorts Gardens

Betterton Street

Shelton Street

Endell Street

Neal's Yard

Neal Street

Seven Dials

Earlham Street

Monmouth Street

Mercer Street

COVENT GARDEN

Long Acre

Bow Street

Drury Lane

Kemble Street

Kean Street

Crown Court

Broad Court

Catherine Street

The Waldorf

Aldwych

Cambridge Circus

Earlham Street

Upr St Martin's Lane

Langley Street

Florral Street

Royal Opera House

Russell Street

Wellington Street

Somerset House

West St

Litchfield St

Newport Ct

Newport St

Little Newport St

Great Newport St

Cranbourn Street

Long Acre

Rose St.

Garrick Street

King Street

Covent Garden

Central Market Hall

Southampton Street

Tavistock Street

Exeter Street

Strand

Lancaster Place

Leicester Square

Bear Street

Cecil Court

St Martin's Lane

New Row

Bedford Street

Henrietta Street

Maiden Lane

Strand

The Savoy

Savoy Street

Savoy Place

Somerset House

Square

The Hampshire

Irving Street

Charing Cross Road

St Martins Lane

Bedfordbury

Hop Gardens

May's Court

Chandos Place

Adam Street

John Adam Street

Ivybridge Lane

Charing Cross

Waterloo Bridge

Orange Street

St Martin's Place

William IV Street

Strand

Victoria Embankment

Cleopatra's Needle

THAMES

National Portrait Gallery

National Gallery

Duncannon St

Pall Mall East

Trafalgar Square

Cockspur Street

Spring Gardens

Charing Cross

Charing Cross Station

Craven Street

Northumberland St.

Northumberland Avenue

Villiers Street

Victoria Embankment Gardens

Embankment

Charing Cross Pier

Admiralty Arch

Gardens

The Mall

Whitehall

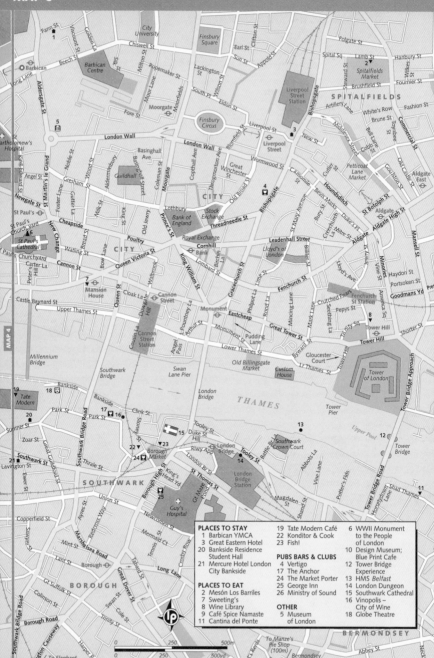

MAP 6

MAP 4

THAMES

PLACES TO STAY
1 Barbican YMCA
3 Great Eastern Hotel
20 Bankside Residence
   Student Hall
21 Mercure Hotel London
   City Bankside

PLACES TO EAT
2 Mesón Los Barriles
7 Sweeting's
8 Wine Library
9 Café Spice Namaste
11 Cantina del Ponte

19 Tate Modern Café
22 Konditor & Cook
23 Fish!

PUBS BARS & CLUBS
4 Vertigo
17 The Anchor
24 The Market Porter
25 George Inn
26 Ministry of Sound

OTHER
5 Museum
   of London

6 WWII Monument
   to the People
   of London
10 Design Museum;
   Blue Print Cafe
12 Tower Bridge
   Experience
13 HMS *Belfast*
14 London Dungeon
15 Southwark Cathedral
16 Vinopolis –
   City of Wine
18 Globe Theatre

A Cub Scout attempting to qualify for his pigeon-feeding badge

Mr Punch up to his old tricks, Covent Garden

Sixties nostalgia lives on, Carnaby St

MAP 7

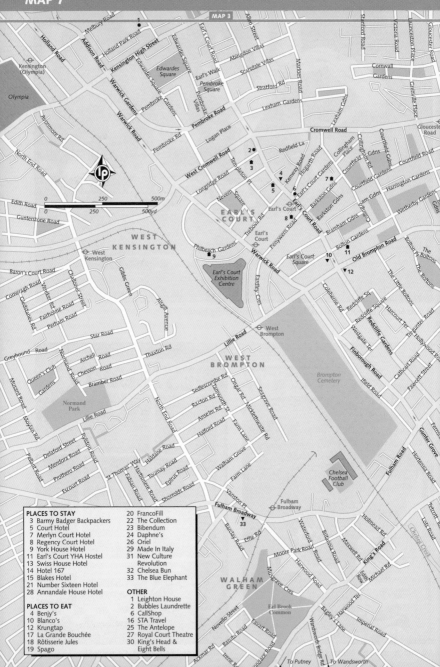

MAP 3

Kensington (Olympia)

Olympia

Cornwall Gardens

Cromwell Road

EARL'S COURT

WEST KENSINGTON

Earl's Court Exhibition Centre

WEST BROMPTON

Brompton Cemetery

Normand Park

Chelsea Football Club

Fulham Broadway

WALHAM GREEN

Earl Brook Common

To Putney   To Wandsworth

PLACES TO STAY
3 Barmy Badger Backpackers
5 Court Hotel
7 Merlyn Court Hotel
8 Regency Court Hotel
9 York House Hotel
11 Earl's Court YHA Hostel
13 Swiss House Hotel
14 Hotel 167
15 Blakes Hotel
21 Number Sixteen Hotel
28 Annandale House Hotel

PLACES TO EAT
4 Benjy's
10 Blanco's
12 Krungtap
17 La Grande Bouchée
18 Rôtisserie Jules
19 Spago
20 FrancoFill
22 The Collection
23 Bibendum
24 Daphne's
26 Oriel
29 Made In Italy
31 New Culture Revolution
32 Chelsea Bun
33 The Blue Elephant

OTHER
1 Leighton House
2 Bubbles Laundrette
6 CallShop
16 STA Travel
25 The Antelope
27 Royal Court Theatre
30 King's Head & Eight Bells

MAP 7

MAP 3

een's Gate Ter

Imperial College Road

Science Museum

Natural History Museum

Victoria & Albert Museum

aston Place

Queen's

rdens

een's
Gate

Brompton Square

Brompton Road

Beaufort Gdns

Beauchamp Place

Place

Hans St

Hans St

Ovington Square

Yeoman's Row

Pont Street

Cromwell Road

Cromwell Place

Queensberry Place

Thurloe Place

Thurloe Square

Egerton Terrace

Egerton Gardens

Walton Street

Ovington Street

Lennox Gardens

Clabon Mews

Cadogan Square

Pavilion Road

Sloane Street

Cadogan Lane

Cadogan Place

Chesham St

Thurloe St

South Terrace

peo▼

Brompton Road

Hasker Street

First Street

Milner Street

Moore St

Halsey St

Cadogan Gardens

Cadogan Pl

Ellis St

Sloane Ter

25 ▮

Stanhope

Queen's Gate

Harrington Road

20 ▼

17 ▼ ▮ ▼ **18** **19**

South Kensington

Pelham Street

22 ▼

24
▼

Pelham Street

Onslow Square

Dunne Pl

Denyer St

Draycott Avenue

Moxon Street

Rawlings St

Cadogan Gardens

Cadogan

26 ▮
27 ▮

Sloane
Square

Sloane Sq

Stanhope Gdns

23 ▼

Sloane Avenue

Lucan Place

Elystan Street

Pelham St

Whitehead's Gro

Draycott Place

Peter Jones

Cliveden▮

Lower Sloane St

Holbein Pl

SOUTH
KENSINGTON

16 ●

Gloucester Rd

Old Brompton Road

Cranley Pl

Summer Place

Onslow Gardens

Pond Place

Ixworth Place

Petyward St

Elystan Place

King's Road

Duke of York's Territorial Army Headquarters

28 ▮

Gardens

21 ▼

Onslow Gardens

Onslow Gdns

Fulham Road

Fawcett St

Neville St

Cale Street

St Luke's Street

Markham St

Elystan Place

Cheltenham Ter

Franklin's Row

Turk's Row

13 ▮ **14** ▮

Roland Gardens

15 ▮

Drayton Gardens

Cranley Gardens

South Parade

Chelsea Manor Street

Sydney Street

Britten Street

Astell Street

Jubilee Pl

Markham Square

Smith St

Radnor Walk

Shawfield Street

Walpole St

Royal Avenue

St Leonard's Ter

CHELSEA

Burton's Court

Royal Hospital Road

Chelsea
Royal
Hospital

Gilston Road

Priory Walk

Evelyn Gardens

Elm Park Gardens

Dovehouse Street

Chelsea Manor Road

Chelsea Old Town Hall

Flood Street

Flood St

Alpha Pl

Redburn Street

Smith Ter

Tedworth Square

Ormonde Gate

Christchurch St

West Road

National Army Museum

Tite Street

MAP 8

Callow St

Beaufort Street

Elm Park Road

The Vale

Mallord Street

Carlyle Square

29 ▼

Bramerton St

Glebe Place

Oakley Street

Phene St

Cheyne Gdns

Royal Hospital Road

Swan Walk

Chelsea
Physic
Garden

Park Walk

Limerston Street

Chelsea Park Gardens

Old Church Street

31 ▼

Paultons Square

Upper Cheyne Row

Cherry Row

Cheyne Walk

30 ▮

Cheyne

Walk

Chelsea Embankment

lhelton Gr

Gertrude Street

Langton St

Lamont Road

32 ▼

Beaufort Street

Milman's Street

Ann Lane

Cheyne Walk

Cadogan Pier

Chelsea Reach

The Parade

Children's Zoo

Grove

Slaidburn St

Ashburnham Rd

Cremorne Road

Battersea Bridge

Albert Bridge

THAMES

BATTERSEA PARK

Radmor Rd

verdale Road

sby Street

Lots Road

Hester Road

Battersea Church Road

Westbridge Road

Elcho St

Parkgate Road

Juer Street

Worfield Street

Albert Bridge Road

Carriage Drive North

Asphalt Road

Carriage Drive West

BATTERSEA
PARK

Thames Ave

Harbour Ave

Chelsea Harbour

Cambridge Rd

Parkham Street

Surrey Lane

Orbel Street

Octavia St

Ursula St

Elria St

Petworth St

Rosenau Road

Prince of Wales Drive

Carriage Drive South

Warriner Gdns

Battersea Park Road

PAUL DOYLE

Midriffs on display at the Notting Hill Carnival, the largest annual street festival in Europe

JULIET COOMBE

An abundance of superior souvenirs on Petticoat Lane

MAP 8

MAP 4

PLACES TO STAY
1 Rubens at the Palace
7 Woodville House Hotel
8 Morgan House Hotel
11 Winchester Hotel
12 Brindle House Hotel
13 Romany House Hotel
16 Luna-Simone Hotel

PLACES TO EAT
6 Jenny Lo's Tea House

14 UNo 1
15 O Sole Mio

OTHER
2 American Express
3 easyEverything
4 Tourist Information Centre (Main Office)
5 usit Campus
9 Victoria Coach Station Arrivals
10 Dial-a-Bike

MAP 9 - GREENWICH

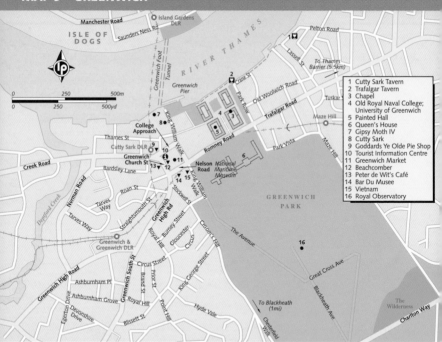

1 Cutty Sark Tavern
2 Trafalgar Tavern
3 Chapel
4 Old Royal Naval College;
  University of Greenwich
5 Painted Hall
6 Queen's House
7 Gipsy Moth IV
8 Cutty Sark
9 Goddards Ye Olde Pie Shop
10 Tourist Information Centre
11 Greenwich Market
12 Beachcomber
13 Peter de Wit's Café
14 Bar Du Musee
15 Vietnam
16 Royal Observatory

WESTMINSTER ABBEY

1 Innocent Victims Memorial
2 Statues of 20th-Century
  Martyrs
3 Churchill Memorial
4 Tomb of the Unknown
  Warrior
5 Screen; Scientists' Corner
6 Musicians' Aisle
7 Quire
8 The Lantern
9 Statesmen's Aisle
10 Disraeli Monument
11 Gladstone's Tomb
12 Robert Peel Monument
13 High Altar
14 Crewe Chapel

15 Edward I's Tomb
16 Chapel of St Edward
   the Confessor
17 Henry III's Tomb
18 Eleanor of Castile's Tomb
19 Coronation Chair
20 Queen Elizabeth Chapel

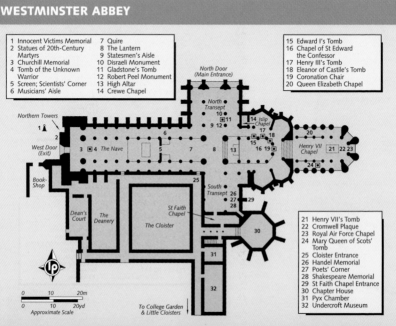

21 Henry VII's Tomb
22 Cromwell Plaque
23 Royal Air Force Chapel
24 Mary Queen of Scots'
   Tomb
25 Cloister Entrance
26 Handel Memorial
27 Poets' Corner
28 Shakespeare Memorial
29 St Faith Chapel Entrance
30 Chapter House
31 Pyx Chamber
32 Undercroft Museum

[continued from page 160]

these cover jobs, cheap tickets, shipping services and accommodation.

Loot (£1.30), which appears five times a week, is a paper made up of classified ads placed free by sellers. It's the best place to look for flats and house-share ads.

Tourist Offices

London is a major travel centre, so along with information on London, tourist offices can help with England, Scotland, Wales, Ireland and most countries worldwide.

Britain Visitor Centre The Britain Visitor Centre, 1 Regent St SW1 (Map 5; ⊖ Piccadilly Circus), is a comprehensive information and booking centre, with the tourist boards of Wales, Scotland, Northern Ireland, the Republic of Ireland and Jersey all represented; there's also a map and guidebook shop on the ground floor. On the mezzanine level are a Thomas Cook outlet where you can arrange accommodation and tours, as well as train, air and car travel; a theatre ticket agency; a bureau de change; international telephones; and computer terminals for accessing tourist information on the Internet. It can get *very* busy. It opens 9 am to 6.30 pm Monday to Friday and 10 am to 4 pm at the weekend (from 9 am to 5 pm on Saturday from late June to September). The centre deals with direct queries and walk-in customers only; it doesn't take telephone enquiries. If you're not in the area and need information about Britain or Ireland ring the British Tourist Authority (BTA) general enquiries line on ☎ 8846 9000. Check out the Web site at www.visitbritain.com.

Tourist Information Centres As well as providing information, London's main tourist information centre (TIC), which is in Victoria train station (Map 8; ⊖ Victoria), handles accommodation bookings. It opens 8 am to 8 pm Monday to Saturday and to 6 pm on Sunday, April to October; and 8 am to 7 pm Monday to Saturday and to 6 pm on Sunday during the rest of the year. It too can get positively mobbed in the peak season.

There's also a TIC in the arrivals hall at Waterloo International Terminal (Map 4; ⊖ Waterloo), open 8.30 am to 10.30 pm daily, and one in Liverpool Street station (Map 6; ⊖ Liverpool Street), open 8 am to 6 pm daily. There are TICs at Heathrow Terminal 3 (arrivals concourse), open 6 am to 11 pm daily, and in the Heathrow Terminals 1, 2 & 3 Underground station, open 8 am to 6 pm. Gatwick, Stansted, Luton and London City airports, Paddington train station and Victoria Coach Station also all have information desks.

Written enquiries should be sent to the London Tourist Board & Convention Bureau, Glen House, Stag Place, London SW1E 5LT (fax 7932 0222). You can also use its Visitorcall system – you simply dial ☎ 09064 123 and then add another three digits, depending on what information you're looking for. These are premium-rate numbers costing 60p per minute and can only be dialled within the UK. You can also visit www.londontown.com on the Web.

Money

Banks and ATMs abound across central London. Whenever possible, avoid using bureaux de change such as Chequepoint to change your money. If you must use them, check their commission rates carefully first.

There are 24-hour bureaux de change in Heathrow Terminals 1, 3 and 4. Terminal 2's bureau opens 6 am to 11 pm daily. Thomas Cook has branches at Terminals 1, 3 and 4. There are 24-hour bureaux in Gatwick's South and North Terminals and one at Stansted. Luton and London City airports have desks open during their operating hours. The airport bureaux are actually good value; they don't charge commission on sterling travellers cheques, and on other currencies it's 1.5% with a £3 minimum.

The main American Express (AmEx) office (Map 5; ☎ 7930 4411), 6 Haymarket SW1 (⊖ Piccadilly Circus), opens for currency exchange 9 am to 5.30 pm Monday to Friday and 9 am to 4 pm at the weekend. There are slightly longer hours from June to September. There's a welter of slightly shorter hours for services like mail. AmEx has offices scattered throughout London. The one at 96 Victoria St SW1 (Map 8), near Victoria train station, opens 9 am to 5.30 pm weekdays and to 4 pm on Saturday.

The main Thomas Cook office (Map 4; ☎ 7853 6400), 30 St James's St SW1 (✪ Green Park), opens 9 am (10 am on Wednesday) to 5.30 pm weekdays and to 4 pm on Saturday. There are branches throughout central London. The one on the 1st floor of the Victoria Place shopping centre at Victoria train station opens 7.30 am to 8 pm Monday to Saturday and 8 am to 6 pm on Sunday.

Discounts
If you plan to do a lot of sightseeing, the London GoSee card (£10/16/26 for one/three/seven days) can be purchased at and is valid for entry to 17 museums and galleries. Family cards, offering free admission for up to two adults and four children, cost £30/50 for three/seven days.

The participating museums are: Apsley House (Wellington Museum), Barbican Art Gallery, BBC Experience, BFI London IMAX Cinema, Design Museum, Globe Theatre, Hayward Gallery, Imperial War Museum, London Transport Museum, Museum of London, National Maritime Museum, Natural History Museum, Royal Academy of Arts, Science Museum, Theatre Museum, Tower Bridge Experience and Victoria & Albert Museum.

Post & Communications
Poste Restante Unless you (or the person writing to you) specify otherwise, poste restante mail sent to London ends up at the Trafalgar Square post office (Map 5), 24–28 William IV St, London WC2N 4DL (✪ Charing Cross). It opens 8 am to 8 pm weekdays and 9 am to 8 pm on Saturday. Mail will be held for four weeks; ID is required.

Telephone See Telephone in the Facts for the Visitor chapter for details of beating

BT's high prices on international calls using special cards such as Lonely Planet's eKno card.

The private company CallShop offers cheaper international calls than BT. You can find it open 9 am to 11.30 pm at 181a Earl's Court Rd SW5 (Map 7; ☎ 7390 4549; ✪ Earl's Court). You phone from a metered booth and then pay the bill. You can also send and receive faxes.

Email & Internet Access EasyEverything, a sister company of the no-frills airline easyJet, is opening numerous, huge, 24-hour Internet cafes around London. Charges vary according to how busy the location is: £1 buys you from 40 minutes to six hours of access. Locations include:

Kensington (Map 3)
  160–166 Kensington High St W8 (☎ 7938 1841; ✪ High Street Kensington)
Oxford St (Map 4)
  358 Oxford St W1 (☎ 7491 8986; ✪ Bond Street)
Trafalgar Square (Map 5)
  457–459 Strand WC2 (☎ 7930 4094; ✪ Charing Cross)
Victoria (Map 8)
  9–13 Wilton Rd SW1 (☎ 7233 8456; ✪ Victoria)

Travel Agencies
London has always been a centre for cheap travel. Refer to the Sunday papers (especially the *Sunday Times*), *TNT Magazine* and *Time Out* for listings of cheap flights, but beware of sharks.

Long-standing and reliable firms include:

Council Travel (Map 5; ☎ 7437 7767) 28a Poland St W1 (✪ Oxford Circus)
  Web site: www.counciltravel.com
STA Travel (☎ 7361 6161 for European enquiries, ☎ 7361 6262 for worldwide enquiries, ☎ 7361 6160 for tours, accommodation, car hire or insurance) 86 Old Brompton Rd SW7 (Map 7; ✪ South Kensington); and 117 Euston Rd NW1 (Map 2; ✪ Euston)
  Web site: www.statravel.co.uk
Trailfinders (Map 3; ☎ 7938 3939 for long-haul travel, ☎ 7938 3444 for 1st- and business-class flights) 194 Kensington High St W8 (✪ High Street Kensington), which also has a visa and passport service (☎ 7938 3848), immunisation centre (☎ 7938 3999), foreign exchange (☎ 7938

3836) and information centre (☎ 7938 3303) Web site: www.trailfinders.com

usit Campus (Map 8; ☎ 7730 3402 for European travel, ☎ 7730 8111 for worldwide enquiries) 52 Grosvenor Gardens SW1 (⊖ Victoria) Web site: www.usitcampus.co.uk

Bookshops
See Books in the Shopping section for bookshops in London that have good ranges of useful travel books and maps.

Laundry
Many hostels and some hotels have self-service washing machines and dryers, and virtually every high street has its own laundrette – with rare exceptions, a disheartening place to spend much time. The average cost to wash and dry a single load is £2.50 to £3. Hours vary but are usually 7 or 8 am to 8 or 9 pm daily.

The following is a selected list of laundrettes (your hotel or hostel should always be able to steer you towards a local laundry):

Bloomsbury (Map 2)
Red & White Laundrette, 78 Marchmont St WC1
Earl's Court (Map 7)
Bubbles, 113 Earl's Court Rd SW5
Bayswater (Map 3)
Laundrette Centre, 5 Porchester Rd W2

Left Luggage
All the train stations and Victoria Coach Station have left-luggage offices or lockers, as do the airports (see the Getting There & Away section later in the chapter). They cost between £2 and £6 a day, depending on the size of the bag or locker.

The London Baggage Company (☎ 0800 378254) is inside Victoria train station (Map 8). It can arrange long-term baggage storage as well as ship excess baggage all over the world.

Medical Services
For the address of a local doctor or hospital, look in the phone book or phone ☎ 100 (free). The following hospitals have 24-hour accident and emergency departments:

Charing Cross Hospital (Map 1; ☎ 8383 0000) Fulham Palace Rd W6 (⊖ Hammersmith)

Guy's Hospital (Map 6; ☎ 7955 5000) St Thomas St SE1 (⊖ London Bridge)
Royal Free Hospital (Map 1; ☎ 7794 0500) Pond St NW3 (⊖ Belsize Park)
University College Hospital (Map 2; ☎ 7387 9300) Grafton Way WC1 (⊖ Euston Square)

To find an emergency dentist phone the Dental Emergency Care Service on ☎ 7955 2186 weekdays between 8.45 am and 3.30 pm or call into the Eastman Dental Hospital (Map 2; ☎ 7915 1000), 256 Gray's Inn Rd WC1 (⊖ King's Cross).

The travel agency Trailfinders (Map 3; ☎ 7938 3999) has a clinic at 194 Kensington High St W8 with a full range of travel vaccines available. Nomad (☎ 8889 7014), 3–4 Wellington Terrace, Turnpike Lane N8 (⊖ Turnpike Lane), sells travel equipment and medical kits and gives immunisations on Thursday and Saturday evenings.

Emergency
Dial ☎ 999 (free) for fire, police or ambulance.

Dangers & Annoyances
Crime Considering its size and the disparities in wealth, London is remarkably safe; most visitors will spend their time in the capital without anything worse happening to them than being overcharged for an ice-cream cone. That said, you should take the usual precautionary measures against pickpockets, who operate in crowded public places such as the Underground, pubs and major tourist attractions. The area around King's Cross as well as Soho both call for caution after dark.

Take particular care at night. When travelling by tube, choose a carriage with other people in it and avoid some of the deserted suburban stations; a bus or a taxi is a safer choice.

Terrorism London remains the occasional target of terrorists trying to make a point. There is a much higher sense of security here than in, say, Sydney or even New York, and precautions are taken regularly – and seriously. *Never* leave your bag unattended in case you trigger a security alert. If you see an unattended package, keep calm and alert those in authority and anyone nearby as quickly as possible; whatever you do, do *not* touch it.

Touts & Scams Hotel and hostel touts descend on backpackers at tube and main-line stations such as Earl's Court, Liverpool Street and Victoria. Treat their claims with scepticism and don't accept any offers of free lifts unless you know exactly where you're going.

Every year foreign men are lured into Soho strip clubs and hostess bars and are efficiently separated from huge amounts of money; refuse to pay and things may rapidly turn nasty. Do yourself a favour and give them a wide berth.

Finally, when you're in high-traffic places such as Oxford St you may smell the overwhelming odour of frying onions. These emanate from one of the many unlicensed hot-dog carts that lurk around Lon-

don. Resist the urge (if there's one at all); the sanitary conditions are dubious.

CENTRAL LONDON
Trafalgar Square (Map 5)

Trafalgar Square WC2 (⊖ Charing Cross) is the heart of visitors' London. This is where many great marches and rallies take place, and where the new year is seen in by thousands of drunken revellers. It's also where you'll fight for space with flocks of pigeons – those dirty flying rats.

The square was designed by John Nash in the early 19th century on the site of the King's Mews and executed by Sir Charles Barry, who was also partly responsible for the Houses of Parliament. The 43.5m-high **Nelson's Column**, which incorporates granite from Cornwall to the Scottish Highlands, was completed in 1843. It was built to commemorate Admiral Nelson's victory over Napoleon off Cape Trafalgar in Spain in 1805. The four bronze lions at its base were designed by Edwin Landseer and

---

Lottery Bonanza

Visitors who think they know London are in for a delightful shock: the capital's cultural heritage has been given an almost complete makeover.

Thanks to the National Lottery, which funds cultural projects (among other things), a windfall of hundreds of millions of pounds has rained down on London, much of it tied in with the new millennium. This has led to much private money being invested as well.

Here's a list of the major projects; details are given in the text:

British Museum – The dramatic new glass roof has opened up the Great Court; there are also new galleries for African art.
Hungerford Bridge – Smart new walkways link the South Bank with the West End.
Imperial War Museum – A new permanent exhibition on the Holocaust has opened.
Millennium Bridge – This new pedestrian footbridge links Tate Modern with the City.
National Maritime Museum – This museum has undergone a complete revamp and has new galleries.
National Portrait Gallery – Expansion has eased access to the wonderful galleries on the higher floors.
Science Museum – The new Wellcome Wing celebrates the latest discoveries.
Somerset House – The gleam has been restored to this London gem and the Gilbert Collection has opened.
Southwark Cathedral – The cathedral has undergone restoration and also has a new visitor centre.
Tate Modern – This huge new museum on the Thames is dedicated to modern art.
Wallace Collection – This fabulous museum has undergone restoration and has new galleries.

added in 1867. If you glance up at the statue of the good admiral, you'll see that he is facing to the south-west, surveying (some say) his fleet of ships atop the lampposts lining The Mall.

Trafalgar Square is flanked by many imposing buildings and important thoroughfares fan out from it. To the north is the **National Gallery** and behind it the **National Portrait Gallery**; Pall Mall runs south-west from the north-western corner. The church of **St Martin-in-the-Fields** is to the northeast. To the south, the square opens out and you catch glimpses down Whitehall through the traffic. To the south-west stands **Admiralty Arch**, erected in honour of Queen Victoria in 1910, with The Mall leading to Buckingham Palace beyond it.

The traffic swirling past makes it difficult to appreciate Trafalgar Square. Plans are being considered to pedestrianise much of the square – a splendid idea.

National Gallery With some 2300 western paintings on display, the National Gallery (☎ 7747 2885), Trafalgar Square WC2, is one of the world's largest – and finest – art galleries. The lovely Sainsbury Wing on the western side was added in 1991.

The paintings in the National Gallery are hung in a continuous time-line; by starting in the Sainsbury Wing and progressing eastwards you can take in a collection of pictures painted between the mid-13th and early 20th centuries in chronological order. If you're keen on the real oldies (1260–1510), head for the Sainsbury Wing; for the Renaissance (1510–1600), go to the West Wing in the museum's main building. Rubens, Rembrandt and Murillo are in the North Wing (1600–1700); if you're after Gainsborough, Constable, Turner, Hogarth and the impressionists visit the East Wing (1700–1900). For a larger collection of paintings by British artists you should visit Tate Britain (see the following Westminster & Pimlico section) or Tate Modern (see the South of the Thames section).

The highlights listed in the boxed text will give you an idea of the *crème de la crème* at the gallery, but if you want to

---

National Gallery Highlights

- *Arnolfini Wedding* – Van Eyck
- *Rokeby Venus* – Velásquez
- *Wilton Diptych*
- *Bathers* – Cézanne
- *Venus & Mars* – Botticelli
- *Virgin of the Rocks* – da Vinci
- *Virgin & Child with St Anne & St John the Baptist* – da Vinci
- *Battle of San Romano* – Uccello
- *The Ambassadors* – Holbein the Younger
- *Charles I* – Van Dyck
- *Le Chapeau de Paille* – Rubens
- *The Hay-Wain* – Constable
- *Sunflowers* – Van Gogh
- *The Water Lily Pond* – Monet
- *The Fighting Temeraire* – Turner

---

know a lot more, borrow an audioguide (contribution suggested) from the central hall. Each painting is numbered; punch this into the machine and it will skip to the appropriate place on the CD-ROM. There are also highlights audioguide tours (featuring 30 paintings) and activity sheets for kids (50p). Free one-hour guided tours, which introduce you to a manageable half-dozen paintings at a time, leave at 11.30 am and 2.30 pm on weekdays and at 2 and 3.30 pm on Saturday (additional tour at 6.30 pm on Wednesday). The Micro Gallery has interactive screens where you can plan your own tour and then print out a plan.

The National Gallery opens 10 am to 6 pm daily (until 9 pm on Wednesday). Admission is free. You can visit its Web site at www.nationalgallery.org.uk.

National Portrait Gallery A visit to the National Portrait Gallery (☎ 7312 2463), St Martin's Place WC2, is not so much about art as history – putting faces to the famous and infamous names in British history from the Middle Ages to the present day. The gallery, founded in 1856, houses a primary collection of some 10,000 works on five floors, and there is a great variety of media, including watercolours, drawings, oil paintings, miniatures, sculptures, silhouettes, photographs and even electronic art.

The pictures are displayed roughly in chronological order, starting with the early Tudors on the top floor and descending to the late 20th century. The portraits of Elizabeth I from 1575 in all her finery and of Byron in romantic oriental garb (1813) by Thomas Phillips are as wonderful as the more recent works: Elizabeth II as seen by Andy Warhol; Prince Charles posing under a banana tree; photographs of Oscar Wilde, Virginia Woolf and more.

A major revamp of the gallery was completed in 2000. There are now expanded galleries, and escalators in the new Ondaatje Wing whisk visitors to the top floor, where any sensible tour begins and where there is a restaurant with a great view. Watch for various special exhibitions.

The National Portrait Gallery opens 10 am to 6 pm Monday to Saturday (until 9 pm on Thursday and Friday, from noon on Sunday). Admission is free. Check out the Web site at www.npg.org.uk.

St Martin-in-the-Fields An influential masterpiece by James Gibbs (1682–1754), the 'royal parish church' of St Martin-in-the-Fields (☎ 7930 0089), Trafalgar Square WC2, occupies a prime site at the northeastern corner of the square. There's an adjoining craft market, and in the crypt you'll find a brass-rubbing centre (☎ 7930 9306), bookshop and popular cafe (see Trafalgar Square in the Places to Eat section later). The church opens 8 am to 6.30 pm daily, the brass-rubbing centre 10 am (noon on Sunday) to 6 pm.

Westminster & Pimlico (Maps 4 & 8)

While the City of London (known simply as 'the City') has always concerned itself with trade and commerce, Westminster is the centre of political power and most of its places of interest are linked with the monarchy, parliament or the Church of England.

Pimlico, to the south and south-west, has never been as smart as, say, neighbouring

Belgravia, but contains some wonderful early-19th-century houses and the incomparable Tate Britain.

Whitehall Whitehall SW1 (Map 4; ✆ Charing Cross or Westminster), together with its southern extension Parliament St, is the wide avenue that links Trafalgar Square with Parliament Square. Once the administrative heart of the British Empire, it remains the focal point for British government. It is lined with so many government buildings, statues, monuments and other historical sights that the best way to take it all in is to follow this short walking tour.

Start at the southern end of Trafalgar Square as it leads into Whitehall. As you walk south you'll see **Admiralty Arch** and the **Old Admiralty** on the right and farther along on the left the **Ministry of Defence**.

Just in front of the latter is **Banqueting House** (☎ 7930 4179), the only surviving part of the Tudor Whitehall Palace, which once stretched most of the way along Whitehall but burned down in 1698. Designed by Inigo Jones in 1622, it was England's first purely Renaissance building. Its claim to fame is that it was on a scaffold built against a 1st-floor window that Charles I, accused of treason by Cromwell, was executed on 30 January 1649. Inside there's a video account of the house's history and on the 1st floor a huge, virtually unfurnished hall whose ceiling displays nine panels painted by Rubens in 1634. It opens 10 am to 5 pm Monday to Saturday. Admission costs £3.60/2.30.

Opposite Banqueting House is **Horse Guards Parade**, where the mounted troopers of the Household Cavalry are changed at 11 am Monday to Saturday and at 10 am on Sunday, offering a more accessible version of the ceremony than the one outside Buckingham Palace.

South of Horse Guards Parade is **Downing St. No 10** has been the site of the British prime minister's official residence since 1732, although Tony Blair and his family actually live in the larger apartments at No 11. During Margaret Thatcher's time in office the gates were erected and the street closed off to the public for fear of IRA terrorist attacks.

A short distance farther on, in the middle of Whitehall, is the **Cenotaph** (Greek for 'empty tomb'), a memorial to Commonwealth citizens who were killed during the two world wars.

To the west of the Cenotaph is the restored **Foreign & Commonwealth Office** (1872), designed by Sir George Gilbert Scott and Matthew Digby Wyatt.

If you walk west along King Charles St, you'll reach the **Cabinet War Rooms** (☎ 7930 6961), where the British government took refuge underground during WWII, conducting its business from beneath 3m of solid concrete. They open 9.30 am to 6 pm daily (from 10 am, October to March). Admission costs £4.80 (free for children).

Whitehall ends at **Parliament Square**, where swirling traffic makes it hard to appreciate the statues of past prime ministers such as **Winston Churchill**. To the northeast along Bridge St is the new, ultramodern and ultra-expensive Parliament extension, **Portcullis House**.

You're now in place to explore the following sights.

Westminster Abbey One of the most visited churches in Christendom, Westminster Abbey (Map 4; ☎ 7222 5152), Dean's Yard SW1 (⊖ Westminster), has played a pivotal role in the history of both England and the Anglican church. With the exception of Edward V and Edward VIII, every sovereign has been crowned here since William the Conqueror in 1066. All the monarchs from Henry III (died 1272) to George II (1760) were buried here as well, but since the death of George III in 1820 they have been laid to rest in St George's Chapel in Windsor.

The abbey's popularity means that certain areas are cordoned off to protect the floors and the northern transept now serves as the main entrance.

The abbey, though a mixture of various architectural styles, is the finest example of Early English Gothic (1180–1280) still standing. The original church was built by

JANE SMITH

His finest hour: Churchill in thoughtful mood during WWII

the 11th-century King (later Saint) Edward the Confessor, who is buried in the chapel behind the main altar. Henry III (reigned 1216–72) began work on the new building but didn't complete it; the French Gothic nave was finished in 1388. Henry VII's huge and magnificent chapel was added in 1519.

Unlike St Paul's, Westminster Abbey has never been a cathedral but is a 'royal peculiar', administered directly by the Crown.

Orientation Immediately past the entrance barrier you come to the **Statesmen's Aisle**, where politicians and eminent public figures are commemorated. The Whig and Tory prime ministers who dominated late-Victorian politics, Gladstone (who is buried here) and Disraeli (who is not), have their monuments uncomfortably close together. Nearby is a monument to Sir Robert Peel who, as home secretary in 1829, created the metropolitan police force. Above them is a rose window, designed by James Thornhill and depicting 11 of the Apostles (Judas is omitted).

On your left as you turn and walk eastwards are several small chapels with fine 16th-century monuments, including a lovely Madonna and Child in alabaster in the Crewe Chapel. Opposite the Islip Chapel, in the northern ambulatory, are three wonderful medieval tombs. Farther on are the tombs of Edward I and Henry III.

At the eastern end of the sanctuary, opposite the entrance to the Henry VII Chapel, is the rather ordinary-looking **Coronation Chair**, upon which almost every monarch is said to have been crowned since 1066. In fact, the oaken chair dates from the late 13th century – another chair must have been used prior to this.

Up the steps in front of you and to your left is the narrow **Queen Elizabeth Chapel**. Here Elizabeth I, who gave the abbey its charter, and her half-sister 'Bloody Mary' share an elaborate tomb.

In the easternmost part of the abbey you'll find the **Henry VII Chapel**, an outstanding example of late perpendicular architecture (a variation of English Gothic) with spectacular circular vaulting on the ceiling. Behind the chapel's altar, with a 15th-century *Madonna and Child* by Vivarini, is the elaborate sarcophagus of Henry VII and his queen, Elizabeth of York. Beyond this is the **Royal Air Force Chapel** and the Battle of Britain stained-glass window. Next to it a plaque marks the spot where Oliver Cromwell's body lay until the Restoration.

The chapel's southern aisle contains the **tomb of Mary Queen of Scots** (beheaded on the orders of her cousin Elizabeth and with the acquiescence of her son, the future James I) and the stunning tomb of Lady Margaret Beaufort, mother of Henry VII. Also buried here are Charles II, William and Mary, and Queen Anne.

The **Chapel of St Edward the Confessor**, the most sacred spot in the abbey, lies just east of the sanctuary and behind the high altar; access may still be restricted to protect the 13th-century floor. St Edward was the founder of the abbey.

Some of the surrounding tombs in the chapel – those of Henry III, Edward I, Edward III, Richard II, Henry V and four queens – are visible from the northern and southern ambulatory. **Eleanor of Castile**, the wife of Edward I, lies in one of the oldest bronze tombs. The abbey's southern transept contains **Poets' Corner**, where many of Eng-

land's finest writers are buried, a precedent established with Geoffrey Chaucer.

In front of medieval wall-paintings of St Christopher and the doubting apostle St Thomas on the eastern wall stands the **William Shakespeare memorial** (although like Byron, Tennyson, William Blake, TS Eliot and various other luminaries, he wasn't actually buried here). Here, too, you'll find memorials to Handel (holding a score of the *Messiah*), Edmund Spenser and Robert Browning, as well as the graves of (or memorials to) Charles Dickens, Lewis Carroll, Rudyard Kipling and Henry James. St Faith's Chapel (entrance to the east) is reserved for private prayer.

Just north of Poet's Corner is the **Lantern**, the heart of the abbey, where coronations take place. If you face east while standing in the centre, the **sanctuary** is in front of you. The ornate **high altar** was designed in 1897. Behind you (ie, to the west) Edward Blore's mid-19th-century **quire** (or chancel) is a breathtaking structure.

The entrance to the **Cloister** dates from the 13th century. East down a passageway off the Cloister, the octagonal **Chapter House** has one of Europe's best-preserved medieval tile floors and retains traces of religious murals. The state still runs the Chapter House and the adjacent **Pyx Chamber**, once the Royal Treasury and containing the pyx, a chest with standard gold and silver pieces for testing coinage weights. It now contains the abbey's treasures and liturgical objects, as well as the oldest altar in the abbey.

The **Undercroft Museum** (or the Abbey Museum) exhibits the death masks of generations of royalty as well as armour and stained glass.

To reach the 900-year-old **College Garden**, the oldest in England, enter Dean's Yard and the **Little Cloisters** off Great College St. There are free lunch-time concerts in the College Garden on Thursday in July and August.

Set in the floor at the western end of the nave is the **Tomb of the Unknown Warrior** in remembrance of those who died in WWI. Just before it is a stone commemorating **Winston Churchill**.

Straight up the aisle is the 1834 screen separating the nave from the choir. Against this stand monuments to Sir Isaac Newton, Darwin, Lord Stanhope, Michael Faraday and four Nobel laureates, including Lord Kelvin and Ernest Rutherford – a veritable **Scientists' Corner**.

The northern aisle of the nave is known as the **Musicians' Aisle**, with memorials to music-makers such as Henry Purcell, who served the abbey as an organist.

The two towers above the western door, through which you exit, were completed in 1745. Just above the door, perched in 15th-century niches, are the latest sacred addition to the abbey: 10 stone statues of the **20th-century martyrs**. To the right as you exit is a memorial to victims of oppression, violence and war around the world. 'All you who pass by, is it nothing to you?' it asks poignantly.

Hours & Tickets The abbey opens 9 am to 4.45 pm weekdays and 9 am to 2.45 pm on Saturday. Last admission is one hour earlier. The Chapter House opens 9.30 am to 5.30 pm April to October and to 4 pm the rest of the year. The Pyx Chamber and Undercroft Museum open 10 am to 4.30 pm daily. The College Garden opens 10 am to 6 pm Tuesday to Thursday, April to September (to 4 pm the rest of the year). The Cloisters open 8 am to 6 pm daily.

Admission to Westminster Abbey costs £5/2. Admission to just the Chapter House, Pyx Chamber and Undercroft Museum costs £2.50 (£1 with an abbey ticket); it's free for English Heritage (EH) members. Admission to the Cloisters is free.

One of the best ways to visit the abbey is to attend a service, particularly evensong (5 pm weekdays, 3 pm at the weekend). Sunday Eucharist is at 11 am.

Guided Tours Guided tours (☎ 7222 7110) of the abbey cost £3 and last about 1½ hours. They depart between three and six times a day, Monday to Saturday.

Houses of Parliament The Houses of Parliament (Map 4; ☎ 7219 4272), comprising the House of Commons and the

House of Lords, are in the Palace of Westminster, Parliament Square SW1 (⊖ Westminster). It was built by Sir Charles Barry and Augustus Pugin in 1840 when the neo-Gothic style was all the rage, and a thorough cleaning has revealed the soft golden brilliance of the original structure. The most famous feature *outside* the palace is the clock tower, commonly known as **Big Ben** (the real Ben, a bell named after Benjamin Hall, who was commissioner of works when the tower was completed in 1858, hangs inside).

The **House of Commons** is where Members of Parliament (MPs) meet to propose and discuss new legislation and to question the prime minister and other ministers. Although the Commons is a national assembly of 659 MPs, the chamber has seating for only 437 of them. Government members sit to the right of the Speaker and Opposition members to the left.

Visitors are admitted to the **Strangers' Gallery** of the House of Commons via St Stephen's Entrance after 4.15 pm Monday to Thursday and from 10 am on Friday; expect to queue for at least an hour. Admission is free. Parliamentary recesses (holidays) last for three months over the summer and another few weeks over Easter and Christmas, so it's best to ring in advance to check whether Parliament is in session. However, recent experimental opening during the summer recess (with tours for £3.50) may become a regular event, so check. Handbags and cameras must be checked at a cloakroom before you enter the gallery, and no large suitcases or backpacks are allowed through the airport-style security gate.

Originally built in 1099, **Westminster Hall** is the oldest surviving part of the Palace of Westminster, the seat of the English monarchy from the 11th to the early 16th centuries. Added between 1394 and 1401, the roof is the earliest known example of a hammer-beam roof and has been described as 'the greatest surviving achievement of medieval English carpentry'.

Jewel Tower Once part of the Palace of Westminster, the Jewel Tower (Map 4;

☎ 7222 2219; EH), opposite the Houses of Parliament and beside Westminster Abbey, was built in 1365 to house Edward III's treasury. Now it houses exhibitions describing the history of Parliament and showing how it works. The Jewel Tower opens 10 am to 6 pm daily, April to September; 10 am to 5 pm daily in October; and 10 am to 4 pm daily, November to March. Admission costs £1.50/80p.

Westminster Cathedral Completed in 1903, Westminster Cathedral (Map 8; ☎ 7798 9064), Victoria St SW1 (⊖ Victoria), is the headquarters of the Roman Catholic Church in Britain and is the only good example of neo-Byzantine architecture in London. Its distinctive candy-striped red-brick and white-stone tower features prominently on the west-London skyline.

The interior is part splendid marble and mosaic and part bare brick; the money ran out and the cathedral was never completed. It features the highly regarded stone carvings of the *14 Stations of the Cross* (1918) by Eric Gill. The cathedral opens 7 am to 7 pm daily. For £2 you can take a lift up the tower for panoramic views of London.

Tate Britain Tate Britain (Map 1; ☎ 7887 8008), Millbank SW1 (⊖ Pimlico), built in 1897, is being spruced up and expanded in conjunction with the high-profile opening of its sister gallery, Tate Modern, down the Thames at Bankside (see the South of the Thames section). But this museum has suffered from the millennium curse and the opening of huge new galleries (and a new entrance on Atterbury St) has been delayed until at least late 2001 due to a flood.

Calamities aside, Tate Britain serves as the historical archive of British art from the 16th century to the present. You'll find works by notables such as William Blake, Hogarth, Gainsborough, Whistler, Spencer and many more. Adjoining the main building is the quirky **Clore Gallery**, where the bulk of JMW Turner's paintings can be found.

Tate Britain opens 10 am to 5.50 pm daily and only major special exhibitions have an admission fee. Guided tours of the museum are available at 11.30 am, 2.30 pm and 3.30 pm weekdays, and at 3 pm on Saturday. The gallery's Web site is at www .tate.org.uk.

St James's & Mayfair (Map 4)

St James's is a mixture of exclusive clubs, historic shops and elegant buildings; indeed, there are some 150 historically noteworthy buildings within its 36 hectares. It has largely escaped the redevelopment that has taken place in much of London.

Mayfair is the area bordered by Oxford St to the north, Piccadilly to the south, Park Lane and Hyde Park to the west and Regent St to the east. It's one of London's most exclusive neighbourhoods – as everyone who's played the British version of Monopoly will know. At the heart of the district is **Grosvenor Square**, dominated by the hideous US embassy on the western side and with a **memorial to Franklin D Roosevelt** in the centre.

Institute for Contemporary Arts The Institute for Contemporary Arts (ICA; ☎ 7930 3647), The Mall SW1 (⊖ Charing Cross), has a reputation for being at the cutting edge of all kinds of art. In any given week this is the place to come for obscure films, dance, photography, art, theatre, music, lectures, multimedia works and book readings. The ICA opens noon to 7.30 pm daily. A day pass costs £1.50 (£2.50 at the weekend.

St James's Park & St James's Palace St James's Park, The Mall SW1 (⊖ St James's Park or Charing Cross), is the neatest and most royal of London's royal parks and has the best vistas, including Westminster, Buckingham Palace, St James's Palace, Carlton Terrace and Horse Guards Parade. In summer, the flower beds are sumptuous and colourful. But what makes St James's Park so particularly special is its large lake and the waterfowl that inhabit it, including a group of pelicans.

The striking Tudor gatehouse of **St James's Palace**, the only surviving part of a building initiated by the palace-mad Henry VIII in 1530, is best approached from St James's St to the north of the park. It is the residence of Prince Charles and his sons, the princes William and Harry, and is never open to the public. Foreign ambassadors to the UK are still accredited to 'the Court of St James's'. Next door is **Clarence House** (1828), the residence of the Queen Mother.

Buckingham Palace Buckingham Palace (☎ 7830 4832; ⊖ St James's Park or Victoria) is at the end of The Mall, where St James's Park and Green Park meet at a large roundabout. In the centre is the **Queen Victoria Memorial**, close to where Marble Arch stood until it was moved to its present location in 1851.

Buckingham Palace was built in 1803 for the Duke of Buckingham and has been the royal family's London home since 1837 when St James's Palace was judged too old-fashioned and insufficiently impressive. A total of 18 rooms (out of 661) is open to visitors for a brief period each year, but don't expect to see the Queen's bedroom. She and the Duke of Edinburgh share a suite of 12 rooms in the northern wing overlooking Green Park; there is a tour of the state apartments only. Many people find the visit overpriced and disappointing.

The tour includes **Queen Victoria's Picture Gallery** (a full 76.5m long, with works by Rembrandt, Van Dyck, Canaletto, Poussin and Vermeer) and the **Throne Room**, with his-and-hers pink chairs initialled 'ER' and 'P' sitting smugly under what looks like a theatre arch.

The palace opens 9.30 am to 4.30 pm daily, early August to early October, and admission costs £10.50/5.

Changing of the Guard This is a London 'must see' – though you'll probably go away wondering what all the fuss was about. The old guard (Foot Guards of the Household Regiment) comes off duty to be replaced by the new guard on the forecourt of Buckingham Palace, which gives tourists a chance to gape at the bright red uniforms, bearskin hats (synthetic alternatives are being looked at), shouting and marching. The ceremony takes place at 11.30 am daily, April to June, and at the same time on odd dates (eg, 1, 3, 5 July and so on) the rest of the year. For any schedule changes phone ☎ 0839 123411.

Queen's Gallery The Queen's Gallery, with its extensive Royal Collection of art, is closed for renovation until late 2002. Call the palace for the latest details.

Royal Mews South of the palace, the Royal Mews, Buckingham Palace Rd SW1 (⊖ Victoria), started life as a falconry but now houses the flashy vehicles the royals use for getting around on ceremonial occasions, including the stunning Gold State Coach of 1762. The Royal Mews opens noon to 4.30 pm Monday to Thursday, August and September, and to 4 pm the rest of the year. Admission costs £4.30/2.10.

Green Park Green Park adjoins St James's Park to the north-west across The Mall, and is a less fussy, more naturally rolling park, with trees and open space, sunshine and shade. Note the serene **Memorial to Canadian War Dead** near Buckingham Palace.

The West End: Piccadilly, Soho & Chinatown (Maps 4 & 5)

No two Londoners ever agree on the exact borders of the West End but let's just say it takes in Piccadilly Circus and Trafalgar Square to the south, Oxford St and Tottenham Court Rd to the north, Regent St to the west and Covent Garden and the Strand to the east. A heady mixture of consumerism and culture, the West End is where outstanding museums and galleries rub shoulders with tacky tourist traps.

Piccadilly Circus Piccadilly Circus (Map 5; ⊖ Piccadilly Circus) is home to the statue of the *Angel of Christian Charity*, commonly known as **Eros** and dedicated to Lord Ashley, the Victorian Earl of Shaftesbury, who championed social and industrial reform.

Piccadilly Circus used to be the hub of

London, where flower girls flogged their wares and people arranged to meet or simply bumped into each other. Nowadays it's fume-choked and pretty uninteresting, overlooked by Rock Circus and Tower Records.

Rock Circus Brought to you by the Madame Tussaud's people, the revamped Rock Circus (☎ 7734 7203), London Pavilion, Piccadilly Circus W1, is one of the capital's most popular attractions. You're whipped back to rock's cotton-picking origins so fast you barely have time to take in what's happening, after which you're treated to a succession of animated models who lip-sync to their music while jerking their limbs around like puppets. It opens 10 am to 10 pm daily (from 11 am on Tuesday). Admission costs £8.25/6.25.

London Trocadero The Trocadero (☎ 09068 881100), 1 Piccadilly Circus W1, is a huge indoor entertainment complex on six levels with several high-tech attractions, anchored by the **Segaworld** indoor theme-park. It's a good place to take youngsters who can't be sold on London's more cultural attractions, but don't expect a peaceful – or cheap – night or day out. There's no admission charge to Segaworld, but you must pay £3 for each of the eight rides. Check for discounts on multiple ticket purchases. **Funland** has upwards of 400 video games to keep even the most hyperactive active. The centre opens 10 am to midnight daily (to 1 am on Friday and Saturday).

Piccadilly Piccadilly (Map 5), the road running south-west from Piccadilly Circus, is home to **St James's Piccadilly**, a church designed by Sir Christopher Wren after the Great Fire of 1666.

The **Royal Academy of Arts** (☎ 7300 8000), Burlington House, Piccadilly W1 (⊖ Green Park), has traditionally played poor relation to the Hayward Gallery. But in recent years exhibitions here have broken all records. Each summer, the academy holds its traditional Summer Exhibition, an open show that anyone can enter. It opens

10 am to 6 pm daily (often to 8.30 pm on Friday). Admission costs depend on what's on, but expect to pay around £6.

Regent St Regent St (Map 5) is lined with elegant shop-fronts but they date back only to 1925. Here you'll find Hamley's (☎ 7734 3161), London's premier toy and game store, and the upmarket department store Liberty. Go east along Great Marlborough St and you'll reach the northern end of **Carnaby St**, which runs parallel to Regent St. It was the street for fashion in the 'swinging London' of the 1960s, and this lives on in the Union Jack-emblazoned gewgaws it offloads to tourists.

The BBC Experience North of Oxford Circus is **Broadcasting House** (Map 4; ⊖ Oxford Circus), from which the BBC began broadcasting in 1932. The basement now houses the BBC Experience (☎ 0870 603 0304), where you can watch clips of popular BBC programs and see the Marconi Collection of early wireless equipment. It opens 10 am (from 11 am on Monday) to 5.30 pm daily. Admission costs £6.95/4.95. There's a shop stocking any number of videos, tapes and books relating to BBC programs.

Oxford St Once London's finest shopping street, Oxford St (Maps 4 & 5) is a big disappointment for most visitors, especially if you emerge from Oxford Circus tube and head east towards Tottenham Court Rd. Things are much better if you head west towards Marble Arch; this is where you'll find the famous department stores, including Selfridges.

Soho East of Regent St and south of Oxford St, with Shaftesbury Ave and Charing Cross Rd to the south and the east, is Soho (Map 5), one of the liveliest corners of London and the place to come for fun and games after dark. A decade ago it was known mostly for strip clubs and peepshows. The sleaze is still there, of course, but these days it rubs shoulders with some of London's trendiest clubs, bars and restaurants. But remember that all manner of disreputable types lurk in the shadows, so be careful.

Leicester Square Despite efforts to smarten it up and the presence of four huge cinemas, various nightclubs, pubs and restaurants, pedestrianised Leicester (**les**-ter) Square (Map 5) still feels more like a transit point between Covent Garden and Piccadilly Circus than its own world.

Chinatown Immediately north of Leicester Square are Lisle and Gerrard Sts, the heart of London's Chinatown (Map 5), where street signs are in both English and Chinese. This is the place to come for an after-hours Chinese meal (see Chinatown in the Places to Eat section).

Covent Garden In the 1630s Inigo Jones converted something that had started life as a vegetable field belonging to Westminster Abbey into the elegant square – or piazza – at Covent Garden (Map 5; ⊖ Covent Garden). But by Victorian times a fruit and vegetable market had been set up (immortalised in *My Fair Lady*, the 1964 screen adaptation of George Bernard Shaw's play *Pygmalion*). When the market moved out in the 1980s, Covent Garden was transformed into one of central London's liveliest hubs, with shops built into the old arcades.

Covent Garden gets horribly overcrowded in summer, but remains one of the few bits of London where pedestrians rule, and there's always a corner of relative peace where you can listen to the licensed buskers.

Beyond the piazza are lively streets of clothes shops and bars, restaurants and designer gift shops. To the north, Floral St is where swanky designers have their outlets.

London Transport Museum Tucked into the corner of Covent Garden between the Jubilee Hall and Tutton's restaurant, the London Transport Museum (☎ 7836 8557) tells how London made the transition from streets choked with horse-drawn carriages to the arrival of the Docklands Light Railway (DLR) and the modern Jubilee Line

Just two of the army of buskers, jugglers and other performers you'll see in Covent Garden

extension – a more interesting story than you might suspect. It opens 10 am to 6 pm daily (from 11 am on Friday) and admission costs £5.50/2.95. There's an excellent shop with merchandise and books.

Theatre Museum A branch of the Victoria & Albert Museum, the Theatre Museum (☎ 7836 7891), Russell St WC2, displays costumes and artefacts relating to the history of the theatre. The museum opens 10 am to 6 pm Tuesday to Sunday. Admission costs £4.50 (free for children).

The Strand At the end of the 12th century nobles built sturdy houses of stone with gardens along the 'beach' of the Thames. The Strand (Maps 4 & 5) linked Westminster, the seat of political power, with the City, London's centre of industry and trade, and became one of the most prestigious places in London to live; in the 19th century Disraeli pronounced it the finest street in Europe. Today this ¾-mile (1.25km) long thoroughfare is a hotchpotch of shops, fine hotels, theatres and offices, in whose doorways the homeless lay out their sleeping bags for the night.

Somerset House This splendid Palladian masterpiece (Map 4; ⊖ Temple), designed by William Chambers in 1775, contains two fabulous museums: the Courtauld Gallery and the new Gilbert Collection of decorative arts. In 2000 the central courtyard reopened after a long restoration that saw a car park banished and one of London's most elegant spaces returned to its former glory. It has tables outside in the summer as well as fountains and occasional live open-air theatre. There are hopes that an ice-skating rink will be installed during the winter. At the back of the building there's a great terrace overlooking the Thames with a cafe and tables for picnickers.

The new **Hermitage Rooms** opened in late 2000 and host rotating exhibitions of rarely seen treasures from the Hermitage museum in St Petersburg. Call ☎ 7845 4630 for the current opening times and ticket details.

Courtauld Gallery Housed in the North Wing (or Strand Block), the Courtauld Gallery (☎ 7848 2526) displays some of the Courtauld Institute's marvellous collection of paintings in grand surroundings following a £25 million architectural refurbishment. Exhibits include works by Rubens, Bellini, Velásquez and Botticelli. However, for many visitors the most memorable display is of impressionist and postimpressionist art by Van Gogh, Cézanne, Rousseau, Gauguin, Toulouse-Lautrec, Manet, Pissarro, Sisley, Renoir, Degas and Monet.

The gallery opens 10 am to 6 pm daily (from noon on Sunday). Admission costs £4 (free for children). Between 10 am and 2 pm on Monday it's free for everyone. Joint admission with the Gilbert Collection costs £7.

Gilbert Collection One of London's newest museums, the Gilbert Collection (☎ 7240 5782) includes such treasures as European silver, gold snuffboxes and Italian mosaics bequeathed to the nation by London-born US businessman Arthur Gilbert.

Worth over £100 million, the collection is housed in the vaults beneath the South Terrace. Opening hours and admission charges are the same as for the Courtauld Gallery.

Bloomsbury (Maps 2 & 4)

East of Tottenham Court Rd and north of High Holborn, south of Euston Rd and to the west of Gray's Inn Rd, Bloomsbury is a peculiar mix of the University of London, the British Museum and beautiful Georgian squares. **Russell Square** (Map 4), the very heart of Bloomsbury, is London's largest square. It was laid out in 1800. At night it becomes a very busy gay cruising area.

Between the world wars these pleasant streets were colonised by a group of artists and intellectuals who became known collectively as the Bloomsbury Group. The novelists Virginia Woolf and EM Forster and the economist John Maynard Keynes are perhaps the best-known members. The centre of literary Bloomsbury was **Gordon Square** (Map 2), where many writers lived. Look for the blue plaques on the buildings. Lovely **Bedford Square** (Map 4) is the only completely Georgian square still surviving in Bloomsbury and was once home to many publishing houses.

British Museum The British Museum (Map 4; ☎ 7636 1555), Great Russell St WC1 (⊖ Tottenham Court Road or Russell Square), is Britain's largest museum and one of the oldest in the world. It's also the most visited tourist attraction in London with more than six million annual visitors.

Late in 2000, the museum's inner courtyard, hidden from the public for almost a century and a half, reopened as the **Great Court**, covered with a spectacular glass roof designed by Sir Norman Foster. This grand new space, which has cost almost £100 million in lottery money, opens up the labyrinth that is the British Museum. Set beneath the sinuous green-tinged glass supported by a seductive lattice of steel frames, the new space is reason enough to visit the museum. The old round reading room – which dates from when the British Library was based in the museum – stands dramatically at the centre. Inside, the reading tables are resplendent under the huge dome, which is larger than the one at St Paul's. This is the place where George Bernard Shaw and Mahatma Gandhi studied and Friedrich Engels and Karl Marx wrote *The Communist Manifesto*. The northern end of the courtyard's lower level is to house the museum's Sainsbury African Galleries and will be linked with new galleries for the American, Asian, Middle Eastern, European and Pacific ethnographical collections on the ground floor of the main hall. These should be open by the time you read this.

While you're in the Great Court, check out the new south portico, which is much lighter than the surrounding stone because it was incorrectly built using French rather than Portland limestone.

In the surrounding museum, the collection is vast, diverse and amazing – so much so that it can seem pretty daunting. To make the most of the museum don't plan on seeing too much in one day; the fact that admission is still free means you can come back several times and appreciate the museum's exhibits at your leisure.

The following are some of the top highlights in the museum. However, it can be equally rewarding to get away from the crowds, pick an exhibit at random and read the usually excellent explanatory material to learn all sorts of surprising things.

Room 25 has Egyptian sculptures and the **Rosetta Stone**, written in two forms of ancient Egyptian (hieroglyphics and demotic) and in Ancient Greek. The Rosetta Stone was the key to deciphering Egyptian hieroglyphics, which had stymied scholars up to that time. The famous mummies have been moved to the new **Mummies Gallery** on the 2nd floor.

Rooms 1 to 15 feature finds from the classical Greek, Roman and Hellenistic empires. Best known of the exhibits here are the **Elgin Marbles**, pilfered from the walls of the Parthenon on the Acropolis in Athens by Lord Elgin from 1801 to 1806. They are thought to show a great procession to the temple but have been pretty battered and beaten over the centuries (not least by the

British Museum Highlights

- Benin Bronzes
- Elgin Marbles
- Egyptian mummies
- Rosetta Stone
- Sutton Hoo Treasure
- Lewis chess-set
- Mildenhall Treasure
- Battersea shield & Waterloo helmet
- Lindow Man
- Oxus Treasure
- Portland Vase

British Museum; see the boxed text 'Hey! We Want Our Marbles Back!').

Upstairs in rooms 51 and 52 is the stunning **Oxus Treasure**, a collection of 7th- to 4th-century BC pieces of Persian gold. Rooms 49 and 50 contain artefacts from Roman Britain and from the Bronze Age and Celtic Europe (approximately 900 to 100 BC). This is where you'll see the stunning **Mildenhall Treasure**, a 28-piece silver dinner service dating from the 4th century.

This is also where you'll find **Lindow Man**, an Iron Age unfortunate who seems to have been struck on the head with a narrow axe (there are holes in the skull) and then garrotted.

The British Museum has two entrances: the imposing, Smirke-designed, porticoed main entrance off Great Russell St, and a back entrance off Montague Place, which tends to be less congested. The Great Court has a good cafe.

Hours & Tickets The British Museum opens 10 am to 5 pm Monday to Saturday and noon to 6 pm on Sunday. Admission is free. There are plans to hold special events and lectures at night in the Great Court.

Guided Tours The museum offers visitors a 1½-hour tour of the collection's highlights at 10.30 am and 1 pm Monday to Saturday and several times on Sunday. It costs £7/4. Focus tours, which are based around particular objects, are usually given in the

Hey! We Want Our Marbles Back!

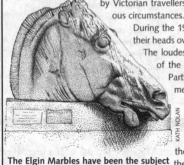

Wonderful though it is, the British Museum can sometimes feel like one vast repository for stolen booty. Much of what you're looking at wasn't just 'picked up' along the way by Victorian travellers and explorers, but stolen, or purchased under dubious circumstances.

During the 1990s, restive foreign governments occasionally popped their heads over the parapet to demand the return of 'their' property. The loudest voice was that of the Greeks calling for the return of the so-called Elgin Marbles to their original home on the Parthenon in Athens. However, successive British governments have been intransigent.

All along, the British Museum has sniffed that the marbles are better off under its protective care. This arrogance proved tragicomic when it emerged in 1999 that earlier in the century the museum had 'cleaned' the marbles using chisels and wire brushes. As a result, the finishes applied to the marbles by the ancient Greeks were destroyed.

The Elgin Marbles have been the subject of some dubious horse-play...

KATH NOLAN

---

afternoon daily. They last an hour and cost £5/3. Audio tours cost £2.50. The reading room is now open for people seeking more information on any part of the collection. It has a wealth of printed and online material.

Dickens' House Charles Dickens' House (Map 2; ☎ 7405 2127), 49 Doughty St WC1 (⊖ Russell Square), is the only surviving residence of the many the great Victorian novelist occupied before moving to Kent. While living here, from 1837 to 1839, he wrote *Pickwick Papers*, *Nicholas Nickleby* and *Oliver Twist*.

The house has 11 reasonably interesting rooms, including a complete Victorian kitchen and lots of memorabilia. Keep an eye out on the stairwell for a goldsmith's shop sign of an arm and hammer that once graced Manette St in Soho and is mentioned in *A Tale of Two Cities*.

Dickens' House opens 10 am to 5 pm Monday to Saturday. Admission costs £4/2.

Holborn & Clerkenwell (Maps 2 & 4)

Holborn (**hoe**-bun), the area north of the Strand and Fleet St and wedged between the City to the east, Covent Garden to the west

and High Holborn to the north, includes several of the Inns of Court, where London's barristers practise, and the wonderful Sir John Soane's Museum. It is the smallest of London's former metropolitan boroughs and takes its name from a tributary of the River Fleet.

Immediately north-west of the City, Clerkenwell has become a very trendy corner of the capital, with the usual batch of pricey restaurants and expensive property. The area around Clerkenwell Green is very attractive.

Sir John Soane's Museum Sir John Soane's Museum (Map 5; ☎ 7405 2107), 13 Lincoln's Inn Fields WC2 (⊖ Holborn), is partly a beautiful – if quirky – house and partly a small museum representing one man's personal taste. Some visitors consider it their favourite 'small' sight in London.

Sir John Soane (1753–1837) was a leading architect who had a real passion for collecting. His eclectic acquisitions include an Egyptian sarcophagus and the original *Rake's Progress*, William Hogarth's set of cartoon caricatures of late-18th-century London lowlife. The museum opens 10 am to 5 pm Tuesday to Saturday and also 6 to

9 pm on the first Tuesday of every month. Admission is free.

The City (Maps 4 & 6)

The City of London is the 'square mile' on the northern bank of the Thames where the Romans first built a walled community 2000 years ago. The boundaries of today's City haven't changed much, and you can always tell when you're within them because the Corporation of London's coat of arms appears on the street signs, and the small statue of a griffin emblazoned with the motto *Domine Dirige Nos* (God Direct Us) marks the City's borders. This is the business heart of London where you'll find not only the Bank of England, but also the headquarters of many British and overseas banks, insurance companies and other financial institutions. Under 10,000 people actually live in the City but around 300,000 commute there to work every day.

A quiet weekend stroll when the banks and offices are closed offers a unique chance to appreciate the architectural richness of its many famous buildings and the atmospheric little alleyways that now separate futuristic office towers.

Fleet St Ever since Wynkyn de Worde moved Caxton's printing press from Westminster to a shop beside St Bride's Church in 1500, Fleet St (Map 4; ⊖ Blackfriars) has been ink-splattered. In the 20th century it earned the nickname 'London's Street of Shame', where printing presses stoked by gossip and lies churned out their scurrilous product: the UK's tabloid newspapers. Then the mid-1980s brought Rupert Murdoch, new technology and the Docklands redevelopment and all the papers moved away.

Temple Church Temple Church (Map 4; ☎ 7353 1736), Inner Temple, King's Bench Walk EC4 (⊖ Temple or, on Sunday, Blackfriars), is just off Fleet St under the archway beyond No 17. Duck under it and you'll find yourself in the Inner Temple, one of the Inns of Court. Temple Church was originally planned and built by the secretive Knights Templar between 1161 and 1185. They modelled it on the Church of the Holy Sepulchre in Jerusalem.

Temple Church opens 10 am to 4 pm Wednesday to Saturday. Westminster Abbey and St Paul's Cathedral aside, this is possibly London's most interesting and architecturally important church. Don't miss it. The surrounding area comprises part of the Inns of Court and the many narrow alleys make for a fascinating wander.

St Bartholomew-the-Great One of London's oldest churches, St Bartholomew-the-Great (Map 4; ☎ 7606 5171), West Smithfield EC1 (⊖ Barbican), is a stone's throw from the Barbican and certainly worth more than a fleeting visit. The authentic Norman arches and details lend this holy space an ancient calm; approaching from nearby Smithfield Market through the restored 13th-century archway is like walking back in time.

The church opens 8.30 am to 5 pm Monday to Friday, 10.30 am to 1.30 pm on Saturday and 8 am to 8 pm on Sunday.

Central Criminal Court (Old Bailey) All Britain's major gangsters and serial killers eventually find themselves at the Central Criminal Court (Map 4), better known as the Old Bailey after the street on which it stands. Look up at the great copper dome and you'll see the figure of justice holding a sword and scales in her hands; oddly she is *not* blindfolded, which has sparked many a sarcastic comment from those being brought in here.

The court's public gallery (☎ 7248 3277), on Newgate St, opens 10.30 am to 1 pm and 2 to 4 pm weekdays.

St Paul's Cathedral St Paul's Cathedral (Map 6; ☎ 7236 4128; ⊖ St Paul's) was built, amid much controversy, by Sir Christopher Wren between 1675 and 1710. It stands on the site of four previous cathedrals, the first of which dated from 604.

The dome still dominates the City and the only church dome that exceeds it in size is that of St Peter's in Rome. Pictures of the cathedral miraculously surviving the devastation of WWII bombing can be seen in a glass case in the southern choir aisle and the images have become an icon of the Blitz.

Before you enter, take a moment to walk around to the north of the cathedral (that's to the left as you face the large stairway). A long-overdue **monument to the people of London** – not all those warmongers, sabre-rattlers and heroes at rest in the crypt – has been unveiled in the small garden just outside the northern transept in St Paul's Churchyard. Simple and elegant, it honours the 32,000 civilians killed in London during WWII.

From the main entrance, proceed up the northern aisle, past the **Chapel of St Dunstan**, dedicated to the 10th-century archbishop of Canterbury, and the grandiose **Duke of Wellington Memorial** (1875), until you reach the central pavement area under the dome. Some 30m above the paved area is the first of three domes – actually a dome, inside a cone, inside a dome – supported by eight massive columns. The walkway around its base is called the **Whispering Gallery**, because if you talk close to the wall it carries your words around to the opposite side 32m away.

In the northern transept chapel is Holman Hunt's celebrated painting *The Light of the World*, which depicts Christ knocking at an overgrown door that, symbolically, can only be opened from the inside. Beyond are the **choir** (or chancel), whose ceilings and arches dazzle with green, blue, red and gold mosaics, and the high altar. Walk around the altar, with its massive gilded oak canopy, to the **American Chapel**, a memorial to the 28,000 Americans based in Britain who lost their lives during WWII.

On the eastern side of the southern transept, a staircase leads down to the Crypt, Treasury and OBE Chapel, where services (weddings, funerals etc) reserved for members of the Order of the British Empire are held. The **Crypt** has memorials to up to 300 military demigods, including Wellington, Kitchener and Nelson, who is below the dome in a black sarcophagus.

The most poignant memorial of all is to Sir Christopher himself. It is south of the **OBE Chapel** and is just a simple slab with his name, the year of his death (1723) and his age ('XCI'). The **Treasury** displays some of the cathedral's plate. There is also a cafe and a shop in the crypt open 9 am to 5 pm Monday to Saturday (from 10.30 am on Sunday).

Back upstairs in the nave, the Whispering Gallery as well as the **Stone Gallery** and the **Golden Gallery** can be reached by a staircase on the western side of the southern transept. All in all there are 259 steps to the first gallery, another 116 to the Stone Gallery and 155 more steps to the top gallery; that's a total of 530 steps to climb up and down. Even if you can't make it right up to the Golden Gallery, it's worth struggling as far as the Stone Gallery for one of the best views of London.

The cathedral opens 8.30 am to 4 pm Monday to Saturday. Admission costs £5/2.50. Audioguide tours lasting 45 minutes are available for £3. Guided 90-minute tours (£2.50/2) leave the tour desk at 11 and 11.30 am, and 1.30 and 2 pm. There are organ concerts at St Paul's at 5 pm most Sundays. Evensong takes place at 5 pm most weekdays and at 3.15 pm on Sunday.

Guildhall The Guildhall (Map 6; ☎ 7606 3030), off Gresham St EC2 (◉ Bank), which sits exactly in the centre of the square mile, has been the City's seat of government for nearly 800 years. The present building dates from the early 15th century.

Visitors can see the **Great Hall** where the mayor and sheriffs are still elected, a vast empty space with church-style monuments and the shields and banners of the 12 principal livery companies of London.

The **Guildhall Art Gallery** to the southeast in Guildhall Yard opened in 1999 and brings together the Corporation of London's huge art collection for the first time since WWII. Over 250 works are on display at any time.

Admission to the Guildhall's art gallery costs £2.50/1; otherwise it is free. It opens 10 am to 5 pm daily (to 4 pm on Sunday), but is closed on Sunday from October to April.

Barbican Tucked into a corner of the City of London where there was once a watchtower (or 'barbican'), the Barbican (Map 6; ☎ 7638 4141), Silk St EC2 (◒ Barbican or Moorgate), is a vast urban development built on a large bomb site from WWII.

The original ambitious plan was to create a terribly smart, modern complex for offices, housing and the arts. Perhaps inevitably, the result was a forbidding series of wind tunnels with a dearth of shops, plenty of expensive high-rise apartments and an enormous cultural centre lost in the middle. Here you'll find the London home of the Royal Shakespeare Company, the London Symphony Orchestra and the London Classical Orchestra. There are also smaller theatrical auditoriums, the Museum of London and the wonderful **Barbican Art Gallery** (☎ 7588 9023) on Level 3, with among the best photographic exhibits in London. The hours vary for each exhibit, but be warned – even Londoners get to the Barbican early to make sure of finding their way to the right spot at the right time.

For details of the theatres and concert halls, see the Entertainment section.

Museum of London Despite it's unprepossessing setting amid the concrete walkways of the Barbican (look for gate 7), the Museum of London (Map 6; ☎ 7600 3699, 7600 0807 for a recording), London Wall EC2 (◒ Barbican), is one of the city's finest museums, showing how the city has evolved from the Ice Age to the Internet.

The sections on Roman Britain and Roman Londinium make use of the nearby ruins of a Roman fort discovered during road construction. Otherwise, the displays work steadily through the centuries, using audiovisual materials to show such events as the Great Fire of London.

Part of the museum's collection dealing with London's port and the Thames will be transferred to a new museum in the Docklands when it opens in 2001.

The museum opens 10 am to 5.50 pm Monday to Saturday and from noon on Sunday. Admission costs £5 (free for children). Tickets are valid for a year. The fine shop has a wide selection of fictional and factual accounts of London.

Tower of London One of London's three World Heritage Sites (the others are Westminster Abbey and its surrounding buildings and Maritime Greenwich), the Tower of London (Map 6; ☎ 7680 9004), Tower Hill EC3 (◒ Tower Hill), has dominated the south-eastern corner of the City of London since 1078 when William the Conqueror laid the first stone of the White Tower to replace the earth and timber castle he'd already built on the site.

In the early Middle Ages, the Tower of London acted not just as a royal residence but also as a treasury, a mint, an arsenal and a prison. After Henry VIII moved to Whitehall Palace in 1529, the Tower's role as a prison became increasingly important, with Thomas More, queens Anne Boleyn and Catherine Howard, and Lady Jane Grey just some of the most famous Tudor prisoners.

These days the Tower is visited by more than two million people a year, with impressive crowds even on cold winter afternoons. However, the queues move quickly.

Orientation The most striking building in the Tower is undoubtedly the huge **White Tower**, in the centre of the courtyard, with its solid Romanesque architecture and four turrets. It was whitewashed during the reign of Henry III and thus got its name. It now houses a collection from the Royal Armouries. On the 2nd floor is the **Chapel of St John the Evangelist**, which dates from 1080 and is therefore the oldest church in London.

Facing the White Tower to the north is the **Waterloo Barracks**, which now contains the Crown Jewels: orbs, sceptres and the centrepiece, the Imperial State Crown, set with diamonds (2868 of them to be exact), sapphires, emeralds, rubies and pearls.

Beside the Waterloo Barracks stands the **Chapel Royal of St Peter ad Vincula** (St Peter in Chains) – unfortunately, it can only be visited on a group tour or after 4.30 pm. It's a rare example of ecclesiastical Tudor architecture.

What looks quite a peaceful, picturesque corner of the Tower is in fact one of its most tragic. On the small green in front of the church stood the **scaffold**, set up during Henry VIII's reign and where seven people were beheaded. On it were executed his two allegedly adulterous wives, Anne Boleyn and Catherine Howard.

Beside Wakefield Tower stands the **Bloody Tower**, probably the best-known part of the complex. On the 1st floor you can see the windlass that controlled the portcullis, the grating that could be dropped down to guard the gateway. A 17th-century wooden screen separates it from a room where Sir Walter Raleigh was imprisoned and where he wrote his *History of the World* (a copy is on display).

Once called the Garden Tower, the Bloody Tower acquired its unsavoury nickname from the story that the 'princes in the Tower', Edward V and his younger brother, were murdered here. The blame is usually laid at the door of their uncle Richard III, but there are those who prefer to finger Henry VII for the crime.

Don't leave the Tower without taking a look at the stretch of green between the Wakefield and White Towers, where the Great Hall once stood. Here you'll find the Tower's famous ravens, the departure of whom, according to legend, would cause the White Tower to collapse. Their wings are clipped to avoid the problem.

Hours & Tickets The Tower opens 9 am to 6 pm Monday to Saturday and from 10 am on Sunday. It closes at 5 pm November to March. Last admission is an hour before closing. Entry costs £11/7.30.

Guided Tours Hugely entertaining, hour-long tours led by the Yeoman Warders, or 'Beefeaters', leave from the Middle Tower every 30 minutes from 9 am (from 10 am on Sunday) to 3.30 pm daily.

Tower Bridge Tower Bridge (Map 6; ☎ 7378 1928; ⊖ Tower Hill) was built in 1894 when London was still a thriving port and the bridge had to allow ships to pass

through. The bridge's walkways afford excellent views across the City and the Docklands.

For the **Tower Bridge Experience**, a lift takes you up from the modern visitors facility in the northern tower where the story of its building is recounted. It opens 10 am to 6.30 pm daily, April to October; and 9.30 am to 6 pm daily, November to March. Admission costs £6.25/4.25.

South of the Thames

As recently as a decade ago, the southern part of central London was the city's forgotten underside – run-down, neglected and offering little for visitors once they'd visited the South Bank arts venues. Recently, however, all that has changed and parts of London immediately south of the river can seem as exciting as anywhere farther north.

Bermondsey (Maps 1 & 6) Although parts of Bermondsey still look pretty dejected, there are pockets of refurbishment and even gentrification.

Design Museum The sparkling white Design Museum (Map 6; ☎ 7403 6933), 28 Shad Thames SE1 (⊖ Bermondsey or Tower Hill), has displays on how product design has evolved over time and how it can make the difference between success and failure for items intended for mass production. The galleries on the 2nd floor look at the past and future development in design of everyday things: from televisions and washing machines to chairs and tableware.

The museum opens 11.30 am to 6 pm daily. Admission costs £5.50/4. There's a coffee shop and gift shop, while the adjacent Blue Print Café offers sky-high river views and prices to match (see Bermondsey in the Places to Eat section).

Southwark (Maps 4 & 6) Originally settled by the Romans, Southwark (**suth**-erk) became an important thoroughfare for people travelling to London in the Middle Ages. For centuries London Bridge was the only place to cross the Thames.

Although Southwark is still pretty run-down it's on the up and up; some say it's London's new Left Bank. There are numerous sights to be found along the Thames in Bankside, an area that's home to popular destinations such as the new Tate Modern art gallery.

HMS Belfast HMS *Belfast* (Map 6; ☎ 7407 6328), Morgan's Lane, Tooley St SE1 (⊖ London Bridge), is a large, light cruiser built with 16 six-inch guns that was launched in 1938. It saw much action during WWII. It's now preserved by the Imperial War Museum. You can visit the ship 10 am to 6 pm daily, March to October (to 5 pm the rest of the year). Admission costs £5 (free for children).

London Dungeon Under the arches of London Bridge station, the London Dungeon (Map 6; ☎ 7403 7221), 28–34 Tooley St SE1 (⊖ London Bridge), is long on gore and short on substance. The reconstruction of the French guillotine in action is gruesome but doesn't hold a candle to the section dealing with Victorian serial killer Jack the Ripper. Kids, of course, love it.

The dungeon opens 10 am to 5.30 pm daily, October to March; 10 am to 6.30 pm daily, April to June and in September; and 10 am to 9 pm daily, July and August. Admission costs £9.95/6.50. Beware of touts selling fake tickets.

Southwark Cathedral There was already a church on this site in 1086, but it was rebuilt in 1106 and then for a third time in the 13th century. By the 1830s it had fallen into decay and much of what you see today is actually Victorian – the nave was rebuilt in 1897 – although the central tower dates from 1520 and the choir from the 13th century. In 1905 the old church became Southwark Cathedral (Map 6; ☎ 7407 3708), Montague Close SE1 (⊖ London Bridge), with its own bishop. It emerged from a major clean-up during 2000, complete with a new visitor centre.

There are monuments and details galore inside and it's worth picking up one of the small guides. On the choir floor are tablets marking the **tomb of Edmond Shakespeare**, actor-brother of the Bard, who died in 1607. Along the southern aisle of the nave, stop and look at the green alabaster **monument to William Shakespeare**, whose great works were originally written for the Bankside playhouses.

The cathedral opens 8 am to 6 pm daily. Admission is free although a £2.50 donation is requested. Evensong is sung at 5.30 pm on Tuesday and Friday, 4 pm on Saturday and 3 pm on Sunday.

Vinopolis – City of Wine Vinopolis (Map 6; ☎ 0870 444 4777), 1 Bank End, Park St SE1 (⊖ London Bridge), in a hectare of Victorian railway vaults in Bankside, cashes in on Londoners' love affair with things red, white and rosé. The high-tech exhibits introduce visitors to the history of wine-making and, more importantly, there are tastings of five wines as you tour. It opens 10 am to 5.30 pm daily (to 8 pm at the weekend) with last entry two hours before it closes. Admission costs £11.50/5 (children don't get any wine).

Globe Theatre & Exhibition The Globe Theatre (Map 6; ☎ 7401 9919), 21 New Globe Walk SE1 (⊖ London Bridge), consists of the reconstructed Globe Theatre and, beneath it, an exhibition focusing on Elizabethan London and the struggle by US actor (later film director) Sam Wanamaker to get the theatre rebuilt.

The original Globe (known as the 'Wooden O' after its circular shape and roofless centre) was erected in 1599. It was burned down in 1613 and was immediately rebuilt. In 1642 it was finally closed by the Puritans, who regarded theatres as dreadful dens of iniquity. The new Globe opened in 1997 and is meant to replicate the original, right down to the thatched roof and lack of seats for the 500 'groundlings', who stand to watch performances.

The Globe opens to visitors 10 am to 5 pm daily. A visit to the exhibition, which also includes a guided tour of the Globe Theatre itself (except on days with a matinee performance, when tours are in the morning only), costs £7.50/5. Performances run from mid-May to late September.

Tate Modern The vast Bankside Power Station, designed by Sir Giles Gilbert Scott after WWII but decommissioned in 1986, is home to Tate Modern (Maps 4 & 6; ☎ 7887 8000), Queen's Walk SE1 (⊖ Blackfriars or London Bridge), London's most popular new attraction. The collections cover art from 1900 in all of its many forms, from paintings to videos to bits of rock piled up on the floor.

The galleries are spread over five floors, all of which open onto the cavernous old **Turbine Hall**. The machinery is gone – although a piped-in hum recalls it – and in its place are some rather huge works of art, including a giant spider by Louise Bourgeois.

The policy of organising the works by theme (rather than ordering them chronologically, for example) has come in for much criticism; the *Evening Standard*'s art critic Brian Sewell called it 'shallow and capricious'. However, the curators have wisely placed the section titled 'Nude/ Action/Body' on the top gallery floor, which means that salacious hordes are drawn well into the building.

Tate Modern opens 10 am to 6 pm Sunday to Thursday and to 10 pm Friday and Saturday. It's free, although special exhibitions charge admission. The £1 audioguides are worthwhile for their descriptions of some of the works.

Millennium Bridge Of all the projects conceived to help usher in the third millennium, this footbridge (Map 6) over the Thames is arguably the most important to the people of London: it is beautiful and will do much to bring London back to the Thames, its birthplace, and link its two banks. Designed by the ubiquitous Sir Norman Foster to look like a 'blade of light', it links Tate Modern and Bankside with the City and St Paul's.

That said, the opening of the bridge in June 2000 turned into the cock-up of all cock-ups when – not surprisingly – mobs arrived to try it out. As the span filled with people it began rocking to such an extent that people had to clutch the rails and each other to keep from toppling over. It was promptly closed, even though it was generally agreed to be safe, albeit wobbly. Sadly, at the time of writing the bridge remained closed as the hand-wringing and finger-pointing continued.

The South Bank (Map 4) North of Waterloo station and across the Thames from Embankment tube station, the South Bank is a labyrinth of arts venues strung out on rain-stained concrete walkways from Hungerford Bridge to just beyond Waterloo Bridge. Almost no-one has a good word to say about the indescribably ugly architecture and a complete overhaul is on the cards so expect a lot of work to be going on here.

The **Royal Festival Hall** hosts classical, opera, jazz and choral music. Alongside a range of pricey cafes and restaurants and a good music shop, it also has a foyer where free recitals take place most evenings. The smaller **Queen Elizabeth Hall**, to the northeast, and the **Purcell Room** host similar concerts. A full-scale refurbishment of the Royal Festival Hall began in 1999.

Tucked almost out of sight under the arches of Waterloo Bridge is the **National Film Theatre**, built in 1958 and screening some 2000 films a year. The popular **Museum of the Moving Image** is closed for redevelopment until 2003.

The **Hayward Gallery** (☎ 7928 3144), Belvedere Rd SE1 (⊖ Waterloo), built in 1968, usually hosts blockbuster modern art exhibitions. Hours and prices for these vary. The **Royal National Theatre**, a love-it-or-hate-it complex of three theatres (Olivier, Lyttleton and Cottesloe), is the nation's flagship theatre.

Hungerford Bridge This once mundane railway bridge (⊖ Embankment or Charing Cross) linking Charing Cross station with south London was recently due to receive a long-overdue rehabilitation. The narrow but vital pedestrian walkway on the northern side was supposed to be replaced by two new dramatically suspended walkways on both sides of the bridge. But right after work began all sorts of engineering cock-ups occurred and at the time of writing the project was postponed indefinitely. For some reason London is having problems doing what the Romans had no problem accomplishing nearly 2000 years ago: bridging the Thames.

British Airways London Eye London's newest landmark and right on the Thames, the British Airways London Eye (⊖ Waterloo) is, at 135m tall, the world's largest Ferris wheel. It is a thrilling experience to be in one of the 32 enclosed glass gondolas, enjoying views across the capital of some 25 miles (40km) on (rare) clear days. The 'Millennium Wheel' (as it's also known) takes 30 minutes to rotate completely.

The wheel operates 9 am to 10 pm daily, April to October (10 am to 6 pm the rest of the year), but such is its popularity that the hours keep lengthening. Tickets cost £8.50/5. It's wise to plan ahead: you can order tickets in advance (☎ 0870 500 0600) for a set date and time and then pick them up before your ride. Alternatively you can buy tickets in person at the wheel; however, at the weekend and during summer, don't expect just to turn up and spin as the entire day is often sold out. For same-day riding you have to either show up before opening to nab some of the few same-day tickets sold, or avail yourself of a ticket-hawker (beware of fake tickets, huge mark-ups etc).

London Aquarium The London Aquarium (☎ 7967 8000), County Hall, Westminster Bridge Rd SE1 (⊖ Westminster or Waterloo), is one of the largest in Europe but curiously disappointing, partly because its location on three basement levels is so dark but also because the fish on display are generally of the less colourful variety. The new coral-reef display, however, is not bad. The aquarium opens 10 am to 6 pm daily. Admission costs £8/5.

Lambeth (Maps 1 & 4) Lambeth is the district immediately south of Westminster Bridge.

Imperial War Museum The Imperial War Museum (Map 1; ☎ 7416 5000), Lambeth Rd SE1 (⊖ Lambeth North), is housed in a striking building dating from 1815.

Although there's still plenty of military hardware on show, these days the museum places more emphasis on the social cost of war. This point is driven home in the **Holocaust Exhibition**, a heartbreaking permanent exhibition that opened in 2000. Artefacts and survivors' recollections are used to tell the story of the Nazis and the genocide they orchestrated. Little is held back and it is not recommended for those aged under 14. Get one of the free timed-admission tickets after you enter the museum.

Other exhibits are only a bit less grim and include the Blitz Experience and the WWI Trench Experience, which depicts the grim day-to-day existence of a WWI infantryman in a frontline trench on the Somme. In addition, there are always several special exhibits. The museum opens 10 am to 6 pm daily. Admission costs £5.50 (free for children, and for everyone after 4.30 pm).

Chelsea, South Kensington & Earl's Court (Map 7)

Much of west London is high-class territory; indeed, Kensington & Chelsea enjoys the highest average gross income of all London boroughs (over £485 a week). Go a bit farther west, though, and you'll reach Earl's Court and Barons Court, less prosperous areas that seem to have been dropped here by accident.

Thanks to the 1851 Great Exhibition, a huge display of technology, South Kensington is first and foremost museumland, boasting the Natural History, Science and Victoria & Albert Museums all on one road.

Victoria & Albert Museum The Victoria & Albert Museum (☎ 7942 2000), Cromwell Rd SW7 (⊖ South Kensington), universally known as 'the V&A', is a vast, rambling, wonderful museum of decorative art and design, part of Prince Albert's legacy to Londoners in the aftermath of the Great Exhibition.

Here you can see a mixed bag of ancient

Chinese ceramics and modernist architectural drawings, Korean bronze and Japanese swords, samples from William Morris' 19th-century Arts and Crafts movement, cartoons by Raphael and Asian watercolours, Rodin sculptures, gowns from the Elizabethan era and dresses straight from this year's Paris fashion shows, ancient jewellery, a 1930s wireless set, an all-wooden Frank Lloyd Wright study and a pair of Doc Martens. Think of it as the nation's attic.

Like the British Museum, this is one that needs careful planning if you're to get the most out of your visit. As soon as you're through the turnstile look at the floor plan and decide what you're most interested in; then stick to that plan unless you want to find the time has flown by and you're still inspecting the plaster casts of classical statues. See the boxed text on this page for the museum's highlights.

There are plans to open the new £31 million British Galleries by 2002. These will be a celebration of British design and will greatly expand the galleries. There's also a controversial scheme kicking about to build a bizarre new entrance based on spiral stairs.

The museum opens 10 am to 5.45 pm daily and also 6.30 to 9.30 pm on Wednesday. Admission costs £5/3. There are free

---

V&A Museum Highlights

- Raphael cartoons
- Music Room from Norfolk House
- Morris, Gamble and Poynter Refreshment Rooms
- Tippoo's tiger
- Shah Jahan's wine cup
- Throne of Maharaja Ranjit Singh
- Becket casket
- Ironwork Gallery
- *Board and Bear Hunt* tapestry
- Henry VIII's writing desk
- Burghley Nef
- Gloucester candlestick
- Pagoda
- Ardabil carpet

---

introductory tours of some of the museum's galleries lasting between one and 1½ hours between 10.30 am and 4.30 pm.

Natural History Museum The Natural History Museum (☎ 7938 9123), Cromwell Rd SW7 (✆ South Kensington), has collections divided between adjoining Life and Earth Galleries. Where once the former was full of dusty glass cases of butterflies and stick insects, there are now wonderful interactive displays on themes such as Human Biology and Creepy Crawlies. Plus there's the crowd-pulling exhibition on mammals and dinosaurs, which includes animatronic movers and shakers such as the 4m-high Tyrannosaurus Rex.

In some ways, though, it's the Earth Galleries that are the most staggering. Enter from Exhibition Rd and you'll find yourself facing an escalator that slithers up and into a hollowed-out globe. Upstairs there are two main exhibits: Earthquake and the Restless Surface, which explains how wind, water, ice, gravity and life itself impact on the earth.

The museum opens 10 am to 5.50 pm daily (from 11 am on Sunday). Admission costs £6.50 (free for children, and for everyone after 4.30 pm weekdays and after 5 pm at the weekend).

Science Museum The Science Museum (☎ 7942 4455), Exhibition Rd SW7 (✆ South Kensington), has had a complete makeover since the days when it was a rather dreary place for eggheads and reluctant school children. The ground floor looks back at the history of the Industrial Revolution via examples of its machinery and then looks forward to the exploration of space. There are interactive and fascinating exhibits on five floors dealing with aeroplanes, the impact of science on food, computers, the history of medicine and much more.

The new £50 million Wellcome Wing focuses on contemporary science, medicine and technology and includes a 450-seat IMAX cinema. The latest scientific breakthroughs will be presented and there is an ongoing, on-site study involving DNA titled 'What Am I?'

The museum opens 10 am to 6 pm daily. Admission costs £6.95 (free for under-17s, and for everyone after 4.30 pm).

Knightsbridge, Kensington & Holland Park (Map 3)

Knightsbridge is where you'll find some of London's best-known department stores, including Harrods and Harvey Nichols. To the west and north-west is Kensington, another thoroughly desirable London neighbourhood where you'll not get much change from a million pounds if you want to buy a sizeable house. Its main thoroughfare, Kensington High St, is another shoppers' paradise. Holland Park is another of London's priciest neighbourhoods.

Albert Memorial On the southern edge of Hyde Park facing Kensington Gore, the Albert Memorial (⊖ South Kensington or Gloucester Road) is an over-the-top monument to Queen Victoria's German husband Albert (1819–61), which was unwrapped in 1998 after an eight-year renovation costing £11 million.

Kensington Palace Sometime home to Princess Margaret and the late Diana, Princess of Wales, Kensington Palace (☎ 7937 9561), Kensington Gardens W8 (⊖ High Street Kensington), dates from 1605 when it was home to the 2nd Earl of Nottingham. Hour-long tours of the palace take you round the small, wood-panelled State Apartments dating from the time of William of Orange and the much grander, more spacious apartments of the Georgian period.

The **Sunken Garden** near the palace is at its prettiest in summer. Also nearby is **The Orangery**, designed by Hawksmoor and Sir John Vanbrugh and with carvings by Grinling Gibbons. Taking tea here is a pricey treat.

The State Apartments open 10 am to 5 pm daily. Admission costs £9.50/7.10. The park and gardens open 5 am to 30 minutes before dusk.

Leighton House Near Holland Park and Kensington but frequently overlooked is Leighton House (Map 7; ☎ 7602 3316), 12 Holland Park Rd W14 (⊖ Kensington Olympia or High Street Kensington), a gem of a house designed in 1866 by George Aitchison. It was once the home of Lord Leighton (1830–96), a painter who belonged to the Olympian movement and decorated parts of the house in Middle Eastern style. Finest of all the rooms is the exquisite **Arab Hall**, added in 1879 and densely covered with blue and green tiles from the Middle East. The house contains notable pre-Raphaelite paintings by Burne-Jones, Millais and Lord Leighton himself.

The house (free, donations welcome) opens 11 am to 5.30 pm Monday to Saturday.

Hyde Park & Notting Hill (Map 3)

The huge popularity of the Notting Hill Carnival (in late August) reflects the multicultural appeal of this area of west London. Notting Hill became a focus for immigrants from Trinidad in the 1950s. Today it's a thriving, vibrant corner of London separated from the West End by the expanse of Hyde Park. It also echoes with the footsteps of tourists drawn by the eponymous film.

Hyde Park At 145 hectares, Hyde Park is central London's largest open space. Expropriated from the Church by Henry VIII in 1536, it became a hunting ground for kings and aristocrats, and then a venue for duels, executions and horse racing. In 1851 the Great Exhibition was held here and during WWII it became an enormous potato field. More recently, it has served as a concert venue. The park is a riot of colour in spring, and full of lazy, milk-white to pink sunbathers in summer. Boating on the Serpentine is an option for the relatively energetic.

Along with sculptures by Henry Moore and Jacob Epstein, and the statue of Peter Pan by George Frampton, Hyde Park boasts its own art gallery. The **Serpentine Gallery** (☎ 7402 6075; ⊖ Hyde Park Corner or Lancaster Gate), beautifully located south of the lake and just west of the main road

LONDON

that cuts through the park, holds temporary exhibitions and specialises in contemporary art. It opens 10 am to 6 pm daily. Admission is free.

Near Marble Arch, **Speakers' Corner** (⊖ Marble Arch) started life in 1872 as a response to serious riots. Every Sunday anyone with a soapbox – or anything else to stand on – can hold forth on whatever subject takes their fancy. It's an entertaining experience.

Hyde Park opens 5.30 am to midnight daily.

Marble Arch In the north-eastern corner of Hyde Park is Marble Arch (⊖ Marble Arch), a huge arch designed by John Nash in 1827 that was moved here from in front of Buckingham Palace in 1851. There is actually a one-room flat inside.

Marylebone & Regent's Park (Maps 2, 3 & 4)

Marylebone Rd is north of Oxford St and home to the capital's No 1 tourist trap, Madame Tussaud's. It's also close to Regent's Park, which provides a haven of peace in the city and is home to London Zoo.

Wallace Collection The Wallace Collection (Map 4; ☎ 7935 0687), Hertford House, Manchester Square W1 (⊖ Bond Street), is London's finest small gallery and relatively unknown. It houses a treasure-trove of high-quality paintings from the 17th and 18th centuries – including works by Rubens, Titian, Poussin and Rembrandt – in a splendid Italianate mansion. Yet another recipient of National Lottery cash, parts of the house have been restored to their original splendour and new space has been created to display the entire reserve collection.

The collection opens 10 am to 5 pm daily (from 2 pm on Sunday) and admission is free. Free guided tours take place daily; phone for the exact times.

Madame Tussaud's Madame Tussaud's (Map 3; ☎ 7935 6861), Marylebone Rd NW1 (⊖ Baker Street), lures in some 2.7 million visitors a year to see its waxworks.

In order to avoid the long queues (particularly in summer), arrive early in the morning or late in the afternoon or – better still – don't go.

Much of Madame Tussaud's is made up of the **Garden Party** exhibition where you can have your picture taken alongside stars-of-the-moment. (The heads of those whose 15 minutes of fame have passed are kept in a cupboard just in case their star ever rises again.) The **Grand Hall** is where you'll find models of world leaders past and present and the royal family.

It opens 10 am to 5.30 pm weekdays and from 9.30 am at the weekend. Admission costs £11/7.50. A combined ticket allowing entry to the London Planetarium as well costs £13.95/9.

London Planetarium Attached to Madame Tussaud's, the London Planetarium (Map 3) presents 30-minute spectaculars on the stars and planets livened up with special effects. The hours are the same as for Madame Tussaud's. Admission costs £6.30/4.20.

Regent's Park Regent's Park (Maps 1 & 2; ⊖ Baker Street or Regent's Park), north of Marylebone and south-west of Camden, was, like many other London parks, once used as a royal hunting ground, subsequently farmed and then revived as a place for fun and leisure during the 18th century.

Today, the roses in **Queen Mary's Gardens** (Map 2) are particularly spectacular and there's live Shakespeare performed in the summer. Phone ☎ 7486 2431 for more information.

London Zoo One of the oldest zoos in the world, London Zoo (Map 2; ☎ 7722 3333), Regent's Park NW1 (⊖ Camden Town), is – like the London Underground – a victim of its great age; it was founded in 1828. The zoo is saddled with many buildings that are historically interesting but don't meet the expectations of animal-rights-minded modern visitors. After a long period in the doldrums, the zoo has embarked on a 10-year, £21-million program to prepare it for the third millennium. The emphasis is now firmly on conservation and education, with fewer species kept, wherever possible in breeding groups.

The zoo opens 10 am to 5.30 pm daily March to October and to 4 pm the rest of the year. Admission costs £8.50/6.

NORTH LONDON

The northern reaches of central London stretch in a broad arc from St John's Wood in the west to Islington in the east. Those two districts exemplify the great economic divide that exists in the capital: the former is all moneyed gentility, the latter the run-down opposite in areas around Angel, where less than 10% of the area is open public space. In between, Regent's Park and its Primrose Hill northerly extension offer the largest expanse of greenery. The Grand Union (Regent's) Canal winds round the north of the park, offering a pleasant way to avoid the traffic en route to Camden Market. North London's other main attractions include Hampstead Heath, where it's as easy to forget you're in a big city as it is to get completely lost.

Euston & King's Cross (Map 2)

Euston Rd links Euston train station to St Pancras and King's Cross stations. This is not an especially inviting area to visit although it's one that you're likely to pass through en route to or from the north of England.

British Library After 15 years and £500 million (the most expensive building in the UK after the Millennium Dome), the British Library (☎ 7412 7000), 96 Euston Rd NW1 (✆ King's Cross St Pancras), opened its doors in 1998. It is the nation's principal copyright library and stocks one copy of every British publication as well as historical manuscripts, books and maps from the British Museum.

Although most of the complex is devoted to storage and scholarly research (access is limited and there is a stringent application procedure), there are some public displays. Subtitled 'Treasures of the British Library',

the **John Ritblat Gallery** spans almost three millennia and every continent. Among the most important documents here are the Magna Carta (1215); the Sherborne Missal (1400–07); a Gutenberg Bible (1455); Shakespeare's First Folio (1623); manuscripts by some of Britain's best-known authors (eg Lewis Carroll, Jane Austen, George Eliot and Thomas Hardy); and *Summer Is Icumen In*, the earliest known example of poetry in English (13th century).

The British Library opens to visitors 9.30 am to 6 pm weekdays (to 8 pm on Tuesday), 9.30 am to 5 pm on Saturday and 11 am to 5 pm on Sunday. Admission is free.

Camden (Map 2)

From Euston station you can walk up Eversholt St to Camden, a tourist mecca that is especially lively at the weekend. In just over 20 years **Camden Market** has developed into London's most visited 'unticketed' tourist attraction, with some 10 million visitors a year. What started out as a collection of attractive craft stalls by Camden Lock on the Grand Union Canal now extends most of the way between Camden Town and Chalk Farm tube stations.

Hampstead

Perched on a hill 4 miles (6km) north of the City, Hampstead is an exclusive suburb, attached to an enormous, rambling heath, that just about gets away with calling itself a village.

Hampstead Heath Hampstead Heath (✆ Hampstead; Gospel Oak or Hampstead Heath station) covers 320 hectares, most of it woods, hills and meadows, and is home to some one hundred species of bird. Some sections of the heath are laid out for sports such as football and cricket. Walk up Parliament Hill or the hill in North Wood, and on a clear day you'll see Canary Wharf and beyond.

Kenwood House This magnificent neoclassical mansion (☎ 8348 1286), Hampstead Lane NW3 (✆ Archway or Golders Green, then bus No 210), on the northern side of the heath, was remodelled by Robert Adam from 1764 to 1779. It is crammed with paintings by Gainsborough, Reynolds, Turner, Lely, Hals, Vermeer and Van Dyck. It is arguably the finest small collection of European art in London. It opens 10 am to 6 pm daily, April to September, closing at 5 pm in March and October and 4 pm the rest of the year. Admission is free.

EAST LONDON

The eastern reaches of central London are taken up by the East End – the London of old Hollywood films and Christmas pantomimes – and the sprawl of the Docklands, where the shockingly new is fast replacing the old and decaying.

East End (Maps 1 & 6)

The East End districts of Shoreditch, Hoxton, Spitalfields and Whitechapel may lie within walking distance of the City, but the change of pace and style is extraordinary. Traditionally this was working-class London, an area settled by wave upon wave of immigrants, giving it a curious mixture of Irish, French Huguenot, Bangladeshi and Jewish culture, all of which can still be felt to varying degrees today. Run-down and neglected in the early 1980s, the East End is starting to look up in places, especially in Spitalfields, where it rubs right up against the City and Liverpool Street station; in the *nouveau* trendy district of Hoxton, including Hoxton Square; and in the area around Old St.

For anyone interested in modern, multicultural London, it's well worth venturing a look at the East End.

The Docklands

The Port of London was once the world's greatest port, the hub of the British Empire and its enormous global trade. In the 16th century there were 20 cargo quays to the east of London. By the 18th and 19th centuries these were hard-pressed to cope with the quantity of cargo flowing through, and new docks were opened throughout the 19th century. But after the Blitz of WWII the docks were in no state to cope with the post-war technological and political changes as the Empire evaporated. From the mid-1960s dock closures followed each other as fast as they had opened.

In 1981 the London Docklands Development Corporation (LDDC) was set up to rejuvenate the area by encouraging new office and housing development. The builders moved in and the Docklands Light Railway (DLR) was built to link the area with the rest of London.

When the recession of the early 1990s hit, the Docklands' bubble burst. Offices stood empty, people lost their jobs, flats wouldn't sell and shopping arcades emptied as trendy shops hung up 'For Sale' signs. Over it all towered the flagship development of Canary Wharf on the Isle of Dogs, bankrupted by the recession and falling property prices.

Things have turned round since then and buildings are full of tenants and more are going up. The Docklands' Achilles heel, transportation, has been largely solved through expansion of the DLR and the building of the Jubilee Line extension on the Underground.

Things to See A ride on the DLR towards Greenwich will take you over and through the heart of the Docklands. **Canary Wharf** is dominated by Cesar Pelli's 500m-high **tower** (1991), described as a 'square prism with a pyramidal top'. **Cabot Square**, at the centre of the Canary Wharf complex, features a shopping centre and hosts arts and cultural events. Sir Norman Foster's Jubilee Line tube station is very impressive.

The Museum of London plans to open a **Docklands Museum**, focusing on the history of the Thames, its port and its industries, in 2001. Phone ☎ 7600 3699 for an update on the museum's progress. There are also plans for a new visitor centre in Sugar House, a 19th-century warehouse at **West India Quay**, to the north of Canary Wharf.

The last DLR station on the Isle of Dogs is **Island Gardens**, from where there are exquisite views of Greenwich's architectural heritage. If you'd like to carry on south to Greenwich, take the DLR to Cutty Sark station or, alternatively, use the historic 390m-long **foot tunnel** running under the Thames.

SOUTH LONDON

Greenwich is a south London highlight for many. Brixton, with its colourful market, is another fine stop.

Greenwich (Map 9)

Packed with splendid architecture, Greenwich has strong connections with the sea, science, sovereigns and – of course – time.

Greenwich (**gren**-itch) lies to the southeast of central London, where the Thames widens and deepens, and there's a sense of space that is rare in the city. Quaint and village-like, and boasting the magnificent *Cutty Sark* clipper ship and the fabulous National Maritime Museum, Greenwich is a delightful place that has been on Unesco's list of World Heritage Sites since 1997. A trip there will be one of the highlights of any visit to London, and you should certainly allow a day to do it justice.

Greenwich is home to an extraordinary interrelated cluster of classical buildings; all the great architects of the Enlightenment made their mark here, largely due to royal patronage. Henry VIII and his daughters Mary and Elizabeth were all born here. Charles II was particularly fond of the area and had Sir Christopher Wren build both the Royal Observatory and part of the Royal Naval College, which John Vanbrugh then completed in the early 17th century.

Information The TIC (☎ 8858 6376, fax 8853 4607), 46 Greenwich Church St SE10, opens 10 am to 5 pm daily.

A Greenwich Passport ticket covers admission to the three main sights – the *Cutty Sark*, National Maritime Museum and Royal Observatory – for £12/2.50. It can be purchased at any of those sights. Unless indicated otherwise, most Greenwich sights are free for children.

Cutty Sark The *Cutty Sark* clipper ship (☎ 8858 3445) is in Cutty Sark Gardens at the top of King William Walk, right beside Greenwich Pier. It was the fastest ship that

had ever sailed the seven seas when launched in 1869.

You can stroll on the decks, check out the progress of the ongoing restoration and then read up on the history below deck and inspect maritime prints, paintings and the world's largest collection of ship's figureheads in the hold.

It opens 10 am to 5 pm daily. Admission costs £3.50/2.50.

Gipsy Moth IV Just next to the *Cutty Sark* is *Gipsy Moth IV* (☎ 8858 3445), the 16m-long sailing ketch in which Sir Francis Chichester made the world's first single-handed circumnavigation of the globe (1966–67). Chichester was 64 at the time and endured 226 days in this bathtub-sized craft. Unfortunately visitors are no longer allowed on board.

Old Royal Naval College If you walk south along King William Walk from the *Cutty Sark* you'll come to the entrance of the Old Royal Naval College (☎ 8858 2154) on the left. This Wren masterpiece has been largely taken over by the University of Greenwich since the Royal Navy baled out in 1998, but visitors are allowed to view the fabulous **Painted Hall** and the **Chapel** in the buildings on the southern side. They open 10 am to 5 pm daily (from 12.30 pm on Sunday) and admission costs £5.

National Maritime Museum Farther south along King William Walk, you'll come to the National Maritime Museum (☎ 8312 6565), Romney Rd SE10, a massive collection of boats, maps, charts, uniforms and marine art designed to tell the long and convoluted history of Britain as a seafaring nation.

As part of a major redevelopment, Neptune Court, the brightly lit central courtyard, has been covered with a huge single-span glass roof to provide easy access to some 16 new themed galleries on two of the museum's three levels. The galleries have interactive displays and video art that focus on such things as marine ecology and the future of the sea, the tea trade and slavery, and imperialism and white settlement. Don't miss the Nelson section, including his tunic with a hole from the bullet that killed him (they also have the bullet on display).

The museum opens 10 am to 5 pm daily. Admission costs £7.50.

Queen's House The Palladian Queen's House (☎ 8858 4422) is attached to the National Maritime Museum on its eastern side. Inigo Jones started work on the house in 1616, but it wasn't completed until 1635. It's been restored to a representation of how it might have looked and opens 10 am to 5 pm daily. Admission costs £7.50.

Royal Observatory In 1675 Charles II had the Royal Observatory (☎ 8858 4422) built on a hill in the middle of Greenwich Park, intending that astronomy be used to establish longitude at sea. The preserved rooms are intriguing and you can see the actual timepieces described in Dava Sobel's *Longitude*, the best-selling book about the fascinating quest to measure longitude. You can place one foot either side of the meridian line and straddle the two hemispheres. It opens 10 am to 5 pm daily. Admission costs £6.

Getting There & Away Greenwich is now most easily accessible on the DLR; Cutty Sark is the station closest to the TIC and most of the sights.

There are fast, cheap trains from Charing Cross to Greenwich station via London Bridge about every 15 minutes. Maze Hill station is more convenient for most of the sights than Greenwich station.

The most pleasant way to get to/from Greenwich if the weather is fine is by boat. Westminster Passenger Services Association (☎ 7930 4097) operates boats between Westminster Pier (Map 4) and Greenwich. There are departures every 30 minutes to one hour daily. The one-way fare is £6.30/3.30 and the trip takes 50 minutes. Return fares are £7.60/3.80.

Catamaran Cruisers (☎ 7987 1185) operates between Embankment Pier (Map 5) and Greenwich via Tower Pier (Map 6). There are departures every 30 minutes to

one hour daily and the trip lasts an hour. The return fare is £8/5.

Around Greenwich

Millennium Dome The Millennium Dome (☎ 0870 606 2000; ✪ North Greenwich), which opened on the first day of 2000, garnered almost as many column inches of coverage in the newspapers as visitors. Hugely controversial from the beginning, it cost upwards of £1 billion; an astonishing sum given that visitors to its vaguely educational displays most often rated it as merely 'enjoyable'.

A huge construction designed by Richard Rogers and with the largest roof in the world, at the time of writing the Dome's future was in the hands of future investors. However, just finding future investors has been a problem as every time a potential investor sees the Dome's books, they run off in fright.

The Dome gobbled up millions more pounds of National Lottery cash limping to the end of 2000. What the future holds for it is highly uncertain.

Dulwich

Tucked away in the wide expanse of south London that the tube fails to reach, Dulwich (**dull**-itch) is a leafy, quiet suburb with some fine architecture and an air of gentility.

Dulwich Picture Gallery Sir John Soane designed the Dulwich Picture Gallery (☎ 8693 5254), College Rd SE21 (North Dulwich station), the country's oldest public art gallery, in 1811 to house paintings collected by dealer Noel Desenfans and painter Francis Bourgeois. Perhaps uniquely, the gallery doubles as this august pair's mausoleum, lit by a moody *lumière mystérieuse* created with stained glass. The gallery, which has emerged from a £9 million refurbishment and extension, contains masterpieces by Rembrandt, Rubens, Reynolds, Gainsborough, Lely and others. Temporary exhibitions by modern artists generally get more space.

The gallery opens 10 am to 5 pm Tuesday to Friday, and at the weekend from 11 am.

Admission costs £3/1.50 (£5 for special exhibitions) but is free on Friday. To get there from North Dulwich station, turn left out of the station, cross over East Dulwich Grove and walk down Dulwich Village until the road divides. Take the left fork (College Rd); the entrance is on the right, opposite Dulwich Park.

Brixton (Map 1)

After WWII immigrants from the West Indies settled in Brixton giving it a palpable Caribbean flavour that can still be found in the exotic fruits and vegetables on sale at Brixton Market (see the Shopping section later). Whatever edge is left from the dark days of the 1980s when there were riots has only added to the excitement of the nightlife, which like the district itself is being tempered by ongoing gentrification.

Wimbledon

This leafy southern suburb will be forever associated in most minds with the lawn tennis championships that have been taking place here every June since 1877. The rest of the year you can still visit the Wimbledon Lawn Tennis Museum. Wimbledon Common is a great place for a picnic.

Wimbledon Lawn Tennis Museum

This museum (☎ 8946 6131), Gate 4, Church Rd SW19 (⊖ Southfields or Wimbledon Park), is for real tennis fans, dwelling as it does on the minutiae of the history of tennis playing, traced back here to the invention of the all-important lawn-mower in 1830 and of the India-rubber ball in the 1850s.

It opens 10.30 am to 5 pm Tuesday to Saturday and from 2 pm on Sunday. During the tournament the museum only opens to those attending the event. Admission costs £4/3. There's a tea room and a shop selling all kinds of tennis memorabilia.

Down House

Charles Darwin, the great Victorian evolutionary theorist, lived at Down House (☎ 01689-859119; EH), Luxted Rd, Downe, near Orpington, Kent, for over 40 years.

The stunning Victorian interior of this fine Georgian house has been restored to show his study, where he wrote the seminal *On the Origin of Species* (1859), to best effect. Temporary exhibitions are housed upstairs, and you can also explore the garden.

Down House opens 10 am to 6 pm Wednesday to Sunday, mid-April to September, to 5 pm in October, and to 4 pm during the rest of the year, except in January when it is closed. Admission costs £5.50/2.80 for adults/children.

Though it has a Kent postal address, Down House is in south-east London. To get there take a train from Victoria to Bromley South and then catch bus No 146.

WEST LONDON
The Wetlands Centre

One of the most interesting natural areas in or near London is this bird sanctuary near the Thames in Barnes. Run by the Wildfowl & Wetlands Trust, the Wetlands Centre (☎ 8409 4400), Queen Elizabeth's Walk SW13 (⊖ Hammersmith; Barnes station), is built on the site of some old reservoirs and boasts a variety of habitats within its 42 hectares. There is an excellent visitor centre as well as viewing areas and some fine interpretative trails. Over 130 species of bird regularly stop by.

It opens 9.30 am to 6 pm (to 5 pm October to March) and is closed to nonmembers on Sunday. Admission is £6.50/4. From the tube, take the No 283 'Duck Bus'; from Barnes station, it's a 1-mile walk north along Rocks Lane, or you can catch bus No 33 or 72.

Chiswick

Despite the abomination of the A4, which cuts off the riverside roads from the centre, Chiswick (**chiz**-ick) is still a pleasant suburb, with cafes and restaurants with pavement tables on Chiswick High Rd.

Chiswick House Chiswick House (☎ 8995 0508; EH), Chiswick Park W4 (⊖ Turnham Green), is a fine Palladian pavilion with an octagonal dome and colonnaded portico. It was designed by the 3rd Earl of Burlington

(1694–1753) when he returned from his grand tour of Italy, fired up with enthusiasm for all things Roman. Lord Burlington used it to entertain friends and to house his library and art collection.

Inside, some of the rooms have been completely restored to a grandeur some will find overpowering. The dome of the main salon has been left ungilded and the walls are decorated with eight enormous paintings.

Chiswick House opens 10 am to 6 pm daily, April to September, closing at 5 pm in October; and 10 am to 4 pm Wednesday to Sunday, November to March. Admission costs £3/1.50 (free for EH members).

The house is about a mile from the tube station, but bus No E3 from under the bridge outside the station will drop you nearby.

Hogarth's House Robbed of its setting by the thundering traffic on the A4, Hogarth's House (☎ 8994 6757), Hogarth Lane, Great West Rd W4 (☻ Turnham Green), nevertheless offers an opportunity to see inside a small 18th-century house.

William Hogarth lived here from 1749 to 1764 and although very little original furniture remains, the pistachio-coloured walls are decorated with his evocatively titled engravings of life in Georgian London (see the boxed text 'Of Rakes & Harlots: Hogarth's World').

The house (free) opens 1 to 5 pm Tuesday to Friday and to 6 pm at the weekend, closing an hour earlier November to March.

Kew Gardens

The Royal Botanic Gardens (☎ 8332 5000), Kew Rd, Kew (☻ Kew Gardens), is one of the most visited sights on the London tourist itinerary, which means it can get very crowded during summer, especially at the weekend. Spring is probably the best time to visit, but at any time of year this 120-hectare expanse of lawns, formal gar-

---

Of Rakes & Harlots: Hogarth's World

William Hogarth (1697–1764) was an artist and engraver who specialised in satire and moralising on the wages of sin. His plates were so popular in his day that they were actually pirated, leading Parliament to pass the Hogarth Act of 1735 to protect copyright. They provide us with an invaluable look at life (particularly among the lowly) in Georgian London. They are also generally quite delightful and are loaded with detail.

The *Marriage à la Mode* series satirises the wantonness and marriage customs of the upper classes and features a pathetic couple whose marriage of convenience ends in suicide and death. *Gin Lane* was produced as part of a campaign to have gin distillation made a crime (as it became under the Gin Act of 1751). It shows drunkards lolling about in the parish of St Giles, with the church of St George's Bloomsbury clearly visible in the background. In contrast, life on *Beer Street* is good and prosperity reigns. Beer was thought to be good for people and this was Hogarth's effort to encourage consumption.

His eight-plate series *The Harlot's Progress* traces the life of a country lass from her arrival in London to imprisoned whore; some of the plates are set in Drury Lane. In *The Rake's Progress*, the debauched protagonist is seen at one stage being entertained in a Russell St tavern by a bevy of prostitutes, one of whom strokes his chest while the other relieves him of his pocket watch. The women's faces are covered with up to half a dozen beauty marks, which were all the rage at the time. By the last frame the lad has lost his mind.

Hogarth's works have mostly remained in London. *Marriage à la Mode* can be found in the National Gallery, *Gin Lane* and *Beer Street* (see the special section 'Pubs') in Hogarth's House, *The Harlot's Progress* in the British Museum and *The Rake's Progress* in Sir John Soane's Museum. Tate Britain is also home to a range of Hogarth's work.

dens and greenhouses has delights to offer. Don't miss the enormous **Palm House**, a hothouse of metal and curved sheets of glass that houses all sorts of exotic tropical greenery. The stunning **Princess of Wales Conservatory** houses plants in 10 different computer-controlled climatic zones – everything from a desert to a cloud forest.

Kew Gardens opens at 9.30 am daily but closes at different times throughout the year: from 4.30 to 7.30 pm depending on the season. Admission costs £5/2.50.

In addition to the tube, Kew can be reached by Westminster Passenger Services Association river boat (☎ 7930 2062) from Westminster Pier (Map 4) from April to September, with reduced sailings in October. The boats depart several times a day and take about 1½ hours. Single tickets cost £7/3 and returns £11/7.

Hampton Court Palace

Hampton Court (☎ 8781 9500; Hampton Court station) was the favourite palace of Henry VIII, who expanded it with a passion. By 1540 it was one of the grandest and most sophisticated palaces in Europe. In the late 17th century, William and Mary employed Sir Christopher Wren to build extensions. The result is a beautiful blend of Tudor and 'restrained Baroque' architecture.

Today the palace is England's largest and grandest Tudor structure, knee-deep in history and with superb gardens and a famous 300-year-old maze. You should set aside plenty of time to do it justice, bearing in mind that if you come by boat from central London the trip will have eaten up half the day already. Among the highlights are **Henry VIII's State Apartments**, including the Great Hall, the largest single room in the palace; the **Tudor Kitchens**, which could rustle up meals for a royal household of some 1200 people; the wonderful **gardens**; and the **maze**.

Hampton Court Palace opens 9.30 am (from 10.15 am on Monday) to 6 pm daily, mid-March to October. It closes at 4.30 pm the rest of the year. An all-inclusive ticket costs £10.50/7.

There are trains every 30 minutes from Waterloo to Hampton Court station. The palace can also be reached by Westminster Passenger Services Association river boat (☎ 7930 2062) from Westminster Pier (Map 4) to Hampton Court Pier via Kew April to September, with reduced sailings in October. Ferries depart at 10.30 am, 11.15 am and noon and take about 3½ hours. One-way tickets cost £10/4 and returns £14/7.

Osterley Park & House

Run by the National Trust (NT) and set in 120 hectares of landscaped park and farmland, Osterley House (☎ 8568 7714) started life in 1575 as the country retreat of Thomas Gresham, the man responsible for the Royal Exchange, but was extensively remodelled in the 18th century by Robert Adam. The wonderful plasterwork, furniture and paintings are all well worth seeing, but many people rate the downstairs kitchen as being even more interesting.

It opens 1 to 4.30 pm Wednesday to Sunday, April to October, and admission costs £4.20/2.10 (free for NT members; family £10.50). A discount for Travelcard-holders encourages people to arrive by public transport. The park, with its ornamental lake, opens 9 am to sunset and entry is free. To get there from Osterley tube station, walk along the Great West Rd and turn left into Thornbury Rd, which will bring you to the park entrance.

ORGANISED TOURS

The Original London Sightseeing Tour (☎ 8877 1722), the Big Bus Company (☎ 7233 9533) and London Pride Sightseeing (☎ 7520 2050) offer tours of the main sights on double-decker buses that allow you either to go straight round without getting off or to hop on and off along the way. They're all expensive (around £12) and probably only worth considering if you're only going to be in London for a day or two. All of the companies mentioned above can sell you advance tickets to the biggest attractions to save wasting time in queues.

Convenient starting points are in Trafalgar

Square in front of the National Gallery; in front of the Trocadero on Coventry St between Leicester Square and Piccadilly Circus; and in Wilton Gardens opposite Victoria train station.

London Pride Sightseeing includes the Docklands and Greenwich in one of its tours, while the Original London Sightseeing Tour has an express tour for those with limited time.

River trips are always recommended; see the Greenwich, Kew Gardens and Hampton Court Palace sections earlier in the chapter as well as the later Getting Around section.

PLACES TO STAY

Wherever you stay in London accommodation is going to take a great wad out of your pocket. Demand can outstrip supply – especially at the bottom end of the market – so it's worth booking at least a few nights' accommodation before arriving, particularly in July and August. Remember too that single rooms are in short supply, and places are reluctant to let a double room to one person, even during quiet periods, without charging a hefty supplement or even the full double rate.

Booking Offices

It's possible to make same-day accommodation bookings for free at most of the TICs. The telephone bookings hotline (open 8.30 am to 6 pm Monday to Friday) is ☎ 7604 2890 and charges £5 per booking. The British Hotel Reservation Centre (☎ 0800 282888) on the main concourse of Victoria train station opens 6 am to 11.30 pm and charges £3 per booking.

The YHA operates its own central reservations system (☎ 7373 3400, fax 7373 3455, e lonres@yha.org.uk). Although you still pay the individual hostel directly, the staff will know what beds are available where and when.

If you want to stay in a B&B, bookings for a minimum of three days can be made free through London Homestead Services (☎ 8949 4455, fax 8549 5492), Coombe Wood Rd, Kingston-upon-Thames KT2 7JY. London Bed & Breakfast Agency Ltd

(☎ 7586 2768, fax 7586 6567, e stay@ londonbb.com), 71 Fellows Rd, London NW3 3JY, specialises in central London.

Places to Stay – Budget

Camping Camping is not a realistic option in the centre of the capital but there are a few possibilities within striking distance.

Tent City Hackney (☎ 8985 7656, Millfields Rd E5; Hackney Central station, then bus No 236 or 276). In north-east London, Tent City Hackney has a hostel tent with 90 beds and 200 tent pitches for £5 per person. It opens June to August.

Abbey Wood Caravan Park (☎ 8311 7708, fax 8311 6007, Federation Rd SE2; Abbey Wood station). South of the river and east of Greenwich, Abbey Wood has 360 pitches and opens year round. Tent/caravan pitches cost £2/8.50 plus £4/1.20 per adult/child. Electricity costs £1.50.

YHA/HI Hostels Seven hostels in the central London area are members of Hostelling International (HI), known as the Youth Hostels Association (YHA) in England.

The YHA hostels in central London can get very crowded in summer. All the hostels take advance credit-card bookings by phone and will hold some beds for those who show up on the day (arrive early and be prepared to queue). Most offer 24-hour access, facilities for self-catering and relatively cheap meals (eg, £3.20 for a full English or continental breakfast, £3.50 for a large packed lunch, £4.70 for a three-course evening meal).

City of London (Map 4; ☎ 7236 4965, fax 7236 7681, e city@yha.org.uk, 36 Carter Lane EC4; ✪ St Paul's). This excellent hostel (193 beds) stands in the shadow of St Paul's Cathedral. Rooms have mainly two, three or four beds though there are a dozen rooms with five to eight beds. There's a licensed cafeteria but no kitchen. Rates are £23.50/19.90 for adults/under-18s. Remember: this part of town is pretty quiet outside working hours.

Earl's Court (Map 7; ☎ 7373 7083, fax 7835 2034, e earlscourt@yha.org.uk, 38 Bolton Gardens SW5; ✪ Earl's Court). This hostel (154 beds) is a Victorian town house in a shabby, though lively, part of town. Rooms are mainly 10-bed dorms with communal showers. There's a cafe, a kitchen for self-catering and a small garden courtyard for summer barbecues. B&B rates are £18.50/16.60 for adults/under-18s.

Hampstead Heath (☎ 8458 9054, fax 8209 0546, ℮ *hampstead@yha.org.uk, 4 Wellgarth Rd NW11;* ✆ *Golders Green).* This hostel (190 beds) has a beautiful setting with a well-kept garden, although it's rather isolated. The dormitories are comfortable and each room has a washbasin. There's a licensed cafe and a kitchen. Rates are £19.90/17.70 for adults/under-18s.

Holland House (*Map 3;* ☎ *7937 0748, fax 7376 0667,* ℮ *hollandhouse@yha.org.uk, Holland Walk W8;* ✆ *High Street Kensington).* This hostel (201 beds) is built into the Jacobean wing of Holland House in the middle of Holland Park. It's large, very busy and rather institutional, but the position can't be beaten. There's a cafe and kitchen. Rates are £20.50/18.50 for adults/under-18s.

Oxford St (*Map 5;* ☎ *7734 1618, fax 7734 1657,* ℮ *oxfordst@yha.org.uk, 14 Noel St W1;* ✆ *Oxford Circus or Tottenham Court Road).* This most central of the hostels (75 beds) is basic but clean and welcoming. It has a large kitchen but no meals are served apart from breakfast (£2.30). Rates are £21.50/17.50 for adults/under-18s in rooms with three or four beds and £22 per person in twin rooms, which make up the majority.

Rotherhithe (*Map 1;* ☎ *7232 2114, fax 7237 2919,* ℮ *rotherhithe@yha.org.uk, 20 Salter Rd SE16;* ✆ *Rotherhithe).* The YHA flagship hostel (320 beds) in London was purpose-built in 1993. It's right by the River Thames and recommended, but the location is a bit remote and quiet. Most rooms have four or six beds, though there are also 22 doubles (four of them adapted for disabled visitors); all have an attached bathroom. There's a bar and restaurant as well as kitchen facilities and a laundry. B&B rates are £23.50/19.90 for adults/under-18s.

St Pancras International (*Map 2;* ☎ *7388 9998, fax 7388 6766,* ℮ *stpancras@yha.org.uk, 79-81 Euston Rd NW1;* ✆ *King's Cross St Pancras).* This central place has 152 beds. The area isn't great, but the hostel itself is up-to-date, with kitchen, restaurant, lockers, cycle shed and lounge. Rates are £23.50/19.90 for adults/under-18s (or £25/26.50 per person for a twin/premium room).

Independent Hostels

London's independent hostels tend to be more relaxed and cheaper than the YHA ones though standards can be pretty low; some of the places are downright grotty.

Most hostels have at least three or four bunk beds jammed into each small room, a kitchen and some kind of lounge. Some have budget restaurants and a bar attached. Be careful with your possessions and deposit your valuables in the office safe, safe-deposit box or secure locker if provided. Check that fire escapes and stairwells are accessible.

Ashlee House (*Map 2;* ☎ *7833 9400, fax 7833 9677,* ℮ *ashleehouse@tsnxt.co.uk, 261-265 Gray's Inn Rd WC1;* ✆ *King's Cross St Pancras).* This hostel is a clean and well maintained backpackers' hostel on three floors close to King's Cross station. Dorm rooms (most with bunks) can be very cramped, but there's double-glazing on the windows, a laundry and a decent-sized kitchen. Rooms with between four and 16 beds cost £15 per person in the low season and £19 in the high season. There are a few twins for £44 (£48).

Barmy Badger Backpackers (*Map 7;* ☎/fax *7370 5213,* ℮ *barmy_badger.b@virgin.net, 17 Longridge Rd SW5;* ✆ *Earl's Court).* This place is a basic dormitory with dorm beds from £13 per person, including breakfast. Twins without/with facilities cost £32/34. There's a big kitchen and safe-deposit boxes.

Court Hotel (*Map 7;* ☎ *7373 0027, fax 7912 9500, 194-196 Earl's Court Rd SW5;* ✆ *Earl's Court).* This place is under Australasian management and has well-equipped kitchens and TVs in most rooms. Dorm beds cost £13, singles/doubles are £30/40 a night.

The Generator (*Map 2;* ☎ *7388 7666, fax 7388 7644,* ℮ *generator@lhdr.demon.co.uk, Compton Place, 37 Tavistock Place WC1;* ✆ *Russell Square).* This is one of the grooviest budget places in central London and the futuristic decor looks like an updated set from Terry Gilliam's film *Brazil.* Along with 207 rooms (830 beds), it has a bar open to 2 am, a large lounge for eating, watching TV or playing pool, a room with Internet kiosks, safe-deposit boxes and a large eating area, but no kitchen. Depending on the season, a place in a dorm with seven or eight beds costs £15 to £20 and with three to six beds £19 to £22. Singles are £38 while twins are £45 to £48. All prices include breakfast.

International Students House (*Map 2;* ☎ *7631 8300, fax 7631 8315, 229 Great Portland St W1;* ✆ *Great Portland Street).* This Marylebone hostel feels more like a university hall of residence. The single and double rooms are ordinary but clean, and there are excellent facilities and a friendly, relaxed atmosphere. It's open year-round. Prices range from £9.99 for a place in an eight-bed dorm without breakfast to £29.50 for a single with washbasin and breakfast. En-suite singles/doubles cost £30/47.

Leinster Inn (*Map 3;* ☎ *7229 9641, fax 7229 5255,* e *astorhotels@msn.com, 7–12 Leinster Square W2;* ✪ *Bayswater).* In a large old house north-west of Bayswater tube station and close to Portobello Market, this place (100 beds) has a bar, cafe and laundry. Rates in dorms with up to 10 beds are £17, doubles are £22 to £25 per person.

Student Accommodation University halls of residence are let to nonstudents during the holidays, usually from the end of June to mid-September and sometimes over the Easter break. They're a bit more expensive than the hostels, but you usually get a single room (there are a few doubles) with shared facilities, plus breakfast.

University catering is usually reasonable and includes bars, self-service cafes, takeaway places and restaurants. Full-board, half-board, B&B and self-catering options are usually available.

The London School of Economics and Political Science (☎ 7955 7370), Room B508, Page Building, Houghton St, London WC2A 2AE, lets half a dozen of its halls in summer and sometimes during the Easter break. These include:

Carr Saunders Hall (*Map 4;* ☎ *7323 9712, fax 7580 4718, 18–24 Fitzroy St W1;* ✪ *Warren Street).* The hall is well located and was recently refurbished. It charges £27/46 for singles/doubles with breakfast.

Bankside Residence (*Map 6;* ☎ *7633 9877, 24 Sumner St SE1;* ✪ *Southwark or Blackfriars).* This hall, with its enviable location near the Globe Theatre and Tate Modern, has beds in four-bed rooms for £20 to £35 and entire quads for £80, including breakfast.

Other halls of residence that are let outside of term-time include:

Goldsmid House (*Map 4;* ☎ *7493 8911, fax 7491 0586, 36 North Row W1;* ✪ *Marble Arch).* This

centrally located hall has 10 singles (£16) and 120 twins (£24) available mid-June to mid-September.

John Adams Hall (*Map 2;* ☎ *7387 4086, fax 7383 0164,* e *jah@ioe.ac.uk, 15–23 Endsleigh St WC1;* ✪ *Euston).* This is quite a grand residence in a row of Georgian houses. It opens at Easter and from July to September. B&B costs from £24/42 for singles/doubles, depending on the time of year.

YMCAs YMCA England (☎ 8520 5599), 640 Forest Rd, London E17 3DZ, can supply you with a list of all its hostels in the Greater London area. Some of the main ones are:

Barbican YMCA (*Map 6;* ☎ *7628 0697, fax 7638 2420,* e *admin@barbican.ymca.org.uk, 2 Fann St EC2;* ✪ *Barbican).* This place has 240 beds, and has singles/doubles for £25/42 including breakfast.

Indian Student YMCA (*Map 4;* ☎ *7387 0411, fax 7383 4735,* e *indianymca@aol.com, 41 Fitzroy Square W1;* ✪ *Warren Street).* Bed plus breakfast and supper costs £33/46 for a single/double.

B&Bs, Guesthouses & Hotels This may come as a shock, but anything below £30/50 for a single/double with shared facilities and below £40/60 with private bathroom is considered 'budget' in London. In July, August and September prices can jump by 25% or more, and it's advisable to book ahead. Prices can differ greatly from those listed below, according to demand. It's always worth asking for any special offers. Be warned: some of the cheaper B&Bs don't accept credit cards.

Pimlico & Victoria (Map 8) Victoria may not be the most attractive part of London, but you'll be very close to the action. Pimlico is more residential and is convenient for Tate Britain at Millbank.

Luna-Simone Hotel (☎ *7834 5897, fax 7828 2474, 47 Belgrave Rd SW1;* ✪ *Victoria).* If all of London's budget hotels were like this central, spotlessly clean and comfortable place, we would all be happy campers (or perhaps not). Singles/doubles without bathroom start at about £35/50; a double with facilities ranges from £60 to £75. A full English breakfast is included, and there are free storage facilities if you want to leave bags while travelling. If the Luna-Simone is full, there are a lot more B&Bs on Belgrave Rd.

Brindle House Hotel (☎ 7828 0057, fax 7931 8805, 1 Warwick Place North SW1; ⊖ Victoria). This place is in a renovated old building in a quiet street; the rooms are small but clean. Singles are £38 (shared facilities), doubles are £50/45 (with/without bathroom), triples are £69.

Romany House Hotel (☎ 7834 5553, fax 7834 0495, 35 Longmore St SW1; ⊖ Victoria). Part of this hotel is built into a 15th-century cottage that boasts tales – real or imagined – of highwaymen. You'll share a bathroom, but breakfasts are good and singles/doubles cost from £30/40.

Bloomsbury (Maps 2 & 4) Bloomsbury is very convenient, especially for the West End. There are lots of places on Gower and North Gower Sts.

Hotel Cavendish (Map 4; ☎ 7636 9079, fax 7580 3609, 75 Gower St WC1; ⊖ Goodge Street). This is a clean and pleasant family-run place, with singles/doubles without bathroom for £34/48 and with en-suite facilities for £42/66, including breakfast. Its nearby sister hotel, **Jesmond Hotel** (Map 4; ☎ 7636 3199, fax 7323 4373, 63 Gower St WC1; ⊖ Goodge Street), is similar and charges the same rates.

Alhambra Hotel (Map 2; ☎ 7837 9575, fax 7916 2476, 17–19 Argyle St WC1; ⊖ King's Cross St Pancras). One of the better finds in this area and very convenient for King's Cross St Pancras tube and the two main-line stations, the Alhambra is a simple but spotlessly clean place with 55 rooms. Simple singles/doubles/triples are £32/45/65; with shower they're £43/50/72. Particularly good value is the quad with shower and toilet for £90. All prices include English breakfast.

Southwark (Map 4) The former home of the Greater London Council, County Hall is now home to one of the many chain hotels cropping up south of the river.

Travel Inn Capital (☎ 7902 1600, fax 7902 1619, Belvedere Rd SE1; ⊖ Waterloo). This is one of those one price, one room deals (in this case £69.95 for up to two adults and two children). It's fairly bare bones, but the rooms are large and reasonable.

Earl's Court (Map 7) Earl's Court is not really within walking distance of many places of interest, but the tube station is a busy interchange, so getting around is easy. It's also an area used to dealing with lots of people in transit.

Regency Court Hotel (☎ 7244 6615, 14 Penywern Rd SW5; ⊖ Earl's Court). This hotel has undergone a much needed renovation and its 15 bright rooms, all with en-suite facilities, cost £35 to £45 for singles, £50 to £60 for doubles and £65 to £75 for triples. Beds in a dormitory cost from £18.

York House Hotel (☎ 7373 7519, fax 7370 4641, 27-28 Philbeach Gardens SW5; ⊖ Earl's Court). This place is good value for what and where it is – on a quiet crescent – and the welcome is warm. The rooms are basic, although some have showers. Singles/doubles/triples without facilities are £34/52/69; with shower and toilet they're £48/74/86.

Merlyn Court Hotel (☎ 7370 1640, fax 7370 4986, 2 Barkston Gardens SW5; ⊖ Earl's Court). This unpretentious place has a nice atmosphere and a lovely location close to the tube. Small but clean singles/doubles/triples with bathroom cost £60/70/80; without they're £35/50/65.

Bayswater & Paddington (Map 3) Bayswater is an extremely convenient location though some of the streets immediately to the west of Queensway, which has a decent selection of restaurants, are run down and depressing. Paddington has lots of cheap hotels and it's a good transit location.

Royal Hotel (☎ 7229 7225, 43 Queensborough Terrace; ⊖ Bayswater). The dormitory accommodation here once attracted backpackers, but it's now just another budget guesthouse with affordable rates: £36/45/52 for a single/double/ triple with shower.

Manor Court Hotel (☎ 7792 3361, fax 7229 2875, 7 Clanricarde Gardens W2; ⊖ Queensway). Though not a spectacular place, this hotel is in a good location just off Bayswater Rd. Singles/doubles with private shower or toilet are from £50/60, depending on the season.

Garden Court Hotel (☎ 7229 2553, fax 7727 2749, 30-31 Kensington Gardens Square W2; ⊖ Bayswater). One of Bayswater's best options and just barely in this category, the Garden Court is a well-run and maintained family hotel cobbled from two town houses (1870), and all its 34 rooms have phone and TV. Singles/doubles without bathroom are £36/58, with bathroom £54/86.

Norfolk Court & St David's Hotel (☎ *7723 4963, fax 7402 9061, 16-20 Norfolk Square W2; ❺ Paddington*). Right in the centre of the action, this place with the long-winded name is clean, comfortable and friendly with the usual out-of-control decor. Basic singles/doubles/triples have washbasin, TV and phone and cost £39/59/70; with shower and toilet they cost £49/69/80, including a huge breakfast.

Balmoral House Hotel (☎ *7723 7445, fax 7402 0118, 156 & 157 Sussex Gardens W2; ❺ Paddington*). This immaculate and very comfortable hotel, with two properties directly opposite one another, is one of the better places to stay along Sussex Gardens, a street lined with small hotels but unfortunately a major traffic artery. Singles without/with bathroom cost £35/45, doubles with facilities are £65 (breakfast included and all rooms have TVs).

Marylebone (Map 3)
Marylebone is very handy for some of London's most popular sights, such as Madame Tussaud's and the London Planetarium. It's also a nice area in its own right.

Glynne Court Hotel (☎ *7262 4344, fax 7724 2071, 41 Great Cumberland Place W1; ❺ Marble Arch*). Fairly typical for this price range and location, the Glynne Court has 15 rooms. Singles are £50 to £60, and doubles £60 to £75. All rooms come with TV and phone.

Places to Stay – Mid-Range
The B&Bs, guesthouses and small hotels in this category charge from £50/70 for a single/double without private facilities and £70/90 with your own bathroom.

Pimlico & Victoria (Map 8)
Pimlico is for the most part an attractive area with some good-value accommodation, while Victoria has an excellent range of transport options.

Winchester Hotel (☎ *7828 2972, fax 7828 5191, 17 Belgrave Rd SW1; ❺ Victoria*). This clean, comfortable and welcoming place is also good value for the area: doubles and twins with private bathroom and TV cost £85.

Woodville House (☎ *7730 1048, fax 7730 2574, 107 Ebury St SW1; ❺ Victoria*). The Woodville has 12 simple but comfortable rooms with shared bathroom, use of a kitchen and a lovely back patio. Basic singles/doubles cost £42/62. Family rooms cost from £80 to £115. It's a friendly, good-value place.

Morgan House (☎ *7730 2384, fax 7730 8842, 120 Ebury St SW1; ❺ Victoria*). This hotel is owned by the same people who run the nearby Woodville House. Singles/doubles without facilities are £42/62, those with bathroom £68/80. You'll find many more places to stay on this street.

Covent Garden (Map 5)
Nothing could be more central than Covent Garden but the buzz continues well into the wee hours.

Fielding Hotel (☎ *7836 8305, fax 7497 0064, 4 Broad Court, Bow St WC2; ❺ Covent Garden*). This place, on a pedestrianised street a block away from the Royal Opera House, is remarkably good value, clean and well run. All rooms have private bathroom, TV and phone. Singles/doubles start at £76/100.

Bloomsbury (Maps 2 & 4)
Tucked away in leafy Cartwright Gardens (Map 2) to the north of Russell Square, within walking distance of the West End, you'll find some of London's best-value hotels. The hotels along nearby Gower St (Map 4) are also pretty good value, but not all of them have double-glazing, which is essential if you're sensitive to traffic noise.

Jenkins Hotel (*Map 2;* ☎ *7387 2067, fax 7383 3139,* ✉ *reservations@jenkinshotel.demon.co .uk, 45 Cartwright Gardens WC1; ❺ Russell Square*). This no-smoking place has attractive, comfortable, stylish rooms with washbasin, TV, phone and fridge. Basic singles are £52; singles/doubles with private facilities are £72/85 (all prices include breakfast). Guests get to use the tennis courts in the gardens across the road.

Crescent Hotel (*Map 2;* ☎ *7387 1515, fax 7383 2054, 49-50 Cartwright Gardens WC1; ❺ Russell Square*). This friendly, family-owned operation, maintained at a very high standard, has basic singles from £43 to £45 and en suite singles/doubles/triples/quads from £70/82/93/102.

Arran House Hotel (*Map 4;* ☎ *7636 2186, fax 7436 5328, 77-79 Gower St WC1; ❺ Goodge*

Street). This welcoming place has a lovely garden and laundry facilities. Singles range from £45 with no facilities to £55 with shower, doubles from £55 to £75, triples from £73 to £93. Prices include breakfast. The front rooms are sound-proofed, and all have TV and phone.

Ridgemount Hotel (Map 4; ☎ 7636 1141, fax 7636 2558, 65-67 Gower St WC1; ✪ Goodge Street). Readers have sent favourable comments about the old-fashioned Ridgemount. Basic singles/doubles are £32/48; with shower and toilet they're from £43/62 (including breakfast). It also has a laundry room (£2 per wash).

Haddon Hall (Map 4; ☎ 7636 2474, fax 7580 4527, 39 Bedford Place WC1; ✪ Russell Square or Holborn). This fairly basic place has simple singles/doubles without bathroom for £50/65, and doubles with bathroom for £90.

Southwark (Maps 4 & 6) Spurred on by gentrification south of the Thames as well as by Tate Modern, a few chain hotels have appeared.

Holiday Inn Express Southwark (Map 4; ☎ 7401 2525, fax 7401 3322, 103–109 Southwark St SE1; ✪ Southwark). Cheap and modern, this fairly anonymous hotel has good rates, with singles/doubles at £50/87.

Mercure Hotel London City Bankside (Map 6; ☎ 7902 0808, fax 7902 0810, 75–79 Southwark St SE1; ✪ Southwark). This outpost of the French mid-range hotel chain has comfortable, modern rooms that will appeal to business travellers. Ask about the many special offers that mean prices average £90/110 for a single/double.

Chelsea & South Kensington (Map 7) Classy Chelsea and 'South Ken' offer easy access to the museums and some of London's best shops.

Annandale House Hotel (☎ 7730 5051, fax 7730 2727, 39 Sloane Gardens SW1; ✪ Sloane Square). This discreet, traditional hotel just south of Sloane Square is a good choice for the noise-sensitive. Rooms, all with en-suite facilities, phone and TV, cost £60 to £70 for singles and £95 to £105 for doubles.

Hotel 167 (☎ 7373 0672, fax 7373 3360, 167 Old Brompton Rd SW5; ✪ Gloucester Road). This small hotel is stylish and has an unusually uncluttered and attractive decor. All 19 rooms have private bathrooms. Singles are from £72, doubles from £90 to £99.

Swiss House Hotel (☎ 7373 2769, fax 7373 4983, ✉ recep@swiss-hh.demon.co.uk, 171 Old Brompton Rd SW5; ✪ Gloucester Road). The Swiss House is a clean and welcoming hotel that has something of a country feel about it. And it's good value: singles with shower start at £48, singles/doubles with shower and toilet start at £68/85, including continental breakfast.

Kensington (Map 3) These hotels are well placed for Kensington Gardens, Notting Hill and Kensington High St.

Vicarage Hotel (☎ 7229 4030, fax 7792 5989, ✉ reception@londonvicaragehotel.com, 10 Vicarage Gate W8; ✪ High Street Kensington). The Vicarage is pleasant and well kept, with good showers and rooms slightly larger than normal. Singles/doubles with shared facilities are £46/76, doubles with private bathroom £99.

Abbey House (☎ 7727 2594, 11 Vicarage Gate W8; ✪ High Street Kensington). Abbey House is a particularly good-value small hotel, with pretty decor and very high standards. Singles/doubles/triples/quads with washbasin and shared bathrooms are £45/74/85/100, including English breakfast.

Bayswater, Paddington & Notting Hill (Map 3) Bayswater is residential and convenient for busy Queensway. Though central, Paddington is a bit scruffy. Notting Hill is relatively expensive, but has lots of good bars and restaurants.

Pavilion Hotel (☎ 7262 0905, fax 7262 1324, 34-36 Sussex Gardens W2; ✪ Paddington). This place boasts 30 individually themed rooms (Moorish, 1970s, all-red) to reflect its slogan/motto: 'Fashion, Glam & Rock 'n' Roll'. If you're feeling somewhat B-list, you might look elsewhere. Singles/doubles cost from £60/90 and include breakfast.

Inverness Court Hotel (☎ 7229 1444, fax 7706 4240, Inverness Terrace W2; ✪ Queensway). This impressive hotel was commissioned by Edward VII for his 'confidante' (ie mistress), the actress Lillie Langtry, and comes complete with a private theatre, now the cocktail bar. The panelled walls, stained glass and huge open fires of the public areas give it a Gothic feel but most of the 183 rooms – some of which overlook Hyde Park – are modern and pretty ordinary. Singles/doubles cost £84/108.

Gate Hotel (☎ 7221 0707, fax 7221 9128,

e gatehotel@aol.com, 6 Portobello Rd W11; ⊖ *Notting Hill Gate).* The rooms in this old town house with classic frilly English decor and lovely floral window boxes all have private facilities and cost £55 to £70 for singles and £80 to £90 for doubles, including continental breakfast.

Marylebone (Map 3) Both of these are within striking distance of Hyde Park.

Edward Lear Hotel (☎ 7402 5401, fax 7706 3766, 28–30 Seymour St W1; ⊖ *Marble Arch).* Once the home of the eponymous Victorian painter and poet, the rooms in this small, comfortable place have TV, tea & coffee facilities and phone. Singles/doubles without bathroom cost from £48/68, with bathroom £75/93.

Bryanston Court Hotel (☎ 7262 3141, fax 7262 7248, e *hotel@bryanstonhotel.com, 56–60 Great Cumberland Place W1;* ⊖ *Marble Arch).* This place has something of a club atmosphere, with leather armchairs, sepia-toned lighting and a formal feel (though it's a Best Western hotel). All rooms have private bathroom, TV and phone and singles/doubles cost £95/120.

Places to Stay – Top End
In this section you'll find the pricier hotels, where doubles cost from £150 – and more. Of course, in this category you can always count on a private bath/shower and toilet.

Victoria (Map 8) The following place is (probably) as close as you'll ever get to staying with the Queen.

Rubens at the Palace (☎ 7834 6600, fax 7233 6037, e *reservations@rubens.redcarnationhotels .com, 39 Buckingham Palace Rd SW1;* ⊖ *Victoria).* This branch of the Rubens chain has a brilliant position overlooking the walls of the Royal Mews and Buckingham Palace. Singles/doubles start at £135/150 without breakfast. It's popular with groups.

The West End & Covent Garden (Map 5)
Unfortunately, staying in such central locations doesn't come cheap.

Hazlitt's (☎ 7434 1771, fax 7439 1524, 6 Frith St W1; ⊖ *Tottenham Court Road).* Built in 1718 and comprising three original Georgian houses, this is one of central London's finest hotels, with efficient personal service. All 23 rooms are

named after former residents or visitors to the house and are individually decorated with antique furniture and prints. Singles/doubles start at £140/175. Booking is advisable – especially since Bill Bryson let the cat out of the bag and introduced it to the world in his bestselling *Notes from a Small Island.*

Strand Palace (☎ 7836 8080, fax 7836 2077, Strand WC2; ⊖ *Charing Cross).* This monstrous place (783 rooms) has improved following renovation. Its position, close to Covent Garden, is excellent and there are a number of snappy bars and restaurants, but the prices (from £100/150 for a single/double without breakfast) are still pretty steep, although there are many special deals.

Clerkenwell (Map 4) This area is not blessed with a wealth of quality accommodation; however there is a notable exception.

The Rookery (☎ 7336 0931, fax 7336 0932, e *reservations@rookery.co.uk, Peter's Lane, Cowcross St EC1;* ⊖ *Farringdon).* This 33-room hotel has been built within a row of once derelict 18th-century Georgian houses and fitted out with period furniture (including a museum-piece collection of Victorian baths, showers and toilets), original wood panelling shipped over from Ireland and open fires. Its singles/doubles start at £170/200.

South Kensington (Map 7) South Kensington presents London at its elegant best.

Blakes Hotel (☎ 7370 6701, fax 7373 0442, e *blakes@easynet.co.uk, 33 Roland Gardens SW7;* ⊖ *Gloucester Road).* For classic style, one of your first choices in London should be this place: five Victorian houses knocked into one and decked out with four-poster beds, rich fabrics and antiques on stripped floorboards. Singles/doubles start at £165/240.

Number Sixteen Hotel (☎ 7589 5232, fax 7584 8615, e *reservations@numbersixteenhotel .co.uk, 16 Sumner Place SW7;* ⊖ *South Kensington).* Number Sixteen has comfortable and well-equipped rooms. It was undergoing a complete renovation at the time of writing but should have reopened by the time you read this, with singles/doubles starting at about £140/200.

Kensington & Knightsbridge (Map 3) The theme of top-end hotels in this part of London seems to be antiques.

The Gore (☎ 7584 6601, fax 7589 8127, e reservations@gorehotel.co.uk, 189 Queen's Gate SW7; ✪ High Street Kensington or Gloucester Road). This splendid hotel is a veritable palace of polished mahogany, Turkish carpets, antique-style bathrooms, aspidistras and portraits and prints (some 4500 of them). The attached Bistrot 190 is a fine place for brunch. Singles/doubles cost from £140/175.

Basil St Hotel (☎ 7581 3311, fax 7581 3693, e thebasil@aol.com, Basil St SW3; ✪ Knightsbridge). This antique-stuffed hideaway in the heart of Knightsbridge is perfectly placed for carrying back the shopping from Harrods, Harvey Nichols or Sloane St. Its singles/doubles start at £128/190.

Bayswater & Notting Hill (Map 3)

You'll get more for your pound at top-end places in these two areas than you would to the south and east.

Queen's Park Hotel (☎ 7229 8080, fax 7792 1330, e parksales1@compuserve.com, 48 Queensborough Terrace W2; ✪ Bayswater). With 86 rooms, the Queen's Park is a somewhat functional top-end place popular with groups, but the rates are good for the location: £98/130 for singles/doubles.

Portobello (☎ 7727 2777, fax 7792 9641, 22 Stanley Gardens W11; ✪ Notting Hill Gate). This beautifully appointed place is in a great location and one of the most attractive hotels in London. Most people consider the £145/185 for a single/double to be money well spent.

East End (Map 6)

This area's top option is a classic Victorian railway hotel.

Great Eastern Hotel (☎ 7618 5010, fax 7618 5011, e sales@great-eastern-hotel.co.uk, Liverpool St EC2; ✪ Liverpool Street). A major addition to the East End and the City, the Great Eastern adjoins Liverpool Street station and has received a lavish overhaul from the Conran organisation. It's stylish and elegant and *the* place to stay for literally miles around. Rates start at £195/225 for rooms boasting everything you could want.

Places to Stay – Deluxe

Some of central London's hotels are so luxurious and well established that they're tourist attractions in their own right. Despite their often old-world splendour, all are well prepared for the needs of business travellers.

Claridges (Map 4; ☎ 7629 8860, fax 7499 2210, e info@claridges.co.uk, Brook St W1; ✪ Bond Street). Claridges is one of the greatest of London's five-star hotels, a leftover from a bygone era. Many of the Art Deco features of the public areas and suites were designed in the late 1920s and some of the 1930s furniture once graced the staterooms of the lost SS *Normandie*. Expect to pay £315/370 for a single/double.

The Ritz (Map 4; ☎ 7493 8181, fax 7493 2687, e enquire@theritzhotel.co.uk, 150 Piccadilly W1; ✪ Green Park). What can you say about a hotel that has lent its name to the English lexicon? Arguably London's most celebrated hotel, the ritzy Ritz has a spectacular position overlooking Green Park and is the royal family's 'home away from home'. Singles/doubles cost from £295/345. The Long Gallery and the Restaurant are decked out like a rococo boudoir.

St Martins Lane (Map 5; ☎ 7300 5500, 0800 634 5500 toll-free, 45 St Martin's Lane; ✪ Leicester Square). A designer hotel, providing what it calls a 'slice of New York urban chic' just a stone's throw from Covent Garden, St Martins was created by international hotelier Ian Schrager and French designer Philippe Starck. It's the place to check into if you want to bump into supermodels in the lift and have great views of the pulsating West End. Indulging in its late-1990s minimalism costs from £245/265 for a single/double.

The Savoy (Map 5; ☎ 7836 4343, fax 7240 6040, e info@the-savoy.co.uk, Strand WC2; ✪ Charing Cross). This hotel stands on the site of the old Savoy Palace, which was burned down during the Peasants' Revolt of 1381. The 207 rooms are so comfortable and have such great views that some people have been known to take up permanent residence. Singles/doubles start at £290/340. The forecourt is the only street in the British Isles where motorists drive on the right.

Airport Hotels

If you have a very early flight out of Heathrow, you might want to stay at one of the anonymous hotels that ring its periphery. The extortionate Hotel Hoppa shuttle bus (☎ 01293-507099; £2.50 for adults, free for children) links the airport's terminals and bus, tube and rail stations with the

LONDON

hotels; see the later Getting There & Away section for details.

Hotel Ibis Heathrow Airport (☎ 8759 4888, fax 8564 7894, 112/114 Bath Rd, Hayes UB3 5AL). The rooms are clean and serviceable and the restaurant is relatively cheap, but when you first wake up you may not know where you are in the world. Singles/doubles are £60/68.

Novotel Heathrow Airport (☎ 01895-431431, fax 431221, Cherry Lane, West Drayton UB7 9HB). There's more anonymous corporate comfort at this hotel near the M4 and M25. The large atrium boasts a pool. Rooms are £90/110.

Serviced Apartments

Families or groups may prefer to rent a flat rather than stay in a hotel or B&B. Several agencies can help track something down. Holiday Serviced Apartments (☎ 7373 4477, fax 7373 4282, e reservations@ holidayapartments.co.uk), 273 Old Brompton Rd SW5 (⊖ Gloucester Road), and Aston's Budget & Designer Studios (☎ 7590 6000, fax 7590 6060), 39 Rosary Gardens SW7 (⊖ Gloucester Road), both have a range of holiday flats on their books.

PLACES TO EAT

London is England's undisputed culinary capital, and the growth in the number of restaurants and cafes – some 8500 at the last count, representing 70 different cuisines – has made the city much more international. No matter what you fancy eating, there's bound to be a restaurant with it on the menu.

Restaurants and other eateries in London have extremely varied opening hours. Many in Soho are closed on Sunday, for example, and in the City for the entire weekend. We have tried to note when restaurants stray from the standard 'open daily for lunch and dinner', but it's always safest to call and check. Also note that many of the pubs listed in the Entertainment section serve food.

Trafalgar Square (Map 5)

You won't find a tremendous number of eateries directly on the square, but there are a couple of cafes within striking distance

and the ***Brasserie*** (☎ 7747 2885), on the 1st floor of the National Gallery's Sainsbury Wing, gets good reviews.

Café in the Crypt (☎ 7839 4342, St Martin-in-the-Fields, Duncannon St WC2; ⊖ Charing Cross). The food in this atmospheric crypt is good, with plenty of offerings for vegetarians, but the place can be hectic and noisy at lunch time. Most main dishes cost from £5 to £6 and there are 'quick meals' from £3.95. It opens 10 am to 8 pm (to 6 pm on Sunday).

ICA Café (Map 4; ☎ 7930 8619, ICA, The Mall SW1; ⊖ Charing Cross). You can lunch at this bohemian magnet for less than £10 but for considerably more in the evening (£36 for two with wine). It's no-smoking, there are lots of vegetarian dishes and it's licensed to serve alcohol until 1 am.

Westminster & Pimlico (Map 8)

We wonder where all those MPs lunch, given the dearth of restaurants in Westminster, but Pimlico has a wide assortment.

Jenny Lo's Tea House (☎ 7259 0399, 14 Eccleston St SW1; ⊖ Victoria). This simple Asian place has soup and fried noodles from £3.50 to £6.50 and rice dishes from £4.50.

O Sole Mio (☎ 7976 6887, 39 Churton St SW1; ⊖ Victoria). This standard, decent-value Italian restaurant has pizzas and pastas for around £6.

UNo 1 (☎ 7834 1001, 1 Denbigh St SW1; ⊖ Victoria). Pastas cost from £5.50 to £8 in this cheery dining room brightly decorated with reds and yellows.

St James's & Mayfair (Map 4)

Shepherd Market is popular with locals and is lined with a fine variety of restaurants.

Shepherd Café Bar (☎ 7495 5509, 7 Shepherd Market W1; ⊖ Green Park). A long list of pastas under £4 is but one of the attractions at this friendly Italian cafe, which also has outdoor tables.

Hard Rock Café (☎ 7629 0382, 150 Old Park Lane W1; ⊖ Hyde Park Corner). This, the original Hard Rock Café, has been here since 1971 and is as popular with tourists as ever – just check out the queues that form every day of the year (no bookings taken). It serves a tried and tested diet of burgers and fries (from £7.25). The rock memorabilia is memorable.

Rasa W1 (☎ 7629 1346, 6 Dering St W1; ⊖ Bond

Street). This South Indian vegetarian restaurant has wonderful food that should cost about £10 per person.

The Little Square (☎ 7355 2101, 3 Shepherd Market W1; ⊖ Green Park). This small restaurant has a good menu of modern British food at lunch and dinner. Main courses cost from £8 to £11 and there is a good wine list. There are a couple of tables outside.

The West End: Piccadilly, Soho & Chinatown (Map 5)

These days Soho is London's gastronomic heart with numerous restaurants and cuisines to choose from. The liveliest streets tend to be Greek, Frith, Old Compton and Dean Sts. Gerrard and Lisle Sts are chocka-block with Chinese eateries of every description.

Chinese If you're with several people and want a proper sit-down meal in Chinatown (⊖ Leicester Square) but are overwhelmed by the choice, consider any of the following three. They've been tested again and again and have always come up trumps:

Fung Shing (☎ 7437 1539, 15 Lisle St WC2)
Gerrard's Corner (☎ 7437 0984, 30 Wardour St WC2)
Mr Kong (☎ 7437 7341, 21 Lisle St WC2)

A particularly good way to sample the best of Chinese cuisine is to try Cantonese dim sum where you select numerous small dishes and wash them down with a pot of jasmine tea.

Chuen Cheng Ku (☎ 7437 1398, 17 Wardour St W1). This place is ideal for the uninitiated as all the dishes (dumplings, noodles, paper-wrapped prawns etc) are trundled around on trolleys.

Wong Kei (☎ 7437 3071, 41-43 Wardour St W1). Wong Kei is famous for the rudeness of its waiters. Some find this adds to the experience, but even if you don't – like us – you might be tempted by the cheap Cantonese food (main dishes from £4.50 to £7.50, rice dishes from £3, set menus from £6).

Japanese & South-East Asian Asian food in the West End is not restricted to Chinese. There are many other fine estab-

---

Tea for Two or More

Given the important role that tea has always played in English culture and society, it should be no surprise that going out for 'afternoon tea' is something dear to the heart of many Londoners.

The following are three of the best places to go for afternoon tea:

Brown's Hotel (Map 5; ☎ 7493 6020, 30 Albemarle St W1; ⊖ Green Park) dispenses tea in the Drawing Room 3 to 6 pm daily, with a pianist to soothe away any lingering stress from the bustling streets outside. A sizeable tea will set you back £17.95 a head.

Fortnum & Mason (Map 5; ☎ 7734 8040, 181 Piccadilly W1; ⊖ Piccadilly Circus) serves afternoon tea for £13.50 and high teas for £16.50 and £18.50 (with champagne) between 3 and 5 pm Monday to Saturday.

The Orangery (Map 3; ☎ 7376 0239; ⊖ High Street Kensington or Queensway) in Kensington Gardens is a superb, graceful place to have a relatively affordable set tea; prices range from £6.50 with cucumber sandwiches or scones to £12.50 with champagne. It opens 10 am to 6 pm daily, April to September (to 4 pm the rest of the year).

---

lishments offering an impressive range of Asian cuisines.

Tokyo Diner (☎ 7287 8777, 2 Newport Place WC2; ⊖ Leicester Square). The Tokyo Diner is a good-value place to stop for a quick bowl of noodles or a plate of sushi before the cinema or theatre. A meal is likely to cost from £8 to £10, although their set *bento* boxes start at £10.50.

Soba (☎ 7734 6400, 38 Poland St W1; ⊖ Oxford Circus). Soba is always our first choice for an easy (and cheap) bowl of Japanese noodles for around £5.

YO! Sushi (☎ 7287 0443, 52-53 Poland St W1; ⊖ Oxford Circus). YO! Sushi is one of London's livelier sushi bars, where diners sit around the bar and the dishes come to them on a 60m-long conveyor belt (drinks, on the other hand, arrive on a robotic trolley). Sushi costs from

£1.50 to £3.50; you should be able to get away with around £10 a head.

Melati (☎ 7437 2745, 21 Great Windmill St W1; ⊖ Piccadilly Circus). This Indonesian/Malaysian/Singaporean restaurant has good food and a respectable range of vegetarian options. Various noodle and rice dishes cost from £6 to £8 and the fish in chilli sauce (£7.25) is excellent.

Cam Phat (☎ 7437 5598, 12 Macclesfield St W1; ⊖ Leicester Square). Cam Phat is a cheap and cheerful Vietnamese place that serves well-prepared dishes such as roast pork with vermicelli noodles (£4.50) and *pho* (£3.50), the Vietnamese soup staple of beef and noodles in a stock flavoured with lemon grass.

Other Innumerable other cuisines are also represented in the West End.

Franx Snack Bar (☎ 7836 7989, 192 Shaftesbury Ave WC2; ⊖ Tottenham Court Road). Franx is as authentic a London 'caff' as you'll find in these parts, with eggs and bacon and other one-plate specials for around £3.

Gaby's (☎ 7836 4233, 30 Charing Cross Rd WC2; ⊖ Leicester Square). This Middle Eastern snack bar beside Wyndham's theatre has been here forever and attracts queues for staples such as hummus and felafel (£3.20) and couscous royale (£7.50).

Mildred's (☎ 7494 1634, 58 Greek St W1; ⊖ Tottenham Court Road). Mildred's is so small (and popular) that you may have to share a table. It's worth it, however, because the vegetarian food – including stir-fried vegetables and beanburgers – is both good and well priced (from £5 to £7 for a large main course).

Pollo (☎ 7734 5456, 20 Old Compton St W1; ⊖ Leicester Square). This Italian cheapie attracts a student crowd with its pastas, risottos, pizzas and chicken dishes for under £4.

Spiga (☎ 7734 3444, 84–86 Wardour St W1; ⊖ Tottenham Court Road). This is where to head if you want authentic pizza (from £6), pasta or an Italian main dish in sleek, pleasant surroundings but don't want to pay the earth for it.

Garlic & Shots (☎ 7734 9505, 14 Frith St W1; ⊖ Leicester Square). Whether or not you'll want to risk eating at this place depends on your tolerance for garlic – and your plans for later in the evening. Everything, including the cheesecake, ice cream and vodka, is spiked with the stuff. Main courses clock in at £9 to £13. It opens daily for dinner only.

Gopal's of Soho (☎ 7434 0840, 12 Bateman St W1; ⊖ Tottenham Court Road). Gopal's is cramped and run-down, but it offers reasonably authentic Indian food at affordable prices. *Thalis* (set meals served on circular metal trays) are good value: £11.75 for vegetarian and £1 more for the meat equivalent.

Rasa Samudra (☎ 7637 0222, 5 Charlotte St W1; ⊖ Goodge Street). This place just north of Oxford St is one of many restaurants on this street, but its emphasis on excellent South Indian vegetarian cuisine and seafood sets it apart. Count on about £15 per person.

L'Odéon (☎ 7287 1400, 65 Regent St W1; ⊖ Piccadilly Circus). This upmarket French restaurant is worth a visit just for the views of Regent St from its lofty windows. The food also comes in for good reports, especially if you go for the £15.50/19.50 two/three-course set lunch or dinner (from 5.30 to 7 pm only).

Cafes Soho's cafes are great for whiling away the hours inside or – depending on the weather – outside.

Pâtisserie Valerie (☎ 7437 3466, 44 Old Compton St W1; ⊖ Tottenham Court Road or Leicester Square). You can't beat this Soho institution for coffee or tea and something sweet (calorie-crunching cakes around £2.50), though you'll be lucky to get a seat. It also does filled croissants and club sandwiches (from £4 to £5.50).

Maison Bertaux (☎ 7437 6007, 28 Greek St W1; ⊖ Tottenham Court Road). Bertaux has been turning out confections for 130 years, and they're still as exquisite as ever.

Bar Italia (☎ 7437 4520, 22 Frith St W1; ⊖ Leicester Square). This great favourite opens round the clock and has a wonderful 1950s decor. It's always packed and buzzing (from the caffeine, no doubt); your best chance for a seat might be sometime after 1 am.

Covent Garden & the Strand (Map 5)

Right beside Soho and technically part of the West End, Covent Garden (⊖ Covent Garden) is also densely packed with places to eat.

Rock & Sole Plaice (☎ 7836 3785, 47 Endell St WC2). This no-nonsense fish and chips shop has basic Formica tables and delicious cod or haddock in batter (£3.50 or £4.50 with chips). It's unlicensed but you can bring your own (BYO).

Food for Thought (☎ 7836 0239, 31 Neal St WC2). This tiny, no-smoking vegetarian cafe features spicy dishes for under £4.

Calabash (☎ 7836 1973, 38 King St WC2). This simple eatery in the Africa Centre serves food from all over Africa and has a menu for the uninitiated describing each dish. Typical dishes are *egusi* (£6.95), a Nigerian meat stew with tomatoes and spices, and *yassa* (£6.50), chicken marinated with lemon juice and peppers, hailing from Senegal.

Café Pacifico (☎ 7379 7728, 5 Langley St WC2). Pacifico serves Mexican food in a cheerful dining room, with main courses for about £7.50 and great margaritas.

Belgo Centraal (☎ 7813 2233, 50 Earlham St WC2). Taking the lift down to the basement and walking through the kitchens is all part of the fun at Belgo, where the waiters dress up as 16th-century monks. This being a Belgian restaurant, *moules et frites* (mussels and chips/french fries) and spit roasts are the specialities and beer (100 different flavoured Pilsners, including banana, peach and cherry) is the drink. There's a set lunch menu for £5; a set dinner of a starter, mussels and chips and a beer costs £13.95.

Café des Amis du Vin (☎ 7379 3444, 11-14 Hanover Place WC2). This brasserie is handy for pre- or post-theatre meals with good, affordable French fare. Starters cost from £4.95 to £6.50, main courses from £10 to £13.50 and set lunches of two/three courses £9.95/12.50.

Orso (☎ 7240 5269, 27 Wellington St WC2). An established Italian eatery popular with media types, Orso is relatively expensive for dinner (about £25 per head), but does a cheaper two/three-course lunch for £14/16 including – as any journalist would expect – a Bloody Mary or a glass of champagne.

Simpson's-in-the-Strand (☎ 7836 9112, 100 Strand WC2). For traditional English roasts, Simpson's is where to go – it's been dishing up hot meats in a fine panelled dining room since 1848. Main courses average £15.

The Admiralty (☎ 7845 4646, Somerset House, Strand WC2; ⊖ Covent Garden or Temple). The flagship restaurant of the restored Somerset House has a traditional interior and modern French food. Expect to pay at least £22 each. There's a lovely terrace outside overlooking the Thames.

Cafes There's a cluster of enjoyable New Age cafes – some of them vegetarian – in Neal's Yard, including the two listed below. All offer a similar diet of wholesome dishes such as cheese breads and home-made noodles in pleasing surroundings, but space fills up quickly. Lunch in any of these places should cost about £5 to £6 if you choose carefully.

World Food Café (☎ 7379 0298, 14 Neal's Yard WC2)

Neal's Yard Salad Bar (☎ 7836 3233, 2 Neal's Yard WC2).

Bloomsbury (Maps 2, 4 & 5)

If you're visiting the British Museum it's worth knowing that Museum St (Map 5) is packed with cafes and simple lunch places where you'll get better value than in the museum cafe.

Ruskins Café (Map 5; ☎ 7405 1450, 41 Museum St WC1; ⊖ Tottenham Court Road). This place does soup and filled jacket potatoes from £2.95.

North Sea Fish Restaurant (Map 2; ☎ 7387 5892, 7-8 Leigh St WC1; ⊖ Russell Square). The North Sea sets out to cook fresh fish and potatoes – a simple ambition in which it succeeds admirably. Cod, haddock and plaice, deep-fried or grilled, and a huge serving of chips will cost you between £6.95 and £7.95.

Coffee Gallery (Map 5; ☎ 7436 0455, 23 Museum St WC1; ⊖ Tottenham Court Road). This tremendously popular place serves pasta dishes and main courses (lots under £7), such as grilled sardines and salad, in a bright, cheerful room with modern paintings on the walls.

Mille Pini (Map 4; ☎ 7242 2434, 33 Boswell St WC1; ⊖ Russell Square or Holborn). This well regarded place is a true, old-fashioned Italian restaurant and pizzeria with reasonable prices. You'll waddle out, but will only have spent about £6/10 for a two-course lunch/dinner.

Mandeer (Map 5; ☎ 7405 3211, 8 Bloomsbury Way WC1; ⊖ Holborn). Vegetarian purists will rejoice at Mandeer, where meat, fish, preservatives and colourings are not used in the food. This Ayurvedic (an Indian holistic tradition) restaurant has numerous vegetarian and vegan meals for about £6. It opens daily except Sunday.

Holborn & Clerkenwell (Maps 2 & 4)

Holborn has a few restaurants and night spots to recommend it but is generally dead after dark. On the other hand, Clerkenwell has well and truly arrived on the eating-out map. These places are mostly accessible from Farringdon tube station.

The Greenery (Map 4; ☎ 7490 4870, 5 Cow-cross St EC1). This small vegetarian cafe, hanging on for the moment amid all the gentrification of Clerkenwell, has salad platters for £3.95 and chickpea and coriander chapatis for £1.80.

St John (Map 4; ☎ 7251 0848, 26 St John St EC1). St John is the place to come if you fancy sampling old-fashioned British staples in new guises, such as tripe and sausage soup (£5), pigeon and Jerusalem artichoke (£11.80) and sweetbreads, peas and broad beans (£12.80). While there are some fish dishes, this place is all about meat, and offal in particular (after all, it is right next to Smithfield Market).

Gaudí (Map 4; ☎ 7608 3220, 63 Clerkenwell Rd EC1). This restaurant takes its cue from the Catalan architect's designs to provide a backdrop for a classy restaurant specialising in what has been dubbed New Spanish cuisine. Fish plays a big role, and first courses start at about £6, main courses at £14. Set lunch midweek costs £12.50/15 for two/three courses. It's got a good Spanish wine list.

Cicada (Map 2; ☎ 7608 1550, 132-136 St John St EC1). Cicada is a lovely, modern restaurant that mingles Asian tastes and flavours with great success. Starters cost from about £5, main dishes from £6 to £10.

Club Gascon (Map 4; ☎ 7253 5853, 57 West Smithfield EC1). Right next to glorious St Bartholomew's-the-Great (of *Four Weddings and a Funeral* fame), Club Gascon serves the food of south-western France. Book well in advance and expect to pay at least £30 each.

The City (Maps 4 & 6)

The City can be an irritating place in which to try to find a decent, affordable restaurant that stays open after office hours. The following recommendations are the pick of the crop.

Ye Olde Cheshire Cheese (Map 4; ☎ 7353 6170, Wine Office Court EC4; ☻ Blackfriars). Rebuilt six years after the Great Fire and popular with Dr Johnson, Thackeray, Dickens and the visiting Mark Twain, the Cheshire Cheese is touristy but always atmospheric and enjoyable for a pub meal (£6).

Dim Sum (Map 4; ☎ 7236 1114, 5-6 Deans Court EC4; ☻ St Paul's). A budget traveller's delight and convenient for St Paul's and the City of London YHA hostel, Dim Sum serves Peking and Sichuan dishes for £3 to £6, but the best deal is the £9.99 all-you-can-eat buffet (mini-mum four people) available 6 to 10.30 pm weekdays.

Wine Library (Map 6; ☎ 7481 0415, 43 Trinity Square EC3; ☻ Tower Hill). This is a great place to go if you want a light but boozy lunch. Buy a bottle of wine retail (no mark-up; £2 corkage fee) from the large selection on offer and then snack on patés, cheeses and salads for £9.95. The shop opens 10 am to 6 pm weekdays and for lunch from 11.30 am to 3 pm.

Da Vinci (Map 4; ☎ 7236 3938, 42-44 Carter Lane EC4; ☻ St Paul's). Here's a rare bird indeed: an affordable neighbourhood Italian place in the City. Starters are from £3.95 to £6.95, pastas £3.80 to £5.95 and main courses £8.50 to £14. A two-course set lunch is £11.50 and there's a 'cheap lunch' for £4.50 available 11.30 am to 1 pm.

Café Spice Namaste (Map 6; ☎ 7488 9242, 16 Prescot St E1; ☻ Tower Hill). One of our favourite Indian restaurants in London, the Namaste serves Goan and Keralan cuisine (with South-East Asian hints) in an old courthouse that has been decorated in 'carnival' colours. Try *frango piri-piri* (£7.75), a fiery hot chicken tikka marinated in red *masala*.

Sweeting's (Map 6; ☎ 7248 3062, 39 Queen Victoria St EC4; ☻ Mansion House). Sweeting's is an old-fashioned place, with a mosaic floor and waiters in white aprons standing behind narrow counters serving up all sorts of traditional fishy delights. Something as wild smoked salmon costs £8.50; main courses run from £8 to £19.

Bermondsey (Map 6)

This area's culinary highlights include Terence Conran's gastronomic palaces at Shad Thames (☻ Bermondsey or Tower Hill).

Blue Print Café (☎ 7378 7031, Design Museum, Butlers Wharf, Shad Thames SE1). Modern European cooking is the order of the day at this flagship Conran restaurant, with starters from £5 to £6.50 and main courses from £11 to £16.50. There are spectacular views of the river from here and the Design Museum is next door.

Cantina del Ponte (☎ 7403 5403, Butlers Wharf, 36c Shad Thames SE1). This is a more affordable riverside Conran restaurant serving Italian/Mediterranean food. Starters are from £5, main courses from £13, with pizzas about £7 and pastas from £7.50 to £12.50. At lunch during the week and at dinner on Sunday there's a two/three-course meal for £12/15. There's fabulous outside seating in warm weather.

Southwark (Map 6)

The number of options in this part of town should increase, thanks in no small part to Tate Modern.

Manze's (☎ 7407 2985, 87 Tower Bridge Rd SE1; ⊖ London Bridge). This pie shop, the oldest still trading in London, has been going strong for over a century and is handy for Bermondsey Market. In its pleasantly tiled interior jellied eels cost £2, pie and mash £2.20, and pie and liquor £1.50.

Konditor & Cook (☎ 7620 2700, 10 Stoney St SE1; ⊖ London Bridge). The original location of arguably the best bakery in London serves excellent hot and cold lunches. There are tables outside and everything is available for takeaway. Most items are under £3.

Tate Modern Café (☎ 7401 5020, Bankside SE1; ⊖ Southwark). The food is, well, artful at this trendy cafe with superb views. The menu – like the galleries below – draws on influences from around the world and features salads, sandwiches and various main courses; a meal can cost from £5 to £20. It opens 10.15 am to 5.30 pm daily and for dinner on Friday and Saturday (although these hours may be extended).

The Tall House (Map 4; ☎ 7401 2929, 134 Southwark St SE1; ⊖ Southwark). Cantonese cuisine is the inspiration for the fresh and lively fare offered at this sleek restaurant. Two courses will cost about £12. It opens noon to midnight (closed on Sunday).

Fish! (☎ 7836 3236, Cathedral St SE1; ⊖ London Bridge). Situated in an all-glass Victorian pavilion overlooking Borough Market and Southwark Cathedral, Fish! serves fresher-than-fresh fish and seafood prepared simply: steamed or grilled swordfish, cod, skate, squid (or whatever is ticked off on the placemat) served with one of five sauces. Expect to pay anything from £8.50 to £15.95 for a main course.

Waterloo & Lambeth (Map 4)

This part of south London is not immediately attractive as a place for eating out, although the cafes and restaurants in the Royal Festival Hall, the Royal National Theatre and the National Film Theatre are popular places to meet, with reasonable food.

Konditor & Cook (☎ 7620 2700, 66 The Cut SE1; ⊖ Waterloo). This cafe branch of the famous Southwark bakery at the Young Vic Theatre serves meals 8.30 am to 11 pm Monday to Friday and from 10.30 am on Saturday.

Mesón Don Felipe (☎ 7928 3237, 53 The Cut SE1; ⊖ Waterloo). This tapas place gets recommended more often than most for its wide choice, affordability (£3 to £4 per dish) and attractive surroundings.

Tas (☎ 7928 1444, 33 The Cut SE1; ⊖ Southwark). This is an excellent Turkish place with plush surroundings and fine food. The choban kavurma lamb casserole (£6.95) has many fans.

Fish! (☎ 7234 3333, 3B Belvedere Rd SE1; ⊖ Waterloo). A new branch of the Southwark original (see earlier in this section), this Fish! maintains the commitment to fresh seafood.

Oxo Tower Restaurant & Brasserie (☎ 7803 3888, Barge House St SE1; ⊖ Waterloo). The conversion of the old Oxo Tower on the South Bank into housing with this restaurant on the 8th floor helped spur much of the restaurant renaissance south of the river. The food – a bit Mediterranean, a bit French, some Pacific Rim – is quite good. Starters cost from £5.50 to £13.50, main courses average £18 and there's a three-course set lunch for £24.50.

Pizzeria Castello (Map 1; ☎ 7703 2556, 20 Walworth Rd SE1; ⊖ Elephant & Castle). Ask any south Londoner to direct you to the best pizzeria on this side of the Thames and you'll find yourself here. Castello has been going for years, is family owned, very friendly and prices are low (under £6). Book or count on a long wait for a table.

Chelsea, South Kensington & Earl's Court (Map 7)

These three areas boast an incredible array of eateries – from Michelin-starred restaurants to trendy noodle bars to French patisseries – to suit all budgets.

Benjy's (☎ 7373 0245, 157 Earl's Court Rd SW5; ⊖ Earl's Court). Though Benjy's is nothing more than a fairly traditional cafe, it's always bustling and the food is cheap and filling. Serious breakfasts, with as much tea or coffee as you can drink, cost around £3.50, while lunch is £4.95.

Krungtap (☎ 7259 2314, 227 Old Brompton Rd SW10; ⊖ Earl's Court). Krungtap (the Thai name for Bangkok) is a busy, friendly cafe open for dinner only. Most dishes are in the £3.50 to £5 range.

Blanco's (☎ 7370 3101, 314 Earl's Court Rd SW5; ⊖ Earl's Court). Blanco's is a lively, authentic tapas (from £2.25 to £4.95) bar that serves good Spanish beer. It stays open until midnight.

Chelsea Bun (Map 7; ☎ 7352 3635, 9a Lamont Rd SW10; ✪ Fulham Broadway or Earl's Court). This London version of an American diner is a great-value place in the area known as World's End. Breakfast is served all day, and there's seating on an upstairs veranda. Main dishes cost between £4 and £7.

Oriel (☎ 7730 2804, 50-51 Sloane Square SW1; ✪ Sloane Square). With its comfortable wicker chairs and mirrors, and tables overlooking Sloane Square, the Oriel makes the perfect place to meet before going shopping in King's Rd or Sloane St. Main dishes cost from £5 to £10, lighter fare, such as pasta and salads, costs from £6 to £8.50.

The Collection (☎ 7225 1212, 264 Brompton Rd SW3; ✪ South Kensington). The Collection has a wonderful location in a converted gallery, with the main restaurant on a balcony overlooking the bar – great for people-watching. Starters are from £3.50 to £7, main courses £11 to £14.50, and there are set meals for £10/13 for two/three courses.

Spago (☎ 7225 2407, 6 Glendower Place SW7; ✪ South Kensington). This excellent-value Italian restaurant, with a good range of pastas and pizzas from £4.50, is convenient for the South Kensington museums. It opens late for dinner only, and there is live music on Saturday.

New Culture Revolution (☎ 7352 9281, 305 King's Rd SW3; ✪ Sloane Square). This trendy, good-value dumpling and noodle bar has main dishes for around £6.

Made in Italy (☎ 7352 1880, 249 King's Rd SW3; ✪ Sloane Square). This family-run restaurant is like a trip to southern Italy without the hassle of the trip. Pizzas (£6) are great, as is the changing menu of pastas and fresh fish (£6 to £12). Families are catered for and it's a just-plain-fun place.

Daphne's (☎ 7589 4257, 112 Draycott Ave SW3; ✪ South Kensington). This place, popular with celebrities and their followers, is small enough to be intimate but large enough not to be claustrophobic. It serves delicious Mediterranean-style food, with main courses from £12.50 to £19, pastas from £9.

Bibendum (☎ 7581 5817, 81 Fulham Rd SW3; ✪ South Kensington). This Conran establishment is in one of London's finest settings for a restaurant, the Art Nouveau Michelin House (1911). The popular Bibendum Oyster Bar (£3.60 to £10.20 for half a dozen) is on the ground floor, where you really feel at the heart of the architectural finery. Upstairs it's all much lighter and brighter. A full meal with wine is likely to set you back around £55 a head.

Casual French A large number of French people live in South Kensington, and you'll find a lot of French-operated businesses here, particularly along Bute St, just southwest of South Kensington tube station, including a delicatessen called *La Grande Bouchée* (☎ 7589 8346) at No 31 and the *Rôtisserie Jules* (☎ 7584 0600) at Nos 6 to 8, a simple French-style cafeteria with flame-roasted chicken (from £4.95 to £9.75) and *gigot d'agneau*.

Around the corner, *FrancoFill* (☎ 7584 0087, 1 Old Brompton Rd SW7) is a delightful cafe-restaurant serving meals for around £10.

Kensington & Knightsbridge (Maps 3 & 4)

The restaurants, cafes and bars in these posh 'villages' of west and south-west London cater for a very well-heeled clientele, but there's always something good (and affordable) off the high streets.

Pizza on the Park (Map 4; ☎ 7235 5273, 11 Knightsbridge SW5; ✪ Hyde Park Corner). This place is as popular for its nightly jazz in the basement as for its pizza. There's also a spacious restaurant upstairs and, if you're lucky, a few tables overlooking Hyde Park. Pizzas average £6.50. Breakfast is available all day from 8.15 am (£4 for continental, £4.95 for English) and afternoon tea (£6.95) at 3.15 pm.

Bellini's (Map 3; ☎ 7937 5520, 47 Kensington Court W8; ✪ High Street Kensington). This stylish restaurant with a few pavement tables and views of a flower-bedecked alley serves two/three-course lunches for £6.75/7.90.

Fifth Floor (Map 3; ☎ 7235 5250, Harvey Nichols, 109–125 Knightsbridge SW1; ✪ Knightsbridge). This restaurant, bar and cafe is the perfect place to drop after you've shopped. It's expensive, averaging £30 per head at dinner, but there's a three-course set lunch for £23.50 served noon and 3 pm weekdays (to 3.30 pm at the weekend).

Notting Hill & Bayswater (Map 3)

Notting Hill, so popular ever since *that* film, has all sorts of interesting places to eat, and there are literally dozens of places lining Queensway and Westbourne Grove, with everything from cheap takeaways to good quality restaurants.

Market Thai (☎ 7460 8320, 240 Portobello Rd; ⊖ Ladbroke Grove). Fresh and delicious Thai cuisine is on offer here one floor above a bar and way above the market crowds. Specials for £5 are good value.

Geales (☎ 7727 7528, 2 Farmer St W8; ⊖ Notting Hill Gate). This popular fish restaurant prices everything according to weight and season. Fish and chips costs about £8.50 and it's worth every penny.

Café Grove (☎ 7243 1094, 253a Portobello Rd; ⊖ Ladbroke Grove). Head here for gigantic and imaginative breakfasts as well as cheap and cheerful vegetarian food at around £5. The large balcony overlooking the market is great for watching all the action on a weekend morning.

Mandola (☎ 7229 4734, 139–141 Westbourne Grove W2; ⊖ Bayswater). Mandola offers something entirely different: vegetarian Sudanese dishes such as tamia (£4.50), a kind of felafel, or fifilia (£6.95), a vegetable curry. Meat dishes such as chicken halla are around £7.

Osteria Basilico (☎ 7727 9372, 29 Kensington Park Rd W11; ⊖ Notting Hill Gate or Ladbroke Grove). This neighbourhood restaurant offers a good mix of Italian rustic charm and west London chic, with an authentic menu and a lively, relaxed atmosphere. The tables by the window are best, but you will need to book. Pasta (from £6) and fish dishes (from £8) are recommended.

Kalamaras Micro (☎ 7727 5082, 66 Inverness Mews W2; ⊖ Bayswater). The surroundings aren't mega, but the food is macro in this Greek spot in a quiet mews off Queensway. Main courses average about £7.50 and you can BYO.

Manzara (☎ 7727 3062, 24 Pembridge Rd W11; ⊖ Notting Hill Gate). This simple place offers cheap but fresh and well-prepared Turkish food for less than £10.

The Standard (☎ 7229 0600, 21–23 Westbourne Grove W2; ⊖ Bayswater). The Standard serves excellent and very good-value Indian food. Count on about £10 per person.

Brasserie de Marché aux Puces (☎ 8968 5828, 349 Portobello Rd; ⊖ Ladbroke Grove). On a quiet stretch of street north of the market, this delightful brasserie has French classics at good prices (most under £12) and tables outside should the sun shine.

Inaho (☎ 7221 8495, 4 Hereford Rd W2; ⊖ Bayswater). This tiny Japanese restaurant has a tempura set dinner comprising an appetiser, soup, mixed salad, yakitori, sashimi, tempura, rice and seasonal fruits for £20 and a teriyaki equivalent for £22. A tonkatsu is £7, and rice and noodle dishes cost from £4 to £6.

Bali Sugar (☎ 7221 4477, 33a All Saints Rd W11; ⊖ Westbourne Park). This lovely restaurant is filled with flowers and charm. The excellent food is described as 'fusion' (average £27 per person) and leans slightly on the Asian side.

Euston (Map 2)

Drummond St (⊖ Euston Square or Euston) has a number of good South Indian vegetarian restaurants. **Diwana** (☎ 7387 5556) at No 121, the first (and some say still the best) of its kind on the street, specialises in Bombay-style bel poori (a kind of 'party mix' snack) and dosas (a kind of filled pancake) and has an all-you-can-eat lunch-time buffet for £3.95. Nearby at No 124, **Chutneys** (☎ 7388 0604) has a better lunch buffet (available all day on Sunday) for £4.95.

Camden (Map 2)

Camden High St is lined with good places to eat, although to watch the Sunday daytrippers snacking on takeaway sausages and chips you'd hardly believe it.

Café Delancey (☎ 7387 1985, 3 Delancey St NW1; ⊖ Camden Town). The granddaddy of French-style brasseries in London, Café Delancey offers the chance to get a decent cup of coffee with a snack or a full meal in relaxed European-style surroundings complete with newspapers. Main dishes cost from £8 to £13, wine starts at £6.90 for a half-bottle. The cramped toilets, bickering staff and Charles Aznavour crooning in the background seem suitably Parisian too.

El Parador (☎ 7387 2789, 245 Eversholt St NW1; ⊖ Mornington Crescent). El Parador is a quiet Spanish place where the selection of some 15 vegetarian dishes and tapas includes empanadillas de espinacas y queso (a spinach and cheese dish) for £3.80, with meat and fish dishes just a little more expensive (about £5).

Bar Gansa (☎ 7267 8909, 2 Inverness St NW1; ⊖ Camden Town). This arty bar/cafe has tapas for around £3 and more elaborate Spanish main courses from £6.50 to £7.95. Service is good and the Spanish staff are very friendly. Breakfast costs £3.95. It serves drinks until 12.30 am (1 am on Friday and Saturday).

Lemon Grass (☎ 7284 1116, 243 Royal College St; ⊖ Camden Town). Lemon Grass is one of the better Thai eateries in Camden with authentic food and charming decor and staff. Main dishes cost around £6.

Thanh Binh *(☎ 7267 9820, 14 Chalk Farm Rd NW1; ⊖ Camden Town)*. A quiet little eatery opposite Camden Market, Thanh Binh serves decent Vietnamese dishes for between £4.50 and £6.50 and there's a set lunch for £5.

Sauce *(☎ 7482 0777, 214 Camden High St NW1; ⊖ Camden Town)*. This young and trendy place makes much of the fact that it uses organic ingredients. The food is broad ranging – from salads to burgers – and averages £6 to £11.

The Engineer *(☎ 7722 0950, 65 Gloucester Ave NW1; ⊖ Chalk Farm)*. A pretty Victorian place converted into a highly successful pub and gastropub restaurant, which upstairs attracts a groovy north-London set. The modern British food is top of the mark and averages about £12 per person.

Lemonia *(Map 1; ☎ 7586 7454, 89 Regent's Park Rd NW1; ⊖ Chalk Farm)*. This upmarket and very popular Greek restaurant offers good-value food and a lively atmosphere. Meze costs £13.50 per person and both the vegetarian and meat moussakas for £7.50 are particularly tasty. There's a set weekday lunch for £7.50.

Islington (Map 2)

Islington is an excellent place for a night out. At the last count there were more than 60 cafes and restaurants between Angel and Highbury Corner, with most of the action on Upper St.

The Duke of Cambridge *(☎ 7359 3066, 30 St Peter's St N1; ⊖ Angel)*. London's 'first organic gastropub' provides good, solid food in welcoming surroundings. Prices range from £4 to £14

Ravi Shankar *(☎ 7833 5849, 422 St John St EC1; ⊖ Angel)*. This small, inexpensive restaurant has some of the best Indian vegetarian food in London.

Afghan Kitchen *(☎ 7359 8019, 35 Islington Green N1; ⊖ Angel)*. This small, simple yet trendy place serves simple Afghan fare – spiced meats and vegetables – that goes well with the basmati rice. It's quick and cheap (about £5).

Angel Mangal *(☎ 7359 7777, 139 Upper St N1; ⊖ Angel or Highbury & Islington)*. Excellent and cheap Turkish food makes this a hard act to beat. A huge array of meat is grilled on command and served with platters of fresh vegetables and salads. Expect to pay under £10 per person.

Tartuf *(☎ 7288 0954, 88 Upper St N1; ⊖ Angel)*. Classic Alsatian *tartes flambeés* are the stars at this fun and casual place. The wafer-thin crusts come with a variety of toppings and cost about £6. The all-you-can-eat deal for £10 per person guarantees an unstoppable flow of hot *tartes* from the kitchen.

Lola's *(☎ 7359 1932, The Mall, 359 Upper St N1; ⊖ Angel)*. This award-winning restaurant is celebrated for its lovely decor, changing menu and popular Sunday brunch with live jazz. Starters range from £5 to £7, main courses from £10.50 to £14.

Hampstead

Hampstead, London's most authentic village, has loads of good restaurants within easy walking distance of its tube station.

Café Base *(☎ 7431 3241, 70-71 Hampstead High St NW3)*. This bright and clean cafe has unusual ciabatta sandwiches and wraps for £2.60 to £4.95 and salads and pastas for £2.95 to £3.95.

La Gaffe *(☎ 7794 7526, 107 Heath St NW3)*. This comfortable, family-run Italian restaurant in an 18th-century cottage has been going forever. The prices are quite reasonable.

Giraffe *(☎ 7435 0343, 46 Rosslyn Hill NW3)*. This delightful cafe offers breakfast in the morning (banana pancakes £4.25) and an eclectic menu the rest of the day. It's comfy and casual and great if you're checking out the village or the heath.

East End (Maps 1 & 6)

From the Indian and Bangladeshi restaurants of Brick Lane to the trendy eateries of Hoxton and Shoreditch, the East End has finally made it onto the culinary map of London. Spitalfields Market (Map 6) is home to a diverse range of casual and fun eateries.

Brick Lane Beigel Bake *(Map 1; ☎ 7729 0616, 159 Brick Lane E2; ⊖ Shoreditch)*. More of a delicatessen than a cafe, the Beigel Bake is at the Bethnal Green Rd end of Brick Lane and opens 24 hours. You won't find fresher or cheaper bagels anywhere in London. Filled bagels are a snip at 45p to 65p (the salmon and cream cheese version is a whopping 95p).

Mesón Los Barriles *(Map 6; ☎ 7375 3136, 8a Lamb St E1; ⊖ Liverpool Street)*. This tapas bar and restaurant in Spitalfields Market has an excellent selection of fish and seafood. Tapas range from £2 to £4.90, main courses average £6.50.

The Real Greek (Map 1; ☎ 7739 8212, 15 Hoxton Market N1; ✆ Old Street). Hoxton Market is one of the trendiest areas of London and this restaurant is justifiably popular. The Greek food is like nothing you've had before and is wonderfully creative. Located in an old pub, it opens for lunch and dinner (closed on Sunday). Expect to pay about £25 per person.

Viet Hoa (Map 1; ☎ 7729 8293, 70–72 Kingsland Rd E2; bus No 67 or 149). This simple canteen-style eatery serves excellent and authentic Vietnamese dishes. A full meal should cost you less than £10 and it's always full.

Indian Brick Lane (Map 1; ✆ Aldgate East or Shoreditch) is lined wall-to-wall with cheap Indian and Bangladeshi restaurants – not all of them very good. *Aladin* (☎ 7247 8210) at No 132, a favourite of many, and *Nazrul* (☎ 7247 2505) at No 130 may be worth a try; both are unlicensed but you can BYO and should eat for around £8. More upmarket are *Le Taj* (☎ 7247 4210) at No 134 and *Sheraz* (☎ 7247 5755) at No 13.

Greenwich (Map 9)

Beautiful Greenwich has both old-style eateries and trendy new restaurants from which to choose. Greenwich Market has several small places for breakfast and lunch and the market itself operates from Friday to Sunday. The Cutty Sark DLR station is convenient for all of the following. See the Entertainment section for some pubs with good food in Greenwich.

Greenwich Church St has a few decent and inexpensive cafes, including *Peter de Wit's* (☎ 8305 0048) at No 21 with cream teas for about £4.

Goddards Ye Olde Pie Shop (☎ 8692 3601, 45 Greenwich Church St SE10). Goddards is truly a step back into the past: a real London caff with wooden benches and things such as steak and kidney pie with liquor and mash, and shepherd's pie with beans and a rich brown gravy (all under £2.50). Sweet pies are from 50p. It opens 11 am to 3 or 4 pm most days except Monday.

Bar Du Musee (☎ 8858 4710, 17 Nelson Rd, SE10). More cafe than pub, this relaxed French place has a good wine selection by the glass and a fine menu of salads, tarts and the like for about £5. It also has a nice garden.

Vietnam (☎ 8858 0871, 18 King William Walk SE10). Vietnam has inexpensive lunch plates such as spring rolls with noodles or rice (£3.95) available from noon to 5 pm.

Beachcomber (☎ 8853 0055, 34 Greenwich Church St SE10). This old stalwart festooned with flower baskets and potted plants does set two/three/four-course lunches for £5.90/7.95/9.90 and full breakfasts for £3.90. It's a very pleasant place on a sunny afternoon.

Brixton (Map 1)

If you're coming for the market (✆ Brixton), don't restrict yourself to the eateries in the covered market itself. The surrounding streets (eg, Atlantic Rd and Coldharbour Lane) have a number of excellent places.

Eco Brixton (☎ 7738 3021, 4 Market Row SW9). This restaurant is one of the best in south London for pizzas (from £5.50), antipasti (£7.50) and cappuccino. It opens to 5 pm daily (except on Wednesday and Saturday).

El Pilon Quindiano (☎ 7326 4316, Granville Arcade SW9). This Colombian cafe serves such authentic delicacies as *arepa* (small maize pancakes with various fillings), yucca and *empañadas* for around £3. A full lunch costs £6. This is the place to come if you want to try cheap South American dishes.

Satay Bar (☎ 7326 5001, 447-450 Coldharbour Lane SW9). One of our favourite Asian eateries, the Satay Bar serves surprisingly authentic Indonesian food: *rendang ayam* (£5.95), laksa (£5.25), mixed satays (£5.95) and *mee goreng* (£4.25). *Rijsttafel* is £11.95 per person. Even more authentic are all the doors that open on to the busy street – you could easily be in a *warung* in Yogyakarta.

Bah Humbug (☎ 7738 3184, St Matthew's Peace Garden, Brixton Hill SW2). In the crypt of St Matthew's Methodist Church, Bah Humbug is one of the best vegetarian restaurants in London with quite a global range – from Thai vegetable fritters (£3) to Cantonese mock duck and *masala* curry (under £6.50).

Fulham (Map 1 & 7)

Fulham Rd is a good place for a meal and a night out.

The Gate (Map 1; ☎ 8748 6932, 51 Queen Caroline St W6; ✆ Hammersmith). This may be the place to convert your carnivorous counterparts to the kinder, gentler world of vegetarianism.

The beautifully presented, unusual main courses go for around £8.50; the dining room with its high ceilings and wall of glass is equally fine.

The Blue Elephant *(Map 7;* ☎ *7385 6595, 4–6 Fulham Broadway SW6;* ⊖ *Fulham Broadway).* This Fulham institution serves upmarket (and very pricey) Thai food in jungle-like surroundings – you can't see the trees for the forest. The best time to come is between noon and 2.30 pm on Sunday when it does a fab Sunday set brunch for £16.75.

The River Café *(Map 1;* ☎ *7381 8824, Thames Wharf, Rainville Rd W6;* ⊖ *Hammersmith).* The very buzzy, see-and-be-seen River Café owes its fame as much to the cookbooks it has spawned as to the food actually served here, but it does have the best modern Italian cuisine in London. Main dishes start at £16.50 and you're unlikely to have much change from £40 once you've added a starter or dessert and wine.

Kew

A short distance north of Victoria Gate, the main entrance to Kew Gardens, is a historic cafe.

Newens Maids of Honour *(*☎ *8940 2752, 288 Kew Rd;* ⊖ *Kew Gardens).* This old-fashioned tearoom that wouldn't seem out of place in a Cotswolds village owes its fame to a special dessert supposedly concocted by Henry VIII's second wife, the ill-fated Anne Boleyn, from puff pastry, lemon, almonds and curd cheese. A 'maid of honour' will cost you £1.40, but don't plan on sampling it on Monday afternoon or Sunday when the tearoom is closed (otherwise it opens 9.30 am to 6 pm). Set teas (£4.65) are served from 2.30 to 5.30 pm.

ENTERTAINMENT
Pubs & Bars

For a selection of London's best pubs and bars, see the boxed text 'Where to Drink in London' on pages 234 and 235.

Clubs

Though the majority of London's pubs still close at 11 pm, there are clubs where you can carry on partying. Admission costs vary from £10 to £15 for most clubs, plus at least £3 per drink. The most happening clubs don't kick off until after midnight and stay open until 4 or 5 am; some are all-nighters. Dress can be smart (no suits) or casual; the more outrageous you look – within reason – the better your chances of getting in.

Bagley's Studios *(Map 2;* ☎ *7278 2777, King's Cross Freight Depot, York Way N1;* ⊖ *King's Cross St Pancras).* A huge converted warehouse with five dance floors, four bars and an outside area in the summer.

The End *(Map 5;* ☎ *7419 9199, 16a West Central St WC1;* ⊖ *Holborn).* Modern industrial decor with a free water-fountain. For serious clubbers who like their music underground.

The Fridge *(Map 1;* ☎ *7326 5100, 1 Town Hall Parade, Brixton Hill SW2;* ⊖ *Brixton).* The Fridge offers a wide variety of club nights in an excellent venue that is not too big, not too small. Saturday is gay night.

Fabric *(Map 4;* ☎ *7490 0444, 77a Charterhouse St EC1;* ⊖ *Farringdon).* This latest feather in Clerkenwell's well-plumed cap boasts three dance floors in a converted meat cold-store.

Ministry of Sound *(Map 6;* ☎ *7378 6528, 103 Gaunt St SE1;* ⊖ *Elephant & Castle).* This cavernous place, arguably London's most famous club, attracts hard-core clubbers as well as people who just want to chill out. It's open until 9 am.

Velvet Room *(Map 5;* ☎ *7439 4655, 143 Charing Cross Rd WC2;* ⊖ *Tottenham Court Road).* An intimate, friendly club swathed in red velvet.

Gay & Lesbian London

The best starting point is to pick up the free *Pink Paper* (very serious, politically correct) or *Boyz* (more geared towards entertainment) available from most gay cafes, bars and clubs. The four-page gay section of *Time Out* is another excellent source of information. The Lesbian & Gay Switchboard (☎ 7837 7324) answers calls 24 hours.

London's bars and clubs cater for every predilection, but there's a growing trend towards mixed gay and straight clubs.

Soho In the 'gay village' of Soho (⊖ Tottenham Court Road or Piccadilly Circus) – particularly along Old Compton St – bars and cafes are thick on the ground. All of the following places are on Map 5.

The ***Old Compton Café*** *(*☎ *7439 3309, 34 Old Compton St W1)* is a friendly, sometimes frantic, 24-hour place while ***Balans*** *(*☎ *7437 5212),* at No 60, is a popular, moderately priced, continental-style cafe.

Piss-elegant **Rupert St** (☎ *7734 5614, 50 Rupert St W1)*, London's trendiest gay bar, is on a corner and has large glass windows for looking, being looked at, looking at being looked at, and so on. Lots of looking, little cruising.

Near Tottenham Court Road tube station, the long-established, friendly **First Out** (☎ *7240 8042, 52 St Giles High St WC2)* is a mixed lesbian-gay cafe that serves vegetarian food and has rotating exhibitions. Close by, the **Astoria** (☎ *7434 9592, 157-165 Charing Cross Rd WC2)* is a dark, sweaty and atmospheric club, with good views of the stage and a huge dance floor.

Retro Bar (☎ *7321 2811, 2 George Court WC2)* is a friendly place down a small lane off the Strand, with a host of theme nights in the upstairs bar during the week.

North There are gay places around King's Cross and in Islington and Camden. The ever popular **Central Station** (Map 2; ☎ *7278 3294, 37 Wharfdale Rd N1; ✪ King's Cross St Pancras)* has a bar with special one-nighters and the UK's only gay sports bar. The **Black Cap** (Map 2; ☎ *7428 2721, 171 Camden High St NW1; ✪ Camden Town)* is a late-night bar famous for its drag shows.

South Brixton is one of south London's gay centres. The laid-back **Fridge Bar** (Map 1; ☎ *7326 5100)*, next to the huge Fridge club (see the previous Clubs section), serves not-so-laid-back absinthe and other libations to 11 pm daily. It also has a good cafe.

Comedy

London plays host to a number of clubs whose *raison d'être* is comedy; there are even more venues – especially pubs – that set aside specific nights for stand-up comedy acts. The place to look for day-to-day details is *Time Out*, but the following are very popular venues:

Comedy Café (Map 1; ☎ *7739 5706, 66 Rivington St EC2; ✪ Old Street)*. There's something for everyone at this Hoxton club, just off

Shoreditch High St. Wednesday is Try Out Night when anyone can give it a go.

Comedy Store (Map 5; ☎ *7344 0234, 1A Oxendon St SW1; ✪ Piccadilly Circus)*. Mostly big acts appear at London's longest-established comedy club, now in its third decade (from £12 to £15). Shows start at 8 pm Tuesday to Sunday with a midnight show on Friday and Saturday.

Live Music

Rock & Pop London's music scene is so vibrant that we can only scratch the surface with the following recommendations. You'll need to check the press to see what's on. The following are some of the best venues:

Brixton Academy (Map 1; ☎ *7771 2000, 211 Stockwell Rd SW9; ✪ Brixton)*. Enormous and very popular venue with a good atmosphere.

Garage (Map 2; ☎ *7607 1818, 20–22 Highbury Corner N5; ✪ Highbury & Islington)*. Good venue for rock, industrial and punk.

Borderline (Map 5; ☎ *7734 2095, Orange Yard W1; ✪ Tottenham Court Road)*. Small, relaxed venue with a reputation for big-name bands playing under pseudonyms.

Underworld (Map 2; ☎ *7482 1932, 174 Camden High St NW1; ✪ Camden Town)*. Beneath the huge World's End pub, a small venue featuring new bands.

Jazz The jazz scene is diverse and spread throughout the city.

Jazz Café (Map 2; ☎ *7344 0044, 5 Parkway NW1; ✪ Camden Town)*. Very trendy restaurant venue; it's best to book a table. Acts cost from £8 to £15 at the door, cheaper in advance.

100 Club (Map 5; ☎ *7636 0933, 100 Oxford St W1; ✪ Oxford Circus)*. Legendary venue, once showcasing the Stones and at the centre of the punk revolution, now concentrating on jazz (tickets from £6 to £10).

Classical Music London is Europe's classical-music capital, with several symphony orchestras, various smaller outfits, brilliant venues, reasonable prices and high standards of performance.

The **Royal Festival Hall**, **Queen Elizabeth Hall** and **Purcell Room** (Map 4; ☎ *7960 4242; ✪ Waterloo)* are three of

Where to Drink in London

Sampling a range of pubs and bars is part of the fun of visiting London. The following list includes most of our favourites, but there's no substitute for individual research. Many of the pubs listed below serve good food.

Westminster & Mayfair (Maps 4 & 5)

Sherlock Holmes (Map 5; 10 Northumberland St WC2; ✪ Charing Cross). Tucked away just off Northumberland Ave, this pub filled with Holmes memorabilia doesn't get quite as busy as it might and is never touristy.

Westminster Arms (Map 4; 9 Storey's Gate SW1; ✪ Westminster). This pleasant, atmospheric place is great for a quick one after a tiring tour of Westminster Abbey, which is a two-minute walk away. Think of the convenience.

Ye Grapes (Map 4; 16 Shepherd Market W1; ✪ Green Park). A middle-of-the-road pub that combines good beer, period decor, a friendly crowd and views of life on Shepherd Market.

West End (Maps 4 & 5)

Scruffy Murphy's (Map 5; 15 Denman St W1; ✪ Piccadilly Circus). This little place is the most authentic – snugs, brogues, Guinness and drunks – of the Irish pubs in Soho.

O Bar (Map 5; 83–85 Wardour St W1; ✪ Piccadilly Circus). This upbeat bar has two main drinking floors with a DJ downstairs nightly (£5 cover charge). It also serves half-price pitchers of cocktails till 8 pm (till closing on Monday, to midnight on Wednesday).

Cork & Bottle Wine Bar (Map 5; 44-46 Cranbourn St WC2; ✪ Leicester Square). Hidden downstairs on the left as you head towards Leicester Square from the tube station, the Cork & Bottle is always packed to the hilt after work, but the food's good, the wine list commendable and there are several hideaway alcoves.

Lamb & Flag (Map 5; 33 Rose St WC2; ✪ Covent Garden). Everyone's 'find' in Covent Garden and therefore always jammed, the pleasantly unchanged Lamb & Flag was once known as the Bucket of Blood.

Bloomsbury (Maps 4 & 5)

The Queen's Larder (Map 4; 1 Queen Square WC1; ✪ Russell Square). In a lovely square east of Russell Square, the Queen is a handy retreat, with outside benches and pub grub.

Museum Tavern (Map 5; 49 Great Russell St WC1; ✪ Tottenham Court Road). After a hard day's work poring over books in the British Museum Reading Room, Karl Marx used to repair to this capacious pub, where you too can sup your pint.

The City (Maps 4 & 6)

Ye Olde Cheshire Cheese (Map 4; Wine Office Court EC4; ✪ Blackfriars). The entrance to this celebrated historic pub is via a picturesque alley at 145 Fleet St. Cross the threshold and you'll find yourself in a wood-panelled interior (the oldest bit dates from the mid-17th century) with sawdust on the floor and divided up into various bars and eating areas (for more on the food, see The City in the Places to Eat section).

Ye Olde Mitre (Map 4; 1 Ely Court EC1; ✪ Chancery Lane). One of our absolute favourites, the Mitre is one of London's oldest and most historic pubs, although the 18th-century-sized rooms can be a bit tight for early-21st-century punters like us.

Cock Tavern (Map 4; East Poultry Ave EC1; ✪ Farringdon). This legendary pub will serve you a pint between 6.30 and 10.30 am when it serves the workers from Smithfield Market.

Vertigo (Map 6; Bishopsgate EC2, ✪ Liverpool Street). The 373m-tall NatWest Tower is a soaring albeit bland component of the London skyline. Vertigo occupies the 42nd floor at the top and has excellent views on a clear day. It's pricey but you're paying for the view. Booking, even for a drink, is essential (☎ 7877 7842).

South of the Thames (Maps 4 & 6)

George Inn (Map 6; Talbot Yard, 77 Borough High St SE1; ✪ London Bridge or Borough). The George is London's last surviving galleried coaching inn, dates from 1676 and is mentioned in Dickens' Little Dorrit. Here too is the site of the Tabard Inn (hence the Talbot Yard address), where the pilgrims gathered in Chaucer's Canterbury Tales before setting out.

The Anchor (Map 6; 34 Park St SE1; ✪ London Bridge). This 18th-century place just east of the Globe Theatre has superb views across the Thames from its terrace.

Where to Drink in London

The Market Porter (Map 6; 9 Stoney St SE1; ✪ London Bridge). There's a good range of beers on offer at this old classic right across from Borough Market.

The Fire Station (Map 4; 150 Waterloo Rd SE1; ✪ Waterloo). This immensely popular gastropub (from £7 to £10 for main courses) is in a part of town that was once a culinary desert but is now always jammed. There's jazz on Sunday afternoon.

Chelsea (Map 7)

King's Head & Eight Bells (50 Cheyne Walk; ✪ Sloane Square). This attractive corner pub, pleasantly hung with flower baskets in summer, has a wide range of beers and was a favourite of the painter Whistler and the writer Carlyle.

The Antelope (22-24 Eaton Terrace SW1; ✪ Sloane Square). This charming pub has been around longer than any of its neighbouring buildings, and it's music-free so a perfect place for a tête-à-tête.

Kensington & Holland Park (Map 3)

The Churchill Arms (119 Kensington Church St W8; ✪ Notting Hill Gate). This traditional English pub is renowned for its Winston memorabilia, chamber pots suspended from a great height and excellent-value Thai food (around £6) served in a lovely conservatory in the back.

Windsor Castle (114 Campden Hill Rd W11; ✪ Notting Hill Gate). The Windsor has one of the nicest walled gardens (with heaters in winter) of any pub in London.

Notting Hill & Bayswater (Map 3)

The Market Bar (240a Portobello Rd W11; ✪ Ladbroke Grove). Convenient for the market, this place has an interesting, eclectic decor and an entertaining crowd.

The Bridge House (13 Westbourne Terrace Rd W2; ✪ Warwick Avenue). This is in a lovely location just opposite the Grand Union Canal.

Camden (Maps 1 & 2)

Crown & Goose (Map 2; 100 Arlington Rd NW1; ✪ Camden Town). This is a new-style pub attracting a youngish crowd with decent, no-nonsense food.

Pembroke Castle (Map 1; 150 Gloucester Ave NW1; ✪ Chalk Farm). We love this light, airy retro place with lovely stained glass and a refined, sportsman's theme.

Oh! Bar (Map 2; 111-113 Camden High St NW1; ✪ Camden Town). This large pub plays good music that's enjoyed by happy crowds. It's a good place to get your vibe right before heading off elsewhere.

Islington (Map 2)

Old Queen's Head (44 Essex Rd N1; ✪ Angel). Loud, popular and packed to the rafters, the Old Queen's Head was the first pub to introduce the stripped-down, open-plan look to trendy Islington.

East End & Wapping (Maps 1 & 6)

Cantaloupe (Map 1; 35-43 Charlotte Rd EC2; ✪ Old Street or Liverpool Street). This cool pub manages to feel arty without being overwhelming. There's a decent restaurant (main courses from £7 to £14) at the back.

Captain Kidd (Map 1; 108 Wapping High St E1; ✪ Wapping). The Kidd, with its large windows, fine beer-garden and mock scaffold recalling the hanging of the eponymous pirate in 1701, is our favourite riverside pub on the northern bank of the Thames.

Prospect of Whitby (Map 1; 57 Wapping Wall E1; ✪ Wapping). Farther afield than the Kidd, the Whitby dates from 1520 and is one of London's oldest surviving drinking houses, once known as the Devil's Tavern. It's firmly on the tourist trail, but there's a terrace overlooking the Thames, a decent restaurant upstairs and open fires in winter. Check out the pewter bar – Samuel Pepys once sidled up to it.

Greenwich (Map 9)

Trafalgar Tavern (Park Row SE10; DLR Cutty Sark). This cavernous pub with big windows looking onto the Thames and the Millennium Dome has a lot of history. It stands above the site of the old Placentia Palace where Henry VIII was born. The current incarnation dates from 1837. The long menu averages £6.

Cutty Sark Tavern (4-6 Ballast Quay SE10; DLR Cutty Sark). A relaxed riverside pub with tables right along the Thames. The fish and chips are very good and cost £6.

London's premier venues for classical music concerts. All are located on the South Bank. Depending on who's performing and where you sit, prices vary from £5 to £50, but they are usually in the £13 to £30 range. The box office opens from 9 am to 9 pm daily.

The Art Nouveau *Wigmore Hall (Map 4; ☎ 7935 2141, 36 Wigmore St W1; ✆ Bond Street)*, one of the best concert venues in London, offers a great variety of concerts and recitals. The Sunday recitals at 11.30 am (from £7) are particularly good. There are Monday lunch-time concerts (from £7 to £16) at 1 pm.

The *Barbican (Map 6; ☎ 7638 8891, Silk St EC2; ✆ Barbican)* is home to the London Symphony Orchestra. Prices can go as high as £32, but stand-by tickets for £6.50 and £9 are sometimes available just before the performance to students and over-60s.

The *Royal Albert Hall (Map 3; ☎ 7589 8212, Kensington Gore SW7; ✆ South Kensington)* is a splendid-looking Victorian concert hall that hosts all kinds of performances, usually costing from £5 to £40. From mid-July to mid-September it stages the Proms – one of the world's biggest and most democratic classical-music festivals. Seats cost from £5 to £35 depending on what's on, but the real Prom experience means queuing for one of the thousand or so standing (or 'promenading') tickets that go on sale one hour before the start of each concert for £3 each. You can choose to be in the gallery or the arena; there are two separate queues. The box office (door No 7; collect pre-paid tickets at door No 9) opens daily 9 am to 9 pm.

Cinema

Leicester Square is where many British films are premiered, but you'll find cinemas throughout London. As well as scores of multiplexes showing the latest Hollywood output, there are also scores of cinemas showing off-beat, artistic, classic, non-English and all other manner of films. This is one category of entertainment where you really do need *Time Out*.

The following two places are of special note:

National Film Theatre (Map 4; ☎ 7928 3232, South Bank; ✆ Waterloo). This film-lover's heaven screens an impressive range of films.

BFI London IMAX Cinema (Map 4; ☎ 7902 1234, Tenison Way SE1; ✆ Waterloo). This stunning structure houses Europe's largest IMAX screen. Film showings begin at noon daily and cost from £6.75/4.75.

Theatre

London is one of the world's great centres for theatre-lovers, and there's a lot more here than just *Cats*, *Art* and *Chicago*. With tickets so plentiful and reasonably priced, it would be a shame not to take in at least one or two of the best productions. See the boxed text 'Buying Theatre Tickets' for tips.

Royal National Theatre The nation's flagship theatre is the *Royal National Theatre (Map 4; ☎ 7452 3000, South Bank; ✆ Waterloo)*, with three auditoriums: the Olivier, the Lyttleton and the Cottesloe. It showcases classics and contemporary plays, and hosts appearances by the world's best companies.

Tickets for evening performances at the Olivier and Lyttleton cost from £10 to £32.50. Visitors to the box office can sometimes buy one or two tickets for same-day performances for £10 or £13.50. Stand-by tickets are sometimes available two hours before the performance for £16; students with ID pay just £8 but must wait until 45 minutes before the curtain goes up. You can save money by going to a weekday matinee performance, when prices range from £10 to £22.

Under-18s pay from £8 to £10 for matinees and seniors from £11 to £13. Registered disabled visitors are eligible for discounts at all performances.

Most tickets at the smaller Cottesloe cost £22, although some seats with restricted views cost £12.

Barbican The *Barbican (Map 6; ☎ 7638 8891, Silk St EC2; ✆ Barbican)* is the London home of the Royal Shakespeare Company, with two auditoriums – the Barbican Theatre and the smaller Pit. Midweek matinee tickets are from £6 to £30 at the Barbican and £12 to £22 at the Pit. Tickets are half-price for anyone aged under 25 on the day of the performance. There are also price reductions for anyone aged over 60 at matinees and Wednesday evening performances.

Royal Court The *Royal Court (Map 7; ☎ 7565 5000; ⊖ Sloane Square)* has two theatres, the Upstairs and the Downstairs. It tends to favour the new and the anti-establishment – various *enfants terribles*, from John Osborne to Caryl Churchill, got their start here.

Globe Theatre The *Globe Theatre (Map 6; ☎ 7401 9919, 21 New Globe Walk SE1; ⊖ London Bridge)*, a replica of Shakespeare's 'Wooden O' that opened in 1997, now dominates Bankside where several Elizabethan theatres once stood. Come here for a very different theatrical experience. Although there are wooden-bench seats in tiers around the stage, many people emulate the 17th-century 'groundlings' who stood in front of the stage, shouting, cajoling and moving around as the mood took them. The Globe makes few concessions to modern sensibilities. With no roof, it is open to the elements; you should wrap up warmly and bring a flask (thermos); no umbrellas are allowed. Performances of plays by Shakespeare and his contemporaries are staged from May to September only. Two pillars holding up the stage canopy (the 'Heavens') obscure much of the view in section D; you'd almost do better to stand.

Tickets for seats cost from £10 to £26. The 500 standing spaces per performance cost £5 each and can be booked, although you may find a few unsold on the day. The box office opens 10 am to 8 pm Monday to Saturday (to 6 pm when the theatre is closed). Check out the theatre's Web site at www.shakespeares-globe.org.

West End Theatres Every summer the dozens of West End theatres stage a new crop of plays, musicals and other performances. For full details, consult *Time Out*. Addresses and box office phone numbers of the West End theatres are given below; all are on Map 5:

Adelphi (☎ 7344 0055, Strand WC2; ⊖ Charing Cross)
Albery (☎ 7369 1740, St Martin's Lane WC2; ⊖ Leicester Square)
Aldwych (☎ 7416 6075, Aldwych WC2; ⊖ Holborn)
Ambassadors (☎ 7836 6111, West St WC2; ⊖ Leicester Square)
Apollo (☎ 7494 5070, Shaftesbury Ave W1; ⊖ Piccadilly Circus)
Cambridge (☎ 7494 5083, Earlham St WC2; ⊖ Covent Garden)
Comedy (☎ 7369 1741, Panton St SW1; ⊖ Piccadilly Circus)
Criterion (☎ 7369 1737, Piccadilly Circus W1; ⊖ Piccadilly Circus)
Dominion (☎ 7656 1857, Tottenham Court Rd W1; ⊖ Tottenham Court Road)
Drury Lane (☎ 7494 5000, Theatre Royal, Catherine St WC2; ⊖ Covent Garden)
Duchess (☎ 7494 5075, Catherine St WC2; ⊖ Covent Garden)
Duke of York's (☎ 7565 5000, St Martin's Lane WC2; ⊖ Leicester Square)
Fortune (☎ 7836 2238, Russell St WC2; ⊖ Covent Garden)
Garrick (☎ 7494 5085, Charing Cross Rd WC2; ⊖ Charing Cross)
Gielgud (☎ 7494 5065, Shaftesbury Ave W1; ⊖ Piccadilly Circus)
Haymarket (☎ 7930 8800, Haymarket SW1; ⊖ Piccadilly Circus)
Her Majesty's (☎ 7494 5400, Haymarket SW1; ⊖ Piccadilly Circus)
London Palladium (☎ 7494 5030, Argyll St W1; ⊖ Oxford Circus)
Lyceum (☎ 7656 1800, Wellington St WC2; ⊖ Covent Garden)
Lyric (☎ 7494 5045, Shaftesbury Ave W1; ⊖ Piccadilly Circus)
New London (☎ 7405 0072, Drury Lane WC2; ⊖ Holborn)
Palace (☎ 7434 0909, Shaftesbury Ave W1; ⊖ Leicester Square)
Phoenix (☎ 7369 1733, Charing Cross Rd WC2; ⊖ Tottenham Court Road)
Piccadilly (☎ 7369 1734, Denman St W1; ⊖ Piccadilly Circus)
Prince Edward (☎ 7447 5400, Old Compton St W1; ⊖ Leicester Square)
Prince of Wales (☎ 7839 5987, Coventry St W1; ⊖ Piccadilly Circus)

Queen's (☎ 7494 5040, Shaftesbury Ave W1; ⊕ Piccadilly Circus)

St Martin's (☎ 7836 1443, West St WC2; ⊕ Leicester Square)

Shaftesbury (☎ 7379 5399, Shaftesbury Ave WC2; ⊕ Tottenham Court Road or Holborn)

Savoy (☎ 7836 8888, Strand WC2; ⊕ Charing Cross)

Strand (☎ 7930 8800, Aldwych WC2; ⊕ Covent Garden)

Vaudeville (☎ 7836 9987, Strand WC2; ⊕ Charing Cross)

Wyndham's (☎ 7369 1736, Charing Cross Rd WC2; ⊕ Leicester Square)

Other Theatres On a sunny day it's fun to take in a Shakespearean play or musical at the **Open Air Theatre** (Map 1; ☎ 7486 2431; ⊕ Baker Street) in Regent's Park.

And as if all of that wasn't enough, at any time of the year London's many off-West End and fringe theatre productions offer a selection of the amazing, the boring, the life-enhancing and the downright ridiculous. Some of the better venues include:

Almeida (Map 2; ☎ 7359 4404, Almeida St N1; ⊕ Angel or Highbury & Islington)

Bridewell Theatre (Map 4; ☎ 7936 3456, Bride Lane, Fleet St EC4; ⊕ Blackfriars)

Donmar Warehouse (Map 5; ☎ 7369 1732, Earlham St WC2; ⊕ Covent Garden)

Hampstead Theatre (Map 1; ☎ 7722 9301, 98 Avenue Rd NW3; ⊕ Swiss Cottage)

King's Head Islington (Map 2; ☎ 7226 1916, 115 Upper St N1; ⊕ Angel)

Old Vic (Map 4; ☎ 7494 5372, Waterloo Rd SE1; ⊕ Waterloo)

Tricycle Theatre (Map 1; ☎ 7328 1000, 269 Kilburn High Rd NW6; ⊕ Kilburn)

Young Vic (Map 4; ☎ 7369 1736, 66 The Cut SE1; ⊕ Waterloo)

Opera & Dance

Culture at this level can cost anywhere from £5 to £100 or more.

Following a £213 million redevelopment, the **Royal Opera House** (Map 5; ☎ 7304 4000, Covent Garden WC2; ⊕ Covent Garden) has welcomed home the peripatetic Royal Opera and Royal Ballet. As a result of the makeover, it has become much more egalitarian: the renovated Floral Hall is now open to the public during the day,

with free lunch-time concerts, exhibitions and daily tours.

The home of the English National Opera, the **Coliseum** (Map 5; ☎ 7632 8300, St Martin's Lane WC1; ⊕ Leicester Square) presents opera in English.

London is home to five major dance companies and a host of small and experimental ones. The Royal Ballet is the best classical-ballet company in the UK. Its lead ballerina, Sylvie Guillem, is easily the most famous in the world.

Sadler's Wells (Map 2; ☎ 7863 8000, Rosebery Ave EC1; ⊕ Angel), which reopened in 1998 after a total refurbishment, has been associated with dance ever since Thomas Sadler set up a 'musick house' next to his medicinal spa in 1683. Its ultramodern theatre attracts classical- and contemporary-dance troupes from around the world.

Spectator Sports

Football Tickets for Premier League football matches start at around £15 (although tickets for the top clubs are almost always sold out well in advance). Some of the big teams worth watching include:

Arsenal (☎ 7704 4040, Avenell Rd N5; ⊕ Arsenal)

Chelsea (Map 7; ☎ 7385 5545, Stamford Bridge, Fulham Rd SW6; ⊕ Fulham Broadway)

Tottenham Hotspur (☎ 8365 5000, White Hart Lane N17; White Hart Lane station)

West Ham United (☎ 8548 2748, Green St E13; ⊕ Upton Park)

The legendary **Wembley Stadium** (☎ 8900 1234; ⊕ Wembley Park), ground zero for many an English football fan, is undergoing a massive reconstruction lasting until 2003.

Rugby Twickenham Rugby Stadium (☎ 8892 2000, Rugby Rd, Twickenham; ⊕ Hounslow East, then bus No 281; Twickenham station) is the shrine of English rugby union. Tickets cost around £30. The ground also boasts a Museum of Rugby (£5). It opens 10 am to 5 pm Tuesday to Saturday, and from 2 pm on Sunday.

Buying Theatre Tickets

There's a bewildering number of options not only for buying theatre tickets but also for getting into shows that otherwise may be sold out. Always carefully check the details printed on tickets you're thinking of buying. Also note that many theatres will sell some cut-rate restricted-view tickets; these tickets are just that and you may find that key action is out of your view.

For simple ticket purchases, you've got two choices. On the day of the performance you can buy half-price tickets for West End productions (for cash only) from the Leicester Square Half-Price Ticket Booth, on the southern side of Leicester Square (Map 5; ⊖ Leicester Square). It is the one with the clock tower – beware of imitations that may rip you off. It opens noon to 6.30 pm daily and charges £2 commission per ticket. Don't expect to find over-hyped musicals but do expect to find many of the more serious and artistically heralded productions.

Your other choice is to go to the theatre box office itself – yes, you can buy tickets the old-fashioned way and if you do it in person, you won't pay any service fees and you can peruse the seating charts for the theatre. Otherwise you can call in advance (from anywhere in the world) and buy the tickets with a credit card for collection on the night of the performance. Expect to pay a service charge of a few pounds. You can also check to see if there are stand-by student tickets made available about an hour before performances. These can be cheap, but you'll need a student card and these tickets aren't always offered.

To get tickets to a popular show, try going on a Monday night or to a Wednesday matinee. Otherwise you can try purchasing through a theatre ticket agency – like those around Leicester Square – or through a hotel concierge, but expect to pay a possibly enormous premium.

The Society of London Theatre (☎ 7836 0971) offers the following advice for people buying tickets from an agency:

- Find out the normal prices for the show first.
- Ask the agent what the ticket's face value is and how much commission is being added.
- Ask to be shown where you'll be sitting on a seat plan.
- Don't pay for the tickets until you've actually seen them and checked the face value.
- Don't agree to pick the tickets up later or have them sent to you.

Finally, be extremely dubious of tickets offered while you are standing in a queue.

Cricket Cricket continues to flourish, despite the fluctuating fortunes of the England team. Test matches in London take place at one of the cricket grounds: *Lord's (Map 1; ☎ 7289 1300, St John's Wood Rd NW8; ⊖ St John's Wood)* and *The Oval (Map 1; ☎ 7582 6660, Kennington Oval SE11; ⊖ Oval)*. Tickets are expensive (from £15 to £45).

Tennis Tennis and *Wimbledon (☎ 8944 1066, 8946 2244 for a recording; ⊖ Southfields or Wimbledon Park)* are almost synonymous; the All-England Lawn Tennis Championships have been taking place here every June since 1877. But the queues, exorbitant prices, limited ticket availability and cramped conditions may have you thinking Wimbledon is just a – well – racket. Although a limited number of seats for the Centre Court and Court Nos 1 and 2 go on sale on the day of play, the queues are painfully long. The nearer to the finals it is, the higher the prices; a Centre Court ticket that costs £25 a week before the final will cost twice that on the day. Prices for the outside courts cost less than £10 and are reduced (£5) after 5 pm.

Between 1 September and 31 December each year there's a public ballot for tickets for the best seats at the following year's tournament. Between those dates you can send a stamped addressed envelope to the All England Lawn Tennis & Croquet Club, PO Box 98, Church Rd, London SW19 5AE, to try your luck.

SHOPPING

London is a mecca for shopaholics from the UK and continental Europe, and if you can't find it here, it probably doesn't exist.

If you're looking for something with a British 'brand' on it, eschew the Union Jack-emblazoned kitsch of Carnaby and Oxford Sts and go for things that the Brits themselves know are of good quality, sometimes stylish and always solid: Dr Marten boots and shoes, Burberry raincoats and umbrellas, tailor-made shirts from Jermyn St and costume jewellery (be it for the finger, wrist, nose, eyebrow or navel).

What to Buy

Books London is the book-buying capital of the world. There is seemingly a special-interest store for every interest and the following are just a few examples.

General For those who read the book or saw the film *84 Charing Cross Road*, Charing Cross Rd (Map 5; ☻ Tottenham Court Road or Leicester Square) will need no introduction. This is where to go when you want reading material old or new.

Foyle's (☎ 7437 5660), 113–119 Charing Cross Rd WC2, is one of the biggest and by far the most confusing of London's bookshops, but it often stocks titles you may not find elsewhere.

Waterstone's (☎ 7434 4291), 121–129 Charing Cross Rd WC2, is a chain that is a bit more serious in its selection than its competitors. Its mega-branch (Map 5; ☎ 7851 2400), the biggest bookshop in Europe, is at 203–206 Piccadilly W1 (☻ Piccadilly Circus).

Special Interest From aardvarks to Zeus there's a bookstore in London for every interest. Here's a sample:

Blackwell's (☎ 7292 5100) 100 Charing Cross Rd WC2. This place stocks a lot of academic titles but has an excellent range of general books as well.

The European Bookshop (Map 5; ☎ 7734 5259) 5 Warwick St (☻ Piccadilly Circus). This shop has a wide range of books and periodicals from the Continent.

French's Theatre Bookshop (Map 2; ☎ 7387 9373) 52 Fitzroy St W1 (☻ Warren Street). This place has thousands of printed plays and other theatrical books.

Motor Books (Map 5; ☎ 7836 5376) 33–36 St Martins Court (☻ Leicester Square). Motor Books has shelves jammed with books covering everything that sails, flies and runs on roads and rails.

Gay's the Word (Map 2; ☎ 7278 7654) 66 Marchmont St WC1 (☻ Russell Square). This shop stocks guides and literature for, by and about gay men and women.

One of the best places for half-price second-hand books is the book market (Map 4) on the South Bank under the arches of Waterloo Bridge. It opens 10 am to 5 pm at the weekend, though a few stalls open throughout the week. Cecil Court (Map 5) has a number of antiquarian bookshops.

Travel The major chains are adequate sources of guidebooks and maps, but there are also several specialist travel bookshops:

Daunt Books (Map 4; ☎ 7224 2295) 83 Marylebone High St W1 (☻ Baker Street). Daunt has a wide selection of travel guides and books on other subjects in a beautiful old sky-lit shop.

Stanford's (Map 5; ☎ 7836 1321) 12–14 Long Acre WC2 (☻ Covent Garden). Stanford's has one of the largest selections of maps, guides and travel literature in the world.

Travel Bookshop (Map 3; ☎ 7229 5260) 13 Blenheim Crescent W11 (☻ Ladbroke Grove). This is London's best 'boutique' travel bookshop and was apparently the inspiration for the shop in *Notting Hill*. It has all the new guides, plus out-of-print and antiquarian gems.

Music For the largest collections of CDs and tapes in London check out any of the following three Goliath-sized music shops, all in the West End (Map 5):

HMV (☎ 7631 3423) 150 Oxford St W1 (☻ Oxford Circus). Open 9.30 am to 8 pm weekdays,

9 am to 7.30 pm on Saturday, and noon to 6 pm on Sunday.

Tower Records (☎ 7439 2500) 1 Piccadilly Circus W1 (✆ Piccadilly Circus). Open 9 am to midnight Monday to Saturday, and noon to 6 pm on Sunday.

Virgin Megastore (☎ 7631 1234) 14–30 Oxford St W1 (✆ Tottenham Court Road). Open 9 am to 9 pm Monday to Saturday, and noon to 6 pm on Sunday.

London also has a wide range of excellent music-shops specialising in everything from jazz and big band to world music. The following (Map 5) are particularly worth trying:

Black Market Records (☎ 7437 0478) 25 D'Arblay St W1 (✆ Oxford Circus)
Trax (☎ 7734 0795) 55 Greek St W1 (✆ Tottenham Court Road)

For second-hand and rare vinyl try either of the following (Map 5):

Division One (☎ 7637 7734) 36 Hanway St W1 (✆ Tottenham Court Road)
On the Beat (☎ 7637 8934) 22 Hanway St W1 (✆ Tottenham Court Road)

Travel Gear The YHA Adventure Shop (Map 5; ☎ 7836 8541), 14 Southampton St WC2 (✆ Covent Garden), is an excellent place to stock up on all sorts of camping and walking gear.

Where to Shop

Although most things can be bought throughout London, there are also streets known for their own specialities. Tottenham Court Rd, for example, is full of electronics and computer shops, while Denmark St has musical instruments, sheet music and books about music (both of these streets are on Map 5).

Some shopping streets rest on their laurels, their claim to fame having more to do with their past than what they have to offer today – Carnaby Street is an obvious example. The twee shops and stalls inside the old market building at Covent Garden (Map 5) tend to be pricey and tourist-oriented, but

the streets running off it remain a happy hunting-ground for shoppers, with Neal St and Neal's Yard in particular offering an interesting range.

Oxford St (Maps 4 & 5) can be a great disappointment. Selfridges is up there with Harrods as a place to visit, but the farther east you go, the tackier and less interesting it gets. Nearby Regent St is much more upmarket. Kensington High St (Map 3) is a good alternative to Oxford St. In the City check out some of the lovely boutiques in Bow Lane (Map 6), which runs between Cheapside and Cannon St.

Many tourist attractions have shops selling good-quality souvenirs: war books and videos at the Imperial War Museum, excellent art books at the National Gallery, tube merchandise at the London Transport Museum (we know someone who loves the 'Mind the Gap' T-shirts) and so on.

Department Stores London's main department stores have a variety of cafes, bars and more. They are great places to pause for afternoon tea.

Harrods (Map 3; ☎ 7730 1234) 87 Brompton Rd SW1 (✆ Knightsbridge). Harrods is always crowded, there are more rules than at an army training camp and it's hard to find what you're looking for, but tourists flock here like lemmings. Items bearing the logo seem to be proliferating.
Harvey Nichols (Map 3; ☎ 7235 5000) 109–125 Knightsbridge SW1 (✆ Knightsbridge). This is the city's heart of high fashion. It has a great food hall on the 5th floor, an extravagant perfume department and jewellery worth saving up for.
Fortnum & Mason (Map 5; ☎ 7734 8040) 181 Piccadilly W1 (✆ Piccadilly Circus). This place is noted for its exotic, old-world food hall on the ground floor, but it also carries plenty of fashion wear on the next four floors.
Selfridges (Map 4; ☎ 7629 1234) 400 Oxford St W1 (✆ Bond Street). Selfridges is arguably the grandest shop on Oxford St and the one with the longest history. It's what Harrods was before it became a self-parody.
Liberty (Map 5; ☎ 7734 1234) 214–220 Regent St W1 (✆ Oxford Circus). Liberty has high fashion, a wonderful luxury-fabrics department and those inimitable Liberty silk scarves.

Markets Believe it or not, London has more than 350 markets selling everything from antiques and curios to flowers and fish. Some, such as Camden and Portobello Rd, are well known to visitors. But others exist just for the locals, who go there to buy everything from dinner to underwear.

The following is a highly selective list of the more noteworthy markets (note that they only operate on certain days). The larger ones can occupy an entire day of browsing, snacking and strolling.

Bermondsey Market (Map 6; ☎ 7351 5353) Bermondsey Square SE1 (⊖ Borough). This is the place to come if you're after old opera glasses, bowling balls, hatpins, costume jewellery, porcelain or any other 'antique'. The main market on Friday (4 am to 2 pm) takes place outdoors on the square, although adjacent warehouses shelter the more vulnerable furnishings and bric-a-brac.

Borough Market (Map 6; ⊖ London Bridge). Borough Market is on the site of a market that's been operating since at least the 13th century. Until recently it served only the wholesale trade, but now from noon to 6 pm on Friday and 9 am to 5 pm on Saturday retailers from around the country sell edibles ranging from English farm cheeses and specialist sausages to gourmet patisserie and fresh fish to the public. At any time it's an atmospheric place and is surrounded by good pubs. A small open-air stand operated by a local Mediterranean grocery sells sensational grilled chorizo sandwiches.

Brick Lane Market (Map 1) Brick Lane E1 (⊖ Shoreditch or Aldgate East). This place is fun. Activity kicks off at around 8 am on Sunday and spreads out along Bethnal Green Rd to the north. By 2 pm it's all over. There's a mix of stalls selling clothes, fruit and vegetables, household goods, paintings and bric-a-brac.

Brixton Market (Map 1; ⊖ Brixton). This place is a cosmopolitan treat that mixes everything from the Body Shop and reggae to slick Muslim preachers, South American butcher shops and exotic fruits. On Electric Ave and in the covered Granville Arcade you can buy wigs, unusual foods and spices and homeopathic root cures. The market opens 8 am to 5.30 pm Monday to Saturday (to 1 pm only on Wednesday).

Camden Market (Map 2). Camden Market stretches north from Camden Town tube station to Chalk Farm Rd. It's busiest at the weekend between 10 am and 6 pm, although there are a few stalls up and running most days. Here you'll find 1960s clothes, army-surplus goods, ceramics, furniture, oriental rugs, musical instruments, designer clothes and so on. The bridge over the Grand Union Canal and Camden Lock offers great views.

Camden Passage (Map 2; ☎ 7359 9969; ⊖ Angel). This is a cavern of almost three dozen antique shops and stalls that has nothing to do with Camden Market. The stalls sell pretty much everything to which the moniker 'antique' or 'curio' could reasonably be applied, and the stallholders know their stuff so real bargains are rare. Wednesday is the busiest day when the action kicks off at 7.30 am and is all over by 2 pm; on Saturday it's worth coming along until about 5 pm. There's a second-hand book market on Thursday from 7 am to 4 pm.

Petticoat Lane (Map 6; ⊖ Aldgate, Aldgate East or Liverpool Street). This is east London's long-established Sunday market (8 am to 2 pm) on Middlesex St, on the border between the City and Whitechapel. These days, however, it's full of run-of-the-mill junk and tourists.

Portobello Rd (Map 3; ☎ 7727 7684; ⊖ Notting Hill Gate, Ladbroke Grove or Westbourne Park). London's most famous (and crowded) weekend street market starts near the Sun in Splendour pub in Notting Hill and wends its way northwards to just past the Westway flyover. Antiques, handmade jewellery, paintings and ethnic stuff are concentrated at the Notting Hill Gate end of Portobello Rd (roughly from Chepstow Villas as far as Elgin Crescent to the west and Colville Terrace to the east). The stalls dip downmarket to the north (second-hand clothing, bric-a-brac).

Spitalfields (Map 6; ☎ 7247 6590; ⊖ Liverpool Street). This large market between Bishopsgate and Commercial St is in a huge covered Victorian warehouse. There's a great mix of arts and crafts, organic fruit and veg, stylish and retro clothes, and second-hand books, with interesting ethnic shops ringing the central area. Most of the shops in the market are open 10.30 am to 5 pm weekdays. The market itself takes place from about 9.30 am to 5.30 pm on Sunday. There is an array of excellent cafes.

GETTING THERE & AWAY

London is the major gateway to England, so further transport information can be found in the Getting There & Away and Getting Around chapters.

Air

Airports *Heathrow* Fifteen miles (24km) west of central London, Heathrow (LHR) is the world's busiest commercial airport, handling upwards of 60 million passengers a year. It now has four terminals. The tube and Heathrow Express each have two stations serving Heathrow: one for Terminals 1, 2 and 3 and one for Terminal 4. Make certain you know from which terminal your flight departs as airlines and flights can shift around the airport.

Unfortunately Heathrow is chaotic, overcrowded and remarkably ugly. BAA, the company that operates the airport, seems to have decided to run a third-rate shopping centre instead of a world-class travel facility. Where there were once peaceful public spaces where you could wait for your flight, now there are all manner of shops; the departure area of Terminal 3 is one of the worst offenders. BAA has also added shops after customs, impeding your escape. The pubs, bars and restaurants are of minimal quality.

On the plus side, each terminal has competitive currency-exchange facilities, ATMs, information counters and accommodation desks.

There are several large international hotels – none particularly cheap or noteworthy – at or near Heathrow, should you be leaving or arriving at a peculiarly early or late hour. See the Places to Stay section for details. To reach them you must take the Heathrow Hotel Hoppa bus (☎ 01293-507099) costing £2.50 (free for children). The buses run between 6 am and 11 pm, with a service every 10 minutes at peak times, every 15 minutes otherwise, for Terminals 1, 2 and 3. Services for Terminal 4 run every 30 minutes.

There are left-luggage facilities at Terminal 1 (☎ 8745 5301), Terminal 2 (☎ 8745 4599), Terminal 3 (☎ 8759 3344) and Terminal 4 (☎ 8745 7460). They usually open at least 6 am to 10 pm. The charge is £3 per item for the first 12 hours and £3.50 per item for up to 24 hours. All can forward baggage.

For general enquiries and flight information phone ☎ 0870 000 0123. The Hotel Reservation Service (☎ 8564 8808) is useful if you need a room near the airport.

Gatwick Although large, Gatwick (LGW) is a much smaller airport than Heathrow and in many ways is easier and more pleasant to use. The northern and southern terminals are linked by an efficient monorail service; check which terminal you will use. There are all the predictable shops, and several eating and drinking areas.

The left-luggage office at the North Terminal (☎ 01293-502013) opens 6 am to 10 pm daily, the one in the South Terminal (☎ 01293-502014) round the clock.

For British Airways flight information, phone ☎ 0870 000 0123. For airport and all other flight information, phone ☎ 01293-535353.

Stansted Some 35 miles (56km) north-east of central London, Stansted (STN), London's third international gateway, handles many of the discount airlines such as Buzz, Go and Ryanair. The futuristic terminal building was designed by Sir Norman Foster. There's a single number (☎ 01279-680500) for general enquiries, hotel reservations and rail information.

Luton The other major airport for the discount airlines, Luton (LTN; ☎ 01582-405100 for general enquiries, hotel reservations and car-park information) is 35 miles (56km) north of the city. It is the home of easyJet and has recently opened an airy new terminal.

London City London City (LCY; ☎ 7646 0088), 6 miles (10km) east of central London, is in the Docklands. Seen as a businessperson's airport and under-utilised until recently, London City now has flights to numerous European destinations.

Airline Offices See the Getting There & Away chapter for airline telephone numbers for flight, booking and office information.

Bus

Most long-distance express coaches leave London from Victoria Coach Station (Map 8; ☎ 7730 3466), an attractive 1930s-style building at 164 Buckingham Palace Rd

SW1 (⊖ Victoria, then about 10 minutes' walk). The arrivals terminal is in a separate building across Elizabeth St from the main coach station.

Train

London has 10 main-line terminals, all linked by the tube. Each serves a different geographical area of the UK:

Charing Cross (Map 5)
  South-eastern England
Euston (Map 2)
  Northern and north-western England, Scotland
King's Cross (Map 2)
  North London, Hertfordshire, Cambridgeshire, northern and north-eastern England, Scotland
Liverpool Street (Map 6)
  East and north-east London, Stansted airport, East Anglia
London Bridge (Map 6)
  South-eastern England
Marylebone (Map 3)
  North-west London, the Chilterns
Paddington (Map 3)
  South Wales, western and south-western England, southern Midlands, Heathrow airport
St Pancras (Map 2)
  East Midlands, southern Yorkshire
Victoria (Map 8)
  Southern and south-eastern England, Gatwick airport, Channel ferry ports
Waterloo (Map 4)
  South-west London, southern and south-western England

In recent years a lot of work has been done to make the terminals more attractive and efficient. Liverpool Street station has been restored to its Victorian splendour, while Brunel's Paddington station is getting a much needed overhaul.

Most stations now have left-luggage facilities and lockers, toilets (20p) with showers (around £3), newsstands and bookshops, and a range of eating and drinking outlets. Victoria and Liverpool Street stations have shopping centres attached.

Car

See the Getting Around chapter for the reservations numbers of the major car rental firms, all of which have airport and various city locations.

GETTING AROUND

Transport for London (TfL), a new organisation under the control of London's mayor, is responsible for much of London's public transport. By the time you read this it should have taken over responsibility for the tube.

To/From the Airports

Bear in mind that some airlines offer their passengers special deals on transport to/from the airport and that return tickets are often cheaper than two singles.

Heathrow The airport is accessible by bus, the Underground (between 5 am and 11 pm) and main-line train.

The Heathrow Express (☎ 0845 600 1515) rail link whisks passengers from Paddington station to Heathrow in just 15 minutes. Single/return tickets cost an exorbitant £12/22 (£14/24 on the train). Trains leave every 15 minutes from around 5 am to 10.30 pm. Many airlines have advance check-in desks at Paddington.

The Underground station for Terminals 1, 2 and 3 is directly linked to those terminals; there's a separate station for Terminal 4. Check which terminal your flight uses when you reconfirm. The adult single fare is £3.50, or you can use an all-zone One Day Travelcard, which costs £4.70. The journey time from central London is about an hour.

The Airbus (☎ 7222 1234) services are prone to traffic congestion. There are two routes: the A1, which runs from Victoria along Cromwell Rd; and the A2, which runs from Russell Square along Bayswater Rd and Notting Hill Gate. Buses run every half-hour and cost £7.

Heathrow and Gatwick airports are linked by various bus services. Speedlink (☎ 0870 574 7777) has offices in the arrivals areas of Heathrow Terminals 1, 3 and 4 and both Gatwick terminals. Buses leave about every 30 minutes and the cost is £17/9 per adult/child. The journey takes about one hour.

A minicab to/from central London will cost from around £25, and a metered black cab around £35.

Gatwick The Gatwick Express train (☎ 0870 530 1530) runs nonstop between Victoria train station and the South Terminal 24 hours daily. Gatwick's North and South Terminals are linked by monorail; check which terminal your flight uses. Some airlines have check-in desks at Victoria. Singles are £10.20 and the journey takes about 30 minutes. The normal train service from Victoria takes a little longer and costs £8.20.

Thameslink trains to Gatwick travel via London Bridge, Blackfriars, City Thameslink and King's Cross. Singles are £9.20 and trains take 30 to 45 minutes.

Jetlink 777 buses (☎ 8668 7261) from Victoria Coach Station cost £8 but take 90 minutes to get to Gatwick.

A minicab to/from central London will cost around £35, and a metered black cab around £50.

See the previous Heathrow section for details on buses linking the two airports.

Stansted The airport is served by the Stansted Express (☎ 0845 748 4950) from Liverpool Street station, which costs £11 and takes 45 minutes. The trains depart every 15 to 30 minutes.

Luton The airport (☎ 01582-405100) is connected by frequent shuttle bus to Luton Airport Parkway station. Several trains (☎ 0845 748 4950) an hour go to/from central London, stopping at King's Cross Thameslink station among others. The fare is £9 and the journey takes 35 minutes.

London City The airport (☎ 7646 0000) is two minutes' walk from Silvertown & City Airport train station, which is linked by train to Stratford. A frequent shuttle bus also connects the airport with the Canning Town tube, DLR and train station. The Airbus connects the airport with Liverpool Street station (£5; 30 minutes) and the Canary Wharf area (£2; 10 minutes).

London Underground

The London Underground, or 'tube', first opened in 1863 (it was then essentially a roofed-in trench) and sometimes it feels as if not a whole lot has changed since then; it is slow, unreliable and, as the ageing system has suffered from decades of underfunding, breakdowns are common.

Still, the tube is normally the quickest and easiest way of getting around London; an estimated 3 million tube journeys are made every day.

Information TfL and the Underground operate information centres that sell tickets and provide free maps. There are centres at all four terminals at Heathrow and at Victoria, Piccadilly Circus, Oxford Circus, St James's Park, Liverpool Street, Euston and King's Cross tube and main-line train stations. There are also information offices at Hammersmith and West Croydon stations. For general information on the Underground, buses, the DLR or trains within London ring ☎ 7222 1234, or you can visit the TfL Web site at www.londontransport .co.uk.

Network Greater London is served by 12 tube lines, along with the independent (though linked) and privately owned DLR and an interconnected railway network (see the later DLR & Train section). The first tube train is at around 5.30 am Monday to Saturday and around 7 am on Sunday; the last train leaves between 11.30 pm and 12.30 am depending on the day, the station and the line.

Remember that any train heading from left to right on the map is designated as eastbound, any train heading from top to bottom is southbound. If your two stations are not on the same line, you need to note the nearest station where the two lines intersect, where you must change trains (transfer).

The biggest change to the Underground in recent years was the completion of the 10-mile Jubilee Line extension in 1999, from Westminster to Stratford via Canary Wharf. The 11 new Jubilee Line stations were all designed by different architects and many are ultramodern works of art in themselves.

If you're caught on the Underground without a valid ticket (and that includes crossing into a zone that your ticket doesn't cover) you're liable for an on-the-spot £10 fine. If you do get nabbed, do us all a favour: shut up and pay up. The inspectors – and your fellow passengers – hear the same stories every day of the year.

Fares TfL divides London into six concentric zones. The basic fare for adults/under-16s for Zone 1 is £1.50/60p, for Zones 1 & 2 £1.90/80p, for three zones £2.20/1, for four zones £2.70/1.20, for five zones £3.30/1.40 and for all six zones (including Heathrow) £3.60/1.50. But if you're travelling through a couple of zones or several times in one day, consider a travel pass or some other discounted fare.

Travel Passes & Discount Fares A Travelcard valid all day offers the cheapest way of getting about in London and can be used after 9.30 am on weekdays and all day at the weekend on all forms of transport in London: the tube, suburban trains, the DLR and buses (but *not* night buses).

Most visitors will find that a Zones 1 & 2 card (£4) will be sufficient. A card to cover all six zones costs £4.90, just £1.30 more than a one-journey all-zone ticket – and you get to use it all day. A One Day Travelcard for those aged five to 15 costs £2 regardless of how many zones it covers, but those aged 14 and 15 need a Child Rate Photocard to travel on this fare. You can buy Travelcards several days ahead but not on buses.

If you plan to start moving before 9.30 am on a weekday, you can buy a Zones 1 & 2 LT Card for £5.10/2.50 (£7.70/3.30 for all six zones), valid on the tube, the DLR and buses (but *not* suburban trains) for one day with no time restrictions.

Weekly Travelcards are also available but require an identification card with a passport-sized photo. A Zone 1 card for adults/those aged five to 15 costs £15.90/6.60 and a Zones 1 & 2 card £18.90/7.70. These allow you to travel at any time of day and on night buses as well.

At £6 for Zones 1 & 2, Weekend Travelcards valid on Saturday and Sunday are 25% cheaper than two separate one-day cards. Family Travelcards are also available for one or two adults and up to four children aged under 16 (who need not be related to them); they start at £2.60 per adult and 80p per child for Zones 1 & 2.

If you will be making a lot of journeys within Zone 1 *only*, you can buy a carnet of 10 tickets for £11.50, a considerable saving of £3.50.

There are plans to introduce electronic smartcards on the system in 2002. These will hold a certain stored value – say £20 – with the appropriate fare deducted for each journey.

Bus

If you're not in much of a hurry, travelling round London by double-decker bus can be more enjoyable than using the Underground. The All London bus map, available free from most TfL information centres, is an essential planning tool. For short journeys in London, it's often more efficient to take a bus than to struggle with the tube for a couple of stops.

Useful Routes The following are two examples of scenic bus routes where the ride can be an attraction in itself. The buses run in both directions.

No 24
Beginning at South End Green near Hampstead Heath, it travels through Camden and along Gower St to Tottenham Court Rd. From there it goes down Charing Cross Rd, past Leicester Square to Trafalgar Square, then along Whitehall, past the Palace of Westminster, Westminster Abbey and Westminster Cathedral. It reaches Victoria station and then carries on to Pimlico, which is handy for Tate Britain.

No 8
From Bow in east London, it goes along Bethnal Green Rd and passes the markets at Spitalfields and Petticoat Lane, Liverpool Street station, the City, the Guildhall and the Old Bailey. It then crosses Holborn and enters Oxford St, travelling past Oxford Circus, Bond St, Selfridges and the flagship Marks & Spencer store at Marble Arch before terminating at Victoria.

The Tube: Fun Facts to Know & Tell

The tube is the oldest (1863), most extensive (254 miles/408km of track) and busiest (nearly 1100 million journeys a year) underground transport system in the world. With breakdowns occurring every 16 minutes on average, it is also the most unreliable, and for the journey between Covent Garden and Leicester Square (£1.50 for 250m), the per km price makes taking the tube more expensive than flying first class. But those aren't the tube's only superlatives and oddities:

- The longest line is the Central Line (46 miles/74km), with the Piccadilly Line running a close second at 44.6 miles (71.3km); the shortest is the Waterloo & City Line (1.4 miles/2.2km), known as 'the Drain' that links Bank with Waterloo.
- With its 10-mile (16km) extension now completed, the Jubilee Line is the only one in the entire system to connect with all the other lines as well as the Docklands Light Railway.
- The longest journey possible without changing trains is from West Ruislip to Epping on the Central Line (31.1 miles/54.9km).
- The longest distance between stations is from Chesham to Chalfont & Latimer on the Metropolitan Line (3.6 miles/6.3km); the shortest is between Leicester Square and Covent Garden (250m).
- The deepest station is Hampstead on the Northern Line (58.5m).
- The District Line has the most stations with 60, followed by the Piccadilly (52) and Central (49) Lines; the Waterloo & City has a mere two.
- The busiest stations are Victoria (86 million passengers a year), Oxford Circus (85 million), King's Cross (69 million), Liverpool Street (44 million) and Baker Street (43 million).
- The stations with the most platforms are Moorgate and Baker Street; each has 10.
- There are 303 escalators on the Underground. Bank has the most (15, not including its two moving walkways) while the one at Angel on the Northern Line is the longest (60m, up a vertical rise of 27.5m).
- There are some 40 'ghost' (disused) stations on the Underground, including British Museum on the Central Line (closed in the 1930s); Down Street near Hyde Park Corner on the Piccadilly Line, used by Churchill and his family during WWII; Marlborough Street on the Metropolitan Line near Lord's, now a Chinese restaurant; South Kentish Town near Camden on the Northern Line, which closed during a power cut and never reopened; and poor Hounslow Town on the District Line, which functioned from 1883 to 1886 and then again from 1903 to 1909, when it closed permanently through lack of use.
- You will never hear 'Mind the gap' on the Jubilee Line extension as all platforms have 'platform-edge doors' to cut out draughts and bridge gaps; the gappiest gaps – caused by curvatures in the platform – are at Embankment and Bank.
- The famous tube map was designed by Henry Beck, an engineering draughtsman for whom the map was a labour of love. From his first version in 1931, Beck continued to work at improving its clarity and detail right up to 1960 when he was 'fired' from a job that had only ever paid him a total of £5.25! A new version of the map was drawn by the Underground's publicity department, who sneered at Beck's classic. This 'improvement' was a disaster and a few years later Beck's design principles – but not Beck – were back guiding the tube map.

The wheelchair-accessible Stationlink buses, which have a ramp operated by the driver, follow a similar route to that of the Underground Circle Line, joining up all the main-line stations. People with mobility problems and those with heavy luggage may find this easier to use than the tube, although it only operates once an hour. From Paddington there are services clockwise (the SL1) from 8.15 am to 7.15 pm, and anticlockwise (the SL2) from 8.40 am to 6.40 pm.

Trafalgar Square is the focus for all but six of TfL's network of 50 night buses (pre-fixed with the letter 'N'). They run from about midnight to 7 am but services can be infrequent. TfL publishes a free credit-card-sized timetable that lists all the routes. Only Travelcards valid for a week or longer are valid on night buses; everyone else pays.

Fares London's bus fares are simple to get to grips with. As far as fares are concerned, there are two zones: the first is the same as Zone 1 on the tube, the second covers the rest of London. Travel within Zone 1 or in both zones costs £1; travel outside Zone 1 only costs 70p. Children pay 40p no matter where they ride. Night buses cost £1.50. Travelcards and other tube passes are good on buses.

DLR & Train
The independent, driverless Docklands Light Railway (DLR) links the City at Bank and Tower Gateway with Canary Wharf, Greenwich and Stratford. It provides good views of development at this end of town. The fares operate in the same way as those on the tube.

Several rail companies operate the thicket of suburban rail services in and around London. These are especially important south of the river where there are few tube lines. Once again, fares operate in the same way as those on the tube.

Car & Motorcycle
Avoid bringing a car into London. The roads are horribly clogged, drivers are aggressive in the extreme and parking space is at a premium. There are car parks, but they can cost £12 or more per day.

Traffic wardens and wheel clampers operate with extreme efficiency, and if your vehicle is towed away you won't see much change from £100 to get it back. If you do get clamped, ring the 24-hour Clamping & Vehicle Section hotline on ☎ 7747 4747 to find out what to do next.

Taxi
London's famous black cabs (☎ 7272 0272) are excellent, but not cheap. A cab is available for hire when the yellow sign is lit. Fares are metered and a 10% tip is expected. They can carry five people.

Minicabs can carry four people and are cheap, freelance competitors to the black cabs. Anyone with a car can work as a minicab driver and, although they can supposedly only be hired by phone, hawkers abound in busy places such as Soho. Beware: some have a very limited idea of how to get around efficiently (and safely). Also, they don't have meters, so it's essential to get a quote before you start. Women are advised to use black cabs.

Small minicab companies are based in particular areas. Ask a local for the name of a reputable company or phone one of the large 24-hour operations (☎ 7272 2612, ☎ 8340 2450 or ☎ 8567 1111). Women can phone Lady Cabs (☎ 7254 3501). Gays and lesbians can choose Freedom Cars (☎ 7734 1313).

Bicycle
Cycling around London is one way of cutting transport costs, but it can be a grim business, with heavy traffic and fumes detracting from the pleasure of getting a little exercise. It's advisable to wear a helmet and increasingly Londoners wear face-masks to filter out pollution.

Bikepark (Map 5; ☎ 7430 0083), 11 Macklin St WC2 (⊖ Holborn), rents out bikes and has bicycle parking. The minimum charge is £10 for the first day, £5 for the second day and £3 for subsequent days.

Dial-a-Bike (Map 8; ☎ 7828 4040), 18 Gillingham St SW1 (⊖ Victoria), rents out bikes from £6.99 per day and £29.90 per week.

Boat
There is a myriad of boat services on the Thames, with more being announced all the time. By boat you avoid the traffic while enjoying great views.

From Westminster Pier (Map 4), City Cruises (☎ 7930 9033) operates a popular service to/from the Tower of London. The adult fare is £4.80/6 single/return and the child fare £2.40/3. The journeys take 30 minutes and operate several times an hour, April to October, less often at other times.

Crown River Cruises (☎ 7936 2033) op-erates a circular cruise from Westminster Pier that calls at piers at London Bridge and St Katharine's (just east of the Tower of London). A ticket costs £5.80/3 and is good all day so you can hop on and hop off. Boats run through the year, usually once an hour.

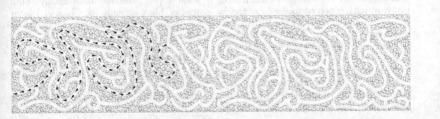

South-Eastern England

The towns and villages of the counties covered in this chapter – Berkshire, Surrey, Kent, East and West Sussex, Hampshire, Isle of Wight, Hertfordshire, Buckinghamshire and Essex – provide peace and solitude away from the capital for a significant number of London's workforce.

The South-East is also a region exceptionally rich in beauty. It caters for those unshakeable traditional images of England – picturesque towns and villages with welcoming old pubs (Rye, Lewes, Winchester and St Albans), spectacular coastline (the white cliffs of Dover and Beachy Head), impressive castles (Dover, Hever, Ightham Mote and Leeds), magnificent historic houses (Knole, Penshurst and Beaulieu), crafted gardens (Sissinghurst and Stowe), great cathedrals (Canterbury and Winchester) and kitsch seaside resorts (Eastbourne, Brighton and Southend).

Consequently, these places are some of the country's most popular tourist destinations. The crowds of holidaymakers during late spring and summer can be a real pain in the neck and prices, particularly south of London, tend to be high.

HISTORY

The South-East's proximity to the rest of Europe means that the region has been a hot spot for much of England's formative history. The town of Deal on the Kent coast is where the Romans first set foot in England in 55 BC. Norman invaders from across the Channel also set their ships on the shores of the South-East in the 11th century. Portsmouth has been home to the British Navy, which has played such a large part in the spread and defence of the British Empire, since 1194. For most of its history, British royalty has preferred the South-East as the site of some of its greatest castles.

With the French coast a mere 20 miles (32km) away, the South-East has always been Britain's front line. During WWII the South-East, particularly Portsmouth and

Highlights

- Exploring Anne Boleyn's childhood home – the fairy-tale Hever Castle in Kent
- Treating yourself to some great shopping, wonderful food and unstoppable nightlife in Brighton
- Taking a trip back in time on HMS *Victory* in Portsmouth – Admiral Nelson's flagship at the Battle of Trafalgar
- Visiting the site of William the Conqueror's victory of 1066 at Battle in East Sussex
- Wandering around the beautifully eerie ruins of Waverley Abbey, a 12th-century monastery in Surrey
- Seeing the wonderful mish-mash of Roman, Saxon, Norman and Victorian architecture of St Albans Cathedral

Southampton, suffered many enemy bomb attacks. More recently the Channel Tunnel has facilitated travel between England and the rest of Europe.

CLIMATE

The South-East of the country has the warmest climate. Being close to the sea means that the counties of the south as well as Essex tend not to drop below 0°C in winter, though temperatures rarely go above 30°C in summer. There are more sunny days on average in the South-East than elsewhere in the country. The region also has less rainfall than the rest of England. Parts of Essex and Kent have recorded an annual rainfall of less than 600mm while some of the most northern and western parts of England can get as much as 4500mm per year.

ORIENTATION

South of London, chalk country runs through the region along two hilly east–west ridges, or downs as they are referred to. The North Downs curve from Guildford across the Kent countryside, to Dover where they become the famous white cliffs. The South Downs run from north of Portsmouth to end spectacularly at Beachy Head near Eastbourne. Lying between the two is the Weald, once an enormous stretch of forest, now orchards and market gardens.

North-west of London, the hilly countryside known as the Chilterns is home to the stunning Ridgeway trail and remains forested and largely unspoiled. Moving east towards the coast, the forests of Essex give way to a flatter and less remarkable countryside, with networks of motorways the more prominent feature until you reach the coast.

INFORMATION

Being such a heavily visited region, the South-East has plenty of Tourist Information Centres (TICs), all with relatively long opening hours. There are YHA youth hostels in most of the larger towns and cities. Many of the universities rent out rooms during summer but booking ahead is advised. Some local TICs charge a B&B reservation fee. You'll find banks, post offices, Internet access and laundrettes in all main cities covered in this chapter.

GETTING AROUND

All the places mentioned in this chapter are quite easy to get to by train or bus, and each town or village could possibly be visited as a day trip from London. Information on public transport options is included throughout the chapter.

Bus

A number of different bus companies operate regular services from London and between all towns and most villages. Explorer tickets (£6/4 for adults/children aged under 16), giving unlimited travel for the day, can be used on most buses throughout the region. These can be bought from the bus drivers or from bus stations. Country Rover tickets (£5/2.50) can be used after 9 am from Monday to Friday and all day at the weekend. Diamond Rover Tickets (£7/5) can also be used on most Arriva (☎ 0870 688 2608) buses in Buckinghamshire, Hertfordshire and Essex. A pass giving you one week unlimited travel on Stagecoach Coastline and Sussex Bus Services (☎ 01903-237661) costs £12.50 and can be purchased on any of these buses.

Train

For rail information call ☎ 0845 748 4950. If you are considering extensive rail travel, a Network Card (£20, giving a 34% discount on tickets) which lasts for one year is a good idea, though you can only travel after 10 am on weekdays (anytime at the weekend). It allows accompanying children up to the age of 15 to travel for £1. A BritRail SouthEast Pass allows unlimited rail travel for three or four days out of seven, or seven days out of 15, but it must be purchased outside the UK. See Train in the Getting Around chapter.

Travelling between the counties north of London (Essex, Hertfordshire and Buckinghamshire) by rail is not so simple as the towns of interest are not necessarily linked by rail to London or to each other.

Berkshire

Long regarded as the stomping ground for some of England's conservative 'old money', Berkshire does indeed have some gorgeous villages, stately homes and stunning countryside, although industrial towns such as Slough and the very ordinary Reading (the county's administrative centre) leave a lot to be desired.

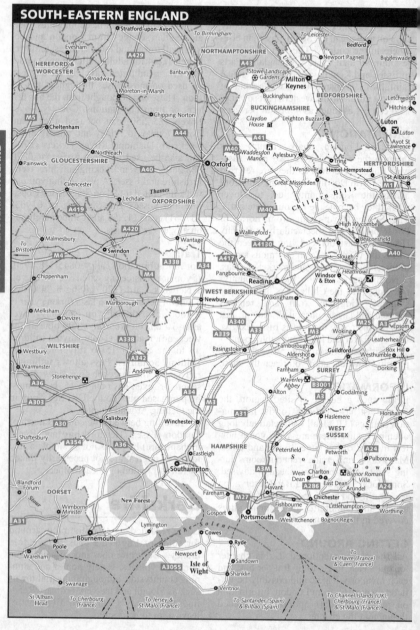

SOUTH-EASTERN ENGLAND

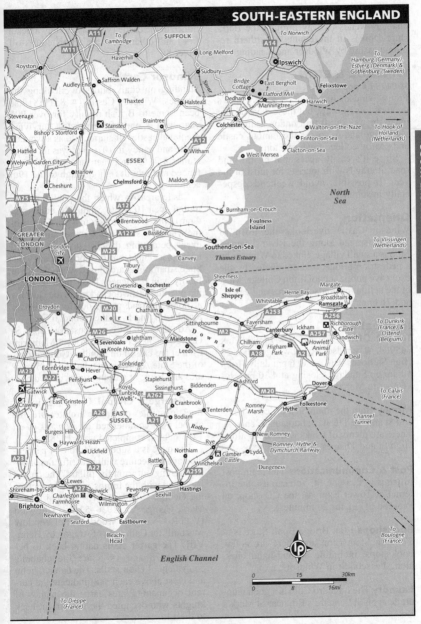

The Thames Path (see the Activities chapter) wends its way through the Berkshire Downs in the county's northern region, passing by Windsor and Reading.

WINDSOR & ETON
☎ 01753 • pop 31,000

Pretty Windsor has long been Berkshire's greatest tourist draw, but these days people make the trek out from London as much to visit Legoland as to see the famous castle and nearby college town of Eton.

Since it's easily accessible by rail and road, it crawls with tourists for most of the year. If possible, avoid weekends, especially in summer.

Orientation

Windsor Castle overlooks the town of Windsor spread along the River Thames. Eton is a small village, linked to Windsor by a pedestrian bridge, and dominated by the exclusive public school, Eton College. Most of the action in Windsor centres on Peascod and Thames Sts.

Information

Tourist Office The TIC (☎ 743900, fax 743904, e windsor.tic@rbwm.gov.uk), 24 High St, opens 9.30 am to 6 pm daily (from 10 am on Sunday), closing at 4.30 pm November to March.

Money Both the main post office in Peascod St and the TIC have bureaux de change. There are plenty of banks with ATMs along High St and Thames St.

Post & Communications The main post office is in Peascod St. You can use the Internet at Tower Express, the CD shop, on Peascod St (£1 for 20 minutes).

Bookshops Eton Bridge Book Store is at 77 High St in Eton and there are a few bookshops, including second-hand ones, along Peascod St in Windsor.

Laundry The Laundro Coin is a good laundrette at 56 St Leonard's Rd, near St Mark's Rd.

Toilets There are public toilets near the entrance to the castle (you have to buy a ticket first) and others near the tennis courts off River St.

Windsor Castle

Standing on chalk bluffs overlooking the Thames, Windsor Castle (☎ 831118) has been home to British royalty for over 900 years and is one of the greatest surviving medieval castles. It started life as a wooden motte and bailey in 1070, but was rebuilt in stone in 1165 and then successively extended and rebuilt right through to the 19th century.

Castle areas to which the public are admitted open 10 am to 5 pm (last admission 4 pm), March to October; to 4 pm the rest of the year. In summer, weather and other events permitting, the changing of the guard takes place at 11 am (not on Sunday). The State Apartments are closed when the royal family is in residence. The Union Jack flying over the castle doesn't mean the Queen's at home; instead watch out for the Royal Standard flying from the Round Tower.

Admission to the castle costs £10.50/5. St George's Chapel and the Albert Memorial Chapel are closed on Sunday. Guided tours of the State Apartments take about 45 minutes and leave at varying times each day.

St George's Chapel One of Britain's finest examples of Gothic architecture, the chapel was commenced by Edward IV in 1475 but not completed until 1528.

The nave is a superb example of perpendicular architecture with beautiful fan vaulting arching out from the pillars. The chapel is packed with the **tombs of royalty** including George V (ruled 1910–36) and Queen Mary, George VI (1936–52), and Edward IV (1461–83). The **wooden oriel window** was built for Catherine of Aragon by Henry VIII. The **garter stalls** dating back to between 1478 and 1485 are the chapel's equivalent of choir stalls. The banner, helm and crest above each stall indicate the current occupant. Plates carry the names of knights who occupied the stalls right back to the 14th century.

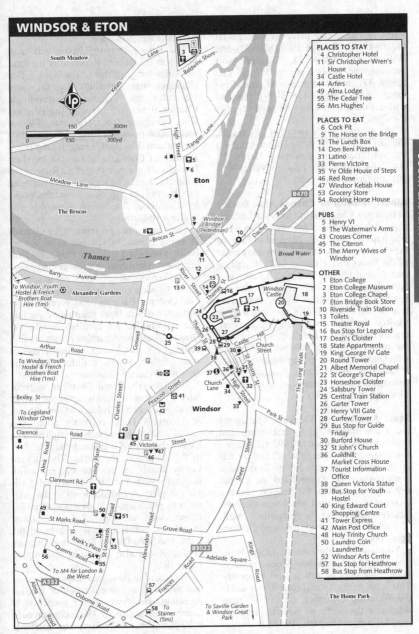

WINDSOR & ETON

SOUTH-EASTERN ENGLAND

PLACES TO STAY
- 4 Christopher Hotel
- 11 Sir Christopher Wren's House
- 34 Castle Hotel
- 44 Arfers
- 49 Alma Lodge
- 55 The Cedar Tree
- 56 Mrs Hughes'

PLACES TO EAT
- 6 Cock Pit
- 9 The Horse on the Bridge
- 12 The Lunch Box
- 14 Don Beni Pizzeria
- 31 Latino
- 33 Pierre Victoire
- 35 Ye Olde House of Steps
- 46 Red Rose
- 47 Windsor Kebab House
- 53 Grocery Store
- 54 Rocking Horse House

PUBS
- 5 Henry VI
- 8 The Waterman's Arms
- 43 Crosses Corner
- 45 The Citeron
- 51 The Merry Wives of Windsor

OTHER
- 1 Eton College
- 2 Eton College Museum
- 3 Eton College Chapel
- 7 Eton Bridge Book Store
- 10 Riverside Train Station
- 13 Toilets
- 15 Theatre Royal
- 16 Bus Stop for Legoland
- 17 Dean's Cloister
- 18 State Apartments
- 19 King George IV Gate
- 20 Round Tower
- 21 Albert Memorial Chapel
- 22 St George's Chapel
- 23 Horseshoe Cloister
- 24 Salisbury Tower
- 25 Central Train Station
- 26 Garter Tower
- 27 Henry VIII Gate
- 28 Curfew Tower
- 29 Bus Stop for Guide Friday
- 30 Burford House
- 32 St John's Church
- 36 Guildhill; Market Cross House
- 37 Tourist Information Office
- 38 Queen Victoria Statue
- 39 Bus Stop for Youth Hostel
- 40 King Edward Court Shopping Centre
- 41 Tower Express
- 42 Main Post Office
- 48 Holy Trinity Church
- 50 Laundro Coin Launderette
- 52 Windsor Arts Centre
- 57 Bus Stop for Heathrow
- 58 Bus Stop from Heathrow

In between the garter stalls, the **Royal Vault** is the burial place of George III (1760–1820), George IV (1820–30) and William IV (1830–37). Another **vault** between the stalls contains Henry VIII (1509–47), his favourite wife Jane Seymour, and Charles I (1625–49), reunited with his head which was chopped off after the Civil War.

The gigantic **battle sword** of Edward III, founder of the Order of the Garter, hangs on the wall near the **tombs** of Henry VI (1422–61 and 1470), Edward VII (1901–10) and Queen Alexandra.

Albert Memorial Chapel After leaving St George's Chapel, don't miss the fantastically elaborate Albert Memorial Chapel. It was built in 1240 and dedicated to Edward the Confessor. It became the original chapel of the Order of the Garter in 1350, falling into disuse when St George's Chapel was built. It was completely restored after the death of Prince Albert in 1861. A major feature of the restoration is the magnificent vaulted roof whose mosaic pieces were crafted in Venice. There's a monument to the prince, although he's actually buried with Queen Victoria in the Frogmore Royal Mausoleum in the castle grounds. A detailed guide to the chapel can be bought for £1 at the chapel entrance.

State Apartments The State Apartments are a combination of formal rooms and museum-style exhibits. In 1992 a disastrous fire destroyed St George's Hall and the adjacent Grand Reception Room. Restoration work has now been completed and a small **exhibition** describes the process. Take a moment to think about which was more destructive, the fire or the restoration. In all, 350 oak trees were used to rebuild the damaged rooms.

You will enter through the Grand Staircase and Grand Vestibule which are decorated with suits of armour and weaponry. This leads to the Ante Throne Room and to the Waterloo Chamber, created to commemorate the Battle of Waterloo and still used for formal banquets. The walls display

Sir Thomas Lawrence's portraits of the men who defeated Napoleon.

The King's Drawing Room was once known as the Rubens Room, after the three paintings hanging there. The King's Bed Chamber has paintings by Giovanni Canaletto and Thomas Gainsborough. Charles II actually slept in the adjacent King's Dressing Room, and some of Windsor's finest paintings hang here, including Sir Anthony Van Dyck's magnificent *Triple Portrait of Charles I* and works by Hans Holbein, Rembrandt, Peter Paul Rubens and Albrecht Dürer. The King's Closet was used by Charles II as a study and contains works by Canaletto, Sir Joshua Reynolds and William Hogarth.

From here you pass through the Queen's Drawing Room, which has paintings by Holbein and Van Dyck, into the King's Dining Room. Here there is a fine ceiling painting by Verrio – one of only three to survive – and woodcarvings by Grinling Gibbons. The Queen's Ballroom has a remarkable collection of Van Dyck paintings, including one of Charles I's children, while the Queen's Audience Chamber boasts another ceiling by Verrio. More Gobelins tapestries and another Verrio ceiling adorn the Queen's Presence Chamber.

The Queen's Guard Chamber is decorated with armoury and weapons as well as a bust of Churchill. It leads to the restored St George's Hall, currently a bit too squeaky new to have much atmosphere. The hammerbeam roof is painted with the arms of the Knights of the Garter. The Lantern Lobby stands on the site where the fire originally started and is used to display silver gilt plate. A corridor leads to the magnificent plush-and-gold Crimson Drawing Room, with the smaller Green Drawing Room visible through a door on the right. The State Dining Room and Octagon Dining Room also had to be thoroughly restored.

After passing through a hallway lined on one side with a fine collection of English porcelain, you come to the French-style Grand Reception Room. The ceiling caved in in 1992, but has now been replaced and leads through to the Garter Throne Room, used for investing new Knights of the Garter.

The State Apartment circuit eventually winds up back in the Waterloo Chamber. Note that some of the smaller rooms are not always open to the public at busy times – an excellent reason for visiting out of season!

Queen Mary's Dolls' House The work of architect Sir Edwin Lutyens, the dolls' house was built in 1923 on a 1:12 scale with the aim of raising money for children's charities. There are occasional special exhibitions here such as displays of the Queen's childhood toys.

Windsor Great Park Stretching south of Windsor Castle almost all the way to Ascot, Windsor Great Park covers about 40 sq miles. There is a lake, walking tracks, bridleway and gardens. The Savill Garden (☎ 860222), which opens 10 am to 6 pm daily (to 4 pm November to February), is particularly lovely; admission costs £3.80/3.30.

Around Town

Windsor's fine **Guildhall** stands on High St beside Castle Hill. It was built between 1687 and 1689, the construction completed under the supervision of Sir Christopher Wren. The council insisted that central columns were required to support the 1st floor even though Wren thought them unnecessary. The few centimetres of clear air proved him right.

The visibly leaning **Market Cross House** of 1768 is right next to the Guildhall. Charles II kept Nell Gwyn, his favourite mistress, in **Burford House** on Church St.

The **Long Walk** is a 3-mile (5km) walk along a tree-lined path from King George IV Gate to the Copper Horse statue (of George III) on Snow Hill, the highest point of Windsor Great Park. There are some great views of the castle along here. The walk is signposted from the town centre.

Eton College

Cross the Thames by the pedestrian Windsor Bridge to arrive at another enduring symbol of Britain's class system: Eton College (☎ 671177), a famous public (meaning private) school that was founded by Henry VI in the mid-15th century. It has educated no fewer than 18 prime ministers and counts Prince William and Prince Harry among its former and current pupils.

The college opens to visitors from 2 to 4.30 pm during term and from 10.30 am during the holidays from April to September. Admission costs £2.50/2. One-hour guided tours at 2.15 and 3.15 pm cost £3.50/3. If you're thinking of sending your offspring to join the 1200 to 1300 pupils at Eton, be prepared to set aside around £14,000 per year for the basic fees.

Legoland Windsor

Visitors with children are unlikely to escape from Windsor without a trip to this fantasia mix of model masterpieces and white-knuckle rides. The idea is family fun with the emphasis on the two to 12 age group. But you'll have to dig deep into your pockets to entertain the family. Tickets are a whopping £17.50/14.50 for adults/children. If you prebook (☎ 0870 504 0404) it costs a whole £1 less per ticket.

It opens 10 am to 6 pm daily, mid-March to October (to 8 pm from mid-July to August). Buses run regularly throughout the day from Thames St.

Places to Stay

As Windsor is one of the most popular tourist destinations year-round, book your accommodation well ahead of your visit.

Hostels A mile west of Riverside train station is *Windsor Youth Hostel* (☎ 861710, fax 832100, e yhawindsor@compuserve .com, Edgworth House, Mill Lane). Catch bus No 50A/B from outside Barclays bank in Thames St, or follow Arthur Rd or Barry Ave (along the riverbank) from the centre. The nightly cost is £10.85/7.40 for adults/under-18s. It closes for one week over the New Year period.

B&Bs & Hotels The Windsor TIC charges £3 to make accommodation bookings. The cheaper B&Bs can be found in the area south of Clarence Rd, between Alma and St Leonards Rds.

Mrs Hughes' (☎ *866036, 62 Queens Rd)* B&B has one single room with kitchenette for £30, a double for £45 and a family room that sleeps six for £20/10 per adult/ child. All rooms have fridges and en-suite facilities.

The Cedar Tree (☎ *860362, 90 St Leonards Rd)* is clean and cosy and decorated in a cottage style. It costs £18/36 for singles/doubles and £40 for a double en suite. *Rocking Horse House* (☎ *853984, 88 St Leonards Rd)*, next door, is better value for two people than for one as rooms cost £38/44.

Alma Lodge (☎ *854550, fax 855620, 58 Alma Rd)* has nicely decorated rooms for £55 a double. Singles are negotiable but you may be out of luck in summer and school holidays. *Arfers* (☎ *855062, 48 Clarence Rd)* charges £50 to £55 for a double. Singles are not often taken but if business is slow you might be lucky. It'll cost you around £35 though.

Castle Hotel (☎ *852359, 10 High St)* is popular with well-to-do American tourists. Rooms go for £150/175. *Sir Christopher Wren's House* (☎ *861354, fax 860172, Thames St)* was built by Wren in 1676 and is one of the more upmarket hotels in town. Rooms cost £145/185.

Christopher Hotel (☎ *852359, 10 High St, Eton)*, across the river, dates from 1511. Rooms cost £98/108 plus £9.95 for a cooked breakfast. Rooms in the old building have more character than those in the newer, motel-style building.

Places to Eat

With such a steady flow of visitors it's hardly surprising that Windsor is bursting with eateries, though they tend to be pricey and rather disappointing. For self-caterers there's a *grocery store* on St Leonards Rd and a *supermarket* at King Edward Court Shopping Centre.

The Lunch Box (☎ *833323, 48 Dachet Rd)* is a takeaway sandwich shop but it does have a couple of tables where you can sit.

Sandwiches are made fresh on the spot and cost from £1.30 to £1.95.

Ye Olde House of Steps (☎ *855334, 1 Church Lane)* serves everything from cream teas to hamburgers to pastries. Fish and chips with salad is very reasonable at £4.95. *Latino* (☎ *857711, 3 Church Lane)* is a cosy and friendly Greek/Continental restaurant with live music on Friday and Saturday nights.

Pierre Victoire (☎ *833009, 6 High St)* is a casual but elegant bistro serving French and Italian food. The early dinner (in before 7.30 pm) costs only £7.95 for two courses.

Don Beni Pizzeria (☎ *622042, 28 Thames St)* is lively and loud and always full of people which suggests that the food is good. Their lunch special gives you the choice of a small pizza or pasta dish with garlic bread for £4.95. Book or be early if you want a table here.

Windsor Kebab House (☎ *622022, 67 Victoria St)* is a cheap alternative. Medium-sized doner kebabs are £2.80 and burgers cost from £1.80. *Red Rose* (☎ *620180, 69 Victoria St)* is an Indian restaurant with main courses for £5 to £8; side dishes for £2.25. A newspaper article in the window claims that orders are regularly picked by members of the royal household.

Along Eton High St places to eat jostle shoulders with antique shops. The rickety *Cock Pit* (☎ *860944, 47–49 High St, Eton)* dates back to 1420 and serves good, simple Italian food. The fireplaces and exposed beams give this place a cosy atmosphere.

The House on the Bridge (☎ *790197, 67 High St, Eton)* is an elegant and pricey restaurant, overlooking the river and the castle. The food is modern French and Spanish and the set menu costs £29.95 for three courses.

Entertainment

Windsor and Eton are simply packed with pubs, though only a few offer live entertainment. *The Merry Wives of Windsor* (☎ *861860, 65 St Leonards Rd)* has long been a favourite with locals and visitors. *Criterion* (☎ *866139, 72 Peascod St)* is more of a men's pub, while *Crosses Corner*

(☎ 862867, 73 Peascod St) is frequented by the upwardly mobile set.

The Waterman's Arms (☎ 861006, Brocas St), in Eton, is a small and intimate pub tucked away to the west of the High St, and is popular with rowers. **Henry VI** (☎ 866051, 37 High St, Eton) has an outdoor terrace and live music in the evenings from Thursday to Sunday.

Windsor Arts Centre (☎ 859336), on the corner of St Leonards Rd and St Marks Rd, contains a bar, theatre and live music venue and attracts a young crowd. **Theatre Royal** (☎ 853888, Thames St) is the town's main theatre.

Getting There & Away

Windsor is 21 miles (34km) west of London between the M4 and the M25, and about 15 minutes by car from Heathrow airport.

Bus Greenline Bus (☎ 0870 608 7261) Nos 700 (express service) and 702 depart for Windsor and Legoland from opposite London's Victoria Coach Station hourly (£7/ 3.50 day return, 65 minutes or 50 minutes express). Bus No 192 (Monday to Saturday) or Nos 190 and 191 (Sunday) connect Windsor with Heathrow airport and run twice an hour.

Train There are two Windsor and Eton train stations – Central station on Thames St, directly opposite the Windsor Castle entrance gate, and Riverside station near the bridge to Eton.

From London Waterloo, trains run to Riverside station every 30 minutes during the week and hourly on Sunday (£6, 55 minutes). Services to Central leave from Paddington twice an hour and require a change at Slough, five minutes from Windsor (£6, 60 minutes).

Getting Around

Guide Friday (☎ 01789-294466) open-top double-decker bus tours of the town operate from late March to October. Tickets costing £6.50/2 are available from the TIC. From Easter to October, French Brothers (☎ 851900) operate 35-minute riverboat

trips from Windsor. Tickets cost £3.80/1.90. Longer trips go to Runneymeade, Maidenhead and Staines. Rowing and motorboats are also available for hire. Their office is on Clewer Court Rd, a mile west of Riverside station (near the youth hostel), or you can ask at the TIC for details.

BEALE PARK

This place in the east of Berkshire, 1¼ miles (2km) from Pangbourne train station, is a lifesaver for parents wanting to entertain children. Here the nippers can touch all kinds of animals in the petting zoo, take a miniature steam train ride, use the adventure playground or swim in the paddling pool. There's a coffee shop and nice walks around the grounds. We hear from good sources that kids just want to keep coming back here again and again. It opens 10 am to 6 pm daily, March to December; admission is very reasonable at £3/2. Direct trains leave every 30 minutes from London Paddington to Pangbourne station (£10.30, 1 hour). From Oxford, trains leave for Pangbourne every 30 minutes and hourly on Sunday (£10.30, 30 minutes).

Surrey

It's said that if Kent is the 'Garden of England' then Surrey is the patio. But among the sprawling dormitory towns for London commuters this much-derided county has some lovely corners that are easy to reach on a day out from the capital. It's also home to the Epsom Downs Racecourse which hosts the Derby, one of Britain's premier horse races.

GUILDFORD
☎ 01483 • pop 130,000

The administrative centre of Surrey, Guildford lies on the high ridge of the North Downs. At the time of the Norman invasion, Guildford was one of the most important towns in England. This was due to its proximity to London (only one day by horse) and its position on the River Wey.

Guildford is still an affluent town, being

a haven for London commuters, though it is decidedly ugly at first glance. A bit of exploration will reveal an attractive old town with a cobbled High St, the ruins of a Norman castle and an unusual modern cathedral. A day trip or an overnighter is all you will need here, as the sights can easily be covered in a day.

Orientation

The old part of Guildford is compact and, with the exception of the cathedral, all the sights mentioned here can easily be covered on foot.

Information

Tourist Office The TIC (☎ 444333, ⓔ tourism@guildford.gov.uk) is at 14 Tunsgate, but they don't have much useful information that is free of charge. Opening hours are 9 am to 6 pm Monday to Saturday, and 10 am to 5 pm on Sunday, May to September; and 9.30 am to 5.30 pm Monday to Saturday, the rest of the year. Free guided walks of the town depart from Tunsgate Arch on High St at 2.30 pm on Sunday, Monday and Wednesday, May to September.

Money There is a bureau de change on the

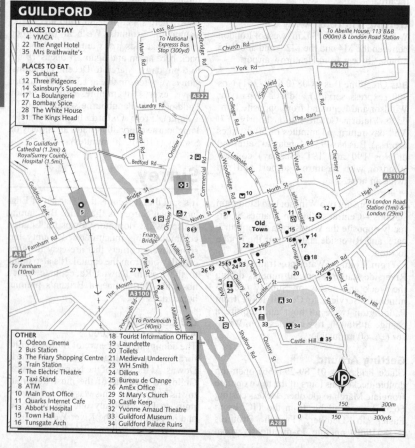

GUILDFORD

PLACES TO STAY
4 YMCA
22 The Angel Hotel
35 Mrs Braithwaite's

PLACES TO EAT
9 Sunburst
12 Three Pidgeons
14 Sainsbury's Supermarket
17 La Boulangerie
27 Bombay Spice
28 The White House
31 The Kings Head

OTHER	
1 Odeon Cinema	18 Tourist Information Office
2 Bus Station	19 Laundrette
3 The Friary Shopping Centre	20 Toilets
5 Train Station	21 Medieval Undercroft
6 The Electric Theatre	23 WH Smith
7 Taxi Stand	24 Dillons
8 ATM	25 Bureau de Change
10 Main Post Office	26 AmEx Office
11 Quarks Internet Cafe	29 St Mary's Church
13 Abbot's Hospital	30 Castle Keep
15 Town Hall	32 Yvonne Arnaud Theatre
16 Tunsgate Arch	33 Guildford Museum
	34 Guildford Palace Ruins

corner of Quarry and High Sts and an AmEx office (☎ 551601) at 38 High St.

Post & Communications The main post office is at 15 North St in the centre. Quarks (☎ 451166) is an Internet cafe at 7 Jeffries Passage. It's expensive – £3 for 30 minutes.

Bookshops Dillons and WH Smith can both be found on High St near the corner of Quarry St.

Laundry There is a laundrette at 1b Sydenham Rd, just a couple of minutes' walk south of the TIC.

Medical Services The Royal Surrey County Hospital (☎ 571122) on Egerton Rd, about 2 miles (3km) north-west of the old town, has an accident and emergency department.

Toilets Public toilets are on Tunsgate, opposite the TIC.

The Old Town

On High St near the TIC is the landmark **Town Hall** (☎ 444035), a Tudor building with a 17th-century facade. You will recognise it by the huge clock which juts out over the street. It opens for guided tours at 2, 3 and 4 pm on Tuesday and Thursday. Admission is free.

On the other side of the street is a **Medieval Undercroft** (☎ 444750), sitting under 72 High St. It opens 2 to 4 pm Tuesday and Thursday, and noon to 4 pm on Saturday, May to September. Admission is free.

Abbot's Hospital (☎ 562670), on High St, was founded in 1619 by George Abbot who was the archbishop of Canterbury from 1611 to 1633. The place is still used as a hospice for the elderly and tours are by arrangement.

To the south of High St, set within landscaped gardens, is the **Castle Keep** which is believed to have been built by William I soon after his great victory. The keep never saw much defensive action and its main role was as the administrative centre of Guildford.

Walk to the south-western corner of the gardens to see the remains of **Guildford Palace**, which dates from the late 12th century. The room left here may have been Henry III's Great Chamber, which he would have stayed in on trips between London and Winchester in the 13th century.

Guildford Museum (☎ 444750), on Quarry St, begins with an archaeological display and moves through the ages until the 19th century. There is a special display on Lewis Carroll who spent a lot of time in Guildford and actually died in his sisters' house at 5 Castle Hill. The museum opens 11 am to 5 pm, Monday to Saturday. Admission is free.

St Mary's Church, in Quarry St, dates from around 1040. The tower, which may have originally been built as a fortress, is pre-Conquest and made of flint. The transept is early Norman and the chapels of St John and St Mary were added in the 12th century. Parts of the church were renovated in the Early English Gothic style in the 13th century. The stone arched roof at one end is evidence of this.

Guildford Cathedral

About 2½ miles (4km) north-west of the centre, atop Stag Hill, is the remarkable Guildford Cathedral (☎ 565287). Its construction was begun in 1935, then interrupted by WWII, and completed in 1961. It is the work of Sir Edward Maufe who won a competition to design the cathedral in 1932. Whether you view it as a monstrous piece of retro architecture or a brilliantly executed Gothic building, you must admit it's quite awesome. The interior is a combination of Gothic austerity and 1960s minimalism. Its starkness makes a change from cathedrals such as Canterbury and Winchester, which are so densely packed with tombs, statues, plaques and stained glass.

It opens 8.30 am until after Evensong. A free floor plan and guide is on your left as you enter the cathedral. Guides of the human kind will be happy to show you around if they are there. Services are at 9 am and 5.30 pm and on Sunday at 8, 9.45 and 11.30 am and 6.30 pm.

SOUTH-EASTERN ENGLAND

Places to Stay

If you decide to stay here be warned that accommodation in or near the old town is very expensive, and prices farther out in very ordinary areas are not much better. Even the **YMCA** (☎ 532555, fax 537161, e admin@ guildford.ymca.org.uk, Bridge St) costs an exorbitant £30 per night, not including breakfast.

Mrs Braithwaite's (☎ 563324, 11 Castle Hill) B&B is the pick of the bunch. It's in a beautiful spot near the castle gardens and the centre, and the rate is very reasonable at £20 per person.

Abeille House (☎ 532200, 119 Stoke Rd) charges £28/40 for singles/doubles. **113 B&B** (☎ 302394, 113 Stoke Rd) charges £26/40. Both places are basic and bland and are about a 15-minute walk along busy roads to the centre.

The Angel Hotel (☎ 564555, fax 533770, 91 High St) is an expensive olde worlde hotel in the old posting house and livery building. Luxurious rooms cost £135 (single or double).

Places to Eat

We recommend you make your own meals as much as possible. Eating out in Guildford is not cheap. There's a **Sainsbury's** on High St and **La Boulangerie** (☎ 561050, 142 High St) nearby has fresh bread as well as pies (£1.25) and quiches (£1.50).

Three Pigeons (☎ 504227, 169 High St) is a dingy pub downstairs but the restaurant upstairs is much nicer and serves rump steak for only £4.95. **The Kings Head** (☎ 575004, Quarry St) is a pleasant pub with exposed beams, an open fireplace, outdoor seating in a leafy courtyard and good pub grub.

Sunburst (☎ 454970, 53 North St) has all kinds of takeaway fare. Baguettes cost from £2.15, pizza is around £5 and chicken fajitas are £3.80. **The White House** (☎ 302006, 8 High St) is on the other side of the River Wey from the centre. It's a spacious, barn-like pub with a big menu. Meals are served all day and there's an outdoor seating area overlooking the river.

Bombay Spice (☎ 454272, 17 Park St) is an Indian restaurant with comfortable surroundings and good service. It costs around £7.95 for main courses and £2.50 for side dishes.

Entertainment

Guildford is big on theatres, the main ones being **The Electric Theatre** (☎ 444789, e electrictheatre@guildford.gov.uk, Onslow St) and the **Yvonne Arnaud Theatre** (☎ 440000, e yat@yvonne-arnaud.co.uk, Millbrook). The **Odeon Cinema** (☎ 578017, Bedford Rd) has nine screens.

Getting Around

The main local bus service is Arriva (☎ 505693). The office at the bus station on Commercial Rd has timetables of local services in and around Guildford. There is a taxi stand on North St, near the corner of Onslow St.

Getting There & Away

Guildford is 29 miles (47km) south-west of London off the A3. Being largely a commuter town, there are plenty of regular rail and bus services from the capital.

Bus National Express (☎ 0870 580 8080) coach No 30 departs London Victoria every two hours and stops in Guildford on Woodbridge Rd, about 1½ miles north of the centre; the journey costs £5.50. Arriva bus Nos 4, 16, 20 and 28 run between the bus station and the National Express stop. Tellings Golden Miller (☎ 020-8897 6131) bus No 740 leaves regularly from the Greenline bus station at London Victoria for Guildford (£4.60, 1 hour). Stagecoach Hampshire (☎ 01256-359142) bus No X64 runs from Guildford bus station to Farnham (£2.75, 30 minutes) and on to Winchester hourly (£4.30, 1 hour 50 minutes).

Train The main train station is on Guildford Park Rd, a few minutes' walk east of the centre. London Rd station is about a 15-minute walk from the centre but is just a five-minute walk to the Stoke Rd B&Bs. There are services from London Waterloo to Guildford every 15 minutes (£8, 35 minutes). Trains go to Farnham twice hourly (£3.80, 22 minutes) and to Portsmouth three times an hour (£11.80, 50 minutes).

FARNHAM
☎ 01252 • pop 38,000

Farnham is an attractive Georgian market town nestled in the valley of the River Wey, on the border with Hampshire. At first glance it seems a conservative place, populated mainly by well-to-do London commuters, but dig a little deeper and you'll find an interesting, artistic town. This may have something to do with the fact that it's home to the West Surrey College of Art and Design.

Farnham's favourite son is William Cobbett (1762–1835), the farmer turned radical social commentator who was the first person to publish parliamentary debates (now done by Hansard).

Orientation & Information

The centre of town can be explored easily on foot. The Borough is the main shopping street and the train station is on South St.

Staff at the TIC (☎ 715109, fax 725083, e info@waverley.gov.uk), in the council offices building on South St, are very helpful. They have an excellent booklet detailing B&Bs in the area, and the free *Farnham Heritage Trail*. It opens 9.30 am to 5.15 pm Monday to Thursday, until 4.45 pm on Friday and until noon on Saturday.

You'll find an ATM on The Borough, near the corner of Castle St. The main post office and a bureau de change are on West St, which is the continuation of The Borough. There are public toilets in the car park on The Hard which runs off West St, near the main post office.

Farnham Castle

Farnham Castle (☎ 713393), owned by English Heritage (EH; see Useful Organisations in the Facts for the Visitor chapter), consists of a castle keep and a residential Palace House, built in the 13th century for the Bishops of Winchester as a place to stop on their travels to London. It was used as such until 1926. From then until the 1950s

it was used by the Bishops of Guildford. It is now the Centre for International Briefing, giving courses to people going to live abroad. It's for this reason that you can only see the place by guided tour.

The house has been changed and altered on a massive scale over the centuries with most of the changes undertaken by Bishop Morley in the 1660s. Admission costs £1.50/ 80p, though it's only open between 2 and 4 pm on Wednesday.

The **Castle Keep** was built in 1138 by Henri de Blois, the grandson of William the Conqueror. (He was also responsible for the founding of Wolvesey Castle and St Cross Hospital in Winchester.) The keep has fallen into ruin over the centuries, but it is possible to get to the top for some great views. It opens 10 am to 6 pm daily, April to October. Admission costs £2/1. The castle can be reached by steps from the end of Castle St.

Other Things to See

Any further exploration of Farnham should begin at historical Castle St. Among the Georgian frontages you'll find the **Almshouses**, recognisable by their blue doors. They were built in 1619 by Andrew Windsor 'for the habitation and relief of eight poor honest old impotent persons'.

Take a stroll around the cobbled Middle, Lower and Upper Church Lanes, where you'll find a string of 15th- and 16th-century **timber-framed houses**. Their original facades are hidden behind 18th-century brickwork.

The excellent **Museum of Farnham** (☎ 715094), at 38 West St, has a special exhibit on the 20th-century architect Falkner, a local boy who was responsible for much architecture around town, including the **Town Hall building** on the corner of Castle St and The Borough. It also covers the history of Farnham from prehistory, through Roman, Saxon and Norman times and up to the present. Its pride and joy is a nightcap belonging to Charles I who stopped overnight at Vernon House (now the Library) on his way to trial in the Tower of London in 1498. He made a gift of the cap to the inn keeper.

If you walk along Castle St and up past the castle for about half a mile you will come to **Farnham Park**, which spreads itself over 130 hectares. It was once a deer park for the bishops. As well as offering some great walks, the park contains a golf course, cricket pitch, football ground and children's playground.

Places to Stay
The hotels in the centre are all very expensive and most of Farnham's cheaper B&Bs are about a 15-minute walk from the centre. You'll need to book ahead, especially at the weekend.

Mrs Burland's B&B (☎ 723047, 15 Vicarage Lane) is great value, but it's 1½ miles from the centre. If you can manage the distance then you are in for a treat. Large, comfortable rooms with en suite and views over the valley cost £18 per person; £16 if you stay for more than one night. There are a few short walks around the country lanes in this area – just ask Mrs Burland.

Sandiway (☎ 710721, 24 Shortheath Rd) is about the same distance from town (about a 20-minute walk) but it is very comfortable and clean and rooms are only £20 per person.

Mrs Williams' (☎ 715430, Wingate, 8 Trebor Ave) B&B is more expensive at £30 for a single en suite and £35 for a double with shared bathroom, but it's only a few minutes' walk from the centre.

The Bishop's Table (☎ 710222, fax 733494, 27 West St) is a nice old Georgian hotel and is a little more affordable than other hotels in the centre at £90/110.

Places to Eat
For self-caterers there's a *Sainsbury's* on South St, near the corner of East St.

Downing St is home to a number of excellent eateries. *The Banaras* (☎ 734081, 40 Downing St) is an Indian restaurant that has earned a very good reputation locally. The lamb tikka masala (£7.95) is supposedly excellent.

The Stirling Sandwich Shop (☎ 711602, 49a Downing St) makes generous sandwiches for £1.30 to £2. This place is very popular and at lunch time the queue stretches the length of Downing St.

The Traditional Plaice (☎ 718009, 50 Downing St) is a fish and chip shop with a restaurant out the back. A seafood meal for two with a bottle of wine can be had for under £20.

Caffè Piccolo (☎ 723277, 84 West St), across the road from the museum, is a casual Italian restaurant in an atmospheric timber-framed building. Excellent pasta and pizza dishes cost around £7.

The Nelson Arms (☎ 716078, 50 Castle St) is an old timber-framed pub with an open fireplace. It escaped a brick makeover but was stuccoed instead. Meals cost around £5.

Getting There & Away
Farnham is 39 miles (63km) from London and only 10 miles (16km) from Guildford on the A31.

Bus National Express (☎ 0870 580 8080) has a service from London Victoria (£5.50, 1¾ hours). Stagecoach Hampshire (☎ 01256-359142) bus No X64 runs between Winchester and Guildford via Farnham twice an hour (hourly on Saturday, no service on Sunday). It takes 70 minutes from Winchester (£4.30) and 30 minutes from Guildford (£2.75). Stagecoach Coastline (☎ 01903-237661) bus No 38 goes to Portsmouth every hour from Monday to Saturday (£3.20, 2¼ hours).

Train The train station is at the end of South St, on the other side of the A31 from the old town (five minutes' walk south-east from the centre). There are half-hourly services from London Waterloo (£9.50, 50 minutes) and Guildford (£3.80, 22 minutes) via Woking. To get to Portsmouth you need to change at Woking (£13, 1½ hours).

WAVERLEY ABBEY
The first Cistercian abbey to be built in England, Waverley dates from 1128. Like Beaulieu Abbey in the New Forest in Hampshire, it was based on a parent abbey at Cîteaux in France. It's easy to see why

these beautiful ruins, sitting sadly on the banks of the River Wey, inspired Walter Scott's novel, *Waverley Abbey*.

The Cistercian monks believed in a simple and hardworking life. They tilled the land and carried out all kinds of manual labour, something that was greatly appreciated by the local community. Waverley suffered the same fate of many other ecclesiastical institutions in the country at the hands of Henry VIII in 1536. Although many of the buildings were destroyed, the ruins are still in remarkable condition and it's a really beautiful spot to wander around. The abbey is off the B3001, 2 miles (3km) south-east of Farnham.

BOX HILL

This hill on the North Downs, 2½ miles (4km) north-east of Dorking, was famous as a beauty spot long before Jane Austen's *Emma* came here for her disastrous picnic. For everyone else it's an excellent place for a long walk, with 20-mile views from the top of the hill. Great stretches of sloping grassland are interspersed with heavily wooded areas. This is also a good area to come for mountain biking, and there are a number of bridle trails.

On top of the hill is a visitor information centre where you'll find trail maps, and a kiosk. Behind them are the remains of a fort and arsenal, built in 1899 as one of 13 immobilisation centres in case of attack by the French. There are trains twice an hour between London Victoria and Box Hill & Westhumble station (£6.30, 50 minutes).

Kent

Kent is one of the most diverse and attractive counties of the region. The history of the coastal towns is long and interesting (see the boxed text 'Cinque Ports' below). It is the opinion of many that the character of most coastal towns was spoiled by the arrival of the railway and mass tourism in the 19th century, not to mention the kitsch video arcades and fun parks of the 20th. It could be argued, however, that this metamorphosis has only endowed these towns with a new character – more modern perhaps, definitely tackier in some cases, but still unique and very distinctive.

The inland area has some stunning countryside and some of the most English of England's villages. Probably the most distinctive feature of the fertile, rolling hills of inland Kent are the white, cone-shaped

Cinque Ports

Due to their proximity to Europe, the coastal towns of south-east England were the frontline against Viking raids and invasions during Anglo-Saxon times. In the absence of a professional army and navy, these towns were frequently called upon to defend themselves, and the kingdom, at land and sea.

In 1278, Edward I formalised this already ancient arrangement by legally defining the Confederation of Cinque (pronounced sink, from the Old French for 'five') Ports. The five Head Ports – Sandwich, Dover, Hythe, Romney (now New Romney) and Hastings – were granted numerous privileges in exchange for providing the king with ships. The number of Cinque Ports gradually expanded to include about 30 coastal towns and villages.

By the end of the 15th century most of the Cinque Ports' harbours had become largely unusable thanks to the shifting coastline, and a professional navy was based at Portsmouth.

As is often the case in England, while real importance and power has evaporated, the pomp and ceremony remains. The Lord Warden of the Cinque Ports is a prestigious post now given to faithful servants of the Crown – they get an apartment at Walmer Castle in Deal and a chance to wear ceremonial clothes and a big, gold chain. The current warden is the Queen Mother; previous incumbents have included the Duke of Wellington, Sir Winston Churchill and Sir Robert Menzies, former prime minister of Australia.

roofs of oast houses (see the boxed text 'Oast Houses'). It's possible to see woods that are still being managed with traditional coppicing (the process of cutting down a tree to the stump to encourage regrowth of multiple stems).

The trails along the North and South Downs attract walkers from all over the world (see the boxed text 'The North Downs Way'). Between the North and South Downs lies an area known as the Weald, much of it designated an Area of Outstanding Natural Beauty.

GETTING AROUND
Bus & Train
Stagecoach East Kent (☎ 01424-440770) has a good network around the region. Its Kent Compass 100 bus runs hourly (less frequently on Sunday) on a circuit taking in Canterbury, Dover, Deal, Sandwich, Ramsgate, Broadstairs, Margate, Herne Bay, Whitstable and back to Canterbury. The 200 bus does the same circuit in the opposite direction.

All the main towns and cities are served at least several times a day by direct trains to London.

Bicycle
A marked cycle route wends its way between Dover, Deal, Sandwich, Canterbury and Whitstable. The countryside is mostly flat and there are plenty of quiet country lanes. Depending on how circuitous the

Oast Houses

Oast houses were basically giant, housed kilns (ovens) for drying hops which were used to brew beer. They sprang up in the early 15th century when beer was introduced to the region. (Ale, which uses malt as a prime ingredient, had been brewed for centuries before this.) The reason oast houses are so common in Kent is that the soil here was ideal for growing hops. Surrey and Hampshire were also successful hop-growing regions.

An oast house is made up of four rooms; the kiln, the drying room (located above the kiln), the cooling room, and the storage room where hops were pressed and put into bales, ready to go to the local inn brewery. The cone-shaped roof was necessary to create a draught for the fire. The bits sticking out from the top of the cone are cowls. They could be moved to regulate the airflow to the fire.

Many oast houses have been converted into homes now (some are B&Bs), and are becoming more and more sought after as prime real estate.

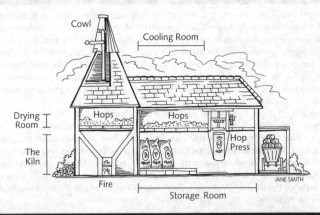

JANE SMITH

The North Downs Way

The North Downs Way is a walking trail that begins near Dorking in Surrey and ends near Dover in Kent. It runs along chalk ridges, through woodlands and valleys. The entire route covers 153 miles (240km) and some sections are suitable for cyclists and horse riders. Much of the North Downs trail follows the Pilgrims Way, mentioned by Chaucer in his Canterbury Tales, and in use for over 2000 years.

The *North Downs Way Practical Handbook* costs £1.95 and is available from most tourist information centres (TICs) in the region. It details routes, distances and places to stay and eat. There are a number of free leaflets detailing smaller sections of the North Downs Way, also available from TICs. For more information contact the North Downs Way National Trail Office (☎ 01622 696185, e jim .walker@kent.gov.uk).

route, it is approximately a 40-mile (64km) ride. TICs stock a good map (£6) detailing cycling routes in Kent.

CANTERBURY
☎ 01227 • pop 38,670

The city of Canterbury was severely damaged by bombing during WWII and parts, especially to the south of the cathedral, have been rebuilt insensitively. Even though parts outside the centre are quite ugly, there's plenty to see in the attractive and atmospheric old town. The town crawls with tourists and there's not much chance of escaping queues in summer.

Canterbury's greatest treasure is its magnificent cathedral, the successor to the church St Augustine built after he began converting the English to Christianity in 597. After the martyrdom of Archbishop Thomas à Becket in 1170, the cathedral became the centre of one of the most important medieval pilgrimages in Europe, immortalised by Geoffrey Chaucer in *The Canterbury Tales* (see the boxed text 'The Murder of Becket' later).

Canterbury can easily be visited on a day trip from London. It makes an ideal stopover on the way to or from Dover or the Cinque Ports farther north. A one or two night stay should be enough to cover all the sights mentioned in this book.

Orientation

The old centre of Canterbury is enclosed by a medieval city wall and a modern ring road. It's easy to get around on foot, which is really the only mode of transport, as cars are not permitted to enter the old town.

Information

Tourist Office At No 34 on St Margaret's St, the TIC (☎ 766567, fax 459840, e canterburyinformation@canterbury.gov.uk) opens 9.30 am to 5 pm daily, to 4 pm on Wednesday. It has a free booking service for local B&Bs (available until half an hour before closing time).

Money There's a bureau de change at 28 St Margaret's St. You'll find all the major banks and ATMs on High St, near the corner of St Margaret's St.

Post & Communications The main post office is on the corner of Stour and High Sts. The Library at the Royal Museum on High St has free Internet access for up to one hour but you'll need to book ahead on ☎ 463608.

Bookshops Chaucer Bookshop on Beer Cart Lane is a cluttered, chaotic used-book shop that also sells histories of Canterbury and rarities of the book world. If you want more organisation, there's a Waterstones bookshop at 20 St Margaret's St.

Laundry There is a laundrette at 36 St Peter's St. It opens 8.30 am to 5.45 pm Monday to Saturday.

Medical Services The Canterbury Health Centre (☎ 452444) is at 26 Old Dover Rd. In the case of an emergency go to Kent & Canterbury Hospital (☎ 766877) on Etherbert Rd, about a mile south of the centre.

SOUTH-EASTERN ENGLAND

The Murder of Becket

In 597 St Augustine arrived in Canterbury and successfully converted the king and many of his subjects to Christianity. He founded a Benedictine monastery and abbey, and the city was established as the centre of the English church. A power struggle between Church and State gradually grew more and more intense. In the 12th century this tension reached breaking point when Henry II refused to accept the independence of the Roman Church and the authority of a foreign pope. Before Henry made him archbishop in 1162, Thomas à Becket had been a loyal friend of the king and was famed for his luxurious lifestyle. Henry thought Becket would be an ally in his battle against the pope – but he was wrong. From the time he became archbishop, Becket completely renounced his old lifestyle and his friend the king. In 1170 the personal and political conflict reached a tragic culmination when four of Henry's knights, apparently without the king's knowledge, killed the archbishop in the cathedral.

Within hours of the murder rumours of miracles spread and a few years after his death Becket was made a saint. His jewel-encrusted shrine became the most important place of pilgrimage in England and was famous throughout Europe. As Chaucer observed, Canterbury's merchants thrived on the pilgrim/tourist trade, and still do.

Toilets You'll find public toilets inside the cathedral grounds.

Canterbury Cathedral

Canterbury Cathedral (☎ 762862) evolved in stages over many years and it reflects a number of architectural styles.

St Augustine's original cathedral burned down in 1067. Construction of a new cathedral by the first Norman archbishop began in 1070, but only fragments of this remain. In 1174 most of the eastern half of the building was destroyed by fire, but fortunately the magnificent crypt beneath the choir survived.

The fire presented the opportunity to create something in keeping with the cathedral's new status as the most important pilgrimage site in England. In response, William of Sens created the first major Gothic construction in England, a style now described as Early English. Most of the cathedral east of Bell Harry tower dates from this period.

In 1391 work began on the western half of the building, replacing the south-western and north-western transepts and nave. The new perpendicular style was used, and work continued for over 100 years, culminating in the completion of Bell Harry in 1500. Subsequently, more has been subtracted than added, although the exterior has not changed substantially.

The main entrance is through the **southwest porchern** (1), which was built in 1415 to commemorate the English victory at Agincourt. From the centre of the nave there are impressive views east down the length of the church, with its ascending levels, and west to the **window** (2) with glass dating from the 12th century.

From beneath **Bell Harry** (3), with its beautiful fan vault, more glass that somehow survived the Puritans is visible. A 15th-century screen, featuring six kings, separates the nave from the choir.

Becket is believed to have fallen in the north-western transept. A modern **altar and sculpture** (4) mark the spot. The adjoining **Lady Chapel** (5) has beautiful perpendicular fan vaulting. Descend a flight of steps into the Romanesque crypt, the main survivor of the Norman cathedral.

The **Chapel of Our Lady** at the western end of the crypt has some of the finest Romanesque carving in England. St Thomas was entombed in the Early English eastern end (6) until 1220. This is where Henry was whipped for Becket's murder and is reputed to be the site of many miracles. The **Chapel of St Gabriel** (7) features 12th-century paintings, and the **Black Prince's Chantry**

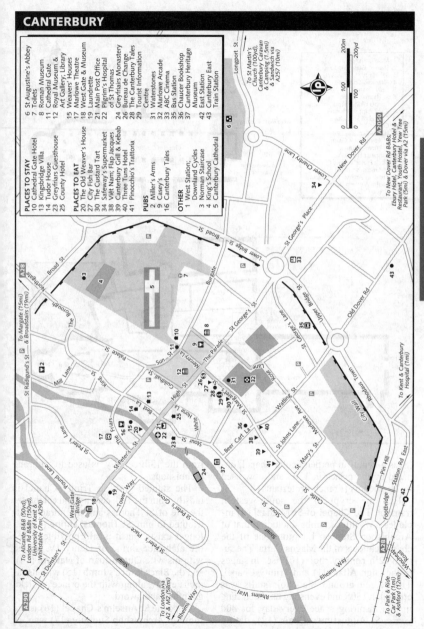

CANTERBURY

PLACES TO STAY
10 Cathedral Gate Hotel
13 Kingsbridge Villa
14 Tudor House
23 Greyfriars Guesthouse
25 County Hotel

PLACES TO EAT
20 The Old Weaver's House
27 Tiny Fish Bar
30 The Custard Tart
34 Safeway's Supermarket
38 Việt Nam; Flap Jacques
39 Canterbury Grill & Kebab
40 Three Tuns Hotel
41 Pinocchio's Trattoria

PUBS
2 Miller's Arms
9 Casey's
16 Canterbury Tales

OTHER
1 West Station;
3 Downland Cycles
4 Norman Staircase
5 King's School
6 Canterbury Cathedral
7 St Augustine's Abbey
8 Toilets
11 Roman Museum
12 Cathedral Gate
15 Royal Museum & Art Gallery, Library
17 Weavers' Houses
18 Marlowe Theatre
19 West Gate & Museum
21 Laundrette
22 Main Post Office
24 Pilgrim's Hospital of St Thomas
26 Greyfriars Monastery
28 Bureau de Change
29 The Canterbury Tales
31 Tourist Information Centre
32 Waterstones
35 Marlowe Arcade
36 ABC Cinema
37 Bus Station
42 Chaucer Bookshop
43 Canterbury Heritage Museum
   East Station
   Canterbury East Train Station

SOUTH-EASTERN ENGLAND

CANTERBURY CATHEDRAL

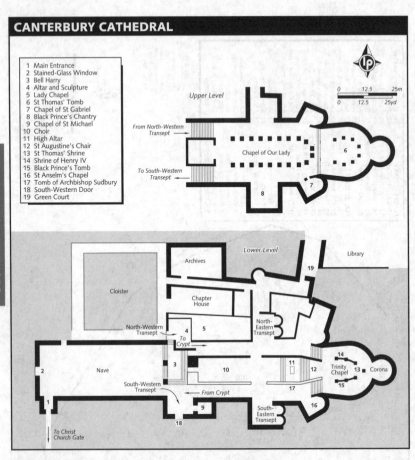

1 Main Entrance
2 Stained-Glass Window
3 Bell Harry
4 Altar and Sculpture
5 Lady Chapel
6 St Thomas' Tomb
7 Chapel of St Gabriel
8 Black Prince's Chantry
9 Chapel of St Michael
10 Choir
11 High Altar
12 St Augustine's Chair
13 St Thomas' Shrine
14 Shrine of Henry IV
15 Black Prince's Tomb
16 St Anselm's Chapel
17 Tomb of Archbishop Sudbury
18 South-Western Door
19 Green Court

(8) is a beautiful perpendicular chapel, donated by the prince in 1363 and now used by Huguenots (French Protestants).

Exit the crypt to the south-western transept. The **Chapel of St Michael** (9) includes a wealth of tombs, including that of Archbishop Stephen Langton, one of the chief architects of the Magna Carta. The superb **12th-century choir** (10) rises in stages to the **High Altar** (11) and Trinity Chapel. The screen around the choir stalls was erected in 1305 and evensong has been sung in this inspiring space every day for 800 years. **St Augustine's Chair** (12), dating

from the 13th century, is used to enthrone archbishops.

The stained glass in Trinity Chapel is mostly from the 13th century and celebrates the life of St Thomas and the miracles attributed to him. **St Thomas' shrine** (13) no longer exists, but it is still possible to see the alabaster shrine of Henry IV, buried with his wife **Queen Joan of Navarre** (14), and the **Black Prince's tomb** (15) with its famous effigy, along with the prince's shield, gauntlets and sword.

Opposite **St Anselm's Chapel** (16) is the **tomb of Archbishop Sudbury** (17) who, as

Chancellor of the Exchequer, was held responsible for a hated poll tax – he was beheaded by a mob during the Peasants' Revolt of 1381. His body was buried with a ball of lead; his head is in a Suffolk church.

Leave the cathedral by the **south-west door** (18) and turn left towards the city wall. Queningate is a small door through the wall which, according to tradition, Queen Bertha used on her way to the Church of St Martin before the arrival of Augustine.

Go round the eastern end of the cathedral and turn right into Green Court (19), which is surrounded on the eastern (right) side by the Deanery and the northern side (straight ahead) by the early-14th-century Brewhouse and Bakehouse, which now house part of the very exclusive King's School. In the north-western corner (far left) is the famous **Norman Staircase** (1151).

Touring the complex can easily absorb half a day. There are treasures tucked away in corners and a trove of associated stories, so a one-hour tour is recommended. They take place at 10.30 am, noon and 2 pm (£3.50), or if the crowd looks daunting you can take a Walkman tour (£2.95, 30 minutes). Admission to the cathedral is £3/2; free for kids under five. There is an excellent guidebook available for £1. The cathedral opens 9 am to 7 pm Monday to Saturday, Easter to September; and 9 am to 5 pm, October to Easter; choral evensong is at 5.30 pm, 3.15 pm on Saturday. It opens 12.30 to 2.30 pm and 4.30 to 5.30 pm on Sunday; choral evensong is at 3.15 pm. If you're visiting in July, phone ahead to check that it's not closed for the two days of university graduation.

The Canterbury Tales

The Canterbury Tales (☎ 479227), in St Margaret's St, provides an entertaining introduction to Chaucer's classic tales. The general concept, however, is strange: jerky, hydraulic puppets seem an inefficient way to recreate history. Perhaps the promoters feel they need something in three dimensions to justify the £5.50/4.60 ticket. The centre opens 9 am to 5.30 pm (to 4.30 pm

November to March) and is usually crammed with school children.

Museums

The **Royal Museum & Art Gallery** (☎ 452747), High St, has military memorabilia and works by local artists; admission is free. It opens 10 am to 5pm Monday to Saturday. The city's three other museums can all be visited with one passport ticket costing £4/2. Individual admission charges are given below.

West Gate & Museum, dating from the 14th century, is the only remaining city gate. It survived because it was used as a prison and therefore it underwent some maintenance; it is now a small museum featuring arms and armour. It opens 11 am to 12.30 pm and 1.30 to 3.30 pm Monday to Saturday year-round. Admission costs £1/65p/50p.

On Stour St, the **Canterbury Heritage Museum** (☎ 452747) is in a converted 12th- and 13th-century building. It gives good though rather dry coverage of the city's history and local characters – who include Rupert Bear and Joseph Conrad. The building, once the Poor Priests' Hospital, is worth visiting in its own right. It opens 10.30 am to 5 pm (last entry 4 pm), Monday to Saturday year-round; and 1.30 to 5 pm on Sunday, June to October. Admission costs £2.40/1.60/1.20.

At the interesting **Roman Museum** (☎ 785575), built underground around the remains of a Roman town house in Butchery Lane, you get to visit the marketplace, smell the odours of a Roman kitchen and handle artefacts. Also on display are large sections of a mosaic floor from a Roman townhouse that was discovered in 1946 during a clean up after WWII bombing. Much of the house is still buried under buildings in Butchery Lane. There's a lot to see here and a visit is a must. It opens 10 am to 5 pm (last entry 4 pm) Monday to Saturday year-round; and 1.30 to 5 pm on Sunday, June to October. Admission costs £2.40/1.60.

Pilgrim's Hospital of St Thomas

Founded in 1180, the Pilgrim's Hospital (☎ 471688) is well worth a visit. Originally built as a hospice for pilgrims to Becket's shrine in the cathedral, it is still used today to house elderly folk (they live behind the doors marked 'Private'). You will see here a Norman undercroft, a refectory hall and, on the upper level, the Pilgrims' Chapel. The building was extensively restored in the 16th century and again in the 20th century, but the roof of the chapel is original.

The hospice opens 10 am to 5 pm Monday to Saturday. Admission costs £1/50p.

St Augustine's Abbey

Henry VIII acted with thoroughness when St Augustine's Abbey (☎ 778000; EH) was demolished in 1538 – only foundations remain. It opens 10 am to 6 pm daily, April to October, and 10 am to 4 pm daily, November to March. Admission costs £2.50/1.30 and includes an audio tour.

St Martin's Church

Believed to be the oldest parish church in England, St Martin's predates St Augustine and is possibly Roman in origin. To reach the church, continue 250m past St Augustine's Abbey and take the first road left; the church is on the right after 100m.

Greyfriars Monastery

This was the first Franciscan (the Grey Friars) monastery in England, founded in 1267. The picturesque building spans a small branch of the River Stour, and includes an upstairs chapel that opens to the public 2 to 4 pm Monday to Saturday, mid-May to September. Eucharist is celebrated every Wednesday at 12.30 pm.

Weavers' Houses

Just off St Peter's St, along the River Stour, are a number of Tudor-style houses dating from around AD 1500. Most of them are inhabited and not open to the public, but if you want to know what they are like inside, stop for a bite at The Old Weaver's House (see Places to Eat later).

Things to Do

There are guided walks from the TIC on St Margaret's St at 2 pm daily, April to October and at 11.30 am Monday to Saturday in July and August. The cost is £3.50/3. The walks take 1½ hours and explore the cathedral and museum precincts, King's School and the town's medieval centre. There is also a range of specialist tours available covering architecture, literature and pilgrimage.

As with most of the major tourist towns in England, Ghost Tours are proving to be more and more popular in Canterbury. At 6.30 pm every Friday, Saturday and Sunday during April, June, July and August you can attend a frightening guided walk around the old town, but you'll need to book ahead on ☎ 454888.

From May to September there are chauffeured punt trips (☎ 07885 318301) along the River Stour at 10 am from the West Gate Bridge. For four adults and two children the charge is £18.

You can also take a rowboat tour from behind The Old Weaver's House (see Places to Eat later in the section) during summer for £4 per person.

Places to Stay

Most Canterbury accommodation is quite expensive, particularly in July and August. In some cases prices almost double; ring ahead to avoid nasty surprises.

Camping Off the A257, *Canterbury Caravan and Camping Site* (☎ 463216, Bekesbourne Lane) is just under 2 miles (3km) east of the centre and charges from £9 to £10 for two people and a tent.

Yew Tree Park (☎ 700306, Stone St, Petham), 5 miles (8km) south of Canterbury off the B2068 (take New Dover Rd out of the centre and turn right just after the youth hostel), has a large swimming pool for guests. It opens from April to October and charges are £4 for one adult and a tent, £6 for two. A bus from Canterbury to Petham village (a half-mile walk to the camp site) leaves hourly from the bus station.

Hostels The *Youth Hostel* (☎ 462911, 54 New Dover Rd), in an old Victorian villa, is just under a mile east of the centre. It's closed from late December to the end of January. The nightly charge is £9.75 and there is one twin room for £28.

Let's Stay (☎ 463628, 26 New Dover Rd) is more homy and better value than the youth hostel. The owner charges £10 per person in four-bed dorms with a cooked breakfast. Men and women are accommodated separately. Couples and families may be able to stay, but will need to call ahead to check on availability.

The University of Kent (☎ 828000, Tanglewood) is a 20-minute walk north-east of the centre and open only when students are away (in April and from July to September). B&B is from £14.50 per person.

B&Bs In the centre of town just off High St, *Kingsbridge Villa (☎ 766415, 15 Best Lane)* is a quiet, comfortable B&B. There are no single rooms; doubles go for £42 or £45 to £50 with en suite. Parking is available.

Tudor House (☎ 765650, 6 Best Lane) is also central, and very good value. This quaint (and slightly eccentric) 450-year-old building has singles/doubles for £18/36. In addition to the usual facilities, it has canoes and boats for guests to hire at £10 per day.

Greyfriars Guesthouse (☎ 456255, 6 Stour St) is right in the heart of the centre and offers large en-suite rooms from £25/45.

Alicante B&B (☎/fax 766277, 4 Roper Rd) is not quite in the centre but just a minute's walk from Canterbury West station. Big double rooms cost £40; singles are negotiable. Thoughtful touches, such as hairdryers in each room, make this place appealing.

The London Rd B&Bs are a 10-minute walk from the centre. *Acacia Lodge* and *Tanglewood B&B (☎ 769955, 39 London Rd)* are actually the same place. Cottagey, cute and very tidy rooms cost £26/38.

London Guest House (☎ 765860, fax 456721, 14 London Rd) is slightly closer to town and has rooms for £20 per person with shared bathroom. The double room has a shower.

Magnolia House (☎/fax 765121, 36 St Dunstan's Terrace), off London Rd, is very

luxurious but so is the price – singles/doubles cost £38/78 and the room with a four-poster bed and spa bath costs £110.

There's a string of decent B&Bs along New Dover Rd, all about a 10-minute walk to the centre.

Charnwood Lodge B&B (☎/fax 451712, 64 New Dover Rd) (the sign out front just says 'B&B') is the best value in town and we can highly recommend it. For £35 you get a clean, self-contained flat that can sleep up to three people. Breakfast is included, which you may cook yourself if you prefer.

Hampton House (☎ 464912, 40 New Dover Rd) is run by a friendly couple who have a strict no smoking policy. Rooms offer a touch of luxury and cost £28/40 with shared bathroom or £45 for an en-suite double. In winter the rates drop to £20/40.

Alverstone House (☎/fax 766360, 38 New Dover Rd) is a gorgeous old manor house with wooden panelling. It's very popular with young travellers and rooms are reasonable at £20/35.

Hotels In the heart of the city, *Cathedral Gate Hotel (☎ 464381, fax 462800, e cgate@cgate.demon.co.uk, 36 Burgate)* has singles/doubles from £23/44 with shared bathroom and £52.50/79 with en-suite facilities. Although the walls are on the thin side and some of the floors slope alarmingly, the rooms are comfortable and the views of the cathedral are magnificent.

County Hotel (☎ 766266, High St) is centrally located and offers true English olde worlde charm with its 15th-century bar and 12th-century cellars. Rooms cost £90/106 and breakfast will set you back £7.50 per person for continental, £10.50 for cooked.

A few cheaper hotels can be found on New Dover Rd. *The Ebury Hotel (☎ 768433, fax 459187, e info@ebury-hotel .co.uk, 65–67 New Dover Rd)* has the feel of an upmarket B&B minus the familiarity or warmth. There is an indoor, heated pool here and singles cost £45 to £50, doubles £65 to £75, depending on their size.

Canterbury Hotel (☎ 450551, fax 780145, e canterbury.hotel@btinternet.com, 71 New Dover Rd) has a jovial atmosphere and helpful staff, but the rooms are not quite as good as those at The Ebury. Singles/doubles/triples go for £55/75/95.

Places to Eat

The crowds of visitors and students ensure that there's a good range of reasonably priced eating places in Canterbury. Bookings are recommended, especially at the weekend. For self-caterers there's a *Safeway* on the corner of New Dover Rd and Lower Chantry Rd, just south-east of the centre.

The Old Weaver's House (☎ 464660, 1 St Peter's St), built around AD 1500, is very cosy and serves everything from salads and pies to fish and chips and curries. Starters cost £2.25 to £3.95 and main courses £6.75 to £9.95. There's an outdoor terrace overlooking the River Stour which is lovely in spring and summer.

You'll find a great variety of cuisines for various budgets along Castle St. *Flap Jacques* (☎ 781000, 71 Castle St) is an inexpensive French bistro serving traditional Breton (buckwheat) pancakes.

Next door is *Việt Nam* (☎ 760022, 72 Castle St) with a modern Vietnamese menu. Prawns with french beans and garlic costs £5.95. The very tempting Vietnamese tapas menu features dishes costing £2.75 to £3.50.

Pinocchio's Trattoria (☎ 457538, 64 Castle St) is more expensive but cheerful with a superb Italian wine selection and a terrace out the back. Pasta costs £5.60 to £8.95 and pizzas go for £4.70 to £7.30.

Canterbury Grill & Kebab (☎ 765458, 66 Castle St) is where you can sample that wonderful British contribution to world cuisine, the chip buttie (French fries sandwich) for £1.30. Kebabs cost from £3 and burgers from £2.20.

Three Tuns Hotel (☎ 456391), at the end of St Margaret's St, stands on the site of a Roman theatre and itself dates from the 16th century. It serves good-value pub meals from around £4.

The Custard Tart (☎ 785178, 35a St Margaret's St) is extremely popular and serves delicious baguettes from £2.30 and cream teas for £2.95. The downstairs take-away counter is excellent value with sausage rolls for £1 and sandwiches for £1.30. Get in before the 1 pm lunch rush.

City Fish Bar (☎ 760873, 29a St Margaret's St) has fish and chips from £3.60 and pie and chips for £2.80.

Canterbury Hotel (☎ 450551, 71 New Dover Rd) has an excellent French restaurant though the atmosphere might be a little quiet and stiff for some. Starters cost from £7 to £8.50 and main courses are £12 to £16.

Entertainment

What, Where & When, a free guide to what's on in Canterbury, is available from the TIC. The Web site www.wwevents.com has a calendar of events listing all kinds of activities in Canterbury.

Pubs Being a university town and favourite tourist haunt, Canterbury has a number of lively pubs. The *Miller's Arms* (☎ 456057, Mill Lane) is a classic student hang-out, while *Casey's* (☎ 463252, 5 Butchery Lane), near the main gate to the cathedral, has a large selection of Irish ales and stouts. *Canterbury Tales* (☎ 768594, 12 The Friars) is a real ale pub just across from Marlowe Theatre.

Theatre & Cinema *Marlowe Theatre* (☎ 787787, fax 479622, ⓔ boxoffice@ canterbury.gov.uk, The Friars) puts on a variety of plays, dances, concerts and musicals year-round. The box office opens 10 am to 8 pm Monday to Saturday. *ABC Cinema* (☎ 453577), on the corner of Upper Bridge St and St George's Place, shows the latest mainstream movies.

Getting There & Away

Canterbury is 58 miles (93km) from London and approximately 15 miles (24km) from Margate, Sandwich and Dover.

Bus The bus station is just within the city walls between St George's Lane and Upper Bridge St. National Express (☎ 0870 580 8080) coaches to Canterbury leave every 30 minutes from London Victoria (£7/9 one way/day return, 1 hour 50 minutes). Its shuttle service from Canterbury to Dover (£2.50, 30 minutes) runs hourly every day.

See Getting Around under Kent at the beginning of this section for stops on Stagecoach East Kent's (☎ 01424-440770) 100/200 service. These buses run every 30 minutes (hourly on Sunday) – Canterbury to Margate takes 40 minutes, to Broadstairs it's 1¼ hours and to Ramsgate it's 1½ hours. Services to Sandwich and Deal run Monday to Saturday only. The fare to each place is £6 so an Explorer ticket would be better value if you intend to make more than one trip.

Train There are two train stations: East (for the youth hostel), accessible from London Victoria; and West, accessible from London's Charing Cross and Waterloo (£14.80 day return or £19.99 for two people, 1½ hours). There are regular trains between Canterbury East and Dover Priory (£4.50, 45 minutes). Trains for Margate, Broadstairs and Ramsgate leave from Canterbury West every hour (£4.70) and take around 30 minutes. For Deal change trains at Ramsgate. Trains to the south coast go via Ashford.

Getting Around

Car Cars are not permitted to enter the centre of town. There are car parks at various points along and just within the ring road.

Alternatively you can make use of the city's Park & Ride service which is free if you have paid the £1.40 fee to leave your car for the day at the Sturry Rd or Wincheap car parks, about 1 mile south of the centre. Shuttle buses run every eight minutes between 7.30 am and 6.30 pm. On Saturday they also run to and from the university.

Taxi Try Laser Taxis (☎ 464422) or Cabwise (☎ 712929).

Bicycle Downland Cycles (☎ 479643) is based at Canterbury West station. Mountain bikes are £10 per day or £50 per week with a £25 deposit. They have maps for the 21 mile (34km) ride to Dover or the 7 mile (11km) ride north to the coastal town of Whitstable.

AROUND CANTERBURY

Higham Park (☎ 830830) is a Palladian mansion set in magnificent Italianate gardens. The park is on the A2, 3 miles (5km) south of Canterbury, and can be reached by catching bus No 16 or 17 towards Folkestone. It opens 11 am to 6 pm Sunday to Thursday, April to September.

Howlett's Animal Park (☎ 721410) covers 70 acres of parkland and has the largest captive gorilla breeding program in the world. You'll also see elephants, tigers, monkeys, wolves and small wild cats. Located 4 miles (6km) east of Canterbury, it opens 10 am to 5 pm (last entry 4 pm) daily year-round. Admission costs £9.80/7.80 or £28 for a family of four. To get there by car take the A257 and turn right at the sign for Bekesbourne, then follow the signs to the Animal Park. From the main bus station you can catch Stagecoach bus Nos 111/211 or 611–14 to Littlebourne, from where it's an 8-minute walk to the park.

Five miles (8km) south-west of Canterbury on the A252, **Chilham** is a medieval village built in true feudal fashion around a square at the gate of a castle. The Norman-style church here was originally built in the 13th century, but sections were added or rebuilt in the 15th century and again in Victorian times. There are several Tudor and Jacobean timber-framed and thatched houses and a couple of friendly pubs. Chilham lies on the North Downs Way and would make a pleasant day's walk from Canterbury. Alternatively you can catch Stagecoach East Kent (☎ 01424-440770) bus No 400 from Canterbury (£1.60, 15 minutes).

Ickham is also 5 miles (8km) from Canterbury, to the east off the A257. Take Stagecoach bus Nos 111/211 or 611–14 to Littlebourne from where it's a 1½-mile (2.5km) walk to the north-east. It is a typical Kentish village with some lovely views of the surrounding countryside. The main focus is a 14th-century church that was built on the site of another church dating from AD 791. The houses, some of which date from 1200, are very well preserved and the town has an eerie, quiet feel about it. One

JANE SMITH

A fistful of ferrets

tourist pamphlet notes the remarkable feat of one of Ickham's residents – he broke a world record when he put two live ferrets down his trousers for over four hours!

MARGATE
☎ 01843 • pop 38,535

Margate was one of the earliest and most popular seaside resorts in England and, even though it's become shabby over the years, the town does have a unique historical appeal. You can almost picture the well-to-do Victorians promenading with their parasols or lunching on the large terraces that line the esplanade. The old town makes for a pleasant stroll with its interesting old houses, antique shops, museum, pubs and cafes. At the time of writing a huge casino was under construction on the esplanade. Hopefully the money derived from this dubious endeavour will result in the cleaning up of Margate's much maligned sea

frontage and restore the town to some of its well-deserved glory.

There's a TIC (☎ 220241, fax 230099) on Marine Dr, four doors down from the sex shop. It opens 9 am to 5 pm (to 4 pm at the weekend).

If you'd like to experience Margate's charms, a well-run *youth hostel* (☎/fax 221616, e margate@yha.org.uk, The Beachcomber, 3–4 Royal Esplanade) charges £10.85/7.40 for adults/under-18s. It's open mid-April to November. Among the many B&Bs and hotels along the esplanade is *Malvern Private Hotel* (☎ 290192, Eastern Esplanade, Cliftonville). Although it could do with a little sprucing up, it's friendly and perfectly adequate at £21 to £23 per person.

For a taste of some local seafood try *Newbys Wine Bar* (☎ 292888, Market Place). A main dish of scampi costs £8.90 and whole sea bass is £12.25, while snacks are around £4.

Getting There & Away
National Express (☎ 0870 580 8080) coach No 22 runs from London Victoria to Margate and on to Broadstairs and Ramsgate about five times a day (£9/10 one way/day return, 2¼ hours). Stagecoach East Kent's (☎ 01424-440770) 100/200 service runs from Canterbury to Margate (40 minutes) and on to Broadstairs 1¼ hours), Deal and Dover.

Trains run hourly from London Victoria or Charing Cross to Margate (£18.20, 2 hours). From Canterbury West trains go via Broadstairs and Ramsgate (£4.70, 30 minutes) and on to Dover (£6.50, 50 minutes) every hour.

BROADSTAIRS
☎ 01843 • pop 23,691

Broadstairs developed later than Margate (late Regency/early Victorian times) and has managed to preserve itself much better. The old part of town, by the sea, is small and intricate and still has the peculiar fascination of a real English resort that has remained unaffected by time. The TIC (☎ 862242, fax 865650) is at 6b High St.

Charles Dickens had a series of holiday homes here and he's the town's claim to fame these days. There's even an annual week-long Dickens Festival in June, which culminates in a ball in Victorian dress.

Between 1837 and 1859 he wrote parts of *Bleak House* and *David Copperfield* in the house on top of the cliff above the pier. It's now a museum – **Bleak House** (☎ 862224). Privately run by its enthusiastic owners, the museum is well worth a visit. There are several rooms arranged as they would have been in Dickens' time, a display on local wrecks and, in the cellars, an entertaining display about local smuggling. If the Kentish Giant looked anything like his mannequin here he must have been absolutely terrifying. The museum opens 10 am to 6 pm daily, March to November (to 9 pm in July and August). Admission costs £3/2.

The **Dickens House Museum** (☎ 862853), 2 Victoria Parade, wasn't actually his house but the home of Mary Pearson Strong, on whom he based Betsey Trotwood. Dickensiana on display includes personal possessions and letters; it opens 2 to 5 pm daily, April to October. Admission costs £1.20/60p.

Places to Stay & Eat

For decent, reasonably priced B&Bs with sea views head for Eastern Esplanade.

Broadstairs Youth Hostel (☎ 604121, fax 604121, [e] broadstairs@yha.org.uk, Thistle Lodge, 3 Osborne Rd) is run by helpful people who charge £9.80/6.75 for adults/under-18s. From the station, turn right under the railway and continue for nearly 30m to a crossroads with traffic lights, then turn left into The Broadway.

Bay Tree Hotel (☎ 862502, fax 860589, 12 Eastern Esplanade) has lovely rooms for £24 per person, or £26 with a sea view. We can highly recommend it.

Gull Cottage Hotel (☎ 861936, 5 Eastern Esplanade) also has decent rooms for £22 per person. *Sunnydene Hotel* (☎/fax 863347, 10 Chandos Rd) is east of the High St, set back from the beach, and is good value at £19 to £21 per person.

There's a wide range of places to eat. *York Gate Café* (☎ 862408, Harbour St),

near the beach, is a wonderful traditional seaside cafe. You can get an egg and bacon sandwich or a cream tea for £2.

Sea Chef (☎ 867964, 17 Albion St) serves good fish and chips for £2.50 or a serving of fried scampi for £2. *Amigos* (☎ 862651, 36 Albion St), a Mexican restaurant, is the place to go if seafood isn't your thing. A huge plate of spicy chicken, rice and salad costs £6.95.

Getting There & Away

Both the train station and the Stagecoach stop are on High St in the centre. Stagecoach East Kent's (☎ 01424-440770) 100/200 bus runs hourly from Canterbury to Broadstairs via Margate, then on to Ramsgate, Sandwich, Deal and Dover. An Explorer ticket is your best bet on this route.

Trains run hourly from London Victoria, London Bridge or Charing Cross to Broadstairs (£18.20, 2½ hours) but you may have to change trains at Ramsgate. Trains run from Margate to Dover (£6.50, 50 minutes) via Broadstairs and Deal.

SANDWICH
☎ 01304 • pop 6000

Sandwich is literally a backwater, but a beautiful one. Once a thriving Cinque Port on the sheltered Wantsum Channel, it has been deserted by the sea and is now a sleepy, medieval village. Due to its location 2 miles (3km) inland it escaped being turned into a seaside resort in the 19th century.

Modern-day interest has centred on the three golf courses on the sand dunes east of the town. The very exclusive Royal St George, perhaps the finest course in England, is sometimes host to the British Open. The town's sedateness and upmarket reputation is reflected in its accommodation. There are a number of very exclusive hotels and the B&Bs are not cheap.

Orientation & Information

The town sits on the southern bank of the River Stour and is mostly surrounded by an earthen embankment dating from the 14th century. Everything is within easy walking distance and there are signs to point you to the sights. You'll find a useful town map on the notice board in the car park opposite the Bell Hotel. It's also available from the TIC (☎ 613565) which is on the New St side of the Guildhall. It opens 11 am to 3 pm daily, May to September. They sell an information pack detailing seven walks around the area.

The post office is on the corner of King and St Peter's Sts.

Things to See & Do

It is said that **Strand St** has more half-timbered houses than any other street in England. Elsewhere, a number of buildings have Dutch or Flemish characteristics (note the stepped gables in some buildings), the legacy of Protestant Flemish refugees who settled in the town in the 16th century. The impressive **Barbican** is a tollgate dating from the 16th century.

The exterior of the **Guildhall** (☎ 617197) was substantially altered in 1910, but the interior is little changed since the 16th century. It is now home to a museum that proudly tells a very detailed history of Sandwich. It opens 10 am to 4 pm Monday to Saturday (it closes between 12.30 and 2 pm on Tuesday, Wednesday and Friday), and 2 to 4 pm on Sunday, April to September. The rest of the year it opens 2 to 4 pm daily (10.30 am to 4 pm Thursday and Saturday). Admission costs £1/50p.

The **Church of St Clement** has one of the finest surviving Norman towers in England. **St Peter's Church** on King St is the earliest of Sandwich's churches, though its tower was rebuilt in 1661.

The **Prince's Golf Club** (☎ 611118) is recommended for visiting golfers, but green fees are steep at around £40 for 18 holes.

Guided tours of the town can be arranged by contacting Frank Andrews on ☎ 611925 (evenings only).

Places to Stay & Eat

The range of places to stay is quite limited and few are cheap.

Sandwich Leisure Park (☎ 612681, *Woodnesborough Rd*), open from March to October, charges £6.80 for one person and a tent.

New Inn (☎ 612335, fax 619133, 2 Harnet St), near the Guildhall, has tiny rooms with private shower for £25 per person. *Fleur de Lis* (☎ 611131, fax 611199, 6–8 Delf St) is a half-timbered place and has nice rooms for £35/50.

The Bell Hotel (☎ 613388, fax 615308, The Quay), overlooking the river, is the town's posh hotel with rooms that are only just OK for the price of £75/100.

Strands (☎ 621611, 19 Strand St) is a coffee shop serving light, hot meals from £4.95 and sandwiches from £2.75. For a splurge, visit the *Fisherman's Wharf* (☎ 613636, The Quay) near the Barbican where a hearty turkey and ham pie costs £6.95 or roast salmon costs £8.95. In summer you can sit outside and enjoy the river view.

Getting There & Away

Sandwich is about 15 miles (24km) east of Canterbury and 10 miles (16km) north of Dover. Stagecoach East Kent's (☎ 01424-440770) 111 and 211 hourly services connect Sandwich with Dover (£3.30, 45 minutes), Deal and Canterbury. Bus No 93 runs between Sandwich and Dover and No 94 runs from Ramsgate to Dover via Sandwich.

Trains run every 30 minutes from Dover Priory (£4, 25 minutes) or from London Charing Cross to Deal from where a bus takes you to Sandwich (£18.20, 2 hours). The train station is off New St, south of the river.

AROUND SANDWICH

One and a half miles north of Sandwich, off the A256, are the remains of **Richborough Castle** (☎ 01304-612013), a Roman hilltop fort whose imposing and vast walls overlook the surrounding countryside. The fort was built around AD 275, but the site was an important town well before this. In AD 43 the Roman army landed at Richborough and established a military supply base. Some of the relics found here are on display in the Guildhall museum in Sandwich.

The castle opens 10 am to 6 pm daily, April to September; to 5 pm during October; to 4 pm Wednesday to Sunday in No-

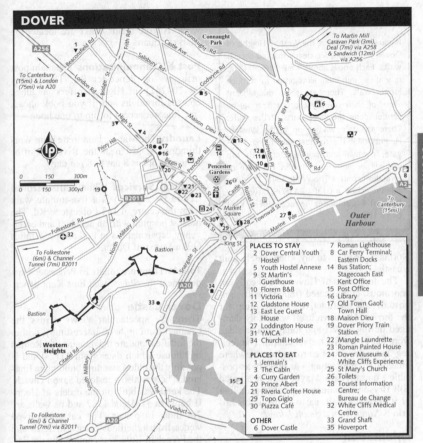

DOVER

PLACES TO STAY
2 Dover Central Youth Hostel
5 Youth Hostel Annexe
9 St Martin's Guesthouse
10 Florern B&B
11 Victoria
12 Gladstone House
13 East Lee Guest House
27 Loddington House
31 YMCA
34 Churchill Hotel

PLACES TO EAT
1 Jermain's
3 The Cabin
4 Curry Garden
20 Prince Albert
21 Riveria Coffee House
29 Topo Gigio
30 Piazza Café

OTHER
6 Dover Castle

7 Roman Lighthouse
8 Car Ferry Terminal; Eastern Docks
14 Bus Station; Stagecoach East Kent Office
15 Post Office
16 Library
17 Old Town Gaol; Town Hall
18 Maison Dieu
19 Dover Priory Train Station
22 Mangle Laundrette
23 Roman Painted House
24 Dover Museum & White Cliffs Experience
25 St Mary's Church
26 Toilets
28 Tourist Information Centre; Bureau de Change
32 White Cliffs Medical Centre
33 Grand Shaft
35 Hoverport

vember and March; and weekends only from December to February. The area is very exposed and it gets pretty windy up here. The Stour River Bus, which runs from the northern side of the tollgate to Richborough, may be in operation (☎ 01304-820171 for details).

The nearby town of **Deal** was the place where Julius Caesar and his armies landed in 55 BC. It's a peaceful town with a great stretch of beach and an unusual circular castle – another link in Henry VIII's chain of defence on the south coast. Also here is Walmer Castle, the official residence of the

Warden of the Cinque Ports (see the earlier boxed text 'Cinque Ports').

DOVER
☎ 01304 • pop 37,826

Dover may be England's 'Gateway to Europe' but the place has just two things going for it: a spectacular medieval castle and the famous white cliffs.

There is evidence of an Iron Age settlement, and the Romans identified the strategic importance of the site. Dubrae, as Dover was known, was a fortified port in the chain of defences along the Saxon shore. The

Dover's Heights

If you want to explore the Western Heights of Dover, there are three clearly marked circular walks. Each one is about 4 miles (6km) long, or you can join them all together for a much longer walk. There are some magnificent views of chalk country and coastline but be careful along the steep parts of the route. There are stairs leading up to the Western Heights near the roundabout linking Snargate, Townwall and York Sts. Once at the top you will see signs for the walks. For more information contact The White Cliffs Countryside Project on ☎ 01304-241806, or write to them at 6 Cambridge Terrace, Dover, Kent CT16 1JT.

Normans, needless to say, immediately built a castle.

The foreshore of Dover is basically an enormous, complicated (though well signposted) and unattractive vehicle ramp for the ferries. The town itself was badly damaged during WWII and today, under siege from heavy traffic, has no charm. The feeling that everyone is en route to somewhere much more interesting – as quickly as possible – doesn't help. Maybe they've all read Bill Bryson's account of a rather gruelling visit to Dover in the early 1970s, in his hilarious *Notes from a Small Island*.

Orientation

Dover is dominated by Henry VIII's enormous castle which sits on a hill top to the east of the centre. The town itself runs back from the sea along a valley formed by the unimpressive River Dour (in Roman times, this formed a navigable estuary).

Information

Tourist Office The TIC (☎ 205108, fax 225498, [e] tic@doveruk.com) is on Townwall St near the seafront and opens 9 am to 6 pm daily. It has an accommodation and ferry-booking service.

Money There is a bureau de change next door to the TIC, which opens seven days a week. All the major banks are located on Market Square.

Post & Communications The main post office is on Pencester Rd. The library (☎ 204241) on High St offers language courses for adults and, if you book ahead, free Internet access for up to one hour.

Laundry The Mangle laundrette is on Worthington St, just near the Riveria Coffee House. It opens 8 am to 8 pm daily.

Medical Services White Cliffs Medical Centre (☎ 201705) is a five-minute walk from the centre at 143 Folkestone Rd. The nearest hospital with an accident and emergency department is in Folkestone, 8 miles (13km) west of Dover.

Toilets There are toilets in Pencester Gardens near the Stagecoach East Kent office.

Dover Castle

There are spectacular views across the Channel from up here. Interestingly, within the fortifications are the remains of a Roman lighthouse which dates from AD 50 and is possibly the oldest standing building in England. There is also a restored **Saxon church**. The **keep** was built on the orders of Henry II between 1181 and 1187 and its walls are 7m thick in places. The castle survived sieges from rebellious barons in 1216 and the French in 1295, was captured by the Parliamentarians in 1642, was the headquarters for operations against German submarines in WWI, and served as the command post for the evacuation of Dunkirk in 1940.

The excellent tour of **Hellfire Corner** covers the castle's role during WWII, and takes you along tunnels beneath the castle.

Dover Castle (☎ 211067; EH) opens 10 am to 6 pm daily; to 4 pm November to March. Admission costs £6.90/3.50. The price includes a 55-minute guided tour of Hellfire Corner; there is a worthwhile audio tour of the keep. You can take Stagecoach bus No 90 from Dover Priory train station to the castle.

Dover Museum & White Cliffs Experience

The Dover Museum (☎ 201066) is one of the best around and definitely shouldn't be missed. The displays are well designed with information being presented in an absorbing way through scale models, artefacts, videos and interactive displays. The pride of the museum is a perfectly preserved Bronze Age boat, discovered off the Dover coast in 1992. At 3600 years old it's the oldest known sea-going vessel in the world and measures 9.5m by 2.4m.

The White Cliffs Experience (☎ 210101) is perfect if you have kids in tow. Robots, dioramas, actors and light-and-sound shows present two periods in Dover's history – Roman times and 1940s Dover.

From April to October the Experience and the museum open 10 am to 5.30 pm daily (last admission 5 pm). Admission costs £5.75/3.95 for both or £1.80/90p for the museum only. You'll find them between Market Square and York St.

Other Things to See

Dover's oldest guesthouse is the **Roman Painted House** (☎ 203279), New St, but there's actually little to see beyond the foundations and the 1800-year-old wall paintings are fragmentary. It opens 10 am to 5 pm daily, April to September. Admission costs £2/80p.

Guided tours of the cells and Victorian court room at the **Old Town Gaol** (☎ 242766) take 45 minutes and leave on the half hour. Located in the town hall on High St, it opens 10 am to 4.30 pm, Tuesday to Saturday, and 2 to 4.30 pm on Sunday. Admission costs £3.50/2.10.

Next door is the **Maison Dieu**, which was built as a hospice for pilgrims and wounded soldiers in 1203. It then became a home for monks and when they were evicted in 1544 it was given to the Royal Navy. It now belongs to the city of Dover and contains a collection of arms, armour, portraits of England's kings and dignitaries, and magnificent stained-glass windows showing events in England's history. It opens most days of the year from 10 am. Admission is free.

Beginning at Snargate St, the **Grand Shaft** is a 43m triple staircase that was cut into the white cliffs as a short cut to town for troops stationed on the Western Heights during the Napoleonic Wars. According to tradition, one staircase was for officers and their ladies, the second for the NCOs and their wives, and the third for soldiers and their women!

Places to Stay

Accommodation in Dover is nothing to write home about. It's worth looking around a bit if you can. Finding any accommodation at all can be tough in high summer, so booking is advisable. For information on what's available call ☎ 401571.

Camping *Martin Mill Caravan Park* (☎ 852658) is at Hawthorn Farm, 3 miles (5km) north-east of Dover, off the A258. It opens March to November and charges £6/7 for one/two people and £7/9 with a car.

Hostels *Dover Central Youth Hostel* (☎ 201314) is at 306 London Rd, but it also has an annexe at 14 Godwyne Rd. Beds costs £10.50.

The *YMCA* (☎ 225500, 4 Leyburne Rd) was closed for refurbishment at the time of writing but may well be open by now for overnight accommodation.

B&Bs & Hotels Most B&Bs are along Folkestone Rd (the A20), but there are others on Castle St and Maison Dieu Rd.

East Lee Guest House (☎ 210176, 108 Maison Dieu Rd) is friendly and luxurious and rooms (no TV) cost from £24/48.

St Martin's Guesthouse (☎ 205938, fax 208229, 17 Castle Hill Rd) is highly recommended. The landlady is helpful and friendly and rooms are spotless and cosy. It costs £45 for two (single rates vary). In early spring and winter this rate can drop as low as £30.

Florern B&B (☎ 206408, 8 Castle Hill Rd) is rather shabby, but rooms with showers are relatively cheap at £20 per person.

Victoria (☎ 205140, 3 Laureston Place) is an attractive Victorian home with lots of tiring stairs. Rooms cost £22 per person with shared bathroom; £18 in the quieter months. *Gladstone House* (☎ 208457, 3 Laureston Place) is very similar and charges £25/35 for rooms with shared bathroom.

Most of the B&Bs along Marine Parade are grotty and run down, and they aren't even super-cheap to make up for it. *Loddington House* (☎/fax 201947, 14 East Cliff, Marine Parade), however, is more upmarket; singles cost £45, doubles £52 to £56.

Churchill Hotel (☎ 203633) is one of the best-value places on the waterfront. It's popular with business travellers and charges range from £37.50 to £50.50 per person.

Places to Eat

Despite its size, Dover is short on decent places to eat. There are plenty of pubs around Market Square offering decent meals though. *Prince Albert* on Biggin St is one of them.

Curry Garden (☎ 206357, 24 High St) is a cheap Indian restaurant with plush decor where you can get a prawn korma for £4.20, or dhal for £1.95.

Riveria Coffee House (☎ 201766, 9–11 Worthington St) is very good value with cream teas for £1.80, or sandwiches and light meals from £1.20.

Jermain's (☎ 205956, 18 Beaconsfield Rd) is a clean, efficient eatery near the hostel. It has a range of good value traditional lunches such as roast beef for £5 and pudding for £1.

There are several places in and around Market Square. *Topo Gigio* (☎ 201048, 1–2 King St) is an Italian place with pasta from £3.45 and pizzas from £5.20. *Piazza Café* (☎ 202195, 12 King St) nearby has a range of interesting snacks (for example, ciabatta sandwiches from £1.85) as well as more substantial fare.

The Cabin (☎ 206118, 91 High St) is one of the few offerings for gourmets. This small but cosy restaurant specialises in traditional English and game dishes but vegetarians are catered for too. Haunch of wild boar with red wine and fresh herbs costs £11.70 while haggis in whisky sauce as a starter is £2.95.

Getting There & Away

Dover is 75 miles (121km) south-east of London and 15 miles (24km) south-east of Canterbury.

Ferry departures are from the Eastern Docks (accessible by bus) south-east of the castle, but the Hoverport is below the Western Heights. Dover Priory train station is a short walk to the west of the town centre. The bus station is closer to the centre of things on Pencester Rd.

Bus Stagecoach East Kent has an office on Pencester Rd (☎ 240024). It has a Canterbury to Dover shuttle service (£2.50, 30 minutes). National Express (☎ 0870 580 8080) coaches leave hourly from London Victoria (£9/11 one way/day return, 2 hours 20 minutes). A few times a day this service goes via Deal.

There's an hourly bus to Brighton but you'll need to change at Eastbourne. Later in the evening it's a direct service. An Explorer ticket (£6) is better value on this route. Stagecoach South Coast (☎ 01424-433711) bus No 711 will take you to Hastings (£4.50, 2 hours 40 minutes). Bus Nos 111 and 211 go to Canterbury via Sandwich and Deal.

Train There are over 40 trains a day from London Victoria and Charing Cross stations to Dover Priory via Ashford and Sevenoaks (£18.20, 1 hour 30 minutes). Trains leave hourly from Canterbury East (£4.40, 28 minutes). There are also regular services north to Deal, Margate and Broadstairs.

Boat Call ☎ 401575 for information on day trips to France and special offers. Ferries depart from the Eastern Docks. P&O Ferries (☎ 0870 242 4999) leaves for Calais every three-quarters of an hour for £24/48 one way/return. With Seafrance (☎ 0870 571 1711) the trip costs £15/30 and ferries leave every 1½ hours. The hourly Hoverspeed (☎ 0870 524 0241) to Calais or Ostende costs £19.50/39 and, if you want to take your car, the Channel Tunnel costs £29/59.

Getting Around

Bus Fortunately, the ferry companies run complimentary buses between the docks and the train station as they're a long walk apart. There are infrequent buses to the Eastern Docks from the Pencester Rd bus station. A trip from one side of town to the other will cost about £1.50.

Taxi Central (☎ 240441) and Heritage (☎ 204420) have 24-hour services. You could also try Star Taxis on ☎ 228822. A one-way trip to Deal costs about £8, to Sandwich about £12.

ROMNEY MARSH & AROUND

Romney Marsh is a flat, fertile plain that was once under water. Parts of it are still below sea level. It is, somehow, a landscape in microcosm, which makes it an appropriate location for the world's smallest public railway. The **Romney, Hythe & Dymchurch Railway** (☎ 01797-362353) runs 13½ miles (22km) from Hythe to Dungeness lighthouse daily from Easter to September; weekends only in March and October.

Hythe, once a Cinque Port, is a low-key seaside resort with an attractive old town. In the crypt of St Leonard's Church is a ghoulish attraction – 8000 thigh bones and 2000 skulls, some arranged on shelves like pots of jam in a supermarket. Stagecoach East Kent (☎ 01424 440770) bus No 558/559 goes to Hythe from Canterbury five times a day, Monday to Saturday (£4.20) and Stagecoach South Coast bus No 711 goes from Dover to Eastbourne via Hythe every hour (every two hours on Sunday).

Dungeness is a low shingle spit dominated by a nuclear power station and a lighthouse. There's a strange magic here that transcends the apocalyptic bleakness. The area supports the largest seabird colony in the South-East. There's an RSPB Nature Reserve visitor centre (☎ 01797-320588), which opens 9 am to sunset daily.

The Romney Marsh Countryside Project (☎ 01304-241806) arranges guided walks and bicycle rides around the area. Pick up a pamphlet from the RSPB Nature Reserve visitor centre in Dungeness.

SISSINGHURST CASTLE GARDENS

Sissinghurst (☎ 01580-715330), a National Trust property (NT; see Useful Organisations in the Facts for the Visitor chapter) off the A262 between Biddenden and Cranbrook, is an enchanted place. Vita Sackville-West and her husband Harold Nicholson (of the infamous Bloomsbury Group) discovered a ruined Elizabethan mansion in 1930 and created a superb series of gardens in and around the buildings. The castle and gardens are surrounded by a moat and rolling wooded countryside. All the elements come together to create an exquisite, dreamlike English beauty. Anyone who doubts the rich seductiveness of the English landscape has not been to Sissinghurst in spring or summer.

Sissinghurst gets very crowded at the weekend, and it's almost impossible from May to August, so avoid weekends in summer if you can. The gardens open 1 to 6.30 pm Tuesday to Friday, 10 am to 5.30 pm Saturday and Sunday, 1 April to 15 October. Admission costs £6.50/3.

It's possible to stay in the substantial estate manager's house, 100m from Sissinghurst Castle. Every room (including the bathroom) has stunning views over the famous gardens and surrounding countryside. *Sissinghurst Castle Farm* (☎ 01580-712885) is deservedly popular and costs from £26 per person; £29 per person for en suite. Booking is advised.

Getting There & Away

The nearest train station is Staplehurst on the line between Tonbridge and Ashford. Arriva Kent & Sussex's (☎ 01634-281100) bus No 4/5 runs from Maidstone to Hastings via Sissinghurst every hour (reduced services on Sunday).

SEVENOAKS

☎ 01732 • pop 19,000

Although of only mild interest in itself, this pleasant town on the north-western edge of Kent is in a perfect position for those intending to visit nearby sights (namely Chartwell, Hever Castle, Penshurst Place,

Knole House and Ightham Mote) by car. Unfortunately for those using public transport, getting around is a little complicated. Although Knole House is just a short stroll from the town, the only place that is serviced directly by bus from Sevenoaks is Chartwell. This situation could change so check with the TIC in the library building on Buckhurst Lane (☎ 450305, fax 461959, e tic@sevenoakstown.co.uk).

Sevenoaks does have a literary claim to fame or two. Apparently HG Wells wrote *The Time Machine* while living at 23 Eardly Rd and two of Charles Dickens' daughters are buried in St Nicholas churchyard.

Places to Stay & Eat

Sevenoaks is not short of accommodation. Two-and-a-half miles (4km) south of town on the A225, **Morley's Farm Camping Ground** (☎ 463309) is open Easter to October. From the bus station head along Tonbridge Rd until you get to the large roundabout. Take the turn for 'Sevenoaks Weald'. The camp site is 100m along here on your left. Bus No 402 from Sevenoaks passes by the front gate hourly. Charges are £4 per person with tent.

Beechcombe (☎ 741643, e anthonytait@ hotmail.com, Vine Lodge Court, Holly Bush Lane) is in a pleasant family home and rooms cost £20/38 with continental breakfast. Rates drop by a few pounds for stays of two nights or more.

Hornshaw House (☎ 465262, 47 Mount Harry Rd), run by Mr & Mrs Bates, is a 10-minute walk from the station. Double rooms with garden views cost £45 with breakfast. Singles are not usually accommodated but it's worth asking anyway.

The Royal Oak Hotel (☎ 451109, fax 740187, Upper High St) restaurant is excellent and reasonably priced, serving such delicacies as baked leek and stilton tart for £6.35, or breast of pheasant with chestnut stuffing for £13.35.

Asia Cuisine Tandoori Restaurant (☎ 453153, 107 London Rd) is a popular place where starters cost from £2 to £4 and main courses from £4 to £7.

Bar 115 (115 London Rd, ☎ 740115) is understated and rather funky. Burgers here cost £4.95 and pastas are around £7.95. There are £5 specials on Sunday nights.

Cheaper eats of the coffee and sandwich shop variety can be found along High St and light meals here will set you back £2 to £4.

Getting There & Away

There are no direct bus services from London to Sevenoaks so you're better off catching the train. From nearby Tonbridge however, Arriva Kent & West Sussex bus Nos 402 and 704 run to Sevenoaks and take 30 minutes.

Sevenoaks station is on London Rd. Trains leave three times an hour from London Charing Cross (£6.20, 35 minutes) and continue to Tunbridge Wells (£4, 20 minutes) and Hastings (£11.40, 1 hour 10 minutes).

KNOLE HOUSE

Graceful Knole House (☎ 01732-450608; NT), just a 1½-mile walk south of Sevenoaks, is a beautiful example of Elizabethan/Jacobean simplicity. Substantially dating from 1456, it is not as old as some of the great houses that incorporate medieval fortresses, but it is more coherent in style.

Little has been changed since early in the 17th century, including the furniture. It is the Sackville family, owners of the house since 1566, who can take credit for resisting the temptation to rebuild and redecorate according to 'modern' fashions. After all, there are some things that just cannot be improved.

Vita Sackville-West, co-creator of Sissinghurst, was born in the house in 1892, and her friend Virginia Woolf based the novel *Orlando* on the history of the house and family.

The house is vast, with seven courtyards, 52 staircases and 365 rooms, so the excellent guidebook is recommended. There is public access 11 am to 5 pm on Wednesday, Friday, Saturday and Sunday; and 2 to 5 pm on Thursday. Admission costs £5/2 and last entry is at 4 pm. Parking is £2.50 (free for NT members). The grounds are open year-round.

CHARTWELL

Chartwell (☎ 01732-866368), just north of Edenbridge, was Winston Churchill's family home from 1924 until his death in 1965.

Filled with memorabilia and the statesman's paintings, the house opens 11 am to 5 pm Wednesday to Sunday, April to October. It also opens on Tuesday in July and August. Admission costs £5.50/2.75.

The Chartwell Explorer bus (☎ 0870 608 2608) runs six times a day between Sevenoaks train/bus stations and Chartwell at the weekend and bank holidays from mid-May to mid-September, and Wednesday to Friday during July and August. The trip takes 30 minutes and the £3/1.50 ticket includes a pot of tea at Chartwell. A combined ticket, including return rail travel from London to Sevenoaks, bus transfer to Chartwell and entry costs £13/6.50; enquire at Charing Cross train station.

HEVER CASTLE

Idyllic Hever Castle (☎ 01732-861702) near Edenbridge, a few miles west of Tonbridge, was the childhood home of Anne Boleyn, mistress to Henry VIII and then his doomed queen. Walking through the main gate into the courtyard of Hever is like stepping onto the set of a period film. It's a truly fairytale place and one of the highlights of the area. The moated castle was built in the 13th and 15th centuries and was restored by the American diplomat William Waldorf Astor, who acquired the house in 1903. The exterior is unchanged from Tudor times, but the interior now has superb Edwardian carved wooden panelling. Among the Astor family memorabilia on display is part of a relief from the Arch of Claudius (built in AD 51), which was brought from Rome by Astor.

The castle is surrounded by a garden, again the creation of the Astors, that incorporates a number of different styles, including a formal Italian garden with classical sculptures.

One of the more interesting items on display is Boleyn's last impassioned letter to the King before she lost her head. The lower level of the gatehouse is home to a horrifying collection of torture and execution instruments. Our particular favourite – the flesh gouger!

Hever opens 11 am to 5 pm daily, March to November. Admission to the castle and gardens costs £7.80/4.20; gardens only is £6.10/4. From London Victoria trains go to Hever (change at Oxted), a mile's walk from the castle (£7.10, 52 minutes). Alternatively you could take the train to Edenbridge, from where it's a 4-mile (6km) taxi ride. Metrobus East Surrey (☎ 01342-893080) No 234 goes from Edenbridge to Hever Brook Corner which is just half a mile from the castle. Their service runs only four times a day (twice on Saturday and no service on Sunday) and takes 35 minutes (95p).

A nice idea would be to cycle from Edenbridge to Hever. From Edenbridge High St the route to Hever is signposted. You could then continue another 6 miles (10km) to Penshurst Place & Gardens. Unfortunately there are no bicycle hire facilities in Edenbridge itself so you would have to bring a bike from elsewhere.

PENSHURST PLACE & GARDENS

Penshurst Place (☎ 870307) is the family home of Viscount De l'Isle and is surrounded by sculptured Tudor-style gardens. The main feature of the house is the splendid Barons' Hall where many of England's monarchs, including Henry VIII, have entertained over the centuries. Built in

---

Penshurst Place Walks

There are a number of circular walks you can do around the vast grounds of Penshurst Place in Kent. Taking in parkland, gardens and riverside, the walks vary from 2 to 4 miles (3km to 6km) in length and can be completed in one to two hours. You can pick up a leaflet detailing these walks from the ticket office at Penshurst, and there are signs on the estate to point you in the right direction. For more information contact Penshurst Place on ☎ 01892-870307.

1341, this medieval hall with its 60ft-high chestnut wood roof has been very well preserved.

With the exception of the State Dining Room, the other rooms in the castle were added in the early 15th century, with further modifications continuing into the 19th century. Furniture and decor from all over Europe date from the 16th to the 18th centuries. An information page at the entrance to each room will tell you about the main features.

Penshurst opens noon to 5 pm daily (gardens from 10.30 am to 6 pm), April to October and at the weekend in March. Admission costs £6/4. It's in the village of the same name, on the B2176. On Sunday and bank holiday Mondays only there is a bus service to Penshurst from Edenbridge (10 miles away) which can be reached by train from London Victoria. Metrobus East Surrey No 231, 232 and 233 from Edenbridge to Tunbridge Wells goes via Penshurst every hour (£2.75, 25 minutes). If you are feeling energetic you could cycle the 10 miles (16km) to Penshurst. A route map is available from Edenbridge TIC (☎ 01732-868110) on Station Rd, although there are no bicycle hire facilities in Edenbridge.

IGHTHAM MOTE

For six and a half centuries Ightham (**eye**-tam) has survived wars, storms, changes in ownership, and generation after generation of occupants. This is all the more remarkable since it is not an aristocratic mansion full of priceless treasures, just a small medieval manor house surrounded by a moat.

Although parts date from around 1340, the building today is an architectural jigsaw puzzle, and you need a detailed guide to unravel which bit belongs to what century. Some of the additions and alterations seem haphazard, but the materials (wood, stone, clay), the building's scale and the frame of water together combine to create a harmonious whole.

Ightham Mote (☎ 01732-811145; NT) is 6 miles (10km) east of Sevenoaks off the A25, 2½ miles south of Ightham off the A227. There is a bus six times a day from Sevenoaks to Ivy Hatch, which is 1 mile from Ightham Mote. It opens 11 am to 5.30 pm daily except Tuesday and Saturday, April to October. Admission costs £5/2.

LEEDS CASTLE

Just to the east of Maidstone, Leeds Castle (☎ 01622-765400) is one of the most famous – and also one of the most visited – castles in the world.

The castle stands on two small islands in a lake surrounded by a huge estate that contains woodlands, an aviary and a really weird grotto that can be entered once you've successfully negotiated your way through a hedge maze.

The building dates from the 9th century. Henry VIII transformed it from a fortress into a palace, and it was privately owned until 1974 when Lady Baillie, the castle's last owner, died. Paintings, furniture and other decor in the castle date from the last eight centuries.

A private trust now manages the property and, as part of a requirement that the castle serve a function other than that of a tourist attraction, some of the rooms are used for conferences and other events. This creates a problem for the visitor in that some of the rooms are closed to the public quite regularly. If you want to be sure you can see all the rooms and get your money's worth, ring ahead. Another problem is the sheer number of people to be negotiated – at the weekend it's the families, during the week it's the school groups.

The castle opens 10 am to 5 pm daily March to October, and 10 am to 3 pm November to February. Admission is expensive at £9.50/6. National Express (☎ 0870 580 8080) has one direct coach a day from Victoria Coach Station in London, leaving at 9 am and returning at 3.50 pm (1¼ hours). It must be prebooked and the combined cost of admission and travel is £12.50/9.50. Greenline Buses (☎ 0870 608 7266) has the same deal costing £13/7 (leave London Victoria at 9.35 am, return at 4 pm).

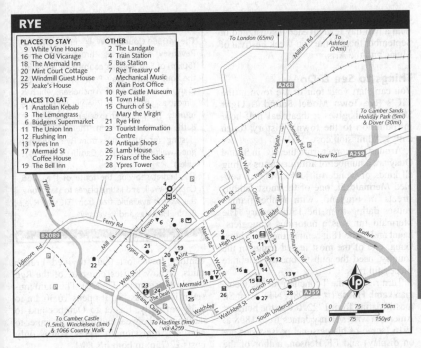

RYE

PLACES TO STAY
9 White Vine House
16 The Old Vicarage
18 The Mermaid Inn
20 Mint Court Cottage
22 Windmill Guest House
25 Jeake's House

PLACES TO EAT
1 Anatolian Kebab
3 The Lemongrass
6 Budgens Supermarket
11 The Union Inn
12 Flushing Inn
13 Ypres Inn
17 Mermaid St
   Coffee House
19 The Bell Inn

OTHER
2 The Landgate
4 Train Station
5 Bus Station
7 Rye Treasury of
   Mechanical Music
8 Main Post Office
10 Rye Castle Museum
14 Town Hall
15 Church of St
   Mary the Virgin
21 Rye Hire
23 Tourist Information
   Centre
24 Antique Shops
26 Lamb House
27 Friars of the Sack
28 Ypres Tower

To London (65mi)
To Ashford (24mi)
Military Rd
A268
To Camber Sands Holiday Park (5mi) & Dover (30mi)
Fishmarket Rd
New Rd
A259
Landgate
Rope Walk
Tower St
Conduit Hill
Hilder Cliff
Cinque Ports St
Market Rd
High St
East St
Lion St
Fishmarket Rd
Rother
The Mint
West St
The Market
Church Sq
Church St
South Underclift
A259
Mermaid St
Watchbell
Watchbell St
Strand Quay
The Deals
Wish Ward
Wish St
Cyprus Pl
Mill La
Ferry Rd
Crown Fields
Tillingham
B2089
Udimore Rd

To Camber Castle (1.5mi), Winchelsea (3mi) & 1066 Country Walk
To Hastings (9mi) via A259

0   75   150m
0   75   150yd

East Sussex

East Sussex has some superb countryside along the spine of the South Downs, and some great coastal areas. Although touristy, Rye and Battle have a certain magic. Lewes is as historically interesting but seems to be bypassed by the crowds. Eastbourne and Brighton are two of England's most entertaining seaside towns; with its extraordinary mix of tackiness and pure groove, Brighton is in a category of its own.

RYE
☎ 01797 • pop 5400

The medieval town of Rye, once a Cinque Port, is the epitome of Ye Cute Olde Englishe Village. It's a desperately picturesque town with half-timbered buildings, winding cobbled streets, hundreds of flower pots and a number of literary associations. The buildings, a mixture of Tudor and Georgian styles, snuggle cosily into each other.

The town is claimed by many to be the most beautiful in Britain and, as a result, it's full of tourists. If you do visit – and you should – avoid summer weekends.

Orientation & Information

Rye is small, so it can easily be covered on foot. The River Tillingham passes through the south-western edge of the town. The Rye Heritage Centre and TIC (☎ 226696, fax 223460, ⓔ ryetic@rother.gov.uk) is on Strand Quay and opens 9 am to 5.30 pm daily, June to August; and 10 am to 4 pm the rest of the year. *Rye Town Walk* gives a detailed history of the town's buildings and costs £1. There's also an audio tour costing £2/1. For guided walks around town phone ☎ 01424-882343.

The main post office is on Cinque Ports St, but most of the action is along High St where you'll find ATMs and a few bookshops.

The town celebrates its medieval heritage with a two-day festival each August, and in September there is the two-week Festival of Music and the Arts.

Things to See & Do

You can start your tour of the town at the TIC's **Rye Town Model Sound & Light Show**, which gives a theatrical half-hour introduction to the town's history (open daily). Admission costs £2/1.

Around the corner from the TIC in Strand Quay are a number of **antique shops** selling all kinds of wonderful junk. Walk up cobbled **Mermaid St**, one of the most famous streets in England, with timber-framed houses dating from the 15th century. The Mermaid Inn was a notorious smugglers' haunt and in the 18th century the Hawkhurst Gang, one of the most feared gangs in the country, used the pub to openly celebrate successful runs.

Turn right at the T-junction for the Georgian **Lamb House** (☎ 224982; NT), West St, mostly dating from 1722. It was the home of American writer Henry James from 1898 to 1916 (some of his personal possessions are on display) and EF Benson, author of the Mapp & Lucia stories, from 1919 to 1940. It opens 2 to 6 pm Tuesday and Saturday, April to October; admission costs £2.50/1.25.

Continue round the dogleg until you come to Church Square, which is surrounded by a variety of attractive houses, including the **Friars of the Sack** on the southern side at No 40. Now a private residence, it was once part of a 13th-century Augustinian friary. The **Church of St Mary the Virgin** is on the highest point in Rye and incorporates a mixture of ecclesiastical styles. The church actually dates from the 12th century but was rebuilt in the 15th. The turret clock is the oldest in England (1561) and still works with its original pendulum mechanism. The two gilded cherubs, known as the Quarter Boys, strike bells on the quarter hour only. There are great views from the church tower.

Turn right at the eastern corner of the square for **Ypres Tower** (pronounced 'wipers' locally), which is part of the 13th-

The 1066 Country Walk

The 1066 Country Walk links Rye to Pevensey and passes through 31 miles (50km) of East Sussex's countryside and joins the South Downs Way. From Rye it's 3 miles (5km) to the village of Winchelsea, which is almost as attractive as Rye yet without the tourists. The path is an excellent way to reach Battle (15 miles or 24km). There are links to Hastings (about 15 miles from Rye). Another good walk from Rye is to Camber Castle (1½ miles).

A leaflet showing the route of the 1066 Country Walk and listing places to stay along the way is available free from TICs at Rye, Battle, Hastings and Pevensey.

century town fort that survived French raids. It now houses one part of the **Rye Castle Museum** (☎ 226728). The main museum is at 3 East St. It opens 10.30 am to 5.30 pm daily, Easter to October and to 4.30 pm at the weekend from November to March. Admission to Ypres Tower only costs £2/75p; to both it's £3/1.

The **Rye Treasury of Mechanical Music** (☎ 223345) is at 20 Cinque Ports St. The enthusiastic owner gives interesting demonstrations of the workings of some of his phonographs, pianolas and other instruments 10 am to 5 pm daily. Admission costs £3/1.25.

At the north-eastern edge of the village is the **Landgate**. Built in 1329 to fortify the town, it's the only remaining gate of four that were originally built in the 14th century.

Places to Stay

As you would expect, there are dozens of places to stay in Rye. Most are not cheap, but then Rye is one place where it's really worth spending a bit more and staying somewhere special.

Camber Sands Holiday Park (☎ 225555) runs alongside a marvellously remote and rugged stretch of beach, 5½ miles (9km) south of Rye. It opens from March to October and rates vary from week to week so it's best to call for latest charges.

The Mermaid Inn (☎ 223065, fax 225069, Mermaid St) has been around since 1420. Visited by royalty and proud of its resident ghost, the hotel charges from £68 per person for bed and breakfast.

White Vine House (☎ 224748, fax 223599), on High St, is another luxurious place to stay. This Tudor-style house, built in 1560, has tasteful decor without the frills and fuss of most B&Bs. Service is impeccable and rooms range from £40/70, and up to £130 for the family room (sleeps five).

The Old Vicarage (☎ 222119, fax 227466, 66 Church Square) is next to St Mary's Church and is very quaint with a lovely garden. Rooms costs £64 for a double or £22 per person for a three- or four-bed room.

Jeake's House (☎ 222828, fax 222623, e jeakeshouse@btinternet.com), on the corner of Mermaid St and Wish Ward, is an atmospheric old place with lots of frills and drapery. Rooms costs £26.50/51 with shared bathroom or £53/66 with en suite. At the weekend there's a minimum two-night stay.

Windmill Guest House (☎ 224027, Mill Lane), off Ferry Rd, is one of the cheaper options. The rooms are in the extension by the windmill. A double with bathroom is around £22 per person. *Mint Court Cottage* (☎ 227780, The Mint), behind the Bell Inn, has one converted attic room plus a private sitting room downstairs for £25 per person, or £23 from November to March.

Places to Eat

There's a surprisingly diverse range of eateries for such a small English town. For self-caterers there's a *Budgens* supermarket near the train station.

Mermaid St Coffee House (☎ 224858), on the corner of Mermaid and West Sts, has a veritable smorgasbord of coffee and snacks. Cake and coffee costs £2.90.

Tudor Room Bar & Bistro (☎ 223065, Mermaid St), at the Mermaid Inn (see Places to Stay), is a tiny, low-ceilinged, half-timbered pub with an outdoor terrace. Baguettes are around £5, or you can have

something more substantial, such as baked local fish pie with smoked cheese, for £7.50. *The Union Inn* (☎ 222334, East St) also has some interesting dishes – anyone for squirrel pie at £9.95?

The Bell Inn (☎ 222232) in The Mint and the *Ypres Inn* (☎ 227460, Gungarden), behind the Ypres Tower, have nice outdoor areas; light meals begin at around £3.50.

Anatolian Kebab (☎ 226868, Landgate), besides offering what you'd expect, is also a takeaway pizza place. Huge kebabs cost £2.90 and pizzas are around £5.

The Lemongrass (☎ 222327, 1 Tower St) is the only Thai restaurant in town and curries cost £6.50.

Flushing Inn (☎ 223292, 4 Market St), at the dearer end of the scale, offers a '1066 Maritime Menu' and local wines. Main courses range from £8.80 to £13.50.

Getting There & Away

Stagecoach Coastline (☎ 01903-237661) bus No 711 runs hourly from Dover to Brighton via Hythe, Romney marshlands, Rye, Hastings and Eastbourne. Bus No 710 runs from Brighton to Rye via Eastbourne and Hastings and on to Camber. Local Rider No 344/345 links Rye with Hastings, and Rambler Coaches bus No 44 runs every two hours (not at the weekend) from Hastings to Rye and takes 50 minutes.

Rye can be reached from London's Charing Cross, via Ashford (£7.60, 1¾ hours). Trains leave Ashford hourly from Monday to Saturday and there are five services on Sunday. The service continues to Hastings (£3.20, 21 minutes).

Getting Around

For a taxi try Rye Motors Taxis (☎ 223176) or Rother (☎ 224554). Alternatively, you could rent bikes from £9 per day from Rye Hire (☎ 223033), Cyprus Place. A cycling map of East Sussex is available from the TIC.

HASTINGS

☎ 01424 • pop 80,820

In spite of the fact that Hastings' seafront – with its tacky fun parks and guesthouses – is run down, the sorry looking pier has been closed, and the new town centre is grey and depressing, the town still attracts around 3½ million holiday-makers each year. In all fairness the old town of Hastings could be described as atmospheric (in a decaying sort of way) with its half-timbered buildings and antique shops, and the nightlife here is much better than in Eastbourne farther down the coast. Still, we are unconvinced that the town actually has any real appeal other than the remains of a castle erected by William I. As the town sits on the coast between Eastbourne and Dover and has good rail and bus connections, it makes a good base for exploring nearby Rye, Battle and Pevensey.

The TIC (☎ 781111, fax 781133, e hic_info@hastings.gov.uk), beside the town hall at Priory Meadow, opens 9.30 am to 5 pm daily (from 10 am on Sunday). There's another branch on the foreshore near the Stade.

Places to Stay & Eat
The cheapest B&Bs can be found along Cambridge Gardens.

The Apollo (☎ 444394, 25 Cambridge Gardens) is recommended and rooms are £15 per person, going up to £20 from June to August. *Senlac B&B (☎ 430080, e senlac@1066-country.com, 47 Cambridge Gardens)* also gets a big tick and charges £16 per person and £18 for en suite.

Jenny Lind Hotel (☎ 421392, 69 High St), in the Old Town, has double rooms with bath for £30/45, including breakfast.

Fresh seafood is the most appropriate choice, and there are plenty of places selling fish and chips, particularly in the Old Town. *Gannets (☎ 439678, 45 High St)* is open for breakfast, lunch and afternoon tea. A roast lunch costs £5.25, spaghetti Bolognese with salad is £5.50 and puddings cost from £1.75 to £2.50.

Getting There & Away
Stagecoach South Coast bus No 711 runs hourly (less frequently on Sunday) from Dover to Brighton via Hastings and Eastbourne (£4.50 from Dover). Bus No 710 also runs hourly from Brighton to Hastings via

Eastbourne, but does not continue to Dover. Most buses use the stop on Queens Rd.

There are regular trains to/from London Charing Cross (£17.60 return, 1½ hours) via Battle and to/from Ashford via Rye. Every 15 minutes trains head west around the Sussex coast from Hastings to Portsmouth (£20, 2½ hours) via Brighton (£8.60, 1 hour). The train station is about 350m west of the TIC, off Cornwallis Terrace.

BATTLE
☎ 01424 • pop 5732

1066 and all that...Battle, 6 miles (10km) north of Hastings, is built around the site where Duke William of Normandy defeated Harold II in the last successful invasion of Britain. The highlight of any visit is the 1½-mile walk around the battlefield.

Orientation & Information
The train station is a short walk from High St, and is well signposted. The TIC (☎ 773721, fax 773436) on High St opens 10 am to 6 pm daily, until 4 pm in winter. The post office and banks are also on High St.

Battlefield & Battle Abbey
The guided walk around the battlefield is a really pleasant way to spend a few hours. The audio tour gives blow-by-blow descriptions of the famous battle and it's easy to absorb yourself in the event, as you wander the field. See the boxed text 'The Battle'.

Construction of the abbey began in 1070. It was occupied by Benedictines until the dissolution of the monasteries in 1539. Only foundations of the church can now be seen and the altar's position is marked by a plaque. A few monastic buildings survive and the whole scene is very painterly.

Battle Abbey and Battlefield (☎ 773792; EH) open 10 am to 6 pm and to 4 pm daily, November to March. Admission costs £4/2 which includes a 1½ hour audio tour.

Places to Stay & Eat
There are not many cheap places to stay within easy walking distance, so you may want to use Hastings as a base.

Clematis Cottage (☎ 774261, 3 High St) is right opposite the abbey entrance and has singles/doubles for £35/45 or £40/50 with en suite.

Abbey View (☎ 775513, Caldbec Hill, Mount St) is a five-minute walk to High St, but it's one of the cheaper options and there are lovely views over the surrounding countryside. Rooms are £30 per person from May to October; £25 the rest of the year.

The King's Head (☎ 772317), on the corner of Mount and High Sts, claims to be Battle's oldest pub and is a small and intimate place for a quiet beer.

Pilgrim's Rest (☎ 772314, 1 High St) is a home-style restaurant opposite the abbey with hearty English meals for around £5.

Getting There & Away

From Battle you can reach Pevensey (£2.10, 45 minutes) and Bodiam (£1.30, 20 minutes) on Eastbourne Bus (☎ 01323-416416) No 19, which runs six times a day from Monday to Saturday. Local Rider (☎ 01273-482006) bus No 4/5 runs hourly to Hastings (£2.15, 30 minutes) with only four services on Sunday. National Express' (☎ 0870 580 8080) London to Hastings service (No 067) passes through Battle.

Battle is on the main train line between London's Charing Cross and Hastings. Trains run every 30 minutes during the week, hourly on Sunday. A cheap day return from London is £15.40 and it takes 1½ hours. From Hastings the fare is £2.30 and the trip takes 15 minutes.

PEVENSEY CASTLE

William the Conqueror's first stronghold, Pevensey Castle is 12 miles (19km) west of Hastings, just off the A259 to Eastbourne. The Norman castle sits within a Roman defensive wall and on the site of a Roman fort, which was built between AD 280 and 340. In 1066, William landed here and occupied the abandoned fort for 17 days before his victory at Hastings. At this time the site would have been much closer to the sea. The castle is mostly in ruins now, but enough is left standing to indicate what each part of the castle was used for. It opens

---

The Battle

Harold's army arrived first on the scene of the Battle of Hastings and occupied a strong defensive position. There were around 7000 infantry and archers, making one of the most formidable armies of the time.

Hearing of Harold's arrival, William marched north from Hastings and took up a position about 400m south of the English. His army also numbered around 7000 men, but included 2000 to 3000 cavalry.

After several unsuccessful uphill attacks against the English shield wall, William's knights feigned retreat, drawing many English after them. This was a disastrous move for the English, as the rift in the wall of soldiers left them vulnerable to attack. Among the English casualties was King Harold who was struck in or near the eye. While he tried to pull the arrow from his head he was struck down by Norman knights. At the news of his death the last of the English resistance collapsed.

---

10 am to 6 pm, Wednesday to Sunday, from April to October; 11 am to 4 pm from November to March. Admission costs £2.50/1.30.

The Mint House, just across the road from the castle, dates from 1342 and is absolutely bursting with one of the biggest and weirdest collections of antiques and bits and pieces you may ever see. The atmosphere is decidedly nutty and admission costs £1/50p.

Regular train services between London and Hastings via Eastbourne stop at Westham, which is half a mile from Pevensey. Eastbourne Bus No 18 also stops at Westham and bus Nos 7 and 19 stop at Pevensey.

BODIAM CASTLE

Moated Bodiam Castle (☎ 01580-830436; NT) could be the most picturesque castle in the country. It was built as a defensive home in the late 14th century by Sir Edward Dalyngrigge after the English lost control of the Channel to the French in 1372. Ironically, the style is that of a French Gothic fortress, with round towers at each corner. Unfortunately what you see is what you get – inside it's mainly ruins and not really worth the £3.60/1.80 entrance fee. It is possible to climb to the top of the battlements for some great views however. The small museum here is free and has some pottery and iron tools dating from the 15th to the 18th century.

The castle opens 10 am to 6 pm daily, late February to October, and to 4 pm at the weekend, November to February. Ryder bus No 326 from Hastings, and Eastbourne bus No 19 from Battle both stop at the gate three times a day; twice at the weekend. Stagecoach South Coast bus No 349 goes from Hastings to Bodiam five times a day, Monday to Saturday. The Kent and East Sussex steam railway (☎ 01580 765155) runs from Tenterden in Kent through 10½ miles (17km) of beautiful countryside to the village of Bodiam from where a bus takes you to the castle. It operates daily during July and August and at the weekend and school holidays the rest of the year.

EASTBOURNE
☎ 01323 • pop 81,395

Friendly and slightly eccentric Eastbourne makes a nice change from some of the tackier seaside resorts in Sussex. Never mind that it's gained a reputation as the foremost holiday spot for octogenarians, it still has plenty of youthful character with its student hangouts, bars and amusements for kids. The beaches are clean, gardens and parks are dotted throughout the town and there are plenty of places to stay, although you will need to book well ahead. Large groups of holiday-makers tend to fill up most of the hotels and B&Bs.

Orientation

The town centre is just north-west of the pier. The old town (though not much is left of it now except a few interesting old buildings and a couple of antique shops) is about a mile north-west of the new town. To the west the stunning chalk cliffs steer the way to Beachy Head, just a 3-mile (5km) walk.

Information

On Cornfield Rd, the TIC (☎ 411400, fax 649574, ℮ eastbournetic@btclick.com) has a number of free leaflets on the town. A 3D map of town costing £1 is available from an automatic dispenser outside.

There's a Thomas Cook office and a Barclays bank on Terminus Rd. The main post office is on Langney Rd, just round the corner from the Arndale Centre. Internet access is available from Wired Cafe (☎ 646436), 2d Pevensey Rd, for 7p per minute with a minimum charge of £1.

Rainbows Laundrette is at 47 Seaside Rd and there are public toilets on the foreshore next to the Wishtower Puppet Museum.

Things to See & Do

Eastbourne's **pier** is home to an amusement arcade, trinket shops, a bar, a disco and lots of birdshit. It's a nice place to watch the sun set over the water though. And you can hire fishing rods from the end of the pier for £2.

Eastbourne Heritage Centre (☎ 411189) on Carlisle Rd, west of the centre, explores the development of the town from 1800 to the present. It opens 2 to 5 pm daily, May to September and bank holiday weekends. Admission costs £1/50p.

Wishtower Puppet Museum (☎ 417776), on King Edward's Parade, could be a great place to take the kids. It has a collection of traditional puppets from all over the world, including Punch and Judy. It opens 10.30 am to 5 pm, daily, Easter to November; admission costs £1.80/1.25.

The Museum of Shops (☎ 737143), at 20 Cornfield Terrace, has an enormous collection of Victorian and early-20th-century memorabilia – antiques, books, toys, you name it – though admission is a little steep at £3/2. It opens 10 am to 5.30 pm daily, but may close a little earlier in winter.

Set inside beautiful **Manor Gardens** is the **Towner Art Gallery & Local History Museum** (☎ 411688), about a mile's walk from the centre. It has a great collection of 20th-century British art as well as diverse temporary exhibitions. It opens noon to 5 pm, Tuesday to Saturday, and 2 to 5 pm on Sunday and bank holidays (closes an

SOUTH-EASTERN ENGLAND

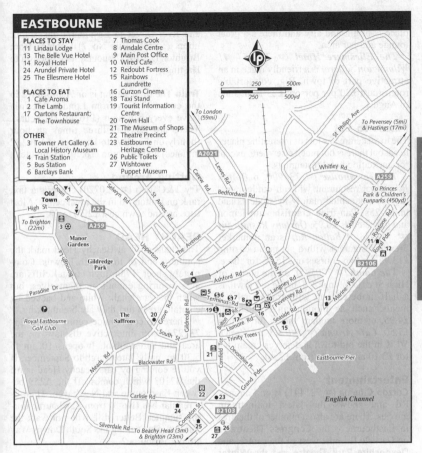

EASTBOURNE

PLACES TO STAY
11 Lindau Lodge
13 The Belle Vue Hotel
14 Royal Hotel
24 Arundel Private Hotel
25 The Ellesmere Hotel

PLACES TO EAT
1 Cafe Aroma
2 The Lamb
17 Oartons Restaurant;
   The Townhouse

OTHER
3 Towner Art Gallery &
  Local History Museum
4 Train Station
5 Bus Station
6 Barclays Bank
7 Thomas Cook
8 Arndale Centre
9 Main Post Office
10 Wired Cafe
12 Redoubt Fortress
15 Rainbows
   Laundrette
16 Curzon Cinema
18 Taxi Stand
19 Tourist Information
   Centre
20 Town Hall
21 The Museum of Shops
22 Theatre Precinct
23 Eastbourne
   Heritage Centre
26 Public Toilets
27 Wishtower
   Puppet Museum

hour earlier from November to March). Admission is free but special exhibitions attract an entry fee.

Places to Stay

Accommodation is difficult to find in Eastbourne unless you book ahead.

Lindau Lodge (☎ 640792, 71 Royal Parade) is a five-minute walk to the centre and is the best choice around here. B&B is £19 per person and a three-course evening meal costs £8.

Royal Hotel (☎ 724027, 8-9 Marine Parade) is on the waterfront, a stone's throw

from the pier. If money is your main concern then you won't do better than this. Somewhat grotty rooms with sea views cost just £15 per person with breakfast.

The Belle Vue Hotel (☎ 649544, 2–4 Grand Parade) is a friendly hotel in a nice old building. It too is very close to the action and rooms cost £25 per person (£19.95 November to March). At the weekend in July and August the rates may be higher.

There are a number of lovely B&Bs and hotels just west of the centre. *Arundel Private Hotel* (☎ 639481, fax 431683, 43–47 Carlisle Rd) is very reasonably priced at £25 per person for its huge rooms. The place is bright and airy and there's a great lounge and bar area.

The Ellesmere Hotel (☎ 731463, 11 Wilmington Square) is a friendly place in an attractive part of town. Big, comfortable rooms cost £20 per person; £23 from June to August.

Places to Eat
The town centre has lots of interesting places to eat but there is not much elsewhere, except for unexciting hotel restaurants.

The Townhouse (☎ 734900, 6 Bolton Rd), a bar/restaurant with an outdoor terrace, is frequented mainly by students and under-25s. Pan-fried crayfish with lemon and garlic costs £6.95. *Oartons Restaurant (☎ 731053, 4 Bolton Rd)* is an upmarket French restaurant with a set menu costing £13.95 for two courses or £15.95 for three.

The Lamb (☎ 720545), on the corner of High St & Ocklynge Rd, in the old town, is a half-timbered pub with traditional bar meals, such as ploughman's lunch for £4.95, or more modern meals for around £7.50. *Cafe Aroma (☎ 640263, 54 Crown St)* is in the old town and serves cream tea for £2.10 and snacks from £2.40.

Entertainment
Curzon Cinema (☎ 731441) is on Langney Rd and shows the latest mainstream movies. There are also a number of theatres in Eastbourne – the **Congress Theatre** is on Carlisle Rd, just west of the centre, and **Devonshire Park Theatre** and the **Winter Garden** are on Compton St. Phone ☎ 412000 to find out what's playing.

Getting There & Away
Eastbourne is 75 miles (121km) from London, making it a bit far for a day trip. It's 23 miles (37km) from Brighton.

Bus Buses stop in the pedestrian strip on Terminus Rd. There are two National Express (☎ 0870 580 8080) services per day to Eastbourne from London Victoria (£8, 2½ hours). Stagecoach Coastline (☎ 01903-237661) bus No 711 runs hourly from

Dover to Brighton via Eastbourne, Hastings and Rye. Dover to Eastbourne takes four hours (£5.50). Bus No 710 comes from Brighton (£2.20, 1½ hours) then goes on to Hastings.

Train The train station is on Ashford Rd in the centre. Trains from London Victoria leave every half-hour (£16.90, 1½ hours). There are services three times an hour (hourly on Sunday) to Hastings (£4.40, 32 minutes) and Brighton (£6.70, 45 minutes).

Getting Around
Try T&C Taxi (☎ 720720). There's a taxi rank on Bolton Rd in the town centre. Most trips around town cost £2.50 to £3.

BEACHY HEAD
The chalk cliffs at Beachy Head mark the southern end of the South Downs. Completely sheer, 175m-high coastal cliffs are awe inspiring enough in themselves, but when they are chalk white and backed by emerald green turf they are breathtaking.

There's a countryside centre (☎ 01323-737273) with interactive displays on the area and a restaurant. It opens 10 am to 5.30 pm daily, late March to September. If you're coming by car, Beachy Head is off the B2103 which comes off the A259 between Eastbourne and Newhaven. There is a regular bus (No 3) from Eastbourne during summer. Better still, why not walk the 3 miles (5km) along the South Downs Way from Eastbourne?

CHARLESTON FARMHOUSE
Charleston (☎ 01323-811265) is a fascinating memorial to the Bloomsbury Group. It's a Tudor/Georgian farmhouse at the foot of the South Downs, just south of the A27 between Lewes and Eastbourne. Vanessa Bell (Virginia Woolf's sister, and an important painter) moved into the farmhouse in 1916 with her lover Duncan Grant and they set about decorating and painting the house, a process that continued into the 1960s. Clive Bell, Vanessa's husband, added his collection of furniture and paintings in 1939. There's also a lovely garden

and interesting outbuildings, including a medieval dovecote.

The house opens 2 to 5 pm, Wednesday to Sunday, from April to October (and bank holiday Mondays) but ring in advance as schedules change. Admission costs £5.50/3.50 and is by guided tour only except on Sunday (£6.50 for special extended guided tours on Friday afternoon). The nearest train station is at Berwick, on the Brighton to Eastbourne line, a 2-mile (3km) walk from the farmhouse.

LONG MAN OF WILMINGTON

If you are travelling along the A27 between Eastbourne and Charleston Farmhouse by car or bus, be sure to look out the window towards the south, just east of the town of Wilmington, to see this amazing sight. The image of this man drawn into a hillside of the South Downs may well be familiar to you. No-one really knows how this 70m-high man got here. He may be an Iron Age agricultural fertility figure, but the shape has similarities to those on Roman coins suggesting later origins. The original markings in the grass have been replaced by white concrete blocks to preserve the image.

There is a turnoff for the Long Man at the town of Wilmington from where you can get a better view. Wilmington is 7 miles (11km) north-west of Eastbourne and 10 miles (16km) south-east of Lewes. If you are walking this section of the South Downs you will pass him and get a close-up view.

LEWES

☎ 01273 • pop 16,000

Lewes, an attractive old town that occupies a ridge above the River Ouse, is the administrative capital of East Sussex. From 1768 to 1774, Thomas Paine, the author of *The Rights of Man* and *The Age of Reason*, lived in The Bull on High St (now Bull House, opposite St Michael's). Paine was eventually sacked from his job as an excise officer and he went to America. His books advocated universal voter franchise, a progressive income tax, old-age pensions, family allowances and a national system of education!

Much of the town is Georgian, but there are also much older styles (sometimes hidden behind Georgian facades). A large variety of materials have been used – timber beams, brick, flint, stone, weatherboards and wooden tiles – creating an absorbing architectural mosaic.

Orientation & Information

The town is built on a steep ridge between the river and the castle ruins, with High St climbing the spine and a number of *twittens* (steep streets and passages) running off it.

The TIC (☎ 483448, fax 484003), 187 High St, opens 9 am to 5 pm Monday to Friday, 10 am to 5 pm on Saturday, and 10 am to 2 pm on Sunday; there are reduced hours in winter. Pick up the free *Town Guide*, which includes a walking tour.

The main post office is on High St, near the corner of Watergate Lane, and there's a Lloyds TSB ATM at the eastern end of the centre on Cliff High St. There's an interesting collection of craft shops in the Old Needlemakers on West St, and there are public toilets on Market Lane.

Lewes Castle & Museum

Building first began on the castle (☎ 486290) just after the Battle of Hastings by William de Warenne to protect his town. Over the next 300 years bits and pieces were added – the keep in the 13th century, the barbican in the 14th century. There isn't much left now, but the views make a visit memorable. The adjacent museum portrays the impact on the region of various invaders and has a collection of prehistoric, Roman, Saxon and medieval objects. Don't miss the Lewes Living History Model, an entertaining 22-minute audiovisual introduction to the town and its history.

The complex opens 10 am to 5.30 pm, Monday to Saturday, and 11 am to 5.30 pm on Sunday and bank holidays. Admission costs £3.70/1.90. The audio tour costs £1. You can buy a combined ticket that includes entry to Anne of Cleves House Museum for £5/2.60.

Anne of Cleves House Museum

Dating back at least to the early 16th century, Anne of Cleves House (☎ 474610), Southover High St, was given to Anne of Cleves by Henry VIII as part of the settlement for their divorce, although Anne never lived here.

It now houses a folk museum that includes all sorts of amazing things. At the prosaic end of the spectrum there's furniture, toys, musical instruments, tapestry, pottery and an extensive collection relating to the Sussex iron industry. At the fantastical end, there's a witch's effigy (complete with pins) and an ancient marble tabletop that miraculously prevented Archbishop Becket's murderers eating from it.

Both the house and the museum are highly recommended. Admission costs £2.50/1.20, or £5/2.60 including Lewes Castle. Anne of Cleves House opens 10 am to 5 pm Monday to Saturday, March to November, and noon to 5 pm on Sunday.

St Michael's Church

The church on High St, just west of the Castle, is a striking building due to its mishmash of architectural styles. The flint tower is from the 12th century and the arcade was built in the 14th century. The facade is Georgian and built of knapped flint and the stained glass is Victorian.

Places to Stay

Reflecting Lewes' status as a tourist backwater, there is not a huge choice of accommodation, and what there is isn't especially cheap.

Felix Gallery (☎ 472668, 2 Sun St) is for those mad about cats. There's one single (£35) and one twin room (£43). If you can afford to pay a little more, *Berkeley House Hotel* (☎ 476057, fax 479575, e www.berkeleyhousehotel.co.uk, 2 Albion St) is a carefully restored Georgian town house with a roof terrace and a licence to serve alcohol. Singles cost £39 to £49, doubles

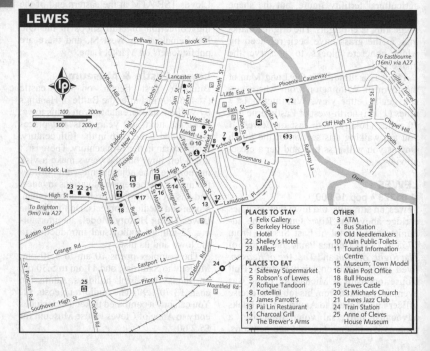

LEWES

PLACES TO STAY	OTHER
1 Felix Gallery	3 ATM
6 Berkeley House Hotel	4 Bus Station
22 Shelley's Hotel	9 Old Needlemakers
23 Millers	10 Main Public Toilets
	11 Tourist Information Centre
PLACES TO EAT	15 Museum; Town Model
2 Safeway Supermarket	16 Main Post Office
5 Robson's of Lewes	18 Bull House
7 Rofique Tandoori	19 Lewes Castle
8 Tortellini	20 St Michaels Church
12 James Parrott's	21 Lewes Jazz Club
13 Pai Lin Restaurant	24 Train Station
14 Charcoal Grill	25 Anne of Cleves House Museum
17 The Brewer's Arms	

£49 to £59, depending on the size of the room.

Shelley's Hotel (☎ *472361, fax 483152, High St)* was originally built in the 1520s, but was converted to a manor house in the 1590s. Antiques adorn the place and the atmosphere is very posh and olde worlde. Singles cost from £100 to £126 and doubles are £140 to £165.

Millers (☎ *475631, 134 High St)* is a 16th-century, timber-framed town house. Double en-suite rooms cost £47/52 for one/two people.

Places to Eat

For self-caterers there's a *Safeway* near Phoenix Causeway.

Robson's of Lewes (☎ *480654, 22A High St, School Hill)* is a popular coffee shop serving snacks and ice cream. A Devonshire tea costs £2.75.

Charcoal Grill (☎ *471126)* on High St is a takeaway joint with plenty of the greasy stuff. Large kebabs cost £3.30 and burgers cost from £1.90. *Tortellini* (☎ *487766, 197 High St)* is a stylish Italian place with pastas for £7 and more substantial dishes for £7.95 to £9.50.

The Brewer's Arms (☎ *479475, 91 High St)* is a traditional old pub with bar meals for under £5. *Rofique Tandoori* (☎ *475817, 205 School Hill)* is an Indian restaurant with very cheap meals – vegetarian dishes cost £3.10, meat dishes cost from £3.20 and a serving of naan is £1.20.

James Parrott's (☎ *472223, 15 Station St)* is a very reasonably priced coffee shop with baguettes for £1.50 and homemade slices for 90p. *Pai Lin Restaurant* (☎ *473906, 20 Station St)* is a cosy Thai restaurant where you can have chicken penang for £5.50 and hot prawn salad for £6.50.

Entertainment

Lewes Jazz Club (☎ 473568, 139 High St) features jazz every Thursday evening from 8 pm. Tickets are £4; £3 for students.

There are a few quiet pubs on the High St that are eminently suitable for enjoying a pint.

Getting There & Away

Lewes is 50 miles (80km) south London, 9 miles (14km) south-east Brighton and 16 miles (26km) north-west Eastbourne.

Bus The bus station is off Eastgate St. Stagecoach South bus No 28 runs hourly from Brighton to Lewes (£2.65, 37 minutes). The No 729 runs hourly between Brighton and Royal Tunbridge Wells via Lewes.

Train Lewes is well served by rail, being on the main line between London Victoria and Eastbourne and on the coastal link between Eastbourne and Brighton. Trains leave every 15 minutes from Brighton (£2.50, 15 minutes), three times an hour from Eastbourne (£4.20, 20 minutes) and every half-hour from London Victoria (£13.20, 55 minutes).

GLYNDEBOURNE

Located 4 miles (6km) east of Lewes off the B2192, Glyndebourne (☎ 01273-812321, e info@glyndebourne.com) is a remarkable English phenomenon. In 1934, John Christie, a science teacher from Eton, inherited a large Tudor mansion and indulged both his and his opera-singer wife's love of opera by building a 1200-seat opera house in the middle of nowhere. The Archive Gallery here houses an exhibition of Glyndebourne's development since the 1930s.

The season runs from late May until the end of August, with performances beginning around 5 pm. In October the company tours other theatres in England. There is a dress code – black tie and evening dress. Tickets range from £23 to £130; standing-only tickets are £10, but you must be on the mailing list to get these. Tickets entitle you to enjoy the estate's landscaped gardens from 3 pm onwards. Call the box office on ☎ 01273-813813 for bookings.

The trip from London takes about 2½ hours by car. Coaches can be arranged for pick up at Lewes station (☎ 01273-815000). See the earlier Lewes section for train services from London.

BRIGHTON
☎ 01273 • pop 188,000

> 'How did England ever produce a town
> with the fizz and craziness of Brighton? It
> is a marvellous mystery – like a family of
> duffers producing a babe of Mozartian
> genius.'
>
> **Nigel Richardson**
> *Breakfast in Brighton – Adventures
> on the Edge of Britain*

Brighton is deservedly England's number
one seaside town – a fascinating mixture of
seediness and sophistication. Londoners
have been travelling here since the 1750s,
when a shrewd doctor suggested that
bathing in, and drinking, the local sea water
was good for them. It's still fine to swim
here, though a little on the cool side; drinking the sea water, however, is definitely not
recommended.

The essential flavour of the town dates
from the 1780s when the dissolute, music-
loving Prince Regent (later George IV) built
his outrageous summer palace for lavish
parties by the sea. Brighton still has some of
the hottest clubs and venues outside London, and the largest gay club scene in
England. There's a vibrant population of
students and travellers, excellent shopping,
a thriving arts scene and countless restaurants, pubs and cafes.

Orientation
Old Steine (pronounced steen) is the major
road running from the pier to the city centre. The interesting (read more bohemian)
part of Brighton lies to the east of Queens
Rd in the area known as North Laine.
Brighton train station is a 15-minute walk
north of the beach. The tiny bus station is
tucked away in Poole Valley, south-east of
the area known as The Lanes.

To the west of Brighton, and now part of
the same administrative unit, is slightly
snobbish Hove. It's jokingly referred to as
'Hove Actually' in Brighton because most
Hove residents, when asked where they
live, will reply 'Hove, actually', to emphasise that they don't live in Brighton!

Information
Tourist Office The TIC (☎ 292599,
℮ tourism@brighton.co.uk), 10 Bartholomew Square, opens 9 am to 5 pm Monday
to Friday, 10 am to 5 pm Saturday and
10 am to 4 pm Sunday, June to August.
The rest of the year it opens 9 am to 5 pm
Monday to Saturday. Copies of Brighton's
what's-on magazines, *The Brighton Latest*
(30p), *Brighton & Hove Scene* (25p) and
New Insight (45p) are available. *Brighton
Town Centre Map-Guide* costs £1. For information on everything from shopping to
nightclubs to eating out in Brighton go to
the Web site at www.brighton.co.uk.

Money There's a branch of American
Express at 82 North St (☎ 321242) and
a Thomas Cook bureau de change
(☎ 328154) on North St, near the Clocktower. You'll find a convenient NatWest
ATM on Castle St, near the entrance to the
Royal Pavilion.

Post & Communications The main post
office is on Ship St and there's a smaller
post office on Western Rd. For Internet access go to Riki Tik (☎ 683844) at 18a Bond
St. You could also go to Brighton Media
Centre (☎ 384200), at 68 Middle St, though
it's expensive at £3 for 30 minutes.

Bookshops Borders Books (☎ 731122), in
Churchill Square Shopping Centre, also
has CDs, a cafe and the occasional live
event. There are a number of specialist
and second-hand bookshops in North
Laine, including David's Book Exchange
(☎ 690223), at 3 Sydney St. The larger
chain bookshops can be found on North St
in the centre.

Laundry Bubbles Laundrette is at 75 Preston St.

Medical Services Wiston's Clinic
(☎ 506263) is at 138 Dyke Rd, just under a
mile from the centre. There's an accident
and emergency department at the Royal Sussex County Hospital (☎ 696955) on Eastern
Rd, 2 miles (3km) east of the centre.

BRIGHTON

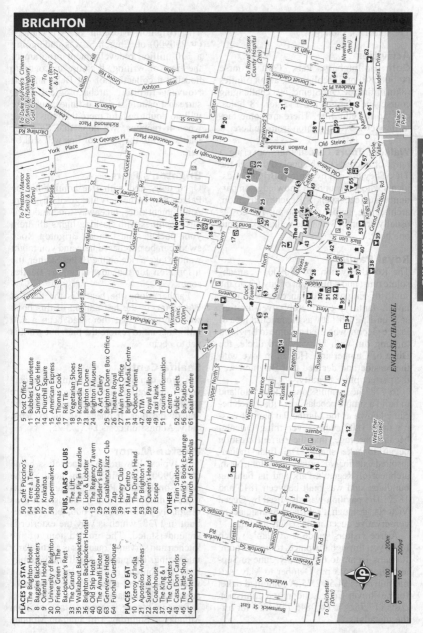

SOUTH-EASTERN ENGLAND

PLACES TO STAY
7   The Brighton Hotel
8   Baggies Backpackers
9   Oriental Hotel
20 University of Brighton
30 Friese Green – The Backpacker's Rest
33 The Grand
35 Walkabout Backpackers
36 Brighton Backpackers Hostel
40 Old Ship Hotel
60 The Amalfi Hotel
63 Genevieve Hotel
64 Funchal Guesthouse

PLACES TO EAT
10 Viceroy of India
21 Apostolos Andreas
22 Sushi Box
28 Coachhouse
37 The King & I
42 The Cricketers
43 Casa Don Carlos
45 The Little Shop
46 Donatello's
50 Café Pucino's
54 Terre à Terre
55 Fishbowl
57 Krakatoa
58 Supermarket

PUBS, BARS & CLUBS
3   The Lift;
    The Pig in Paradise
6   Lion & Lobster
13 The Regency Tavern
29 Fiddler's Elbow
32 Casablanca Jazz Club
38 Zap
39 Honey Club
41 Bar Centro
44 The Druid's Head
53 Dr Brighton's
59 Queen's Head
62 Escape

OTHER
1   Train Station
2   David's Book Exchange
4   Church of St Nicholas
5   Post Office
11 Bubbles Laundrette
12 Sunrise Cycle Hire
14 Churchill Square
15 American Express
16 Thomas Cook
17 Riki Tik
18 Vegetarian Shoes
19 Komedia Theatre
23 Brighton Dome
24 Brighton Museum & Art Gallery
25 Brighton Dome Box Office
26 Theatre Royal
27 Main Post Office
31 Brighton Media Centre
34 Odeon Cinema
47 ATM
48 Royal Pavilion
49 Taxi Rank
51 Tourist Information Centre
52 Public Toilets
56 Bus Station
61 Sealife Centre

Toilets You'll find public toilets behind the TIC on Black Lion St.

Activities

Golf Hollingbury Park Golf Course (☎ 500086) on Ditchling Rd, about 5 miles (8km) from the Old Steine, is a challenging course and charges are £12 for 18 holes, plus £5 for club hire. There are some fantastic views over Brighton from up here.

Walking Tours Guided tours covering a range of interests can be booked through the TIC. They are run by various Brighton residents who have a broad knowledge on particular subjects such as Regency Brighton, architecture, gardens and so on. The cost is usually around £3 and the walks take about one hour.

Royal Pavilion

The Royal Pavilion (☎ 290900) is an absolute must and a highlight of any trip to the south of England. It's an extraordinarily lavish fantasy; completely over-the-top; so...'un-English'! It was the fanciful idea of Prince George who used to come to Brighton to hang out with his wayward uncle, the Duke of Cumberland. He fell in love with the seaside and decided that Brighton was the perfect place to party.

In 1787 he commissioned Henry Holland to build a simple neoclassical villa which became known as the Marine Pavilion. It wasn't until 1802, when everything Oriental became the rage, that the current creation began to take shape. The final Indian-inspired exterior was produced by John Nash, architect of Regent's Park and its flanking buildings, and was built between 1815 and 1822. The pavilion was also used by Queen Victoria, although it's difficult to imagine the conservative queen in these surroundings.

A free visitors' guide is available which takes you through the place, room by room. It opens 10 am to 6 pm daily, June to September, and to 5 pm October to May. Admission costs £4.50/2.75. A combined ticket for rail travel from London and admission costs £17.75/3.75 (☎ 0845 748 4950 for further details).

Brighton Museum & Art Gallery

The Brighton Museum & Art Gallery (☎ 290900) on Church St was undergoing a £10-million redevelopment program at the time of writing. It's sure to continue housing a collection of Art Deco and Art Nouveau furniture, archaeological finds, surrealist paintings and costumes, but there will no doubt be a lot more than this to see when it reopens. We hope that Salvador Dali's sofa in the shape of lips will still be here.

Brighton's Piers

Open daily and with free admission, the **Palace Pier** is the very image of Brighton. Amusement rides, takeaway food and various machines with flashing lights all drain your pocket. The famous Brighton Rock sweet can be purchased here and you might want to take a ride on the Helter Skelter, the inspiration for the now infamous Beatles song.

Farther along the beach is the derelict **West Pier**. In the last edition of this book we mentioned that there had been a £20 million grant to restore the pier, but work is yet to begin.

Sealife Centre

Yes, you can see sharks from the underwater observation tunnel here. The centre (☎ 604234) is on Marine Parade, near the end of the pier. It opens 10 am to 5 pm daily. Admission costs £4.95/3.25.

Preston Manor

This typical Edwardian, upper-class home (☎ 290900), 2½ miles (4km) north of the centre on London Rd, is brimful with antiques, ornaments and paintings. It was originally built around 1600, but was rebuilt in 1738, which is why the exterior is so understated. The guided tour of the kitchen and servants' quarters is particularly interesting. The place is small and you may have to contend with school groups on weekdays so call ahead if you want to be sure of a bit of space.

Preston Manor is open 10 am to 5 pm Monday to Saturday, 1 to 5 pm on Monday and 2 to 5 pm on Sunday. Admission costs £3.10/1.95. You can get there on bus No 5 or 5a from the centre.

Special Events

Brighton Festival (☎ 292961), the largest arts festival outside Edinburgh, runs for three weeks every May; though it's mostly mainstream, there are fringe events too. Check out the Web site at www.brighton-festival.org.uk for details.

Places to Stay

There's plenty of accommodation in Brighton to suit all budgets. You should book ahead for weekends in summer and during the Brighton Festival in May.

Hostels Brighton's independent hostels provide a more relaxed alternative to the inconveniently located YHA hostel.

Baggies Backpackers (☎ 733740, 33 Oriental Place) is a friendly, homy place with beds for £10 per night (plus £5 deposit for a room key) and double rooms for £25. There are two lounges, a communal kitchen and a laundry. It's well situated in a quiet area close to the seafront and plenty of cheap restaurants.

Brighton Backpackers Hostel (☎ 777717, fax 887778, e stay@brightonbackpackers .com, 75–6 Middle St) seems to be trying very hard to cultivate a lackadaisical atmosphere. Charges are £10 per night (or £11 in the seafront annexe). Weekly rates are £55/60. Travellers have painted the murals here.

Friese Green – The Backpacker's Rest (☎ 747551, 20 Middle St) charges £9 for a bed and £30 for a double room. *Walkabout Backpackers* (☎ 770232, 79–81 West St) is not exclusively for Australians and New Zealanders but it might seem that way. Beds in ordinary, bland dorms cost £10 or £12 in a double room. This place doesn't take reservations.

The *University of Brighton* (☎ 643167, fax 642610) has flats for two to eight people available in various locations near the university from July to September. Prices start at £60 per person per week.

B&Bs & Hotels The biggest cluster of cheap B&Bs is to the east of Palace Pier. Cross the Old Steine roundabout and walk up St James's St. *Funchal Guesthouse* (☎/fax 603975, 17 Madeira Place) tries very hard to please with cosy, clean rooms that are serviced daily. Prices begin at £20 per person, but these rates may go up a few pounds in summer.

Genevieve Hotel (☎ 681653, 18 Madeira Place) is clean and everything seems quite new. Rooms cost £20 to £25 per person with continental breakfast.

The Amalfi Hotel (☎ 607956, 44 Marine Parade) is right on the seafront and rooms are quite reasonable at £23 to £30 per person with en suite.

Oriental Hotel (☎ 205050, fax 821096, e info@orientalhotel.co.uk, 9 Oriental Place) is a real breath of fresh air among B&Bs. Decorated with bright colours, homemade furniture and cool decor, it's very funky. Doubles go for £54/70 weekdays/weekends. There are no single occupancy rates.

The Grand (☎ 321188, Kings Rd) was built in the 1860s and was completely refurbished following the IRA bombing during the Tory party conference of October 1984. Prices are hefty, with elegant rooms from £145/180. Package deals are available throughout the year.

Old Ship Hotel (☎ 329001, fax 820718), also on Kings Rd, is the doyen of Brighton's hotels. In the 1830s, Thackeray stayed there while writing *Vanity Fair*. It costs from £75/99 for singles/doubles.

The Brighton Hotel (☎ 820555, fax 821555, 145 Kings Rd) is better than most that are in the same price range along this stretch. Singles/doubles cost from £60/80.

Places to Eat

Brighton has it all as far as food goes. Wander around The Lanes or head down to Preston St, which runs back from the seafront near West Pier, and you'll turn up all sorts of interesting, affordable possibilities. Vegetarians, vegans and healthfoodies won't be left out in the cold either. For self-caterers, there's a *supermarket* in St James's St.

Krakatoa (☎ 719009, 7 Poole Valley), near the bus station, is a small, casual restaurant with a modern Oriental fusion menu. It's for serious foodies. Main courses are around £7 or £8.

Fishbowl (☎ 777505, 74 East St) is a groovy place with a small but interesting menu offering everything from Malaysian satays to paella.

Terre à Terre (☎ 729051, 71 East St), a little farther along, is a relatively expensive vegetarian restaurant with a huge menu. Starters are around £5 and main courses are about £9.50. This place is very popular so book ahead, especially at the weekend.

Sushi Box (☎ 818040, 181 Edward St) is close to the university and charges £3 to £4 for a takeaway lunch box of sashimi and/or California rolls.

Apostolos Andreas (☎ 687935, George St) is a Greek coffee-house with English-style food. It's extremely popular with students because it's such good value. If you can get a seat in this tiny place you will pay about 65p for a coffee, 95p to £1.45 for a sandwich and from £1.35 for a hot meal.

The King & I (☎ 773390, 2 Ship St) is a Thai restaurant and there's a lunch menu which comprises one main course with rice plus tea or coffee for £4.99.

Casa Don Carlos (☎ 327177 or 303274, 5 Union St, The Lanes) is an intimate Spanish tapas house and restaurant with a large selection of Spanish plonk. A large serve of paella costs £4.25 and a Spanish omelette is £3.10.

Donatello's (☎ 775477, 1–3 Brighton Place, The Lanes) is an enormous place that almost takes up a whole block. There is a bistro, a pizzeria and a more upmarket restaurant. It offers very good value – two courses for £6.60 and three courses for £7.90 – but it's not the place for a quiet, intimate meal.

The Little Shop (☎ 325594, 48a Market St, The Lanes) has apparently won awards for its sandwiches. They *are* delicious, and very chunky, and cost from £2.25.

Café Puccino's (☎ 204656, fax 206915, 1 Bartholomews) has an enormous range of coffee with names such as 'Mocha Melt-

down' and 'Wham Bam'. Meals and snacks are also available for a reasonable price.

Viceroy of India (☎ 324733, 13 Preston St) is one of the best-value Indian restaurants along this street and serves a range of cuisines – Kashmir, Madras, Ceylon, Balti and Tandoor. Main courses are £3 to £3.50.

Coachhouse (☎ 719000, 59a Middle St) is a relaxed cafe/bar with a studenty atmosphere and live music on Friday. The Thai curry with crispy noodles for £7 is absolutely delicious.

The Cricketers (☎ 329472, Black Lion St) is the place for old fashioned pub grub. Steak and mushroom pie costs £4.95. Note the decorative ceiling in this 16th-century pub.

Entertainment

Ever since the 1960s, Brighton has had a reputation as the club and party capital of the south, if not the whole country. In the late 1970s this reputation was enshrined in the cult movie *Quadraphenia*. For those who don't remember those good old days you will remember Fat Boy Slim. He hails from Brighton; other DJs guest quite regularly at various places around town. Pubs, bars and clubs are constantly opening, closing and changing their themes – check *The Brighton Latest*, *New Insight* and bar and cafe walls for places of the moment. There is a huge gay scene in Brighton and most of the gay bars and clubs can be found around St James's St and the Old Steine. Go to the Web site at www.gay.brighton.co.uk for information on Brighton's gay scene.

Pubs Decorated with skulls and votive offerings, *Druid's Head* (☎ 325490, 9 Brighton Place) is recommended. The *Lion & Lobster* (☎ 776961, 24 Sillwood St) has live music most nights. *Fiddler's Elbow* (☎ 325850, Boyces St) is an Irish pub with live music on Friday evenings.

Gay pubs include *Dr Brighton's*, King's Rd, and *Queen's Head*, on the small side street off Marine Parade. Recognise the bloke on the pub sign here?

No pub could be more Brighton than *The Regency Tavern* (☎ 325652, 32 Russell

Square) – very plain outside, inside it's pure Regency, like an extension of the Pavilion with its striped green wallpaper and painted cameos.

Clubs All are open until at least 2 am, some as late as 5 am. Door charges range from between £4 and £10.

Some of the long-standing clubs worth investigating include *Zap (☎ 821588, Kings Rd Arches)* which is midway between the two piers. *Honey Club (☎ 07000 446639, 214 Kings Rd Arches)* plays 70s and 80s disco classics on Monday and Thursday (£4 admission) and has guest DJs on Saturday (£12).

Bar Centro (☎ 206580), on Ship St, is a drum and bass club and admission is free. Sunday night is for members only.

The punters at *Casablanca Jazz Club (9 Middle St)* are mainly aged 25 to 35. There is no live music but a DJ plays a range of music for £5 admission 9 pm to 2 am, Tuesday to Saturday.

There's also *Escape (☎ 606906, 10 Marine Parade)*, a laid-back place. *The Pig in Paradise* and *The Lift (☎ 724639, 11 Queens Rd)* have live music every night, mostly alternative and experimental stuff with some jazz and blues as well (£2 to £3 admission).

Theatre & Cinema There are a number of theatres in Brighton. The Art Deco *Brighton Dome (☎ 709709, e tickets@brighton-dome .org.uk, 29 New Rd)*, next to the Royal Pavilion, was once the stables and exercise yard of George IV and is the largest theatre complex in Brighton.

Others are *Theatre Royal (☎ 328488, New Rd)*, which hosts plays, musicals and operas, and *Komedia Theatre (☎ 647101, Gardner St, North Laine)*, which is home to comedy and cabaret as well as fringe theatre.

The huge *Odeon Cinema (☎ 207977)* is on the corner of King's Rd and West St and shows mainstream films. *Duke of York's Cinema (☎ 602503, Preston Circus)*, about a mile north of North Rd, is the home of art-house films.

Things to Buy

Just south of North St (and north of the TIC) you'll find **The Lanes**, a maze of narrow alleyways crammed with jewellery, antiques and clothes shops. Some of the best restaurants and bars are around here, too.

For second-hand clothes, records and CDs, bong shops, local craft and new age places (and a slightly less touristy feel), explore **North Laine**, a series of streets north-west of The Lanes, including Bond, Gardner, Kensington and Sydney Sts. On Gardner St check out Vegetarian Shoes for animal-friendly footwear. The flea market on Upper Gardner St on Saturday morning is also worth visiting.

Getting There & Away

Transport to and from Brighton is fast and frequent. London is 53 miles (85km) to the north and Eastbourne is 23 miles (37km) to the east.

Bus National Express (☎ 0870 580 8080) has an office at the bus station, though tickets can also be bought at the TIC. There is a shuttle service hourly from London Victoria (£7 one way; £5 off-peak which means you must leave London after 9.30 am).

Stagecoach Coastline (☎ 01903-237661) bus No 711 runs between Brighton and Dover via Hastings and Rye. Bus No 712 runs every half-hour from Eastbourne to Brighton (£2.20, 1¼ hours). Bus No 710 goes from Brighton to Hastings (£4.30, 2½ hours). Bus No 702 goes to Chichester every 30 minutes (£3.20, 2 hours 50 minutes) and bus No 700 runs along the south coast from Brighton to Portsmouth every 30 minutes (£3.20, 3 hours 20 minutes).

Airlinks (☎ 0870 574 7777) is a daily coach service between Brighton bus station and all London airports. Buses leave for Gatwick and Heathrow roughly every 30 minutes.

Train There are twice-hourly services to Brighton from London Victoria and King's Cross stations (£13.70/14.60 one way/day return, 50 minutes). For £1 on top of the rail fare to Brighton you can have unlimited travel on local Brighton and Hove buses for the day. There are hourly services between Brighton and Portsmouth (£11.70, 1 hour 20 minutes), and frequent services to Eastbourne (£6.70, 37 minutes) and Hastings (£8.60, 1¼ hours).

Getting Around

Bus The local bus company is Brighton & Hove (☎ 886200). A day ticket costs £2.60 from the driver. Guide Friday open-top buses (☎ 746205) take you around the main sights of Brighton. You can get on and off as much as you like. Tickets are available from the driver and cost £6.50/2.50.

Car All we can say is – don't bother. Parking is a nightmare and driving is even more difficult due to the one-way and pedestrian-only systems. If you decide to bring a car be prepared to pay plenty for parking. To park in any street space you will need a voucher. They can be purchased from garages and various shops around town marked with a tick. It usually costs about £1 an hour but prices do vary.

Taxi Try Radio Cars (☎ 414141), Yellow Cab Company (☎ 884488) or Brighton Streamline Taxis (☎ 747474).

Bicycle You can hire from Sunrise Cycle Hire (☎ 748881) by West Pier. Rates start at £10 a day. There are cycle routes along the seafront and throughout the city centre, but traffic is very unpredictable so be careful. For more information on cycling in and around Brighton call ☎ 292475.

West Sussex

West Sussex doesn't offer as many picturesque villages, castles and great houses as East Sussex and Kent, but it is home to the historical town of Chichester, which is worth a visit. Arundel makes a good base for exploring the county's rolling hills and the small villages that are tucked away within them.

ARUNDEL
☎ 01903 • pop 4000

Arundel is a lovely little tourist trap that sits on the River Arun at the foot of a romantic-looking castle. Despite its ancient appearance and history, however, most of the town dates from Victorian times. It can easily be explored on foot and you really only need half a day to do it.

The TIC (☎ 882268, fax 882419), 61 High St, opens 9 am to 5 pm weekdays, and 10 am to 5 pm at the weekend from Easter to October; the rest of the year it opens 10 am to 3 pm daily. *A Walk Around Arundel* is available from here for 25p, although everything to see in the town is pretty well signposted. Next door is the **Museum & Heritage Centre** with a small exhibition showing the history of Arundel; it opens 10.30 am to 5 pm Monday to Saturday, and 2 to 5 pm on Sunday. Admission costs £1/50p.

Arundel Castle (☎ 882173) has been the ancestral home of the dukes of Norfolk for over 700 years. Originally built at the end of the 11th century, it sits at the top of a hill and overlooks the town and the River Arun. It opens noon to 5 pm (last entry 4 pm) Sunday to Friday, April to October. Admission costs £7/4.50.

Set within 25 acres, the **Waterfowl Park** (☎ 883355) on Mill Rd, a mile from the centre, is a nice place to visit for those keen on a spot of birdwatching, but others may find it a little lacklustre for the price. It opens 9.30 am to 5.30 pm (4.30 pm in winter) daily. Admission costs £5/3.

Arundel Cathedral (☎ 882297) is a Roman Catholic church which was built around 1870 in the French Gothic style. It's a stunning piece of architecture and was commissioned by Henry, the 15th Duke of Norfolk. It opens 9 am until dusk daily.

Places to Stay & Eat

There are a number of B&Bs and hotels, all very different in character and price, so look around a bit.

Warningcamp Youth Hostel (☎ 882204, *Sefton Place, Warningcamp*) is 1 mile from the station and is signposted on the A27. A dorm bed costs £7.70 and camping is

£3.85 per person. It's closed January and February.

Arden Guesthouse (☎ 882544, 4 Queens Lane) is signposted on the left as you come into the town from the A27. This clean, bright place is good value at £18 per person, or £20 for en suite.

Dukes of Arundel (☎ 883847, fax 889601, 65 High St) is a luxurious B&B and the pick of the bunch. Notice the Italian Renaissance ceiling in the cafe downstairs, which, according to the owner, may have been pilfered a long time ago from the Medici Palace in Florence. Rooms cost £25 to £32 per person, but the beautiful Venetian-style honeymoon suite is the place to be if you have £80 to blow.

Norfolk Arms (☎ 882101, fax 884275, High St) was built by the 10th Duke of Norfolk around 1800. The antiques in the lobby suggest that this place is expensive and it is – £65/100 for singles/doubles.

The Country Kitchen (☎ 882438, 31 Tarrant St) is a simple coffee shop offering very good value – a pot of tea is 80p and sandwiches cost from £1.75. *Pappardelle (☎ 882025, 41a High St)* is a casual Italian restaurant with pastas for around £6.95 and pizza for £5.95.

Getting There & Away

Rail is the most efficient way of getting to/from Arundel; it's 55 miles (89km) from London (£15.90, 1 hour 25 minutes), 20 miles (32km) from Brighton (£6.30, 50 minutes) and 11 miles (18km) from Chichester (£3.40, 20 minutes). Stagecoach Coastline (☎ 01903-237661) bus No 702 runs from Brighton to Chichester via Arundel every 30 minutes (every hour on Sunday). It takes 1¾ hours from Brighton (£3.20) and one hour from Chichester (£2.80).

BIGNOR ROMAN VILLA

Discovered in 1811 by a farmer, this villa (☎ 01798-869259) dates from AD 240, although some findings date from 2000 to 600 BC. Only the mosaic floors and a hypocaust (the Roman version of duct heating) remain of the villa but the mosaics are some of the best preserved in the country.

One particularly intricate piece depicts Venus and gladiators.

The amazing thing is that relics are still being discovered around the villa. In 1999 the complete skeleton of an infant who lived sometime between the 3rd and 4th centuries AD was found here.

The villa opens 10 am to 6 pm daily, June to September, and to 5 pm October to May. Admission costs £3.50/1.50. It's 6 miles (10km) north of Arundel, off the A29, but getting there is a bit of a problem if you don't have your own car (a fact that is bemoaned by the attraction's owners). You can take the rather slow and infrequent bus from Chichester to the village of Bignor and walk the 300m to the villa. You could also get there from Petworth House & Park (see Around Chichester later in this chapter), 6 miles to the north, on the Sutton Village bus from Worthing.

CHICHESTER

☎ 01243 • pop 28,000

Chichester is the thriving administrative centre for West Sussex and was founded soon after the Roman invasion of AD 43. It lies on the flat meadows between the South Downs and the sea and was once a port.

East, West, North and South Sts were laid out by the Romans for their town, Noviomagus, and the foundations for an enormous Roman villa and its beautiful mosaics, survive at Fishbourne on the town outskirts (see Around Chichester later in this chapter). The Norman castle has long disappeared but the cathedral survives. The City Cross at the centre of town dates from 1501 (built by Bishop Story for the 'comfort of the poore people there') and is one of the finest in the country. A substantial part of the town centre is dominated by classic Georgian architecture.

Orientation & Information

Much like Canterbury and Winchester, there's a ring road outside the old city walls and the centre is easily covered on foot.

The TIC (☎ 775888, fax 539449, e helpline@chichester.gov.uk), 29a South St, opens 9.30 am to 5.30 pm Monday to

Saturday, and 10 am to 4 pm on Sunday, Easter to October.

The main post office is on the corner of Chapel and West Sts. You'll find an AmEx office at 81 East St as well as a number of bureaux de change a little farther along the street.

There are a few public loos around the centre – next to the Guildhall Museum in Priory Park and off West St, near the corner of Tower St.

Chichester Cathedral

The Chichester Cathedral of today has evolved over 900 years, but it remains substantially Norman, or Romanesque, and is more harmonious in appearance than most other churches of similar antiquity. Artworks inside range from Norman stone carvings to 20th-century paintings.

Work began in 1075 and continued for over 100 years – the nave survives; at the beginning of the 13th century the inside of the clerestory, the retrochoir, sacristy and porches were built in the Early English Gothic style; the side chapels and Lady Chapel date from the beginning of the 14th century and are in the Decorated style; and, finally, the cloisters, bell tower and unique detached belfry were built in perpendicular style around the turn of the 15th century.

There are a number of treasures on display in the cathedral and the building's story is best revealed by an expert: guided tours operate at 11 am and 2.15 pm, Monday to Saturday from Easter to October. In particular, don't miss the beautiful Lady Chapel ceiling by Lambert Barnard, the exquisite 12th-century stone carvings, said to be among the finest masterpieces of Romanesque sculpture, the shrine of St Richard, the window designed by Marc Chagall, and the poignant tomb of the Earl of Arundel and his countess. The two are shown holding hands, with their feet resting

CHICHESTER

CHICHESTER

PLACES TO STAY
1   Chichester Institute
3   11 Cavendish St
6   The Ship
8   Suffolk House Hotel & Restaurant
23 Whyke House
24 Encore

PLACES TO EAT
5   Clinches Coffee Shop & Restaurant

9   Café Metro Brasserie
10 The Nag's Head
11 Little London Indian Tandoori
12 Shepherd's Tea Rooms
14 St Martin's Tea Room
22 Home Bake Café
27 Waitrose Supermarket

OTHER
2   Chichester Festival Theatre
4   Public Toilets
7   Church of the Greyfriars

13 Chichester District Museum
15 Main Post Office
16 Public Toilets
17 Chichester Cathedral
18 City Cross
19 AmEx
20 Tourist Information Centre
21 Pallant House
25 Bus Station
26 Train Station

SOUTH-EASTERN ENGLAND

on their pet dogs (this in 1376) – which inspired Philip Larkin to write *An Arundel Tomb*, but also shows the English have been peculiar about dogs for a long time.

Chichester Cathedral (☎ 782595) opens 7 am until 7 pm daily during summer and until 6.30 pm the rest of the year. It has a fine choir, which sings daily at evensong. Evensong is at 5.30 pm Monday to Saturday, 3.30 pm on Sunday. Admission to the cathedral is free but there is a suggested donation of £2/1.

Pallant House

Of the many fine Georgian houses in town, Pallant House (☎ 774557), 9 North Pallant, is outstanding. It was built by a wealthy wine merchant who spared no expense. It has since been carefully restored and now houses an excellent collection of 20th-century, mainly British art in the form of paintings, furniture, sculpture and porcelain. Among them are works by Picasso, Moore, Sutherland and Cézanne. There are also a lot of works by a German artist named Feibusch. He escaped the Nazis in Germany in 1933 and lived in London until he died in 1998. In his will he left the contents of his studio to Pallant House. It opens 10 am to 5 pm Tuesday to Saturday, and from noon to 5 pm on Sunday. Admission is £4/free.

Church of the Greyfriars

The Franciscans established a church here in 1269 on the old site of the castle – now Priory Park, in the eastern corner of the town. The simple, but quite beautiful building that remains was their choir and now overlooks the local cricket pitch. After dissolution in 1538, the building became the guildhall and later a court of law, where William Blake was tried for sedition in 1804. It opens noon to 4 pm Saturdays only from June to September, but visits at other times can be made by arrangement (☎ 784683). Admission is free.

Chichester District Museum

Here we learn all about the history and the people of West Sussex. The Museum (☎ 784683) is at 29 Little London Rd and opens 10 am to 5.30 pm Tuesday to Saturday. Admission is free.

Special Events

Chichester's Festival Theatre (☎ 781312, e box-office@cft.org.uk), built in 1962, is a striking modern building in parkland to the north of the ring road. Sir Laurence Olivier was the theatre's first director and other famous names to have played here include Ingrid Bergman, John Gielgud, Maggie Smith and Anthony Hopkins. It is now at the centre of an important arts festival, the Chichester Festivities (☎ 780192, e info@chifest.org.uk), which is held every July.

Places to Stay

We found most accommodation in Chichester to be inexplicably expensive. It pays to look around a bit.

Chichester Institute (☎ 816070, College Lane) rents out rooms from July to September from £23 per person, or £32 with en suite. There are 218 rooms and they are all singles.

Encore (☎ 528271, 11 Clydesdale Ave) is a short walk from the centre. It costs from £20 per person for a double room with shared bathroom; singles are not usually taken in.

11 Cavendish St (☎ 527387) is a non-smoking B&B, with one double and one single at £17 per person.

Whyke House (☎ 788767, 13 Whyke Lane) is run by a helpful couple and they charge £45 per night for a minimum of two nights in a self-contained flat. Breakfast is not included.

The Ship (☎/fax 778000, North St), an attractive hotel dating from the 18th century, has a good restaurant and is convenient for the theatre. Singles/doubles are £75/114.

Suffolk House Hotel & Restaurant (☎ 778899, fax 787282, e suffolkhshotel .demon.co.uk, 3 East Row) is a Georgian house in the heart of the city with a range of comfortable rooms; prices start from £59/89.

Places to Eat

There's a *Waitrose* supermarket near the train station.

Home Bake Café (☎ 533785, The Hornet) is the best place for a cheap feed. Its yorkie (Yorkshire pudding), sausage, mash and beans dish is great value at £3.70.

Clinchs Coffee Shop & Restaurant (☎ 789915, 4 Guildhall St) is reasonably priced and close to the theatre. Main courses cost from £6 to £8.

St Martin's Tea Room (☎ 786715, 3 St Martin's St) and *Shepherd's Tea Rooms (☎ 774761, 35 Little London)* both serve tea and cakes in comfortable surroundings.

Café Metro Brasserie (☎ 788771, St Pancras St) does set lunches for £4.50 and there's live jazz on Tuesday evening.

The best curry house in town is the *Little London Indian Tandoori (☎ 537550, 38 Little London)*. Chicken tikka masala costs £8.95 and a vegetarian dish such as sag paneer costs £2.95.

The Nag's Head (☎ 785823, 3 St Pancras St) is a great place for a meal and the menu is large and varied. There's also an outdoor seating area.

Getting There & Away

Chichester is 60 miles (97km) from London and 18 miles (29km) from Portsmouth.

Bus Chichester is served by Stagecoach Coastline (☎ 01903-237661) bus No 700/701 which runs between Brighton (£3.20, 2 hours) and Portsmouth (£3, 1 hour), from Monday to Saturday every 30 minutes (hourly on Sunday). Bus No 702 runs from Brighton to Chichester via Arundel every 30 minutes, hourly on Sunday (£3.20, 2 hours 40 minutes). National Express (☎ 0870 580 8080) has a rather protracted daily service from London Victoria (£10.50/£14 one way/day return, 3 hours).

Train Chichester can be reached easily from London Victoria (£16, 1¾ hours) on an hourly service via Gatwick airport and Arundel. It's also on the coast line between Brighton (£7.60, 45 minutes) and Portsmouth (£4.50, 25 minutes).

Getting Around

If you have a car we recommend you use the long-stay car parks, all of which are within easy walking distance of the town centre. Parking within the ring road requires vouchers, which cost 20p per 20 minutes.

AROUND CHICHESTER

To the south of Chichester lies the popular Chichester Harbour, which has been declared an Area of Outstanding Natural Beauty. North of the harbour lie the beautiful South Downs, and several unspoiled villages – like East and West Dean and Charlton (6 miles/10km from Chichester).

From Itchenor, you can take a 1½-hour cruise around the harbour with Chichester Harbour Water Tours (☎ 786418). The price of £5/2 includes refreshments. To get to Itchenor you could take a 4-mile canal tour from Chichester or you could just enjoy the walk along the towpath. Phone ☎ 771363 or 671051 for details.

Fishbourne Roman Palace & Museum

Discovered in 1960, the palace at Fishbourne (☎ 01243-785859), Salthill Rd, is the largest known Roman residence in Britain. It is believed to have been built around AD 75 for a local king who allied himself to the Romans. It was spectacular in size and luxury – its bathing facilities would still put most contemporary British arrangements to shame. Although all that survive are foundations and some extraordinary mosaic floors and hypocausts, the ruins still convey a vision of 'modern' style and comfort.

The pavilion that shelters the site is an ugly creation, but there are some excellent reconstructions and the garden has been replanted as it would have been in the 1st century. It opens 10 am to 5 pm, May to September (to 6 pm in August). Admission costs £4.40/2.30.

Bus Nos 11 and 700 leave hourly Monday to Saturday (No 56 on Sunday) from outside Chichester Cathedral and stop at the bottom of Salthill Rd (a five-minute walk away). The museum is a 10-minute walk south-east from Fishbourne train station, on the line between Chichester and Portsmouth.

Petworth House & Park

Twelve miles (19km) north-east of Chichester, Petworth House (☎ 01798-342207; NT) dates primarily from 1688. The architecture is impressive (especially the western front), but the art collection is extraordinary. JMW Turner was a regular visitor and the house is still home to the largest collection (20) of his paintings outside Tate Britain in London. There are also many paintings by Van Dyck, Reynolds, Gainsborough, Titian and Blake. Petworth is, however, most famous for its park, which is regarded as the supreme achievement of Lancelot (Capability) Brown's natural landscape theory. It's also home to herds of deer.

The house opens 1 to 5.30 pm daily (last admission 4.30 pm) Saturday to Wednesday, April to October. Admission costs £5/2.50. The car park and Pleasure Ground, a part of the landscaped grounds that features a number of classical follies, are open noon to 6 pm. The park opens 8 am to sunset daily throughout the year. Admission is free.

Petworth is 6 miles (10km) from the train station at Pulborough. Trains from London Victoria leave hourly (£12.80, 1¼ hours). There is a limited bus service (No 1/1A) from the station to Petworth Square, Monday to Saturday.

Hampshire

Hampshire has plenty to slow down visitors on their way to the West Country. First there's Winchester with its important cathedral; then, the important maritime centres of Portsmouth and Southampton; and finally, the beautiful New Forest – the largest remaining relict (ie still original) area of forest in England.

WINCHESTER
☎ 01962 • pop 96,000

Winchester is a beautiful cathedral city on the River Itchen, interspersed with water meadows. It has played an important role in the history of England, being both the capital of Saxon England and the seat of the powerful Bishops of Winchester from AD 670. In modern times it's most famous for the magnificent Winchester Cathedral.

The Romans built Venta Bulgarum on the present-day site; part of their defensive wall can still be seen incorporated into a later medieval defence. Alfred the Great and many of his successors, including Canute and the Danish kings, made Winchester their capital, and William the Conqueror came to the city to claim the crown of England. The Domesday Book was also written here. However, much of the present-day city dates from the 18th century, by which time Winchester had settled down as a prosperous market centre.

Orientation

Winchester can be covered in a day trip from London. The city centre is compact and easily negotiated on foot. The train station is a five-minute walk north-west of the city centre while the bus and coach station is right in the centre, directly opposite the Guildhall and TIC. High St, partly pedestrianised, is the main shopping street. Jewry St borders the western side of the centre and was once the city's Jewish quarter.

Information

In the Guildhall on Broadway, the TIC (☎ 840500, fax 850348, e tourism@ winchester.gov.uk) opens 10 am to 6 pm Monday to Saturday year-round; and 11 am to 2 pm on Sunday, June to September. It produces the excellent *Winchester Visitor's Guide*, which includes information on sights and places to stay and eat.

The main post office is on Middle Brook St and there is a smaller one on Kingsgate St near the college. You won't be able to miss the banks, ATMs and money changers on High St. There are public toilets in the park off Broadway.

Winchester Cathedral

Winchester's first church, the Old Minster, was built by King Kenwahl in AD 648. Its site, with subsequent enlargements, is

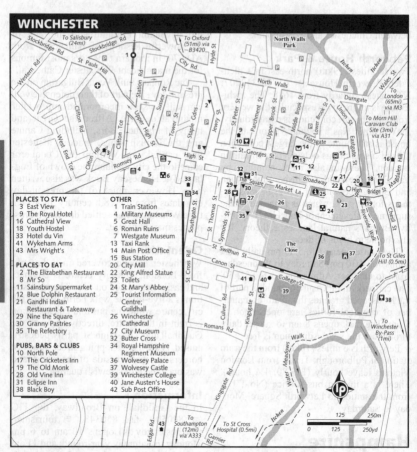

WINCHESTER

PLACES TO STAY
3 East View
9 The Royal Hotel
16 Cathedral View
18 Youth Hostel
33 Hotel du Vin
41 Wykeham Arms
43 Mrs Wright's

PLACES TO EAT
2 The Elizabethan Restaurant
8 Mr So
11 Sainsbury Supermarket
12 Blue Dolphin Restaurant
21 Gandhi Indian
    Restaurant & Takeaway
29 Nine the Square
30 Granny Pastries
35 The Refectory

PUBS, BARS & CLUBS
10 North Pole
17 The Cricketers Inn
19 The Old Monk
28 Old Vine Inn
31 Eclipse Inn
38 Black Boy

OTHER
1 Train Station
4 Military Museums
5 Great Hall
6 Roman Ruins
7 Westgate Museum
13 Taxi Rank
14 Main Post Office
15 Bus Station
20 City Mill
22 King Alfred Statue
23 Toilets
24 St Mary's Abbey
25 Tourist Information
    Centre;
    Guildhall
26 Winchester
    Cathedral
27 City Museum
32 Butter Cross
34 Royal Hampshire
    Regiment Museum
36 Wolvesey Palace
37 Wolvesey Castle
39 Winchester College
40 Jane Austen's House
42 Sub Post Office

marked out in the churchyard adjacent to the current Winchester Cathedral. Old Minster was supplanted by New Minster, where Alfred the Great (AD 871–99) was eventually interred after a short period in Old Minster. By around 1000, Old Minster was one of England's largest Saxon churches, but the Norman Conquest in 1066 brought sweeping changes and the foundations for a new cathedral were laid in 1079.

The New Minster was also demolished, around 1110. The completed cathedral was the longest in Britain at the time but it faced problems, in part due to the soggy ground

upon which its inadequate foundations were laid. In the 13th century the eastern end of the cathedral was extended in the Early English style to make the retrochoir, along with the central choir and presbytery. From the mid-14th century the Norman nave, suffering from severe subsidence, was completely rebuilt in the perpendicular style.

The Priory of St Swithun was demolished at the time of the dissolution of the monasteries. The cathedral also suffered some damage at the hands of Cromwell's armies during the Reformation. You can still see sword and axe marks on walls and statues and some stained-glass windows were replaced in the 19th century

Near the entrance, in the northern aisle is the **grave of Jane Austen**, who died a stone's throw from the cathedral in 1817. The transepts are the most original part of the cathedral. Note the early Norman rounded arches and painted wooden ceiling. The **Holy Sepulchre Chapel** has wall paintings dating from 1120 and 1240.

Crypt tours normally commence from the northern transept but are often suspended if the crypt is flooded. They take place at 10.30 am and 2.30 pm Monday to Saturday, Easter to September. You can get access to the first part of the crypt where a rather spooky modern sculpture is displayed.

The choir features amusingly carved wooden choir stalls, the work of William Lyngwode from 1307. The **pulpit** was provided by Prior Silkstede around 1520 and the carved folds of silk are a visual pun on his name!

At the end of the presbytery is the magnificent **Great Screen**, built around 1470. During the Reformation the figures in the screen were removed and broken up. The current figures are 1890 replacements,

which is how Queen Victoria (2nd level, 3rd row from right of minor figures) has managed to sneak in among the Saxon royalty. **Mortuary chests**, high up under the arches on both sides of the presbytery, contain the bones of Saxon royalty (including King Canute) and bishops.

The retrochoir has a number of **chantry chapels** – small chapels each devoted to one person. Note the unusual skeletal effigies of Bishop Gardiner and, on the other side of the cathedral, Bishop Fox. They wanted their images to be preserved like this to remind onlookers of their own human mortality and frailty.

The particularly original **Guardian Angels Chapel** has wall paintings dating from 1240. Twentieth-century reproductions of 16th-century paintings can be seen in the **Lady Chapel**, along with a modern sculpture of the *Pietà*. Just outside this chapel is a small bronze **statue** to the memory of William Walker, the diver who spent five years shoring up the submerged cathedral footings in the early 20th century. The **wavy floor** each side of the retrochoir is a reminder of the subsidence problems the cathedral faced.

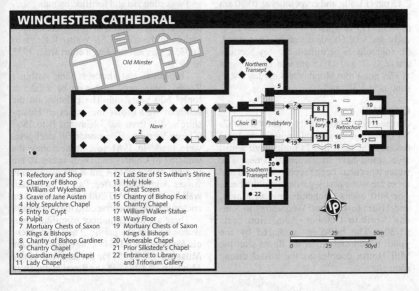

WINCHESTER CATHEDRAL

Old Minster

Northern Transept

Nave

Choir Presbytery Feretory Retrochoir

Southern Transept

1 Refectory and Shop
2 Chantry of Bishop William of Wykeham
3 Grave of Jane Austen
4 Holy Sepulchre Chapel
5 Entry to Crypt
6 Pulpit
7 Mortuary Chests of Saxon Kings & Bishops
8 Chantry of Bishop Gardiner
9 Chantry Chapel
10 Guardian Angels Chapel
11 Lady Chapel
12 Last Site of St Swithun's Shrine
13 Holy Hole
14 Great Screen
15 Chantry of Bishop Fox
16 Chantry Chapel
17 William Walker Statue
18 Wavy Floor
19 Mortuary Chests of Saxon Kings & Bishops
20 Venerable Chapel
21 Prior Silkstede's Chapel
22 Entrance to Library and Triforium Gallery

0   25   50m
0   25   50yd

In the middle of the retrochoir is the **last site of St Swithun's shrine**. From 1150 to 1476 St Swithun's shrine featured a **Holy Hole**, a tunnel beneath the shrine for keen pilgrims to crawl through. The entrance can still be seen.

In the southern transept, **Prior Silkstede's Chapel** has the grave of Izaak Walton (1593–1683) and a window dedicated to this patron saint of the pastime of fishing and author of *The Compleat Angler*. Note the comic faces in the carvings on either side of the **Venerable Chapel** entrance which may have been a little artistic licence by the wood workers. The south transept Library and Triforium Gallery house a display of cathedral treasures, including damaged figures from the Great Screen and the illuminated, 12th-century Winchester Bible. Opening hours are somewhat variable. Admission costs £1/50p. In the southern aisle of the nave is the **chantry of Bishop William of Wykeham**, founder of New College, Oxford, and of Winchester College.

Enthusiastic local volunteers run tours of the cathedral at 11 am and 2 pm daily except Sunday. There are tower tours on Wednesday at 2.15 pm, Saturday at 11.30 am and 2.15 pm (£1.50), and crypt tours at 10.30 am and 2 pm daily except Sunday. The cathedral (☎ 853137) is open 7.30 am to 6.30 pm daily, and a £2.50/50p donation is requested. Photography is permitted. Sunday services are at 8, 10 and 11.15 am and Evensong is at 3.30 pm. From Monday to Saturday Evensong is at 5.30 pm.

City Mill

On the river bank the City Mill (☎ 870057; NT), which once ground grain for the local bakers, was built in 1743, although a mill also stood here in medieval times. The water wheel has been recently restored and there are some pretty gardens out the back. The mill opens weekends only in March, and 11 am to 4.30 pm, Wednesday to Sunday April to October. Admission costs £1/50p. The building is shared by the youth hostel and when the doors shut the Mill House doubles as the hostel dining room.

Museums

The **City Museum** (☎ 863064) on The Square has interesting displays on Roman ruins on the top floor, a collection of Winchester shopfronts on the middle floor, and the story of Saxon and Norman Winchester on the ground floor. It opens 10 am to 5 pm, Monday to Saturday (closed from 1 to 2 pm on Saturday), and 2 to 5 pm on Sunday from April to September. The rest of the year it closes on Monday. Admission is free.

The **Westgate Museum** (☎ 869864), on High St, is in the old medieval gateway, at one time a debtors' prison. The displays include a macabre set of gibbeting irons, last used to display the body of an executed criminal in 1777. You can also see graffiti carved into the walls by prisoners. It opens 10 am to 5 pm (closed between 1 and 2 pm on Saturday), Monday to Saturday, and 2 to 5 pm Sunday, April to September. The rest of the year, apart from November to January when it's closed all week, it closes on Monday. Admission costs 30/20p.

The **Great Hall** (☎ 845610) was the only part of Winchester Castle that Oliver Cromwell did not destroy. The castle was begun by William the Conqueror in 1067 and was added to and fortified by many successive kings of England. It was the site of many dramatic moments in English history, including the trial of Sir Walter Raleigh in 1603. It was last used as a court from 1938 to 1978.

The Great Hall houses King Arthur's Round Table, now known to be a fake at 'only' 600 years old. The painting on the southern wall shows the names of Hampshire's MPs from 1283 (Edward I) to 1868 (Queen Victoria). The wonderful steel gates were made in 1981 to commemorate the wedding of Charles and Di. It opens 10 am to 5 pm daily and to 4 pm at the weekend in winter. Admission is free. Part of the **Roman wall** built around AD 200 can be seen in an enclosure near the entrance to the Great Hall.

There are also a number of military museums open to the public. The **Green Jackets Museum** (☎ 828549), the **Royal Hussars Museum** (☎ 828541), the **Light Infantry Museum** (☎ 828550), the **Royal Hampshire**

Regiment Museum (☎ 863658) and the Gurkha Museum (☎ 828536). Opening hours vary and admission prices range from free entry to £2.

Wolvesey Castle & Palace

Wolvesey Castle's (☎ 854766; EH) name, so the story goes, comes from a Saxon king's demand for an annual payment of 300 wolves' heads. Commenced in 1107, the castle was completed by Henry de Blois, grandson of William the Conqueror, over half a century later. In the medieval era it was the residence of the Bishop of Winchester. Apparently Queen Mary I and Philip of Spain had their wedding breakfast here. It was largely demolished in the 1680s and today the bishop lives in the adjacent Wolvesey Palace. The castle opens 10 am to 6 pm daily, April to November. Admission costs £1.80/90p.

Winchester College

Winchester College (☎ 621217), on College St, was founded in 1382 by Bishop Wykeham whose idea it was to educate 70 poor scholars and prepare them for a career in the church. Students are still known as Wykehamists. It was the model for the great public (meaning private) schools of England. The chapel and cloisters open to visitors 10 am to 1 pm and 2 to 5 pm (except Sunday morning). From April to September, one-hour guided tours leave at 11 am (except Sunday) and 2 and 3.15 pm (£2.50/2) from the Porter's Lodge in College St; there's no need to book.

Nearby on College St is Jane Austen's house. Well, it's referred to as her house, but it's just the place where she spent the last six weeks of her life.

St Cross Hospital

The Hospital of St Cross (☎ 851375), on St Cross Rd one mile south of the High St off Kingsgate Rd, was founded in 1132 by Henri du Blois to provide sustenance and a bed for pilgrims, the poor and the crusaders, who prayed and ate here before taking off to conquer the heathens. The hospital is the oldest charitable institution in the country

and is still home to 25 brothers and continues to provide alms. Within the complex you can see the church, the brethren hall, the kitchen and the master's garden. It opens 9.30 am to 5 pm, Monday to Saturday from April to October; from 10.30 am to 3.30 pm the rest of the year. Admission costs £2/50p, which entitles you to the Wayfarer's Dole (a crust of bread and horn of ale), sustenance doled out to any itinerant passer-by.

St Mary's Abbey

Although just a few relics in an enclosure off High St, this place has an interesting history. The nunnery was founded by Alfred the Great's wife in AD 903. In its heyday it was one of the foremost centres of learning in the country. It was rebuilt after the Norman conquests and lasted well into the 16th century, at which time it was demolished by Henry VIII.

Walks

From the Wolvesey Castle entrance the Water Meadows Walk goes for one mile to the Hospital of St Cross. The Riverside Walk runs from the castle along the bank of the River Itchen to High St. The half-mile walk up to St Giles Hill, the site of an Iron Age settlement, is rewarded by great views over the city.

There are also guided walks around Winchester's main sights at 11 am and 2.30 pm Monday to Saturday and 11.30 am on Sunday, May to September. From November to March they are on Saturday only at 11 am and in October and April at 2.30 pm Monday to Friday and 11 am and 2.30 pm on Saturday. Tours leave from the TIC and cost £3/50p.

If you prefer you can take the Phantasm Ghostwalk, which leaves from outside the cathedral at sunset each day and lasts for one hour. You'll need to book on ☎ 07990 876217.

Places to Stay

B&Bs in Winchester tend not to hang signs out the front. You'll have to get a list from the TIC.

Camping The *Morn Hill Caravan Club Site* (☎ 869877, *Morn Hill*) is 3 miles (5km) east of the city centre off the A31. There are tent sites for £2.50 plus £3.90 per person.

Hostels The *Youth Hostel* (☎ 853723, *City Mill, 1 Water Lane*) is in the beautiful 18th-century water mill. It's on the other side of the river from the mill entrance. The nightly cost is £8.80/5.95 for adults/under-18s. The dining room is actually part of the City Mill.

B&Bs & Hotels There are plenty of small B&Bs, most with only one or two rooms.

Cathedral View (☎ 863802, *9a Magdalen Hill*) is a friendly place with nice rooms, a lounge and a sunny breakfast room conservatory. It costs £30/40 for singles/doubles with shared bath and £40/50 for en suite. *Mrs Wright's* (☎ 855067, *56 St Cross Rd*) B&B is a five-minute walk from the centre and charges are £22/40.

East View (☎ 862986, *16 Clifton Hill*) is conveniently located and there are three small but comfortable rooms from £35/45. Each room has its own bathroom. The *Wykeham Arms* (☎ 853834, fax 854411, *75 Kingsgate St*), near the college, has some fine en-suite rooms from £70/80.

The Royal Hotel (☎ 840840, fax 841582, *St Peter St*) is right in the heart of the city, on a quiet side street. The interiors are lovely and there's an attractive garden. Rooms cost from £82.50/89.50 but they also have special weekend deals (not in summer) for two nights including dinner, bed and breakfast.

Hotel du Vin (☎ 841414, fax 842458, e *admin@winchester.hotelduvin.co.uk, Southgate St*) is very luxurious and rather decadent – each room has a minibar, VCR and CD player. Each room is sponsored by a different French winehouse, which is why room numbers have been replaced by names such as Courvoisier. Rooms cost from £90 to £125.

Places to Eat

There are several supermarkets in the centre of the town. The best is *Sainsbury's*, on Middle Brook St.

Granny Pastries (☎ 878370, *The Square*) is deservedly popular and the pies are to die for. Try a Thai green curry chicken pie or a Stilton and celery pasty. They also do huge baguettes with all kinds of exotic fillings for around £2.

The Refectory, near the entrance to the cathedral, is recommended. Sandwiches cost from £1.70 and a cream tea is £3.45.

Blue Dolphin Restaurant (☎ 853804) on Broadway does fish and chips for £3.10. *Gandhi Indian Restaurant & Takeaway* (☎ 863940, *163 High St*) is opposite the Guildhall. Chicken masala costs £5.25 and sag paneer costs £3.95.

Nine the Square (☎ 864004, *8 Great Minster St*) is a wine bar and elegant restaurant. There's excellent homemade pasta for around £6 and interesting dishes, such as roast guinea fowl with garlic and rosemary, for around £14.

Mr So (☎ 861234, *3 Jewry St*) specialises in Peking, Szechuan and Cantonese food and main courses cost from £6 to £7.50. *The Elizabethan Restaurant* (☎ 853566, *18 Jewry St*) is in a Tudor-style house dating from 1509. The menu is traditional English and French and a set three-course dinner costs £10.50.

The *Wykeham Arms* (see Places to Stay) looks authentically olde Englishe with school desks as tables and tankards hanging from the ceiling. This is an excellent place to eat, with restaurant dishes from £9 to £13 and a cheaper bar menu; no food is served on Sunday.

The bistro at the *Hotel du Vin* (see Places to Stay) has a very good reputation but will set you back about £13.50 for a main course such as roast cod with a pea pancake and sauce ravigote.

Pubs *Black Boy* (☎ 861754, *1 Wharf Hill*) is on the other side of the river and has the atmosphere of an art-house pub, if there is such a thing. Bookshelves line the wall and there is an outdoor terrace. A Sunday roast here costs £5.

The Cricketers Inn (☎ 862603, *Bridge St*) is dedicated to the game and no matter how hard you try not to talk about cricket, that's just the way the conservation seems to go in this place.

The Old Monk (☎ *855111, 1 High St)* has a pleasant outside seating area overlooking the river and the food is excellent.

Close to the City Museum there's the tiny but atmospheric *Eclipse Inn* (☎ *865676, The Square)* and the popular *Old Vine Inn* (☎ *854616, 8 Great Minster St)*. The *North Pole* (☎ *878315, 9a Parchment St)* is a small bar that's popular with students and has live music on Wednesday, Friday and Saturday evenings.

Getting There & Away

Winchester is 65 miles (105km) south-west of London and 15 miles (24km) north-east of Southampton.

Bus National Express (☎ 0870 580 8080) coach No 32 leaves every two hours from London Victoria via Heathrow (£7/9, 2 hours), and there are less frequent services to Oxford.

Solent Blue Line (☎ 023-8022 6235) bus No 47 runs from Southampton to Winchester (£2.05, 50 minutes) every 30 minutes, and hourly on Sunday. Bus No 29 runs hourly to Southampton (£2.35, 1½ hours). Stagecoach Hampshire (☎ 01256-359142) bus No 69 runs hourly (every two hours on Sunday) between Winchester and Portsmouth (£3.50, 1 hour 50 minutes). The No 68 service goes farther west to Salisbury (£3.50, 1½ hours) hourly (not on Sunday).

Train There are fast links with London Waterloo station and the south coast. Trains depart about every 15 minutes from London (£17.30, 1 hour), Southampton (£3.60, 18 minutes) and Portsmouth (£6.70, 1 hour). To get to Salisbury you'll need to change at Southampton; for Oxford change at Reading.

Getting Around

Your feet are the best form of transport. If you want a taxi try the stand outside Sainsbury's on Middle Brook St or phone Wintax Taxis on ☎ 854838 or 866208 or Wessex Cars on ☎ 853000.

There is plenty of day parking within a five-minute walk of the centre. The Park and Ride service costs £1.50.

PORTSMOUTH & SOUTHSEA
☎ 023 • pop 190,000

For much of British history, Portsmouth has been the home of the Royal Navy and it is littered with reminders that this was, for hundreds of years, a force that shaped the world. Portsmouth's major attractions are the historic ships in the Naval Heritage Area, but it is still a busy naval base and the sleek, grey killing machines of the 20th century are also here.

Largely due to bombing during WWII, the city is not a particularly attractive place but Old Portsmouth has some interesting spots, and the adjoining suburb of Southsea is a lively seaside resort.

Orientation

The bus station, Portsmouth Harbour train station and the passenger ferry terminal for the Isle of Wight are conveniently grouped together, a stone's throw from the Naval Heritage Area and the TIC. The quay here is known as The Hard.

Southsea, where the beaches are, as well as most of the accommodation and restaurants, is about 2 miles (3km) south of Portsmouth Harbour. Old Portsmouth is on the old harbour, known as the Camber, half a mile south of Portsmouth Harbour.

There is not really anything to see in the rest of Portsmouth, so most of your sightseeing and activities are likely to be concentrated along the water's edge.

Information

Tourist Office The TIC (☎ 9282 6722) on The Hard provides guided tours, an accommodation service and plenty of brochures. In summer the office opens 9.30 am to 5.45 pm daily. The main TIC office is at 102 Commercial Rd (☎ 9283 8382, fax 9273 0116, e tic@portsmouthcc.gov.uk) and in summer there is one next to the Sea Life Centre in Southsea (☎ 9283 2464, fax 9282 7519); both have the same opening times as the one on The Hard.

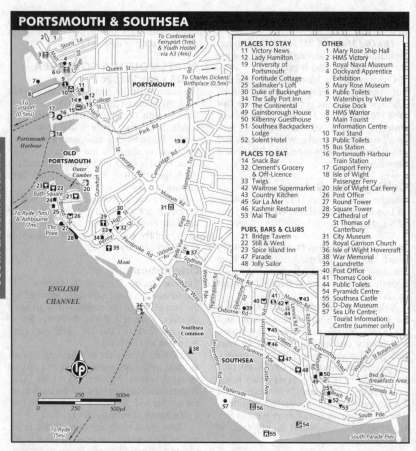

PORTSMOUTH & SOUTHSEA

PLACES TO STAY
11 Victory News
15 Lady Hamilton
19 University of Portsmouth
24 Fortitude Cottage
25 Sailmaker's Loft
30 Duke of Buckingham
34 The Sally Port Inn
37 The Continental
49 Gainsborough House
50 Kilbenny Guesthouse
51 Southsea Backpackers Lodge
52 Solent Hotel

PLACES TO EAT
14 Snack Bar
32 Clement's Grocery & Off-Licence
33 Twigs
42 Waitrose Supermarket
43 Country Kitchen
45 Sur La Mer
46 Kashmir Restaurant
53 Mai Thai

PUBS, BARS & CLUBS
21 Bridge Tavern
22 Still & West
23 Spice Island Inn
47 Parade
48 Jolly Sailor

OTHER
1 Mary Rose Ship Hall
2 HMS Victory
3 Royal Naval Museum
4 Dockyard Apprentice Exhibition
5 Mary Rose Museum
6 Public Toilets
7 Waterships by Water Cruise Dock
8 HMS Warrior
9 Main Tourist Information Centre
10 Taxi Stand
13 Public Toilets
15 Bus Station
16 Portsmouth Harbour Train Station
17 Gosport Ferry
18 Isle of Wight Passenger Ferry
20 Isle of Wight Car Ferry
26 Post Office
27 Round Tower
28 Square Tower
29 Cathedral of St Thomas of Canterbury
31 City Museum
35 Royal Garrison Church
36 Isle of Wight Hovercraft
38 War Memorial
39 Laundrette
40 Post Office
41 Thomas Cook
44 Public Toilets
54 Pyramids Centre
55 Southsea Castle
56 D-Day Museum
57 Sea Life Centre; Tourist Information Centre (summer only)

Money In Southsea you'll find Thomas Cook on Palmerston Rd, and there are various ATMs on Osborne Rd. In Portsmouth the banks and ATMs are concentrated along Commercial Rd, about 1½ miles (2.5km) east of the Hard.

Post & Communications There's a post office at 42 Broad St in Old Portsmouth and another in Southsea on Palmerston Rd. There is Internet access at Southsea Backpackers Lodge (see Places to Stay later) for £2.50 per 30 minutes. You don't have to be a guest to use it.

Laundry In Southsea there's a laundrette on Osborne Rd. There are no laundrettes near The Hard or Old Portsmouth.

Toilets You'll find public toilets in the Naval Heritage Area, next to the ticket office, and at the bus station on The Hard.

Flagship Portsmouth (Naval Heritage Area)

The Naval Heritage Area (☎ 9286 1512) has three classic ships and a few museums. Prepare yourself though – it's a very expensive day out. There are individual entry fees for each ship (around £6) or you can buy an All-Ships ticket for £11.90/8.90 that includes the three ships plus the Royal Naval Museum and the Mary Rose Museum. You don't have to see everything on the same day – the ticket is valid for two years. Maybe this is the Navy's way of making the cost of the tickets seem more justified – if you want to get your money's worth, you can come back the next day and do it all again. A Passport ticket (£14.90/10.90) includes all the above plus the Dockyard Apprentice exhibition and a Warships by Water cruise. Even though the Royal Naval Museum is very interesting, the real highlight is HMS Victory, so if money's a problem, we suggest you just pay for this tour.

The area opens 10 am to 5.30 pm daily, March to October, and 10 am to 5 pm from November to February.

The Ships HMS Victory was Lord Nelson's flagship at the Battle of Trafalgar in 1805. Nelson died on board during the battle. Commissioned in 1765, the Victory was already 40 years old at the time of its great battle. She carried 850 crew and her greatest speed was 16km/h. She was still afloat, though in tatty condition, when she was converted to a museum in 1922.

Exploring HMS Victory, and walking in the footsteps of Lord Nelson and his multicultural crew of ruffians and gentlemen, is about as close as you can get to time travel – an extraordinary experience. This is a popular tourist attraction, and entry is by 45-minute guided tour with a timed entry ticket. The tours are conducted at high speed although with considerable humour, and none of the gory details of life on the ship are left out. Astounding facts about life at sea will stay in your mind forever, such as the liquor ration of one gallon of beer and half a pint of rum per day. When you consider that the water ration was usually much less, you wonder how any of the crew survived the inevitable dehydration. There are lots of steep, narrow stairs to negotiate, and make sure you keep your head ducked. Photography is not allowed inside the ship. Admission costs £6.50.

Nearby are the carefully conserved remains of the Mary Rose. Built in 1509 under the orders of Henry VIII, the 700-tonne ship sank in shallow water off Portsmouth in 1545. There was much speculation about why she sank. At the time it was put down to 'human folly and bad luck'. Its time-capsule contents were raised to the surface in 1982, after 437 years underwater. Finds from the ship are displayed in the Mary Rose museum. Entry to the shiphall is £5.95.

Dating from 1860, and at the cutting edge of the technology of the time, HMS Warrior was a transition ship, as wood was forsaken for iron and sail for steam. The four decks of the ship illustrate life in the navy in the Victorian era. You are free to wander around at your leisure. Admission costs £5.95.

Royal Naval Museum Housed in five separate galleries, this huge museum has an extensive collection of ship models, dioramas of naval battles, exhibits on the history of the Royal Navy, medals and paintings. Audiovisual displays recreate the Battle of Trafalgar and one even lets you take command of a battleship – see if you can cure the scurvy and avoid mutiny and execution. One gallery is entirely devoted to Lord Nelson and, among many other things, there are personal items from his private ship quarters – life at sea must have been pretty tough for the officers who had their own wine coolers! Admission costs £6.50.

Mary Rose Museum This is an excellent museum where you can find out about the discovery of the Mary Rose and the successful salvage mission through exhibits, audiovisuals and great sound effects. It also recounts the failed salvage attempt made in the late 16th century by two hopeful Venetians and the massive underwater excavation mission of 1965. Considering the length of time the ship was at the bottom of the ocean, it's surprising just how many artefacts were recovered. A 15-minute film about the raising of the Mary Rose is shown every 30 minutes. Admission costs £5.95.

Dockyard Apprentice Exhibition This museum covers everything to do with ship-building, dockyard work and dockyard workers. Entry (not included with the All-Ships ticket) is £2.50.

Waterships by Water Cruise To be able to see all the ships, old and new, from a different angle you can take a 40-minute guided cruise around the harbour for £3.50/2. If you have a Passport ticket the cruise is included.

Old Portsmouth to Southsea

On a sunny day it's very pleasant to sit at **The Point**, beside the cobbled streets of Old Portsmouth, and sip a pint at one of the pubs while watching the car ferries and naval ships pass by.

Only fragments of the original 1180 **Cathedral of St Thomas of Canterbury** in Old Portsmouth remain. The nave and tower were rebuilt around 1690 and more additions and extensions were made in 1703 and between 1938 and 1939. Immediately south of Old Portsmouth is the **Round Tower**, originally built by Henry V, a stretch of old fort walls and the **Square Tower** of 1494.

Continue south to the ruins of the **Royal Garrison Church**, which started life in 1212, was closed in 1540, then restored between 1866 and 1868 before being damaged in a WWII air raid in 1941. A **moat** runs beside the waterfront and the Isle of Wight hovercraft slipway. Harbour cruises also operate from here and the anchor of HMS *Victory* is on display.

At the Southsea end of the waterfront there's a cluster of attractions, old and new, on Clarence Esplanade. The **Sea Life Centre** (☎ 9287 5222) has aquarium displays and opens 10 am to 5 pm daily (11 am to 3 pm in winter). Admission costs £5.50/ 3.50. Portsmouth was a major departure point for the Allied D-Day forces in 1944 and the **D-Day Museum** (☎ 9282 7261) recounts the story of the Normandy landing with the 83m Overlord Embroidery (inspired by the Bayeux Tapestry) and other exhibits. It opens 10 am to 5 pm daily. Admission costs £4.75/2.85.

Southsea Castle (☎ 9282 7261) was built by Henry VIII to protect the town against French invasion. It was altered in the early 19th century to accommodate more guns and soldiers, as well as a tunnel under the moat. It's said that Henry VIII watched the *Mary Rose* sink from the castle. It opens 10 am to 5.30 pm daily. Admission costs £2/1.20.

The **Pyramids Centre** (☎ 9279 9977) on Clarence Esplanade is a pool and waterslide complex. Opening times vary throughout the year, but it usually opens 10 am to 6 pm daily. **South Parade Pier** is a typical British seaside pier with amusements.

Other Things to See

The **Royal Navy Submarine Museum** (☎ 9252 9217) is across the water in Gosport (see Getting Around later). It opens 10 am to 5.30 pm daily, April to October, and to 4.30 pm November to March. Admission costs £3.75/2.50.

On Museum Rd is the **City Museum** (☎ 9282 7261) which tells the history of Portsmouth through audiovisual displays, reconstructions of various rooms in typical houses from the 17th century to the 1950s, and other exhibits. It opens 10 am to 5.30 pm. Admission is free.

Charles Dickens' Birthplace (☎ 9282 7261) is at 393 Old Commercial Rd. It's furnished in a style appropriate to 1812, the year of his birth, but the only genuine piece of Dickens' furniture is the couch on which he died in 1870! The house opens 10 am to 5.30 pm daily, April to October. Admission costs £2/1.20.

Places to Stay

The biggest concentration of cheap B&Bs is in Southsea, but the most pleasant area to stay in is The Point in Old Portsmouth. There are lovely views, a historical atmosphere and it's just a 10-minute walk to the ships. Unfortunately, rooms fill up quickly so book well ahead if you want to be sure of a room around here.

Hostels The *Youth Hostel* (☎ 9237 5661, fax 9221 4177, Wymering Manor, Old*

Wymering Lane, Cosham) is well to the north, about 4 miles (6km) from the main sights. The nightly cost is £8.80/5.95 for adults/under-18s. Local buses Nos 5 and 41 operate to Cosham from Southsea Parade Pier via Commercial Rd in Portsmouth while Stagecoach bus No 38 goes there from The Hard every hour.

Southsea Backpackers Lodge (☎ 9283 2495, 4 Florence Rd, Southsea) is far more convenient, and charges £10 for a bed in a dorm, £15 for singles and £22 to £25 for doubles. The owners are very friendly and have worked at making the place homy and comfortable.

University of Portsmouth (☎ 9284 3178) offers B&B-style accommodation in summer, overlooking Southsea Common, from £16.75 per person, or six-person flats at the Nuffield Centre, St Michael's Rd.

B&Bs & Hotels *Sailmaker's Loft (☎ 9282 3045, fax 9229 5961, 5 Bath Square)* is very tasteful and we can highly recommend it. The place is run by a retired merchant seaman who can tell you a lot about Portsmouth. He charges £20/22 per person for rooms with shared bathroom/en suite. There are great views across the harbour and one room has its own balcony.

Fortitude Cottage (☎ 9282 3748, 51 Broad St), around the corner, has en-suite rooms for £23 per person. *Duke of Buckingham (☎ 9282 7067, fax 9282 3397, 119 High St, Old Portsmouth)*, nearby, has very basic rooms for a reasonable £17.50/25.

The Sally Port Inn (☎ 9282 1860, fax 9282 1293, High St) is a well-run, 16th-century place with sloping floors. Rooms cost £37/55; there are no en-suite facilities but doubles have showers in the room.

Lady Hamilton (☎ 9287 0505, fax 9283 7366, 21 The Hard) is right by the bus station and Naval Heritage Area, and B&B costs £18/32 or £25/38 for en suite.

Victory News (☎ 9282 5158, 11 The Hard) is your cheapest bet. Rooms go for £14/24, although we were unable to check them to verify the standard.

The Continental (☎ 9282 2783, 2 Belle Vue Terrace) is between Southsea and Old Portsmouth, and a few minutes' walk from the beach. Singles cost from £18 to £25 and doubles from £30 to £36. It's basic but clean.

The main accommodation area is Southsea. Due to the competition prices tend to be very reasonable. It's best just to wander around checking vacancy signs, but there are a few we can recommend.

Gainsborough House (☎ 9282 2322, 9 Malvern Rd) is very good value at £17 per person (no en-suite facilities). *Kilbenny Guesthouse (☎ 9286 1347, 2 Malvern Rd)* is very similar in standard and costs £16/35 for clean, large rooms. En-suite facilities are a few pounds dearer. *Solent Hotel (☎ 9287 5566, 14–17 South Parade)* fronts onto Southsea Common and has rooms (some with sea views) for £25 to £50 per person.

Places to Eat

On High St in Old Portsmouth there's *Clement's Grocery & Off-Licence* and there's a *Waitrose* supermarket on Marmion Rd in Southsea.

The *snack bar* near the bus station on The Hard has tasty, greasy morsels from 80p. *Lady Hamilton* (see Places to Stay) is a large pub with roast lunch for £4.95.

Twigs (☎ 9282 8316, 39 High St) is a small coffee shop with sandwiches, baguettes and baps from £1.80 to £3.30.

Osborne Rd and Palmerston Rd are the main restaurant strips in Southsea.

Kashmir Restaurant (☎ 9282 2013, 91 Palmerston Rd) is relatively cheap and you can get a prawn vindaloo for £4.30, chicken tikka for £5.75 and chapati for 75p.

Sur La Mer (☎ 9287 6678, 69 Palmerston Rd) is a French bistro/cafe with snacks from £2.95 to £3.50 and main courses from £9.20 to £13. *Country Kitchen (☎ 9281 1425, 59a Marmion Rd)* is a wholefood restaurant, open during the day from Monday to Saturday. A two-course lunch with a soft drink costs £4.95.

Mai Thai (☎ 9273 2322, 27A Burgoyne Rd) is a good Thai restaurant, just off South Parade. A four-course meal is £11, chicken coconut curry costs £4.95.

Entertainment

Pubs On a warm summer's evening there can be no better place for a drink than outside the *Still & West* (☎ *9282 1567, 2 Bath Square*), or the *Spice Island Inn* (☎ *9287 0543, 65 Broad St*) at The Point. *Bridge Tavern* (☎ *9275 2992, 54 East St*), overlooking the Camber, is a real old salts' hangout and is also very popular.

Along Clarence Parade in Southsea there's a variety of discos, clubs and pubs such as the *Parade* (☎ *9282 4838*) and the *Jolly Sailor* (☎ *9282 6139*).

Getting There & Away

Portsmouth is 75 miles (120km) south-west of London and is well connected by rail and bus to the capital and the rest of the south-east and south-west.

Bus There are numerous National Express (☎ 0870 580 8080) coaches from London, some via Heathrow airport (£9/11 one way/day return, 2½ hours). There's also a daily service from Brighton (£6.75). One bus a day heads west as far as Penzance in Cornwall via Plymouth (£30 and £35 on Saturdays in July and August, 11 hours).

Stagecoach Coastline (☎ 01903-237661) bus No 700 runs between Brighton and The Hard in Portsmouth (£3.20, 3 hours 20 minutes) via Chichester every 30 minutes Monday to Saturday (hourly on Sunday). Stagecoach Hampshire (☎ 01256-359142) bus No 69 goes to Winchester hourly (every two hours on Sunday) and takes 1 hour 50 minutes (£3.50).

Train There are over 40 trains a day from London Victoria and Waterloo stations (£17.80, faster from Waterloo, 1½ hours). There are hourly services to Brighton (£11.70, 1 hour 20 minutes) and to Winchester (£6.70, 1 hour). There are three trains an hour to Chichester (£4.50, 25 minutes).

For the ships at Flagship Portsmouth get off at the final stop, Portsmouth Harbour.

Boat See the Isle of Wight section later in the chapter for information on getting to the island.

Condor Ferries (☎ 0845 345 2000) runs a car-and-passenger service from Portsmouth to Jersey and Guernsey but these trips are very expensive. It costs around £76/38 return for adults/children. Don't even consider taking your car. P&O Ferries (☎ 0870 242 4999) sail twice a week to Bilbao in Spain and daily to Cherbourg and Le Havre in France. Brittany Ferries (☎ 0870 901 2400) has overnight services to St Malo, Caen and Cherbourg in France. It has a Web site at www.brittanyferries .co.uk. The Continental Ferryport is on Wharf Rd, about a mile north of Flagship Portsmouth.

Getting Around

Local bus No 6 operates between Portsmouth Harbour bus station and South Parade Pier in Southsea. Bus No 17 or 6 will take you from the station to Old Portsmouth.

For a taxi try MPS Taxis on ☎ 9261 1111. Ferries shuttle back and forth between The Hard and Gosport (£1.10 return, bicycles travel free).

SOUTHAMPTON

☎ 023 • pop 216,031

Southampton developed as a major medieval trading centre with important connections to France and other European countries. When its trading role declined, the city took up a new life as an important shipbuilding centre (the *Titanic* sailed from here in 1912) and later as an aircraft manufacturing centre. These pursuits were its downfall in WWII when over two nights in late 1940 over 30,000 bombs rained down on the city.

Unfortunately, little remains of Southampton's medieval old town. For this reason, and the fact that the bulk of the new city is rather unattractive, Southampton doesn't attract a great number of tourists. However, recent developments, which include a huge waterfront shopping and entertainment complex, are attempting to raise the city's tourist quota. The impressive city walls still remain, however, and there is a signposted walk around the top of them. The **Tudor House** (☎ 8063 5904), on Bugle

St in the Old Town, dates from 1495 and across the way, on French St, is another timbered house known as the **Medieval Merchant's House** (☎ 8022 1503), which was originally built in 1290.

The TIC (☎ 8022 1106), on Civic Centre Rd (at the northern end of the pedestrian stretch of Above Bar St), opens 9 am to 5 pm, Monday to Saturday. Free guided walks of the old town take place on Sunday and bank holidays at 10.30 am; and at 10.30 am and 2.30 pm daily, late June to mid-September. Meet at the Bargate on High St.

Getting There & Away

Air Southampton International Airport has flights to Brussels, Paris, Zurich, Amsterdam, Dublin and major holiday resorts in Spain. Phone ☎ 8062 0021 for information on flights.

Bus National Express (☎ 0870 580 8080) coaches run to Southampton from London and Heathrow several times a day (£9, 2½ hours). Stagecoach bus No 700 runs between Portsmouth and Southampton. Solent Blue Line (☎ 8022 6235) bus Nos X34 and X35 run from Southampton to Lyndhurst (£2.60, 1½ hours) in the New Forest and on to Bournemouth (£4.10, 2 hours) every hour during the week and every two hours on Sunday. Bus Nos 47 and 29 run between Southampton and Winchester (£1.95, 40 minutes) every 30 minutes with reduced services on Sunday. Wilts & Dorset bus No 56/56A goes to all the main towns in the New Forest hourly (every two hours on Sunday). Explorer tickets are valid on these routes.

Train From London's Waterloo there are twice-hourly train services to Southampton Central (£20.30, 1 hour 20 minutes). Trains from Portsmouth run three times an hour (£6.20, 50 minutes). Trains for Bournemouth (£7.60, 30 minutes) and Winchester (£3.70, 17 minutes) leave about every 15 minutes.

Boat Red Funnel (☎ 8033 4010) ferries go to the Isle of Wight and there is a ferry service to Hythe in the New Forest (see Getting There & Away in the New Forest

section). Channel Hoppers (☎ 01481-728680, e info@channelhoppers.com) has a ferry service between Southampton and the Channel Islands and France.

NEW FOREST
☎ 023 • pop 160,456

The New Forest is not a national park, but it has been designated an area of Outstanding Natural Beauty. Outside the Highlands of Scotland this is the largest area of relatively natural vegetation in Britain. It's been that way since 1079 when William the Conqueror founded the area as a royal hunting ground.

The New Forest covers 145 sq miles, of which 105 sq miles is forest and heathland. The rest is occupied by villages and farmland. It's a pretty area to drive through, but even better when you get off the roads and onto the cycling and walking tracks.

Information

The Lyndhurst TIC (☎ 8068 9000, fax 8028 4404) is on High St, next to the main car park, and opens 10 am to 6 pm daily (to 5 pm November to February). It sells a wide variety of information on the New Forest including cycling maps ranging from £2 to £3.50, a map of the area showing walking tracks for £1.50, a more comprehensive Collins map for £5.99 and a free camping and caravanning guide. The Ordnance Survey (OS) map (No 22, £5.95) covers the area in greatest detail.

Places to Stay

You cannot simply camp anywhere, but there are a number of commercial camp sites detailed in a free brochure from the TIC.

There are numerous B&Bs in the New Forest towns, but we recommend you use Lyndhurst as a base. The Lyndhurst TIC makes free bookings. We can highly recommend *South View B&B* (☎ 8028 2224, Gosport Lane, Lyndhurst), with its friendly atmosphere and lovely dog, for £22 per person for B&B. *The Fox & Hounds* (☎ 8028 2098, 22 High St, Lyndhurst) is a 400-year-old coaching inn. Double rooms go for £50 per night, with breakfast. It's a nice place for a beer and a game of pool too.

New Forest Ponies

One of the first things you will notice as you travel into the New Forest is the ponies. While much of the rest of England was being fenced off and ploughed to grow crops and graze stock, the New Forest area remained relatively untouched due to the unsuitability of the soil for agriculture. The ponies were effectively forced into the area. Even though they are wild, each one of the 3000-odd ponies is owned by a commoner who has the right to graze their stock on the Open Forest. The Agisters, as these people are known, pay for grazing rights.

Visitors are requested not to feed the ponies; they are wild animals and feeding will attract them onto the roads. To protect the ponies, as well as cyclists and walkers, there is a 40-mph speed limit on unfenced roads. If you come across an injured pony phone Lyndhurst Police on ☎ 023-8028 2813 and state the location and, if possible, the registration number of any vehicle involved in an accident. You should try to stay with the animal (but don't touch it) to protect it from further injury.

Getting There & Away

Southampton and Bournemouth bracket the New Forest and there are regular bus services from both to New Forest towns. Wilts & Dorset (☎ 01202-673555) bus No 56/56A goes from Southampton to all the main towns in the New Forest hourly (every two hours on Sunday). Nos X34 and X35 go to Lyndhurst from Southampton (£2.60, 1½ hours) and on to Bournemouth hourly during the week and every two hours on Sunday.

Trains run every 30 minutes from London Waterloo station via Brockenhurst (£22.70, 1½ hours) to Bournemouth, Poole and Weymouth. There is a Brockenhurst–Lymington connection every 30 minutes known as the Lymington Flyer (£2, seven minutes).

White Horse Ferries (☎ 023-8084 0722) operates a service from Southampton to Hythe every 30 minutes (£3.60 return, 12 minutes).

Getting Around

The New Forest can be explored in a variety of ways.

Bus Busabout tickets offer unlimited travel on main bus lines for seven days and cost £19/10. The Solent Blue Line (☎ 023-8022 6235) X1 service goes through the New Forest taking the Bournemouth–Burley–Lyndhurst–Southampton route. Wilts & Dorset bus No 56 links Lyndhurst, Brockenhurst and Lymington.

Bicycle The New Forest is a great place to cycle and there are several rental shops. AA Bike Hire (☎ 023-8028 3349) is at Fern Glen, Gosport Lane in Lyndhurst, and charges £8/42 per day/week. The New Forest Cycle Experience (☎ 01590-624204), 2–4 Brookley Rd, Brockenhurst, charges £9.50/53.20. Rentabike in Brockenhurst (☎ 01590-681876) offers free local delivery from 8 am to 8 pm and charges £9 per day. You can pick up cycling route maps from TICs and bicycle shops.

Horseback This is a nice way to explore the New Forest but we're not talking about saddling up one of the wild ponies here. There are a couple of trail riding set-ups where you can arrange a one- or two-hour ride. Sandy Balls (honestly!) is at Godshill in Fordingbridge (☎ 01425-654114), and the Burley-Villa School of Riding (☎ 01425-610278) is off the B3058, just south of New Milton. Both places welcome beginners.

Beaulieu & National Motor Museum

If you go to the New Forest, a visit to Beaulieu (**bew**-lee) is a must. Beaulieu Abbey was another victim of Henry VIII's great monastic land grab in the mid-16th century. The king sold the 3200 hectare estate to the ancestors of the Montague family around 1538.

It is Lord Montague's collection of 250

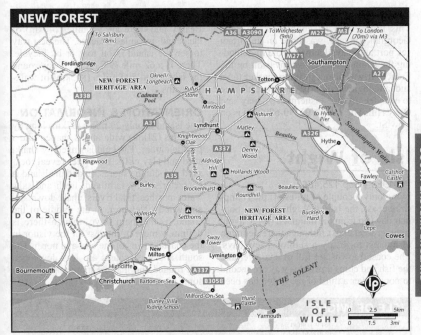

NEW FOREST

vehicles that makes the **Motor Museum** one of the biggest tourist attractions in the country. There are cars, motorbikes, buses, as well as number of land speed record-holders, like the jet-powered Bluebird that broke the land speed record (403 mph) in 1964. This is not just a place for rev heads.

The **Palace House** was once the abbey gatehouse and is an odd combination of 14th-century Gothic and 19th-century Scottish baronial architecture, as converted by Baron Montague in the 1860s. Unlike other manor houses you might visit, this place really feels like a home and therefore exudes a certain warmth. All through the house are family mementos – paintings, photos, furniture – accompanied by explanations of the history of the house and the family.

The **abbey** was founded in 1204 when King John gave the land to the Cistercian monks. It was one of the first buildings in England to incorporate Gothic pointed arches. In keeping with the Cistercian credo,

there are no elaborate decorative elements such as stained glass, and the interiors are austere and cold. There is an excellent exhibit on everyday life in the monastery, and a plaque in the courtyard tells us that the European resistance movement used the abbey as a training camp during WWII.

Beaulieu (☎ 01590-612345) opens 10 am to 6 pm daily, Easter to September, and to 5 pm the rest of the year, though the Palace House doesn't open until 11 am. Entry to the whole complex is expensive at £9.25/6.75, or £29.50 for a family of four, but it is definitely worth it.

Getting There & Away Stagecoach Hampshire (☎ 01256-359142) bus No 66/X66 runs to Beaulieu from Winchester via Lyndhurst. You can also get here from Southampton by taking a ferry to Hythe and catching bus No 112 or X9. Solent Blue Line buses run between all the major towns in the New Forest.

Lymington

This town, with its cobbled streets and Georgian cottages, was once an important sea port and played a major role in defending the south coast against invasion by the French. It was also a thriving market town and, although very touristy in parts, it's nice to wander around Fisherman's Quay and Quay Hill. The TIC (☎ 01590-689000) is on New St.

Isle of Wight

☎ 01983 • pop 125,466

Lying only a couple of miles off the Hampshire coast, the Isle of Wight makes a popular day trip from the mainland (try to avoid summer weekends), although there's enough of interest to justify a stay of a few days. The coastal towns are full of character and the fish and chips down this way are second to none. Over a third of the island has been designated an Area of Outstanding Natural Beauty and there are 25 miles (40km) of clean and unspoiled beaches. The best way to see the island is on foot or by bicycle. There is a 62 mile (99km) cycleway round the island and 500 miles (805km) of walking paths.

ORIENTATION & INFORMATION

The island is only 23 miles (37km) long by 13 miles (21km) wide and is shaped like a parallelogram. The land is ringed by chalk, sand and clay cliffs. Low tides reveal rock, sand and shingle shores. Inland the island is characterised by farmland, fresh and saltwater marshes, tidal rivers, chalk downland and woods. Newport, in the middle of the island, is the main town, though there is definitely more of interest for the visitor in the coastal towns of the east and north. The south and west coasts are less developed and rugged and may be more appealing to some visitors.

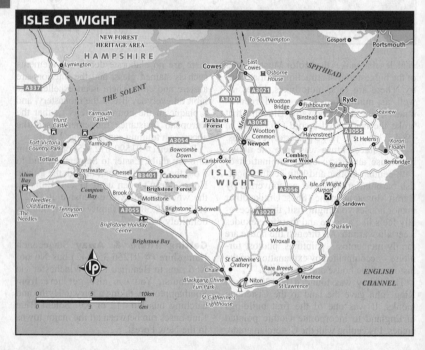

ISLE OF WIGHT

The merry-go-round of Brighton in summer: a heady mix of seediness and sophistication

The sylvan tranquility of the New Forest

Dover's lighthouse stands guard over the legendary white cliffs.

RICHARD I'ANSON

Brighton's Royal Pavilion at dusk: not to be mistaken for an over-the-top Indian restaurant

JON DAVISON

Indulging in sandwiches and champagne at the Royal Regatta, Henley-on-Thames

You can pick up the *Official Pocket Guide* to the island from TICs in most towns. There are numerous camping grounds and a brochure is available from TICs. There are various Web sites with information on the island – try www .wightonline.co.uk.

COWES

Located at the northern tip of the island, Cowes is a hilly, Georgian harbour town. This is a major yachting centre and the late-July/early-August Cowes Week is an important international yachting event. The TIC (☎ 913818, fax 280077) is at Fountain Quay and opens 9.30 am to 4.30 pm, Tuesday to Saturday.

Since its appearance in the film *Mrs Brown*, **Osborne House** (☎ 200022; EH) has become one of English Heritage's most visited attractions. The house was built between 1845 and 1851 and Queen Victoria died here in 1901. Osborne House has an antipodean connection: Victoria's Government House in Melbourne's Botanic Gardens is a copy, built in 1872. The house is in East Cowes, which is separated from the rest of the town by the River Medina, and linked by a chain ferry. It opens 10 am to 5 pm daily, mid-March to October. Admission costs £6.90/3.50. At other times it opens 10 am to 2.30 pm Sunday, Monday, Wednesday and Thursday for guided tours only (£5/3).

With its well-to-do yachting fraternity, Cowes attracts a number of wealthy tourists. As a result, accommodation is expensive, but there are some beautiful places to stay. *Rawlings Hotel* (☎ 297507, 30 Sun Hill) has a restaurant, bar and swimming pool. It has doubles only from £45, which goes up to £120 from June to August. A five-minute walk from the centre is *Villa Rothsay* (☎ 295178, fax 290352, Baring Rd), which was built in 1878 and is full of wood panelling and antiques. Luxurious double rooms cost £90.

RYDE

Victorian Ryde is the most important entry point to the island and the busiest of the resort towns. There is a TIC (☎ 562905) on Western Esplanade which opens 9.30 am to 4.30 pm Thursday to Monday.

At **St Cecilia's Abbey** on Appley Rise, you can hear Gregorian chants by Benedictine nuns every day during Mass at 9.15 am (10 am on Sunday).

A few doors down from the TIC is the *Seahaven Hotel* (☎ 563069, fax 563570, St Thomas St), which has sea views and charges £24/42 for clean, comfortable en-suite rooms. These rates go up a couple of pounds in July and August. Make sure you ask for a room at the front. *Georgian House* (☎ 563588, 22 George St) is clean and bright, if a little on the frilly side, and costs £19 per person.

AROUND RYDE

Quarr Abbey at Binstead, 2½ miles (4km) south-west of Ryde, was founded in 1132 and destroyed in 1536. A Benedictine monastery was built here in 1908.

Brading, 4 miles (6km) to the south of Ryde, has a Roman villa (☎ 406223) with fine mosaic floors. It opens 9.30 am to 5 pm, Monday to Saturday, and 10.30 am to 5 pm Sunday, April to September. Admission costs £2.50/1.25. The town also has two interesting old houses – Morton Manor and Nunwell House – and a wax museum (yes, there's a chamber of horrors).

About 5 miles (8km) from Ryde, at the easternmost tip of the island is **Bembridge**. There's a Shipwreck Centre & Maritime Museum (☎ 872223), open 10 am to 5 pm daily, April to October. Admission costs £2.50/1.35. The only windmill on the island (☎ 873945; NT), dating from 1700, can also be seen here. The three-storey windmill exhibits artefacts and opens 10 am to 5 pm (last entry 4.30 pm), Sunday to Friday, April to October, and daily in July and August. Admission costs £1.50/75p. A fine 5-mile coastal walk leads from Bembridge to Sandown.

For something different you might want to stay at the *Xoron Floatel* (☎ 874596, Embankment Rd) in Bembridge. This houseboat is surprisingly roomy and en-suite rooms cost £20 per person.

VENTNOR

Ventnor is a typical fishing town that doesn't try too hard, nor does it need to. There is a real peace here which is very appealing. One mile south of the town, off the A3055, is the **Rare Breeds Park** (☎ 852582) which is home to a large array of rare and not so rare farm animals, including llamas, African cattle and Falabella miniature horses. There's a petting zoo for kids and a coffee shop and it opens 10 am to 5.30 pm daily, late March to end of October. Admission costs £3.70/2.20 and free for under-fives. Bus Nos 7, 7a and 31 will get you there from Ryde or Ventnor.

We can highly recommend *The Spy Glass Inn* (☎ 855338), at the western end of the Esplanade, for somewhere to stay and eat. Decked out with all kinds of seafaring memorabilia, the place has an outdoor seating area with great views of the town and live music most nights. This is a really fun pub and the atmosphere is charged and friendly. Accommodation is in self-contained flats above the hotel and costs £50 for two people (no kids, no dogs).

SOUTH COAST

The south coast of the Isle of Wight, from Ventnor to Alum Bay, is the quietest stretch of the island circuit. The southern point of the island is marked by **St Catherine's Lighthouse**, which was built between 1837 and 1840 and usually opens to the public 1 to 6 pm, Monday to Saturday, Easter to mid-September.

Looking like a stone rocket, **St Catherine's Oratory** is a lighthouse dating from 1314 and marks the highest point on the island. It's perched on a hilltop overlooking **Blackgang Chine Fun Park** (☎ 730330), which opens 10 am to 5.30 pm daily, April to October (to 10.15 pm in July and August), and costs £5.95/4.95.

A great place to stay on the south coast is the **Brighstone Holiday Centre** (☎/fax 740244), which is on the A3055, 6 miles (10km) south-east of Freshwater. This caravan park/B&B, perched high on the cliffs overlooking the island's most stunning stretch of coastline, is also close to walking trails. Tents cost £5 per night, caravans are

£10, self-catering cabins cost from £126 per week for two people and B&B (continental breakfast) is £18 per person.

WEST WIGHT

Yarmouth Castle (☎ 760678; EH) was Henry VIII's last great fortress. Its facade dates from 1547 and there are a few paintings and photos of the island on display inside. It opens 10 am to 6 pm April to September and to 5 pm in October. Admission costs £2.10/1.10.

One mile west of Yarmouth, off the A3054, is **Fort Victoria Country Park**, which is home to an Aquarium, a Marine Museum, a Planetarium and the Sunken History Exhibition. Entry prices to each of these costs around £1.50/80p, though the exhibitions only just warrant a fee.

The **Needles**, at the western tip of the island, are three towering rocks that rise out of the sea to form the postcard symbol of the island. A lighthouse, topped by an ugly helicopter landing pad, stands at the end of the final rock. At one time there was another rock, a 37m-high spire, which really was needle-like, but it collapsed into the sea in 1764.

The road and bus service to this end of the island ends at **Alum Bay**, famed for its coloured sands. There's an unappealing melange of amusement park rides and souvenir shops here and a chairlift to take you down to the beach. From Alum Bay a walking path leads a mile (buses every hour, every 30 minutes in peak season) to the **Needles Old Battery** (☎ 754772; EH), a fort established in 1862 and used as a lookout during WWII. The fort directly overlooks the Needles and there's a 200 foot tunnel leading down the cliff to a searchlight lookout. The fort is open 10.30 am to 5 pm, Sunday to Thursday, April to October; daily during July and August; it costs £2.50/1.60.

Nearby **Brighstone** is a quaint village with rows of thatched cottages, cobbled streets and walks to Brighstone Forest. The **Tennyson Trail** runs from Carisbrooke near Newport, across Bowcombe Down, through Brighstone Forest to the Needles; Lord Tennyson, son of the poet, lived near here.

The only cheap place to stay around here is the *Totland Bay Youth Hostel* (☎ 752165, fax 756443, Hirst Hill), which charges £10/7 for adults/juniors.

GETTING THERE & AWAY

Wightlink (☎ 0870 582 7744) operates a passenger ferry from The Hard in Portsmouth to Ryde pier (15 minutes) and a car-and-passenger ferry (35 minutes) to Fishbourne. They run about every 30 minutes (£7.40 day return). Car fares start at about £38 for a day return. The passenger day return on the Wightlink car ferry between Lymington (in the New Forest) and Yarmouth is £7; for a car it's about £37. The trip takes 30 minutes and ferries run every 30 minutes. You can get more information from the Wightlink Web site at www.wightlink.co.uk.

Hovertravel (☎ 023-9281 1000) hovercrafts zoom back and forth between Southsea (near Portsmouth) and Ryde (£8.60 day return, 10 minutes).

Red Funnel (☎ 023-8033 4010) operates car ferries between Southampton and East Cowes (£7 day return, car from £46, 55 minutes) and high-speed passenger ferries between Southampton and West Cowes (£7, 10 minutes). Children travel for half-price on all these services.

GETTING AROUND
Bus & Train

Southern Vectis (☎ 827005) operates a comprehensive bus service around the island. It has an office in Cowes at 32 High St. Buses circumnavigate the island hourly, and run between the towns on the eastern side of the island about every 30 minutes. It costs £3 from Cowes to Ryde and £3.05 from Ryde to Ventnor. You can pick up a bus route map and timetable from the Southern Vectis office or from TICs. Trains run twice an hour from Ryde to Shanklin and the Isle of Wight Steam Railway branches off from this line at Havenstreet and goes to Wootton.

Rover Tickets give you unlimited use of buses and trains for £6.25 for a day, £9.95 for two days and £25.50 for a week.

Bicycle

Bicycles can be rented in most major towns on the island. Offshore Sports (☎ 290514), Birmingham Rd, Cowes charges £9 for the day, or £5 for four hours. You could hire here and drop off at their other store in Shanklin (☎ 866269), 19 Orchardleigh Rd. Wavells (☎ 760219), on The Square, Yarmouth, charges £12 for their newest bikes and £10 for older rental bikes.

Essex

Despite being one of England's largest counties, Essex lacks major sights. It boasts a long coastline, a number of seaside resorts and the oldest recorded town in England, but it doesn't attract the tourist numbers of other counties in the South-East. If you find yourself in Essex (which will happen if you arrive at Stansted airport or Harwich ferry terminal) you should certainly try to visit the medieval villages of Saffron Walden and Thaxted, and the countryside around Dedham, which inspired the painter Constable. If you want to explore a typical, tacky English seaside resort then head for Southend.

The good thing about Essex is that, compared with the rest of south-eastern England, it's very cheap.

SOUTHEND-ON-SEA
☎ 01702 • pop 172,300

Spreading itself along the Thames Estuary, Southend is not only the most popular seaside resort in Essex, it's also the county's largest town. At just under 50 miles (80km) east of central London, it's an appealing holiday spot for many of London's East Enders. It has the longest pleasure pier in the world and there's a major focus on entertainment, although this usually translates into funparks, amusement arcades, tattoo parlours and sleazy nightspots. Southend does have more cerebral attractions, however, and there's a busy program of plays and concerts throughout the year.

More recently Southend has taken on the task of housing many Eastern European refugees. What this means for the visitor is

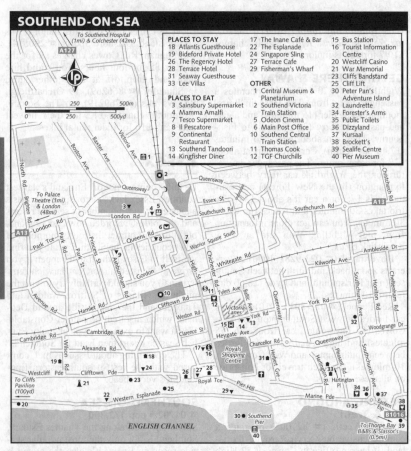

SOUTHEND-ON-SEA

PLACES TO STAY
18 Atlantis Guesthouse
19 Bideford Private Hotel
26 The Regency Hotel
28 Terrace Hotel
31 Seaway Guesthouse
33 Lee Villas

PLACES TO EAT
3 Sainsbury Supermarket
4 Mamma Amalfi
7 Tesco Supermarket
8 Il Pescatore
9 Continental Restaurant
13 Southend Tandoori
14 Kingfisher Diner

17 The Inane Café & Bar
22 The Esplanade
24 Singapore Sling
27 Terrace Cafe
29 Fisherman's Wharf

OTHER
1 Central Museum & Planetarium
2 Southend Victoria Train Station
5 Odeon Cinema
6 Main Post Office
10 Southend Central Train Station
11 Thomas Cook
12 TGF Churchills

15 Bus Station
16 Tourist Information Centre
20 Westcliff Casino
21 War Memorial
23 Cliffs Bandstand
25 Cliff Lift
30 Peter Pan's Adventure Island
32 Laundrette
34 Forester's Arms
35 Public Toilets
36 Dizzyland
37 Kursaal
38 Brockett's
39 Sealife Centre
40 Pier Museum

that a large number of guesthouses and some seafront hotels are now boarding houses so don't be surprised if you're turned away from a few places.

Orientation

Southend is large and spread out. The central shopping and business district is on and around High St. To the east of the pier is Marine Parade, which leads to Thorpe Bay where you'll find the quieter and cleaner stretches of sandy beach. Sitting atop the hill west of the pier is Westcliffe, the upmarket residential district with its Regency period homes and expensive though somewhat shabby hotels. When the tide goes out here it goes right out, leaving about half a mile of grey, sandy, mudflats around the pier.

Information

Tourist Office The TIC (☎ 215120, fax 431449, ✉ marketing@southend.gov.uk) is at 19 High St and opens 9.30 am to 5 pm Monday to Saturday and 11 am to 4 pm on Sunday in August.

Money You'll find ATMs on High St, and a Thomas Cook (☎ 573700) at No 92.

Post & Communications The main post office is on the corner of High St and Queens Rd. The only public Internet cafe in Southend had just closed at the time of writing so ask at the TIC if any new ones have opened up.

Bookshops All the major book store chains are on High St in the centre.

Laundry There's a laundrette at 87 Southchurch Ave, close to the Hartington Rd B&Bs but a bit of a walk from the centre.

Medical Services Southend Hospital (☎ 435555) Prittlewell Chase, Westcliffe is the place to go in the case of an accident. It's about a mile north-west of the centre, between the A13 and the A127.

Toilets There are public toilets on Marine Parade between the pier and the Sealife Centre.

Southend Pier

Not as exciting as Brighton's, but this is the longest pleasure pier in the world at 1.3 miles (2.1km). There are a couple of restaurants and a bar at the end. You can ride on the **Pier Railway** (£2/1), or walk if it's not too cold and windy. The pier opens 8 am to 5 pm (3 pm in winter), Monday to Friday; to 7 pm at the weekend (5 pm in winter). The **Pier Museum** (☎ 611214) opens 11 am to 5 pm at the weekend, Tuesday and Wednesday, May to October; admission is free.

Other Things to See

The **Central Museum & Planetarium** (☎ 215640) is on Victoria Ave, next to Southend Victoria train station. At the time of writing the museum was undergoing some expansion and reorganisation. It opens 10 am to 5 pm daily and the planetarium shows are at 11 am and 2 and 4 pm. The museum is free; the planetarium costs £2.25/1.60.

Victorian Lanes is an open market where stallholders sell antiques, bric-a-brac, shoes, clothes, flowers and food. It gets going at about 9.30 am and closes around 5 pm (4 pm in winter).

The **Sealife Centre** (☎ 462400) is an aquarium with everything from starfish to sharks. It's small and may not be exciting enough to warrant the £5.25/3.50 admission price. It opens 10.30 am to 3.30 pm Monday to Friday; 10 am to 5 pm at the weekend.

Places to Stay

There is no youth hostel in Southend but there are dozens of B&Bs. You ought to book ahead for summer weekends though. The cheaper B&Bs are concentrated along Hartington Place and Hartington Rd, which runs off Marine Parade, but the best value B&Bs are along the seafront in Thorpe Bay, about 1½ miles (2.5km) east of the pier.

Seaway Guesthouse (☎ 615901, 15 Herbert Grove) is clean, close to the centre and very good value at £15 per person. We recommend it before the Hartington Rd B&Bs, although it's not in a particularly interesting street. *Lee Villas (☎ 317214, 1–2 Hartington Place)* is the best choice of the cheap B&Bs around here at £15 per person.

The Regency Hotel (☎ 340747, 18 Royal Terrace) is very central and sits on the hill above the pier. It's run by an expat New Yorker with a passion for naval history. This friendly place has basic but large rooms from £20/35 for singles/doubles and £55 for the triple en suite. *The Terrace Hotel (☎ 348143, 8 Royal Terrace)* is very reasonable at £21/34 for nice rooms. En-suite facilities cost £30/40.

Atlantis Guesthouse (☎ 332538, fax 392736, 63 Alexandra Rd) is one of the newer places in town and is only a few minutes' walk from the station. Spacious rooms cost £25/40 or £25/50 with en-suite facilities.

Bideford Private Hotel (☎ 345007, 7 Wilson Rd) is one of the cheaper options, but it is a 15-minute walk to the centre and the pier. Rooms cost from £17.50/35 with shared bathroom.

Thorpe Bay Pebbles Guesthouse (☎/fax 582329, e *pebbles.guesthouse@virgin.net, 190 Eastern Esplanade)* is a tasteful, clean place at £35/50 for a single/double; £60 for the sea-view room with a balcony.

Beaches Hotel (☎ 586124, fax 588377) is similar with freshly decorated and tasteful rooms. Rooms cost £25/50. *The Moorings* (☎ 587575, fax 586791, 172 Eastern Esplanade) is a pleasant B&B on the way to Thorpe Bay and we can highly recommend it. Rooms are £30/42.50.

The Camelia Hotel (☎ 587917, fax 585704, 178 Eastern Esplanade) is an up-market place and clean, luxurious rooms all have satellite TV and phones. It charges £46/60, less for a stay of two nights or more.

Places to Eat

Southend has lots of cafes, fish and chip shops and Italian restaurants. You'll find most of these places in the sidestreets off High St and along the seafront. There is a *Sainsbury's* supermarket on London Rd and a *Tesco* supermarket on High St.

Fisherman's Wharf (☎ 346773, Western Esplanade) claims to have the best fish and chips in town, and they're not wrong. Huge fillets of juicy, delicate fish, chips, salad and a variety of condiments will cost you about £7. There's an extensive seafood menu and it's licensed.

Terrace Cafe (☎ 344158, 15 Royal Terrace) is a popular and reasonably priced cafe with an al fresco feel. Bagels and baguettes are £1.75, omelette and salad is £4.25, and fish and chips are £4.

The Inane Cafe & Bar (☎ 332889, 19 Alexandra Rd) is a brightly decorated place with snacks and pasta dishes for around £4.95. There's a wine bar downstairs.

Il Pescatore (☎ 341892, 4 Queens Rd) is a dimly lit Italian restaurant with pasta dishes for £6 and pizza from £4.95.

Continental Restaurant (☎ 330175, 75 Queens Rd) is a rather odd place, or maybe it's just that it's very old fashioned. The menu covers Spanish, Italian and German dishes and the lacy curtains and table clothes give the place a homy feel. Dishes are very good value at around £5, or £8 for steaks.

Mamma Amalfi (☎ 341353, 5–6 London Rd) is a modern, sophisticated Italian restaurant where Chardonnay is consumed in great quantities. The set two-course lunch is good value at £6.25.

Singapore Sling (☎ 431313, 12 Clifftown Parade) is a modern-looking restaurant and bar serving Chinese, Japanese, Malaysian and Thai food. Prices vary depending upon the cuisine, but most main courses are under £7.

The Esplanade (☎ 353180, Western Esplanade), below the bandstand, is a huge pub and bistro but it does manage to create a cosy and welcoming atmosphere.

Kingfisher Diner (☎ 610306, 34 York Rd) is a greasy spoon which serves good food at very good prices. Burgers are £2.40, fish and chips are £3.50 and kids meals are only £1.70.

Southend Tandoori (☎ 463182, 36 York Rd), next door, is an Indian restaurant with curries from £3.50 and Malayan prawns for £4.50. Their three-course lunch for £4.25 is amazing value.

Slassor's (☎ 614880, 145 Eastern Esplanade) has won various food awards and is very well known locally. It serves mainly seafood dishes in its maritime, gingham-decked surroundings. Starters cost from £2.95 to £5 and main courses are £8.50 to £11. BYO allowed.

Entertainment

Kids will probably want to go to *Adventure Island* (☎ 468023) on the foreshore on either side of the pier. It opens 11 am until late daily, Easter to mid-September. Admission is free but you pay for each ride. There's also *Dizzyland*, a funpark on the corner of Southchurch Ave and Eastern Esplanade. *Kursaal* (☎ 322322), across the road, is a rather disappointing amusement arcade with 10-pin bowling (£3.70 per game), bars and restaurants.

The *Odeon Cinema* (☎ 0870-505 0007) is on the corner of London Rd and High St. The huge and rather rowdy *TGF Churchills* (☎ 617866, Tylers Ave) has a number of different bars as well as a nightclub, but the place does feel a bit like a meatmarket. For night owls there's the rundown *Brockett's* (☎ 559137, Eastern Esplanade), opposite the Sealife Centre. DJs play mainly 50s, 60s and 70s music, and there's the occasional live act. *Forester's Arms* (☎ 467927, 65 Marine Parade), behind Dizzyland, with a DJ and jazz is the call of the day.

Cliffs Bandstand, on Clifftown Parade, has concerts from time to time. Phone ☎ 343605 for information or ask at the TIC. *Cliffs Pavilion (☎ 351135, Westcliffe Parade)* presents concerts, plays and musicals, as does the *Palace Theatre (☎ 342564, London Rd)*.

You can try your luck at the *Westcliff Casino (☎ 352919, Western Esplanade)*.

Getting There & Away

Southend is 50 miles (80km) east of London on the A127.

Bus Greenline (☎ 0870 608 7266) runs bus No 721 every 30 minutes from Bulleid Way Coach Stop, opposite London's Victoria Coach Station, to Southend but stops just about everywhere along the way (£4.50 day return, 2 hours 40 minutes).

Train There are several trains each hour from London Liverpool Street to Southend Victoria station (£10.30, 1 hour) and from London Fenchurch Street station to Southend Central station.

Getting Around

Distances are quite large in Southend and it's difficult to cover everything on foot.

Bus Local bus companies are Arriva (☎ 442444) and First Thamesway (☎ 01245-262828), which are both based at the bus station on York Rd. The Southend Day Rover ticket gives you unlimited travel in and around Southend on First Thamesway or First Eastern National Buses (☎ 01245-256159) for £2.75/1.80.

Taxi If you need a taxi try Southend Taxis (☎ 334455) or ARC Taxis (☎ 611611).

COLCHESTER
☎ 01206 • pop 142,000

Britain's oldest recorded town, Colchester was founded by the Roman emperor Claudius in AD 49. It was the capital of Roman Britain when London was just a minor trading post. It's a fairly interesting place with a castle, several museums and the remains of Roman walls, but a half-day is all you'll need to explore the sights.

Orientation & Information

There are two train stations – most services stop at North station, about half a mile north of the town centre. The bus station (☎ 282645) is in the centre of town, near the TIC and the castle.

The TIC (☎ 282920, fax 282924) is at 1 Queen St and opens 9.30 am to 6 pm Monday to Saturday; 10 am to 5 pm on Sundays and weekdays during winter. There are guided walking tours (£2.50/1.25) of the town at 11 am daily, June to September, but times may vary so phone first. You can also take an open-top bus tour mid-July to September for £4.95/2.95 (tickets available from the TIC).

There's a post office on North Hill and another on Longe Wyre St. Banks, ATMs and a Thomas Cook office can be found on Culver St West.

Things to See

Colchester Castle (☎ 282939) was built by William I on the foundations of a Roman fort. Construction began in 1076 and was completed in 1125. It boasts the largest castle keep in Europe – bigger than the keep at the Tower of London. During the 14th century it was used mainly as a prison. The museum contains Roman mosaics and statues. It opens 10 am to 5 pm Monday to Saturday (last admission 4.30 pm); 1 to 5 pm on Sunday. Admission costs £3.80/2.50. For another £1.20/70p you can take a guided tour of the Roman vaults, the Norman chapel on the roof and the top of the castle walls.

In Tymperleys – a magnificent, restored, 15th-century building – is the **Clock Museum**. It opens 10 am to 5 pm Tuesday to Saturday; admission is free. It's also interesting to walk around the **Dutch Quarter**, just north of the High St, established in the 16th century by Protestant refugee weavers from Holland.

The **Natural History Museum** (☎ 282931), on High St, opposite the Castle, was closed at the time of writing. When it opens again the hours should be 10 am to 5 pm, Tuesday to Saturday, and 1 to 5 pm on Sunday.

SOUTH-EASTERN ENGLAND

Places to Stay

Colchester doesn't have a great number of B&Bs, though there are plenty of reasonably priced small hotels.

Colchester Camping (☎ 545551) is on Cymberline Way in Lexden, a 30-minute walk from the city centre, or you can catch bus No 5 from the bus station (twice hourly). It's £6.90 for a tent and one person.

The Old Manse (☎ 545154, fax 545153, 15 Roman Rd), a few minutes' walk from the centre, offers comfortable accommodation for nonsmokers. It's in a quiet square beside Castle Park and part of the Roman wall is at the bottom of the garden. Singles/doubles with shared bathroom are £30/42.

Scheregate Hotel (☎ 573037, 36 Osborne St) offers adequate rooms right in the town centre. It costs £22/34, or £30/42 for en-suite facilities.

Peveril Hotel (☎ 574001, 51 North Hill) is also conveniently located on the road to the train station. There are 17 rooms, mostly without bathroom, from £25/36.

The *Rose & Crown Hotel* (☎ 866677, East St) is probably the best place to stay. There are 30 rooms – all doubles have bathrooms – from £62.50 to £99. There are cheaper deals for weekend stays.

Places to Eat

There are plenty of places to eat in Colchester, though fast-food places seem to outnumber just about anything else.

The Lemon Tree (☎ 767337, 48 St John's St) is very good value and has an enticing menu. Provencale potato salad with seared fillet of mackerel is only £3.95 as a starter. Vegetarians are well catered for here.

Picasso's (☎ 561080, 2 St John's St) must be the best value in town. It's a colourful and casual cafe with sandwiches from £1.70, burgers from £1.40 and hot main meals for around £4.

Akash (☎ 578791, 40 St Botolph's St) is an Indian restaurant recommended by locals. Lamb vindaloo costs £4.10 while their special balti chicken makhani is £7.95.

The *Foresters Arms* (☎ 542646, Castle Rd), off Roman Rd, is a nice old pub in a quiet part of town, behind the castle. It has seating outside in the warmer months.

Getting There & Away

Colchester is 62 miles (100km) north-east of London. There are daily National Express (☎ 0870 580 8080) coaches from London (£7.50/8.50 one way/day return). First Eastern National (☎ 0870 608 2608) bus No 103 goes to Harwich hourly (1 hour). There is no direct bus service to Colchester from Southend.

There are train services every 15 minutes or so from London Liverpool Street (£9.90, 55 minutes). There are hourly services north to Norwich (£15.50, 1 hour 10 minutes) and more frequent services to Ipswich (£3.70, 20 minutes).

HARWICH

☎ 01255 • pop 15,374

Although the old harbour is interesting, the only real reason to come here is to catch a ferry to Holland with Stena Line (☎ 0870 570 7070) or to Hamburg or Esbjerg (Denmark) with Scandinavian Seaways (☎ 0870 533 3000). See Sea in the Getting There & Away chapter. There are direct train services to Harwich from London Liverpool Street (£16.70, 1 hour 10 minutes).

DEDHAM VALE

'I love every stile and stump and lane...
these scenes made me a painter.'

John Constable

If Dedham Vale in the Stour Valley, near the border with Suffolk, looks strangely familiar it's because you've probably already seen the romantic, bucolic images on the canvases of early 19th-century painter, John Constable. Constable country, as the area is known, centres on the villages of Dedham, East Bergholt (in Suffolk; where the painter was born) and Flatford. The area is best explored by car but there are bus and train services around the area from Colchester.

Flatford Mill (not the original) was once owned by Constable's father, but is now owned by the National Trust and used as a

Field Studies Centre where you can take an art course (phone ☎ 01206-298283 for information). **Bridge Cottage** (☎ 01206-298260; NT) features in some Constable landscapes and houses a display about the famous painter. It opens 10 am to 5.30 pm daily, April to September; Tuesday, Thursday and Saturday in March and weekends only the rest of the year. Guided tours operate three times a day from May to September. Entry (with a tour) is £1.80/free. Willy Lott's House, of *Haywain* fame, is nearby. Willy was a neighbour and friend of Constable's.

First Eastern National (☎ 0870 608 2608) bus No 93 from Colchester operates every hour Monday to Saturday (three services only on Sunday) to East Bergholt, which is three-quarters of a mile from Bridge Cottage. It's better to come by train (get off at Manningtree), as you get a nice 1¾-mile (3km) walk along footpaths through Constable country. If you do find yourself in Manningtree, make a quick diversion and walk up the hill to the town of Mistly for a wonderful view over the estuary of the River Stour. These walks are well signposted.

SAFFRON WALDEN
☎ 01799 • pop 14,300

Saffron Walden was the biggest market town in the area from the 15th century until the first half of the 20th century. It is named after the saffron crocus which was cultivated in the surrounding fields. The town is a treasure trove for antique lovers. Try also to visit the nearby Tudor village of Thaxted. You can get there on First Eastern National (☎ 0870 608 2608) bus No 5, which stops on Church St in Saffron Walden.

The TIC (☎ 510444, fax 510445) is at 1 Market Place and sells a useful town trail leaflet as well as information on Thaxted. You can use the Internet (£1.25 for 15 minutes) at AS1 (☎ 528045) on Lime Tree Court in the centre.

The **Museum** (☎ 510333) has a wealth of material and is well worth a visit. It includes a very interesting exhibit on local history and has an eclectic collection of objects from all over the world, including a mummy from Thebes. It opens 10 am to 5 pm, Monday to Saturday and 2 to 5 pm Sunday. Admission costs £1/50p. The ruins of **Walden Castle Keep**, built around 1125, are next to the museum.

The church of **St Mary the Virgin**, off Museum St, dates mainly from between 1450 and 1525, when the town was at the height of its prosperity. It's one of the largest in the county and has some very impressive Gothic arches, decorative wooden ceilings and a 200-foot spire which was added in 1832. On the eastern side of the town is an ancient earthen **maze**; a path circles for almost a mile, taking you to the centre if you follow the right route.

Places to Stay & Eat
Most of the B&Bs are in tiny houses and have only one or two rooms but there aren't too many tourists and you shouldn't have any problems finding somewhere to stay.

Saffron Walden Youth Hostel (☎ 01799-523117), on the corner of Myddylton Place and Bridge St, is in the best-preserved 15th-century building in town. Beds are £9/6.20 for adults/under-18s.

The Sun Inn and the *Queen Elizabeth Inn* (☎ 520065 or 5214894, 23 Fairycroft Rd), where singles/doubles cost £20/38, is recommended. Rooms in The Sun Inn can be noisy on Friday and Saturday night until about 11 pm, due to the disco downstairs.

Mrs Skipper (☎ 527857, 53/55 Castle St) has two double rooms for £20 per person in her tiny house. *Archway Guesthouse* (☎ 501500, 11 Church St) is an odd place, with an unusual mix of decor and a huge collection of what can only be described as 'stuff'. The rooms are lovely and cost £30/50.

Dorringtons (☎ 522093, 9 Cross St) is a bakery and sandwich shop with delicious, fresh pastries. Sandwiches cost from 70p to £1.40. There are some lovely old pubs around town including the 16th-century *Eight Bells* (☎ 522790, 18 Bridge St), about three minutes' walk from the centre.

Getting There & Away
Stagecoach Cambus (☎ 01223-423554 or 717740) bus No 102 runs hourly between

Cambridge and Saffron Walden (£2.70, 1 hour). Biss Brothers (☎ 681155) commuter bus No 38 leaves London Victoria coach station at 5 pm each weekday, and comes back from Saffron Walden at 6.55 am (£7.35, 2 hours).

The nearest train station is Audley End, 2½ miles (4km) to the west. Trains leave from London Liverpool Street every 20 minutes (£10.70, 1 hour).

AUDLEY END HOUSE

Built in the early 17th century, this Jacobean mansion was used as a royal palace by Charles II, and was described by James I as 'too large for a king'. The 30 rooms on display house a fine collection of painting, silverware and furniture. It's set in a magnificent landscaped park, the handiwork of Capability Brown.

One mile west of Saffron Walden on the B1383, Audley End House (☎ 01799-522399; EH) opens 1 to 6 pm (last entry 5 pm), Wednesday to Sunday, April to September. The gardens open from 11 am. Admission costs £6.50/3.30. Audley End train station is 1¼ miles (2km) from the house. Stagecoach Cambus bus No 102 from Cambridge to Saffron Walden stops here.

Hertfordshire

The small county of Hertfordshire isn't the most exciting of places, with its mixture of commuter-belt housing estates in the south and rolling farmland in the north. The highlight of a visit is the predominantly Georgian town of St Albans, which dates back to Roman times and has a magnificent cathedral well worth seeing. About 6 miles (10km) east of St Albans is Hatfield House, one of Britain's most important stately homes and Hertfordshire's top attraction.

ST ALBANS

☎ 01727 • pop 120,700

Just 25 minutes by train from central London, the cathedral city of St Albans makes a pleasant day trip. To the Romans, St Albans was Verulamium, and their theatre and parts of the ancient wall can still be seen to the south-west of the city. There's also lots you can't see, buried under farmland on the outskirts of St Albans.

St Albans is an attractive and cheerful place with some beautiful old Georgian houses, although many of the buildings here actually date back to the 15th century. There are lots of antique shops and furniture crafters here and on Wednesday and Saturday mornings the market place in the centre of town really comes alive.

Orientation

St Peter's St, a 10-minute walk west of St Albans train station, is the focus of the town. The market place is next to the TIC building. The cathedral lies to the west, off High St, with the ruins of Verulamium even farther to the west, on St Michael's St. All the sights can be covered on foot, but you'll need at least a day.

Information

Tourist Office The TIC (☎ 864511, fax 863533, e tic@relaxion.co.uk) is in the grand Town Hall on Market Place and opens 9.30 am to 5.30 pm, Monday to Saturday, Easter to October; and 10.30 am to 4 pm on Sundays, July to mid-September. It opens 10 am to 4 pm, Monday to Saturday only November to Easter. It sells the useful *Discover St Albans* town trail (95p). The *Official Visitors Guide* is free and features a detailed town walk that covers all the sights. There are free guided walks of the town at 11.15 am on Sundays and 3 pm from Easter to September. Meet at the clocktower on High St.

Money All the major banks and ATMs are on Chequer St and St Peter's St, a stone's throw from the TIC. The Thomas Cook office is at 65 St Peter's St.

Post & Communications The main post office is on St Peter's St. There were no Internet cafes at the time of writing, but this situation may have changed so ask at the TIC.

Bookshops There is a Waterstone's bookshop at 10 Catherine St. Paton Books, at 34

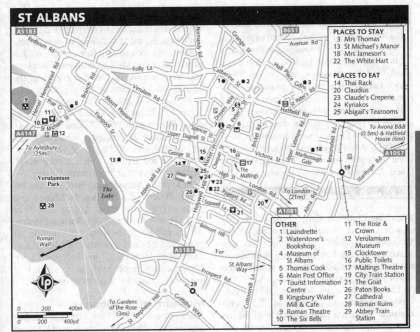

ST ALBANS

PLACES TO STAY
3 Mrs Thomas'
13 St Michael's Manor
18 Mrs Jameson's
22 The White Hart

PLACES TO EAT
14 Thai Rack
20 Claudius
23 Claude's Creperie
24 Kyriakos
25 Abigail's Tearooms

OTHER
1 Laundrette
2 Waterstone's Bookshop
3 Museum of St Albans
5 Thomas Cook
6 Main Post Office
7 Tourist Information Centre
8 Kingsbury Water Mill & Cafe
9 Roman Theatre
10 The Six Bells
11 The Rose & Crown
12 Verulamium Museum
15 Clocktower
16 Public Toilets
17 Maltings Theatre
19 City Train Station
21 The Goat
26 Paton Books
27 Cathedral
28 Roman Ruins
29 Abbey Train Station

Holywell Hill, is in a lovely 17th-century building and stocks new and second-hand books as well as some rare and out-of-print titles.

Laundry There's a laundrette at 13 Catherine St.

Toilets There are public toilets next to the Maltings Theatre, off Chequer St in the centre, and some more at the Verulamium Museum off St Michael's St.

St Albans Cathedral

In AD 209, a Roman citizen named Alban was beheaded for his Christian beliefs, becoming Britain's first Christian martyr. In the 8th century, King Offa of Mercia founded an abbey for the Benedictine monks on the site of his martyrdom. The first Norman abbot, Paul, rebuilt the church in 1077, incorporating parts of the Saxon building. You can see remnants of a **Saxon archway** in the southern

aisle alongside the presbytery. Many Roman bricks were also used and they sit conspicuously in the central tower. Considerable restoration took place in 1877.

As you enter the cathedral (☎ 860780) you will notice the **murals** that decorate the Norman columns. They were painted by monks in the 13th century. One mural depicts Thomas à Becket (southern side of the first two pillars) and above him is St Christopher. These paintings were hidden by whitewash after the Reformation and were not rediscovered until 1862.

The painted wooden panels of the **choir ceiling** date from the 15th century. The **tower ceiling** is decorated with the red and white roses of the houses of Lancaster and York. The **altar screen** is mainly 16th century, although some statues were added in the 19th century.

In the heart of the cathedral is **St Alban's shrine**, immediately behind the presbytery and overlooked by a beautifully carved oak

The Alban Way

The Alban Way is a 6½-mile (10km) path running from St Albans to Hatfield (where you can visit the Jacobean Hatfield House). It is suitable for both walkers and cyclists. The path follows the route of an old railway line that opened in 1865, but was closed in 1951 after roads in the area were improved and buses became the preferred mode of transport between the two towns. A pamphlet entitled *The Alban Way* is available for free from the TIC in St Albans. It includes a map and details all there is to see along the way.

Watching Chamber, dating from 1400. This is where monks would stand guard to ensure pilgrims didn't pilfer relics. As you leave the shrine, turn to your left to see an ancient **marble slab** embedded with marine fossils which was once an altarpiece.

The cathedral opens 9 am to 5.45 pm. Admission is free but a donation of £2.50 is requested. There are guided tours at 11.30 am and 2.30 pm. In the southern aisle you can watch an audiovisual account of the cathedral's history. There are screenings from 11 am to 4 pm, Monday to Friday, with the last showing at 3.30 pm on Saturday (2 to 5 pm on Sunday). The cost is £1.50/1.

Verulamium Museum & Roman Ruins

Britain's best museum (☎ 819339) of everyday life under the Romans, in St Michael's St, displays wonderful mosaic pavements and murals. There are lots of interactive displays, audiovisuals and re-creations of how rooms would have looked in a Roman house. Displays include models of craftsmen working and women cooking. You can even hear the citizens of Verulamium talking about their lives. Kids will love it. The museum opens 10 am to 5.30 pm daily (2 to 5.30 pm on Sunday). Tickets are £3.05/1.75 and allow you a return visit on the same day. You can take a free guided walk of the city of Verulamium, that is, of the area on which it once stood, from the museum at 3 pm every Sunday.

In adjacent **Verulamium Park** you can inspect remains of a basilica, bathhouse and parts of the city wall. Across the busy A4174 are the remains of a **Roman theatre**, which appear to be just a collection of grassy ditches and mounds and a few ruins. They open 10 am to 5 pm daily for £1.50/50p, but they're probably only worth it if you're seriously keen on the Romans.

Museum of St Albans

The museum (☎ 819340), Hatfield Rd, begins with an exhibition of tools used between 1700 and 1950 by English tradesmen – coopers, wheelwrights, blacksmiths, lumberjacks and cabinet makers. It gives a rundown of the city's market and trade history and has good displays of Victorian memorabilia. It opens 10 am to 5 pm, Monday to Saturday and 2 to 5 pm on Sunday. Admission is free.

Other Things to See

The medieval **clocktower** on High St was

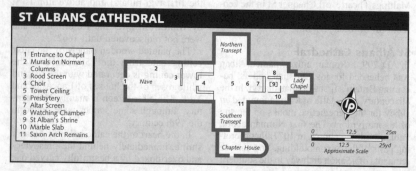

ST ALBANS CATHEDRAL

1 Entrance to Chapel
2 Murals on Norman Columns
3 Rood Screen
4 Choir
5 Tower Ceiling
6 Presbytery
7 Altar Screen
8 Watching Chamber
9 St Alban's Shrine
10 Marble Slab
11 Saxon Arch Remains

Northern Transept

Nave

Lady Chapel

Southern Transept

Chapter House

Approximate Scale

built between 1403 and 1412. It's the only medieval belfry in England and the original bell is still there. You can climb to the top for great views over the town between 10.30 am and 5 pm at the weekend and bank holidays Easter to October.

The **Kingsbury Water Mill**, St Michael's St, was used for milling grain until 1936. It dates back to Saxon times, but the current mill buildings are actually Elizabethan with a Georgian facade. There is a small museum here and a lovely coffee shop with home-cooking and outdoor seating. It opens 11 am to 6 pm, Tuesday to Saturday, and noon to 6 pm on Sunday (5 pm in winter). Admission costs £1.10/60p.

With about 30,000 specimens, the **Gardens of the Rose** (☎ 850461), 3 miles (5km) south of St Albans, contain the world's largest rose collection. They open 9 am to 5 pm, Monday to Saturday, mid-June to mid-October. Admission is £4/free.

Places to Stay

The following are within a five-minute walk of the centre.

Mrs Jameson's (☎ 865498, fax 854136, 7 Marlborough Gate), off Upper Latimore Rd, is convenient to the train station and charges £18 per person for rooms with shared bathroom.

Mrs Thomas' (☎ 858939, 8 Hall Place Gardens) is highly recommended. Lovely singles/doubles with garden views are £25/40 with shared bathroom.

Avona (☎ 842216, fax 07956 857353, 478 Hatfield Rd) is good value at £20/40 or £50 for the double room with en suite. It's a 10-minute walk from the centre.

The White Hart (☎ 853624, fax 840237, 25 Holywell Hill), a half-timbered hotel with exposed beams and creaky floors, is just a couple of minutes' walk from the centre of town. En-suite rooms cost £54/70 (cheaper at the weekend) and breakfast is £5 extra.

St Michael's Manor (☎ 864444, fax 848909, e smmanor@globalnet.co.uk, Fishpool St) is St Albans' best. It's peaceful and elegant with beautiful gardens. Rooms start at £110/145 and go up to £225/295.

St Albans Beer Festival

Each year in late September or early October, the South Hertfordshire branch of CAMRA (Campaign for Real Ale) holds a four-day beer festival at the Civic Centre in St Peter's St. Around 4000 people attend the event whose purpose is to support the smaller local breweries and increase the appreciation of traditional beers and ciders as part of the national culture. About 180 ales, brewed locally and farther afield in the UK and overseas, are on show. Some beers are specially brewed for the festival. Food is available and in the evenings there is usually some musical entertainment. Depending on the day you go, tickets range from free to £3. For more information contact CAMRA on ☎ 01727-867201 or e realales@ yahoo.com.

Weekend deals, including dinner and champagne, are available.

Places to Eat

St Albans has no shortage of places to eat, and they all offer pretty good grub at reasonable prices.

Abigail's Tearooms (☎ 856939, 7 High St), with its lacy curtains and cream teas, is in the Village Arcade. *Claudius* (☎ 850527, 116 London Rd) is a fun Italian restaurant that is cluttered with the owner's football memorabilia collection. Ask him to show you one of his card tricks. Meals are simple and delicious and cost around £6.

Kyriakos (☎ 832841, 3 Holywell Hill) is an atmospheric Greek restaurant with starters from £3 and main courses from £8.95.

Claude's Creperie (☎ 846424, 15 Holywell Hill), with its rustic interior, has a huge menu combining French and Italian regional cooking. Main courses are £6 to £8.50.

Thai Rack (☎ 850055, 13 George St) has a peaceful, leafy interior and the three-course lunch costs £9.50. A la carte main courses are around £6.20.

The Goat (☎ 833934, 37 Sopwell Lane) is a nice old pub in a Tudor-style building. It's just a few minutes' walk from the

Wendover Woods

About a mile north-east of the town of Wendover (off the B4009) are the Wendover Woods (☎ 01296-625825 for the Forest Ranger), 325 hectares of beech and conifer forest lining the northern edge of the Chiltern hills. There are a number of walks you can do, ranging from the ½-mile walk to the top of Coombe Hill, the highest point in the Chilterns at 260m, to the 2-mile (3km) Firecrest Trail. There are cycling routes and bridleways but if you don't want to be too active you can just come to this peaceful spot for a picnic. The TIC (☎ 01296-696759) in the clocktower, High St, Wendover, has information on the Chilterns, the Ridgeway Path and the Wendover Woods. You can pick up a walking map from the information stand at the woods themselves.

Aylesbury Bus No 54 goes to Wendover every 30 minutes (15 minutes). There are half-hourly train services to Wendover from London Marylebone (£7.30, 45 minutes).

centre and there's live jazz on Sunday from 12.30 to 3 pm. *The Rose & Crown* (☎ 851903, 10 St Michaels St) and, a little farther along, *The Six Bells* (☎ 856945, 16–18 St Michaels St) are both popular and cosy pubs with exposed beams, low ceilings and open fireplaces. Both offer traditional pub grub as well as more modern fare.

Getting There & Away
Rail is the most direct way to get to St Albans, although if you are coming from Heathrow you can catch Greenline (☎ 0870 608 7266) bus No 724 which leaves hourly (£4.20, 1 hour).

St Albans City station is on Stanhope Rd, a 10-minute walk east of St Peter's St. Thameslink trains depart every 15 minutes from London Kings Cross to St Albans City station (£6.20, 23 minutes). St Albans Abbey station (for trains to Watford) is a 15-minute (uphill) walk to the centre. For this station you'll need to change trains at Watford, 6 miles (10km) south of St Albans.

HATFIELD HOUSE
Hatfield House (☎ 01707-262823) is England's most impressive Jacobean house. This red-brick and stone mansion, built between 1607 and 1611 for Robert Cecil, 1st Earl of Salisbury and secretary of state to both Elizabeth I and James I, is full of treasures. It was modelled on an earlier Tudor palace, built around 1497, where Elizabeth I spent much of her childhood. Only one wing of the Royal Palace survives and it can be seen in the gardens.

Inside, the house is extremely grand with a wonderful Marble Hall and famous portraits of Elizabeth and numerous English kings. The oak Grand Staircase is decorated with carved figures, including one of John Tradescant, the 17th-century botanist responsible for the gardens.

Five-course Elizabethan banquets, complete with minstrels and court jesters, are held in the great hall at 7.45 pm on Tuesday (£31.50 per head), Friday (£33) and Saturday (£35.50). Phone ☎ 01707-262055 to book tickets.

It opens 1 to 4 pm at the weekend and bank holidays; noon to 4 pm Tuesday to Thursday for guided tours only. Admission is £6.20/3.10; for the park only it's £1.80/90p. Hatfield House is 21 miles (34km) from London and 6 miles (10km) from St Albans. It's opposite Hatfield train station, and there are numerous trains from London King's Cross station (£6.30 day return, 25 minutes). Greenline Bus (☎ 0870 608 7266) No 797 runs from London to Hatfield hourly and Greenline bus (☎ 0870 608 7266) No 724 runs between St Albans and Hatfield every hour.

Buckinghamshire

Buckinghamshire is uneventful commuter country, a pleasant mix of urban and rural landscapes. Among the many commuters drawn here were the influential Rothschilds, who constructed several impressive houses around Aylesbury. Other well-known figures who have lived in Buckinghamshire include the poets John Milton, TS Eliot and Shelley (Marlow), and Robert Frost (Beaconsfield).

Stretching across the south of Buckinghamshire, the Chilterns are a range of chalk hills famous for their beech woods. The countryside is particularly attractive in autumn.

The 85-mile (137km) Ridgeway path follows the Chiltern hills to Ivinghoe Beacon in the east of the county. There are forest trails in the Chilterns and along the Grand Union Canal, which cuts across the county's north-eastern edge on its way from London to Birmingham.

AYLESBURY
☎ 01296 • pop 51,497

Affluent Aylesbury has been the county town since 1725. Yet apart from being a transport hub with half-hourly trains to/from London Marylebone (£8.60, 54 minutes), it has little to offer visitors. However, the TIC (☎ 330559), 8 Bourbon St, can provide general information on the county.

AROUND AYLESBURY
Waddesdon Manor

Designed by a French architect for Baron Ferdinand de Rothschild, Waddesdon Manor (☎ 01296-651282; NT) was completed in 1889 in French Renaissance style to house the baron's art collection, Sèvres porcelain and French furniture. There are a number of paintings by Gainsborough and Reynolds as well as some by 17th-century Dutch masters. The family's wine cellar is open for viewing but unfortunately tastings are out of the question. An aviary houses a collection of exotic birds.

It opens 11 am to 4 pm, Thursday to Sunday, April to October; also on Wednesday in July and August. Entry is by timed ticket and costs £6. You can book in advance but must pay a £2.50 booking fee. The grounds open 10 am to 5 pm, Wednesday to Sunday, March to mid-December. Admission to the grounds costs £3/1.50.

The chateau is 6 miles (10km) north-west of Aylesbury. From Aylesbury bus station, take Red Rose bus No 16 or 17.

Claydon House

The decoration of Claydon's grand rooms is said to be England's finest example of the light, decorative rococo style that developed from the more ponderous Baroque in early-18th-century France. Florence Nightingale lived here for several years and a museum houses mementos of her Crimean stay. Some scenes from the 1995 film *Emma* with Gwyneth Paltrow were filmed here.

Claydon House (☎ 01296-730349; NT) opens 1 to 5 pm, Saturday to Wednesday from April to October. Admission costs £4.20. It's 13 miles (21km) north-west of Aylesbury and Red Rose bus Nos 16 and 17 can take you there, but you'll need to tell the driver.

Stowe Landscape Gardens

About 4 miles (6km) north of the pleasant county town of Buckingham, Stowe is the sort of private school so exclusive its driveway is half a mile long. The greatest British landscape gardeners, Charles Bridgeman, William Kent and Capability Brown, all worked on the grounds.

The Georgian gardens (☎ 01280-822850; NT) cover about 400 hectares. They are known for their 32 temples, created in the 18th century by the wealthy owner Sir Richard Temple, whose family motto was *Templa Quam Delecta* (How Delightful are your Temples). There are also arches, lakes and a Palladian bridge.

The gardens open to the public 10 am to 5 pm (last entry 4 pm), Wednesday to Sunday, April to October; closed Monday in July and August. Admission costs £4.60/ 2.30. There are no buses that go past the gardens. It's a 3-mile (5km) walk or a £6 taxi ride from the nearby town of Buckingham, which is one hour from Aylesbury and can be reached on Arriva bus No 66.

Wessex

Together the counties of Somerset, Dorset and Wiltshire form the historic kingdom of Wessex, long vanished into history but given fresh form by the pen of Thomas Hardy, the region's best-known son.

Nowhere have the footprints of the past left such an enduring mark on the landscape as in Wessex. Some truly great monuments fly the flag for English civilisation: the Stone Age left Stonehenge and spellbinding Avebury; Iron Age Britons created Maiden Castle, just outside Dorchester; the Romans (and later the Georgians) developed Bath; the legendary King Arthur is supposedly buried at Glastonbury; the Middle Ages left the great cathedrals at Salisbury and Wells; and the 16th- and 17th-century landed gentry left great houses like Montacute and Wilton.

The west is densely packed with things to see and the countryside, though varied, is a classic English patchwork of hedgerows, stone churches, thatched cottages, great estates and emerald green fields. Lacock in Wiltshire, Dunster in Somerset and Corfe Castle in Dorset are all perfect little villages that look to have stepped out of a film set.

Towns such as Bath and Salisbury are honey-pot tourist attractions on every first-time visitor's hit list. Bristol is often overlooked by visitors in a hurry to explore Bath, but the biggest city in the south-west has excellent nightlife and, in the suburb of Clifton, has architecture to rival anywhere. The charms of Dorset, Somerset and North Devon are more low-key and you can happily wander around without too many plans and without stumbling over too many people, but the beauty of Exmoor National Park draws the crowds in summertime.

Walkers make for the South West Coast Path, a long-distance walk that follows the coastline from Minehead in Somerset, around the Cornish peninsula, to Poole, near Bournemouth in Dorset, giving spectacular access to some of the best and most untouched sections of England's coastline.

Highlights

- Strolling the streets of Georgian Bath
- Exploring the mysteries of Avebury and Stonehenge
- Pausing for thought in the wonderful Wells Cathedral
- Pubbing & clubbing 'till the wee hours in Bristol
- Snapping pretty Lacock, home of photography
- Walking the pony-dotted wilds of Exmoor

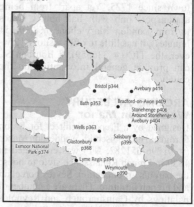

ORIENTATION & INFORMATION

From the windswept beauty of Exmoor and the Somerset cliffs, across the blustery plains of Wiltshire to England's green and pleasant landscape in slumbering Dorset, Wessex is a region of dramatic scenery and pleasant towns. The chalk downs centred on Salisbury Plain run across Wiltshire and down through central Dorset to the coast. Granitic Exmoor dominates the Somerset landscape.

There are several YHA youth hostels in Exmoor National Park, as well as popular ones in Salisbury, Bath and Bristol, and several along the coast, for example, in

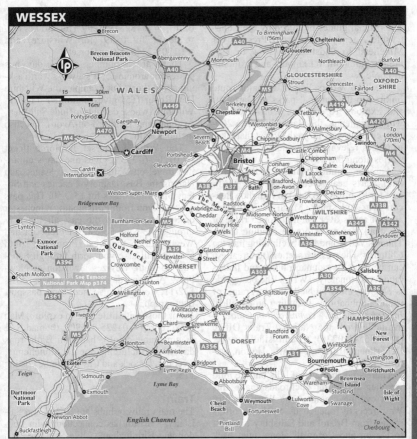

WESSEX

To Birmingham (56mi)

WALES

Brecon Beacons National Park

English Channel

Swanage and Lulworth. There are many independent hostels in this part of the country including ones in Bath, Bournemouth, Bristol, Glastonbury and Salisbury. When it comes to B&Bs and hotels, the choice is limitless.

WALKING & CYCLING

The south-west has plenty of beautiful countryside but the walks in Exmoor National Park and round the coastline are the best known. Exmoor covers some of the most beautiful countryside in England, and the coastal stretch from Ilfracombe to Mine-

head is particularly spectacular. See the Exmoor section later in this chapter for more information.

The South West Coast Path, England's longest national trail, is not a wilderness walk – villages with food, beer and accommodation are generally within easy reach. It follows truly magnificent coastline, and completing a section of the path should be considered by any keen walker but it's best to avoid busy summer weekends.

The South West Coast Path Association (☎ 01364-73859) has an accommodation guide, as well as detailed route descriptions. The official guides produced by the Countryside Agency and Aurum Press cover Minehead to Padstow, Padstow to Falmouth, Falmouth to Exmouth and Exmouth to Poole.

The Two Moors Way is a major route linking up the national parks of Dartmoor and Exmoor. To combine a bit of culture with a challenge, the Hardy Way is a 200-mile circular walk through Dorset that takes in places relevant to the author's life and stories along the way.

Another famous walk, the Ridgeway Path, starts near Avebury and runs northeast for 85 miles (137km) to Ivinghoe Beacon near Aylesbury. Much of it follows ancient roads over the high, open ridge of the chalk downs before descending to the Thames Valley and finally climbing into the Chilterns. The western section (to Streatley) can be used by mountain bikes and horses (and, unfortunately, 4WDs). The best guide is *The Ridgeway* by Neil Curtis. A range of useful publications, including an excellent *Information and Accommodation Guide*, is available from the National Trails Office (☎ 01865-810224), Countryside Service, Department of Leisure & Arts, Holton, Oxford OX33 1QQ.

There's no shortage of hills but the mild weather and quiet backroads make this great cycling country. The West Country Way, recently opened by Sustrans, offers routes from Bristol and Salisbury out west to Devon and Cornwall along quiet back roads.

GETTING THERE & AROUND

Bus

National Express (☎ 0870 580 8080) provides reasonable connections between the main towns. Transport around Exmoor can be difficult in winter, but is not too bad for those sticking to the coastal areas of the park. Generally, Exmoor tends to favour those who can get around using their own transport.

Local bus services are fairly comprehensive, particularly given how rural it soon gets. Phone numbers for regional timetables include ☎ 0117-955 5111 (for Bristol and Bath), ☎ 01823-358299 (for Somerset), ☎ 0845 709 0899 (for Wiltshire) and ☎ 01305-224535 (for Dorset).

There are a number of one-day bus passes for around £5; it's always worth asking about them. For example, the Wiltshire Day Rover (£5) gives unlimited travel in Wiltshire (whose delights include Salisbury, Avebury and Bradford-on-Avon), but also includes Bath.

The Wilts & Dorset Explorer ticket (☎ 01202-673555) gives one day's unlimited travel on Wilts & Dorset, Stagecoach Hampshire Bus, Damory Coaches and Solent Blue Line buses for £5/2.50. This pass will take you from Portsmouth, Winchester or Southampton in the east all the way through the New Forest to Dorchester and Weymouth in the west. From the south coast it will take you north through Salisbury to Bath, Devizes, Swindon or Newbury. A seven-day Busabout pass costs £22/11; you will also need one passport photograph.

For those with little time to explore, Mad Max Tours (☎ 01225-325900, e maddy@madmax.abel.co.uk), based in Bath, runs day trips, including one to Stonehenge, Avebury, Lacock and Castle Combe costing £15.

Train

The main railway hubs are Bristol and Salisbury – Bristol has connections with London and Birmingham, while Salisbury is a link between the capital and the south-west. Train services in the west are reasonably comprehensive, linking Bristol, Bath, Salisbury, Weymouth and Exeter. For more information phone National Rail Enquiries on ☎ 0845 748 4950 or visit www.railtrack.co.uk and www.thetrainline.com on the Web.

Several regional rail passes are available, including the Freedom of the SouthWest Rover, which, over 15 days, allows eight days' unlimited travel west of a line drawn through (and including) Salisbury, Bath, Bristol and Weymouth (£71.50 in summer, £61 in winter).

Bristol & Bath

BRISTOL

☎ 0117 • pop 414,000

Bristol is far and away south-western England's largest and liveliest city, home to music maestros Portishead, Tricky and Massive Attack, as well as clay chums Rocky the Rooster, and Wallace and Gromit. It really is a happening place to be and new restaurants, bars and clubs are popping up all over town.

Unfortunately WWII bombing raids destroyed much of the centre, which was rebuilt with scant regard for aesthetics in the 1950s and '60s. The city does, however, have pockets of magnificent architecture, docks and warehouses that have been rescued from ruin, and plenty of pubs and restaurants. Charming Clifton is every bit the equal of Bath when it comes to Georgian grandeur but, thankfully, lacks the crowds.

Although it's 6 miles (10km) from the Severn estuary, Bristol is most famous as a port. However, by the late-19th century changing trading needs had rendered the docks obsolete and they were relocated from the city centre to nearby Avonmouth and Portishead. Work has finally started on restoring the last pocket of dereliction around the old Floating Harbour and new developments include an Imax cinema.

Bristol is an important transport hub, with connections north to the Cotswolds and the Midlands, south-west to Devon and Cornwall, and east to Bath (an easy day trip). South Wales is linked to Bristol across the Severn Bridge and the unimaginatively named Second Severn Crossing.

History

Little is known about Bristol until the 10th century, but in the Middle Ages a town grew up around a castle near what is now Bristol Bridge. The centre of town was then around Wine, High, Broad and Corn Sts.

Several religious houses were established on high ground above the marshes, commemorated in the name of Temple Meads station. The importance of choosing high ground is shown by a look at Bristol's own leaning tower, attached to Temple Church in Victoria St.

Soon Bristol's wealth was dependent on the triangular trade in slaves, cocoa, sugar, tobacco and manufactured goods with Africa and the New World. William Canynges, a wealthy merchant, paid for the original church on the site of St Mary Redcliffe and it was from Bristol that John Cabot sailed to discover Newfoundland in 1497.

By the 18th century the city was suffering from competition from Liverpool in particular, and the Avon Gorge made it hard for large ships to reach the city-centre docks. By the 1870s, when new docks were opened at Avonmouth and Portishead, Britain's economic focus had shifted northwards.

Orientation

The city centre, to the north of the Floating Harbour, is easy to get around on foot but is very hilly. Glorious Clifton lies to the north-west, accessible by bus from the centre. Bristol's main shopping centre is in and around the undercover Galleries shopping mall in Broadmead, but the shops lining Park St, Queens Rd and Whiteladies Rd, and those in Clifton, are more interesting.

The mainly Afro-Caribbean suburb of St Paul's, just north-east of the centre, remains a run-down, occasionally tense part of town with a heavy drug scene, best not visited alone at night.

The main train station is Bristol Temple Meads, a mile south-east of the centre and linked to it by regular buses. Some trains use Bristol Parkway, 5 miles (8km) to the north, just off the M4 and accessible from the centre by bus and train. A taxi costs about £8.

The bus station in Marlborough St to the north of the city centre serves National Express coaches, and Badgerline buses to surrounding towns and villages.

Information

Tourist Offices Bristol's TIC (☎ 926 0767, fax 922 1557, ⓔ bristol@tourism.bristol.gov.uk) is in The Annexe, Wildscreen Walk, Harbourside. The comprehensive *Visitors*

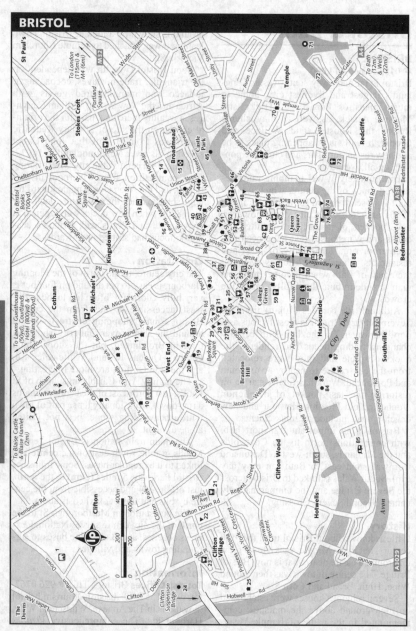

BRISTOL

BRISTOL

PLACES TO STAY
8   Tyndales Park Hotel
9   Oakfield Hotel
10 Washington Hotel
11 The Hawthorns (University)
16 Hotel du Vin
25 Avon Gorge Hotel
42 Grand Thistle Hotel
54 Bristol Backpackers
60 Marriot Royal Hotel
70 City Inn
77 Jurys
78 Bristol Youth Hostel
85 Baltic Wharf Caravan
     Club

PLACES TO EAT
3   Thai Classic; Cartier Vert
18 Brown's
22 Bouboulinos
28 The Boston Tea Party
29 Vincenzo's
30 Melbourne's
32 Le Chateau
33 Pastificio
35 Woode's Café
39 Arc
48 The Glass Boat
50 St Nicholas Market
51 Via Vita; All Bar One
52 San Carlo
57 Harvey's Restaurant;
     Harvey's Wine Museum
65 Aqua

68 Belgo
74 Riverstation; Severnshed
76 Mud Dock

PUBS, BARS & CLUBS
4   Maze
5   Club Loco
6   Lakota
7   The Highbury Vaults
21 The Albion
23 Coronation Tap
31 All in One; Brasserie Pierre
34 Queenshilling; Silent Peach
43 Bierkeller
49 Fez Club; Las Iguanas
53 Tantric Jazz
62 Renato's Taverna dell Artista
64 The Old Duke
66 Llandoger Trow
67 The Famous Royal Navy
     Volunteer
75 Thekla
80 Evolution; Brasshouse

OTHER
1   Bristol Zoo Gardens
2   Train Station (Bristol Parkway)
12 Bristol Royal Infirmary
     Casualty
13 Bus & Coach Station
14 John Wesley's New Room
15 Galleries Shopping Centre
17 City Museum & Art Gallery
19 usit Campus

20 STA Travel
24 Observatory; Camera Obscura
26 Georgian House
27 St George's
36 Red Lodge
37 Colston Hall
38 Bus Stop (for Clifton)
40 Net Gates
41 YHA Adventure Shop
44 Bakers Dolphin Travel
45 Floating Harbour
46 Bristol Bridge
47 St Nicholas Church
55 Hippodrome
56 Taxi Rank
58 Lord Mayor's Chapel
59 Bristol Cathedral
61 Watershed Media Centre
63 Old Vic (Theatre Royal & New
     Vic);
69 Temple Church
71 Train Station (Bristol Temple
     Meads)
72 Bristol Old Station
73 St Mary Redcliffe
79 Arnolfini Arts Centre
81 Tourist Information Centre
82 Explore-at-Bristol;
     Wildscreen-at-Bristol
83 The Matthew
84 SS Great Britain
86 Maritime Heritage Centre
87 SS Waverley
88 Industrial Museum

Guide is worth buying, as are the booklets describing the *Bristol Heritage Trail* and the *Slave Trade Trail*. The TIC is open 10 am to 6 pm daily in summer; phone for other opening times. For more details check out the Web site at www.visitbristol.co.uk.

Internet Resources On Broad St, Net Gates is a sophisticated Internet cafe with more to offer than just terminals.

Travel Agencies STA Travel (☎ 929 4399), 43 Queen's Rd, has just opened a new branch near the university. Just over the road is usit Campus (☎ 929 2494, 37 Queens Rd), offering similar discounted deals for those aged under 26.

For travel publications or equipment, head to the YHA Adventure Shop at 10 Fairfax St.

Bookshops Bristol Books (☎ 924 5458), 180b Cheltenham Rd, is excellent for purchasing second-hand books.

Newspapers & Magazines The fortnightly listings magazine *Venue* gives comprehensive details of what's on in both Bristol and Bath; check it out before you arrive at www.venue.co.uk. You can get more news and information, including theatre, cinema and restaurant guides, in the *Bristol Evening Post,* or see their on-line version at www.thisisbristol.com.

Museums
The **City Museum & Art Gallery** (☎ 922 3571), at the top of Park St, houses a mixed bag of exhibits ranging from Egyptian mummies through natural history and local

history to fine art. It's open from 10 am to 5 pm daily; admission is free.

Those interested in Bristol's links with the aerospace industry should head for the **Industrial Museum** (☎ 925 1470) at Princes Wharf in the docks. It's open from 10 am to 5 pm Saturday to Wednesday from April to October (weekends only in winter). Admission is free.

Explore-at-Bristol (☎ 915 5000), Harbourside, is Bristol's interactive science museum for the 21st century. Among other things, natural phenomena such as twisters and whirlpools are explained. Admission costs £6.50/4.50. Neighbouring **Wildscreen-at-Bristol** (☎ 915 5000) is along similar lines but with the emphasis on nature and the environment. See also the Web site at www.at-bristol.org.uk.

SS *Great Britain*

Bristol was home to the Victorian engineering genius Isambard Kingdom Brunel (1806–59), known for, among many other things, the Clifton Suspension Bridge. In 1843, he designed the first ocean-going iron ship, the SS *Great Britain*, the first large ship to be driven by a screw propeller.

For 43 years the ship served as a cargo vessel and a liner, carrying passengers as far as Australia. Then in 1886 it was badly damaged passing Cape Horn. The cost of repairs was judged too high so it was sold for storage. In 1970 it was returned to Bristol and since then has been undergoing restoration in the dry dock where it was originally built.

The ship (☎ 926 0680) is off City Dock and is open from 10 am to 5.30 pm (to 4.30 pm in winter); admission costs £6.25/3.75. Nearby is a replica of John Cabot's ship *Matthew*, which undertook the journey from Bristol to Newfoundland in 1497.

Entrance is via the **Maritime Heritage Centre**, which celebrates Bristol's shipbuilding past (same opening hours as the ship; admission is free).

Clifton & the Suspension Bridge

The north-western suburb of Clifton boasts some splendid Georgian architecture, including the Cornwallis and Royal York crescents, as well as some of Bristol's most attractive shopping streets. In many ways Clifton is as grand as Bath but, thankfully, lacks the tourists.

The spectacular 75m-high **Clifton Suspension Bridge**, designed by Brunel, spans a dramatic stretch of the Avon Gorge. Work on the bridge began in 1836 but wasn't completed until 1864, after Brunel's death. The bridge is an inevitable magnet for stunt artists. More poignantly, it's also a favoured suicide spot. A famous story relates how Sarah Ann Hedley jumped from the bridge in 1885 after a lovers' tiff. Her voluminous petticoats parachuted her safely to earth and she lived to be 85. More recently the car of Richey James Edwards of the Manic Street Preachers was found abandoned near here before his disappearance, but his body has never been found. A bridge visitors centre is open daily from 10 am to 6 pm for £1.50/1.

On Durdham Downs, overlooking the bridge, an **observatory** houses a fascinating **camera obscura** (£1/50p), which offers some incredible views of the suspension bridge – and an illuminating insight into what folks did for entertainment in the days before television. There is also access to a nearby **cave** (£1/50p) with a viewing platform in the side of the gorge to get that extra special view of the bridge.

Nearby is **Bristol Zoo Gardens** (☎ 970 6176), one of the country's best-known zoos, which includes a well-known group of West African gorillas, part of an ongoing conservation project in Cameroon, as well as a major area for seals and penguins. It is open 9 am to 5.30 pm (to 4.30 pm in winter). Admission costs £8.20/4.60.

Bus Nos 8/9 and 508/9 run to Clifton from the city centre.

Georgian House & Red Lodge

The Georgian House (☎ 921 1362), 7 Great George St, was home to 18th-century sugar merchant John Pinney and retains complete eriod fixtures and fittings. It was here that Wordsworth and Coleridge had their first meeting with poet laureate Robert Southey, a Bristol lad himself.

The Elizabethan Red Lodge (☎ 921 1360) with walled garden in Perry Rd, was much altered in the 18th century. One room is preserved as a memorial to Mary Carpenter who set up the first women's reformatory here in 1854.

Both places are open 10 am to 5 pm daily except Thursday and Friday. Admission is free.

Bristol Cathedral

Originally founded as the church of an Augustinian monastery in 1140, Bristol Cathedral (☎ 926 4879) on College Green gained cathedral status in 1542. One of its most striking features is its Norman chapter house. The choir dates back to the 14th century but much of the nave and the west towers were designed by George Street in 1868. The south transept shelters a rare Saxon carving of the 'Harrowing of Hell'.

St Mary Redcliffe

Described as 'the fairest, goodliest and most famous parish church in England' by Queen Elizabeth I in 1574, St Mary Redcliffe (☎ 929 1487) is a stunning piece of perpendicular architecture with a grand hexagonal porch that easily outdoes the cathedral in splendour. It's open daily from 8 am to 8 pm, closing at 5.30 pm in winter.

Lord Mayor's Chapel

Once the chapel of St Mark's Hospital, the Lord Mayor's Chapel (☎ 929 4350) in Park St is a medieval gem squeezed in between shops opposite the cathedral and packed with stained-glass windows, medieval monuments and ancient tiles. The church-loving poet John Betjeman dubbed it 'for its size one of the very best churches in England...'. It's open 10 am to noon and 1 to 4 pm daily except Monday.

New Room

Tucked away in Broadmead Shopping Centre, the **New Room** (☎ 926 4740), 36 The Horsefair, was the world's first Methodist chapel when it opened in 1739. John Wesley, whose equestrian statue stands in the courtyard, preached from its double-decker pulpit. Upstairs, visit the old living quarters, with rooms for John and Charles Wesley and Francis Asbury. It's open 10 am to 4 pm daily except Sunday (and Wednesdays in winter). Admission is free.

Blaise Castle House Museum

In the northern suburb of Henbury lies Blaise Castle (☎ 950 6789), a late-18th-century house that contains a fine museum of West Country rural and urban life. It's open 10 am to 5 pm Saturday to Wednesday and admission is free.

On a hill stands a mock castle, in grounds laid out by Humphrey Repton. Across the road is **Blaise Hamlet**, a cluster of thatched cottages designed for estate servants in 1811 by John Nash; with its neatly kept green and flower-filled gardens, it's everyone's fantasy of a 'medieval' English village.

Bus Nos 1/501 pass this way from the city centre.

Bristol Old Station

Before rushing for their train, visitors to Temple Meads station should pause to look at what is the oldest surviving major railway terminus in the world, built to yet another Brunel design in 1839–40. The original terminus stands to the left of the modern one; the Great Train Shed, with its mock hammerbeam roof, last saw a train in 1966. Try the door of the **Brunel Centre** and you may be able to look around.

Organised Tours

From June to the end of September, hop-on, hop-off open-top bus tours circle 14 points in Bristol daily except Saturday. Tickets (£7/5) can be bought on board the bus or from the TIC. Pick up the bus in St Augustine's Parade, outside the Hippodrome.

Special Events

St Paul's Carnival, a smaller version of London's Notting Hill Carnival, livens up the first Saturday of each July. There's a regatta in the harbour in July, and not-to-be-missed hot-air balloon and kite festivals in Ashton Court, across Clifton Suspension Bridge, in August and September. The 2000 balloon

WESSEX

festival saw a world record for consecutive take-offs as several hundred floated skyward.

Places to Stay

Camping The *Baltic Wharf Caravan Club* site (☎ 926 8030, *Cumberland Rd*), 1½ miles (2.5km) from the centre, charges £2 a pitch and £4 a person. It's near the A370, A369, A4 and A3029 junctions. They no longer take bookings so arrive early at the weekend as there are just three pitches.

Hostels Bristol has little cheap accommodation, but the 129-bed *Bristol Youth Hostel* (☎ 922 1659, fax 9273789, ℮ bristol@ yha.org.uk, 14 Narrow Quay St) in a converted warehouse, five minutes from the town centre, is an excellent place to stay. The nightly charge is £11.90/8.20 for adults/children. The location is right in the thick of things when it comes to nightlife.

Conveniently near the bus station, *Bristol Backpackers* (☎ 925 7900, kate&martin @bristolbackpackers.co.uk, 17 St Stephen's St) is a new place in a charming, old house with beds for £12.50 a night, including free tea and coffee. This also has a fine location for exploring Bristol, day or night.

University Accommodation Outside term times the university rents out rooms. *The Hawthorns* (☎ 954 5900, fax 923 7188, ℮ central-catering@bris.ac.uk, Woodland Rd, Clifton) is the best located and charges from £25/38 a room, including a continental breakfast.

B&Bs & Hotels The *Lawns Guest House* (☎ 973 8459, 91 Hampton Rd), in the leafy suburb of Redland, offers room for £24/40.

Most of the other cheap B&Bs tend to be a fair distance from the centre. Clifton, 1½ miles (2.5km) from the centre, is a very attractive suburb and a good place to stay, but most of the B&Bs here cost at least £25 per person. Just off Whiteladies Rd, the attractive *Oakfield Hotel* (☎ 973 5556, fax 974 4141, 52 Oakfield Rd) has rooms for £28.50/38.50.

In Tyndalls Park Rd, *Tyndalls Park Hotel* (☎ 973 5407) charges from £40/50.

Washington Hotel (☎ 973 3980, fax 973

4740, St Paul's Rd) is midway between the city centre and Clifton Suspension Bridge. During the week, rooms are £53 or £67 with bathroom, £36/46 at the weekend.

About a mile north of the centre, *Courtlands Hotel* (☎ 942 4432, fax 923 2432, 1 Redland Court Rd, Redland) is a family-run place with a bar and restaurant. There are 25 rooms, most with bathroom, for £50/60.

Most of the city centre hotels bag their profits from their business clientele midweek and then slash prices at the weekend. However, *City Inn* (☎ 925 1001, fax 907 4116, ℮ bristolreservations@cityinn.com, Temple Way) is cheap throughout the week with comfortable if characterless rooms from £51.50.

A classic option is the *Avon Gorge Hotel* (☎ 973 8955, fax 923 8125, Sion Hill, Clifton), which has a terrace overlooking the suspension bridge. It's expensive (£99/109) during the week, but prices drop to £44 a head, provided you stay two nights, at the weekend. See the Web site at www .peelhotel.com.

The *Grand Thistle Hotel* (☎ 929 1645, fax 922 7619, ℮ bristol@thistle.co.uk, Broad St) is a Victorian hotel in the heart of the city. During the week rooms are £84/93, without breakfast. At the weekend B&B costs £94 per room.

Jurys (☎ 923 0333, fax 923 0300, ℮ con ring@jurys.com, Prince St) has a splendid position overlooking the Floating Harbour but charges £120 for a room midweek, falling to £54/69 at the weekend.

Hotel du Vin (☎ 925 5577, fax 925 1199, Narrow Lewins Mead) is the new kid on the block and has sumptuous rooms in a former warehouse complex. Rooms are £99/125 (excluding breakfast) and the bistro here is very well regarded.

Fanciest of the lot is the 19th-century *Marriot Royal Hotel* (☎ 925 5100, fax 925 1515, College Green) beside the cathedral. Swish B&B costs £129/139 during the week, £89/110 at the weekend.

Places to Eat

If you're dining on a shoestring, one of the cheapest places to eat in the city centre is inside *St Nicholas Market* where classics such as bangers and beans, jacket spuds and toasties are all cheap.

Nearby Broad St is home to *Arc* (☎ 922 6456, 27 Broad St), a cool little cafe that has tasty soups, bargain pizzas and main dishes such as Thai curry for £4. By night it's a bar and club.

Other popular lunch spots include the cafe-bars in the *Watershed* (☎ 921 4135) and the *Arnolfini* (☎ 937 9191), both arts complexes on St Augustine's Reach, overlooking the waterfront; quick, tasty meals in either cost around £5 and they also make pleasant spots for a tipple by night.

Not far away the *Mud Dock* (☎ 934 9734, 40 The Grove), above a bike shop, is a bit pricier but very popular, with more water views. By night it doubles as a bar that draws a crowd.

The nearby *Riverstation* (☎ 914 4434, Harbourside) is housed in a designer building and has excellent food (scrumptious desserts) that costs less downstairs than upstairs. Next door is *severnshed* (☎ 925 1212, Harbourside, The Grove), a light, bright cafe-bar specialising in organic, Middle Eastern cuisine in Tapas-type portions or mezes for around £7. By night, expect Belgian beers, live jazz and higher prices on the a la carte menu.

Sticking with the waterfront area, *Aqua* (☎ 915 6060, Welsh Back) is *the* place for Bristol's city slickers on the business schmooze, with an excellent menu and a nice atmosphere. Figure on £15 upwards for the full experience.

Nearby is a branch of *Belgo* (☎ 905 8000, The Old Granary, Queen Charlotte St), the place for mussel lovers, seafood platters and bountiful Belgian beers. They claim to have more than 100 brands available, but most kick off at 6% volume and above so tread carefully or the beer will tread upon your dreams.

In the past few years, the grand old bank buildings along Corn St have been given new life as pubs, cafe-bars and restaurants. There are branches of *All Bar One* (☎ 946 8751) and *Via Vita*, while *San Carlo* (☎ 922 6586) does sound pizzas.

For a splurge, the place to go is *Harvey's Restaurant* (☎ 927 5034, 12 Denmark St) above Harvey's Wine Museum; three-course dinners cost near enough £40, lunch less at £17.95.

In a prettier setting is *The Glass Boat* (☎ 929 0704), a converted barge on Welsh Back, where dinner will cost around £20.

Heading towards Clifton, Park St is lined with reasonably priced pizzerias: try *Pastificio* (☎ 949 9884, 39 Park St) or *Vincenzo's* (☎ 926 0908, 71a Park St). *Woode's Café* (☎ 926 4041, 18 Park St) sells excellent sandwiches and light meals in sophisticated surroundings.

Le Chateau (☎ 929 7298, 64 Park St) doles out reasonably priced French food and wine, in the vein of the Pierre Victoire chain, but the real draw is the licence until 2 am.

Hottest spot of all, *The Boston Tea Party* (☎ 929 8601, 75 Park St) serves good lunches; there's a larger branch in Lewins Mead.

Melbourne's (☎ 922 6996, 74 Park St) keeps prices down by pitching itself as an authentic Australian BYO and is popular with Cliftonites by night.

Brown's (☎ 930 4777, 38 Queens Rd) serves excellent food in the classy surroundings of the neo-Venetian ex-university refectory and is always busy.

Heading even further out up Whiteladies Rd are several interesting options. *Thai Classic* (☎ 973 8930, 87 Whiteladies Rd) has a balanced menu of Thai and Malaysian food and offers a good lunchtime deal of two courses for £6.50. Neighbour *Cartier Vert* is an impeccable modern French restaurant and a good lunch will cost around £15 (more for dinner).

Moving into Clifton village proper is the remarkable *Bouboulinos* (☎ 973 1192, 9 Portland St), a Greek restaurant with famous fish, meat and vegetarian mezes of 15 dishes for £12.95. You can BYO wine.

Entertainment

Venue magazine (£1.90) has comprehensive listings with details of theatre, music, gigs – the works basically – for both Bristol and Bath.

Pubs & Bars Most pubs in and around St Augustine's Parade (the city centre) are best avoided, especially at the weekend. Instead, head down King St to the *Llandoger Trow* (☎ 926 0783), a pub that has been around for centuries and may have provided the inspiration for the Admiral Benbow in *Treasure Island*. It also may have been where Daniel Defoe met Alexander Selkirk, a real-life Robinson Crusoe who inspired the book.

Popular student hang-outs include *The Albion* (☎ 973 3522, *Boyces Ave, Clifton*) and the *Highbury Vaults* (☎ 973 3203, *St Michael's Hill*), which has a courtyard for alfresco tippling.

Cider-lovers shouldn't miss *The Coronation Tap* (☎ 973 9617, *Sion Place, Clifton*) up near the suspension bridge, which usually has five varieties of the adult apple juice available. The rash of Irish pubs between Baldwin St and Corn St are cheerful enough but no more 'Irish' than those with fewer shamrocks on display.

Liberal late licences are a fresh feature of Bristol. *Riverstation*, *severnshed* and *Arc*, all recommended restaurants, play late. *All in One* and *Brasserie Pierre* masquerade as restaurants, but are primarily tacky late-night boozers on Park St. They may be brash but they are also the only places to really push it up a gear in this part of town.

Brasshouse (☎ 922 0330, *Canons Rd*), down by the docks, sells itself as all style but has no substance; it's one of many McBar chains that are insidiously taking over Bristol and beyond.

Las Iguanas (☎ 927 6233, *10 St Nicholas St*) by St Nicholas Market has a healthy range of Latino tunes, and beers to accompany them.

Best of the late-night drinking haunts by a mile is *Renato's Taverna dell Artista* (☎ 929 7712, *33 King St*), next door to the Old Vic Theatre. It may look like an Italian restaurant, but don't be misled as this is the place to get a drink after the witching hour and the atmosphere is great.

Opposite is the *Famous Royal Navy Volunteer* (☎ 929 1763, *King St*), an ale pub once favoured by pressgangs that dragged young men off to sea – Royal Navy recruitment tactics are apparently more professional these days so we can drink freely without fear of waking up in East Timor, Kosovo or Sierra Leone.

The Queen's Shilling (☎ 926 4342, *9 Frogmore St*) is arguably the city's most popular gay bar and opposite is a happening little club, the *Silent Peach* (☎ 929 1181, *1 Unity St*), which draws a mixed crowd with low cover charges.

Clubs Trendy nightspots come and go with alarming frequency. The popular *Lakota* (☎ 942 6208, *2 Upper York St*) stays open until 6 am, whereupon you can move on to *Club Loco* (☎ 942 6208, *Hepburn Rd*) off Stokes Croft, which has a 24-hour licence.

Other happening clubs right now include the chilled-out *Fez Club* (☎ 925 9200, *St Nicholas St*), *Maze* (☎ 923 2920, *84 Stokes Croft*), *Thekla* (☎ 929 3301, *The Grove*) with big beats and house, and infinitely tacky *Evolution* (☎ 922 0330, *The Waterfront, Canons Rd*) down by the docks.

Live Music Near the Llandoger Trow is the excellent *Old Duke* (☎ 927 7137, *45 King St*), which hosts regular jazz sessions. *Tantric Jazz* (☎ 940 2304, *39 St Nicholas St*) has live jazz every night of the week and is a welcome escape from the soulless theme bars in the Corn St area.

The legendary *Bierkeller* (☎ 926 8514, *All Saints St*) has played host to plenty of rock luminaries and still has regular world-music nights. Admission costs from £1 to £12 depending on the night of the week and who's playing.

Theatre, Cinema & Concerts Among the theatres, the *Hippodrome* (☎ 0870 607 7500, *St Augustine's Parade*) hosts ballet, musicals and pantomimes. The *Old Vic* (☎ 987 7877, *King St*) sticks with straight drama and occasional comedy. The *Colston Hall* (☎ 922 3686, *Colston St*) stages everything from wrestling bouts to concerts.

St George's (☎ 923 0359, *Great George St*) is an incredible old converted church that plays host to regular classical concerts and has a cafe set in the crypt below.

The *Arnolfini Arts Centre (☎ 929 9191, 16 Narrow Quay, Harbourside)* is more avant garde, staging performance art and contemporary dance, as well as housing one of the city's most lively cinemas.

Another cinema with a steady diet of foreign films is the nearby *Watershed Media Centre (☎ 925 3845, 1 Canon's Rd, Harbourside)*.

Getting There & Away

Bristol is 115 miles (185km) from London, 75 miles (121km) from Exeter and 50 miles (81km) from Cardiff. See the fares tables in the Getting Around chapter for more details.

Air Bristol International Airport (☎ 01275-474444) is 8 miles (13km) south-west of town, off the A38. There are buses to the airport from Marlborough St bus station and less frequently from Temple Meads train station. A taxi to the airport costs around £13.

Bus National Express (☎ 0870 580 8080) has services every 1½ hours to Heathrow Airport (2½ hours, £24) and Gatwick Airport (three hours, £28). Services into central London are equally regular (2½ hours, £11). Bakers Dolphin (☎ 972 8000) has cheaper tickets to London (£10 one way, £18 period return) – visit the Bakers Dolphin travel agencies around town.

National Express also has frequent buses to Cardiff (1¼ hours, £5). There are a couple of buses a day to Barnstaple (2¾ hours, £14) and regular buses south to Truro in Cornwall (4½ hours, £25.75), Exeter in Devon (1¾ hours, £9.75), Oxford (2½ hours, £12.75) and Stratford-upon-Avon (2½ hours, £13).

Local Badgerline buses (☎ 955 3231) also operate out of Marlborough St bus station. There are frequent services to Bath, Wells and Glastonbury. Hourly buses to Bath can also be picked up outside Temple Meads train station. There are hourly services to Salisbury (X4) and north to Gloucester. Bus No 376 heads to Wells and Glastonbury hourly every day.

Day Rambler tickets (£5.30/3.75) let you use Badgerline and City Line buses all day, all over the region.

Train Bristol is an important rail hub, with regular connections to London Paddington (1½ hours, £21.00). Most trains (except those to the south) use both the Temple Meads and Parkway stations.

Only 20 minutes away, Bath makes an easy day trip (£4.80 day return). There are frequent links to Cardiff (¾ hour, £6.90), Exeter (one hour, £15.60), Fishguard (3½ hours, £21.50), Oxford (1½ hours, £9.90) and Birmingham (1½ hours, £19).

Boat Between July and October you can travel by boat along the Bristol Channel from Bristol to Clevedon, Penarth, Ilfracombe, Barry and Lundy Island. Sailings are on the SS *Balmoral* or the SS *Waverley*, the world's last seagoing paddle steamer. Prices start at £12.95 to Clevedon. Ring Waverley Excursions on ☎ 01446-720656 for full details.

Getting Around

Bus City Line (☎ 955 3231) bus fares aren't cheap, but Dayrider tickets are available on the bus after 9 am from Monday to Friday and at any time at the weekend, allowing multiple journeys for a discount.

Clifton is a long walk from the town centre. Catch bus Nos 8/9 (508/509 at the weekend) from bus stop 'Cu' on Colston Ave, or from Temple Meads train station. In summer, half-hourly bus No 511 loops from Baltic Wharf to Broadmead, through Clifton Triangle and Hotwells, and back to Baltic Wharf, linking many of the major attractions and shopping centres.

Taxi The taxi rank on St Augustine's Parade is central but not a good place to hang around late at night. To call a cab, ring Premier Taxis free on ☎ 0800 716777.

Boat The nicest way to get around is to use the ferry (☎ 927 3416) that plies the Floating Harbour every 20 minutes (weekends only in winter), April to September, stopping at the SS *Great Britain*, Hotwells, the Baltic Wharf, the Centre, Bristol Bridge (for Broadmead Shopping Centre) and Castle Park. A short hop is £1/60p, a complete circuit £3/1.50.

WESSEX

BATH
☎ 01225 • pop 84,400

Bath is the grandest town in England, in reputation as much as reality, and visitors throng here in their thousands. For more than 2000 years, the city's fortune has revolved around its hot springs and the tourism that the water has attracted. It was the Romans who first developed a complex of baths and a temple to the goddess Sulis-Minerva on the site of what they called Aquae Sulis. Today, however, Bath is just as famous for its glorious Georgian architecture that has won it Unesco World Heritage Site status.

Throughout the 18th century, Bath was the fashionable haunt of English society. Aristocrats flocked here to gossip, gamble and flirt. Fortunately they had the good sense and fortune to employ the brilliant architects who designed the Palladian terraced housing, the circles, crescents and squares, that dominate the city.

Like Florence, Bath is an architectural gem. It too has a shop-lined, much-photographed bridge. Like Florence, it can also seem at times like little more than an upmarket shopping mall for wealthy tourists. However, when sunlight brightens the honey-coloured stone, and buskers and strollers fill the streets and line the river, only the most churlish would deny its charm. Head up some of the steep hills and you can even find pockets of Georgiana that only the residents seem to appreciate.

Bath looks wealthier than Bristol, in part because its beauty attracts moneyed residents, in part because the sheer crush of visitors ensures the good life to those involved in tourism. The best-known sites in and around Abbey Courtyard receive too many visitors for their own good. Away from the centre, however, smaller museums fight for the droppings from their more famous neighbours' tables and are genuinely pleased to see those who trouble to seek them out. Inevitably, Bath also has its share of residents for whom affluence is somebody else's success story. For all the glitzy shops, you'll still see beggars on the streets.

The big news in Bath is that at long last the city is to have a spa again. A grant from the Millennium Fund is funding the restoration of the old Hot and Cross Baths and the building of a brand-new spa complex designed by Nicholas Grimshaw, the architect behind the Eurostar Terminal at Waterloo. It is due for completion by the end of 2001.

History

Prehistoric camps on the hills around Bath indicate settlement before the Romans arrived, and legend records King Bladud founding the town after being cured of leprosy by a bath in the muddy swamps. The Romans established the town of Aquae Sulis (named after the Celtic goddess Sul) in AD 44 and it was already a spa, with an extensive baths complex, by the reign of Agricola (AD 78–84).

When the Romans left, the town declined and was captured by the Anglo-Saxons in 577. In 944 a monastery was set up on the site of the present abbey and there are still traces of the medieval town wall in Upper Borough Walls. Throughout the Middle Ages, Bath served as an ecclesiastical centre and a wool-trading town. However, it wasn't until the 18th century that it really came into its own, when the idea of taking spa water as a cure for assorted ailments led to the creation of the beautiful city visitors see today. Those were the days when Ralph Allen developed the quarries at Coombe Down and employed the two John Woods (father and son) to create the glorious crescents and terraces; when Doctor William Oliver established the Bath General Hospital for the poor and gave his name to the Bath Oliver biscuit; and when the gambler Richard 'Beau' Nash became the arbiter of fashionable taste.

By the mid-19th century, sea bathing had become more popular than spas and Bath fell out of fashion. Curiously, even in the 1960s, few people appreciated its architecture and many houses were pulled down to make way for modern replacements before legislation was introduced to protect what remains.

Orientation

Although hemmed in by seven hills, Bath still manages to sprawl quite a way (as

WESSEX

BATH

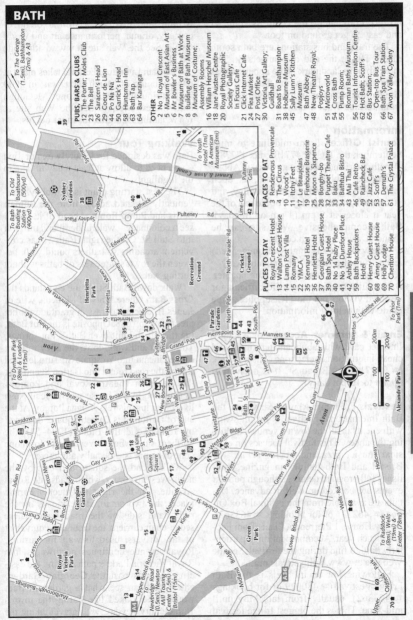

PUBS, BARS & CLUBS
12 The Porter; Moles Club
23 The Bell
26 Saracen's Head
29 Coeur de Lion
44 Po Na Na
50 Garrick's Head
58 Huntsman Inn
63 Bath Tap
64 Bar Karanga

OTHER
2 No 1 Royal Crescent
5 Museum of East Asian Art
6 Mr Bowler's Business
7 Museum of Bath at Work
8 Building of Bath Museum
9 Museum of Costume;
   Assembly Rooms
16 William Herschel Museum
18 Jane Austen Centre
20 Royal Photographic
   Society Gallery;
   In Focus Cafe
21 Click Internet Cafe
24 Flea Market
27 Post Office
30 Victoria Art Gallery;
   Guildhall
31 Boats to Bathampton
38 Holburne Museum
45 Sally Lunn's Kitchen
   Museum
47 Bath Abbey
48 New Theatre Royal;
   Popjoys
51 Microworld
54 Cross Bath
55 Pump Room;
   Roman Baths Museum
56 Tourist Information Centre
62 Hot Bath; Scoff's
65 Bus Station;
   Open-top Bus Tour
66 Bath Spa Train Station
67 Avon Valley Cyclery

PLACES TO EAT
3 Rendezvous Provencale
4 The Circus
10 Wood's
11 Itchy Feet
17 Le Beaujolais
19 Firehouse Brasserie
25 Moon & Sixpence
28 Bonghy-bo
32 Puppet Theatre Cafe
33 Baku
34 Bathtub Bistro
43 Mai Thai
46 Café Retro
49 Raincheck Bar
52 Jazz Cafe
57 Demuth's
61 The Crystal Palace

PLACES TO STAY
1 Royal Crescent Hotel
13 Walton's Guest House
14 Lamp Post Villa
15 Romany
22 YMCA
35 Kennard Hotel
36 Henrietta Hotel
37 Georgian Guest House
39 Bath Spa Hotel
40 No 14 Raby Place
41 No 14 Dunsford Place
42 Ashley House
59 Bath Backpackers
   Hotel
60 Henry Guest House
68 Amey Guest House
69 Holly Lodge
70 Cheriton House

visitors discover if they stay at the youth hostel). Fortunately, the centre is compact and easy to get around on foot.

The train and bus stations are both south of the TIC at the end of Manvers St. The most obvious landmark is the abbey, across from the Roman Baths and Pump Room. Guided tours and open-top bus tours leave from Terrace Walk nearby.

Information

Tourist Offices From mid-June to mid-September, the TIC (☎ 477101, fax 477787, e bath_tourism@bathnes.gov.uk), in Abbey Chambers, Abbey Churchyard, is open 9.30 am to 7 pm Monday to Saturday, and 10 am to 6 pm on Sunday. For the rest of the year it closes at 5 pm (4 pm on Sunday). Bath's comprehensive Web site can be found at www.visitbath.co.uk.

Free walking tours (highly recommended) leave from the Abbey Churchyard daily – see Organised Tours later in this chapter. Bath's hilly terrain makes life difficult for disabled visitors but the TIC supplies a free guide with helpful information.

Email & Internet Access For a handy Internet cafe with abundant terminals and cheap international telephone calls try Click (☎ 337711), 19 Broad St. It is open from 10 am to 10 pm daily.

Festivals From mid-May to early June the Bath International Festival is in full swing with events in all the town's venues, including the abbey. This festival focuses on classical music, jazz and opera. *Venue*, the Bristol and Bath listings magazine, publishes full program details, although popular events are booked up well in advance. Details are available from the Festival Box Office (☎ 462231 or for bookings ☎ 463362), Linley House, 1 Pierrepont Place, from February each year. Accommodation is particularly hard to find during the festival. See the Web site at www.bathfestivals.org.uk.

Following hot on its heels is the Bath Fringe Festival (☎ 480079 or for bookings ☎ 463362), usually from late May until mid-June. This is the biggest fringe festival

in England, second only to Edinburgh in Britain, and involves a similar blend of comedy, drama, performance art and world music. See the Web site at www.bathfringe.co.uk.

The Bath Literature Festival takes place at the beginning of March each year; in 2000 its contributors included Roger McGough and Andrew Motion. See the Web site at www.bathlitfest.org.uk for more details.

Walking Tour

Bath was designed for leisurely exploration – you need to allow at least a day to take in the highlights.

The best starting point is the **abbey**, conveniently situated across from the **Roman Baths** and **Pump Room**. Ahead of it, you'll see a colonnade – walk under it and turn left into Stall St. On the right, Bath St has convenient arcading so bathers could walk between the town's three sets of baths without getting wet.

Walk down Bath St. At the end stands the **Cross Bath** where Mary of Modena, wife of James II, erected a cross in gratitude for her pregnancy in 1688. Opposite is the **Hot Bath**, the third bath built over Bath's hot springs. Turn right and walk down the alley in front of the cinema into Westgate St. Turn left and follow the road round into Barton St and past the Georgian **Theatre Royal** and **Popjoys Restaurant**, in the house where Beau Nash lived with his mistress Juliana Popjoy. At the end of Barton St is **Queen Square**, designed by John Wood the Elder (1704–54); the northern side, where seven houses form one cohesive unit, is especially attractive.

Walk round the square and exit by the north-western corner, which leads into Royal Avenue. On the right is Queen's Parade Place; the two small, stone kiosks on the right-hand side of the road were where sedan-chair carriers, the Georgian equivalent of taxi drivers, used to wait for custom. Royal Avenue continues northwards into Royal Victoria Park; a path skirting the eastern side runs past the **Georgian Garden**, where you can see what a garden in Bath would have looked like during the town's 18th-century heyday, with gravel taking the place of grass to protect women's long dresses from staining. Follow the path round the perimeter and you'll emerge on the lawn in front of the famous **Royal Crescent**, designed by John Wood the Younger (1728–1801).

After inspecting the Crescent's superb architecture, turn right along Brock St and walk down to the **Circus**, a circle of 30 houses designed by John Wood the Elder. Plaques on the houses commemorate famous residents such as Thomas Gainsborough, Clive of India and David Livingstone. A left turn out of the Circus will take you down Bennett St to the **Assembly Rooms** and **Museum of Costume**. Walk in front of the museum into Alfred St, where houses retain fine 18th-century metal fittings, including snuffers to put out footmen's torches. Continue down Alfred St and turn right into Bartlett St, then right into George St and left down Milsom St, Bath's main shopping drag. About halfway down you'll pass the **Royal Photographic Society Gallery** in what was once the Octagon Chapel.

At the bottom of Milsom St, bear left into New Bond St until you reach the grand colonnaded post office. Cross the road and turn right along busy Northgate St, then left along Bridge St (passing the **Victoria Art Gallery** on the right), to the River Avon and **Pulteney Bridge**, designed by Robert Adam in 1774. From the bridge, there are views over terraced Pulteney Weir.

Continue straight ahead across Laura Place and along Great Pulteney St. At the far end is the **Holburne Museum**. A plaque opposite, at No 4 Sydney Place, commemorates Jane Austen, the author who lived here for three not particularly happy years. She wrote *Persuasion* and *Northanger Abbey* in Bath and both vividly describe fashionable life in the city around 1800. Walking back along Great Pulteney St, take any turning on the right to get to Henrietta Park, the perfect place for a rest.

Roman Baths Museum

Between the 1st and 4th centuries, the Romans built a bath and temple complex over one of Bath's three natural hot springs.

In the Middle Ages, the baths crumbled and it wasn't until the 17th century that anyone paid the spring much more heed. However, by the end of the century, Mary of Modena was only one of a growing number of visitors coming to 'take the cure' in Bath. In 1702 the visit of Queen Anne set the seal on the trend and the town began to expand.

Nowadays, a raised walkway gives visitors their first glimpse of the **Great Bath**, complete with Roman paving and lead base and surrounded by 19th-century arcading. A series of excavated passages and chambers beneath street level lead off in several directions and let you inspect the remains of other smaller baths and hypocaust (heating) systems. One of the most picturesque corners of the complex is the 12th-century **King's Bath**, built around the original sacred spring; through a window there are views of the pool, complete with niches for bathers and rings for them to hold on to; 1.5 million litres of hot water still pour into the pool every day.

The museum outlines the history of the baths and displays finds made during excavations, including the fine gorgon head found on the site of the temple of Sul and the gilt-bronze head from the cult statue.

The Roman Baths (☎ 477791), Abbey Courtyard, are one of England's most popular attractions and can be uncomfortably congested in summer when the museum's enclosed corridors can also feel very claustrophobic. Visit early on a midweek morning and you'll probably have a much better time.

The baths open 9 am to 6 pm daily (to 9 pm in August, 5 pm in winter and on Sunday); allow an hour to fully appreciate them. Admission costs £6.90/4, but a combined ticket giving entry to the Costume Museum as well costs £8.90/5.30.

Pump Room

The elegant, 18th-century Pump Room (☎ 444477) is attached to the Roman Baths Museum, and a fountain from the King's Bath dispenses tepid spa water, which is on sale in the classy restaurant. Since Georgian times, diners have been serenaded by a Palm Court trio, a tradition that continues today. Pictures on the wall depict Georgian luminaries, including Sir Robert Walpole and Ralph Allen, whose quarries at Coombe Down provided much of the Bath stone used to build the town's squares and crescents. There's also a statue of Richard 'Beau' Nash (1674–1761), the uncrowned 'king' of Georgian Bath, a gambler who laid down the rules of etiquette for the town's fashionable visitors.

The Pump Room does the best cream teas in town and is also open for stylish dining; see Places to Eat for more Information.

Bath Abbey

Edgar, the first king of united England, was crowned in a church in Abbey Courtyard in 973, but the present abbey, more glass than stone, was built between 1499 and 1616, making it the last great medieval church raised in England. The nave's wonderful fan vaulting was erected in the 19th century.

The most striking feature of the abbey's exterior is the west facade, where angels climb up and down stone ladders, commemorating a dream of the founder Bishop Oliver King. The abbey boasts 640 wall monuments, the second-largest collection after Westminster Abbey; among those buried here are the Reverend Thomas Malthus, the Victorian philosopher famous for his views on population control; Sir Isaac Pitman, who devised the Pitman method of shorthand; and Beau Nash, who is buried at the eastern end of the south aisle.

Bath Abbey (☎ 422462) is open 9 am to 6 pm (to 4.30 pm in winter) (afternoon only on Sunday); a donation of £2 is requested.

On the abbey's southern side, steps lead down to a vault in which a small **museum** describes the abbey's history and its links with the baths and fashionable Georgian society. It's open from 10 am to 4 pm Monday to Saturday; admission is £2/free.

Assembly Rooms & Museum of Costume

In the 18th century, fashionable Bath visitors gathered to play cards, dance and listen to music in the Assembly Rooms in Bennett St. Nowadays, the basement museum (☎ 477789) displays costumes worn from the 16th to late-20th centuries, including alarming crinolines that would have forced women to approach doorways side on.

The museum is open 10 am to 5 pm daily (from 11 am on Sunday); admission costs £4/2.90. Combined tickets with the Roman Baths Museum are better value at £8.90/5.30.

No 1 Royal Crescent

Superbly restored to the minutest detail of its 1770 magnificence, this grand Palladian town house (☎ 428126) in the Royal Crescent is well worth visiting to see how people lived during Bath's glory days.

It's open 10.30 am to 5 pm Tuesday to Sunday, March to October (to 4 pm in November). Admission costs £4/3.

Jane Austen Centre

Located in a Georgian town house, the Jane Austen Centre (☎ 443000), 40 Gay St, is a fitting tribute to one of the city's most famous residents. The displays include period pieces and personal items.

The centre is open 10 am to 5 pm daily. Admission costs £3.95/2.95. See also the Web site at www.janeaustin.co.uk.

Building of Bath Museum

Housed in the 18th-century chapel of the Countess of Huntingdon in the Paragon, the Building of Bath Museum (☎ 333895) details how Bath's Georgian splendour came into being, a more interesting story than you might imagine.

It's open 10.30 am to 5 pm Tuesday to Sunday, March to November; admission costs £3.50/1.50.

Holburne Museum

The fine 18th-century Holburne Museum in Great Pulteney St (☎ 466669) was originally designed as the Sydney Hotel. It now houses a collection of porcelain, antiques, and paintings by great 18th-century artists such as Gainsborough and Stubbs.

It's open 11 am to 5 pm Monday to Saturday and 2.30 to 5.30 pm on Sunday, mid-February to mid-December (closed Monday, mid December to Easter). Admission costs £3.50/1.50.

Living in the past: the legendary hippy-fest at Glastonbury, Somerset

GUY MOBERLY

Living it up in a beach hut, Poole, Dorset

EDWARD AM SNIDERS

Pulteney Weir, Bath – just a stone's throw from some of England's finest Georgian architecture

A stroll by the sea, Poole, Dorset

A rural idyll: the rustic delights of Castle Combe, Wiltshire

Museum of Bath at Work

Tucked away in Julian Rd, the Museum of Bath at Work (☎ 318348) is Bath's industrial heritage centre housed in what was originally an 18th-century 'real' tennis court. Most of the fittings belonged to Jonathan Burdett Bowler's 19th-century mineral-water bottling plant and brass foundry.

It's open from 10 am to 5 pm daily (weekends only, November to Easter); admission costs £3.50/2.50.

William Herschel Museum

William Herschel arrived in Bath as an organist but was to become most noteworthy for his achievements in the field of astronomy. In 1781, he discovered the planet Uranus from the garden of his home, now housing this museum. Inside is a re-creation of how the house might have looked during the city's heyday in the 18th century. The museum (☎ 311342, 19 New King St) is open 2 to 5 pm daily (weekends only, November to February). Admission costs £2.50/1.

Sally Lunn's Kitchen Museum

Round the corner from the abbey in North Parade Passage, Sally Lunn's Kitchen Museum (☎ 461634) consists mainly of exposed foundation stones, but a commentary describes how Sally Lunn, a 17th-century Huguenot refugee, used to bake brioche. Similar brioche are still on sale in the cafe upstairs.

It's open 10 am to 6 pm Monday to Saturday and noon to 6 pm on Sunday. Admission costs 30p.

Victoria Art Gallery

Opposite Pulteney Bridge, the Victoria Art Gallery (☎ 477772) contains two Thomas Rowlandson cartoons belonging to a series entitled *The Comforts of Bath*. It also has paintings by Walter Sickert who lived nearby.

It is open from 10 am to 5.30 pm daily, closing at 5 pm on Saturday and opening at 2 pm on Sunday. Admission is free.

Royal Photographic Society Gallery

In Milsom St, the Royal Photographic Society Gallery (☎ 462841) contains exhibits illustrating the history of photography, a bookshop and the excellent In Focus cafe. It's open 9.30 am to 5.30 pm daily; admission is £4/free.

Museum of East Asian Art

The Museum of East Asian Art (☎ 464640), 12 Bennett St, contains more than 500 jade, bamboo, porcelain and bronze objects from Cambodia, Korea and Thailand, but the main emphasis is on China and Japan. It's open 10 am to 5 pm daily except Monday (from 12 pm on Sunday; shorter hours in winter). Admission costs £3.50/2.50.

Microworld

This unlikely museum (☎ 333033), 4 Monmouth St, houses a collection of microscopic sculptures such as Tower Bridge in the eye of a needle and Mount Rushmore in a match head. This quirky exhibition is open 10 am to 6 pm daily and admission costs £3.95/1.95.

Organised Tours

Free two-hour walking tours (☎ 477786) leave from outside the Pump Room at 10.30 am and 2 pm Sunday to Friday (at 10.30 am and 7 pm on Saturday, May to September). There are additional 7 pm tours on Tuesday and Friday during summer.

There are also tours of Jane Austen's Bath for those on the literary trail. They leave from the TIC at 11 am daily, last 1½ hours and cost £3.50/2.50.

Two-hour ghost walks (☎ 463618) depart from the Nash Bar in the Garrick's Head pub, off Saw Close, at 8 pm Monday to Saturday, May to October (Friday only in winter). Walks cost £4/3.

Bizarre Bath comedy walks (☎ 335124) offer an irreverent look at the city that definitely makes a change from the cultural tours normally encountered. They leave nightly from the Huntsman Inn in North Parade Passage at 8 pm and cost £4.50.

Guide Friday (☎ 444102), at the train station, runs open-top, hop-on, hop-off bus tours 9.15 am to 5.25 pm daily, Easter to October (shorter hours for the rest of the year). The buses pass Terrace Walk behind the abbey, and Bath bus station. Tickets cost £8.50/3.

WESSEX

The Classic Citytour (☎ 424157) is a similar sort of deal with locally based Ryan Coaches and is cheaper at £6/1.50.

Places to Stay

Finding somewhere to stay during busy periods can be tough and you might want to pay the TIC's £2.50 booking fee for its help. Bath Visitor Call can fax you an accommodation list; call ☎ 0891 194601 (calls cost at least 45p a minute).

Camping About 3 miles (5km) west of Bath, at Newton St Loe, the *Newton Mill Touring Centre* (☎ 333909, fax 461556, Newton Rd) charges £11.50 for a tent and two people. It's open year-round. To reach it, take the B3310 off the A4.

Hostels The wonderfully decorated, 52-bed *Bath Backpackers Hotel* (☎ 446787, e backpackers_uk@hotmail.com, 13 Pierrepont St) is Bath's most convenient budget accommodation, less than 10 minutes' walk from the bus and train stations. B&B in nonsmoking dorm rooms with up to eight beds costs £12. There's a lounge, cooking facilities and Internet access. Some readers find the atmosphere a little more Woodstock, USA than Bath, England, but if it's not to your taste there are other options. Also central, the *YMCA* (☎ 460471, International House, Broad St Place) takes men and women and has no curfew, but is often full, especially in summer. Approaching from the south along Walcot St, look out for an archway and steps on the left about 180m past the post office. Rooms with continental breakfast are £15/28; dorm beds cost £11.

Bath Youth Hostel (☎ 465674, fax 482 947, e bath@yha.org.uk, Bathwick Hill) is out towards the University of Bath, a good 25-minute walk from the city centre, or a short hop on Badgerline bus No 18 from the bus station. There are compensatory views and the building is magnificent. It has 117 beds. It's open all day, all year, and charges £10.85/7.40 for adults/children.

B&Bs & Hotels Staying in Bath doesn't come cheap, particularly during summer when many establishments hike up their prices. Bath is a popular place to spend the weekend and prices also reflect this. The main areas for B&Bs are along Newbridge Rd to the west, Wells Rd to the south, and around Pulteney Rd in the east.

Considering its location, just a few minutes' walk from the bus and train stations, *Henry Guest House* (☎ 424052, e Cox@ TheHenryBath.freeserve.co.uk, 6 Henry St) is reasonable at £22 per person. The eight rooms all have shared bathrooms.

Romany (☎ 424193, 9 Charlotte St) is also dead central and reasonable value at from £40 for a double.

There are numerous B&Bs on and around Pulteney Rd. *Ashley House* (☎ 425027, 8 Pulteney Gardens) has eight rooms, some with shower, for £26.50/50. Low-season discounts are available.

Nonsmoking *14 Raby Place* (☎ 465120, fax 465283, 14 Raby Place), off Bathwick Hill just after you turn off Pulteney Rd, charges from £25/42 with a healthy breakfast thrown in.

There are several places along Henrietta St, near Henrietta Park. The handsome nonsmoking *Georgian Guest House* (☎ 424103, fax 425279, e georgian@georgian-house .co.uk, 34 Henrietta St) has a range of rooms from £38/55.

Henrietta Hotel (☎ 447779, fax 444150, 32 Henrietta St), next door, charges from £30/50; at the weekend, this rises to £50/75!

Across the road, the classy *Kennard Hotel* (☎ 310472, fax 460054, e kennard@ dircon.co.uk, 11 Henrietta St) has rooms with baths from £48/88.

In an idyllic location beside the River Avon, the *Old Boathouse* (☎ 466407, Forester Rd) is an Edwardian boating station within walking distance of the centre. Comfortable nonsmoking rooms with bathrooms cost £55.

The B&Bs west of the centre along Upper Bristol Rd (A4), just south of the Crescent, mostly cost at least £25 a head, more if you're travelling alone. On Crescent Gardens, try *Lamp Post Villa* (☎ 331221, fax 426783, 4 Crescent Gardens), which has very comfortable doubles for £55.

At *Walton's Guest House* (☎ 426528, fax 420350, 17 Crescent Gardens), some singles/doubles go for £27/£50, suggesting the singles are a pretty fair deal compared to most in Bath.

Wells Rd (A367) also harbours B&Bs. *Arney Guest House* (☎ 310020, 99 Wells Rd) has three rooms and charges from £25/45 with shared bath. There are numerous other places nearby.

Holly Lodge (☎ 424042, fax 481138, e george.h.hall@btinternet.com, 8 Upper Oldfield Park), a 10-minute walk from the centre, has views over the city. Rooms in this nonsmoking, award-winning hotel are from £48/97.

Readers have also recommended the welcoming *Cheriton House* (☎ 429862, fax 428403, e cheriton@which.net, 9 Upper Oldfield Park), across the road, which has big rooms from £42/64.

Bath's top place to stay is on the grandest of grand crescents. The *Royal Crescent Hotel* (☎ 739955, fax 339401, 16 Royal Crescent) has 46 rooms in the two central houses. There's a garden behind the hotel and an excellent restaurant. Decorated with period furnishings, rooms are officially from £195, but if it's low season and mid-week you can usually negotiate a lower price. See the Web site at www.royalcrescent.com.

Similarly exclusive is the five-star *Bath Spa Hotel* (☎ 444424, fax 476825, Sydney Rd), which has elegant rooms from £140/224, excluding breakfast! See also the Web site at www.bathspahotel.com.

If you can afford prices like that and have a car it's worth considering staying outside Bath at *Ston Easton Park* (☎ 01761-241631, fax 01761-241377, e stoneastonpark@stoneaston.co.uk), a stunning Georgian mansion in landscaped grounds with wonderful rooms for £155/320. The village of Ston Easton is 10 miles (16km) south-west of Bath.

Places to Eat

Bath has a range of eateries to suit every budget. Self-catering is covered by the covered market and local supermarkets; pubs and cafes offer value dining, while those who are flush can find plenty of top-class restaurants.

Itchy Feet (☎ 337987, fax 337986, 4 Bartlett St) has a small menu for travellers on the move, with a sandwich, packet of crisps, brownie and soft drink for £4.95. Even if that doesn't catch your eye, it is worth checking out the well-stocked travel shop, chockablock full of everything from clothing to guidebooks.

Near the abbey, wannabee retro *Café Retro* (☎ 339347, York St) does three-course meals for around £10, although light bites are much less. Good cakes are on offer in the *In Focus* cafe in the Royal Photographic Society Gallery (see that section earlier).

Just east of Pulteney Bridge is *Baku* (☎ 444440, Argyle St), a small, cosy diner offering gourmet sandwiches and the like. Nearby, the good-value *Bathtub Bistro* (☎ 460593, 2 Grove St) serves interesting dishes such as spinach, lentil and apricot filo parcel.

The *Jazz Café* near Westgate has no music but a great selection of traditional greasy-spoon fare.

Demuth's (☎ 446059, North Parade Passage) serves vegetarian and vegan food to die for and has two-course specials for £6.95. Vegetarians might also like to try one of the two *Scoff's*, including the Arts Café in the Hot Bath Gallery where the hot dishes start from around £3.

Alternatively, pop into *Sally Lunn's*, which has been baking brioche for over 300 years and has a selection of very traditional English meals like toad-in-the-hole (made with a sausage, rather than a fat frog in case anyone is worrying) and roast meals. See also Sally Lunn's Kitchen Museum earlier.

The *Moon & Sixpence* (☎ 460962, 6 Broad St) offers pleasant two-course eat-all-you-can lunches for £5. Pubs are also the best bet for cheap evening meals, too. *The Crystal Palace* (☎ 423944, Abbey Green), south of Abbey Churchyard, has a beer garden, traditional ale and standard pub fare.

The Raincheck Bar (☎ 444770, 34 Monmouth St) is a popular cafe-bar with good food, an intimate atmosphere and some streetside tables. By night it is for drinking rather than dining.

The *Firehouse Brasserie* (☎ 482070, *Queen St)* offers classic Mediterranean food and what are considered the best pizzas in town. Prices are higher than some of the competition (£10 for a pizza), but that doesn't seem to stop locals from congregating here in numbers. *Wood's* (☎ 314812, *9 Alfred St)* is more reasonable – prices for two-course lunches start at around £5.

Bonghy-bo (☎ 462276, *2–3 Barton Court, Upper Borough Walls)* is a small cafe with an eclectic mix of Asian dishes and the prices are pretty sensible, even if the name provokes a smirk. *Mai Thai* (☎ 445557, *6 Pierrepoint St)* is a good Thai restaurant with some excellent lunchtime offers including two courses for £7.

Good French restaurants include *Le Beaujolais* (☎ 423417, *5 Chapel Row)*, with express three-course lunches for £8.50 and a selection of regional favourites. The fact that this is always busy is a statement on the quality of the food. *Rendezvous Provencal* (☎ 310064, *Upper Church St)* is another French restaurant with a similar lunchtime deal, cosy atmosphere and good location near the Crescent.

The Circus (☎ 318918, *Brock St)* has a good reputation, but is a step up in price. Expect to pay more like £20 a head.

The best place for cream teas is the *Pump Room* (see also that section earlier). Here one sips one's tea and heaps one's scones with jam and cream while being serenaded by the Pump Room Trio. Starting at £6.95, it's hardly cheap but is very much part of the Bath experience. It's open 9.30 am to 10 pm. Dinner is served 7 to 10 pm; two courses cost £16.50 or three courses £18.95. The menu is pretty lively including such delights as fillet of salmon with grilled asparagus and a lemon cream dressing.

Entertainment

Venue magazine (£1.90) has comprehensive listings with details of theatre, music, gigs – the works basically – for Bristol and Bath.

Pubs & Clubs Bath has lots of atmospheric pubs and, thanks to a healthy student population, some reasonable clubs.

Pubs worth a drink include the intimate *Coeur de Lion* (*17 Northumberland Place)*, off the High St, *The Bell* (☎ 460426, *103 Walcot St)* and the *Saracen's Head* (☎ 426518, *Broad St)*, the city's oldest pub. Work up a thirst by following the canal 1½ miles (2.5km) north-east out of Bath to Bathampton village, where the ever-popular *George* (☎ 425079) is beside the towpath.

The *Bath Tap* (☎ 404344, *19–20 St James Parade)* is the most popular place among Bath's gay community. Pre-club hotspots at the moment include *The Porter* (☎ 424104, *2 Miles's Bldgs, George St)*, a pub-bar with a cool atmosphere just above the popular *Moles* club (☎ 404445, *14 George St)*.

Another place attracting attention is *Bar Karanga* (☎ 446546, *8–10 Manvers St)*, a trendy spot named in honour of the city's most popular club night that rocks on at *Babylon* (☎ 400404, *Kingston Rd)*, a club that is otherwise not really worth a visit.

Po Na Na (☎ 401115, *8–9 North Parade)* is a popular bar-club that hits 2 am at the weekend, one of a chain that has slowly stamped its identity on cities from Oxford to Bristol.

Theatre The sumptuous *Theatre Royal* (☎ 448844, *Barton St)* often features shows on their pre-London run.

Classical Music A regular program of lunchtime recitals is featured at *Bath Abbey* (☎ 422462); the price depends on who is appearing.

Shopping

Much of the city centre, including the maze of passageways just north of Abbey Churchyard and Shire's Yard off Milsom St, is given over to shops of the pricey 'novelty' kind, but the Saturday and Sunday morning flea market (antiques and clothes) in Walcot St, near the YMCA, is popular with bargain hunters. The covered Guildhall Market in High St has excellent second-hand bookstalls.

Itchy Feet (☎ 337987, fax 337986), 4 Bartlett St, is an excellent travel shop stocking books, maps, clothing and supplies. They also have a cafe; see Places to Eat for more details.

Getting There & Away

Bath is 106 miles (171km) from London, 19 miles (31km) from Wells and only 12 miles (19km) from Bristol. See the fares tables in the Getting Around chapter.

Bus There are National Express (☎ 0870 580 8080) buses every two hours from London (three hours, £11.50). There's also a link with Oxford (two hours, £9.75), and Stratford-upon-Avon via Bristol (2½ hours, £15.75).

There is an hourly bus (X4) between Bristol and Salisbury (£3.90) via Bath. Several buses serve the Bath to Bristol route, but most frequent is the X39, which runs every 15 minutes (30 minutes Sundays) and takes 50 minutes. Wells is served by hourly Bus No 173 (1¼ hours).

The useful Cotswold Shuttle (X55) offers two daily services to Stratford-upon-Avon via Cotswold honeypots like Cirencester, Bourton-on-the-Water, Stow-on-the-Wold, Moreton-in-Marsh, Chipping Campden and so on. See the Cotswolds section for more details. Some excellent map-timetables are available from the bus station (☎ 464446) on Manvers St. The Badgerline Day Rambler (£5.30/3.75) gives you access to a good network of buses in Bristol, Somerset (Wells, Glastonbury), Gloucestershire (Gloucester) and Wiltshire (Lacock, Salisbury, Bradford-on-Avon).

Train There are numerous trains from London Paddington (1½ hours, £30), and also plenty of trains to Bristol for onward travel to Cardiff, Exeter or the north. Hourly trains link Portsmouth and Bristol via Salisbury and Bath. A single ticket from Bath to Salisbury is £10. A day return to Bristol is £4.60.

Getting Around

Car Bath has a bad traffic problem and parking space is hard to find. In the city centre, you must display a parking disc on your windscreen. It will cost you 50p for quarter of an hour and can be bought from local shops. Clamping is big business in

Bath and release fees are around £110. Take care about where you park. Sainsbury's supermarket and Homebase DIY store have a huge free car park for customers (two hours) near Charles St and the River Avon.

Bicycle Bikes can be hired from Avon Valley Cyclery (☎ 461880), behind the train station, for £14 per day. See the Web site at www.bikeshop.uk.com. Cyclists can use the 12-mile Bristol and Bath Railway Path that follows a disused railway line.

Boat Hourly passenger boats sail from beneath Pulteney Bridge to Bathampton from April to October. Alternatively, you can hire canoes, punts or rowing boats to propel yourself along the Avon from £4.50 an hour (£1.50 for additional hours); try Bath Boating station (☎ 466407) in Forester Rd.

AROUND BATH
Prior Park

This recently restored, beautiful 18th-century park (☎ 833422), owned by the National Trust (NT), with spectacular views of Bath was created for Ralph Allen by Capability Brown. It's in Ralph Allen Drive, accessible only by bus No 2, 4 or 733, or on foot. Admission costs £3.80/1.90 (£1 refund if you show your bus ticket); it's open noon to 5.30 pm daily except Tuesday.

American Museum

Claverton Manor (☎ 460503), 3 miles (5km) south-east of Bath, is an 1820s mansion housing re-created 17th- to 19th-century American home interiors, a collection of quilts and other American memorabilia. There is also a recreation of an 18th-century Massachusetts tavern.

Bus No 18 to the university drops you half a mile from the entrance. The house is open 2 to 5 pm daily except Monday, March to October (the grounds from 1 to 6 pm). Admission costs £5.50/3, although you can buy a grounds-only ticket for £3/2.

Dyrham Park

On the A46 8 miles (13km) north of Bath, Dyrham Park (☎ 0117-937 2501; NT) is a

105-hectare deer park surrounding the fine 17th-century house of William Blathwayt, secretary of state to William III.

The house is open noon to 5.30 pm Friday to Tuesday, April to October; admission costs £7.50/3.70. The park is open noon to 5.30 pm daily year-round; admission costs £1.80/90p. On Friday and Saturday Ryans Coaches connect Dyrham with Bath; phone ☎ 424157 for times.

Somerset

A largely agricultural county, Somerset is known for its cider-making, cricket club and Cheddar cheese. The most interesting towns are Wells, with its superb cathedral, and mystical Glastonbury, a magnet for druids and New Age hippies. Bath or Wells make good bases to the east of Somerset, as do Lynton and Lynmouth to the west.

Somerset is good walking country. The Mendip Hills are cut by gorges where caves were inhabited from prehistoric times. The Quantocks to the west are less cultivated, while to the far west of the county, the wilder Exmoor National Park (see later in this chapter) spans the border with Devon.

WALKING & CYCLING

The 613-mile (987km) South West Coast Path begins in Minehead and follows the West Country coast round to Poole in Dorset. See the Activities chapter for information. TICs stock the free *Cycle Round South Somerset* describing an 80-mile (129km) cycle route, and *The Somerset Cycle Guide*.

GETTING AROUND

The Somerset transport inquiry line is ☎ 01823-358299, but you can also phone the bus companies direct: the region is roughly split between First Badgerline (☎ 0117-955 3231) north of Bridgwater, and First Southern National (☎ 01823-272033) to the south. First Southern National has a day explorer pass that covers Somerset, North Devon and West Dorset for £5.30/3.75. First Badgerline's explorer covers much of Somerset, Bristol, Salisbury and Berkeley, and costs the same.

WELLS

☎ 01749 • pop 9400

Wells is a must for anyone in this part of the world. Taking its name from three springs that emerged near the medieval Bishop's Palace, Wells is England's smallest cathedral city. It has managed to guard much of its medieval character and the cathedral is one of England's most beautiful, with one of the best surviving examples of a full cathedral complex.

Wells is 22 miles (35km) south-west of Bath, on the edge of the Mendips. As well as being a good base for touring the Mendips, it's within easy reach of Cheddar, Wookey Hole and Glastonbury.

Orientation & Information

The city centre is compact and easy to get around. The TIC (☎ 672552, fax 670869, ⓔ wellstic@ukonline.co.uk) is at the Town Hall, on the picturesque Market Place near the cathedral. It is open 9.30 am to 5.30 pm daily.

Wells Cathedral Clock

High up in the north transept is a wonderful mechanical clock dating from 1392 – the second-oldest surviving in England after the one in Salisbury Cathedral.

The complex-looking dial shows the hours in two sets of 12 on the outer circle, with the sun rotating round the earth to mark the hours. The minutes are shown on the inner circle, each indicated by a rotating star.

The clock also shows the position of the planets and the phases of the moon, but it's the entertaining cabaret act performed above it by jousting knights on horseback that draws a small crowd on the hour (the quarter-hour in summer).

Quarterjacks in the shape of 15th-century knights use poleaxes to hit a bell to mark the time on the clock's exterior face.

There are lots of interesting walking and cycling routes nearby; the TIC has details. Markets are held in Market Place on Wednesday and Saturday.

Wells Cathedral

The cathedral (☎ 674483) was built in stages from 1180 to 1508 and incorporates several Gothic styles. Its most famous feature is the wonderful **west front**, an immense sculpture gallery with over 300 figures, that was built between 1230 and 1250 and restored to its original splendour in 1986. Apart from the figure of Christ, installed in 1985 in the uppermost niche, all the other figures are original.

Inside, the most striking feature is the pair of **scissor arches**, separating the nave from the choir, a brilliant solution to the problem posed by the subsidence of the central tower; they were added in the 14th century, shortly after the tower's completion. Just before the hour, make sure you're standing in front of the intriguing **mechanical clock** in the north transept.

Among other things to look out for in the cathedral are the elegant **Lady Chapel** at the eastern end; the seven **effigies** of Anglo-Saxon bishops ringing the choir; and the **chained library** upstairs from the south transept. The library is open 2.30 to 4.30 pm Tuesday to Saturday, April to October. Admission costs 50p.

Reached by worn steps leading off the north transept is the glorious mid-13th-century **Chapter House**, the ceiling ribs of which sprout like a palm from a central column. Externally, look out for the **Chain Bridge** built from the northern side of the cathedral to Vicars' Close to enable clerics to reach the cathedral without getting their robes wet. The **cloisters** on the southern side surround a pretty courtyard.

The cathedral is open 7 am to 7 pm (to 8.30 pm in July and August); visitors are asked to donate £4/1. Guided tours are free.

Cathedral Close

Wells Cathedral is the focal point of a cluster of buildings whose history is inextricably linked to its own. Facing the west front,

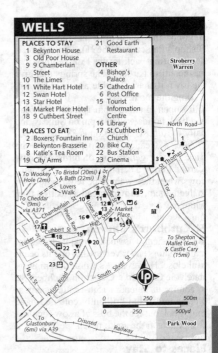

WELLS

PLACES TO STAY	21	Good Earth
1 Bekynton House		Restaurant
3 Old Poor House		
9 Chamberlain	OTHER	
Street	4	Bishop's
10 The Limes		Palace
11 White Hart Hotel	5	Cathedral
12 Swan Hotel	6	Post Office
13 Star Hotel	15	Tourist
14 Market Place Hotel		Information
18 9 Cuthbert Street		Centre
	16	Library
PLACES TO EAT	17	St Cuthbert's
2 Boxers; Fountain Inn		Church
7 Bekynton Brasserie	20	Bike City
8 Katie's Tea Room	22	Bus Station
19 City Arms	23	Cinema

on the left are the 15th-century **Old Deanery** and a salmon-coloured building housing **Wells Museum** (☎ 673477), with exhibits about caving in the Mendips, local life and the cathedral architecture. The museum is open 10 am to 5.30 pm daily, April to October (to 8 pm in July and August); and 11 am to 4 pm daily except Monday and Tuesday, November to April. Admission costs £2/1.

Further along on the left, **Vicars' Close** is a cobbled street of uniform houses dating back to the 14th century with a chapel at the end; members of the cathedral choir still live here. It is thought to be the oldest complete medieval street in Europe. Passing under the Chain Bridge inspect the outside of the Lady Chapel and a lovely medieval house called **The Rib**, before emerging at a main road called The Liberty. In the Middle Ages this marked the boundary of the cathedral precincts within which a refugee could take sanctuary.

WESSEX

Bishop's Palace

Beyond the cathedral is the moated Bishop's Palace (☎ 678691), a private residence dating back to the 13th century that has beautiful gardens. The springs that give the town its name bubble and babble here, feeding the moat.

It's open 11 am to 6 pm Tuesday to Friday and bank holidays, 2 to 6 pm on Sunday and daily in August; admission is £3/free.

After a decade when no swans knew the trick, a new generation of birds has now learned to ring a bell outside one of the windows when they want to be fed. If you want to feed them, brown bread is better than white.

St Cuthbert's Church

Wells Cathedral is such a major draw that many visitors never venture beyond its beautiful close. However, it's worth dropping by stately **St Cuthbert's Church** in Cuthbert St, to admire its splendid 15th-century perpendicular tower and brilliantly coloured nave roof. Look out for the boss of a sow suckling five piglets in the south porch.

Places to Stay

There are plenty of B&Bs but most have only a few rooms so advance booking is advised. **9 Chamberlain St** (☎ 672270, e number9@ukf.net) is well located near the cathedral and charges £22/38. Nearby is **The Limes** (☎ 675716, fax 674874, e john @thelimes.uk.com, 29 Chamberlain St), with two rooms. For the four-poster bed, B&B costs £20 per person; in the twin room it's £18. Singles are £30.

The B&B at **19 St Cuthbert St** (☎ 673166) overlooks the cathedral in a quiet part of town and charges from £16.50 per person.

The **Old Poor House** (☎/fax 675052, e bookings@wells-poorhouse.co.uk, 7a St Thomas St) is a comfortable 14th-century cottage just outside the cathedral precincts. The nightly charge is £25 per person. Slightly further out, **Bekynton House** (☎ 672222, e desmond@bekynton.freeserve .co.uk, `7 St Thomas St) charges £36/52 for comfortable lodgings.

There's a cluster of hotels near the cathedral. The **Star Hotel** (☎ 670500, fax 672654, 18 High St) has good-value triple rooms for £65. Singles/doubles cost £50/55. The **White Hart Hotel** (☎/fax 672056, e white hart@wells.demon.co.uk, Sadler St) has rooms for £57.50/75 with bathrooms.

The **Swan Hotel** (☎ 678877, fax 677647, e swan@heritagehotels.co.uk, Sadler St) is a fine 15th-century inn with some four-poster beds; some of the rooms look straight onto the cathedral's west front. Room prices are £75/95, but ask about special deals.

The newest establishment is the **Market Place Hotel** (☎ 672616, fax 679670, e marketplace@heritagehotels.co.uk, Market Place), actually housed in one of the oldest buildings. Rooms here are £75/95, but it works out much cheaper to book a two-night half-board break from £49.50 per night in winter, £65 in summer.

Places to Eat

The most atmospheric place to eat is the **Refectory** in the cathedral cloisters where you can lunch on soup and a roll or sandwiches, overlooked by 18th-century monuments. It's open daily for lunch and afternoon tea. **Katie's Tea Room** (Sadler St), opposite the White Hart Hotel, does a good cream tea.

Near the bus station is the **Good Earth Restaurant** (☎ 678600, 4 Priory Rd), an excellent vegetarian place to eat. The courgette and stilton lasagne is recommended and the soups are a bargain.

Bekynton Brasserie (☎ 675993, 21 Market Place) is a good place for standard lunch fare, and is popular with locals.

The **City Arms** (☎ 673916, 69 High St) serves good pub grub and also has a restaurant open in the evening. Part of the pub used to be a jail in Tudor times.

The town's best restaurant is probably **Boxers** (☎ 672317, 1 St Thomas St), upstairs in the Fountain Inn; expect to pay about £20 for a three-course meal and drinks.

Entertainment

A year-round program of lunchtime recitals and evening concerts gives the chance to hear the historic cathedral choir in full voice. For details, phone ☎ 674483.

Getting There & Around

Badgerline (☎ 0117-955 3231) operates hourly buses from Bristol (Nos 376/976) and Bath (No 173). No 163 runs to Wells from Glastonbury and Street. Bus Nos 161/2 travel from Frome via Shepton Mallet. Coming from the coast, bus Nos 126 and 826 travel hourly (every two hours Sunday) from Weston-Super-Mare via Cheddar.

There's no train station in Wells; the nearest is 15 miles (24km) away at Castle Cary.

Bike City (☎ 343111, 91 Broad St) has bikes for hire from £8 per day.

WOOKEY HOLE

Wookey Hole, the site of a sequence of caves carved out by the River Axe, one of them containing a spectacular lake, is just 2 miles (3km) east of Wells. The striking shape of one particular stalagmite gave rise to the legend of the Witch of Wookey. Nowadays the caves are the focal point of a series of other attractions, including an ancient handmade-paper mill, an Edwardian fairground, a maze of mirrors and an arcade of vintage amusement machines.

The Wookey Hole attractions (☎ 01749-672243) are open 10 am to 5 pm daily, April to September (10.30 am to 4.30 pm in winter); admission costs £7.20/4.20. Bus No 171 offers an hourly service between Wells and Wookey Hole (10 minutes, £1.20/1.60 one way/return). A 3-mile walk to Wookey is signposted from New St in Wells.

CHEDDAR GORGE
☎ 01934

The Mendips' most dramatic scenery can be found along its southern side where the Cheddar Gorge cuts a mile swathe through the landscape, exposing great swathes of 138m-high grey stone cliff. Approaching on foot from the north or walking along the cliff-top paths, it's possible to imagine how wild and spectacular Cheddar must have been before the stalactite and stalagmite-filled Cox's and Gough's caves started to suck in the crowds; however, the area immediately around the caves can be very off-putting in summer when the place heaves with visitors. It's probably best to visit out

---

Cheddar Cheese

The country's most famous cheese only began to become widely known when people started visiting Cheddar Gorge and taking home some of the local cheese. Cheddar was just one of many Somerset villages that produced this type of cheese.

Over the years, and with mass production not only all over Britain but in several other countries as well, Cheddar has become a generic name for any pale yellow, medium-hard cheese. The name covers a wide range of qualities, from soapy supermarket Cheddar to the delicious farmhouse variety, which is mature and tangy.

If you're interested in the process of making genuine Cheddar Cheese, the Cheddar Gorge Cheese Company (☎ 01934-742810) is open daily. You can watch the cheese-maker at work and on the hour there's a short talk. It's part of the Rural Village (just off the B3135) that also includes demonstrations of lace-making, pottery, fudge-making and spinning. Entry to the village is £1.50/1.

---

of season, bearing in mind that most of the teashops and fish and chip shops only open over winter weekends.

The **Cheddar Showcaves** (☎ 742343) are open 10 am to 5 pm daily, Easter to September, and 10.30 am to 4.30 pm in winter. Admission costs £7.50/5, which covers entry to the heritage centre, lookout tower and cliff-top walk.

The TIC (☎ 744071, fax 744614) in the gorge is open 10 am to 5 pm daily, Easter to October, and Sunday only for the rest of the year. **Cheddar village**, to the south-west of the gorge, has an elegant church and an ancient market cross but is otherwise disappointing. A mile from the caves on a road off The Hayes, the *Cheddar Youth Hostel* (☎ 742494, fax 744724, e cheddar@yha .org.uk, Hillfield), on the western side of the village, charges £10.85/7.40 per night.

Badgerline bus Nos 126/826 run between Wells (9 miles; 14km) and Weston-Super-Mare via Cheddar (20 minutes, £2.45/3.40

WESSEX

one way/return), hourly Monday to Saturday and every two hours on Sunday.

AXBRIDGE
☎ 01934

Just 1½ miles (2.5km) from Cheddar, the pretty village of Axbridge is light years away from Cheddar's tackiness, and makes a much nicer, albeit pricier, place to stay.

One corner of the central square is dominated by the striking half-timbered **King John's Hunting Lodge** (☎ 732012; NT), a Tudor merchant's house now housing the local museum. It's open 2 to 5 pm daily, Easter to September.

Another corner is occupied by the huge late-Gothic church of St John with a 17th-century plaster ceiling. The rest of the square is ringed with hotels and restaurants.

Places to Stay & Eat

For somewhere to stay, try *The Lamb Inn* (☎ 732253, fax 733821, ℮ lambinn@ax bridge.org.uk) where rooms cost £40/50 with bath. *The Oak House Hotel (*☎ 732444, fax 733122, The Square)* is another with rooms for £45/65.

To eat, choose between the *Spinning Wheel Restaurant (*☎ 732476, The Square)* where a three-course dinner midweek costs £17.95, and the 15th-century *Almshouse Bistro (*☎ 732493).

Getting There & Away

You can easily walk or cycle to Axbridge from Cheddar. Badgerline bus No 126 from Cheddar to Burnham-on-Sea also passes through the centre.

MENDIP HILLS

The Mendips are a ridge of limestone hills about 25 miles (40km) long and 5 miles (8km) wide in northern Somerset. These are not lofty hills – their highest point is Black Down (326m) to the north-west – but they stand out in an area that is otherwise very flat, giving way in the south to the Somerset Levels where roads often run on causeways above flood level.

Nowadays the Mendips form a densely cultivated agricultural area, but in the past they were more famous for coal mining, traces of which can be seen round Radstock and Midsomer Norton to the east. The Romans are known to have mined for lead around Charterhouse and Priddy; lead mining continued throughout the Middle Ages and right up until 1900.

Pubs that loom up out of the middle of nowhere are survivors from a time when mining brought plenty of thirsty drinkers. You can see the remains of St Cuthbert's lead mines near Priddy, and scruffy hollows around Charterhouse mark the sites of shallow mine workings. Quarrying for stone is an important (and controversial) industry to this day.

Local TICs in the surrounding towns stock leaflets with information on walking and cycling opportunities in the area, including village trails that take in points of interest.

The A371 skirts the southern side of the Mendip Hills, and any of the towns along it – Axbridge, Cheddar, Wells, Shepton Mallet or Frome – would make good touring bases, though Wells has got the best range of facilities.

Mendip Villages

The Mendip villages are not renowned for particularly striking buildings, although you might be interested in the 19th-century **Downside Abbey**, established by English monks driven from France by the French Revolution. Downside is now a famous Roman Catholic boys' school.

Otherwise, many of the villages are pretty, in a low-key way, and several have fine perpendicular church towers. Especially impressive is that at **Chewton Mendip** (off the A37 from Bristol to Wells), where there's an attractive medieval churchyard cross. Further west, the village of **Priddy**, the highest in the Mendips, has a massive sheep fair on the green that locals flock to from around the region.

The village of **Compton Martin** has a Norman church with a 15th-century tower. A mile to the east, **West Harptree** is a prettier village with two 17th-century former manor houses. Near **East Harptree** are the remains of Norman Richmont Castle, captured from supporters of Matilda by those of King Stephen in 12th-century skirmishing.

Getting There & Away

Badgerline buses (☎ 0117-955 3231) serve this area, although don't expect services to be very frequent off the major roads. Apart from the buses to Wells and Glastonbury, Nos 126/826 run between Wells, Cheddar and Axbridge. Nos 160/162 regularly link Wells with Shepton Mallet, No 161 links Wells and Frome, while No 173 runs between Bath, Radstock, Midsomer Norton and Wells.

By car, the Mendip Hills are squeezed in between the A38 Bristol to Burnham-on-Sea and the A37 Bristol to Wells roads.

FROME
☎ 01373

Frome (pronounced froom) is a town that owes its existence to sheep and the wool off their backs. This is a pretty town with a liberal smattering of historic buildings and narrow alleys, although the suburbs sprawl rather, as this is now the fourth-largest town in Somerset. **Cheap St** is home to Tudor houses, while **Catherine Hill** is a tumbling road of arts and antiques shops that are good for browsing. There is nothing else compelling, but its location to the east of the Mendips makes it a clear alternative to the towns of the west.

The TIC (☎ 467271, fax 451733, **e** frome .tic@ukonline.co.uk), The Round Tower, 2 Bridge St, is open 10 am to 5 pm Monday to Saturday.

Bus No 161 runs to Shepton Mallet and Wells.

SHEPTON MALLET
☎ 01749

Shepton Mallet also grew from the wool and cloth trades and was at its height of importance in the 17th century. In the 21st century it finds itself rather less important, but could offer a useful base to explore the Mendips if Wells feels overrun. There is an ornate **market cross** in the centre of town dating from the 16th century, but otherwise little to keep you.

The TIC (☎ 345258, **e** sheptonmallet .tic@ukonline.co.uk), 70 High St, shares a home with the Heritage Centre. It is open 10 am to 4 pm Monday to Friday (to 2 pm on Saturday), and 10 am to 1 pm in winter (to noon on Saturday).

Bus No 161 runs here regularly from Wells and on to Frome.

GLASTONBURY
☎ 01458 • pop 6900

Little more than an extended village, Glastonbury is the New Age capital of the country – the place to come if you want your runes read, if you want to find out about English paganism or to buy crystals, candles or incense sticks. The juxtaposition of Somerset's gentrified classes, white witches and the soap-dodging brigade make for a pretty heady mix.

Myths and legends about Glastonbury abound. One story tells how Jesus came here with his great-uncle Joseph of Arimathea, while another reports Joseph bringing the chalice from the Last Supper with him. Later legends also made Glastonbury the burial place of King Arthur and Queen Guinevere, and the tor (the nearby hill), the Isle of Avalon. Finally, the tor was thought to guard a gateway to the underworld. Over time, these different tales became entangled with each other in a potent mixture that has left Glastonbury important to Christians, pagans and atheists alike, as a glimpse in the shop windows of the various bookshops confirms.

Whatever you choose to believe, Glastonbury has the ruins of a 14th-century abbey, a couple of museums, mystic springs and superb views from the tor to make it well worth a visit.

Orientation & Information

The main bus stop is opposite the town hall in Magdalene St, within sight of the market cross and the abbey ruins.

Glastonbury's TIC (☎ 832954, fax 832949, **e** glastonbury.tic@ukonline.co.uk), at Tribunal, 9 High St, is open 10 am to 5 pm daily (10 am to 5.30 pm on Friday and Saturday). It stocks free maps and accommodation lists, and sells leaflets describing local walks and village trails.

There is Internet access at Café Galatea (see Places to Eat). From Easter to October you can hire bikes for £7/30 a day/week at Pedalers (☎ 834562) opposite the town hall on Magdalene St.

Glastonbury hosts a market on Tuesday.

Glastonbury Abbey

Legend suggests that there has been a church on this site since the 1st century, but the first definite traces date back to the 7th century when King Ine gave a charter to a monastery here. The first abbey church seems to have reached the height of its importance under the abbacy of St Dunstan, later an archbishop of Canterbury. During his time in office, King Edgar, the first king of a united England, died and was buried at Glastonbury.

In 1184 the old church was destroyed by fire; reconstruction began in the reign of Henry II. In 1191 monks claimed to have had visions confirming hints in old manuscripts that the 6th-century warrior-king Arthur and his wife Guinevere were buried in the grounds. Excavations to the south of the old church uncovered what was said to be their tomb, and a lead cross recording that fact, which has since disappeared. The

couple were reinterred in front of the high altar of the new church in 1278 and the tomb survived until 1539 when Henry VIII dissolved the monasteries.

The last abbot was hanged, drawn and quartered on the tor. After that, the abbey complex gradually collapsed, its component parts scavenged to provide building materials. It wasn't until the 19th century that Romanticism brought renewed interest in King Arthur and the sites associated with him.

The ruins you see at Glastonbury today are mainly of the church built after the 1184 fire. They include a **Lady Chapel**, built, unusually, at the western end of the church; some nave walls; parts of the crossing arches, which may have been scissor-shaped like those in Wells Cathedral; some **medieval tiles**; and remains of the choir. The site of the supposed **tomb of Arthur and Guinevere** is marked in the grass. A little to the side of the main site, don't miss the flagstone-floored **Abbot's Kitchen** with its soaring chimney; later use as a Quaker meeting house allowed it to survive intact.

An excellent **Visitors Centre** describes the history of the site and contains a model showing what the ruins would have looked

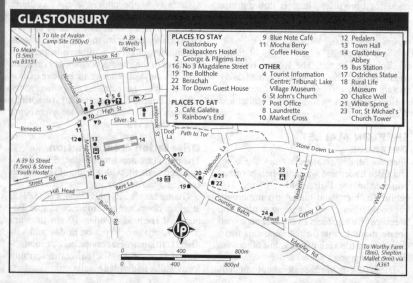

GLASTONBURY

To Isle of Avalon Camp Site (350yd)

To Meare (3.5mi) via B3151

A 39 to Wells (6mi)

Manor House Rd

Northload St

High St

Silver St

Benedict St

Magdalene St

A 39 to Street (1.5mi) & Street Youth Hostel

Street Rd

Hill Head

Butleigh Rd

Bere La

Lambrook St

Dod La

Chilkwell St

Wellhouse La

Path to Tor

Stone Down La

Coursing Batch

Ashwell La

Basketfield La

Gypsy La

Edgarley Rd

Wick La

To Worthy Farm (8mi), Shepton Mallet (9mi) via A361

PLACES TO STAY
1 Glastonbury Backpackers Hostel
2 George & Pilgrims Inn
16 No 3 Magdalene Street
19 The Bolthole
22 Berachah
24 Tor Down Guest House

PLACES TO EAT
3 Café Galatea
5 Rainbow's End

9 Blue Note Café
11 Mocha Berry Coffee House

OTHER
4 Tourist Information Centre; Tribunal; Lake Village Museum
6 St John's Church
7 Post Office
8 Laundrette
10 Market Cross

12 Pedalers
13 Town Hall
14 Glastonbury Abbey
15 Bus Station
17 Ostriches Statue
18 Rural Life Museum
20 Chalice Well
21 White Spring
23 Tor; St Michael's Church Tower

0   400   800m
0   400   800yd

WESSEX

like in their heyday. Behind it, and easy to overlook, are tiny **St Patrick's Chapel** and a **thorn tree** supposedly grown from the original that sprouted on Wearyall Hill when Joseph of Arimathea stuck his staff into the ground. It flowers in spring and at Christmas.

The site (☎ 832267) is open from 9.30 am (9 am, June to August) to 5.30 pm or dusk daily; admission costs £3/2.50.

Lake Village Museum

A small museum devoted to the prehistoric village that flourished near Glastonbury when the surrounding lowlands had not yet been drained is upstairs in the Tribunal, the medieval courthouse that dates back to 1400 and now houses the TIC. Wet conditions have allowed an unusually large quantity of wooden artefacts to survive – even a dugout canoe (in a separate room at the back). The museum (☎ 832949), owned by English Heritage (EH), is open 10 am to 5 pm Sunday to Thursday, April to September (to 5.30 pm on Friday and Saturday; to 4.30 pm, October to March). Admission costs £2/1.

St John's Church

Set back from the High St is this stunning open-plan perpendicular church that has a spectacular 15th-century wooden roof and pillars so thin it's hard to believe they can support the weight of the walls. Look out for the egg-timer attached to the pulpit to guard against overlong sermons. Vandalism means the church must be kept locked when there's no one to supervise visitors. You're most likely to find it open on market day (Tuesday).

Glastonbury Tor

Tor is a Celtic word used to describe a hill shaped like a triangular wedge of cheese, and Glastonbury Tor is open to walkers year-round. On the 160m-high summit stands a tower, all that remains of the medieval church of St Michael, a saint frequently associated with high places. You can see a carving of St Michael weighing the souls of the dead in a giant scale on the tower front.

It takes three-quarters of an hour to walk up and down the tor; there are short-stay car parks at the bottom of both paths. A Tor Bus runs there every 30 minutes from Magdalene St from May to September (£1/50p).

White Spring

This spring flows out into a cave at the foot of the tor in Wellhouse Lane, and has been dressed up with a cafe and mock medieval and Tudor house facades; atmospheric or Disneyfied depending on your mood and the number of other visitors.

Chalice Well

The Chalice Well has become entwined in Glastonbury myths and legends, even though its name probably relates to its site in Chilkwell St rather than to real links with the Holy Grail. The well has a long association with traditions of healing and you can drink from it as the water pours out through a lion's head spout. It then runs through brick channels into the gardens below, eventually cascading down a series of ceramic dishes into two interlocking basins surrounded by flowers.

It's a beautiful, peaceful spot to spend a few hours and is open 10 am to 5 pm daily. Admission costs £2.75/1.

Rural Life Museum

Partially housed in a late-14th-century tithe barn, the Rural Life Museum (☎ 831197) in Bere Lane exhibits artefacts associated with farming, cider-making, cheese-making and other aspects of Somerset country life. In the grounds, you can see rare breeds of sheep and chicken, and apple trees. Upstairs, don't miss the three-seater toilet, with holes for Mum, Dad and Junior. The barn has fine carvings on the gables and porch, and an impressive timber roof; it now houses a collection of old agricultural machinery.

The museum opens 10 am to 5 pm weekdays, except Monday, Easter to October, and 2 to 6 pm at the weekend. The rest of the year it opens 10 am to 3 pm Tuesday to Saturday. Admission costs £2.50/1.

Glastonbury Festival

In the Glastonbury Festival, the spirit of Woodstock lives on. This three-day summer extravaganza of music, theatre, circus, natural healing and so on, is a massive affair with more than 1000 acts, which doesn't always go down well with the locals. It takes place at Worthy Farm, Pilton, 8 miles (13km) from Glastonbury. Admission is by advance ticket only (about £90 for the whole festival).

The 2001 festival was cancelled after the large number of people jumping the fence in 2000 prompted concerns about safety, but the festival is planned to go ahead in 2002, complete with new high-security fences to deter gatecrashers. See the Web sites at www.glastonburyfestivals.co.uk and www.efestivals.co.uk/glastonbury.

Places to Stay

Camping There are several camp sites in and around Glastonbury. *Isle of Avalon* (☎ 833618, fax 833618, Godney Rd) is a 10-minute walk from the centre, off the B3151. A pitch costs from £5.95, plus £1.90 per person.

Hostels Worth a try is the *Glastonbury Backpackers Hostel* (☎ 833353, fax 835988, e glastonbury@backpackers-online.com, Crown Hotel, Market Place). Dorm beds are £10, there are also a few doubles (£26) and even an en suite (£30). There's a kitchen, TV room and popular cafe downstairs that draws locals as well as backpackers.

The nearest HI hostel is in nearby Street (see Around Glastonbury).

B&Bs Glastonbury has B&Bs from around £20 a night and many establishments offer aromatherapy, muesli breakfasts, vegetarian meals and so on. The TIC has a complete list.

Nonsmoking *Tor Down Guest House* (☎ 832287, fax 831100, e torangel@aol.com, 5 Ashwell Lane) has singles/doubles from £20/42.

The Bolthole (☎ 832800, 32 Chilkwell St) is near the foot of the tor, and has two doubles and a twin for £19 per person. There are a couple of similar B&Bs in the same street.

Berachah (☎ 834214, fax 832252, Well House Lane) is convenient for the tor and the wells, and has beds for £25 per person.

The *George & Pilgrims Inn* (☎ 831146, fax 832252, 1 High St) has a history dating back to the reign of Edward III. Rooms cost from £45/70 but two-night special breaks including dinner are better value.

Travellers with money to spend may be interested in peaceful *No 3 Magdalene St* (☎ 832129, fax 834227, e info@numberthree.co.uk), a wonderful house whose owners have seen a bit of the world themselves, hence the Indian fabrics and wall hangings. Comfortable rooms with private bathrooms cost £55/75.

Places to Eat

If you've ever considered becoming a vegetarian, Glastonbury would be an ideal place to start since it's one of the few places in England where nut roasts are more common than pot roasts.

A good place for a coffee is the *Mocha Berry Coffee House* (☎ 832149, 14 Market Place), near the Market Cross.

The *Blue Note Café* (☎ 832907, 4a High St) has courtyard tables and a plentiful selection of light lunches.

Across the way, *Café Galatea* (☎ 834284, 5a High St) does nutritious salads and wholesome main dishes. It's also a sculpture gallery, and a cybercafe.

Rainbow's End (☎ 833896, 17a High St) has delicious leek and mushroom pie, and huge chunks of chocolate cake. It's in an alley with shops selling second-hand books and shoes, and is open 10 am to 5 pm. A three-course lunch at the *George & Pilgrims Inn* (☎ 831146, 1 High St) costs around £10.

Getting There & Away

There's a daily National Express bus to London (£19.50, 4¼ hours) and also a service to Bath.

Badgerline runs buses from Bristol (No 376) to Wells, Glastonbury and Street. It continues to Ilchester and Yeovil. Glastonbury is only 6 miles (10km) from Wells – a 15-minute bus journey on No 163. Bus No 29 goes to Taunton every two hours (No 929 on Sunday).

There is no train station at Glastonbury.

AROUND GLASTONBURY
Street

Street found its name from an ancient causeway that ran across the River Brue to Glastonbury. These days it is little more than a sideshow to the Glastonbury circus, but it is well known for its factory outlets. Clarks, the shoemaker, began life in Street in 1825, but stopped production in 1996 only for Dr Martens to step in and take over the factory. **Clarks Village** is a dedicated discount outlet that sells branded clothes as well as Clarks shoes.

The *Street Youth Hostel* (☎ *442961, fax 442738, The Chalet, Ivythorn Hill*) is about one mile from the town centre. Beds cost £9/6.20 for adults/children. Bus No 376 from Glastonbury stops at Marshalls Elm, from where the hostel is a 500m walk.

QUANTOCK HILLS

The Quantocks, in western Somerset, are a ridge of red sandstone hills, 12 miles (19km) long, not much more than 3 miles (5km) wide and running down to the sea at Quantoxhead.

Like the Mendips, the Quantocks are lowly hills – just 385m high at their highest point – but they're less cultivated and can look much more bleak. The narrow country lanes and woody dells make this enjoyable walking country.

Some of the most attractive country is owned by the NT, including the Beacon and Bicknoller hills, which offer views of the Bristol Channel and Exmoor to the north-west. In 1861, red deer were introduced to these hills from Exmoor and there's a local tradition of stag hunting.

A road runs across the bleaker part of the Quantocks from Over Stowey to Crowcombe, and there's a walkers' track as well. At Broomfield, 6 miles (10km) north of Taunton, Fyne Court houses the Somerset Trust for Nature Conservation (☎ 01823-451587), open 9 am to 6 pm daily, where you can pick up information.

Bridgwater or Taunton would make reasonable bases for exploring the Quantocks, but it's more atmospheric to stay in one of the villages.

Getting There & Away

To appreciate the lanes and woods of the Quantocks at their peaceful best, aim to arrive on a weekday when the Bridgwater and Taunton weekend visitors are back at their desks. Coming by car, the M5 linking Bristol and Exeter skirts the eastern edge of the Quantocks. The A358 then runs along the western side of the hills, linking Taunton to Williton in the north.

Trains from Bristol, Bath and Exeter call at Taunton and Bridgwater, and infrequent Southern National (☎ 01823-272033) buses serve the main roads. Its No 28 bus runs along the southern edge from Minehead to Taunton. Southern National also has one bus a day (No 23) between Taunton and Nether Stowey. No 15 runs between Minehead and Bridgwater. No 29 from Bristol continues to Bridgwater and Taunton after Wells and Glastonbury on Sunday and bank holidays only.

Nether Stowey & Holford

One of the Quantocks' most famous residents was the poet Samuel Taylor Coleridge, who lived in **Nether Stowey** from 1769 to 1796. You can visit **Coleridge Cottage** (☎ 01278-732662; NT) where he wrote *The Rime of the Ancient Mariner*; it's open 2 to 5 pm Tuesday to Thursday and Sunday, April to October; admission costs £2.60/1. Some of the rooms have been recently restored to their original bright colours.

Coleridge's friend William Wordsworth, and Wordsworth's sister Dorothy, also spent 1797 at nearby Alfoxden House in **Holford** – a pretty village near a wooded valley. *Lyrical Ballads*, published in 1798, was the joint product of Coleridge's and Wordsworth's stays.

Set in a wooded area 2 miles (3km) west of Holford is the *Quantock Hills Youth Hostel* (☎ *01278-741224, fax 01278-741224, Sevenacres, Holford*). It's open daily in July and August, and daily except Sunday from April to June. The nightly charge is £8.10/5.65 for adults/children. Southern National bus No 15 from Bridgwater gets you to Nether Stowey, No 28

WESSEX

from Taunton or Minehead will drop you at Williton; in either case it's then a 3½ mile walk.

West Somerset Railway

Trains on Britain's longest privately run railway steam between Bishops Lydeard and Minehead, a seaside town 20 miles (32km) away. There are stops along the line at Crowcombe, Doniford Beach, Stogumber, Williton, Watchet, Washford, Blue Anchor and Dunster.

Trains run daily from May to September, and at weekends only in winter. A single/return from Bishops Lydeard to Minehead costs £6.20/9.10. Phone ☎ 01643-707650 for 24-hour talking timetables, ☎ 01643-704996 for other information. Or visit the Web site at www.west-somerset-railway .co.uk.

Southern National bus Nos 28 and 28A from Taunton and Minehead pass through Bishops Lydeard.

Crowcombe

One of the prettiest Quantock villages, Crowcombe still has cottages built of stone and cob (a mixture of mud and straw), many with thatched roofs. There's a pleasant church with 16th-century bench ends, and part of its spire still in the churchyard where it fell when struck by lightning in 1725. The 16th-century Church House has mullioned windows and a Tudor door. Crowcombe Court is a fine Georgian house.

A large country house with 50 beds, The *Crowcombe Heathfield Youth Hostel* (☎ *01984-667249, fax 667249, Denzel House, Heathfield)* is 2 miles (3km) from the village and half a mile from Crowcombe station on the West Somerset Railway. It's a 7-mile (11km) hike over the Quantocks from the hostel in Holford (see Nether Stowey & Holford earlier in the chapter). You can also get here on bus No 28C from Taunton station, getting off at Triscombe Cross and walking almost a mile. The hostel is open daily from April to August (but closed on Thursday in May and June). Beds cost £9/6.20 for adults/children.

TAUNTON
☎ 01823 • pop 35,000

Taunton is the relatively uninspiring administrative capital for Somerset. The town's most famous landmark is the **Church of St Mary Magdalene**, with its 50-metre tower carved from the red rock of the nearby Quantocks. The tower was first erected in the 15th century, but dismantled due to safety concerns in 1858 before being rebuilt. Taunton is the transport hub for central Somerset as well as a gateway to the Quantocks.

The TIC (☎ 336344, fax 340308, Paul St) is by the library and is open 9.30 am to 5.30 pm Monday to Saturday (to 5 pm on Saturday).

Somerset County Museum (☎ 355455) is housed in part of **Taunton Castle**. It is open 10 am to 5 pm Tuesday to Saturday; admission costs £2.50/1. The Great Hall, part of which is occupied by the museum, was where Judge Jeffries held one of his bloodiest assizes in 1685 (see boxed text 'The Bloody Assizes' under Dorchester).

Should hunger strike during a fleeting visit, *Pain et Vin (☎ 324412, 51a St James St)* does a formidable range of sandwiches and rolls, eat in or takeaway. More sophisticated is *Café Mamba (☎ 354955, 61 High St)*, with a selection of light lunches from home and abroad.

Taunton is on a main National Express coach route, with services to London (3½ hours, £11), Bristol (1¾ hours, £5), Bridgwater (30 minutes, £2.75) and Exeter (50 minutes, £4.50). First Southern National buses Nos 28 and 28A cross the Quantocks to Minehead. Bus No 29 goes to Glastonbury hourly (No 929 on Sunday).

It's also on the main West Country rail line, which links Exeter and Plymouth with London.

MONTACUTE HOUSE

Montacute House (☎ 01935-823289; NT), 22 miles (35km) south-east of Taunton and 4 miles (6km) west of the market town of Yeovil, is an impressive Elizabethan mansion built in the 1590s for Sir Edward Phelips, a Speaker of the House of Commons.

The Long Gallery displays Tudor and Jacobean portraits on loan from London's National Portrait Gallery. Formal gardens and a landscaped park surround the house.

Visitor numbers have shot up since it was used as a major location in *Sense and Sensibility*, starring Kate Winslet and Alan Rickman, so anticipate crowds at the weekend.

It's open noon to 5.30 pm daily except Tuesday, April to October. Admission costs £5.50/2.80 (£3.10/1.80 for the garden only). The garden remains open in winter from 11.30 am to 4 pm and costs £1.50. Bus No 681 (☎ 01460-240309) from Yeovil to South Petherton passes close by.

HAYNES MOTOR MUSEUM

To British people the name Haynes is a familiar one, for the owner of this car collection also owns a publishing empire that specialises in servicing and repair manuals for almost any car you could care to imagine. Charity shops throughout the country stock classics such as Austin Allegro or Ford Cortina Mark III manuals. This museum (☎ 01963-440804), in Sparkford, near Yeovil, brings together more than 250 cars from around the world, including some of the legendary vehicles of the racing world.

The museum is open from 9.30 am to 5.30 pm, March to October (to 6.30 pm during July and August) and 10 am to 4.30 pm the rest of the year. Admission costs £4.95/2.95.

Exmoor National Park

Covering parts of West Somerset and North Devon, Exmoor is a small national park (265 sq miles; 687 sq km) enclosing a wide variety of beautiful landscapes. Along the coast the scenery is particularly breathtaking with humpbacked headlands giving superb views across the Bristol Channel. Exmoor's cliffs are the highest in England, rising in places to 366m.

A high plateau rises steeply behind the coast, but is cut by steep, fast-flowing streams. The bare hills of heather and grass run parallel to the coast; the highest point is Dunkery Beacon at 519m. On the southern side the two main rivers, the Exe and Barle, wind their way along wooded valleys.

Horned sheep, Exmoor ponies (descended from ancient hill stock) and England's last wild red deer still roam the moors. The symbol of the park is the antlered head of a stag, and depending on the season you may see people hunting. Although the sport is supported by many local farmers who see the deer as a pest, it's equally strongly opposed by others, including the NT (who have banned it on their land), causing conflict in the hunting season.

There are several particularly attractive villages: Lynton and Lynmouth, joined by a water-operated railway; Porlock, on the edge of the moor in a beautiful valley; Dunster, dominated by its partly medieval castle; and Selworthy, with traditional thatched cottages.

Arguably the most dramatic section of the South West Coast Path runs from Minehead, just outside the north-eastern boundary of the park, to Padstow in Cornwall.

ORIENTATION

From west to east the park measures only about 21 miles (34km) and north to south just 12 miles (19km). It's accessible from the west through Barnstaple, from the south-west through South Molton, from the south via Tiverton, from the south-east through Taunton, and from the east through Minehead.

Within the park boundaries, the main centres are Dulverton on the southern edge; Exford in the centre; Dunster in the east; and Porlock, Lynton and Lynmouth on the coast.

There are over 600 miles (966km) of public footpaths and bridleways, most of them waymarked.

INFORMATION

The National Park Authority (NPA) has five information centres in and around the park, but it's also possible to get information in the TICs at Barnstaple, Ilfracombe, Lynton and Minehead. The NPA centres at Dunster (☎ 01643-821835), Lynmouth (☎ 01598-752509), County Gate (☎ 01598-741321), and Combe Martin (☎ 01271-883319) are open daily from the end of March to October. For the rest of the year, some of these offices are closed or operate limited opening hours.

The main visitors centre and the Exmoor NPA headquarters (☎ 01398-323841) in Dulverton are open all year but for limited hours in winter.

The *Exmoor Visitor* is a free newspaper listing useful addresses, accommodation and a program of guided walks and bike rides from the villages offered by the NPA and local organisations. Most walks are in the summer but there are some throughout the year.

The visitors centres and TICs stock a wide range of walking guides and Ordnance Survey maps. There are also two comprehensive Web sites covering Exmoor. For information on the national park, head to www.exmoor-nationalpark.gov.uk. For general tourist information on the Exmoor area, see www.exmoortourism.org.

Most of the villages on Exmoor are tiny so ATMs are few and far between. Try Dulverton, Lynton or Minehead, or come prepared.

ACTIVITIES
Walking
Although over 70% of Exmoor is privately owned, there are numerous waymarked paths. The best-known routes are the Somerset and North Devon Coast Path (part of the South West Coast Path) and the Exmoor section of the Two Moors Way, which starts in Lynmouth and follows the River Barle through Withypool and on to Dartmoor.

Part of the 180-mile (290km) Tarka Trail (based on the countryside that inspired Henry Williamson's *Tarka the Otter*) is in the park. Join it in Combe Martin and walk to Lynton/Lynmouth, and then inland to Brayford and Barnstaple.

Exmoor's main walking centres are Lynton, Porlock, County Gate, Oare, Horner, Exford, Simonsbath, Withypool and Dulverton. The *Exmoor & West Somerset Public Transport Guide*, free from TICs, also includes detailed route descriptions of a dozen walks that are accessible by public transport.

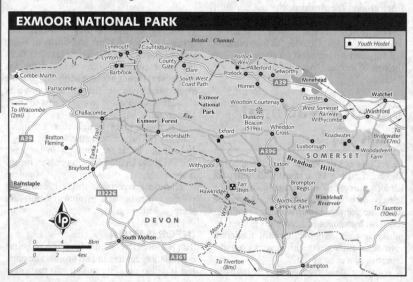

EXMOOR NATIONAL PARK

Cycling

Cyclists are not allowed on public footpaths or the open moor, and horse riders and walkers have priority on public bridleways and roads used as public paths. The visitors centres can advise on regulations.

Official places for cyclists include a coastal route – along the old Barnstaple railway line, parts of the Tarka Trail, the Brendon Hills and Crown Estate woodland. The West Country Way runs through Exmoor from Padstow to Bristol.

Pony Trekking & Horse Riding

Exmoor is popular riding country and stables scattered round the park offer ponies and horses for all abilities for rides from a few hours to a full day. Wet weather gear is recommended – it can turn cold and wet very quickly. Charges are from about £9 per hour.

Contact Pine Lodge Riding & Holidays (☎ 01398-323559), Higher Chilcott Farm, Dulverton; Doone Valley Riding Stables (01598 741278), Cloud Farm, Lynton; or Burrowhayes Farm (☎ 01643-862463), West Luccombe, Porlock.

Red Deer Tracking

Several companies offer Exmoor safaris – tracking wild red deer. Moorland Wildlife Safaris (☎ 01398-323699) charge from £10 per person for three-hour excursions.

Fishing

To fish for salmon and trout, you need a licence, usually obtainable from the main shop or village post office. Sea fishing is possible from harbour walls, and boats can be hired in the larger coastal villages.

PLACES TO STAY & EAT

There are youth hostels in Minehead and Ilfracombe (outside the park), and Lynton and Exford in the park. Camping is allowed with the landowner's permission; local shops will usually know who owns the surrounding land. Along the coast, there are regular camping grounds with all the usual facilities.

There are also camping barns (bring your own sleeping bag) at Woodadvent Farm in Roadwater (£3.75) and Northcombe, a mile from Dulverton (£4.50). For bookings call ☎ 01200-428366.

There's no shortage of B&Bs and hotels in this holiday area. There are plenty of places to eat in Exmoor – old country pubs with low beams to hit your head on and log fires in the winter, little shops serving cream teas, as well as more upmarket restaurants.

For those who are thinking of staying for a week or more, hiring a cottage might be fun. The Exmoor Holiday Group (☎ 01398-323722) is the specialist in this area. See the Web site at www.exmoor-holidays.co.uk.

GETTING THERE & AWAY
Bus

National Express coaches go from London to Barnstaple (5 hours) and Ilfracombe (5½ hours) daily. There are also buses from Plymouth and Bristol to Barnstaple, both via Taunton.

First Red Bus (☎ 01271-345444) and First Southern National (☎ 01823-272033) run services from Minehead, Barnstaple, Ilfracombe, Dunster and Williton. You could also do part of this journey on the privately run West Somerset Railway (see Somerset earlier in this chapter).

Train

From London Paddington, InterCity services stop at Taunton (2¼ hours), Tiverton Parkway (2½ hours) and Exeter (2¾ hours). These places can also be reached from Bristol (on the Bristol–Plymouth line). From Exeter, the scenic Tarka Line runs to Barnstaple; the journey takes about 1½ hours and there are about four trains a day.

GETTING AROUND

It's easiest to get around with your own transport, on foot or horseback, because bus services are limited. Some services are based on school runs, some are operated by volunteer drivers, most are seasonal and few operate on Sunday. On the other hand, the narrow streets of Exmoor villages quickly clog up in peak season and parking can be tricky.

WESSEX

Bus

The *Exmoor & West Somerset Public Transport Guide*, free from TICs, is invaluable. It also includes information on day walks.

The Exmoor Bus Service's three-day ticket costs £9.50/6.50 and allows unlimited travel on Red Bus and Southern National services.

Bicycle

Tarka Trail Cycle Hire (☎ 01271-324202), Train Station, Barnstaple, has all kinds of bikes for hire. Charges start from £6.50 per day for touring bikes, £8.50 for mountain bikes.

DULVERTON

☎ 01398 • pop 1300

This attractive village, south of the moor in the Barle Valley, is the local 'capital' and home to the park's head office. Dulverton's narrow streets get choked with traffic in summer so if you can try to visit out of season.

The Exmoor National Park Visitors Centre (☎ 323841, 7–9 Fore St) is open 10 am to 5 pm (closed 1.15 to 1.45 pm) daily from Easter to October and 10.30 am to 3 pm in winter.

Walks

The four-hour circular walk along the river from Dulverton to Tarr Steps – an ancient stone clapper bridge across the River Barle – is recommended. Add another three or four hours to the walk by continuing from Tarr Steps up Winsford Hill for distant views over Devon.

While at the Tarr Steps, be sure to stop at *Tarr Farm* (☎ 01643-851507), an old riverside inn with cream teas and a popular restaurant.

Places to Stay & Eat

About one mile from Dulverton is *Northcombe Farm Camping Barn* (☎ 323118). There is space for up to 35 people here and places cost £4.50 per night.

Breakfast in bed and log fires at atmospheric *Town Mills* (☎ 323124) costs from £19 per person. The driveway is just off the High St.

Springfield Farm (☎/fax 323722, Ashwick Lane) is 4 miles (6km) from Dulverton on the Exford road; and just 1½ miles (2.5km) from Tarr Steps. B&B costs £22.50 per person, or £26 in rooms with a bath. Evening meals are served from mid-May, when the lambing season is over.

Right on the edge of the moor, award-winning *Highercombe Farm* (☎/fax 323 616) is 3 miles (5km) north of Dulverton at the end of a no-through road. B&B in rooms with a bathroom costs from £22, plus there is a three-bedroom cottage for rent in the grounds.

Crispins Restaurant (☎ 323397, 26 High St) serves decent vegetarian food and also has a few meaty choices. There is also an attractive vine-decked garden for summer days.

The Lion Hotel (☎ 323444, 2 Bank Square) has generous servings of good bar food.

Getting There & Away

Devon Bus No 398 runs from Minehead to Tiverton via Dulverton eight times daily except Sunday. Change in Tiverton for the No 55 on to Exeter.

Devon Bus No 307 links Dulverton to Barnstaple and Taunton every couple of hours, daily except Sunday.

DUNSTER

☎ 01643 • pop 800

Promoted as the most attractive Exmoor village, Dunster can be teeming with people in summer. The main attraction is the castle but there's also St George's Church, a working water mill, an old packhorse bridge, the nearby beach and the 17th-century octagonal Yarn Market – a relic of a time when the people of Dunster made their living from weaving, rather than tourism.

The Exmoor National Park Visitors Centre (☎ 821835), Dunster Steep, is open 10 am to 5 pm daily, Easter to October (at the weekend only in winter; closed January and February).

Dunster Castle

Heavily restored to the Victorian ideal of how castles should look – turrets, crennellations and all – Dunster Castle (☎ 821314; NT) dates back to Norman times, although only the 13th-century gateway of the original structure survives. Inside are Tudor furnishings and portraits of the Luttrell family, including a bizarre 16th-century portrait of Sir John skinny-dipping.

It's open 10.30 am to 4.40 pm Saturday to Wednesday, April to October (to 4 pm in October). Admission costs £5.50/3. The surrounding garden and park are open most of the year. It's a short, steep walk up from the village.

Places to Stay

The nearest youth hostel is 2 miles (3km) away at Minehead (see Minehead later in this section).

Woodville House (☎ 821228, West St) is one of the cheapest places to stay in the village, charging from £19 per person for friendly B&B.

The Old Priory (☎ 821540) is a medieval house in walled gardens opposite the dovecote. It charges from £27.50 per person for B&B (£50 for a room with a four-poster bed).

Dollons House (☎ 821880, Church St) does luxury B&B charging £27.50 in nonsmoking rooms, all with bathroom.

Exmoor House Hotel (☎ 821268, 12 West St) is a very comfortable, nonsmoking hotel, which charges £25/45 for B&B in rooms with a bathroom.

The *Yarn Market Hotel* (☎ 821425, fax 821475, e yarnmarket.hotel@virgin .net, High St) has some pretty good value rooms available. Singles start from just £30, while doubles are £60 or £70 with a four-poster bed.

Dunster's most comfortable hotel is *The Luttrell Arms* (☎ 0870 400 8110, fax 0870 382 1567, 32 High St), one of the Forte Heritage group with rates starting from £85 per person.

Places to Eat

The *cafe* (☎ 821759, Dunster Watermill, Mill Lane) is a good place to go for lunch or tea in summer; for £2.10/1.10 you can also watch flour being ground in the active mill.

The Tea Shoppe (☎ 821304, 3 High St) does morning coffee, lunches and cream teas in its 15th-century tearooms. By night, it is an acclaimed restaurant. If it's full there are several other places along the High St, including *Willow Tearooms* (☎ 821414), set in a period premises with a small garden.

Locks (☎ 822032) dresses its staff in period costume, and while it can't be much fun for the employees, it seems to draw the nostalgia crowd.

The Luttrell Arms (☎ 821555, 36 High St), opposite the Yarn Market, does good bar snacks including filled baguettes and main dishes for around £5.

Getting There & Away

Devon Bus runs No 398 from Minehead to Dunster and on to Dulverton eight times a day, except Sunday. First Southern National runs an hourly service (No 928) between Minehead and Dunster on Sundays and public holidays – there are just six buses. You can also get here by steam train on the West Somerset Railway (see the Somerset section).

MINEHEAD

☎ 01643 • pop 8500

Somerset's largest seaside resort is just outside the park's eastern border. During summer, it's packed with British holidaymakers, many of them escapees from Somerwestworld, a vast holiday camp. Visit in May, however, and the town still enacts medieval May Day ceremonies with a hobbyhorse performing a fertility dance through the streets.

The TIC (☎ 702624, fax 707166, e mineheadtic@visit.org.uk), 17 Friday St, is open 9.30 am to 5.30 pm Monday to Saturday and 10 am to 1 pm on Sunday.

Places to Stay & Eat

In a secluded spot 2 miles (3km) south of Minehead is the *Minehead Youth Hostel* (☎ 702595, fax 703016) at Alcombe Combe. It's open daily in July and August; daily

WESSEX

except Monday from April to June; and daily except Monday and Tuesday in September and October. The nightly charge is £9.80/6.75 for adults/children.

Getting There & Away
From Minehead, Southern National operates hourly service No 28 (No 928 Sunday) to Taunton (1¼ hours), No 38 to Porlock Weir and No 300 to Lynton (three times a day). Minehead is the northern terminus for the West Somerset Railway.

EXFORD
☎ 01643
This tiny village in the centre of the park makes a good base for walks, especially to Dunkery Beacon, the highest point on Exmoor, 4 miles (6km) from Exford.

Places to Stay & Eat
Right in the village centre, *Exford Youth Hostel* (☎ 831288, fax 831650, Exe Mead) is set in a Victorian house by the River Exe. It is open daily in July and August, and daily except Sunday in April, May and June (phone for other opening hours). A bed costs £9.80/6.75 for adults/children.

Just outside Exford, off the Porlock road, *Westermill Farm Campsite* (☎ 831238, fax 831660) is open from April to October and charges £6 for tents. There are also cottages to rent.

Exmoor House Hotel (☎ 831304, Chapel St) overlooks the village green, and offers B&B from £25/50 for a single/double.

The *White Horse Inn* (☎ 831229), a 16th-century inn right by the bridge, does B&B from £35 per person for rooms with a bathroom. There's bar food during the week and a carvery on Sunday.

Getting There & Away
Over the moor, it's a 7-mile (11km) walk to Exford from Porlock, 10 miles (16km) from Minehead Youth Hostel, 12 miles (19km) from Dunster and 15 miles (24km) from Lynton.

During summer, Bus No 285 (☎ 01823-358232) links Porlock, Minehead and Exford (Bus No 985 on Sunday). Bus No 398

operates year-round (except Sunday), linking Exford to Dulverton or Dunster and Minehead every two hours.

PORLOCK
☎ 01643 • pop 1500
This attractive village of thatched cottages lies in a deep valley, reached by a steep lane. The charming harbour of Porlock Weir is 2 miles (3km) farther west.

The picturesque NT-owned village of **Selworthy** is 2½ miles (4km) east of Porlock. Its cream-painted cob-and-thatch cottages make this a popular movie location; Thomas Hardy's *The Return of the Native* was filmed here.

Porlock's tiny visitor centre (☎ 863150, fax 863014), West End, High St, is open 10 am to 6 pm (to 1 pm on Sunday) during summer.

Places to Stay & Eat
Well signposted and in the centre of Porlock is *Sparkhayes Farm Campsite* (☎ 862470). Charges are £3.50 per person.

Most places to stay are on the High St. For B&B, cosy, thatched *Myrtle Cottage* (☎ 862978, High St) charges from £30/43 for rooms with a bath.

The *Lorna Doone Hotel* (☎ 862404, High St) charges £25/50 for a single/double with bathroom, with reductions for stays of three or more days.

The Ship Inn (☎ 862507, High St) is a 13th-century thatched hostelry mentioned in *Lorna Doone*. B&B starts at £25 per person, and the pub overlooks the harbour, offering crab sandwiches and pub classics on the menu. Try the inn's country wines – damson is good.

Open every evening, *Piggy in the Middle* (☎ 862647, 2 High St) does good steak and seafood. A salmon steak is under £10, the seafood platter more like £20.

There are several tearooms in the High St that serve lunch as well.

Getting There & Away
Southern National (☎ 01823-272033) runs service No 300 along the coast from Barnstaple through Lynton and Porlock to

Minehead and Bridgwater. Bus No 38 runs to Minehead.

LYNTON & LYNMOUTH
☎ 01598 • pop 2075

Lynmouth has the looks, Lynton the height, but an incredible water-operated cliff railway links the villages so it is easy to commute between them. The picturesque, steeply wooded gorge of the West Lyn River, which meets the sea at Lynmouth, can be delightful out of season. This is a good base for walks along the coast and in the northern part of the park.

There's a TIC (☎ 752225, fax 752755), Lynton Town Hall, Lee Rd, which is open 9.30 am to 5.30 pm daily (closed Sunday in winter).

On The Esplanade by Lynmouth harbour there's a National Park Visitors Centre (☎ 752509). It is open 10 am to 5 pm daily, Easter to October (open weekends only in winter).

Biketrail (☎ 753987, ℮ info@biketrail .co.uk) has mountain bikes for hire in Lynton.

Things to See

In 1952, storms caused the East and West Lyn rivers to flood, destroying 98 houses and claiming the lives of 34 people. The disaster is recorded at the **Lyn & Exmoor Museum** (☎ 752317) in haunted St Vincent's Cottage, Market St, Lynton. The museum is open daily except Sunday morning and Saturday, late March to late October, but closes 12.30 to 2 pm for lunch. Admission costs £1/20p.

The **cliff railway** is a simple piece of environmentally friendly Victorian engineering. Two cars linked by a steel cable descend or ascend the slope according to the amount of water in their tanks. For £1/50p it's the best way to get between the two villages between Easter and November and the views across to the Exmoor cliffs are incredible as you descend.

Walking

Lynton TIC and Lynmouth Visitors Centre have information about the many local walks. The South West Coast Path and the Tarka Trail pass through the villages, and the Two Moors Way, linking Exmoor with Dartmoor, starts in Lynmouth.

Leaving Lynmouth look out for signs to **Glen Lyn Gorge**, which is open year-round and has a small exhibition centre, open in summer only. It costs £2/1 to walk along the gorge.

The **Valley of the Rocks**, which is believed to be where the River Lyn originally flowed, was described by the poet Robert Southey as 'rock reeling upon rock, stone piled upon stone, a huge terrifying reeling mass'. It's just over a mile west of Lynton and makes a pleasant walk along the coastal footpath. East of Lynmouth, the lighthouse at **Foreland Point** is another good focus for a walk.

Watersmeet, 2 miles (3km) along the river from Lynmouth, makes another popular walk. The old hunting lodge houses a NT teashop.

Places to Stay & Eat

Lynton Youth Hostel (☎ 753237, fax 753 305), at Lynbridge, is roughly a mile outside Lynton. It's a Victorian house in the gorge, and is open daily in July and August (phone for other times). The nightly charge is £9.80/6.75 for adults/children. Also up in Lynton, for those who prefer to look down on Lynmouth, *Valley House* (☎ 752285, Lynbridge Rd) charges £24/40.

St Vincent House Hotel (☎ 752244, fax 753971) is right next door to the museum in Lynton and charges £31 a double, or £38 with bathroom. Out the front is an attractive garden, popular for teas in summer.

The *Orchard House Hotel* (☎ 753247, fax 753855, Watersmeet Rd, Lynmouth) just about has views of the sea, depending on which room you have, and charges from £24 per person.

The *Rising Sun* (☎ 753223) is a 14th-century inn beside Lynmouth harbour. Rooms cost from £52 per person, and there are also two-night packages available, including dinner. This is an excellent place for a pub lunch or evening meal. The poet Shelley brought his 16-year-old bride to the adjoining rose-clad cottage for their honeymoon, and you can stay here for £70/140 (singles/doubles; book through the hotel).

Those looking to put together a picnic might like to try *Gourmet Organix* (☎ 752 228, 4 Queen St) in Lynton, a specialist shop with heaps of tasty food.

Getting There & Away

First Red Bus (☎ 01271-345444) services No 309 and 310 run between Barnstaple and Lynton (one hour, 10 daily), Monday to Saturday (one daily on Sunday). Lyn Valley Bus (☎ 01598-752225) has a Tuesday service from Lynton to Minehead (two daily).

Driving from Porlock, note that Porlock Hill is notoriously steep; look out for the old AA box at the top where motorists could phone to report overheated radiators. There are two alternative toll roads (£1), both of them scenic and less steep.

Dorset

In spite of its natural beauty and attractive towns and villages, most of Dorset manages to avoid inundation by tourists. The impressively varied coast includes the large resort towns of Bournemouth and Weymouth, as well as Lyme Regis, a particularly attractive spot with famous literary connections. The Dorset Coast Path, part of the longer 613-mile South West Coast Path, runs for most of the length of the coast.

Inland is Dorchester, the heart of Thomas Hardy's fictional Wessex and once the author's home. Dorset also boasts famous earthworks (Maiden Castle), castles (Corfe Castle), stately homes (particularly Kingston Lacy), a string of Lawrence of Arabia connections, some fine churches (Christchurch Priory, Wimborne Minster and Sherborne Abbey) and one of England's best-known chalk hill figures (the Cerne Giant).

GETTING THERE & AROUND

Dorchester makes a good base for exploring the best of Dorset, but Lyme Regis or Weymouth will suit those who prefer the coast.

One of the reasons for Dorset's backwater status is that no major transport routes cross it. A rail loop runs west from Southampton to Dorchester, then north to Yeovil, and the main westbound InterCity trains stop at Axminster (East Devon).

For general bus enquiries in Dorset call ☎ 01305-225165. The main operators in east and central Dorset are Wilts and Dorset (☎ 01202-673555). They offer an explorer ticket for £5/2.50 that includes Wiltshire and Bath.

For western Dorset and on to Devon, First Southern National (☎ 01305-262992) are the main operators and their day explorer costs £5.30/3.75.

BOURNEMOUTH
☎ 01202 • pop 265,000

Bournemouth has been a popular beach resort since the mid-19th century and continues to exude an air of Victorian seaside prosperity. The town is young by English standards as it was only founded in 1810, and it is a young crowd that continues to flock here during summer weekends. The nightlife rivals Brighton's, but is rather more raucous, with the emphasis on stag nights and serious drinking. Revellers might find it a useful base for exploring the New Forest without compromising the nightlife.

An artificial reef is currently under construction, which could see Bournemouth become a surfer destination.

In a survey by a well-known condom manufacturer, Bournemouth beach was voted the most popular place in Britain for open-air sex.

Orientation & Information

Bournemouth is a vast, sprawling town that spreads along the coast towards Poole to the west and Christchurch to the east. The pier marks the central seafront area and northeast from there is the town centre and railway station.

Bournemouth's TIC (☎ 0906-802 0234, fax 451743, ⓔ info@bournemouth.gov.uk), on Westover Rd, is open 9.30 am to 6 pm Monday to Saturday and 10 am to 4 pm

Sunday. Note that telephone calls are charged at 50p a minute so it may be cheaper to check out the Web site at www.bournemouth.co.uk.

There are free guided walks departing the TIC at 10.30 am on weekdays and 2.30 pm on Sunday, in summer only. Guide Friday (☎ 01789-294466) operates an open-top bus tour leaving every 30 minutes from outside Bournemouth Pier from 10 am until 4.30 pm. It only operates late April to September and costs £5.50/1.50.

Things to See & Do

Bournemouth is noted for its beautiful *chines* (sharp-sided valleys running down to the sea).

The wonderful **Russell-Cotes Art Gallery & Museum** (☎ 451800) looks out to sea from Russell-Cotes Rd and has a varied collection, much of it garnered from its namesake's travels, including an exquisite Japanese collection. It is open 10 am to 5 pm daily except Monday

In Shelley Park, Beechwood Ave, in Boscombe, the **Shelley Rooms** (☎ 303571) house a collection of Shelley memorabilia. They're open from 2 to 5 pm Tuesday to Sunday, and admission is free. *Frankenstein* author Mary Shelley is buried at St Peters.

Compton Acres (☎ 700778) is a cluster of gardens in a sheltered cliff chine. It's open 10 am to 5.15 pm daily, March to October. Admission costs £5.45/2.45. Bus Nos 150 and 151 go there from the centre.

Right next to Bournemouth Pier is the **Oceanarium** (☎ 311933), an expensive aquarium with sealife on display. It is open 10 am to 5 pm daily and costs £5.75/3.75.

Places to Stay

Bournemouth is bursting with places to stay and the TICs make free bookings (calls cost 50p a minute, however). Bournemouth may have hundreds of options, but during summer weekends it fills up fast so book ahead. Heading up Priory Rd to the West Cliff area, B&Bs and hotels fan out in every direction. There are also plenty of camping grounds in the area, but nothing in town itself.

Bournemouth Backpackers (☎ 299491, e bournemouth.backpackers@virgin.net, 3 Frances Rd) has a good location near the bus and train stations and beds start from £12.

Cartrefle Guest House (☎ 297856, 45 St Michael's Rd) has B&B from £17 per person, £25 with en suite facilities. *Denbry Hotel* (☎ 558700, 179 Holdenhurst Rd) has something similar from £18/20 per person.

Parklands Hotel (☎ 552529, 4 Rushton Crescent) has rooms for £28/50 for singles/doubles, more with a four-poster bed.

Places to Eat

Amid the fish-and-chip shops are more interesting, if a bit pricier, places to eat. Try *Sala Pepe* (☎ 291019, 43 Charminster Rd) where fresh fish dishes include monkfish with crabmeat and prawns.

There is a branch of the ever-popular *Cafe Rouge* (☎ 757472, 67 Seamoor Rd). *Mr Pang's* (☎ 553748, 234 Holdenhurst Rd) is the place to head to for fine Chinese food. For the best Indian food on offer, seek out *Bournemouth Tandoori* (☎ 296204, 8 Holdenhurst Rd), before or after the pub as it stays open until midnight.

For something completely different, the *Helvetia* (☎ 555447, 61 Charminster Rd) specialises in Swiss food such as fondues and schnitzels.

Entertainment

Nightlife can be pretty full-on in Bournemouth so be prepared to go the distance. Long queues are the norm for most clubs at the weekend, plus bouncers that can't understand anything but smart dress.

The *Moon in the Square* (☎ 314940, 48 Exeter Rd), near the Victorian Pleasure Gardens, is the cheapest pub in town, but lacks music. However, service is always fast, even on a busy night.

Liquids at the Landsdowne is getting a good reputation as somewhere to warm-up for Bournemouth's clubbing scene. The best-known club is *Urban* and, upstairs, pre-club bar *Slam* (☎ 55512, Firvale Rd).

In an incredible converted theatre, *Opera House* (☎ 399922, 570 Christchurch Rd) is

Bournemouth's answer to the super club if you like that sort of thing.

The Zoo & Cage (☎ 311178, Firvale Rd) is a long-established favourite that continues to pull a crowd at the weekend.

Getting There & Away

There are regular bus connections from London with National Express. Bus X3 runs regularly from Salisbury and the X33 heads from Southampton. Bus Nos 121/2/3/4 run from Lymington frequently. There are plenty of buses between Bournemouth and Poole.

Trains run every 30 minutes from London Waterloo (£30, two hours). There are also regular services from Bristol and Bath, changing at Southampton.

POOLE
☎ 01202

The medieval port of Poole is now a container dock and yachting centre. This is also one of the most popular places in the southwest to arrange fishing trips.

Poole's TIC (☎ 253253, fax 684531), The Quay, on the waterfront, is open 10 am to 6 pm daily.

Things to See & Do

Poole Old Town has attractive 18th-century buildings, including a wonderful **Customs House**.

The **Waterfront Museum** (☎ 683138) recounts the town's history, including the prosperity brought by its Newfoundland fishing trade. It's open 10 am to 5 pm Monday to Saturday, and noon to 5 pm on Sunday. Admission costs £2/1.35, except in August when the £4/2.85 charge also includes nearby **Scaplen's Court Museum**. Open for the rest of the year to school parties only, this museum is in a medieval merchant's house.

Poole Pottery (☎ 666200), The Quay, draws huge numbers of visitors and the complex includes a gift shop with seconds – a whole lot more affordable than collectable Poole in antique shops throughout Britain.

Both **deep-sea fishing** and **mackerel fishing** are possible in Poole and a lot of English lads end up on trips after a night of

fishing for lasses on a stag night in Bournemouth. Poole Sea Angling Centre (☎ 676597), 5 High St, has half-day mackerel trips for £10 and evening bass trips for £12. Sea Fishing (☎ 679666), The Quay, can arrange a deep-sea trip.

Brownsea Island

Brownsea Island is an NT nature reserve at the mouth of Poole Harbour where the first Boy Scout camp was held in 1907. From April to October boats from Sandbanks (on the peninsula between Bournemouth and Poole) cost £3/2 return, plus a landing fee of £2.60/1.30. During winter the RSPB operates sporadic Birdboats to watch the harbour bird life; phone ☎ 666226 for boat information.

Places to Stay & Eat

There are plenty of B&Bs in Poole, but it is more fun to stay in Bournemouth.

Poole has become something of a centre for seafood restaurants, perhaps not surprising given its location.

Corkers (☎ 681393, 1 High St) is open as a cafe-bar all day, and as a restaurant for lunch and dinner.

John B's (☎ 672440, High St) adds a Gallic touch to the predominantly seafood menu for fans of French food. *Storm (☎ 674970, 16 High St)* is another good spot for seafood with flair.

For something more simple, the *Custom House (☎ 676767, The Quay)* is a gracious building with an outdoor area and the menu includes afternoon tea and cakes.

Getting There & Away

Wilts & Dorset (☎ 673555) runs bus Nos 101/2/3/4/5 to Bournemouth.

A ferry shuttles across from Sandbanks to Studland. This is a short cut from Poole to Swanage, Wareham and the west Dorset coast, but summer queues can be horrendous.

CHRISTCHURCH
☎ 01202 • pop 30,000

An attractive small town that might make a pleasant alternative base to Bournemouth is Christchurch, about 5 miles (8km) east of Bournemouth.

The TIC (☎ 471780, fax 476816, e tic@christchurch.gov.uk), 23 High St, is open 9.30 am to 5.30 pm Monday to Saturday and 10 am to 2 pm on Sunday.

Opposite the Priory is the **Red House Museum & Gardens** (☎ 482860), a workhouse now accommodating a local history museum. It's open 10 am to 5 pm Tuesday to Saturday and 2 to 5 pm on Sunday. Admission costs £1.50/80p.

The magnificent **Christchurch Priory** (☎ 485804) stands between the Avon and Stour rivers. The Norman nave had a new choir added to it in the 15th century, when the tower was also built. Among the wonderful misericords in the choir, look for a carving of Richard III and another of a fox 'friar' preaching to a flock of geese. In summer you can climb the tower for views and learn about priory life in the **St Michael's Loft Museum**. Visitors are asked for a £1 donation.

Bus Nos 121/2/3/4 run to Bournemouth and Lymington frequently.

WIMBORNE
☎ 01202 • pop 14,000

The attractive small town of Wimborne is centred around its interesting old church, or minster. The TIC (☎ 886116, fax 841025, e wimbornetic@eastdorsetdc.gov.uk), 29 High St, is near the minster. It is open 9.30 am to 5.30 pm Monday to Saturday (to 4.30 pm winter).

Near the minster is the 16th-century Priest's House Museum (☎ 882533), an interesting local history museum with a series of reconstructed period rooms. It's open 10.30 am to 5 pm Monday to Saturday, April to October, and 2 to 5 pm on Sunday, June to September. Admission costs £2.20/1.

Wilts & Dorset (☎ 673555) bus Nos 132/3 and 182/3 serve Wimborne from Bournemouth and Poole.

Wimborne Minster
Founded around 1050, the minster was considerably enlarged in Decorated style in the 14th century and became the parish church in 1537 when Henry VIII began attacking monasteries. It's notable for its twin towers and for the varied colours of its stonework. The mid-15th-century perpendicular-style west tower was added when there were fears for the strength of the simple Norman-style 12th-century central tower. Those fears were realised when the crossing spire fell in 1600.

Inside, the nave columns, the piers of the central tower and the north and south transepts are the main Norman survivors. Traces of 13th- to 15th-century painted murals can be seen in a Norman altar recess in the north transept. In the presbytery is a 1440 brass of King Ethelred who was killed in battle in 871, the only brass commemorating a king in England.

In Holy Trinity Chapel is the tomb of Ettricke, the 'man in the wall'. A local eccentric (but obviously one with some influence), he refused to be buried in the church or in the village and was interred in the church wall. Confidently expecting to die in 1693, Ettricke also had his memorial engraved. When he survived his prediction by 10 years, the 1693 was rechiselled to 1703.

Above the choir vestry is a **chained library** established in 1686.

Kingston Lacy
Kingston Lacy (☎ 01202-842913; NT), 2 miles (3km) north of Wimborne, is a fine 17th-century house with 18th-century landscaped gardens. It's unusual in that it didn't decline into genteel poverty and then have to be completely refurbished. The last occupant lived in the house until 1981 without selling a thing, so the house is dense with furniture and art, much of it collected by William Bankes, who was responsible for major renovations in the 1830s.

The house is open noon to 5.30 pm (last admission 4.30 pm) Saturday to Wednesday, April to October. Admission costs £6/3 (grounds only £2.50/1.25).

SOUTH-EAST DORSET
The south-eastern corner of Dorset – the Purbeck peninsula – is crowded with pretty

WESSEX

Lawrence of Arabia

The green fields and pretty villages of Dorset are a long way from the sandy wastes of Arabia, but there are numerous Lawrence connections to this area. The TIC in Wareham even produces *The Lawrence of Arabia Trail* leaflet.

Born in 1888 in Wales, TE Lawrence was the son of Sir Thomas Chapman, who had abandoned his first wife and their daughters in Ireland to run off with the girls' governess. As Mr and Mrs Lawrence they had five boys; Thomas Edward was the second. Lawrence studied history at the University of Oxford, specialising in the Middle East. He travelled extensively in the region between 1909 and 1914, and his expertise led to a Cairo army posting at the outbreak of WWI.

Turkey, still known as the Ottoman Empire at the time, was allied with Germany and, as Arab unrest began to develop, Lawrence led a brilliant guerrilla campaign against the Ottoman forces, culminating in the capture of Aqaba in mid-1917. After the war, he was disgusted to find his Arab visions discarded at the bargaining table as the old Ottoman Empire was carved up between Britain and France. Refusing military honours, he spent several years shuttling between Europe and the Middle East, while at the same time revelations of his dramatic exploits earned him the epithet 'Lawrence of Arabia'.

Lawrence was always an enigmatic character and in 1922 he clandestinely joined the Royal Air Force as a low-ranking enlisted man under the assumed name of John Hume Ross. At the same time he published, in a very limited edition, his immense work *Seven Pillars of Wisdom*. Newspapers soon broke the story of his RAF hideaway but a year later he joined the army as Private TE Shaw, a name he later assumed legally. He was stationed at Bovington Camp in Dorset and bought Clouds Hill, a nearby cottage. In 1925 he transferred to the RAF and spent the next 10 years in India and England before his discharge in 1935. Retiring to Clouds Hill at the age of 46, he was killed two months later in a motorbike accident.

Lawrence connections in Dorset include Bovington Camp, where the tank museum has a small Lawrence display. He died at Bovington Military Hospital six days after his accident, which took place between the camp and Clouds Hill, only a mile away. His grave is in the cemetery of St Nicholas Church, Moreton. The Wareham Museum houses more Lawrence memorabilia, and the small Saxon church in Wareham has a stone effigy of Lawrence.

thatched villages and crumbling ruins. The Dorset Coast Path, part of the South West Coast Path, runs through wonderful scenery along this stretch. There are plenty of camping grounds around and B&Bs in almost every village.

Tolpuddle

Tolpuddle, on the A35, played a historic role in the development of trade unions. In 1834, a group of farm workers met to discuss a cut in their wages and were promptly arrested, convicted of holding an illegal meeting (striking was not illegal) and sentenced to transportation to Australia. Public support for the 'Tolpuddle Martyrs' resulted in their pardon in 1836.

A memorial stands by a tree under which they are thought to have gathered. The **Tolpuddle Martyrs Museum** (☎ 01305-848237) on the town's western outskirts recounts the tale. It's open 10 am (11 am on Sunday) to 5.30 pm daily except Monday; in winter it closes at 4 pm. Admission is free.

Athelhampton House

Athelhampton House (☎ 01305-848363), built in 1485, was a new home in the days when Tudor was a new dynasty, but the house has lasted a little longer. It contains some impressive panelling and heraldic glass, although the most popular features are the gardens outside. The gardens are open 10.30 am to 5 pm (to dusk from November to February) daily except Saturday. The house is open 11 am to 4.30 pm. Admission costs £5.40/1.50 or £3.50 gardens only.

Wareham
☎ 01929 • pop 2800

The pretty village of Wareham forms a neat square, bounded by the River Frome on its southern side and by a remarkably intact Saxon wall on the other three sides. To complete the pattern, North, East, South and West Sts run in the four cardinal directions from The Cross in the centre. The village was badly damaged by a succession of fires, most disastrously in 1762, after which thatched buildings were banned.

Purbeck TIC (☎ 552740, fax 554491, e purbecktic@compuserve.com), Holy Trinity Church, South St, stocks an excellent guide and walking-tour map (free). It is open 9.30 am to 5 pm Monday to Saturday and 10 am to 4 pm on Sunday. It closes for lunch between 1 and 2 pm.

Things to See The recently refurbished **Wareham Museum** (☎ 553448), on East St, adjacent to the town hall, is open 11 am to 1 pm and 2 to 4 pm daily, Easter to mid-October. A Lawrence of Arabia collection supplements the usual local items.

You can rent rowing boats from **Abbots Quay**, once a busy port on the River Frome.

The sturdy **earth banks** around the town were built after a Viking attack in 876. A stretch on the West Wall is known as Bloody Bank, after Monmouth rebels were executed here in 1685 following the Bloody Assizes (see the boxed text in the Dorchester section later in this chapter).

Standing on the wall beside North St is Saxon **St Martin's Church**, which dates from about 1020. Although the porch and bell tower are later additions, and larger windows have been added over the centuries, the basic structure is unchanged. Inside there's a 12th-century wall painting on the northern wall and a marble effigy of Lawrence of Arabia.

Places to Stay & Eat Several camping grounds can be found around Wareham. Convenient B&Bs include *Belle Vue*

(☎ 552056, West St) right on top of West Wall, which costs from £42 for doubles.

The *Black Bear Hotel* (☎ 553339, fax 552846, 14 South St) is fronted by a life-size figure of a bear. Rooms with bathroom cost from £25/40 for singles/doubles.

The picturesque *Old Granary* (☎ 552 010, fax 552482, The Quay) charges £45 for a room and has a good restaurant. The nearby *Quay Inn* (☎ 552735) is a popular local pub with food.

Getting There & Away Bus Nos 142/3/4 run frequently between Poole and Swanage via Wareham.

Bovington Camp Tank Museum
The Tank Museum (☎ 01929-405096), 6 miles (10km) from Wareham, houses an extensive collection from the earliest WWI prototypes, to WWII tanks from both sides, and on to examples from Cold War days. From more recent times, there's also a collection of Iraqi tanks from the Gulf War. It's open 10 am to 5 pm daily, and admission costs £6.90/4.50. Lawrence of Arabia was stationed here in 1923 and there's a small museum in the shop.

Monkey World
Monkey World (☎ 0800 456600) was set up in 1987 to provide a sanctuary for abused beach chimpanzees from Spain. Most of the animals have been rescued from exploitation, whether as pets or in laboratories. The chimpanzees here form the largest group outside of Africa, plus there are orangutans, lemurs and macaques. It is open 10 am to 5 pm year-round (to 6 pm in July and August; last admission one hour earlier); admission costs £5.50/4.

Clouds Hill
The former home of Lawrence of Arabia (☎ 01929-405616; NT) opens noon to 5 pm Wednesday to Friday and Sunday, April to October. Admission costs £2.30.

Corfe Castle
Corfe Castle's (☎ 01929-481294; NT) magnificent ruins tower above the pretty

stone village, offering wonderful views over the surrounding countryside. Even by English standards, the 1000-year-old castle had a dramatic history. In 978, 17-year-old King Edward was greeted at the castle gate by his stepmother, Queen Elfrida, proffering a glass of poisoned wine; even before the poison could take effect he was stabbed to death. His half-brother, Ethelred the Unready, succeeded him, as the wicked queen had planned, but the martyred boy king was canonised as St Edward in 1001.

The castle was besieged twice during the Civil War, being reduced to the present picturesque ruin after the second assault in 1646. It's open 10 am to 5.30 pm daily, February to October (to 4.30 pm in March), and 11 am to 3.30 pm the rest of the year. Admission costs £4/2.

The village has several pubs and B&Bs, and there are camping grounds nearby.

The *Greyhound* is a good pub by the castle moat, with a pleasant garden, while the *Fox Inn* is a homely locals' pub.

Bus Nos 142/3/4 run frequently between Poole and Swanage via Corfe Castle.

The Blue Pool Designated a site of special scientific interest (SSSI), the Blue Pool's water has a chameleon-like tendency to change colour. Admission to this popular local beauty spot, signposted from the A351, costs £3/1.50.

Swanage
☎ 01929

In Victorian times local quarryman John Mowlem made a fortune supplying stone from Swanage for the huge rebuilding projects in booming London. The firm bearing his name is still a major building contractor. He also judiciously chose buildings in London that were due for demolition and shipped material back to Swanage. As a result there are City of London bollards dotted around town, the town hall has a grandiose stone front removed from the Wren-influenced Cheapside Mercers Company building and the Wellington Clock Tower was rescued from London Bridge and stands on the pier. There is a small heritage centre on the waterfront recounting the story of Swanage and the Isle of Purbeck beyond. It is open 10 am to 5 pm (closed 1 to 2 pm) daily, Easter to October. Admission is free.

The TIC (☎ 422885, fax 423423, e mail @swanage.com), White House, Shore Rd, is open 10 am to 5 pm daily.

The *Swanage Youth Hostel (☎ 422113, fax 426327, e swanage@yha.org.uk, Cluny Crescent)* has a pretty central location and beds for £10.85/7.40. There are many B&Bs to confirm Swanage's popularity as a beach resort.

Ricky's (☎ 424476, 15 High St) is a popular upmarket cafe with decent, if expensive, breakfasts and two-course evening meals for £10.95.

Bus No 150 runs to Bournemouth every half an hour, while Bus Nos 142/3/4 go frequently to Poole via Corfe Castle and Wareham.

Lulworth Cove & the Coast
☎ 01929

The lovely Dorset coast is at its most spectacular (and crowded) between Lulworth Cove and Durdle Door. Lulworth Cove is almost perfectly circular and nearly enclosed by towering cliffs. Durdle Door has a fine beach, a dramatic cove and an impressive natural archway. It's about a mile west of Lulworth Cove with fine cliff-top walks in both directions. The beach at Lulworth Cove is nothing to get excited about, but those to the east and west of Durdle Door are impressive. See also the Web site at www.lulworth.com for more information about the area.

Stumpy **Lulworth Castle** (☎ 400352) is in the village of East Lulworth, about 3 miles (5km) inland. The castle is 'modern' compared with many in England, built in 1608, but was devastated by fire in 1929. The exterior is fully restored, while the interior continues to undergo work. The grounds are open 10 am to 6 pm (to 4 pm November to March) daily, while the castle is only open from 1 to 4.30 pm Wednesday, April to September. Admission costs £4.50/2.50.

There are a number of places to stay at

The Bloody Assizes

In 1685 the Duke of Monmouth, illegitimate son of Charles II, landed at Lyme Regis intending to overthrow James II and become king. His rebellion ended in defeat at the Battle of Sedgemoor in Somerset, and the duke was beheaded in the Tower of London – it took four swings of the axe to sever his head. Judge Jeffreys, the chief justice, tried the rebels in Dorchester in a barbaric trial known as the Bloody Assizes.

Over 300 rebels were hanged and their gruesome drawn-and-quartered remains were displayed in towns and villages all over the region. Nearly 1000 more rebels were transported to Barbados and many more were imprisoned, fined or flogged.

Lulworth Cove, and more just back from the coast in West Lulworth.

Durdle Door Holiday Park (☎ 400200, fax 400260) has a prime location on the fields above the cliffs, and has sites for £15 for a tent and car. For non-campers it costs £3 to bring a car in here.

Lulworth Cove Youth Hostel (☎ 400564, fax 400640, School Lane, West Lulworth) costs £9.80/6.75 for adults/children.

Shops in Lulworth Cove serve up some very fine ice cream, including such delicate flavours as raspberry pavlova or ginger. Be sure to indulge.

First Southern National (☎ 01305-783 645) runs irregular bus Nos 101/2/3/4 from Dorchester to Lulworth Cove. Bus No 29 comes from Wareham.

DORCHESTER
☎ 01305 • pop 14,000
Famous as the home of novelist Thomas Hardy, Dorset's administrative centre is rather a sleepy place and lively Weymouth or pretty Cerne Abbas would make equally good bases for exploring the local attractions.

Orientation & Information
Most of Dorchester's action takes place along South St, which runs into pedestrianised Cornhill and then emerges in the High St, divided into East and West parts at St Peter's church.

The TIC (☎ 267992, fax 266079), Unit 11, Antelope Walk, is just off Trinity St. It is open 9.30 am to 5.30 pm Monday to Saturday. It sells the *Historical Guide – Dorchester* with interesting walks around town, and lots of Hardy literature, including a set of leaflets that retraces the scenes of individual novels.

Max Gate (Hardy's Home)
Those on the Hardy trail should check out this house, designed by the novelist, where he lived from 1885 until his death in 1928. It was here that he wrote several of his most famous works including *Tess of the D'Urbervilles* and *Jude the Obscure*, but there's not exactly a wealth of memorabilia.

Max Gate (☎ 262538; NT), on Alington Ave, is open 2 to 5 pm Monday, Wednesday and Sunday, April to September. Admission costs £2.10/1.10. The house is one mile east of the town centre on the A352. Bus D comes this way; hop off at the Max Gate roundabout.

Dorset County Museum
The Dorset County Museum (☎ 262735), on High West St, houses the study where Hardy did his writing. The museum also contains interesting sections on the archaeological excavations at Maiden Castle, fossil finds from Lyme Regis and a rural craft collection.

It's open 10 am to 5 pm Monday to Saturday (on Sunday too in July and August), and admission costs £3.30/1.50.

Tutankhamun Exhibit
The Tutankhamun Exhibit (☎ 269571) in High West St may seem out of place in Dorset but it's nevertheless an interesting place to visit. The discovery of the tomb and its contents have been recreated in montages complete with sounds and smells.

It's open 9.30 am to 5.30 pm daily; admission costs £4.50/2.95.

Other Things to See

The **Keep Military Museum** (☎ 264066), beyond the Bridport Rd roundabout, traces Dorset military valour overseas. It is open 9.30 am to 5 pm Monday to Friday (closed 1 to 2 pm on Saturday) and 10 am to 4 pm on summer Sundays. Admission costs £2.50/1.50.

There's also a small **Dinosaur Museum** (☎ 269880), Icen Way, which is open from 9.30 am to 5.30 pm daily. Admission costs £4.50/2.95.

The **Barclays Bank building** at No 10 South St provided the fictional home for Hardy's *Mayor of Casterbridge*. Hardy himself worked for a time at an architect's office at No 62. A **statue** of Hardy watches the traffic from a seat by the West Gate roundabout.

Places to Stay

The cheaper B&Bs in Dorchester have only a few rooms. *Hillfort View* (☎ 268476, fax 269233, 10 Hillfort Close) has a single for £18 and a double for £36.

Maumbury Cottage (☎ 266726, 9 Maumbury Rd) is convenient for the stations and charges £34 for a double. *Mountain Ash* (☎ 264811, e peewheet@cixcompulink.co .uk, 30 Mountain Ash Rd) charges £20/36 for a single/double.

The *Casterbridge Hotel* (☎ 264043, fax 260884, reception@casterbridgehotel .co.uk, 49 High East St) is a luxurious small hotel where B&B costs £42/72 in summer.

There are two comfortable Georgian hotels in High St West. The *Westwood House Hotel* (☎ 268018, fax 250282, 29 High St West) charges £49/69. Nearby, *Wessex Royale Hotel* (☎ 262660, fax 251941, 32 High St West) has the same tariff.

Places to Eat

An atmospheric place to take tea or a bigger meal, provided you're not squeamish about the gruesome historical associations (see the boxed text 'The Bloody Assizes' earlier in the chapter), is the half-timbered *Judge Jeffreys' Lodgings* (☎ 264369, 6 High West St). Main dishes are £7 to £10.

Allow around £20 a head for a three-course meal at the *Mock Turtle* (☎ 264011, High West St).

The Old Tea House (High West St) across the road serves cream teas and light meals.

The *Kings Arms* (☎ 265353, High East St) has associations with Hardy's *Mayor of Casterbridge*. There's good pub grub and a coffee shop.

The *Royal Oak* (High West St) and the nearby *Old Ship Inn* (the oldest pub in town) are also atmospheric places for a meal or drink.

Getting There & Away

Bus Connections tend to be much slower than trains – buses from London take four hours. Local bus operators include First Southern National (☎ 783645) from Lyme Regis and Taunton, Wilts & Dorset (☎ 01202-673555) from Salisbury, and Dorchester Coachways (☎ 262992) from Weymouth.

Train There are two train stations, Dorchester South and unstaffed Dorchester West, both south-west of the town centre. Dorchester South is linked seven times daily to London's Waterloo (three hours, £32.40) via Bournemouth (£7.10) and Southampton (£14.60). There are numerous services from Weymouth (10 minutes, £2.50). Dorchester West has connections from Bath (two hours, £10.30) and Bristol.

Getting Around

Dorchester Cycles (☎ 268787), at 31b Great Western Rd, rents bikes for £10 a day (£50 a week).

AROUND DORCHESTER
Maiden Castle

The earthwork ramparts of Maiden Castle, 1½ miles (2.5km) south-west of Dorchester, stretch for 3 miles (5km) and enclose nearly 20 hectares. The site has been inhabited since Neolithic times but the first fort was built here around 800 BC. It was subsequently abandoned, then rebuilt around 500 BC. The earth walls were later extended and enlarged in 250 and 150 BC. Despite the addition of more defences, the Romans still

Charlieville

Taking shape on Dorchester's western outskirts is Poundbury, a model town designed to immortalise Prince Charles' conservative ideals, and known locally as Charlieville. The estate will eventually house 5000 people, although only 135 houses have been built so far. They're all based on traditional designs but with modern conveniences such as double glazing and central heating.

Central to the Prince's concept of a modern town is that different social groups should be mixed, living on the same street, rather than separated onto different parts of the estate. Another idea was to make the town as pedestrian-friendly as possible. Planning controls are strict, however. Window surrounds may only be painted white, and telephone wires, TV aerials and satellite dishes must be kept out of sight.

Although the project has had many critics, it's quite obviously a success. Houses are sold as quickly as they are put up and property prices have increased dramatically.

captured it in AD 43, finally abandoning it in the 4th century. The sheer size of the walls and ditches and the area they enclose is stunning, and there are wonderful views. Dorset County Museum displays finds from the site.

Hardy's Cottage

The cottage (☎ 01305 262366) where Thomas Hardy was born and where he wrote *Far from the Madding Crowd* is at Higher Bockhampton, about 3 miles (5km) north-east of Dorchester and reached by a 10-minute walk from the car park. Despite the absence of Hardy memorabilia, the cottage is a popular attraction.

It's open 11 am to 5 pm Sunday to Thursday, April to October; admission costs £2.60.

Cerne Abbas & the Cerne Giant

Delightful little Cerne Abbas has several fine 16th-century houses and a medieval church. The much-rebuilt abbey house is now a private residence, although the ruins behind the house can be visited. The Abbot's Porch (1509) was once the entrance to the whole complex.

Just north of the village is the Cerne Giant, one of Britain's best-known chalk figures. The giant stands 55m tall and wields a 37m-long club. He's estimated to be anything between a few hundred and a couple of thousand years old. One thing is obvious – this old man has no need of

Viagra! The poor fellow only regained his manhood this century after the prudish Victorians allowed grass to grow over his vital parts.

With several B&Bs, Cerne Abbas would make a good alternative to staying in Dorchester (20 minutes by bus, eight miles; 13km). There's good pub food at the *Red Lion* (☎ *01300-341441*) and *Royal Oak* (☎ *01300-341797*), both on Long St.

WEYMOUTH

☎ 01305 • pop 40,000

This bustling, endearing seaside resort makes a good alternative to Dorchester as a base for exploring Hardy country – Weymouth was 'Budmouth' in the novels.

It was George III's experimental dip in Weymouth waters in 1789 that sparked the British passion for the seaside. Despite the shock of emerging from his 'bathing machine' to hear a band strike up in his honour, the king revisited Weymouth 13 times.

Orientation & Information

Central Weymouth, between the beach and the Inner Harbour, is only a few blocks wide. The Esplanade is the main walk along the beach, but each block of the road has a different secondary name. St Mary St is the pedestrianised shopping centre but Hope Square, on the far side of the pretty Old Harbour, is more inviting.

The TIC (☎ 785747, fax 788092, e tour ism@weymouth.gov.uk), on The Esplanade,

WESSEX

WEYMOUTH

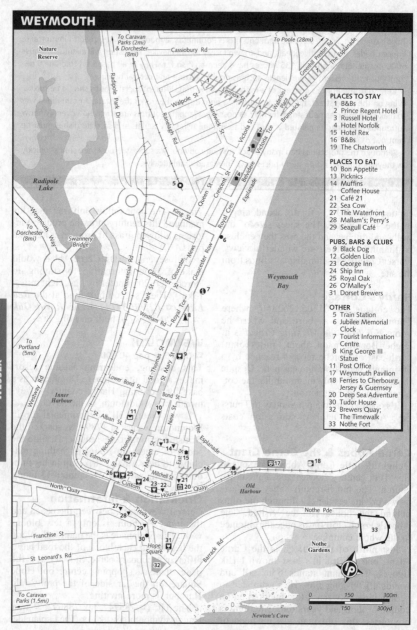

PLACES TO STAY
1 B&Bs
2 Prince Regent Hotel
3 Russell Hotel
4 Hotel Norfolk
15 Hotel Rex
16 B&Bs
19 The Chatsworth

PLACES TO EAT
10 Bon Appetite
13 Picknics
14 Muffins
   Coffee House
21 Café 21
22 Sea Cow
27 The Waterfront
28 Mallam's; Perry's
29 Seagull Café

PUBS, BARS & CLUBS
9 Black Dog
12 Golden Lion
23 George Inn
24 Ship Inn
25 Royal Oak
26 O'Malley's
31 Dorset Brewers

OTHER
5 Train Station
6 Jubilee Memorial
   Clock
7 Tourist Information
   Centre
8 King George III
   Statue
11 Post Office
17 Weymouth Pavilion
18 Ferries to Cherbourg,
   Jersey & Guernsey
20 Deep Sea Adventure
30 Tudor House
32 Brewers Quay;
   The Timewalk
33 Nothe Fort

WESSEX

is opposite the statue of King George III. It is open from 9.30 am to 5 pm daily.

Esplanade & Old Harbour

Weymouth is a fine example of the archetypal English seaside resort and a summer walk along The Esplanade will reveal garish beach-equipment stands, deck chairs for hire, donkey rides and Punch & Judy shows. Look for the brightly painted Jubilee Memorial Clock of 1888 and the equally vivid statue of King George III, patron saint of Weymouth tourism.

The less brash Old Harbour inlet is lined with attractive old buildings used as shops, restaurants and pubs, and packed with fishing trawlers and fancy yachts from around the world.

Deep Sea Adventure

The Deep Sea Adventure (☎ 760690), in an old grainstore at 9 Custom House Quay, traces the history of diving, with exhibits on local shipwrecks, the *Titanic*, and the £40-million gold recovery from HMS *Edinburgh*, sunk while part of a convoy from Russia. William Walker, the Winchester Cathedral diver (see Winchester in the South-Eastern England chapter) plays his part, as does the intriguing story of John Lethbridge and his pioneering 'diving engine' of 1715.

The exhibit is open 9.30 am to 6.30 pm daily (to 8 pm in July and August). Last entry is 1½ hours before closing time. Admission costs £3.75/2.75.

Brewer's Quay & the Timewalk

Brewer's Quay on Hope Square has a shopping centre and plentiful attractions, including the Timewalk (☎ 777622) that takes you through the town's early history as a trading port, the disaster of the Black Death plague years, the drama of the Spanish Armada and Weymouth's development as a resort. You even see a figure of the portly George III emerging from his famous bathing machine.

This excellent tour ends with the story of the Devenish brewery, in which it is housed.

It's open 10 am to 5.30 pm daily (to 9 pm in July and August). Admission to the Timewalk costs £4.25/3.

Tudor House

When Tudor House (☎ 812341), 3 Trinity St, was built around 1600, the waterfront would have lapped at the front door. Furnished in Tudor style, it's open 11 am to 3.45 pm Tuesday to Friday, June to September; first Sunday afternoon of the month only October to May. Admission, including a guided tour, costs £2/50p.

Nothe Fort

Perched on the end of the promontory, 19th-century Nothe Fort (☎ 766626) houses a museum on Britain's coastal defence system. It's open 10.30 am to 5.30 pm daily, early May to late September (from 2 pm only on Sunday in winter). Admission costs £3/free.

Places to Stay

There's a freephone number (☎ 0800 765223) for accommodation bookings.

Camping There are caravan parks between Overcombe and Preston, north along the Dorchester Rd and south near Sandsfoot Castle and Chesil Beach.

B&Bs & Hotels Weymouth has an awesome number of places to stay. Cheaper B&Bs, typically costing £14 to £18 per person, can be found all over town. Good hunting grounds include Brunswick Terrace, on the northern stretch of The Esplanade. The pretty B&Bs along this stretch look straight over the beach.

Lennox St, just north of the train station, and Waterloo Place, the stretch of The Esplanade from the Lennox St junction, are both packed with cheaper B&Bs. At the other end of The Esplanade, just before Weymouth Quay, there are also ranks of B&Bs from Nos 1 to 34.

The Chatsworth (☎ 785012, fax 766342, ⓔ dave@chatsworth.freeserve.co.uk, 14 The Esplanade) looks out to sea in one direction and across the Old Harbour in the

WESSEX

other. Rooms with bathroom run from £25 per person.

Most of the places along the central part of The Esplanade are expensive but *Hotel Norfolk* (☎ 786734, fax 766250, 125–6 The Esplanade) is reasonable, charging from £30 per person.

The *Russell Hotel* (☎ 786059, fax 775723, e admin@russell-hotel.co.uk, 135–8 The Esplanade) has singles/doubles for £32/64. Next door, the *Prince Regent Hotel* (☎ 771313, fax 778100, e hprwey@aol.com, 139 The Esplanade) charges from £55/85.

Hotel Rex (☎ 760400, fax 760500, 29 The Esplanade) was the Duke of Clarence's summer residence; these days anyone can stay for £54.50/96.

Places to Eat

A good place for takeaways is *Bon Appetite* (☎ 777375, 32 St Mary St), offering filled baguettes and gourmet pizza slices.

North of the Old Harbour, *Picknics* (☎ 761317, 31 Maiden St) prepares a variety of takeaway sandwiches and filled rolls (closed Sunday).

Café 21 (☎ 767848, 21 East St) is a funky little vegetarian place with healthy, tasty food and low prices. Dishes such as mushroom and leek crepes and seasonal fruit crumbles make this a must.

Muffins Coffee House (☎ 783844, St Albans St) is popular for lunches, with specials chalked on boards outside.

Weymouth is a good place to sample that most British of fast foods – fish and chips. On the southern side of the harbour, *The Waterfront* (☎ 781237, 14 Trinity Rd) does takeaway cod, haddock, skate and plaice for around the £3 mark. Round the corner, the *Seagull Café* (10 Trinity St) is another cheap chippie.

On the southern side of the Old Harbour, *Perry's* (☎ 785799, 4 Trinity Rd) and *Mallam's* (☎ 776757, 5 Trinity Rd) both make imaginative use of local seafood. At Perry's, dishes on the a la carte menu range from £12.50 to £22.50 (lobster). Mallam's has a fixed price menu – two courses for £18.90.

In the Old Harbour, *The Sea Cow* (☎ 783524, 7 Custom House Quay) has a good range of seafood, including more exotic local fish such as John Dory. Count on £15 to £25 for a three-course meal with wine.

Entertainment

Weymouth is packed with pubs. The *Dorset Brewers* (☎ 786940, Hope St) has a nautical theme and serves good pub grub.

O'Malley's (☎ 761020) and the *Royal Oak*, on Custom House Quay by the bridge, or the *Ship Inn* (☎ 773879) and the *George Inn* (☎ 773301), towards the sea, are all popular.

Back from the harbour, there's the *Golden Lion* (☎ 786778), on the corner of St Mary and St Edmund Sts.

The *Black Dog* (☎ 771426), on pedestrianised St Mary St, is said to be the oldest pub in town, and is named after the first black Labrador brought into England on a ship from Newfoundland.

Weymouth Pavilion (☎ 783225), on the quay, has a busy schedule of events year-round. It's pretty highbrow stuff – highlights have included Australian male strippers and Ronnie Corbett.

Getting There & Away

Bus Buses stop along the Esplanade; phone ☎ 224535 for local bus information). Dorchester Coachways (☎ 262992) has daily buses to London. Wilts & Dorset has services to Dorchester, Salisbury, Taunton, Poole and Bournemouth. First Southern National (☎ 01305-783645) operates the X53 hourly to Exeter via Lyme Regis. Bus No 1 runs frequently to Portland.

Train Weymouth station is conveniently located at the junction of Ranelagh Rd and King St. There are hourly services to London (£33.70, 3½ hours) via Bournemouth (£8.80, 1 hour) and Southampton (£15.90, 1½ hours). Services to other centres in the south-west include nearby Dorchester (£2.50, 12 minutes).

Boat Condor (☎ 761551) high-speed catamaran car ferries whizz across to Cherbourg, France in 4¼ hours. A day trip costs £29.90 return. Condor also runs ferries to Jersey and Guernsey.

WEYMOUTH TO LYME REGIS
Portland
South of Weymouth, Portland is joined to the mainland by the long sweep of Chesil Beach. Many famous buildings have been made from locally quarried Portland stone.

The sturdy **Portland Castle** (☎ 820539; EH) is one of the finest examples of the defensive castles constructed during Henry VIII's castle-building spree, spurred by fear of an attack from France. It is open 10 am to 6 pm daily, April to September; and 10 am to 5 pm daily in October). Admission costs £2.80/1.40.

There are superb views from the lighthouse, which houses the summer-only TIC (☎ 01305-861233) at the end of **Portland Bill**. The lighthouse is open 11 am to 5 pm daily in summer, but Saturday only, October to April. It costs £2/1.50 to climb the 41m-high tower. An earlier, smaller lighthouse now acts as a bird observatory.

Chesil Beach
Chesil Beach is a long curving sandbank (except that it's made of pebbles rather than sand) stretching along the coast for 10 miles (16km) from Portland to Abbotsbury. The bank encloses the slightly stagnant waters of the Fleet Lagoon, a haven for water birds including the famed Abbotsbury swans.

The stones vary from pebble size at Abbotsbury in the west to around 15cm in diameter at Portland in the east; local fishermen can supposedly tell their position along the bank by gauging the size of the stones. In places the stone bank reaches 15m high. Although winter storms can wash right over the top, it has never been broken up. The bank is accessible at the Portland end and from just west of Abbotsbury.

Abbotsbury
☎ 01305
Abbotsbury is one of the prettiest coastal villages in Dorset and now boasts several attractions to keep the visitors coming.

Things to See The huge, 83m-long **tithe barn** (☎ 871817), at one time a communal storage site for farm produce, was used for a harvest supper scene in Polanski's *Far from the Madding Crowd*. It houses an interesting country museum and recent exhibits include a partial recreation of the terracotta army from Xian, China.

It is open 10 am to 6 pm daily April to October, Sunday only the rest of the year. Admission costs £4/3.

On the coast, and offering fine views of the Fleet Lagoon, is **Abbotsbury Swannery** (☎ 871130), on New Barn Rd. Swans have been nesting here for 600 years and the colony can number up to 600, plus cygnets. The walk through the swannery and reed beds will tell you all you ever wanted to know about swans. Come in May for the nests, or in late May and June for the cygnets. It's open 10 am to 6 pm daily (to dusk in winter), and admission costs £5/3.

The swannery was founded by Abbotsbury's Benedictine monastery, which was destroyed in 1541. Traces of the monastery remain by the tithe barn. The energetic can walk up to 14th-century **St Catherine's Chapel**, overlooking the swannery, the village and Chesil Beach.

Abbotsbury Subtropical Gardens (☎ 871 387) were laid out in 1765 as a kitchen garden, but have a few more exotic plants today. They are open 10 am to 6 pm daily, March to October (to 4 pm in winter; last admission one hour earlier). Admission costs £4.50/3.

Places to Stay & Eat Abbotsbury has several comfortable B&Bs and places to eat.

The old *Ilchester Arms* (☎ 871243, 9 Market St), right in the village, has interesting pub food such as Dorset sausage baguette, and also has a restaurant. It doubles as a hotel with double rooms from £45.50 excluding breakfast.

Chesil House (☎ 871324) is a friendly place with rooms from £22.50 a person.

Getting There & Away Abbotsbury is 9 miles (14km) north-west of Weymouth on the B3157 and during summer buses run this route at least three times daily, Monday to Saturday.

LYME REGIS
☎ 01297 • pop 4600

The attractive, delicate seaside town of Lyme Regis marks the end of Dorset – Devon begins just beyond the pier known as the Cobb. The Cobb is a famous literary spot: not only did Louisa Musgrove's accident in Jane Austen's novel *Persuasion* take place here, but it was also where *The French Lieutenant's Woman* stood and stared out to sea in John Fowles' novel (and where Meryl Streep stood in the film).

The town's other claim to fame is prehistoric. The limestone cliffs on either side of town are some of Britain's richest sources of fossils, and the first dinosaur skeletons were discovered here.

In 1685 the Duke of Monmouth landed on Monmouth Beach, west of the town, to start his abortive rebellion against James II. See the boxed text 'The Bloody Assizes' in the Dorchester section earlier in the chapter for further details.

Orientation & Information

The A3052 drops precipitously into Lyme Regis from one side and climbs equally steeply out on the other. From Bridge St, where the A3052 meets the coast, Marine Parade runs west to the harbour.

Lyme Regis' TIC (☎ 442138, fax 443773), Guildhall Cottage, Church St, is situated where Church St becomes Bridge St. It is open 10 am to 6 pm daily (to 5 pm at the weekend).

Museums

In Bridge St is the **Lyme Regis Philpot Museum** (☎ 443370), with displays of fossils and local history. The cliffs west of the harbour and Monmouth Beach are still prone to fossil-exposing landslips; the museum has

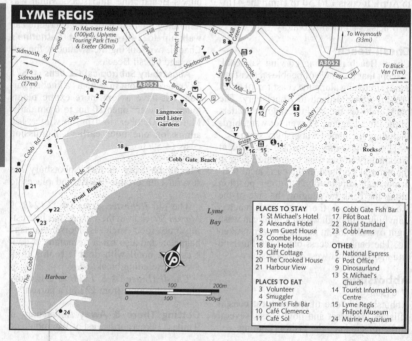

LYME REGIS

PLACES TO STAY
1 St Michael's Hotel
2 Alexandra Hotel
8 Lym Guest House
12 Coombe House
18 Bay Hotel
19 Cliff Cottage
20 The Crooked House
21 Harbour View

PLACES TO EAT
3 Volunteer
4 Smuggler
7 Lyme's Fish Bar
10 Café Clemence
11 Café Sol

16 Cobb Gate Fish Bar
17 Pilot Boat
22 Royal Standard
23 Cobb Arms

OTHER
5 National Express
6 Post Office
9 Dinosaurland
13 St Michael's Church
14 Tourist Information Centre
15 Lyme Regis Philpot Museum
24 Marine Aquarium

details of the Dowlands Landslip on Christmas Day 1839, when a stretch of cliff top three quarters of a mile long slid away, taking with it farms and houses. It's open 10 am to 5 pm daily (closed noon to 2.30 pm on Sunday); admission costs £1/40p.

Dinosaurland (☎ 443541), on Coombe St, is an eclectic mix of science, fossils and local folklore. It's open 10 am to 5 pm daily, Easter to November; admission costs £3.20/1.90.

The Cobb

The Cobb is a 183m-long stone jetty-cum-breakwater. The small **Marine Aquarium** (☎ 443678) has interesting displays of local marine life. It's open 10 am to 5 pm (later in peak season) daily, April to October. Admission costs £1.40/90p.

From Cobb Gate towards East Cliff runs **Gun Cliff Walk**. The superstructure ingeniously conceals the town's sewage system.

Places to Stay

Lyme Regis has plenty of hotels, guesthouses and B&Bs. Two people with a tent can camp at **Uplyme Touring Park** (☎ 442801, Hook Farm, Uplyme) for £9 in summer. To get there, walk up Silver St/Uplyme Rd (towards Exeter) for about 15 minutes.

Lym Guest House (☎ 442164, 1 Mill Green) at the junction of Hill Rd and Sherborne Lane, has good B&B from £22 per person.

At **Coombe House** (☎/fax 443849, 41 Coombe St), you'll pay £16 in a room with private bathroom.

Perched above the harbour, there's **Harbour View** (☎ 443910, Cobb Rd), housed in a comfortable, modern home. It charges £17 excluding breakfast.

A little further up the hill is **The Crooked House** (☎/fax 444741, 6 Cobb Rd), which hasn't earned its name for nothing. Beams and stairways abound, and bed with a wholesome breakfast is £20 per person.

Cliff Cottage (☎ 443334, Cobb Rd) has doubles for £38 including breakfast, and there are some impressive panoramas across the bay below.

St Michael's Hotel (☎ 442503, Pound St) has nice views and costs £35 for rooms with bathroom, £30 without the sea view.

Nearby is the **Alexandra Hotel** (☎ 442 010, fax 443229, e alexandra@lymeregis .co.uk, Pound St), one of the town's finest hotels, which charges £50/85 for singles/doubles.

The 17th-century **Mariners Hotel** (☎ 442 753, fax 442431, Silver St) is full of history and atmosphere, with rooms from £42 a head.

The **Bay Hotel** (☎ 442059, Marine Parade) has a seafront location and costs from £45 per person.

Places to Eat

For fish and chips try **Lyme's Fish Bar** (34 Coombe St) or the **Cobb Gate Fish Bar** on the waterfront.

Café Sol on Coombe St has a varied and light menu for any time of day and a welcoming vibe.

Around the corner in the old mill complex is popular **Café Clemence** (Mill Lane).

The **Smuggler** (☎ 442795, 30 Broad St) does all-day breakfasts, lunches, cream teas, and early suppers, closing at 8 pm.

Many of the pubs do food – try the **Cobb Arms** or the **Royal Standard**, both on Marine Parade by the Cobb.

Other possibilities include the **Volunteer** (Broad St) and the **Pilot Boat** (Bridge St).

Getting There & Away

Lyme Regis makes a convenient midway point between Dorchester or Weymouth and Exeter. Southern National Bus No 31 links Lyme Regis to Taunton and Weymouth via Axminster. Hourly Bus X53 goes west to Exeter and east to Weymouth.

AROUND LYME REGIS
Parnham

Parnham (☎ 01308-862204) is both a home and a showroom for owner John Makepeace's contemporary furniture. You might pick up a chair for £600, but most pieces are in the £3000 to £10,000 range.

It's near Beaminster, 5 miles (8km) north of Bridport, and is open 10 am to 5 pm

Tuesday to Thursday and Sunday, April to October. Admission costs £5/2.

Forde Abbey

Set in 12 hectares of magnificent gardens, Forde Abbey (☎ 01460-220231) is a monastery converted into a private home. It's 6 miles (10km) north-east of Axminster, and is open 1 to 4.30 pm on Wednesday and Sunday, April to October. Admission is £5/free, which includes admission to the gardens. The gardens are open 10 am to 4.30 pm daily, year-round, and admission is £4/free.

SHERBORNE

☎ 01935 • pop 7500

Sherborne is an appealing country town, home to a wonderful abbey church with a colourful history. On the edge of town, remains of the Old and New Castles face each other across Sherborne Lake.

Sherborne's TIC (☎ 815341, fax 817210, e tourism@westdorset-dc.gov.uk) is opposite the abbey entrance at 3 Tilton Court, Digby Rd. It is open 9 am to 5 pm from Monday to Saturday.

Sherborne Abbey

The abbey started life as a small Saxon church early in the 8th century, and became a Benedictine abbey in 998. After further expansion and decoration, it was seized by the Crown in 1539, whereupon the townsfolk clubbed together and bought it as their parish church.

Simmering unrest between monastery and town flared up in 1437. At that time, the monks used the chancel of the church while the townspeople used the nave. When the monks attempted to narrow a doorway between the abbey and the connected All Hallows Church (now gone), a pitched battle broke out and a flaming arrow shot across the church from town end to monastery end and set the roof alight.

The abbey is entered via a Norman porch built in 1180. Immediately on the left is the Norman door, built in 1140, which was the cause of the 1437 riots and fire. The remains of All Hallows are to the west of the Saxon wall; a Saxon doorway from 1050 survives. The superb fan vault above the choir dates from the early 15th century and is the oldest ceiling of this type and size in the country. The similar vault over the nave is from later in the century. Solid Saxon–Norman piers support the abbey's soaring central tower. The monk's choir stalls also date from the mid-15th century and are carved with amusing figures.

The abbey has a cathedral-like close where you'll find the 1437 St John's Almshouses. They open 2 to 4 pm on Tuesday and Thursday to Saturday, May to September; admission costs £1. The museum (☎ 812252) in Half Moon St has a model of the Old Castle before it was slighted. It's open 10.30 am to 4.30 pm Tuesday to Saturday, and 2.30 to 4.30 pm on Sunday, April to October; admission is £1/free. Sherborne School, a private school, dates back to 1550 and occupies various buildings from the monastery.

Old Castle

East of the town centre stand the ruins of the Old Castle (☎ 812730; EH), originally constructed from 1107. In the late 16th century, Sir Walter Raleigh took a fancy to the castle, and Elizabeth I negotiated its purchase for him. Before Sir Walter could move in, he incurred the queen's displeasure by marrying one of her ladies-in-waiting and Sir Walter and his new bride paid a short visit to the Tower of London. Later he spent large sums of money modernising the castle, before deciding it wasn't worth the effort and moving across the River Yeo to start work on the new castle. Cromwell destroyed the castle after a 16-day siege in 1645. 'A malicious and mischievous castle, like its owner [the Earl of Bristol]', he thundered. The castle is open 10 am to 6 pm daily; admission costs £1.60/80p.

Sherborne Castle

Sir Walter Raleigh commenced his New Castle (☎ 813182) in 1594 but by 1608 he was back in prison, this time at the hands of James I. The king first gave the castle away, then took it back, and in 1617 sold it to Sir

John Digby, the Earl of Bristol. It's been the Digby family residence ever since.

The castle is open 12.30 to 4.30 pm on Thursday, Saturday and Sunday, Easter to September; admission costs £5/2.50.

Places to Stay & Eat

There are few budget B&B places in Sherborne. The *Britannia Inn (☎ 813300, Westbury St)* charges from £20 per person in the week, £25 at the weekend.

Clatcombe Grange (☎ 814355, Bristol Rd) has comfortable accommodation in a converted barn, for £25/50 per single/double.

Antelope Hotel (☎ 812077, fax 816473, Greenhill) is a pub that offers B&B for £44/65.

In Milborne Port, 2 miles (3km) from Sherborne, is *The Old Vicarage (☎ 01963-251117, Sherborne Rd)*. B&B costs from £25 to £45 per person, depending on the room. There are weekend breaks also including dinner, from £41 to £63 per person. It's a listed building in an attractive country setting.

For light meals try the *Three Wishes (☎ 817777, 78 Cheap St)*, where they also stock a good selection of cakes.

The *Cross Keys Hotel (☎ 812492)*, at the junction of Cheap and Long Sts, right by the abbey, has an extensive pub-food menu. Also near the abbey is the *Digby Tap (☎ 813148, Cooks Lane)*, a pub offering a wide range of ales and good-sized portions of traditional fare.

Getting There & Away

Sherborne is out on a limb when it comes to transport services, but nearby Yeovil is a handy hub. Bus Nos 57/58 run frequently from Yeovil, while No 216 goes regularly from Dorchester. From Shaftesbury, catch No 58/A.

SHAFTESBURY
☎ 01747 • pop 4900

Shaftesbury is an atmospheric if slow-paced country town and is worth a stop just to see the charming Gold Hill, a tumbling street of cosy cottages, which affords some great views of the surrounding plains.

The TIC (☎ 853514), 8 Bell St, is open 10 am to 5 pm daily during summer. It opens Wednesday morning and Thursday to Saturday in winter.

Things to See

Situated on a 240m-high ridge, **Shaftesbury Abbey** (☎ 852910) was founded in 888 by Alfred the Great and was at one time England's richest nunnery. Today, only scant signs of the foundations remain, situated off Park Walk with fine views over the surrounding countryside. St Edward (see Corfe Castle in the South-East Dorset section earlier in this chapter) was said to have been buried here, and King Canute died at the abbey in 1035.

It's open 10 am to 5 pm daily, April to October and admission costs £1.50/60p.

Perched at the top of the hill, **Shaftesbury Museum** (☎ 852157) is open 10.30 am to 4.30 pm daily, Easter to October. Admission is £1.20/free.

The picturesquely steep cobbled street known as **Gold Hill** tumbles down the ridge from beside the abbey ruins and on a clear summer's evening you might just get a photo as rich and textured as the postcards.

Places to Stay & Eat

Set in a sweet little cottage nestled at the base of Shaftesbury's finest and most famous hill is *Thatch Cottage (☎ 853318, e info@thatchcottage.co.uk, 15 Gold Hill)*. There is one double room with a bathroom and classic English furnishings for £22.50 per person, and guests can use the garden and terrace.

Those who like a meal with a view should make for *The Salt Cellar (☎ 851 838, 2–3 Gold Hill Parade)*. It's a cosy cafe at the top of Gold Hill, although it is generally open only during the day and not by night.

The *Ship Inn* and *King's Arms* pubs, by the central car park, both serve food.

Getting There & Away

Wilts and Dorset (☎ 01202-673555) run Bus Nos 182/3 regularly from Wimborne

WESSEX

Chalk Figures

Wiltshire's rolling fields are a green cloak over a chalk substructure, and the practice of cutting pictures into the hillsides has a long history. The technique is simple: mark out your picture and cut away the green grass and topsoil to reveal the white chalk below. The picture will need periodic maintenance, but not much – some of the chalk figures may date back to prehistoric times, although the history of the oldest figures is uncertain. Although Wiltshire has more chalk figures than any other county, the best are probably the 55m-tall Cerne Abbas Giant (with his even more notable 12m penis) in Dorset and the 110m-long Uffington White Horse in Oxfordshire (which really requires a helicopter or hot-air balloon for proper inspection).

Horses were particularly popular subjects for chalk figures in the 18th century and noteworthy ones can be seen in Wiltshire at Cherhill near Calne, Alton Barnes and Hackpen, and at Osmington near Weymouth in Dorset.

During WWI a series of regimental badges were cut into a hillside outside Fovant in Wiltshire. A New Zealand WWI regiment left a gigantic kiwi on a hillside at Bulford, near Amesbury in Wiltshire. Get a copy of Kate Bergamar's *Discovering Hill Figures* (Shire Publications) for the complete lowdown on England's chalk figures.

and Blandford (except on Sunday). Bus Nos 26 and 27 run from Salisbury (approx nine per day), from Monday to Saturday.

Wiltshire

Wiltshire boasts wonderful rolling chalk downs, Britain's most important prehistoric sites at Stonehenge and Avebury, a fine cathedral at Salisbury and a number of the stateliest of stately homes at Wilton, Stourhead and Longleat. The Ridgeway Path, taking walkers along a crest of the downs, has its western end in Wiltshire. Salisbury is the best base for exploring the area.

For information on bus services throughout the county, call the Wiltshire Bus Line on ☎ 0845 7090899.

ACTIVITIES

The Ridgeway Path starts near Avebury and runs north-east for 85 miles (137km) to Ivinghoe Beacon near Aylesbury. For more details, see Walking & Cycling at the start of this chapter.

The **Wiltshire Cycleway** comprises six circular routes ranging from 70 to 160 miles (113km to 258km). TICs stock the *Wiltshire Cycleway* brochure that details the routes and lists cycle shops and rental outlets.

Wiltshire Cycleway Campsites lists camping grounds along the routes.

Stretching from Bristol to Reading, the 87-mile-long **Kennet & Avon Canal** was re-opened in 1990 after standing derelict for 40 years. Built by the brilliant engineer John Rennie between 1794 and 1810, it's now used by narrowboats and has some fine stretches of towpath. The stretch from Bath to Bradford-on-Avon passes a notable aqueduct. The flight of 29 locks just outside Devizes is an engineering marvel. The Kennet & Avon Canal Museum (☎ 01380-721279) on the wharf in Devizes has information on the canal.

SALISBURY
☎ 01722 • pop 37,000

Salisbury is deservedly famous for its cathedral and accompanying close, but it's still very much a bustling market town, not just a tourist trap. Markets have been held in the town centre twice weekly for over 600 years and the jumble of stalls still draws a cheery crowd. The town's architecture mixes every style since the Middle Ages and includes some beautiful, half-timbered, black-and-white buildings.

Salisbury makes a good base for visiting attractions throughout Wiltshire and for excursions to the coast.

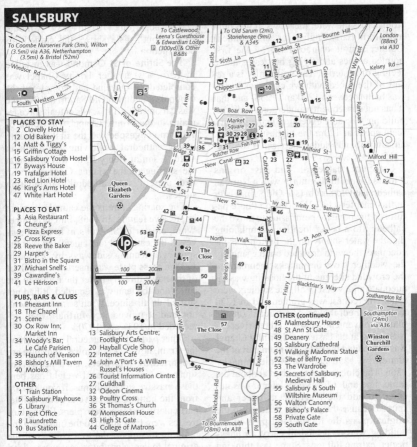

SALISBURY

PLACES TO STAY
2 Clovelly Hotel
12 Old Bakery
14 Matt & Tiggy's
15 Griffin Cottage
16 Salisbury Youth Hostel
17 Byways House
19 Trafalgar Hotel
21 Red Lion Hotel
46 King's Arms Hotel
47 White Hart Hotel

PLACES TO EAT
3 Asia Restaurant
4 Cheung's
9 Pizza Express
25 Cross Keys
28 Reeve the Baker
29 Harper's
31 Bistro in the Square
37 Michael Snell's
39 Cawardine's
41 Le Hérisson

PUBS, BARS & CLUBS
11 Pheasant Inn
18 The Chapel
21 Scene
30 Ox Row Inn;
   Market Inn
34 Woody's Bar;
   Le Café Parisien
35 Haunch of Venison
38 Bishop's Mill Tavern
40 Moloko

OTHER
1 Train Station
5 Salisbury Playhouse
6 Library
7 Post Office
8 Laundrette
10 Bus Station

13 Salisbury Arts Centre;
   Footlights Cafe
20 Hayball Cycle Shop
22 Internet Café
24 John A'Port's & William
   Russel's Houses
26 Tourist Information Centre
27 Guildhall
32 Odeon Cinema
36 Poultry Cross
36 St Thomas's Church
42 Mompesson House
43 High St Gate
44 College of Matrons

OTHER (continued)
45 Malmesbury House
48 St Ann St Gate
49 Deanery
50 Salisbury Cathedral
51 Walking Madonna Statue
52 Site of Belfry Tower
53 The Wardrobe
54 Secrets of Salisbury;
   Medieval Hall
55 Salisbury & South
   Wiltshire Museum
56 Walton Canonry
57 Bishop's Palace
58 Private Gate
59 South Gate

WESSEX

Orientation & Information

Salisbury's town centre is a 10-minute walk to the east of the train station or just a couple of minutes down Endless St from the bus station. Everything is within easy walking distance of Market Square, the town centre, which is dominated by its impressive guildhall.

Directly behind the guildhall, the TIC (☎ 334956, fax 422059) on Fish Row is open 9.30 am to 5 pm Monday to Saturday, and 10.30 am to 5 pm on Sunday in summer. It sells *Seeing Salisbury*, a useful pamphlet that outlines walks around the town and across the water meadows for classic views of the cathedral.

Excellent one-hour walking tours of Salisbury (£2.50/1) leave from the TIC at 11 am and 6 pm daily from May to September. On Friday, an 8 pm ghost walk replaces the 6 pm tour.

Internet Café on Milford St is a swish little Internet centre with iMacs only.

Salisbury Cathedral

The Cathedral Church of the Blessed Virgin Mary (☎ 555100) is one of the most beautiful and cohesive in Britain, an inspiration to the artist John Constable who painted it from across the water meadows. It was built in uniform Early English (or early pointed) Gothic, a style characterised by the first pointed arches and flying buttresses and a feeling of austerity. The uniformity is a result of the speed with which the cathedral was built (between 1220 and 1258) and that it has not subsequently undergone major rebuilding. The sole exception is the magnificent spire, at 123m the highest in Britain, an afterthought added between 1285 and 1315.

Salisbury cathedral had its origins 2 miles (3km) further north with a Norman cathedral at Old Sarum (see Old Sarum later in this chapter). In 1217, Bishop Poore petitioned the pope for permission to move the cathedral to a better location, complaining that the water supply on the hilltop was inadequate, the wind drowned out the singing, the weather gave the monks rheumatism, the crowded site meant the housing was inadequate and, worst of all, the soldiers were rude. His request was granted and in 1220 a new cathedral was constructed on the plains, conveniently close to three rivers.

Starting at the eastern end, **Trinity Chapel** was completed by 1225, the main part of the church by 1258 and the whole thing by 1266. The cloisters were added at about the same time and a few years later it was decided to add the magnificent tower and spire. Because this had not featured in the original plans the four central piers of the building were expected to carry an unexpected extra 6400 tons. Some fast thinking was required to enable them to do this.

The highly decorative West Screen was the last part of the cathedral to be completed and provides a fine view from across the close. The cathedral is entered via the cloister passage and the **south-west door**. The 70m-long nave, with its beautiful Purbeck marble piers, was 'tidied up' by James Wyatt from 1789 to 1792; among other things he lined up the tombs in the nave neatly. At the south-western end of the nave is the **grave slab of Bishop Joscelyn** (1141–84), at one time thought to be the tomb of Bishop Roger, who completed the

final cathedral at Old Sarum where he was bishop from 1107 to 1139. A **model** in the south aisle shows the cathedral's construction.

The **Shrine of St Osmund** was installed in 1226, a year after Trinity Chapel was completed. St Osmund had completed the original cathedral at Old Sarum in 1092 and was canonised in 1457. His actual grave remains in the Trinity Chapel. The **Tomb of William Longespée** was the first new tomb in the cathedral, following his death in 1226. A son of Henry II, he was present at the signing of the Magna Carta and also laid one of the cathedral's foundation stones.

The soaring spire is the cathedral's most impressive feature. In 1668, Sir Christopher Wren, creator of St Paul's in London, surveyed the cathedral and calculated that the spire was leaning sideways by 75cm. In 1737, a **brass plate** was inserted in the floor of the nave, directly under the centre of the spire, and the lean was recorded. It had not shifted at all since Wren's measurement, nor had it moved any further when rerecorded in 1951 and 1970.

Other parts of the cathedral clearly show the strain, however. The tower and spire are supported by four **piers**, each nearly 2m square, but the additional weight has bent these massive stone columns. If you look up from the bottom, the curve is quite visible, particularly on the eastern piers. Flying buttresses were later added to the outside of the building to support the four corners of the original tower. More buttresses were added internally and the openings to the eastern transepts were reinforced with **scissor arches** as in Wells Cathedral. Reinforcement work on the notoriously 'wonky spire' continues to this day.

Not everything in the cathedral requires looking upwards. The **tomb of Sir Richard Mompesson**, who died in 1627, and his wife Catherine, is a brilliantly colourful tomb. The grandiose **tomb of Edward Seymour** (1539–1621) and **Lady Catherine Grey**, sister of Lady Jane Grey, is at the eastern end of the ambulatory. The first part of the cathedral to be built, **Trinity Chapel**, at the eastern end, has fine Purbeck marble pillars; the vivid blue **Prisoners of Conscience** stained-glass window was installed in 1980.

The Sudan chapel contains a magnificent 14th-century **memorial brass** to Bishop Robert Wyvil showing him praying in Sherborne castle, and a **prism memorial** to artist Rex Whistler who lived in the close. The **clock** displayed in the north aisle is the oldest in England and one of the oldest in the world. It was certainly in existence in 1386 when funds were provided for maintenance of a 'clocke'. Restored in 1956, it continues to operate, maintaining the 600-year-old tradition of having a clock in this position.

The cloisters lead to the beautiful Gothic **Chapter House** of 1263–84, which houses one of the four surviving original versions of the **Magna Carta**, the agreement made between King John and his barons in 1215. The delicate fan-vaulted ceiling is supported by a single central column. A frieze around the room recounts Old Testament tales.

The cathedral is open 8 am to 6.30 pm daily; a donation of £3/1 is requested. The Chapter House is open 9.30 am to 4.45 pm Monday to Saturday, and 1 to 4.45 pm on Sunday. There are tower tours at 11 am, 2 pm, 3 pm and 6.30 pm Monday to Saturday (4.30 pm only on Sunday), which cost £3/2. These offer a unique opportunity to come to grips with medieval building practices and are highly recommended.

Cathedral Close

Salisbury Cathedral has England's largest, and arguably most beautiful, cathedral close. Many of the buildings were constructed at the same time as the cathedral although it owes most of its present appearance to Wyatt's late-18th-century clean-up of the cathedral. The Close was actually walled in, physically separating it from the town, in 1333, using the old cathedral at Old Sarum as a source of building material. To this day it remains an elite enclave, with the gates in the wall still locked every night. Residents have their own gate keys. The most famous current resident is former prime minister Edward Heath.

Wyatt also cleared the close grounds of gravestones and demolished the late-13th-century external belfry, by then in a ruinous condition. Striding across the close lawns on the western side of the cathedral is Elizabeth Frink's **Walking Madonna** (1981).

The close has several museums and houses open for inspection, most of them with cafe facilities.

The **Salisbury & South Wiltshire Museum** (☎ 332151) in the King's House has exhibits on local prehistory, including Stonehenge and Old Sarum. It's open 10 am to 5 pm Monday to Saturday year-round and 2 to 5 pm on Sunday during July and August. Admission costs £3/75p.

A half-hour audiovisual performance, **Secrets of Salisbury**, is on in the Medieval Hall (☎ 412472), which is open 11 am to 5 pm daily. Admission costs £1.50/1.

Home to the military museum, **The Wardrobe** (☎ 414536) shows paraphernalia associated with the Royal Gloucestershire, Berkshire and Wiltshire Regiment. It is open 10 am to 4.30 pm daily, April to October; and weekdays only in November, February and March. Admission costs £2.50/50p.

Built in 1701, **Mompesson House** (☎ 335 659; NT) is a fine Queen Anne house with a walled garden that served as Mrs Jenning's London home in the film of *Sense and Sensibility*. It's open noon to 5.30 pm Saturday to Wednesday, April to October. Admission costs £3.40/1.70.

Malmesbury House (☎ 327027) was originally a 13th-century canonry and later the residence of the earls of Malmesbury. It can be visited by guided tour (£5). Phone ahead for times.

From High St, the close is entered by the narrow High St Gate. Just inside is the **College of Matrons**, founded in 1682 for widows and unmarried daughters of clergymen. South of the cathedral is the **Bishop's Palace**, now the Cathedral School, parts of which date back to 1220. The **Deanery** on Bishop's Walk mainly dates from the 13th century.

Izaak Walton, patron saint of fishermen (see Winchester Cathedral in the South-Eastern England chapter), lived for a time in the **Walton Canonry**, and no doubt dropped a line in the nearby Avon.

St Thomas's Church

Were it not for Salisbury Cathedral, splendid St Thomas's Church would attract much more attention. The light, airy edifice seen today dates mainly from the 15th century and its principal drawcard is the superb 'doom', or judgement-day painting, which spreads up and over the chancel arch. Painted around 1475, it was whitewashed over during the Reformation and uncovered again in 1881. In the centre, Christ sits in judgement astride a rainbow with scenes of heaven on the left and hell on the right; hell is supervised by a hairy devil whose foot pokes out onto the chancel arch. On the hell side look out for a bishop and two kings, naked except for their mitre and crowns, and for a miser with his moneybags and a female alehouse owner, the only person allowed to hang on to her clothes.

Market Square

Markets were first held here in 1219, and since 1361 have been held every Tuesday and Saturday. The market once spread much further than the present car-park area and street names like Oatmeal Row, Fish Row or Silver St indicate their medieval specialities. The square is dominated by the late-18th-century guildhall.

Facing the guildhall are two **medieval houses**: John A'Port's of 1425 and William Russel's of 1306. Russel's looks newer because of a false front, but inside its age is revealed. The present shop owners, Watson's of Salisbury, are used to sightseers and produce a leaflet about what is probably the town's oldest house.

Immediately behind Market Square look out for Fish Row, with some fine old houses, and for the 15th-century **Poultry Cross**.

Places to Stay

Camping The *Coombe Nurseries Park* (☎ 328451) is about 3 miles (5km) west of Salisbury at Netherhampton. A tent site for two costs £9. There are other sites in the vicinity.

Hostels The *Salisbury Youth Hostel* (☎ 327572, fax 330446, e salisbury@ yha.org.uk, Milford Hill) is an attractive old building in large gardens, an easy 10-minute walk along Milford St from the centre of Salisbury, just beyond the ring road. The nightly cost is £10.85/7.40.

Close to the bus station, *Matt & Tiggy's* (☎ 327443, 51 Salt Lane) is an independent hostel-like guesthouse with several houses around town. A bed costs £10, including a light breakfast, and they can hook you up with Internet access, bike hire and the like.

B&Bs & Hotels Castle Rd, the A345 continuation of Castle St north from Salisbury, has a wide choice of B&Bs between the ring road and Old Sarum.

Leena's Guesthouse (☎/fax 335419, 50 Castle Rd) has six singles/doubles from £25/46. *Castlewood* (☎ 421494, fax 421494, 45 Castle Rd) charges £25/45 for rooms in this Edwardian house. Large *Edwardian Lodge* (☎ 413329, fax 503105, e richard white@edlodge.freeserve.co.uk, 59 Castle Rd) charges £30/45 for rooms with bath (less off-season).

Follow Milford St out of the centre and, just beyond the ring road and the youth hostel, turn right to *Byways House* (☎ 328364, fax 322146, e byways@bed-breakfast-salis bury.co.uk, 31 Fowlers Rd). Rooms cost from £35/55, almost all of them with a private bathroom. This is a pleasantly quiet area and is only a short walk from the centre of town.

On the other side of the centre, near the train station, *Clovelly Hotel* (☎ 322055, fax 327677, e clovelly.hotel@virgin.net, 17–19 Mill Rd) has rooms for £38/58, most with bathroom.

The *Old Bakery* (☎ 320100, 35 Bedwin St) is a small B&B in a 16th-century house with rooms from £18/38. It is a convivial and comfortable place to stay.

Another B&B that has been recommended is 17th-century *Griffin Cottage* (☎/fax 328259, e mark@brandonasoc .demon.co.uk, 10 St Edmunds Church St), a small comfortable place where even the bread is home-baked. There are just two doubles at £38.

Red Lion Hotel (☎ 323334, fax 325756, e *reception@the-redlion.co.uk, Milford St*), with rooms from £84/104, is very comfortable and of great historical interest. Dating from 1230, it's said to be the oldest purpose-built hotel in England.

The characterful *King's Arms Hotel* (☎ 327629, 9–11 St John's St) has rooms from £50/75.

Five hundred years old, the *Trafalgar Hotel* (☎ 338686, 33 Milford St) has 18 rooms, all with bathroom, costing from £55/65 excluding breakfast.

Concealed behind a grand portico near the cathedral close is Salisbury's plushest hotel, the *White Hart Hotel* (☎ 327476, fax 412761, 1 St John's St). There are 68 rooms at £95/135; breakfast is extra. Cheaper B&B deals are available at the weekend. Its Web site is at www.heritage-hotels.com.

Places to Eat

In Market Square in the centre, *Reeve the Baker* has an upstairs tearoom, popular for lunch and snacks. *Michael Snell's*, near St Thomas's Church, does light lunches and teas. *Cawardine's* (☎ 320619, 3 Bridge St) is a cafe immensely popular with local residents and includes some vegetarian options. French-run *Le Café Parisien* (☎ 412356, Oatmeal Row) has some tasty patisseries and good coffee.

The *Pheasant Inn* (see Entertainment) serves lunches from around £5, and there's a good vegetarian menu. Cheap lunches are also available at the *Footlights Café* (☎ 321744) in Salisbury Art Centre from Tuesday to Saturday. Nearby is *Harper's* (☎ 333118), which has reasonably priced set lunches at under £10 for three courses. The a la carte dinner menu includes dishes such as roast Barbary duck with plum and ginger sauce and salmon with fennel.

On Market Square is *Bistro in the Square* (☎ 328923), which of breakfasts, light meals, soups and filled baguettes. Also very centrally located is a branch of *Pizza Express* (☎ 415191, 50 Blue Boar Row).

Le Hérisson (☎ 333471, Crane St) is a thriving deli and restaurant business that draws people with flamboyant food at modest prices. Modern British main courses are around £8.

Fisherton St, between the centre and the station, features a choice of reasonably priced Asian restaurants. *Cheung's* (☎ 327 375, 60 Fisherton St) is a popular Chinese restaurant. The *Asia Restaurant* (☎ 327628, 90 Fisherton St) is good for spicy Indian food.

Entertainment

Pubs & Bars The *Haunch of Venison* (☎ 322024, 1–5 Minster St) is an atmospheric old pub with panelled walls and oak beams. There's an interesting range of pub food and more than 100 malt whiskies on offer. Finish your meal *before* asking to see the 200-year-old mummified hand of the card player.

The *Pheasant Inn* (☎ 327069), an old pub on the corner of Salt Lane and Rollestone St, attracts a young crowd and also serves food. Also atmospheric is the 14th-century *Cross Keys*, complete with beams and good pub food.

Trendy *Moloko* (☎ 507050, 5 Bridge St) and *Woody's Bar* (12 Minster St) are both lively hangouts, and Moloko often has a late licence.

The *Ox Row Inn* and the *Market Inn* are dead central on Market Square, while *Bishop's Mill Tavern* has an outdoor area with river views.

Scene (Milford St) is a minimalist cafe-bar that is an 'in' place right now. *The Chapel* (Milford St) is a tacky sort of pub/club that has cheap drinks during the week and a cover charge at the weekend.

Theatre There is often interesting live entertainment including high-quality contemporary music and performances in the *Salisbury Arts Centre* (☎ 321744, Bedwin St), set in a converted church. It's open 10 am to 4 pm Tuesday to Saturday.

It's also worth checking out what's on at the *Salisbury Playhouse* (☎ 320333) in Malthouse Lane.

Cinema The *Odeon Cinema (☎ 0870 505 0007, New Canal)* must be one of the few cinemas in the world with a medieval foyer.

Getting There & Away

Salisbury is 88 miles (142km) west of London, 52 miles (84km) east of Bristol and 24 miles (39km) from Southampton.

There are excellent walking and cycling routes to and from Salisbury; Hayball Cycle Shop (see Getting Around) has the useful *Cycling Around Salisbury* (free). The Clarendon Way is a 26-mile walking route to Winchester.

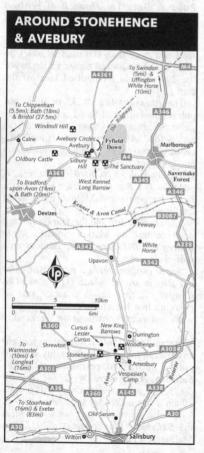

AROUND STONEHENGE & AVEBURY

Bus Three National Express (☎ 0870 580 8080) buses a day run from London via Heathrow to Salisbury (three hours, £12). National Express has a daily Portsmouth–Salisbury–Bath–Bristol service, but it's more expensive than local operators Wilts & Dorset (☎ 336855). Salisbury–Bath costs £6.25 with National Express, but just £3.90 with the local operator.

There are roughly hourly services from Bath via Bradford-on-Avon and Wilton (two hours), from Bournemouth and Poole (1½ hours) and from Southampton (1¼ hours).

Wilts & Dorset operates bus No 3 from Stonehenge; Nos 5 (Monday to Saturday) and 6 (Sunday only) from Avebury, Marlborough and Swindon; and No 184 (and X84 in summer) from Dorchester. Hampshire Bus operates X68 from Winchester.

Train Salisbury is linked by rail to Portsmouth (£11.10, 1¼ hours, numerous), Bath (£9.80, two hours, numerous) and Exeter (£20.10, two hours, 10 per day). There are 30 trains a day from London's Waterloo station (£21.80, 1½ hours). To get to Salisbury from Winchester (£9.50) requires a change at Basingstoke or Southampton.

Getting Around

Bikes can be hired from Hayball Cycle Shop (☎ 411378, 26–30 Winchester St) for £9 per day. It is closed on Sunday.

AROUND SALISBURY
Old Sarum

Once an Iron-Age hillfort, Old Sarum (☎ 01722-335398; EH) became a town with its own cathedral in the Middle Ages. Today, the 22-hectare site consists of impressive earthworks offering fine views of Salisbury, with ruins of the Norman fortifications and the foundations of the old cathedral nestling inside.

Bishop Osmund completed the first 53m-long cathedral in 1092, but it was immediately struck by lightning and badly damaged. Around 1130 it was rebuilt and extended, but this cathedral was abandoned with the shift to Salisbury and finally demolished in 1331 to provide building material for the walls of the cathedral close.

By 1540 the last real voter had disappeared but Old Sarum continued to elect two members to parliament until 1833 – a classic example of the sort of 'rotten borough' the 1832 Reform Act was designed to abolish.

Old Sarum is 2 miles (3km) north of Salisbury, and from Monday to Saturday there are up to four buses an hour. It is open 10 am to 6 pm daily and admission costs £2/1 (more if a special event is taking place).

Wilton House

Henry VIII gave Wilton House (☎ 01722-746720) to William Herbert in 1541. Herbert became the Earl of Pembroke in 1551, a title the colourful family has held since. After a fire destroyed most of the house it was redesigned by Inigo Jones and completed when the fifth earl took over. The present Earl of Pembroke is the seventeenth.

A visit to Wilton House and its 8 hectares of grounds starts with a video, followed by a tour of the kitchen and laundry. The hall has a statue of Shakespeare, who dedicated the first folio edition of his plays to the third earl. Inigo Jones was responsible for the Single and Double Cube Rooms, with their magnificent painted ceilings, elaborate plaster work and paintings by Van Dyck.

Wilton House is 2½ miles (4km) west of Salisbury on the A30 and buses depart up to six times hourly. It's open 10.30 am to 4.30 pm daily, April to October. Admission to the house costs £6.75/4. Bus Nos 60/61 pass this way.

While in Wilton, carpet fanciers might like to visit the **Wilton Carpet Factory** (☎ 01722-744919) on King St, which is open 9 am to 5 pm Monday to Saturday and 11 am to 5 pm on Sunday, year-round (except 10 days over Christmas and the New Year). Admission costs £4/2.50.

Old Wardour Castle

Just north of the A30 between Salisbury and Shaftesbury, the Old Castle (☎ 01747-

870487; EH) was built around 1393 and suffered severe damage during the Civil War. Admission to the picturesquely sited ruins costs £2/1. It is open 10 am to 5.30 pm daily.

STONEHENGE

Stonehenge (☎ 01980-624715; EH/NT) is Europe's most famous prehistoric site. It consists of a ring of enormous stones (some of which were brought from Wales), built in stages beginning 5000 years ago. Reactions vary, some feeling that the car park, gift shop and crowds of tourists swamp the monument, and that the two roads surging past rob it of atmosphere. Avebury, 19 miles (31km) to the north, is more isolated and recommended for those who would like to commune with the ley lines in relative peace (see Avebury later in this chapter).

The Site

Stonehenge was built and rebuilt over a 1500-year period. Construction started around 3000 BC when the outer circular bank and ditch were constructed. An inner circle of granite stones, known as bluestones from their original colouring, was erected 1000 years later. The stones weighed up to 4 tons each and were brought from the Preseli Mountains in South Wales, nearly 250 miles (403km) away.

Around 1500 BC, the huge stones that make Stonehenge instantly recognisable were dragged to the site, erected in a circle and topped by equally massive lintels to make the sarsen (the type of sandstone) trilithons (the formation of vertical and horizontal stones). The sarsens were cut from an extremely hard rock found on the Marlborough Downs about 20 miles (32km) from the site. It's estimated that dragging one of these 50-ton stones across the countryside to Stonehenge would require about 600 people.

Also around this time, the bluestones from 500 years earlier were rearranged as an inner horseshoe. In the centre of this horseshoe went the altar stone, a name given for no scientific reason in the 18th century. Around the bluestone horseshoe was a sarsen horseshoe of five trilithons. Three of these trilithons are intact, the other two have just a single upright. Then came the major circle of 30 massive vertical stones, of which 17 uprights and six lintels remain.

Further out was another circle delineated by the 58 Aubrey Holes, named after John Aubrey who discovered them in the 1600s. Only a handful of the stones remain in this circle. In the same circle are the South Barrow and North Barrow, each originally topped by a stone. Between them are two other stones, though not quite on the east-

west axis. Outside the Aubrey Holes circle was the bank and then the ditch.

The inner horseshoes are aligned along the sun's axis on rising in midsummer and setting in midwinter. From the midsummer axis, approximately NNE, the Avenue leads out from Stonehenge and today is almost immediately cut by the A344. The gap cut in the bank by the Avenue is marked by the Slaughter Stone, another 18th-century name tag. Beyond the ditch in the Avenue, the Heel Stone stands on one side, and recent excavations have revealed that another Heel Stone stood on the other. Despite the site's

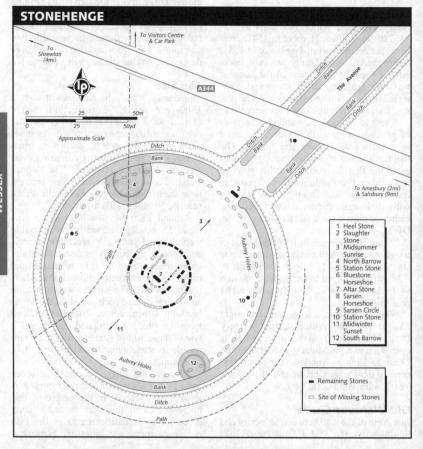

STONEHENGE

To Visitors Centre & Car Park

To Shrewton (4mi)

A344

The Avenue

Ditch
Bank
Bank
Ditch

0   25   50m
0   25   50yd
Approximate Scale

Ditch
Bank

Ditch
Bank
Bank
Ditch

1 ●

To Amesbury (2mi) & Salisbury (9mi)

4

2

3

5

Aubrey Holes

Path

6
7   8
9

10 ●

11

12

Aubrey Holes

Bank
Ditch

Path

1 Heel Stone
2 Slaughter Stone
3 Midsummer Sunrise
4 North Barrow
5 Station Stone
6 Bluestone Horseshoe
7 Altar Stone
8 Sarsen Horseshoe
9 Sarsen Circle
10 Station Stone
11 Midwinter Sunset
12 South Barrow

■ Remaining Stones
▫ Site of Missing Stones

WESSEX

sun-influenced alignment, little is really known about Stonehenge's purpose.

The site is open 9.30 am to 6 pm daily, April to October (to 7 pm, June to August, and to 4 pm the rest of the year). Admission costs £4/2, including audio tour. Some feel that it is unnecessary to pay the admission fee because you can get a good view from the road, and even if you do enter you are kept at some distance from the stones. If you can afford it, the most atmospheric way to see the stones is with an hour-long private view outside the standard opening hours. This must be arranged well in advance and a pass (£8/4) obtained from English Heritage (☎ 01980-623108).

Getting There & Away

Stonehenge is 2 miles (3km) west of Amesbury on the junction of the A303 and A344/A360. It's 9 miles (14km) from Salisbury (the nearest train station). Buses leave Salisbury bus station for Stonehenge, picking up at the train station, up to nine times a day in summer from 10 am. Buy a Wilts & Dorset Explorer ticket for £5/ 2.50.

Guide Friday (☎ 01225-444102) operates

The Battle for Stonehenge

Despite its World Heritage Site status, the 20th century wasn't kind to Stonehenge, which is hemmed in by the busy A303 to the south and the A344 to the north. Instead of being encouraged to let their imaginations rip, visitors have to put up with being funnelled through a tunnel under the A344 and then staring at the stones from behind a barbed-wire barricade with a constant backdrop of roaring traffic.

For a relatively small site, Stonehenge has always received a daunting number of visitors... over 700,000 per year at the last count. To make matters worse, in the 1980s latter-day Druids and New Age travellers began to descend on Stonehenge for the summer solstice en masse, often lingering for weeks afterwards. Archaeologists claimed that they would damage not just the stone circle but the lesser monuments in the surrounding fields as well. The ensuing police clampdown on solstice visits turned into an annual stand-off, culminating in the infamous Battle of the Beanfield when television viewers were treated to pictures of women and children being tipped out of a motley assortment of ancient vehicles in a none-too-gentle fashion. The barbed wire is one legacy of the clash; the 1994 Criminal Justice and Public Order Act, aimed at making it harder for convoys to assemble, is another.

'A national disgrace' is how the Public Accounts Committee of the House of Commons described the situation at Stonehenge back in 1992. But what hope for a brighter future? Ideally English Heritage (EH) and the National Trust (NT) would like to see both roads moved back from the site, and the A303 rerouted through a tunnel – at a cost of £300 million.

The NT and EH have plans for a Stonehenge Millennium Park, which would at least see the A344 closed and the visitor centre repositioned a mile away to give the site back some of its mystique.

It's still not clear where the money's coming from but Culture Secretary Chris Smith has made it clear that he would like Stonehenge to be restored to its natural setting sooner rather than later.

LPP

WESSEX

two-hour tours to Stonehenge from Salisbury. They depart up to three times daily in mid-summer and cost £13.50/6.50, including entry to the site; this is one way to avoid the queues in peak season. There are various minibus tours to Stonehenge, including some that also go to Avebury. Contact AS Tours (☎ 334956, e astours@globalnet.co .uk) for more information.

AROUND STONEHENGE

Stonehenge is surrounded by a collection of mysterious prehistoric sites, several of them only recently revealed by aerial surveys. Only the sites within the NT boundaries are open to the public; others are on private property. The *Stonehenge Estate Archaeological Walks* leaflet details walks around these sites.

Just north of Amesbury and 3 miles (5km) east of Stonehenge is **Woodhenge**, where concrete posts mark the site of a concentric wooden structure that predates Stonehenge.

North of Stonehenge and running approximately east–west is the **Cursus**, an elongated embanked oval, once thought to have been a Roman hippodrome; in fact it is far older, although its purpose is unknown. The **Lesser Cursus** looks like the end of a similar elongated oval. Other prehistoric sites around Stonehenge include a number of burial mounds, like the **New King Barrows**, and **Vespasian's Camp**, an Iron-Age hillfort.

STOURHEAD

Stourhead (☎ 01747-841152; NT) is another of England's fine stately homes, but here the house is merely an adjunct to the stunning garden. If it's a choice between house and garden, opt for the outdoors.

Wealthy banker Henry Hoare built the house between 1721 and 1725, while his son, Henry Hoare II, created the garden in the valley beside the house. Subsequent Hoares enlarged and enriched the house: traveller and county historian Sir Richard Colt Hoare added wings between 1790 and 1804, and the house was rebuilt after a fire in 1902. Landscapes by Claude and Gas-

pard Poussin betray the inspiration for the Stourhead gardens.

A 2-mile (3km) circuit takes you around a garden and a lake created by Henry Hoare II out of a series of medieval fish ponds. From the house, the walk leads by an **ice house**, where winter ice would be stored for summer use. At the **Temple of Flora** it continues around the lake edge, through a **grotto** and past a **Gothic cottage** to the **Pantheon**. There's a climb up to the **Temple of Apollo**, copied from a temple at Baalbek in Lebanon, which has fine views down the length of the lake. From the temple, you descend to the 15th-century **Bristol Cross**, acquired from the city of Bristol in 1765, past **St Peter's Church** and the **Spread Eagle Inn** back to the starting point. From near the Pantheon, a 3½-mile (5.5km) side trip can be made to **King Alfred's Tower**, a 50m-high folly overlooking Wiltshire, Somerset and Dorset.

The garden is open 9 am to 7 pm (or sunset) daily. The house is open noon to 5.30 pm Saturday to Wednesday, April to October. Admission costs £4.60/2.60 to the house, and another £4.60/2.60 to the garden (£3.30/1.50 in winter). A combined house and garden ticket costs £8/3.80. King Alfred's Tower is another £1.50/70p.

LONGLEAT

Longleat (☎ 01985-844400) is the English stately home turned circus act. Following Henry VIII's monastic land grab, Sir John Thynne picked up the priory ruins and Longleat's 360 hectares for the princely sum of £53 in 1541. Having acquired the 13th-century Augustinian priory, he turned 16th-century architecture on its head to produce a house that looked out onto its magnificent park rather than in towards its courtyards. It was still under construction when he died in 1580, but although its external appearance hasn't changed since, there have been many internal alterations. The rooms are sumptuously furnished and feature seven libraries with 40,000 books. Capability Brown landscaped the surrounding park in 1757–62, planting woods and creating the Half Mile Pond.

After WWII, taxation started to nibble away at the English nobility's fortunes, just as maintenance costs skyrocketed and servants became scarce and expensive. The sixth Marquess of Bath responded by pioneering the stately home business at Longleat, going on to add new, less-serious attractions in the grounds. These days Longleat boasts a pub, a narrow-gauge railway, a Dr Who exhibit, a pets' corner, a butterfly garden and a safari park with lions, as well as the magnificent old house. The eccentric seventh Marquess has even added a series of murals, some depicting his numerous 'wifelets', in his private apartments.

Longleat House is open 11 am to 4 pm daily (to 5.30 pm, Easter to September). The safari park is open 11 am to 5.30 pm, mid-March to October; the other attractions open an hour later. Admission to the grounds costs £2/1, to the house £6/4, to the safari park £6/5, and there are entry charges to 13 other features. An all-inclusive ticket costs £13/11. In summer, a daily Lion Link bus leaves Warminster station at 11.10 am for the safari park's entrance gate, a 2½-mile (4km) walk from Longleat House through marvellous grounds.

BRADFORD-ON-AVON
☎ 01225 • pop 9000
Bradford-on-Avon is a beautiful old town with fine stone houses and factories rising like a series of terraced paddy fields from the river. Bath, with a much wider range of accommodation and eating options, is only 8 miles (13km) away, making a day trip a good alternative to staying here. Sadly, the extension of the Bath bypass has had the effect of displacing unwanted excess traffic onto little Bradford.

Orientation & Information
The Town Bridge is Bradford's most important landmark. The crowded buildings rise up from the River Avon on the northern side. The Kennet and Avon Canal passes through Bradford-on-Avon, and there's a pleasant 1½-mile walk or cycle ride along it to neighbouring Avoncliff, with its impressive Victorian aqueduct.

The TIC (☎ 865797, fax 868722, 34 Silver St) is across the bridge from the train station. It is open 10 am to 5 pm daily (to 4 pm, January to March).

Things to See & Do
Although Bradford-on-Avon dates back to Saxon times, it reached its peak as a weaving centre in the 17th and 18th centuries. The magnificent factories and imposing houses were the showpieces of the town's wealthy clothing entrepreneurs. The soothing honey colour of the solid stone buildings encourages wandering.

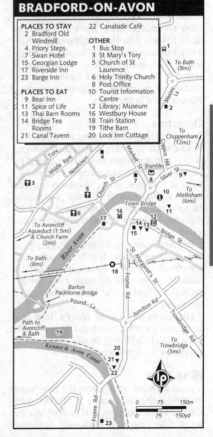

BRADFORD-ON-AVON

PLACES TO STAY
2 Bradford Old Windmill
4 Priory Steps
7 Swan Hotel
15 Georgian Lodge
17 Riverside Inn
23 Barge Inn

PLACES TO EAT
9 Bear Inn
11 Spice of Life
13 Thai Barn Rooms
14 Bridge Tea Rooms
21 Canal Tavern
22 Canalside Café

OTHER
1 Bus Stop
3 St Mary's Tory
5 Church of St Laurence
6 Holy Trinity Church
8 Post Office
10 Tourist Information Centre
12 Library; Museum
16 Westbury House
18 Train Station
19 Tithe Barn
20 Lock Inn Cottage

WESSEX

Start at the **Shambles**, the original marketplace, check out adjacent **Coppice Hill** and wander up Market St to the terrace houses of **Middle Rank** and **Tory**, a name probably derived from the Anglo-Saxon word 'tor', meaning a high hill. Across the river, by the **Town Bridge**, is **Westbury House**, where a riot against the introduction of factory machinery in 1791 led to three deaths.

The first bridge across the Avon at the Town Bridge site was constructed around the 12th century, but the current bridge dates from 1610. The small room jutting out was originally a chapel and then a lock-up.

The **Bradford-on-Avon Museum** (☎ 863 280), on Bridge St, is open 10.30 am to 12.30 pm and 2 to 4 pm Wednesday to Saturday (afternoon only on Sunday). During winter it is open afternoons only, except Saturday. It is in the library by the river and contains a rehoused Victorian pharmacy that operated in the town.

Churches

One of Britain's finest Saxon churches, tiny **St Laurence** probably dates from around 1001. Later it was put to secular use and by the 19th century was no longer even recognised as a church. It has now been restored to its original condition; note particularly the lofty walls, narrow arches and stone angels above the chancel arch. It's open year-round.

Bradford quickly outgrew St Laurence and the new **Holy Trinity Church** was completed in 1150. The original church is virtually submerged beneath 14th-century extensions and 15th- and 19th-century rebuilding.

Higher up the hill, **St Mary's Tory** was built as a hermitage chapel about 1480. Used as a cloth factory in the 18th century, it has now been restored.

Tithe Barn

A pleasant short walk along the river bank leads from the town centre to the barn used to store tithes (taxes in kind) in the Middle Ages. The imposing 50m-long structure was built in 1341 with 100 tons of stone tiles to roof it.

Places to Stay

For campers, **Church Farm** (☎/fax 722246, e churchfarmcottages@compuserve.com, Winsley) is the nearest option. Staying here is only £2.50 per person, plus 50p for vehicles.

The **Barge Inn** (☎ 863403, 17 Frome Rd), in a pleasant setting by the canal, has singles/doubles for £25/35.

Close to the bridge, the **Riverside Inn** (☎ 863526, 49 St Margaret's St) has a pleasant riverside setting and simple rooms with bathroom for £35/47.50.

Georgian Lodge (☎ 862268, fax 862218, e georgian_lodge_hotel@btinternet.com, 25 Bridge St) has rooms with bath for £30/68, including breakfast.

If you can afford more, this is a good town for a splurge. The **Swan Hotel** (☎ 868686, 1 Church St), right in the town centre, has singles/doubles for £50/80.

Priory Steps (☎ 862230, fax 866248, e priorysteps@clara.co.uk), at Newtown, is only a few minutes' walk from the town centre but has wonderful views from its hillside position. Rooms, all with a bathroom, are from £58/78.

The **Bradford Old Windmill** (☎ 866842, fax 866648, e distinctly.different@virgin .net, 4 Masons Lane) is a beautifully converted old windmill overlooking the town, with luxury rooms from £79, £10 less for single occupancy.

Places to Eat

Olde-worlde **Bridge Tea Rooms** (☎ 865537, 24a Bridge St), beside the Town Bridge, serves excellent lunches and teas, including wholesome soups and popular cream teas. Another option for lunch or tea is the tiny **Spice of Life** (☎ 864351, 33 Silver St) behind the TIC, which has vegetarian and organic choices on the menu.

The **Canalside Café** in the Lock Inn Cottage, near where Frome Rd crosses the canal, does a good range of snacks at reasonable prices.

The **Swan Hotel** in the centre does bar

food for under a fiver and has a restaurant with set meals. Other pub food possibilities include the *Bear Inn (26 Silver St)* and the nonsmoking *Canal Tavern (49 Frome Rd)*, which promotes its fish dishes.

The *Georgian Lodge*, beside the Town Bridge is altogether fancier with dishes such as oak-smoked salmon with capers and lime for around £10.

For something more exotic, try *Thai Barn (☎ 866433, 24 Bridge St)* with an authentic Siamese feel and a varied menu.

Getting There & Away
There is a train service from Bath (£3.60 return, 14 minutes, at least hourly) but there are also hourly buses (No X4, £3.40 return) that continue to Salisbury. Once a week there are also buses to Devizes; phone ☎ 0845 709 0899 for details.

Getting Around
Bicycles can be hired for £12 a day from the Lock Inn Cottage (☎ 868068), at 48 Frome Rd, by the canal. Canoes can also be hired here for a paddle along the canal.

CHIPPENHAM & AROUND
☎ 01249 • pop 22,000
Chippenham is an unexceptional market town, with a newly pedestrianised centre, which makes a touring base for several nearby attractions.

The town's TIC (☎ 657733, fax 460776, e tourism@northwilts.gov.uk), The Citadel, Bath Rd, stocks a town trail map and can advise on accommodation costing from £15 per person. The museum in the 15th-century *Yelde Hall* is open 10 am to 12.30 pm and 2 to 4.30 pm daily except Sunday from March to October. While waiting for a bus you could pop into the delightfully old-fashioned *Waverley Restaurant*, opposite the Bear Hotel, for a cheap cup of tea and cake.

Bus No 92 from Chippenham passes through Malmesbury hourly, on its way to Cirencester. There are regular buses to Bristol and Bath.

Frequent trains from London Paddington (£31.50, 1 hour 20 minutes) pass through Chippenham on the way to Bath (£3.60, 12 minutes) and Bristol (£6.20, 24 minutes).

Castle Combe
A Cotswold village that's strayed, Castle Combe is as close to the English ideal as you can get. There's a 13th-century market cross and a packbridge with weavers' cottages reflected in a pool, and the main street is lined with flower-covered stone cottages, pubs and tasteful shops. Pretty, medieval St Andrew's Church also contains a remarkable 13th-century monument of Sir Walter de Dunstanville.

Gates Tea Shop (☎ 782111), by the market cross, has two double rooms costing £45 or £55 depending on the style of bed. Cream teas are served during the day.

At the opposite end of the price spectrum, the cheapest bed at the grand *Manor House Inn (☎ 782206)* is £145. Both the charming *Castle Inn* and the olde-worlde *White Hart* do quality pub lunches.

Bus No 35 leaves Chippenham train station for Castle Combe every two hours – it is easiest visited with a car.

Corsham Court
An Elizabethan mansion dating from 1582, Corsham Court (☎ 01249-701610) was enlarged and renovated in the 18th century to house an art collection accumulated by Paul Methuen and his descendants.

The house is 3 miles (5km) south-west of Chippenham and is open 11 am to 5 pm Tuesday to Sunday, Easter to October; shorter hours and days the rest of the year. Admission costs £4.50/2.50.

Bowood House
This stately house (☎ 01249-812102) is home to the Marquis of Landsdowne and includes a picture gallery with several old masters, as well as the laboratory where Dr Joseph Priestly discovered oxygen in 1774. The gardens are an attraction in themselves, designed by Capability Brown, and include a terraced rose garden. The house is 3 miles (5km) south-east of Chippenham and is open 11 am to 5.30 pm daily, April to October. Admission costs £5.70/3.50.

LACOCK

☎ 01249

Exquisitely attractive little Lacock lays claim to being the birthplace of photography and has many buildings from an extensive medieval monastic complex. The village dates back to the Saxon era, well before the foundation of Lacock Abbey. Many of the buildings date from medieval times and are owned by the NT; few were built after the 18th century.

The NT's free *Lacock Village* leaflet plots a route round the most interesting buildings. King John's **Hunting Lodge** dates in part from the 13th century, while the adjacent **St Cyriac's Church** is mainly late 15th century; note the brass in the south transept to Robert and Elizabeth Baynard and their 18 children (1501). The **At the Sign of the Angel** hotel dates from 1480. WH Fox Talbot of Lacock Abbey founded the village **primary school** in High St in 1824. His **grave** is in the village cemetery. Also check out the 14th-century **tithe barn & lock-up**.

Lacock provided the setting for many scenes in the BBC's acclaimed production of *Pride and Prejudice*.

Lacock Abbey & the Fox Talbot Museum of Photography

Lacock Abbey (☎ 730459; NT) was established as a nunnery in 1232, then sold to Sir William Sharington by Henry VIII in 1539. Sharington converted the nunnery into a home, demolished the church, tacked a tower onto the corner of the abbey building and added a brewery, while retaining the abbey cloister and other medieval features. Despite his three marriages he died childless and the house passed to the Talbot family, who bequeathed the whole village to the NT in 1944.

In the early 19th century, William Henry Fox Talbot, a prolific inventor, conducted crucial experiments in the development of photography here. Inside the entrance to the abbey a museum (☎ 730459) details his pioneering photographic work in the 1830s, when Louis Daguerre was also undertaking similar work in France. Fox Talbot's particular contribution was the photographic neg-

ative, from which further positive images could be produced. Before that a photograph was a one-time, one-image process. A picture of the abbey's oriel window may be the first photograph ever taken.

The abbey and museum open 11 am to 5.30 pm Wednesday to Monday, April to October. Admission costs £5.80/3.20, although if you just want to see the cloister, museum and grounds it's £3.70/2.20.

Places to Stay & Eat

Lacock makes a wonderful place to stay although accommodation is both limited and relatively pricey.

King John's Hunting Lodge (☎/fax 730313, 21 Church St) has two lovely rooms with exposed beams costing £32.50 per person for B&B. It also houses a weekend and summer-season tearoom. Pretty *Lacock Pottery* (☎ 730266, fax 730948, e simone@lacockbedandbreakfast.com, 1 The Tanyard) offers rooms for £37/59, with good healthy breakfasts and the chance to sign up for a pottery course thrown in.

Pricier but highly atmospheric are rooms in the 15th-century *At the Sign of the Angel* (☎ 730230, fax 730527, e angel@lacock .co.uk, Church St); beds beneath exposed beams cost from £68/99, more on a Saturday.

All three village pubs do food. *At the Sign of the Angel* does formal dinners, which cost around £20 to £25. The charming *George Inn* is cheaper and hugely popular, a great local for those who like proper pubs. The *Carpenters Arms* is the most reasonably priced of the lot and spacious, but has less character than the George.

In season, teas are served in *The Stables* opposite the abbey.

Getting There & Away

Monday to Saturday, bus No 234 operates a roughly hourly service from Chippenham (15 minutes).

DEVIZES

☎ 01380 • pop 12,500

An attractive market town, Devizes was once an important coaching stop and several old coaching inns survive in the market square. Interesting buildings nearby include the **Corn Exchange**, topped by a figure of Ceres, goddess of agriculture, and the **Old Town Hall** of 1750–52. The town is also home to the **Wadworth brewery**, and their popular 6X can be sampled in local pubs. Shire horses are still used to deliver their beer to local pubs on weekday mornings.

The TIC (☎ 729408, 39 St John's St) is right by the market square and is open 9.30 am to 5 pm daily except Sunday.

Things to See
Just beyond the TIC, **St John's Alley** has a wonderful collection of Elizabethan houses, their upper storeys cantilevered over the street. The new **town hall**, dating from 1806, is at this end of St John's St. **St John's Church** displays elements of its original Norman construction, particularly in the solid crossing tower.

The **Wiltshire Heritage Museum** (☎ 727 369, 41 Long St) has interesting displays on the development of Avebury and Stonehenge, a section on Roman history and, upstairs, a social history room. It's open 10 am to 5 pm Monday to Saturday. Admission costs £3/75p (free on Monday).

The **Kennet & Avon Canal Exhibition** (☎ 729489) in The Wharf just north of the town centre is open 10 am to 5 pm daily (to 4 pm in winter); admission costs £1.50/50p. The **Caen Hill** flight of 29 successive locks raises the water level 72m in 2½ miles (4km) on the western outskirts of Devizes.

Places to Stay & Eat
Lower Foxhangers Farm (☎ 828254, fax 828254), 2½ miles (4km) west of Devizes near the Caen Hill locks, offers camping for £6 a pitch plus £1 for electricity. It's conveniently near the canal for walkers and cyclists – public transport is a non-starter.

Dating back to 1558, the ***Bear Hotel*** (☎ 722444, fax 722450, Market Place) charges £59/86 for bed and breakfast. In a 17th-century coaching inn, the ***Black Swan Hotel*** (☎ 723259, fax 729966, Market Place) has rooms for £50/70.

Healthy Life (Little Britox) is a new organic vegetarian restaurant above a health-food shop just off the Market Place.

The popular Wiltshire Kitchen has been replaced by *Quintessence* (☎ 724840, 11–12 St John's St).

Otherwise the pubs around Market Place are your best bet for reasonably priced fare, especially on market days.

Getting There & Away
Bus Nos 33/X33 run from Chippenham (£2.70, 25 minutes, every 2 hours), and No X71 runs from Bath (£3.40, 1 hour, hourly).

AVEBURY
☎ 01672
Avebury stone circle stands at the hub of a prehistoric complex of ceremonial sites, ancient avenues and burial chambers. It's a bigger site and is less visited than Stonehenge, and many find it more atmospheric and impressive. It is also even older, dating from around 2500 BC. The impact of Neolithic people on the environment is so dramatic you can almost feel them breathing down your neck. Avebury itself is a pretty village where even the church walls are thatched. Silbury Hill and West Kennet Long Barrow are close by, and the Ridgeway Path ends here.

Orientation & Information
The Avebury stones encircle much of the village, but don't drive into it as the car park on the A4361 is only a short stroll from the circle.

At the time of writing, the TIC (☎ 539425, fax 539494) was due to move into new premises in the great barn by summer 2001. It is open 10 am to 5 pm Wednesday to Sunday.

Stone Circle
The stone circle dates from around 2600 to 2100 BC, between the first and second phase of construction at Stonehenge. With a diameter of about 348m, it's one of the largest stone circles in Britain. The site originally consisted of an outer circle of 98 standing stones from three to six metres in length, many weighing up to 20 tons. These

WESSEX

had been selected for their size and shape, but had not been worked to shape like those at Stonehenge. The stones were surrounded by another circle formed by a 5½m-high earth bank and a 6 to 9m-deep ditch. Inside were smaller stone circles to the north (27 stones) and south (29 stones).

The circles remained largely intact through the Roman period. A Saxon settlement grew up inside the circle from around 600 but in medieval times, when the church's power was strong and fear of paganism even stronger, many of the stones were deliberately buried. As the village expanded in the late 17th and early 18th centuries, the stones were broken up for building material. Fortunately, William Stukeley (1687–1765) surveyed the site around this time so some record survives of what had existed.

In 1934, Alexander Keiller supervised the re-erection of the buried stones and the placing of markers to indicate those that had disappeared. The wealthy Keiller eventually bought Avebury in order to restore 'the outstanding archaeological disgrace of Britain'.

Modern roads into Avebury neatly dissect the circle into four sectors. Start from High St, near the Henge Shop, and walk round the circle in a counter-clockwise direction. There are 12 standing stones in the south-west sector, one of them known as the **Barber Surgeon Stone**, after the skeleton of a man found under it; the equipment buried with him suggested he was a medieval travelling barber-surgeon, killed when a stone accidentally fell on him.

The south-east sector starts with the huge **portal stones** marking the entry to the circle from West Kennet Ave. The **southern inner circle** stood in this sector and within this circle was the **Obelisk** and a group of stones known as the **Z Feature**. Just outside this smaller circle, only the base of the **Ring Stone** remains. Few stones, standing or

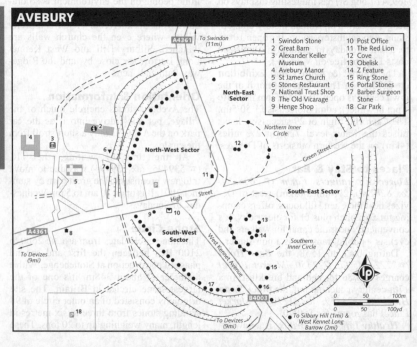

AVEBURY

1 Swindon Stone	10 Post Office
2 Great Barn	11 The Red Lion
3 Alexander Keiller	12 Cove
Museum	13 Obelisk
4 Avebury Manor	14 Z Feature
5 St James Church	15 Ring Stone
6 Stones Restaurant	16 Portal Stones
7 National Trust Shop	17 Barber Surgeon
8 The Old Vicarage	Stone
9 Henge Shop	18 Car Park

To Swindon (11mi)

North-East Sector

Northern Inner Circle

Green Street

North-West Sector

High Street

South-East Sector

A4361

South-West Sector

West Kennet Avenue

Southern Inner Circle

To Devizes (9mi)

To Devizes (9mi)

B4003

To Silbury Hill (1mi) & West Kennet Long Barrow (2mi)

0   50   100m
0   50   100yd

WESSEX

fallen, are to be seen around the rest of the south-east or north-east sectors. Most of the northern inner circle was in the north-east sector. The **Cove**, made up of three of the largest stones, marked the centre of this smaller circle.

The north-west sector has the most complete collection of standing stones, including the massive 65-ton **Swindon Stone**, the first stone encountered and one of the few never to have been toppled.

Alexander Keiller Museum

Alexander Keiller, who made his fortune out of Dundee marmalade, not only bought the Avebury Circle but most of the village, West Kennet Ave, Windmill Hill and virtually everything else that was up for sale. The Alexander Keiller Museum (☎ 539250), in the former stables of Avebury Manor, explains the history of the Avebury Circle and houses finds from the sites. It's open 10 am to 6 pm (to 4 pm in winter). Admission costs £1.80/80p.

The Village

St James Church contains round Saxon windows, a Norman font and a rare surviving rood (cross) loft. The National Trust plan to develop a new museum in the thatched **Great Barn**. It will exhibit information on the local landscape and the rediscovery of the stone circle. Note the 16th-century circular **dovecote** close by.

Graceful **Avebury Manor** (☎ 539388; NT) dates back to the 16th century but was altered in the early 18th century. It's open 2 to 5 pm Tuesday, Wednesday and Sunday, April to October. Admission costs £3.20/1.60. The gardens (£2.25/1) are open 11 am to 5 pm daily except Monday and Thursday.

Places to Stay & Eat

The cheapest B&B is available at *The Old Vicarage (☎ 539362, High St)* from £22 per person. *The Red Lion (☎ 539266, fax 539618)* is a charming country pub where doubles cost £30 per person.

Beside the Great Barn, the popular *Stones Restaurant* offers 'megaliths' (hot dishes) for around £6.

Getting There & Away

Avebury is just off the A4 between Calne and Marlborough, and can be reached easily by Wilts & Dorset Bus No 5, which operates a Salisbury–Marlborough–Avebury–Swindon route three times daily. Tour buses also operate from Salisbury. A better connection for those coming from London or Bristol is the hourly bus No 49 running between Swindon and Devizes that passes this way.

Coming from Bath, you'll have to change at Devizes; check connections with the county inquiry line (☎ 0845 709 0899). Thamesdown (☎ 01793-428428) operates from Swindon to Avebury regularly Monday to Saturday, less frequently on Sunday. Its buses also link Avebury to Marlborough and Devizes on weekdays.

AROUND AVEBURY

Several excellent walks link the important sites around Avebury, starting with the stroll across the fields to Silbury Hill and West Kennet Long Barrow. The Ridgeway Path starts near Avebury and runs westward across Fyfield Down, where many of the sarsen stones at Avebury (and Stonehenge) were collected.

Windmill Hill

The earliest site around Avebury, Windmill Hill was a Neolithic enclosure or 'camp' dating from about 3700 BC. Ditches confirm its shape.

The Avenue & Sanctuary

The 1½-mile-long West Kennet Ave, lined by 100 pairs of stones, connects the Sanctuary with the Avebury Circle. Today, the B4003 road follows the same route and at its southern end the A4 virtually overrides the avenue. The stone shapes along the avenue alternate between column-like stones and triangular-shaped ones; Keiller thought they might have been intended to signify male and female.

Only the site of the Sanctuary remains, although the post and stone holes indicate there was a wooden building surrounded by a stone circle. The possible route of Beckhampton Ave, a similar 'avenue' into

Going Round in Circles

Wiltshire is the crop-circle capital of the world. Crop circles are a curious phenomenon that encourage passion and scepticism in equal measure. More than 5000 circles have appeared throughout the world, and while they are usually associated with cereals such as barley and wheat, they have also appeared in grass and heather. They range from simple circles to highly complex fractals. Romantics claim they represent an extra-terrestrial message from alien lifeforms, but realists argue they are a very terrestrial message from farmers, artists or practical jokers in the countryside.

Scientists have studied the circles in some detail, and have found them to alter the molecular structure of the plants and the chemical composition of the soil, but the crops continue to grow. Some say they also have an effect on electrical equipment, although this can usually be explained by the presence of high-voltage power lines nearby. A decade ago, the debate gripped England with a series of documentaries on contending theories, but eventually many of the circles were attributed to local cider drinkers looking to cause some mischief.

The best areas to spot the circles are the Marlborough Downs and Pewsey Vale. Remember that many of the circles are on private land so always ask the farmer before ploughing in!

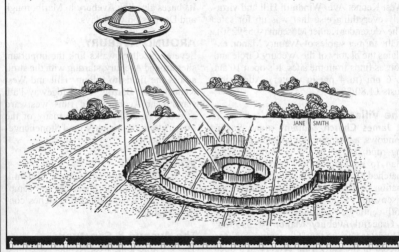

JANE SMITH

Avebury from the south-west, is mainly guesswork.

Silbury Hill

Rising abruptly from the surrounding fields, Silbury Hill is one of the largest artificial hills in Europe, similar in size to the smaller Egyptian pyramids. Like a truncated cone, its 40m-high summit ends in a flat top measuring 30m across. It was constructed in stages from around 2500 BC but its purpose is a mystery. Certainly no one seems to have been buried here.

The hill has been greatly eroded by many pairs of feet, despite signs and fences asking visitors to enjoy the hill from a distance.

West Kennet Long Barrow

Across the fields south of Silbury Hill stands West Kennet Long Barrow, England's finest burial mound, dating from around 3500 BC and measuring 104m by 23m. Its entrance is guarded by huge sarsens, massive stones like those at Stonehenge, and its roof is constructed of gigantic overlapping capstones. About 50 skeletons were found when it was excavated. The finds are displayed in Devizes Museum.

MARLBOROUGH

☎ 01672 • pop 5400

Marlborough is a pleasant shire town with a famous public school. It started life as a Saxon settlement at The Green, and the main street extended westward from there to an 18m-high prehistoric mound where the Normans later erected a motte and bailey fortification. To make more room for a market as the town grew, the houses along High St were pushed back until the road reached its present extraordinary width. At either end of the High St stands a church, St Mary's to the east, St Peter's to the west.

Today's High St makes for an interesting stroll, particularly on Wednesday and Saturday, which are market days. The 17th-century **Merchant's House** (☎ 511491) at No 132 is now a museum. It opens 10 am to 4 pm on Saturday, April to September. The exclusive Marlborough College now occupies the site of the **old Norman castle**. Just to the west is a small white horse cut into the hillside by schoolboys in 1804.

The TIC (☎ 513989), George Lane Car Park, is just off the High St. It is open 10 am to 5 pm daily (to 4.30 pm Sunday). There's plenty of accommodation along High St and George Lane, but there is no compelling reason to spend a night here.

Best of the teashops is *Harpers (High St)*, across the road from St Peter's church, although service may be quicker at the *Polly Tea Rooms*, also in the High St. *Options*, behind the Ivy House Hotel, has some vegetarian dishes on its menu. Pubs with good food along High St include the *Green Dragon (☎ 512366)*, the 15th-century *Sun Inn (☎ 512081)* and the *Wellington Arms (☎ 512954)*.

Regular bus services run to Marlborough from Swindon, Salisbury, Amesbury and Pewsey.

MALMESBURY

☎ 01666 • pop 4300

Perched on top of a hill, Malmesbury has a superb semi-ruined abbey church, a late-

15th-century market cross and several pleasant pubs and restaurants.

The town's well-stocked TIC (☎ 823748, e malmesbury@northwilts.go.uk) is in the town hall on Market Lane and is open 9 am to 4.50 pm Monday to Thursday (to 4.20 pm Friday and 4 pm Saturday). It's round the corner from the small **Athelstan Museum** (☎ 829258), which is open 10 am to 2 pm Monday to Saturday in summer and 10 am to noon Thursday to Saturday in winter (check ahead). Admission is free.

Malmesbury Abbey

Malmesbury Abbey is a wonderful blend of ruin and living church. Construction began in the 12th century, and by the 14th a massive edifice 100m long had been built, with a tower at the western end and a tower and spire at the crossing. In 1479, a storm brought the tower and spire crashing down; its fall destroyed the crossing and the eastern end of the church.

When the monastery was suppressed in 1539, the abbey was sold to a local clothier who initially moved looms into the nave. Later he changed his mind and gave it to the town to replace the ruinous parish church of St Paul's. In about 1662, the west tower fell, destroying three of the west bays of the nave. Today's church consists of the remaining six bays – about a third of the original church – framed by ruins at either end.

The church is entered via the magnificent south porch, its doorway a Norman work with stone sculpture illustrating Bible stories. The huge carved Apostles on each side of the porch are some of the finest Romanesque carvings in Britain. Looking out over the nave from the south side is a watching loft the purpose of which is obscure. In the north-eastern corner of the church is a medieval cenotaph (empty tomb) commemorating Athelstan, king of England from 925 to 939 and grandson of Alfred the Great.

Steps lead up to the parvise, a small room above the porch, which contains a collection of books including a four-volume, illuminated-manuscript Bible of 1407. A window at the western end of the church

WESSEX

shows Elmer the Flying Monk. In 1010, he strapped on wings and jumped from the tower. Remarkably, he survived, and blamed his crash-landing on aerodynamic problems.

In the churchyard, the 14th-century steeple of St Paul's, the original parish church, now serves as the belfry. Towards the south-eastern corner of the churchyard is the **gravestone of Hannah Twynnoy** who died in 1703, aged 33. Her headstone reads: 'For tyger fierce, Took life away, And here she lies, In a bed of clay.' The tiger belonged to a visiting circus and she was killed in the White Lion pub where she was a serving maid.

The abbey is open 10 am to 5 pm daily. Donations are appreciated.

Places to Stay & Eat

A 10-minute walk along the river, **Burton Hill Camping Park** (☎ 826880) has sites at £5 for one, £7.50 for two.

Bremilham House (☎ 822680, Bremilham Rd) is an easy walk from the town centre and costs £19.50/34 for singles/doubles. **King's Arms Hotel** (☎ 823383, fax 825327, High St) is a charming old coaching inn with rooms for £30/50. The historic **Old Bell Inn** (☎ 822344, fax 825145, e info@oldbellhotel.com, Abbey Row) by the abbey, charges from £75/95 for luxurious rooms.

The cheerful **Whole Hog** (☎ 825845) wine bar is right behind the market cross

and serves hogburgers (vegetarian version available) and pigwitch sandwiches.

Getting There & Away

Malmesbury has hourly connections from Swindon on Bus No 31. Bus No 92 between Cirencester and Chippenham passes through Malmesbury hourly. There are no buses to Malmesbury in the evening or on Sunday.

SWINDON
☎ 01793 • pop 182,000

Swindon has a proud place in the history of railways in Britain, providing a home to the massive Great Western Railway works for a century and a half until its closure in 1986. These days it's a fast-growing town with a burgeoning IT sector, but hardly the most inspiring place in the south-west. It is quite well located, however, for forays into the Cotswolds and Britain's pre-history around Wiltshire.

The TIC (☎ 530328, fax 434031), 37 Regent St, is open 9.30 am to 5.30 pm daily except Sunday.

STEAM – Museum of the Great Western Railway (☎ 466646, Kemble Drive) is a new museum telling the story of the Great Western Railway and Swindon's place in its success. It is open 10 am to 6 pm daily and admission costs £4.80/3.

Swindon is on the main train line from London Paddington (£26.50, 1 hour, 2 per hour) to Bristol (£10.70, 40 minutes, 2 per hour) or south Wales.

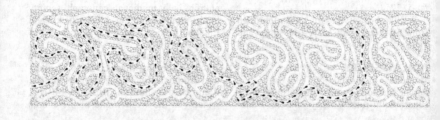

Devon & Cornwall

Devon and Cornwall boast some of the most beautiful countryside and spectacular coastline in England. They are littered with the evidence of successive cultures and kingdoms that have been swept away by one invader after another.

Devon and particularly Cornwall were once England's Wild West, a remote refuge for smugglers and pirates. Cornwall even had its own language, and although the last speaker of Cornish died in the 1770s, efforts are being made to rediscover it.

The weather in this part of England is milder than elsewhere and some of the beaches boast golden sand and surfable waves. Despite the competition from cheap holidays abroad, the 'English Riviera' still seethes with sunburned suburbanites every summer. For those who want to catch some waves, Devon and Cornwall are also the top surfing regions in England, particularly the town of Newquay in Cornwall. However, it's wise to steer clear of the coastal towns in July and August, not least because the narrow streets are choked with traffic.

Dotted here and there along the coast are some of England's prettiest coastal villages. Clovelly in Devon and Mousehole in Cornwall are among the best known. The towns aren't bad either; St Ives in Cornwall is the embodiment of the picture-postcard seaside resort, and Dartmouth in Devon is a classic estuarine town.

Walkers aren't short-changed in this beach-oriented corner of England, with a large portion of the South West Coast Path, a long-distance walking route, winding through the best and most untouched sections of the coastline.

WALKING & CYCLING

Devon and Cornwall have plenty of beautiful countryside, but walks in the Dartmoor National Park and round the coastline are the best known. The barren, open wilderness of Dartmoor can be an acquired taste, especially compared with Exmoor (for Ex-

Highlights

- Admiring modern art at Tate St Ives
- Taking in the breathtaking views along the South West Coast Path in West Cornwall
- Watching a play in the Minack Theatre
- Day-tripping to remote Lundy Island
- Walking on wild Dartmoor
- Exploring Tresco Abbey Gardens, Isles of Scilly
- Braving the surf in Newquay
- Treading the cobbles of charming Clovelly

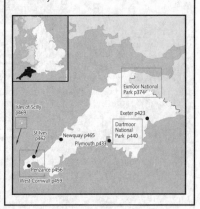

moor see the Wessex chapter). The Two Moors Way links these national parks.

The South West Coast Path, England's longest national trail, is not a wilderness walk – villages with food, beer and accommodation are generally within easy reach. It follows truly magnificent coastline. Completing a section of the path should be considered by any keen walker; if possible, avoid busy summer weekends. The South West Coast Path Association (☎ 01364-73859) publishes an accommodation guide, as well as detailed route descriptions. The

DEVON & CORNWALL

official guides (published by Aurum Press) cover Minehead to Padstow, Padstow to Falmouth, Falmouth to Exmouth and Exmouth to Poole. Lonely Planet's *Walking in Britain* also has detailed information.

Bikes can be hired in most major regional centres, including Exeter, Plymouth, Penzance, Padstow and Barnstaple, and the infrequent bus connections make cycling a sensible option. There's no shortage of hills, but the mild weather and quiet back roads make this great cycling country. The West Country Way, recently opened by Sustrans (see Cycling in the Activities chapter), runs from Penzance, St Ives or Padstow in Cornwall to Bristol, via Bodmin Moor and Exmoor. It follows disused railway tracks and quiet back roads.

SURFING

The capital of English surfing is Newquay on the west Cornish coast, which comes complete with surf shops, dreadlocks and Combis. The surfable coast runs from Porthleven (near Helston) in Cornwall, west around Land's End and north to Ilfracombe. The most famous reef breaks are at Porthleven, Lynmouth and Millbrook; though good, they are inconsistent, and it's very cold in winter!

GETTING AROUND

Look out for the excellent *Car-Free Days Out* leaflet in tourist information centres (TICs), which has comprehensive public-transport listings and advice on using them to get to places of interest. Alternatively, visit the Web site at www.carfreedaysout .com for lots of advice on getting around by public transport.

Bus

National Express (☎ 0870 580 8080) buses provide reasonable connections between the main towns, particularly in the east, but the farther west you go the more dire the situation becomes. Transport around Dartmoor is very difficult in summer, and nigh on impossible at any other time. This is territory that favours those with their own transport. Phone numbers for regional

timetables are ☎ 01392-382800 (Devon) and ☎ 01872-322142 (Cornwall).

There are a number of one-day Explorer passes available for around £5; these are described in the relevant sections throughout the chapter. First Western National (☎ 01752-402060) and First Red Bus (☎ 01271-345444) have a joint Explorer covering Cornwall, Dartmoor, north Devon and parts of south Devon. A one-day ticket costs £6/3.50, a three-day ticket £15/8.50 and a seven-day ticket £27/15.

Train

Train services are pretty limited in this part of the world, so buses are needed to fill in the gaps. Beyond Exeter, a single line follows the south coast as far as Penzance, with spurs to Barnstaple, Gunnislake, Looe, Falmouth, St Ives and Newquay. The line from Exeter to Penzance is one of England's most beautiful. For information on services phone ☎ 0845 748 4950.

Several regional rail passes are available, including the Freedom of the South-West Rover, which, over 15 days, allows eight days' unlimited travel west of a line drawn through (and including) Salisbury, Bath, Bristol and Weymouth (£71.50 in summer, £61 in winter). There are also separate Devon and Cornish Rail Rovers – see the relevant following sections for further information.

Devon

Devon is one of the most popular holiday destinations in England. It is where the English come for a traditional family holiday by the seaside, and the coastal resorts continue to draw the crowds in the summer.

Devon's history is inextricably bound up with the sea; from Plymouth, Drake set out to fight the Spanish Armada and the Pilgrim Fathers sailed to America. Little country lanes lead to idyllic villages of thatched cottages; tearooms serve traditional cream teas; and you can buy rough cider from local farms. Inland, there's superb walking country in two national parks – wild

Dartmoor in the centre and Exmoor in the north, which extends into Somerset.

GETTING AROUND

Contact the Devon County Public Transport Help Line (☎ 01392-382800) 9 am to 5 pm weekdays for information. They can send you the invaluable *Devon Public Transport Map* and the useful *Dartmoor Bus Services Timetable*. Stagecoach Devon (☎ 01392-427711) is an important operator in south Devon.

Devon's rail network skirts along the south coast through Exeter and Plymouth to Cornwall. There are some picturesque stretches where the line travels right beside the sea. Two branch lines run north – the 39-mile (63km) Tarka Line from Exeter to Barnstaple, and the 15-mile (24km) Tamar Valley Line from Plymouth to Gunnislake. The Devon Rail Rover allows three days' travel in a week for £30 (£24 in winter) or eight days' travel in 15 days for £46.50 (£39.50 in winter).

Away from the main roads, Devon is good cycling country. TICs have a free leaflet – *Making Tracks!* – which gives details of the main routes. Sustrans' West Country Way route crosses north Devon through Barnstaple and continues via Taunton to Bristol. The award-winning Bike Bus (☎ 01392-383223), with a Web site at www.devon.gov.uk/tourism/ncn, is a summer bus service that carries bikes in addition to passengers. At the time of writing its route was under review, but from 2001 it will probably run between Barnstaple and Plymouth via Okehampton, also connecting with Exeter. Contact Bike Bus directly for the latest details.

EXETER

☎ 01392 • pop 89,000

Exeter is the heart and soul of the West Country, home to one of the finest medieval cathedrals in the region. More mundanely, it is the main transport hub for Devon and Cornwall, and a good starting point for Dartmoor.

Until the 19th century, Exeter was an important port, and the waterfront is slowly being restored. Many of the older buildings were destroyed in the air raids of WWII and much of the city is modern and architecturally uninspiring. It is, however, a thoroughly liveable university city with a thriving nightlife.

History

Exeter was founded by the Romans in about AD 50 to serve as the administrative capital for the Dumnonii of Devon and Cornwall. There was, however, a settlement on the banks of the River Exe long before the arrival of the Romans.

By the 3rd century, the city was surrounded by a thick wall, parts of which can still be seen although most of it has either been buried or incorporated into buildings.

The fortifications were battered by Danish invaders and then by the Normans in the 11th century. In 1068, William the Conqueror took 18 days to break through the walls. He appointed a Norman seigneur (feudal lord) to construct a castle, the ruins of which can still be seen in Rougemont Gardens.

Exeter was a major trading port until Isabel, Countess of Devon, built a weir across the river, halting river traffic. It was not until 1563, when the first ship canal in Britain was dug to bypass the weir, that the city began to re-establish itself as a trading centre.

Exeter has been closely involved in many of England's greatest battles. Three of the ships sent to face the Spanish Armada were built here and some of the greatest sea captains of the time, including Drake, Raleigh and Frobisher, lived in the area for part of their lives. In 1942 heavy German bombing reduced large areas of Exeter to rubble.

Orientation

The old Roman walls enclose a hill in a bend of the River Exe, and the cathedral's great square towers dominate the skyline. Most of the sights are accessible on foot; long-stay car parks are well signposted. There are two main train stations, Central and St David's; most long-distance trains use St David's, a 20-minute walk west of the city centre.

Information

The TIC (☎ 265700, fax 265260, ℮ tic@exeter.gov.uk), in the Civic Centre, Paris St, is just across the road from the bus station (for which there have been provisional redevelopment plans for some time). It's open 9 am to 5 pm Monday to Saturday year-round, and also 10 am to 4 pm on Sunday, May to September. Its Web site is at www.exeter.gov.uk.

Free guided tours led by the volunteer Exeter 'Redcoats' are well worth joining. They last 1½ to two hours and cover a range of subjects, from a standard walking tour

(daily) to a ghost walk (7 pm on Tuesday). Tours leave from outside the Royal Clarence Hotel or from Quay House several times a day in summer. Ask at the TIC for details.

The List is a new, free magazine with details of events in the Exeter area. The Exeter Festival (☎ 265198) takes place in early July and involves the expected blend of music, dance and other arts and entertainment.

There are several supermarkets, including a Tesco on Sidwell St. Convenient laundrettes include Soaps beside St David's

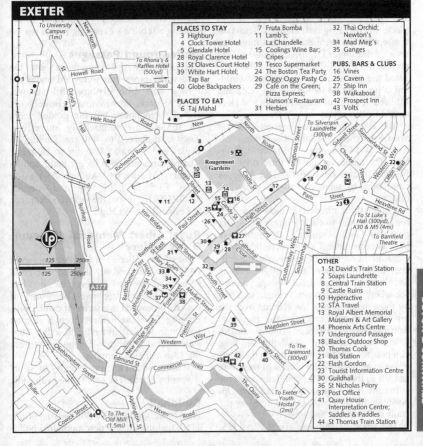

EXETER

PLACES TO STAY		7 Fruta Bomba	32 Thai Orchid;
3 Highbury		11 Lamb's;	Newton's
4 Clock Tower Hotel		La Chandelle	34 Mad Meg's
5 Glendale Hotel		15 Coolings Wine Bar;	35 Ganges
28 Royal Clarence Hotel		Cripes	
33 St Olaves Court Hotel		19 Tesco Supermarket	PUBS, BARS & CLUBS
39 White Hart Hotel;		24 The Boston Tea Party	16 Vines
Tap Bar		26 Oggy Oggy Pasty Co	25 Cavern
40 Globe Backpackers		29 Café on the Green;	27 Ship Inn
		Pizza Express;	38 Walkabout
PLACES TO EAT		Hanson's Restaurant	42 Prospect Inn
6 Taj Mahal		31 Herbies	43 Volts

OTHER
1 St David's Train Station
2 Soaps Laundrette
8 Central Train Station
9 Castle Ruins
10 Hyperactive
12 STA Travel
13 Royal Albert Memorial Museum & Art Gallery
14 Phoenix Arts Centre
17 Underground Passages
18 Blacks Outdoor Shop
20 Thomas Cook
21 Bus Station
22 Flash Gordon
23 Tourist Information Centre
30 Guildhall
36 St Nicholas Priory
37 Post Office
41 Quay House Interpretation Centre; Saddles & Paddles
44 St Thomas Train Station

DEVON & CORNWALL

train station and Silverspin on Blackboy Rd. For Internet access visit Hyperactive in Central Station Crescent.

Exeter Cathedral

Exeter's jewel is the Cathedral Church of St Mary & St Peter, a magnificent building that has stood largely unchanged for the last 600 years. Unlike many of the cathedrals in England, it was built within a relatively short time, which accounts for its pleasing architectural unity.

There's been a church on this spot since 932. In 1050 the Saxon church was granted cathedral status and Leofric was enthroned as the first bishop of Exeter. Between 1112 and 1133, a Norman cathedral was built in place of the original church. The two transept towers were built at this time – an unusual design for English cathedrals of the period. In 1270, Bishop Bronescombe instigated the remodelling of the whole building, a process that took about 90 years and resulted in a mix of Early English and Decorated Gothic styles.

You enter through the impressive Great West Front, with the largest surviving collection of 14th-century sculpture in England. The niches around the three doors are filled with statues of Christ and the Apostles surrounded by saints and angels, kings and queens.

Inside, the cathedral is light and airy, roofed with the world's longest single expanse of Gothic vaulting. It might have been even brighter if a controversial plan to clean all the stonework and repaint the ceiling bosses in their original bright colours hadn't been stopped. Looking up, you can see where restoration was brought to a halt by those who thought the scheme over the top, even though much of the medieval cathedral would have been brightly painted.

Walking clockwise round the building, you pass the **astronomical clock** in the north tower, which shows the phases of the moon as well as the time. The dial dates from the 15th century but the works are modern. Opposite is the **minstrels' gallery**, used by the choir at Christmas and Easter.

The **Great Screen** was erected in 1325.

Behind is the choir, which features some interesting misericords including the earliest representation of an elephant in England. The **Bishop's Throne** was carved in 1312.

In the Lady Chapel, at the eastern end, are the **tombs** of Bishop Bronescombe and Bishop Leofric, and a memorial to the author of *Lorna Doone*, RD Blackmore. Cathedral staff will point out the famous sculpture of the **lady with two left feet**.

The cathedral (☎ 255573) opens from 8.30 am daily and a £2.50 donation is requested from visitors. There are guided tours (free) at 11 am and 2.30 pm Monday to Friday and 3 pm only on Saturday, April to October, which last 45 minutes and are highly recommended. It's also worth attending a service – evensong is at 5 pm.

Underground Passages

The medieval maintenance passages for the lead water pipes that were laid under the city in the 14th century still survive. They're dark, narrow and definitely not for claustrophobes but the guided tours (☎ 265887) are surprisingly interesting. They take place 2 to 4.30 pm Tuesday to Friday and 10 am to 4.30 pm on Saturday. The passages are open longer hours and on Monday in July and August. Admission costs £3.50/2.50 in July and August, £2.50/1.50 the rest of the year. The entrance is beside Boots on High St.

Royal Albert Memorial Museum & Art Gallery

Most of the galleries in this large museum (☎ 265858) are laid out in classic Victorian style, with crowded display cases and lots of dusty hunting trophies. The history of the city is covered in a series of exhibitions, ranging from prehistory through Roman Exeter to modern times. The gallery upstairs includes works by Devon artists from the 18th and 19th centuries.

It opens 10 am to 5 pm Monday to Saturday; entry is free. The cafe is good value too.

Guildhall

Parts of the Guildhall (☎ 265500) date from 1160, making it the oldest municipal building in the country that is still in use. It was, however, mainly built in the 14th century and the impressive portico that extends over the pavement was added at the end of the 16th century. Inside, the city's silver and regalia are on display.

It opens (as long as there are no functions) 10.30 am to 1 pm and 2 to 4 pm Monday to Friday, in the morning only on Saturday. There's no entry charge.

St Nicholas Priory

Originally built as accommodation for overnight visitors, the guest wing of the Benedictine St Nicholas Priory (☎ 265858), off Fore St, became the house of a wealthy Elizabethan merchant. It's now preserved, with period furniture and plaster ceilings, as it might have looked when inhabited by the merchant and his family.

It opens 3 to 4.30 pm on Monday, Wednesday and Saturday, Easter to October; entry costs 50p.

Quay House Interpretation Centre

Down by the river, this display and audio-visual presentation offers a painless résumé of the city's history and its commercial reliance on the river. There's no charge, and it's open 10 am to 5 pm daily, Easter to October.

Walking & Cycling Routes

The 11-mile (18km) walk to the *Steps Bridge Youth Hostel* (see the Moretonhampstead section later in the chapter for details) on Dartmoor follows country lanes through Shillingford St George and Doddiscombsleigh. Ask at the TIC for details.

Drop in at the *Nobody Inn* (☎ 01647-252394, fax 252978, e inn.nobody@virgin .net) in Doddiscombsleigh – we think it's one of the best pubs in south-western England.

A 30-mile (48km) cycling tour of Dartmoor takes you from Exeter through Doddiscombsleigh and Bovey Tracey to Widecombe-in-the-Moor and back to Exeter. You can get full details of the tour from the TIC.

Places to Stay

Hostels In a large house overlooking the River Exe, *Exeter Youth Hostel* (☎ 873329, fax 876939, e exeter@yha.org.uk, 47 Countess Wear Rd) is 2 miles (3km) south-east of the city towards Topsham. It's open year-round and the nightly charge is £10.85/7.40 for adults/juniors. From High St, catch minibus J, K or T (10 minutes) and ask for Countess Wear post office. Bus No 57 will get you there from the bus station.

At new *Globe Backpackers* (☎ 215521, fax 215531, e caroline@globebackpackers .freeserve.co.uk, 71 Holloway St), a welcome addition to the budget scene, there are 60 beds (£11), free tea and coffee, and Internet access, with a good vibe to top it off. If you stay six nights, the seventh is free.

University Accommodation Some of the best-value accommodation in Exeter is the university's *St Luke's Hall* (☎ 211500, fax 263512, e conferences@exeter.ac.uk) on its St Luke's campus – rates start at just £13.50/22.50 for a single/double including breakfast. The catch is that it's available only in university holidays.

B&Bs & Hotels The cheapest B&Bs are on the outskirts of the city. The *Old Mill* (☎ 259977, Mill Lane, Alphington), in a quiet residential suburb, is excellent value, with B&B for £12.50 a person. It's easy to reach by bus.

Most B&Bs and cheaper hotels lie in the area east of St David's train station and north of Central train station. There are several reasonable B&Bs on St David's Hill. The *Highbury* (☎/fax 434737, 85 St David's Hill) is good value from £20/35. *Glendale Hotel* (☎/fax 274350, 8 St David's Hill) has rooms from £20 per head, some with showers.

The *Clock Tower Hotel* (☎ 424545, fax 218445, e reservations@clocktower-hotel.com, 16 New North Rd) is a handsome place with a few singles from £30, doubles from £45. There are several other places along this road and more on Blackall Rd and Howell Rd. *Rhona's* (☎ 277791, 15 Blackall Rd) has singles/doubles from

£15/29. More upmarket is **Raffles Hotel** (☎ 270200, ℮ raffleshtl@btinternet.com, 11 Blackall Rd); all rooms have a bathroom and charges are £34/48.

The **Claremont** (☎ 274699, ℮ geoffself@ conscribe.com, 36 Wonford Rd) is a comfortable B&B for nonsmokers, in a posh suburb on the eastern side of the city. Ensuite singles/doubles are £34/44.

The **White Hart Hotel** (☎ 279897, fax 250159, South St) is an old coaching inn, and the cobbled courtyard through which the coachmen drove their horses is still the focal point. It's an interesting place to stay, with rooms with a bath from £49/64 at the weekend, £61/94 during the week.

The centrally located **St Olaves Court Hotel** (☎ 217736, fax 413054, Mary Arches St) has 15 comfortable rooms, each with a bathroom. Prices are from £65/90 at the weekend, £75/100 during the week. Some rooms come with a Jacuzzi.

Dating back to the 14th century, the **Royal Clarence Hotel** (☎ 319955, fax 439423) has the best location of all, right in Cathedral Yard. Its weekend B&B deals are good value at £65 a head per night for two nights; pay the extra £10 for a front room with a superb view of the cathedral. During the week, these rooms cost £99/125; breakfast is extra. Former guests include Tsar Nicholas I and Lord Nelson.

Places to Eat

Herbies (☎ 258473, 15 North St) is an excellent vegetarian restaurant raved about by locals. Its home-made soups, chilli dishes and apple pie are highly recommended.

Not so far away on Queen St is the **Oggy Oggy Pasty Co** with a great range of pasties from vegetarian to beef and stilton. Also on Queen St **Fruta Bomba** (☎ 412233) has an impressive array of Latin American food. Lunch and a drink costs about £6; by night it's a popular cocktail bar.

In an alley off Queen St is **The Boston Tea Party** (☎ 201181), open from 8 am daily and in the evenings from Thursday to Saturday. All meals cost under £5.

In Cathedral Close there are several places to choose from. **Café on the Green** (☎ 310130) has a jolly menu that includes a British Buttie (soda bun with bacon, fried egg and lashings of HP Sauce). There are also salads, pasta, pizzas and steaks. **Hanson's Restaurant** (☎ 276913) is the place for a cream tea or traditional lunch in a nonsmoking environment. Also in Cathedral Close is a branch of **Pizza Express**.

Nearby, on the other side of the cathedral green, is **Thai Orchid** (☎ 214215), which does good set lunches for £8.50 and is also open for dinner. Next door is sophisticated **Newton's** (☎ 411200, 3 Cathedral Yard) with a more expensive modern British menu.

There are several bistro-style places around Gandy St. **Coolings Wine Bar** (☎ 434184, 11 Gandy St) has a good range of main dishes and an extensive wine list. **Cripes** (☎ 491411, 21 Gandy St) specialises in sweet and savoury Brittany pancakes.

The **Ganges** (☎ 272630, Fore St) is reputed to be the best of Exeter's Indian restaurants for those that like to turn up the heat. The **Taj Mahal** (☎ 258129, 50 Queen St) is also good value and does an all-you-can-eat Sunday buffet for £6.95.

Said to have terrorised the kitchens of the Sheriff of Exeter, Mad Meg now lends her name to a Middle Ages theme restaurant with long wooden tables and bare flagstones. **Mad Meg's** (☎ 221225, Fore St) serves English baronial fare – steaks, ribs, pheasant, rabbit and the like. Main courses range from £6 to £16.

The city's top restaurants include **Lamb's** (☎ 254269, 15 Lower North St), under the old iron bridge, serving modern British fare. The three-course set dinner costs about £20. A couple of doors down is **La Chandelle** (☎ 435953), where the accent is decidedly French and the set menu is more like £15.

Michael Caine's (☎ 319955), at the Royal Clarence Hotel, has nothing to do with the actor who thought he only told us to 'blow the bloody doors off'. This time it is a famous chef and the food is highly regarded. The restaurant at **St Olaves Court Hotel** is also popular: two courses cost £11.50, three courses £14.50.

Entertainment

Pubs & Clubs Sir Francis Drake's favourite local is said to have been the **Ship Inn** (☎ 270891, Martin's Lane), in the alley between High St and the cathedral. The place trades heavily on its famous customer, but it's atmospheric and the food's good value. The **Tap Bar** at the White Hart Hotel feels more authentic with sawdust on the floor and jugs of real ale.

Vines (Gandy St) is a heaving place, and is particularly packed with locals when it has live music on Sunday night.

The **Prospect Inn** is a cosy pub down on the redeveloped Quay, and is a nice place to sit outside on a summer evening. The **Double Locks** (☎ 256947) is a popular pub right beside the Exeter Shipping Canal, with good food, great puddings and daily barbecues in summer. It's a 20-minute walk south along the canal from The Quay.

The **Walkabout** on Fore St might send Aussies weak at the knees, but it hardly offers the real thing. There's live music or DJs each night in the excellent subterranean **Cavern** (☎ 495370, 83 Queen St). Most nights have a nominal entry fee.

Nightclubs come and go. Down on The Quay **Volts** is remarkably popular with students.

Theatre Exeter's **Phoenix Arts Centre** (☎ 667080, Gandy St) stages dance, theatre, film and music events and is open Monday to Saturday. At the time of writing it was under renovation.

There are two theatres: the **Northcott** (☎ 493493), on the university campus, and the smaller **Barnfield** (☎ 270891, Barnfield Rd), which features programs from touring companies and local groups.

Getting There & Away

Exeter is 172 miles (277km) from London, 75 miles (121km) from Bristol, 45 miles (72km) from Plymouth and 120 miles (193km) from Land's End. If you're driving down from London, follow the M3 and then the A303, not the congested A30. It's even faster to take the M4 to Bristol and then the M5 south to Exeter.

Air Scheduled services run between Exeter airport (☎ 367433) and Birmingham, Ireland, the Channel Islands and the Isles of Scilly.

Bus The booking office at the bus station is open 7.45 am to 6.30 pm daily.

National Express runs coaches between Exeter and numerous towns, including London (3¾ hours, £16.50) via Heathrow airport (3½ hours), Bath (2¾ hours, £12.50), Bristol (1½ hours, £9.75), Salisbury (two hours, £12.50) and Penzance (five hours, £16). There's a daily National Express south-coast service between Brighton and Penzance (via Portsmouth, Weymouth, Dorchester, Bridport, Exeter and Plymouth), which departs from Exeter for Brighton (seven hours, £22.50).

Stagecoach Devon (☎ 427711) runs the hourly No X38 to Plymouth (1¼ hours). First Western National (☎ 01752-222666) has buses to Okehampton (one hour) and Torquay (45 minutes).

Stagecoach Devon produces a useful *Smugglers' Trail* leaflet with details of walks accessible by bus. The area covered includes Sidmouth, Exeter, Torquay and Dartmouth. An Explorer ticket costs £5.65/14.30/24.20 for one/three/seven days of unlimited bus travel.

Train The fastest trains between London and Exeter use Paddington station and take two hours (hourly, £39). Trains from London Waterloo also leave hourly but take three hours, following a more scenic route via Salisbury.

Exeter is at the hub of lines running from Bristol (1½ hours, £15.60), Salisbury (two hours, £20.10) and Penzance (three hours, £18.60).

The 39-mile (63km) branch line to Barnstaple (1½ hours, £9.70) is promoted as the Tarka Line, following the valleys of the Rivers Yeo and Taw and giving good views of traditional Devon countryside with its characteristic, deep-sunken lanes. There are nine trains a day, throughout the year. Most intercity trains use St David's station.

Getting Around

Bus Exeter is well served by public transport. A one-day Freedom Ticket on the Exeter bus system might be useful. Bus N links St David's and Central train stations and passes near the bus station.

Taxi There are taxi ranks outside the train stations. Alternatively, try Capital Taxis (☎ 433433).

Bicycles & Canoes You can hire bikes at Flash Gordon (☎ 424246), 15 Clifton Rd, as well as camping equipment and canoes. Three-speed bikes cost £5/20 per day/week, mountain bikes cost £12 daily and tandems are £25 per day.

Saddles & Paddles (☎ 424241) on The Quay rents out bikes (£12/9 per day for adults/children) and Canadian canoes (from £8/27 per hour/day). It also organises 'paddling parties' with a barbecue at the Double Locks (see Entertainment later). Visit its Web site at www.saddlepaddle.co.uk.

AROUND EXETER
Powderham Castle

The castle (☎ 01626-890243) is on the estuary of the River Exe, 8 miles (13km) south of Exeter. It dates from the 14th century but was considerably altered in the 18th and 19th centuries. The home of the Courtenay family, it contains collections of French china and Stuart and Regency furniture, and features some garish rococo ceilings.

It's open 10 am to 5.30 pm daily except Saturday, April to September; entry costs £5.85/2.95.

A la Ronde

Jane and Mary Parminter planned to combine the magnificence of the Church of San Vitale, which they'd visited in Ravenna, with the homeliness of a country cottage, to create the perfect dwelling place. The result is an intriguing 16-sided house (☎ 01395-265514), owned by the National Trust (NT), whose bizarre interior decor includes a shell-encrusted room, a frieze of feathers, and sand and seaweed collages.

It's open 11 am to 5.30 pm Sunday to Thursday, April to October; entry costs £3.30/1.65. It's 2 miles (3km) north of Exmouth on the A376; Stagecoach Devon bus No 57 runs close by en route to Exeter.

SOUTH DEVON COAST
Sidmouth
☎ 01395 • pop 11,000

A busy fishing port in the Middle Ages, Sidmouth became a fashionable holiday resort when the future Queen Victoria visited with her parents in 1819. The town still retains a certain grandeur, with many gracious Regency buildings. To the east, a steep path climbs Salcombe Hill, with superb views from the top.

The TIC (☎/fax 516441) on Ham Lane shares a home with the public swimming pool. It is open 9.30 am to 6 pm daily (to 5 pm on Sunday). There are guided strolls around the town leaving **Sidmouth Museum** at 10.15 am on Tuesday and Thursday, Easter to October.

Sidmouth International Festival Sidmouth is best known for its folk-music festival, which has grown from a small gathering to a major event on the international folk scene. The festival takes over the town for a week in late July or early August.

Tickets covering all the events cost £140/84, plus £40/16 to camp; a day's ticket is £29/19 plus £8 if you're camping. Phone ☎ 01296-433669 for information.

Places to Stay The nearest camp site is *Salcombe Regis Camping and Caravan Park* (☎/fax 514303, e info@salcombe-regis.co.uk), about 2 miles (3km) east of Sidmouth, which charges from £6.75 a pitch.

The nearest hostel is the *Beer Youth Hostel* (☎ 01297-20296, fax 23690, e beer@yha.org.uk, Bovey Combe, Townsend) in a large house half a mile west of the village of Beer, itself 6 miles (10km) east of Sidmouth. It's open daily in July and August, and daily except Sunday from April to June and in September and October. The nightly charge in summer is £10.85/7.40.

When it comes to B&Bs and hotels, there are an incredible number in Sidmouth, but try to book ahead during the international festival.

Getting There & Away There are two buses an hour from Exeter (45 minutes, £3.15) to Sidmouth. Axe Valley (☎ 01297-625959) runs the X53 to Beer village.

Torbay Resorts
☎ 01803

The contrasting towns set around Torbay – Torquay, Paignton and Brixham – describe themselves as the English Riviera, and while it's true that the climate here is appealing for England, if you're expecting the Med, think again.

Torquay Torquay, with a population of over 60,000, is the largest and boldest of the three towns. There's a long seaside promenade, hung with coloured lights at night, and streets of hotels and cheap B&Bs, all hoping to vanquish the ghost of the BBC sitcom *Fawlty Towers*, which took Torquay as its location.

The TIC (☎ 297428, fax 214885, e torbay .tic@torbay.gov.uk) on Vaughan Parade is near the harbour. It is open 9.30 am to 5.30 pm Monday to Friday, and to 5 pm on Saturday.

Things to See Agatha Christie was born here and **Torquay Museum** (☎ 293975) at 529 Babbacombe Rd has a display on the author. In summer it's open 10 am to 4.45 pm Monday to Saturday, and from 1.30 pm on Sunday; in winter it's open weekdays only. Entry costs £2/1.25.

Torre Abbey (☎ 293593), in the park set back from the beach, was a monastery converted into a country house. Admiral Horatio Nelson stayed here in 1801. It now houses a collection of furniture, glassware and more Agatha Christie mementos. It's open 9.30 am to 5 pm daily, April to October. Entry costs £2.75/1.50.

Kent's Cavern (☎ 215136) is a surprising stalactite cave underneath the modern town. It is open 10 am to 4.30 pm year-

round (to 5 pm in July and August, to 4 pm in winter). Entry costs £4.75/3. There are also evening 'chiller' tours during July and August.

Pretty **Babbacombe Beach** is at the base of what must be one of England's steepest roads, so whether on a bicycle or in a car, check your brakes first! The beach is about 2 miles (3km) north of the town centre.

Places to Stay & Eat Near the town centre and the beach is *Torquay Backpackers* (☎ 299924, e torquay.backpackers@ btinternet.com, 119 Abbey Rd), charging £8 per night or £48 per week. During summer, there are sometimes beach barbecues or night trips onto Dartmoor.

There are literally hundreds of B&Bs and hotels in the Torquay area, but so far none have been brave enough to take the name Fawlty Towers. For B&B, *The Wilsbrook* (☎ 298413, 77 Avenue Rd) is pleasant with rooms from £17 per person. At the other end of the spectrum, the *Palace Hotel* (☎ 200200, fax 299899, e info@ palace torquay.co.uk, Babbacombe Rd) was built for the Bishop of Exeter. It has everything, including swimming pools and a golf course, and costs from £61 per person.

The *Tudor Rose* (14 Victoria Parade) is a good place for light lunches and teas. For something more substantial, *Capers* (☎ 291177, 7 Lisburne Square) has a fine array of international food with the emphasis on French; expect to spend £10 and up.

For the best Indian food in this neck of the woods, catch the *Bombay Express* (☎ 380060, 98 Belgrave Rd), with friendly service and a range of buzzing baltis. You can bring your own booze.

Claire's (☎ 292079, Torwood St) is the club to check out for a late one.

Paignton Around the bay to the south, Torquay merges into Paignton, which promotes itself as a family seaside resort. Roundham Head separates the two main beaches. **Paignton Zoo** (☎ 527936), on Totnes Rd, sells itself as an environmental park and is considered to have better standards than some of the other zoos in

England. It is open 10 am to 6 pm (to dusk in winter); entry costs £7.50/5.40.

The TIC (☎ 558383, fax 551959) on The Esplanade is open 9.30 am to 6 pm daily in summer, and 9.30 am to 5 pm Monday to Saturday in winter.

Places to Stay & Eat At *Riviera Backpackers* (☎/fax 550160, e alan@riviera-backpackers.ssnet.co.uk, 6 Manor Rd, Preston Sands), a short walk from the beach, dorm beds are £8, including free tea and coffee. Call from the train station and they'll meet you.

The Natural Break (☎ 526220, 41 Torquay Rd) is an excellent vegetarian restaurant open all day. *Thai Paradise* (☎ 551166, 4a Parkside Rd) is a reliable Thai restaurant.

Brixham Now a fishing town crowded round a small harbour, in the middle of the 19th century Brixham was the country's busiest fishing port and is still the place to come for a fishing expedition. **Brixham Heritage Museum** (☎ 856267) in the Old Police Station, New Rd, gives a lively introduction to the town's history and its connection to the sea. It is open from 10 am to 5 pm Monday to Friday (to 1 pm Saturday) and costs £1.50/50p.

The TIC (☎ 852861) in the Old Market House, The Quay, is open 9.30 am to 5.30 pm Monday to Saturday.

Fishing Trips Kiosks line the harbour touting boat trips. It costs around £20 for a half-day trip to fish for conger, ling and coalfish around the wrecks in the bay, less to fish for mackerel. Before parting with your money, it's worth asking whether there are any mackerel shoals about. To arrange a trip, contact the boats' skippers directly – try *Boy Richard* (☎ 521986) or *Our Jenny* (☎ 854444).

Places to Stay Four miles (6km) from Brixham and across the water from Dartmouth, the attractively located *Maypool Youth Hostel* (☎ 842444, fax 845939) is a mile south-west of Galmpton. Beds are

£9/6.20 for adults/juniors and it's open daily, April to August. Stagecoach Devon bus No 12 stops at Churston Pottery, a mile away beside Churston train station.

Getting There & Away The No X46 bus service runs hourly from Exeter to Torquay (one hour, £4.10). Service No 12 operates five times an hour along the coast from Torquay to Paignton and Brixham.

A branch railway line runs from Newton Abbot via Torquay to Paignton. The Paignton & Dartmouth Steam Railway (☎ 555872) runs from Paignton along the coast on the scenic 7-mile (11km) trip to Kingswear on the River Dart, linked by ferry (six minutes) to Dartmouth; a combined rail/ferry ticket from Paignton to Dartmouth costs £5.50/3.70 for an adult/child one-way, £7.50/5 return.

Dartmouth
☎ 01803 • pop 5300

Dartmouth is an extremely attractive port with a long history, on the River Dart estuary. The deep natural harbour has sheltered trading vessels since Norman times, fishing boats for many more centuries, the Pilgrim Fathers in 1620 on their way to Plymouth, and D-Day landing craft bound for France in 1944. Today, it's filled with yachts, but naval associations continue with the Royal Navy's officer training college located on the edge of town.

The TIC (☎ 834224, fax 835631, e enquire@dartmouth-tourism.org.uk), in the Engine House, Mayor's Ave, is open 9 am to 6 pm Monday to Saturday and 10 am to 4 pm on Sunday. Alternatively, visit its Web site at www.dartmouth-tourism.co.uk.

Dartmouth Castle Three-quarters of a mile (1km) outside the town, Dartmouth Castle (☎ 833588) dates from the 15th century and was designed so that a chain could be placed across to the companion castle at Kingswear to block off the estuary. It's run by English Heritage (EH).

The castle is open 10 am to 6 pm daily in summer, and 10 am to 4 pm Wednesday to

Sunday in winter; admission costs £2.90/1.50. There's a ferry along the estuary to the castle from the town every 15 minutes (£1).

Other Things to See Narrow streets wind through the town. In the centre, the **Butterwalk** is a row of timber-framed houses built in the 17th century, with a **museum** featuring a large collection of model boats. The museum (☎ 832923) is open 11 am to 5 pm Monday to Saturday (noon to 3 pm in winter); entry is free.

Places to Stay The nearest youth hostel is about 5 miles (8km) away in Maypool; see the previous Brixham section for details.

There are cheap B&Bs along Victoria Rd. *Galleons Reach* (☎ 834339) at No 77 costs £16 per person, or £20 for a room with a bath. Near the waterfront is the charming *Captain's House* (☎/fax 832133, 18 Clarence St) with rooms from £22.50 per person.

The *Little Admiral Hotel* (☎ 832572, fax 835815, e info@little-admiral.co.uk, 29 Victoria Rd) offers a luxurious base with impeccable rooms from £45/90.

Places to Eat *Dartmouth Castle Tea Rooms*, at the castle, do cream teas and light lunches, and there are excellent views over the water from here. *Dartmouth Bakery (Smith St)* has an exceptional range of cakes and pies.

The town has something of a reputation for gourmet dining. The *Royal Castle Hotel* (☎ 833033, 11 The Quay) has a popular restaurant. Better known is the *Carved Angel* (☎ 832465, 2 South Embankment), where a memorable feast will cost £48 for three courses. Run by the same people but with a cheaper menu, the *Carved Angel Café* (☎ 834842, 7 Foss St) offers bistro-style main courses from £7.50; fish is a speciality. *Hooked* (☎ 832022, 5 Higher St) is another well-known fish restaurant: expect to pay from £25 per head.

The *Cherub Inn* (☎ 832571, 13 Higher St) claims to be the oldest building in the town and is a good place for a pint or a bar meal.

Getting There & Away The best way to approach Dartmouth is by boat, either on the ferry from Kingswear (six minutes, £2 for a car and four people, 50p for a foot passenger) or downstream from Totnes (1¼ hours, £5.20/£6.90 single/return). River Dart Cruises (☎ 832109) is one operator. From Exeter, take a train to Totnes and a boat from there.

For details of the popular Paignton & Dartmouth Steam Railway, see Getting There & Away in the previous Torbay Resorts section.

Totnes
☎ 01803 • pop 7500

Totnes was once one of the most prosperous towns in Britain, a centre for the tin and wool industries. It's now a trendy market town ('the Glastonbury of the west') with a thriving arts community. It's a pleasant place to wander round, with interesting shops, numerous Elizabethan buildings and a busy quay. There are cruises on the river with frequent departures to Dartmouth in summer. It is 9 miles (14km) inland from Torquay and 10 miles (16km) upriver from Dartmouth.

The TIC (☎ 863168, fax 865771) is in The Plains and is open 9.30 am to 5 pm Monday to Saturday, 10 am to 1 pm on Sunday.

Things to See In a Tudor building on Fore St is **Totnes Museum**. It's open Monday to Saturday. The £3 admission ticket also covers the **Guildhall** and the **Museum of Period Costume**.

Totnes Castle (☎ 864406; EH), nothing more than a ruin these days, is open 10 am to 6 pm daily in summer; entry costs £1.60/80p.

Places to Stay The *Dartington Youth Hostel* (☎ 862303, fax 865171, Lownard, Dartington) is 2 miles (3km) from Totnes off the A385 near Week. It's open daily in July and August, Tuesday to Sunday from April to June, and Wednesday to Sunday in September and October; the nightly charge is £9/6.20 for adults/juniors. First Western

National bus No X80 from Torquay to Plymouth via Totnes passes close by.

Just off High St, *Alison Fenwick* (☎ *866917, 3 Plymouth Rd)* offers B&B from £15 to £19 per person, and can arrange private tours of Dartmoor. A couple of minutes' walk from the Totnes train station, there's a comfortable B&B on Queen's Terrace at *No 4 (☎ 867365)*, with singles/doubles for £25/40 including vegetarian breakfast.

The 600-year-old *Old Forge (☎ 862174, Seymour Place)* is the most atmospheric place in town and even has its own old lockup. Rooms cost from £54.

Places to Eat Totnes High St is lined with interesting places to eat. *Munchmania* is an organic juice bar that draws a healthy crowd. *Anne of Cleves Tearoom* has some mouthwatering cakes, as well as the classic cream tea. *Willow Vegetarian Restaurant* (☎ *862605)* at No 87 does main dishes from about £4 and has a nice garden.

Tolivers Vegetarian Bistro (65 Fore St) is more expensive but has live music at the weekend and good food at all times.

Getting There & Away Buses run only a few times a week to Exeter, but National Express coaches stop here.

There are frequent rail connections to Exeter (45 minutes, £7.10) and Plymouth (25 minutes, £5.50). The train station is a 15-minute walk from the town centre.

A short walk from Totnes main-line train station, the private South Devon Railway (☎ 01364-642338) runs to Buckfastleigh (25 minutes, £6.50/4 return for adults/children, £6/3.50 if you book at the TIC) on the edge of Dartmoor.

PLYMOUTH
☎ 01752 • pop 239,000

Plymouth was renowned as a maritime centre long before Drake's famous game of bowls on Plymouth Hoe in 1588, but this history is difficult to appreciate as you approach Devon's largest city through its extensive modern suburbs. Devastated by WWII bombing raids, most of Plymouth has been rebuilt, although the Barbican (the old quarter by the harbour where the Pilgrim Fathers set sail for the New World) has been preserved.

History

Plymouth really began to expand in the 15th century, with the development of larger ships; the Plymouth Sound provided a perfect anchorage for warships.

The seafarer most commonly associated with Plymouth is Sir Francis Drake, who achieved his knighthood through an epic voyage around the world; setting out from Plymouth in 1577 in the *Golden Hind* and returning three years later.

In 1588, Drake played a prominent part in the defeat of the Spanish Armada, the fleet sent to invade England by Philip II, who wanted to restore Catholicism to the country. On the way home from a Caribbean raid in 1586, Drake had taunted the Spanish king with an attack on some ships in Cadiz harbour.

Whether Drake really was playing bowls on the Hoe at the time is debatable, but the English fleet certainly did set sail from here. Drake was vice admiral and John Hawkins (who had sailed with him on the 1586 raid) was rear admiral. The Armada was chased up the English Channel to Calais, where the troops they were supposed to collect for the planned invasion of Britain failed to arrive. The English then attacked the fleet with fire ships. Many of the Spanish vessels escaped but were blown off course and wrecked off Scotland. Losses were England nil, Spain 51.

Thirty-two years later, the Pilgrim Fathers' two ships, the *Mayflower* and the *Speedwell*, put into Plymouth. Because the second ship was badly damaged, only the *Mayflower* set sail for America on 16 September 1620. Some of the 102 passengers and crew spent their last night on English soil in Island House, now the TIC. Another famous Plymouth mariner is Captain James Cook, who set out from the Barbican in 1768 in search of a southern continent.

The royal dockyard was established at

Devonport beside the River Tamar in 1690, and there's still a large naval base here.

Orientation & Information

The train station is about a mile north of Plymouth Hoe, the grassy park overlooking the sea. Between them is the pedestrianised city centre, with shopping streets branching off Armada Way, and the bus station. To the east of the Hoe is the Barbican, the interesting old quarter, by Sutton Harbour.

The TIC (☎ 264849, fax 257955), in Island House, 9 The Barbican, is open 9 am to 5 pm Monday to Saturday, and 10 am to 4 pm on Sunday in summer. If you're driving into Plymouth there's another TIC (☎ 266030) next to the Sainsbury's supermarket at Marshall's Roundabout (off the A38).

There are laundrettes on Notte St and Pier St.

Plymouth Hoe

This famous promenade gives wonderful, breezy views over Plymouth Sound. In one corner there's even a bowling green; the one on which Drake finished his game was probably where his statue now stands.

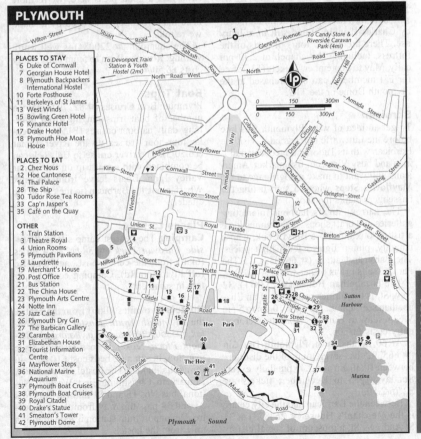

PLYMOUTH

PLACES TO STAY
6 Duke of Cornwall
7 Georgian House Hotel
8 Plymouth Backpackers International Hostel
10 Forte Posthouse
11 Berkeleys of St James
13 West Winds
15 Bowling Green Hotel
16 Kynance Hotel
17 Drake Hotel
18 Plymouth Hoe Moat House

PLACES TO EAT
2 Chez Nous
12 Hoe Cantonese
14 Thai Palace
28 The Ship
30 Tudor Rose Tea Rooms
33 Cap'n Jasper's
35 Café on the Quay

OTHER
1 Train Station
3 Theatre Royal
4 Union Rooms
5 Plymouth Pavilions
9 Laundrette
19 Merchant's House
20 Post Office
21 Bus Station
22 The China House
23 Plymouth Arts Centre
24 Notte Inn
25 Jazz Café
26 Plymouth Dry Gin
27 The Barbican Gallery
29 Caramba
31 Elizabethan House
32 Tourist Information Centre
34 Mayflower Steps
36 National Marine Aquarium
37 Plymouth Boat Cruises
38 Plymouth Boat Cruises
39 Royal Citadel
40 Drake's Statue
41 Smeaton's Tower
42 Plymouth Dome

DEVON & CORNWALL

The Hoe's most obvious landmark is the red-and-white-striped **Smeaton's Tower**, originally the Eddystone Lighthouse but rebuilt here in 1882. This may look like just another lighthouse but it was actually the first scientifically designed jointed masonry lighthouse in the world. Open in summer, it costs 75p to climb the 93 steps.

The **Plymouth Dome** (☎ 603300), below Smeaton's Tower, details Plymouth's history through high-tech audiovisual shows. There's also a Tudor street with rowdy locals to liven things up, and a harbour observation deck with interactive computers and radar. It opens 9 am to 5 pm daily (to 4 pm in winter); entry costs £4.10/2.60.

East of the Hoe is the **Royal Citadel**, built by Charles II in 1670 and still in military use. There are guided tours of parts of the fortress, including the chapel, at 2.30 pm daily, May to September. Tickets (£3/2; free for EH members) can be purchased at the Plymouth Dome or the TIC.

Barbican

To get an idea of what Plymouth was like before the Luftwaffe redesigned it, visit the Barbican with its Tudor and Jacobean buildings and busy Victorian fish market. Americans will want to make a pilgrimage to the **Mayflower Steps** where a sign listing the passengers marks the spot.

The narrow streets harbour interesting galleries and craft shops. One famous local artist to look out for is Beryl Cook, whose naughty, plump figures fetch high prices. The Barbican Gallery (☎ 661052), 15 The Parade, sells prints of her work.

The **Elizabethan House** (☎ 253871), 32 New St, is the former residence of an Elizabethan sea captain. It's open 10 am to 5 pm Wednesday to Sunday, April to October; entry costs £1/50p.

At 60 Southside St, **Plymouth Dry Gin** (☎ 665292) has seven tours of the distillery between 10.30 am and 3.45 pm daily except Sunday, April to December; tickets are £2.75/2.50.

Between the Barbican and the city centre is the **Merchant's House** (☎ 264878) at 33 St Andrews St, a museum of social history

open 10 am to 1 pm and 2 to 5.30 pm Tuesday to Saturday, April to October; entry costs £2/1.

National Marine Aquarium

Opened in 1998 in an impressive building opposite the Barbican, the aquarium is a nonprofit-making venture designed to educate as well as amuse. Following a route along ramps winding through the building, visitors can examine aquatic life in a range of habitats – moorland stream, river estuary, shore and shallow sea, and deep reef. There's also the mandatory shark pool but Jaws gets a good press here: we're more likely to die from a coconut dropping on our head than from being savaged by a shark, we're told.

The aquarium (☎ 220084) is well worth visiting. It's open 9 am to 5 pm daily; entry costs £6.50/4.

Boat Trips

Plymouth Boat Cruises (☎ 822797) offers a number of boat trips ranging from hour-long, daily harbour cruises (£4/2) to irregular four-hour cruises up the River Tamar (£6.50/3). The river cruise to Calstock can be combined with a rail trip on the Tamar Valley Line. Boats leave from Phoenix Wharf, along the Barbican (to the east of the citadel).

Places to Stay

Camping The nearest camp site is *Riverside Caravan Park* (☎ 344122), 4 miles (6km) from the centre on Longbridge Rd (off Plympton Rd). Camping costs £7 per tent in summer.

Hostels Two miles (3km) from the centre, the *Plymouth Youth Hostel* (☎ 562189, fax 605360, ✉ plymouth@yha.org.uk, Belmont Place, Stoke) is in a Grecian-style mansion. In summer, beds cost £10.85/7.40 for adults/juniors. The hostel is open daily, January to Christmas. First Western National bus Nos 15 and 81 and Citybus Nos 33 and 34 pass this way from the city centre. Devonport train station is a quarter of a mile from the hostel.

Plymouth Backpackers International Hostel (☎ 225158, fax 207847, 172 Citadel Rd) is a friendly place. There are 48 dorm beds starting from £8.50 per night, with cheaper weekly rates. There are also some double rooms (£20). Showers are free (baths cost £1.50) and there's a laundry service.

B&Bs & Hotels Try the north-western corner of the Hoe for B&Bs and hotels. Citadel Rd is lined with places to stay. *West Winds* (☎ 0800 731 5717, fax 662158) at No 99 charges £20/40 for singles/doubles; the doubles have showers. The large, friendly *Kynance Hotel* (☎ 266821, fax 254076) at No 107 has en-suite rooms from £25/40. A continental breakfast is provided if you're leaving early on the ferry to France.

Slightly more upmarket is the *Georgian House Hotel* (☎ 663237, fax 253953, e georgianhousehotel@msn.com, 51 Citadel Rd), where rooms with a bath cost from £24/38. In winter prices drop to £21/36.

Berkeleys of St James (☎/fax 221654, 4 St James Place East) is a comfortable, nonsmoking guesthouse charging from £25/40 for rooms with a bath.

The *Bowling Green Hotel* (☎ 667485, fax 209092, 9 Osborne Place, Lockyer St) is, as the name suggests, located right beside the Hoe bowling green. It's a small, comfortable place run by friendly people. Rooms with a shower cost from £38/50. Also on Lockyer St is the *Drake Hotel* (☎ 229730, fax 255092, e drakehotel@themutual.net, 1 Windsor Villas) with en-suite rooms for £42/52.

The *Forte Posthouse* (☎ 0870 400 9064, fax 660974, Cliff Road) charges £89 for a double at the weekend. It has good views over Plymouth Sound.

Plymouth Hoe Moat House (☎ 639988, fax 673816, Armada Way) charges £115/130. It's a fairly spiritless place but offers good views of the Sound.

The *Duke of Cornwall* (☎ 266256, fax 600062, e duke@bhere.co.uk, Millbay Rd) is an impressive Victorian Gothic hotel situated between the Hoe and the ferry terminal. Rooms start from £84.50/99.50 without breakfast.

Places to Eat

The Barbican area makes the best hunting ground for interesting places to eat, especially along Southside St and New St behind the TIC.

The *Tudor Rose Tea Rooms* (☎ 255502, New St) have a pleasant garden at the back where teas and lunches are available. The beef and Guinness pie is tasty. *Café on the Quay* by the aquarium has light lunches, including baked potatoes filled with tuna – dolphin-friendly, of course. *Cap'n Jasper's* is a popular snack stand that does breakfasts and burgers near the Mayflower Steps. Half a yard of hot dog is available for junk-food junkies. *The Ship* (☎ 667604), beside the marina near the Barbican, offers good-value carvery meals.

There are few restaurants in the Lockyer St/Citadel Rd area but *Hoe Cantonese* (☎ 661895, 14 Athenaeum St) is a good exception and stays open late most evenings. Also up in this part of town is *Thai Palace* (☎ 255770, Elliot St), a decent-enough Thai restaurant to keep chilli fiends content.

The city's top restaurant is the predominantly French *Chez Nous* (☎ 266793, 13 Frankfort Gate), a short walk from the Theatre Royal. Seafood is a speciality, and main courses are around £18; a three-course set lunch or dinner costs £30. Book in advance.

Entertainment

For an introduction to music and arts in Plymouth, pick up a copy of the free monthly magazine *Scene* with its comprehensive listings.

Pubs & Clubs The Barbican is a good place to drink in the evening; the *Dolphin*, on Southside St, and the *Ship*, on the Barbican, are both popular.

The *Union Rooms* (Union St) have the cheapest drinks, but no music, while the *Notte Inn* (Notte St) is part-pub, part-restaurant, with a touch of history.

The *China House* (☎ 260930, Marrowbone Slip, off Sutton Rd), overlooking Sutton

DEVON & CORNWALL

Harbour, is a popular pub in a converted warehouse. There's live jazz on Sunday at lunch time and bands on Friday and Saturday evening.

Jazz Café on Southside St dabbles in all sorts of music and has jazz, bands or DJs most nights.

Candy Store (*67 Hyde Park Rd*) and *Club Fandango* are lively clubs, while *Dance Academy* is the big one.

Theatre Plymouth's fine *Theatre Royal* (*☎ 267222, Royal Parade*) attracts surprisingly big names for a regional theatre. The *Pavilions* (*☎ 229922, Millbay Rd*) host everything from Tom Jones to the Bolshoi Ballet.

Plymouth Arts Centre (*☎ 206114, 38 Looe St*) has a cinema, art galleries and a vegetarian restaurant.

Getting There & Away
Plymouth is 211 miles (340km) from London, 90 miles (145km) from Land's End and 46 miles (74km) from Exeter.

Bus First Western National (*☎ 402060*) runs three buses an hour to Yelverton (35 minutes) on the edge of Dartmoor, with an hourly service on Sunday and bank holidays. For details of Explorer tickets covering much of the region, see Getting Around near the start of this chapter.

Stagecoach bus No X38 runs to Exeter every 90 minutes (1¼ hours, £5.45). Stagecoach Explorer tickets for one/three/seven days cost £5.50/13.40/22.65, but Stagecoach offers far fewer services.

National Express (*☎ 0870 580 8080*) has direct connections to numerous cities including London (4½ hours, £20.50) and Bristol (2½ hours, £18).

Train The fastest way to get to London is by train (3½ hours, £44). There are also direct services to Bristol (1½ hours, £29) and Penzance (two hours, £10.30).

There's a scenic route to Exeter (one hour, £10) – the line follows the River Exe estuary, running beside the sea for part of the way. The Tamar Valley Line, through

Bere Ferrers, Bere Alston and Calstock to Gunnislake, is another scenic route. In summer, it's possible to travel to Calstock by train (£3.90) and return by boat, or the other way round; see the earlier Boat Trips section.

Getting Around
You can hire bikes from the conveniently located Caramba (*☎ 201544*) at 9 Quay Rd for £10 per day or £60 per week. Its Web site is at www.carambabikes.co.uk.

AROUND PLYMOUTH
Mount Edgcumbe
The 400-year-old home of the Earls of Mount Edgcumbe lies across the water in Cornwall. Although the house is open to the public and filled with 18th-century furniture, it's the French, Italian and English gardens that draw visitors. The gardens are open daily and admission is free.

The house opens 11 am to 4.30 pm Wednesday to Sunday, April to September; entry costs £4.50/2.25. You get there from Plymouth on the Cremyll foot ferry.

Buckland Abbey
Eleven miles (18km) north of Plymouth, Buckland Abbey (*☎ 01822-853607; NT*) was a Cistercian monastery, transformed into a family residence by Sir Richard Grenville and bought in 1581 by Sir Francis Drake. Among the memorabilia is Drake's Drum, used to summon sailors onto the deck of the *Revenge* before battle with the Armada. When Britain is in danger of being invaded, the drum is said to beat by itself.

It's open 10.30 am to 5.30 pm daily except Thursday, April to October; and 2 to 5 pm at the weekend in winter; entry costs £4.50/2.20. From Plymouth, bus Nos 83 and 84 will take you to Yelverton, from where bus No 55 will get you to Buckland Abbey.

NORTH DEVON
North Devon has some incredibly attractive stretches of coastline, including the disturbingly pretty Clovelly and the twin

towns of Lynton and Lynmouth (see Exmoor National Park in the Wessex chapter).

Barnstaple
☎ 01271 • pop 24,500

Barnstaple is a large town and transport hub – a good starting point for north Devon and Exmoor (see the Wessex chapter). The **Museum of North Devon** (☎ 346747) in The Square aside, there's no compulsion to stay. It is open 10 am to 4 pm Tuesday to Saturday.

The TIC (☎ 375000) at 36 Boutport St is open 9.30 am to 5.30 pm Monday to Friday, and from 10.30 am on Saturday.

Bikes are available from Tarka Trail (☎ 324202) at the train station from £6.50 per day (£8.50 for mountain bikes) and they can suggest some trails to follow.

Barnstaple is at the north-western end of the Tarka Line railway from Exeter and connects with a number of bus services around the coast. First Red Bus (☎ 345444) No 310 runs every two hours to Lynton (see Exmoor National Park in the Wessex chapter), but the most interesting option is the excellent DevonBus No 300 scenic service that heads across Exmoor to Bridgwater, going through Lynton and Minehead.

The Bike Bus connects with Barnstaple; see Getting Around at the beginning of the Devon section.

Ilfracombe
☎ 01271 • pop 10,471

Rising above its little harbour, Ilfracombe is north Devon's largest seaside resort, although the best beaches are 5 miles (8km) west at Woolacombe, and at Croyde Bay, 2 miles (3km) beyond.

In 1998, the striking **Ilfracombe Pavilion** (☎ 865655) opened, comprising the 500-seat Landmark Theatre and a circular ballroom. They're housed in two white brick cones that look a bit like enormous lampshades.

The TIC (☎ 863001, fax 862586) on The Promenade is open 10 am to 6.30 pm daily.

Both Woolacombe and Croyde Bay beaches are popular with surfers, particularly the beach break at Croyde – check out *The Thatch* bar here for all the surf gossip.

Places to Stay & Eat The *Ilfracombe Youth Hostel* (☎ 865337, fax 862652, e ilfracombe@yha.org.uk, 1 Hillsborough Terrace) stands above the town, overlooking the harbour. The nightly charge is £9.80/ 6.75 for adults/juniors, and it's open Monday to Saturday, April to September (daily in July and August).

Ocean Backpackers (☎/fax 867835, 29 St James Place) is a fine, friendly hostel opposite the bus station with lively food, good tunes and beds for £9 for the first night, £8 thereafter, including tea and toast. It used to be a hotel so there are more bathrooms than in the average hostel. Downstairs is the *Atlantis Restaurant*, a vegetarian cafe that draws locals as well as guests.

Rendezvous Cafe in the Ilfracombe Pavilion complex is a very popular place to lunch.

Getting There & Away First Red Bus Nos 1 and 2 operate four services an hour (two on Sunday) between Ilfracombe and Barnstaple (35 minutes). DevonBus No 300 links Ilfracombe to Lynton and Minehead twice a day daily. Bus No X85 goes to Plymouth on Saturday.

Lundy Island

Ten miles (16km) out in the Bristol Channel, Lundy is a granite mass, 3 miles (5km) long, half a mile wide and up to 122m high. There's a resident population of just 19 people, one pub (the *Marisco Tavern*), one church and no roads.

People come to climb the cliffs, watch the birds, dive in the marine nature reserve or escape from the world in one of the 23 holiday homes.

Interesting properties that can be rented include the lighthouse, the castle and a converted pigsty, but they need to be reserved months in advance. You can also camp for £4 to £7 per person, depending on the season. For further information phone ☎ 01237-431831; to make a booking phone ☎ 01628-825925.

Otherwise you can day trip from Ilfracombe or Bideford. There are between two

Puffin Pence

Martin Harman, owner of Lundy Island from 1925 to 1954, was a typical English eccentric. Not satisfied with owning the remote island, he was determined to make it independent from the rest of the UK, closing the post office and issuing his own stamps. Given that Lundy took its name from the old Norse word for puffin, the stamps were denominated in 'puffinage' instead of sterling.

The stamps were ignored but in 1930 Harman carried things a step further and issued a Lundy coinage, with his own head in place of the king's and a puffin on the reverse. These, too, were denominated in 'puffins' instead of shillings and pence. Such defiance couldn't be overlooked and Harman was duly convicted of counterfeiting under the 1870 Coinage Act.

Sadly, Lundy's once-common puffins are now a thoroughly endangered species; you'll be lucky to see any at all.

and five sailings (two hours, £25/12.50 for adults/juniors) a week from these ports during the summer season. For bookings, phone ☎ 01237-470422 or on the Web visit www.lundyisland.co.uk.

It is also possible to make day trips from Clovelly – the *Jessica Hettie* (☎ 431042) makes irregular day trips during the summer, which include a full day on the island. A ticket costs £22.50.

If you are feeling very affluent or are very prone to seasickness, you could always charter a chopper from Lomas Helicopters (☎ 01237-421054).

Bideford
☎ 01237 • pop 14,000

Charles Kingsley based his epic novel *Westward Ho!* on the town of Bideford, not on the nearby tacky resort of the same name – the latter was actually named after the book and it is the only town in England whose name contains an exclamation mark! Bideford's a pleasant enough place but there's no need to stay here. Several

useful bus services pass through the town, though, and boats to Lundy Island leave from the quay.

Find the TIC (☎ 477676, fax 421853, e bidefordtic@visit.org.uk) by the quay in Victoria Park. It is open 10 am to 5 pm (to 4 pm on Sunday).

Bicycles can be hired from Bideford Bicycle Hire (☎ 424123) on Torrington St for £7 a half-day, £9.50 all day.

There are frequent buses to Barnstaple (30 minutes). Bus No 2A runs to Appledore (15 minutes).

Appledore

This attractive little town with its narrow streets and olde-worlde charm is the complete antithesis of terribly tacky Westward Ho! nearby. Appledore was long associated with boat-building, but the industry declined in the early part of the 20th century. Revived in 1963, it continues to this day.

The **North Devon Maritime Museum** (☎ 01237-422064) tells the story of local boat-building, shipwrecks and smuggling and is open 11 am to 1 pm and 2 to 5 pm daily, Easter to October; entry costs £1/30p (free on Sunday). The *Seagate Hotel* (☎ 01237-472589) is a friendly waterside pub that offers B&B in singles/doubles for £29/50. Bus No 2A runs regularly to Bideford (15 minutes).

Clovelly
☎ 01237

Looking for all the world like an oil painting, Clovelly has turned itself into a living gallery and charges visitors £3.50 for the experience, although technically this is for the visitor centre (☎ 431781) and the car park above. If you arrive in the evening there is no charge and you can let yourself in through a gate to the right of the visitors centre. The tiny village, with its one cobbled street (flat shoes advisable), is certainly attractive and the best way to appreciate it is to stay here, as the atmosphere is very different once the daily invaders depart. If that's not possible, try to visit early morning or late afternoon.

The village clings to a steep slope above a picturesque harbour, and has to be Devon's most photographed village. From Easter to October, Land Rovers regularly ferry visitors up and down the slope (£1/1.50 single/return) between 9.30 am and 5.30 pm.

Places to Stay & Eat Several places do B&B, but it is advisable to book ahead. *Mrs Golding's (☎ 431565, 104 High St)* is the cheapest at £15 per person. *Temple Bar (☎ 431438)* charges £19 per person and has a fine location above the harbour. *Donkey Shoe Cottage (☎ 431601, 21 High St)* is a homely B&B charging £18 per person.

The *New Inn (☎ 431303, fax 431636, High St)* has rooms for £60 during peak season, less for longer stays. Its restaurant has a pub-style menu including classics such as bangers and mash. It also has a catch of the day and other seafood favourites such as half a pint of prawns.

Right by the harbour, the *Red Lion Hotel (☎ 431237, fax 431044)* charges £83 for a double, less if you stay a while. Food is a far more formal affair than at the New Inn with an a la carte restaurant with an emphasis on seafood. Expect to pay around £20 for a full meal.

Both stop serving by 9 pm so keep an eye on the clock if you want to avoid going hungry.

Getting There & Away There are three departures a day on First Red Bus (☎ 01271-345444) No 319 to Bideford (40 minutes).

Hartland Abbey

Hartland Abbey (☎ 01237-441264) dates from the 12th century, but has been a private home since the monastery was dissolved in 1539 and given to the sergeant of Henry VIII's wine cellar. It is open 2 to 5 pm on Wednesday, Thursday and Sunday, May to September (plus Tuesday in July and August). Entry costs £4.50/1.50.

Hartland Abbey is 15 miles (24km) west of Bideford, off the A39 between Hartland and Hartland Quay.

Dartmoor National Park

Dartmoor encloses some of the wildest, bleakest country in England – suitable terrain for the Hound of the Baskervilles (one of Sherlock Holmes' more notorious foes). The landscape and weather (mist, rain and snow) can make this an eerie place in which to be – try not to think of the opening scenes of *An American Werewolf in London* on a dark, misty evening. The park is about 365 sq miles in area.

Dartmoor lies within the county of Devon and is named after the River Dart, which has its source here; the West Dart and East Dart rivers merge at Dartmeet. The park covers a granite plateau punctuated by distinctive tors (high rocks), which can look uncannily like ruined castles, and is cut by deep valleys, or combes, and fast-flowing rivers and streams. Some tors, such as Vixen Tor, are almost 30m high. The moorland is covered by gorse and heather, and is grazed by sheep, cattle and semi-wild Dartmoor ponies. The countryside in the southeast is more conventionally beautiful, with wooded valleys and thatched villages.

There are plenty of prehistoric remains – Grimspound is possibly the most complete Bronze Age village site in England and the many cairns and tumuli mark the burial places of ancient chieftains.

The area was once rich in minerals such as tin, copper, silver, lead and china clay and the remains of old mines and quarries are scattered about. Most of Dartmoor's prehistoric monuments are built of rough grey local granite. The quarries at Haytor produced stone for Nelson's Column, London Bridge and many other monuments. The wealth generated by these enterprises has left the moor's small communities with attractive churches and buildings. Dartmoor's best-known building, however, is the high-security prison at Princetown.

Most of the park is around 600m high. The highest spot is High Willhays, at 621m, near Okehampton. About 40% of Dartmoor

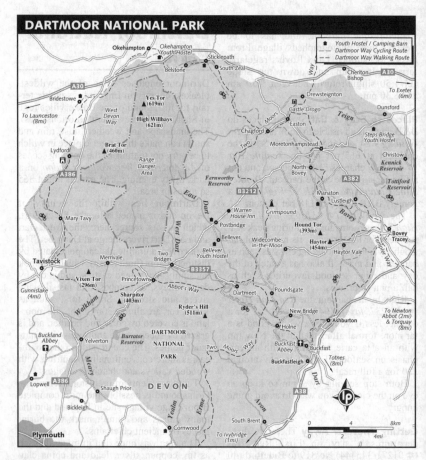

DARTMOOR NATIONAL PARK

is common land but 15% of the park (the north-western section, including High Willhays and Yes Tor) is leased to the Ministry of Defence (MOD) and is closed for firing practice for part of the year.

This is wonderful hiking country, but you'll be far from alone in the summer on the most popular routes. It's essential to have a good map as it's easy to get lost, particularly if the mist comes down.

ORIENTATION

Dartmoor is 10 miles (16km) from Exeter and 7 miles (11km) from Plymouth. It's ringed by a number of small market towns and villages, including Ashburton, Buckfastleigh, Tavistock and Okehampton. Buses link these towns with Princetown, Postbridge and Moretonhampstead on the moor itself. The two main roads across the moor meet near Princetown, the only village of any size on Dartmoor.

Two Bridges, with its medieval clapper bridge, is the focal point for car and coach visitors, and can be extremely crowded in summer. Most of the places to see are on the eastern side; the western side is for serious walkers.

INFORMATION

You can get information about Dartmoor at the TICs in Exeter and Plymouth, and there are other visitor centres in and around the park. The National Park Authority (NPA) runs the High Moorland Visitors Centre (☎ 01822-890414), Old Duchy Hotel, Princetown, which is open daily all year.

The other visitor centres are generally open 10 am to 5 pm daily, April to October, and are at Haytor (☎ 01364-661520), Postbridge (☎ 01822-880272), New Bridge (☎ 01364-631303), Okehampton (☎ 01837-53020), Ivybridge (☎ 01752-897035) and Tavistock (☎ 01822-612938).

These information centres have useful publications, including the *Dartmoor Visitor*, free and updated annually. They also stock walking guides and Ordnance Survey (OS) maps. The *Dartmoor Public Transport Guide* gives information on walks accessible by bus.

The following Web sites are also worth trying: www.dartmoor-guide.co.uk; www.dartmoor-npa.gov.uk; and www.dartmoorway.org.uk.

Guided walks focusing on local wildlife, bird-watching, archaeology or legends and folklore are arranged from April to October. Charges are from £2.50 for two hours to £4.50 for six hours. Details appear in the *Dartmoor Visitor*. If you arrive at the start of a walk by bus you can join it free of charge.

Don't feed the Dartmoor ponies as this encourages them to move dangerously near to the roads.

WALKING

Dartmoor offers excellent walking country. Postbridge, Princetown and Chagford are all good centres, and south of Okehampton there is a high, wild area around Yes Tor and High Willhays (but note that this is within the MOD firing range). Haytor is also a popular hiking destination.

There are several waymarked routes. The Abbot's Way runs along an ancient 14-mile (23km) route from Buckfast to Princetown. The West Devon Way is a 14-mile (23km)

> ### Warning
>
> Access to the north-western Ministry of Defence (MOD) training area, where there's good walking and some of the highest tors, is restricted when there's live firing. The areas are marked by red and white posts and notice boards at the main approaches. When firing is in progress, there are red flags (red lights at night) in position.
>
> Always check the firing schedules with the MOD (☎ 0800 458 4868) or a TIC.

walk between Tavistock and Okehampton along old tracks and through pretty villages on the western edge of Dartmoor. You can always take a bus for part of this route as the walk runs parallel to the No 187 bus route.

Youth hostels are conveniently placed a day's walk apart across the moor, so a five-day circuit from either Exeter or Plymouth is possible.

The Templer Way is an 18-mile (29km) hike from Teignmouth (on the coast east of the moor) to Haytor, following the route originally designed to transport Dartmoor granite down to the docks.

The Two Moors Way runs from Ivybridge, on the southern edge of the moor, 103 miles (166km) north to Lynmouth in Exmoor. The *Two Moors Way* (£3.70 including postage) is available from the Ramblers' Association (☎ 020-7339 8500), 1 Wandsworth Rd, London SW8 2XX.

The Dartmoor Way is a 90-mile (145km) circular route round the outer edge of the national park, stretching from Buckfastleigh in the south, up through Moretonhampstead, north-west to Okehampton and south through Lydford to Tavistock. Pick up the *Escapes on Foot* leaflet from TICs for more details.

The Tarka Trail (see Exmoor National Park in the Wessex chapter) circles north Devon and links with Dartmoor, south of Okehampton.

It's always wise to carry a map, compass and rain gear since the weather can change very quickly and not all walks are

DEVON & CORNWALL

waymarked. OS Outdoor Leisure Map No 28 shows the park boundaries as well as the MOD firing-range areas.

CYCLING

Cycling is only allowed on public roads, byways open to all traffic, public bridlepaths and Forestry Commission roads.

The Plym Valley Cycle Way follows the disused Great Western Railway between Plymouth and Yelverton, on the edge of the moor. Other cycle routes include a 3-mile (5km) stretch of forest track from Bellever; the 26-mile (42km) West Devon Tavistock Cycle Route, along country lanes; and the 30-mile (48km) Sticklepath Cycle Route, also along lanes. The Dartmoor Way (see the previous Walking section) is also the name of a 90-mile (145km) circular cycling route round the edge of the moor, including Okehampton, Chagford, Buckfastleigh, Princetown and Tavistock. Pick up the *Escapes by Bike* leaflet from TICs for more details.

Bikes can be hired in Exeter (see Getting Around in the earlier Exeter section), and also from Tavistock Cycles (☎ 01822-617630), Paddons Row, Brook St, Tavistock, and Mountain Bike Hire (☎ 01364-631505), beside the pub in Poundsgate.

OTHER ACTIVITIES
Pony Trekking & Horse Riding

There are riding stables all over the park. Lydford House Riding Stables (☎ 01822-820321), Lydford House Hotel, Lydford, charges from £10/18 for one/two hours.

Near Widecombe-in-the-Moor, Babery Farm Stables (☎ 01364-631296) offers half-day rides and pub rides (three hours riding, one hour in the pub) from £20.

Climbing

Rock climbing can only be done where there is a right of access – on private land you must ask the owner's permission first. Popular climbing areas are at Haytor, owned by the NPA, and the Dewerstone near Shaugh Prior, owned by the NT. Groups need to book in advance. Ask at a visitor centre or TIC for details.

Fishing

You can fish on certain stretches of the East and West Dart (with a Duchy of Cornwall permit), and on the Rivers Tavy, Walkham, Plym, Meavy and Teign, as well as on seven reservoirs in the park. A permit is usually needed; phone the Environment Agency (☎ 01392-444000, fisheries department) for information.

PLACES TO STAY & EAT

If you're backpacking, the authorities and owners of unenclosed moorland don't usually object to campers who keep to a simple code: don't camp on moorland enclosed by walls or within sight of roads or houses; don't stay on one site for more than two nights; don't light fires; and leave the site as you found it. With large tents, however, you can only camp in designated camping grounds. There are several camping and caravan parks around the area, many on farms.

There are youth hostels at Postbridge (Bellever), bang in the middle of the moor, and at Steps Bridge, near Dunsford (between Moretonhampstead and Exeter), as well as at Okehampton, Exeter, Plymouth and Dartington.

There are youth hostel camping barns at Manaton (Great Houndtor), Postbridge (Runnage), Sticklepath (Sticklepath Halt), Cornwood (Watercombe), Bridestowe (Fox & Hounds) and Lopwell (Lopwell Dam). These are 'stone tents' that sleep up to about 15 people. Cooking and shower facilities and a wood burner are provided. You sleep on the floor or on a bunk bed; bring your own bedding. Charges are from £3.75 per person. For more information and centralised booking, phone ☎ 01200-428366. There are also some independent barns and bunkhouses.

The larger towns on the edge of the park (such as Okehampton and Tavistock) all have plentiful supplies of B&B and hotel accommodation. Within the park itself, accommodation is sometimes limited, so it is wise to book ahead in summer. There are also several comfortable country-house hotels in the park.

The Dartmoor Tourist Association (☎ 01822-890567) produces an accommodation guide; there's a service charge of £2.75 if you book rooms through any of the national park's visitor centres. TICs have details of farm B&Bs.

The old pubs and inns provide a focus for local communities and are sometimes the only places you can get anything to eat in small villages.

GETTING THERE & AWAY

Exeter and Plymouth are the best starting points for the park, but Exeter has the better transport connections to the rest of the country. Totnes, Exeter, Newton Abbot and Plymouth all have train services to London, Bristol and the Midlands. National Express has coach services between London and Exeter, Newton Abbot, Okehampton and Plymouth.

There's a Sunday service between Okehampton and Exeter (40 minutes). The only other train stations near the park are at Ivybridge and South Brent on the Exeter/Plymouth line. Ivybridge is useful for people who want to walk the Two Moors Way. The return fare from Exeter is £9.60 (40 minutes).

The most useful bus that actually crosses Dartmoor is DevonBus No 82, the Transmoor Link, running between Exeter and Plymouth via Steps Bridge, Moretonhampstead, Warren House Inn, Postbridge, Princetown, Sharpitor and Yelverton. It runs daily from late May to late September, but on Saturday and Sunday only the rest of the year. For more information phone ☎ 01752-402060.

DevonBus No 359 runs regularly from Exeter through Steps Bridge to Moretonhampstead (Monday to Saturday). The No 173 is a regular service through Drewsteignton to Chagford. The No X39 (operated by Stagecoach Devon) goes along the A38 between Plymouth and Exeter, stopping at Buckfastleigh and Ashburton. First Western National bus Nos 83 and 84 operate from Plymouth via Yelverton to Tavistock every 20 minutes.

The summer-only Dartmoor Sunday Rover ticket (£5/3) entitles you to unlimited travel on most bus routes within the area and to rail travel on the Tamar Valley Line from Plymouth to Gunnislake.

On Sunday in summer, DevonBus No 187 loops round from Plymouth, through Gunnislake, Tavistock, Mary Tavy and Lydford, to Okehampton; you could do part of this journey on the Tamar Valley Line or even by boat (see Plymouth earlier in the chapter).

Since buses are infrequent and subject to change, it's best to work out what you want to do and then contact the Devon County Public Transport Help Line (☎ 01392-382800, 8.30 am to 5 pm weekdays). They can send you the *Dartmoor Public Transport Guide* with suggestions for walks connected to bus routes.

GETTING AROUND

The Dartmoor Rover (☎ 01392-383800) is a popular Sunday-only ticket that costs £5/3. It covers all services on Dartmoor as well as those to Exeter, Plymouth and other centres.

PRINCETOWN
☎ 01822

At an altitude of 420m, Princetown is England's highest settlement, as well as being Dartmoor's largest community. With the infamous prison located here, it's not Dartmoor's most beautiful town, but it is close to excellent walking country.

The town was created in the late 18th century by Thomas Tyrwhitt, who wanted to convert large areas of the moorland into arable farmland. When this failed, he came up with another plan to create employment for the people who had moved into the area, suggesting that a prison be built to house prisoners of war. In the first half of the 19th century, the prison housed both French and American POWs. When hostilities with those countries ceased, British prisoners were transferred there. There are now about 600 inmates in the maximum-security prison.

The High Moorland Visitors Centre (☎ 890414) was once the Duchy Hotel. It has displays on Dartmoor and an information centre that stocks maps. Donations of 25p are appreciated.

Places to Stay & Eat

The *Plume of Feathers Inn (☎ 890240, fax 890780, The Square)*, Princetown's oldest building, is a pub near the visitor centre, with all sorts of cheap accommodation. The camping ground (from £2.50 per person) is open year-round, the camping barn costs from £3.50 and there's bunkhouse accommodation from £5.50 (including rooms for two and four people). You need to book well in advance. There's also B&B from £15.50 per person.

Across from the visitor centre, the *Railway Inn (☎/fax 890232, e railwayinnpl20@ aol.com, Two Bridges Rd)* is a pub offering B&B for £20/35 (singles/doubles).

Getting There & Away

DevonBus No 82 (the Transmoor Link) runs here from both Exeter and Plymouth (both 50 minutes). It runs daily from late May to late September, but on Saturday and Sunday only the rest of the year. Bus No 98 links Princetown with Tavistock.

POSTBRIDGE
☎ 01822

Right in the middle of the park, Postbridge makes a popular starting point for local walks. It's known for its granite clapper bridge, which crosses the East Dart. Clapper bridges date from the 13th century and are made of large slabs of granite supported at each end by short, stone pillars.

Local legend tells of the landlady of an 18th-century temperance house who took to serving alcohol – much to the horror of her husband who poured it into the river. A dog that paused to quench its thirst was driven mad by the potent mixture and died. Its tormented spirit is still said to haunt Dartmoor – this is one version of the story that gave Conan Doyle the idea for *The Hound of the Baskervilles*.

From April to October, there's an NPA visitor centre in the car park. There's also a post office and shop in the village.

Places to Stay & Eat

The *Bellever Youth Hostel (☎ 880207, fax 880302)* is a mile south of Postbridge on the western bank of the river. It's open daily in July and August, daily except Sunday April to June, and Tuesday to Saturday in September and October. A bed costs £9.80/6.75 for adults/juniors.

Runnage Farm (☎ 880222) has a camping barn – the nightly charge is £4 per person. To reach the farm, take the small road off the B3212 just before you reach Postbridge coming from the Moretonhampstead side.

A former coaching inn, the *East Dart Hotel (☎ 880213, fax 880313)* is 100m from the clapper bridge and has B&B from £26/48.

The *Lydgate House Hotel (☎ 880209, fax 880202)* is a quarter of a mile from the village centre in an attractive, sheltered valley. It's an excellent place to stay, with beds from £30.50 per person; a good three-course dinner is also available.

Headland Warren Farm (☎ 880206) is an ancient farm on the moor, 5 miles (8km) from Postbridge and convenient for walkers as it's by the Two Moors Way. B&B costs from £25 per person for the first night, £20 per additional night.

Two miles (3km) north-east of Postbridge, along the B3212 towards Moretonhampstead, is the *Warren House Inn (☎ 880208)*. It's a good place to come after a walk, and you can warm yourself by a fire they claim has been burning continuously since 1845. There's real ale, and pub food including home-made rabbit pie.

Getting There & Away

DevonBus No 82 (the Transmoor Link) runs through Postbridge between Plymouth and Exeter.

BUCKFASTLEIGH
☎ 01364

On the park's south-eastern edge, Buckfastleigh is an old market town near the valley of the upper Dart. Nearby is Buckfast Abbey, Britain's last working monastery.

For centuries, Buckfastleigh was a centre

for the manufacture of woollen cloth. Above the town is the parish church, and in the graveyard in a heavy tomb, built by villagers to ensure he could not come back to life, lies Sir Richard Cabell, the most hated man in Dartmoor. When this evil landowner died in the 17th century, it's said that black phantom hounds were seen speeding across the moor to howl beside his grave.

Buckfast Abbey

Buckfast Abbey, 2 miles (3km) north of Buckfastleigh, was founded in 1016 and flourished in the Middle Ages through its involvement in the wool trade. With the dissolution of the monasteries in 1539, it was abandoned. In 1806, the ruins were levelled and a mock-Gothic mansion erected; the house was purchased in 1882 by a group of exiled French Benedictine monks. The abbey church was built between 1906 and 1932 by the monks, and an impressive, modern, stained-glass figure of Christ dominates the eastern end chapel.

The abbey (☎ 645500) is a popular tourist attraction. Entry is free. The monks augment their income by keeping bees and making tonic wine.

Places to Stay & Eat

About 3 miles (5km) north-west of Buckfastleigh, in Holne, there's budget accommodation in a stone barn at *Holne Court Farm* (☎ 631271) from £3.50 per person.

Furzeleigh Mill Hotel (☎/fax 643476, e furzeleigh@eclipse.co.uk, Old Ashburton Rd, Dartbridge) has singles/doubles for £33.75/57.50.

Dartbridge Inn (☎ 642214, fax 643839, Totnes Rd) offers B&B from £45/60 for a room with bath.

The restaurant and tearooms at *Buckfast Abbey* are good for lunch or tea.

Getting There & Away

First Western National bus No 88 runs between Plymouth and Buckfastleigh three times a day, Monday to Saturday (one hour). It continues to Newton Abbot (30 minutes). Bus No X39 runs from Buckfastleigh to Exeter (one hour).

The South Devon Railway (☎ 642336) links Totnes and Buckfastleigh (25 minutes) every 1½ hours with a 7-mile (11km) journey beside the River Dart on a steam-operated branch line. The adult/child return fare is £6.50/4.00. The service operates daily mid-May to September. Trains run on Wednesday, Saturday and Sunday in April and October; and on Tuesday, Wednesday, Saturday and Sunday in May.

WIDECOMBE-IN-THE-MOOR
☎ 01364

Uncle Tom Cobbleigh and all still flock to this popular little Dartmoor village, and not just on the second Tuesday of September when the fair, commemorated in the folk song *Widdicombe Fair*, still takes place. The fine 14th-century granite church, known as the Cathedral in the Moor, was funded by prosperous tin miners and has a 37m-high tower.

There's a Visitor Information Point at Sexton's Cottage, adjacent to the Church House. Built in 1537 as a brewhouse, the Church House is now the village hall.

Five miles (8km) from Ashburton is *Cockingford Farm Campsite* (☎ 621258), 1½ miles (2.5km) south of Widecombe. It costs £2.50 per person to camp here.

Dartmoor Expedition Centre (☎ 621249) is about 1½ miles (2.5km) outside Widecombe. There are 32 beds in two old barn bunkhouses starting from £7 (including bedding), but it is best to book well in advance during the high season.

On the edge of Widecombe, there's B&B at *Sheena Tower* (☎ 621308) for £17 per person, or £18 in a room with a bath.

MORETONHAMPSTEAD
☎ 01647

Moretonhampstead is a pleasant market town at the junction of the B3212 and the A382, 14 miles (22km) north-east of Princetown.

Just inside the park's north-eastern border, 4½ miles (7km) east of Moretonhampstead, along the B3212, is *Steps Bridge Youth Hostel* (☎ 252435, fax 252948). Beds

Letterboxing

If you see a walker acting furtively and slipping an old Tupperware box into a tree stump or under a rock, you may be witnessing someone in the act of letterboxing. This wacky pastime has more than 10,000 addicts and involves a never-ending treasure hunt for several thousand 'letterboxes' hidden all over Dartmoor.

In 1844 the railway line reached Exeter, and Dartmoor started to receive visitors, for whom this was a chance to imagine themselves as great explorers. One guide for these intrepid Victorian gentlefolk was James Perrott of Chagford. In 1854, he had the idea of getting them to leave their calling cards in a glass jar at Cranmere Pool – the most remote part of the moor accessible at that time. It was not until 1938 that the second 'box' was established, and the idea really took off after WWII. Originally, people left their card with a stamped addressed envelope in a box and if someone else found it they would send it back.

There are now about 4000 boxes, each with a visitors' book for you to sign and a stamp and ink pad (if they haven't been stolen) to stamp your record book. Although it's technically illegal to leave a 'letterbox' – because in effect you're leaving rubbish on the moor without the landowner's permission – as long as the boxes are unobtrusive, most landowners tolerate them. Now there are even German, French, Belgian and American boxes, not to mention 'mobile boxes', odd characters who wander the moors waiting for a fellow letterboxer to approach them with the words 'Are you a travelling stamp?'!

Once you've collected 100 stamps, you can apply to join the '100 Club', whereupon you'll be sent a clue book with map references for other boxes. Contact Godfrey Swinscow (☎ 015488-21325), Cross Farm, Diptford, Totnes, Devon TQ9 7NU, for more information.

Inevitably, as more people go letterboxing, a downside (other than general nerdiness) has been identified. A code of conduct now prohibits letterboxers from disturbing rocks, vegetation or archaeological sites in their zeal. Even so, there have been mutterings about the disturbance caused to nesting golden plovers and ring ouzels.

JANE SMITH

cost £7.20/4.95 for adults/juniors and it's open daily April to September. It's a 10-mile (16km) walk from here to the hostel in Exeter.

You can camp at *Clifford Bridge Park* (☎ 24226, fax 24116, Clifford) from Easter to September, from £3.50 for a person and tent. The site is by the River Teign, 3 miles (5km) west of Steps Bridge, and there's even a heated swimming pool.

Moretonhampstead is on the Transmoor Link bus route (DevonBus No 82).

CHAGFORD
☎ 01647 • pop 1500

This delightful country town by the River Teign makes a more attractive base for the park's north-eastern area than Moretonhampstead. In the 14th century, it was a Stannary town, where the tin mined on the moor was weighed and checked, and the taxes paid. It's an excellent walking and riding centre.

Places to Stay & Eat
Glendarah House (☎ 433270, fax 433483, **e** enquiries@glendarah-house.co.uk, Lower St) has rooms with bath for £26 per person, including the single room. *Lawn House* (☎ 433329, Mill St) offers B&B from £20 per person.

Opposite the church, the pretty *Three Crowns Hotel* (☎ 433444, fax 433117, High St) dates from the 13th century. Beds here cost from £32.50.

Evelyn Waugh stayed at *Easton Court Hotel* (☎ 433469, fax 433654, **e** stay@ easton.co.uk) while writing *Brideshead Revisited*. It's a lovely thatched 15th-century building, just off the A382 at Easton, on the opposite side from the turning to Chagford. B&B costs from £78/136.

Getting There & Away
From Exeter (one hour), bus No 173 goes through Moretonhampstead. From Okehampton, bus No 179 provides a daily service.

CASTLE DROGO
Just over a mile from Chagford and run by the National Trust (NT), **Castle Drogo**

(☎ 01647-433306) is a medieval-looking granite fortification that was designed by Sir Edwin Lutyens, and constructed between 1910 and 1930 for a wealthy businessman, Julius Drewe, who died shortly after moving in. It overlooks the wooded gorge of the River Teign with fine views of Dartmoor. Once you've been round what must be the most comfortable castle in the kingdom, you can rent croquet sets for a game on the lawn. It opens 11 am to 5.30 pm daily except Friday, April to October; entry costs £5.40/2.70.

OKEHAMPTON
☎ 01837 • pop 4200

Bustling Okehampton is divided from Dartmoor by the A30, the main route to Cornwall. Some of the wildest walking on the moor lies directly south of Okehampton, but since it's within the MOD's firing area, you should phone in advance to check that it's open. The part of the park to the south of Belstone is also good, and is outside the MOD zone.

The TIC (☎ 53020, fax 55225, **e** oketic@ visit.org.uk) at 3 West St is by the museum. It's open 10 am to 5.30 pm daily. Look out for the free, comprehensive *Okehampton Area Discovery Map*.

Things to See & Do
Okehampton has several attractions to delay hikers. The ruined **castle** (☎ 52844; EH) above the town charges £2.30/1.20 for admission. It is open 10 am to 6 pm daily, April to September, and to 5 pm in October.

The **Museum of Dartmoor Life** (☎ 52295) on West St has interactive exhibits, displays and photographs about the moor and its inhabitants. It's open 10 am to 5 pm daily, June to September; phone ahead for other opening times. Entry costs £2/1.

It's a pleasant three- to four-hour walk along part of the Tarka Trail from Okehampton to Sticklepath, where the **Finch Foundry** (☎ 840046; NT) has three working water wheels. It's open 11 am to 5.30 pm daily except Tuesday, April to October; entry costs £2.80. The *Two Museums Walk* leaflet, available from the TIC, has information on this hike. Bus No X10 (no service on Sunday) links Sticklepath with Okehampton and Exeter.

Places to Stay & Eat

Yertiz Caravan & Camping Park (☎ 52281, e yertiz@dial.pipex.com) is three-quarters of a mile (1km) east of Okehampton on the B3260. The charge is £4 for one person and a tent in the summer, £5 for two.

Olditch Caravan & Camping Park (☎ 840734) is on the edge of Sticklepath, 4 miles (6km) east of Okehampton, and charges £5 for one person and a tent year-round, and from £7 to £9 for two depending on the season.

Okehampton Youth Hostel (☎ 53916, fax 53965, e okehampton@yha.org.uk, Klondyke Rd) is in a newly converted goods shed at the train station. It has 64 beds in small dormitories and the nightly charge is £10.85/7.40. There's also a kitchen and laundry.

The *Fountain Hotel (☎ 53900, Fore St)* charges £16 per person for rooms with shared bathrooms.

Heathfield House (☎ 54211, Klondyke Rd) offers B&B in en-suite singles/doubles for £35/50.

The *Coffee Pot (14 St James St)* does teas and lunches.

Getting There & Away

Okehampton is 23 miles (37km) west of Exeter, 29 miles (46km) north of Plymouth. There's a daily National Express bus from London via Heathrow.

First Western National bus Nos X9 (hourly) and X10 run between Exeter and Okehampton (one hour). There are fewer buses on Sunday. Bus No 86 runs every two hours between Plymouth and Okehampton (1½ hours).

The Bike Bus connects with Okehampton; see Getting Around at the beginning of the Devon section.

In 1997, Okehampton train station was reopened and there's now a Sunday service to Exeter (40 minutes).

The Tarka Trail passes through Okehampton and Sticklepath on a 180-mile (288km) route through north Devon.

LYDFORD
☎ 01822 • pop 1800

Lydford is a picturesque village on the western edge of the moor. There's evidence of both Celtic and Saxon settlements here, and the ruins of a Norman castle. It was also the administrative centre for the Stannary towns (see the earlier Chagford section). Courts trying recalcitrant tin workers were particularly harsh; it was said that perpetrators of offences punishable by death would be hanged in the morning and tried in the afternoon.

Lydford is best known, however, for the 1½-mile (2.5km) **Lydford Gorge**. An attractive but strenuous riverside walk leads to the 28m-high White Lady waterfall and past a series of bubbling whirlpools, including the Devil's Cauldron. It's owned by the NT and is open 10 am to 5.30 pm daily, April to October (10.30 am to 3 pm in winter); entry costs £3.50.

There's a riding stable in the grounds of the Lydford House Hotel (see the following Places to Stay & Eat section), which charges £10/18 for one/two hours.

Widgery Cross

From Lydford it's possible to take a 5-mile (8km) walk to one of Dartmoor's best-known monuments, the Widgery Cross on Brat Tor, which was erected for Queen Victoria's golden jubilee in 1887. The scenery along the way is classic Dartmoor, rugged and windswept.

Places to Stay & Eat

The 16th-century *Castle Inn (☎ 820242, fax 820454, e castleinnlyd@aol.com)* was featured in *The Hound of the Baskervilles* and is right beside the castle and half a mile from Lydford Gorge. It's a good place to stay, as well as a truly atmospheric place for a pint and an excellent place to eat, offering seasonal dishes such as venison and juniper-berry pie and wild boar, as well as bar snacks that are considerably better than the average pub's. B&B costs £35/62 for a single/double with bathroom.

At *Lydford House Hotel (☎ 820347, e relax@lydfordhouse.co.uk)*, on the edge of the village, B&B starts at £39.50 per person.

By the main entrance to the White Lady waterfall, **Manor Farm Tea Rooms** is a good place to go for cream teas and light lunches.

Getting There & Away

First Western National bus No 86 crosses Devon from Barnstaple to Plymouth via Lydford, every two hours, Monday to Saturday. DevonBus No 187 operates between Exeter and Tavistock via Lydford six times a day on Sunday in the summer.

TAVISTOCK
☎ 01822 • pop 8700

Tavistock's glory days were in the late 19th century, when it was one of the world's largest copper producers. Until the dissolution of the monasteries, Tavistock Abbey controlled huge areas of Devon and Cornwall; only slight ruins remain.

On the town's outskirts is a **statue of Sir Francis Drake**, who was born in Crowndale, just over a mile from Tavistock. Buckland Abbey, the mansion he bought after circumnavigating the globe, can be visited (see the Around Plymouth section earlier in the chapter).

There's a TIC (☎ 612938, fax 610909, e tavistocktic@visit.org.uk) on Bedford Square, underneath the town hall. It is open 9.30 am to 5.30 pm daily, Easter to October (to 4.30 pm and closed on Sunday in winter).

Bikes can be rented from Tavistock Cycles (☎ 617630) at Paddons Row, Brook St, opposite Goodes Café, for £12 for the first day, £8 for each subsequent day.

Getting There & Away

First Western National bus Nos 83, 84 and 86 run up to three times an hour between Tavistock and Plymouth (50 minutes). The Sunday No 187 bus service links Okehampton and Tavistock with Gunnislake train station for connections to Plymouth. Sunday service No 23 links Tavistock to Exeter via Princetown, Postbridge, Chagford and Moretonhampstead.

Cornwall

Clinging on to the south-western corner of England, Cornwall has been described as a beautiful frame around a plain picture. The metaphor is a good one, for the coastline is wonderful – a mix of high, jagged cliffs and pretty inlets sheltering little fishing villages. The interior, however, is much less attractive, even desolate in places.

Cornwall likes to emphasise its separateness from the rest of the country and the county's cultural roots are indeed different, for this was the Celts' last bastion in England after they were driven back by the Saxons. The Cornish language survived until the late 18th century. Efforts are being made to revive it, but Cornish mainly lives on in place names – every other village name seems to be prefixed with *tre-* (meaning settlement).

In the 18th and 19th centuries Cornwall dominated the world's tin and copper markets. Most of the mines have now closed but the industrial past has left scars on the landscape. China clay is still mined around St Austell but tourism has largely replaced the mining industry. Unfortunately, though, it offers mainly low-paid, seasonal work and Cornwall is now one of the poorest parts of England.

In summer, Cornwall's seaside resorts are packed but don't let this put you off, since the holiday-makers tend to congregate around the larger resorts of Bude, Newquay, Falmouth, Penzance and St Ives, and even at the height of the season some of these towns are still worth a visit. Newquay is England's surfing capital, and one can't fail to be impressed by beautiful St Ives.

Some people find Cornwall disappointing. You'll certainly feel cheated if you expect the extreme south-western tip of the island to be full of untouched, undiscovered hideaways. Thanks to thoughtless development, Land's End – a veritable icon – has been reduced to a commercially minded tourist trap, and inland much of the peninsula has been devastated by generations of mining. However, many of the coastal

When Did Cornish Die?

A Celtic language akin to Welsh, Cornish was spoken west of the Tamar until the 19th century. Written evidence indicates that it was still widely spoken at the time of the Reformation but after a Cornish rising against the English in 1548, the language was suppressed. By the 17th century only a few people living in the peninsula's remote western reaches still spoke nothing but Cornish.

Towards the end of the 18th century linguistic scholars foresaw the death of Cornish and fanned out round the peninsula in search of people who still spoke it. One such scholar, Daines Barrington, visited Mousehole in 1768 and recorded an elderly woman called Dolly Pentreath abusing him in Cornish for presuming she couldn't speak her own language.

Dolly died in 1769 and has gone down in history as the last native speaker of Cornish. However, Barrington knew of other people who continued to speak it into the 1790s, and an 1891 tombstone in Zennor commemorates one John Davey as 'the last to possess any traditional considerable knowledge of the Cornish language'.

Recently efforts have been made to revive the language. Unfortunately there are now three conflicting varieties of 'Cornish' – Unified, Phonemic and Traditional – and there's no sign that it can regain its former importance.

villages retain their charm, especially out of season.

Cornish churches lack the splendour of those in Devon and Somerset and even Truro cathedral is a relative newcomer. However, the names of the churches speak loudly of Cornwall's separateness. Where else would you cross paths with St Non, St Cleer, St Keyne and the many others whose lives are detailed in *The Cornish Saints* by Peter Berresford Ellis?

Cornwall is great at self-promotion and seems to produce more brochures and leaflets than the rest of England put together. Some are useful, but many are little more than advertising and you'd do better to ignore them. For general information on the Internet, take a look at www.cornwall-online.co.uk.

WALKING & CYCLING

The Cornwall Coast Path is the most scenic section of the long-distance South West Coast Path. The Saints' Way is a 26-mile (42km) waymarked trail that runs from Fowey across the centre of the county to Padstow on the northern coast. It was used in the 6th century as a route for Celtic missionaries between Brittany (France) and Wales or Ireland, saving a long sea trip around Land's End.

Youth hostels are well placed along the coast for stops on a walk or cycle ride around Cornwall. In the north, the 17-mile (27km) Camel Trail follows an old railway line from just outside Padstow through Bodmin and along the River Camel.

GETTING AROUND

For information about buses, there's an efficient helpline (☎ 01872-322142). The main bus operator is First Western National (☎ 01209-719988); an Explorer ticket gives a day's travel on its network for £6/3.50 and there are several other passes.

For rail information, phone ☎ 0845 748 4950. The main rail route from London terminates in Penzance, but there are branch lines to St Ives, Falmouth, Newquay and Looe. A Cornish Rail Rover ticket costs £40.50 (£33 in winter) for eight days' travel in a 15-day period, or £25.50 (£18 in winter) for three days in seven. Plymouth is included in this price.

The TICs stock the county council's annual *Public Transport Timetable* (with a map), listing all the air, bus, rail and ferry options in Cornwall.

SOUTH-EAST CORNWALL

Southern Cornwall is very different in character from the wild northern and central parts of the county. It's a more gentle area of farms, wooded inlets and pretty fishing villages – some overrun by tourists in the summer but worth visiting at quieter times.

The mild climate favours many plants that thrive nowhere else in England and there are several gardens worth visiting, with rhododendron trees growing almost as tall as in their natural Himalayan habitat. TICs stock the free *Gardens of Cornwall* map and guide with full details.

One of the most famous gardens in the area is **Heligan** (☎ 01726-845100), 4 miles (6km) south of St Austell, which was lost to the world for many years before an ambitious restoration was begun a decade ago. It is open 10 am to 6 pm daily (to 5 pm in winter; last admission 1½ hours before). Entry costs £5.50/2.50.

Trelissick Garden (☎ 01872-862090; NT) is 4 miles (6km) south of Truro, beside King Harry's Ferry. It is open 10.30 am to 5.30 pm (from 12.30 pm on Sunday, to 5 pm in winter). It is closed November to mid-February. Entry costs £4.30/2.10.

Cotehele

Seven miles (11km) south-west of Tavistock, on the western bank of the Tamar, the river that forms the boundary between Devon and Cornwall, the Cotehele estate comprises a small stately home with a splendid garden, a quay with a museum, and a working water mill.

One of Britain's finest Tudor manor houses, Cotehele has been the Edgcumbe family home for centuries. The hall is particularly impressive, and many rooms are hung with great tapestries; because of their fragility, there's no electric lighting. Visitor numbers are limited, so you may have to wait. Pick up a timed ticket when you arrive.

Cotehele Quay is part of the National Maritime Museum and has a small museum with displays on local boat-building and river trade. The *Shamrock*, the last surviving River Tamar barge, is moored nearby.

Cotehele Mill is a 15-minute walk away and can be seen in operation; there's also an adjoining cider press.

The Garden of Eden

One of England's most spectacular botanical gardens is located in a disused china-clay pit near St Austell. The Eden Project (☎ 01726-811911) is a scientific foundation (online at www.edenproject.com) that aims to highlight the human race's dependency on plant life.

Masterminded by Tim Smit, the man responsible for the gardens at Heligan, the project comprises a vast geodesic dome structure 1km long and 60m high. It is heated to 35°C and filled with 10,000 species of plant from around the world. The structure was designed by Nicholas Grimshaw, architect of the Eurostar terminal at Waterloo International. Trees such as teak and mahogany will have enough space to grow to their full size, although this will take up to 50 years.

The Eden Project should be fully open by the time you read this, and although the plants may not have had time to grow much by then, the structure is sure to impress. Opening hours are 10 am to 6 pm daily (last admission 5 pm).

The estate (☎ 01579-351346; NT) is open 11 am to 5.30 pm daily except Friday, April to October; entry costs ·£6/3, or £3.20/1.60 for the garden and mill only. You can get here by bus from Tavistock to Calstock, a mile from Cotehele, on First Western National bus No 79.

East & West Looe
☎ 01503

A bridge connects these twin towns, on either side of their river. They make up the county's second-largest fishing port, the place to come if you're into shark fishing.

East Looe is the main part of the town, with narrow streets and little cottages; the wide, sandy beach is to the east. There are boat trips from the quay to tiny Looe Island, a nature reserve, and to Fowey and Polperro.

The TIC (☎ 262072, fax 265426) in the Guildhall on Fore St is open 10 am to 5 pm Monday to Saturday (closed for lunch on

DEVON & CORNWALL

Friday and Saturday), and 2 to 5 pm on Sunday, Easter to September.

Shark Fishing If you like the idea of trying this, contact the Tackle Shop (☎ 265444) for details of day trips (around £25, depending on numbers and the quarry).

Oceana This exhibit in the South-East Cornwall Discovery Centre (☎ 262777), Millpool, West Looe, gives an interactive insight into the Cornish coastline. It is open 10 am to 4 pm (to 6 pm in summer) Monday to Friday, and 11 am to 3 pm on Sunday, March to December. It is also open on Saturday afternoon in summer and entry is free.

Walking An excellent 5-mile (8km) walk links Looe to the nearby village of Polperro via beaches, cliffs and the old smuggling village of Talland. You should allow around two hours; buses connect the villages every day in summer.

Getting There & Away Trains travel the scenic Looe Valley Line from Liskeard (30 minutes, £2.40), on the main London-Penzance line, at least six times a day.

Polperro

Much prettier than Looe, Polperro is an ancient fishing village around a tiny harbour, best approached along the coastal path from Looe or Talland. Unfortunately, it's very popular with day-trippers so you should try to visit in the evening or during low season.

The village is a picturesque jumble of narrow lanes and fishing cottages, and was once heavily involved in pilchard fishing by day and smuggling by night – there's a small smuggling museum in the centre. There's no TIC.

Fowey

☎ 01726 • pop 2600

Unspoiled Fowey (pronounced foy) lies on the estuary of the same name. The town has a long maritime history and in the 14th century conducted its own raids on coastal

towns in France and Spain. This led to the Spanish launching an attack on Fowey in 1380. The town later prospered by shipping Cornish china clay, which it still does, although yachts mainly fill its harbour today. Although there are no specific sights (apart from a small museum and aquarium), Fowey is a good base for walks around the estuary.

The TIC (☎/fax 833616, e foweytic@visit.org.uk) is in the post office at 4 Custom House Hill. It is open 9 am to 5.30 pm Monday to Friday, 9.30 am to 4 pm on Saturday and 10 am to 5 pm on Sunday.

Walking Fowey is at the southern end of the Saints' Way (see Walking & Cycling Routes under Cornwall earlier in the chapter). Ferries operate across the river to Bodinnick to access the 4-mile (6km) Hall Walk to Polruan. You can catch a ferry from Polruan back to Fowey.

Places to Stay & Eat Four miles (6km) north of Fowey, in Golant, is the *Golant Youth Hostel* (☎ 833507, fax 832947, e golant@yha.org.uk, Penquite House). It's open daily, February to September, and daily except Friday, October to early November. The nightly charge is £10.85/7.40 for adults/juniors. First Western National bus No 24 from St Austell to Fowey stops in Castle Dore, 1½ miles (2.5km) from the hostel.

In Bodinnick, the *Old Ferry Inn* (☎ 870237, fax 870116) has pleasant rooms with river views and bathrooms; charges range from £20 to £35 per person for B&B.

The delightful *Marina Hotel* (☎ 833315, fax 832779, e marina.hotel@dial.pipex.com) is right on the waterfront on the Esplanade. Rooms with sea view, bathroom and breakfast are £84. It also has an excellent restaurant.

Recommended pubs in Fowey include the big *King of Prussia*, on the quay, and the *Ship* and the *Lugger*, back from the water on Lostwithiel St.

Getting There & Away There are frequent departures from St Austell (50 min-

A magnet for walkers, the South West Coast Path offers mile after mile of stunning views.

A (one-time) smugglers' haven: the ancient fishing village of Polperro, Cornwall

Walking to St Michael's Mount, Cornwall

Wholesome fare: traditional Cornish pasties

LARGE TRADITIONAL P
16oz
Chuck Steak (17.5%), Turnip, Po
and onion in Flakey Pastry

Summer in Torquay (Fawlty Towers not shown)

A stormy day on the Cornish coast

utes) on First Western National bus No 24, which also passes Par, the closest train station to Fowey.

Lanhydrock House
Amid parkland above the River Fowey, 2½ miles (4km) south-east of Bodmin, this grand country house (☎ 01208-73320; NT) was rebuilt after a fire in 1881. The impressive gallery, with its fine plaster ceiling, survived the fire, but the house is mainly of interest for its portrayal of the type of *Upstairs Downstairs* divisions of life in Victorian England. The kitchens are particularly interesting, complete with all the gadgets that were mod cons 100 years ago.

The house is open 11 am to 5 pm daily except Monday, April to October. Entry costs £6.60, or £3.60 for the garden and grounds only. The garden is open year-round and entry is free in winter. Bodmin Parkway train station is 1¾ miles (3km) from the house.

Charlestown
☎ 01726
Despite its size, St Austell is not particularly exciting and most people will pass straight through. However, it's worth making a detour south to visit the port of Charlestown, a marvellously picturesque village and harbour built by Charles Rashleigh between 1790 and 1815. On the best days the harbour will be filled with magnificent square-rigged ships. However, these are sometimes away taking part in worldwide film assignments. The film of Daphne Du Maurier's *Frenchman's Creek* was partly shot here in 1998.

The **Shipwreck and Heritage Centre** (☎ 69897) has exhibits on many aspects of Cornish sea life, with animated models illustrating 19th-century village life. It's open 10 am to 5 pm daily, March to October (to 6 pm in high season) and costs £4.45 (free for children). The attached *Bosun's Bistro* does teas, coffees and lunches.

T'Gallants (☎ 70203) is a fine Georgian house with B&B singles/doubles for £30/45. Alternatively, the *Pier House Hotel* (☎ 67955, fax 69246), right on the quayside, charges £40/63 including breakfast.

TRURO
☎ 01872 • pop 18,000
Truro was once the distribution centre for Cornwall's tin mines and its prosperity dates from this time. Lemon St has some fine Georgian architecture, and the cathedral is worth a visit if you're passing through, even though it only dates back to the late 19th century. Built in neo-Gothic style, it was the first new cathedral to be built in England since St Paul's in London.

The TIC (☎ 274555) on Boscawen St is in the municipal buildings near the covered market. It's open 9 am to 5.30 pm Monday to Friday, to 5 pm on Saturday, and is closed on Sunday.

The **Royal Cornwall Museum** (☎ 272205) on River St has exhibits on Cornish history, archaeology and mineralogy. It's open 10 am to 5 pm daily except Sunday and costs £3 (free for children).

Places to Stay & Eat
There's no hostel but cheap B&Bs can be found near the train station on Treyew Rd. *The Fieldings* (☎/fax 262783, e ukrab@ globalnet.co.uk, 35 Treyew Rd) charges from £18/32 for singles/doubles.

The *Royal Hotel* (☎ 270345, fax 242453, e reception@royalhotelcornwall.co.uk, Lemon St) is a fine Georgian building convenient for the cathedral. Rooms cost from £35/55 at the weekend, a heftier £67/90 in the week.

Charlotte's Tea House in the old coinage hall building is an institution among Truro folk, popular for its delicious cakes and period costume.

The *Old Ale House* is a decent pub on Quay St. Pub grub includes generously sized sandwiches and main dishes served in a choice of portions.

Saffron (Key St) is a bistro-style restaurant with a good-looking menu.

Getting There & Away
Truro is 246 miles (394km) from London, 26 miles (42km) from St Ives and 18 miles (29km) from Newquay.

National Express (☎ 0870 580 8080) has buses to numerous destinations, sometimes requiring a change at Plymouth. There are four direct daily services to London (6½ hours, £27.50), St Ives (one hour, £3) and Penzance (1½ hours, £3.25). First Western National (☎ 01209-719988) covers many local bus routes.

Truro is on the main rail line between London Paddington (4¾ hours, £53) and Penzance (45 minutes, £6.10). There's a branch line from here to Falmouth (20 minutes, £2.60) and to St Ives (£6, change at St Erth).

ROSELAND PENINSULA

South of Truro, the Roseland Peninsula gets its intriguing name not from flowers (although there are plenty of them) but from the Cornish word *ros*, meaning promontory. Villages worth visiting include **Portloe**, a wreckers' hang-out on the South West Coast Path, and **Veryan**, which is awash with daffodils in spring.

St Mawes has a castle (☎ 01326-270526; EH) that was built by Henry VIII to guard the Fal estuary. It's open 10 am to 6 pm daily, April to September, 10 am to 5 pm daily in October, and 10 am to 4 pm (closed for lunch) Friday to Tuesday in winter. Entry costs £2.50/1.30.

St Just-in-Roseland boasts what must be one of the most beautiful churchyards in the country, full of flowers and tumbling down to a creek with boats and wading birds.

SOUTH-WEST CORNWALL
Falmouth
☎ 01326 • pop 18,000

Falmouth has a refreshingly 'real' feel, as it has not sold its soul to tourism – sole perhaps, but not its soul. It has an interesting castle with a youth hostel in its grounds. There are also several worthwhile boat trips from the pier. The art college here attracts students from all over the country, so Falmouth feels a little more sophisticated than many other parts of the county.

The port came to prominence in the 17th century as the terminal for the Post Office Packet boats, which took mail to America. The dockyard is still important for ship repairs and building.

The TIC (☎ 312300, fax 313457) at 28 Killigrew St is by the bus station in the town centre. It is open 9.30 am to 5.30 pm Monday to Saturday, and 10 am to 4 pm on Sunday. Try the Web site at www.falmouth-sw -cornwall.co.uk.

Things to See On the end of the promontory is **Pendennis Castle** (☎ 316594; EH), which is Cornwall's largest, worth visiting for the displays inside and the superb views from the ramparts. It was an operations centre in WWII. It is open 10 am to 6 pm daily (to 4 pm in winter); entry costs £3.80/1.90.

Boat Trips From the Prince of Wales pier, there are ferries to St Mawes. In summer, boat trips run to Truro (£5 return) and there are excursions to a 500-year-old smuggler's cottage upriver. For information, contact Enterprise Boats (☎ 374241) or St Mawes Ferries (☎ 313201).

Places to Stay & Eat At the castle, three-quarters of a mile (1km) from Falmouth train station is *Pendennis Castle Youth Hostel (☎ 311435, fax 315473)*. It's open daily mid-February to September, and Tuesday to Saturday in October and November; beds cost £9.80/6.75 for adults/juniors.

There are B&Bs and small hotels lining Melvill Rd, convenient for the train station. Try *Ivanhoe (☎ 319083, 7 Melvill Rd)* with B&B for £22 per person. *Tudor Court Hotel (☎/fax 312807,* e *peter@tudor -court-hotel.freeserve.co.uk, 55 Melvill Rd)* charges from £21 per person.

De Wynn's, in pretty, cobbled Church St, is a 19th-century tearoom with dainty cakes and seafood pies. Nearby *Citrus* is a bright cafe-gallery with tasty snacks, opposite the parish church.

No 33 (☎ 211914, High St) is a very popular restaurant with lots of fancy fish on the menu, but anticipate paying £20 per head.

The only fix you'll get at *Smack Alley's* is late-night fish and chips – it's open until at least 1 am most nights. It's opposite Finn M'Couls on Market Strand.

Good local pubs include the *Mason*

Arms (Killigrew St) for St Austell ales and the *Chain Locker*, on the waterfront, for that genuine fisherman feel.

Finn M'Couls (Market Strand) is one of those 'Irish pubs' but is certainly the most popular in town and full of art students. Nearby *Paradox* is Falmouth's nightclub and the paradox is clear – it's a cracking little club in a tiny little town. There's no entry charge and drinks are cheap. Most nights it is open until 1 am or later.

Getting There & Away National Express has buses from Falmouth to numerous destinations, including London (6¼ hours, £27.50) and Penzance (one hour). For St Ives, you must change at Penzance or Truro; this also applies to Newquay (except on Sunday).

Falmouth is at the end of the branch line from Truro (20 minutes, £2.60). In summer, you can also travel by boat to Truro (one hour, £2.50); at low tide, when boats can only get as far as Malpas, there's a bus service to Truro.

The Lizard

The Lizard peninsula is England's most southerly point and is also good walking country since much of the coastline is owned by the NT. The mild climate guarantees that several rare plant species flourish, and there are stretches of unusual red-green serpentine rock. For more information on this unique area, visit www.lizardpenisula.co.uk.

In 1901 Marconi transmitted the first transatlantic radio signals from Poldhu. The Lizard is still associated with telecommunications and the centre is dominated by the white satellite dishes of the Goonhilly Earth Station (☎ 0800 679593). Overseas visitors can rest assured that every call home they make goes through Goonhilly, the largest satellite station on earth. It is open to visitors 10 am to 5 pm daily and admission costs £4/2.50.

Across the north of the Lizard is the beautiful **River Helford**, lined with ancient oak trees and hidden inlets – the perfect smugglers' hideaway. Secluded **French-man's Creek**, the inspiration for Daphne Du Maurier's romantic novel of the same name, can be reached on foot from the car park in **Helford** village.

On the northern bank of the river is **Trebah Garden** (☎ 01326-250448), dramatically situated in a steep ravine filled with giant rhododendrons, huge Brazilian rhubarb plants and Monterey pines. It's open 10.30 am to 5 pm daily; entry costs £3.50/1.75.

Near Gweek, at the western end of the river, is the **National Seal Sanctuary** (☎ 01326-221361), which treats injured marine animals and is open to visitors 9 am to 4 pm daily; entry costs £6.50/4.25.

Cadgwith is the quintessential Cornish fishing village, with thatched, whitewashed cottages and a small harbour. *Cadgwith Cove Inn* serves delicious crab sandwiches. **Lizard Point** is a 3½-mile (6km) walk along the South West Coast Path from here.

It's about 8 miles (13km) in the opposite direction to the *Coverack Youth Hostel (☎ 01326-280687, fax 280119, Parc Behan, School Hill, Coverack)*, which is open April to October and costs £9.80/6.75 for adults/juniors.

Helston The gateway to the Lizard, on 8 May Helston is also home to the **Furry Dance**, when the town takes to the streets for a dance that has pagan roots. **Helston Folk Museum** (Church St) has informative displays on the history of these strange happenings.

The TIC (☎ 01326-565431, fax 572803, e info@helstontic.demon.co.uk) at 79 Meneage St is open 10 am to 1 pm and 2 to 4.30 pm Monday to Saturday during summer. In winter, it is closed on Monday and Saturday afternoon and all day Wednesday.

The *Blue Anchor (Coinagehall St)* is a 15th-century tavern that brews its own ales (Spingo) with local well-water. It's more like a home than a pub and is worth a detour.

Getting There & Away The Lizard's transportation hub is Helston, which is served by Truronian buses (☎ 01872-273453). Bus No T1 runs from Truro via

Helston to the village of Lizard (1½ hours, £2.75); there are four buses daily, Monday to Saturday. It's just under a mile from the village to Lizard Point.

St Michael's Mount

In 1070 St Michael's Mount (☎ 01736-710507; NT) was granted to the same monks who built Mont St Michel off the Normandy coast. It was an important place of medieval pilgrimage. Since 1659 the St Aubyn family has lived in the ex-priory buildings.

Though not in such a dramatic location as the French version, St Michael's Mount is still impressive. High tide cuts the island off from the mainland, and the priory buildings rise loftily above the crags.

At low tide, you can walk across from Marazion, but at high tide in summer a ferry (☎ 01736-710265; £1/50p) lets you save your legs for the stiff climb up to the house. The best way to appreciate the house is to use the Walkman tour. The house is open 10.30 am to 5.30 pm (last admission 4.45 pm) Monday to Friday, April to October; entry costs £4.40/2.20. Phone for other opening times.

The *Fire Engine Inn* in Marazion has great views across to the mount for those feeling thirsty.

First Western National bus No 2 passes Marazion as it travels from Penzance to Falmouth.

PENZANCE
☎ 01736 • pop 19,000

For train travellers from London, Penzance is the end of the line. It is a pleasant if uninspiring small town in which to linger (and shop) alongside a curious mix of seaside holiday-makers, locals, artists and New Age hippies. Newlyn, out on the western edge of Penzance, was the centre of a community of artists in the late 19th century.

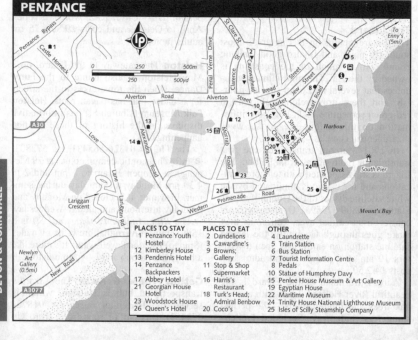

PENZANCE

PLACES TO STAY	PLACES TO EAT	OTHER
1 Penzance Youth Hostel	2 Dandelions	4 Laundrette
12 Kimberley House	3 Cawardine's	5 Train Station
13 Pendennis Hotel	9 Browns; Gallery	6 Bus Station
14 Penzance Backpackers	11 Stop & Shop Supermarket	7 Tourist Information Centre
17 Abbey Hotel	16 Harris's Restaurant	8 Pedals
21 Georgian House Hotel	18 Turk's Head; Admiral Benbow	10 Statue of Humphrey Davy
23 Woodstock House	20 Coco's	15 Penlee House Museum & Art Gallery
26 Queen's Hotel		19 Egyptian House
		22 Maritime Museum
		24 Trinity House National Lighthouse Museum
		25 Isles of Scilly Steamship Company

Orientation & Information

The harbour spreads along Mount's Bay, with the ferry terminal to the east, the train and bus stations just to the north and the main beach to the south. The town itself spreads uphill towards the domed Lloyds TSB building that has a statue of local man Humphrey Davy, inventor of the miner's lamp, in front. Part of the building now houses craft shops.

The TIC (☎ 362207) on Station Rd is in the car park by the train and bus stations. It is open 9 am to 5 pm Monday to Friday, 9 am to 4 pm on Saturday and 10 am to 1 pm on Sunday. There's a laundrette nearby, opposite the train station.

Pedals (☎ 360600, e pedalsbikes@ hotmail.com, Wharf Rd) hires out mountain bikes (£10.50 for 24 hours, including helmet and tool kit).

Things to See & Do

Penzance has some attractive Georgian and Regency houses in the older part of town around Chapel St, where you'll also find the exuberant early-19th-century **Egyptian House**. Farther down towards the harbour, by the Georgian House Hotel, is the **Maritime Museum** (☎ 368890), which opens 10 am to 5 pm Monday to Saturday.

Trinity House National Lighthouse Museum (☎ 360077), Wharf Rd, relates the history of the lighthouses that have helped keep ships off this dangerous coast. It's open 10.30 am to 4.30 pm daily, March to October; entry costs £2.50/1.50.

Some examples of the Newlyn school of painting are exhibited in the **Penlee House Museum & Art Gallery** (☎ 363625) on Morrab Rd. It's open daily except Sunday; entry costs £2 (free on Saturday). The **Newlyn Art Gallery** (☎ 363715) in New Rd features contemporary art only and is open 10 am to 5 pm Monday to Saturday; entry is free.

Walking

The 25-mile (40km) section of the South West Coast Path around Land's End between Penzance and St Ives is one of the most scenic parts of the whole route. The walk can be broken at the youth hostel at St Just-in-Penwith (see later in the chapter), and there are also plenty of cheap farm B&Bs along the way.

Places to Stay

The **Penzance Youth Hostel** (☎ 362666, fax 362663, e penzance@yha.org.uk, Castle Horneck, Alverton) is an 18th-century mansion on the outskirts of town. Bus Nos 5B, 6B and 10B run from the train station to the Pirate Inn, from where it's a 500m walk. The nightly charge is £10.85/7.40 for adults/juniors.

The friendly **Penzance Backpackers** (☎ 363836, e pzbackpack@ndirect.co.uk, The Blue Dolphin, Alexandra Rd) has 30 bunk beds for £10 each (£9 for additional night), and there are two double rooms at £22. There's also a kitchen and washing machine (£3). It's all spotlessly clean – 'the bed sheets smell great,' wrote one reader! Bus Nos 1A, 5A and 6A go there from the TIC or train station.

Penzance has lots of B&Bs and hotels, especially along the Promenade, Alexandra Rd and Morrab Rd. **Pendennis Hotel** (☎/fax 363823, Alexandra Rd) charges from £15 to £21, depending on the season. **Kimberley House** (☎ 362727, 10 Morrab Rd) has rooms from £16 to £18 per person. Friendly **Woodstock House** (☎/fax 369049, e woodstocp@aol.com, 29 Morrab Rd) charges from £18 to £24.50 per person for rooms with a shower or bath.

In the older part of Penzance, the **Georgian House Hotel** (☎/fax 365664, 20 Chapel St) has beds from £21 with a bathroom, from £18 without.

The noble **Queen's Hotel** (☎ 362371, fax 350033, e enquiries@queens-hotel.co .uk) on the Promenade charges £54 per person with a sea view, £48 without.

The **Abbey Hotel** (☎ 366906, fax 351163, e glyn@abbeyhotel.zetnet.co.uk, Abbey St) is owned by sixties supermodel Jean Shrimpton, and is the top place to stay. Singles/doubles cost from £75/100.

Alternatively you could rent a floor of the **Egyptian House** (see Things to See & Do) from the Landmark Trust (☎ 01628-825925).

Costs range from around £123 for a four-day winter break to £419 for a week in summer.

There's excellent farmhouse accommodation at *Enny's* (☎ *740262, fax 740055,* e *ennys@zetnet.co.uk, St Hilary*) about 5 miles (8km) east of Penzance. Rooms have a bath or shower and B&B costs from £30 to £40 per person. There's a heated swimming pool.

Places to Eat

Cawardine's (10 Causewayhead) has a range of speciality teas and coffees, and does good-value meals. A crispy-bacon and melted-cheese baguette or cod and chips cost around £3 to £4. *Dandelions*, nearby at No 39a, is a small vegetarian cafe and takeaway with fine fare. *Browns* in Bread St is similar, and also has an art gallery attached.

Chapel St has several cheap places to eat as well as two well-known pubs: the kitsch *Admiral Benbow* (☎ *363448)* and the *Turk's Head* (☎ *363093)*, which has a good reputation for its food. Across the road from these is *Coco's* (☎ *363540)*, a flamboyant Spanish restaurant with an 'if you can't beat them, join them' response to the tourism challenge from Costa del Sol.

For a splurge, head for *Harris's Restaurant* (☎ *364408, 46 New St)*, in a narrow, cobbled street opposite Lloyds TSB. Smoked salmon cornets with fresh crab or venison should sate the appetite.

Getting There & Away

Penzance is 281 miles (450km) from London, 9 miles (14km) from Land's End and 8 miles (13km) from St Ives.

There are five buses a day from Penzance to London (five hours, £27.50) and Heathrow airport, one direct bus a day to Exeter (five hours, £16) and three buses a day to Bristol via Truro and Plymouth. There are at least two services an hour to St Ives (20 minutes). There are daily First Western National services to Land's End (one hour) on bus No 1, hourly during the week, less frequently at the weekend.

The train offers an enjoyable if pricey way to get to Penzance from London. There are five trains a day from London Paddington (five hours, £54). There are frequent trains from Penzance to St Ives between 7 am and 8 pm (20 minutes, £2.90).

For ferries to the Isles of Scilly, see later in the chapter.

WEST CORNWALL
Mousehole
☎ 01736

Mousehole (pronounced mowsel) is another idyllic fishing village that's well worth seeing outside the high season. It was once a pilchard-fishing port, and tiny cottages cluster round the edge of the harbour. Like St Ives, the village attracts artists and there are several interesting craft shops.

The *Old Coastguard Hotel* (☎ *731222, fax 731720,* e *bookings@oldcoastguard hotel.co.uk)* has singles/doubles from £32/36 per person.

The excellent *Ship* (☎ *731234)* does good seafood and fresh fish; beds cost £35/50, the views are free. *Annie's Eating House* serves delicious teas with lashings of clotted cream.

Infrequent buses run the 20-minute journey to Penzance.

Minack Theatre

Surely the world's most spectacularly located open-air theatre, Minack perches on the edge of the cliffs overlooking the bay. It was built by Rowena Cade, an indomitable local woman who did much of the construction herself, until her death in 1983. The idea came to her when her family provided the local theatre group with an open-air venue for a production of *The Tempest*. The place was so well suited that annual performances were instituted.

There are performances at the theatre (☎ 01736-810181) from late May to late September; tickets cost £6.50/3.25. Seats are hard, so bring a cushion or hire one there. There's also an exhibition centre open 9.30 am to 5.30 pm daily, Easter to September (it's sometimes closed if there's a performance on); tickets are £2.50 (free for children).

The theatre is south of the village of Porthcurno, 3 miles (5km) from Land's End and 9 miles (14km) from Penzance. First Western National bus No 1 from Penzance to Land's End stops at Porthcurno, Monday to Saturday.

Land's End
☎ 01736

The coast on either side of Land's End is some of the most spectacular in England, but the theme-park development (☎ 01736-871501) is a Thatcherite monument to the triumph of crass commerce over culture. Peter de Savary was the man who outbid the NT to inflict this monstrosity on Britain's most westerly point. He's long since cashed in and moved on but the damage is done.

There are five separate exhibits to visit, including the *Air-Sea Rescue* film in a moving cinema, and Miles of Memories, which commemorates the various methods of transport used to get between Land's End and John o'Groats. Entry to each costs £2.50/1.50 or there are all-inclusive tickets for £8. Tackiness aside, the complex does provide 250 jobs in an unemployment black spot. If you walk from Sennen Cove, about a mile to the north, you escape the car-parking charge (£3).

In summer, the place is extremely crowded, with stands selling everything from burgers to strawberry-and-clotted-cream crepes. To have your picture taken by the signboard listing your home town and its distance from this famous spot costs £5.

Places to Stay & Eat The *Land's End Youth Hostel* is near St Just-in-Penwith (see the next section), 5 miles (8km) north of Land's End.

The comfortable *Land's End Hotel* (☎ 871844, fax 871599, e info@landsend-landmark.co.uk), the 'first and last hotel in England', is part of the complex and is the

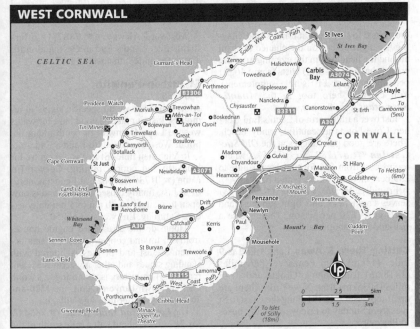

WEST CORNWALL

End-to-End Records

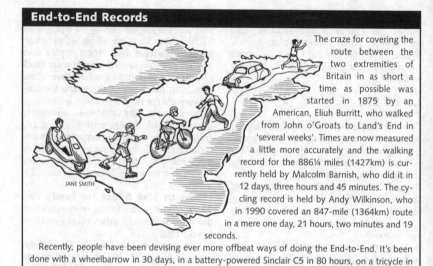

The craze for covering the route between the two extremities of Britain in as short a time as possible was started in 1875 by an American, Eliuh Burritt, who walked from John o'Groats to Land's End in 'several weeks'. Times are now measured a little more accurately and the walking record for the 886¼ miles (1427km) is currently held by Malcolm Barnish, who did it in 12 days, three hours and 45 minutes. The cycling record is held by Andy Wilkinson, who in 1990 covered an 847-mile (1364km) route in a mere one day, 21 hours, two minutes and 19 seconds.

JANE SMITH

Recently, people have been devising ever more offbeat ways of doing the End-to-End. It's been done with a wheelbarrow in 30 days, in a battery-powered Sinclair C5 in 80 hours, on a tricycle in 5½ days and on roller skates in 9½ days. In 1990, it was run in 26 days and seven hours by Arvind Pandya – no great record in itself, apart from the fact that he was running backwards!

only place to stay right at Land's End. Staying the night gives you the chance to stroll around the headland in the evening after the crowds have gone. B&B costs from £46 per person (there's a £10 single supplement). You can eat here too, in the *Atlantic Restaurant* or in the bar.

Just over a mile north of Land's End, Sennen Cove boasts a beautiful, sandy beach. There are good pub lunches at the *Old Success Inn* (☎ *871232, fax 871457)*, where rooms cost from £26 for the cheap single to £39 per person in rooms with a bath.

Friendly *Myrtle Cottage* (☎ *871698)* serves cream teas and light lunches, and B&B costs £20 per person. There's also a fish-and-chip shop nearby.

Getting There & Away Land's End is 9 miles (14km) from Penzance, 886 miles (1418km) from John o'Groats and 3147 miles (5035km) from New York. There are open-top buses (No 15) along the coast to St Ives from Sunday to Friday, and daily buses to Penzance.

Westward Airways (☎ 788771) offers flights over Land's End in Cessna aircraft; a seven-minute hop costs £19/17.

St Just-in-Penwith
☎ 01736

Although there are no specific sights in remote St Just, it makes a good base for walks west to Cape Cornwall or south along the South West Coast Path to Land's End.

In Victorian times St Just was a centre for local tin and copper mining. **Geevor Tin Mine** (☎ 01736-788662), at Pendeen, north of St Just, finally closed in 1990 and is now open to visitors 10.30 am to 5 pm daily except Saturday. Entry costs £5/2.50.

Alongside the abandoned engine houses from old tin and copper mines, the area between St Just and St Ives is littered with standing stones and other mysterious ancient remains. If prehistory is your thing, it's worth tracking down **Lanyon Quoit**, the **Mên-an-Tol** and **Chysauster Iron Age Village**.

The *Land's End Youth Hostel* (☎ *788437, fax 787337)* is about half a mile south of the

DEVON & CORNWALL

village at Letcha Vean. It's open daily from April to October; phone for other times. The nightly charge is £9.80/6.75 for adults/ juniors.

You can stay at the independent *Whitesands Lodge* (☎ 871776, ⓔ *whitesan@ globalnet.co.uk*) backpackers hostel in Sennen village; dorm beds cost £10, and there's also a double for £29. Breakfast costs £4.

At *Kelynack Caravan & Camping Park* (☎ 787633), a mile south of St Just, a bed in the bunk barn costs £6, but book ahead in summer as there is room for just eight. Camping costs £3 per person.

At Botallack, north of St Just, there's comfortable farmhouse accommodation at *Manor Farm* (☎ 788525). B&B costs £23 per person.

Zennor

There's a superb 6-mile (10km) walk along the South West Coast Path between St Ives and the little village of Zennor, where DH Lawrence wrote part of *Women in Love*. The interesting church has a mermaid carved on one of its bench ends, and there's a small museum.

There are 32 beds costing £10 per head at the *Old Chapel Backpackers Hostel* (☎/*fax* 01736-798307), plus full breakfasts for £4 and continental breakfasts for £2.50. The *Tinners Arms* serves good food and cream teas.

At least four buses a day run to Zennor from St Ives. A taxi from St Ives should cost about £5.

ST IVES
☎ 01736 • pop 9500

St Ives is the ideal to which other seaside towns can only aspire. The omnipresent sea, the extraordinary brightness of the light, the harbour, the beautiful sandy beaches, the narrow alleyways, steep slopes and hidden corners are all captivating. Artists have been coming here since Turner visited in 1811, and in 1993 Tate St Ives, a branch of the London art gallery, opened here. These days countless galleries and craft shops line its narrow streets.

Unfortunately in summer St Ives is un-believably crowded – avoid July and August weekends.

Orientation

The area above St Ives' harbour is very built up and merges into Carbis Bay. Fore St, the main shopping street, is set back from the wharf and crammed with eating places. The north-facing section of the town, overlooking Porthmeor Beach, comprises Tate St Ives and many guesthouses. The train station is by Porthminster Beach, with the bus station nearby, up Station Hill.

Information

The TIC (☎ 796297, fax 798309) in the Guildhall on Street-an-Pol is open 9 am to 5.30 pm Monday to Saturday and, in summer, 10 am to 1 pm on Sunday.

In summer, a Park & Ride service operates from the Park Ave car park above the town.

Windansea (☎ 794830) on Fore St rents out wet suits and 7-foot boards (£5 per day).

Tate St Ives

Opened in 1993 in a £3 million building designed by Evans and Shalev (architects of the award-winning Truro Law Courts), Tate St Ives (☎ 796226) is a showcase for the St Ives school of art. The impressive building replaced an old gasworks, and has wide central windows framing the surfing scene on Porthmeor Beach below. The collection is small and exclusive, with works by Ben Nicholson, Barbara Hepworth, Naum Gabo, Terry Frost and other local artists.

The gallery is open 10.30 am to 5.30 pm Tuesday to Sunday all year, and daily in July and August. Entry costs £3.95, or you can buy a £6.50 ticket that also includes admission to the Barbara Hepworth Museum. The cafe on the roof is almost as popular as the gallery itself.

Barbara Hepworth Museum

Barbara Hepworth was one of the 20th century's greatest sculptors. In the 1930s, with Henry Moore and Ben Nicholson (her then-husband), she was part of the leading group of artists with an interest in abstraction. While Moore's sculpture remained close to

DEVON & CORNWALL

the human form, Hepworth avoided representational works. She moved to Cornwall in 1939 and lived here from 1949 until her death in a fire in 1975.

The museum (☎ 796226) is on Ayr Lane, across town from Tate St Ives, and has the same opening times and the same charges. The beautiful garden forms a perfect backdrop for some of Hepworth's larger works.

Leach Pottery

Bernard Leach travelled to Japan in 1909 to teach etching, but soon discovered a talent for pottery. When he returned in 1920, his Japanese-inspired work had a profound influence on British ceramics. He died in 1979 but the pottery he established is still used by several craftspeople (including his wife, Janet, until her death in 1997).

The showroom (☎ 796398) is open 10 am to 5 pm weekdays and on Saturday in summer. It's along the road to Zennor, on the outskirts of St Ives.

Beaches

There are several excellent, clean beaches in the area. **Porthmeor** is the surfing beach to the north of the town, below Tate St Ives.

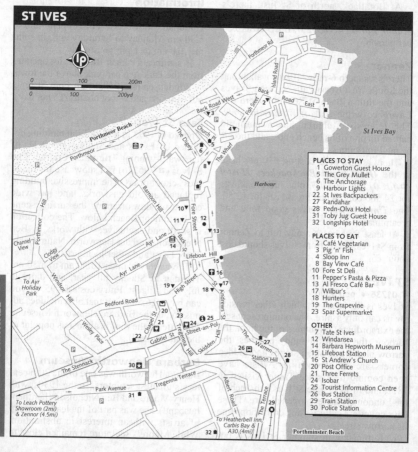

ST IVES

St Ives Bay

Porthmeor Beach

Harbour

Porthminster Beach

PLACES TO STAY
1 Gowerton Guest House
5 The Grey Mullet
6 The Anchorage
9 Harbour Lights
22 St Ives Backpackers
27 Kandahar
28 Pedn-Olva Hotel
31 Toby Jug Guest House
32 Longships Hotel

PLACES TO EAT
2 Café Vegetarian
3 Pig 'n' Fish
4 Sloop Inn
8 Bay View Café
10 Fore St Deli
11 Pepper's Pasta & Pizza
13 Al Fresco Café Bar
17 Wilbur's
18 Hunters
19 The Grapevine
23 Spar Supermarket

OTHER
7 Tate St Ives
12 Windansea
14 Barbara Hepworth Museum
15 Lifeboat Station
16 St Andrew's Church
20 Post Office
21 Three Ferrets
24 Isobar
25 Tourist Information Centre
26 Bus Station
29 Train Station
30 Police Station

To Ayr Holiday Park

To Leach Pottery Showroom (2mi) & Zennor (4.5mi)

To Heatherbell Inn, Carbis Bay & A30 (4mi)

DEVON & CORNWALL

Just to the east is the tiny, sandy cove of **Porthgwidden**, with a car park nearby.

There are sandy areas in the sheltered harbour, but most families head south to **Porthminster**, which has half a mile of sand and a convenient car park. **Carbis Bay**, to the south-east, is also good for children. **Porth Kidney Sands**, the next beach along, is only safe for swimming if you stay between the flags. It's dangerous to swim in the Hayle estuary.

Places to Stay

Camping There's no camp site by the beach, but *Ayr Holiday Park (☎ 795855, fax 798797, e andy@ayr-holiday-park .demon.co.uk)* is only half a mile to the west in Higher Ayr. It costs £12.30 for a tent.

Hostels At the *St Ives Backpackers (☎ 799444, e st-ivesbackpackers@dial .pipex.com, Lower Stennack)*, a converted chapel with a range of excellent facilities, beds cost £12 per night, or £8 out of season.

Two miles (3km) out of town in the Carbis Bay area is *Heatherbell Inn (☎ 298604, Longstone Hill)*, a pub with dorm beds available for £10. It's not far to the bar and there is a National Express stop nearby.

B&Bs & Hotels The main road into St Ives from Penzance, above Carbis Bay, is lined with B&Bs in the £15 to £18 bracket, but the closer you are to the town centre the better.

The *Toby Jug Guesthouse (☎ 794250, 1 Park Ave)*, convenient for the bus station, is good value with B&B for £15 per person. There are 10 rooms, each with a toby jug as a teapot.

On Sea View Place, in an excellent location right by the sea, is *Gowerton (☎ 796805, 6 Sea View Place)*, offering pleasant enough rooms for £17 per person.

The *Grey Mullet (☎ 796635, 2 Bunkers Hill)* is an excellent guesthouse in the old part of town, close to the harbour. Rooms cost from £20 to £24 per person, with a bath. Opposite is an attractive cottage called *The Anchorage (☎/fax 797135, 5 Bunkers*

Hill) with rooms from £20 per person. They can do a vegie breakfast.

Harbour Lights (☎/fax 795525, Court Cocking) is right in the centre. B&B costs around £21 per person in summer.

There are a few rooms available at the *Sloop Inn (☎ 796584, fax 793322, e sloop@ connexions.co.uk, The Wharf)* by the harbour, although this location could be noisy in summer. B&B costs from £34 per person.

Kandahar (☎ 796183, e cortina@21 .com, 11 The Warren) is right on the rocks by the water. It charges £21 to £28 per person. It's ideally located for the bus and train stations, but closes mid-November to mid-February.

Nearby is the more upmarket *Pedn-Olva Hotel (☎ 0796222, fax 797710, Porthminster Beach)*, which has a similar waterside location. Beds cost from £45 for B&B to £60 for half-board and there's a small swimming pool and sun deck.

To the south, overlooking Porthminster Beach, is the comfortable *Longships Hotel (☎ 798180, fax 798180, Talland Rd)*, where rooms with sea views and bathrooms cost from £27 per person.

Places to Eat

Fish and chips is an obvious choice and a favourite with local seagulls, who have learned to dive-bomb anyone eating outdoors. It's fun to watch – less fun if it's your grub they're making off with.

The *Café Vegetarian* is a small vegie restaurant just off Back Rd East with an impressive array of wholesome dishes.

The *Fore St Deli* is a useful stop for self-caterers, full of goodies for a picnic on the beach. For a pizza, *Pepper's Pasta & Pizza* just off Fore St is good.

Hunters (☎ 797074, St Andrews St) is a seafood and game restaurant that the local crowd likes. Nearby is *Wilbur's (☎ 796663)*, serving lobster and local fish. *The Grapevine (☎ 794030)* on nearby High St is an informal bistro with speciality seafood and a basement bar.

Best of the pubs is the 14th-century *Sloop Inn* next to the harbour where the bar is hung with paintings by local artists. Its seafood is very popular; fresh fish (cod, sole, plaice) costs £6 to £9.

There are several other places to eat along the Wharf, including the *Bay View Café*, unsurprisingly offering a view of the bay. A place to be seen in St Ives is the Italian *Alfresco Café Bar* (☎ 793737), also on the Wharf, offering a Mediterranean-style menu.

The top place to eat is the *Pig 'n' Fish* (☎ 794204, Norway Lane), renowned for its seafood. Main dishes range from about £11 to £17, with turbot, monkfish, bass, red mullet and mussels usually featuring on the menu.

Entertainment

Isobar, on Tregenna Hill, is a cafe-bar with a nightclub open until 1 am. This is about as happening as St Ives gets.

For a no-nonsense local pub, try the *Three Ferrets*, where you can even bring along your own food.

Getting There & Away

St Ives is 8 miles (13km) from Penzance and 277 miles (443km) from London. National Express (☎ 0870 580 8080) has three buses a day to London (7½ hours, £27.50). There are also buses to Newquay (1¼ hours), Truro (one hour) and Plymouth (three hours). For Exeter, you must change at Plymouth.

There's a three-times-daily bus service from St Ives to Land's End via Zennor, St Just-in-Penwith and Sennen Cove in summer, open-top if the weather allows. An Explorer ticket allowing a day's travel on the route costs £6/3.50. In winter, you must go via Penzance.

St Ives is easily accessible by train from Penzance and London via St Erth.

NEWQUAY
☎ 01637 • pop 14,000

The original Costa del Cornwall, this bold and brash town was drawing them in long before the British learnt to say Torremolinos. Today it is a confused, if enjoyable, blend of surf gossip, family holidays and testosterone-driven lad hell. Until they moved to Seignosse in France in 1998, the World Surfing Championships were held here each summer.

Little that predates the 19th century survives in Newquay, but on the cliff north of Towan Beach stands the whitewashed **Huer's House**, where a watch was kept for approaching pilchard shoals. Every Cornish fishing village had a watchtower like this and the netting operation was directed by the huer. Until they were fished out early in the 20th century, these shoals were enormous – one St Ives catch of 1868 netted a record 16.5 million fish.

Orientation & Information

The TIC (☎ 871345, fax 852025, ⓔ info@ newquay.co.uk) on Marcus Hill is near the bus station in the town centre. It is open 10 am to 5.30 pm daily (to 3.30 pm on Sunday), late May to mid-September. The rest of the year it is open to 4.30 pm (to noon on Saturday, closed on Sunday).

If you don't have a tattoo, at least get yourself a temporary one before hitting the beach. Cut Snake on Fore St has a range and they'll last for up to four weeks.

Cyber Surf (☎ 875497, 2 Broad St) provides Internet access. There's a laundrette on Beach Rd.

Beaches

Fistral Beach, to the west of the town, round Towan Head, is the most famous British surfing beach. There are fast hollow waves, particularly at low tide, and good tubing sections when there's a south-easterly wind.

Watergate Bay is a 2 mile-long sandy beach on the east side of Newquay Bay. At low tide it's a good place to learn to surf. A mile south-west of Newquay, **Crantock** is a small north-west-facing sheltered beach, where the waves are best at mid- to high tide.

Surfing

The surf shops all hire out fibreglass boards and wet suits for around £5 each per day. Try Fistral Surf Co on Beacon Rd, or Tunnel Vision Surf Shop opposite the Somerfield supermarket on Alma Place.

If you don't know how to surf, contact

Offshore Surfing (☎ 877083), on Tolcarne Beach, for an all-inclusive, half-day beginner's lesson (around £20), or Winter Brothers' Surf School (☎ 879696), also £20 a time. The Sunset Surf Shop (☎ 877624) at 106 Fore St also runs in-shop 'soft' tuition.

Places to Stay

Camping There are several large caravan parks/camp sites in the area. *Trenance Caravan & Chalet Park* (☎ 873447, fax 852677) at the southern end of Edgcumbe Ave charges £6.75 per person in summer, £4.75 at other times.

Hostels Several independent hostels cater for surfers in particular. Newcomer *Home Surf Lodge* (☎ 873387, e home.surflodge@ btinternet.com, 18 Tower Rd) is a great place to stay. Facilities include free Internet access and beds start from just £10; book ahead during summer.

The nearest to Fistral Beach is *Fistral Backpackers* (☎ 873146, 18 Headland Rd), with a cinema screen for film buffs. Dorm beds range from £5.50 to £10 (depending on the season) and there are doubles for £18.

In an excellent central position, *Newquay Cornwall Backpackers* (☎ 874668, e stevenpark@aucom.net, Beachfield Ave) overlooks Towan Beach and has dormitory beds for £7 a night or £39 per week.

Newquay International Backpackers (☎ 879366, e backpackers@dial.pipex.com, 69 Tower Rd) has been in the business for years and charges £12 for a dorm bed in peak season, £8 off-season. It has a good range of facilities and can arrange discounts for board hire and entry to the clubs.

Rick's (☎ 851143, 8 Springfield Rd) only rents out by the week in summer (£70 in August). Outside the peak season it's £6 per night or £30 per week.

Matt's Surf Lodge (☎/fax 874651, 110 Mount Wise) has dorm beds for £10 including continental breakfast.

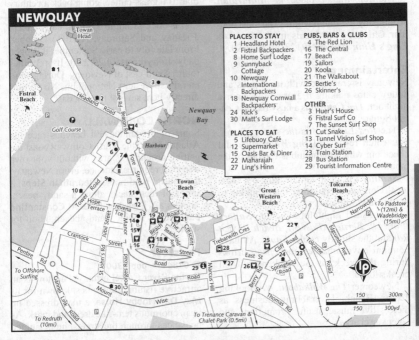

NEWQUAY

PLACES TO STAY
1 Headland Hotel
2 Fistral Backpackers
8 Home Surf Lodge
9 Sunnyback Cottage
10 Newquay International Backpackers
18 Newquay Cornwall Backpackers
24 Rick's
30 Matt's Surf Lodge

PLACES TO EAT
5 Lifebuoy Café
12 Supermarket
15 Oasis Bar & Diner
22 Maharajah
27 Ling's Hinn

PUBS, BARS & CLUBS
4 The Red Lion
16 The Central
17 Beach
19 Sailors
20 Koola
21 The Walkabout
25 Bertie's
26 Skinner's

OTHER
3 Huer's House
6 Fistral Surf Co
7 The Sunset Surf Shop
11 Cut Snake
13 Tunnel Vision Surf Shop
14 Cyber Surf
23 Train Station
28 Bus Station
29 Tourist Information Centre

DEVON & CORNWALL

B&Bs & Hotels Book ahead in July and August! Trebarwith Crescent, Mount Wise, Dane Rd, Tower Rd, Cliff Rd and Narrowcliff are all packed with places to stay. *Sunnyback Cottage* (☎ 879403, e rose@ sunnyback26.freeserve.co.uk, 26 Sydney Rd) is a homely B&B costing £15 per person with full breakfast served throughout the morning.

The huge *Headland Hotel* (☎ 872211, fax 872212, e office@headlandhotel.co .uk) is the best located of Newquay's large hotels. As the name suggests it's out on the headland above Fistral Beach. Rooms cost £76 per person during peak season.

Places to Eat

Lifebuoy Café, at the junction of Fore St and Beacon Rd, does good cheap breakfasts and meals.

Oasis Bar & Diner, Fore St, does all-day breakfasts and burgers, and turns into a bar by night.

The top Indian place is *Maharajah* (☎ 877377, 39 Cliff Rd), with fine views to accompany the fine flavours. The most popular Chinese with locals in the know is *Ling's Hinn* (☎ 877439, 28–30 East St).

Entertainment

Newquay is crammed with local pubs and dodgy clubs making it a great place for a night out. *The Central* is a busy bar on Central Square.

The *Red Lion* pub is *the* surfers' hangout: catch re-runs of *Big Wednesday* and check out which nightclub is flavour of the month.

Skinner's is a pub for checking out some local Cornish beers rather than sticking to the faceless imported stuff.

Established nightclubs include *Sailors* (Fore St), *Bertie's* (East St), *Beach* (Beach Rd) and the slightly cooler *Koola*. All have nominal cover charges and cheap drinks during the week; at the weekend all hell breaks loose.

Newcomer *The Walkabout*, overlooking Towan Beach, is grabbing business as there's live music, useful promotions and no cover charge.

Getting There & Away

Newquay is 32 miles (51km) from St Ives and 252 miles (403km) from London. National Express provides connections via Plymouth to most places in England and has two direct buses daily to London (six hours, £27.50). There are four buses to Plymouth (1¼ hours) and one direct service to Exeter.

There are four trains a day between Newquay and Par, which is on the main London to Penzance line.

AROUND NEWQUAY
Trerice

If the cultural void of Newquay starts to take its toll, take a trip to Trerice (☎ 01637-875404; NT), an Elizabethan manor house without a surfboard or nightclub in sight. Much of the plasterwork is original and there is some fine furniture from the 17th and 18th centuries. Strangest of all is a lawnmower museum in the barn, with more than 100 grass-cutters going back a century or more.

It is open 11 am to 5.30 pm daily except Tuesday and Saturday, April to October. From late July to early September it is open daily. Entry costs £4.20/2.10. It is 3 miles (5km) south-east of Newquay. During summer, First Western National bus No 50 runs directly here several times a day.

NORTH CORNWALL

Some of England's best beaches face the Atlantic along the North Cornwall coast but getting around this area without your own transport requires patience. From Newquay, the coastal road passes **Bedruthan Steps**, a series of rock stacks along a sandy beach. There's a NT teashop here. At **Constantine Bay**, there's a wide, sandy beach, good for surfing.

Padstow
☎ 01841 • pop 2300

On the River Camel estuary, Padstow is an attractive fishing village best known for its **May Day Hobby Horse**, a man dressed up in an enormous tent-like dress and mask. As he dances through the streets, he is taunted by the local women; if he catches one, he pulls her under the tent and pinches her – to ensure future motherhood, of course.

Above the village is **Prideaux Place** (☎ 532411), a lavish manor house built in 1592 by the Prideaux-Brune family and used by the US army during WWII. It's open 1.30 to 5 pm Sunday to Thursday, Easter to September; entry costs £4/1.50.

The poet Sir John Betjeman is buried at St Enodoc Church, across the river and north of **Rock**, a small village that is the posh kids' answer to Newquay during summer. A regular ferry (£1.60 return) runs between Padstow and Rock.

The TIC (☎ 533449, fax 532356, ⓔ padstowtic@visit.org.uk) in Red Brick Building on North Quay is open 9.30 am to 5 pm Monday to Saturday and 10 am to 3.30 pm on Sunday.

Bicycles can be hired from Padstow Cycle Hire (☎ 533533) on South Quay from £5 to £7 a day (weekly discounts are available).

Places to Stay & Eat The nearest budget accommodation is *Treyarnon Bay Youth Hostel (☎/fax 520322, Tregonnan)*, located above a popular surfer's beach about 4½ miles (7km) west of Padstow. Beds cost £9.80/6.75 for adults/juniors. Bus No 55 passes nearby on the B3274.

There are umpteen B&Bs in Padstow. *Althea Library (☎/fax 532717, 27 High St)* is a snug little house with B&B for £26 per person.

For pampering, consider the *Tregea Hotel (☎ 532455, fax 533542, ⓔ tim@ tregea.co.uk, 16 High St)*, which gained the prestigious gold award from the British Tourist Authority and has super rooms for £80.

Padstow has several restaurants worth a gastronomic detour, but the most famous is television chef Rick Stein's *Seafood Restaurant (☎ 532485)* on the harbour front, which serves all manner of fish dishes. Expect to pay at least £30 per head. Rick Stein is now so well known in England that you'll need to book months in advance. When his restaurant is closed on Sunday you can eat bistro-style at *St Petroc's House (☎ 532485, 4 New St)*.

Tintagel
☎ 01840

Tintagel sold out to tourism long ago and has adopted King Arthur and the Knights of the Round Table to fight its corner in the battle for tourists' cash. That said, even the summer crowds and the grossly commercialised village can't entirely destroy the surf-battered grandeur of Tintagel Head. The scanty castle ruins are not King Arthur's castle, since they mainly date from the 13th century, but there's no reason to disbelieve the theory that he was born here in the late 5th century. The ruins (☎ 770328; EH) are open 10 am to 7 pm daily, April to October (to 4 pm in winter); entry costs £2.90/1.50. There are exhilarating walks along the cliffs.

Back in the village, **Tintagel Old Post Office** (☎ 770024; NT) is a higgledy-piggledy 14th-century house that served as a post office in the 19th century. It's open 11 am to 5.30 pm daily, April to October; entry costs £2.20/1.10.

Tintagel TIC (☎ 779084) on Bossiney Rd is open 10 am to 5 pm daily.

Places to Stay The *Tintagel Youth Hostel (☎ 770334, fax 770733, Dunderhole Point)* is in a spectacular setting on the South West Coast Path, three-quarters of a mile (1km) west of the village. It's open daily, April to September; beds cost £9.80/6.75 for adults/juniors.

Cornishman Inn (☎ 770238, fax 770078, ⓔ jeremy@cornishmaninn.freeserve.co.uk) in the centre of Tintagel charges from £25 per head for rooms with a bath. Or if it's kitsch you crave, try *King Arthur's Castle Hotel (☎ 770202, fax 770978)*, a pseudo-castle with rooms from £39 per person, including breakfast.

With a car, you might prefer to follow the signs to Trebarwith to stay in the *Old Mill-floor (☎ 770234)*, a B&B in a delightful setting charging from £18 per person.

Getting There & Away First Western National bus No 122 runs from Wadebridge, and the No X4 comes from Bude. There are occasional buses from Plymouth.

Boscastle
☎ 01840

Nearby Boscastle also draws visitors in the thousands, as it is absurdly picturesque. In particular, hunt out Minster church in a wonderful wooded valley. The harbour wall dates from 1584 and was built on the orders of Sir Richard Grenville, captain of Elizabeth I's ship *The Revenge*.

There's a well-stocked visitor centre in the car park (☎/fax 250010). It is open 10 am to 5 pm daily.

The *Boscastle Harbour Youth Hostel* (☎ 250287, fax 250615) is open mid-April to late September and costs £9.80/6.75. It's perfectly positioned right on the edge of the harbour.

For B&Bs, try *Sunnyside* (☎ 250453) right beside the harbour, with beds from £17 without bath, or £21 with.

For bus information, see the previous Tintagel section.

Bodmin Moor

Cornwall's 'roof' is a high heath pockmarked with bogs and with giant tors like those on Dartmoor rising above the wild landscape – Brown Willy (419m) and Rough Tor (400m) are the highest.

The A30 cuts across the centre of the moor from **Launceston**, which has a castle perched above it like the cherry on a cake (☎ 01566-772365; EH) and a granite church completely covered in carvings. The castle is open 10 am to 6 pm daily, April to September, 10 am to 5 pm daily in October, and 10 am to 1 pm and 2 to 4 pm Friday to Sunday in winter; entry costs £1.80/90p.

At **Bolventor** is *Jamaica Inn* (☎ 01566-86250), made famous by Daphne Du Maurier's novel of the same name. Stop for a drink on a misty winter's night and the place still feels atmospheric. In summer, it's full of day-trippers queuing to view the author's desk and the bizarre Mr Potter's **Museum of Curiosities**, a collection of stuffed kittens and rabbits in the best of Victorian bad taste. Bolventor is a good base for walks on the moor. About a mile to the south is **Dozmary Pool**, said to have been where Arthur's sword, Excalibur, was thrown after his death. It's a 4-mile (6km) walk north-west of Jamaica Inn to Brown Willy.

Bodmin itself lies to the south-west of the moor and the TIC (☎/fax 01208-76616, e bodmintic@visit.org.uk) in Shire House on Mount Folly Square has plenty of leaflets on exploring the moor.

Bodmin has bus connections with St Austell, as well as Bodmin Parkway, a station on the London to Penzance line farther

---

The Daphne Du Maurier Trail

Daphne Du Maurier, author of a number of bestselling thriller romances set in Cornwall, has probably done more to publicise the county than anyone else. For many years she lived on the Fowey estuary, originally in Ferryside (a house in Bodinnick) and later in Menabilly.

Her first big success was *Jamaica Inn*, an entertaining tale of a smuggling ring based at the famous inn. The idea for the story is said to have come when she and a friend got lost in the mists of Bodmin Moor, eventually stumbling upon the inn. The local vicar entertained them with gripping yarns of Cornish smugglers. The Jamaica Inn has a small display about the author. The vicar was from nearby Altarnun, where the church receives a steady flow of Du Maurier fans.

The author's next book was *Rebecca*, written in 1938. Manderley, the house in the book, was based on Menabilly, where the author lived – it's not open to the public. *Frenchman's Creek* was set around the inlet of the same name on the River Helford. Lanhydrock House and Falmouth's Pendennis Castle both feature in *The King's General*.

The West Country Tourist Board produces a useful *Daphne Du Maurier in Cornwall* leaflet. The Daphne Du Maurier Festival of Arts & Literature (☎ 01726-74324) takes place in May.

south. Launceston has bus connections with Plymouth and Bodmin.

Bude
☎ 01288 • pop 2700

Five miles (8km) from Devon, Bude is another resort that attracts both families and surfers. Crooklets Beach is the main surfing area, just north of the town. Nearby Sandymouth is good for beginners, and Duckpool is also popular. Summerleaze Beach, in the centre of Bude, is a family beach. This is part of the so-called Atlantic Heritage Coast; visit www.atlantic-heritage-coast .co.uk on the Web for further details on this and the Bude area.

The Bude Visitor Centre (☎ 354240, fax 355769, budetic@visit.org.uk), The Crescent, is open 9.30 am to 5 pm Monday to Friday and 10 am to 4 pm on Sunday.

Bude is well served by buses, including a daily National Express coach to London (6½ hours, £31).

ISLES OF SCILLY
☎ 01720 • pop 2000

The Isles of Scilly, a group of 140 rocky islands with an extremely mild climate caused by the warm Gulf Stream, are 28 miles (45km) south-west of Land's End and home to plants and trees that grow nowhere else in England. One of the main objectives for visitors is the subtropical garden at Tresco Abbey. Growing flowers for the mainland is an important industry.

Of the islands, St Mary's, Tresco, St Martin's, St Agnes and Bryher are inhabited. St Mary's is the largest (3 miles by 2 miles; 5km by 3.5km) and is home to most of the population. Most of the islands have white, sandy beaches and gin-clear water that attracts divers. The pace of life is slow and gentle – forget any idea of Newquay-style nightlife.

Whatever you do, remember not to make any 'silly' jokes – the locals have heard them all before.

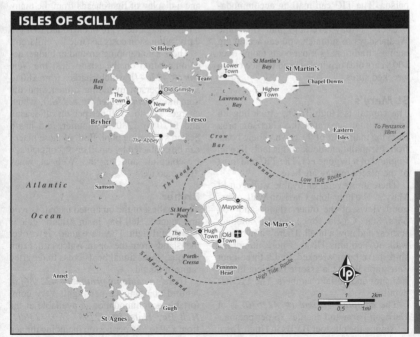

ISLES OF SCILLY

DEVON & CORNWALL

Information

The Isles of Scilly Tourist Board (☎ 422536, fax 422049), Wesleyan Chapel, Porthcressa Bank, is on St Mary's. It is open 8.30 am to 6.30 pm Monday to Thursday, 8.30 am to 5.30 pm on Friday and Saturday, and 10 am to 2 pm on Sunday, May to September. The rest of the year it closes at 5 pm most weekdays, on Saturday afternoon and all day on Sunday. The *Standard Guidebook, Isles of Scilly* is the best in-depth guide to the islands.

For general Internet information on the islands, visit www.scillyonline.co.uk. The TIC's has a Web site at www.simplyscilly.co.uk.

Accommodation should be booked in advance, particularly in summer, and tends to be more expensive than on the mainland. Many places close between November and March.

All the islands except Tresco have camping grounds that charge from £3 to £6 per person. The TIC can mail an accommodation list.

Every Friday evening, and on some Wednesdays in summer, you can watch gig racing – traditional six-oar boats (some over 100 years old) originally used to race out to wrecked ships.

St Mary's

The capital is Hugh Town, straddling an isthmus that separates the Garrison area from the main part of the town, where boats from the mainland dock and it feels like an England of a bygone era. The TIC and most of the places to stay are here.

There are several enjoyable walks on St Mary's. The hour-long Garrison Walk offers good views of the other islands and you pass Star Castle, once an Elizabethan fortress and now a hotel. There's a two-hour walk to Peninnis Head, where numerous ships have been wrecked, and a three-hour Telegraph Walk via assorted ancient historical sites and burial chambers. The TIC has details.

The *camping ground* (☎ 422670) is at Garrison Farm and charges £6 per person.

Among the cheaper B&Bs in Hugh Town

is *Lyonnesse Guest House* (☎ 422458, The Strand), which costs £25 for B&B or £36 for half board. *The Wheelhouse* (☎/fax 422719, Porthcressa) has well appointed rooms from £42 for half board.

Atlantic Hotel (☎ 422417, fax 423009, e atlantichotel@btinternet.com) is right by the water in Hugh Town, and has a good restaurant. It costs £82.50 per person with a sea view or £70 without, including B&B and dinner.

The top place to stay on St Mary's is the *Star Castle Hotel* (☎ 422317, fax 422343). Luxuries include a heated swimming pool and four-poster beds. Rooms cost from £72 to £105 per person for B&B and dinner. Its Web site is at www.starcastlescilly.co.uk.

Tresco

The second-largest island is best known for Tresco Abbey Gardens, laid out in 1834 on the site of a 10th-century Benedictine abbey. There are more than 5000 subtropical plants and a display of figureheads from the many ships that have been wrecked off these islands. The gardens are open 10 am to 4 pm daily; admission costs £6 (free for children).

There's no camping ground or budget accommodation on the island, just the *New Inn* (☎ 422844), which charges from £80 to £92 per person including dinner, and the upmarket *Island Hotel* (☎ 422883), which charges £90 to £130 per person off-season and £120 to £230 in summer, and has a heated swimming pool. Both of these places can be contacted by email on e contactus@ tresco.co.uk and on the Web at www.tresco.co.uk.

Bryher

The smallest of the inhabited islands is wild and rugged; Hell Bay in an Atlantic gale is a powerful sight. There are good views over the islands from the top of Watch Hill. From the quay, occasional boats cross to deserted Samson Island.

There's a *camping ground* (☎ 422886) in Jenford charging £5 per night. Very comfortable accommodation is available at the *Hell Bay Hotel* (☎ 422947, fax 423004) from £59 to £94 per person including dinner.

St Martin's

Known for its beautiful beaches, St Martin's is the most northerly of the main islands. There's cliff scenery along the north shore, a good walk on Chapel Downs up to the Day Mark and long stretches of sand on both the northern and southern coasts.

The *camping ground (☎ 422888)* is near Lawrence's Bay.

B&Bs include *Polreath (☎ 422046)*, which offers half board from £28 to £39.50 per person.

The only hotel is the posh *St Martin's on the Isle (☎ 422092, fax 422298)* on Tean Sound, where half board costs from £85 to £135 per person. It has an excellent seafood restaurant.

St Agnes

A disused lighthouse overlooks the bulb fields of England's most southerly community. To the west are striking granite outcrops, including one that resembles Queen Victoria. At low tide, you can walk across the sand to the neighbouring island of Gugh. The islanders call themselves Turks.

The *camping ground (☎ 422360)* is near the beach at Troy Town Farm. There's B&B and evening meals at *Covean Cottage (☎ 422620)* from £36.50 to £39.50 per person.

Getting There & Away

There's no transport to or from the islands on a Sunday.

Air Isles of Scilly Skybus (☎ 0845 710 5555) is the islands' airline. It has frequent flights in summer (daily except Sunday) between Land's End aerodrome and St Mary's. The flight takes 15 minutes and for an adult/child costs £49/25 one way (£36/18 stand-by), £57/28 for a day return and £68/34 for a short break of one to three nights. There's a free car park at the Land's End aerodrome, or a free shuttle bus from Penzance train station, which should be booked in advance. There are also flights from Exeter and Newquay (Monday to Saturday from both), Plymouth (Monday, Wednesday and Friday), Bristol (Monday, Tuesday, Thursday and Friday) and Southampton (Monday and Friday).

Scotia Helicopter Services (☎ 01736-363871) has flights to St Mary's, daily except Sunday, from Penzance heliport. The journey takes 20 minutes and for an adult/child costs £47/23.50 one way, £62/31 for a day return, £69/34.50 for a five-day excursion and £62/31 for a 'late saver return' for a one- to three-night stay (you can book only one day in advance). There are also flights to Tresco, daily except Sunday, from Penzance; prices are the same as those for St Mary's. It costs £2 per day to leave your car at the heliport and there's a bus link to Penzance train station.

Boat From April to October, the Isles of Scilly Steamship Company (☎ 0845 710 5555) has one departure a day, Monday to Saturday, between Penzance and St Mary's. The trip takes 2¾ hours and costs £72/36 in high season for an adult/child return ticket. One- to three-night breaks cost £52/26 return. In Penzance, the reservations office is by the south pier.

Getting Around

There are regular departures to the other four main islands from St Mary's harbour. A return trip to any island costs £5.60. Boat trips to see the seals and sea birds cost £5.60.

On St Mary's, you can hire bikes from Buccabu Hire (☎ 422289), near the TIC, from £5 per day. There's also an infrequent circular bus service, and tours of St Mary's by minibus.

From the Thames to the Wye

The counties lying between Oxford and the Welsh borders have some of the most lush countryside in England, as well as a glut of postcard-perfect villages and some resolute market towns.

In the south-east, Oxford remains extremely beautiful, albeit extremely busy, and close by is magnificent Blenheim Palace. The nearby Cotswolds to the west embody the popular image of the English countryside. The prettiness can seem artificial, and few of the villages are strangers to mass tourism, but there will be moments when you'll be transfixed by the combination of golden stone, flower-draped cottages, church spires, towering chestnut trees and oaks, rolling hills and emerald-green fields.

Cheltenham is a gracious Regency town that makes a good western base for the Cotswolds, as does historic Tewkesbury with its assortment of architecture.

In the south-west the Bristol Channel and the wide Severn Valley form a natural border with agricultural Herefordshire, Worcestershire and the region known as the Welsh Marches. This is great touring country as it boasts beauty without the numbers. Worcester is the easiest base for Worcestershire, although Great Malvern, nestled in the Malvern Hills, may be preferable for walkers. Hereford or Ross offer good facilities for rural adventures near Wales, although literature buffs will prefer secondhand-bookshop capital Hay-on-Wye, straddling the border.

Oxfordshire

Oxfordshire is famous worldwide for the university town of Oxford, a mecca for tourists who come to admire the lovely honey-coloured colleges and riverside views.

Highlights

- Seeing the honey-hued stone villages of the Cotswolds in spring
- Picking a favourite Oxford college
- Admiring Gloucester Cathedral and Tewkesbury Abbey
- Exploring the Wye Valley and Symonds Yat
- Deciphering the Mappa Mundi in Hereford Cathedral
- Messing about on the river at Henley-on-Thames
- Checking out the Regency splendour of Cheltenham

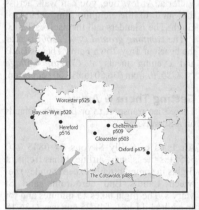

The surrounding countryside has the gentle, unspectacular charm of central England. Major features are the River Thames, which flows through the centre and south of the county; the chalk Chilterns, a wooded ridge running across the south-eastern corner of the county; and the limestone Cotswolds, extending from the west across Gloucestershire.

As well as the colleges, museums and gardens of England's oldest university, no one should miss nearby Blenheim Palace, the spectacular birthplace of Sir Winston Churchill. There are good walks in the hills, and many pretty villages whose character stems from the use of local building materials.

WALKING & CYCLING

Oxfordshire is crossed by three long-distance paths. The ancient ridge track known as the Ridgeway runs along the county's southern border. If you want to walk it look out for either the *Ridgeway National Trail Information & Accommodation* leaflet or for the official National Trail Guide by Neil Curtis. For further information, see the Activities chapter.

The Oxfordshire Way is a 65-mile (105km) waymarked trail connecting the Cotswolds with the Chilterns and runs from Bourton-on-the-Water to Henley-on-Thames. The leaflet *Oxfordshire Way* divides the route into 16 individual walks of between 2 and 8 miles (3km to 13km) in length.

The Thames Path follows the river 175 miles (282km) from its mouth near the Thames Barrier in London, across the centre of Oxfordshire, to its source at Thames Head in Gloucestershire. Look out for the *Thames Path National Trail Information & Accommodation* leaflet or for the official National Trail Guide.

Oxfordshire is also good cycling country. There are few extreme gradients and Oxford offers cheap bike hire. The *Oxfordshire Cycleway* map covers Woodstock, Burford and Henley.

GETTING AROUND

Oxfordshire has a reasonable rail network, with Oxford and Banbury the main stations. There are services on the Cotswolds and Malvern line between London Paddington

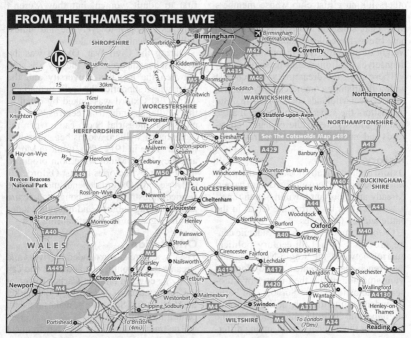

FROM THE THAMES TO THE WYE

and Hereford, and between London Euston and Birmingham.

Oxford is the hub of a fairly comprehensive bus service. Tourist Information Centres (TICs) stock a useful free *Bus & Rail Map* showing routes and giving contact numbers for each operator. The main companies are Stagecoach (☎ 01865-772250) and the Oxford Bus Company (☎ 01865-785400).

OXFORD
☎ 01865 • pop 115,000

The poet Matthew Arnold described Oxford as 'that sweet city with her dreaming spires', a phrase that still has much resonance today – although it helps to add to the mood by visiting out of season.

Oxford is one of the most important towns in England, and its graduates are some of the most self-important people in the country. For some, Oxford University is synonymous with academic excellence, for others it's an elitist club whose members unfairly dominate many aspects of British life. That sense of elitism is taking on new life as the colleges, sinking under the weight of mass tourism, increasingly close themselves off from would-be sightseers.

These days the dreaming spires coexist with a flourishing commercial city that has some typical Midlands social problems. But for visitors the superb architecture and the unique atmosphere of the colleges, courtyards and gardens remain major drawcards.

History

Oxford is strategically located at the point where the River Cherwell meets the Thames. Already an important town in Saxon times, it was fortified by Alfred the Great in the battle against the Danes.

Oxford's importance as an academic centre grew out of a 12th-century political quarrel between the Anglo-Normans and the French that prevented Anglo-Normans from studying at the then centre of European scholastic life, the Sorbonne in Paris.

Students came to study at the Augustinian abbey in Oxford, which soon became known for theological debate among different religious orders. When such debates were conducted in an academic setting all was well, but discussions among students occasionally spilled over into violence. Eventually universities at Oxford and Cambridge were given royal approval, so that future student rebellions would take place far from London. To help the authorities keep an eye on student activity, the university was broken up into colleges, each of which developed its own traditions.

The first colleges, built in the 13th century, were Balliol, Merton and University. At least three new colleges were built in each of the following three centuries. More followed, though at a slower rate, and some of the older colleges were redesigned in Baroque or neoclassical style. New colleges, like Keble, were added in the 19th and 20th centuries to cater for a growing student population. There are now about 14,500 undergraduates and 36 colleges. Lady Margaret's Hall, built in 1878, was the first to admit women, but they weren't awarded degrees until 1920. These days the colleges are open to everyone and almost half the students are female.

During the Civil War, Oxford was the Royalist headquarters, and the city was split between the Royalist university and the town, which supported the Parliamentarians.

In 1790 Oxford was linked by canal to the Midlands industrial centres, but the city's real industrial boom came when the industrialist William Morris began producing cars here in 1912. The Bullnose Morris and the Morris Minor were both produced in the Cowley factories in east Oxford.

These days Oxford depends more on the service industries, but its congested centre and sprawling suburbs and housing estates are the legacy of its manufacturing past.

Orientation

The city centre is surrounded by rivers and streams to the south, east and west and can easily be covered on foot. Carfax Tower, at the intersection of Queen St, Cornmarket St, High St and St Aldate's, makes a useful central landmark.

The train station to the west has frequent

buses to Carfax Tower. Alternatively, turn left into Park End St and it's a 15-minute walk. The bus station is nearer the centre, off green-less Gloucester Green.

University buildings are found throughout the city, with the most important and architecturally interesting at its centre. It takes more than a day to do justice to them all, but if pushed for time try to visit Christ Church, New and Magdalen Colleges.

Information

The TIC (☎ 726871, fax 240261), The Old School, Gloucester Green, right next to the bus station, can be pretty hectic in summer. It opens 9.30 am to 5 pm Monday to Saturday and 10 am to 3.30 pm on Sunday in summer. For further information before arriving here, try the Web site at www .oxford.gov.uk/tourism.

College opening hours are increasingly restrictive; some don't open at all, some only accept guided groups, many close in the morning and others charge visitors for admission.

The TIC stocks the *Welcome to Oxford* brochure, which has a walking tour with college opening times. Two-hour guided

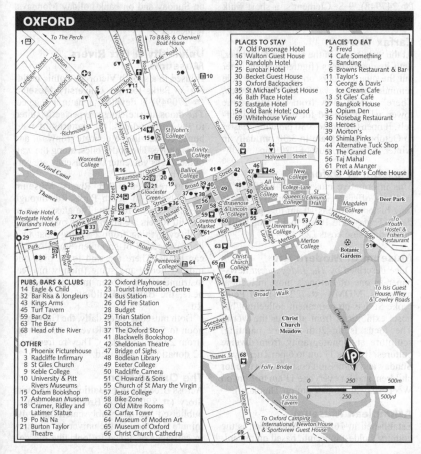

OXFORD

PLACES TO STAY
7 Old Parsonage Hotel
16 Walton Guest House
20 Randolph Hotel
25 Eurobar Hotel
30 Becket Guest House
33 Oxford Backpackers
35 St Michael's Guest House
46 Bath Place Hotel
52 Eastgate Hotel
54 Old Bank Hotel; Quod
69 Whitehouse View

PLACES TO EAT
2 Frevd
4 Cafe Something
5 Bandung
6 Browns Restaurant & Bar
11 Taylor's
12 George & Davis' Ice Cream Cafe
13 St Giles' Café
27 Bangkok House
34 Opium Den
36 Nosebag Restaurant
38 Heroes
39 Morton's
40 Shimla Pinks
44 Alternative Tuck Shop
53 The Grand Cafe
56 Taj Mahal
61 Pret a Manger
67 St Aldate's Coffee House

PUBS, BARS & CLUBS
14 Eagle & Child
32 Bar Risa & Jongleurs
43 Kings Arms
45 Turf Tavern
59 Bar Oz
63 The Bear
68 Head of the River

OTHER
1 Phoenix Picturehouse
3 Radcliffe Infirmary
8 St Giles Church
9 Keble College
10 University & Pitt Rivers Museums
15 Oxfam Bookshop
17 Ashmolean Museum
18 Cramer, Ridley and Latimer Statue
19 Po Na Na
21 Burton Taylor Theatre
22 Oxford Playhouse
23 Tourist Information Centre
24 Bus Station
26 Old Fire Station
28 Budget
29 Trian Station
31 Roots.net
37 The Oxford Story
41 Blackwells Bookshop
42 Sheldonian Theatre
47 Bridge of Sighs
48 Bodleian Library
49 Exeter College
50 Radcliffe Camera
51 C Howard & Sons
55 Church of St Mary the Virgin
57 Jesus College
58 Bike Zone
60 Old Mitre Rooms
62 Carfax Tower
64 Museum of Modern Art
65 Museum of Oxford
66 Christ Church Cathedral

walking tours of the colleges leave the TIC at 10.30 and 11 am and 1 and 2 pm; they cost £4.50/2.50. Inspector Morse tours, around sites associated with Colin Dexter's fictional detective, leave the TIC every Saturday at 1.30 pm (£5/3).

Oxford is a free listings guide produced every couple of months; it includes ideas for wining and dining throughout the city.

For Net access, try Internet Exchange (☎ 241601), 12 George St; charges start at 3p per minute.

Those in need of travel supplies might like to check out the YHA Adventure Shop (☎ 247948), 9 St Clement's, a short walk east of the town centre.

Carfax Tower
At the very centre of the city, Carfax Tower, with its quarterjacks (figures who hammer out the quarter hours on bells), is the sole reminder of medieval St Martin's Church. There's a fine view from the top of the tower, which is good for orientating yourself. It opens 10 am to 5.30 pm daily, Easter to October, and 10 am to 3.30 pm daily in winter. Admission costs £1.20/60p.

Museum of Oxford
This informative museum (☎ 815559), St Aldate's, offers an introduction to the city's long history. It opens 10 am to 4 pm Tuesday to Friday, and 10 am to 5 pm on Saturday. Admission costs £2.

Museum of Modern Art
Once described by *The Independent* newspaper as one of Europe's most influential museums, MOMA (☎ 722733), 30 Pembroke St, has no permanent collection, but hosts exhibitions from all over the world. The focus is on 20th-century painting, sculpture and photography from diverse cultures. It opens 11 am to 6 pm Tuesday to Sunday and admission costs £2.50 (free for children, and for everyone 11 am to 1 pm on Wednesday and 6 to 9 pm on Thursday).

Ashmolean Museum
Established in 1683, the Ashmolean is the country's oldest museum, based on the collections of the gardening Tradescant family and Dr Elias Ashmole, who presented their possessions to the university.

The building, on Beaumont St, is one of England's best examples of neo-Grecian architecture, and dates from 1845. It houses extensive displays of European art (including works by Raphael and Michelangelo) and Middle Eastern antiquities. Other exhibits include Guy Fawkes' lantern and a unique Saxon enamel portrait of Alfred the Great.

The museum (☎ 278000) opens 10 am to 5 pm Tuesday to Saturday and 2 to 5 pm on Sunday and on bank holiday Mondays. Admission is free, but a £3 donation is requested.

University & Pitt Rivers Museums
Housed in a superb Victorian Gothic building on Parks Rd, the **University Museum** (☎ 270949) is devoted to natural science. The dinosaur skeletons are perfectly suited to the surroundings, the patterns of their bones echoed in the delicate ironwork and glass above. The dodo relics, along the wall to the left as you enter the museum, are particularly popular.

You reach the **Pitt Rivers Museum** (☎ 270949), on South Parks Rd, through the University Museum. The glass cases at the Pitt Rivers are crammed to overflowing with everything from a sailing boat to a gory collection of shrunken South American heads. There are said to be over one million items, and some (mainly musical instruments) have been moved to an annexe, the Balfour Building, on Banbury Rd.

Both museums open daily, the University noon to 5 pm, the Pitt Rivers 1 to 4.30 pm (from 2 pm on Sunday). They're free but a £2 donation is requested.

The Oxford Story
Across Broad St from Balliol is The Oxford Story (☎ 790055), 6 Broad St, a much-publicised and reasonably entertaining 40-minute ride through the university's history in carriages designed to look like old col-

lege desks. It opens 9.30 am to 5 pm, April to October (to 6 pm in July and August), and 10 am to 4.30 pm the rest of the year (to 5 pm at the weekend). Tickets cost £5.70/4.70.

Punting

There's no better way to soak up Oxford's atmosphere than to take to the river in a punt. The secret to propelling these flat-bottomed boats is to push gently on the pole to get the punt moving, then to use it as a rudder to keep on course.

Punts are available from Easter to September and hold five people, including the punter. Both the Thames and the Cherwell are shallow enough for punts, but the best advice is to bring a picnic and head upstream along the Cherwell. Alternatively, follow the Cherwell downstream from Magdalen Bridge for views of the colleges across the Botanic Gardens and Christ Church Meadow.

You can rent a punt from C Howard & Sons (☎ 761586) by Magdalen Bridge (£7 per hour, £20 deposit), or from the Cherwell Boat House (☎ 515978) farther upstream at the end of Bardwell Rd (£8 per hour, £40 deposit; £10 and £50 at the weekend).

Boat Trips

Salter Bros (☎ 243421) offers several interesting boat trips from Folly Bridge between May and September, including a two-hour trip to Abingdon (£6.80/10.40 one-way/return).

Colleges and University Buildings

Pembroke College On St Aldate's, Pembroke College (☎ 276444) was founded in 1624. Sir Roger Bannister, the first man to run a mile in under four minutes, was a former master, and the dictionary-writer and wit Dr Samuel Johnson a past student.

Christ Church College Opposite Pembroke is Christ Church College (☎ 276150), the grandest of all Oxford colleges. It was founded in 1525 by Cardinal Thomas Wolsey and refounded by Henry VIII in 1546. Illustrious former students include John Wesley, William Penn, WH Auden and Charles Dodgson – better known as Lewis Carroll – who wrote *Alice's Adventures in Wonderland* and also went on to teach mathematics here.

The main entrance is below Tom Tower, which is so called because it was dedicated to St Thomas of Canterbury. The upper part of the tower, designed by Sir Christopher Wren (architect of St Paul's Cathedral) in 1682, rests on a Tudor base. Great Tom, the tower bell, chimes 101 times each evening at 9.05 pm, the time when the original 101 students were called in. Since Oxford is five minutes west of Greenwich, this is actually 9 pm Oxford time. The visitors' entrance is farther down St Aldate's, via the Memorial Gardens.

The cloisters lead to **Christ Church Cathedral**, the smallest cathedral in the country, which has been the city's Anglican cathedral since the reign of Henry VIII. It was founded on the site of the nunnery of St Frideswide, whose shrine was a focus of pilgrimage until it was partly destroyed on Henry VIII's orders. The shrine was reconstructed in the 19th century. Beside it is a **Watching Loft** for the guard, who made sure no one walked off with the saint's relics. The Lady and Latin Chapels boast some particularly fine windows.

From the cathedral, you enter **Tom Quad**, whose central pond served as a water reservoir in case the college caught fire. To the south side is the **Great Hall**, the college's grand dining room, with an impressive hammerbeam roof. You can also explore another two quads and the **Picture Gallery**.

The college opens 9.30 am to 5.30 pm (from 1 pm on Sunday). The Great Hall closes between noon and 2 pm, the cathedral at 4.45 pm and the Chapterhouse at 5 pm. There's an admission charge of £3/2.

Merton College One of the original three colleges founded in 1264, Merton College (☎ 276310), Merton St, represents the earliest form of collegiate planning. The 14th-century **Mob Quad** was the first of the college quadrangles. The **library** leading off it is the oldest medieval library still in use, with some books still chained up, an ancient anti-theft device. The library owns several 15th-century astrological instruments, and an astrolabe that may have been used by Chaucer. TS Eliot was a former student, and JRR Tolkien was a professor of English here.

The college opens 2 to 4 pm Monday to Friday and 10 am to 4 pm at the weekend.

Magdalen College Magdalen (**maud**-lin) College is on the High St, near the handsome bridge over the River Cherwell. One of Oxford's richest colleges, it has the most extensive and beautiful grounds, including a deer park, river walk and superb lawns. It's also a popular location for film-makers – part of *Shadowlands*, the story of CS Lewis, was filmed here.

The college was founded in 1458 by William of Waynflete, the bishop of Winchester. The chapel, with its 43m-high bell tower, dates from the late 15th century. Each year, the college choir ushers in May Day at 6 am by singing a hymn from the top of the tower to the crowds below. Pubs open before breakfast, ensuring that this is a well supported tradition. Magdalen alumni include Oscar Wilde, Sir John Betjeman and Dudley Moore.

The college (☎ 276000) opens noon to 6 pm daily. There's an admission charge of £2/1, April to September.

Opposite Magdalen are the **Botanic Gardens** (☎ 276920), founded in 1621 by Henry Danvers for the study of medicinal plants. It opens 9 am to 4.30 pm daily.

St Edmund Hall On Queen's Lane, St Edmund Hall (☎ 279000) became a college in 1957 but has been in existence since at least the early 13th century; it is the sole survivor of the original medieval halls – the teaching institutions that preceded colleges in Oxford. Its small chapel was decorated by William Morris and Edward Burne-Jones.

Queen's College On the High St, Queen's College (☎ 279121) was founded in 1341

but the current buildings are all classical in style. Like most colleges, Queen's preserves some idiosyncratic traditions: students are summoned to meals with a trumpet call and at Christmas a boar's head is served to commemorate a time when a scholar fought off an attacking boar by thrusting a volume of Aristotle down its throat! How appropriate, then, that Rowan Atkinson (aka Mr Bean) once studied here. To visit the college, you must join an official tour.

University College University College (☎ 276602), High St, has acquired notoriety as the college where Bill Clinton didn't inhale noxious substances. Despite claims for King Alfred as a founder, the college actually started life in 1249. A romantic memorial commemorates the poet Percy Bysshe Shelley, who was sent down (ie, expelled) for publishing *The Necessity of Atheism* in 1811. You need a private invitation to visit the college.

All Souls College All Souls College (☎ 279379), High St, was founded in 1438, the souls in question being those of soldiers who died in the Hundred Years' War. No undergraduates are admitted to All Souls, a small college of just 70 fellows.

The college chapel, open 2 to 4 pm weekdays, is worth seeing.

Church of St Mary the Virgin At the junction of High and Catte Sts, the Church of St Mary the Virgin has a 14th-century tower offering splendid views (£1.60/80p).

It opens 9 am to 7 pm daily in July and August, and to 5 pm the rest of the year.

Radcliffe Camera The Radcliffe Camera is a spectacular circular library ('camera' means room) built in 1748 in the Palladian style. Unfortunately, it's not open to the public.

Brasenose College Dating from the 16th century, Brasenose College (☎ 277830) is entered from Radcliffe Square and takes its name from an 11th-century snout-like door knocker that now graces the dining room.

Author William Golding *(Lord of the Flies)* is one of its best-known graduates.

It opens 10 to 11.30 am and 2 to 4.30 pm daily.

New College To reach New College (☎ 279555) from Catte St, turn down New College Lane under the **Bridge of Sighs**, a 1914 copy of the famous bridge in Venice. New College was founded in 1379 by William of Wykeham, bishop of Winchester, and its buildings are fine examples of the perpendicular style. Don't miss the chapel, which has superb stained glass, much of it from the 14th century. The west window is a design by Sir Joshua Reynolds, and Sir Jacob Epstein's disturbing statue of Lazarus is also here. The gardens contain a section of Oxford's medieval wall.

A former college warden was William Spooner, whose habit of transposing the first consonants of words made his name part of the English language. It's claimed that he once reprimanded a student with the words, 'You have deliberately tasted two worms and can leave Oxford by the town drain'.

The college opens 11 am to 5 pm daily, Easter to October, and 2 to 4 pm daily in winter. Admission costs £2 in summer; it's free in winter.

Sheldonian Theatre In Broad St stands the Sheldonian Theatre (☎ 277299), the university's main public building. Commissioned by Gilbert Sheldon, archbishop of Canterbury, it was Sir Christopher Wren's first major work and was built in 1667 when he was professor of astronomy.

It opens 10 am to noon and 2 to 4.30 pm (to 3.30 pm in winter) Monday to Saturday. Admission costs £1.50/1.

Bodleian Library One of England's three copyright libraries, the **Bodleian Library** is off the Jacobean-period **Old Schools Quadrangle**. Library tours (☎ 277000) take place at 10.30 and 11.30 am, and 2 and 3 pm daily and show off Duke Humfrey's library (1488). They book up fast and cost £3.50 (no children aged under 14).

Also not to be missed is the **Divinity School**, with its superb vaulted ceiling. Renowned as a masterpiece of 15th-century English Gothic architecture, it opens 9 am to 5 pm weekdays, to 12.30 pm on Saturday.

Trinity College On Broad St, Trinity College (☎ 279900) was founded in 1555, but the existing buildings mostly date from the 17th century.

It opens 10.30 am to noon and 2 to 4 pm daily, and admission costs £1.

Balliol College Also on Broad St, Balliol College (☎ 277777) was founded in 1263, but most of the present buildings date from the 19th century. The wooden doors between the inner and outer quadrangles still bear scorch marks from when Protestant martyrs were burnt at the stake in the mid-16th century. Matthew Arnold, Aldous Huxley and Graham Greene were all students here. The college also churned out two Conservative prime ministers last century, Harold Macmillan and Edward Heath.

It opens 2 to 5 pm daily and charges £1.

Lincoln College Founded by bishop Richard Fleming in 1427 to defend the faith against medieval heresy, one of Lincoln's most famous past fellows is John Wesley, the founding father of Methodism, a latter-day heretic (or he would have been in the bishop's eyes). Wesley's former rooms in the college (☎ 279800) open 2 to 5 pm daily, to small groups only.

Illustrious graduates include Dr Seuss and John Le Carré.

Exeter College This college (☎ 279600) is known for its elaborate 17th-century dining hall. The chapel includes a William Morris tapestry and he was also an undergraduate, along with his Arts and Crafts friend Edward Burne-Jones, in 1853. Other notables to have passed through here include the actor Richard Burton. It opens 2 to 5 pm daily.

Jesus College This college (☎ 279700) in Turl St was originally established in 1571 to train Welsh scholars in 'good letters'. Many of today's students are still drawn from Wales. Famous folk from here include TE Lawrence (aka Lawrence of Arabia) and former Labour prime minister Harold Wilson. It opens 2.30 to 4.30 pm daily.

Organised Tours

Guide Friday (☎ 790522) runs a hop-on, hop-off city bus tour every 15 minutes from 9.30 am to 7 pm in summer, and less frequently in winter. It leaves from the train station or can be joined at various sights along the way. Tickets cost £8.50/2.50. The company's Web site is at www.guidefriday .com.

The Oxford Classic Tour (☎ 240105) offers the same sort of thing, but is a little cheaper at £7/2. It runs from both the bus and train stations between about 10 am and 6 pm (5 pm in winter).

Cotswold Roaming (☎ 250640/308300) runs guided bus tours to several places around Oxford, including Bath on Wednesday and Saturday, Stonehenge and Salisbury on Thursday and Sunday, and Stratford-upon-Avon and Warwick Castle on Friday. These cost about £30 per person. It also offers half-day tours to the Cotswolds four times a week; these trips cost £18.

Places to Stay

Finding a place to stay in summer can be difficult; arrange things in advance or join the queues in the TIC and pay £2.75 for their help.

Camping One-and-a-half miles south of the centre, *Oxford Camping International* (☎ 244088, 426 Abingdon Rd) is conveniently located by the Park & Ride car park. Charges are relatively high for nonmembers at £5.30 per person and £4.30 for a pitch.

Hostels The most convenient hostel is *Oxford Backpackers* (☎ 721761, fax 315038, ⓔ oxford@hostels.demon.co.uk, 9A Hythe Bridge St), which is less than 500m from the train station. There are 120 beds, mostly in dorms. From April to September you need to book a week in advance and leave

a deposit. Beds in dorms cost £11 each. Facilities include a large kitchen, a bar, a laundry and Internet access.

The *Oxford Youth Hostel* (☎ 762997, fax 769402, ⓔ oxford@yha.org.uk, 32 Jack Straw's Lane) gets booked up quickly in summer although it's hardly central. Get there on bus No 14 or 14A from the High St. It's open all year and beds cost £10.85/7.40 for adult/juniors.

University Accommodation Over the holidays it is possible to find a room in empty student accommodation.

From July to September, St Edmund Hall provides accommodation in the guise of the *Isis Guest House* (☎ 248894, fax 243492, 45–53 Iffley Rd), offering student digs as superior B&B accommodation. Rooms with a bathroom cost £26 per person, those without cost £24 per person.

Otherwise, try the *Old Mitre Rooms* (☎ 279821, fax 279963, 4B Turl St), which lets singles/doubles for £25/46 in July and August only.

B&Bs & Hotels – Central In the peak season, figure on around £20 per person for a room in a B&B. The main areas are on Abingdon Rd to the south, Cowley and Iffley Rds to the east and Banbury Rd to the north. All are on bus routes, but Cowley Rd has the best selection of places to eat.

The fairly basic *Becket Guest House* (☎ 724675, fax 724675, 5 Becket St) is near the train station and has singles/doubles costing from £30/45. West of the station, the small *River Hotel* (☎ 243475, fax 724306, 17 Botley Rd) by Osney Bridge is a popular business hotel with rooms starting at £60/70. The *Westgate Hotel* (☎ 726721, fax 722078, 1 Botley Rd) charges £36/48 for a room (£39/56 with a bath).

St Michael's Guest House (☎ 242101, 26 St Michael's St), just off Cornmarket St, couldn't be more central. Rooms with shared bath cost £32/48, but you need to book weeks in advance.

The closest B&B to the bus station is basic *Walton Guest House* (☎ 552137, 169 Walton St) with bathless rooms for £18 per person. **Eurobar Hotel** (☎ 725087, fax 243367, e eurobarox@aol.com, 48 George St) is very convenient for the bus station. The comfortable rooms start at £45/58.

Oxford's choicest accommodation is Forte's centrally located **Randolph Hotel** (☎ 0870 400 8200, fax 791678, Beaumont St), opposite the Ashmolean Museum. It was built in 1864 in neo-Gothic style; rooms cost from £140/170 but there are reductions at the weekend. You can make a reservation on the company's Web site at www.heritage-hotels.com. Delightful **Old Parsonage Hotel** (☎ 310210, fax 311262, 1 Banbury Rd) has well equipped rooms for £130/165 and is highly recommended by the tourist board.

Bath Place Hotel (☎ 791812, fax 791834, 4 & 5 Bath Place) is a luxurious 10-room retreat in which all the rooms have different styles, and some have four-poster beds. Rooms cost from £90/140. It is ina quiet but central part of town near New College. Its Web site is at www.bathplace.co.uk.

Old Bank Hotel (☎ 799599, fax 799598, e oldbank@bestloved.com, 92 High St) brings the designer hotel to Oxford at designer prices. Plush, lush rooms start at £135/155, excluding (!) breakfast.

B&Bs & Hotels – East There are several B&Bs in the student area east of the centre on Cowley Rd and numerous ones along Iffley Rd to the south. Another cluster lies to the north along Headington Rd.

The **Bravalla Guest House** (☎ 241326, fax 250511, e bravalla.guesthouse@virgin .net, 242 Iffley Rd) is a homely place and charges £35 for en suite rooms.

The **Athena Guest House** (☎ 243124, 253 Cowley Rd) is within walking distance of shops and restaurants and has beds for £18 a head. A bit farther out, the comfortable **Earlmont** (☎ 240236, fax 434903, e beds@earlmont.prestel.co.uk, 322 Cowley Rd) offers nonsmoking B&B for £35/50.

B&Bs & Hotels – North There are several B&Bs along Banbury Rd, north of the centre. **Cotswold House** (☎/fax 310558, 363 Banbury Rd) is very comfortable; rooms with bathroom cost from £41/66. **Burren Guest House** (☎ 513513, 374 Banbury Rd) is more basic and offers B&B starting at £33/48.

B&Bs & Hotels – South Closest to the city centre is the good-value **Whitehouse View** (☎ 721626, 9 Whitehouse Rd) on a side road off Abingdon Rd, with rooms costing from £18/34.

There are numerous other places along Abingdon Rd. **Newton House** (☎ 240561, fax 244647, e newton.house@btinternet .com, 82 Abingdon Rd) is quite large (it's actually two houses joined together) and rooms cost £46/48. At No 106 the **Sports-view Guest House** (☎ 244268, fax 249270, e stayatsportsview_guest_house@freeserve .co.uk) has rooms from £30/52 (£35/60 with bath).

Places to Eat

Many Oxford eateries are aimed at the wallets of wealthy parents and tourists. To eat cheaply, track down the places that draw the student trade.

Self-caterers should visit the **covered market**, on the north side of High St at the Carfax Tower end, for snacks, fruit and vegetables. Among the stalls, **Palm's Delicatessen** offers a good range of patés and cheeses. **Brown's Café** has cheap fodder of the sausage and beans variety. Otherwise, the **Alternative Tuck Shop** (Holywell St) does excellent filled rolls and sandwiches at lunch time.

A popular place for snacks is **St Giles' Café** (St Giles) with cheap fry-ups and toasted sandwiches. Those who love to spoil themselves must check out **Taylor's** (☎ 558853, 31 St Giles), a delightful deli with an impeccable selection of olives, salads and pastries. The apricot and ginger slices are amazing. The popular **George & Davis' Ice Cream Café** (☎ 511294, Little Clarendon St) serves light meals (bagels from £1) as well as delicious home-made ice cream.

There are some excellent sandwich bars throughout the centre and many a student debate has centred on which is best. *Morton's* (☎ *200867, 22 Broad St*) can't be faulted for its tasty baguettes and at the back there's an attractive garden for sunny days. Just a block behind Morton's on Ship St is *Heroes*, which builds to order with a fine selection of fillings.

The nonsmoking *Nosebag Restaurant* (☎ *721033, 6 St Michael's St*) does good soups and has a fine selection of cakes. It opens daily for lunch and dinner (closed on Monday evening).

St Aldate's Coffee House, nestled under St Aldate's Church, is a favourite with students and has a decent selection of sandwiches and cakes. Light lunches, teas and coffees are available in the *Convocation Coffee House* attached to the Church of St Mary. If you're at the TIC around lunch time, the adjoining *Old School* pub does snack meals such as filled baguettes at reasonable prices.

The Grand Café (☎ *204463, 84 High St*) is right in the thick of things opposite Queen's College and offers luxury sandwiches and salads in suitably grand surroundings, amid pillars and mirrors. The food makes it well worth a visit. Just as inviting is *Freyd* (☎ *311171, Walton St*), a cafe-bar inside an old church with an impressive neoclassical facade. There's Latin dancing here on Sunday evening.

Stylish *Browns* (☎ *511995, 5 Woodstock Rd*) looks more expensive than it is and offers a good selection of dishes from Europe and beyond. *Café Something* (☎ *559782, Walton St*) is a trendy little place specialising in reasonably priced pizzas and some delicious desserts.

Shimla Pinks (☎ *244944, 16 Turl St*) is a particularly good Indian restaurant, part of a growing nationwide chain, with buffets from around £6 and a wide range of a la carte dishes. Out towards the station, *Bangkok House* (☎ *200705, 42a Hythe Bridge St*) does set Thai meals for £15.50, assuming two diners, with cheaper options at lunch time. It is pretty convenient for those staying at Oxford Backpackers. Sticking to South-East Asia, *Bandung* (☎ *511668, 124 Walton St*) offers Malaysian and Indonesian cuisine with daily specials for £7. Satay is a speciality here and can be washed down with a *Bintang* beer flown in from Java. *The Opium Den* (☎ *248680, 79 George St*) is considered one of the best Chinese restaurants in town and offers a series of set menus for those who like to pick and mix. Most main courses cost £5.30.

Quod (☎ *202505, 92–94 High St*) is incredibly popular with the local set for stylish Italian cuisine in comfortable surroundings. It is best to book ahead, and reckon on £15 a head and up. The wine list is even more extensive than the menu.

If fish is your thing, then *Fishers Restaurant* (☎ *243003, 36 St Clement's*) is Oxford's favourite seafood restaurant. The menu includes Whitstable oysters at £12.50 a dozen for those feeling amorous.

Entertainment

Pubs & Bars Oxford has some excellent city-centre pubs as well as others within stumbling distance along the Thames.

The *Head of the River*, ideally situated by Folly Bridge, is very popular and an excellent place to be on a warm summer's day. Less prominent is the tiny *Turf Tavern*, a perennial student favourite, which is hidden down a city-centre alley (Bath Place) and was featured in the *Inspector Morse* TV series. There are several beer gardens for outdoor enthusiasts. The *Kings Arms* is a crowded student pub in the heart of the city, opposite the Sheldonian Theatre on Parks Rd. *Bar Risa* (*3–5 Hythe Bridge St*) has Jongleurs comedy club attached.

Academics loosen up in the 17th-century *Eagle & Child* (*49 St Giles*), where JRR Tolkien and CS Lewis used to meet for readings from *The Hobbit* and the chronicles of Narnia. Locals refer to it affectionately as the 'Bird & Baby'.

Just off the High St, opposite Turl St, *The Bear* is thought to be the oldest pub in the city and has a snug, intimate atmosphere thanks to its tiny size.

Homesick antipodeans might seek solace in *Bar Oz*, tucked down an alley off Cornmarket St behind the covered market, although it's still pints and halves rather than schooners and midis.

The *Isis Tavern*, a 1½-mile (2.5km) walk along the towpath from Folly Bridge, is the perfect place to go on a sunny day provided you don't mind the crowds. Thatch-roofed *The Perch* by the river in Binsey is a 25-minute walk from the city centre; from Walton St, take Walton Well Rd and cross Port Meadow. This is a very popular pub for food as well as ale, and has the most pleasant garden in the Oxford area.

For something a little less conventional, try venturing out to *Baba* (☎ 203011, 240 Cowley Rd), a sort of Indian restaurant that makes its money as a bar and stays open into the early hours. There is some token food in the takeaway-style front, but beer is the real order of the day. Also out this way is *The Zodiac (190 Cowley Rd)*, a small student club that livens up at the weekend.

Po Na Na (13 Magdalen St) is probably the best of Oxford's unimpressive clubs, but is more a bar where people start shaking their stuff in the early hours.

Music Most weekends see Irish bands playing at the *Bullingdon Arms (162 Cowley Rd)*, a lively Irish local with live jazz or blues on Wednesday evening.

Roots.net (27 Park End St) has a great selection of tunes from around the world and the complex includes a bar and club with live performances most nights.

Theatre, Cinema & Comedy The *Oxford Playhouse* (☎ 798600, Beaumont St) puts on a mixed bag of theatre, music and dance. The *Old Fire Station* (☎ 794490, George St) stages mainly classical plays while the *Burton Taylor Theatre* (☎ 798600, Gloucester St) goes in for more offbeat productions.

The most interesting films tend to be shown at the *Phoenix Picturehouse* (☎ 554909, Walton St).

For comedy, try *Jongleurs* (see Bar Risa under Pubs & Bars), one of a fast-growing national chain of clubs. Weekends sometimes see a big name coming to town.

Getting There & Away

Oxford is 57 miles (92km) from London, 74 miles (119km) from Bristol and 33 miles (53km) from Cheltenham. If you're driving, the M40 provides fast access from London, but Oxford has a serious traffic problem and finding somewhere to park can be difficult. It's best to use the Park & Ride system; as you approach the city follow the signs for the four car parks. Parking is free but the buses to the city centre cost £1.30 return. They leave every 10 minutes throughout the day, Monday to Saturday.

Bus Several bus companies compete for business on the route to London. The Oxford Tube (☎ 772250) goes to Victoria Coach Station but stops at Shepherd's Bush, Notting Hill Gate and Marble Arch en route. A next-day return to Victoria costs £7.50; the journey takes around 1½ hours and the service operates 24 hours a day. Departures are extremely frequent and it is unlikely you'll have to wait more than 15 minutes. The Oxford Tube also stops on St Clement's, near Cowley Rd.

National Express (☎ 0870 580 8080) has numerous buses to central London and Heathrow airport. There are three buses daily to Cambridge (three hours, £14), two or three services to Bath (two hours, £9.75) and Bristol (2¼ hours, £12.75), and two to Gloucester (1½ hours, £8) and Cheltenham (one hour, £7.75).

Citylink (☎ 785400) is the third major operator, with frequent departures to London (X90), Heathrow (X70), Gatwick (X80), Birmingham and Stratford-upon-Avon.

Train Oxford has a snazzy modern station with frequent services to London Paddington (1½ hours, £13).

There are regular trains north to Coventry and Birmingham, the main hub for transport farther north, and north-west to Worcester and Hereford via Moreton-in-Marsh (for the Cotswolds).

To connect with trains to the south-west you have to change at Didcot Parkway (15 minutes). There are plenty of connections to

Bath (1½ hours). Change at Swindon for another line running to the Cotswolds (Kemble, Stroud and Gloucester).

Getting Around

Bus Oxford was among the world's first cities to introduce battery-operated electric buses. They run every 12 minutes from the train station into the city centre for a flat fare, 8 am to 6 pm Monday to Saturday.

The city has fallen victim to the worst excesses of bus deregulation, with so many competing buses plying Cornmarket St that it can be difficult to cross the road. The biggest companies are the Oxford Bus Company (☎ 785410) and Stagecoach (☎ 772250). Oxford Bus Company bus No 4 serves Iffley Rd and No 5 serves Cowley Rd. The information office in the bus station has full details.

Car For car hire, Budget (☎ 724884) is handily located near the station on Hythe Bridge St.

Taxi There are taxis outside the train station and near the bus station.

Bicycle Students have always espoused pedal power and there are cycle lanes along several streets. The *Cycle into Oxford* map shows all the local cycle routes. Bikes for hire in Oxford are usually of the three-speed town type and are much better value by the week than by the day.

Warlands (☎ 241336), Botley Rd, is near the station and charges £8 per day or just £15 for the week (plus £35 deposit). Bike Zone (☎ 728877), 6 Market St, is right in the centre of town and has bikes for £10 per day or £20 for a week (plus £100 deposit).

WOODSTOCK
☎ 01993

Woodstock is easy day-tripping territory from Oxford and owes its fame and prosperity to glove-making and the Churchill family. Although people usually come here en route to Blenheim Palace, there's also a fine collection of 17th- and 18th-century buildings, particularly the Bear Hotel and

the town hall, built at the Duke of Marlborough's expense in 1766. The church has an 18th-century tower tacked onto a medieval interior. Opposite the church, Fletcher's House accommodates **Oxfordshire County Museum** (☎ 811456), open 10 am to 5 pm daily except Monday; admission costs £2.50/50p.

Woodstock's TIC (☎ 813276, e tourism@ westoxon.gov.uk), Hensington Rd, opens 9.30 am to 5.30 pm Monday to Saturday and 1 to 5 pm on Sunday.

Places to Stay & Eat

Staying in Woodstock is expensive when compared with the cheap options in Oxford. Best value is *The Lawns (☎/fax 812599, 2 Flemings Rd)*, which offers singles/doubles for £25/35, and includes free local rides for trains, buses and Blenheim Palace. It also has a free laundry service, making it as good as unique!

Moving upmarket, *Pinetrees (☎ 813300, fax 01608-678877, 44 Green Lane)* has an attractive garden, and singles cost from £30, doubles £48. *Plane Tree House (☎ 813075, 48 Oxford St)* is an upmarket B&B in the middle of things with three rooms available for £60.

There are two opulent hotels in town for those with money to burn. Cheaper of the two is the *Feathers Hotel (☎ 812291, fax 813158, Market St)* with luxurious rooms for £88/105. The *Bear Hotel (☎ 0870 400 8202, fax 813380, e woodstockbear@ fortehotels.com, Park St)* is a historic 13th-century coaching inn with rooms starting at £115/140.

Harriet's Tearooms (Park St) is a nice little teashop with some of the best French patisserie this side of Calais. *Brotherton's Brasserie (Park St)* has a fair selection of Mediterranean favourites, plus a healthy wine list. Bar food at the popular *Black Prince* includes Mexican dishes and pizzas.

Getting There & Away

To get to Woodstock from Oxford, catch Stagecoach bus No 20 from Oxford bus station.

The honey-hued charm of the Cotswolds

The dignified Sheldonian Theatre, Oxford

Beware of the shark: New High St, Oxford

A day at the races: a college boathouse, Oxford

Of dreaming spires: the exquisite quad of Brasenose College, Oxford

Christ Church: the largest and one of the most beautiful of Oxford's colleges

AROUND WOODSTOCK
Oxford Bus Museum
Public-transport purists might like to see one of the largest collections of public buses in England. There are more than 50 buses, some of which are still undergoing restoration. It opens 1.30 to 4.30 pm on Saturday and 10.30 am to 4.30 pm on Sunday and bank holidays. Admission costs £3/1.50. The museum is right next to Long Hanborough train station, just 10 minutes from Oxford.

Blenheim Palace
One of Europe's largest palaces, Blenheim was a gift to John Churchill, the first Duke of Marlborough, from Queen Anne and Parliament as a reward for his role in defeating Louis XIV. A vast baroque fantasy, it was built by Sir John Vanbrugh and Nicholas Hawksmoor between 1704 and 1722. It's now a Unesco World Heritage Site.

You enter the house through the great hall where – 20m above – the ceiling is decorated with a painting by Sir James Thornhill showing the Duke of Marlborough presenting Britannia with his plan for the Battle of Blenheim. West of the great hall, apartments once used by the domestic chaplain now house the Churchill Exhibition; in the room where Winston was born you can view the great prime minister's slippers and a lock of his hair.

The windows of the sumptuous state dining room offer a glimpse of the tower of Bladon church, where Churchill and his parents are buried. Between the saloon and library are three state rooms, hung with tapestries commemorating Marlborough's campaigns.

You can also visit the chapel and grounds, which cover over 800 hectares, some of it parkland landscaped by Capability Brown. Blenheim Park railway leads to the herb garden, the butterfly house and a large maze. A separate ticket lets you look round the current duke and duchess's private apartments.

Blenheim Palace (☎ 01993-811325) opens 10.30 am to 5 pm mid-March to October and admission costs £9/4. The park opens from 9 am daily, all year. Cotswold Roaming (☎ 01865-250640/308300) offers organised tours to Blenheim from Oxford. Alternatively a taxi from Oxford to Blenheim will cost around £15.

OXFORDSHIRE COTSWOLDS
For details of Oxfordshire's share of the beautiful Cotswolds, see the Cotswolds & Around section later in this chapter.

SOUTH OF OXFORD
Abingdon
☎ 01235 • pop 30,000
Pretty Abingdon is a market town 6 miles (10km) south of Oxford. The impressive County Hall building was designed in 1678 by Christopher Kempster, who worked on St Paul's Cathedral in London. It now houses Abingdon Museum (☎ 523703), which opens 11 am to 5 pm daily (to 4 pm in winter). Admission is free, but it costs £1/50p for the view from the roof. Wider than it is long, St Helen's Church is a fine example of perpendicular architecture.

The TIC (☎ 522711), 25 Bridge St, is near the river, and opens 10 am to 5 pm Monday to Saturday and 1.30 pm to 5 pm on Sunday in summer.

On St Helen's Wharf, overlooking the Thames, is the *Old Anchor Inn*, a friendly pub that also serves meals.

The nicest way to reach Abingdon from Oxford is by boat (see Boat Trips in the earlier Oxford section). Alternatively, Stagecoach bus No 31 links Abingdon with Oxford and Wantage.

Didcot Railway Centre
Didcot Railway Centre (☎ 01235-817200, ⓔ didrlyc@globalnet.co.uk) is where the Great Western Railway (GWR) lives on. Designed by Isambard Kingdom Brunel, the line ran from London to Bristol on an extremely broad gauge and retained its independence until the nationalisation of the railways in 1948. The centre houses a range of steam engines and opens 10 am to 5 pm daily, April to September, and 10 am to 4 pm at the weekend in winter. Admission charges vary from £4 to £12, depending on the event.

The centre is in Didcot, which is on the A34, or may be reached by train from Oxford (15 minutes).

Dorchester-on-Thames

A street of old coaching inns and a magnificent medieval church are more or less all there is of Dorchester-on-Thames, although in Saxon times there was a cathedral here. In the 12th century an abbey was founded on the site. Following the Reformation it became the parish church of Saints Peter and Paul, and it's worth stepping inside to see the rare Norman lead font with figures of the apostles; a wonderful Jesse window with carved figures and stained glass tracing Christ's ancestry; and a 13th-century monument of a knight. There's a small museum and cafe in the *Abbey Guest House* (☎ *340703)*, which also dates back to the Middle Ages. The museum opens 11 am to 5 pm Tuesday to Saturday and 2 to 5 pm on Sunday and bank holiday Mondays; admission is free. Thames Travel (☎ 01491-874216) bus No X39 connects Dorchester with Oxford and Abingdon.

Wantage
☎ 01235 • pop 9700

Wantage lies at the foot of the Berkshire Downs, 15 miles (24km) south-west of Oxford. Alfred the Great was born here in 849, and his statue dominates the main square. The Ridgeway national trail is less than 3 miles (5km) to the south.

The TIC (☎/fax 760176), 19 Church St, opens 10 am to 4.30 pm Tuesday to Saturday, and 2.30 to 5 pm on Sunday. It's located in a converted 16th-century cloth-merchant's house together with the **Vale & Downland Museum Centre** (☎ 771447), which has information about King Alfred and life around the Ridgeway. The museum keeps the same hours as the TIC and admission costs £1.50/1.

Places to Stay & Eat About 2 miles (3km) south of Wantage, the *Ridgeway Youth Hostel (☎ 760253, fax 768865, Court Hill)* was created out of several old barns set around a courtyard. It opens daily May to early September (phone for further details). The nightly charge is £9/6.20 for adults/juniors.

The Chalet (☎ 769262, 21 Challow Rd) has basic B&B starting at £16 per person. A pricier option is the *Bell Inn (☎ 763718, fax 224392, e thebellwantage@aol.com, Market Square)* at £22.50/45, or £55 for an en suite double, but it's more central.

The *Flying Teapot*, beside the church, does traditional English snacks like jacket potatoes with the usual toppings. You can get bar meals in *The Shears (Mill St)*.

Getting There & Away Stagecoach (☎ 01865-772250) operates regular buses to Didcot and Swindon. A Sunday Rover ticket lets you travel throughout the area for £5.

The White Horse

About 6 miles (10km) west of Wantage, a stylised image of a horse cut into the hillside is probably the most famous chalk figure in Europe. Why this mysterious figure (114m long and 49m wide) was carved into the turf about 2000 years ago is unclear. How the artist managed to get the lines and perspective exact when the whole horse can only be seen from a distance is a mystery.

Above the chalk figure are the grass-covered earthworks of Uffington Castle. From the Ridgeway Youth Hostel, near Wantage, a wonderful 5-mile (8km) walk leads along the Ridgeway to the White Horse.

Thomas Hughes, author of *Tom Brown's Schooldays*, was born in **Uffington** village. His house is now a simple **museum** (☎ 01367-820259), open 2 to 5 pm at the weekend, Easter to September; admission costs 60/30p.

The Craven (☎ 01367-241846) is a thatched farmhouse offering B&B from £25/48 and up.

HENLEY-ON-THAMES
☎ 01491 • pop 11,000

Henley is world famous for its rowing regatta, one of those oar-fully English occasions of boaters and blazers, strawberries and cream, that these days tend to be commandeered by the high ranks of the corporate entertainers.

The TIC (☎ 578034, fax 411766) is in the basement of the town hall on Market Place. It opens 10 am to 6 pm daily, Easter to September. During winter it opens 10 am to 5 pm Monday to Saturday and 10 am to 4 pm on Sunday. In summer there's also a booth in Mill Meadows.

The stately High St is dominated by **St Mary's Church**, which dates back to the 13th century. Above the arches of Henley Bridge, built in 1786, are sculptures of Isis and Father Thames. Two fine coaching inns, the Red Lion and the Angel, stand sentinel at the High St end of the bridge. Both predate their 18th-century heyday, and have played host to many eminent people, from the Duke of Wellington to James Boswell.

Henley Royal Regatta

In 1829, the first Oxford and Cambridge boat race took place between Hambledon Lock and Henley Bridge. Ten years later the regatta was developed to enhance Henley's growing reputation.

Each year, in the first week of July, the regatta still plays host to the beau monde. Despite its peculiar mix of pomposity and eccentricity, it's a serious event that attracts rowers of the highest calibre.

There are two main areas for spectators – the stewards' enclosure and the public enclosure – although most people appear to take little interest in what's happening on the water. Epicurean picnics are consumed, large quantities of Pimm's and champagne are drunk, and it's still a vital fixture in the social calendar.

Those with contacts in the rowing or corporate worlds can get tickets to the stewards' enclosure; others pay £6 for a day ticket for the public enclosure on Wednesday and Thursday or £10 Friday to Sunday.

River & Rowing Museum

Henley recently acquired a purpose-built museum designed by minimalist architect David Chipperfield in which to display paintings and artefacts associated with the history of Henley and with the River

Thames and rowing. Like all the best modern museums, the River & Rowing Museum (☎ 415600) harnesses modern technology to liven up its story. The views from the building are lovely, and there are, of course, a cafe and shop.

It opens 10 am to 6 pm daily (from 10.30 am on Sunday) and admission costs £4.95/3.75. The museum is in Mill Meadows, with its own car park.

Brakspear Brewery Tour

Fans of English bitter should not pass up the opportunity to take a tour around the Brakspear Brewery (☎ 570224), New St, based in the town since 1779. The tours take around 45 minutes and must be booked in advance (the minimum is six people, so find some friends). The charge is £5 and this includes the obligatory bottle of Brakspear bitter.

Boat Trips

Henley is the perfect place to indulge in a bit of messing about on the river, and plenty of boat companies near the bridge are ready to help you enjoy yourself. On summer Sundays Hobbs & Son (☎ 572035) organises cruises starting at £20 a head. Shorter trips to Hambledon Lock and back cost about £4/3. To hire a five-seater rowing boat for an hour costs £10, a four-seater motor boat £18.

Places to Stay

If you want to stay anywhere near Henley during the regatta you need to book weeks in advance. Even at quiet times B&Bs are relatively pricey.

Camping The *Swiss Farm International Camping* (☎ 573419, Marlow Rd) site is a quarter of a mile out of Henley on the road to Marlow. Camping costs £4 per adult and £1 for the pitch.

B&Bs and Guesthouses Handsome *No 4 Riverside* (☎ 571133, fax 413651, 4 River Terrace) is in a very nice location and has rooms facing the river costing from £40/50. Or try *Alftrudis* (☎ 573099, fax 411747,

e *b&b@alftrudis.fsnet.co.uk, 8 Norman Ave)*, a friendly B&B about a five-minute walk from the centre; rooms cost from £40 to £55 with bath. *Avalon (☎ 577829, 36 Queen St)* is one of the cheaper places in town and charges from £25/40.

Lenwade (☎ 573468, e lenwadeuk@ compuserve.com, 3 Western Rd) has three doubles starting at £55 (£45 for single occupancy!). *Abbotsleigh (☎/fax 572982, 107 St Marks Rd)* has doubles with a bath for £56 in a large family home.

Places to Eat
Several pubs offer reasonably priced food. Near the TIC, the *Three Tuns (5 Market Place)* is a proper, old-fashioned pub with good bar meals, including Sunday lunch. *The Angel* is a pub with a view on Thames Side, next to Henley Bridge, but is expensive whether for food or drink. The bar snacks are more affordable than the restaurant.

Alternatively, branches of *Café Rouge (☎ 411733)* and *Caffe Uno (☎ 411099)* face each other in the High St, and nearby is a *Pizza Express (35 Market Place)*. *Henley Tea Rooms* faces onto the river on River Terrace, and you can get high tea with all the trimmings at the *Old Rope Walk (High St)*. *Thai Orchid (☎ 412227, Hart St)* has a pretty standard menu of Thai favourites and most main courses cost around £7.

Getting There & Away
Henley is 21 miles (34km) south-east of Oxford on the A423 and 40 miles (64km) west of London. Thames Travel (☎ 874216) bus No X39 links Henley with Oxford and Abingdon hourly (every two hours on Sunday).

To get from Henley to Oxford by train you must change at Twyford or Reading. Henley to London Paddington takes about one hour and costs £7.20.

AROUND HENLEY-ON-THAMES
Stonor Park
Stonor Park (☎ 01491-638587) has been occupied by the Stonor family, an unrepentant Catholic family that has suffered much in-

dignity since the Reformation, for more than 800 years. The Tudor mansion has a fine collection of paintings, including works by Tintoretto and Caracci.

Stonor Park is 5 miles (8km) north of Henley. You need your own transport to get there. It opens 2 to 5.30 pm on Sunday in April; on Wednesday and Sunday in May, June and September; on Wednesday, Thursday and Sunday in July; and Wednesday, Thursday, Saturday and Sunday in August. Admission costs £4.50.

The Cotswolds & Around

The Cotswold Hills – a limestone escarpment overlooking the Severn Vale between Bath and Chipping Campden – are the source of the traditional picture of rustic, rosy-cheeked England. It's a region of stunningly pretty, honey-coloured stone villages and remarkable views. Some of the villages are extremely popular, and can feel overrun during summer; the best way to escape the commercialism is to explore on foot or by bike. Accommodation can be pricey, with hostels and camping grounds thin on the ground.

The Severn Vale nurtures Cheltenham (one of Britain's best-preserved Regency towns), Tewkesbury (with a beautiful abbey) and Gloucester (with a historic cathedral), as well as Berkeley Castle and the Wildfowl & Wetlands Trust at Slimbridge. To the west, and geographically part of Wales, are the Forest of Dean, and, bordering Wales, the beautiful Wye Valley.

WALKING & CYCLING
The Cotswolds and the surrounding areas are perfect for walking and cycling, with plenty of quiet roads, mild but rewarding gradients and fine pubs. Look out for the handy leaflets *Walking in Gloucestershire* and *Cycling in Gloucestershire* in TICs.

The 100-mile (161km) Cotswold Way (see Walking in the Activities chapter) runs from Bath to Chipping Campden. TICs stock walking guides and a useful pack called *Cycle Touring Routes in Gloucestershire*. Bartholomew's *Cycling in the Cotswolds* (£8.99) gives full details.

Campus Holidays (☎ 01242-250642) organises mountain-bike tours of the region, starting from Cheltenham, while Cotswold Country Cycles (☎ 01386-438706) rents out bikes for £10 per day from Chipping Campden.

Several companies offer guided or unguided walking tours; for example, try Cotswold Walking Holidays (☎ 01242-254353, **e** walking@star.co.uk), 10 Royal Parade, Cheltenham GL50 3AY.

Part of the 210-mile (338km) Severn Way runs south through Gloucestershire along the edge of the Severn.

GETTING AROUND

Some TICs stock local bus timetables, or you can phone the Gloucestershire public-transport enquiry line for details (☎ 01452-425543). Limited as it is, the Cotswolds' bus service is still more comprehensive than the rail network, which skims the northern and southern borders.

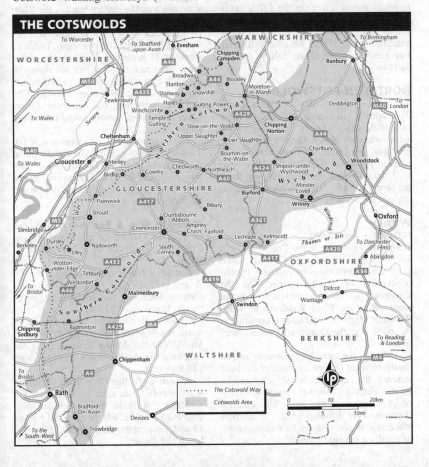

THE COTSWOLDS

The Cotswold Way
Cotswolds Area

The Cotswold Link (bus No X55) is a useful bus service to keep in mind. It links up the tourist meccas of Stratford-upon-Avon and Bath via the picturesque villages of the Cotswolds and runs every day of the year, leaving Bath at 9.30 am and 3.30 pm and Stratford at 10 am and 3.30 pm (10 minutes later in winter). Stops (going towards Bath) are Mickleton, Hidcote Manor Garden, Chipping Campden, Moreton-in-Marsh, Stow-on-the-Wold, Bourton-on-the-Water, Northleach, Cirencester, Kemble, Tetbury, Westonbirt Arboretum, Old Sodbury and, during summer, Dyrham Park. A one-way/return ticket for the full journey costs £7.70/13, and you can jump on and off all day. A three-day Rover ticket is available for £15/7.50 for adults/children. For further information, call ☎ 01225-464446.

NORTHERN COTSWOLDS

The northern Cotswolds are characterised by charming villages of soft, mellow stone built in the folds between the rolling wolds. Although they owed their being to the medieval wool industry, most now rely on tourism for a living. A handful have been well and truly overwhelmed, but even these are worth a look – they didn't become so popular for nothing.

Witney
☎ 01993 • pop 22,000

Witney is a gateway to the Cotswolds, just 10 miles (16km) west of Oxford. Since 1669, the town has specialised in the production of blankets. Sheep on the Cotswolds and the local downs provide the wool, while the River Windrush provides the water. High-quality blankets continue to be made and the Queen still orders hers from Early's of Witney.

Although the town has grown to absorb the demands of Oxford commuters and light industry, the centre retains some character. In the High St, blankets were formerly weighed and measured in the 18th-century Baroque-style Blanket Hall. In Market Place stands the 17th-century Buttercross, originally a covered market.

There is a small town **museum** (☎ 775915), Gloucester Court Mews, High St, but there's not much on show. It opens 2 to 5 pm Tuesday to Friday, and 10.30 am to 5 pm on Saturday (plus Sunday in July and August). Admission costs £1 (free for children).

The TIC (☎ 775802, fax 709261), 51 Market Square, is in the 18th-century town hall and opens 9.30 am to 5.30 pm Monday to Saturday (10 am to 4.30 pm, November to February).

Cogges Manor Farm Museum Clearly signposted on the eastern bank of the River Windrush, Cogges Manor Farm Museum (☎ 772602) allows you to glimpse what life was like in Witney 100 years ago. There's a working 18th-century hand loom on display, and domestic farm animals roam the grounds of the 13th-century manor house, which was drastically altered in the 17th and 18th centuries. You can even sample cakes and scones freshly baked on the old range.

The museum opens 10.30 am to 4.30 pm Tuesday to Friday, and noon to 4.30 pm at the weekend, late March to October. Admission costs £4/2. If you're coming by bus from Oxford, get off at the Griffin Pub and walk down Church Lane.

Places to Stay & Eat Most will choose to stay in Oxford or the heart of the Cotswolds, but there are a few options in Witney.

Cassidy's Guest House (☎/fax 779445, e mc1351@aol.com, Puck Lane) is a comfortable B&B not far from the centre of things. Rooms cost £30/40.

If you prefer a room in the middle of town, the *Marlborough Hotel* (☎ 776353, fax 702152, 28 Market Square) is an old coaching inn with rooms costing from £49.50/69.50.

Browns Café Bar (☎ 709788, Waterloo Walk) serves a nice selection of dishes. For something a little more sophisticated, *Bistro 35* (☎ 703540, 35 High St) has an adventurous menu and opens daily for lunch and dinner.

Getting There & Away There are frequent buses to Oxford.

Minster Lovell

This village in the valley of the River Windrush was said to have been a favourite of William Morris – after his beloved Bibury (see later in this section). There are lovely walks along the river from here.

The handsome ruins of **Minster Lovell Hall**, Lord Lovell's 15th-century manor house, are looked after by English Heritage (EH). The Lovells were an ill-fated family. Francis Lovell was on the losing side at the Battle of Bosworth in 1485, and made matters worse by championing pretender Lambert Simnel's tenuous claim to the throne against Henry VII. He is said to have fled the Battle of Stoke in 1487 and spent the rest of his years living in a secret room in the house.

In the centre of the tiny village is *The Swan*, a beautiful pub and hotel with an excellent menu.

Minster Lovell is 3 miles (5km) west of Witney, off the A40, and 5 miles (8km) south-east of Burford.

Burford
☎ 01993

One of the loveliest of the Cotswold villages, Burford has a wide, flowing high street of handsome stone houses and attracts huge throngs of tourists in summer. Once an important coaching town, it boasts fine 14th- to 16th-century houses and a medieval bridge over the River Windrush.

The TIC (☎ 823558, fax 823590), The Brewery, Sheep St, is by the Lamb Inn. It opens 9.30 am to 5.30 pm Monday to Saturday and 10 am to 3 pm on Sunday.

Things to See The 16th-century **Tolsey Museum** (Toll House), in the High St, houses a small museum on Burford's history. It opens 2 to 5 pm Monday to Friday and 11 am to 5 pm at the weekend, April to September. Admission costs 50p/10p.

Just outside Burford is **Cotswold Wildlife Park** (☎ 823006), a long-established zoo in the grounds of a Gothic mansion. It opens 10 am to 5 pm (to 4 pm in winter) daily. Admission costs £6/4.

Places to Stay & Eat Burford is no place for those on a tight budget; most of the cheaper accommodation is 4 miles (6km) north-east at Leafield.

In Burford, *Priory Tearooms* (☎ 823249, High St) has five rooms with bargain B&B at just £15 per person. The cafe has tables outside during the summer, although fellow visitors may well end up tripping over them when it gets busy. *Chevrons* (☎ 823416, Swan Lane) is another of the cheaper B&Bs, with singles/doubles with bathroom starting at £25/35.

Burford's oldest pub, the 15th-century *Lamb Inn* (☎ 823155, Sheep St), is now a very comfy place to stay, with beamed ceilings and creaking stairs. Rooms with bathroom cost from £52.50 per person during the week, £57.50 at the weekend. Short breaks are better value.

Burford House (☎ 823151, fax 823240, e stay@burfordhouse.co.uk, 99 High St) is arguably the most elegant accommodation in town. Rooms in this timber-frame town house are not cheap, costing from £75/90.

Burford has several good pubs in which to get a meal or a drink. On the High St, the characterful *Mermaid* and the *Golden Pheasant* do bar snacks and full meals. In Witney St, the *Angel* is popular, not only for its real ale but also for its award-winning food. The restaurant is pricey but meals in the bar are more reasonable.

The High St has several tearooms: *Huffkins* has the most incredible selection of cakes and is always crowded during the peak season.

Getting There & Away From Oxford, Swanbrook (☎ 01452-712386) runs four buses daily (two on Sunday) to Burford via Witney.

Chipping Norton
☎ 01608

Chipping Norton is an attractive market town, the highest in Oxfordshire, and makes a useful base for touring nearby villages. As with its neighbours, its wealth was built on the backs of sheep and tweed took over where wool left off by the 19th century. The **Church of St Mary** is a classic example of the wool churches seen throughout the Cotswolds, while the old **glove factory** off the road to Moreton-in-Marsh is a striking monument to industrial architecture of the 19th century. There is a small local history museum (☎ 658518), 4 High St, in an old hall opposite the town hall. It opens 2 to 4 pm Tuesday to Sunday, Easter to October. Admission costs £1/50p.

The TIC (☎ 644379) is located in the Guildhall. It opens 9.30 am to 5.30 pm Monday to Saturday, but is sometimes closed for half-an-hour at lunch time.

Northleach
☎ 01451 • pop 1000

Northleach clusters around an attractive market square. The village is a marvellous mixture of architectural styles and evocative names and is home to perhaps the finest of the wool churches, a masterpiece of the Cotswold perpendicular style with an unrivalled collection of medieval memorial brasses.

The TIC (☎ 860715, fax 860091) is housed in the old prison. It opens 10 am to 5 pm Monday to Saturday and 2 to 5 pm on Sunday in summer.

Things to See Near the square is Oak House, a 17th-century wool house that contains **Keith Harding's World of Mechanical Music** (☎ 860181), a collection of clocks and musical boxes. It opens 10 am to 6 pm daily; admission costs £5/2.50.

Just as interesting is the **Cotswold Heritage Centre** in the old Northleach House of Correction on the Fosse Way, once a model 19th-century prison. It opens 10 am to 5 pm Monday to Saturday and 2 to 5 pm on Sunday, April to October, and costs £2.50/80p.

Chedworth Roman Villa This villa (☎ 01242-890256), owned by the National Trust (NT), lies about 4 miles (6km) southwest of Northleach in a peaceful setting. Built around AD 120 for a wealthy landowner, it contains some wonderful mosaics illustrating the seasons.

It opens 10 am to 5 pm daily except Monday, May to September, and 11 am to 4 pm Wednesday to Sunday, March April, October and early November. Admission costs £3.60.

Places to Stay & Eat B&B at *Market House* (☎ 860557, *Market Square*) costs £20/36 in singles/doubles (£24/44 en suite).

An attractive old pub, the *Red Lion Inn* (☎ 860251, e steveheath@redlion46 .freeserve.co.uk, Market Place) offers beds as well as beers. Rooms cost £25/45.

The Red Lion, the *Sherborne Arms* and the *Wheatsheaf*, all around the main square, are the readiest sources of solid or liquid sustenance.

Getting There & Away Northleach is 9 miles (14km) from Burford and 13 miles (21km) from Cheltenham. Swanbrook (☎ 01452-712386) runs several buses daily between Cheltenham and Oxford via Northleach. The Cotswold Link (bus No X55) passes this way.

Bibury
☎ 01285 • pop 500

Described by William Morris as 'the most beautiful village in England', Bibury is a delightful place that manages to retain some dignity despite the hordes of visitors.

The River Coln flows alongside the road and is filled with trout, which you can pay to fatten at the local trout farm. There are some lovely houses, most notably **Arlington Row**, a picturesque line of NT-owned weavers' cottages. Opposite is Rack Isle, where cloth was once dried after weaving and fulling (compressing) in the 17th-century **Arlington Mill**, now a folk museum (☎ 740368). The mill opens 10 am to 5.30 pm; admission costs £2/1.20.

A 5½-mile (9km) walk winds its way near the River Coln. Starting at Arlington Row, head over the clapper bridge and head south for pretty **Coln St Aldwyns**, where the *New Inn* can provide liquid refreshment, before veering north back to Bibury mill and the village centre.

Places to Stay & Eat The *William Morris* (☎ 740555, fax 850648, e *alex@ ndva2000.freeserve.co.uk, 11 The Street*) has three rooms decorated after its namesake and a great location opposite Arlington Row. Double rooms start at £55. If you want to splash out, try the famous *Swan Hotel* (☎ 740695, fax 740473, e *swanhot1@ swanhotel-cotswolds.co.uk)*, where singles/ doubles cost £99/180.

Jenny Wren's Tearoom offers afternoon tea that's so filling you won't need dinner.

Getting There & Away There are two buses daily (except Sunday) between Cirencester and Lechlade-upon-Thames that pass through Bibury.

Bourton-on-the-Water
☎ 01451 ● pop 2600

There can be no doubting Bourton's charms, with the River Windrush passing beneath a series of low bridges in the village centre and an array of handsome houses in Cotswold stone, but why it's become such a honey pot is a mystery.

To justify the large area set aside for coaches and cars, a number of attractions (model railway and village, perfume exhibition, maze) have opened in the village. The model village has been around since 1937 and is built at a scale of 1:9, including the trees. Admission costs £2/1.50.

Birdland (☎ 820480), a serious bird conservation project, started after the owner purchased two of the Falkland Islands to save the local penguin colonies. It opens 10 am to 5 pm (to 3 pm in winter) daily and costs £4.25/2.50.

Places to Stay & Eat There is an overwhelming number of places to stay in Bourton and nearby Lansdowne. However, it makes sense to spend a night or two here as most of the tourists that drown the atmosphere by day disappear by night.

Fairlie (☎ 821842, Riverside) is in a pretty location overlooking the river and costs £19 per person. Lovely *Manor Close* (☎ 820339, High St) is also in the centre of the village, offering nonsmoking B&B

in a classic Cotswold house for £45 for a double.

Back at the river is the *Kingsbridge Inn* (☎ 820371, fax 810179, e *lionheart@ lionheartinns.demon.co.uk, Riverside)*, a pleasant pub with rooms for £64.

Bourton's *Old Manse Hotel* (☎ 820082, fax 810381, Victoria St) is the most venerable hotel in the village and has 15 en suite rooms, which go for £75.

Tearooms and restaurants line the main street.

Getting There & Away The Cotswold Link (bus No X55) passes through the village twice a day.

The Slaughters

Along with Bourton-on-the-Water, the Slaughters, Upper and Lower, are the most famously picturesque villages of the Cotswolds. Their repellent name is actually a corruption of a Saxon word meaning 'place of sloe trees'.

The best way to enjoy the Slaughters is to spend an hour walking to them from Bourton. Following part of the Warden's Way will take you across the Fosse Way from Bourton, over a meadow and along a path into Lower Slaughter. Continuing past the Victorian flour mill, the route crosses meadows and goes behind the Manor House into Upper Slaughter.

The **mill** opens 10 am to 6 pm daily, March to October; admission costs £1.50/ 75p. It is possible to stay in *Old Mill Lodge* (☎ 01451-822127, Mill Lane), a B&B born from this famous landmark. The rooms are extremely nice and cost £50/70.

Stow-on-the-Wold
☎ 01451 ● pop 2000

At almost 240m, Stow-on-the-Wold is the highest town in the Cotswolds. It is the windswept meeting point of eight routes and the site of the last battle of the Civil War. The pretty main square resembles an Italian piazza. The Royalist Hotel claims to be England's oldest inn; some of its timbers have been carbon-dated to the 10th century.

The TIC (☎ 831082, fax 870083), Hollis House, is on the central square and opens 9.30 am to 5.30 pm Monday to Saturday and 10 am to 4 pm on Sunday.

Places to Stay & Eat The *Stow-on-the-Wold Youth Hostel (☎ 830497, fax 870102, Market Square)* occupies a handsome building in the centre of town and charges £10.85/7.40 for adults/juniors. It opens daily, April to early September – phone for other opening times.

Apart from the hostel, cheap accommodation is scarce. The *White Hart Inn (☎ 830674, The Square)* charges from £22 per person. Attractive *Gate Lodge (☎ 832103, Stow Hill)*, half a mile out of the centre, has rooms for £27/40. Another good option, charging from £40/52, is delightful *Number Nine (☎ 870333, fax 870445, 9 Park St)*. There are just three en suite rooms and a log fire warms the lounge in winter. The *Royalist Hotel (☎ 830670, fax 870048, Digbeth St)*, possibly established in 947, has rooms for £45/95.

Peggums (☎ 830102, Church St) is a tiny tearoom with Cotswold character.

There is a substantial number of inns in Stow, dating from its days as a coaching crossroads. The *Talbot Inn (Market Square)* is a Wadworth pub with a good selection of ale. The *Queen's Head Inn (Market Square)* is a very pretty little pub adorned with flowers, every bit the embodiment of the Cotswold ideal.

Getting There & Away Pulhams Coaches (☎ 820369) operates a daily service linking Stow with Moreton-in-Marsh (15 minutes) and a Monday to Saturday service to Cheltenham (45 minutes). The Cotswold Link (bus No X55) comes through this way.

The nearest train stations are 4 miles (6km) away at Kingham and Moreton-in-Marsh.

Moreton-in-Marsh
☎ 01608 • pop 2600

Straddling the Fosse Way, the old Roman road between Cirencester and Leicester, Moreton may not be the most attractive Cotswold town, but it has some of the best transport connections. It's nowhere near a marsh (Marsh is a corruption of 'March', meaning boundary) and grew first as a staging post and then as a railway town. Its Tuesday market, an old-fashioned affair with over 200 stalls, is worth a look.

Sezincote House About 2 miles (3km) from Moreton is spectacular, Mogul-style Sezincote House, built in 1805 by Charles Cockerell of the East India Company and thought to have inspired the Royal Pavilion in Brighton.

There are tours of the house on Thursday and Friday afternoon in May, June, July and September. The garden opens 2 to 6 pm on the same days, January to November. Admission costs £5 for the house (no children) and garden, £3.50/1 for the garden only. There is no telephone number for the house; for further information contact the TIC in Stow-on-the-Wold.

Places to Stay & Eat The nearest youth hostel is in Stow-on-the-Wold, 4 miles (6km) to the south. B&Bs in Moreton include *Treetops (☎ 651036, London Rd)*, which offers singles/doubles with bathroom for £30/42. *Moreton House Guest House (☎ 650747, fax 652747, High St)* has a restaurant and a range of rooms costing from £24/44, or £62 for a four-poster bed.

Manor House Hotel (☎ 650501, High St) has luxurious rooms starting at £70/98.

Pubs include the atmospheric *White Hart Royal*, the *Bell Inn*, with its large patio for summer dining, and the *Black Bear*, known for its excellent hot beef sandwiches.

Getting There & Away Pulhams Coaches (☎ 01451-820369) operates a daily service (limited on Sunday) between Moreton and Cheltenham (one hour) via Stow-on-the-Wold (15 minutes) and Bourton-on-the-Water. Many surrounding villages put on market-day buses. Stratford Blue (☎ 01789-292085) bus No 569 runs hourly to Stratford-upon-Avon via Broadway or Chipping Campden alternately. The Cotswold Link (bus No X55) serves Moreton.

There are trains roughly every two hours to Moreton from Oxford (35 minutes, £7.20), Worcester (30 minutes, £7.60) and Hereford (one hour, £10.40).

Chipping Campden
☎ 01386 • pop 2000

In an area filled with exquisite villages, Chipping Campden, with its thatched roofs, neatly clipped hedges and gorgeous gardens, is a contender for the prettiest. The unspoilt main street is flanked by a succession of golden-hued terraced cottages, each subtly different from the next.

The TIC (☎ 841206, fax 841681) is just off the High St in Noel Arms Courtyard and opens 10 am to 5.30 pm daily (to 5 pm in winter, when this is the only TIC in this part of the Cotswolds open on Sunday). Across the road, the gabled Market Hall dates back to 1627.

Things to See At the west end is **St James**, one of the finest Cotswold wool churches with some splendid 17th-century monuments. Nearby are the Jacobean lodges and gateways of the vanished manor house, and opposite is a remarkable row of **almshouses**.

Above the town, **Dover's Hill** is named after Robert Dover, who instigated the 17th-century Cotswold Olimpick Games, recently reinstated. The games take place on Spring Bank Holiday and include sports such as slippery-pole climbing and welly wanging, and culminate in a torch-lit procession and dancing in the square. Transport is available from The Square.

Hidcote Manor Gardens These gardens (☎ 438333; NT), a series of six lovely gardens designed to complement each other, lie about 4 miles (6km) north-east of Chipping Campden, in secluded Hidcote Bartrim. The gardens open 11 am to 7 pm daily (except Tuesday and Friday), April to September; admission costs £5.60/2.80.

The Cotswold Link (bus No X55) serves Hidcote Manor Gardens from Chipping Campden or Stratford-upon-Avon (£2.40) twice daily.

Places to Stay & Eat None of the numerous B&Bs near Chipping Campden is cheap. *Sparlings* (☎ 840505, fax 841676, Leysbourne) has a double and a twin, both with bath, for £50 and £53 respectively. Fifteenth-century *Badgers Hall* (☎ 840839, 🖃 badgershall@talk21.com, High St) has just two rooms available for £45/50. Readers have recommended staying at award-winning *Marnic* (☎ 840014, fax 840441, 🖃 marnic@zoom.co.uk) in nearby Broad Campden. Rooms at this nonsmoking establishment cost from £36/44.

The *Cotswold House Hotel* (☎ 840330, fax 840310, 🖃 reception@cotswold-house.demon.co.uk, High St) is the town's most sumptuous pad and the prices reflect this. Rooms start from £75/170, but prices can be negotiated down during the week or in winter.

When it comes to dining in Chipping Campden, there are a lot of choices for such a small place. The *Eight Bells* in Church St does delicious dishes, such as braised lamb in a caper dressing. *Badger Bistro* (☎ 840520, The Square) does Sunday lunch for under £6. *Joel's Restaurant* (☎ 840598, High St) has a selection of pastas and a modern British menu. For a cream tea try *Badgers Hall* in the High St where the restored tearoom has exposed beams and an open fire lit winter.

Getting There & Away Stratford Blue (☎ 01789-292085) bus No 569 runs hourly to Stratford-upon-Avon or Moreton. The Cotswold Link (bus No X55) has two services heading north to Stratford and two going south to Bath daily. On Tuesday the market bus runs from Moreton.

Getting Around You can hire a bike from Cotswold Country Cycles (☎ 438706), Longlands Farm Cottage, for £10 a day or £60 a week.

Broadway
☎ 01386 • pop 2000

Just over the border in Worcestershire, this well-known and much-visited village is strung out along two sides of a broad street, beneath the crest of an escarpment. Undeniably handsome, and largely unspoilt despite its fame, it has inspired artists and writers from JM Barrie to Edward Elgar. A new bypass has brought some relief from through traffic although coaches still manage to cause maximum chaos in high summer.

The friendly TIC (☎ 852937), 1 Cotswold Court, is staffed by volunteers and opens 10 am to 1 pm and 2 to 5 pm Monday to Saturday, March to mid-December.

Things to See The most striking building is the Lygon Arms, now a famous hotel. The unspoilt medieval **Church of St Eadburgha**, a 30-minute walk away, is signposted from the village.

For a longer walk, take the footpath opposite the church, which leads up to **Broadway Tower** (☎ 852390), a crenellated 18th-century folly that stands above the town with a small **William Morris** exhibition on one floor. On a clear day you can see 12 counties from the top. It opens 10.30 am to 5 pm daily (later on Sunday); admission costs £3/2.20.

Places to Stay & Eat Broadway has lots of high-quality accommodation but the luxury is inevitably pricey. The excellent *Cinnibar Cottage* (☎ 858623, 45 Bury End) is about half a mile from the centre and charges £40 for its one room – book ahead. The *Olive Branch Guest House* (☎ 853440, fax 859070, e clive@theolivebranch.u-net .com, 78 High St) is in a delightful 16th-century home and has rooms costing from £35/55.

The best place to stay is the *Lygon Arms* (☎ 852255, fax 858611, info@the-lygon -arms.co.uk, High St) – if your plastic will stretch to £99/159. Its restaurant, *Olivers*, has a good reputation and does dishes such as fish cakes in sorrel sauce. For cheaper meals try *Roberto's Coffee House*, one of the few places open on Sunday.

Getting There & Away Broadway is 6 miles (10km) from Evesham (see the Worcestershire section later in this chapter)

and 9 miles (14km) from Moreton-in-Marsh. Castleways Coaches (☎ 01242-602949) runs bus No 559 to Evesham and No 606 to Cheltenham.

Snowshill

Snowshill Manor (☎ 01386-852410; NT) is furnished with an extraordinarily eclectic collection of items, from Japanese armour to Victorian perambulators, gathered by the eccentric Charles Paget Wade. The walled gardens are particularly delightful and the restaurant has wonderful views. It opens noon to 5 pm Wednesday to Sunday, April to October; admission costs £6/3. Timed tickets are issued for the cramped house. It's a 3-mile (5km) walk uphill to get here from Broadway.

Stanton & Stanway

Stanton is a tiny Cotswold village that many people miss as it isn't really on the road to anywhere. This is a pity as not only is it an attractive village, but it also has one of the region's finest summer pubs, the *Mount Inn* (☎ 01386-584316), with commanding views across the village and the surrounding hills. Locally brewed beer is available from Donnington Ales and there is a small but interesting menu. However it isn't worth making the diversion on a rainy day.

Stanway House (☎ 01386-584469) is in the nearby blink-and-you'll-miss-it hamlet of Stanway. It is a handsome Jacobean property with a most elaborate gatehouse and a recently restored water garden that includes a 25m fountain. It opens 2 to 5 pm on Tuesday and Thursday; admission costs £3/1.

Winchcombe
☎ 01242 • pop 5000

Saxon Winchcombe was the capital of its own county and the seat of Mercian royalty. Its Benedictine abbey was one of the country's main pilgrimage centres. Splendid **St Peter's Church** is noted for its fine gargoyles, including one that looks like Lewis Carroll's Mad Hatter.

An excellent 2½-mile (4km) hike along

the Cotswold Way leads to **Belas Knap**, a false-entrance burial chamber built about 5000 years ago. The TIC (☎ 602925), Town Hall, High St, has information on other local walks. It opens 10 am to 5 pm daily (to 4 pm on Sunday).

Sudeley Castle Winchcombe's main attraction is Sudeley Castle (☎ 604357). Its chapel houses the tomb of Catherine Parr, Henry VIII's last wife. The castle was popular with a succession of royalty, including Prince Rupert, nephew of Charles I, who used it as his Civil War headquarters, precipitating its later sacking by Cromwell's men. Parts of the original building have been left in ruins, but the rest was restored in the 19th century.

The castle opens 10.30 am to 5.30 pm daily, Easter to October; admission costs £6.20/3.20. The gardens are especially beautiful.

Gloucestershire Warwickshire Railway This cunningly named steam railway has appropriated the initials of the most famous railway line in Britain, the GWR (Great Western Railway). Unfortunately this GWR (☎ 621405) doesn't travel such a useful route as Bristol to London; instead it goes from Toddington to Toddington via Winchcombe. The railway is operated totally by volunteers. Ring ahead for more details as the schedule is patchy, or visit its Web site at www.gwsr.plc.uk. Tickets cost £7/4.

Places to Stay & Eat There are plenty of options in Winchcombe, or it is easy to daytrip from Cheltenham or Tewkesbury. The *Courtyard House* (☎ 602441, High St) has two double rooms for £45. Half-timbered *Wesley House* (☎ 602366, fax 602405, High St) charges £48/70 for a single/double (dinner in the excellent restaurant costs from £15.50). It also accepts credit cards. Farther out, friendly *Blair House* (☎ 603626, fax 604214, 41 Gretton Rd) has some of the cheapest beds in Winchcombe, starting at £25/42.50.

Wincelcumbe Tearooms (☎ 603578, 7 Hailes St) does soup with tasty rosemary-and-raisin bread and classic cream teas. *Poachers Restaurant* (☎ 604566, 6 North St), round the corner from the TIC, has main dishes from £8 to £11. The *Old White Lion* in North St is an inviting 15th-century pub. The *Plaisterers Arms*, near the church, does good meals and real ales.

Getting There & Away Castleways Coaches (☎ 602949) runs several buses a day from Winchcombe to Cheltenham or Broadway, Monday to Saturday.

Hailes Abbey

About 3 miles (5km) north-east of Winchcombe along the Cotswold Way, this former Cistercian abbey, now a romantic ruin, was once an important place of pilgrimage; people came from all over Europe to see the phial of Christ's blood kept here. After the dissolution of the monasteries, the blood was exposed as a mixture of honey and saffron.

Hailes Abbey (☎ 01242-602398; EH/NT) opens 10 am to 6 pm daily, Easter to October, but at the weekend only for the rest of the year; admission costs £2.60/1.30.

The small neighbouring **church**, with medieval stained glass, murals and heraldic tiles, is delightful. A short walk away are the organic *Hayles Fruit Farm* (which sells good cider) and *Orchard Tea Room*.

Guiting Power
☎ 01451

Guiting Power lies about 4 miles (6km) east of Winchcombe. It's an attractive place, set around a green with a shop, post office and two pubs. It even has its own music festival in July, and a remarkable Norman doorway to its church.

Nearby, **Cotswold Farm Park** (☎ 850307) preserves endangered species of farm animal such as the Gloucester old spot pig. It opens 10.30 am to 5 pm (to 6 pm on Sunday) daily, April to October, and costs £4.50/2.30.

Farmers Arms (☎ 850358, fax 850724) is a traditional pub complete with skittles, a favourite game in this part of the world –

like tenpin bowling for technophobes, but played with just nine pins. There is a good selection of real ales and home-cooked food. If you want to stay, there are three rooms available for £30/45.

SOUTHERN COTSWOLDS

The southern Cotswolds are quite different in character to the northern area: the stone is more soberly coloured, the valleys are steeper and the area is less reliant on tourism. If you want to get away from the Cotswold honey pots, it's worth exploring some of these villages.

Painswick

☎ 01452 • pop 2800

Often called the 'Queen of the Cotswolds', Painswick is a picture-perfect Cotswold village. St Mary's Church is particularly interesting, its graveyard bristling with the table-top tombs of rich wool merchants who made the village prosperous from the 17th century. The yew trees are said to be uncountable but certainly number no more than 99; if the 100th should grow, legend claims the devil will shrivel it. The church tower still bears cannonball scars from the Civil War.

The streets behind the church are lined with handsome merchants' houses. Bisley St, with several 14th-century houses, was the original thoroughfare, while New St is a medieval addition. Rare iron spectacle stocks stand in the street just south of the church.

The TIC (☎ 813552), The Library, Stroud Rd, is staffed by dedicated volunteers and opens 10 am to 4 pm Tuesday to Friday, and 10 am to 1 pm at the weekend, Easter to October.

Painswick Rococo Garden The gardens of Painswick House (☎ 813204), half a mile north of the village, open 11 am to 5 pm Wednesday to Sunday (daily in summer), mid-January to November. They're best visited in February or March for the spectacular snowdrop displays. Admission costs £3.30/1.75. There are also a restaurant and tearooms here.

Places to Stay & Eat Pleasant *Hambutts Mynd* (☎ 812352, Edge Rd) caters especially for Cotswold Way walkers, with doubles for £45. Centrally positioned, *Cardynham House* (☎ 814006, The Cross) has nine rooms starting at £36/46; it dates back to the 15th century. Sixteenth-century *Thorne* (☎ 812476, Friday St) has two doubles for £50. *Painswick Hotel* (☎ 812160, Kemps Lane) is the best hotel, with luxurious rooms costing from £85/110, many with views over the valley.

The *Royal Oak* (☎ 813129, St Mary's St) is a popular local, as is the *Falcon*. The *Country Elephant* (☎ 813564, New St) does great food but allow £25 per head for dinner. *Bertram's Café-Bistro*, opposite the church, offers more hope for those on a budget, with simple fare such as ploughman's lunches.

Getting There & Away Bus No 46 connects Cheltenham and Stroud with Painswick hourly. Swanbrook (☎ 712386) has a better service for Gloucester. Those with their own vehicles should watch out – the streets are extremely narrow.

Stroud

☎ 01453 • pop 37,800

The narrow, steep-sided Stroud Valley stands out from the rest of the southern Cotswolds and was the scene of the Cotswold wool industry's final fling.

Stroud is built around a spur above the River Frome. Very little cloth is produced today, although Stroudwater Scarlet used to be famous throughout the world. Many of the old mill buildings remain, though most now have new uses. A walk around Stroud's hilly streets should take in the old Shambles market (on Wednesday, Friday and Saturday), the Tudor town hall and the Stroud Museum.

The TIC (☎ 765768, fax 755658), Stroud Subscription Rooms, George St, opens 10 am to 5.30 pm Monday to Saturday. Cotswold Experience Tours (☎ 767574), 84 Horns Rd, is a local travel agency that specialises in organising tours of the Cotswolds.

Places to Stay & Eat The *London Hotel* (☎ 759992) does B&B starting at £29/42 (£39/50 with a bathroom) and is opposite the town centre car park. *Fern Rock House* (☎ 757307, 72 Middle St) charges £20/35 for rooms. Nonsmoking *Deben House* (☎ 766573), off the London Rd, charges from £20/45.

In Union St, the *Pelican* serves pub lunches, or there are several cafes in the pedestrianised High St, behind the TIC. Try *Woodruff's Organic Café*, which was one of the first 100% organic cafes in England, or *Mills Café*, which is down an alley and has a few outdoor tables for catching the sun in summer.

Getting There & Away Stagecoach Stroud Valleys (☎ 763421) is the main local operator; bus No 46 runs hourly to Painswick and Cheltenham, and No 93 operates half-hourly to Gloucester.

Around Stroud

Owlpen Manor Owlpen (☎ 01453-860261) is a romantic medieval manor house, dating from 1450, near the picturesque village of Uley. Throughout much of the 19th century it was abandoned and empty, and only in 1926 was it refurbished under the eyes of Norman Jewson, a Cotswolds Arts and Crafts architect and follower of William Morris. It is possible to visit the house and 17th-century gardens from 2 to 5 pm daily except Monday, April to mid-October; admission costs £4.50/2.

It is also possible to stay here in one of several cottages. Prices start from £20 per person in the smallest and rise considerably for the largest, which sleeps nine. There is also a restaurant here, the *Cyder House*, specialising in pheasant as well as cream teas. The village of Uley also has a number of B&Bs.

The Owlpen Manor Web site is at www.owlpen.com.

Woodchester Mansion Architects and the curious might want to make the journey to Woodchester Mansion (☎ 01453-750455), a massive Victorian house that

was never completed. In 1868, the workers walked out after 16 years and left many of the 27 rooms unfinished. The result is certainly weird, with doors going nowhere, fireplaces stuck halfway up a wall and a gaggle of gruesome gargoyles.

The house generally opens 11 am to 5 pm on Sunday, June to September, but phone ahead to check. Tours take at least two hours and cost £4/2.50. The house is 5 miles (8km) south of Stroud, one mile north of Uley.

The Woodchester Mansion Web site is at www.the-mansion.co.uk.

Getting There & Away There are hourly buses to Uley from Stroud, daily except Sunday.

Tetbury

☎ 01666 • pop 4500

Tetbury has an interesting 18th-century Gothic church with a graceful spire and a wonderful interior. The 17th-century Market House was used for wool trading.

In the Old Court House on Long St, the TIC (☎/fax 503552, @ tetburytourism@ yahoo.co.uk) opens 9.30 am to 4.30 pm Monday to Saturday and 10.30 am to 2.30 pm on Sunday.

Westonbirt Arboretum Westonbirt Arboretum (☎ 880220) is a huge arboretum with a magnificent selection of temperate trees, located 2½ miles (4km) south-west of Tetbury. Walks among the trees are particularly stunning in spring and autumn. There are thought to be more than 4000 species of plant here, spread over an area of 240 hectares that includes 17 miles (27km) of paths.

It opens 10 am to dusk daily. Admission costs £4/1.

Places to Stay & Eat *Gordon House* (☎ 503383, @ dh20@fdn.co.uk, 12 Silver St) has comfortable B&B in an 18th-century property near the centre. Rooms cost £22/40.

The *Snooty Fox* (☎ 502436, fax 503479, @ res@snooty.fox.co.uk, Market Place) is probably Tetbury's fanciest place and has luxurious rooms for £67.50/90.

Tetbury Gallery Tearoom (☎ 503412, 18 Market Place) has a reputation far beyond the Cotswolds for teas and cakes.

For food with flavour, *The Mad Hatters (☎ 832615, 3 Cossack Square)* is an interesting organic restaurant with a famous fish soup.

Getting There & Away East of Wotton, on the A433, Tetbury has regular bus connections with Cirencester and Stroud.

Lechlade-upon-Thames
☎ 01367

At the highest navigable point of the River Thames, Lechlade is graced by the spire of **St Lawrence's Church**, described as an 'aerial pile' by Shelley in 1815 in his poem *A Summer Evening Churchyard, Lechlade, Gloucestershire*. A wool church, it was rededicated to the Spanish saint by Catherine of Aragon, who held the manor in the 16th century. It also has a famous toll bridge dating from 1792, known as the **Ha'penny Bridge**, recalling the sum charged to cross.

Kelmscott Manor About 3 miles (5km) east of Lechlade, off the Faringdon road, Kelmscott Manor (☎ 252486) was home to poet and artist William Morris, founder of the Arts and Crafts movement in 1871, and its leader until his death in 1896 (see the boxed text 'The Pre-Raphaelites & the Arts and Craft Movement' in the Birmingham section of the Midlands chapter).

It opens 11 am to 1 pm and 2 to 5 pm on Wednesday only, plus occasional summer Saturdays, April to September; admission costs £6/3. The Memorial Cottages nearby feature a beautiful carving of Morris seated under a tree.

Buscot Park This 18th-century neoclassical mansion is home to the Faringdon collection of paintings and furniture, which includes work by the pre-Raphaelites. The house opens 2 to 6 pm on Wednesday, Thursday and Friday, plus every other weekend, April to September. Admission

costs £4.40/2.20. It is 2¾ miles (4km) from Lechlade.

Places to Stay The *New Inn Hotel (☎ 252296, fax 252315, e newinnlech@ aol.com, Market Square)* is a Georgian coaching inn right in the middle of town. Singles/doubles cost £45/55.

Getting There & Away There are a couple of buses a day from Lechlade to Cirencester via Bibury.

Fairford

Fairford's claim to fame is **St Mary's Church**, which houses Britain's only complete set of medieval stained-glass windows. The gift of wealthy wool merchant John Tame, who also rebuilt the church, the windows are thought to be by Barnard Flower, master glass-painter to Henry VII. Tiddles, the church cat, is buried in the churchyard. The High St largely consists of graceful 18th-century houses.

CIRENCESTER
☎ 01285 ● pop 17,500

About 12 miles (19km) south of Cheltenham, Cirencester is the self-styled capital of the Cotswolds and the largest town in the region. The town was originally founded as a military base at the junction of the Roman Akeman St, Fosse Way and Ermin Way, starting life as Corinium, the second-largest Roman town after London. Eventually it was one of the principal towns of north-west Europe. The 2nd-century amphitheatre, on Cotswold Ave, is mostly grassed over, but was one of the largest in the country. The Saxons destroyed the town in the 6th century and built smaller settlements outside the walls, renaming it Cirencester. It only really regained its status in the Middle Ages when it became the most important Cotswold wool town.

Today it's an affluent medium-sized town with several worthwhile sights. Weekly markets still take place every Monday and Friday.

The centre clusters round the parish church on the Market Square. Here you'll find the TIC (☎ 654180, fax 641182), Corn Hall, Market Place, open 9.30 am to 5.30 pm Monday to Saturday (from 9.45 am on Monday).

Brewery Arts is a popular arts and craft centre (☎ 657181) in Brewery Court that has been around since 1979. There's a number of artisans based here and the quality of work is impressive.

Church of St John the Baptist

One of England's largest churches, St John's seems more like a cathedral. It has a magnificent perpendicular-style tower, built with the reward given by Henry IV to a group of earls who foiled a rebellion. The highlight of the exterior, however, is the three-storey south porch, which faces the square. Built as an office by late-15th-century abbots, it subsequently became the medieval town hall.

Inside the church several memorial brasses record the matrimonial histories of important wool merchants. A 15th-century painted stone pulpit comes complete with an hourglass and the east window contains fine medieval stained glass. A wall safe displays the Boleyn Cup, made for Anne Boleyn, second wife of Henry VIII, in 1535. The church is also notable for the oldest 12-bell peal in the country and continues to observe the ringing of the 'pancake bell' on Shrove Tuesday and the celebration of the Restoration on 29 May.

Corinium Museum

This museum (☎ 655611) in Park St shows local Roman finds in tableaux complete with impressive mosaics, including the famous *Hunting Dogs* and *Four Seasons*. It opens 10 am to 5 pm Monday to Saturday, and 2 to 5 pm on Sunday; it closes on Monday in winter. Admission costs £2.50/80p.

Cirencester Park

On the western edge of town, this park features magnificent geometrical landscaping, designed with the help of the poet Alexander Pope. The Broad Ride makes an excellent short walk.

Cirencester House was built by the first Earl of Bathurst between 1714 and 1718 and hides behind one of the world's highest yew hedges. It's not open to the public.

Places to Stay

If you're prepared to put up with a lack of facilities for a cheap stay, there's camping space for £1 per person on bicycle or on foot, £2 if you come by car, at *Abbey Home Farm* (☎ 656969/652808 daytime/evening), an organic farm a mile north of Cirencester on the Northleach road.

The *Duntisbourne Abbots Youth Hostel* (☎ 821682, fax 821697, e duntisbourne@ yha.org.uk, Old Rectory) is 5 miles (8km) north-west of Cirencester in a Victorian vicarage. It opens daily (except Sunday), April to October. The nightly charge is £9/6.20 for adults/juniors and the hostel is renowned for its good food. You need your own transport to get here.

During college holidays, rooms are available at the *Royal Agricultural College* (☎ 652531) on the northern outskirts. Rooms cost from £24.50/45 for a single/ double.

Victoria Rd has several B&Bs and guesthouses. The *Apsley Villa Guest House* (☎ 653489, 16 Victoria Rd) has five rooms costing from £25/40. *Wimborne House* (☎/fax 653890, 91 Victoria Rd), which is nonsmoking, has rooms with a bath from £30/40.

White Lion Inn (☎ 654053, fax 641316, e roylion@aol.com, 8 Gloucester St) is a 17th-century coaching inn five minutes' walk from the town centre. Rooms with bath cost from £39.50/47.

The *Golden Cross* (☎ 652137, Black Jack St) has good-value rooms from £20/30 and is about as central as it gets in Cirencester. The comfortable *Kings Head Hotel* (☎ 01942-824824, Market Place) is opposite the church. Rooms cost £65/85, less for two days or more.

Places to Eat

Cirencester has plenty of good places to eat. There's an excellent *cafe* inside Brewery Arts, just off Cricklade St, that some say does the best coffee in Cirencester, as well as some tasty cakes; it opens Monday to Saturday. Opposite is *The Café-Bar (Brewers Courtyard)*, which has a range of filled baguettes and ciabatta rolls, making it a good stop for a light lunch. *Black Jack Coffee House (Black Jack St)* is a good place to pause for refreshment. The *Swan Yard Café (6 Swan Yard)* does mouthwatering cakes.

For putting together a picnic you could hardly better *Jeroboams*, beside the church, where they claim to 'build' sandwiches rather than make them.

Those who savour the flavour of the sub-continent should make for the *Rajdoot Tandoori* (☎ 652651, Castle St), which has Sunday all-you-can-eat lunches for £6.95 (£4.95 for vegetarians), as well as a full menu of the usual favourites. For those that prefer a taste of the Orient, *Tatyans* (☎ 653529, Castle St) does the sort of Chinese that makes the pages of good-food guides.

The Mad Hatter Wine Bar and *MacKenzie* in Castle St serve cafe-bar-style lunches and are also popular places for a drink. *Somewhere Else* on Castle St has global food and a good courtyard for the summer.

There's real ale at the very local *Twelve Bells*, out on Lewis Lane, and good pub food at *The Black Horse* in Castle St.

Getting There & Away

National Express buses run from Cirencester to London (2¼ hours, £10.75).

Stagecoach (☎ 01242-522021) bus No 51 runs to Cheltenham. The less frequent No 52 runs to Gloucester. There are two buses daily to Lechlade-upon-Thames via Bibury. Bus No 92 runs to Chippenham (for Lacock) hourly, passing through Malmesbury.

GLOUCESTER
☎ 01452 • pop 106,600

Despite being a county capital, Gloucester (**glos**-ter) is less than the sum of its past and these days finds itself in the shadow of its more glamorous neighbour Cheltenham. Approaching the city, its physical location is impressive, nestled in the vale beneath the Cotswold escarpment and beside the River Severn. The city suffered greatly

from WWII bombing but is still well worth visiting, particularly for its wonderful Gothic cathedral and the cluster of museums in the restored docks. It also has some of the cheapest accommodation around, making it a good base for exploring the surrounding area.

History

To the Romans, Gloucester was Glevum, founded as a retirement home for Cirencester's centurions. It remained important to the Saxons as a garrison town at the junction of the kingdoms of Mercia and Wessex and grew to become a major monastic centre.

When Ethelred, Alfred the Great's brother, was buried in the Saxon royal palace near the cathedral, Gloucester equalled Winchester in importance and it remained as important to the Normans.

In 1216, Henry III's coronation took place in St Peter's Abbey. After murdered Edward II was buried here, Gloucester became an important place of pilgrimage, which helped develop its commercial importance.

During the Civil War, the city was a Puritan stronghold and withstood a 26-day siege. In the 18th century Gloucester flourished on the back of the Forest of Dean's iron, coal and timber industries. Throughout the 20th century it has been an industrial centre, producing at various times railway rolling stock, aircraft and motorcycles.

Orientation & Information

The city centre is based around Northgate, Southgate, Eastgate and Westgate Sts, which all converge on The Cross.

Gloucester's TIC (☎ 421188, fax 504273, e tourism@gloscity.gov.uk), 28 Southgate St, is located in a handsome building, and sells the *Via Sacra* town trail and a leaflet outlining the route of the 26-mile (42km) Glevum Way round the city outskirts. It opens 10 am to 5 pm Monday to Saturday and 11 am to 3 pm on Sunday.

Intercafe (☎ 305303), 124 Barton St, offers Internet access.

The Laundry Centre (☎ 300306), 104

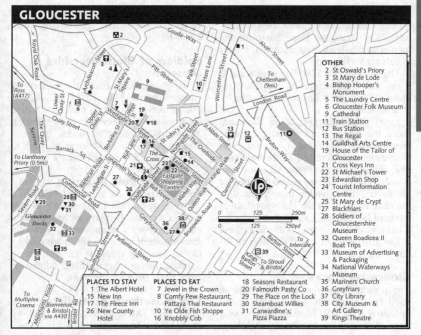

GLOUCESTER

OTHER
2 St Oswald's Priory
3 St Mary de Lode
4 Bishop Hooper's Monument
5 The Laundry Centre
6 Gloucester Folk Museum
9 Cathedral
11 Train Station
12 Bus Station
13 The Regal
14 Guildhall Arts Centre
19 House of the Tailor of Gloucester
21 Cross Keys Inn
22 St Michael's Tower
23 Edwardian Shop
24 Tourist Information Centre
25 St Mary de Crypt
27 Blackfriars
28 Soldiers of Gloucestershire Museum
32 Queen Boadicea II Boat Trips
33 Museum of Advertising & Packaging
34 National Waterways Museum
35 Mariners Church
36 Greyfriars
37 City Library
38 City Museum & Art Gallery
39 Kings Theatre

PLACES TO STAY	PLACES TO EAT	18 Seasons Restaurant
1 The Albert Hotel	7 Jewel in the Crown	20 Falmouth Pasty Co
15 New Inn	8 Comfy Pew Restaurant;	29 The Place on the Lock
17 The Fleece Inn	Pattaya Thai Restaurant	30 Steamboat Willies
26 New County	10 Ye Olde Fish Shoppe	31 Carwardine's;
Hotel	16 Knobbly Cob	Pizza Piazza

Westgate St, can clean up your life and opens daily.

Gloucester Cathedral

The gorgeous Gothic cathedral is still Gloucester's focal point, one of the earliest examples of the English perpendicular style. Built as part of St Peter's Abbey, the cathedral's foundation stone was laid in 1089. When the abbey was dissolved in 1541, the church became the centre of the new Gloucester diocese. The nave has some wonderful Norman arcading, with the last two bays at the western end rebuilt in perpendicular style in 1420. Note how the southern wall of the southern aisle leans out of true because of the defensive ditch of the Roman town beneath.

The magnificent 69m-high tower was constructed from 1450 to replace the 13th-century spire.

The newly restored east window, made in 1349 to commemorate local participation in the Battle of Crecy, is the largest in England, while the wooden choir stalls date from 1350. Above them soars wonderfully elaborate lierne vaulting. The late-15th-century Lady Chapel represents the final flowering of the perpendicular style.

In the south ambulatory is an effigy of Robert, William the Conqueror's eldest son. Edward II's magnificent tomb, surmounted by an alabaster effigy, is in the northern ambulatory.

The northern transept, containing a 13th-century reliquary, leads into the treasury and also gives access to the tribune gallery, with an exhibition on the cathedral's history (summer only). In the northern aisle is a memorial to John Stafford Smith, a Gloucester composer who wrote the tune for the US national anthem.

At the western end stands a statue of Edward Jenner (1749–1823), who discovered how to vaccinate people against smallpox at nearby Berkeley.

The Great Cloister has the country's oldest fan vaulting, dating from the 14th century. Don't miss the stone basin for the monks to wash at, with niches for their towels across the way.

The cathedral (☎ 528095) opens 8 am to 6 pm daily. Donations of £2.50 are requested. Guided tours are available by arrangement.

Every third year Gloucester Cathedral hosts the Three Choirs Festival (www.3choirs.org), an event it shares with Worcester and Hereford Cathedrals (see later in this chapter). Gloucester's next turn is in 2004. The cathedral is also destined for the silver screen, having been selected as the main location for the Hollywood adaptation of JK Rowling's Harry Potter stories. It has always been popular with visitors, but is likely to draw droves of devotees in future years.

Gloucester Docks
The present quay was first recorded in 1390. Direct trade with foreign ports started in 1580 and by 1780 some 600 ships a year were docking at Gloucester, although large ships generally got only as far as Bristol. The 15 warehouses in the dock area were built for the 19th-century corn trade. Now redundant, they've been refurbished and most house museums, offices and restaurants.

National Waterways Museum
Llanthony, the largest warehouse, houses the excellent National Waterways Museum (☎ 318054), which has a varied collection of historic vessels and imaginative displays. It opens 10 am to 5 pm daily; admission costs £4.75/3.75.

Museum of Advertising & Packaging
The Albert Warehouse, part of the Victoria Dock, which specialised in salt transhipment, houses the Museum of Advertising & Packaging (☎ 302309), Robert Opie's nostalgia-provoking collection of packaging ephemera. Everything is here from beer bottles to biscuit barrels, a real trip through

consumerism in the 20th century. It opens 10 am to 6 pm daily; admission costs £3.50/1.25.

Soldiers of Gloucestershire Museum
In the old Custom House, the Soldiers of Gloucestershire Museum (☎ 522682) is livelier than most military museums, telling the story of the county's brave boys during 300 years of conflict. It opens 10 am to 5 pm Tuesday to Sunday (daily, June to September); admission costs £4/2.

Gloucester Folk Museum
The Gloucester Folk Museum (☎ 526467), 99 Westgate St, is in a 16th-century former clothier's house. Displays include a dairy, an ironmonger's shop and a Victorian schoolroom. It opens 10 am to 5 pm Monday to Saturday (plus 10 am to 4 pm on Sunday, July to September); admission costs £2.00 (free for children).

City Museum & Art Gallery
The City Museum & Art Gallery (☎ 524131), Brunswick Rd, is worth visiting to see the beautiful Birdlip Mirror, which dates back to the 1st century AD. The museum opens 10 am to 5 pm daily (to 4 pm on Sunday). Admission costs £2.00 (free for children).

Other Things to See
St Nicholas House, next door to the Folk Museum, was the family home of the Whittingtons of pantomime fame, and one of those places where Elizabeth I slept. Nearby are the remains of St Oswald's Priory and St Mary de Lode, Gloucester's oldest church.

At 5 Southgate St, an Edwardian shop boasts a curious mechanical clock with figures representing the four countries of the United Kingdom. Along Eastgate St are 15th-century St Michael's Tower, Eastgate Market (pop inside to inspect the Beatrix Potter clock) and the remains of the East Gate itself.

If you're a fan of Beatrix Potter you'll love the House of the Tailor of Gloucester

The Tailor of Gloucester

Beatrix Potter's own favourite story was apparently *The Tailor of Gloucester*, the famous children's story she wrote and illustrated in 1901 as a Christmas present for a friend.

While visiting cousins at Harescombe Grange, near Stroud, she heard a story about a real-life tailor, John Prichard of Gloucester. As in her tale, he'd been asked to make a waistcoat for the city's mayor. He was so busy that the Saturday before the Monday when the garment was due, he'd only reached the cutting stage. But when he returned to the shop on Monday, he found it complete, bar a single buttonhole. A note pinned to it read, 'No more twist'.

Mystified (but commercially minded), he placed an advert in his window imploring people to come to Prichard's, where the 'waistcoats are made at night by the fairies'. Later it transpired that the tailor's assistants had finished the waistcoat after sleeping in the shop because they'd stayed out too late to get home.

John Prichard died in 1934 and his tombstone at Haresfield records that he was the Tailor of Gloucester. In Potter's version, the young tailor became an old one and the fairies became mice. She spent hours sketching on the streets of Gloucester and in local cottages. The house in Gloucester's College Court, which she chose as the tailor's fictional premises, is now a gift shop-cum-museum.

(☎ 422856), established in the shop that inspired the story of the same name. Open 10 am to 5 pm Monday to Saturday, admission costs £1 (free for children). The exhibition includes a very popular gift shop. **Blackfriars**, Ladybellgate St, is England's finest surviving example of a Dominican friary. Admission is free and it opens daily.

In Hempsted Lane, across Llanthony Bridge from the dock area, are the remains of **Llanthony Priory**, one of the richest Augustinian houses in England when it was dissolved in 1538.

Places to Stay

Many people prefer to day-trip from nearby Cheltenham. A dependable B&B is *Bienvenue (☎ 523284, 54 Central Rd)*, which starts at £18 per person, but gets cheaper the longer guests stay.

Much nearer the centre and in a charming old listed property is *The Albert Hotel (☎ 502081, 56-58 Worcester St)*, which charges £37/54 for B&B.

Historic *New Inn (☎ 522177, fax 301054, 16 Northgate St)*, reckoned to have been in the hospitality business more than 500 years, has reopened and offers good-value rooms for such a central location. Singles start at £29.95, doubles at £49.95, family

rooms are £59.95 and some romantic suites with four-poster beds are £79.95.

Similarly olde worlde is *The Fleece Inn (☎ 522762, fax 385371, Westgate St)*, which has singles/doubles starting at £26/33 including breakfast, or £35/40 with en suite facilities. Look out for the old telephone exchange behind reception.

The *New County Hotel (☎ 307000, fax 500487, 44 Southgate St)* is a clean, comfortable and characterful three-star hotel, a five-minute walk from the centre, and has doubles with en suite facilities costing from £65.

Places to Eat

Orchids at the Undercroft, in part of the former monastery great hall next to the cathedral, is a good place for lunch or tea. Also near the cathedral is the *Comfy Pew Restaurant (☎ 415648)*, housed in a delightful timber-framed building, which does teas and cakes, light lunches and a la carte dinners. Next door, *Pattaya Thai Restaurant (☎ 520739)* has set lunches for about £5 and a lengthy a la carte menu by night. It too is housed in an attractive black-and-white building, the sort of house the city was full of before bombing raids did their damage. Opposite the Beatrix Potter shop is the *Seasons Restaurant*

(☎ 307060), which does a two-course lunch for £5.95.

For fish and chips, go to *Ye Olde Fish Shoppe (☎ 522502, Hare Lane)*, just east of the cathedral; prices are relatively high for the national dish, but it has held a licence since 1535 so inflation has played its part. The *Falmouth Pasty Co (Westgate St)* rustles up fresh pasties. Another cheap option for sandwiches on the run is the *Knobbly Cob*, also on Westgate St.

For a curry, consider the *Jewel in the Crown (☎ 310666)*, which has all the popular subcontinent standards for around £5.

Gloucester Docks has several good places to eat. *The Place on the Lock (☎ 330253)*, on the 1st floor of the Glouc-ester Docks Antiques Centre, is cheaper than it might appear. *Steamboat Willies (☎ 300990)* has Tex-Mex dishes and pasta from £5.95. *Pizza Piazza (☎ 311951)*, overlooking the water in Merchants Quay shopping centre, does pizzas. There's also a *Carwardine's* coffee shop here.

Entertainment

The Regal (St Aldate St) is one of Gloucester's cheapest pubs, but for something with more character try the *Cross Keys Inn (Cross Keys Lane)*.

Getting There & Away

Gloucester is 16 miles (26km) from Cirencester, 45 miles (72km) from Bath, 49

Surfing the Severn Bore

A 'bore' is a tidal phenomenon that occurs when flood tides pour into the wide mouth of an estuary in greater volume than can easily flow along the normal channel of the river. The incoming tide then sweeps over the slower river flow and pushes upstream, flooding the riverbanks as it goes.

In England the most striking bore occurs on the River Severn, the country's longest river, which has one of the highest tides anywhere in the world. At its deepest point the Severn Bore can be 2.75m deep, although in October 1966 a bore measuring 2.82m and travelling at 13 miles (21km) an hour was recorded.

In recent years a new sport of bore-surfing has developed, with surfers, body-boarders and canoeists lining up to catch the wave. If they time it right they can ride for 1½ miles (2.5km) upriver, much to the irritation of traditionalists who think that the surfers are spoiling this amazing natural phenomenon.

The best places to see the Severn Bore are between Awre, where the estuary narrows, and Gloucester. Gloucester TIC can tell you the best dates to go bore-watching. Wear wellies, as the water floods the surounding roads.

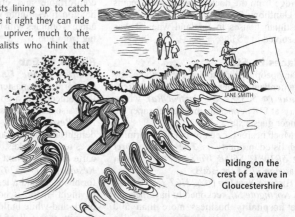

JANE SMITH

Riding on the crest of a wave in Gloucestershire

miles (79km) from Oxford and 105 miles (169km) from London. National Express has all the usual connections, and buses every two hours to London (3½ hours, £11). Stagecoach operates most local bus services; phone ☎ 01242-522021 for details. An Explorer ticket to use the Gloucestershire bus network for a day costs £4.50/3. There are buses every 15 minutes to Cheltenham, but the quickest way to get there is by train (10 minutes, £2.30).

AROUND GLOUCESTER
Slimbridge
☎ 01453

The renowned **Slimbridge Wildfowl & Wetlands Centre** (☎ 891900) was established in 1946 by the late Sir Peter Scott as a breeding ground for wildfowl, notably geese and swans. It is 11 miles (18km) south-west of Gloucester. Open 9.30 am to 5 pm daily (9.30 am to 4 pm in winter), the centre is as interesting in winter – when Arctic 'visitors' arrive – as it is in summer. Admission costs £5.75/3.50, and is discounted if you stay the night before at *Slimbridge Youth Hostel* (☎ 890275, fax 890 625, e slimbridge@yha.org.uk), half a mile south across the Sharpness Canal. The hostel opens March to August; phone for other times. The nightly charge is £9.80/ 6.75 for adults/juniors.

Badgerline (☎ 0117-955 5111) bus No 308 service links Bristol with Gloucester and passes by the Slimbridge crossroads, 2 miles (3km) from the centre. On Sunday, Stagecoach operates three buses to and from the sanctuary; phone ☎ 01452-527516 for exact times.

BERKELEY
☎ 01453

This quiet Georgian town is best known as the place where Edward II met his grisly end in Berkeley Castle. His last days must have been as awful as his death (he was supposedly impaled on a red-hot poker); the ventilation shaft in the murder room was connected to a pit in which the rotting carcasses of dead animals were thoughtfully kept.

Berkeley Castle
The beautiful medieval castle (☎ 810332) is set in terraced Elizabethan gardens surrounded by lawns. It was built by Lord Maurice Berkeley in 1153 and has remained in the family ever since.

It opens 2 to 5 pm Tuesday to Sunday in April and May; 11 am to 5 pm Tuesday to Saturday (plus Monday in July and August) and 2 to 5 pm on Sunday, June to September; and 2 to 4.30 pm on Sunday in October. Admission costs £5.40/2.90, or £2/1 just for the grounds. The **Butterfly Farm** across the car park opens one hour after the castle and closes at 5.30 pm; admission costs £2/1.

A path winds through **St Mary's** churchyard, with its unusual detached bell tower, to the **Jenner Museum** (☎ 810631), in the house where Edward Jenner performed the first smallpox vaccination in 1796. Opening hours are similar to the castle's, but it's closed on Monday. Admission costs £2.50/1.

Getting There & Away
Berkeley is 6 miles (10km) south-west of Slimbridge. Badgerline bus No 308 from Bristol to Gloucester passes this way.

CHELTENHAM
☎ 01242 • pop 88,000

Cheltenham is, like its more illustrious sibling Bath, one of England's definitive spa towns. These days, though, it is not so much known for its waters as for its racecourse and its public school, Cheltenham Ladies' College. The planners haven't been quite as kind to what is essentially a Regency town as they have to Bath – the town's handsome squares, colourful public gardens and elegant early-19th-century architecture are interspersed with obtrusive and incongruous slabs of modernity – but it nonetheless exudes a certain culture and class.

With plenty of restaurants and accommodation, Cheltenham makes an ideal base for exploring the western Cotswolds. As it's also a city of gracious parks and gardens there's no need to go far to relax. **Imperial Gardens**, outside the Queen's hotel, are a floral riot, while nearby **Montpellier Gardens** have an old Victorian bandstand.

Cheltenham is also the scene of four important festivals: the National Hunt Meeting in March, during which the Cheltenham Gold Cup is run; the Music and Cricket festivals in July; and the Literature Festival in October. At these times, the odds on your finding a room are worse than those on your winning the National Lottery.

History
As a village midway between Gloucester and Tewkesbury, and on the road to Winchcombe and Oxford, Cheltenham received its market charter in 1226, when it was little more than a row of houses each side of the current High St. It remained important after the Civil War, when the area of the southern Cotswolds became associated, briefly, with tobacco production, but it really started to flourish after 1788, when George III visited to take the waters.

In 1716, pigeons pecking in a field under what is now the Ladies' College turned out to be eating salt crystals from a spring. Following fashion, the owner's son-in-law built a substantial pump room and opened it to the public. The king's visit sealed the spa's future and several new wells were built, as well as houses to accommodate the hordes of visitors, among them Handel and Jane Austen.

Modern visitors usually find the architecture more interesting than the waters. The elegant Regency style is evident around town in beautifully proportioned terraces, mostly creamy white and decorated with wrought-iron balconies and railings. Believe it or not, many of these attractive, imposing terraces were the prefabs of the early 19th century, built by property speculators with an eye for a quick buck. By the 1960s, many were sinking under their own weight and many millions of pounds had to be spent just to keep them standing.

Orientation
Cheltenham train station is out on a limb to the west; bus F or G will run you to the centre for 65p. The bus station is more conveniently positioned immediately behind The Promenade in the town centre.

Central Cheltenham is eminently walkable. The High St runs roughly east-west and south from it is The Promenade, the most elegant shopping area ('the Bond St of the West'). The Promenade extends into Montpellier, a 19th-century shopping precinct, beyond which lie Suffolk Square and Lansdown Crescent. Pittville Park and the old Pump Room are a mile north of the High St.

Information
The helpful TIC (☎ 522878, fax 255848, e tic@cheltenham.gov.uk), 77 The Promenade, opens 9.30 am to 5.15 pm Monday to Saturday. It sells all sorts of Cotswold walking and cycling guides, as well as *The Romantic Road*, a guide to a 30-mile (48km) circular driving tour of the southern Cotswolds. It also stocks a leaflet listing public transport options to the most popular tourist destinations around Cheltenham.

There are guided tours of the town that leave the TIC at 11 am Monday to Friday in July and August; the charge is £2.50.

The Promenade
The Promenade is the heart of Cheltenham and is at its best in summer, when its hanging baskets are full of flowers.

The **Municipal Offices**, built as private residences in 1825, are one of the best features of one of Britain's most beautiful thoroughfares. In front of the offices stands a **statue of Edward Wilson** (1872–1912), a Cheltenham man who went on Captain Scott's ill-fated second expedition (1910–12) to the South Pole and died in Antarctica.

Following The Promenade towards Montpellier, you come to the **Imperial Gardens**, originally built to service the Imperial Spa but covered by the Winter Gardens in 1902. The iron-and-glass structure was dismantled during WWII in case its reflection attracted German bombers.

Pittville Pump Room
Set in a delightful area of villas and park a mile from the town centre, the Pump Room

is the town's finest Regency-style building. Built between 1825 and 1830, it was constructed as a spa and social centre for Joseph Pitt's new estate. Upstairs, there are occasional art exhibitions in the former library and billiard rooms.

It opens daily (except Tuesday), but times vary; admission is free. Downstairs (where it's still possible to try the spa water), the former ballroom is used for concerts.

The park itself is also used for concerts ('Pittville on Sunday') throughout the summer.

Art Gallery & Museum

Cheltenham's history is well displayed at the Art Gallery & Museum (☎ 237431), Clarence St, with excellent sections covering Edward Wilson, William Morris and the Arts and Crafts movement, and Dutch and British art. There's a temporary exhibition gallery on the ground floor and a cafe on the first floor. It opens 10 am to 5.20 pm Monday to Saturday; admission is free.

Gustav Holst Birthplace Museum

The Victorian house (☎ 524846) at 4 Clarence Rd where composer Gustav Holst

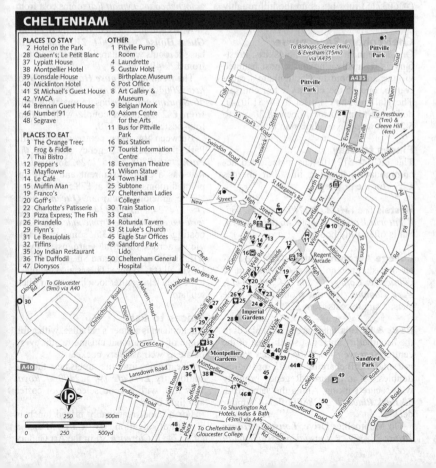

CHELTENHAM

PLACES TO STAY
2 Hotel on the Park
28 Queen's; Le Petit Blanc
37 Lypiatt House
38 Montpellier Hotel
39 Lonsdale House
40 Micklinton Hotel
41 St Michael's Guest House
42 YMCA
44 Brennan Guest House
46 Number 91
48 Segrave

PLACES TO EAT
3 The Orange Tree; Frog & Fiddle
7 Thai Bistro
12 Pepper's
13 Mayflower
14 Le Café
15 Muffin Man
19 Franco's
20 Goff's
22 Charlotte's Patisserie
23 Pizza Express; The Fish
26 Pirandello
29 Flynn's
31 Le Beaujolais
32 Tiffins
35 Joy Indian Restaurant
36 The Daffodil
47 Dionysos

OTHER
1 Pitville Pump Room
4 Laundrette
5 Gustav Holst Birthplace Museum
6 Post Office
8 Art Gallery & Museum
9 Belgian Monk
10 Axiom Centre for the Arts
11 Bus for Pittville Park
16 Bus Station
17 Tourist Information Centre
18 Everyman Theatre
21 Wilson Statue
24 Town Hall
25 Subtone
27 Cheltenham Ladies College
30 Train Station
33 Casa
34 Rotunda Tavern
43 St Luke's Church
45 Eagle Star Offices
49 Sandford Park Lido
50 Cheltenham General Hospital

(1874–1934) was born displays Holst memorabilia alongside descriptions of life 'below stairs' at the turn of the century. You get to listen to the music as you go round too (*The Planets*, usually). It opens 10 am to 4.15 pm Tuesday to Saturday; admission costs £2.50/1.25.

Cleeve Hill

About 4 miles (6km) north of Cheltenham, Cleeve Hill, at 325m (1066 feet), is the highest point of the Cotswolds and lowland England, and offers fine views over Cheltenham. On weekdays, Castleways (☎ 603715) runs buses up the hill roughly once an hour from the town centre.

Cheltenham Racecourse

On Cheltenham's northern outskirts, Prestbury is reputedly England's most haunted village and home to Cheltenham's racecourse, one of the country's top courses. The Hall of Fame museum (☎ 513014), dedicated to its history, opens 8.30 am to 5.30 pm weekdays; admission is free.

Places to Stay

The TIC (☎ 517110) has a dedicated accommodation booking line, but charges £2.75 for the privilege.

Hostels The *YMCA (☎ 524024, fax 232635, 6 Vittoria Walk)* has some singles for £15, but is often fully booked.

College Accommodation Over the Easter and summer holidays, *Cheltenham & Gloucester College (☎ 532774, fax 543412, Park Campus)* lets out rooms at its three sites; a single costs from £25.

B&Bs & Hotels There are several places in the Montpellier area, just south-west of the centre. *Segrave (☎ 523606, 7 Park Place)* is a small B&B charging £16/35 for singles/doubles, set in a sturdy Regency property with secure parking. Along the same road, *32 Park Place (☎ 582889)* offers a similar deal.

On Montpellier Drive, *Lonsdale House (☎/fax 232379, e lonsdalehouse@hotmail .com)* is a comfortable B&B set in a charming town house and has well appointed singles/doubles starting at £21/42. *St Michael's Guest House (☎/fax 513587, 4 Montpellier Drive)* is smaller but equally popular and charges £28/40 for homely rooms in a nonsmoking Edwardian property.

Number 91 (☎ 579441, 91 Montpellier Terrace), where Wilson of the doomed 1910–12 Antarctic expedition was born, has lovely rooms for £26/50.

At the sophisticated *Lypiatt House (☎ 224994, fax 224996, e lypiatthouse@ gofornet.co.uk, Lypiatt Rd)* rooms cost from £55/65.

Also centrally located, friendly *Brennan Guest House (☎ 525904, 21 St Lukes Rd)* has six rooms with shared bathroom costing from £22/40.

The *Beaumont House Hotel (☎ 245986, fax 520044, e rocking.horse@virgin.net, 56 Shurdington Rd)* has rooms with bath from £42/60, and a couple with opulent four-poster beds for £78.

Between the town centre and Pittville Park, the luxurious Regency *Hotel on the Park (☎ 518898, fax 511526, 38 Evesham Rd)* has a good restaurant and well appointed rooms starting at £78.50/96.50.

The gracious Victorian *Queen's* hotel (☎ 514724, fax 224145, e gm1050@ forte-hotels.com, The Promenade)* has rooms costing from £100/135, some with fine views across Imperial Gardens. Edward VII, Sir Edward Elgar and Sir Arthur Conan Doyle all stayed here. This is also the place to be seen taking afternoon high tea in Cheltenham.

Places to Eat

Cheltenham is a diner's paradise, with a full range of international cuisine to suit every palate as well as every pocket.

Cheap cafes litter the streets near the bus station; try *Le Café (☎ 522400, 1 Royal Well Rd)*, with a good selection of coffee and light bites.

For a good, reasonably priced lunch in a central location try *Café Museum (☎ 237431, Clarence St)* in the Art Gallery

& Museum: soup, a roll and a cake will cost less than £4. Another popular place with the local movers and shakers is *Tiffins* (☎ 222492, 4 Montpellier Walk), where there is a dazzling array of sandwiches to eat in or take away.

If cakes alone are in order, *Charlotte's Patisserie* (☎ 575144, 112 The Promenade) can deliver. The *Orange Tree* (☎ 234232, 317 High St) is an inviting vegetarian restaurant and even serves up organic wine and beer to accompany the fare. *Axiom Centre for the Arts* (☎ 253183, 57 Winchcombe St) also has a vegetarian cafe serving veggie shepherd's pie.

The excellent *Indus* (☎ 516676, 226 Bath Rd) is possibly the best of the town's Indian restaurants and specialises in tandoori. It recently made the Top 100 in the *Good Curry Guide*. For a more central location, classy *Joy Indian Restaurant* (☎ 522888, Lansdown Rd) is hard to beat, overlooking Montpellier Gardens.

For a taste of China, head to the *Mayflower* (☎ 522426, 32 Clarence St), an established favourite, with some incredible set menus and a great selection of vegetarian food including 'mock duck'. Most main courses are in the £6 to £8 range. For something with a little more spice, *Thai Bistro* (☎ 244590, 8 Well Walk) serves up a wide range of Siam favourites.

Franco's (☎ 224880, 49 Rodney Rd) is a traditional Italian restaurant where a three-course meal costs about £15. They don't serve pizza. Another new Italian is *Pirandello* (☎ 234599, The Promenade), but the menu is expensive so expect to spend £20 for the works.

Pizza Express (☎ 253896, Imperial Square), inside Belgrave House, has live jazz on Wednesday evening and the usual excellent pizzas. For those who prefer the more south-easterly reaches of the Mediterranean, *Dionysos* (☎ 227277, 8 Suffolk Parade) is a Greek Cypriot restaurant that has won local awards. Try a meze for the full experience.

Pepper's (☎ 573488, Regent St) is a brasserie with an outdoor area for summer drinks.

Two of the finest dining places in Cheltenham are *Le Beaujolais* (☎ 525230, 15 Rotunda Terrace) and *Le Petit Blanc* (☎ 266800, Queen's, The Promenade). Le Beaujolais is a small, slick French restaurant offering sumptuous set menus for £15.95 for lunch and £18.95 for dinner. Le Petit Blanc is a not-so-poor-man's introduction to the sort of food the other half eat – it has fantastic, entry-level three-course meals for £15, but hearty eaters will not find the portions up to the presentation.

One more place definitely worth considering is *The Daffodil* (☎ 700055, 18 Suffolk Parade), housed in a sympathetically restored Art Deco cinema. The menu is modern British with a hint of France and the Mediterranean, and the *Independent* newspaper described it as 'Cheltenham's hottest restaurant' – perhaps they didn't have the air-conditioning on that day.

Entertainment

Pubs & Clubs For a sophisticated cafe-bar try *Casa* (Montpellier Walk); it's where some of Cheltenham's bright young things like to gather for drinks as well as fine food. *The Fish* (Imperial Square) is a pretty funky little place tucked away next to Pizza Express that plays some good tunes.

For those more worried about beer than atmosphere, the *Belgian Monk* (Clarence St) has an excellent array of strong and fruity stuff. The *Rotunda Tavern* (The Promenade) is more like the pub visitors expect from England and is housed in one of Cheltenham's landmark buildings. One last place worth a stop is the *Frog & Fiddle* down at the architecturally challenged end of the High St, an up-and-coming part of town.

Dedicated clubbers might find Cheltenham lacking, but *Subtone* (☎ 575925, 117 The Promenade) gets a steady crowd and draws occasional big-name DJs from London.

Theatre & Music The *Everyman* theatre (☎ 572573, Regent St) stages everything from comedy and panto to Shakespeare. *Pittville Pump Room* often hosts classical music concerts, while the *Town Hall* (☎ 227979, Imperial Square) goes for the more popular stuff. The *Axiom Centre for the Arts* (☎ 690243, 57 Winchcombe St) also has a regular program of less mainstream musical and theatrical events.

Getting There & Away

Cheltenham is 9 miles (14km) from Gloucester, 40 miles (64km) from Bristol, 43 miles (69km) from Oxford and 100 miles (161km) from London.

Bus National Express (☎ 0870 580 8080) runs buses between Cheltenham and London (2¾ hours, £11), Oxford (1¼ hours, £7.75) and all the other places on the National Express network. Swanbrook Coaches (☎ 01452-712386) also has buses to Oxford (1½ hours, £5).

Stagecoach (☎ 522021) runs buses every 10 minutes to Gloucester (30 minutes). Monday to Saturday it has buses (No 51) every two hours to Cirencester (30 minutes). It also runs weekday buses to Tewkesbury; phone for details.

Pulhams Coaches (☎ 01451-820369) runs daily buses to Moreton-in-Marsh (one hour) via Bourton-on-the-Water and Stow-on-the-Wold. Castleways Coaches (☎ 602949) operates regular services between Cheltenham and Broadway (45 minutes) via Winchcombe, Monday to Saturday.

Train Cheltenham is on the Bristol to Birmingham line, with hourly trains to London (2½ hours, £31.50), Bristol (45 minutes, £7.20) and Bath (one hour, £11.20), and frequent departures for Gloucester (10 minutes, £2.30).

Getting Around

Compass Holidays (☎ 250642) have bicycles for hire for £11 per day at Cheltenham train station.

TEWKESBURY

☎ 01684 • pop 9500

Just 8 miles (13km) north-west of Cheltenham, Tewkesbury is a charming country town liberally endowed with timber-framed buildings and dominated by its magnificent, partly Norman abbey church. The Battle of Tewkesbury took place here in May 1471, one of the most savage of the Civil War, in which the Yorkist Edward IV reclaimed his throne from the Lancastrian Henry VI. It was the final flourish of Margaret of Anjou, the scheming queen of the incompetent Henry, and her forces were routed. The site of the battle – off Lincoln Green Lane, south-west of the abbey – is known as Bloody Meadow to this day.

It's well worth wandering in and out of the narrow alleys and courts, down one of which you'll find an old **Baptist chapel** in a building dating back to the 15th century. Church St, Mill St and Mill Bank are particularly worth exploring.

The TIC (☎ 295027, fax 292277), 64 Barton St, shares the same building as the town's museum (admission 70/25p). It opens 9 am to 5 pm Monday to Saturday and 10 am to 4 pm on Sunday.

Tewkesbury Abbey

The town's focal point is the church of the former Benedictine abbey, the last of the monasteries to be dissolved by Henry VIII. Stone to build it was brought by sea and river from Normandy in the 12th century. Tewkesbury's fortunes depended on the wool industry because the abbey owned land and sheep all over the Cotswolds. When the abbey was dissolved, the church survived because the townspeople bought it.

One of England's largest churches, with a 40m-high tower, the abbey has some spectacular Norman pillars lining the nave, 14th-century stained glass above the choir and an organ dating from 1631. Don't miss the tombs of Edward, Baron Le Despenser, who fought at Poitiers in 1356, and John Wakeman, the last abbot, who is shown as a vermin-ridden skeleton. Also here beneath the chancel is Edward, Prince of Wales, son of Henry VI and the most notable victim of the Yorkist massacre that took place in the abbey after the Battle of Tewkesbury.

A new visitors centre by the gate houses the Abbey Refectory, which does tea, coffee and lunches. Abbey visitors are asked for donations of £2.

Other Things to See & Do

The **John Moore Countryside Museum** (☎ 297174), in a 15th-century house at 41 Church St, has a nature conservation collection. It opens 10 am to 1 pm and 2 to 5 pm Tuesday to Saturday, April to October; admission costs £1/50p.

During the summer, daily cruises on the Kingfisher Ferry along the River Avon to the Fleet Inn are available with Telstar (☎ 294088), Riverside Walk. It also offers self-drive cruisers starting at £30 for two hours, holding up to six passengers.

Places to Stay

The nicest places to stay are all near the abbey in Church St. Cheapest is *Crescent Guest House (☎ 293395, 30 Church St)*, which charges £19 per person.

Abbey Hotel (☎ 294247, fax 297208, 67 Church St) charges from £45/60. Opposite the abbey entrance, the *Bell Hotel (☎ 293293, fax 295938, 52 Church St)* has doubles with bath costing from £75. Attractive *Jessop House Hotel (☎ 292017, fax 273076, 65 Church St)* charges £45/75.

There are a couple of cheaper places in Barton Rd, east of the TIC. *Barton House (☎ 292049, 5 Barton Rd)* charges £18 per person in a double, and rooms in *Hanbury House (☎ 299911, Hanbury Terrace, Barton Rd)* start at £36 for a double. However these places are a little farther from the town centre.

Places to Eat

My Great Grandfather's (☎ 292687, 85 Church St) is a homely restaurant and tearoom. Cream teas cost under £3 and there's roast beef, pork or lamb for weekday lunches. The *Hen & Chickens Eating House (☎ 292703, 73 Church St)* does dishes such as smoked fish and seafood crumble. Nearby, the *Abbey Tea Rooms (☎ 292215, 59 Church St)* does roasts for around a fiver. *Aubergine (☎ 292703, 73 Church St)* is an elegant cafe with a fresh menu.

Le Bistrot André (☎ 290357, 78 Church St) is a reasonably priced French restaurant. Starters cost around £3; main dishes range from £8 to £13. For those desiring cuisine from further afield, *New World (☎ 292225, 61 High St)* is a superb Vietnamese restaurant run by a former resident of Hanoi; the food is very authentic and reasonably priced.

Entertainment

The *Royal Hop Pole (Church St)*, mentioned in Dickens' *Pickwick Papers*, is a popular pub, restaurant and hotel. Alternatively, try the incredibly old *Berkeley Arms (Church St)* or the historic *Ye Olde Black Bear (High St)* for a drink.

Getting There & Away

The easiest way to get to Tewkesbury is on Stagecoach's hourly bus No 41 from Clarence St in Cheltenham. Stagecoach also has weekday bus services to Tewkesbury from Gloucester and Worcester; phone ☎ 01242-522021 for details.

You can also get from Cheltenham to Tewkesbury by train, but Ashchurch station is about 3 miles (5km) out of town.

FOREST OF DEAN
☎ 01594

Formerly a royal hunting ground, the Forest of Dean occupies a triangular plateau between Gloucester, Ross and Chepstow, and comprises an area of 42 sq miles (including 28 sq miles of woodland) subject to ancient forest law. It is a rewarding part of Gloucestershire to explore as its relative isolation keeps visitor numbers well below those of the Cotswolds. It's also an excellent area for walking or cycling.

Information

The main TIC (☎ 812388, **e** tourism@ fdean.gov.uk), on the High St in Coleford, stocks walking and cycling guides. It opens 10 am to 5 pm Monday to Saturday and 10 am to 1.30 pm on Sunday. It offers a free bed-booking service.

Forest Adventure (☎ 834661), 5 Brummels Drive, Coleford, offers activities such as rock climbing, caving, abseiling and kayaking.

Miners of the Forest of Dean

From before Roman times the Forest of Dean was an important source of timber, iron and stone. A coal seam covering thousands of acres also runs under the forest. By a curious anomaly, for the past 700 years a select band of foresters from St Briavels has retained the right to mine this coal, a right won by their forefathers as a reward for their skill in tunnelling under castle fortifications. Although many men could still lay theoretical claim to this right after working for a year and a day in a mine, only two full-time 'free mines' are still in operation and they are one-man operations.

Things to See & Do

The **Clearwell Caves** (☎ 832535), near Coleford, have been mined for iron since the Iron Age, and you can wander through nine dank, spooky caves and inspect the paraphernalia of the mine workings alongside pools and rock formations. Every Halloween something akin to an underground rave takes place in Barbecue Churn, the largest cave; you need to book ahead for this. The caves open 10 am to 5 pm daily, March to October. Admission costs £3/2.20.

Less than 3 miles (5km) away is the pretty village of **Newland**, dominated by **All Saints**, the so-called 'Cathedral of the Forest'. In the Greyndour Chantry look for the brass depicting a free miner (see the boxed text 'Miners of the Forest of Dean') with a *nelly*, or tallow candle, in his mouth, a pick in his hand and a *billy*, or backpack, on his back.

Also near Coleford is the **Hope Colliery Museum**, a working free mine open to the public 10 am to 4.30 pm daily, Easter to October. Admission costs £3/2.

At the Beechenhurst Enclosure near Cinderford you can follow the easy Forest of Dean **sculpture trail**.

The **Dean Heritage Centre** (☎ 822170), in an old mill at Soudley, near Cinderford, recounts the history of the forest and the free miners. It opens 10 am to 6 pm daily, April to September, and 10 am to 5 pm daily in February, March and October. Admission costs £3.50/2. The **Dean Heritage Kitchen** does lunches and teas.

Places to Stay & Eat

Imposing **St Briavel's Castle Youth Hostel** (☎ 530272, fax 530849, e stbriavels@yha .org.uk, Lydney) has a moat and was once a hunting lodge used by King John. It's west of the forest above the Wye Valley and charges £10.85/7.40 for adults/juniors.

In Clearwell village the **Tudor Farmhouse Hotel** (☎ 833046, fax 837093, e reservations@tudorfarmhouse.u-net.com) has excellent double rooms with bath starting at £65. **Scatterford Farm** (☎ 836562, fax 836323, Newland) offers comfortable B&B for £27/44 in an ancient country farmhouse. **Cherry Orchard Farm** (☎ 832212, Newland) has B&B costing from £20 per person on a working dairy farm. They have two rooms, but phone ahead for directions. There are also a couple of camping pitches available. **Tan House Farm** (☎ 832222, fax 833561, e christie.arno3@virgin.net, Newland) hardly looks like a farm, more like a small French chateau, and B&B in these lovely surroundings costs £25 per person for the first night, £22 thereafter.

Getting There & Away

Buses run from Gloucester and Monmouth to Coleford, Lydney and the smaller villages. Cirencester and Ross-on-Wye are the other options for beginning a trip into the area. Phone the Gloucestershire public transport enquiry line for details on ☎ 01452-425543.

Trains run to Lydney Junction. On Wednesday, Thursday, Saturday and Sunday, April to September, steam trains run on the Dean Forest Railway from Lydney to Norchard (£4.20/2.20). For details phone ☎ 845840.

Getting Around

With relatively little traffic on most of the roads this is sound cycling country. Pedalabikeaway (☎ 860065), at Cannop Valley on the B4234, hires out bicycles for £10 a day, but only does day rents. Forest Cycle Centre (☎ 832121, e pkendall@compuserve.com), 44 Park Rd, Coleford, is in an easier location and rates start from £6 for half a day. You could think about bringing a bike from somewhere nearby, such as Ross-on-Wye.

NEWENT
☎ 01531 • pop 5160
The unspoilt, small town of Newent feels a little like the land that time forgot, perennially caught in 1950s England – or perhaps an even earlier era given the popularity of the Shambles Museum of Victorian Life.

The TIC (☎ 822468), 7 Church St, is almost opposite the museum. It opens 9 am to 12.30 pm and 1.30 to 4 pm Monday to Friday, and 10 am to 4 pm on Saturday.

Shambles Museum of Victorian Life
The Shambles Museum (☎ 822144) is a sort of living museum with assorted Victorian-style shop fronts around a tearoom. It opens 10 am to 6 pm Tuesday to Sunday, Easter to December. Admission costs £3.50/1.95.

National Birds of Prey Centre
At the National Birds of Prey Centre (☎ 820286), on the outskirts of Newent, you can watch hawks and owls in free flight during daily displays. It opens 10.30 am to 5.30 pm daily, February to November; admission costs £5.50/3.25.

Museum of Crime Through Time
This museum (☎ 821888) in Nicholson House depicts criminals and their crimes through the ages and is housed in a former police station. The exhibits are generally gruesome and include a guillotine, torture instruments and personal artefacts of notorious criminals such as hardman Charles Bronson. It opens 10 am to 5 pm daily and admission costs £3/2.

Places to Stay & Eat
The *George Hotel (☎ 820203, Church St)* is an old coaching inn with very reasonable rates starting at just £16 per person in a double.

The *Singing Kettle (☎ 822941, 1 Cheapside)* is a cafe and restaurant just off Church St. The cafe has light lunches, while the restaurant serves up fish and game into the evening. Good food and English wine can be sampled at the *restaurant* at the Three Choirs Vineyard (☎ 890223), where self-guided tours are available for £2.50/1.50.

Getting There & Away
National Express (☎ 0870 580 8080) has daily services linking Newent to Hereford and London. Stagecoach bus No 32 runs here from Gloucester.

Herefordshire

Bounded by the Malverns to the east and Wales to the west, Herefordshire is a sleepy county of fields and hedgerows, virtually untainted by tourism. The River Wye winds its way through the countryside, and dotted about are several attractive market towns and pretty black-and-white villages. Hereford, Ross-on-Wye and Hay-on-Wye all make good bases for exploration.

Herefordshire has its own Web site at www.herefordshiretourism.com.

WALKING
Several long-distance paths pass through this area. The Offa's Dyke Path runs along the western border with Wales. The 107-mile (172km) Wye Valley Walk begins in Chepstow (Wales) and follows the river's course upstream into England through Herefordshire and back into Wales to Rhayader. The Three Choirs Way links Hereford to Worcester and Gloucester.

GETTING AROUND
First Midland Red (☎ 01905-763888) is the region's biggest bus company. A Day Rover pass costs £4.60/3.60 and allows travel anywhere on its system and on routes run by most other smaller companies. For general bus information, phone ☎ 0845 712 5436. The Wye Valley Wanderer is a popular bus

THE THAMES TO THE WYE

linking Ross-on-Wye and the Wye Valley with Worcestershire on summer Sundays and bank holiday Mondays; call ☎ 01432-260948 for more details.

There are rail links from Hereford to Shrewsbury, Worcester, Birmingham and Cardiff.

HEREFORD
☎ 01432 • pop 48,400

At first, Hereford might feel like the back of beyond, but stay a while and it is a town of warmth and spirit, home to one of the world's most famous maps, a potent (if patched-together) cathedral and some fine historic architecture.

Hereford owes its importance to its position on the River Wye on the border with Wales, where it became a garrison protecting the Saxons from the Welsh tribes. It was the capital of the Saxon kingdom of Mercia, and has been a cathedral city since the beginning of the 8th century.

Orientation & Information

The High Town shopping centre is at the heart of the city on the north bank of the River Wye, with the cathedral a few blocks south along Church St. The bus station lies to the north-east, off Commercial Rd, with the train station a little farther out, behind the Safeway supermarket.

The ever-helpful TIC (☎ 268430), 1 King St, is opposite the cathedral. It opens 9 am to 5 pm Monday to Saturday, plus 10 am to 4 pm on Sunday in summer. There are guided walking tours (☎ 266867) at 10.30 am Monday to Saturday and at 2.30 pm on Sunday, June to September (£2/1).

The Pi Shop (☎ 377444), 17 King St, is an excellent Internet cafe charging £4 an hour.

Hereford Cathedral

The purple-red cathedral (☎ 374200) is less aesthetically satisfying than many of the

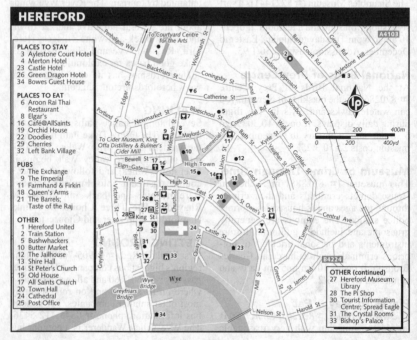

HEREFORD

PLACES TO STAY
3 Aylestone Court Hotel
4 Merton Hotel
23 Castle Hotel
26 Green Dragon Hotel
34 Bowes Guest House

PLACES TO EAT
6 Aroon Rai Thai
 Restaurant
8 Elgar's
16 Café@AllSaints
19 Orchid House
22 Doodies
29 Cherries
32 Left Bank Village

PUBS
7 The Exchange
9 The Imperial
11 Farmhand & Firkin
18 Queen's Arms
21 The Barrels;
 Taste of the Raj

OTHER
1 Hereford United
2 Train Station
5 Bushwhackers
10 Butter Market
12 The Jailhouse
13 Shire Hall
14 St Peter's Church
15 Old House
17 All Saints Church
20 Town Hall
24 Cathedral
25 Post Office

OTHER (continued)
27 Hereford Museum;
 Library
28 The Pi Shop
30 Tourist Information
 Centre; Spread Eagle
31 The Crystal Rooms
33 Bishop's Palace

great English cathedrals, partly because of the reconstruction after the west tower collapsed into the nave in 1786, and partly because the stonework is a bit too frilly.

Although parts of the cathedral date back to the 11th century and the 50m-high central sandstone tower was built in the 14th century, the west front is less than 100 years old. Inside the cathedral, much of the Norman nave, with its arches, remains. In the choir is the 14th-century bishop's throne and King Stephen's chair, said to have been used by the king himself. In the northern transept is the shrine of St Thomas Cantilupe, a 13th-century Hereford bishop whose tomb became an object of veneration and pilgrimage. The south transept contains three tapestries showing the tree of life designed by John Piper in 1976.

The cathedral is best known for two ancient treasures: the 13th-century **Mappa Mundi** and the **chained library** of 1500 volumes, some of them dating back to the 8th century. To house them, an impressive 'high-tech medieval building' has been erected to the south-west of the cathedral. It opens 10 am to 4.15 pm Monday to Saturday and 11 am to 3.15 pm on Sunday (11 am to 3.15 pm Monday to Saturday in winter). Admission costs £4/3.

The cathedral will next host the Three Choirs Festival, an event it shares with Gloucester and Worcester Cathedrals, in 2003. Visit www.3choirs.org on the Web for more details.

Old House

Stranded in the pedestrianised High Town, the Old House (☎ 260694) is a marvellous black-and-white three-storey wooden house, built in 1621 and fitted with 17th-century wooden furnishings. Note the murals of the Muses on the 1st floor.

It opens 10 am to 5 pm Tuesday to Saturday, and 10 am to 4 pm on Sunday and bank holiday Mondays, April to September. Admission is free.

Hereford Museum

This museum and art gallery (☎ 260692) is located above the library on Broad St and contains Roman antiquities, English watercolours and traditional farming implements. It opens 10 am to 5 pm Tuesday to Saturday and 10 am to 4 pm on Sunday.

Other Things to See

Near the cathedral, the **Bishop's Palace** contains one of England's oldest timber halls. East of the cathedral are the ancient Cathedral School and Castle Green, site of a castle that was pulled down in 1652. Narrow streets and alleys lead from Cathedral Close to the shopping area.

In the High St, **All Saints Church** has a slightly bent 65m-high tower surmounted by England's largest weathercock. More unusually, it also contains a medieval carving of a man mooning and exposing himself; it's on a beam immediately above the excellent cafe (see Places to Eat).

Cider Factory Tours

Just off the A438 to Brecon, the **Cider Museum & King Offa Distillery** (☎ 354207) is in Pomona Place in a former cider works. In 1984 production of cider brandy recommenced after a 250-year gap. The museum and distillery open 10 am to 5.30 pm daily, April to October, and 11 am to 3 pm Tuesday to Sunday in winter; admission costs £2.40/1.90.

Bulmers Cider Mill (☎ 352000) has been making cider since 1887. It offers two-hour factory tours (£3.95/2) Monday to Friday, leaving at 10.30 am, and at 2.15 and 7.30 pm. Telephone a week ahead to make a booking.

Places to Stay

Bowes Guest House (☎ 267202, 23 St Martin's St), just north of the Wye Bridge, has rooms starting at £18.50/34.

Merton Hotel (☎ 265925, fax 354983, [e] sales@mertonhotel.co.uk, 28 Commercial Rd) is convenient for the station and charges £45/60. Just off the main street, across from the train station, the comfortable *Aylestone Court Hotel (☎ 341891, Aylestone Hill)* has rooms with a bathroom costing from £55/85.

Castle House (☎ 356321, fax 266460,

@ *info@castlehse.co.uk, Castle St)*, close to the cathedral, was once the bishop's residence and has recently undergone a major upgrade; well equipped rooms with a bathroom now cost a severe £90/165. The hotel's Web site is at www.castlehse.co.uk.

Comfort is more affordable at the **Green Dragon** (☎ *272506, fax 352139, Broad St)*, where rates start at £56/84 in a handsome, neoclassical building in the very centre of town. Bookings may be made on the Web at www.heritage-hotels.com.

Places to Eat

The most atmospheric place to eat is **Café@All Saints** (☎ *370415)*, tastefully set in the west end of beautiful All Saints Church – a novel way to revive declining attendance. The menu is wholesome and vegetarians are well catered for with dishes such as roast aubergine ratatouille and spiced chickpeas. Lunches are good value and it opens for dinner on Friday.

To put together a picnic, head straight for the covered **Butter Market**, which dates back to 1860, in the High Town.

An impressive new alternative for self-caterers is **Leftbank** (☎ *340200, Bridge St)*, a development that includes a bakery and delicatessen. **Cherries** (☎ *279714, 2 Bridge St)* offers a wide selection of breakfasts starting at 99p. For something a little more sophisticated, **Elgar's** (☎ *266444, 22 Widemarsh St)* has teas and coffees from all over the globe, as well as cream teas and a small selection of hot food, and opens Monday to Saturday.

There are no fewer than two Thai restaurants in Hereford. **Aroon Rai** (☎ *279971, 60 Widemarsh St)* has a wide range of authentic Siamese dishes for around £7 and some big banquets. Located in a characterful building on East St is **Orchid House** (☎ *277668, East St)*; locals rave about the food.

For Indian specialities, **The Taste of the Raj** (☎ *351076, St Owen's)* has a reliable reputation for good food from the subcontinent.

The best restaurant in town is the happening **Doodies** (☎ *269974, 48 St Owen's)*,

which has a wide range of dishes from around the world starting at £10, although with vegetables on top it's likely to be £20 a head. There is a little cafe next door with lighter, cheaper meals available, tapas by night and a popular bar.

Entertainment

Pubs On St Owen's St, **The Barrels** is a must for any visitor to Hereford. It is home to the Wye Valley Brewery and some welcoming locals as permanent as the wallpaper. Leading brews include Butty Back and Dorothy Goodbodys, both of which are prepared in former stables at the back.

Of the other town-centre pubs, the **Spread Eagle** *(King St)* is a popular watering hole with the young crowd. The **Queen's Arms** *(Broad St)* has an older gang of regulars. **The Exchange** *(Widemarsh St)* is noteworthy for its medieval interior with Victorian cladding.

For those who don't believe familiarity can breed contempt, the chain pubs are represented by The **Farmhand & Firkin** *(Commercial St)*.

Clubs Hereford's most prominent nightclub is **The Crystal Rooms** (☎ *267378, Bridge St)*, which sees its share of imported DJs on a Friday night, but don't come expecting Cream. For something even less sophisticated, but sometimes fun, try **Bushwhackers** (☎ *270009, Blue School St)*.

Music & Theatre For live music from local bands, try **The Jailhouse** (☎ *344354, 1 Gaol St)*.

The **Courtyard Centre for the Arts** (☎ *359252)*, off Edgar St, offers a theatre, two cinemas, a gallery and the usual bar and cafe.

Getting There & Away

Hereford is 25 miles (40km) from Worcester, 38 miles (61km) from Brecon (Wales) and 140 miles (225km) from London.

Bus National Express (☎ *0870 580 8080)* operates three services daily from London (four hours, £14.50) via Heathrow, Cirencester, Cheltenham, Gloucester, Newent and Ross-on-Wye.

First Midland Red (☎ 01905-763888) connects Hereford to Worcester (Nos 419 and 420) and Ludlow (No 192). Bus No 476 runs to Ledbury hourly (every two hours on Sunday), while the No 38 serves Ross-on-Wye and Gloucester hourly Monday to Saturday, and just once on Sunday. Six buses a day serve Hereford (one hour, £3.40) Monday to Saturday, and three on Sunday.

For those aiming to continue on into Wales, bus No 20 runs regularly to Abergavenny and No 416 heads to Monmouth five times daily.

Train Hereford is linked by hourly train to London (three hours, £33), usually via Newport or Worcester. From Hereford, there are also rail services to Worcester (one hour, £5.20).

AROUND HEREFORD
Black-and-White Villages

Herefordshire's black-and-white architecture is a big attraction for some visitors and the TICs promote a trail that can be followed through the most popular villages. **Eardisland** is the most picturesque, with a unique 18th-century dovecote, but all of them offer something that is hard to find during peak season in the Cotswolds these days: peace and tranquillity. **Pembridge** is another gem with a huddle of classic houses, and its useful Black & White Villages Centre (☎ 01544-388761) doubles as a TIC; it's open 9 am to 6 pm daily. Bus No 496 runs to these villages regularly Monday to Saturday.

The Golden Valley

The Golden Valley, set in a remote corner of Herefordshire bordering Wales, has been made famous by the author CS Lewis and the film *Shadowlands*. Following the meandering River Dore, this is one of the least visited corners of England, yet it offers some stunning scenery.

Croft Castle

Croft Castle (☎ 01568-780246; NT) is near the Shropshire border, and dates from the

14th century. Much of the interior was refitted in the 18th century, including a sweeping Gothic stairway. A short walk away are the remains of the Iron Age fort of **Croft Ambrey**.

The castle opens 1.30 to 5.30 pm Wednesday to Sunday, May to September, and 1.30 to 5.30 pm (to 4.30 pm in October) at the weekend in April and October; it also opens on bank holidays. Admission costs £3.80/1.90.

HAY-ON-WYE
☎ 01497 • pop 1500

On 1 April 1977 Hay-on-Wye declared independence from Britain – just one publicity stunt this eccentric little bookshop town has used to draw attention to itself. Most of the publicity has been generated by bookseller Richard Booth, the colourful, self-styled King of Hay, who has been largely responsible for Hay's evolution from just another market town on the Welsh-English border to the second-hand bookshop capital of the world.

A day browsing among the shops is definitely recommended. With its small centre made up of narrow sloping lanes, the town itself is also interesting, and the people it attracts certainly are. On the north-eastern corner of Brecon Beacons National Park, Hay makes an excellent base for exploring western Herefordshire and the Black Mountains of Wales.

History

Most events in the history of Hay have been connected with its location in the Marches, on the border of Wales and England. In fact, during the Norman period the town was administered as English Hay (the town proper) and Welsh Hay (the countryside to the south and west of the town).

A castle had already stood in the town before the construction of the present one, built in about 1200 by the treacherous William Breos II (one of the Norman barons, or Lords Marcher, granted vast tracts of land in border country to consolidate conquered territory). From then until the final acquisition of Wales by the English

Crown, Hay changed hands many times. It subsequently became a market town, employing a large number of people in the flannel trade during the 18th century. The first large-scale second-hand bookshop opened in 1961, the vanguard of a new industry.

The castle, complete with the Jacobean mansion built within its Norman walls, was purchased by Booth in 1971 but a fire in 1977 resulted in its present dilapidated state.

Orientation & Information

Hay's compact centre contains the castle and most of the bookshops, within a roughly square perimeter. The main central thoroughfare is Castle St, which links Oxford Rd with Lion St.

The TIC (☎ 820144), on Oxford Rd, is on the edge of town by the main car park. It opens 10 am to 5 pm daily, Easter to October, and 11 am to 4 pm the rest of the year.

Most bookshops stock the useful free town plan that locates and describes all the bookshops in Hay. The annual Festival of Literature takes place in May/June and is a very popular and entertaining affair.

Things to See & Do

There are now over 30 second-hand bookshops in Hay, containing literally hundreds of thousands of books – there are 400,000 in Richard Booth's Bookshop alone. English publishers churn out tens of thousands of new titles each year, and the country has a long history of publishing. According to the experts, quantity rather than quality is what you'll find in most places in Hay.

Some of these bookshops specialise in esoteric fields: **B & K Books** (☎ 820386) in Newport St boasts the world's finest stock of books on apiculture (the breeding and care of bees); **Rose's Books** (☎ 820013) at 14 Broad St stocks rare and out-of-print children's books; **Lion St Books** (☎ 820121) at 1 St John's Place deals in militaria and anarchism; there's theology and church history at **Marches Gallery** (☎ 821451) in Lion St; and **Murder & Mayhem** (☎ 821613) at 5 Lion St is filled with detective fiction, true crime and horror.

Many bookshops, however, cover everything, the most famous being **Richard Booth's** (☎ 820322) at 44 Lion St and the **Hay Cinema Bookshop** (☎ 820071) in Castle St.

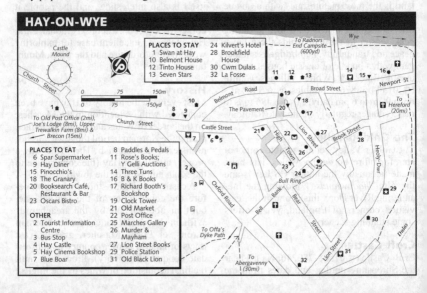

HAY-ON-WYE

PLACES TO STAY		24	Kilvert's Hotel
1	Swan at Hay	28	Brookfield
10	Belmont House		House
12	Tinto House	30	Cwm Dulais
13	Seven Stars	32	La Fosse

PLACES TO EAT		8	Paddles & Pedals
6	Spar Supermarket	11	Rose's Books;
9	Hay Diner		Y Gelli Auctions
15	Pinocchio's	14	Three Tuns
18	The Granary	16	B & K Books
20	Booksearch Café,	17	Richard Booth's
	Restaurant & Bar		Bookshop
23	Oscars Bistro	19	Clock Tower
		21	Old Market
OTHER		22	Post Office
2	Tourist Information	25	Marches Gallery
	Centre	26	Murder &
3	Bus Stop		Mayhem
4	Hay Castle	27	Lion Street Books
5	Hay Cinema Bookshop	29	Police Station
7	Blue Boar	31	Old Black Lion

Some shops will carry out searches to locate out-of-print books. Booksearch, Hay-on-Wye, Hereford HR3 5EA, deals only by post. There are regular book auctions at **Y Gelli Auctions** (☎ 821179) in Broad St.

Canadian canoes (for two/three people) can be hired from Paddles & Pedals (☎ 820604) in Castle St for £15 per canoe for half a day or £25 for a day. Bicycles are also available for hire here.

Places to Stay

Radnors End Campsite (☎ 820780) is 550m from the bridge over the River Wye, on the road to Clyro. The charge is £3 per person.

Hay has a number of B&Bs and hotels, but the nearest **YHA hostel** (☎ 890650) is at Capel-y-ffin in Wales, 8 miles (13km) south; it charges £8.70/5.75 for adults/ juniors. Book ahead if you want to stay at **Joe's Lodge** (☎ 01874-711845, Hay Rd, Talgarth), 8 miles south-west of Hay. It's an independent hostel, and B&B costs £10. Also in Talgarth, there's an upmarket B&B at **Upper Trewalkin Farm** (☎ 01874-711349, Pengenffordd), which charges £20 per person. Evening meals (£13) are excellent. Short-stay specials are also available.

Back in Hay-on-Wye, **Brookfield House** (☎ 820518, Brook St) is a centrally located 16th-century residence. Rooms cost from £18/32 for a single/double. **Belmont House** (☎ 820718, Belmont Rd) is well located, with rooms for £20/32 (£38 for a double with bathroom).

At friendly **Cwm Dulais** (☎ 820640, Heoly-Dwr), also central, there's B&B for £25/38. **La Fosse** (☎ 820613, Oxford Rd) is a comfortable place charging £40 for a double with bathroom. Popular **Kilvert's Hotel** (☎ 821042) is right in the centre on the Bull Ring, with rooms starting at £35/65.

The **Seven Stars** (☎ 820886, Broad St) is an excellent place to stay. As well as comfortable singles/doubles starting at £22/37 (£28/45 with bathroom), it also has a swimming pool and sauna. Booking ahead is advisable. Almost next door, **Tinto House** (☎ 820590, Broad St) is a pleasant place with a secluded garden that charges £30/40.

The **Swan at Hay** (☎ 821188, Church St) is more conventionally luxurious and charges £50 for a single and between £65 and £100 for a double room.

Two miles (3km) from Hay, at Llanigon and near Offa's Dyke Path, is the **Old Post Office** (☎ 820008), an excellent vegetarian B&B with rooms for £17 per person with shared bathroom, £25 with private bathroom.

Places to Eat

For such a small place, there's a lot of variety. There's a **Spar** supermarket on Castle St for picnic material.

Hay Diner, also on Castle St, is good for a coffee, a beer or a full meal – and there's a takeaway next door. It opens 10 am to 10 pm daily, and there's some seating in the garden.

For something informal yet substantial, the **Granary** (☎ 820790, Broad St) is an excellent and popular choice. Hungarian goulash costs £7.50, and there are good vegetarian dishes – the Tibetan roast is recommended. It opens daily in summer and during the festival, and until 5.30 pm in winter.

Booksearch Café, Restaurant & Bar (☎ 821932, The Pavement) is a nice place to have a drink or some food while willing staff search the town's bookshops for requests, or the world's via the Internet. The menu includes dishes such as seared salmon in tarragon butter for £10.50, or you can just have a drink at the bar. It's closed on Monday.

Oscars Bistro (☎ 821193, High Town) is central and offers very reasonably priced dishes (including vegetarian). It also has excellent filled baguettes for £3.50. **Pinocchio's** (☎ 821166, 2 Broad St) is a good Italian restaurant with excellent pizza.

The tiny **Three Tuns** (Broad St) is a wonderful old pub and cider house, popular with locals. The **Blue Boar** (☎ 820884, Castle St) has a wide selection of bar food, and there's upmarket pub grub at the **Old Black Lion** (Lion St). **Kilvert's Hotel** (see Places to Stay) is a cosy place with good pub food and an a la carte restaurant. The pub part can get a bit smoky, though, if you're dining. Escalope of salmon with lemon grass costs £10.95; pizza and pastas start at £4.

Getting There & Away

There are six buses a day to Hereford (one hour, £3.40), Monday to Saturday, and three buses on Sunday. Departures are from Oxford Rd and there are additional services from the clock tower on Broad St. For Brecon (40 minutes), there are also six buses a day, Monday to Saturday, and two on Sunday. The nearest train station is in Hereford.

Offa's Dyke Path passes beside Hay.

ROSS-ON-WYE
☎ 01989 • pop 8300

Built on a dramatic sandstone bluff, Ross-on-Wye makes a pleasant base for exploring the **Wye Valley**, the most scenic part of the river. Winding through a landscape of woods and meadows past Ross, Symonds Yat and then along the border with Wales, the River Wye empties into the Bristol Channel beneath the Severn Bridge.

The TIC (☎ 562768, fax 565057), Swan House, Edde Cross St, opens 9 am to 5.30 pm Monday to Saturday and 10 am to 4 pm on Sunday.

Things to See

There are fine views of the valley and ruined Wilton Castle from the **Prospect**, a cliff-top public garden designed by 17th-century town planner John Kyrle, the 'Man of Ross', who also laid out some of the streets. His philanthropic works were much praised by Pope in *Of the Use of Riches*. Kyrle is buried in the parish church, where the Plague Cross records the burial of 315 victims of the 1637 plague.

A small **Heritage Centre** is on the 1st floor of the stilted Market House.

Places to Stay

The nearest hostel is 6 miles (10km) south of Ross at Welsh Bicknor (see Goodrich in the Around Ross-on-Wye section).

In Ross, the Georgian *Vaga House* (☎ 563024, e vagahouse@hotmail.com, *Wye St)* is in a pretty street near the TIC and does B&B starting at £19 per person, £23 with a bathroom. Next door is the *Radcliffe Guesthouse (☎ 563895, Wye St)*, which charges £25/44 for a single/double.

Nonsmoking *Linden House (☎ 565373, fax 565575, 14 Church St)*, opposite the church, charges £25/42 for a single/double (£36/50 en suite) and can do veggie breakfasts on request.

The *King's Head Hotel (☎ 763174, fax 769578, e enquiries@kingshead.co.uk, 8 High St)* is comfortable and rooms start at £43.50/75. The beautifully positioned *Royal Hotel (☎ 565105, fax 768058, Palace Pound)* is the smartest place to stay and costs £50 per person.

Places to Eat

Ross' High St is full of teashops, the most interesting being the *Antique Teashop (☎ 566123, 40 High St)*, where a cream tea taken on antique chairs costs £3.65. The *Priory Coffee House (☎ 562217, 45 High St)* serves toasties, sandwiches and home-made cakes. *Poppy's Bistro (☎ 564455, 9 High St)* does hot dishes of the day for £4.95.

Oat Cuisine (☎ 566271, 47 Broad St), one of the greatest names to have come out of the wholefood revolution, does inexpensive vegetarian lunches. *Yaks 'n Yetis (☎ 564963, Broad St)* has an extensive list of lively Mexican dishes, rather than the expected Nepalese dhal or Tibetan *momos*, so it's clearly no relation of the Yak 'n Yeti Hotel in Kathmandu.

For a night out, *Le Faisan Dore Brasserie (☎ 565751, 52 Edde Cross St)*, formerly the Pheasant, does fine English cuisine from Tuesday to Saturday; main courses cost around £12.

Alternatively try *Meaders (☎ 562803, 1 Copse Cross St)*, where traditional Hungarian dishes start at about £8.50. Opposite, *Cloisters* wine bar (☎ 567717, 24 High St) has fish specials such as rainbow trout with lime and almonds for £8.50.

Also down in this part of town is *China Boy Jo (☎ 563533, 27 Gloucester Rd)*, an authentic Chinese restaurant with lunchtime specials. It's closed on Monday.

Entertainment

Ross is not known for its nightlife, but the *King Charles II* is an atmospheric enough pub, and the *Hope & Anchor Inn* down by the river is busy throughout the day for dining or drinking.

Getting There & Away

Ross is 14 miles (23km) from Hereford and 16 miles (26km) from Gloucester, with bus links to London via Cheltenham and Cirencester. Stagecoach (☎ 485118) operates an hourly bus service between Hereford and Gloucester via Ross (No 38; only one bus on Sunday), and No 34 from Ross to Monmouth (for Goodrich and Symonds Yat).

Getting Around

Bikes can be rented from Revolutions (☎ 562639), 48 Broad St, from £10 per day.

AROUND ROSS-ON-WYE
Goodrich

Goodrich Castle (☎ 01600-890538; EH) is a red-sandstone castle dating back to the 12th century. A Royalist stronghold during the Civil War, it fell to the Roundheads after a siege lasting 4½ months and was destroyed by Cromwell. It opens 10 am to 6 pm daily; admission costs £3.20/1.60.

Just under 2 miles (3km) from Goodrich is *Welsh Bicknor Youth Hostel (☎ 01594-860300, fax 861276, e welshbicknor@yha.org.uk)*, a Victorian rectory standing in 10 hectares of grounds by the river. Beds cost £9.80/6.75 for adults/juniors. It's open April to October; phone for other times.

Bus No 34, which runs regularly between Ross and Monmouth, passes this way. The infrequent bus No 32 to Gloucester is the only choice on Sunday.

Symonds Yat

Symonds Yat, 2½ miles (4km) south of Goodrich, is a popular beauty spot overlooking the Wye. It's crowded in summer but worth visiting at quieter times. There are good views from Yat Rock (Symonds Yat East), and rare peregrine falcons nest in the rock face. Telescopes enable you to watch them from April to August.

A small rope ferry connects the two sides of the village, and can be picked up at either the *Saracen's Head Inn* on the east bank or *Ye Olde Ferrie Inn* on the west bank.

This area is renowned for canoeing and climbing, among other activities, and the Wyedean Canoe Centre (☎ 01594-833238) has a solid reputation for organising kayaking and white-water trips. It can also arrange caving and climbing in the area. It has a picturesque *camp site* by the river, beneath the famous viewpoint, first established in 1904; it costs £4.50 per person. You can visit the centre's Web site at www.wyedean.co.uk.

Symonds Yat Canoe Hire (☎ 01600-891069) arranges a variety of expeditions along the Wye, from half a day to four days.

LEDBURY
☎ 01531

Ledbury is a handsome market town with a reputation for antiques. Many of its buildings are themselves antique, including a beautiful 17th-century black-and-white timber-framed **market hall**.

Creaky **Church Lane** is the best area to concentrate on for architectural heritage. Here too is the **Ledbury Heritage Centre** (☎ 636147), housed in a timber-framed former grammar school. It opens 10 am to 4.30 pm daily, Easter to October; admission is free. In nearby Church Lane are the **Butcher's Row Houses** (☎ 632040), a sort of folk museum open 11 am to 5 pm daily, Easter to September.

Ledbury's TIC (☎ 636147, fax 634313, e tourism@herefordshire.gov.uk), 3 The Homend, opens 10 am to 5 pm Monday to Saturday.

Bus No 476 runs from Hereford hourly (every two hours on Sunday).

AROUND LEDBURY
Eastnor Castle

Eastnor Castle (☎ 01531-633160) looks like it's escaped from the film *El Cid*, but actually dates from the early 19th century. It has recently undergone much restoration work to improve the interior. The extensive grounds include a deer park and arboretum.

It opens 11 am to 5 pm daily except Saturday in July and August, and on Sunday, mid-April to early October. Admission costs £4.75/2.50 for the castle and £2.75/1.50 for the grounds only.

The castle is a short distance from Junction 2 of the M50 and just a couple of miles outside Ledbury.

Worcestershire

Worcestershire is undoubtedly a county of contrasts, where the rural idyll of little England comes face-to-face with the urban sprawl of big England.

Much of Worcestershire comprises the flattish plains of the Severn Vale and the Vale of Evesham, surrounded by rolling hills, with the Malverns to the west and the Cotswolds to the south. The Rivers Wye, Severn and Avon flow through, and the county boasts many attractive riverside market towns.

The north and east of the county, on the other hand, blend into Birmingham (see the Midlands chapter) and offer few attractions, except for some quirky museums in Redditch and Bromsgrove, and Droitwich Spa, the country's active spa centre.

Binding the county together is Worcester, an interesting enough city famous for its cathedral, china and cricket, and this is the most convenient base.

WALKING & CYCLING

The Severn Way winds its way through Worcestershire, passing through Stourport-on-Severn, Worcester and Upton-upon-Severn. The Three Choirs Way links Worcester to Hereford and Gloucester. Cyclists should pick up *Elgar Ride Variations* from TICs, which has a choice of routes around the Malverns.

GETTING AROUND

First Midland Red (☎ 01905-763888) is the region's biggest bus company. A Day Rover pass costs £4.60/3.60 and allows travel any-where on its system and on routes run by many other smaller companies. For general bus information, phone ☎ 0845 712 5436. The Wye Valley Wanderer is a popular bus linking Pershore and Worcester with Ross and the Wye Valley on summer Sundays and bank holiday Mondays; call ☎ 01432-260948 for more details.

There are rail links to Worcester, Evesham and Pershore. Kidderminster is the southern railhead of the popular Severn Valley Railway.

WORCESTER
☎ 01905 • pop 75,500

Known for centuries as the 'faithful city' after it remained staunchly Royalist during the Civil War, Worcester (**woos**-ter) hasn't always been faithful to its heritage, tearing down the Elgar family's Victorian music shop in an extended moment of ill-considered town planning. World famous for its bone china, as well as for its sauce, it also has an impressive cathedral where King John of Magna Carta fame is buried.

It's a disjointed town, not always immediately inviting, but some streets boast the half-timbered buildings more usually associated with Stratford-upon-Avon and it has far fewer tourists than Shakespeare's birthplace.

Orientation & Information

The main part of the city lies on the east bank of the River Severn, the cathedral rising above it. The High St, just to the north, runs through a bewildering number of name changes as it heads north: The Cross, The Foregate, Foregate St and The Tything.

The TIC (☎ 726311, fax 722481), in the Guildhall on High St, opens 10 am to 5.30 pm Monday to Saturday. Walking tours (£3/1.50) leave from here at 11 am and 2.30 pm on Wednesday, May to August.

Worcester Cathedral

The present cathedral was begun in 1084 by Bishop – later Saint – Wulfstan and the atmospheric crypt dates back to this period. The choir and Lady Chapel were built in 13th-century Early English style, while the

Norman nave was given a makeover in 14th-century Decorated style. Take a close look at the carvings in the ambulatory and transepts and you'll see there are scenes of judgement and hell as well as of the nativity.

Wicked King John, whose treachery towards his brother Richard left the country in turmoil at his death, is buried in the choir. Knowing he stood only a slim chance of making it past the Pearly Gates, the dying king is said to have asked to be buried disguised as a monk. When the tomb was opened in 1797, shreds of a monk's cowl were found over his skull.

An ornate chantry chapel south of the high altar commemorates Prince Arthur, elder brother of Henry VIII, who died while honeymooning with Catherine of Aragon.

The cathedral (☎ 28854) opens 7.30 am to 6 pm daily. A £2 donation is requested. The cathedral choir sings evensong at 5.30 pm daily except Thursday (at 4 pm on Sunday).

Commandery Civil War Centre

Beside Sidbury Lock, south-east of the cathedral, the Commandery (☎ 361821) is

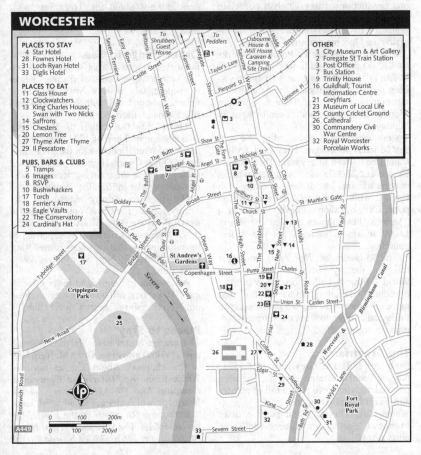

WORCESTER

PLACES TO STAY
4 Star Hotel
28 Fownes Hotel
31 Loch Ryan Hotel
33 Diglis Hotel

PLACES TO EAT
11 Glass House
12 Clockwatchers
13 King Charles House; Swan with Two Nicks
14 Saffrons
15 Chesters
20 Lemon Tree
27 Thyme After Thyme
29 Il Pescatore

PUBS, BARS & CLUBS
5 Tramps
6 Images
8 RSVP
10 Bushwhackers
17 Torch
18 Ferrier's Arms
19 Eagle Vaults
22 The Conservatory
24 Cardinal's Hat

OTHER
1 City Museum & Art Gallery
2 Foregate St Train Station
3 Post Office
7 Bus Station
9 Trinity House
16 Guildhall; Tourist Information Centre
21 Greyfriars
23 Museum of Local Life
25 County Cricket Ground
26 Cathedral
30 Commandery Civil War Centre
32 Royal Worcester Porcelain Works

in a splendid Tudor building used as Charles II's headquarters during the Battle of Worcester. This brought the Civil War to an end in 1651 and the centre details the ins and outs of this and many other battles that raged in 17th-century England.

It opens 10 am to 5 pm Monday to Saturday and 1.30 to 5 pm on Sunday. Admission costs £3.70/2.60.

Royal Worcester Porcelain Works

Worcester has been manufacturing ornate bone china since 1751, the longest continuous production of any English porcelain company. In 1789, the company was granted a royal warrant, and Worcester remains the Queen's preferred crockery.

The Royal Worcester Porcelain Works (☎ 21247) was moved to its current Severn St site in 1840. It now boasts an entire visitors complex, with shops, restaurant and museum, which opens 9 am to 5.30 pm Monday to Saturday and 11 am to 5 pm on Sunday.

Conducted factory tours lasting one hour run Monday to Friday. They cost £5 and should be booked in advance. The Visitors' Centre (£2.25/1.75) lets you see what a potter's life was like at the end of the 19th century, while a film tells the story of the pottery. The gift shop sells everything from a 23-piece 'best' dinner service for nearly £1000 to single seconds for just a few pounds.

The **Museum of Worcester Porcelain** tells the factory's story and houses the world's largest collection of Worcester porcelain, including some of the first pieces. It opens 9.30 am to 5 pm Monday to Friday and 10 am to 5 pm on Saturday. Admission costs £3/2.25.

The Greyfriars

Built in 1480, The Greyfriars (☎ 23571; NT), a Tudor house on Friar St, has been painstakingly restored and is full of textiles and furnishings. It opens 2 to 5 pm on Wednesday, Thursday and bank holiday Mondays, Easter to October. Admission costs £2.60.

Museum of Local Life

The Museum of Local Life (☎ 722349) on Friar St evokes Worcester's past with reconstructed Victorian shops, displays of toys and costumes, and details of daily life during WWII. It opens 10.30 am to 5 pm daily except Thursday and Sunday; admission is free.

Worcester City Museum and Art Gallery

Worcester City Museum and Art Gallery (☎ 25371) on Foregate St features interesting temporary exhibitions and has permanent exhibits about the River Severn. It opens 9.30 am to 5.30 pm Monday to Saturday; admission is free.

Other Things to See

For a general idea of what Worcester looked like before the modern-day planners began to meddle, take a walk down New St or Friar St, both lined with fine Tudor and Elizabethan buildings.

The splendid **Guildhall** in the High St is a Queen Anne building of 1722, designed by a pupil of Wren. Look out for the stone carving of Oliver Cromwell with his ears pinned back just above the main entrance. He wasn't very popular in Royalist Worcester.

Half-timbered **Trinity House** (on The Trinity, just off The Cross) once belonged to the Guild of the Holy Trinity. After the Battle of Worcester Charles II is supposed to have hidden in what was later named **King Charles House**, 29 New St, which is now a restaurant.

Away from museums and historic buildings, cricket fans will no doubt want to check out Worcestershire County Cricket Club.

Places to Stay

The nearest hostel is in Malvern Wells, 8 miles (13km) away (see Great Malvern later in this chapter). About 3 miles north of Worcester is the *Mill House Caravan & Camping Site* (☎ 451283, fax 754143, Hawford), which charges £5.50 for all tents.

Barbourne Rd, north of the centre, has several B&Bs. The *Shrubbery Guest House* (☎ 24871, fax 23620, 38 Barbourne Rd) has a small single with shared facilities for £20, and en suite singles/doubles for £35/45.

Another popular B&B is *Osborne House* (☎/fax 22296, ℮ enquiries@osbornehouse .freeserve.co.uk, 17 Chestnut Walk) and while it's not quite as flash as Queen Victoria's pad on the Isle of Wight, it is very homely with en suite rooms costing from £36.

Loch Ryan Hotel (☎/fax 351143, 119 Sidbury), near the cathedral, has rooms starting at £45/60. Slap bang in the centre of town, right near the station, is the *Star Hotel (☎ 24308, fax 234400, Foregate St)*, which offers well appointed rooms costing from £65/80.

One of the best-situated hotels in town is *Diglis House (☎ 353518, fax 767772, ℮ diglis@england.com, Severn St)*, located on the banks of the River Severn. Rooms start at £60/75, but be sure to try and get one with a river view. The huge *Fownes Hotel (☎ 613151, fax 23742, City Walls Rd)*, in a converted glove factory, is a popular business hotel. Midweek prices of £85 per room fall to £55 at the weekend.

Places to Eat
The Guildhall's elaborate *Assembly Room Restaurant* opens Monday to Saturday for lunch and snacks.

For those in a hurry to see the sights or explore the nearby charity shops, *Clockwatchers (☎ 611662, 21 Mealcheapen St)* is the city's most popular sandwich bar. For those with time to linger, going upstairs reveals a crooked old house, a real contrast with its unassuming exterior, and there is a garden for warm days.

Glass House (☎ 611120, Church St) has an impressive location in an old church and a menu to suit all budgets, including pasta, luxury baguettes and salads at lunch time. The 16th-century *King Charles House (☎ 22449, 29 New St)* offers traditional three-course lunches for £9.95 and is a good place to dine for those of a historical bent. Next door is the cheap and cheerful *Swan with Two Nicks (☎ 28190)*, offering a steady diet of traditional pub food.

Saffrons (☎ 610505, 15 New St) offers a global tour from Thai to modern British,

but high prices may deter some – expect to pay about £25 per head all-in. Nearby *Chesters (☎ 611638, 51 New St)* concentrates on Mexican.

Lemon Tree (☎ 27770, 12 Friar St) offers modern British cooking with a distinctly international flavour in intimate surroundings. The chefs could be moving towards celebrity status after a couple of television appearances. Ten pounds should cover lunch and a drink, and you're looking at £20 for a full dinner.

Il Pescatore (☎ 21444, 34 Sidbury), near the cathedral, is a popular Italian restaurant offering light lunch dishes for about £5. *Thyme after Thyme (☎ 611786, 27 College St)* offers a range of teasing tasters to go with salads, baguettes or in jackets at lunch, all at around £4. At night they turn on the style and prices rise considerably.

Entertainment
RSVP (☎ 723035, The Cross) leads the way in church conversions, with the original pulpit as the staircase and the font in the thick of things. It is a popular bar at night, as well as a lively lunch spot.

The popular *Farrier's Arms (Fish St)*, near the cathedral, has some outdoor seating, while Worcester's oldest pub, the *Cardinal's Hat (Friar St)*, has open fires in winter. *Eagle Vaults (Friar St)* is an original Victorian boozer complete with ornate tiling and elaborate interior.

For cheap drinks and zany promotions, *The Conservatory (Friar St)* is worth a shot. *Bushwhackers (Trinity St)* is an Aussie pub that draws the crowds at night.

Many of the clubs in town have the sort of name that make you wonder if the '80s are back (perhaps they never left Worcester?), such as *Tramps (Angel Place)* and *Images (The Butts)*. *Torch (Hylton Rd)* is possibly the safest bet, although a train to Birmingham might be wiser still.

Music by Elgar is always a highlight of the Three Choirs Festival, hosted by Worcester Cathedral (☎ 616211) every third year. It will next be Worcester's turn in 2002. Visit www.3choirs.org on the Web for more details.

Getting There & Away

Worcester is 25 miles (40km) from Hereford, 57 miles (92km) from Oxford and 113 miles (182km) from London.

Bus National Express (☎ 0870 580 8080) runs at least one coach daily between Worcester, Heathrow and London (3½ hours, £14.50). Another service links Aberdare and Great Yarmouth via Worcester, Great Malvern and Hereford.

First Midland Red (☎ 763888) operates services to Hereford, Tewkesbury and Evesham. A Day Rover ticket costs £4.60/3.60.

Cambridge Coach Services (☎ 01223-423900) has a weekday service linking Worcester with Cambridge via Stratford-upon-Avon and Warwick.

Train Worcester Foregate station – for trains to Hereford (one hour, £5.20) and Birmingham – is more central than Worcester Shrub Hill, which offers regular trains to London Paddington (2¼ hours, £22.80). Shrub Hill is a dismal 15-minute walk from the centre; bus No 30 passes nearby.

Getting Around

Peddlers (☎ 24238), 46 Barbourne Rd, hires out bikes for £8/30 per day/week.

AROUND WORCESTER
Elgar's Birthplace Museum

About 3 miles (5km) west of Worcester is Broadheath, birthplace of Sir Edward Elgar (1857–1934). The cottage (☎ 01905-333224) is now a museum of Elgar memorabilia, including original scores and manuscripts; admission costs £3/50p. Phone ahead for opening times.

Severn Valley Railway

A 20-minute ride from Worcester Foregate Street station to **Kidderminster**, once the carpet capital of Britain, lets you link with the Severn Valley Railway (☎ 01299-403816). See Bridgnorth in the Midlands chapter.

Witley Court

Arguably the most venerable and romantic ruin in England, this mighty house was once one of the most extravagant private homes in the country. A massive fire in 1937 gutted part of the interior, although the fire actually only damaged a small area around the ballroom. Unfortunately, the building was under-insured, so the carpet-magnate owner sold it on to an antiques dealer, who proceeded to take it apart piece by piece, right down to the plasterwork, leaving the immense skeleton that stands today. Pop star George Michael paid a visit to the house not so long ago and was reportedly interested in purchasing it for renovation – until he heard the estimated cost, which is well over £1000 million!

The gardens, originally designed by William Nesfield, have been fully returned to their former glory, as have the famous fountains. One of these, depicting Perseus and Andromeda, used to fire water more than 30m into the air. It has been partially restored and is turned on for bank holidays.

The adjacent **Great Witley Church** is widely considered to be one of the finest Baroque churches in England. It includes exquisite paintings by Antonio Bellucci and some exceptionally ornate carving and glasswork. It was originally designed as the private chapel for Witley Court, but with the demise of the house villagers wisely stepped in to preserve this treasure. All in all it feels more like a music hall than a church and regular classical concerts are held throughout the summer – call ☎ 01299-896437 for details.

Witley Court (☎ 01299-896636; EH) opens 10 am to 5 pm daily, April to October, and 10 am to 4 pm Wednesday to Friday, November to March. Admission costs £3.50/1.80. It is 10 miles (16km) north-west of Worcester on the A443 and the nearest train station is at Droitwich Spa, about 8 miles (13km) away. Buses travelling from Worcester or Kidderminster to Tenbury Wells pass this way infrequently.

Droitwich Spa
☎ 01905

Mention Droitwich Spa to most people in England and a sort of confused look will probably come across their face. It may not be as famous a spa town as Cheltenham or Leamington, but it has what neither of those has any longer: the genuine article, an active health spa that draws the faithful from all over England.

Next door to the spa, the TIC (☎ 774312, fax 794226), St Richard's House, Victoria Square, is open 10 am to 4 pm Monday to Saturday.

By train, Droitwich Spa is less than 10 minutes from Worcester Foregate Street or Worcester Shrub Hill.

Redditch
☎ 01527
Redditch was once the needle capital of the world, churning out sewing needles, knitting needles and fishing hooks destined for the far corners of the British Empire.

Needles may not sound like the ideal subject for a museum, but the **Forge Mill Needle Museum** (☎ 62509), Needle Mill Lane, Riverside, housed in an 18th-century needle factory, manages to carry it off, with informative displays and exhibitions. It opens 11 am to 4.30 pm Monday to Friday and 2 to 5 pm at the weekend, Easter to September. During winter, it opens 11 am to 4 pm Monday to Thursday and 2 to 5 pm on Sunday. It's closed in December and January. Admission costs £3.50/50p, including the **Bordesley Abbey Visitors Centre**, home to a collection of relics excavated from the remains of a nearby 12th-century abbey.

Unfortunately, there's not a lot else of interest to detain you in Redditch. The TIC (☎/fax 60806), Civic Square, Alcester St, opens 9 am to 5.30 pm Monday to Thursday, 9 am to 5 pm on Friday, and 9.30 am to 1.30 pm on Saturday.

Direct trains to Redditch run from Birmingham New Street (35 minutes). If you're coming from Worcester (one hour 15 minutes), you'll need to change at University station.

Bromsgrove
☎ 01527
There's not a lot to draw the visitor to Bromsgrove, but the **Avoncroft Museum of**

Historic Buildings (☎ 831363), Stoke Heath, is certainly a unique place, offering a home to historic buildings that are no longer wanted elsewhere. Famous exhibits include a working windmill from Warwickshire, a church, the national telephone-box collection (ie, the old red ones) and even a Tardis from the popular British TV series *Dr Who*.

The museum generally opens 11 am to 5 pm Tuesday to Sunday (daily in summer); admission costs £4.60/2.30. It's signposted from the A38, and there are regular bus services from Bromsgrove and Droitwich. The museum's Web site is at www.avoncroft .org.uk.

Bromsgrove's TIC (☎ 831809), 26 Birmingham Rd, shares its home with the town museum. Both open 10.30 am to 12.30 pm and 1 to 4.30 pm Monday to Saturday. In the High St there is a statue of the poet AE Houseman, author of *A Shropshire Lad*, who was born near here in 1859.

Bromsgrove train station is served by trains from Birmingham and Worcester.

GREAT MALVERN
☎ 01684 • pop 30,000
The Malvern Hills form a dramatic backdrop for Great Malvern, the biggest and best known of a cluster of settlements whose names invoke the illustrious hills that overshadow them. Famous for mineral water, a music festival in late May, a public school and Morgan motorcars, Great Malvern looks a bit like one of the spa towns of mid-Wales with a mini-version of Gloucester Cathedral and lots of cedars, pines and monkey-puzzle trees. Turner was inspired to paint it – before the grand Victorian piles started to straddle the hills, of course! As it is built into the side of a hill, there are some very steep streets in Great Malvern, so be warned if you're carrying heavy bags.

The TIC (☎ 892289, fax 892872, e malvern.tic@malvernhills.gov.uk), 21 Church St, sells an access guide for disabled visitors (£1), although just getting up the hill to buy it could be a problem. It also stocks a leaflet describing six cycle routes

On the Elgar Trail

Sir Edward Elgar, composer of Britain's near-national anthem *Land of Hope and Glory*, was born in Broadheath, 3 miles (5km) west of Worcester, in 1857 and died in Worcester in 1934. He lived in Hereford for eight years and drew much of the inspiration for pieces of music such as the *Pomp and Circumstance* marches and the *Enigma Variations* from the nearby Malvern Hills. The Hereford, Worcester and Malvern TICs stock a leaflet detailing a signposted 'Elgar Route' that takes you through places associated with his life. He is buried in St Wulstan's church in Little Malvern, just south of Great Malvern.

The Elgar Birthplace Museum (☎ 01905-66224) in Lower Broadheath opens 10.30 am to 6 pm daily except Wednesday, May to September, and 1.30 to 4.30 pm during most of winter (closed 16 January to 15 February). Admission costs £3/50p.

round the Malvern Hills. It opens 10 am to 5 pm daily.

The Malvern Festival Theatre (☎ 892277) is based in the Winter Gardens Complex in Grange Rd.

Great Malvern Priory

The Priory Church, with Norman pillars lining the nave, is famous for its stained glass and tiles. Of particular note are the 15th-century west window, the clerestory windows of the choir and the window in the Jesus Chapel in the north transept, which shows the Joys of Mary. The choir is decorated with 1200 medieval tiles, the oldest and finest such collection in the country.

Other Things to See

For the story of the town, venture into the **Malvern Museum of Local History** (☎ 567811), housed in the impressive Priory Gatehouse (1470) of the town's former Benedictine abbey. It opens 10 am to 5.30 pm daily except Wednesday, Easter to October.

The **Theatre of Small Convenience**, in a converted men's toilet, is in the *Guinness Book of Records* as the smallest theatre in the world – it has seating for 12. Just don't ask where the toilets are.

Walks in the Malvern Hills

Cut up St Ann's Rd for a short, steep walk to the summit of Worcestershire Beacon (419m/1374 feet), offering tremendous views. Herefordshire Beacon (334m/1095 feet), south of Great Malvern, is the site of the British Camp, an Iron Age fort. There's a superb walk along the path that meanders across the summits of the Malverns.

The Malvern Hills provided Elgar with the inspiration for his *Enigma Variations* and the *Pomp and Circumstance* marches (see the boxed text 'On the Elgar Trail').

The TIC stocks the *Malvern Map Set*, with three maps covering the chain of hills.

Places to Stay & Eat

Though there's plenty of accommodation in Great Malvern, much of it very pleasant, this is an upmarket area with prices to match.

Malvern Hills Youth Hostel (☎ 569131, fax 565205, **e** *malvern@yha.org.uk, 18 Peachfield Rd)* is in Malvern Wells, 1½ miles (2.5km) south of Great Malvern (take bus No 675 to British Camp). It opens mid-February to October and costs £9.80/6.75 for adults/juniors.

The *Great Malvern Hotel (☎ 563411, fax 560514, 7 Graham Rd)* is very central, offering singles/doubles with bathroom for £55/80. The *Cottage in the Wood (☎ 575859, fax 560662,* **e** *proprietor@ cottageinthewood.co.uk, Holywell Rd)*, 3 miles (5km) away near Malvern Wells, boasts spectacular views. Rooms cost from £75/95. A formal dinner in the excellent restaurant costs around £30.

Church St hosts frilly *Victoria's*, where you can get tea or a jacket potato from £2. Round the corner from the TIC, *Blue Bird Tearooms* serves cream teas for those who need a treat after a long day's walking in the hills.

Lady Foley's Tearoom (☎ 893033, Imperial Rd) serves lunches and teas in the splendid Victorian train station. On Friday and Saturday night from 7 to 9 pm the station also hosts *Passionata*, serving more elaborate dishes.

The Indian *Baazi Blue Restaurant* (☎ 575744, Church St) is the place to spice up your evening. The *Red Lion* (☎ 564787, St Ann's Rd) includes a traditional pub and a modern restaurant with an excellent menu of contemporary cuisine.

Getting There & Away

Great Malvern is 8 miles (13km) from Worcester and 15 miles (24km) from Hereford. National Express runs a daily bus between Great Malvern and London (four hours, £12.50) via Worcester and Pershore.

The quickest way to get to Great Malvern is by train from Worcester or Hereford. There are trains to London and Birmingham.

VALE OF EVESHAM

Worcestershire's south-eastern corner looks particularly splendid in spring when its myriad fruit trees are in blossom. The Vale's two principal towns are Evesham itself and Pershore.

Evesham

☎ 01386 • pop 15,000

A quiet market town on the River Avon, Evesham was the scene of the battle where Prince Edward, son of Henry III, defeated Simon de Montfort in 1265.

The river flows close to the 16th-century bell tower of the lost Benedictine abbey, which makes a fine grouping with the twin medieval churches of All Saints and St Lawrence. Look out for the beautiful fan vaulting of the Lichfield Chantry in All Saints.

The TIC (☎ 446944, fax 442348), Abbey Gate, in the picturesque Almonry Centre on the south side of town, houses a small heritage centre; admission costs £2 (free for children). Both open 10 am to 5 pm Monday to Saturday and 2 to 4 pm on Sunday.

Places to Stay & Eat Nonsmokers should head for *Berryfield House* (☎ 48214, 172 Pershore Rd, Hampton), where B&B starts

at £15. *Park View Hotel* (☎ 442639, Waterside) has singles/doubles costing from £23/41.

Readers have enjoyed staying at *Brookside Guest House* (☎ 443116, Mill St), which is three-quarters of a mile along the river from the centre in Hampton, with rooms starting at £18 per person. Comfortable *Evesham Hotel* (☎ 765566, Cooper's Lane) has rooms for £63/98. The restaurant here also has a very good reputation.

The best place for a snack or an afternoon tea is *Gateway Cake Shop*, beside the abbey. *Vine Wine Bar* (☎ 446799, 16 Vine St) offers delicacies such as swordfish steak.

Some of the best spots lie just outside Evesham. *The Fleece* (☎ 831178, The Cross, Bretforton) is a historic 16th-century inn left to the NT by landlady Lola Taplin in the 1970s. It specialises in fruit wine – ideal in front of the fire in winter – and has plenty of real ales. Evening meals are served.

Getting There & Away The hourly First Midland Red (☎ 01905-763888) bus No 550 runs to Pershore and Worcester, Monday to Saturday. Bus No 28 runs to Stratford-upon-Avon, Monday to Saturday.

There are frequent trains from Worcester (20 minutes), and from London (two hours, £22.50) via Oxford (one hour).

Pershore

☎ 01386 • pop 6900

A backwater town of graceful Georgian houses, Pershore is chiefly noted for its abbey, founded in 689. The TIC (☎ 554262) is inside a travel agency at 19 High St.

Pershore Abbey When Henry VIII's henchmen moved in to dissolve Pershore Abbey the townsfolk bought the austere Early English choir to serve as their parish church. That, and the earlier south transept, parts of which may predate the Norman Conquest, are all that now remain.

Places to Eat A good spot for morning tea or coffee or a lunch before launching deeper into Worcestershire is *Whistlers* (The Square), which has a fine range of sandwiches and salads. For a taste of some local real ale, try the *Brandy Cask (Bridge St)*, which brews up its own beer.

Getting There & Away About 8 miles (13km) from Worcester and 7 miles (11km) from Evesham, Pershore is best reached by bus from either place. By train, Pershore is on the Cotswold line linking Hereford and Worcester with Oxford and London. However, the train station is 1½ miles (2.5km) north-west of the town centre.

Bredon Hill

This solitary hill guarding the border of Worcestershire and Gloucestershire is excellent walking country and was made famous by the poet AE Houseman's *Summertime on Bredon*. The summit of the hill once supported an Iron Age camp and later a Roman fort, one of a string in the area that helped suppress the natives. Encircling the lower reaches of the hill are small villages that make useful starting points for an assault on the summit; try Ashton-under-Hill, Conderton or Elmley Castle.

The main gateway to the hill is the pretty village of Bredon, which has irregular bus connections to Tewkesbury. From Bredon, it is possible to do a loop up through Bredons Norton and on to the summit, descending to Overbury, through Kemerton, and back to the start. The views across to

the Malvern Hills are tremendous, and even Wales is visible on a clear day.

Upton-upon-Severn
☎ 01684

Upton is a pretty little town on the banks of the Severn, with a pleasing muddle of Tudor and Georgian architecture. The town has a small **heritage centre** housed in a former church known locally as the 'pepperpot'. It opens 2 to 4.30 pm daily (10.30 am to 4.30 pm on Saturday), Easter to September.

The TIC (☎ 594200, fax 594185, [e] upton.tic@malvernhills.gov.uk), 4 High St, opens 10 am to 5 pm daily (to 4 pm in winter). There is a popular jazz festival held in the town at the end of June.

Map fanatics will enjoy The Map Shop (☎ 593146), 15 High St, which has one of the best selections available in England outside London.

Upton has a surprising number of pubs for such a small town, dating back to the days when it was an important river crossing. *Ye Olde Anchor Inn* is a creaking pub complete with beams and fireplace that brews its own beer and has a popular bar menu.

The nearby village of Hanley Castle is home to the *Three Kings Inn* (☎ 592686), a cracking old pub that has picked up several major awards from the Campaign for Real Ale.

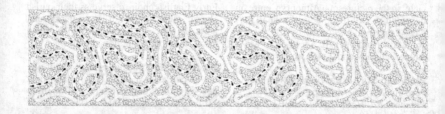

The Midlands

The Midlands is a vast swathe of England that includes some memorable places, as well as a number that are best forgotten. Many of the areas around the M1 corridor can look pretty miserable on a wet and windy day, but some of the region's liveliest cities are also here, such as Nottingham, Leicester, Coventry and Birmingham. What this area lacks in prettiness, it makes up for in personality, and there is an authentic feel to the eastern Midlands that isn't always found in the tourist meccas of Stratford-upon-Avon and Warwick.

The southern Midlands boasts some of England's most popular tourist sites, including Warwick Castle, one of the finest medieval buildings in England, and Stratford-upon-Avon, a place of pilgrimage for Shakespeare lovers from around the world. Nearby Northampton offers a chance to get away from the tourists, but lacks any big attractions.

In contrast, the northern Midlands is often dismissed as England's industrial backyard. The dense motorway network gives forewarning of the claustrophobic development and the continuing economic importance of the region, despite the decline of some traditional industries. This is England's working-class heartland, with a wide gap in living standards between these northern cities and those south of Birmingham. Tucked away amid the urban sprawl of the northern reaches is one of England's finest national parks, the Peak District, with endless opportunities for rambling, cycling and other outdoor activities, and some of the wildest countryside around. Nottingham continues to win friends with some of the best nightlife between London and Manchester.

Lichfield stands out as a beacon of light in Staffordshire, home to a splendid cathedral, while those keen on fine bone china will also want to brave the wastes of Stoke-on-Trent in search of the big-name suppliers.

Out in the west in the Marches are med-

Highlights

- Delving into the Peak District
- Exploring Ironbridge Gorge, cradle of the Industrial Revolution
- Hitting the pubs and clubs of Nottingham
- Watching a Shakespeare performance in Stratford-upon-Avon
- Visiting Warwick Castle or Chatsworth
- Walking the winding passages of medieval Shrewsbury
- Eating fine food in luscious Ludlow
- Catching an adrenaline buzz at Alton Towers

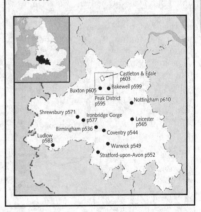

THE MIDLANDS

ieval Shrewsbury and the fascinating Ironbridge Gorge Museum. Also in Shropshire is the beautiful town of Ludlow and some little-visited countryside, great for walking.

For information on transport in the Midlands, see the individual county entries for details. One ticket worth looking out for is the Midland Day Ranger, covering trains in an area from Northampton to Birmingham and Lichfield, and from Hereford to Shrewsbury. It costs £11.50.

533

Birmingham

☎ 0121 • pop 1,014,000

Birmingham is England's second largest city, culturally vibrant, socially dynamic but aesthetically challenged. Birmingham remains a major manufacturing centre, a city of fierce pride and boundless vitality. Although there are no essential sights and the city centre is chopped to pieces by ring roads, there are still some interesting corners, especially in Brindleyplace, the award-winning waterfront development around the old canal network. The city is starting to get a buzz about it once more, so, thankfully, it's no longer regarded with disdain by people from beyond the Black Country.

The city was one of the great centres of the Industrial Revolution, home to inventors such as steam pioneers James Watt (1736–1819) and Matthew Boulton (1728–1809), gas lighting whizz kid William Murdock (1754–1839), printer John Baskerville (1706–75) and chemist Joseph Priestley (1733–1804). But by the mid-19th century, the 'workshop of the world' exemplified

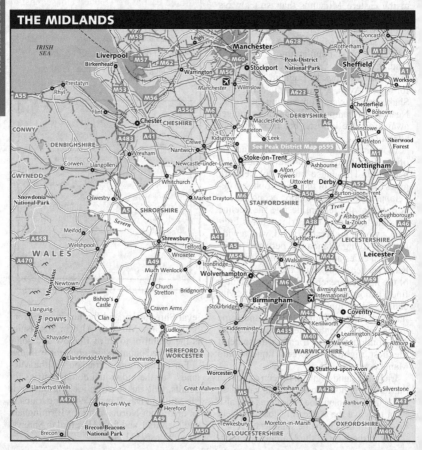

THE MIDLANDS

everything that was bad about industrial development. Under enlightened mayors such as Joseph Chamberlain (1869–1940), father of the unfortunate Neville, the city became a trendsetter in civic development, but WWII air raids undid their good work and post-war town planners completed the vandalism by designing the ring roads and motorways that virtually obliterated the old city centre. The connection between the M5, M6 and M42 is such a mess that it's commonly known as Spaghetti Junction.

The Birmingham accent is consistently rated England's most unattractive. Locally, the city is known as Brum, the inhabitants as Brummies and the dialect as Brummie.

Orientation

The endless ring roads, roundabouts and underpasses make Birmingham a confusing city to navigate, particularly for motorists.

The city centre is the pedestrian precinct in front of the huge Council House. Head west from here to Centenary Square, the International Convention Centre and Symphony Hall, and the Gas St Basin/Brindleyplace development. Head north-west for the Jewellery Quarter.

South-east of the Council House most of Birmingham's shops can be found along pedestrianised New St and in the modern City Plaza, Pallasades and Pavilions shopping centres; the latter is overlooked by the landmark Rotunda office block.

After dark the underpasses linking New Street station to Digbeth coach station can seem very alarming, especially for lone women. The good news is that work is currently underway that will see the whole ghastly Bull Ring mess razed to the ground.

Information

The Tourist Information Centre (TIC; ☎ 693 6300, fax 693 9600, e ticketshop@ bmp.org.uk) at 130 Colmore Row, on Victoria Square, is the most useful. It opens 9.30 am to 6 pm Monday to Saturday and 10 am to 4 pm on Sunday. There's another TIC (☎ 643 2514, fax 616 1038) at 2 City Arcade and a third in the National Exhibition Centre (☎ 780 4321, fax 780 4260), roughly midway between Birmingham and Coventry and near Birmingham airport.

Orange Studio (☎ 634 2800) is a state-of-the-art Internet cafe at 7 Cannon St near New Street station with very reasonable rates. NetAdventure Cybercafe (☎ 693 6655), 68 Dalton St, is an independent option in the centre of town.

Town Centre

The central pedestrian precinct of Victoria and Chamberlain Squares features a statue of Queen Victoria, a fountain, a memorial to Joseph Chamberlain and some of

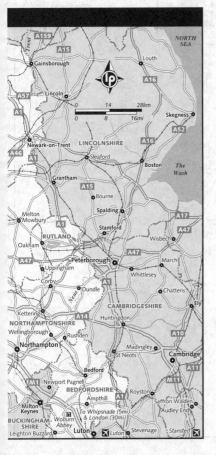

BIRMINGHAM

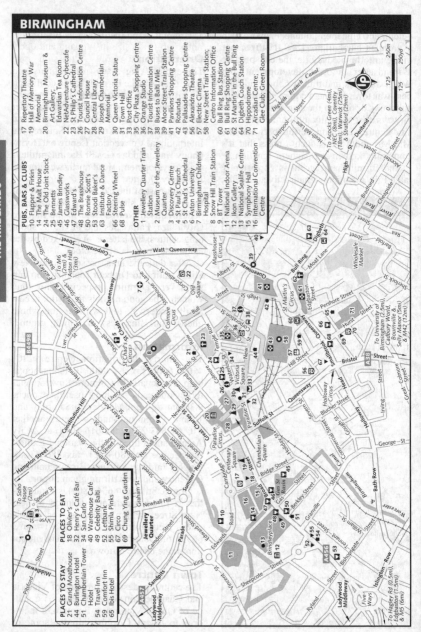

17	Repertory Theatre
19	Hall of Memory War Memorial
20	Birmingham Museum & Art Gallery; Edwardian Tea Room
22	NetAdventure Cybercafe
23	St Philip's Cathedral
26	Tourist Information Centre
27	Council House
28	Central Library
29	Joseph Chamberlain Memorial
30	Queen Victoria Statue
33	Town Hall
34	Post Office
35	City Plaza Shopping Centre
36	Orange Studio
37	Tourist Information Centre
38	Buses to Balti Mile
39	Moor Street Train Station
41	Pavilions Shopping Centre
42	Rotunda
43	Pallasades Shopping Centre
56	Alexandra Theatre
57	Electric Cinema
58	New Street Train Station; Centro Information Office
60	Bull Ring Bus Station
61	Bull Ring Shopping Centre
62	St Martin's in the Bull Ring
64	Digbeth Coach Station
70	Hippodrome
71	Arcadian Centre; Glee Club; Green Room

PUBS, BARS & CLUBS
10	Flapper & Firkin
14	The Malt House
24	The Old Joint Stock
25	Bennetts
45	James Brindley
46	Glassworks
47	Edward's
48	The Brasshouse
53	Ronnie Scott's
53	Stoodi Baker's
55	Institute & Dance Factory
66	Steering Wheel
68	Pulse

OTHER
1	Jewellery Quarter Train Station
2	Museum of the Jewellery Quarter
3	Discovery Centre
4	St Paul's Church
5	St Chad's Cathedral
6	Aston University
7	Birmingham Childrens Hospital
8	Snow Hill Train Station
9	BT Tower
11	National Indoor Arena
12	Ikon Gallery
13	National Sealife Centre
15	Symphony Hall
16	International Convention Centre

PLACES TO STAY
21	Grand Moathouse
44	Burlington Hotel
51	Chamberlain Tower Hotel
54	Travel Inn
59	Comfort Inn
65	Ibis Hotel

PLACES TO EAT
18	Olivier's
32	Henry's Café Bar
34	San Carlo
40	Warehouse Café
49	Celebrity Balti
52	Leftbank
55	Shimla Pinks
67	Circo
69	Chung Ying Garden

Birmingham's most eye-catching architecture. The imposing **Council House** forms the north-eastern face of the precinct. Nearby is the Birmingham Museum & Art Gallery (see later in the section), which is connected by a bridge to the Gas Hall building topped by the Big Brum clock tower. The precinct's north-western corner is formed by the modernist Central Library, reminiscent of an inverted ziggurat with the Paradise Forum shop and cafe complex next to it.

To the south stands the **Town Hall**, designed by Joseph Hansom (creator of the Hansom Cab, a forerunner of black taxis in London) in 1834 to look like the Temple of Castor and Pollux in Rome. For those who won't make it to Gateshead to see Antony Gormley's *Angel of the North* statue (see Newcastle-upon-Tyne in the North-Eastern England chapter), his wingless *Iron Man* of 1993 is a step in the same direction.

West of the precinct, Centenary Square is another pedestrian square closed off at the western end by the International Convention Centre and the Symphony Hall, and overlooked by the Repertory Theatre. In the centre is the Hall of Memory War Memorial and a curious modern statue, *Forward*, depicting a cluster of Brummies.

Canal System

Birmingham sits on the hub of England's canal network, and visiting narrow boats can moor in the Gas St Basin right in the heart of the city.

During the 1990s the creation of Brindleyplace, a waterfront development of trendy cafes and bars alongside the National Indoor Arena and the National Sealife Centre, turned the area where it stands into the most vibrant, attractive part of the city, a must for visitors. Following the towpath north-east along the Birmingham and Fazeley Canal it is easy to see just what a wonder has been worked – the surroundings soon deteriorate into a post-apocalyptic mess. Those with a dedicated interest in the myriad canals should seek out the excellent *City of Canals* leaflet available at the TICs.

The state-of-the-art **National Sealife Centre** (☎ 633 4700) is the only inland aquarium of its size in England and opens 10 am to 5 pm daily. Admission costs £8/5.50 (£5.95/3.95 from the TIC).

St Philip's Cathedral

In Colmore Row, St Philip's was built in neoclassical style between 1709 and 1715 and became a cathedral in 1905. The 19th-century Pre-Raphaelite artist Edward Burne-Jones was responsible for the magnificent stained-glass windows: the *Last Judgement* at the western end, the *Nativity, Crucifixion* and *Ascension* at the eastern end.

Birmingham Museum & Art Gallery

On Chamberlain Square, the newly restored museum (☎ 303 2834) boasts displays on local and natural history, and archaeology. It is the art collection, particularly the Pre-Raphaelite paintings, however, that takes pride of place (see the boxed text 'The Pre-Raphaelites & the Arts and Crafts Movement' later).

People keen on science will have to make do with the Light on Science Gallery here, until the Museum of Science and Industry finds a new home in the Millennium Point development. The museum opens 10 am to 5 pm Monday to Saturday and 12.30 to 5 pm Sunday. Admission is free.

Jewellery Quarter

Birmingham is a major jewellery manufacturing centre and the Jewellery Quarter is packed with manufacturers and showrooms. The *Jewellery Quarter Magazine* has an interesting walking tour map taking you past the 1903 Chamberlain Clock and various other sights.

The Museum of the Jewellery Quarter (☎ 554 3598), 75–79 Vyse St, shows you the Smith & Pepper jewellery factory as it was on the day it closed in 1981 after 80 years of operation. It opens 10 am to 4 pm Monday to Friday and 11 am to 5 pm Saturday. Admission costs £2.50/2.

The Jewellery Quarter is a 15-minute walk from the city centre, or you can catch a train from Moor Street to Jewellery Quarter station.

Soho House

The industrialist Matthew Boulton lived in Soho House (☎ 554 9122), Soho Ave, Handsworth, from 1766 to 1809. It has been restored to let visitors see what such a house would have looked like in the 18th century. It opens 10 am to 4.30 pm Tuesday to Saturday and noon to 4.30 pm Sunday. Admission costs £2.50/2. It is walking distance from the Jewellery Quarter, or bus Nos 70, 74, 78 and 79 pass by.

Aston Hall

Built between 1618 and 1635, this Jacobean mansion (☎ 327 0062) with a fine long gallery is in Aston Park on Trinity Rd, Aston, about 3 miles (5km) north of the city centre. It opens 2 to 5 pm daily, Easter to October, and admission is free. Get there on bus No 65 or 104, or take a train to Aston station.

Barber Institute of Fine Arts

The small collection of old masters at the Barber Institute of Fine Arts (☎ 414 7333) is, for art lovers, the highlight of a visit to Birmingham. The collection has only been assembled since the 1930s and that makes it all the more remarkable as it includes pieces by Rubens, Van Dyck, Gainsborough, Turner, Monet, Van Gogh and Picasso. It opens 10 am to 5 pm Monday to Saturday and to 2 pm Sunday. Admission is free.

Barber Institute is at the University of Birmingham, 2½ miles (4km) south of the city centre (get off at University station). Bus Nos 61, 62 and 63 come this way from the centre.

Ikon Gallery

The Ikon Gallery (☎ 248 0708), Oozells Square, Brindleyplace, features changing exhibitions of modern art, often impressive, often utter nonsense, depending on one's taste. There is also a lively little cafe here featuring a tapas menu.

Organised Tours

Late June to early September Guide Friday (☎ 01789-294466) operates seven daily 90-minute bus tours for £7.50/2.50 per head. Phone the TIC (☎ 693 6300) for details of ghost and graveyard tours (£4.50/4) as well

The Pre-Raphaelites & the Arts and Crafts Movement

The Pre-Raphaelite Brotherhood was formed in 1848 by three young British artists: Dante Gabriel Rossetti, William Holman Hunt and John Everett Millais. Four other artists soon joined them in their rejection of contemporary English art, in favour of the directness of art prior to the High Renaissance, especially the work preceding that of Raphael.

Often unashamedly romantic in its view of the past, their work was characterised by almost photographic attention to detail, a combination of hyper-realism and brilliant colours that ensured the movement's popularity to this day.

Birmingham Museum & Art Gallery has one of the best collections of works by the Pre-Raphaelites. If you get the bug, there are more fine paintings in the Lady Lever Art Gallery at Port Sunlight near Liverpool.

The Arts and Crafts movement followed Pre-Raphaelitism in its rejection of contemporary standards and its yearning for an earlier, purer and more naturalistic style. The socialist William Morris, the movement's leading light, had worked with Rossetti and projected the same ideals into tapestries, jewellery, stained glass and textile prints. Cheltenham Art Gallery & Museum has a fine display of Arts and Crafts furniture, as does Arlington Mill in Bibury, Gloucestershire. Those passing through Birmingham must call on Wightwick Manor, an Arts and Crafts masterpiece, complete with original William Morris wallpaper and fabrics.

as more conventional walking tours of the city centre.

Canal boat trips can be arranged from the Gas St Basin or the Convention Centre quay (☎ 507 0477) for around £5/2.50 per head.

Places to Stay

Birmingham has no YHA hostel. Most accommodation in the centre is aimed at business visitors, and at the weekend or during summer it may be worth asking at the TIC in case there are special deals to fill surplus beds. Day-tripping into Birmingham is an option, but means missing out on the nightlife, something to savour these days. Stratford-upon-Avon and Coventry are short train rides away.

Although one reader recommended the 92-room *YWCA* (☎ 454 8134, Alexandra House, 27 Norfolk Rd, Edgbaston), which has dorm beds for £9 a night, the hostel is clear that 'our priority is to provide accommodation for those people without homes'.

Popular areas for B&Bs include Edgbaston (to the south-west) and Acocks Green (to the south-east). The friendly *Ashdale House Hotel* (☎ 706 3598, fax 706 3958, 39 Broad Rd, Acocks Green) has singles from £22 (£28 with bathroom) and doubles from £42. Vegetarian breakfasts can be arranged.

Birmingham has a full set of mid-range chain hotels – perfectly comfortable although lacking in character. Closest to New Street station is the *Comfort Inn* (☎ 643 1134, fax 643 3209, Station St), with singles/doubles for £45/65. The centrally located *Ibis Hotel* (☎ 622 6010, Arcadian Centre, Ladywell Walk) has double rooms from £39 (breakfast is extra). The *Travel Inn* (☎ 644 5266, 230 Broad St) is ideally placed for exploring the Brindleyplace nightlife. Rooms cost a flat £49.95.

Nearby is the more upmarket *Chamberlain Tower Hotel* (☎ 606 9000, fax 606 9001, e info@chamberlain.co.uk, Broad St) with plush rooms for £55, making them good value. The *Burlington Hotel* (☎ 643 9191, 6 Burlington Arcade) is one of the most pleasant centrally located hotels and has rooms from £135/157 during the week,

a more sensible £65/80 at the weekend. Nicest of the posh places is the *Grand Moathouse* (☎ 607 9988, Colmore Row), overlooking the cathedral, but a room sets you back £110/130.

Places to Eat

Birmingham's contribution to world cuisine is the balti, a uniquely Midlands version of Indian food. England is now engulfed with balti houses but Birmingham remains their homeland. The most down-to-earth prices are in the Birmingham Balti Mile of Sparkbrook, Sparkhill and Balsall Heath, 2 miles (3km) south of the centre, where 50 or more restaurants are squeezed into the area around Ladypool Rd and Stoney Lane. Pick up a complete listings leaflet in the TIC and head out on bus No 4, 5 or 6 from Corporation St.

Luckily there are also a few decent alternatives in the city centre. The *Celebrity Balti* (☎ 632 6074, 44 Broad St) is much glossier than average but the food is delicious. Baltis range from around £6 to £9. Another classic is *Shimla Pinks* (☎ 704 0344, 214 Broad St), one of a growing chain that isn't compromising its reputation and serves some of the best subcontinental specialities in the city centre.

The *cafe* (☎ 248 3226), at the Ikon Gallery in Brindleyplace (see earlier), is a great place to sample some Spanish food. The menu includes a selection of cheap nibbles, such as artichoke hearts, for around £1; larger dishes include the inevitable paella, this time with squid.

Dine in even classier surroundings in the *Edwardian Tea Room* (☎ 303 2834) in the Birmingham Museum & Art Gallery; there are hot meals, as well as sandwiches and cakes. Big, busy and rather brazen *Henry's Café Bar* (☎ 631 3827, Hill St) serves everything from burgers to cashew-nut paella. The *Warehouse Café* (☎ 633 0261, 54 Allison St, Digbeth) specialises in vegan food and opens to 9 pm Monday to Saturday. In the Arcadian Centre in Hurst St, an up-and-coming area like Brindleyplace but with less water and sophistication, the *Green Room* serves a popular pre-theatre menu to Hippodrome punters; specials cost around £5.

Excellent Cantonese cuisine can be had nearby at *Chung Ying Garden* (☎ 666 6622, 17 Thorpe St), which wheels out 70 varieties of dim sum and main courses from £6.50. *Circo* (☎ 643 1400, 6 Holloway Circus) is a popular tapas bar offering a £5 lunch-time special of mussels, french fries, salad and mayonnaise.

San Carlo (☎ 633 0251, 4 Temple St) has a lengthy Italian menu including some impressive pizzas and pastas, along with a selection of Italian country cooking and is well worth sampling. *wineREPublic* (☎ 644 6464, Centenary Square), the Repertory Theatre's restaurant, comes in for plenty of praise. Try the pre-theatre menu for under £10, or go a la carte and pay about £15 – the balti duck is said to be delicious.

Brindleyplace offers wall-to-wall eateries, with many of the big chains represented. More of a one-off is *Tin Tin* (☎ 633 0888), a classy Chinese restaurant where fish dishes are particularly good. *Bank* (☎ 633 4466, 4 Brindleyplace) has a sophisticated atmosphere and draws the punters with pre-concert meals for £15.50 for three courses. It is currently one of the more popular places in the canal area. *Le Petit Blanc* (☎ 633 7333, 9 Brindleyplace) offers entry-level haute cuisine at almost sensible prices. Best value is the set menu at £12 for two courses or £15 for three. Otherwise opt for a la carte with foie gras and other regional French specialities.

Leftbank (☎ 643 4464) takes expensive dining to new heights, but is renowned for well-prepared, well-presented food. Count on £30 and up.

Entertainment

Birmingham is a massive city and each area has its highs and lows. Brindleyplace and the Arcadian Centre are the most popular central areas for a drink, but students often congregate in Edgbaston and Aston. *What's On* (free at the TIC, otherwise 80p) is a fortnightly listings guide to entertainment in and around Birmingham.

Pubs & Bars Pleasant canal-side pubs include the *James Brindley* (Gas St Basin), which is named after the canal pioneer, and the trendy *Glassworks* (Gas St Basin). Facing each other across the canal in Broad St are *The Brasshouse* and *Edward's*, but these are both chain pubs so will not satisfy everyone.

The *Flapper & Firkin* (☎ 236 2421, Cambrian Wharf, Kingston Row), a little farther along the canal at Cambrian Wharf, is decorated in canal style. There is another *Firkin* in the Aston University Quadrant that has live music most nights. *The Malt House* (☎ 633 4171, 75 King Edwards Rd, Brindley Place) has a great position overlooking the canal. Also in this area is *Stoodi Baker's* (☎ 643 5100, 192 Broad St), a trendy bar and club that is popular with students.

Birmingham has several impressive banks-turned-bars. *Bennetts* (☎ 643 9293, Bennetts Hill) serves up tasty food to accompany the drinks in grand surroundings. Alternatively, try *The Old Joint Stock* (Temple Row), facing the cathedral, which serves up fine Fuller's ales and feels more like a traditional pub.

Clubs The *Institute & Dance Factory* (☎ 643 7788, Digbeth High St) is a large nightclub that often has live music. The busy *Steering Wheel* (☎ 622 5700, Wrottesley St, Chinatown) has three dance floors and during the week hosts promotion nights with cheap drinks and entry. *Pulse* (☎ 643 4715, Hurst St) is a similar sort of place, which serves up something different every night of the week. *Birmingham Sanctuary* (☎ 246 1010, 78 Digbeth High St) is another popular club.

The *Que Club* (☎ 472 0777, Corporation St) is an incredible venue housed in a former Methodist church. Club nights and gigs are held here, including some of the big boys from London, such as Return to the Source, who keep the decks spinning until dawn.

The *Glee Club* (☎ 693 2248, Hurst St) hosts stand-up comedians several nights a week. Thursday night's admission (£6.95) includes a balti; at the weekend it is £10 and up (but you do get to dance afterwards).

Music *Ronnie Scott's* famous jazz club (☎ *643 4525, Broad St)* charges £11 to £16 admission depending on the night.

The City of Birmingham Symphony Orchestra plays in the ultramodern *Symphony Hall (☎ 780 3333)*.

Major rock and pop acts appear at the *National Exhibition Centre (☎ 780 4133)*, but if the artists are big enough to play, the price is similarly big at £15 and up. Since the closing of the Hummingbird, the Institute & Dance Factory and Que Club often have bands, but the best venue of all is the *Civic Hall* in Wolverhampton (see the following Around Birmingham section).

Theatre & Cinema The Victoria Square TIC has a ticket shop (☎ 643 2514) where, from 11 am daily, you can buy half-price theatre tickets. Theatres include the *Hippodrome (☎ 689 3000, Hurst St)*, home of the Birmingham Royal Ballet; the *Alexandra Theatre (☎ 0870 607 7533, Station St)*; and the *Repertory Theatre (☎ 236 4455, Centenary Square, Broad St)*.

The fantastically decorated *Electric Cinema (☎ 643 7277, Station St)* often shows cult movies; double bills cost just £4.30.

Getting There & Away

Air Birmingham boasts an increasingly busy international airport (☎ 767 7000) with flights to numerous European destinations and to New York. Trains from New Street station run here constantly.

Bus National Express (☎ 0870 580 8080) has links to most parts of Britain from dreary Digbeth coach station. A single ticket to London costs £10 (3½ hours), to Oxford £8.75 and to Manchester £9.75. Local buses operate from the Bull Ring bus station. Bus No X93 goes to Kidderminster for the Severn Valley Railway.

Train New Street station, one of England's busiest rail interchanges, is underneath the Pallasades shopping centre, which in turn is linked with the Bull Ring bus station and Bull Ring shopping centre. Birmingham International is the station for both the National Exhibition Centre and Birmingham airport.

Most trains run from New Street, including those to London, Oxford, Bristol, Manchester and Scotland. However, certain services, such as those to Worcester and Hereford or Stratford-upon-Avon or Warwick, run from Snow Hill and Moor Street stations.

During summer, special **steam services** (☎ 707 4696) operate between Birmingham Snow Hill and Stratford-upon-Avon six times a day. One-way/return tickets cost £10/15 for adults and £3/5 for children.

Tram Birmingham again has trams running from Snow Hill to Wolverhampton, via the Jewellery Quarter, West Bromwich and Dudley. Fares start at 40p and rise to £1.80 for the full length. A day pass costs £3/2.

Getting Around

Centro (☎ 200 2700), the transport authority for the Birmingham and Coventry area, has an information office in New Street station. They can provide help and advice on planning journeys and they also produce a comprehensive guide to getting around the West Midlands for those with a mobility difficulty. A Daytripper ticket gives all-day travel on buses and trains after 9.30 am and costs £4/2.35.

Local trains, including the Stratford-upon-Avon service, operate from Moor Street station, which is only a few minutes' walk from New Street – follow the red line on the pavement. Other handy stations are at Snow Hill and the Jewellery Quarter.

AROUND BIRMINGHAM
Cadbury World & Bournville Village

Chocoholics should make a beeline for Cadbury World, where you can find out the story behind a creme egg and visit the chocolate-packaging plant where around 800 bars a minute are wrapped and dispatched. Not surprisingly this place is packed over weekends and school holidays when it's best to book ahead by phoning ☎ 0121-451 4159. Opening hours vary throughout the year but are generally 10 am to 5.30 pm daily. Admission costs £6.50/4.50.

To get to Cadbury World take a train to Bournville station from Birmingham New St. Alternatively, bus Nos 83, 84 and 85 run this way from the centre. In summer Guide Friday tours (see Organised Tours earlier in the section) drop off at Cadbury World.

Before returning, follow the signs to pretty Bournville village, designed for early-20th-century factory workers by the Cadbury family with large houses set around a green.

It's also well worth visiting **Selly Manor** (☎ 0121-472 0199), the sort of half-timbered medieval-cum-Elizabethan house you see in Stratford-upon-Avon but without the crowds. It opens 10 am to 5 pm Tuesday to Friday and 2 to 5 pm weekends. Admission costs £2.50/50p. The manor also stocks the excellent *Bournville Trail Guide*.

The Black Country

The area stretching west of Birmingham and out to Wolverhampton was traditionally known as the Black Country because of the smoke and dust generated by the local coal and iron industries. These days things have improved, though it's still not a tourist hotspot. **Walsall** has put itself back on the map with the **New Art Gallery** (☎ 01922-654400), Gallery Square, home to the Garman-Ryan collection, which includes works by Picasso and Van Gogh. It opens 10 am to 5 pm Tuesday to Saturday (from noon Sunday) and admission is free.

Wolverhampton To the west, Wolverhampton has recently been granted city status. If you were having trouble understanding Brummies, you'll find things get harder here.

Wolverhampton TIC (☎ 01902-556110, fax 556111), 18 Queen Square, opens 9 am to 5 pm Monday to Friday (to 4.30 pm Saturday).

As well as having an **art gallery** (☎ 01902-552055), Wolverhampton is also home to **Wightwick Manor** (☎ 01902-761108). Run by the National Trust (NT), it is an Arts and Crafts masterpiece, complete with original William Morris wallpaper and

Running from the Republicans

Charles II, England's merry monarch who 'never said a foolish thing, nor ever did a wise one', was almost captured by parliamentarians following his defeat at the Battle of Worcester in 1651. His father, Charles I, had already lost his head to the House of Commons, and Charles II, had he been captured, would likely have lost his too. However, he escaped to the Continent with help from supporters along the way and two of the houses that harboured him, Boscobel House (☎ 01902-850244), run by English Heritage (EH), and Moseley Old Hall (☎ 01902-782808; NT) are open to visitors.

Boscobel House is home to the so-called Royal Oak, the tree up which Charles hid when parliamentarians searched the house. The timber-framed house opens 10 am to 6 pm daily, April to September (to 5 pm October), and 10 am to 4 pm Wednesday to Sunday at other times (closed January). Admission costs £4/2. It is 8 miles (13km) north-west of Wolverhampton.

Moseley Old Hall was a second house that saved a king and has a small priest-hole where Charles was able to hide. It opens 1.30 to 5.30 pm Wednesday, Saturday and Sunday, June to October; weekends and bank holidays, April and May and Sundays, November and December. Admission costs £4/2. It is 4 miles (6km) north of Wolverhampton.

After his escape, Charles II wandered Europe in exile for many years, scheming and plotting his return with help from Catholic monarchs. A settlement was eventually negotiated returning him as king in 1660. He ruled until 1685, a volatile monarch with a combative view of parliament, unsurprising given the treatment of his father. During the last four years of his rule, parliament was dissolved.

fabrics, Kempe glass and de Morgan tiling. It opens 2.30 to 5.30 pm Thursday and Saturday, March to December. Admission costs £5.50/2.75.

Black Country Museum The 10.5-hectare Black Country Museum (☎ 0121-557 9643) features a re-created coal mine, village and fairground on the banks of the Dudley Canal at Tipton in Dudley. It's a great place for a day out, with a full program of mine trips, Charlie Chaplin films and chances to watch glass cutters and sweet makers in action.

From March to October you can also take a 40-minute boat ride through the Dudley Canal Tunnel to explore assorted caverns (£2.90/2.50).

The museum opens 10 am to 5 pm daily, March to October; and 10 am to 4 pm Wednesday to Sunday in winter. Admission costs £7.95/4.75. The *Stables Restaurant* offers pretty mundane on-site meals, or there's the excellent re-created *fish and chip shop*. The *Bottle & Glass Inn* can help you wash your food down.

To get there from Birmingham city centre, take the No 126 bus from Corporation St and ask to be put off at Tipton Rd. It's a 10-minute walk along Tipton Rd to the museum, or you can catch bus No 311 or 313. A Daytripper ticket will cover the entire journey.

Warwickshire

Warwickshire is home to two of England's biggest tourist attractions: Stratford-upon-Avon, with its Shakespearean connections, and Warwick, with its popular castle. The ruined castle at Kenilworth is also worth a look, as is the modern cathedral in Coventry. Elsewhere the county has plenty of museums, castles, market towns, canals and pleasant countryside.

For bus information throughout the area phone ☎ 01926-414140. Coventry is a good transport hub with rail connections to London Euston, Birmingham New Street and Leicester.

COVENTRY
☎ 024 • pop 318,800

Coventry was once one of England's most important towns, a centre for the wool industry in medieval times and more recently a dynamic manufacturing centre for the motor car. However, between the aerial bombshells of the Luftwaffe and the architectural bombshells of the planners, much of historic Coventry disappeared under a mountain of concrete – although it should be remembered that the pedestrianised areas were among the first in the country.

It is easy to get to from Birmingham or Stratford-upon-Avon and fans of modern architecture will want to drop by to save the new cathedral built beside the bombed-out ruins of the medieval one. Nearby are some fine Georgian town houses and medieval cottages, small clues to the city's beauty prior to its destruction. It's also an escape from the tourist merry-go-round during the summer months.

During the 14th century Coventry was one of the four largest towns in England outside London, its fortune made on the back of sheep, literally. Decline set in and Coventry was still essentially a medieval town when the Industrial Revolution hit it in the 19th century.

Coventry was one of the most inventive of the Victorian industrial centres and claims to be the birthplace of the modern bicycle. The first car made in England was a Daimler built in Coventry in 1896, and in the early years of the 20th century Coventry was England's motor-manufacturing capital as well as a major centre for the manufacturing of aircraft. But steady growth switched to headlong decline in the 1970s and 80s as Sunbeam, Hillman, Singer, Humber and Triumph cars all disappeared. Now only Jaguar remains of the home-grown models (albeit owned by the US giant Ford), although French Peugeots are also assembled in Coventry.

Coventry is probably best known for Lady Godiva, a medieval member of the elite who took off all her clothes to help the poor, a sort of 'Stripping Hood'.

Orientation & Information

Central Coventry is encircled by a ring road with most points of interest tucked inside. Medieval Spon St features several half-timbered buildings relocated from elsewhere in the city.

The TIC (☎ 7683 2303, fax 7683 2370), Bayley Lane, is beside Coventry University and faces the two cathedrals. It opens 9.30 am to 5 pm Monday to Friday and 10 am to 4.30 pm at the weekend.

Cathedrals

Founded in the 12th century and rebuilt from 1373, St Michael's was one of England's largest parish churches when it became a cathedral in 1918, its spire topped only by those of Salisbury and Norwich cathedrals. Then on 14 November 1940, a Luftwaffe raid gutted the cathedral, leaving only the outer walls and the spire standing amid the smoking ruins.

After the war, the ruins were left as a reminder. The new St Michael's Cathedral (☎ 7622 7597) was built beside it. Designed by Sir Basil Spence and built between 1955 and 1962, the cathedral is one of the few examples of post-war British architecture to

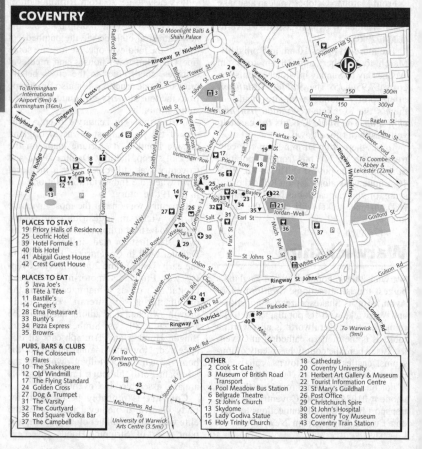

COVENTRY

PLACES TO STAY
19 Priory Halls of Residence
25 Leofric Hotel
39 Hotel Formule 1
40 Ibis Hotel
41 Abigail Guest House
42 Crest Guest House

PLACES TO EAT
5 Java Joe's
8 Tête à Tête
11 Bastille's
14 Ginger's
28 Etna Restaurant
33 Bunty's
34 Pizza Express
35 Browns

PUBS, BARS & CLUBS
1 The Colosseum
9 Flares
10 The Shakespeare
12 Old Windmill
17 The Flying Standard
24 Golden Cross
27 Dog & Trumpet
31 The Varsity
32 The Courtyard
36 Red Square Vodka Bar
37 The Campbell

OTHER
2 Cook St Gate
3 Museum of British Road Transport
4 Pool Meadow Bus Station
6 Belgrade Theatre
7 St John's Church
13 Skydome
15 Lady Godiva Statue
16 Holy Trinity Church
18 Cathedrals
20 Coventry University
21 Herbert Art Gallery & Museum
22 Tourist Information Centre
23 St Mary's Guildhall
26 Post Office
29 Christchurch Spire
30 St John's Hospital
38 Coventry Toy Museum
43 Coventry Train Station

inspire popular affection. It's noted for the soaring etched glass screen wall at the western end, for the Graham Sutherland tapestry above the altar, for Piper's lovely stained glass and for Epstein's sculpture of St Michael subduing the devil beside the entrance steps.

The visitor centre screens an audiovisual presentation on the destruction of the old cathedral and the birth of its replacement for £2/1 (except Sunday). Visitors to the new cathedral are asked for a £2 donation. The old cathedral spire still looks down on the ruins and its 180 steps lead up to magnificent views. Admission costs £1.

Museum of British Road Transport

The museum (☎ 7683 2425), in Hales St, has a huge collection of bicycles, motorcycles, racing cars and rally cars and even Thrust 2 (once the world's fastest car), alongside traditional British family cars. It's a sobering reminder of how to turn a good industry bad when you look at the dazzling array of glamorous models churned out in the 1950s and 60s and the sort of skips-on-wheels that came out of British Leyland by the late 1970s. It opens 10 am to 4.30 pm daily and admission is free.

Other Things to See & Do

The **statue of Lady Godiva** (see the boxed text 'Stripping Away the Myth'), at the edge of The Precinct, is a Coventry meeting spot handily overlooked by the Coventry Clock. A figure of the naked lady parades from the clock each hour, while Peeping Tom peers out from above. Godiva appears again, this time with husband Leofric, on the fairy-tale facade of the Council House on High St.

The **Herbert Art Gallery & Museum** (☎ 7683 2386), in Jordan Well, provides a quick run through Coventry's history. The upstairs art gallery has paintings of the Lady Godiva legend and the original sketches for Sutherland's cathedral tapestry. It opens 10 am to 5.30 pm daily and noon to 5 pm Sunday and admission is free.

The **Coventry Toy Museum** (☎ 7622 7560) is housed in the ancient Whitefriars Gate, which dates from 1352. The museum includes exhibits ranging from 1970s icon, the Raleigh Chopper, to timeless teddy bears. It opens 1 to 4 pm daily (1 to 5 pm at the weekend), April to November, and costs £1.50/1.

Other buildings that have survived Coventry's misfortune include **St Mary's Guildhall**, an elaborate, rambling civic building dating from medieval times. It is possible to visit from April to October, but check with the TIC first as it is sometimes used for civic functions. **Holy Trinity Church** dates from the 12th century and its 67m spire has long been a landmark of the city. It is home to a rare medieval painting located above the chancel arch. Smaller

---

Stripping Away the Myth

Lady Godiva is to Coventry what Robin Hood is to Nottingham, a character based in history whose story has been embellished through the ages. Lady Godiva was the wife of Leofric, the mean-minded earl of Mercia and lord of Coventry, a compassionate woman who begged her husband to relieve the tax burden on the region's poor. Leofric jested that he would do so only if she rode naked on a horse from one end of town to the other. Surprisingly she did just that, although only on agreement from the townsfolk that they remain indoors. One young voyeur called (Peeping) Tom couldn't resist the temptation for an eyeful, but was struck with blindness.

Myths aside, Lady Godiva certainly played an important role in the history of Coventry. Unfortunately for romantics, it is unlikely that Leofric would have allowed his wife of such standing to demean herself in such a way. However, for Coventry it is an excuse for a celebration and every year a parade is held in early June to commemorate the original stripper.

Lady Godiva has an entirely different meaning in London where it is rhyming slang for fiver (£5).

St John's Church is famous for giving the world the expression 'sent to Coventry'. Royalist prisoners of war were interned here during the Civil War, out of touch with their friends and family.

Places to Stay

The TIC makes bookings free of charge (☎ 0800 243748), though many places are uncomfortably close to the noisy ring road.

There's no hostel but in July and August the *Priory Halls of Residence* (☎ 7688 8318, Priory St), at Coventry University, offers accommodation from £15 per person.

The *Crest Guest House* (☎ 7622 7822, e alanharve@aol.com, 39 Friars Rd) offers a good standard of comfort for non-smokers at £26.50 per head. Just around the corner is homely *Abigail Guest House* (☎ 7622 1378, 39 St Patricks Rd) with rooms starting from a very reasonable £18.50.

The *Ibis Hotel* (☎ 7625 0500, Mile Lane) is a stone's throw from the station, as well as the city centre, and offers its standard ensuite rooms for £39.95.

Right next to the Ibis Hotel is a *Hotel Formule 1* (☎ 7623 4560, Mile Lane), one of a chain of basic French hotels making headway in England. Rooms feel a little like ship cabins and showers are shared, but at £19.50 that is hardly grounds for complaint.

For something more comfortable, try the *Leofric Hotel* (☎ 7622 1371, Broadgate), which offers rooms with all the trimmings from £95, though there are cheaper deals at the weekend. Don't be put off by the ugly exterior as it gets better inside.

The city's finest hotel is *Coombe Abbey* (☎ 7645 0450, Brinklow Rd, Binley) out in the suburbs. Once an 11th-century abbey, you no longer need to take the vows to enter. Rooms cost (take a breath) £125 and up.

Places to Eat

Browns (☎ 7622 1100, Jordan Well) has long been a Coventry institution and should not be missed. It has a long menu of huge dishes for £4.50 each and no one leaves hungry. It is a popular bar by night and DJs ply their trade at the weekend. *Bunty's* (☎ 7622 3758, 4 Hay Lane) is a pleasant tearoom serving filled bagels and excellent hot chocolate. Nearby are some hit-and-run sandwich bars for those in a hurry.

Also in renovated Hay Lane is a branch of *Pizza Express* (☎ 7663 3156) serving up the usual favourites. However, for individualised Italian, *Etna Restaurant* (☎ 7622 3183, 57 Hertford St) is hard to beat, with a vast selection of southern European favourites. Expect to eat well for £10 per head and up. *Ginger's* (☎ 7622 3223, 20 Hertford St), on the pedestrian precinct, is a popular place for cheap sandwiches, filled spuds and hearty breakfasts.

Java Joe's (☎ 7622 8898, 50 Corporation St) is a great little coffee bar with the full range of international fixes.

Old-world Spon St has several eateries including the elegant *Bastille's* (☎ 7622 9274, 21 Spon St), in a gorgeous old house, which has excellent-value two-course lunches for a fiver and an extensive dinner menu at around £15 to £20 all said. Nearby *Tête à Tête* (☎ 7655 0938, 18 Spon St) scoops the afternoon-tea trade.

There are some good balti restaurants in Coventry, and the Foleshill Rd remains one of the most popular hunting grounds. Up this way is *Moonlight Balti* (☎ 7663 3414, 196–198 Foleshill Rd) with a regular following and the option of BYO even though it has a licence.

Shahi Palace (☎ 7668 8719, 367 Foleshill Rd) is also in this area and focuses on Bangladeshi cuisine with cheap buffets and banquets pulling in business Sunday to Thursday.

Entertainment

Pubs & Clubs With two universities, Coventry has a thriving nightlife. The *Golden Cross* (☎ 7622 2311, 8 Hay Lane) is home to 'food, drink and scruffy people', rare in this day of strict dress codes and burly bouncers on the door. Nestled beneath the cathedrals in Hay Lane, it is one of Coventry's oldest pubs dating from the 16th century.

For the ultimate student pub, try *The Campbell* (☎ 7623 4831, 122 Gosford St), which now, rather dangerously for some, boasts a 2 am close and a whole host of drinks promotions. *The Varsity (Little Park St)*, in the city centre, is another popular student pub, which is part of a growing chain. It has a late licence at the weekend. For a cheap pub, look no farther than *The Flying Standard* (☎ 7655 5723, 2–10 Trinity St), one of the Wetherspoon chain with absurd bargains but little atmosphere.

Spon St offers a host of further pubs including the pleasantly quiet *Old Windmill*, which locals usually call Ma Browns. They have two beer festivals a year making it a good spot for ale enthusiasts. Nearby is *The Shakespeare* (☎ 7663 4087, Spon St), a timeless traditional pub that draws in a local crowd while the rest of Spon St changes.

For those that prefer a 1970s feel to timeless, the psychedelic *Flares* (☎ 7623 4821, 181 Spon St) is a popular theme bar set in a mock-timber building. On some nights there is a nominal charge. Another popular pub is *The Courtyard* with, as you might expect, a nice courtyard for when the sun shines. It is housed in a building part of which dates back to the 15th century. *Red Square Vodka Bar* is the place to get a vodka fix, although outside of weekends it has more flavours than customers.

When it comes to live music and clubs, *The Dog & Trumpet (Hertford St)* is only really worth a go on Friday night for its alternative music. *The Colosseum* (☎ 7655 4473, Primrose Hill St), in Hillfields, is rated for up-and-coming bands, but take care in this area as it has always had a bit of a reputation for trouble.

The new *Skydome* (☎ 7655 5911, Croft Rd) is promoting itself by saying 'Sorry, Birmingham' but Brum doesn't have to panic just yet. The complex includes ice skating, bowling and cinemas and has a couple of big nightclubs, *Ikon* and *Diva*.

Theatre & Cinema The University of Warwick, 4 miles (6km) south of the city, has the largest *Arts Centre* (☎ 7652 4524) outside London, with a regular program of events and a popular cinema showing the sort of foreign films and cult classics that mainstream cinemas never do. Bus Nos 12 and X12 run here from Coventry. *Belgrade Theatre* (☎ 7655 3055) puts on plays and musicals. It is in Corporation St.

Getting There & Away

Air Birmingham international airport (☎ 0121-767 5511) is actually closer to Coventry than Birmingham.

Bus Pool Meadow bus station is in Fairfax St. West Midlands bus services are coordinated by Centro (☎ 7655 9559). One-way National Express tickets cost £10.50 to London, £8 to Oxford and £16.50 to Bath. Arriva (☎ 0116-251 1411) run bus No X67 to Leicester every hour (except Sunday).

Stagecoach (☎ 01788-535555) has Explorer tickets for £4.50/2.50, allowing a day's bus travel to Birmingham, Evesham, Kenilworth, Leamington, Northampton, Oxford, Stratford-upon-Avon and Warwick. There are plenty of buses to Birmingham (No 900), but the train is much quicker.

Train The train station is just across the ring road, south of the centre. Coventry is on the main rail route to London (£19.50, less than 1½ hours). Birmingham is £2.80 by rail.

Getting Around

Phone ☎ 7655 9559 for local bus service information; a Coventry Daysaver costs £2/1, or a Daytripper ticket gives you a day's use of local bus and train services in the Centro area for £4/2.

KENILWORTH

☎ 01926 • pop 21,000

Kenilworth is famous for its castle, a monstrous medieval work mostly destroyed during the Civil War. Close to Warwick University, the town is pleasant in the parts where planners haven't left their mark and is like one big guesthouse for well-heeled workers in neighbouring Coventry, 4 miles (6km) to the north-east. Old and new Kenilworth are some way apart, with the castle closer to picturesque Old Kenilworth.

The TIC (☎ 852595, fax 864503), The Library, 11 Smalley Place, opens 9 am to 7 pm Monday to Saturday (except Wednesday) and 9.30 am to 4 pm Sunday.

Kenilworth Castle

Dramatic, red-sandstone Kenilworth Castle (☎ 852078), run by English Heritage (EH), was founded around 1120 and enlarged in the 14th and 16th centuries. Edward II was briefly imprisoned here before being transferred to Berkeley Castle and murdered. In 1563, Elizabeth I granted the castle to her favourite, Robert Dudley, earl of Leicester. Between 1565 and 1575 she visited him at Kenilworth on four occasions and the theatrical pageants he arranged for her in 1575 were immortalised in Sir Walter Scott's 1821 work *Kenilworth*. The castle was deliberately ruined in 1644, after the Civil War. The castle opens 10 am to 6 pm daily, April to September, and to 4 pm October to March. Admission costs £3.50/1.80.

Places to Stay & Eat

Abbey Guest House (☎ 512707, fax 859148, 41 Station Rd) has singles/doubles for £26/45. There are several B&Bs concentrated on Priory Rd. *Priory Guest House* (☎ 856173, 58 Priory Rd) has eight rooms and charges from £25/40. Nearby *Ferndale Guest House* (☎ 853214, fax 858336, 45 Priory Rd) has very comfortable rooms from £26/40.

The Peacock Hotel (☎ 851156, fax 864644, ⓔ peacockhotel@rafflesmalaysian .com, 149 Warwick Rd) is a relatively new hotel with a smart interior. It costs from £65/75.

Directly opposite the castle, the *Clarendon Arms* (☎ 852017, 44 Castle Hill), with its large garden, is renowned for serving good food and is a pleasant pub to spend some time in during summer. More or less next door, *Harringtons on the Hill* (☎ 852074, 42 Castle Hill) is more of an up-market restaurant with the emphasis on modern British cuisine. Figure on about £15 per person. Next to that is *Time for Tea* offering inexpensive lunches and teas.

The Virgins & Castle (☎ 853737, 7 High St) claims to be the farthest pub from the coast in England, so street surfing only after too many drinks.

Getting There & Away

To get to Kenilworth take bus No X18 from Coventry or from Warwick. Bus No X14 runs frequently to Leamington Spa and Coventry.

WARWICK
☎ 01926 • pop 22,000

Warwickshire's pleasantly sedate county town is home to Warwick Castle, one of England's major tourist attractions. There are a number of historic buildings around town attesting to its importance in years gone by. It makes a handy base for visits to nearby Stratford-upon-Avon.

Orientation & Information

Warwick is simple to navigate; the A429 runs right through the centre with Westgate at one end and Eastgate at the other. The old town centre lies just north of this axis, the castle just south.

The TIC (☎ 492212, fax 494837), Court House, Jury St, is near the junction with Castle St. It opens 9.30 am to 4.30 pm daily.

Warwick Castle

Warwick Castle (☎ 406600), one of England's finest medieval castles, is owned by Madame Tussaud's and can easily take up half a day to explore in depth.

Warwick was first fortified in Saxon times, but the first real castle was constructed on the banks of the River Avon in 1068, soon after the Norman Conquest. The castle's external appearance principally dates from the 14th and 15th centuries, but the interiors are from the late 17th to late 19th centuries, when the castle changed from a military stronghold to a grand residence. Capability Brown landscaped the magnificent grounds in 1753.

The castle is entered through a gatehouse beside the armoury and the dungeon and torture chamber. Just inside, a sign points to the 'Kingmaker' exhibition. The most powerful of all the castle's powerful owners was Warwick the Kingmaker, Richard Neville, the 16th earl (1428–71). Having replaced the ineffectual Henry VI with the king's son Edward IV in 1461, Neville then fell out with Edward IV and brought Henry VI back in 1470, only to be defeated and killed by Edward IV less than a year later. At one time, he had Henry VI under lock and key in the Tower of London while Edward IV was his prisoner at Warwick. The 'Kingmaker' exhibit uses models to show preparations for one of his many battles.

The Tussaud influence is most strongly felt in the private apartments that are furnished as they would have been in 1898, with a series of waxwork figures attending a weekend house party. As you walk round you bump into various members of the nobility, their servants and attendants as well as historic figures such as the young Churchill and the Prince of Wales, later Edward VII.

The castle opens 10 am to 6 pm daily and to 5 pm in winter. Admission costs £10.95/ 6.50. Phone ahead for details of medieval banquets in the castle.

Collegiate Church of St Mary

Originally built in 1123, this church (☎ 403940) on Old Square was badly damaged by a fire in 1694, and rebuilt in a mishmash of styles. The remarkable perpendicular Beauchamp Chapel was built between 1442 and 1460 at a cost of £2400, a huge sum for the time. Luckily it survived the fire.

The gilded bronze effigy of Richard Beauchamp, 13th earl of Warwick, sits in the centre of the chapel; Richard Neville is the sinister-looking figure on the corner of the tomb.

The church opens 10 am to 6 pm daily and to 4 pm November to March. A £1 donation is requested. Don't miss the 12th-century crypt with remnants of a medieval ducking stool, used to drench scolding wives.

THE MIDLANDS

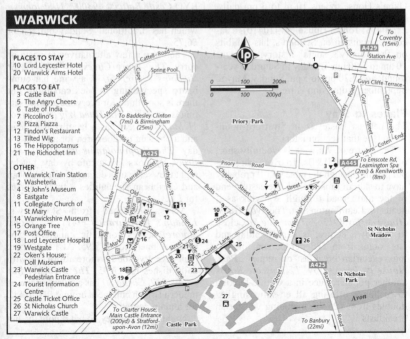

WARWICK

PLACES TO STAY
10 Lord Leycester Hotel
20 Warwick Arms Hotel

PLACES TO EAT
3 Castle Balti
5 The Angry Cheese
6 Taste of India
7 Piccolino's
9 Pizza Piazza
12 Findon's Restaurant
13 Tilted Wig
16 The Hippopotamus
21 The Richochet Inn

OTHER
1 Warwick Train Station
2 Washeteria
4 St John's Museum
8 Eastgate
11 Collegiate Church of St Mary
14 Warwickshire Museum
15 Orange Tree
17 Post Office
18 Lord Leycester Hospital
19 Westgate
22 Oken's House; Doll Museum
23 Warwick Castle Pedestrian Entrance
24 Tourist Information Centre
25 Castle Ticket Office
26 St Nicholas Church
27 Warwick Castle

Lord Leycester Hospital

At the Westgate end of the town, the road cuts through a sandstone cliff. In 1571 Robert Dudley, earl of Leicester, founded the impressive Lord Leycester Hospital (☎ 491422), High St, as an almshouse above the cliff. It has a beautiful courtyard, a 14th-century chapel and a guildhall built by Neville containing a military museum. The hospital opens 10 am to 5 pm Tuesday to Sunday, April to September, and to 4 pm October to March. Admission is £3/free or £1 for the garden only.

Museums

Warwickshire Museum (☎ 412500), in the 17th-century market building in Market Place, has displays on natural history and archaeology. The museum opens 10 am to 5.30 pm Monday to Saturday and 11 am to 5 pm Sunday, May to September. Admission is free.

In Castle St, the **Doll Museum** (☎ 412500), in the half-timbered medieval Oken's House, opens 10 m to 5 pm daily, Easter to September, and admission costs £1/70p. **St John's House** (☎ 410410), a Jacobean mansion on St John's, has exhibits on the county's social history. It opens 10 am to 5.30 pm Tuesday to Saturday year-round; and 2.30 pm to 5 pm Sunday, May to September. Admission is free.

Places to Stay

The nearest hostel is in Stratford-upon-Avon (see that section later).

The centre of Warwick is woefully short of budget-priced B&Bs. To overnight without paying through the nose you'll probably have to stay in Emscote Rd, the eastern end of the main road through Warwick as it heads for Leamington Spa. The *Avon Guest House* (☎/fax 491367, 7 Emscote Rd), close to the town centre, is very popular and has rooms from £20 per person, including vegetarian breakfast on request. *Park House* (☎/fax 494359, 17 Emscote Rd) is another popular place in a Gothic-looking town house offering all en-suite singles/doubles from £25/40, including vegetarian breakfasts.

The *Warwick Arms Hotel* (☎ 492759, fax 410587, 17 High St) has rooms with bathrooms from £40/50, £55/65 during the week. The *Lord Leycester Hotel* (☎ 491481, fax 491561, 17 Jury St) oozes history and offers a reasonable deal from £55/65 per person. There is a popular local bar downstairs.

Charter House (☎ 496965, fax 411910, e penon@charterhouse8.freeserve.co.uk, 87–91 West St) is an outstanding B&B, but outstanding rarely comes cheap. The characterful period rooms include four-poster beds and start from £49.50/75.

Places to Eat

Reasonable pizzas at reasonable prices are served at *Pizza Piazza* (☎ 491641, 33–35 Jury St), which also has lunch-time deals offering discounted main courses. Farther east, *Piccolino's* (☎ 491020, 31 Smith St) is deservedly popular, serving delicious seafood pasta.

For something Indian, try the popular, BYO *Castle Balti* (☎ 493007, 11 St John's), or *Taste of India* (☎ 492151, 35 Smith St), which has 'traditional' Sunday buffets for £6.75.

There are a few alternatives to pasta or curry. *The Angry Cheese* (☎ 400411, St Nicholas Church St) is a wine bar-cum-bistro specialising in Mexican food, but there is something for everyone and the setting is attractive. The *Tilted Wig* (☎ 410466, 11 Market Place) has a lengthy bar menu and a pleasant outdoor area for a summer's day. The *Hippopotamus* (☎ 439504, 48 Brook St) looks like a cafe by day, but by night they serve up a daring array of African and Caribbean specialities – three courses for £12.

Across the road from St Mary's, *Findon's Restaurant* (☎ 411755, 7 Old Square) serves romantic candlelit two-course dinners for £15.95. At lunch time, their inventive food is more affordable with daily dishes for £4.95. *The Ricochet Inn* (☎ 491232, Castle St) has a sturdy menu of modern British cuisine at around £10 to £12 for a main course.

Nightlife is low key, to put it politely, but

the *Orange Tree* (☎ *621821, 62 Market St)* is a lively bar, by Warwick's standards. A bus to Leamington Spa or Coventry might make sense for those with an itch for a bit more action.

Getting There & Away

National Express buses operate from Old Square. Stagecoach buses (☎ 01788-535555) stop in Market Place; a bus to Coventry (No X16/X18) takes one hour, less to Stratford-upon-Avon (No X16). These services are hourly, every two hours on Sunday.

Trains operate to Birmingham, Stratford-upon-Avon and London, but there are more connections from nearby Leamington Spa.

AROUND WARWICK
Baddesley Clinton

Baddesley Clinton (☎ 01564-783294; NT) is an enchanting medieval moated house, which has hardly changed since the death of Squire Henry Ferrers in 1633. The house is known for its Elizabethan interiors. It provided something of a refuge for persecuted Catholics in the 16th century, hence the three priest-holes. The house opens 1.30 to 5 pm Wednesday to Sunday, March to October (to 5.30 pm May to September). Admission costs £5.20/2.60 or £2.60 for the grounds only. Bus No 60 passes nearby travelling between Warwick and Solihull.

LEAMINGTON SPA
☎ 01926 • pop 57,000

Leamington Spa has some fine Regency architecture and classy shops, lending it a very European air when compared with nearby Warwick or Stratford-upon-Avon. It more or less runs into Warwick and can be a useful base during peak season when the more illustrious neighbours are overrun.

The old Pump Rooms on The Parade now house an interesting local **Museum & Art Gallery**, as well as the TIC (☎ 742762, fax 881639, **e** leamington@shakespeare-country.co.uk). The TIC opens 9 am to 5 pm Monday to Friday, 9.30 am to 5 pm on Saturday and 10.30 am to 5 pm on Sunday, Easter to September; and 9.30 pm to 5 pm

Monday to Saturday and noon to 4 pm on Sunday, October to Easter. The Museum & Art Gallery opens 10.30 am to 5 pm on Tuesday, Wednesday, Friday and Saturday; 1.30 pm to 8 pm on Thursday; and 11 am to 4 pm on Sunday.

Places to Stay & Eat

There are several B&Bs handily located on Avenue Rd near the station. Friendly *Charnwood Guest House* (☎ *831074, 47 Avenue Rd)* is one of the cheapest with doubles from £17 per person, £18 en suite. Nonsmoking *Comber House* (☎ *421332, fax 313930,* **e** *b-b@comberhouse.freeserve.co .uk, 2 Union Rd)* is the most atmospheric B&B in town. Set in a handsome residence, singles/doubles start from £40/65.

Adams Hotel (☎ *450742, fax 313110,* **e** *adams22@tinyworld.com, Avenue Rd)* is a comfortable lodging in one of Leamington's large regency villas and has B&B from £54/68.

Sacher's (☎ *421620, 14 The Parade)*, at the top end of town, is an excellent cafe and restaurant serving a selection of daily specials. By night it doubles as a bar and there is live jazz at the weekend. In the Pump Rooms is *Café Hudson* (☎ *742750)*, serving a good selection of light meals, high teas and pretentious pastries.

For a splurge, try *Amor's* (☎ *778744, 15 Dormer Place)* near the TIC. French is the fashion and the food is freshly prepared; lunch costs around £10, dinner £15 or more. At the opposite end of town are several super-cheap balti restaurants, exiles from Balsall Heath in Birmingham so the food is good. The best hunting ground is Bath St, south of the post office.

Getting There & Away

Leamington Spa is well served by public transport. Trains run to Birmingham and London Marylebone, as well as infrequently on a spur line to Stratford-upon-Avon. National Express buses go three times daily from London. Bus Nos X12, X14, X16 and X18 run to Coventry frequently. Bus X16 also serves Stratford-upon-Avon regularly. Bus No X14 serves Kenilworth.

STRATFORD-UPON-AVON

☎ 01789 • pop 22,000

The fortunate, freak chance of being the birthplace of the world-famous Elizabethan playwright William Shakespeare (1564–1616) has brought Stratford-upon-Avon international fame and fortune and tourists in ever-growing numbers – it's now second only to London in popularity. The town today devotes itself to furiously marketing its favourite son. Its position beyond the northern edge of the Cotswolds makes Stratford-upon-Avon a handy stopover en route to or from the north. It's a good base

for visiting the castles at Warwick and Kenilworth.

Orientation & Information

Arriving by coach or train, you'll find yourself within walking distance of the town centre, which is easy to explore on foot. Transport is only really essential for visiting Mary Arden's House.

Close to the river on Bridgefoot, the TIC (☎ 293127, fax 295262, ℮ stratfordtic@ shakespeare-country.co.uk) has plenty of information but gets frantically busy in summer. It opens 9 am to 6 pm Monday to

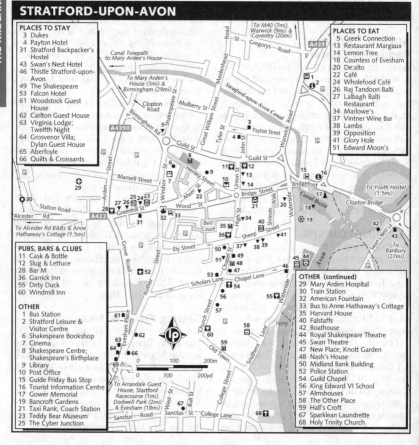

STRATFORD-UPON-AVON

PLACES TO STAY
3 Dukes
4 Payton Hotel
31 Stratford Backpacker's Hostel
43 Swan's Nest Hotel
46 Thistle Stratford-upon-Avon
49 The Shakespeare
53 Falcon Hotel
61 Woodstock Guest House
62 Carlton Guest House
63 Virginia Lodge; Twelfth Night
64 Grosvenor Villa; Dylan Guest House
65 Aberfoyle
66 Quilts & Croissants

PUBS, BARS & CLUBS
11 Cask & Bottle
12 Slug & Lettuce
28 Bar M
36 Garrick Inn
55 Dirty Duck
60 Windmill Inn

OTHER
1 Bus Station
2 Stratford Leisure & Visitor Centre
6 Shakespeare Bookshop
7 Cinema
8 Shakespeare Centre; Shakespeare's Birthplace
9 Library
10 Post Office
15 Guide Friday Bus Stop
16 Tourist Information Centre
17 Gower Memorial
18 Bancroft Gardens
21 Taxi Rank; Coach Station
23 Teddy Bear Museum
25 The Cyber Junction

PLACES TO EAT
5 Greek Connection
13 Restaurant Margaux
14 Lemon Tree
18 Countess of Evesham
20 De:alto
22 Café
24 Wholefood Café
26 Raj Tandoori Balti
27 Lalbagh Balti Restaurant
34 Marlowe's
37 Vintner Wine Bar
38 Lambs
39 Opposition
41 Glory Hole
51 Edward Moon's

OTHER (continued)
29 Mary Arden Hospital
30 Train Station
32 American Fountain
33 Bus to Anne Hathaway's Cottage
35 Harvard House
40 Falstaffs
42 Boathouse
44 Royal Shakespeare Theatre
45 Swan Theatre
47 New Place; Knott Garden
48 Nash's House
50 Midland Bank Building
52 Police Station
54 Guild Chapel
56 King Edward VI School
57 Almshouses
58 The Other Place
59 Hall's Croft
67 Sparklean Laundrette
68 Holy Trinity Church

To M40 (7mi), Warwick (9mi) & Coventry (20mi)

Canal Towpath to Mary Arden's House

To Mary Arden's House (3mi) & Birmingham (29mi)

To Mary Arden's House (3mi & 29mi)

To Youth Hostel (1.5mi)

To Alcester Rd B&Bs & Anne Hathaway's Cottage (1.5mi)

To Banbury (27mi)

To Arrandale Guest House, Stratford Racecourse (1mi), Dodwell Park (2mi) & Evesham (18mi)

Saturday and 11 am to 5 pm on Sunday, April to October; and 9 am to 5 pm Monday to Saturday, November to March.

Every Thursday and Saturday (plus Sunday during July, August and September) two-hour **guided walks** (☎ 412602) depart from outside the Swan Theatre at 10.30 am. Tickets cost £5/4. There are also **ghost tours** (☎ 551702) leaving from the American fountain at 3.30, 5.30 and 7.30 pm April to September (ring ahead during winter). A tour costs £4/2.

Sparklean (☎ 269075), 74 Bull St, is a useful laundrette. The Cyber Junction (☎ 263400), 28 Greenhill St, offers Internet access and game play as well as snacks.

The Shakespeare Properties

The Shakespeare Birthplace Trust (☎ 204016, e info@shakespeare.org.uk) looks after five buildings associated with Shakespeare. In summer the crowds can be horrendous and none of the houses were designed to accommodate such a squash; visit out of season if at all possible. Note that wheelchair access to the properties is very restricted.

Three of the houses are centrally located, one is a short bus ride away, and the fifth a drive or bike ride out. A £12/6 ticket offers access to all five properties, or £8.50/4.20 for just the three town houses. To pay for each place individually would cost nearly twice as much. The properties open 9 or 9.30 am to 5 pm Monday to Saturday and 9.30 or 10 am to 5 pm Sunday, late March to mid-October; and 9.30 or 10 am to 4 pm Monday to Saturday and 10 or 10.30 am to 4 pm Sunday in winter. Visit the trust's Web site at www.shakespeare.org.uk for more information.

Shakespeare's Birthplace The number one Shakespeare attraction, in Henley St, has been so extensively rebuilt over the centuries that Will might have trouble recognising it. It's been a tourist attraction for three centuries; you'll see the evidence of famous 19th-century visitor-vandals who scratched their names on one of the windows. A ticket costing £5.50/2.50 includes admission to the

adjacent **Shakespeare Centre**, which has the lowdown on its famous son.

Across the road the **Shakespeare Bookshop** (☎ 292176) sells the complete works in a multitude of formats.

New Place & Nash's House In retirement, the wealthy Shakespeare bought a fine home at New Place on the corner of Chapel St and Chapel Lane; the house was demolished in 1759 and only the site and grounds remain. An Elizabethan knot garden has been laid out on part of the New Place grounds. The adjacent Nash's House, where his granddaughter lived, tells the town's history and contains an interesting picture of what the house looked like in 1876 and after a complete face-lift in 1911. Admission costs £3.50/1.70.

Hall's Croft Shakespeare's daughter Susanna married the eminent doctor John Hall, and their fine Elizabethan town house stands near Holy Trinity Church. Displays explain medical practice in Shakespeare's time. Admission costs £3.50/1.70. There's a cafe right next door.

Anne Hathaway's Cottage Before their marriage, Shakespeare's wife lived in Shottery, a mile west of Stratford-upon-Avon, in a pretty thatched farmhouse with a garden and orchard. The nearby Tree Garden has samples of all the trees mentioned in Shakespeare's plays. A footpath (no bikes allowed) leads to Shottery from Evesham Place, or catch a bus from Wood St. Admission costs £4.20/1.70.

Mary Arden's House The home of William's mother now houses the Shakespeare Countryside Museum with exhibits tracing local country life over the last four centuries. Since there's also a collection of rare farm animals and a turn-of-the-century farmhouse, you'll probably need more time here than at the other properties. Admission costs £5/2.50.

Mary Arden's House is at Wilmcote, 3 miles (5km) west of Stratford-upon-Avon. If you cycle there via Anne Hathaway's

Cottage, follow the Stratford-upon-Avon Canal towpath to Wilmcote rather than re-tracing your route or riding back along the busy A3400.

Holy Trinity Church

Holy Trinity Church (☎ 266316) has transepts from the mid-13th century, when it was greatly enlarged. It has had frequent later additions; the spire dates from 1763. In the chancel, there are photocopies of Shake-speare's baptism and burial records, his grave and that of his wife, and a bust that was erected seven years after Shakespeare's death but before his wife's and thus as-sumed to be a good likeness. It costs £1/50p to see these legacies. The church opens 8.30 am to 6 pm Monday to Saturday and 2 to 5 pm Sunday in summer.

Harvard House

On High St, the exuberantly carved Har-vard House (☎ 204016, fax 296083) was home to the mother of John Harvard, after whom Harvard University in the USA was named in the 17th century. It now houses a collection of pewter. It opens 10 am to 4 pm Tuesday to Saturday (Sunday from 10.30 am), May to late October, and admis-sion is free.

Next door is the historic timber-framed Garrick Inn, while across the road the Mid-land Bank Building has reliefs illustrating scenes from Shakespeare's plays.

Other Things to See & Do

Erected in 1881, the Gower Memorial fea-tures a statue of Shakespeare surrounded by four of his characters – Falstaff, Hamlet, Lady Macbeth and Prince Hal. It overlooks the canal basin, where the Stratford-upon-Avon Canal meets the River Avon, a popu-lar place to watch narrow boats 'working the lock'.

The Guild Chapel, at the junction of Chapel Lane and Church St, dates from 1269, though it was rebuilt in the 15th cen-tury. Next door is King Edward VI School, which Shakespeare probably attended; it was originally the Guildhall.

The Royal Shakespeare Company

Gallery (☎ 296655), inside the Swan The-atre, exhibits the RSC's collection of props, costumes and theatrical paraphernalia. It opens 9.30 am to 5 pm Monday to Saturday and noon to 4.30 pm Sunday (11 am to 3.30 pm on winter Sundays); admission costs £1.50/1. Theatre tours (☎ 412602) op-erate at 1.30 and 5.30 pm Monday to Friday (except matinee days) and at 12.30, 1.45, 2.45 and 3.45 pm Sunday (one hour earlier in winter). Tours plus admission to the RSC collection cost £4/3.

The Teddy Bear Museum (☎ 293160), 19 Greenhill St, is popular with youngsters and those that never kicked the teddy out of bed. It opens 9.30 am to 6 pm daily (to 5 pm in January and February) and costs £2.25/1.

Falstaffs (☎ 298070), 40 Sheep St, is an obscure little museum offering a step back in time. It opens 10 am to 5.30 pm Monday to Saturday and 11 am to 5 pm Sunday and admission is £2.50/free.

Places to Stay

Camping There are two camp sites on Stratford's western outskirts. *Dodwell Park (☎ 204957, fax 336476, Evesham Rd)* charges £9 for a tent and £1.50 per person. From Easter to September you can camp at *Stratford Racecourse (☎ 267949, fax 415850, Luddington Rd)*. It costs from £7 for two people.

Hostels It's bad news for the YHA that *Stratford Backpackers Hostel (☎ 263838, e stratford@hostels.demon.co.uk, 33 Green-hill St)* has finally brought much-needed centrally located, budget accommodation to Stratford. Beds are £11 in the dorms, £15 in twin rooms, and it is wise to book well ahead in the summer months.

Stratford-upon-Avon Youth Hostel (☎ 297093, fax 205513, e stratford@ yha.org.co.uk, Hemmingford House, Alve-ston) is 1½ miles (2.5km) from the town centre. From the TIC, walk across Clopton Bridge and turn left (north-east) along Tid-dington Rd (B4086). Bus No 18 runs to Alveston from Bridge St. The hostel opens early January to mid-December and charges £14.90/11.20 for adults/juniors.

B&Bs B&Bs can be expensive – and hard to find – during summer. If it's all too much, Leamington Spa and Warwick are worthwhile alternatives. Prime hunting grounds for cheaper places are Evesham Place, Grove Rd and Broad Walk, only a couple of minutes' walk from the town centre. If you're stuck, the TIC charges £3 plus a 10% deposit to help you find something. South Warwickshire Tourism also has a booking hotline (☎ 415061) for credit-card bookings. It operates 9 am to 5 pm Monday to Friday.

On Evesham Rd, south of Evesham Place, is **Arrandale** (☎ 267112, 208 Evesham Rd), the cheapest option in this area, which costs £15.50 per person in a standard room. They take Visa here.

Possibilities in Evesham Place include the cheerful **Grosvenor Villa** (☎ 266192, 9 Evesham Place) at £22 a single or £48 for an en-suite double. The **Dylan Guest House** (☎ 204819, 10 Evesham Place) is a non-smoking Victorian house with period fireplaces; B&B costs £24 per person. **Virginia**

The Old Bard, William Shakespeare

Probably the greatest dramatist of all time, William Shakespeare was born in Stratford-upon-Avon in 1564, the son of a local glove maker. At the age of 18 he married Anne Hathaway, eight years his senior, and their first daughter, Susanna, was born about six months later. Boy and girl twins, Hamnet and Judith, followed two years later, but the son died at the age of 11.

Around the time of the twins' birth, Shakespeare moved to London and began to write for the Lord Chamberlain's Company. This successful company enjoyed the finest theatre (the Globe) and the best actors. It wasn't until the 1590s that Shakespeare's name appeared on his plays. Before that, the company's name was regarded as more important than the dramatist's.

Shakespeare's 37 plays made novel and inventive use of the English language, but also boasted superb plot structures and deep insights into human nature – characteristics that have ensured not only their survival over the centuries

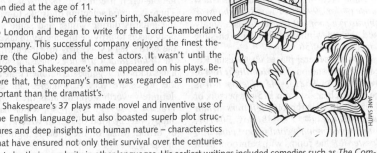

but also their popularity in other languages. His earliest writings included comedies such as The Comedy of Errors, historical accounts such as Henry VI and Richard III and the tragedy Romeo and Juliet. The new century saw his great tragedies, Hamlet, Othello, King Lear and Macbeth.

Around 1610 he retired, moved back to Stratford-upon-Avon, and lived in comfortable circumstances until his death in 1616. He was buried in the parish church. His wife outlived him by seven years.

Despite Shakespeare's prodigious output of plays, no letters or other personal writing have survived and the little that is known about him and his family has been pieced together from birth, death and marriage files and other official records (including the will in which he left his wife his 'second-best bed'!). This paucity of information has bred wild theories that Shakespeare didn't actually write the plays. Since none have survived in manuscript form, there's no handwriting evidence to prove they're his. Nonbelievers speculate that Shakespeare's origins and education were too humble to have provided the background, experience and knowledge to write the plays. Their favourites for the 'real' Shakespeare are the earl of Derby or the earl of Oxford who, they claim, may have had reasons for wanting to remain anonymous.

THE MIDLANDS

Lodge (☎/fax 292157, 12 Evesham Place) has some attractive themed rooms for £24, some including Laura Ashley furnishings and four-poster beds.

Friendly *Aberfoyle* (☎/fax 295703, 3 Evesham Place) is an Edwardian home offering nonsmoking B&B for £21 per person. *Carlton Guest House* (☎/fax 293548, 22 Evesham Place) is £40/48 for doubles with/without bathrooms, including a hefty breakfast to help you survive the day. The welcoming *Quilts & Croissants* (☎ 267629, fax 551651, e rooms@quilt-croissants .demon.co.uk, 33 Evesham Place) charges from £20/35 – no prizes for guessing the bedding and breakfast.

Up in price but definitely worth it for a treat is nonsmoking *Twelfth Night* (☎ 414595, 13 Evesham Place), charging from £27 to £31 per person, including the breakfast served on bone china. In the same area of town, *Woodstock Guest House* (☎/fax 299881, e woodstockhouse@ compuserve.com, 30 Grove Rd) is a highly rated, award-winning B&B with en-suite rooms from £30/56.

There are several places on Alcester Rd, near the train station. The *Moonlight Bed & Breakfast* (☎ 298213, 144 Alcester Rd) is one of the cheapest from £15 per person, or £17.50 with a bathroom. *Hunters Moon Guest House* (☎ 292888, fax 204101, e thehuntersmoon@compuserve.com, 150 Alcester Rd) has rooms with bathroom from £30/48 and can prepare a vegetarian breakfast. Rooms with bathrooms at attractive *Moonraker House* (☎ 299346, fax 295504, 40 Alcester Rd) cost from £45/49, with four-poster bed suites for £75.

Hotels Numerous pricey hotels cater to international package tours. Theatre-goers could hardly do better than stay at the *Thistle Stratford-upon-Avon* (☎ 294949, fax 415874, e stratford.uponavon@thistle .co.uk, Waterside), immediately across the road from the Swan Theatre, but rooms start high at £69/82.

The Shakespeare (☎ 0870 400 8182, fax 415411, Chapel St), with its beautiful historic buildings, is a four-star establishment with rooms from £105/210. The charming *Falcon Hotel* (☎ 279953, fax 414260, Chapel St) has rooms from £80/115 in an old timber-framed building that looks to have been around for almost as long as Shakespeare's plays.

Smaller, more reasonably priced hotels include charming *Dukes* (☎ 269300, fax 414700, e dukes-hotel@freeserve.co.uk, Payton St), a privately run hotel that backs onto the canal and has rooms with bathrooms from £56/69.50. The much smaller *Payton Hotel* (☎ 266442, fax 294410, e info@payton.co.uk, 6 John St), across the road, charges from £28 per person and all the rooms are en suite.

Places to Eat

There's plenty of choice when it comes to eating in Stratford. *Café* is an elegant spot on Meer St, leaving nothing to the imagination when it comes to its *raison d'être*. There is a good selection of drinks to warm the innards during winter and some very tasty cakes to provide the energy to take on the bard's legacy. Nearby on Greenhill St, the *Wholefood Café* does pleasant soups and salads for vegetarians at lunch time and the prices are very reasonable. One cafe definitely worth stopping at is the *Lemon Tree* (☎ 292997, 2 Union St), which has a happy, breezy kind of feel in which to eat or drink. Most of the food is light and modern.

Sheep St is wall-to-wall restaurants, all of them with a similar atmosphere but different menus. The *Glory Hole* (☎ 293546, 21 Sheep St) has olde-worlde English food and furnishings. Main courses mostly fall within the £5 to £10 bracket. *Opposition* (☎ 269980, 13 Sheep St) specialises in good pasta and is pretty popular. *Lambs* (☎ 292554, 12 Sheep St) is regarded as one of the town's better restaurants and the menu is influenced by various world cuisines. An evening meal costs about £15. *Vintner Wine Bar* (☎ 297259, 5 Sheep St) is the best bet for lively vegetarian options.

Edward Moon's (☎ 267069, 9 Chapel St) has a tasty menu from around the globe, and main courses start at about £8 in these stylish surroundings. The desserts are something to savour, including a tempting sticky-toffee pudding. The *Greek Connection* (☎ 292214), on the corner of Birmingham Rd and Shakespeare St, is the place to go for plate-smashing fun; expect to pay from around £15 per head.

Asian restaurants include *Lalbagh Balti Restaurant* (☎ 293563, 3 Greenhill St) and the excellent *Raj Tandoori Balti* (☎ 267067, 7 Greenhill St), where you can eat well for about a tenner.

De:alto (☎ 298326, 13 Waterside) is a trendy, popular Italian restaurant near the river. It is clearly one of the right places to be seen in Stratford these days. *Restaurant Margaux* (☎ 269106, 6 Union St) has a fine variety of expensive French-influenced food – be prepared to spend £20 and up.

The town's most celebrated restaurant is *Marlowe's* (☎ 204999, 18 High St), which reminds diners of its heritage, proclaiming 'newly built 1595'. It is very formal and very expensive, but they do have a cheaper bistro called *Georgie's* within. One last option for water babies is the *Countess of Evesham* (☎ 07836-769499, fax 01789-293477, ℮ countess@tinyworld.co.uk, The Basin), a floating restaurant offering lunch cruises, cream teas and dinner cruises (£20.50). You'd be unlucky to get seasick on the River Avon.

Entertainment
Pubs & Bars A pint at the *Dirty Duck* (☎ 297312, Waterside) – aka the Black Swan – close to the river, is an essential Stratford experience for thespians and theatre-goers alike. The *Slug & Lettuce* (☎ 299700, 38 Guild St) and the *Cask & Bottle* (☎ 267881, 7–9 Union St) remain popular with the younger crowd.

The *Windmill Inn* (☎ 297687, Church St) is reputed to be the oldest pub in town, draws a lively, young crowd most nights and is the unofficial local for those staying at Stratford Backpackers. The *Falcon Hotel* (see Places to Stay earlier) is another bar steeped in history, as is the *Garrick Inn* (☎ 292186, 25 High St), which is worth visiting just to marvel at the building. *Bar M* (Greenhill St), has a late licence most nights.

Theatre Seeing a Royal Shakespeare Company production (☎ 295623) is a must. Performances take place in the main **Royal Shakespeare Theatre**, the adjacent **Swan Theatre** or, nearby, **The Other Place**.

Tickets cost from £12 to £40 and the box office in the Royal Shakespeare Theatre opens 9.30 am to 8 pm Monday to Friday. Stand-by tickets are available to students, under-19s and over-60s on the day of the performance (£13 or £16.50). Over-60s also qualify for £14 tickets for weekday matinees and Wednesday evening shows, provided they book 24 hours in advance. Standing room tickets may be available up to the last moment for just £5.

Getting There & Away
Stratford-upon-Avon is 93 miles (150km) from London, 40 miles (64km) from Oxford and 8 miles (13km) from Warwick. Bus connections are a whole lot better than train connections to most parts of the country.

Bus National Express links Birmingham, Stratford-upon-Avon, Warwick, Oxford, Heathrow and London several times a day. Singles from Stratford include Birmingham (£5, one hour) and Victoria (£11, three hours 10 minutes). The National Express stop is on Bridge St, opposite McDonald's.

Cambridge Coach Services (☎ 01223-423900) has a weekday service linking Worcester with Cambridge via Stratford and Warwick.

Stagecoach Midland Red (☎ 01788-535555) operates to Warwick (X18, 20 minutes), Coventry (X18, 1¼ hours), Birmingham (X20, one hour) and Oxford (X50, 1½ hours). The useful Cotswold Shuttle (X55) offers two daily services to Bath via Cotswold honey pots such as Chipping Campden, Moreton-in-Marsh, Stow-on-the-Wold, Bourton-on-the-Water and Cirencester. See the From the Thames to the Wye chapter for more details. Stratford Blue (☎ 01789-292085) bus No 569 runs hourly to Stratford or Moreton.

Train Stratford-upon-Avon station is on Station Rd, a few minutes' walk west of the centre. There are only a couple of daily services direct from London Paddington (£20, 2½ hours).

Coming from the north, it's sometimes easier to transfer at Leamington Spa, sometimes at Birmingham. Services from Birmingham depart from Moor Street station (£3.50, 50 minutes).

During summer, special **steam services** (☎ 299866) operate between Birmingham Snow Hill and Stratford six times a day. One-way/return tickets are £10/15 for adults and £3/5 for children.

Getting Around

Bus Call Busline (☎ 01788-535555) for local bus information. Bus No X18 operates via the youth hostel at Alveston to Warwick and Leamington Spa, hourly Monday to Saturday.

Guide Friday (☎ 294466) operates open-top buses that do circuits past the five Shakespeare properties every 15 minutes during peak summer months for £8.50/2.50. You can pick them up outside the TIC.

Bicycle Stratford is small enough to explore on foot, but a bicycle is good for getting out to the surrounding country or the rural Shakespeare properties. The canal towpath offers a fine route to Wilmcote.

Off the Beaten Track (☎ 01926-817380, ⒠ offbeatentrack@demon.co.uk) offers bicycles (and a helmet and lock) for hire for £13.50, including delivery and collection from anywhere within a 25-mile (40km) radius of Warwick.

Car If money is no object on the path to enjoyment, consider renting a Jaguar E Type (£200), Lotus Elan (£100) or an MG Roadster (£100) from The Open Road (☎ 01926-624891, ⒠ openroad@attglobal.net).

Boat Punts, canoes and rowing boats are available from the boathouse by Clopton Bridge. There are also frequent half-hour cruises (☎ 267073) leaving from Bancroft Gardens daily between Easter and November. It costs £3/2.

AROUND STRATFORD-UPON-AVON

Stratford-upon-Avon is ringed by pretty villages, atmospheric pubs and stately homes. The popular Cotswold villages of Chipping Campden and Broadway are only a short distance south (see the From the Thames to the Wye chapter), and Warwick, Leamington Spa, Coventry and Birmingham are within day-tripping distance. It is possible to walk or cycle to Birmingham along the Stratford-upon-Avon Canal towpath.

Charlecote Park

Sir Thomas Lucy is said to have caught the young Shakespeare poaching deer in the grounds of Charlecote Park (☎ 01789-470277; NT), around 5 miles (8km) east of Stratford-upon-Avon. The park, which was landscaped by Capability Brown, still has deer. The house was built in the 1550s and rebuilt in a Victorian interpretation of Elizabethan style in the early 19th century. It opens noon to 5 pm daily except Wednesday and Thursday, April to October. Admission costs £5.40/2.70. To get there from Stratford, take bus No 19 or X18.

Ragley Hall

Ragley Hall (☎ 01789-762090) is a Palladian house a couple of miles south-west of Alcester. The house was built between 1679 and 1683, but the over-the-top plaster ceilings and huge portico were added later. The intriguing South Staircase Hall with its murals and ceiling painting was painted between 1968 and 1982. The house opens 12.30 to 5 pm Thursday to Sunday, 11 am to 3.30 pm Saturday, April to September. Admission costs £5/3.50.

Northamptonshire

Northampton itself has just a handful of buildings of interest, but the surrounding area boasts two of England's finest surviving Saxon churches, a fine canal museum, England's most important motor-racing circuit and the shrine to the late Diana, Princess of Wales, in the grounds of Althorp

House. American visitors also derive a certain fascination from Sulgrave Manor, built by an early ancestor of the one and only George Washington. For local bus information phone ☎ 01604-620077.

NORTHAMPTON
☎ 01604 • pop 154,000

Lacking any major attractions, Northampton doesn't see a whole lot of tourists, although that can be a blessing for those who have tired of the frilly feel to nearby places such as Stratford-upon-Avon and Warwick. Although nothing significant remains of it, Thomas à Becket was tried for fraud in Northampton Castle in 1164. A fire in 1675 left few other reminders of medieval Northampton. The Industrial Revolution made the town a shoe-manufacturing centre and around town are numerous factory shops knocking out cheap Docs from the all-conquering Dr Martens factory, or for serious gentlemen, Churches also has some bespoke outlets.

The helpful TIC (☎ 622677, fax 604180, e tic@northampton.gov.uk), 10 Giles Square, is directly across from the Guildhall, and has a huge amount of information about surrounding attractions. Look out for the *Historic Town Trail* leaflet packed full of surprises. The TIC opens 9.30 am to 5 pm Monday to Friday and to 4 pm Saturday.

The town is at its busiest during the annual balloon festival that takes place in the second half of August.

Things to See & Do
Central Museum & Art Gallery (☎ 639415), Guildhall St, has a collection of shoes to make foot fetishists drool. It opens 10 am to 5 pm Monday to Saturday and to 2 pm Sunday. Admission is free. **Holy Sepulchre Church** has curiosity value as one of only four round churches in the country.

Heading out of town on the London Rd, is the **Eleanor Cross**, one of twelve originally erected to mark the places at which the funeral procession of Queen Eleanor (wife of Edward I) camped on the long journey from Lincoln to Westminster Abbey following her death in 1290. The most famous of the three remaining crosses stands in the village of **Geddington**, a short distance from Kettering on the A43.

Australian visitors might like to know that buried in the Billing Rd cemetery is **Caroline Chisholm**, forever known as the immigrant's friend for her work with refugees and once immortalised on the A$5 note.

Places to Stay & Eat
There is not exactly an abundance of accommodation in Northampton. In the middle range, the *Aarandale Regent Hotel* (☎ 631096, 6–8 Royal Terrace, Barrack Rd) is a family-run place with a homely atmosphere where singles/doubles cost £30/44.

The *Coach House Hotel* (☎ 250981, fax 234248, 10 East Park Parade) is set in a row of converted Victorian houses near the racecourse and has well equipped rooms from £55/65.

For the discerning traveller, the *Lime Trees Hotel* (☎ 632188, fax 233012, e info@limetreeshotel.co.uk, 8 Langham Place) is a fine option found in a Georgian House about half a mile (1km) from the centre of town. Rooms here cost £65/77 with discounts at the weekend.

Pumpernickels (☎ 629154, 26–28 The Drapery) is a sandwich bar for those in a hurry to move on. Coffee fiends can find a fix at *Cafe Morandi* (☎ 250062, 5 Gold St), which has some speciality drinks such as espresso with Cornish ice cream. Near the main square, *Laurence's Coffee House* has a good selection of snacks and light meals.

For something more fulfilling, *The Vineyard Restaurant* on Derngate has a good selection of seafood and offers two-course, pre-theatre meals for £10.

Entertainment
Pubs & Bars Nightlife has a very provincial feel to it in Northampton. Real-ale quaffers will enjoy *The Malt Shovel* (☎234212, 121 Bridge St), a pub that comes recommended by none other than the Campaign for Real Ale (CAMRA). There are always guest beers available and for those feeling homesick, they stock a huge selection of bottled beers from around the world.

Cuba Libre (☎621070, 47–49 St Giles St) has beer from a little farther afield, mainly Latin America, while *Bar Soviet* (☎230444, 16 Bridge St) has a cool, intimate vibe to it.

Theatre & Cinema *Derngate* (☎ 624811, Guildhall Rd) is Northampton's arts centre and hosts anything from Tom Jones to Tom Thumb. The *Royal Theatre* (☎ 632533, Guildhall Rd) is an impressive Victorian structure and hosts plays. The *Forum Cinema* (☎ 402833, Weston Favell Centre) is an arts cinema with a good selection of international films as well as gay and lesbian seasons.

Getting There & Away
Stagecoach (☎ 620077) is the major bus operator. Bus X38 serves Oxford every two hours from Monday to Saturday; there are only three buses on Sunday. Bus X7 heads to Leicester hourly, every two hours on Sunday. The bus station is on Lady's Lane, near the Grosvenor shopping centre.

Northampton has excellent rail links with Birmingham and London Euston offering regular services throughout the day. The train station is about half a mile (1km) west of town along Gold St.

AROUND NORTHAMPTON
Althorp
With the late Diana, Princess of Wales, continuing to attract the public's attention from beyond the grave, the memorial and museum in the grounds of her ancestral home, Althorp Park, off the A428 northwest of Northampton, is a popular tourist attraction. But the park is only open in July and August and tickets cost £10/5 (profits go to her Memorial Fund). The limited number of tickets must be booked in advance (☎ 01604-770107). You can also visit www.althorp.com to book. Incidentally, Althorp should be pronounced altrup!

There are four buses a day linking Althorp and Northampton train station.

Stoke Bruerne Canal Museum
On a pretty stretch of the Grand Union Canal at Stoke Bruerne, 8 miles (13km) south of Northampton, the excellent Canal Museum (☎ 01604-862229) explains the development of English canals and displays models of pioneering canal engineering. It opens 10 am to 5 pm daily, Easter to September; and 10 am to 4 pm Tuesday to Sunday in winter. Admission costs £3/2.

If the displays catch your eye, it is possible to rent a narrow boat for the day from the Stoke Bruene Boat Company (☎ 01604-862107), Bridge Rd, for £90.

There are several pleasant pubs serving food on the banks of the canal, as well as the stylish *Old Chapel* restaurant (☎ 01604-863284, Chapel Lane), which stays open until 9 pm. *Wharf Cottage* (☎ 01604-862174) offers B&B overlooking the canal.

Silverstone
The British Grand Prix motor race is held in summer at Silverstone (☎ 01327-857271), just south of the A43. It's still one of the fastest racing circuits in Europe, with a lap record of more than 140mph, despite the extra corners that have been added in to slow cars down.

All Saints, Brixworth
About 8 miles (13km) north of Northampton off the A508, All Saints (☎ 01604-880286) is England's largest relatively intact Saxon church. Built on a basilica plan around AD 680, it incorporates Roman tiles from an earlier building. The tower and stair turret were added after 9th-century Viking raids, and the spire was built around 1350. It usually opens 10 am to 6 pm (10 am to 4 pm in winter). To get to Brixworth from Northampton, take Stagecoach (☎ 01604-620077) bus No X7 or 62.

All Saints, Earls Barton
About 8 miles (13km) east of Northampton, the church at Earls Barton is notable for its solid Saxon tower with patterns seemingly imitating earlier wooden models. It was probably built during the reign of Edgar the Peaceful (959–95) and the 1st-floor door may have offered access to the tower during Viking raids. Around 1100, the Norman

nave was added to the original tower; other features were added in subsequent centuries. To get to Earls Barton from Northampton, take Stagecoach bus No 46, 47 or 48.

Sulgrave Manor

Sold to Lawrence Washington by Henry VIII in 1539, Sulgrave Manor (☎ 01295 760205) would probably be just another handsome country house were it not for the fact that 250 years later a certain family descendant named George Washington became the first president of the USA. The family lived here for 120 years before Colonel John Washington moved to Virginia in 1656. Today American tourists throng here in large numbers for guided tours of this historic property and no doubt find it very quaint. Telephone ahead for opening hours, as they vary widely throughout the year, or visit www.stratford.co.uk/sulgrave on the Web for more information. Admission costs £4/2 and includes the guided tour.

Rushton Triangular Lodge

Northampton's most famous folly is a tribute to the Catholic fervour of one man, Sir Thomas Tresham, who designed a number of buildings in the area to express his beliefs, beliefs that landed him in prison on more than one occasion. The Triangular Lodge (☎ 01536-710761; EH) has three of everything, from sides to floors to gables and is Tresham's enduring symbol of the trinity. Built at the end of the 16th century, today it opens 10 am to 6 pm daily, April to September (10 am to 5 pm in October). Admission costs £1.50/80p. Stagecoach bus Nos 46, 47 and 48 come here from Northampton.

Oundle

Oundle is the most sightly town in the shire, largely thanks to a blend of architecture more readily associated with the more popular Cotswold region. Thankfully, it doesn't attract such numbers so can be rewarding to explore for those with transport.

The TIC (☎/fax 01832-274333, trbaxter@ compuserve.com), 14 West St, opens 9 am to 5 pm Monday to Saturday.

The *Talbot Inn* has associations with both Mary Queen of Scots and her executioner, who may well have stayed here before he gave her the chop, and is a good place for a meal.

There are bus connections with Northampton and Peterborough.

Fotheringhay

Famous for the birth of a notorious king and the death of a notorious queen, Fotheringhay Castle is today little more than a small hillock. Richard III, an infamous victim of the Tudor spin doctors and their literary wizard William Shakespeare, was born here in 1452, while Mary, Queen of Scots was executed here on the wishes of her cousin Elizabeth I in 1587.

Bedfordshire

Bedfordshire is compact, peaceful and largely agricultural. The River Great Ouse winds across the fields of the north and through Bedford; the M1 motorway roars across the uninteresting semi-industrial south.

The unexceptional county town of Bedford is best known to tourists as the home of John Bunyan (1628-88), the 17th-century Nonconformist preacher and author of *The Pilgrim's Progress*. South-east of Bedford lies the much publicised stately home of Woburn Abbey. For information on buses around the county, phone the enquiry line (☎ 01234-228337). Stagecoach (☎ 01604-620077), the main regional bus company, offers an Explorer ticket allowing a day's travel anywhere on its routes for £5/3.50.

BEDFORD
☎ 01234 • pop 77,000

Most visitors to Bedford are on a pilgrimage of their own to follow in the footsteps of Bedford's most famous preacher. Most places with links to John Bunyan are in and around the town, which boasts an attractive

John Bunyan & *The Pilgrim's Progress*

The son of a tinker, John Bunyan was born in 1628 at Elstow, near Bedford. He joined a Nonconformist church and became an accomplished preacher. In 1660, when the monarchy was restored, the government tried to restrain Nonconformist sects by forbidding preaching. Bunyan was arrested and spent the next 12 years in jail.

The allegorical work he started in prison, *The Pilgrim's Progress*, became one of the most widely read books ever written. It has been translated into over 200 languages.

An immediate success when it was published in 1678, its popularity stems from the fact that it's a gripping adventure story as well as a religious text. The pilgrim Christian, with his knapsack full of sins, embarks on a journey to paradise, via the Slough of Despond and Hill of Difficulty. On the way he is tempted by Vanity Fair and imprisoned in a giant's castle, but triumphing over these difficulties, he finally reaches the Celestial City.

riverside setting and an impressive art gallery, but is otherwise just another London satellite.

Information

The TIC (☎/fax 215226, tic@bedford.gov .uk), 10 St Paul's Square, is just off High St. It stocks *John Bunyan's Bedford*, a free guide to places with a Bunyan connection. It opens 9.30 am to 5 pm Monday to Saturday and 11 am to 3 pm summer Sundays. Guided walks depart the TIC at 2.15 pm on summer Sundays.

The Bunyan Meeting

The Bunyan Meeting (☎ 358870), Mill St, was built in 1849 on the site of the barn where Bunyan preached from 1671 to 1678. The church's bronze doors, inspired by Ghiberti's doors for the Baptistry in Florence, show scenes from *The Pilgrim's Progress*. One famous stained-glass window shows Bunyan in jail. There is also a purpose-built museum here that offers an insight into the life of Bunyan and visitors can admire some 169 editions of *The Pilgrim's Progress* from around the world. The church opens to visitors 10 am to 4 pm Tuesday to Saturday, April to October and admission is free.

Cecil Higgins Art Gallery

The **Cecil Higgins Art Gallery** (☎ 353323), Castle Close, houses a splendid collection of glass, porcelain and colourful Victorian fur-niture. **Bedford Museum**, with archaeological and historical exhibits, is next door. Both open 11 am to 5 pm Tuesday to Saturday, and 2 to 5 pm Sunday and admission is £2/free.

Places to Stay & Eat

Bedford makes an easy day trip from London, but if you want to stay overnight there are several hotels and B&Bs along leafy De Pary's Ave, which leads north from High St to Bedford Park. *Bedford Park House* (☎ 215100, 59 De Pary's Ave) has singles/doubles for £22/40. *De Pary's Guest House* (☎ 261982, 48 De Pary's Ave) has nine singles and six doubles. En-suite rooms cost from £29.50/37. Just to confuse things, there is also a *De Pary's Hotel* (☎ 352121, 45 De Pary's Ave), a cut above the other places on this road, which charges from £47.50/57.50. The restaurant here is well regarded locally.

Park View (☎ 341376, 11 Shaftesbury Ave) is very good value, although a little way out of town. Rooms are £17.50 per person. The historic *Swan Hotel* (☎ 346565, fax 212009, The Embankment), right beside the river, has business rates of £76/84.50, but prices drop to £57.50 per person for half-board at the weekend.

The *Bunyan Meeting* (☎ 213722, Mill St) serves tea and coffee in its foyer or in summer you can snack alfresco on filled potatoes or sandwiches in *The Piazza* (☎ 328433, St Paul's Square), immediately behind St Paul's Church. *Green Cuisine* (☎ 305080, 41 St Cuthbert's St) is a real treat for vegetarians with a wide selection of inexpensive, wholesome food from English classics to Indian specials. For coffees from Colombia to Kenya, *Caffe Crema* (☎ 330518, 59 High St) hits the spot and has some fine pastries on the side.

The Orchid (☎ 266766, St Paul's Square) is a Charles Wells pub as well as a Thai restaurant. The food is authentic and the price around £6 a plate. For good Italian food, look no further than *Santaniello's* (☎ 353742, 9 Newnham St), whose Italian owners knock out some of the best pizzas in the area. Sticking to European flavours, *Vol-au-Vent* (☎ 360320, 27 St Peters St) is a well-regarded French restaurant with some good deals during the week, including a three-course meal with coffee for about £10.

Many of Bedford's pubs do cheap meals, including *Hobgoblin* (☎ 356391, 26–28 High St), cheapest of the lot thanks to a mainly student crowd. *Fleur de Lis* is more famous for its beer and has been a real ale centre for many a year.

The *Wellington Arms* (40 Wellington St) is another good pub with a range of guest beers and some of Europe's better brews such as Budvar.

Getting There & Away

Bedford is 50 miles (80km) north of London and 30 miles (48km) west of Cambridge.

National Express has direct links between Bedford and London, Cambridge and Coventry. Cheaper is Stagecoach (☎ 01604-620077), which runs the hourly X5 to Oxford (£4.75) and Cambridge (£2.75) daily. The X2 runs to Northampton hourly Monday to Saturday, irregularly on Sunday. The bus station is half a mile (1km) west of High St.

There are frequent trains from King's Cross Thameslink (£16 day return, one hour) to Midland station, a well-signposted 10-minute walk west of High St.

WOBURN ABBEY & SAFARI PARK

Not an abbey but a grand stately home built on the site of a Cistercian abbey, **Woburn Abbey** (☎ 01525-290666) has been the seat of the dukes of Bedford for the last 350 years. The house dates mainly from the 18th century, when it was enlarged and remodelled into a vast country mansion. Although half the building was demolished in 1950 because of dry rot, it remains well worth visiting and is stuffed with furniture, porcelain and paintings.

The 1200-hectare park is home to the largest breeding herd of Père David's deer, extinct in their native China for a century (although a small herd was returned to Beijing in 1985).

It opens 11 am to 4 pm daily, late March to October; weekends only January to March and in October. Admission costs £7.50/3 (free to under-12s). Although it's easily accessible by car off the M1 motorway, trains from King's Cross Thameslink only run to Flitwick, leaving you to take a taxi for the last 5 miles (8km) to the abbey.

A mile from the house is **Woburn Safari Park** (☎ 01525-290407), the country's largest drive-through animal reserve. It opens daily, late March to October; weekends only in winter. Admission costs £12/9.50. If you visit the abbey first you qualify for a 50% discount.

WHIPSNADE

Whipsnade Wild Animal Park (☎ 01582-872171) is the free-range branch of London Zoo. It was originally established to breed endangered species in captivity, and claims to release 50 animals into the wild for every one captured. The 2500 animals on the 240-hectare site are mostly kept in pleasingly large enclosures and can be viewed by car, on the park's railway or on foot.

It opens 10 am to 6 pm daily (to 4 pm November to March). Admission costs £9.90/7.50, plus £8 for a car if you want to drive around the park.

During the summer you can get to Whipsnade (via Hemel Hempstead) by Green Line bus from Buckingham Palace Rd near Victoria Coach Station (☎ 0870 608 7261) in London.

Leicestershire & Rutland

Leicestershire is often overlooked by tourists as they rush between London and the Lakes or Peaks, but it has several interesting towns and historic sites. Arriva Fox County is the main bus operator; for general bus information phone ☎ 0116-251 1411.

Rutland was merged with Leicestershire in 1974, but in April 1997 regained its 'independence' as a county. It is easy to get around due to its tiny size, although it lacks any major attractions.

LEICESTER
☎ 0116 • pop 320,000

Leicester (**les**-ter) is another Midlands centre that has suffered the triple disasters of wartime damage, uninspired postwar development and catastrophic industrial decline, but has reacted to it better than most, reinventing itself as an environmentally progressive, ethnic melting pot of a city that could teach other, bigger cities a thing or two about multiculturalism. The modern town has a large and vibrant Asian community and there are Hindu, Muslim, Jain and Sikh temples as well as some excellent Indian, Bangladeshi and Pakistani restaurants. Many of the city's most interesting events are staged around festivals like Holi, Diwali and Eid-ul-Fitr.

The city's history dates back to Roman times. Later, it was one of the five Danelaw towns and was the traditional home of Shakespeare's tragic King Lear and his daughters. In 1239 Simon de Montfort, earl of Leicester, captured the castle. Medieval Leicester became a centre for manufacturing stockings but remained a small town until the rapid industrial growth of the 19th century.

Leicester bequeathed the word 'Luddite' to the language, after apprentice Nedd Ludd smashed stocking frames in a protest against modern production methods. The Luddite riots took place from 1811 to 1816.

The modern day package tour as we know it also began life here when, in 1841, Thomas Cook ran his first trip to Loughborough. His company has travelled a whole lot farther since.

Leicester City Football Club (☎ 291 5000), Filbert St, seem to have firmly established itself in the Premier League and you might find it easier to pick up a ticket for a Leicester match than for other clubs. Gary Lineker, now a BBC TV anchorman, is Leicester's most famous old boy.

Orientation & Information

Leicester is initially difficult to navigate as there are few landmarks. For those on wheels, it's plagued by the usual maze of one-way streets and forbidden turns.

The friendly TIC (☎ 299 8888, tic@leicesterpromotions.org.uk), 7–9 Every St, Town Hall Square, opens 9 am to 5.30 pm Monday to Saturday (from 10 am Tuesday and to 5 pm Saturday). There's another office (☎ 251 1301) in St Margaret's bus station during summer.

The centre of the Asian community, Belgrave Rd 'the Golden Mile', is about a mile north-east of the centre. Castle Park, with many of the historic attractions, lies immediately west of the centre, beside De Montfort University.

Leicester's Weightiest Citizen

Born in 1770, Daniel Lambert, the one-time keeper of Leicester Gaol, started life as a normal baby but soon began to tip the scales at ever more alarming totals. Despite eating only one meal a day, by age 23 he weighed 32 stone and by 39 an astounding 52 stone 11lb, making him, as the Dictionary of National Biography puts it, 'the most corpulent man of whom authentic record exists'.

When he died in Stamford in 1809 one wall of the house had to be dismantled to remove the coffin, and 20 pallbearers were needed to carry it to the graveyard. A whole room in Leicester's Newarke Houses Museum is devoted to Lambert's memory.

THE MIDLANDS

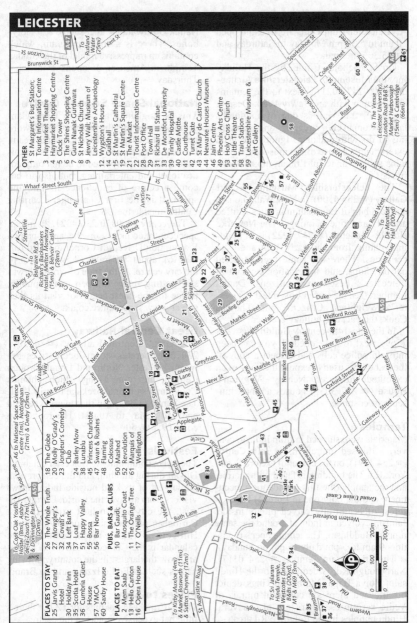

LEICESTER

PLACES TO STAY
25 Jarvis Grand Hotel
30 Holiday Inn
35 Scotia Hotel
36 Cumbria Guest House
57 YMCA
60 Saxby House

PLACES TO EAT
2 Mem Saab
13 Hello Canton
16 Opera House
26 The Whole Truth
27 Mowgley's
32 Covati's
34 Left Bank
37 Loaf
51 Happy Valley
55 Bossa
56 Bar Nova

18 The Globe
20 Molly O'Grady's
23 Jongleur's Comedy Club
24 Barley Mow
38 Lunablu
45 Princess Charlotte
47 Swan & Rushes
48 Flaming Colossus
50 Mashed
52 Revolution
61 Marquis of Wellington

PUBS, BARS & CLUBS
10 Bar Gaudi;
   Mosquito Coast
11 The Orange Tree
17 O'Neills

OTHER
1 St Margaret's Bus Station;
   Tourist Information Centre
3 Haymarket Theatre
4 Haymarket Shopping Centre
5 Clock Tower
6 The Shires Shopping Centre
7 Guru Nanak Gurdwara
8 St Nicholas Church
9 Jewry Wall; Museum of Leicestershire Archaeology
12 Wygston's House
14 Guildhall
15 St Martin's Cathedral
19 St Martin's Square Centre
21 The Market
22 Tourist Information Centre
28 Post Office
29 Town Hall
31 Richard III Statue
33 De Montfort University
39 Trinity Hospital
40 Castle Motte
41 Courthouse
42 Turret Gate
43 St Mary de Castro Church
44 Newarke Houses Museum
46 Jain Centre
49 Phoenix Arts Centre
53 Holy Cross Church
54 Little Theatre
58 Train Station
59 Leicestershire Museum & Art Gallery

Jewry Wall & Museums

All Leicester's museums are free and open 10 am to 5.30 pm Monday to Saturday and 2 to 5.30 pm Sunday.

On St Nicholas Circle, by the Holiday Inn, the **Museum of Leicestershire Archaeology** (☎ 247 3021) is next to the remains of a Roman bath and **Jewry Wall**. Despite its name, this wall is one of England's largest Roman civil structures and has nothing to do with Judaism. Ignore the grim external appearance of the museum; it contains some wonderful Roman mosaics and frescoes.

The **Leicestershire Museum & Art Gallery** (☎ 255 4100), in New Walk, houses a mixed bag of Egyptian mummies, stuffed animals and fine paintings. The **Newarke Houses Museum** (☎ 247 3222) is in buildings dating from the early 16th and 17th centuries. There are some reconstructed period shops, and information on two of Leicester's best-known citizens: Daniel Lambert (see the earlier boxed text 'Leicester's Weightiest Citizen') and Thomas Cook, the package holiday pioneer.

In the late-14th-century **Guildhall** (☎ 253 2569), next to the cathedral, you can peep into old police cells and inspect a copy of the last gibbet used to expose the body of an executed murderer. Nearby **Wygston's House** (☎ 247 3056) houses a small museum of costume.

Temples

Materials were shipped in from India to convert a disused church into a **Jain Centre** (☎ 254 3091), on the corner of Oxford St and York Rd. The building is faced with marble, and the temple (the first outside the subcontinent and the only one in Europe) boasts a forest of beautifully carved pillars inside. Jainism evolved in India at around the same time as Buddhism. The temple opens to visitors 9 am to 5 pm daily (6 pm on Sunday).

The **Sri Jalaram Temple** (☎ 254 0117), Narborough Rd, is dedicated to the Hindu saint Pujya Bapa. Marble carvings depict his life and there are colourful murals of Vedic scriptures. There are also several Hindu temples in the Belgrave Rd area.

Close to the Jewry Wall is the Sikh **Guru Nanak Gurdwara** (☎ 262 8606), at 9 Holybones. There is a small museum, which contains an impressive model of the Golden Temple in Amritsar. It opens 1 to 4 pm Thursday.

National Space Science Centre

This is England's answer to Cape Canaveral. Reflecting the years of hard work put in by Leicester's Space Research Team, Leicester was chosen as the location for this centre, which is expected to be not only educational and entertaining, but also to become a centre of excellence in studying space. It is the first Challenger Learning Centre outside the US.

The centre (☎ 0870 235 4321, ⓔ info@ spacecentre.co.uk) is on the aptly named Exploration Drive, off Corporation Rd (off the A6), about 1½ miles (2.5km) north of the city centre. At the time of writing it was still getting ready to open to the public; phone for the latest details or visit its Web site at www.spacecentre.co.uk.

Great Central Railway

The Great Central Railway (☎ 01509-230726) operates steam locomotives between Leicester North and Loughborough Central, the route along which Thomas Cook ran his original package tour in 1841. The 8-mile (13km) trip runs every weekend and daily, May to August. The round trip costs £9.50/6.50.

Festivals

The Asian community in Leicester celebrate Diwali during autumn, and the celebration, the largest of its kind outside India, draws visitors from all over the world. During August, the city is also host to the biggest Caribbean party outside London's Notting Hill Festival. A more recent addition to the calendar is the Comedy Festival in February, now the largest in the country, drawing names such as Eddie Izzard and Jo Brand.

Places to Stay

The TIC makes bookings for £2 but there's little but expensive hotels in the centre.

The *Copt Oak Youth Hostel (☎/fax 01530-242661, Whitwick Rd, Copt Oak)* is 8 miles (13km) north-west of the centre, near junction 22 on the M1. It opens daily mid-April to September and beds cost £7.35/5.15 for adults/juniors.

Richard's Backpackers Hostel (☎ 267 3107, 157 Wanlip Lane) has beds for the under-30s for just £8.50 (£45 a week), including a basic breakfast. It is £3 for tent space. The *YMCA (☎ 255 6507, 7 East St)* is just across from the train station and has a few single rooms at £12 (£44.79 a week).

There are some cheap places on Saxby St, off London Rd just south of the train station, although this may not be the best area for lone women. Friendly but basic *Saxby House (☎ 254 0504, 24 Saxby St)* is just £13 per person, and there are other cheapies nearby.

The *Scotia Hotel (☎/fax 254 9200, 10 Narborough Rd)* has rooms for £21/42, a little more with en-suite facilities. The *Cumbria Guest House (☎ 254 8459, 16 Narborough Rd)* is slightly cheaper with rooms from £18/32.

Try Westcotes Drive off Narborough Rd for B&Bs.

The centrally located, venerable *Jarvis Grand Hotel (☎ 255 5599, fax 254 4736, Granby St)* has rooms from £92/114 during the week, almost half that at the weekend. Rooms at the *Holiday Inn (☎ 253 1161, fax 251 3169, 129 St Nicholas Circle)* drop from £130 during the week to £75 with breakfast at the weekend.

Places to Eat

The Belgrave Rd area, to the north of the centre (bus is best), is noted for its fine Indian cuisine and excellent vegetarian food. The award-winning but budget-priced *Friends Tandoori (☎ 266 8809, 41–43 Belgrave Rd)* serves excellent northern Indian food, but no baltis as according to them the word means bucket. Other popular vegetarian choices include *Sayonara (☎ 266 5888, 49 Belgrave Rd)*, *Sharmilee (☎ 261 0503, 71 Belgrave Rd)*, where a thali costs £7.50, and *Bobby's (☎ 266 0106, 154 Belgrave*

Rd), where delicious southern Indian food is the speciality.

The ring road location of *Mem Saab (☎ 253 0243, Vaughan Way)* may not be memorable, but the food is and the weekday banquets for £10.75 leave a glow for days.

For stylish Italian dining head for *Covati's (☎ 251 8251, Westbridge Place)*, a well-designed restaurant accessible by footbridge from Castle Gardens, which serves main courses costing from £6. *Bar Nova (☎ 255 4667, 153 Granby St)* is a bargain Italian and a good place to linger over drinks after a meal.

Happy Valley (☎ 255 7700, New Walk) does Chinese business lunches for £5.50. *Hello Canton (☎ 262 9029, Guildhall Lane)* is big and offers set meals from £10.

For budget dining, *The Whole Truth (☎ 254 2722, 19 Belvoir St)* is a lively vegetarian cafe with a creative menu, but only opens for lunch. Just up the road, *Mowgley's* is a sandwich bar to help those on the move survive the urban jungle. *Bossa (☎ 233 4544, 110 Granby St)* has cheap toasted sarnies in a cheerful atmosphere, as well as a range of teas and coffees to keep you warm. Bossa is also a bar that draws a gay crowd.

Opera House (☎ 223 6666, 10 Guildhall Lane), near the cathedral, is very well regarded by Leicester residents. The menu is a mix of French and modern British, and lunch is pretty good value at £8.70/10.25 for two or three courses.

The left bank of the canal is an up-and-coming area of town, although not quite its Parisian namesake just yet, and there are a couple of gastro cafe-bars on Braunstone Gate. *Left Bank (☎ 255 2422, 26 Braunstone Gate)* was first to venture this way and has a fine menu of contemporary cuisine. *Loaf (☎ 299 9424, 58 Braunstone Gate)* has a highly addictive menu and the immortal motto 'it is better to have loafed and lost, than never to have loafed at all'.

Entertainment

Pubs & Bars Leicester has a thriving nightlife due in part to the huge student population at Leicester and De Montfort universities. Places come in and out of fashion by the month. Some of the most popular at the moment include *Revolution (☎ 255 9633, 6b New Walk)* and *Mashed (☎ 255 8181, 8–10 King St)* at the bottom of the laid-back New Walk area, both of which have DJs and a chilled-out atmosphere at any time. *The Orange Tree (☎ 223 5256, 99 High St)* is a cool little cafe-bar that pulls a crowd most nights. It has food, but most are there to see and be seen with a drink.

Over on Left Bank are the aforementioned *Loaf* and the rather stylish *Lunablu*, complete with games area downstairs and funky furniture all over. Lunablu goes on late at the weekend.

Those who prefer a real pub have a fair choice too. The *Barley Mow (☎ 254 4663, 93 Granby St)* has a good location on Granby St. This once run-down area is regaining its pride and the pub is becoming more popular. The *Marquis of Wellington (☎ 255 5833, 139–141 London Rd)* is a good boozer for those aiming to catch a band at De Montfort Hall (see Live Music later). *The Globe (☎ 262 9819, 43 Silver St)* is an alternative pub with good tunes and a quiet room if that's not your thing. They also do very cheap bar snacks.

For a real Irish pub check out the *Swan and Rushes (☎ 233 9167, 19 Infirmary Square, off Oxford St)*, which was around long before *O'Neills (☎ 242 9911, 18–20 Loseby Lane)* or *Molly O'Grady's (☎ 257 8992, 14 Hotel St)* came to town. The Swan serves up decent Guinness and is a welcome change from the synthetic feel of so many 'Irish' pubs in England.

Clubs *Junction 21 (☎ 251 9333, 13 Midland St)* is Leicester's very own superclub and it attracts some big names on a regular basis. More centrally located is *Flaming Colossus (☎ 233 4788, 57 Welford Rd)*, which is always good if you fancy a dance. *Mosquito Coast (☎ 299 0255, 37 St Nicholas Place)* is one of the favourites of the city's student community and beneath it is *Bar Gaudi*, a late-night drinking haunt with some lively decor. *Streetlife (Dryden St)* is the city's leading gay club with regular guest DJs.

Live Music *Princess Charlotte (☎ 255 3956, 8 Oxford St)* is Leicester's legendary venue that has played host to most of the big names over the years, including Oasis and Blur, but before they became megastars. It is a small place, but with a late licence it is one of the Midlands' best venues. Bands that are just too big to squeeze in these days will probably play at *The Venue (Leicester University)* or *De Montfort Hall (☎ 233 3111, Granville Rd)*. Classical concerts are also performed at De Montfort Hall. To get to The Venue head up London Rd and take a right onto University Rd – it's on the left hand side.

Theatre & Comedy *Phoenix Arts Centre (☎ 255 4854, Newarke St)* hosts films, plays and dance events. Plays are also staged at the *Little Theatre (☎ 255 1302, Dover St)* and sometimes at the *Haymarket Theatre (☎ 253 9797, 1 Belgrave Gate)*.

The *Jongleurs Comedy Club (☎ 0800 783 9933, 30 Granby St)* hosts comedians at the weekend.

Getting There & Away

Leicester is 105 miles (169km) from London, 40 miles (64km) from Birmingham, and 25 miles (40km) from Coventry and Nottingham.

Bus National Express operates from St Margaret's bus station in Gravel St, north of the centre, which has left-luggage facilities. There are hourly services to London. The Stagecoach (☎ 01604-620077) Express service No 777 runs to Nottingham hourly (one hour) and Arriva (☎ 0870 608 2608) runs bus No X67 from Coventry to Leicester every hour (except on Sunday). The Busline (☎ 0870 608 2608) offers general bus information.

Train A statue of Thomas Cook stands outside the train station on London Rd, southeast of the centre. Trains from London St Pancras operate every half-hour; the fastest take just over one hour. There are hourly services between Birmingham and Cambridge, or Norwich via Leicester.

AROUND LEICESTER
Bosworth Battlefield
South-west of Leicester at Sutton Cheny, 2 miles (3km) from Market Bosworth, Richard III was defeated by the future Henry VII in 1485, ending the Wars of the Roses. 'A horse, a horse, my kingdom for a horse', was his famous death cry. Richard III may be a villain to most for his supposed role in the murder of his young nephews, the 'princes in the tower', but Leicester has adopted him as something of a folk hero, not the hunchback of Shakespearean spin. History will never be certain who had the princes killed, but most historians would tend to side with the victorious Tudors and blame Richard III. The visitor centre (☎ 01455-290429) opens 11 am to 5 pm daily, April to October. Admission costs £3/1.90.

Ashby-de-la-Zouch
☎ 01530

Driving from Leicester to Derby it's easy to divert via this pleasant little town with its **castle** (☎ 413343; EH). Built in Norman times, and owned by the Zouch family until 1399, the castle was extended in the 14th and 15th centuries and then reduced to its present picturesque ruined state in 1648 after the Civil War. Bring a torch (flashlight) to explore the underground passageway that connects the tower with the kitchen. The castle opens 10 am to 4 pm daily (6 pm in summer). Admission costs £2.60/1.30.

There is also a small **local museum** (☎ 560090) in North St, that houses some basic exhibits on local history. It opens 10 am to noon and 2 to 4 pm Monday to Friday, all day on Saturday and on Sunday afternoon, Easter to September. Admission costs 50/30p.

Ashby-de-la-Zouch TIC (☎ 411767, fax 560660), North St, opens 10 am to 5 pm Monday to Friday and 10 am to 3 pm Saturday.

Melton Mowbray
☎ 01684

Something of a culinary capital, Melton Mowbray not only gave the world the best pork pies under the sun, but more recently lays claim to Stilton cheese. This unassuming Leicestershire town is also the fox-hunting capital of England until such time as legislation is passed to outlaw this most controversial of pastimes.

The TIC (☎/fax 480992), Thorpe End, is in the **Melton Carnegie Museum**. It opens 10 am to 5 pm Monday to Friday (to 4 pm Saturday). The museum keeps the same hours, but also opens Sunday afternoon in summer. Melton Mowbray has a lively market on Tuesday and Saturday. There is also a cattle market on Tuesday.

To get your hands on an authentic pork pie, make for *Ye Olde Pork Pie Shoppe & The Sausage Shop (☎ 482068, Nottingham St)*. The *Anne Of Cleves (☎ 481336, Burton St)* is a popular pub and restaurant located in a historic 14th-century building.

Donington Park
The Donington Park motor-racing circuit at Castle Donington, 20 miles (32km) north-west of Leicester, hosts the annual British Motorcycle Grand Prix. It also features the **Donington Collection** (☎ 01332-811027) of racing cars (including probably the world's best collection of Formula 1 racing cars) and motorcycles. It opens 10 am to 4 pm daily and admission costs £7/2.50. Fans of heavy metal music will know it more for the 'Monsters of Rock' festival formerly held here each year.

Belvoir Castle
North-east of Leicester, Belvoir (**bee**-ver) Castle (☎ 01476-870262) is 6 miles (10km) from Grantham, off the A1. This Baroque and Gothic fantasy was rebuilt in the 19th century after suffering serious damage during the Civil War. It is home to the Duke of Rutland, whose impressive art collection is one of the highlights. It opens 11 am to 5 pm Tuesday to Thursday and at the weekend, April to September; and on Sunday in October. Admission costs £5.25/3.

RUTLAND
☎ 01572

Rutland finally threw off the colonial yoke once more in the late-1990s, after many years of being 'occupied' by neighbouring Leicestershire. The county motto is 'Multum in Parvo' (so much in so little) and it is England's smallest county, much of it formed by **Rutland Water**, a vast and attractive reservoir offering ample opportunity for watersports and walks. The Rutland Belle (☎ 787630), The Harbour, Whitwell Park, offers pleasure cruises every afternoon, May to September, that cost £4/3. The Watersports Centre (☎ 460154), Whitwell, organises canoeing and boating. For cycle hire contact Rutland Water Cycling (☎ 460705), Whitwell Car Park.

The county town of **Oakham** is pleasant, if not compelling, with a famous school, but most people choose to stay in lovely Stamford, over the border in Lincolnshire. Oakham's TIC (☎/fax 724329), 34 High St, opens 9.30 am to 5 pm Monday to Saturday and 10 am to 3 pm Sunday. There is also a branch at Whitwell Rd, Empingham (☎ 653026) on Rutland Water, which opens during the summer.

To the south, **Uppingham** offers more rewards, with its weaving alleys and pretty architecture. The town is known for its art galleries, bookshops and public school.

Oakham has rail connections with Leicester and Peterborough.

Shropshire

Spread across the rolling hills between Birmingham and the Welsh border, Shropshire is a large county with a relatively small population centred on the attractive regional capital of Shrewsbury and the new town of Telford. Just outside Telford is Ironbridge, where a series of remarkable museums commemorate the birthplace of the Industrial Revolution.

Shropshire is bisected by the River Severn, which flows west to east through Shrewsbury. To the north the countryside is largely flat and uninteresting, but to the south lie the Shropshire Hills, the 'blue remembered hills' of local poet AE Houseman, author of *A Shropshire Lad*. The best known of a series of ridges are Wenlock

Edge, the Long Mynd and the Stiperstones. Mostly below 500m, this is excellent walking country that sees relatively few hikers.

With such an array of attractions on offer, it can only be a matter of time before Shropshire draws visitors in coach-loads, but for now its ends-of-the-earth (well, England at least) location has tended to protect it from the shock troops of mass tourism.

CYCLING
Starting from Shrewsbury, a good 100-mile (161km) five- or six-day cycle route takes you round the most scenic parts of Shropshire. You can rent bikes in Church Stretton and Ludlow. The route goes from Shrewsbury via Wroxeter to Ironbridge (14 miles/23km), Ironbridge to Much Wenlock (only 5 miles (8km) but there's a lot to see in Ironbridge), Much Wenlock to Ludlow (20 miles, 32km), Ludlow to Clun (an easy 17-mile (27km) ride), Clun to Church Stretton (15 miles/24km), and Church Stretton to Shrewsbury (16 miles/26km) along side roads parallel to the busy A49.

GETTING AROUND
Public transport between Shropshire's main towns isn't bad, with railway lines and most bus routes radiating from Shrewsbury. Getting to country areas without a car is less easy but the county council has a useful phone line (☎ 0845 705 6785) for bus and rail information. The invaluable *Shropshire Bus & Train Map*, available free from TICs, shows all the bus routes. There is a good Sunday service from Shrewsbury to most major places of interest.

SHREWSBURY
☎ 01743 • pop 60,000
When Charles Dickens was staying at the Lion Hotel in Shrewsbury, he wrote, 'I am lodged in the strangest little rooms, the ceilings of which I can touch with my hands. From the windows I can look all downhill and slantwise at the crookedest black and white houses, of all many shapes except straight shapes.'

The county's capital can still claim to be

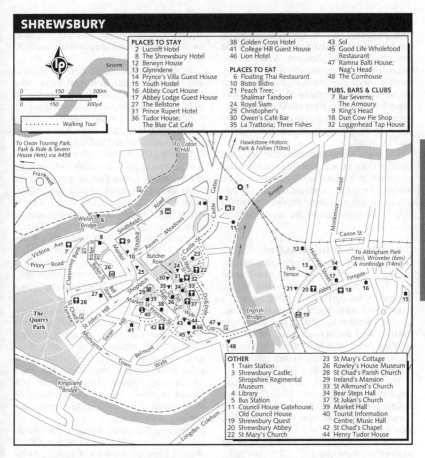

SHREWSBURY

PLACES TO STAY
2 Lucroft Hotel
8 The Shrewsbury Hotel
12 Berwyn House
13 Glynndene
14 Prynce's Villa Guest House
15 Youth Hostel
16 Abbey Court House
17 Abbey Lodge Guest House
27 The Bellstone
31 Prince Rupert Hotel
36 Tudor House;
   The Blue Cat Café

38 Golden Cross Hotel
41 College Hill Guest House
46 Lion Hotel

PLACES TO EAT
6 Floating Thai Restaurant
10 Bistro Bistro
21 Peach Tree;
   Shalimar Tandoori
24 Royal Siam
25 Christopher's
30 Owen's Café Bar
35 La Trattoria; Three Fishes

43 Sol
45 Good Life Wholefood
   Restaurant
47 Ramna Balti House;
   Nag's Head
48 The Cornhouse

PUBS, BARS & CLUBS
7 Bar Severns;
   The Armoury
9 King's Head
18 Dun Cow Pie Shop
32 Loggerhead Tap House

OTHER
1 Train Station
3 Shrewsbury Castle;
   Shropshire Regimental
   Museum
4 Library
5 Bus Station
11 Council House Gatehouse;
   Old Council House
19 Shrewsbury Quest
20 Shrewsbury Abbey
22 St Mary's Church

23 St Mary's Cottage
26 Rowley's House Museum
28 St Chad's Parish Church
29 Ireland's Mansion
33 St Alkmund's Church
34 Bear Steps Hall
37 St Julian's Church
39 Market Hall
40 Tourist Information
   Centre; Music Hall
42 St Chad's Chapel
44 Henry Tudor House

the finest Tudor town in England, famous for its higgledy-piggledy half-timbered buildings and winding medieval streets, crisscrossed with *shuts* (stairways or alleys linking different levels of the city) and passages. There are no vitally important sights here, which has saved Shrewsbury from inundation by tourists, but there is undoubtedly a wonderful atmosphere to much of the town, which makes it a good base for exploring Shropshire and a convenient stop en route to Wales. The town gets very busy during the middle of August when the annual flower show takes place.

History

Strategically positioned within a defensible loop of the River Severn, Shrewsbury has been important since the 5th century; the Saxon town of Scrobbesbryrig was established on the two hills here. After the Norman Conquest, the town came under the control of Roger de Montgomery, who built the castle. The Benedictine abbey was founded in 1083.

For many centuries Shrewsbury played an important part in the control of the Welsh, and in 1283 the Welsh prince David III was executed here after a parliament convened in the abbey chapterhouse. Despite problems with its unruly neighbours, the town prospered from the wool trade with the Welsh hill farmers. Many of the beautiful Tudor buildings were built by wealthy wool merchants in the days when the Severn was navigable all the way from Bristol. Even as the river silted, the town remained an important transit town on the coach route between London and Dublin, via Holyhead.

The town's best-known former resident, Charles Darwin, was born here in 1809 and educated at Shrewsbury's famous public school. His statue stands outside the library. The town has also done him the questionable honour of naming the shopping mall after him.

Orientation & Information

Houseman described Shrewsbury as 'islanded in Severn stream'. The train station now lies across the narrow land bridge formed by the loop of the River Severn, a five-minute walk north of the town centre. The bus station is central and the whole town is well signposted. Many of the old winding streets still have names that reflect the occupations of their former inhabitants – Butcher Row, Fish St, Milk St.

The TIC (☎ 281200, fax 355323, ⓔ tic@ shrewsburytourism.co.uk), Music Hall, The Square, opens 10 am to 6 pm Monday to Saturday year-round, and to 4 pm Sunday, May to September.

One-and-a-half-hour guided walking tours (£2/1) leave the TIC at 2.30 pm daily, May to October. Tours leave at 2.30 pm Saturday only during winter. There are also Brother Cadfael (the medieval monastic sleuth of Ellis Peters' novels) walking tours leaving the TIC at 11 am Sunday during summer. These finish at the abbey and cost £2.50/1.50.

Walking Tour

Start from the TIC, which is in the old **Music Hall** of 1839. Opposite, in the square, is the **Market Hall** (☎ 351067), an open-sided building erected in 1595. Until the mid-19th century trade was carried on in

this square and, on the insides of the pillars at the northern end, you can still see holes for the markers used to record the numbers of fleeces sold.

Walk across the square into the High St and there is a statue to Robert Clive, who laid the foundations for British control of India and was mayor of Shrewsbury in 1762. On your left is the 16th-century **Ireland's Mansion**, most impressive of the town's timber-framed buildings.

Head back along the High St and turn left into narrow Grope Lane with its overhanging buildings. Cross Fish St and go up the steps into St Alkmund's Place, the original town square. The medieval tower aside, **St Alkmund's Church** was completely remodelled at the end of the 18th century. The restored 14th-century **Bear Steps Hall** opens 10 am to 4 pm and is well worth a visit. Nearby St Julian's Church now houses a craft centre. There are several black-and-white houses along **Butcher Row**, including the Abbot's House, built in 1450.

The 'cathedral' of the Churches Conservation Trust, magnificent **St Mary's Church** is no longer used for worship but is worth visiting for its beautiful 15th-century angel roof and stained glass. Best of all is the great Jesse window made from rare mid-14th-century English glass. The spire collapsed in 1894 – because the townsfolk were planning a memorial to Darwin (according to the vicar).

Opposite the northern side of the church, past 17th-century **St Mary's Cottage**, follow Water Lane back down into Castle St. At the far end of the street is **Shrewsbury Castle**, which houses the **Shropshire Regimental Museum** (☎ 358516), open 10 am to 4.30 pm Tuesday to Saturday, and summer Sundays. Admission costs £2/1 but there's no charge to walk around the grounds. The entrance gate is Norman but much of the castle was remodelled by Edward I. The Scottish engineer Thomas Telford added Laura's Tower in 1780.

Down the alley near the entrance to the castle is the Jacobean-style **Council House Gatehouse** dating from 1620. Beyond it is the **Old Council House** where the Council of the Welsh Marches used to meet to administer the area.

Across the road from the castle is the library, surely one of the grandest in the land, with a **statue of Charles Darwin** outside. Returning to St Mary's St, follow it into Dogpole. At the end of Dogpole, turn right onto Wyle Cop, which is Welsh for 'hill top'. The **Lion Hotel** was where Dickens stayed on his visit to the town; a 200-year-old gilded lion marks its entrance. Henry VII is said to have stayed in the **Henry Tudor House**, on the other side of Barracks Passage, before the Battle of Bosworth.

Walk right down Wyle Cop and bear left for the graceful 18th-century **English Bridge**, widened and reconstructed in 1927 and offering magnificent views of the Shrewsbury skyline.

Head back up Wyle Cop and turn left along Barracks Passage. Then turn right up Belmont Bank to **St Chad's Chapel**, all that remains of the medieval church. Turn right again into College Hill and it's a short walk back to the TIC.

Rowley's House Museum

Shrewsbury's main museum (☎ 361196), on Barker St, is housed in a restored 16th-century timber-framed building and an adjoining 17th-century mansion built by a wealthy merchant.

The museum displays some of the finds from the nearby Roman town of Wroxeter (including a particularly beautiful mirror) and has a good section on medieval Shrewsbury, as well as exhibits on costume and local wildlife. It opens 10 am to 5 pm Tuesday to Saturday year-round; and to 4 pm Sunday and Monday, mid-May to September. Admission is free.

Shrewsbury Abbey

This huge red-sandstone church in Abbey Foregate is virtually all that remains of the Benedictine monastery founded by Roger de Montgomery in 1083. The abbey has been drawing tourists since medieval times as St Winifred's bones were brought here from Wales. Inside, the architecture is part pure Norman and part Victorian copy. In

the vestry don't miss the photo of men rowing in the choir after a flood! The churchyard contains a memorial to Wilfred Owen, one of the best known of the WWI poets, killed just a week before the war ended. In the car park opposite, a stranded stone pulpit also survives from the abbey.

Shrewsbury Quest

Across the street from the abbey, the Shrewsbury Quest (☎ 243324), 193 Abbey Foregate, stands on the site of some of the old abbey buildings. It was inspired by the Brother Cadfael detective stories. Visitors look for clues to solve a medieval murder as they wander around displays relating to 12th-century monastery life and a pleasant herb garden. Fans of the Ellis Peters books will love it. It opens 10 am to 6.30 pm (5.30 pm November to March) daily, admission costs £4.50/2.95. There's a good cafe on site.

Places to Stay

Camping *Oxon Touring Park* (☎ 340868, fax 340869, e oxon@morris-leisure.co.uk, Welshpool Rd) is a five-star touring park conveniently located next to Shrewsbury's Park and Ride. Camping here costs from £9. Four miles (6km) north of Shrewsbury, at Montford Bridge on the B4380, *Severn House* (☎ 850229) has a riverside site where you can camp for £5.50 per tent, including showers.

Hostels *Shrewsbury Youth Hostel* (☎ 360179, fax 357423, e shrewsbury@ yha.org.uk, The Woodlands, Abbey Foregate) is a mile from the train and bus stations, just off the roundabout by Lord Hill's Column. It opens Monday to Saturday, April to August, and Tuesday to Saturday, September to October; phone ahead for other times. It's a great place to stay for £9/6.20 for adults/juniors.

B&Bs & Hotels While most hotels are in the town centre (some of them in appropriately historic timber-framed buildings), B&Bs are mainly concentrated in and around Abbey Foregate, to the north up Coton Hill, and to the west along the A458 and A488. As ever, there's a shortage of decent single rooms.

In the Abbey Foregate area, friendly **Glynndene** (☎/*fax 352488, Park Terrace*), overlooking the abbey, has rooms from £20 per person. Nearby is **Berwyn House** (☎ 354858, 14 Holywell St), a comfortable family house with B&B from £20/40 a single/double.

Prynce's Villa Guest House (☎ 356217, 15 Monkmoor Rd), off Abbey Foregate, is a slightly cheaper option from £18/32, and cat lovers will enjoy meeting Bibby.

Abbey Court Guest House (☎ 364416, fax 358359, 134 Abbey Foregate) is a step up in comfort and has rooms without/ with bathrooms from £20/22 per person. Farther along the street, **Abbey Lodge Guest House** (☎ 235832, 68 Abbey Foregate) charges from £18 a head, £20 with ensuite facilities.

About a 10-minute walk north of the train station, the Coton Hill area harbours another group of B&Bs and hotels. **The Bancroft** (☎/*fax 231746, 17 Coton Crescent*) charges from £18 to £22 a person. **The Stiperstones Guest House** (☎ 246720, fax 350303, @ stiperston@aol.com, 18 Coton Crescent) is clean and good value with rooms for £22/37.

Lucroft Hotel (☎ 362421, Castle Gates), on the way into town from the train station, has clean if unexciting rooms for £20/34, including breakfast. **College Hill Guest House** (☎ 365744, 11 College Hill) has an excellent location near the centre of town and has cosy rooms for £21/42.

Dating from 1460, quaint **Tudor House** (☎ 351735, 2 Fish St) is centrally located on a quiet medieval street. Beds in pretty beamed rooms with no straight lines cost from £21 per person with a filling breakfast. Another historic lodging is the **Golden Cross Hotel** (☎ 362507, 14 Princess St), one of the oldest pubs in town, where rooms cost from £20/35.

A couple of affordable mid-range places have emerged in Shrewsbury. **The Shrewsbury Hotel** (☎ 236203, Bridge Place) is a Wetherlodge, a new breed of McHotels looking set for big things, with large, clean rooms from £32, regardless of numbers. Arguably offering a little more character, a little less chain, is **The Bellstone** (☎ 242100, fax 242103, @ admin@bellstone-hotel.co .uk, Bellstone) where all rooms cost £37.50 and are very comfortable.

The **Lion Hotel** (☎ 353107, fax 352744, Wyle Cop) has well-appointed rooms from £70/90. Two-night bed, breakfast and dinner deals offer better value from around £40 a head off-season. Rooms at the luxurious **Prince Rupert Hotel** (☎ 499955, fax 357306, @ post@prince-rupert-hotel.co.uk, Butcher Row) cost £75/85, including access to the Jacuzzi and sauna.

Places to Eat

Shrewsbury has plenty of reasonably priced places to eat during the day but in the evening many of the cheaper places close. On a tight budget, it is best to make for a pub (any excuse!).

For light lunches on the run, **Christopher's** is a swish sandwich bar on Mardol. Just a short way down the road is **Bistro Bistro** (☎ 352214, Mardol), a worthwhile restaurant with set lunches at £5 for two courses, £7 for three and set dinners for £10.

The Blue Cat Café (☎ 232236, Fish St) is a newish place that draws the locals in droves and has a huge range of sandwiches, ciabattas and tortillas, and some tempting desserts such as rhubarb and ginger crumble. Another delightful summer spot for a snack is the little **coffee shop** tucked away in Bear Steps (a medieval building on Fish St), which has tables outside if the sun can be bothered to shine.

The **Good Life Wholefood Restaurant** (☎ 350455), in restaurant-lined Barracks Passage off Wyle Cop, is a fantastic place for lunch with huge portions of righteous food, all at absurdly reasonable prices. Consider it unmissable. Popular with the local crowd, **Owens Café-Bar** (☎ 363633, 18 Butcher Row) has a wide range of wines, bottled and draught beers and interesting dishes such as mixed tapas.

· Opposite in the 14th-century timber-framed **Royal Siam** (☎ 353117, Butcher Row), fans of Thai food can get an atmospheric taste of all the favourites. However, for the ultimate Thai experience in quite strange surroundings, try the *Floating Thai Restaurant* (☎ 243123, Welsh Bridge), which has tasty, authentic food at sensible prices. The Severn is not quite the Chao Praya, but then Shrewsbury is a world away from Bangkok.

Sol (☎ 340560, 82 Wyle Cop) is a splash-out option where three-course meals costing £25 a head are served in classy, colourful surroundings. At the bottom of the hill, *The Cornhouse* (☎ 231991, 59a Wyle Cop) serves beautifully presented modern British cuisine in the £7 to £10 range. At the weekend they have a recovery brunch menu for those who played too hard the night before.

The *Peach Tree* (☎ 355055, 21 Abbey Foregate) also specialises in good modern British cuisine and has had a cool make-over in recent times. Expect to pay around £15 per head at the restaurant and considerably less downstairs in the cafe-bar. If that all sounds too much, have a beer and be one of the beautiful set on the cheap. A meal at the *Shalimar Tandoori* (☎ 366658, 23 Abbey Foregate), two doors down the road, is a cheaper option. Another good option for curry heads is *Ramna Balti House* (☎ 363170, 33 Wyle Cop), which is not only BYO, but also offers inexpensive set meals. For good Italian food try *La Trattoria* (☎ 249490, 7–10 Fish St) – although it's closed Sunday and Monday.

Entertainment

City-centre pubs worth trying include *The Loggerhead Tap House* for its selection of ales (among the best in Shrewsbury) and *The Nag's Head* (☎ 362455, 22 Wyle Cop), which draws the young crowd out and is one of the livelier pubs in town.

For those who like a bit of history in the surroundings, the *Three Fishes* (☎ 344793, 4 Fish St) is worth stopping at for a pint or two, and boasts the distinction of being the first nonsmoking pub in Shropshire. If you thirst for the genuinely yokel-local experience, venture into *King's Head* (☎ 362843, Mardol). Some of the regulars look to have been there as long as the beams. Farther out

the *Dun Cow Pie Shop* (☎ 356408, 171 Abbey Foregate) is full of clutter but manages to be extremely cosy and is something of a Shrewsbury institution.

Sports fans may like to catch some live action at the vast *Bar Severns*, while next door is *The Armoury* (☎ 340525, Welsh Bridge), a huge theme pub that may satisfy some.

In the old Music Hall that houses the TIC, a small *cinema* (☎ 281281) shows recent releases, classics and foreign films to small audiences. The small *theatre* has the same booking office.

Getting There & Away

Shrewsbury is 150 miles (241km) from London, 68 miles (109km) from Manchester, 43 miles (69km) from Chester and 27 miles (43km) from Ludlow.

Bus National Express has two buses a day to and from London (from £12.50, five hours) via Telford and Birmingham.

For information on transport in Shropshire, call the county helpline (☎ 0845 705 6785). Bus No X5 (☎ 01952-200005) runs between Shrewsbury and Telford via Ironbridge regularly. Bus No 420 connects Shrewsbury with Birmingham twice daily. Arriva (☎ 01543-466123) runs Shropshire Link bus No 435 to Ludlow via Church Stretton and Craven Arms (for Stokesay Castle see Around Ludlow later). Bus No 552/553 runs to Bishop's Castle (one hour) every two hours Monday to Saturday.

Train There's one direct train a day to and from London Euston (from £17, three hours), and regular links to Chester (£5.80, one hour). There are also regular trains rom Cardiff to Manchester via Bristol, Ludlow and Shrewsbury. Telford Central to Shrewsbury costs £3.20 and takes 20 minutes.

Two fascinating small railways terminate at Shrewsbury. It's possible to do an excellent rail loop from Shrewsbury around northern Wales to Chester and another famous line, promoted as the Heart of Wales Line (☎ 0845 702 3641), runs south-west to

Swansea (four hours), connecting with the main line from Cardiff to Fishguard.

AROUND SHREWSBURY
Attingham Park

This elegant late-18th-century neoclassical house (☎ 01743-708162; NT) is 4 miles (6km) south-east of Shrewsbury at Atcham on the B4380. Set in a 92-hectare deer park, it's the grandest of Shropshire's stately homes. It features magnificent state rooms with decorated ceilings, a 300-piece collection of Regency silver, and a picture gallery designed by John Nash.

Attingham Park opens 1.30 to 5 pm Friday to Tuesday, late March to October; the grounds open daily in daylight hours. Admission to the house and park costs £4.20/2.10. Bus No X5 stops in Atcham at the end of the lengthy drive.

Wroxeter Roman City

In Roman times Wroxeter was the fourth largest city in Britain, after London, Colchester and Verulamium (St Albans). Much of the site lies under farmland but visitors can explore the extensive remains of the baths. Admission to the ruins (☎ 01743-761330; EH) costs £3.20/1.60.

A short walk along a country lane leads to **Wroxeter church** where a huge font was created out of a column from the Roman site. The church has some fine 17th- and 18th-century woodwork and 17th-century monuments.

Bus No X5 runs to near Wroxeter.

Hawkstone Historic Park & Follies

This restored 40-hectare park (☎ 01939-200611) is an 18th-century fantasia of follies, caves and cliffs, mostly artificially created. A three-hour walking tour takes you up the White Tower (from which a dozen counties are said to be visible), over the Swiss Bridge, into the Hermit's Cave and rhododendron jungle, and through a rocky chasm. Bizarre as it is, fans of Gaudi or even Disneyland will probably find it tame.

Hawkstone Park is about 10 miles (16km)

north of Shrewsbury off the A49, and you need your own transport to get here. It opens 10.30 am to 5 pm daily, April to September, Wednesday to Sunday in winter. Admission costs £4.50/2.50 and £5/3 at the weekend. Disabled access is limited to the tearoom, gift shop and picnic area.

IRONBRIDGE GORGE
☎ 01952

The Silicon Valley of the 1700s, Ironbridge Gorge is blessed not just with a beautiful setting but with a wealth of important industrial relics. Not far from the eminently forgettable Telford, Ironbridge is a Unesco World Heritage Site and an enduring monument to the Industrial Revolution. In 1709 it was here that Abraham Darby pioneered the technique of smelting iron ore with coke that led to the production of the first iron wheels, the first iron rails, the first steam locomotive and the first iron bridge. Readily accessible deposits of iron ore and coal and easy transportation on the River Severn soon made Ironbridge the dynamo driving industrial progress in the 18th century, but by 1810 its glory days were already behind it as the action shifted to Birmingham, Sheffield and Manchester.

The Ironbridge Gorge Museum is England's best industrial archaeology complex, with seven museums and several smaller sites spread over 6 sq miles around the beautiful old iron bridge. It's well worth visiting even if industrial archaeology may not seem the most obvious drawcard.

Orientation & Information

Ideally you need your own transport as the museum sites are so spread out and buses are very infrequent. It's 3 miles (5km) from Blists Hill to the Museum of Iron.

It's best to start your trip at the visitor centre to the west of the centre, where a video provides a good introduction to the site and to the Industrial Revolution in general.

The TIC (☎ 432166, fax 432204, ⓔ info@ironbridge.org.uk), The Wharfage, near the bridge opens 9 am to 5 pm Monday to Friday and from 10 am at the weekend. This is the only place in Ironbridge where money can be exchanged and there are no ATMs in the village!

Ironbridge Gorge Museum

The Ironbridge Gorge Museum (☎ 433522) opens 10 am to 5 pm daily (to 6 pm in summer). Some of the minor sites (Rosehill House, Tollhouse, Broseley Pipeworks, Tar Tunnel) close November to March. A passport ticket (valid indefinitely until you've visited all the sites) allowing entrance to all the museums costs £10/6. Separate tickets to the individual museums cost from £1 (Tar Tunnel and visitor centre) to £7.50/5 (Blists Hill); the combined ticket saves around £15. To see everything properly it takes a good two days.

Ironbridge Visitor Centre An interesting video sets the museum in its historic context, but otherwise the centre mainly focuses on the environmental consequences

of industrialisation. A useful model shows the gorge in its late-18th-century heyday when the River Severn was choked with sailing boats.

Coalbrookdale Museum of Iron On the site where Abraham Darby first succeeded in smelting iron ore with coke, the ruined furnace is lovingly preserved. The museum shows all the uses to which iron has been put. Don't miss the 812kg Deerhound Hall table upstairs in the Glynwed Gallery.

Iron Bridge & Tollhouse As well as providing a crossing point for the river, the world's first iron bridge was constructed in 1779 to draw attention to the new iron-based technology and the local ironworks. It was used by motor vehicles until 1930 but now only pedestrians get to cross.

Blists Hill Open Air Museum This 20-hectare museum re-creates a working

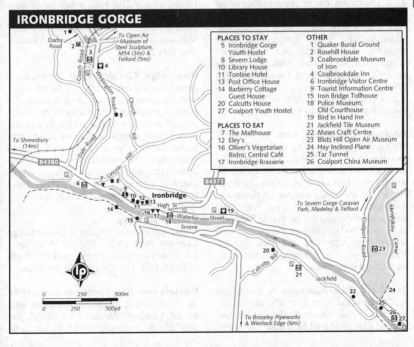

IRONBRIDGE GORGE

PLACES TO STAY	OTHER
5 Ironbridge Gorge Youth Hostel	1 Quaker Burial Ground
8 Severn Lodge	2 Rosehill House
10 Library House	3 Coalbrookdale Museum of Iron
11 Tontine Hotel	4 Coalbrookdale Inn
13 Post Office House	6 Ironbridge Visitor Centre
14 Barberry Cottage Guest House	9 Tourist Information Centre
20 Calcutts House	15 Iron Bridge Tollhouse
27 Coalport Youth Hostel	18 Police Museum; Old Courthouse
	19 Bird in Hand Inn
PLACES TO EAT	21 Jackfield Tile Museum
7 The Malthouse	22 Maws Craft Centre
12 Eley's	23 Blists Hill Open Air Museum
16 Oliver's Vegetarian Bistro; Central Café	24 Hay Inclined Plane
17 Ironbridge Brasserie	25 Tar Tunnel
	26 Coalport China Museum

JANE SMITH

The revolutionary Iron Bridge

community from the 1890s. Visitors first stop at the bank to exchange their pounds and pence for old money at a rate of £1 for 2½d. The money can be spent in the village pub and shops. Blists Hill is staffed by craftspeople in period costume who demonstrate the old skills. You can visit the foundry, sweet shop, church, doctor's surgery, butcher's, candle-maker's and carpenter's. On certain days, the only wrought ironworks still operating in the western world is also set in motion. Allow at least half a day for a visit to the museum.

Coalport China Museum By the early 19th century, iron-making skills had spread to other parts of the world and Ironbridge went into a steep decline, slowed only by the development of the porcelain and decorative tile industries around Coalport and Jackfield. Fine Coalport china was made here until the company moved to Staffordshire in 1926. The museum exhibits all sorts of elaborate pottery but also describes the life of the factory workers and how they carried out their tasks.

Jackfield Tile Museum A footbridge leads across the river to an abandoned factory where you can see displays of the decorative tiles produced here until the 1960s.

Other Things to See & Do About 90m up the hill from Coalbrookdale Museum of Iron, 18th-century **Rosehill House** was built by the Darbys but is maintained as it was when it was home to an early-19th-century ironmaster. There's a **Quaker burial ground** nearby.

The small **Police Museum** (☎ 433838) in Waterloo St shows off original police cells and a birching stool. Admission costs £1.50/1.

Just before Coalport China Museum is the astonishing **Hay Inclined Plane**, designed to transport boats between the River Severn and the Shropshire Canal. Nearby is the **Tar Tunnel**, a natural source of bitumen discovered in 1785.

Across the river, the **Broseley Pipeworks** contains a museum devoted to the clay pipe-making industry.

The newest addition to the many museums of Ironbridge is the **Open Air Museum of Steel Sculpture** (☎ 433152), Moss House, Cherry Tree Hill, which has 60 contemporary sculptures set in landscaped gardens. It opens 10 am to 5 pm, daily except Monday, March to November and admission costs £2/1.50.

Ironbridge Circular Walk Ironbridge's attractions are no secret, but to get away from the crowds, take a walk up to Benthall's Edge, a wood opposite the town. It is easy enough to follow, just cross the bridge and duck into the woods, bearing west then north across the River Severn and back down into Ironbridge. The combination of charming countryside and industrial heritage is impressive. The walk is 6 miles (10km) and should take approximately 2½ hours.

Places to Stay

Camping There's camping at *Severn Gorge Caravan Park* (☎/fax 684789, Bridgnorth Rd, Tweedale), three-quarters of a mile north of Blists Hill. The charge is £3 per adult.

Hostels Ironbridge Gorge has two sites for its youth hostel. Bookings are dealt with at the *Coalport Hostel* (☎ 588755, fax 588722, ⓔ ironbridge@yha.org.uk, John

Rose Building, High Street, Coalport), which is near the China Museum. The second site is the *Coalbrookdale Hostel (Paradise Rd, Coalbrookdale)*, near the Museum of Iron. Lots of school groups visit during term time, but both tend to be quieter in the holidays. Both open daily February to November. Coalport also opens Friday and Saturday, December to January. Beds cost £10.85/7.40.

B&Bs & Hotels Overlooking the famous bridge, *Post Office House (☎ 433201, 6 The Square)* has three rooms (one with a bathroom) costing from £30/40. The historic *Tontine Hotel (☎ 432127, The Square)*, also with a bird's eye view of the bridge, has singles/doubles for £22/40 without a bathroom or £36/56 with a bathroom.

Across the river is the comfortable, friendly *Barberry Cottage Guest House (☎ 882110, 71 Bower Yard)* with rooms for £22/38. Also on this side of the river is *Calcutts House (☎ 882631, fax 882951, Jackfield)*, a Georgian ironmaster's house, with rooms from £29/39 in the coach house and £49/59 en suite in the main house.

Other accommodation in Ironbridge tends to be pricey. The salubrious Georgian *Library House (☎ 432299, fax 433967, e libhouse@enta.net, 11 Severn Bank)*, right in the centre of Ironbridge, has rooms for £45/55. A short walk above the river is the delightful award-winning *Severn Lodge (☎ 432148, e severnlodge@compuserve .com, New Road)*, an attractive Georgian house with a secluded garden. There are two doubles and a twin room, all with bathrooms, for £45/59.

Places to Eat
There are *cafes* at the Museum of Iron, the China Museum, Blists Hill (and a pub too) and Rosehill House, as well as in the Maws Craft Centre. For a snack or a picnic, *Eley's* on the square does an excellent, really porky pork pie, among other pies, pasties and pastries.

The *Old Courthouse (☎ 433838, Waterloo St)* above the Police Museum, is the most interesting of the tea shops, where you sip your drink in what was a Victorian courtroom.

Oliver's Vegetarian Bistro (☎ 433086, 33 High St) opens for lunch and dinner Tuesday to Saturday and has been dishing up top tastes for years; starters cost around £3, main courses more like £6. Nearby, the cheap and cheerful *Central Café (☎ 433147, 32–32a High St)* serves anything with chips.

The *Ironbridge Brasserie (☎ 432716, 29 High St)* goes for modern British cuisine with prices and decor to match, and for the summer months it has a garden area overlooking the bridge. Expect to pay £15 and up for the pleasure, but not on Monday as it's closed. *The Malthouse (☎ 433712, The Wharfage)* has a fine menu of contemporary cooking, and a three-course meal can be had for around £15. It opens daily, handy for those Monday blues when everywhere else seems to close, and speaking of blues, they host regular live jazz performances. The Malthouse is also a hotel.

One reader rated the *Coalbrookdale Inn (☎ 433953, 12 Wellington Rd)*, near the Ironbridge youth hostel, the best pub in the world. It would take some research to verify that claim but the real ale and pub grub (unavailable Sunday) certainly go down a treat. Another decent pub worth a pint is the *Bird in Hand Inn (☎ 432226, Waterloo St)*, with a large garden with views across the gorge.

Getting There & Away
Ironbridge is 14 miles (23km) from Shrewsbury. Coming from the other direction, it's well signposted from the M54. See Getting There & Away under Shrewsbury earlier in the chapter for buses. The nearest train station is at Telford and there are fairly frequent buses (£1.15) to Ironbridge from there.

WENLOCK EDGE
There are great walks along this steep escarpment that stretches 15 miles (24km) from Ironbridge Gorge to Craven Arms, with superb views across to the Long Mynd to the west. It's geologically famous, in particular for its ancient coral reef

exposures. Wenlock limestone was formed 400 million years ago when this area was under the sea.

Housed in an impressive country house 7 miles (11km) south of Much Wenlock, *Wilderhope Manor Youth Hostel (☎ 01694-771363, fax 771520,* e *wilderhope@yha.org.uk)* opens February to October and a bed costs £9.80/6.75 for adults/juniors.

For walkers, there are several trails, including one west along the top of Wenlock Edge. There are infrequent buses from Ludlow; you really need your own transport to get around.

MUCH WENLOCK
☎ 01952
Much Wenlock is a rather idyllic village, home to the ruins of 13th-century **Much Wenlock Priory** (☎ 727466; EH) and an informative little town museum located in the same building as the TIC. Believe it or not, it also has a strong claim to be the birthplace of the modern day Olympic Games, thanks to Dr Brooks and the Wenlock Olympian Games.

The TIC (☎ 727679), High St, opens 9 am to 1 pm and 2 to 4.30 pm Monday to Saturday (closed Wednesday). The museum keeps the same hours.

Mountain bikes are available from Wenlock Bike Hire (☎ 727089) for £10 a day.

Places to Stay & Eat
The cheapest bricks and mortar accommodation available in Much Wenlock is *Stokes Bunkhouse Barn (☎ 727293, fax 728130,* e *c.h.hill.and.son@farmline.com, Newton House Farm)*, which offers bunks for £8 per person. The complex includes a kitchen converted from the old dairy. It is signposted from the main road.

Walton House (☎ 727139) has a warm atmosphere and a great price (from £15), but only opens April to October. *The Old Police Station (☎ 727056)* has got to be a secure base for exploring the area and has comfortable rooms, which cost £42 for an en-suite double.

For those in search of a meal, *The George & Dragon Inn (☎ 727312, 2 High St)* offers classic pub food and good ales. *The Talbot Inn (☎ 727077, 13 High St)* has a more sophisticated menu and a wonderful atmosphere, with colossal beams and cavernous fireplaces – great on a cold or wet day, and there are many of those in Shropshire.

Getting There & Away
Much Wenlock is about 7 miles (11km) north-west of Bridgnorth. Bus Nos 436 and 437 running between Shrewsbury and Bridgnorth stop here.

BRIDGNORTH
☎ 01746
Clinging to a sandstone bluff, Bridgnorth has a dramatic location above the River Severn and is the northern terminus of the Severn Valley Railway. To negotiate the cliffs, the town has one of England's oldest funicular railways dating from 1892, or for the bold or virtuous there is a series of steep stairways. A return fare on the railway (☎ 762052) costs 60p.

The TIC (☎ 763257, fax 766625, e tic@bridgnorthshropshire.com), Listley St, is housed in the library and opens 9.30 am to 5 pm Monday to Saturday except Thursday (plus 10 am to 1 pm and 2 to 5 pm on Thursday, April to October). They stock an excellent map with a town trail to follow.

Severn Valley Railway
The Severn Valley Railway (☎ 01299-403816) is one of England's most popular steam lines connecting Bridgnorth to Kidderminster (Worcestershire), via the pretty village of Bewdley. A return ticket costs £9.60/3.50.

Dudmaston
This country house (☎ 780866; NT) dates from the 17th century and is 4 miles (6km) south-east of Bridgnorth. The gardens are more of an attraction than the house itself. The house opens 2 to 5.30 pm Tuesday, Wednesday, Sunday and bank holiday Monday, April to September. The garden has longer hours: noon to 6 pm, Monday, Tuesday, Wednesday and Sunday. Admission

costs £3.75/2.25, or £2.75/1.30 for the garden only.

Places to Stay & Eat
St Leonard's Gate (☎ 766647, e stewbuch@ aol.com, 6 Church St) is a little B&B with just three rooms. It's a good deal at £18/34 a single/double. The *King's Head Hotel* (☎ 762141, Whitburn St) is an ancient coaching inn with beams running all over the place. Rooms are good value at £19/35. A century younger, the *Friars Inn* (☎ 762396, St Mary's St) is a comfortable 18th-century inn with six en-suite rooms. B&B costs from £30/45. *Severn House* (☎/fax 766976, 38 Underhill St) has a lovely location on the banks of the River Severn. The en-suite rooms set you back £38/55.

Getting There & Away
Bus Nos 436 and 437 run to Shrewsbury via Much Wenlock. Bus No 141 heads to Ludlow and No 297 to Kidderminster.

THE LONG MYND & CHURCH STRETTON
☎ 01694

The Long Mynd is probably the best known of Shropshire's hills – an excellent area for walking. Mynd is an abbreviation of the Welsh *mynydd* (mountain) but since these hills are below 550m they can hardly be called mountains. Nevertheless, there are superb views from the top of the ridges. **The Portway** is an ancient track that runs the full length of the Long Mynd.

The village of Church Stretton makes a good base for walks on the Long Mynd. The Victorians called the area Little Switzerland, bottled the local spring water and promoted Church Stretton as a health resort.

The Shropshire Hills Information Centre (☎ 723133), Library, Church St, opens 10 am to 5 pm daily except Monday and Saturday, Easter to September; Saturday only in October. They stock a lot of useful walking information and leaflets. At other times, enquire in the library itself.

Mountain bikes can be hired from Terry's Cycles (☎ 723302), 6 Castle Hill, All Stretton. They cost from £10 per day and you can also rent a tandem, which costs £20 per day. Bikes can be delivered and collected for an extra charge, paid for in advance.

Walking
Just a 10-minute walk from Church Stretton Market Place, the **Carding Mill Valley** trail leads up to the 517m-high (1695 feet) summit of the Long Mynd, with views of the Stiperstones to the east. You can drive part of the way and in summer a National Trust information centre and tea shop opens in the valley. On the other side of the A49, the walk up **Caer Caradoc** to an ancient fort is less busy. The 5-mile (8km) trip should take about 2½ hours.

Places to Stay
Bridges Long Mynd Youth Hostel (☎ 01588-650656, fax 650531) is 5 miles (8km) from Church Stretton in an old village school at Ratlinghope, in the valley between the Long Mynd and the Stiperstones. It opens year-round (but book ahead in winter). Beds cost £8.10/5.65 for adults/juniors. The walk from Church Stretton train station takes a couple of hours.

Just inside the grounds of the Long Mynd, *Dalesford* (☎ 723228) has blissfully quiet rooms for £20 per person.

Brookfields Guest House (☎ 722314, Watling St North) charges £45 for very comfortable rooms with bathrooms.

The excellent 16th-century *Jinlye Guest House* (☎/fax 723243, Castle Hill) is at the base of the Long Mynd, just outside All Stretton and 2 miles (3km) north of Church Stretton. Rooms with views and showers cost from £27 per person, but book ahead as this place has scooped a number of awards.

Longmynd Hotel (☎ 722244, fax 722718, Cunnery Rd) stands head and shoulders above Church Stretton and boasts a heated swimming pool, sauna and solarium. Rooms cost from £55/100.

Getting There & Away
Shropshire Link bus No 435 takes 45 minutes from Shrewsbury, or 35 minutes from

Ludlow. The train that runs from Ludlow to Shrewsbury via Church Stretton is more than twice as fast, but Church Stretton station is unstaffed. Trains continue north to Shrewsbury.

Getting Around

The National Trust are sensibly trying to discourage drivers from taking their vehicles up on to the Mynd as the road is tiny. At the weekend and bank holidays April to September, they run a circular shuttle bus from Church Stretton station departing five times a day. A single journey is £1.60/80p and a full return is £2.50/1.25. These prices are halved for those arriving by public transport. It's a great service and deserves support.

BISHOP'S CASTLE
☎ 01588

This is wild frontier country, real Shropshire, not the emigre Shropshire of Ludlow. The main reason for visiting Bishop's Castle in the south-western corner of the county is not the castle (which no longer exists) but the Three Tuns (see Places to Stay & Eat), a locally famous pub and brewery that still makes its own beer. **Brewery tours** are also possible on request.

There are good local walks in the area. Eight miles (13km) to the north, the **Stiperstones** are an inhospitable group of ridges topped with rough rocks. When the mist comes down and Satan settles into The Devil's Chair, it can seem a pretty sinister place.

Believe it or not, there are two small museums in town. The **Railway and Transport Museum** (☎ 638446), High St, is a shrine to public transport and opens 2 to 5 pm weekends and bank holidays. The curious **House on Crutches** (☎ 630007) houses the Town Museum, which opens noon to 5 pm weekends and bank holidays, April to September. Admission costs 50p.

Tourist information is available from the excellent, privately run Old Time (☎ 638467, fax 630126, **e** jane@tan-house .demon.co.uk), 29 High St, 10 am to 10 pm

daily (to 2 pm Sunday) – yes, 10 pm, surely a record for England!

Places to Stay & Eat

The *Green Caravan Park* (☎ 650605, Wentnor) is not far beyond Bishop's Castle in the Onny Valley and charges £6.50 for camping.

The aforementioned *Old Time* (see earlier in the section) also offers B&B from £18.50 per person in en-suite rooms and the owners know all that there is to know about the surrounding area.

If you want a taste of rural Shropshire, try *Lower Broughton Farm* (☎ 638393) on the edge of Bishop's Castle. It is a working farm and rooms cost £20/35.

The *Three Tuns* (☎ 638797), Salop St, is legendary in this part of the world and the reputation is drawing punters from beyond Shropshire. The beer is brewed on the premises and the menu is worth sampling if you are feeling peckish. The desserts alone are reason enough for a bite. B&B is also available here for £75 per room. The *Six Bells Inn* (☎ 638930, Church St) has also returned to the brewing business after many years, serving its own beers and a range of traditional pub fare.

Getting There & Away

Bus No 745 runs to Ludlow via Clun and Craven Arms, but it is infrequent on weekdays, just once on Saturday. Bus No 552/553 runs to Shrewsbury (one hour) every two hours Monday to Saturday.

CLUN
☎ 01588

About 6 miles (10km) south of Bishop's Castle is the village of Clun, with a wonderful ruined castle and more good walking country; it's just a few miles east of Offa's Dyke and the Welsh border. Despite the current shortage of trees, this area is known as Clun Forest because it was once a royal hunting ground.

Places to Stay & Eat

Accommodation at *Clun Mill Youth Hostel* (☎/fax 640582), in an old water mill on the outskirts of the village, costs £7.20/4.95 for adults/juniors. It opens daily mid-July to August. Phone to confirm other opening times.

Farm accommodation is the order of the day in Clun. *New House Farm* (*☎ 638314*) has award-winning rooms set in an 18th-century farmhouse from £25 per person.

Famous for its breakfasts is *Hurst Mill Farm* (*☎ 640224*) with rooms for £23. There are also some self-catering cottages here, plus a stables for those who want to explore the area on horseback.

Getting There & Away
Bus 745 runs this way from Ludlow and on to Bishop's Castle. Services to Ludlow leave roughly every two hours, but there are just two on Saturday and none on Sunday.

LUDLOW
☎ 01584 • pop 7500
Ludlow is undoubtedly one of England's most handsome towns, rich in historic architecture. Fortunately geography has helped it coyly guard its charms from flocks of suitors and it remains a lot less crowded than similar towns in the Cotswolds. The Ludlow Festival (see later in the section) is the exception and accommodation can be very hard to find at this time.

The centre, especially along Broad St, boasts fine Georgian town houses interspersed with occasional half-timbered black-and-white buildings. A rambling ruined castle rises above the River Teme.

Ludlow developed around its 11th-century castle. Involved in the medieval wool trade, it prospered from the sale of fleeces and the manufacture of woollen cloth. The town was also an important administrative centre and until 1689 the Council of the Welsh Marches was based here.

Information
The TIC (☎ 875053) is in the 19th-century assembly rooms in Castle St, which has a small museum attached with some diverting exhibits such as the world's oldest known spider (dead, not alive!). It opens 10 am to 5 pm daily (from 10.30 am Sunday) and admission costs £1/50p. Guided tours

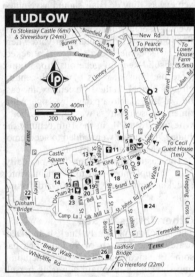

LUDLOW

PLACES TO STAY		
4	Bull Hotel	
5	Feathers Hotel	
17	The Globe	
23	Dinham Hall Hotel	
24	Hen & Chickens Guesthouse	
25	Number Twenty Eight	
26	The Charlton Arms	

PLACES TO EAT	
1	Merchant House; The Unicorn Inn

3	Hibiscus	
7	Ludlow Fish Bar	
10	The Olive Branch	
12	Organza	
13	Ego Café-Bar	
18	De Grey's Café	
22	Mr Underhill's	

OTHER	
2	Train Station
6	Post Office
8	The Centre

9	Laundrette
11	Church of St Laurence
14	Ludlow Castle
15	Castle Lodge
16	Market Place
19	Tourist Information Centre
20	Assembly Rooms
21	Blue Boar Inn

(☎ 874205) leave from outside the castle entrance at 2.30 pm on summer weekends and cost just £1.50 for adults.

Pearce Engineering (☎ 876016), Fishmore Rd, about a mile north-east of the centre, rents out mountain bikes for £12.

The Centre (☎ 874641), 5 Tower St, offers Internet access for about £5 an hour Monday to Saturday.

Ludlow Castle

The impressive castle (☎ 873355) was built around 1090 by Roger de Lacy to control the Welsh, something that took years to achieve as Tony de Blair should have noted before trying to appoint his man to run the Welsh Assembly. It consists of a huge fortification with a large outer courtyard where the townspeople could shelter if attacked, and a solid keep of generous proportions. Note the unusual ruins of a 12th-century circular chapel. In the 14th century, the castle was turned into a palace by Roger Mortimer, whose mistress was Queen Isabella, wife of Edward II. In the 16th century the Judges' Lodgings were added to accommodate the March administrators.

The castle opens 10 am to 5 pm daily, May to September and to 4 pm in winter (weekends only in January). Admission costs £3/1.50.

Other Things to See

The large, mainly Early English and Decorated style **Church of St Laurence** has some fine medieval misericords, including one showing a mermaid admiring herself in a mirror. On the outside wall by the northern entrance is a simple memorial to Houseman. Note the unusual hexagonal porch.

Near the castle, the partially half-timbered **Castle Lodge** (☎ 878098) dates back to the 14th century, although most of what you'll see inside is mainly Elizabethan or later. During its life, it has been a prison and home to the officials of the Council of the Marches, who presided over the Border Lands after the demise of an independent Wales. Inside is some particularly fine plasterwork, although no

furniture these days. Ring the bell for admission, which costs £2.

The waymarked 30-mile (48km) **Mortimer's Trail** to Knighton starts just outside the castle entrance. Phone ☎ 797052 for details.

Ludlow Festival

During June and July the town plays host to the Ludlow Festival, an annual arts bash that includes a Shakespearean epic performed in the castle ruins, an amazing experience for those able to time their visit and find a ticket. Phone ☎ 872150 for full details.

Places to Stay

The youth hostel has closed and there's no camp site, so budget options are limited.

Ludlow's B&Bs tend to be expensive, but about a mile from the centre, *Cecil Guest House* (☎ 872442, Sheet Rd) has 10 rooms from £20 per person or £25 en suite. *The Globe* (☎ 874212, 3 Market St) is a town-centre pub with cheap B&B at £20 per person. Another attractively located pub with good value lodgings is *The Charlton Arms* (☎ 872813, Ludford Bridge) above Ludford Bridge overlooking the river, where singles/doubles cost from £30/45.

Best of the cheaper B&Bs is *Hen and Chickens Guesthouse* (☎ 874318, 103 Old St), which has a good location, ample parking and a homely atmosphere, all from £20 per person.

Those with their own transport can enjoy the comforts of charming, medieval *Lower House Farm* (☎ 823648, Cleedownton), about 5 miles (8km) outside Ludlow, where B&B is £24 per person. Leave Ludlow on the A4117 and take the B4364 to Cleedownton.

For luxury B&B, check out *Number Twenty Eight* (☎ 876996, fax 876860, **e** ross.no28@btinternet.com, 28 Lower Broad St), a collection of small period houses with extremely comfortable rooms from £70. For those who can afford it, the timber-framed Jacobean *Feathers Hotel* (☎ 875261, fax 876030, Bull Ring) has charm and character in abundance. Some rooms have four-poster beds and staying in this beautiful building is a delight. Rooms normally cost from £65/85 but it's worth asking about cheaper leisure breaks.

For a cheaper version of the black and white dream, consider the *Bull Hotel* (☎/fax 873611, 14 Bull Ring), one of the oldest buildings in town, with pleasant enough rooms for £30/45.

Right beside the castle, the Georgian *Dinham Mill Hotel* (☎ 876464, fax 876019) is the most expensive place in town at £65/110.

Places to Eat

Ludlow has emerged as the gastronomic capital of rural England – there are three Michelin-starred restaurants within walking distance of the centre. Those on a budget should steer clear of these places as they can seriously damage your wallet.

Organza (☎ 873366, 6 Church St) is a good lunch time stop-off for those in a hurry, with wholesome sandwiches and cheap soups, the place to 'large it up as nature intended'. For teas and coffees, head for the old-fashioned *De Grey's Café* (☎ 872764, 5–6 Broad St). They have a full restaurant menu by night. *The Olive Branch* (☎ 874314, 2–4 Old St) is undoubtedly the place to sit for lunch, an excellent vegetarian restaurant with plenty of salads and a positively dangerous selection of desserts. It heaves with diners during the peak season.

For anything more substantial the classy *Ego Café-Bar* (☎ 878000, Quality Square), off Castle Square, does exquisite contemporary cuisine at prices a whole lot more accessible than the Michelin mob. They also have tapas nights with the best of Spanish cuisine.

Speaking of which, these high flying restaurants deserve a mention. *Merchant House* (☎ 875438, Lower Corve St) is perhaps the best known. It is run by chef Shaun Hill and offers a set dinner for £32.50. *Mr Underhill's* (☎ 874431, Dinham Weir) is also very highly rated by those in the know, although again the food is very expensive and the menu offers little choice.

The latest addition to the cuisine scene is *Hibiscus* (☎ 872325, 17 Corve St). The set menu is £32.50 and is primarily modern French with flair.

Ludlow Fish Bar hasn't got a Michelin star, but does very passable fish and chips for the staunch traditionalists who just can't get their heads around nouvelle cuisine.

There are several good pubs in Ludlow, including the *Blue Boar Inn* (☎ 872630, 52 Mill St), an atmospheric tavern, popular with the festival crowd; *The Unicorn Inn* (☎ 873555, Lower Corve St), which has a good, local clientele most nights of the week; and *The Globe* (see Places to Stay earlier), which gets a younger crowd at the weekend.

Getting There & Away

Ludlow is 29 miles (47km) from Shrewsbury and 24 miles (39km) from Hereford. For information on First Midland Red buses to Hereford, Birmingham, Kidderminster and Shrewsbury phone ☎ 01905-763888. For specific transport information on southern Shropshire, call ☎ 877717. Bus No 192/292 runs to Hereford (one hour) and Birmingham (2½ hours) regularly, including Sunday. Bus No 435 heads to Shrewsbury, as well as Stokesay Castle and Church Stretton. Bus No 736 goes to Knighton for Wales.

From Ludlow train station there are direct services to Shrewsbury (£6.80, 30 minutes), Church Stretton (£3.70, 15 minutes), Hereford (£5.30, 25 minutes), Cardiff, Liverpool and Manchester.

AROUND LUDLOW
Stokesay Castle

Seven miles (11km) north-west of Ludlow, Stokesay Castle (☎ 01588-672544; EH) is one of the most picturesque 13th-century fortified manor houses in England. The grouping of stout stone walls, half-timbered 17th-century gateway and church tower is one to set a thousand camera shutters clicking – as it does on sunny summer days. It opens 10 am to 6 pm April to September and to 4 pm in winter and admission costs £3.50/1.80.

Teas and light lunches are available in the attractive castle grounds themselves or at *Pottery Cottage* beside the car park; or there's food and accommodation back in lovely Ludlow or uninspiring Craven Arms.

Shropshire Link bus No 435 runs to Stokesay from Shrewsbury and Ludlow; drivers will drop you at the bottom of the lane leading to the castle. It's often quicker to take a train to Craven Arms and walk a mile south to the site.

Staffordshire

Most visitors pass straight through Staffordshire, which stretches from the northern edge of Birmingham nearly to the southern fringes of Manchester. It's worth a stop to see Lichfield's wonderful cathedral, to sample the beer in Burton-upon-Trent or for an adrenaline rush at Alton Towers, Europe's most famous theme park. Lovers of fine porcelain will also want to break their journey in Stoke-on-Trent, heart of the famous Potteries district. To the north-east the Staffordshire moorlands blend into the Peak District National Park.

GETTING AROUND
For information on Staffordshire buses, call the Busline on ☎ 01782-206608. Stoke-on-Trent, Stafford and Lichfield are the best transport hubs in the county.

LICHFIELD
☎ 01543 • pop 25,000
Lichfield is a small, handsome market town of cobbled streets and attractive gardens, topped off with a towering red brick cathedral. It was also home to the famous 18th-century diarist and wit Samuel Johnson and a museum has been established in his honour.

The TIC (☎ 308209, fax 417308, e tic@lichfieldtourist.co.uk), Market Square, opens 9 am to 5 pm Monday to Friday and to 3 pm Saturday.

The Lichfield International Arts Festival

(☎ 306543) takes place in the first half of July and includes classical music, comedy and theatre.

Lichfield Cathedral
The fine red brick cathedral is famous for its three spires although it also boasts a fine west front adorned with exquisitely carved statues of the kings of England from Edgar through to Henry I. Most of what you see dates from the various rebuildings of the Norman cathedral during the Middle Ages. St Chad, the first Bishop of Lichfield, was laid to rest in each building in turn. His gold-leafed skull was once kept in St Chad's Head Chapel, just to the west of the south transept.

The Lichfield Gospels, a superb illuminated manuscript from AD 730, are displayed in the beautifully vaulted mid-13th-century chapterhouse. Don't miss the effigy of George Augustus Selwyn, first Bishop of New Zealand in 1841, in the Lady Chapel, or the poignant memorial to the two daughters of a cathedral prebendary at the east end of the south aisle.

The cathedral opens 7.40 am to 6.30 pm daily. A donation of £3 is requested. Once finished in the cathedral, it's worth walking round **Cathedral Close**, which is ringed with imposing 17th- and 18th-century houses.

Samuel Johnson Birthplace Museum
Samuel Johnson was born here in 1709. His pioneering dictionary together with the biography written by his close friend James Boswell (*The Life of Samuel Johnson*) established him as one of the great scholars, critics and wits of the English language but, like so many modern media superstars, Johnson was mainly famous simply for being famous. Statues of Johnson and Boswell adorn the Market Square. The Samuel Johnson Birthplace Museum (☎ 264972), on the square, opens 10.30 am to 4.15 pm daily and admission costs £2/1.10. You can inspect the famous diary using the computer in the bookshop in the lobby.

Other Things To See & Do

The **Heritage & Treasury Exhibition** (☎ 256611), St Mary's Centre, on the market square, opens 10 am to 4 pm daily and admission costs £2/1.50p. It's possible to climb the tower to get some fine views of the city.

The **Erasmus Darwin Centre** (☎ 306260) commemorates Erasmus Darwin, grandfather of the more famous Charles, and is located in the house where he lived from 1756 to 1781 in Beacon St. It opens 10 am to 4.30 pm (last entry 3.45 pm) Tuesday to Saturday, noon to 4.30 pm Sunday. Admission costs £2.50/2.

Places to Stay

There are several B&Bs charging £18 to £20 a head in Beacon St, round the corner from Cathedral Close. *32 Beacon St* (☎ 262378) is in a cosy town house and offers two en-suite rooms from £21/38 a single/double. Farther away from the town centre is *206 Beacon St* (☎ 262130), a dinky Georgian terrace with a couple of rooms available for £20/36, including breakfast.

For very little more, you can stay on The Close itself; there are three rooms at the excellent *No 8* (☎ 418483) for £22/44 with shared bathroom or £26/52 en suite with a great view of the cathedral. *No 23* (☎ 306140, The Close) may be a big house, but it only has one room available at £26 for one, £45 for two.

The *Angel Croft Hotel* (☎ 258737, fax 415605, Beacon St) has comfortable rooms for £62/75, or £51/62 at the weekend, and is handy for the cathedral.

Places to Eat

The *Cathedral Coffee Shop* (☎ 306125, 19 The Close), set in a charming 18th-century house, serves soup and sandwich lunches for around £3.50. Another popular local spot for coffee is the *Rendezvous Coffee House* (☎ 411633, 10b Market St) and they also have some of the tastiest sandwiches in town. For atmospheric surroundings, *Tudor of Lichfield* (☎ 263951, Bore St) is hard to beat, a real tea shop in a Tudor building.

The Eastern Eye (☎ 414500, 19 Bird St) is a popular Indian restaurant with an award-winning chef. *The Lal Bagh* (☎ 262697, 9 Bird St) also serves up Bangladeshi dishes and comes recommended by none other than the *Good Curry Guide*.

If you want to splash out, try *Colleys Yard* (☎ 416606, 26 Bird St) where a modern British dinner costs from £15 to £20. *Chandlers Grande Brasserie* (☎ 416688), in the old Corn Exchange, is locally renowned for continental cuisine and a fine ambience – but bank on little change from £20 after an evening meal.

Entertainment

Samuel Johnson described Lichfield folk as 'the most sober, decent people in England', but that was 250 years ago and there are pubs-a-plenty these days.

The Sozzled Sausage (☎ 419111, Church St) is a lively pub that has gone well beyond alcopops to bring us alcoholic sausages. Another, more traditional pub worth checking out is *The King's Head* (☎ 256822, Bird St).

Getting There & Away

There are two train stations: Lichfield City and Lichfield Trent Valley. Both are 30 minutes from Birmingham New Street station and trains leave every 15 minutes (£3.30 day return). Intercity trains travelling between London Euston and Manchester Piccadilly often call at Lichfield Trent Valley.

STAFFORD
☎ 01785

The county town of Staffordshire has always been a crossroads for travellers heading north or south, but with cars replacing horses people don't tend to stick around for very long today. The **Ancient High House** (☎ 619619), Greengate St, is the largest timber-framed house left standing today and has period rooms showing the house through the ages. It also houses the TIC (☎ 619619). Both open 9 am to 5 pm Monday to Friday and 10 am to 4 pm Saturday (to 3 pm in winter). **Stafford Castle** (☎ 257698) is no more than a ruin, but has a visitor centre. It opens 10 am to 5 pm (to 4 pm in winter) daily except Monday and admission costs £2.

STOKE-ON-TRENT
☎ 01782

Stoke-on-Trent is not known as England's most glamorous town, nevertheless, it is home to some of England's most glamorous porcelain and the famous factories continue to draw large numbers of visitors. Arguably the most famous of all is Wedgwood. Factory tours generally need to be booked in advance and don't run during factory holiday periods, but the Wedgwood, Spode and Royal Doulton visitor centres are permanently open, as well as the Gladstone and the Potteries museums where it is safe to browse without the temptation to buy.

Arnold Bennett left memorable descriptions of the area in its industrial heyday in his novels *Clayhanger* and *Anna of the Five Towns* – something of a misnomer since Stoke actually consists of six towns!

Orientation & Information

Stoke-on-Trent is made up of Tunstall, Burslem, Hanley, Stoke, Fenton and Longton – which, together, are often called the Potteries. Hanley is the official 'city centre'. Stoke-on-Trent train station is southwest of the city centre, but buses from outside the main entrance will run you there in minutes. The bus station is right in the city centre.

The TIC (☎ 236000, fax 236005, e stoke.tic@virgin.net), Quadrant Rd, Hanley, located in the Potteries shopping centre, opens 9 am to 5 pm Monday to Saturday. The various visitor centres, factories and showrooms are widely scattered about, but the TIC stocks an informative map with their locations. All require entry one hour before closing time. Email e museums@ stoke.gov.uk for specific information on the museums.

Royal Doulton Visitor Centre

The Royal Doulton Visitor Centre (☎ 292434), Nile St, in Burslem, has the biggest collection of Doulton figures around. It opens 9.30 am to 5 pm Monday

Josiah Wedgwood

Born in 1730, Josiah Wedgwood was the twelfth child of parents who were already turning out pots. When he was nine his father died and Josiah went to work in the family business inherited by his older brother Thomas. After a lengthy apprenticeship, he jumped ship and went into partnership with Thomas Whieldon who had a pottery in Fenton. It was there that he started the experiments that eventually led to his own distinctive wares.

Although Wedgwood is best known for his blue and white jasper, and black basalt wares, his first success was in creating a green glaze that could be used to finish off the then-fashionable pots and jugs in the shape of vegetables.

Five years after joining Whieldon, Wedgwood was confident enough to branch out on his own, opening the Ivy House Works in Burslem. In 1765 he was allowed to name his distinctive cream-coloured pottery Queen's Ware after Queen Charlotte, wife of George III. Five years later he completed an order for Catherine II of Russia.

Wedgwood perfected his technique for producing black basalt pottery in 1768, but the distinctive blue and white jasper ware didn't put in an appearance until 1775.

Wedgwood was more than just a master potter. A supporter of the French and American Revolutions, he also worked for the abolition of slavery and found time to devise new machinery for his business at the same time. When he died in 1795, he left a business well on its way to the international success it enjoys today.

to Saturday and 10.30 am to 4.30 pm Sunday. Admission costs £3/2.25. Factory tours take place at 10.30 am and 1.15 and 2.45 pm Monday to Thursday (10.30 am and 1.30 pm Friday) for an extra £3.50/2.75.

Spode Museum & Visitor Centre

The Spode Museum & Visitor Centre (☎ 744011) is conveniently situated near the train station in Church St, Stoke. It opens 9 am to 5 pm Monday to Saturday and 10 am to 4 pm Sunday. Admission costs £2.75/2.25. Factory tours take place at 10 am and 1.30 pm Monday to Thursday, and at 10 am on Friday, costing an extra £2/1.50.

Wedgwood Visitor Centre

The Wedgwood Visitor Centre (☎ 204218), in Barlaston, takes you right through the production process from raw clay to glazing and decorating. You can even get behind the wheel. It opens 9 am to 5 pm daily, from 10 am at the weekend. Admission costs £4.95/3.95. Factory tours are self-guided so have no fixed times.

Potteries Museum

This large museum and art gallery (☎ 232323), Bethesda St, in Hanley, opens 10 am to 5 pm daily, from 2 pm Sunday. Admission is free. Come here to discover the history of the Potteries and to inspect a miscellaneous collection of ceramics.

Gladstone Pottery Museum

Constructed round Stoke's last remaining bottle kiln and its yard, this wonderful museum (☎ 319232), Uttoxeter Rd, in Longton, is great on evoking the hot, unhappy working life of those who worked in the Potteries until the Clean Air Acts of the 1950s changed everything beyond recognition. Particularly fun is the gallery devoted to Victorian sanitaryware – toilet bowls more flowery than you would think possible. It opens 10 am to 5 pm daily and admission costs £3.95/2.50. Make sure you try a Staffordshire oatcake (actually a pancake) in the pleasant cafe.

Etruria Industrial Museum

On the site of the original canalside Wedgwood factory, Stoke's newest museum (☎ 233144), Lower Bedford St, Etruria, incorporates a steam-powered bone and flint mill and a blacksmith's forge, as well as a visitor centre. It opens 10 am to 4 pm Wednesday to Sunday and admission costs £1.50/1.

Places to Stay

It takes more than a day to see all of Stoke's sights properly, which is a shame, since decent accommodation is thin on the ground. Leek Rd, just off Station Rd, is convenient for the train station. *L Beez Guest House* (☎ 846727, 46 Leek Rd) has rooms for £20/35 a single/double. Close by is the *Rhodes Hotel* (☎ 416320, 42 Leek Rd), which offers B&B in a somewhat more comfortable environment, also for £20/35.

For more comfort, the *North Stafford Hotel* (☎ 744477, fax 744580, Winton Square) is right opposite the station and has all the trimmings expected of a three-star place. Rooms are £95/105 in the week, £49 per person half board at the weekend. Doulton fans might want to be closer to their shrine and the *George Hotel* (☎ 577544, fax 837496, e georgestoke@btinternet .com, Swan Square, Burslem) is next door! It is a well-equipped, family run hotel charging £65/85 for a room.

Places to Eat

Cafe-bars and gastro pubs haven't really hit Stoke in a big way, but this is good news for those who worry more about cost than class. For those on a hit-and-run visit, it is probably easiest to eat at the cafes attached to the museums and visitor centres. They all feel more like tearooms than restaurants, but the *Sir Henry Doulton Gallery Restaurant* (☎ 292434), the *Blue Italian Restaurant* (744011, Spode Visitor Centre) and the *Wedgwood Story Restaurant* are the favourites.

Stoke has a good reputation for baltis and there are plenty of places to sample one. *Shaffers Kashmiri Balti* (☎ 206030, 63

Piccadilly) is a good spot for those in Hanley. Those up in Burslem, near the Doulton factory, should look out for **Kismet** *(☎ 834651, 1a Queen St)*. Thai food has also come to town. **Ria** *(☎ 264411, 65 Piccadilly, Hanley)* has a large menu with the emphasis on seafood. For those tired of roast dinners, they also offer a Sunday buffet.

Portofino (☎ 209444, 38 Marsh St, Hanley) is the leading Italian restaurant and does all the pizza and pastas expected as well as some regional specialities. Expect to pay at least £10 a head.

Entertainment

La Bodega (☎ 273322, 66 Piccadilly, Hanley) is a try for those who can't resist a little nibble with their drinks and can't stomach any more crisps, pork scratchings or other English favourites.

Bar la de Dah (☎ 272775, 62–64 Piccadilly, Hanley) is a modern bar that is worth stopping at. For those who like a cheap drink, there is a *JD Wetherspoon* in Piccadilly with its usual blend of budget beer and lack of music. Try a pint of the locally brewed Titanic – they say it goes down well!

The *Regent Theatre (☎ 213800, Piccadilly, Hanley)* is an Art Deco surprise in the centre of modern Hanley. It stages plays and musicals.

Getting There & Away

National Express buses do day returns from London to the Potteries for £15, but you will only have six hours in which to squeeze everything in. There are regular trains to Stoke-on-Trent from Birmingham New Street and from Manchester Piccadilly.

Getting Around

The Wedgwood Express no longer operates. Bus Nos 6, 7 and 8 serve Wedgwood and Gladstone and Nos 20, 21 and 22 serve Doulton and Spode; phone First Bus PMT (☎ 207999) for details of bus routes and times. The Potteries Museum is within walking distance of the centre.

AROUND STOKE-ON-TRENT
Biddulph Grange Gardens

The National Trust has recently restored these gorgeous Victorian gardens (☎ 01782-517999), with their Chinese, Egyptian and Italian corners. The final element of restoration is the Rainbow, a huge bank of rhododendrons that flower simultaneously. The gardens are 7 miles (11km) north of Stoke and open noon to 6 pm Wednesday to Friday and 11 am to 6 pm weekends, April to October. Admission costs £4.40/2.30 but if you also visit Little Moreton Hall, 6 miles (10km) east, a joint ticket costs £6.75/3.30.

Little Moreton Hall

Off the A34 south of Congleton, Little Moreton Hall (☎ 01260-272018; NT) is England's most spectacular black-and-white timber-framed house, dating back to the 15th century. It opens noon to 5.30 pm (from 11 am in August) Wednesday to Sunday, late March to October. Admission costs £4.40/2.30.

Shugborough

This regal, neoclassical mansion is the ancestral home of Lord Lichfield, although he's more famous for his photographs than his house. Construction began in 1693, but it was only with considerable work during the 18th and 19th centuries that the house reached its present immense proportions. The estate is famous for the monuments within its grounds including a Chinese House, Doric temple and the Triumphal Arch, and for a fine collection of Louis XV and XVI furniture. There is also a museum and a farm to explore.

Shugborough (☎ 01889-881388) opens 11 am to 5 pm Monday to Saturday, late March to late September. Admission to the house or museum costs £4/3, or a family ticket, including the museum and farm, goes for £18.

Burton-upon-Trent
☎ 01283

Burton-upon-Trent has been a brewing centre for centuries and the **Bass Museum &**

Visitor Centre (☎ 511000) tells the full story. Founded in 1777, Bass is now England's biggest brewer. The centre opens 10 am to 4 pm daily, and the £4.50 admission fee includes the obligatory free Bass beer. The TIC (☎ 526609, fax 517268, e tic@burtonwindow.com), Unit 40, Octagon Centre, opens 9 am to 5.30 pm Monday to Friday and to 4 pm Saturday.

Alton Towers

Alton Towers (☎ 0870 520 4060) is England's most popular theme park and a must for white-knuckle fiends everywhere. There are over 100 rides, including **Oblivion**, the world's first vertical-drop roller-coaster, which blows the mind. Or if that's not your thing, try **Hex**, which just messes with your brain instead.

Alton Towers costs £19.95/15.95 during peak season/at the weekend or £14.95/11.95 off season. Located between Stoke-on-Trent and Ashbourne, it opens 9.30 am to 6 pm (later in summer) daily, April to October. There is transport to Alton Towers from most major Midlands towns in summer.

Places to Stay There is an expensive hotel within the park, but most visitors opt to stay in nearby villages such as Alton.

For a dependable B&B in Alton, try the *Old School House (☎/fax 01538-702151, e old_school_house@talk21.com, Castle Hill Rd)*, which offers very comfortable rooms for £50.

If you'd prefer something cheaper, *Fields Farm (☎ 01538-752721, fax 757404, Chapel Lane, Threapwood)* is about 2 miles (3km) outside Alton in a lovely ivy-clad farmhouse. B&B starts from £17 per person.

Although it's 12½ miles (20km) south-east of Alton, a number of Lonely Planet readers have recommended *Little Park Holiday Hostel (☎ 01283-812654, 2 Park Lane, Tutbury)*, which has two-bedroomed chalets overlooking the Dove Valley from just £12.50 per night, and offers free pick-up from both Tutbury and Burton train stations.

Drayton Manor Park

This is south Staffordshire's answer to Alton Towers, another massive theme park with massive rides. New rides include **Apocalypse**, a 54m 'stand up' drop from a tower and **Stormforce 10**, a sort of oversized log flume that gets you drenched. The park (☎ 01827-287979) opens 10.30 am to 5 pm (later in summer) Easter to October; admission costs £14/10. The park is near Junctions 9 and 10 of the M42 on the A4091.

LEEK
☎ 01538

Leek is a useful town to browse when journeying between the Potteries and the Peak District. It's a gateway to the Staffordshire moorlands, but there's not enough to justify a stay. **St Edward's Church** (Church St) has a rose window by William Morris, while **All Saint's Church** (Compton) was once described by John Betjeman as 'one of the finest churches in Britain', with its elaborate decoration. The TIC (☎ 483741, fax 483743, e tourism.smdc@staffordshire.gov.uk), 1 Market Place, opens 9.30 am to 5 pm Monday to Saturday.

Derbyshire

Derbyshire is all about the Peak District, one of the wildest, most beautiful areas in England (see the Peak District section later in the chapter), most of which falls within the county boundaries. It also has the industrial town of Derby and some wonderful stately homes, including Haddon Hall, one of England's finest medieval manor houses, and unforgettable Chatsworth.

The Derbyshire Wayfarer ticket covers buses and trains throughout the county and beyond to link up with Sheffield, Macclesfield and Burton-on-Trent. It costs £7.25, or £12 for a family for a day. For general bus information phone ☎ 01332-292200.

DERBY
☎ 01332 • pop 220,000

There is something of an intense rivalry between Derby and Nottingham and Derby usually comes out second best, although when it comes to all-important football, it's Nottingham that's in the doldrums these days. The Industrial Revolution transformed sleepy Derby (**dar**-by) first into a pioneering silk-production centre, then into a major railway centre. In the 20th century it became famous as the home of Rolls-Royce aircraft engines.

Although there are no major tourist attractions in Derby, the town makes a reasonable base for exploring the surrounding area.

The TIC (☎ 255802, fax 256137, **e** tourism@derby.gov.uk), in the Assembly Rooms on Market Place, opens 9.30 am to 5.30 pm Monday to Friday, to 5 pm on Saturday and 10.30 am to 2.30 pm on Sunday.

Things to See & Do

Derby's 18th-century **cathedral** boasts a 64m tower and some magnificent ironwork. Look out for the tomb of Bess of Hardwick (see Hardwick Hall under Around Chesterfield later in the chapter) in the south aisle.

A short walk from the cathedral, in Full St, **Derby Industrial Museum** (☎ 255308) recounts Derby's industrial history with pride of place going, of course, to Rolls-Royce aircraft engines. Other possibilities include the **Museum & Art Gallery** (☎ 716659), The Strand, and **Pickford's House Museum** (☎ 255363), 41 Friar Gate, a museum of Georgian life. All these museums are free and open 11 am to 5 pm Monday, 10 am to 5 pm Tuesday to Saturday and 2 pm to 5 pm on Sunday.

Tours of the **Royal Crown Derby** china factory (☎ 712841), 194 Osmaston Rd, take place at 10.30 am and 1.45 pm Monday to Thursday, and at 1.15 pm on Friday. There is also a museum and seconds shop on the premises. It is worth having a look here if you aren't going to make it to Stoke-on-Trent.

Places to Stay & Eat

Crompton St is central and has several standard B&Bs such as *Chuckles* (☎ 367193, **e** ianfraser@chucklesguesthouse.freeserve .co.uk, 48 Crompton St), a fresh and friendly B&B where singles/doubles cost £19/34. Nearby is the recently reopened *Wayfarer* (☎ 348350, 27 Crompton St), which has rooms for £18/32. The large, modern *International Hotel* (☎ 369321, fax 294430, 288 Burton Rd), just south of the centre, charges £62.50/72, but prices drop at the weekend.

Old Blacksmith's Yard is in an attractive area of town and houses several popular restaurants, including the cafe-bar *Farriers* with a lively little menu. *Steliana's and Sapho's Greek Tavern* (☎ 385200, 7 Old Blacksmith's Yard) is a Hellenic restaurant that has long been a local favourite. Huge *Arkwright's* is a popular cafe-bar on the square by the TIC – the building is hideous, but it's pleasant in the summer when tables are put out front. For a better incarnation of the cafe-bar concept, try *Casa* (☎ 341946, 11 Iron Gate), with a modern, reasonably priced menu and drinks into the night.

For good Indian food, head south down Normanton Rd, where there's a large Asian community. Nearer the centre on Curzon St are *Balti Towers* (☎ 200443) and *Curry Mania* (☎ 344786), both inexpensive, unpretentious curry houses. *Chai Yo Thai* (360207, 8 Bold Lane) has great-value Thai food at lunch time – under a fiver for a main course and two courses plus coffee for £6.30.

For cheap pub grub, *Ye Olde Dolphin Inne* (Queen St), right in the shadow of the cathedral, does the business.

Entertainment

Pubs & Clubs Pubs worth calling into include *The Standing Order* (Babington Lane) for its cheap drinks, one of the 'Spoons' family so no music. Other places include *The Wardwick* (☎ 332677, The Wardwick), a handsome traditional pub, and *The Victoria Inn* (☎ 740091, 12 Midland Place), near the train station, probably the best live music venue in Derby.

If a pub doesn't cut the mustard, *Boom Club* (☎ 200910, 6 Sadlergate) is the liveliest choice for clubbers, including Latin and

70s nights. However, Nottingham has more to offer.

Getting There & Away
Derby is 130 miles (209km) from London, 60 miles (97km) from Manchester, 40 miles (64km) from Birmingham and 30 miles (48km) from Leicester.

The dismal bus station is close to the centre. The TransPeak (☎ 0870 608 2608) TP service operates from Manchester through the Peak District to Derby, taking just 30 minutes to continue to Nottingham. Trains link Derby with London in just under two hours.

AROUND DERBY
Kedleston Hall
Construction of this superb neoclassical mansion (☎ 01332-842191; NT) with its Palladian front was started in 1758 by a trio of architects. The Curzon family has lived at Kedleston since the 12th century and Sir Nathaniel Curzon tore down an earlier house in order to construct this stunning masterpiece. He also moved Kedleston village a mile down the road so it wouldn't interfere with the landscaping! Only the medieval village church beside the house remains.

The entrance to the Marble Hall with its statues of Greek and Roman deities is breathtaking. The 20 alabaster columns were originally plain but from 1776 to 1777 it was decided that the room was too austere and fluting was chiselled into the columns *in situ*. The circular saloon with its domed roof was modelled on the Pantheon in Rome.

The whole house is lavishly decorated and includes the Indian Museum, displaying a later Lord Curzon's oriental collection. From 1898 to 1905 he was the viceroy of India – a century earlier, Government House in Calcutta (now Raj Bhavan) was modelled on Kedleston Hall. The adjacent church houses a collection of family memorials, their increasing magnificence indicating the Curzons' escalating fortunes.

Kedleston Hall is 5 miles (8km) northwest of Derby. It opens noon to 4 pm daily,

except Thursday and Friday, Easter to October. Admission costs £5/2.50.

Calke Abbey
Ten miles (16km) south of Derby in Ticknall is captivating Calke Abbey (☎ 01332-863822; NT), a Baroque mansion built between 1701 and 1703 but left untouched after the last baronet died in 1924. It contains a treasure-trove ranging from natural history to a caricature room. Admission is by timed ticket; at busy periods it's wise to phone and check that you'll be able to get in.

The house opens 1 to 5.30 pm Saturday to Wednesday, April to October and admission costs £5.10/2.50.

CHESTERFIELD
☎ 01246 • pop 70,000
Chesterfield is justly famous for its Leaning Tower of Jesus, the famous twisted spire of **St Mary's & All Saints Church** in Church Way. The 68m-high spire leans nearly 3m to one side and performs a painful-looking twist, the result of heavy lead tiles over a poorly seasoned timber frame. It is open to climb on bank holiday Mondays for £2.50/1.

Located on the eastern edge of the Peak District, nearer to Sheffield than Derby, the town is pleasant enough for a detour, but lacks enough to justify a night. The **Museum & Art Gallery** in St Mary's Gate opens 10 am to 4 pm daily, except Wednesday and Sunday. Those with their own transport heading to Chesterfield up the M1 should check out **Sutton Scarsdale Hall** (☎ 822844; EH), a mansion built by the last earl of Scarsdale to outdo Chatsworth. He died bankrupt and the hall was stripped to nothing. Today it is a moody shell and admission is free.

The TIC (☎ 345777, fax 345770), Low Pavement, opens 9 am to 5.30 pm Monday to Saturday. A market is held on Monday, Friday and Saturday, and there is a flea market on Wednesday.

Buses run from Chesterfield to Sheffield, Derby or Nottingham. Bus No X67 (☎ 250450) runs across the Peak District to Manchester three times a day.

THE MIDLANDS

AROUND CHESTERFIELD
Hardwick Hall

Hardwick Hall (☎ 01246-850430; NT) was Bess of Hardwick's crowning achievement and the ES initials on the walls loudly trumpet her ownership as Elizabeth, Countess of Shrewsbury. Separated from her fourth husband, the earl of Shrewsbury, Bess moved to Hardwick after buying it from her bankrupt brother in 1583. Lacking the means to build a home commensurate with her high opinion of herself, she initially settled for rebuilding Hardwick Old Hall. But as soon as her husband died in 1590, and she got her hands on his fortune, work started on Hardwick Hall.

The house features the very best of late-16th-century design, including vast amounts of glass, a considerable status symbol at the time. It's notable for its many late-16th- to early-17th-century tapestries and for a remarkably thorough inventory taken in 1601; many items from that inventory still exist. Over the centuries the house managed to escape both modernisation and neglect so it retains a wonderfully ancient feel. Despite its airy appearance – 'more glass than wall' – it remains rather austere.

The house opens 12.30 to 5 pm (or sunset if earlier) Wednesday, Thursday, Saturday and Sunday, April to October. Admission costs £6/3. The adjacent ruins of Hardwick Old Hall (EH) open 10 am to 6 pm and admission costs £2.60/1.30 (a joint ticket to both properties is £8/4). Hardwick Hall is about 10 miles (16km) south-east of Chesterfield, just off the M1 between junctions 28 and 29. There is a special heritage bus (☎ 0114-248 9139) running to Chesterfield and Bolsover during summer. It costs £5 round trip.

Peak District

Although the Peak District is principally in Derbyshire it spills over into five adjoining counties. It's a remarkable region – smack-bang in the middle of one of the most densely populated, industrialised parts of England and is one of the country's best-loved national parks. So loved in fact that it is the busiest in Europe, and believed to be the second busiest in the world. Dotted with pretty villages, historic sites and fascinating limestone caves, the Peak District also encompasses some of England's most wild and beautiful scenery. The region is criss-crossed with hundreds of miles of dry stone walls, dividing the hills into a patchwork of fields.

ORIENTATION

Although it's squeezed between Manchester and Sheffield, with the industrial towns of Yorkshire to the north and the northern Midlands to the south, there are no large towns within the Peak District National Park.

Nor are there any actual peaks in the Peak District, just endless rolling hills; the name comes from the ancient people who once inhabited the region. The 555 sq miles of the national park are divided into two areas: the harsher, wilder Dark Peak to the north, and the more pastoral, 'prettier' White Peak to the south. Both areas are limestone but the higher Dark Peak moorlands are on coarse gritstone, while the green fields of the White Peak are patterned with dry-stone walls, much like Ireland, and divided by deep-cut dales.

INFORMATION

There are TICs or National Park Information Offices in Bakewell, Castleton, Edale and other locations. Information for disabled visitors is available by calling ☎ 01629-816200. The Ordnance Survey (OS) *Peak District* map (1:63,360) will be adequate for most users, but there are also separate maps of the White and Dark Peaks.

Pick up a copy of the free *Peak District* from TICs. It lists all sorts of walks guided by National Park rangers.

There are several useful Web sites that can provide you with information on the park. These include www.peakland.com, www.peakdistrict-npa.gov.uk and www.cressbrook.co.uk.

PEAK DISTRICT NATIONAL PARK

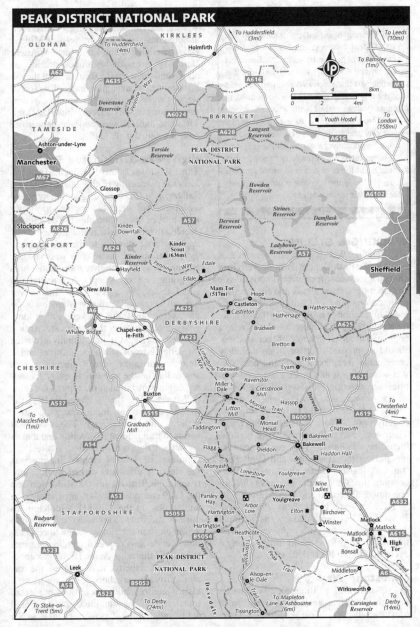

Well-Dressed Derbyshire

Well dressing is an ancient tradition in the Peak District that was condemned as water worship or paganism by early Christians, but was revived 650 years ago in Tissington. It is a unique art that involves decorating the wells of the region with pictures formed from living plants. Villagers start with a board, which they throw into a pond to soak for days, fill with clay and then use to create the picture using wood, flowers, berries and seeds. Well dressings take place from May to September throughout the area and in some villages it is possible to see the dressing in progress. Contact the TICs for the dates.

WALKING & CYCLING

The Pennine Way has its southern end at Edale in the Peak District. See the Activities chapter for more information on this classic British long-distance walk and for essential preparations and precautions. There are many other shorter walks within the park but those intending to explore the Dark Peak or engage in the local practice of 'bog trotting' should be prepared for the often viciously changeable weather; a map and compass, wet-weather gear and emergency food supplies are essential. TICs stock the handy *Walks Around...* and *Walks About...* guides.

The High Peak and Tissington trails are equally popular with walkers and cyclists. There are several Peak cycle hire centres, including the Parsley Hay centre near the junction of the Tissington and High Peak trails. A leaflet details the centres, their opening times and rental charges (£9/6 for one day, £20 deposit and ID required).

TICs also stock the *Peak Park Cycle Route* booklets produced by the national park authorities. Email **e** cyclehire@peakdistrict.org for general information on cycle hire in the Peak District.

Limestone Way

The 26-mile (42km) Limestone Way winds through the White Peak from Castleton to Matlock via Peak Forest, Miller's Dale, Taddington, Flagg, Monyash, Youlgreave, Winster and Bonsall. There are youth hostels at both ends and at Ravenstor (near Miller's Dale), Youlgreave and Elton (near Winster). Camping barns and grounds are dotted about, and there are B&Bs in most of the villages as well as an ample supply of pubs. The walk is signposted with fingerposts, yellow arrows and the walk's Derbyshire Ram logo. TICs and the Bakewell national park office have a detailed walk leaflet.

High Peak & Tissington Trails

The 17½-mile (28km) High Peak Trail follows the pioneering **High Peak & Cromford Railway line**. This was originally envisaged as a canal but when the engineering problems proved insurmountable the developers decided to build a railway line instead. They applied canal thinking to the new technology, labelling the stations as wharves and ending up with a line that surmounted hills by going up them steeply, like a flight of canal locks. As a result the line never worked very well; railway engineers soon discovered that trains worked best on long, gentle inclines rather than short, steep ones. Opened in 1830, the line actually predated the general use of steam locomotives and at first the carriages were hauled by horses and pulled up the steep inclines by stationary engines installed at the tops of the hills.

When the line finally closed in 1967 the tracks were torn up and it was made into a walking and cycling track. The wide, well surfaced trail is ideal for cycling and makes a pleasant day out in rolling White Peak country. The 1-in-14 Hopton Incline was the steepest gradient worked by locomotives in the British Isles. At Middleton Top the 1829 steam winding engine that used to haul trains up the 1-in-8¾ Middleton Incline is still in working order and jolts into action on summer Sundays. The Sheep Pasture Incline also required winding engines to haul the trains up. At the High Peak Junction at the southern end of the trail, the former railway workshop is now used as a visitor centre and museum. Goods were transferred to boats on the Cromford Canal at this point. Later it took trains up to seven hours to cover the distance a cyclist can ride in just a couple.

The 13-mile (21km) Tissington Trail was a much later railway line, opened in 1899, but it never proved economically feasible and, like the High Peak Line, was closed in 1967. The two trails meet just south of Parsley Hay and continue farther north, although not all the way to Buxton.

Bicycles can be hired on the trails at Parsley Hay (☎ 01298-84493), at Middleton Top (☎ 01629-823204), towards the southern end of the High Peak Trail, or at Ashbourne (☎ 01335-343156), at the southern end of the Tissington Trail. If you've got time it's a pleasant 40-mile (64km) round trip from Parsley Hay down the High Peak Trail and up the Tissington Trail, linking the two trails by the B5053 from Matlock Bath to Ashbourne. The B5053 section undulates a lot so make sure you allow plenty of time.

Monsal Trail

Like the High Peak and Tissington trails, the Monsal Trail, along the deep valley of the River Wye, follows a disused railway line. It's used by walkers more than cyclists (unlike the other two).

The 8½-mile (14km) trail starts from the Coombs Rd Viaduct, just east of Bakewell, but there's no view of the viaduct from the trail. You can also walk from Rowsley on the A6 to the beginning of the trail. The old train station at Hassop near Bakewell has been converted into the Country Bookstore. At Monsal Head there's a pub, B&B and a superb view of the **Monsal Viaduct**, a man-made wonder of the Peak District and the subject of considerable controversy when it was first built. **Cressbrook Mill** opened as a water-powered cotton mill in 1783 and continued in operation, powered by steam, from 1890 until 1965. **Litton Mill** opened in 1782 and was infamous for its owner's exploitation of child labourers. Walking west, the final tunnel requires what can be a very muddy, slippery and wet detour. The trail ends at Blackwell Mill Junction, a short walk from the A6, 3 miles (5km) east of Buxton.

Other Walks

The Peak District is crisscrossed with good walks and the TICs are packed with information. Castleton and Bakewell in the White Peak make particularly good centres for short walks. From Edale you can walk in either direction: north to the Dark Peak and nearby Kinder Scout, or south towards Castleton. Hayfield is another good starting point for walks into the Dark Peak.

OTHER ACTIVITIES

The Peak District limestone is riddled with caves including 'showcaves' open to the public in Castleton, Buxton and Matlock Bath. For information on caving trips and courses contact Derbyshire Caving Association (☎ 01629-534775). *The Caves of Derbyshire* by TD Ford has extensive information on the county's caves.

The Peak District has been a training ground for some of England's best-known mountaineers, and cliff faces such as High Tor, overlooking Matlock Bath, are still popular. Jumping off the cliff faces on hanggliders is also popular. Pony treks can offer a less exerting way to explore the area and Ladybooth Trekking Centre (☎ 01433-670205) is conveniently located in Edale. Fishing on most Peak District rivers is private.

There are a host of companies specialising in adventure activities. Look out for the *Peak Pursuits* brochure for the full story. Derwent Pursuits (☎ 01629-824179), Mill Lane, Cromford, has a solid reputation for organising abseiling, caving, climbing and gorge scrambling.

PLACES TO STAY

Walkers may appreciate the ***camping barns*** *(☎ 01629-825850)* that offer a roof over your head for a nightly cost from £3.50 per person. A leaflet shows the locations of the barns and explains how to book a place. Another brochure details camp sites in and around the Peak District.

There is an impressive concentration of youth hostels in and around the park offering more than a thousand beds all said. Those most popular include Bakewell, Castleton, Edale, Eyam and Hartington.

THE MIDLANDS

There is no shortage of B&Bs and farmhouse accommodation throughout the park, and for those who prefer day-trips, Buxton, Nottingham and Sheffield all make good bases.

GETTING THERE & AWAY

The Peak District authorities are trying hard to wean visitors off their cars, and TICs stock the excellent *Peak District Timetable* covering all local bus and train services.

There are train services from Derby to Matlock, at the southern edge of the Peak District, or from Sheffield across the northern part of the district through Edale to New Mills and on to Manchester. There's also a Manchester-New Mills-Buxton service.

The convenient TransPeak (☎ 0870 608 2608) TP bus operates right across the Peak District, linking Nottingham, Derby, Matlock, Bakewell, Buxton, New Mills and Manchester (3½ hours) daily; Matlock to Buxton takes about an hour. Yorkshire Traction has services from Barnsley into the district from the north and down to Castleton and Buxton. The No X67 is a handy service that links Manchester and Chesterfield via Eyam and Tideswell three times a day.

A Derbyshire Wayfarer ticket costs £7.25 (including one child or dog), £12 for a family, for one day's unlimited travel on most train and bus services into and around the Peak District. An Explorer ticket also gives you all-day travel on Trent and Barton buses including the TransPeak TP service. It costs £5 and includes one child. The Busline information service can be contacted on ☎ 01298-23098.

Visitors coming from or continuing on to Manchester can purchase a Manchester Wayfarer (☎ 0161-228 7811) ticket that covers trains as well as certain bus routes in the Peak District. It costs £6.60/3.30 or £10 for the weekend.

BAKEWELL
☎ 01629 • pop 3900

Famous more for its Mr Kipling tarts than the original puddings, this picture-postcard village is the largest population centre

Which Bakewell Pudding?

Bakewell blundered into the cookbooks around 1860 when a cook at the Rutland Arms Hotel misread the strawberry tart recipe and spread the egg mixture on top of the jam instead of stirring it into the pastry, thus creating the Bakewell pudding (pudding mark you, not tart). It features regularly on local dessert menus and is certainly worth sampling.

Bakewell establishments are locked in battle over whose is the original recipe, a dispute so serious it may finally be settled by the European Court in Brussels. Bloomers (☎ 813724), Water St, insists it created 'the first and only Bakewell puddings' and swiftly converted its name to a registered trademark. But the Old Original Bakewell Pudding Shop (☎ 812193) is adamant that its recipe is older, and it pulls more trade thanks to its position on the main thoroughfare.

In a blind tasting, this author preferred Bloomers' version. The pastry was thicker, and the egg mixture less heavy. It was also slightly cheaper.

within the Peak District National Park boundaries and a notorious traffic bottleneck on summer weekends. It is a handsome village and has the best range of facilities of anywhere in the area.

Information

The TIC (☎ 813227, fax 816201), Bridge St, in the 17th-century Market Hall, has an informative display about the national park. It opens 9.15 am to 5.30 pm daily, April to September and 10 am to 5 pm daily, October to March. Bakewell Bicycle Hire (☎ 814004, ⓔ adrianboyes@dial.pipex .com), Station Yard, rents out mountain bikes. There's a lively local market on Monday.

Things to See

All Saints Church has Norman features and a fine octagonal spire. There's a Saxon cross from around AD 800 in the graveyard.

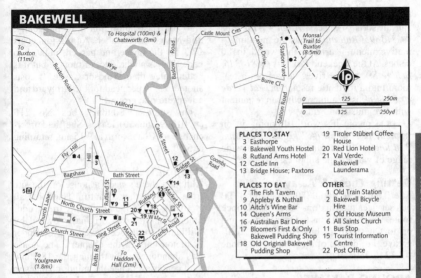

BAKEWELL

To Hospital (100m) &
Chatsworth (3mi)

Castle Mount Cres

Monsal
Trail to
Buxton
(8.5mi)

To
Buxton
(11mi)

Buxton Road

Wye

Milford

Castle Street

Fly Hill

Bagshaw

Bath Street

Rutland St

Bridge St

Coombes
Road

Baslow Road

Castle Drive

Station Yard

Burre Cl

Station Road

0   125   250m
0   125   250yd

PLACES TO STAY		
3 Easthorpe	19 Tiroler Stüberl Coffee	
4 Bakewell Youth Hostel	House	
8 Rutland Arms Hotel	20 Red Lion Hotel	
12 Castle Inn	21 Val Verde;	
13 Bridge House; Paxtons	Bakewell	
	Launderama	

PLACES TO EAT	OTHER
7 The Fish Tavern	1 Old Train Station
9 Appleby & Nuthall	2 Bakewell Bicycle
10 Aitch's Wine Bar	Hire
14 Queen's Arms	5 Old House Museum
16 Australian Bar Diner	6 All Saints Church
17 Bloomers First & Only	11 Bus Stop
Bakewell Pudding Shop	15 Tourist Information
18 Old Original Bakewell	Centre
Pudding Shop	22 Post Office

North Church Street
South Church Street
Church Lane

To
Youlgreave
(1.8mi)

Butts Rd

King Street

Matlock St

Granby Road

Water St

Market St

Rutland

To
Haddon
Hall (2mi)

THE MIDLANDS

The **Old House Museum**, in Cunningham Place near the church, has a local collection housed in a building dating from 1534 but it only opens 2 to 5 pm April to October. Admission costs £2.50/1.

The pretty five-arched **bridge** over the River Wye dates from medieval times. The popular **Monsal Trail** walking and cycling track (see earlier in the chapter), which follows a disused railway line, starts just outside Bakewell, but there are many other good walking routes around the village, including trails to Magpie Mine, Haddon Hall and Chatsworth House.

Places to Stay
Hostels *Bakewell Youth Hostel* (☎/fax 812313, e bakewell@yha.org.uk, Fly Hill) costs £9/6.20 for adults/juniors. It opens daily except Sunday, April to October, Friday and Saturday only the rest of the year.

B&Bs & Hotels *Bridge House* (☎/fax 812867, Bridge St) is not just a fine building, but a fine location and charges from £17.50 per head for a room and continental breakfast, from £20 with full English breakfast. The historic *Castle Inn* (☎ 812103, fax 814830, Castle St) charges £39.50 for rooms accommodating up to four people, good value for those that like it cosy.

Buxton Rd is home to several B&Bs, including Gothic *Easthorpe* (☎ 814929) with bed and breakfast from £23 per person.

The accidentally gastronomically pioneering *Rutland Arms Hotel* (☎ 812812, fax 812309, e rutland@bakewell.demon.co.uk) – see the boxed text 'Which Bakewell Pudding?' – is a fine establishment right on the main square in town, with singles/doubles from £47/79. Front rooms can be a bit noisy.

Places to Eat
Bakewell has lots of tea and coffee shops, most invoking the name of England's most famous tart. The most imaginative is the *Tiroler Stüberl Coffee House* (☎ 813899, Wye Cottage, Water St), a sort of Austrian tearoom attached to *Bloomers First & Only Bakewell Pudding Shop*.

The *Red Lion* and the *Queen's Arms* serve standard pub food; the food at the *Castle* is especially good. *The Fish Tavern* is the place to be for fish and chips.

There are also a few restaurants. In Granby Rd, the *Australian Bar Diner*

(☎ *814909)* has roast meals for around £5 and all sorts of snacks. ***Aitch's Wine Bar*** *(☎ 813895, Rutland St)* has the most imaginative menu – around the world in 80 dishes. At the weekend ***Paxtons*** *(☎ 814336, Bridge St)*, by the river, turns from a tearoom into a romantic restaurant. ***Val Verde*** *(☎ 814404)* is an authentic Italian restaurant with live music on Friday.

For a picnic it's worth dropping in on ***Appleby & Nuthall*** *(☎ 812699, 3 Rutland Buildings, Buxton Rd)*, which has a wide range of wholesome supplies.

Getting There & Away

The TransPeak (☎ 0870 608 2608) TP bus services the Buxton-Bakewell-Matlock route. Bus No 170 runs to Over Haddon and on to Chesterfield, bus No 171 to Youlgreave. For details of all local buses phone ☎ 01246-250450.

AROUND BAKEWELL
Chatsworth

More than two-thirds of sumptuous Chatsworth (☎ 01246-582204), the 'Palace of the Peak', is still occupied by the duke of Devonshire's family.

The original Elizabethan house was started in 1551 by the inimitable Bess of Hardwick (see Hardwick Hall under Around Chesterfield earlier in the chapter) and her second husband. Mary Queen of Scots was imprisoned here several times between 1570 and 1581 at the behest of her cousin Elizabeth I. Mary's jailer, the earl of Shrewsbury, was Bess' fourth husband but her suspicion that the 'knave, fool and beast' was rather more than just a jailer led to their separation. The house was extensively altered between 1686 and 1707 and then enlarged in the 1820s.

The amazing Baroque ceiling paintings are among the house's prime attractions but all the rooms are a treasure-trove of splendid furniture and magnificent artworks.

The house is surrounded by 40 hectares of gardens, beyond which stretch another 400 hectares of parkland landscaped by Capability Brown.

Chatsworth is about 3 miles (5km) north-east of Bakewell. The house opens 11 am to 5.30 pm (last admission 4.30 pm) daily, mid-March to October. Admission costs £7/3 for the house and garden, plus £1 to park. This is a whole lot of money, but it is better value than Windsor Castle. It costs another £3.50 per head for the **farmyard and adventure playground**.

On summer Sundays bus No 210 (☎ 01709-566360) leaves Sheffield Interchange for Chatsworth at 9.15 am, returning at 5.40 pm.

Haddon Hall

Although there's been a house on the site from much earlier, beautiful Haddon Hall (☎ 01629-812855) dates mainly from Tudor times. The site was originally owned by William Peveril (see Peveril Castle under Castleton later in the chapter). The house was abandoned right through the 18th and 19th centuries, hence the minor changes in that period. Highlights include the 14th-century chapel and the medieval kitchens and great hall. Visitor numbers have risen significantly since some scenes from the 1998 film *Elizabeth* were shot here.

Outside, terraced gardens step down to the River Wye near an old stone packhorse bridge. The house is 2 miles (3km) south-east of Bakewell on the A6, offering straightforward bus connections, and opens 10.30 am to 5 pm daily, April to September. Admission costs £5.75/3.

TIDESWELL
☎ 01298

The huge church at Tideswell is sometimes described as the 'cathedral of the Peaks' and is worth visiting to see its brasses, woodwork and fine ceilings.

Ravenstor Youth Hostel *(☎ 871826, fax 871275,* **e** *ravenstor@yha.org.uk, Miller's Dale)* is located in a charming National Trust property near Litton Mill, about 1½ miles (2.5km) south of Tideswell. It only opens during school holidays. Beds cost £10.85/7.40 for adults/juniors.

Poppies *(☎ 871083,* **e** *poptidza@ dialstart.net, Bank Square)* has B&B (closed January) from £17.50, but the tearoom is no longer operating. The *George Hotel* (☎ *871382, Commercial Rd*), beside the church, does good pub food and has rooms from around £25 per person.

The No X67 runs to Manchester (1½ hours) and Chesterfield (30 minutes) three times a day.

EYAM
☎ 01433 • pop 900

The small village of Eyam (ee-em) is famous for all the wrong reasons. A dark shadow fell across the village in 1665, when a consignment of cloth from London delivered to a local tailor brought with it the Black Death. As the dreaded disease spread through Eyam, the village rector, William Mompesson, convinced the villagers that rather than risk spreading it to other villages Eyam should quarantine itself. By the time the plague burnt itself out in late 1666, more than 250 of the village's 350-strong population were dead, including the rector's wife. The *Eyam History Trail* details all the sites associated with the plague.

The **Church of St Lawrence** dates from Saxon times and has many reminders of the events of 1665 and 1666, including a cupboard said to have been made from the wooden box that carried the infected cloth to Eyam. The plague register records the names of those who died during the outbreak. The church also has a leaflet describing some of the monuments and headstones in the churchyard, which has an 8th-century **Celtic cross**, one of the finest in the country. Many of the plague victims were buried in the churchyard but apart from that of Catherine Mompesson, the rector's wife, only one other headstone relating to the plague has survived. Other victims were buried around the village – at the Riley graves, Mrs Hancock buried all seven members of her family one by one.

Next to Eyam's church are the **plague cottages** where the tailor lived. A walk up Water Lane from the village square, or a drive towards Grindleford from Hawkhill Rd, will bring you to **Mompesson's Well**. Food and other supplies were left here by friends from other villages. Back in Eyam,

the 17th-century **Eyam Hall** (☎ 631976) has some impressive tapestries and opens 11 am to 4 pm Wednesday, Thursday and Sunday, Easter to October. Admission costs £4/3.

Places to Stay & Eat
Eyam Youth Hostel (☎ *630335, fax 639202,* e *eyam@yha.org.uk, Hawkhill Rd*) charges £10.85/7.40 for adults/juniors and has 60 beds. *Bretton Youth Hostel* (☎/fax *631856*) is a much smaller place, about one mile north-west of Eyam in the village of Bretton. Beds cost £8.10/5.65 for adults/juniors. *Delf View House* (☎ *631533, Church St*) offers courteous, comfortable B&B in a Georgian house with singles for £25/35 and en-suite doubles for £32 per person.

The *Eyam Tearooms* offers the quintessential cream tea, but can get very busy at the weekend. The *Miner's Arms* (☎ *630853, Water Lane*), overlooking the square, which dates from 1630, turns out good sandwiches and refreshing beers.

Getting There & Away
The bus No X67 runs to Manchester (1½ hours) via Tideswell and to Chesterfield (30 minutes) three times a day. There are also daily buses from Tideswell to Eyam (No 65/66).

CASTLETON
☎ 01433 • pop 900

This tiny village, often referred to as the 'gem of the peaks', is overshadowed by 517m-high (1696 feet) Mam Tor. It is a popular base for exploring the Peaks and features several cave complexes, as well as a ruined castle that gave the town its name. It's also the northern terminus of the Limestone Way. Mam Tor is the boundary between the limestone of the White Peak and the gritstone of the Dark Peak.

Orientation & Information
Castleton nestles at the western end of the Hope Valley. Mam Tor's unstable condition undermined the A625 road through Castleton and it's now bypassed by the spectacular Winnats Pass road, which goes through a steep-sided dale. This is some road to

descend on a bicycle, if traffic is light. Castle St is home to the church, pubs, B&Bs and the youth hostel.

The National Park Information Centre (☎ 620679), Castle St, opens 10 am to 5.30 pm daily, Easter to October; weekends only in winter.

Peveril Castle

Castleton is overlooked by the ruins of Peveril Castle (☎ 620613; EH), built by William Peveril, son of William the Conqueror. The keep, which is about all that remains, was added by Henry II in 1176. From the castle, which sits more or less on top of Peak Cavern, there are superb views north to Mam Tor and the Dark Peak, and south over pretty Cave Dale, directly behind the castle. It opens 10 am to 6 pm daily (5 pm in winter). Admission costs £2.20/1.10.

Caves

The area around Castleton is riddled with caves, four of which are open to the public. Although most of them are natural, the area has also been extensively mined for Blue John, a reddish-pink form of fluorspar, as well as lead, silver and other minerals. Miners often broke into natural chambers during the course of their excavations.

The **Peak Cavern** (☎ 620285), popularly known as the Devil's Arse, is reached by a pretty stream-side walk from the village centre. Unfortunately the ugly wall erected to stop you sneaking a free peek into the yawning 18m-by-30m chasm detracts from the natural beauty. Rope was made here until 1974 and rope-makers' houses used to stand just inside the cave entrance. The cave opens 10 am to 4 pm daily, Easter to October; weekends only in winter. Admission costs £4.75/2.75.

The small, stalactite-filled **Treak Cliff Cavern** (☎ 620571) has a healthy share of Blue John and opens 10 am to 5.30 pm (to 4 pm November to February). Admission costs £5/3. Check out the Web site www .bluejohnstone.com for more information.

Speedwell Cavern (☎ 620512) boasts a long, artificially flooded tunnel along which you travel by electric boat to the 'bottomless'

pit at the end; before electrification the boatman would propel the boat along the tunnel by 'walking' it with his feet on the tunnel roof. It opens 10 am to 4.30 pm daily and costs £5.25/3.25. Visit www.speedwellcavern .co.uk on the Web for more information.

On the other side of the closed section of road by Mam Tor is the impressive **Blue John Cavern** (☎ 620638) where it's thought that Blue John may have been mined in Roman times. One of the cave's chambers has a collection of 19th-century mining equipment. It opens 9.45 am to 5 pm (dusk in winter) daily and admission costs £6/3.

Experienced potholers can explore other caves, including the **Odin Mine** below Mam Tor, and the **Suicide Cave** and **Old Tor Mine** on Winnats Pass. The remains of prehistoric animals have been found in **Windy Knoll Cave**.

Walking

The 26-mile (42km) Limestone Way starts at the narrow, rocky entrance into beautiful Cave Dale behind the castle.

There are many other excellent walks around Castleton. A fine day walk (see the Castleton & Edale map) of about 7 miles (11km) can be taken by going south along the Cave Dale track to a road, where you turn right, and right again to pass by Rowter Farm and meet the Buxton road just beyond Winnats Pass. The route then climbs up to Mam Tor where ditches marking a pre-Roman fort can be distinguished on the top. The trail follows the ridge to Back Tor, but just before reaching that high point there's a path down from the ridge directly into Castleton along Hollowford Lane and Mill Bridge. Another pleasant day walk makes a 7-mile (11km) round trip via Edale, starting point of the Pennine Way.

Places to Stay

Large and impressive *Castleton Youth Hostel* (☎ 620235, fax 621767, e castleton@ yha.org.uk, Castle St), across from the church, costs £10.85/7.40 for adults/juniors.

Just outside Castleton back towards the village of Hope is *Pindale Farm Outdoor Centre* (☎ 620111, e pindalefarm@

tingonline.uk, Pindale Lane, near Hope)
with a whole host of cheap accommodation.
Camping is £3.50 per person including access to the showers. Beds in the bunkhouses
are from £5 to £7, while conventional B&B
in the farmhouse starts at £20 per person.
There's something for everyone basically.

Of the B&Bs, handsome *Cryer House*
*(☎/fax 620244, ℮ fleeskel@aol.com, Castle
St)*, near the youth hostel, charges from £21
– there is a highly popular tearoom downstairs. *Rambler's Rest (☎ 620125, Mill
Bridge)*, set in a 17th-century cottage,
charges from £17.50 or £22 en suite. *Bargate
Cottage (☎ 620201, fax 621739, Market
Place)* is full of character. You'll pay from
£21.50, or £23.50 with a four-poster bed, and
be prepared for convivial breakfasts.

The slightly pricier *Swiss House Hotel
(☎ 621098, How Lane)*, on the main road on
the Hope side of the village, offers pleasant
rooms with bathroom for £35/45 a single
/double. If you want to splash out, *Castle
Hotel (☎ 620578, Castle St)* has rooms with
four-poster beds and Jacuzzis for £65 during the week.

Places to Eat

Castleton is a popular place for a cream tea.
Hilary Beth's Tea Room, in Market Place,
and *Rose Cottage Cafe (☎ 620472, Cross
St)*, beside the Blue John Craft Shop, are
two places that prepare the works.

The pubs are the most obvious places to
eat. Castle Hotel has the best selection of
standard fare. *Ye Olde Cheshire Cheese
(☎ 620330, How Lane)* is a traditional pub

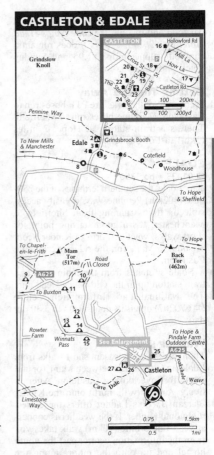

THE MIDLANDS

CASTLETON & EDALE

PLACES TO STAY		24	Bargate Cottage;		12	Treak Cliff Cavern
2	Cooper's Camp		Hilary Beth's Tea Room		13	Old Tor Mine
3	Stonecroft	25	Swiss House Hotel		14	Suicide Cave
4	Rambler Inn				15	Speedwell Cavern
6	Stables Bunkhouse	**OTHER**			17	Ye Olde Chehsire Cheese
	Barn	1	Old Nag's Head		18	Rose Cottage Cafe;
7	Edale Youth Hostel	5	National Park Information			Ye Olde Nag's Head Hotel;
16	Rambler's Rest		Centre; Fieldhead Camp site			Blue John Craft Shop
20	Castle Hotel	8	Edale Train Station		19	National Park Information Centre
21	Cryer House	9	Windy Knoll Cave		23	Church
22	Castleton Youth	10	Odin Mine		26	Peveril Castle
	Hostel	11	Blue John Cavern		27	Peak Cavern

on the Hope side of the village with good bar food and real ale. *Ye Olde Nag's Head Hotel (☎ 620248, Cross St)* does romantic candlelit suppers for £17.95 and Sunday lunches for £12.95.

Getting There & Away
Trent and South Yorkshire PTE buses run to Castleton. Mainline buses run to Sheffield. There's a train station at Hope, 2 miles (3km) east of Castleton.

EDALE
☎ 01433 • pop 350

Tiny Edale, the southern terminus of the 250-mile (402km) Pennine Way, is easily accessible on trains running from Sheffield to Manchester. It's a good starting point for short walks, whether north to Kinder Scout or south to Mam Tor, the ridge overlooking Castleton.

Edale stretches from the main road and train station up to the Old Nag's Head pub. The National Park Information Centre (☎ 670207) opens its doors 9 am to 5.30 pm daily.

Walking
There are several pleasant short walks from Edale up to the ridge between Mam Tor and Back Tor, overlooking Castleton. Alternatively you can walk north onto the Kinder Plateau; Jacob's Ladder offers the easiest route onto Kinder. If the weather is cooperative, a fine 6-mile (10km) walk takes you from the information centre, past the youth hostel and up onto the moors along the southern edge of Kinder before dropping back down to Edale.

Places to Stay & Eat
The small *Fieldhead Camp Site (☎ 670386)* charges £3.25 per person and is right by the information centre. Showers cost 50p and the charge for cars is £1.20. To the north of the village, *Cooper's Camp (☎ 670372)* charges £2.75 per person and 50p for cars. Just outside Edale is the *Stables Bunkhouse Barn (☎ 670235, Ollerbrook Farm)*, which offers 16 bunks spread throughout four rooms for £8 per person.

Linen is provided, but you need your own sleeping bag.

Edale Youth Hostel (☎ 670302, fax 670243, e edale@yha.org.uk, Rowland Cote, Nether Booth) lies about 2 miles (3km) east of the village and charges £10.85/7.40 for adults/juniors.

B&B for £32/52 is available at the *Rambler Inn (☎ 670268, Lane Head Green)*, a popular pub right by the train station. *Stonecroft (☎ 670262)*, beyond the information centre and church, has B&B from £26 per person.

The *Old Nag's Head (☎ 670291, Grindsbrook Booth)* – official starting point of the Pennine Way – and the *Rambler Inn* serve reasonable pub grub. *Cooper's Camp* has a small shop for provisions.

HAYFIELD
Hayfield is famous as the starting point of the 1932 'trespass' on Kinder Scout when people from northern England clashed with gamekeepers over the right to walk through open country. In good weather an excellent 7-mile (11km) walk proceeds east from Hayfield, climbing to the 636m-high (2088 feet) summit of Kinder Scout. Summit is somewhat of a misnomer as there's little difference between the high point and the rest of the Kinder Plateau. From the top, the trail runs north to the Kinder Downfall along the western edge of the Moorland Plateau. It then turns east, still following the plateau edge, before dropping steeply and turning south to Kinder Reservoir near Hayfield.

BUXTON
☎ 01298 • pop 19,500

Buxton has a genteel air to it and is frequently compared to Bath; it even has its own natural spring discovered by the Romans in AD 78. Buxton's heyday was in the 18th century when there were seven sets of baths about town. By the 1950s all of these had closed and, despite all the New Age shops around town, it seems unlikely they will reopen. The town is actually outside the Peak District National Park boundaries, but with its cosmopolitan atmosphere, it makes a fine base for visiting the area.

Orientation & Information

Buses drop off in the Market Place where most of Buxton's eating choices can be found. Those arriving by train will find themselves near pedestrianised Spring Gardens and the Spring Gardens shopping centre. The TIC (☎ 25106, fax 73153, ℯ tourism@highpeak.gov.uk) is beside the Crescent. It opens 9.30 am to 5 pm daily. The Opera House (☎ 72190) is the focus for the annual mid- to late-July Buxton Festival.

Things to See & Do

Renovation of the graceful **Crescent** (1784–88), which was modelled on the Royal Crescent in Bath, is well under way, although no obvious new use has been found for the building as yet. Across from it, the **Pump Room**, which dispensed Buxton's spring water for nearly a century, now hosts temporary art exhibitions. Fill your water bottle with delicious warm mineral water from **St Ann's Well**, next to the Pump Room.

Across the road, the TIC is housed in the old **Natural Mineral Baths** building where

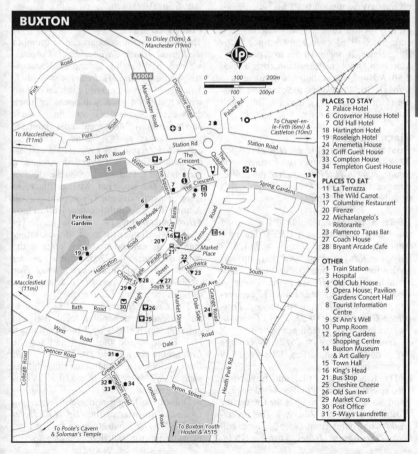

BUXTON

To Disley (10mi) &
Manchester (19mi)

A5004

To Macclesfield
(11mi)

To Chapel-en-le-Firth (6mi) &
Castleton (10mi)

To Macclesfield
(11mi)

To Poole's Cavern
& Soloman's Temple

To Buxton Youth
Hostel & A515

PLACES TO STAY
2 Palace Hotel
6 Grosvenor House Hotel
7 Old Hall Hotel
18 Hartington Hotel
19 Roseleigh Hotel
24 Arnemetia House
32 Griff Guest House
33 Compton House
34 Templeton Guest House

PLACES TO EAT
11 La Terrazza
13 The Wild Carrot
17 Columbine Restaurant
20 Firenze
22 Michaelangelo's
    Ristorante
23 Flamenco Tapas Bar
27 Coach House
28 Bryant Arcade Cafe

OTHER
1 Train Station
3 Hospital
4 Old Club House
5 Opera House; Pavilion
    Gardens Concert Hall
8 Tourist Information
    Centre
9 St Ann's Well
10 Pump Room
12 Spring Gardens
    Shopping Centre
14 Buxton Museum
    & Art Gallery
15 Town Hall
16 King's Head
21 Bus Stop
25 Cheshire Cheese
26 Old Sun Inn
29 Market Cross
30 Post Office
31 5-Ways Laundrette

you can still see the spa water source; a side room tells the full story. On the corner of The Square and The Crescent is the **Old Hall Hotel** where Mary Queen of Scots stayed while visiting to take the waters; the hotel was rebuilt a century later in 1670.

Buxton's fine **Opera House** opened in 1903 and stands in a corner of Pavilion Gardens. Behind it is the glassy **Pavilion** of 1871 and the **Pavilion Gardens Concert Hall** of 1876. The **Buxton Museum & Art Gallery**, in Terrace Rd, round the corner from the town hall, opens 9.30 am to 5.30 pm Tuesday to Friday, to 5 pm Saturday and from 10.30 am on Sunday. Admission costs £1/50p.

Poole's Cavern (☎ 26978), less than a mile from the centre, is a stalactite- and stalagmite-filled cave known since Neolithic times. It opens 10 am to 5 pm daily, March to October. Admission costs £4.75/ 2.50. A 20-minute walk leads from the cave through Grin Low Wood to **Solomon's Temple** (Grin Low Tower), an 1896 folly with fine views over the town.

Places to Stay
Hostels **Buxton Youth Hostel** (☎/fax 22287, e buxton@yha.org.uk, Sherbrook Lodge, Harpur Hill Rd), south of the centre, charges £8.10/5.65 for adults/juniors. It's usually closed on Sunday.

B&Bs & Hotels Compton Rd is a good place to look for cheaper B&Bs. The gastronomic **Griff Guest House** (☎ 23628, 2 Compton Rd) is owned by a chef, and has rooms for £18 per person. Next door, comfortable **Compton House** (☎/fax 26926, 4 Compton Rd) offers beds from £17 per person and can arrange dinner on request. **Templeton Guest House** (☎ 25275, 13 Compton Rd) charges from £18.50 per person.

Arnemetia House (☎ 26125, 14 Grange Rd) is delightful and offers B&B from £19 per person.

The Broadwalk, a pleasant, traffic-free road overlooking the Pavilion Gardens, is a good place to stay. First up is the **Grosvenor House Hotel** (☎/fax 72439, 1 The Broadwalk) with rooms from £45/50. The excellent **Hartington Hotel** (☎/fax 22638,

e harthot@globalnet.co.uk, 18 The Broadwalk) has a very pleasant location and charges from £50/70. The nonsmoking **Roseleigh Hotel** (☎/fax 24904, e enquiries@ roseleighhotel.co.uk, 19 The Broadwalk) has rooms from just £32/44, some with nice views of the lake.

The historic **Old Hall Hotel** (☎ 22841, fax 72437, The Square), which overlooks the Pavilion Gardens and Opera House, charges £62/90. Buxton's finest beds are found in the **Palace Hotel** (☎ 22001, Palace Rd), which boasts an indoor swimming pool – well, it would have to be really. Rooms start from £99/114.

Places to Eat
The cheapest serious meals can be found in the **Bryant Arcade Café** (off Eagle Parade), where a roast lunch is around £4. Vegetarians should try **The Wild Carrot** (☎ 22843, 5 Bridge St), an excellent health food store with a restaurant upstairs. It opens for lunch daily except Sunday, and for dinner Thursday to Saturday. Most meals cost about £5.

La Terrazza (☎ 72364, Unit 11, Cavendish Arcade, The Crescent) is a pleasant cafe upstairs in Cavendish Arcade, a tiled building that used to house the hot baths on The Crescent. Market Place, in front of the town hall, has several places. Among the possibilities are **Michaelangelo's Ristorante** (☎ 26640, 1 Market Place), which goes for meaty dishes, rather than the pizzas and pastas on offer at the popular **Firenze** (☎ 72203, 3 Eagle Parade) across the road. **Flamenco Tapas Bar** (☎ 27392, 7–9 Concert Place) has a range of tapas for around £2.50 each.

The **Coach House** (☎ 71393, 3 Scarsdale Place) is a popular local fish and chippie, which closes by 7 pm. Turn down Hall Bank behind the town hall for the **Columbine Restaurant** (☎ 78752, 7 Hall Bank), which offers traditional English fare, such as Aylesbury duck, for £10.95 in intimate surroundings.

One of the longer and more interesting menus is on offer at the **Old Hall Hotel** (☎ 22841, The Square) where you can get everything from stuffed potatoes to full meals. There's a good choice for vegetarians too. Pre-theatre set meals (for those going on to the Opera House) cost £15.25.

Popular pubs include the ***King's Head*** (☎ 27719, *Market Place*), right beside the town hall, and the ***Old Club House*** *(Water St)*, just across from the Opera House. Down towards the southern end of the High St, the cosy ***Old Sun Inn*** is full of beams and character, and has a small outdoor area at the front. The nearby ***Cheshire Cheese*** (☎ 73135, *37–39 High St)* serves smooth Kimberley's Ales, possibly the farthest west this great Nottinghamshire beer is found.

Getting There & Away

Trains run from Buxton to Manchester (£4.60) via New Mills. Change at New Mills to get to Sheffield via Edale.

The TransPeak (☎ 0870 608 2608) TP bus service between Nottingham and Manchester stops by Market Place. There are also daily buses to Stoke-on-Trent, Bakewell and Chesterfield, as well as three buses a week to Tideswell and Castleton.

AROUND BUXTON
Lyme Park

For those who saw the popular BBC serialisation of *Pride and Prejudice*, Lyme Park (☎ 01663-762319; NT), at Disley, 9 miles (14km) north-west of Buxton, will forever be the site of the lake at Pemberley where Colin Firth (aka Mr Darcy) went bathing. The 18th-century Venetian-style exterior of this Italianate palace conceals a partially Elizabethan core.

The house opens 1 to 5 pm daily, except Wednesday and Thursday, April to October, although the park keeps longer hours. Admission costs £4.50/2.25 and £3.50 for a car.

DOVEDALE

The steep-sided valley of the **River Dove** is one of the most beautiful – and so most crowded – of the Derbyshire Dales. The river flows beneath natural features like Thorpe Cloud, Dovedale Castle, Lovers' Leap, the Twelve Apostles, Tissington Spires, Reynard's Kitchen and Ilam Rock. **Beresford Dale**, upstream from Dovedale,

was a favourite haunt of Izaak Walton, author of *The Compleat Angler*. The 17th-century Fishing Temple is a memorial to him.

Ilam Hall Youth Hostel (☎ 01335-350212, fax 350350, **e** *ilam@yha.org.uk)*, in a Gothic NT mansion, is about one mile south-west of Dovedale. It charges £10.85/7.40 for adults/juniors. It only opens during school holidays.

Hartington Hall Youth Hostel (☎ 01298-84223, fax 84415, **e** *hartington@yha.org .uk)*, a grand, 17th-century hall that has just undergone a refurbishment, is about 5 miles (8km) north of the Dovedale area. Beds cost £9.80/6.75 for adults/juniors. Bus No 442 from Buxton train station goes by regularly.

MATLOCK BATH & MATLOCK
☎ 01629

Tucked away at the south-eastern edge of the Peak District are the twin towns of Matlock and Matlock Bath. Despite its spectacular setting, squeezed into the narrow valley of the River Derwent, Matlock Bath feels more like a displaced seaside resort than a country town, complete with arcades and aquarium, chippies and candyfloss.

The **Venetian Nights** have been a fixture in the Matlock Bath calendar for more than 100 years, first held in honour of Queen Victoria's 60th year on the throne. Each Saturday and Sunday evening, during a six-week period from late August to early October, a procession of boats bedecked in lights and decorations sails along the Derwent, and there are occasional firework displays, which have the gorge for a spectacular backdrop.

The helpful TIC (☎ 55082, fax 56304) is in the pavilion on Grand Parade and opens 9.30 am to 5 pm daily.

Things to See & Do

At the **Peak District Mining Museum and Temple Mine** (☎ 583834), at the same location as the TIC, you can have a go at panning for gold. It opens 10 am to 5 pm daily and costs £2.50/1.50, or £4/2.50 including the mine. Alternatively, for those who like a view, cable cars carry visitors from the centre of Matlock Bath up to the **Heights of**

Abraham (☎ 582365) with its mixture of nature trails and family attractions. It opens 10 am to 5 pm daily, Easter to October, and admission costs £6.50/4.50.

Over weekends and almost daily during August, you can travel by steam train through lovely scenery on the restored **Peak Railway** from Matlock Riverside station to Rowsley South. There are occasional guest appearances by famous trains such as *The Flying Scotsman*. Return fares cost £6/3. For timetable details see the Web site www .peakrail.co.uk or phone ☎ 01629-580381.

Places to Stay & Eat

LettinGo (☎ *580686*, 🇪 *n&j@lettingo .freeserve.co.uk, Byron House, 1 Brunswood Rd)* is an excellent new backpackers pad in an attractive Victorian house near the station with beds from £11.50 per person. Try to book ahead as there is limited space.

Matlock, a couple of miles beyond, has more shops, restaurants and *Matlock Youth Hostel* (☎ *582983, fax 583484,* 🇪 *matlock@ yha.org.uk, 40 Bank Rd)* with beds for £9.75/6.55 for adults/juniors.

The Fishpond (☎ *581000, 204 South Parade)* is the place to check out in Matlock Bath, a pub that has live music most nights, as well as good beer and lively food.

For the traditionalists that like a quieter pub, the *Princess Victoria* (☎ *57462, South Parade)* has decent beer and provides a warm welcome in winter.

About half way between Matlock and Matlock Bath is *The Boathouse* (☎ *583776, 110 Dale Rd)*, popular locally for its seafood specialities.

Getting There & Away

The TransPeak (☎ 0870 608 2608) service covers Matlock, linking it to Buxton and Manchester to the north-west, and Derby and Nottingham to the south-east. There are train links between Matlock Bath and Derby.

AROUND MATLOCK
Derwent Valley

The Derwent Valley has played its part in England's industrial heritage, home as it was to a number of pioneering mills and dams, almost an Ironbridge of the 19th century. **Caudwell's Mill** (☎ 01629-734374), a working example of Victorian ingenuity complete with shops and a popular cafe, is located in Rowsley. It opens 10 am to 6 pm daily, April to October and 10 am to 4.30 pm weekends during winter. Rowsley is on the A6 towards Bakewell.

The combination of beauty and history of the valley has led to a concerted campaign for UNESCO World Heritage Site status and the area is now promoted as the National Heritage Corridor.

Red House Stables Working Carriage Museum

Red House Stables (☎ 01629-733583), Old Road, Darley Dale, is a museum of the horse-drawn carriage. There are more than 40 examples here, including a Hansom Cab, a forerunner of black taxis in London, and a Royal Mail coach. Many have starred in television shows. It opens 10 am to 5 pm daily and admission costs £4/2. It is 2½ miles (4km) from Matlock.

National Tramway Museum

Trams were a major feature of British life until a disastrous policy decision saw them wiped off the landscape of cities throughout the country. Today they are making a comeback from Sheffield to Croydon, but in Crich they never went away. The National Tramway Museum (☎ 01773-852565, fax 852326) is a living museum with a dramatic location in an old quarry. It provides a home to more than 40 trams of all ages. It opens 10 am to 5.30 pm daily, April to October (to 6.30 pm weekends, June to August); 10.30 am to 4.30 pm Sunday and Monday, November to March. Admission costs £6.70/3.30.

Nottinghamshire

Nottinghamshire is most famous for a man in tights, and Robin Hood, his merry men and the Sheriff of Nottingham have been roped into a variety of amusement parks, pubs and restaurants, although there's not actually much left of Sherwood Forest these days. Nevertheless, Nottingham is undoubtedly one of the most happening cities in the Midlands and there are several other worthwhile places around the county.

For bus information, call the Nottinghamshire Buses Hotline on ☎ 0115-924 0000.

NOTTINGHAM
☎ 0115 • pop 275,000

Nottingham is the happening heart of the East Midlands, home to a vibrant fashion, music and sporting scene that competes with the best in England. Designer Paul Smith has picked up where lace left off to keep the city on the clothing map of England, the clubs and bars are some of the liveliest outside London, and while Nottingham Forest and Notts County may no longer be setting the football world alight, Trent Bridge remains a major draw for cricket fans.

The Saxon city bore the less than charming name of Snotingham, but modern Nottingham had its moment of glory in the 19th century when the lace industry transformed the city centre. Nottingham was a centre for the Luddite riots of 1811 to 1816. Lace-making declined during the 1890s and was virtually killed off by WWI, although the tourist industry supports some small-scale lace production. The city remains an industrial centre and is home to Raleigh bicycles.

Nottingham's famed Goose Fair dates back to the Middle Ages, but these days it's just an outsize funfair, which takes place in the Forest Recreation Ground on the first Thursday, Friday and Saturday of October.

The city is also noted for its peculiar Midlands dialect. If someone greets you with a hearty 'eyupmeduck', a suitable response is 'hello'.

Orientation & Information

Like other Midlands cities, Nottingham is chopped in pieces by an inner ring road. The train station is south of the canal on the southern edge of the centre. There are two bus stations: Victoria bus station is hidden away behind the Victoria shopping centre, just north of the city centre, while Broad Marsh bus station is behind Broad Marsh shopping centre to the south.

The TIC (☎ 915 5330, fax 915 5323, e touristinformation@nottinghamcity.gov.uk), Smithy Row, is in the Council House and opens 9 am to 5.30 pm Monday to Friday, and to 5 pm Saturday year-round; and 11 am to 3 pm summer Sundays.

Nottingham Castle Museum, the Brewhouse Yard Museum and Wollaton Hall are all free during the week but have admission charges at the weekend. Anyone planning to visit the Caves of Nottingham, the Tales of Robin Hood and the Galleries of Justice should consider buying an Explorer Pass (£15.95/9.95), which also covers the other museums at the weekend. Passes are available from all the attractions they cover.

Nottingham Castle Museum & Art Gallery

Nottingham Castle was demolished after the Civil War and replaced with a mansion in 1674. This was, in turn, burned out during the Reform Bill Riots of 1831, but a museum was opened inside the shell in 1875. The museum (☎ 915 3651) describes Nottingham's history and houses some of the alabaster carvings for which Nottingham was noted between 1350 and 1550. Upstairs there's also an art gallery.

The castle opens 10 am to 5 pm daily (except Friday November to February). At the weekend admission costs £2/1. Tours of Mortimer's Hole beneath the castle take place at 2 and 3 pm Monday to Friday for £2/1. There's also a stylish cafe and an excellent shop.

Caves of Nottingham

Nottingham stands on a plug of Sherwood sandstone that is riddled with man-made caves dating back to medieval times. Rather surprisingly, you need to go inside Broad Marsh shopping centre to find the entrance to the most fascinating, readily accessible caves (☎ 924 1424). These contain an air-raid shelter, a medieval underground tannery, several pub cellars and a mock-up of

THE MIDLANDS

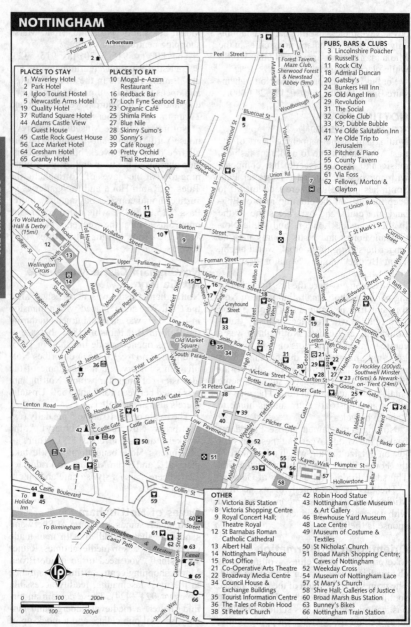

NOTTINGHAM

THE MIDLANDS

Arboretum

Portland Rd
Peel Street

To
Forest Tavern,
Maze Club,
Sherwood Forest
& Newstead
Abbey (9mi)

PLACES TO STAY
1 Waverley Hotel
2 Park Hotel
4 Igloo Tourist Hostel
5 Newcastle Arms Hotel
19 Quality Hotel
37 Rutland Square Hotel
44 Adams Castle View
    Guest House
45 Castle Rock Guest House
56 Lace Market Hotel
64 Gresham Hotel
65 Granby Hotel

PLACES TO EAT
10 Mogal-e-Azam
    Restaurant
16 Redback Bar
17 Loch Fyne Seafood Bar
23 Organic Café
25 Shimla Pinks
27 Blue Nile
28 Skinny Sumo's
30 Sonny's
39 Café Rouge
40 Pretty Orchid
    Thai Restaurant

PUBS, BARS & CLUBS
3 Lincolnshire Poacher
6 Russell's
11 Rock City
18 Admiral Duncan
20 Gatsby's
24 Bunkers Hill Inn
26 Old Angel Inn
29 Revolution
31 The Social
32 Cookie Club
33 K9; Dubble Bubble
41 Ye Olde Salutation Inn
47 Ye Olde Trip to
    Jerusalem
53 Pitcher & Piano
55 County Tavern
59 Ocean
61 Via Foss
62 Fellows, Morton &
    Clayton

Bluecoat St

To Wollaton
Hall & Derby
(15mi)

Wellington
Circus

Old Market
Square

To Hockley (200yd);
Southwell Minster
(16mi) & Newark-
on-Trent (24mi)

To Birmingham

Nottingham
& Beeston
Canal

To
Holiday
Inn

OTHER
7 Victoria Bus Station
8 Victoria Shopping Centre
9 Royal Concert Hall;
   Theatre Royal
12 St Barnabas Roman
    Catholic Cathedral
13 Albert Hall
14 Nottingham Playhouse
15 Post Office
21 Co-Operative Arts Theatre
22 Broadway Media Centre
34 Council House &
    Exchange Buildings
35 Tourist Information Centre
36 The Tales of Robin Hood
38 St Peter's Church

42 Robin Hood Statue
43 Nottingham Castle Museum
    & Art Gallery
46 Brewhouse Yard Museum
48 Lace Centre
49 Museum of Costume &
    Textiles
50 St Nicholas' Church
51 Broad Marsh Shopping Centre;
    Caves of Nottingham
52 Weekday Cross
54 Museum of Nottingham Lace
57 St Mary's Church
58 Shire Hall; Galleries of Justice
60 Broad Marsh Bus Station
63 Bunney's Bikes
66 Nottingham Train Station

0   100   200m
0   100   200yd

The Legend of Robin Hood

In the Middle Ages most of Nottinghamshire was covered in forest. It was here that Robin Hood and his band of merry men were said to have waged their private war on the wicked Sheriff of Nottingham while Richard I was away crusading.

Nottinghamshire is littered with sites associated with Robin. Nottingham Castle obviously played a key role, as did St Mary's Church. Robin is said to have married Maid Marian in Edinstowe church, while Fountaindale, near Blidworth, is the supposed site of his battle with Friar Tuck.

But did Robin ever really exist? As long ago as 1377 William Langland made fleeting reference to him in his poem *Piers Plowman*, but it was only in the early 16th century that the story began to be fleshed out, most notably in the ballad *A Geste of Robyn Hoode*. In 1795 Joseph Ritson collected all the known accounts of Robin into one volume, since when innumerable authors (including Scott and Tennyson) have turned them into torrid novels and poems.

The Robin Hood story has generated many films, the most recent and successful *Robin Hood Prince of Thieves* with Kevin Costner following in the footsteps of Errol Flynn as Robin and Alan Rickman as the Sheriff. Burnham Beeches in Buckinghamshire stood in for Sherwood Forest, while other scenes were filmed in the church of St Bartholomew-the-Great in London, Peckforton Castle in Preston, Lancashire, and also in France.

In spite of all this, researchers have failed to turn up any hard evidence that the outlaw actually existed. He is, for example, said to have been born in Lockesley in Yorkshire or Nottinghamshire, but no such place appears on any map. Optimists point to a Loxley in Staffordshire where Hood's father supposedly owned land. But it may be that 'Robin' is no more than a jumbled memory of ancient ideas about forest fairies, or a character made up to give voice to medieval resentments.

a Victorian slum dwelling. They open 10 am to 4.15 pm Monday to Saturday and from 11 am Sunday. Admission costs £3.25/2.25.

The Tales of Robin Hood

The Tales of Robin Hood (☎ 948 3284), 30–38 Maid Marian Way, is a modern tourist attraction that takes you through models of Nottingham Castle and Sherwood Forest in the days when Robin Hood was battling it out with the Sheriff. Afterwards you have time to find out more about the reality behind the legend or to watch clips from the various film versions in the cafe.

It opens 10 am to 4.30 pm daily. Admission costs £4.95/3.95. Medieval banquets take place here too, but are best booked in advance; they cost about £30.

Wollaton Hall

Built in 1588 by land and coal-mine owner, Sir Francis Willoughby, Wollaton Hall (☎ 915 3900) is a fine example of Tudor architecture at its most extravagant. Architect Robert Smythson was also responsible for the equally avant-garde Longleat. Wollaton Hall now houses the **Nottingham Natural History Museum**.

The **Industrial Museum**, in the estate

buildings, has lace-making equipment, Raleigh bicycles, a gigantic 1858 beam engine and oddities like a locally invented 1963 video recorder that never got off the ground.

Both museums open 10 am to 5 pm Monday to Saturday and from 1.30 pm Sunday, April to September. The Industrial Museum is closed Monday to Wednesday, October to March. Combined admission costs £1.50/1. Wollaton Hall is on the western edge of the city, 2½ miles (4km) from the centre. You can get there on a No 25 bus.

Brewhouse Yard Museum
The Brewhouse Yard Museum (☎ 915 3600) is housed in five 17th-century cottages on Castle Boulevard virtually below the castle. It re-creates everyday life in 19th-century Nottingham with particularly good displays of traditional shops. An underground passageway, known as Mortimer's Hole, leads from the castle to Brewhouse Yard. Roger Mortimer, who arranged Edward II's murder, is said to have been captured by supporters of Edward III who entered via this passage. It opens 10 am to 4 pm daily and admission is free during the week, £1.50/80p at the weekend.

Museum of Costume & Textiles
The Museum of Costume & Textiles (☎ 915 3500), on Castle Gate, has displays of costumes from 1790 to the mid-20th century, arranged in period rooms, as well as tapestries and lace. It opens 10 am to 4 pm Wednesday to Sunday and admission is free.

Museum of Nottingham Lace
Nottingham's lace museum (☎ 989 7365), 3–5 High Pavement, is housed in the city's former lace market. It is a useful introduction to the industry that helped to construct the modern city. It opens 10 am to 5 pm daily (last admission 4 pm). Admission costs £2.95/1.95.

Across from the castle a small **Lace Centre** (☎ 941 3539) is housed in the medieval Severns building in Castle Rd, with locally made lace on sale.

Galleries of Justice
In the impressive Shire Hall building on High Pavement, the Galleries of Justice (☎ 952 0558) has been redeveloped as a National Museum of Law. The interactive Police Galleries let you visit a pretend crime scene and assess the available evidence, while the Crime & Punishment Galleries look at how offences were handled in Victorian times. It opens 10 am to 5 pm Tuesday to Sunday and bank holiday Mondays. Admission costs £7.95/4.95.

Places to Stay
The cheapest accommodation is at the *Igloo Tourist Hostel* (☎ 947 5250, reception@ igloohostel.co.uk, 110 Mansfield Rd), a short walk north of Victoria bus station. It is handy for the city centre and a bunk bed in a dorm costs £11.

A little farther up is the *Newcastle Arms Hotel* (☎ 947 4616, 68 North Sherwood St) with rooms from £17 per person, including breakfast. There are a host of inexpensive B&Bs on the Mansfield Rd as it enters Sherwood.

Just south of the castle, on Castle Boulevard, the *Adams Castle View Guest House* (☎/fax 950 0022, 85 Castle Boulevard) charges £19/30, including breakfast. The *Castle Rock Guest House* (☎ 948 2116, 79 Castle Boulevard) was refurbished in 1999 and rooms start from £18 per head.

South of the centre there are some cheap B&Bs near the train station. The *Granby Hotel* (☎ 958 2158, 19 Station St) has rooms from £20 per night. The *Gresham Hotel* (☎ 950 1234, 109 Carrington St) has singles/doubles from around £22/36 per night.

Pricier places north of the centre include the *Park Hotel* (☎ 978 6299, fax 942 4358, ℮ parkhotel@ic24.net, 5–7 Waverley St), right across from the arboretum. Rooms cost from £48/68. Just off Waverley St, the *Waverley Hotel* (☎ 978 6707, fax 924 4865, ℮ reservation@waverleyhotel.net, 107 Portland Rd) is cheaper at £27/55. It's worth considering the *Quality Hotel* (☎ 947 5641, fax 948 3292, ℮ admin@gb620.net .com, George St) that charges £71/83.

You're never far from a postbox in England.

The imposing Council House, Nottingham

A romantic mist enshrouds magnificent Warwick Castle.

CHRIS MELLOR

The excellent Black Country Museum in Dudley evokes the Midlands' industrial heritage.

CHRIS MELLOR

Forward sculpture, Centenary Square, Birmingham

CHIRS MELLOR

Pottery kiln tower, Staffordshire

JULIET COOMBE

Bang those sticks: morris men dancing in Stratford-upon-Avon

At the weekend and throughout August, Nottingham's business hotels often offer a special discounted 'Robin Hood Rate'. The *Holiday Inn* (☎ *993 5000, fax 993 4000,* e *holidayinn.nottingham@zoom .co.uk, Castle Marina Park)* and *Rutland Square Hotel* (☎ *941 1114, fax 955 9494, St James St)*, for example, suddenly become wholly affordable at about £35 per person. Otherwise avoid them as prices are huge!

The *Lace Market Hotel* (☎ *852 3232, fax 852 3223,* e *admin@lacemarkethotel.co .uk, 31 High Pavement)* is a new designer hotel and charges £89/99 during the week, £65/75 at the weekend.

Places to Eat

The Hockley area, around Carlton St to the east of the centre, is a good place to start looking for something to eat and has become pretty fashionable in recent years.

There's good vegetarian food on Goose Gate where *Organic Café* is a vegan/vegetarian cafe above the Hiziki wholefood store. The Moroccan stew is tasty. Nearby, classy *Sonny's* (☎ *947 3041, 3 Carlton St)* has a bright and imaginative menu, with main dishes (modern British) from around £10. Excellent *Skinny Sumo's* (☎ *952 0188, 11 Carlton St)* offers sushi on a conveyor belt and has cheap speciality nights (Monday for curry, Wednesday for noodles) during the week (main courses cost £6).

The *Broadway Media Centre* (☎ *952 6611, 14–18 Broad St)* has a good, if smoky, cafe where you can get soup, a baguette and endless coffee for £4.50 at lunch time. The *Blue Nile* (☎ *941 0976, 5 Heathcoate St)* is an Egyptian restaurant with vegetarian dishes and belly dancing. Down on Goose Gate is one of the city centre's best Indian restaurants, *Shimla Pinks* (☎ *958 9899, 38 Goose Gate)*, part of an expanding chain. Beside the Theatre Royal, the *Mogal-e-Azam* (☎ *947 2911, 7 Goldsmith St)* is another acclaimed Indian restaurant.

The *Loch Fyne Seafood Bar* (☎ *950 8481, 17 King St)* is a branch of the excellent Scottish oyster and smoked-seafood company. Half a dozen oysters cost £5. Round the corner, the *Redback Bar* (☎ *953*

1531, Queen St) offers good beer and company, plus rooburgers and outback soup.

Bridlesmith Gate is a lively cut-through, with a branch of *Café Rouge* (☎ *958 2230, 31 Bridlesmith Gate)*. Just off it, the *Pretty Orchid Thai Restaurant* (☎ *958 8344)* serves lunches for £4.50, but dinner will cost more like £15.

Entertainment

Pubs & Bars *Ye Olde Trip to Jerusalem* (☎ *947 3171, Brewhouse Yard, Castle Rd)*, tucked into the cliff below the castle, is one of England's best pubs; the upstairs bar is actually cut into the rock. Crusaders are said to have gathered here before setting off to the Holy Land and today pub-crawlers follow in their footsteps before setting out to conquer Nottingham. Just over the ring road, *Ye Olde Salutation Inn* (*Maid Marian Way)* is now part of the Hogshead chain, but has decent beers and some caves beneath.

Real ale fiends must get to the *Lincolnshire Poacher* (☎ *941 1584, 161–163 Mansfield Rd)*, a brilliant pub with well kept beer. Just up the hill is the *Forest Tavern* (☎ *947 5650, 257 Mansfield Rd)*, which has a dangerous selection of Belgian beers and a fancy glass collection to accompany them; the happening little *Maze Club* is in the same spot. Another great ale pub to look out for is *Bunkers Hill Inn* (☎ *910 0114, 36–38 Hockley)*, at the bottom of Goose Gate.

Fellows, Morton & Clayton (☎ *950 6795, 54 Canal St)* is an excellent pub overlooking the redeveloped and re-emergent canalside area of town. Neighbouring *Via Fossa* (☎ *947 3904, Castle Wharf, Canal St)* is one of *the* places to go in town and heaves during summer. Luckily it has a huge interior, as well as plenty of space outside. Opposite the Lace Market is the incredible *Pitcher & Piano* (☎ *958 6081, The Former Unitarian Church, High Pavement)*, surely one of the boldest church conversions in the country, which draws the faithful daily. *Revolution* (☎ *947 4578, 7 Broad St)* remains a cool place to wind down and has spread its wings to nearby Leicester.

THE MIDLANDS

The *Old Angel Inn* *(Woolpack Lane)*, in Hockley, is a popular student pub, as is the cosy *County Tavern* *(☎ 950 1039, 25 High Pavement)*. Another enduringly popular student pub is *Russels* *(☎ 947 3239, 38 Shakespeare St)*.

Gatsby's *(Huntingdon St)* is a busy gay bar, as is the *Admiral Duncan* *(☎ 950 2727, 74 Lower Parliament St)*, down on the ring road, near Goose Gate.

Clubs *The Social* *(☎ 950 5078, 23 Pelham St)* is a remarkably trendy bar and has DJs and live guests, certainly one of the places to be seen in Nottingham. *K9* is a retro cafe-bar that is always rammed and downstairs is *dubble bubble* *(☎ 956 2006, 19 Greyhound St)*, which is one of the city's better clubs.

The *Cookie Club* *(Pelham St)*, on the edge of Hockley, is a friendly little club with alternative nights and fair prices. *Rock City* *(☎ 941 2544, Talbot St)* is a popular rock venue with a £4 to £12 entry charge. This is the major live venue for bands in Nottingham. *Ocean* *(☎ 958 0555, Greyfriar Gate)* is a large club between the Broad Marsh shopping centre and the canal.

Theatre, Cinema & Classical Music
The *Broadway Media Centre* *(☎ 952 6611, 14–18 Broad St)* cinema is the city's arthouse movie centre. Theatrical venues include the *Co-operative Arts Theatre* *(☎ 947 6096, George St)* and the *Nottingham Playhouse* *(☎ 941 9419, Wellington Circus)*. The *Royal Concert Hall* and *Theatre Royal* share a booking office *(☎ 948 2626, Wollaton St)* and an imposing building close to the centre.

Getting There & Away
Nottingham is 135 miles (217km) from London, around 75 miles (121km) from Manchester and Leeds, and 50 miles (80km) from Birmingham.

Bus National Express buses operate from the Broad Marsh bus station. A single to London costs £12.25.

For information on buses serving Nottingham, phone the Buses Hotline on ☎ 924 0000. Sherwood Forester buses (☎ 977 4268) operate to tourist attractions all over Nottinghamshire in summer. An unlimited-travel Ranger Ticket for £4.50/2.50 gives discounted admission to some attractions. Rainbow Route services by Trent & Barton Buses (☎ 01773-712265) operate to Derby and continue through the Peak District to Manchester (TransPeak). They operate from both bus stations and a one-day Explorer Ticket costs £5.95; one child goes free.

Train Nottingham is not on the main railway routes through the Midlands but frequent services to London St Pancras take 1¾ hours.

Getting Around
For information on buses within Nottingham, call ☎ 950 3665. A Day Rider ticket gives you unlimited travel for £2.20.

Bunney's Bikes (☎ 947 2713), at 97 Carrington St near the train station, has bicycles for hire from £8.50 per day (£100 deposit!).

AROUND NOTTINGHAM
Newstead Abbey
Converted into a home after the dissolution of the monasteries in 1539, Newstead Abbey (☎ 01623-455900) is chiefly notable for being the residence of Lord Byron (1788–1824) but the Byronic connections are sparse.

The facade of the ruined priory church is next to the house, which was already in bad shape when Byron inherited it from his great-uncle. The continuing decline of the family fortune forced him to sell it in 1817. The poet used to hold shooting sessions indoors and a friend commented that a visit was so pleasant it 'made one forget that one was domiciled in the wing of an extensive ruin'.

The house opens noon to 4 pm daily, April to September and the garden opens year-round. Admission to house and garden costs £4/1.50. The house is 12 miles (19km) north of Nottingham, off the A60. The Sherwood Forester bus runs right there on summer Sundays; otherwise take bus No 737/747 and walk a mile from the abbey gates.

Southwell Minster

To judge by its magnificent minster, medieval Southwell must have had an importance the modern town just doesn't. For those who love England's Gothic architecture but loathe the crowds, Southwell Minster (☎ 01636-812649) will come as a great relief. The highlight of the building is the lovely, decorated chapterhouse, which is filled with naturalistic carvings of leaves, pigs, dogs and rabbits. Children will also enjoy looking for wooden mice carved by Yorkshire's famous woodcarver, Robert Thompson, for whom they acted as a 'signature'.

Admission is free, but a donation of £2/1 is suggested. You can get to Southwell on regular bus No 61 from Nottingham.

DH Lawrence Birthplace Museum

The birthplace of DH Lawrence (1885–1930; ☎ 01773-763312), 8a Victoria St, Nottingham's controversial author, is in Eastwood, about 10 miles (16km) north-west of the city. It's now a museum, which opens 10 am to 5 pm (to 4 pm in winter) daily, April to October. Admission costs £3.50/1.50.

Sherwood Forest

Only tiny fragments of Robin Hood's mighty forest remain, but a quarter of a million people visit the 180-hectare Sherwood Forest Country Park near the village of Edinstowe every year. At least the **Sherwood Forest Visitor Centre** (☎ 01623-824490) keeps some of the crowds out of the real woods where Robin is supposed to have hidden in the Major Oak. Speaking of the oak, if ever there was a case for euthanasia for plant life, this is it – the tree has almost more supports than branches these days. The visitor centre opens 10.30 am to 5 pm daily (to 4.30 pm November to March) and admission costs £1.50. The Robin Hood Festival is a massive medieval re-enactment that takes place every August.

Sherwood Forest Youth Hostel (☎ 01623-825794, fax 825796, e sherwood@yha .org.uk, Forest Corner, Edwinstowe) is a new hostel just a short distance from the visitor centre. Beds here cost £10.85/7.40 for adults/juniors.

Sherwood Forester buses run the 20 miles (32km) to the park from Nottingham.

Newark-upon-Trent
☎ 01636

This proud market town has many buildings of distinction including the ruins of **Newark castle** (☎ 655765), one of the few to hold out against Cromwell's men during the Civil War. Charles I commanded Lord Bellasis to surrender and soon after the castle was rubble. An impressive Norman gate remains. The castle grounds open until dusk year-round. The castle buildings are sometimes open 10 am to 3 pm Wednesday, Friday and Sunday during summer. Admission is free.

The town has a large, cobbled square overlooked by the medieval White Hart Inn and the Clinton Arms Hotel, from where former prime minister Gladstone made his first political speech and where Lord Byron stayed while his first book of poems was published.

The TIC (☎ 655765, fax 655767, e gilstrap@newark-sherwood.gov.uk), Castlegate, is in the Gilstrap Centre and opens 9 am to 6 pm daily (to 5 pm in winter). If lunch is on the agenda, *Bay Tree Restaurant* (☎ 674000, Castlegate) has set meals for £10, which makes the tasty food more affordable than by night. *Gourmets Café* (☎ 702066, 35 Castlegate) is a cheaper place with the emphasis on light lunch and teas.

There are regular buses to Nottingham.

THE MIDLANDS

Eastern England

When planning a trip to England, the eastern counties included in this chapter – Suffolk, Norfolk, Lincolnshire and Cambridgeshire – rarely find their way into a 'best of' list. With one outstanding exception, there isn't really any town that can rival Bath as a tourist destination, or any museum as famous as London's British Museum. Yorkshire's Castle Howard has no majestic equal here, nor is there a patch of coastline as impressive as, say, the stretch between Land's End and St Ives in Cornwall or that between Scarborough and Saltburn in North Yorkshire. Why visit Lincoln when you can go to York? Why go to the cathedral in Ely when the spires of Canterbury are more renowned?

This area, particularly the part known as East Anglia (Norfolk, Suffolk and east Cambridgeshire), has always been distinct, separated from the rest of England by the reclaimed marshlands known as the fens and the Essex forests. Although motorways, bus routes and train lines have rendered this distinction less tangible over the years, the tourist hordes that swarm all over England's more famous destinations continue to stay away.

Hence your reason for going. Here you will find a softer England, where picturesque medieval market towns are dotted over a gently undulating landscape bordered by some stunning coastlines and criss-crossed by waterways and marshland. It is difficult to believe that this pastoral idyll was once the epicentre of economic power in England, but in the region's more important towns – Cambridge, Norwich, Ely, Bury St Edmunds, King's Lynn and Lincoln – you will find enough evidence of its bustling medieval past, when the trade of cloth brought immense prosperity.

And virtually all of this is accessible without standing in long lines, paying exorbitant admission fees and vying for standing room in churches or museums with hundreds of other visitors.

Highlights

- Visiting medieval Lavenham and Georgian Bury St Edmunds, taking in the art of fine architecture over 800 years
- Boating on the Norfolk Broads
- Dreaming about being a Nobel laureate while strolling around Cambridge University
- Being captivated by choral Evensong at King's College Chapel (and if you can carry a tune...)
- Punting on the River Cam between Cambridge and Grantchester...without toppling in
- Walking up Steep Hill to Lincoln Cathedral, saving enough energy to appreciate the interior
- Sampling Norwich nightlife, from pub to club

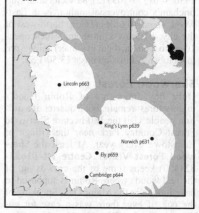

- Lincoln p663
- King's Lynn p639
- Norwich p631
- Ely p659
- Cambridge p644

The one exception is Cambridge, home of the world-famous university and a favourite destination of the caravans of tour coaches. Less than an hour from London, smaller and less developed than its great rival Oxford, Cambridge is not just one of the most famous university towns in the world, but a beautiful town in its own right. Its mix of fine architecture and large tracts of parkland straddling a bend in the River Cam make this one of the most attractive towns in the south of England – as well as one of the most visited.

East of the fens, Norfolk and Suffolk have gentle, unspectacular scenery that can still be very beautiful. Norfolk's county seat, Norwich, has long been considered 'quiet' (read: boring) but an impressive program of urban rejuvenation and the presence of a university have given it a new lease of life. To the east of the city, the Nor-

folk Broads – a boggy area criss-crossed by wide expanses of reed-filled waterways known as 'broads' – has become a popular destination for Britons looking for a relaxing holiday in the countryside.

To the north, Lincolnshire has been dismissed as flat and uninteresting, yet the unspoiled nature of some of the Lincolnshire towns – cobbled streets, solid stone-built houses with red-tiled roofs – has made it a favourite destination of film companies looking for bygone settings for their period films. The county seat, Lincoln, is not nearly as famous as its great northern rival

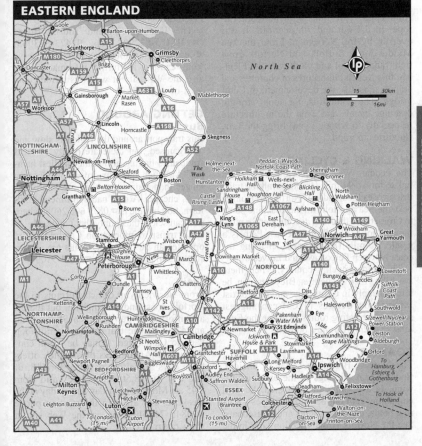

EASTERN ENGLAND

of York, but it is still home to one of the most spectacular cathedrals in Europe.

The distinctive architectural character of the region was determined by the lack of suitable building stone. Stone was occasionally imported for important buildings, but for humble churches and houses three local materials were used: flint, clay bricks and oak. The most unusual of the three, flint, can be chipped into a usable shape, but a single stone is rarely larger than a fist. Often the flint is used in combination with dressed stone or bricks to form decorative patterns.

HISTORY

More than any other part of England, East Anglia has close links with northern Europe. In the 6th and 7th centuries it was overrun by the Norsemen. From the late Middle Ages, Suffolk and Norfolk grew rich trading wool and cloth with the Flemish; this wealth built scores of churches and helped subsidise the development of Cambridge. The windmills, the long, straight drainage canals and even the architecture (especially in King's Lynn) bring the Low Countries to mind.

WALKING & CYCLING

The Peddars Way and Norfolk Coast Path link to form a 94-mile (151km) walking track that crosses the middle of Norfolk to Holme-next-the-Sea and follows the coastline south to Cromer (see the Activities chapter for more information). The Suffolk Coast Path is a gentle, 50-mile (80km) meander along the coast between Felixstowe and Lowestoft.

This is ideal cycling country. Where there are hills, they're gentle. Bicycles can be hired cheaply in Cambridge and the Tourist Information Centres (TICs) can suggest several interesting routes. Ask for the *England's Cycling Country* booklet.

BOATING

The Norfolk Broads, a series of ancient, flooded peat diggings to the east of Norwich, is a popular boating area. Several companies rent out boats of all types – narrow boats, cruisers, yachts and houseboats. See the Norfolk Broads section later in the

chapter for information. Punting on the River Cam in Cambridge is also very popular; see that section for details.

GETTING THERE & AWAY

All the major towns covered in the chapter are easily accessible by train from London. Buses from the capital also serve the major towns, but you're better off getting to the region by train if you want to avoid long bus journeys with plenty of stops. From London, there is a direct train line linking Cambridge, Ely and King's Lynn. To get to Bury St Edmunds, Ipswich and Norwich you'll have to go via Cambridge, while Lincoln usually requires a change at Ely and/or Peterborough.

The East of England Tourist Board (☎ 01473-822922, fax 01473-823063, ⓔ eastofenglandtouristboard@compuserve .com) can provide further information. See also the Web site at www.visitbritain.com /east-of-england.

GETTING AROUND
Bus

Bus transport around the region is slow and disorganised, but there are plenty of local companies linking all but the smallest hamlets. Although bus trips invariably drag on longer than train rides, they are almost always cheaper. A new national timetable information hotline is ☎ 0870 608 2608, where you can select the county that you need.

For transport information, Cambridgeshire operates an 0891 number (calls are expensive at 50p per minute) – ☎ 0891 910910.

Train

From Norwich you can catch trains to the Norfolk coast and Sheringham, but there's an unfortunate gap between Sheringham and King's Lynn that prevents a rail loop back to Cambridge. It may be worth considering an Anglia Plus pass, which offers three days' travel out of seven for £18, or one day for £8.50. These are valid from 8.45 am Monday to Friday and all day at the weekend. For all train information phone ☎ 0845 748 4950 or see the Web site at www.railtrack.co.uk.

Suffolk

Once one of the richest parts of the country, Suffolk is now something of a backwater – and all the better for it as far as the visitor is concerned. Like most of East Anglia, the county is fairly flat, but the landscape has a serene beauty in parts.

Along the border with Essex is the Stour Valley, made famous by the painters Gainsborough and Constable. Constable enthused about the county's 'gentle declivities, its woods and rivers, its luxuriant meadow flats sprinkled with flocks and herds, its well cultivated uplands, with numerous scattered villages and churches, farms and picturesque cottages'. The description still holds true for much of the county today.

The region's economic boom as a wool trading centre lasted until the 16th century and has left the county with its magnificently endowed 'wool' churches, many built to support much larger populations than live here now. Some of the villages have changed little since then and Suffolk buildings are famous for their *pargeting* – decorative stucco plasterwork.

IPSWICH
☎ 01473 • pop 129,600

Poor old Ipswich. In bygone days it was an important Saxon town, and while it still retains a certain importance as a commercial and shopping centre, its major role these days is as Suffolk's county town. A rash and ill-conceived spate of urban development over the last 30 years – seemingly without concern for aesthetics – has made chunks of the city downright ugly. Yet its most recent development, the Wet Dock Quayside, is a testament to more thoughtful modern planning and a pleasant spot to while away a couple of hours.

You might end up here anyway, as Ipswich is a transport hub for the region; if so, make an effort to check out the town's beautiful examples of the Tudor style, the Ancient House and Christchurch Mansion.

Famous children of Ipswich include Cardinal Wolsey, Trevor Nunn (director of the National Theatre), 80s pop singer Nik Kershaw and actress Val Lehman, who played B Smith in the cult classic *Prisoner Cell Block H*. The town also claims to be the spiritual home of the hardcore style of dance music known as drum'n'bass or jungle: one of its early pioneers, LTJ Bukem, is from the town.

Orientation & Information

Ipswich is a pretty compact place that is easy to get around. Most of the action is in and around the ancient market place of Cornhill, now dominated by the Buttermarket Shopping Centre. Everything worth seeing is within a few minutes' walk of here. The train station is a 15-minute walk south-west of the centre along Princes St and across the roundabout. The bus station is closer, about 100 yards south of the TIC on Turret Lane.

The TIC in St Stephen's Church, off St Stephen's Lane (☎ 258070, fax 432017, e tourist@ipswich.gov.uk), is near the bus station and the Ancient House. It opens 9 am to 5 pm from Monday to Saturday. The TIC organises 90-minute guided tours (£1.75/1.25 per adult/child) of the town at 2.15 pm every Tuesday and Thursday.

Things to See

The 17th-century Ancient House at 40 Buttermarket (☎ 214144) is now a branch of the Lakelands kitchen outfitters, and you can wander in to take a look at the exquisite hammer-beam roof on the first floor. The external decor, done around 1670, is an extravagant example of the Restoration style, with plenty of stucco and some of the finest examples of pargeting in the country. The store opens 9 am to 5.30 pm Monday to Saturday. The house is situated about 50 yards north of the TIC, just off Stephen's Lane.

At the Ipswich Museum, on the High St, there's a replica of the Sutton Hoo ship burial found near Woodbridge, east of Ipswich, in 1939. It was the richest archaeological discovery in the country; the original artefacts are now in the British Museum.

Set in a 65-acre park about 300 yards north of town, Christchurch Mansion

(☎ 433554), Soane St, is a fine Tudor mansion built between 1548 and 1550. The exterior is awash with Dutch-style gables, while the enormous interior is decorated with period furniture and the walls adorned with a good collection of works by Constable and Gainsborough. The **Wolsey Art Gallery** hosts contemporary art exhibitions. It opens 10 am to 5 pm Tuesday to Saturday (to 4 pm October to February) and 2.30 to 4.30 pm on Sunday. Admission is free. To get there, walk north from the TIC along Stephen's Lane, which becomes Tower St. Turn right onto St Margaret's St and then take a left at the fork onto Soane St.

Places to Stay & Eat

Dickens used the *Great White Horse Hotel* (☎ 256558, fax 253396, e gwh@keme.co.uk, Tavern St) in *Pickwick Papers*. The 'mouldy, ill-lighted rooms' were recently renovated (no more mould and plenty of light); they cost £45/55 for a single/double.

Cliffden Guest House (☎ 252689, fax 461077, e cliffden@btinternet.com, 21 London Rd) is a 10-minute walk west of the TIC along Tavern St. It charges from £20/34.

There's also very comfortable farmhouse accommodation from £18/42 at *College Farm* (☎/fax 652253, e bryce1@agripro .co.uk, Hintlesham), 6 miles (10km) west of Ipswich, just off the A1071 to Hadleigh.

There are some good places to eat by the Wet Dock. We recommend *Il Punto* (☎ 289748), located aboard a pleasure boat docked along the quayside. The food is French and you can eat well for around £15.

Getting There & Away

National Express (☎ 0870 580 8080) runs daily coaches to Ipswich from several destinations, including London (£8.50, 2¾ hours) and Cambridge (£6.75, 1½ hours). The largest of the several local bus companies is First Eastern Counties (☎ 0845 602 0121). They run eight buses daily, Monday to Friday, to Sudbury (£2.40, one hour). Beestons (☎ 823243) also runs about 10 buses daily, Monday to Saturday (£2.70 return) between the two towns. On Sunday,

Chambers (☎ 01787-227233) runs five buses (£2.40).

Trains run half-hourly to London's Liverpool St station (£18.40, 1¼ hours) and at least hourly to Norwich (£11.50, 50 minutes). There are 12 trains daily to Bury St Edmunds (£4, 30 minutes); and six daily to Lowestoft (£8.40, 1½ hours).

STOUR VALLEY

Running along the border between Suffolk and Essex, the River Stour flows through perhaps the most appealing landscape in the region. It has a soft, pastoral feel that has inspired some of England's most noteworthy painters, including John Constable and Thomas Gainsborough. Although hard to believe today, the sedate villages dotted along the banks of the Stour were once veritable powerhouses in the medieval cloth trade, but with the growth of the bigger towns in the area – Colchester, Norwich and Ipswich – their importance receded dramatically. By the 19th century, southern Suffolk was a rural backwater ignored by the Industrial Revolution and virtually everyone else – a curse for the locals but a godsend for the visitor looking for a genuine experience of the gentle English countryside. While some of the more picturesque towns, such as Lavenham and Sudbury, are attracting visitors in greater numbers, the area is still quiet enough to ensure that you'll be able to explore it. For Dedham Vale, the area known as Constable country, see the Essex section in the South-Eastern England chapter.

Long Melford
☎ 01787 • pop 2800

Known for its long high street (the longest in England, the locals like to claim) and the lovely timber-framed buildings that line it, Long Melford has a magnificent church with some fine stained-glass windows, two stately homes and the obligatory antique shops.

Run by the National Trust (NT), **Melford Hall** (☎ 880286) is a turreted Tudor mansion in the centre of the village, dating from 1578. There's an 18th-century drawing room, a Regency library, a Victorian bedroom and a display of paintings by Beatrix

Potter, who was a distant relative of the Parker family (owners of the house from 1786 until 1960, when it passed to the hands of the Treasury). It opens 2 to 5.30 pm Wednesday to Sunday, May to September, and 2 to 5.30 pm Saturday and Sunday, April and October; phone for other times. Admission costs £4.30/2.15.

On the edge of the village, down a tree-lined avenue, lies **Kentwell Hall** (☎ 310207), another red-brick Tudor mansion described by *Country Life* as 'the epitome of many people's image of an Elizabethan house'. It is too, probably because it is privately owned and makes a big deal of its Tudor origins. It is not a museum, but a fully functioning household whose decor and furnishings have been carefully restored over the last 30 years. The owners are big Tudor fans, and between mid-June and mid-July they host a re-enactment festival, when over 200 Tudor enthusiasts abandon their contemporary cynicism in favour of traditional hose and velvet jacket and descend on Kentwell Hall to recreate and live out a certain year in the Tudor calendar.

The house is surrounded by a moat, and there's a brick-paved Tudor Rose maze and a rare-breeds farm. It opens noon to 5 pm daily, April to October, and entry costs £4.90/2.90 (more during the historical re-enactment period).

Places to Stay & Eat At the northern end of the village, *High Street Farmhouse (☎/fax 375765, High St)* has three doubles for £50; single occupancy is £30. All are en suite.

The George & Dragon (☎ 371285, fax 312428, Hall St) has singles/doubles for £35/60. It also has a pretty good restaurant serving good local specialities and classic English cuisine; mains range from £6.95 to £13.95.

The upmarket *Black Lion (☎ 312356, fax 374557, The Green)* has well appointed, comfortable singles/doubles from £69/90.

Most of the cheaper places to eat are on Hall St. *Chips & Chopstix (☎ 378776)* is a fish and chip-cum-Chinese takeaway. *Melford Valley Indian Cuisine (☎ 310079)* serves good dishes for around £10 each.

The best (and most expensive) eatery in town is *Scutchers Bistro (☎ 310200, West-gate St)*, just west of the Green near the Black Lion. It has a mouth-watering menu famous throughout the region. Mains cost from £8.90 to £15.90. It is closed on Monday.

Entertainment The Great Church of the Holy Trinity has lunchtime recitals at 1.10 pm every Wednesday from mid-May to mid-September. For details on what's on, contact Mrs Jilly Cooper on ☎ 281836.

Shopping The village is littered with antique shops. Across the street from Scutcher's on Westgate St, Country Antiques (☎ 310617) is a treasure trove of 18th- and 19th-century antiques and small, domestic furniture – perfect for sticking in your suitcase or rucksack!

If you like barometers, check out Patrick Marney's shop in the Gate House of Melford Hall (☎ 880533). The shop is so exclusive – and Marney's work so specialised – that viewing appointments are required.

Getting There & Away Chambers Buses (☎ 227233) runs 13 buses Monday to Saturday between Long Melford and Bury St Edmunds (£2, one hour) calling at Sudbury (£1, five minutes). They also run a circular bus route between Long Melford and Sudbury (£1, 10 minutes) at 10 and 40 minutes past the hour from Monday to Saturday.

Sudbury
☎ 01787 • pop 17,800

The most important town in the western half of the Stour Valley, Sudbury is a bustling town that grew up as a result of a roaring medieval trade in wool. The wool industry has been reduced to little more than a whimper these days, but the town continues to maintain a key link with the manufacture of cloth, particularly silk weaving. Although not an unpleasant place to spend an afternoon, most visitors come to visit the birthplace of the town's most famous son, portrait and landscape painter Thomas Gainsborough (1727–88). Charles

Celebrity Duel: Thomas Gainsborough vs Sir Joshua Reynolds

Although Thomas Gainsborough (1727–88) was undoubtedly one of the major English painters, his professional life was marked by a fairly intense but mutually respectful rivalry with the pre-eminent portrait artist of the 18th century, Sir Joshua Reynolds (1723–92).

Although both were extremely accomplished painters, Gainsborough was in many ways the antithesis of Reynolds. Whereas Reynolds was sober-minded and the complete professional, Gainsborough (even though his output was prodigious) was much more easy-going and often overdue with his commissions, writing that 'painting and punctuality mix like oil and vinegar'. Although eager to advance his career, Gainsborough was lazier than Reynolds, who was an expert at currying favour with the rich and powerful. He always ensured that the dignity (and looks) of his sitters were enhanced by basing their poses along classical lines, whereas Gainsborough preferred looser poses, often setting his subjects against a rich landscape which sometimes took the focus away from the subject. Furthermore, Gainsborough was never exclusively a portraitist (the best path towards advancement in the vainglorious 18th century), stating that while he painted portraits by profession he painted landscapes by choice.

Ever mindful of the successes of the other, the two painters' careers took similar strides. In 1768 both were founder members of the Royal Academy, and while Reynolds went on to be its president and George III's Principal Painter, Gainsborough's skill with the brush ensured that he soon became a favourite at the Royal Court. One story has it that at a Royal Academy dinner, Reynolds proposed a toast to 'Gainsborough, the best landscape painter in Britain' to which a fellow academician replied, 'and the best portrait artist too!' Reynolds, whose speciality was portraiture, was suitably incensed.

The two rivals were united, however, at Gainsborough's death bed. The dying man asked specifically for Reynolds to come and see him, and after his death Reynolds paid tribute to his rival in his 14th *Discourse*. Recognising the fluid brilliance of his brushwork, Reynolds praised 'his manner of forming all the parts of a picture together' and wrote of 'all those odd scratches and marks' that 'by a kind of magic, at a certain distance...seem to drop into their proper places'. Gainsborough, who disdained literature and preferred music, would have been grudgingly impressed.

Dickens recreated the town in *Pickwick Papers* as Eatanswill.

The TIC (☎ 881320, fax 374314) is in the town hall. It opens 10 am to 4.45 pm Monday to Saturday, Easter to October (shorter hours the rest of the year). See also the Web site at www.babergh-south-suffolk.gov.uk.

Gainsborough's House The birthplace of Thomas Gainsborough at 46 Gainsborough St has been preserved as a shrine and is now home to a museum (☎ 372958) with the largest collection of his work in the country. The house features a Georgian facade built by Gainsborough's father, while the mulberry tree in the garden features in some of the son's paintings. Inside, the extensive collection features his earliest known work, *A Boy and a Girl in a Land-scape*, now in two separate parts (the author of the separation is unknown), a portrait of *Reverend Tobias Rustat* and the exquisite *Lady Tracy*. This last work is particularly beautiful for its delicate portrayal of drapery and its folds. Gainsborough's studio features original furniture as well as his walking stick and pocket watch. In the parlour is the statue of a horse, the only known sculpture the artist ever produced. The Gallery and Weaving Room are home to constantly changing exhibits of modern art, while in summer the garden hosts a sculpture exhibition. The house opens 10 am to 4 pm Tuesday to Saturday and 2 to 4 pm on Sunday. Admission costs £3/1.50. See also the boxed text, 'Celebrity Duel: Thomas Gainsborough vs Sir Joshua Reynolds'.

Places to Stay If you plan to stay, *The Old Bull Hotel* (☎ *374120, fax 379044, Church St*) is a family-run hotel in a 16th-century building with nine rooms, all decorated differently. Singles/doubles start at £38/52.

Similarly priced is the *Boathouse Hotel* (☎/*fax 379090, Ballingdon Bridge*) – rooms start at £34/52 – but it's on the water and the hotel rents out rowing boats.

Getting There & Away Bus travel in and out of Sudbury is quite tricky. Beestons (☎ 01473-823243) runs nine buses daily, Monday to Friday (seven on Saturday), to Ipswich (£2.70, one hour). To get almost anywhere else involves a few changes. For Cambridge, you first have to get to Haverhill. Beestons has nine buses a day to Haverhill, Monday to Friday (£1.70, 45 minutes). There are seven buses on Saturday and five on Sunday. From Haverhill, Stagecoach Cambus (☎ 01223-423554) runs buses roughly every half hour to Cambridge (£2.40, one hour) from Monday to Saturday and every two hours on Sunday.

Sudbury also has a train station with an hourly service to London (£15.90, 1¼ hours).

LAVENHAM
☎ 01787 • pop 1700

A tourist honey pot, Lavenham can get crowded with bus tours but it's nevertheless worth seeing. It's a beautifully preserved example of a medieval wool town, with over 300 listed buildings. Some are timber-framed, others decorated with pargeting. There are cosy, pink, thatched cottages, crooked houses, antique shops and art galleries, quaint tea-rooms and ancient inns. When the wool industry moved to the west and north of England in the late 16th century, none of Lavenham's inhabitants could afford to build anything more modern. Today, as long as there are not too many tourists around, you can feel as if you're in a time warp while walking through parts of the village.

The Market Place, off the High St, is dominated by the handsome **Guildhall** (☎ 247646; NT), a superb example of a

close-studded, timber-framed building, dating back to the early 16th century. It's now a local history museum with displays on the wool trade and opens 9 am to 5.30 pm daily Easter to October; admission costs £3.

Little Hall, which has soft ochre plastering and grey timber, is a private house that can be visited. It opens 2 to 5.30 pm Wednesday, Thursday and at the weekend, April to October; admission costs £1.75/1.

At the southern end of the village, opposite the car park, is the **Church of St Peter and St Paul**. Its soaring steeple is visible for miles around. The church bears witness to Lavenham's past prosperity at the centre of the local wool trade.

The TIC (☎ 248207), Lady St, has lists of places to stay. It opens 10 am to 5.30 pm. One of the most attractive and atmospheric places is *Lavenham Priory* (☎ *247404, fax 248472,* e *mail@lavenhampriory.co.uk, Water St*). Once the home of Benedictine monks, then medieval cloth merchants, up-market B&B is now offered here for £39 to £59 per person. It's a beautiful place, but you cannot visit it unless you are a guest. You can, however, get a virtual tour of the building at their Web site, www.lavenham priory.co.uk.

The Island House (☎ *248181,* e *island house@dial.pipex.com, Lower Rd*) is beautifully set at the edge of a wood east of Market Square (walk 200 yards to the end of Prentice St to get to the Lower Rd). It has two rooms for £50 per person.

Since most people come just for the day, there are numerous teashops offering light lunches. The *Angel Gallery* (☎ *247388, Market Place*) does a fine venison fillet with juniper and mushrooms for £10.25 – all other mains come in at around £8.

Chambers (☎ 01787-227233) runs hourly buses (until 6 pm Monday to Saturday, no service on Sunday) from Bury St Edmunds (£1.60, 30 minutes), which run through Sudbury (£1.60, 20 minutes), 7 miles (11km) to the south, on their way to Colchester. There are no direct buses from Cambridge; you must go via Sudbury, also the location of the nearest train station (see the Sudbury section earlier in the chapter).

KERSEY

☎ 01473 • pop 240

Lavenham's only rival as the most photogenic village in Suffolk lies 8 miles (13km) south-east, just off the A1141. It's actually little more than a one-street hamlet lined with Tudor-style, timber-framed houses that in recent years have become highly prized by estate agents and property developers looking to flog a bit of 'merry old England' to city folk in search of a weekend getaway home. Hardly surprising considering its genuine charm and appeal, even though there is little to do here save admire the architecture and marvel at the fact that the village's only street (appositely named 'The Street') dips and disappears into a shallow ford before reappearing on the other side!

Once you're done you can go for a pint or a bite to eat at either of the pubs, the *Bell Inn* (☎ 823229) or the *White Horse* (☎ 824418). Both serve a fairly good pub lunch.

Getting There & Away

Galloway European Coachlines (☎ 01449-766323) runs a service three times daily except Sunday between Kersey and Ipswich (£1.90, one hour) and Kersey and Hadleigh (70p, 15 minutes). On Sunday, Chambers (☎ 01787-227233) and First Eastern National (☎ 01245-256159) each run one direct service between Kersey and Ipswich (£1.55, 25 minutes), also serving Sudbury (£1.30, 20 minutes). From Lavenham, the only way to get here is by taxi; the only company is Granger's Cars (☎ 01787-247456 or 0589-409237), operated by a fellow called Cyril, who charges between £6 and £7. The trip takes about 20 minutes.

HADLEIGH

☎ 01473 • pop 6595

Two miles (3km) south-east of Kersey, Hadleigh is a largish town with a wonderful 15th-century **Guildhall** (☎ 827752), topped by a splendid crown post roof. The building has been managed by the Hadleigh Market Feoffment (elected management committee) continuously since 1432. It opens 2.30 to 5 pm Thursday and Sunday only, June to September. Admission to the guildhall costs £1.50, and includes a guided tour. Alternatively, you can wander into the garden for cream teas, served during opening hours (when it's not raining). A scone with cream and strawberry jam, washed down with a cup of tea, will set you back about £2.

Hadleigh is also the headquarters of the East of England Tourist Board (☎ 822922, fax 823063, e eastofenglandtouristboard@ compuserve.com), just off the High St in Toppesfield Hall. It is not a walk-in office, so all enquiries should be by telephone. They can, however, provide comprehensive lists of what to see and do in the region as well as where to stay and eat.

There are a couple of decent pubs in town. The *Cock Inn* (☎ 822879, 89 George St) is a typical country pub that serves a limited menu of bar food.

A number of bus companies serve Hadleigh from Ipswich and Sudbury on an hourly basis, including First Eastern Counties (☎ 0845 602 0121) and First Eastern National (☎ 01245-256159), Beestons (☎ 01473-823243) and Galloway European Coachlines (☎ 01449-766323). It's a 30-minute ride from Ipswich (£1.60) and 35 minutes from Sudbury (£1.40).

BURY ST EDMUNDS

☎ 01284 • pop 30,500

This is easily Suffolk's most attractive large town, straddling the Rivers Lark and Linnet amid gently rolling farmland. The town has a distinct Georgian flavour, with street upon street of handsome, 18th-century facades that hark back to a period of great prosperity. It's now a busy agricultural centre and cattle, vegetable and fruit markets are held every Wednesday and Saturday. Greene King, the famous Suffolk brewer, is based here.

Centrally placed, Bury is a convenient point from which to explore west Suffolk. The ruined abbey is set in a beautiful garden and is worth seeing. There's also a fascinating clock museum, and recommended guided tours of the brewery.

History

Suffolk's most attractive large town is best known today for its grid of elegant Georgian streets and – in summer – the blossoms of its flower gardens. It is within easy reach of Ipswich and Cambridge and is well worth visiting, if only for a day trip.

Bury's motto 'Shrine of a King, Cradle of the Law' recalls the two most memorable events in its history. The Danes decapitated Edmund, a Christian prince from Saxony who was destined to be the last king of East Anglia, in 856 and his body was brought here for reburial in 903. The shrine to the saint became the focal point of a new Benedictine monastery called St Edmundsbury, around which the town grew. The abbey, now ruined, became one of the most famous pilgrimage centres in the country and until the dissolution of the monasteries in 1537 was the wealthiest in the country; for many years St Edmund was patron saint of England.

The second memorable episode in Bury's early history took place at the abbey. In 1214, at St Edmund's Altar, the English barons drew up the petition that formed the basis of the Magna Carta.

Orientation & Information

Bury is an easy place to find your way around because it has preserved Abbot Baldwin's 11th-century grid layout.

The train station is a quarter of a mile north of the town centre; there are regular bus connections (50p) to the centre. The bus station is in the heart of town. The TIC (☎ 764667, fax 757084, ℮ eloise.appleby@burybo.stedsbc.gov.uk), 6 Angel Hill, opens 9 am to 5.30 pm daily, Easter to October, and the same hours daily except Sunday the rest of the year. Phone for information and times of the guided walking tours (£3/free for children) that start from here.

There are tours of the Greene King Brewery (☎ 763222), Crown St, at 2.30 pm Monday to Thursday. Tickets are £6; tours are popular, so you need to book ahead.

The post office (☎ 763954) is at 56–58 St Andrew's St South.

Walking Tour

Outside the TIC on Angel Hill there are many fine Georgian buildings, such as the 18th-century Angel Hotel, which is covered in thick Virginia creeper.

The Abbey & Park Although the abbey is very much a ruin, it's a spectacular one set in a beautiful garden. After the dissolution of the monasteries, the townspeople made off with much of the stone – even St Edmund's grave and bones have disappeared.

To reach the abbey, walk right along Angel Hill until you're opposite the second Abbey Gate, which is still as impressive in its austere regality as it was in Norman times. Cross over and walk around the green, which is home to Elisabeth Frink's statue of St Edmund (1976). From here, you can see the remains of part of the west front and Samson Tower, which have houses built into them.

The abbey opens until sunset daily and admission is free. There's a visitor centre housed in Samson's Tower (once part of the west side of the abbey), where an excellent 45-minute Walkman tour (£1.50) is available. Alternatively, you can guide yourself around the ruins using the information boards, which help to show how large a community this must have been with its chapels and priory, its chapter house and treasury, abbot's palace and garden. The huge church dominated everything in the vicinity. It contains a crypt and St Edmund's Altar, near which is the plaque commemorating the barons' pledge of 1214.

Walk down to the river, past the old dovecote, before turning back to head for the superb formal gardens, with circular flowerbeds set in perfectly manicured lawns. Leave by the Gothic Gate and turn left to reach the cathedral.

St Edmundsbury Cathedral The cathedral dates from the 16th century, but the eastern end was added between 1945 and 1960 and the northern side was not completed until 1990. It was made a cathedral in 1914. The interior is light and lofty with a painted hammer-beam roof. It opens 8.30 am to 8 pm, April to October (until 7 pm the rest of the year). The cathedral was recently granted £10 million-worth of

National Lottery funds by the Millennium Commission that will go towards the cathedral's restoration; the project is expected to last until 2004.

St Mary's Church From the cathedral, turn left out of the west door and walk past the Norman Tower to reach St Mary's. Built around 1430, it contains the tomb of Mary Tudor (Henry VIII's sister and one-time queen of France). A curfew bell is still rung, as it was in the Middle Ages.

Manor House Museum At 5 Honey Hill, near St Mary's, is a magnificent museum of horology, art and costume housed in a Georgian building. It's worth being here around noon, when the clocks strike. Manor House (☎ 757072) opens 10 am to 5 pm Tuesday to Sunday; admission costs £2.85/1.85.

Art Gallery & Moyse's Hall Retrace your steps on Honey Hill and Crown St, then turn left up Churchgate St, turning right at the end onto Guildhall St. Up the street on the right, is Market Cross, remodelled in 1774 by Robert Adam as a theatre and now the Art Gallery (☎ 762081). It opens 10.30 am to 5 pm Tuesday to Sunday; admission costs 50p. Turn right by the Corn Exchange and continue to the Buttermarket, where Moyse's Hall, dating back to the 12th century, is probably East Anglia's oldest domestic building. It is now a local museum (☎ 757488), but at the time of writing was closed for refurbishment until October 2001; call for details.

Activities
Rollerskating At *Rollerbury* (☎ 701216), Station Hill, you can get your skates on at England's home of roller-skating. There are classes, fitness programs, private sessions and roller-discos. At 4 pm on Tuesday there's a class for beginners (£2.75, 2½ hours). Admission costs £5; you can rent ordinary skates for 60p or blades for £2.

Places to Stay
There's B&B at **Hilltop** (☎ 767066, e bandb@hilltop22br.freeserve.co.uk, 22 Bronyon Close, off Flemyng Rd) for £16 per person. **Sheila Keeley Oak Cottage B&B** (☎ 762745, fax 762745, 54 Guildhall St) is a centrally located place with rooms for the same price.

Ounce House (☎ 761779, fax 768315, e pott@globalnet.co.uk, Northgate St) is very comfortable, centrally located and non-smoking. Singles/doubles with bath start at £55/75; ask for a room with a garden view.

Charles Dickens stayed at the **Angel Hotel** (☎ 753926, fax 750092, e sales@ theangel.co.uk, 3 Angel Hill), in the centre of Bury. It's an upmarket place with prices to match, starting at £69/84 for singles/doubles (breakfast extra). Weekend breaks are cheaper at £54 per person B&B, or £67 including dinner.

Places to Eat
The **Scandinavia Coffee House** (☎ 700853, 30 Abbeygate) is by the TIC. A smoked-salmon open Danish sandwich is a good lunch for £5.25. The **Refectory**, at the cathedral, also does teas and light lunches.

Holland & Barrett (☎ 706677, 6 Brentgovel St) is a vegetarian restaurant and cafe; most dishes are around £3. It's open until 4.30 pm Monday to Saturday.

Maison Bleue (☎ 760623, 31 Churchgate St) is a highly recommended seafood restaurant. Main dishes (brill, sea bass, monkfish etc) range from £9 to £14.50, and there's a set menu for £19. It's closed on Sunday.

Entertainment
Pubs Just off Abbeygate, the best known pub in Bury is the **Nutshell** (☎ 764867, 1 The Traverse). It's the smallest pub in the country – it measures 4.80m by 2.25m – and also has a mummified cat.

The Wolf (☎ 755188, 88 St John's St) is one of the newer pubs in town and a favourite with the younger crowd.

Nightclubs The most popular club in town is **Club Brazilia** (☎ 769655, Station Hill), with a mix of hard house, garage, club classics and 70s disco. It opens 9 pm to 3 am Thursday to Saturday. The usual dress code (no trainers and jeans) is enforced pretty strictly except on Friday nights, but you'd better be on the safe side. Admission costs between £3 and £6, depending on the night.

Getting There & Away

Bury is 75 miles (121km) from London, 35 miles (56km) from Norwich and 28 miles (45km) from Cambridge.

There's a daily National Express (☎ 0870 580 8080) bus to London (£12.25, 2 hours and 20 minutes). From Cambridge, Stagecoach Cambus (☎ 01223-423554) runs buses to Bury (£4.20 for a day return, 35 minutes) every two hours Monday to Saturday; the last bus back to Cambridge leaves at 5.05 pm.

Bury is on the Ipswich to Ely line, so trains to London (£23.50, 1¾ hours) go via these towns. From Cambridge, there are trains every two hours to Bury (£5.30, 45 minutes).

AROUND BURY ST EDMUNDS
Ickworth House & Park

Three miles (5km) south-west of Bury on the A143, Ickworth House is the eccentric creation of the Earl of Bristol. It's an amazing structure, with an immense oval rotunda dating back to 1795. It contains a fine collection of furniture, silver and paintings (Titian, Gainsborough and Velasquez). Outside, there's an unusual Italian garden and a park designed by Capability Brown, with waymarked trails, a deer enclosure and a hide.

Ickworth House (☎ 01284-735270; NT) opens 1 to 5 pm, mid-March to October. The park opens 7 am to 7 pm, all year. Admission costs £5.50/2.40 for the house and park, £2.40/80p for the park alone.

To get here by bus, First Eastern Counties runs a twice-daily service (£1.25, 12.35 and 4.10 pm) bound for Garboldisham (No 304), leaving from outside Bury train station.

Pakenham Water Mill

Six miles (10km) north-east of Bury along the A143 is the only parish in England to retain a working water mill and windmill. Corn has been ground here for over 900 years, and the mill makes an appearance in

the Domesday Book survey of 1086. The mill ceased production in 1974, but it was taken over four years later by the Suffolk Preservation Society, who sponsored a painstaking restoration. During the restoration a Tudor mill was uncovered on the site of the present building, which dates from the late 18th century. Visitors get a guided tour of the building and can observe the grinding process from start to finish; you can also buy ground corn produced on the premises. As it is a working mill (☎ 01359-230275), admission is restricted: it opens to the general public 2 to 5.30 pm, Wednesday and weekends, Good Friday to the end of September. Admission costs £2/1.75.

To get here, First Eastern Counties (☎ 0845 602 0121) runs four buses daily from 1.05 pm (No 337 to Thetford), Monday to Friday and three on Saturday (£1.50, 20 minutes). The bus stops in front of the Fox pub; the mill is just up the street.

SUFFOLK COAST

Separated from the rest of the county by a maquis of woodland and swathes of marsh, the Suffolk Coast is one of the most unspoiled coastlines in England, at least by human hand (if you ignore the Sizewell nuclear power plant). Coastal erosion has done its fair of damage – the old section of Dunwich lies underwater – while the demise of the fishing industry, once the main provider for the coastal towns, has brought with it sharp economic depression. Still, this is a coast of contrasts, from the traditional seaside resorts such as Lowestoft in the north, the busy port of Felixstowe (now freight only – passenger ferries all go from Harwich) in the south, and some of the least visited sections of coastline in England in- between. In April 2000 the government declared the coast an Area of Outstanding Natural Beauty, granting it near-preservation status. With public transport virtually nonexistent in places it can be tough to get around if you don't have your own wheels, but an excellent country walk and the quiet serenity of some of the seaside villages make this a good spot to idle away a few lazy days.

EASTERN ENGLAND

Aldeburgh

☎ 01728 • pop 2800

The sea is closing in on Aldeburgh (alde-braw), where the beach is now only yards from the village. The town is best known for the Aldeburgh Festival, an annual program of music and the arts that was begun in 1948 by Benjamin Britten and his lover, the tenor Peter Pears (see Aldeburgh Festival later). The town's other claim to fame is as the 1999 winner of the Small Country Town category of the 'Anglia in Bloom' competition, when the town's gardens and flower arrangements were resplendent, leading one of the judges to remark that 'this beautiful town has become a floral showpiece. We were almost overwhelmed by the experience of judging it.' High praise indeed. Yet even when the flowers are not in bloom the town is quite pleasant and well worth stopping at.

The TIC (☎/fax 453637, ⓔ atic@ suffolkcoastal.gov.uk), on High St, opens 9 am to 5.15 pm daily, Easter to October. The rest of the year it opens 10 am to 4 pm Monday to Saturday.

Things to See Aldeburgh's important building, the 16th-century **Moot Hall**, was once in the middle of town but is now right on the seashore. This elegant, redbrick building is home to the local folk museum with bits and bobs on Aldeburgh's history (contact the TIC for details). It opens 10.30 am to 12.30 pm and 2.30 to 5 pm, July to August (afternoons only, September and October). Admission costs 60p.

The other place worth checking out is the Royal National Lifeboat Institution (RNLI) Lifeboat Station (☎ 452552), opposite Jubilee Hall on the seafront. It was built in 1994 thanks to a generous donation by Russian emigre Eugenie Boucher, who came here in the 1920s. The station is always open, but the best time to visit is during the bi-weekly launch of the lifeboat. Call for exact times, as they vary.

Places to Stay & Eat Try the *Blaxhall Youth Hostel* (☎ 688206), 4½ miles (7km) from Aldeburgh, near Snape Maltings; beds are £8.50/6 for adults/juniors.

Sanviv (☎ 453107, 59 Fairfield Rd) is a chalet bungalow with one large double for £20 per person. It is no smoking.

The *Alde End House* (☎/fax 454755, 90 Saxmundham Rd) is on the edge of town, on the road to Saxmundham. Singles/doubles cost £20/40.

East Cottage (☎/fax 453010, ⓔ anglia55 @hotmail.com, 55 King St) is a period cottage (built in 1892) about 40 yards from the beach. Rooms start at £20 per person. It opens May to September only. It fills up pretty quickly, so you're best off booking well in advance.

At the top end is the *Wentworth Hotel* (☎ 452312, fax 452343, ⓔ wentworth.hotel @anglian.co.uk, Wentworth Rd), close to the water's edge. It's a fancy country house with prices to match: rooms start at £51.50/82 in January, while in August the cheapest rates are £64/103.

Aldeburgh Festival Founded in 1948 by composer Benjamin Britten (who was born in Lowestoft in 1913), eastern England's most renowned cultural event takes place each June in venues around Aldeburgh and in a number of superbly converted malthouses at Snape, 3 miles (5km) up the River Alde (along which runs the B1069). The Snape Maltings (☎ 01728-688303) is now an impressive complex, including a recording studio, a music school, craft shops, galleries and a pub as well as the concert hall.

For festival information and bookings, phone the box office in Aldeburgh on ☎ 453543, or see the Web site at www .aldeburgh.co.uk.

Getting There & Away First Eastern Counties (☎ 0845 602 0121) runs hourly buses between Ipswich and Aldeburgh (£3, one hour and 20 minutes).

Sizewell

Nuclear power stations, like tobacco companies, expend an enormous amount of energy trying to convince people that their product is – despite strong evidence to the contrary – safe. The plant at Sizewell, 4 miles (6km) north of Aldeburgh along the

Tourist hustle and bustle, Great Yarmouth

MANFRED GOTTSCHALK

Traditional windpower in the Norfolk Broads

DAVID ELSE

Punting frenzy: an afternoon on the River Cam, Cambridge

JON DAVISON

The windswept delights of the Norfolk Coast Path

Strolling through the heart of Norfolk on the Weavers Way

Timber-framed houses in Lavenham, Suffolk: just a few of the village's abundance of historic buildings

coast, is no different. In the far-flung days of the 1960s, when the first of the plant's two reactors was built (reactor A), there were few protests save perhaps an objection to the distinctive superstructure topped by what is most kindly described as a huge golf ball. It was the construction of the second reactor (B) in the wake of the Chernobyl disaster that unleashed a storm of protest and was subject to a year-long public enquiry. When it finally went into operation in 1995, a snazzy, super-friendly information centre was opened alongside; here you're assured how impossible it is for an accident to occur.

Whatever your view, if you feel like finding out more (or getting a guided tour of the place), the information centre (☎ 01728-653890) opens to visitors 10 am to 4 pm Monday to Friday and 12 to 4 pm on Sunday, Easter to October. Admission is free. There are 1½-hour walking tours of Reactor A at 11.30 am and 1.30 pm on Wednesday and Thursday (12.15 and 2.15 pm on Sunday).

Reactor B can only be visited by a 45-minute bus tour between 11 am and 3.15 pm Monday to Friday (from 12 pm on Sunday). All tours are free.

To get here, you'll need your own transportation.

Orford

Few visitors get to this little village, 6 miles (10km) south of Snape, but there are several worthwhile attractions. The ruins of **Orford Castle** (☎ 01394-450472), run by English Heritage (EH), date from the 12th century; only the keep has survived. It opens 10 am to 5 pm daily (shorter hours from November to March) and admission costs £2.50/1.30.

The other draw is gastronomic. From Orford Quay, *MV Lady Florence (☎ 0831-698298)* takes diners on all-inclusive, 2½-hour brunch cruises (9 to 11.30 am) or four-hour lunch or dinner cruises year-round. The brunch cruise costs £18.25 all-inclusive (the menu is fixed), while the lunch and dinner cruises cost £10 per person for the boat plus whatever you choose from the menu: mains cost between £6.95 and £8.75.

Norfolk

Noel Coward once famously remarked that Norfolk was very flat. It is, but he didn't just mean the landscape. Although the nightlife has become a lot livelier in Norwich since then, it's still not Monte Carlo. And frankly, that's what is nice about it. Once a busy wool-producing and trading area making use of the ports of King's Lynn and Great Yarmouth, Norfolk is now much quieter and less populated than it was in the Middle Ages. It's a sleepy county, not yet overrun by tourists, with a superb, unspoiled coastline and several nature reserves that attract bird-watchers.

Norwich, the county town, is a very pleasant place with an interesting castle and cathedral and excellent nightlife. The Norfolk Broads is a network of inland waterways that have long been popular for boating holidays, and King's Lynn is a historic port on the River Ouse, with several very well-preserved buildings along the waterfront – even though the newer part of town is best described as 'soulless'. The whole area is easily accessible from Cambridge.

WALKING & CYCLING

Several waymarked walking trails cross the county, the best known being the Peddars Way (see the Activities chapter at the start of the book). The Weavers Way is a 57-mile (92km) walk from Cromer to Great Yarmouth via Blickling and Stalham. The Angles Way follows the valleys of the Waveney and the Little Ouse for 70 miles (113km). The Around Norfolk Walk is a 220-mile (354km) trail linking the Peddars Way, the Norfolk Coast Path, the Weavers Way and the Angles Way. TICs have information leaflets on these walks and on cycle routes. See the Web site at www.visit norfolk.co.uk.

GETTING AROUND

The public transport county phone line (☎ 01603-613613) has information on bus routes; there are several operators, the largest being First Eastern Counties (☎ 0845 602 0121).

Norwich, King's Lynn, Cromer and Great Yarmouth are accessible by rail.

NORWICH
☎ 01603 • pop 170,000

Norfolk's county town (pronounced nor-ridge) was once larger than London. For several centuries, when its prosperity was based on trade with the Low Countries, it was the second-largest town in England.

The East Angles had a fortified centre at Norwich that was burned down twice by marauding Danes. The Normans built the splendid castle keep, now the best-preserved example in the country. Below the castle lies what has been described as the most complete medieval English city. Clustered around the castle and cathedral within the circle of river and city walls are more than 30 parish churches.

Norwich is a surprisingly lively city with a large student population and the best nightlife in the region outside of Cambridge; the University of East Anglia is on the western outskirts.

Orientation
The city centre, where you'll most likely spend most of your time, grew up around the castle and its size is easily manageable. There are two cathedrals – Roman Catholic to the west and Anglican to the east. Most of the cheaper accommodation is west of the centre along the Earlham Rd.

Outside the TIC is the market, a patch-work of stall awnings known as tilts. This is one of the biggest and longest-running markets in the country. It was moved here 900 years ago from its original site in Tombland by the now Anglican cathedral.

Information
Tourist Office The TIC (☎ 666071, fax 765389, e tourism.norwich@gtnet.gov.uk) is in the guildhall, Gaol Hill. It opens 9.30 am to 5 pm Monday to Saturday, June to September (until 4.30 pm the rest of the year). A number of guided walking tours (£2.50/1, 1½ hours) take place at various

times, including the evening – phone the TIC for details. See also the Web site at www.norwich.gov.uk.

Post & Communications There is a post office (☎ 220228) at 13–17 Bank Plain and another (☎ 761635) at 84–85 Castle Mall. UKCybercafés (☎ 612643, e norwich@ukcybercafes.co.uk) is at 46 Magdalen St. It charges £2 for 15 minutes, £3 for half an hour and £6 for an hour. It opens 9 am to 9 pm Monday to Friday, 10 am to 5 pm on Saturday (to 4 pm on Sunday).

Laundry Gaydays Launderette (☎ 624891) is at 24 Earlham Rd, just opposite EdMar Lodge (see Places to Stay later). It opens 7.30 am to 11 pm daily, but if you want to leave a bag in for a service wash you can only do so from 8.30 am to 6 pm daily except Wednesday and Sunday. A 10lb bag will cost you about £5.

Medical Services Superdrug Pharmacy (☎ 619179) is at 25 Gentleman's Walk. It opens 8.30 am to 6 pm Monday to Saturday. Norfolk & Norwich Hospital (☎ 286286) is on Wessex St, about 500 yards south of Unthank Rd.

Emergency The police station (☎ 768769) is on Bethel St, south-west of the market. For all emergencies dial ☎ 999.

Things to See & Do
Norwich Castle Two blocks east of the market square is the massive Norman castle keep. It was built in about 1160 and measures 28m square by 21m high – a solid sentinel on the hill overlooking the medieval and modern cities. It's the best surviving example of Norman military architecture after the Tower of London and has worn pretty well, although it was refaced in 1834.

The castle is now a museum, housing archaeological and natural-history exhibits, as well as providing a gallery for the paintings of the Norwich School. Founded by John Crome in the early 19th century, this group, which included John Cotman, painted local

EASTERN ENGLAND

landscapes and won acclaim throughout Europe. At the time of writing, **Norwich Castle Museum** (☎ 493624) was undergoing a substantial refurbishment, courtesy of funds provided by the Millennium Commission, and is due to reopen in the spring of 2001. Call for details.

Also on the premises, in the Shirehall (entrance opposite the Anglia TV station), is the **Royal Norfolk Regimental Museum** (☎ 493649), detailing the history of the local regiment since 1830. It opens 10 am to 5 pm Monday to Saturday. Admission costs £1.80/90p.

Elm Hill

Thanks to imaginative restoration, this street has retained its medieval charm and atmosphere and is, appropriately enough, the centre of the local antique business. It's one of the most attractive parts of the city. Walk down Wensum St to Tombland, where the market was originally located. 'Tomb' is an old Norse word for 'empty' – hence space for a market.

Norwich Cathedral

The focal point of the city, the Anglican cathedral has retained the appearance and

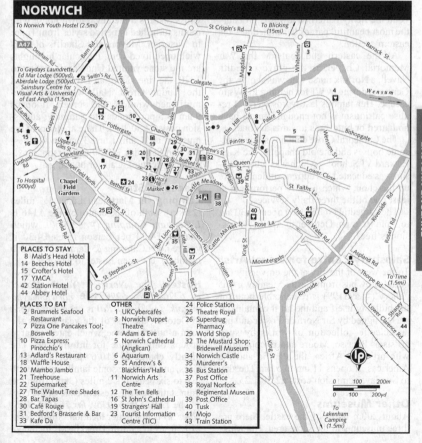

NORWICH

To Norwich Youth Hostel (2.5mi)
To Blicking (15mi)
St Crispin's Rd

To Gaydays Laundrette, Ed Mar Lodge (500yd), Aberdale Lodge (500yd), Sainsbury Centre for Visual Arts & University of East Anglia (1.5mi)

To Hospital (500yd)

EASTERN ENGLAND

PLACES TO STAY
8 Maid's Head Hotel
14 Beeches Hotel
15 Crofter's Hotel
17 YMCA
42 Station Hotel
44 Abbey Hotel

PLACES TO EAT
2 Brummels Seafood Restaurant
7 Pizza One Pancakes Too!; Boswells
10 Pizza Express; Pinocchio's
13 Adlard's Restaurant
18 Waffle House
20 Mambo Jambo
21 Treehouse
22 Supermarket
27 The Walnut Tree Shades
28 Bar Tapas
30 Café Rouge
31 Bedford's Brasserie & Bar
33 Kafe Da

OTHER
1 UKCybercafés
3 Norwich Puppet Theatre
4 Adam & Eve
5 Norwich Cathedral (Anglican)
6 Aquarium
9 St Andrew's & Blackfriars'Halls
11 Norwich Arts Centre
12 The Ten Bells
16 St John's Cathedral
19 Strangers' Hall
23 Tourist Information Centre (TIC)
24 Police Station
25 Theatre Royal
26 Superdrug Pharmacy
29 World Shop
32 The Mustard Shop; Bridewell Museum
34 Norwich Castle
35 Murderer's
36 Bus Station
37 Post Office
38 Royal Norfolk Regimental Museum
39 Post Office
40 Tusk
41 Mojo
43 Train Station

To Time (1.5mi)
To Lakenham Camping (1.5mi)

0   100   200m
0   100   200yd

characteristics of a great Anglo-Norman abbey church more than any other English cathedral, apart from Durham.

The foundation stone was laid in 1096, and the building took 40 years to complete. In 1463 it was made fireproof by means of a magnificent stone lierne vault (an inside roof with many tertiary ribs) that, with its sculpted bosses, is one of the finest achievements of English medieval masonry.

As you enter the cathedral through the west door, the first thing that strikes you is the length of the nave. Its 14 bays are made of yellow-beige stone. Above, on the amazing vault, stories from the Old and New Testament are carved into the bosses. Beyond the richly patterned tower is probably the most beautiful part of the cathedral – the eastern section.

At the eastern end, outside the War Memorial Chapel, is the grave of Edith Cavell, a Norfolk nurse who was shot by the Germans during WWI for helping POWs to escape. Her famous last words were, 'I realise patriotism is not enough. I must have no hatred or bitterness towards anyone.'

The Cathedral Close contains some handsome houses and the old chapel of the King Edward VI School – which was where Nelson was educated. Its current students make up the choir, which usually performs in at least one of the three daily services.

The cathedral (☎ 764385) opens 7.30 am to 7 pm (to 6 pm October to April). Admission is free.

Sainsbury Centre for Visual Arts

To the west of the city at the university (20 minutes by bus from Castle Meadow), this gallery (☎ 593199) is remarkable both for the building itself and the art it contains. It was designed by Sir Norman Foster and has an eclectic collection of works by such artists as Picasso, Moore and Bacon, along with art from Africa, the Pacific and the Americas. It opens 11 am to 5 pm Tuesday to Sunday; admission costs £2.50/1.25.

Other Museums

About 200m north of the castle, there are three museums in the same area. The Mus-

tard Shop, 15 Royal Arcade, has a small museum (☎ 627889) that tells the story of Colman's Mustard, a famous local product. It opens 9.30 am to 5 pm Monday to Saturday and 11 am to 4 pm on Sunday. Admission is free.

Nearby is **Bridewell Museum** (☎ 667227), Bridewell Alley, which has surprisingly interesting displays of local industries throughout the last 200 years. Formerly a merchant's house, in the 14th century it served as an open prison for vagrants (a bridewell). It opens 10 am to 5 pm Monday to Saturday; admission costs £2/1.

Strangers' Hall (☎ 629127) is 250m west of here, along St Andrew's and Charing Cross Sts. It's a medieval town house with rooms furnished in period styles from Tudor to Victorian. Mayors and Sheriffs of Norwich once lived here. Particular highlights are the stone vaulted Undercroft, dating to 1320, the fine Georgian Dining Room and the Tudor Great Hall with its stone-mullioned window and screen. It opens 9 am to 5 pm Monday to Saturday; admission costs £2.50/1.50. There are tours of the museum at 11 am, 1 and 3 pm on Wednesday and Saturday (£2.50 per person, maximum 15 people). Call for bookings.

Places to Stay

Camping On Martineau Lane, 1½ miles (2.5km) south of the centre by the A146 is *Lakenham Camping* (☎ 620060), which charges £4.80 per person (plus £4.30 if you're not a Camping & Caravanning Club member). It's open Easter to October.

Hostels The *Norwich Youth Hostel* (☎ 627647, fax 629075, e norwich@yha .org.uk, 112 Turner Rd) is open daily April to October; the rest of the year it runs the Rent-a-hostel scheme, which caters to large groups only; phone for information. The nightly charge is £10/6.90 for adults/juniors, and there are some family rooms with two to six beds. It's 2 miles (3km) from the train station on the western edge of the city.

The *YMCA* (☎ 620269, fax 762151, 48 St Giles St) is in a better location. Singles cost £13.50; £9 in a dorm. Breakfast is included.

B&Bs. & Hotels Most of the B&Bs and cheaper hotels are outside the ring road, along Earlham and Unthank Rds to the west, and around the train station.

The B&Bs along Earlham Rd become more expensive the closer they are to the centre. *Aberdale Lodge (☎ 502100)*, at No 211, charges £17 per person with shared bath.

EdMar Lodge (☎ 615599, fax 495599, e edmar@cwcom.net, 64 Earlham Rd) is an excellent place, with singles/doubles costing from £26/£34, all with shower.

In the shadow of the Roman Catholic cathedral, *Crofter's Hotel (☎ 613287, 2 Earlham Rd)* has 15 rooms for £44.50/59.50, all with bathrooms. Next door is the comfortable *Beeches Hotel (☎ 621167, fax 620151, e reception@beeches.co.uk, 4–6 Earlham Rd)*. Rooms cost from £59/76 to £64/88. there's a lovely garden.

In the train station area, the *Abbey Hotel (☎/fax 612915, 16 Stracey Rd)* charges £19/38 with shared bath.

The *Station Hotel (☎ 611064, fax 615161, e station_hotel@norwich.netkonect .co.uk, 5–7 Riverside Rd)* has rooms for £30/54.

In the centre is the comfortable and historic *Maid's Head Hotel (☎ 209955, fax 613688, Tombland)*, a 700-year-old former coaching inn. Room charges are £91.75/120.50 (including breakfast) during the week and £46 per person including breakfast at the weekend (minimum two-night stay).

Places to Eat

The large student population ensures that there's a good range of places to eat in Norwich. By the TIC is a convenient *Tesco Metro* supermarket.

Bar Tapas (☎ 764077, 18 Exchange St) describes itself as 'the rhythm of South America and the taste of Spain'. Tapas range from £3 to £6; a jug of sangria is £12.50.

Two streets west is the Mexican-Cajun *Mambo Jambo (☎ 666802, 14–16 Lower Goat Lane)*. A Jambo Dog with chilli, cheese and coleslaw is £5.95.

The *Waffle House (☎ 612790, 39 St Giles St)* specialises in savoury and sweet Belgian waffles. They range in price from £2.50 to £7 and there's a wide selection of fillings. On some nights a classical guitarist entertains diners.

The *Treehouse (☎ 763258, 14 Dove St)*, above the health food shop, is an excellent vegetarian restaurant serving such delicacies as nut and moonbeam paté. Main courses come in two sizes – £4.60 and £6.10. It's closed on Sunday.

In the city centre there's a branch of *Café Rouge (☎ 624230, 31 Exchange St)* and an excellent *Pizza Express* on St Benedict's St. Almost next door is *Pinocchio's (☎ 613318)*, a good Italian place.

Pizza One Pancakes Too! (☎ 621583, 24 Tombland) is near the Anglican cathedral and does exactly as its name says.

The Walnut Tree Shades (☎ 620166, Old Post Office Court) is a fabulous little restaurant that is one of Norwich's best-kept secrets; the steak Diane (£11.95) will have carnivores drooling.

Kafe Da (☎ 622836, 18 Bedford St) is a trendy new cafe themed around international espionage: the subs are named after Bond movies, the sandwiches are named after Russian leaders...and everything costs between £4 and £6.

Almost opposite is *Bedford's Brasserie & Bar (☎ 666869, 1 Old Post Office Yard)*. On the menu are sauteed king prawns with chilli jam and a light puff pastry (£6) – not run-of-the-mill pub grub!

For a splurge, there's *Adlard's Restaurant (☎ 633522, 79 Upper St Giles St)* offering classic French cuisine. It's open on Monday for dinner and from Tuesday to Saturday for lunch and dinner; dinner costs £35 for four courses.

Alternatively, *Brummels Seafood Restaurant (☎ 625555, 7 Magdalen St)* operates on the 'eat fish, live longer' premise. The catch is always fresh and the prices are reasonable: there's a two-course menu for £21.95 (pricey but worth it).

Entertainment

ArtEast is a useful, free Norfolk listings

EASTERN ENGLAND

magazine published bimonthly. You can pick it up in the TIC and in most cafes.

Pubs *Boswells* (☎ 629099, *24 Tombland*) is a wine bar with live jazz or blues most nights. Between midnight and 2 am daily except Monday the DJ takes over and pounds out dance music.

Next door, the *Aquarium* (☎ 630090, *23 Tombland*) advertises itself as the 'classiest joint' on the 'seriously wicked' Tombland. Not quite, but it is a trendy, modern bar housed in a Georgian building.

Serious beer drinkers should head for the *Adam & Eve* (☎ 667423) on Bishopgate. *The Ten Bells* (☎ 667833, *76 St Benedict's St*) is popular with students. Another good spot for a little pre-club action is *Tusk* (☎ 441560, *27 King St*).

Once a prostitute's hangout and site of a gruesome murder in the 18th century, the aptly named *Murderer's* (☎ 621447, *2–8 Timber Hill*) is more sedate these days. It's an old-fashioned bar with a happy hour between 5 and 7 pm weekdays.

Nightclubs Norwich's club scene is second only to Cambridge in East Anglia. *Mojo* (☎ 622533, *62 Prince of Wales Rd*) features soul, breaks, hip hop and R&B. It is open until 2 am; admission costs £3.50. At the time of writing Wednesday nights were home to a soul and funk night, Thursdays a hip hop/R&B night, while Friday and Saturday rocked to the sound of UK garage.

The biggest club in town is the 1700-capacity, ultra-plush *Time* (☎ 767649, *Norwich Riverside Development*), about one mile east of town on the Yare. The music is mostly hard house, garage and other dance anthems. It stays open until 2 am; admission costs between £2 and £5, depending on the night. Tuesday night is student night, with a mixed bag of sounds and £1 admission before 11 pm (£2 after). Trainers, jeans and dressing down are no-nos.

Theatre & Concerts The *Theatre Royal* (☎ 630000, *Theatre St*) features programs by touring drama and ballet companies.

The *Norwich Arts Centre* (☎ 660352,

Reeves Yard, St Benedict's St) features a wide-ranging program of drama, concerts, dance, cabaret and jazz.

St Andrew's and Blackfriars' Halls (☎ 628477, *St George's St*), once home to Dominican Blackfriars, now serve as an impressive civic centre where concerts, antique and craft markets, the Music and Arts Festival and even the annual beer festival are held; there's also a cafe in the crypt.

Norwich Puppet Theatre (☎ 629921, *St James, Whitefriars*) is very popular, particularly with children. Tickets cost around £6/4.

Shopping

Although you will find pretty much everything in Norwich, two spots are worth mentioning. The first is the market in front of the TIC, which opens 8.30 am to around 4 pm daily except Sunday. Here you will find everything from children's clothing to second-hand books.

The other notable is the World Shop (☎ 610993) at 38 Exchange St, a wonderful shop of multicultural bric-a-brac run by Norfolk Education and Action for Development. With a stated aim of raising money for the Third World through the 'free trade' principle – whereby every artisan receives full payment for any work sold – they stock pieces from countries as diverse as Mexico, India, Vietnam and Zimbabwe.

Getting There & Away

Cambridge Coach Services (☎ 01223-423900) has four buses a day to Cambridge (£7, or £8 day return, two hours), and National Express (☎ 0870 580 8080) has a daily bus to Cambridge (£8, two hours) and London (£12.50, three hours). First Eastern Counties (☎ 0845 602 0121) runs hourly buses to King's Lynn (£4.70, 1½ hours) and Peterborough (£4.90, two hours, 40 minutes); and half-hourly buses to Cromer (£1.90, one hour). There's no bus service to Ely, and for Bury St Edmunds you must change in Diss.

By train, there is a half-hourly service to London (£28.20, two hours); hourly to Cambridge (£10.50, two hours), Ely (£9.70,

1¼ hours) and Great Yarmouth (£3.30, ½ hour); and six daily to Cromer (£3.40, 50 minutes).

AROUND NORWICH
Blickling Hall

Anne Boleyn, one of Henry VIII's unfortunate wives, lived in the original Blickling Hall. It's said that on the anniversary of her execution a coach drives up to the house – drawn by headless horses, driven by headless coachmen and containing the queen with her head on her lap.

The house dates from the early 17th century and is filled with Georgian furniture, pictures and tapestries. There's an impressive Jacobean plaster ceiling in the long gallery. The house is surrounded by parkland offering good walks.

Blickling Hall (☎ 01263-733084; NT) is 15 miles (24km) north of Norwich, and opens 1 to 4.30 pm Wednesday to Sunday (and also on Tuesday in August), Easter to October; admission costs £6/3. The gardens open 10.30 am to 5.30 pm Wednesday to Sunday, Easter to October, shorter hours the rest of the year.

Saunder's Coaches (☎ 01692-406020) runs hourly buses here from Norwich in summer (£1.20, 20 minutes). Aylsham is the nearest train station, 1¾ miles (3km) away.

NORFOLK BROADS

The Norfolk Broads is an area of rivers, lakes, marshland, nature reserves and bird sanctuaries on the Norfolk/Suffolk border. The area, measuring some 117 sq miles, has 'national protected status', which is equivalent to it being a national park. Just to make doubly sure that everyone recognises its national value, the government announced in May 2000 that the area is one of a number of protected 'Areas of Outstanding Natural Beauty'.

A broad is a large piece of water formed by the widening of a river. The main river is the Bure, which enters the Broads at Wroxham and is then joined by several other rivers, including the Ant and the Thurne. The Waveney joins the Yare to meet the Bure at Great Yarmouth, where this large network of rivers flows into the sea. What makes this area special is that all these lakes, rivers and their tributaries are navigable. In all, there are 125 miles (201km) of lock-free waterways.

There's little variety of scenery, but the ecology of the area means that it's a wonderful place for nature lovers and for people who like being on or near the water. The habitat includes freshwater lakes, slow-moving rivers, water meadows, fens, bogs and saltwater marshes, and the many kinds of birds, butterflies and water-loving plants that inhabit them.

How Hill, a mere 12m above sea level, is the highest place in the Broads. Since there's nothing to impede the path of sea breezes, this is a good area for wind power. Many wind pumps (which look like windmills) were built to drain the marshland and to return the water to the rivers.

Orientation

The Broads form a triangle with Norwich at the apex, the Norwich–Cromer road as the northern side, the Norwich–Lowestoft road as the southern side and the coastline as the base.

Wroxham, on the A1151 from Norwich, and Potter Heigham, on the A1062 from Wroxham, are the main centres. Along the way, there are plenty of waterside pubs, villages and market towns where you can stock up on provisions, and stretches of river where you can feel you are the only person around.

Information

The Broads Authority (☎ 01603-610734), Thomas Harvey House, 18 Colegate, Norwich NR3 1BQ, can supply information about the conservation centres and RSPB bird-watching hides at Berney Marshes, Ranworth, Bure Marshes, Cockshoot Broad, Hickling Broad, Horsey Mere, How Hill, Strumpshaw Fen and Surlingham Church Marsh.

You can also get information about the Broads from the Norwich TIC. *The Broadcaster* is a visitors' magazine, published annually.

Getting Around

Two companies that operate boating holidays are Blakes (☎ 01603-782911) and Hoseasons (☎ 01502-501010). Costs depend on the boat size, the facilities on the boat, the time of year and the length of the holiday. A boat for two to four people is £500 to £800 for a week, including fuel and insurance. Short breaks (three to four days) during the low season are much cheaper.

Many boat yards (particularly in the Wroxham and Potter Heigham areas) have a variety of boats for hire by the hour, half-day or full day. Charges still vary according to the season and the size of the boat, but they start from £10 for one hour, £28 for four hours and £45 for one day.

No previous experience is necessary, but remember to stay on the right side of the river, that the rivers are tidal, and to stick to

The Origin of the Broads

For many years the origin of the Norfolk Broads was unclear. The rivers were undoubtedly natural and many thought the lakes were too – it's hard to believe they're not when you see them – but no one could explain how they could have formed.

The mystery was solved when records were discovered in the remains of St Benet's Abbey (on the River Bure). They showed that from the 12th century certain parts of land in Hoveton Parish were used for peat digging. The area had little woodland and the only source of fuel was peat. Since East Anglia was well populated and prosperous, peat digging became a major industry.

Over a period of about 200 years, approximately 1040 hectares were dug up. However, water gradually seeped through causing marshes, and later lakes, to develop. The first broad to be mentioned in records is Ranworth Broad (in 1275). Eventually, the amount of water made it extremely difficult for the diggers and the peat-cutting industry died out. In no other area of Britain has human effort changed the natural landscape so dramatically.

the speed limit – you can get prosecuted for speeding. If you don't feel like piloting your own boat, Broads Tours runs 1½-hour pleasure trips April to September, with a commentary, for £5.20/3.95 per person. Broads Tours has two bases: The Bridge, Wroxham (☎ 01603-782207), and Herbert Woods, Potter Heigham (☎ 01692-670711).

NORFOLK COAST
Great Yarmouth
☎ 01493 • pop 54,800

This is one of England's most popular seaside resorts, complete with all the tacky trimmings such as amusement arcades and greasy-spoon cafes, but it's also an important port for the North Sea oil and gas industries.

The TIC (☎ 846345, fax 846221) is in the town hall in the centre of town. It opens 9 am to 5 pm Monday to Friday throughout the year. Easter to the end of September a second office opens on Marine Parade (☎ 842195) 9.30 am to 5.30 pm daily.

As well as a wide, sandy beach, other attractions include a number of interesting buildings in the old town. The **Elizabethan House Museum** (☎ 745526), South Quay, was a merchant's house and now contains a display of 19th-century domestic life. It opens 10 am to 5 pm daily except Saturday; entry costs £2/1.50. The **Old Merchant's House** (☎ 857900), Row 111, South Quay, is a group of typical 17th-century town houses. The house (☎ 857900) opens 10 am to 1 pm and 2 to 5 pm daily 1 April to 1 October; admission costs £1.85/1.40. The **Tolhouse Museum** (☎ 858900), Tolhouse St, was once the town's courthouse and jail; prison cells can be seen and there's a display covering the town's history. The museum opens 10 am to 5 pm Monday to Friday and 1.15 to 5 pm at the weekend. Admission costs £1.10/90p. There's also a small **maritime museum** on Marine Parade near the TIC. Opening hours and admission prices are the same as for the Tollhouse.

There are numerous B&Bs, and *Great Yarmouth Youth Hostel* (☎ 843991, 2 Sandown Rd) is three-quarters of a mile from the train station, near the beach. Charges are £9.20/6.25 for adults/juniors.

Tunstall Camping Barn (☎ 700279, Manor Farm, Tunstall, Halvergate) is an independent hostel with 20 sleeping platforms in a barn for £4 per person. It's about 6 miles (10km) from Great Yarmouth, on the Norwich road.

Great Yarmouth is on main bus and rail routes to Norwich. First Eastern Counties (☎ 0845 602 0121) runs an hourly service between Norwich and Great Yarmouth (£2.65, 40 minutes). Wherry Lines runs trains roughly every half hour to Norwich (£4, 25 minutes) every day except Sunday, when there are hourly departures between 8.20 am and 5.20 pm only.

Cromer
☎ 01263 • pop 4500

In the late Victorian and Edwardian eras, Cromer was transformed into the most fashionable resort on the coast. It's now somewhat run-down, but with its elevated seafront, long, sandy beach and scenic coastal walks, it's still worth visiting. Cromer has long been famous for its crabs, and they're still caught and sold here. The TIC (☎ 512497, fax 513613) is by the bus station, and opens 9.30 am to 6 pm Monday to Saturday (until 5 pm on Sunday), July 18 to August 31. The rest of the year it opens 10 am to 5 pm Monday to Saturday.

Two miles (3km) south-west of Cromer, **Felbrigg Hall** (☎ 837444; NT) is one of the finest 17th-century houses in Norfolk. It contains a collection of 18th-century furniture; outside is a walled garden, orangery and landscaped park. It opens 1 to 5 pm daily except Thursday and Friday, Easter to October; admission costs £5.40/2.10.

Cromer is one of the few coastal resorts with a train station linked to Norwich. There are 13 trains Monday to Saturday and six on Sunday (£3.40, 45 minutes).

Cley Marshes

Between Cromer and Wells-next-the-Sea, Cley Marshes (☎ 740008) is one of the top bird-watching places in England, with over 300 species recorded. There's a visitor centre built on high ground to give good views over the area.

Wells-next-the-Sea
☎ 01328 • pop 2400

Set back from the sea, Wells is both a holiday town and a fishing port. It's a pleasant place, with streets of attractive Georgian houses, flint cottages and interesting shops. The TIC (☎ 710885, fax 711405) is on Staithe St. It opens 10 am to 5 pm Monday to Saturday (to 4 pm on Sunday), Easter to mid-July and September to October; and 9.30 am to 6 pm Monday to Saturday (to 5 pm on Sunday), from mid-July to the end of August.

Holkham Hall (☎ 710227) is a most impressive Palladian mansion situated in a 1200-hectare deer park 2 miles (3km) from Wells. The grounds were designed by Capability Brown. The house opens 1 to 5 pm daily except Friday and Saturday, from late May to September; entry costs £6/3 and includes the Bygones Museum and the park.

A narrow-gauge steam railway runs 5 miles (8km) to **Little Walsingham**, where there's a Catholic shrine that has been an object of pilgrimage for almost 1000 years.

KING'S LYNN
☎ 01553 • pop 37,500

Only 3 miles (5km) from the sea on the River Great Ouse, Lynn (as the locals call it) was one of England's chief ports in the Middle Ages. It was also a natural base for fishing fleets and their crews, and home to a number of religious foundations. The old town is a fascinating mixture of these three elements and Lynn is still a port today, though much less busy than it once was. Away from the port, the modern town is sadly sterile, with the main streets clogged with chain stores and bland architecture.

Orientation & Information

The old town lies along the eastern bank of the river, and the train station is on the eastern side of the town. Modern Lynn and the bus station are between them.

Tourist Office The TIC (☎ 763044, fax 777281, [e] kings-lynn.tic@west-norfolk .gov.uk) is in the Custom House on Purfleet Quay. It opens 9.15 am to 5 pm Monday to

Saturday and 10 am to 5 pm on Sunday, April to October. The rest of the year it opens 10.30 am to 4 pm daily.

Post & Communications The post office (☎ 692185) is at Baxter's Plain. It opens 9 am to 5.30 pm from Monday to Friday and 9 am to 12.30 pm on Saturday.

Laundry Gaywood Launderette (☎ 770078) is east of the town centre, just off Gaywood Rd at 21 St Faith's Drive. It opens 6.30 am to 9 pm daily. Service washes, available daily except Sunday, cost a minimum of £5.

Medical Services Jai Chemists (☎ 772828) is at 68 High St. It opens 9 am to 5.30 pm daily except Sunday. All chemists in town operate on a rota system, whereby once every two weeks or so they are open until 6.30 pm. Check with the TIC for details of whose turn it is. The Queen Elizabeth Hospital (☎ 613613) is on Gayton Rd, at the Hunstanton bypass, about 2½ miles (4km) east of the town centre.

Emergency The police station (☎ 691211) is on St James Rd.

Walking Tour

This walk takes around 2½ hours. Start in the Saturday Market Place at **St Margaret's** parish church, founded in 1100 with a Benedictine priory. Little remains of the original buildings, but the church is impressive for its size (72m long) and contains two Flemish brasses, which are among the best examples in the country. By the west door there are flood-level marks – 1976 was the highest, but the 1953 flood claimed more lives.

Walk south down Nelson St to see a fine collection of domestic and industrial buildings. Their frontages are 17th and 18th century, but their interiors are much older. Retracing steps back, on the corner of St Margaret's Lane, and dating back to the 15th century, is a restored building that was once the warehouse or 'steelyard' of the **Hanseatic League** (the Northern European merchants' group). Now known as St Mar-

garet's House, it is home to a number of civic offices, including the Education League, the Weights & Measures department and the town registrar. In theory access is restricted to those offices alone, but you can wander in and have a look at the interior. If there's a group of you, you're better off seeking permission by calling the Education League on ☎ 669200.

Continue north-west along Margaret Plain to College Lane and the former Thoresby College, which was founded in 1508 to house priests and is now the youth hostel. Across Queen St is the **town hall**, dating back to 1421. Next to it, at 45 Queen St, is the **Town House Museum** (☎ 773450). Inside you will find exhibits charting life in the town from the Middle Ages up to the 1950s. It opens 10 am to 5 pm Monday to Saturday (from 2 pm on Sunday), May to October. The rest of the year it opens 10 am to 4 pm Monday to Saturday. Admission costs £1.80/1.40.

The **Old Gaol House** (☎ 774297), next door, has been converted into a tourist attraction with self-guided Walkman tours. Lynn's priceless civic treasures, including the 650-year-old King John Cup, can be seen in the basement. It opens 10 am to 5 pm daily (last entry at 4.15 pm), Easter to October (same hours, Friday to Tuesday only, the rest of the year). Entry costs £2.40/1.75.

Continuing down Queen St you pass **Clifton House**, with its quirky barley-sugar columns and waterfront tower, which was used by merchants scanning the river for returning ships. Its interior is in dire need of restoration, so access is restricted to groups organised by the TIC. Walk down the lane to the river past the sturdy, red floodgates. The stately Bank House is on your right. Opposite the square is **Purfleet Quay**, in its heyday the principal harbour. The quaint building with the lantern tower is the **Custom House** (housing the TIC), which dates back to 1683.

Turn into King St, where the second medieval town begins. It was planned in the latter half of the 12th century and had its own church, guildhall, market and friary. There are many interesting buildings in King St, especially on the left-hand side, where the wealthier merchants built their homes and warehouses on reclaimed land. **St George's Guildhall** (☎ 767557; NT) is the largest surviving 15th-century guildhall in England. It has served as warehouse, theatre, courthouse and armoury (during the Civil War), and now contains art galleries, a theatre, restaurant and coffee house. This is the focal point of the annual King's Lynn festival.

At the end of King St is the spacious **Tuesday Market Square**, which still fulfils its original weekly role. It's bordered with old buildings, including the Corn Hall (1854) and the Duke's Head Hotel (1689).

Walk diagonally across the Tuesday Market Square and turn right into St Nicholas St to reach the **Tudor Rose Hotel**, a late-15th-century house with some very interesting features, including the original main door. North of here, on the corner of St Ann's St, is **True's Yard**, where the two remaining cottages of the 19th-century fishing commu-

nity that used to be here have been restored and now house a folk museum (☎ 770479) detailing the life of a shellfish fisherman around 1850. It opens 9.30 am to 3.45 pm (closed for Christmas week); admission costs £1.90/1.50.

Return to Chapel St, and on the corner of Market Lane is an attractive building known as **Lattice House** – dating from the 15th century, it is now a restaurant, and a good place to stop.

Places to Stay

Excellently located, the *King's Lynn Youth Hostel* (☎ 772461, Thoresby College, College Lane) opens fully 1 July to 31 August and haphazardly outside that time. A bed costs £9/6.40 for adults/juniors.

Maranatha/Havana Guest House (☎ 774596, fax 763747, 115–17 Gaywood Rd) are two former guesthouses now joined into one under the same proprietors. It offers budget accommodation from £15 per

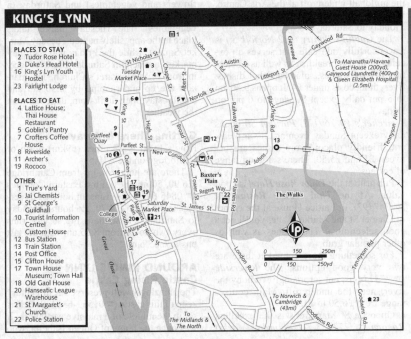

KING'S LYNN

PLACES TO STAY
2   Tudor Rose Hotel
3   Duke's Head Hotel
16 King's Lyn Youth Hostel
23 Fairlight Lodge

PLACES TO EAT
4   Lattice House; Thai House Restaurant
5   Goblin's Pantry
7   Crofters Coffee House
8   Riverside
11 Archer's
19 Rococo

OTHER
1   True's Yard
6   Jai Chemists
9   St George's Guildhall
10 Tourist Information Centrel Custom House
12 Bus Station
13 Train Station
14 Post Office
15 Clifton House
17 Town House Museum; Town Hall
18 Old Gaol House
20 Hanseatic League Warehouse
21 St Margaret's Church
22 Police Station

EASTERN ENGLAND

person, while a double room costs £36 (£40 with a bathroom).

Fairlight Lodge (☎ 762234, fax 770280, 79 Goodwins Rd) is a comfortable guesthouse with seven rooms (four with bathrooms), which charges £25/40 for a single/double with a private bathroom and £20/34 without.

The *Tudor Rose Hotel* (☎ 762824, fax 764894, ℮ kltudorrose@aol.com, St Nicholas St) is a 15th-century house with B&B from £35/60.

The town's top hotel is the *Duke's Head Hotel* (☎ 774996, fax 763556, Tuesday Market Square), a fine classical building overlooking the market. Rooms cost £79/95; there are also special weekend deals at £42/52 per person per night, including breakfast/breakfast and dinner.

Places to Eat

There are several places for teas or light meals. *Crofters Coffee House (King St)*, in the guildhall undercroft at the Arts Centre, is recommended. It opens 9.30 am to 5 pm Monday to Saturday.

The *Goblin's Pantry (122 Norfolk St)* is a wonderfully odd cafe that serves an excellent English breakfast as well as a selection of sandwiches, salads and hot dishes. Everything costs under £4. It opens 9.30 am to 5 pm daily except Sunday (to 6 pm on Friday).

Archer's (☎ 769177, Purfleet St) opens daily except Sunday evening. It's a pleasant, friendly place; many dishes are between £4 and £5.50. There's a good range of coffees.

Pub grub at the *Tudor Rose Hotel* is good value. At the *Thai House Restaurant* (☎ 767397), in Lattice House at the corner of Chapel St and Market Lane, you'll get a good selection of Thai dishes as well as other popular grub.

For something more upmarket there are two very good options. The *Riverside* (☎ 773134) is, not surprisingly, right by the river, near the undercroft. Main courses range from £6.50 to £18.

Opposite St Margaret's is the excellent *Rococo* (☎ 771483, 11 Saturday Market

Place). A two-course lunch costs £9.95 and set dinners range from £22.50 to £32.50.

King's Lynn Festival of Music & the Arts

Celebrating its 50th anniversary in 2000, the King's Lynn Festival (the brainchild of Lady Ruth Fermoy) offers a diverse program of concerts and recitals of all kinds of music, from medieval ballads to Jamaican Jazz. It usually takes place in the last week of July. For details of programmed events, call the administrative office at ☎ 767557 (fax 767688, ℮ enquiries@kl-festival.free serve.co.uk), or the box office at ☎ 764864. See the Web site at www.kl-festival.free serve.co.uk.

Shopping

There are three market days each week – Tuesday (the major market, with everything from clothing to bric-a-brac to fish), Friday (a recent addition with a limited selection of flowers and vegetables) and Saturday (a food market selling fish, fruit, flowers and vegetables). The Tuesday market takes place in the appositely named Tuesday Market Square, while the Friday and Saturday markets are held in Saturday Market Place, in front of St Margaret's Church. The markets are up and running by 8.30 am and usually stay open until 4 pm, depending on the weather.

Getting There & Away

King's Lynn is 43 miles (69km) north of Cambridge on the A10.

There are hourly trains from Cambridge (£6.90, 50 minutes). First Eastern Counties (☎ 0845 602 0121) runs an hourly bus service to Norwich (£4.70, 1½ hours) Monday to Saturday; on Sundays the service runs every two hours from 8.25 am with the last bus at 6.55 pm.

AROUND KING'S LYNN
Castle Rising Castle

The amazingly well-preserved 12th-century keep of this castle (☎ 01553-631330; EH) is set in the middle of a massive earthwork. It was once the home of Queen Isabella, who arranged the murder of her husband Edward II. It opens 10 am to 6 pm (to 4 pm November to March); entry costs £3.25/1.60. First Eastern Counties (☎ 0845 602 0121) bus No 411 runs here (£1.40, 19 minutes) every hour from King's Lynn bus station, 6 miles (10km) to the south.

Sandringham House & Estate

In 1862 Queen Victoria bought a Georgian house set on 8000 hectares of land as the official country residence of the Prince of Wales (later Edward VII). By 1870 the house had been enlarged and completely redesigned in what later became known as the Edwardian style. Today, the Queen's country pile is limited to the house and 25 hectares, which includes two studs, a fruit farm, a country park and landscaped gardens and lakes. The remaining 7975 hectares make up the house's estate, half of which is held by farm tenants (the Queen has to earn money somewhere!). The other half is managed by the Crown Estate as forestry. The royal family usually spends three weeks here from mid-July to early August.

The house itself is home to a museum that contains a collection of vintage cars and other royal trinkets. There are guided tours (£3) of the formal gardens on Friday and Saturday at 2 pm. There is also a yearly program of special events, including a craft fair in September. Check with the office for details of upcoming events or write to Sandringham House, The Estate Office, Sandringham, Norfolk PE35 6EN.

Sandringham House (☎ 01553-772675) opens 11 am to 4.45 pm, April to September (except when the royal family is here). Admission costs £5.50/3.50 (£4.50/3 if you only want to see the grounds and museum). First Eastern Counties bus No 411 (which also goes to Castle Rising Castle, see above) runs here from King's Lynn bus station (£1.80, 25 minutes), 10 miles (16km) south-west.

Houghton Hall

Built for Sir Robert Walpole in 1730, Houghton Hall (☎ 01485-528569) is an example of the Palladian style, and is worth seeing for the ornate state rooms alone. It's 14 miles (23km) north-east of King's Lynn and opens 1 to 5.30 pm Thursday and Sunday only (last admission 5 pm), Easter to September. Admission costs £6/3.

Unfortunately, the house is not served by public transportation; if you don't have your own wheels you'll have to get here from King's Lynn by taxi, which should cost between £10 and £12. A reputable service in King's Lynn is Ken's Taxis (☎ 01553-766166).

Cambridgeshire

The overwhelming majority of visitors come to Cambridgeshire for one reason only: to visit the beautiful university town in the south of the county. Cambridge sits on a bend in the River Cam at the edge of the fens – the flat, fertile, once submerged region that covers the rest of the county. Smaller and more compact than its great rival Oxford, Cambridge's position and lack of heavy industry gives it a rural flavour – cattle and horses graze within a half mile of the city centre.

The lack of hills makes this excellent cycling country. A towpath winds the 15 miles (24km) from Cambridge to Ely, where the superb cathedral, on ground slightly higher than the surrounding plain, is known as the 'ship of the fens'. In the north of the county there's another fine cathedral at Peterborough, which carries the questionable title of England's shopping capital.

GETTING AROUND

Public transport centres on Cambridge. Rather than phoning the costly council transport helpline (☎ 0891-910910, 50p per minute), get the useful *Cambridgeshire and Peterborough Passenger Transport Map* and contact the bus companies directly.

The main bus companies operating in the area are Stagecoach Cambus (☎ 01223-423554) between Cambridge, Ely and Bury St Edmunds; Cambridge Coach Services (☎ 01223-423900) from Cambridge to Norwich; and Stagecoach United Counties

(☎ 01604-620077) from Cambridge to Huntingdon and Peterborough.

Cambridge is only 55 minutes by rail from London. This line continues north through Ely to terminate at King's Lynn in Norfolk. From Ely, a branch line runs east through Norwich, and south-east into Suffolk.

CAMBRIDGE
☎ 01223 • pop 88,000

Ask anyone to name the most famous universities in the world, and it will be a safe bet that Cambridge will make the top five. Along with its great rival Oxford, Cambridge is synonymous with the highest standards of education, both academic and otherwise, so much so that the term 'Oxbridge' was coined to define the very special breed both universities produce. An Oxbridge graduate is popularly characterised as white, male, private-school educated, intelligent and upper class, but the value judgement attached to the term depends on who is using it. To some, it denotes the highest levels of academic excellence, but to others it denotes the spoilt and snobby children of a privileged elite that unfairly dominate the upper strata of English life.

Whatever way you look at it, the truth is that Cambridge is an exceptional university. The honour roll of famous graduates reads like an international who's who of high achievers and a list of their accomplishments in a wide variety of fields could fill a couple of thick volumes. So far, the university has produced 78 Nobel Prize winners (29 from Trinity College alone), 13 British prime ministers, nine archbishops of Canterbury, an immense number of scientists, a healthy host of poets and other scribblers... and Britain's most infamous Cold War spies, the quartet of Kim Philby, Donald Maclean, Guy Burgess and Anthony Blunt. And this is but a limited selection. Today, the university remains at the top of the research league in British universities; it owns a prestigious publishing firm and a world-renowned examination syndicate; it is the leading centre for astronomy in Britain; its Fitzwilliam Museum contains an outstand-

ing art collection; and its library is used by scholars from around the world.

Though brimming with history and antiquity, and with no primary industry of which to speak, Cambridge is hardly rustic. No longer an important market town due to the decline of agriculture, the city (it was granted that status by King George VI in 1951) is a perfect example of the marketing strategist's vision of a contemporary English town. No huge, smoke-spewing factories, but plenty of secondary industry, particularly electronics and computers (Philips Electronic are a major player). The streets are lined with trendy designer shops and fancy boutiques, and there is no shortage of overpriced continental-style cafes and restaurants clamouring for a share of Cool Britannia's bulging wallet. Yet it is Cambridge's tranquil, ageless appearance that is hardest to match, and which the visitor will remember best.

If you have the time, you should visit both Cambridge and Oxford. If you're on a tight schedule and must choose between the two, go for Cambridge. Smaller, more compact and less crowded, its trump card is the choir and chapel of King's College, which should not be missed by any visitor to England.

History
Neolithic tools and weapons, circa 3000 BC, and ancient burial grounds have been found around Cambridge. There is also an Iron Age fort, Wandlebury, in the Gog Magog hills nearby. In AD 43, when the Romans needed a road from Colchester to Godmanchester, the River Cam was forded just below Magdalene Bridge and a fort was built on the small hill overlooking it.

The camp became a town, and trading took place by road and river. In the 5th century the Romans withdrew and there followed a series of invasions from Europe – first by the Anglo-Saxons, who didn't do much to develop the town: Ely monks in the 7th century described it as 'desolate'. It was kick-started back into life in the 9th century by the Norse/Danish invaders, who were great traders.

Next, in 1066, came the Normans who replaced the fort with a castle (now a mere mound on Castle Hill) in order to campaign against the bold Saxon leader Hereward the Wake, who lurked in the marshy fens round Ely. The 1086 Domesday Book records 400 'burgesses' (full citizens) in Cambridge.

In 1209 the university town of Oxford exploded into a riot between scholars and townspeople, with the result that three students were hanged. A number of scholars decided enough was enough, packed their books and arrived in Cambridge to found the nucleus of a new university. The facts surrounding the foundation are a little hazy, undoubtedly due to another riot in 1261 between 'town and gown', when the university records were burned. At the rioters' trial, the judges ruled in favour of the students, setting a precedent that would last for centuries. The new university had found favour with the law and began to establish a firm footing within the town.

The collegiate system, unique to Oxford and Cambridge, came into being gradually with the first college, Peterhouse, founded in 1284 by Hugh de Balsham (later Bishop of Ely). The plan was for tutors and students to live together in a community, much as they would in a monastery.

From the 14th century onwards, a series of colleges was founded by royalty, nobility, leading church figures, statesmen, academics and trade guilds – all for men only. In 1869 and 1871, however, there was a breakthrough for women when Girton and Newnham were founded, though it was only in 1948 that women were actually permitted to graduate. Now, 29 of the 31 colleges are co-residential – two still choosing to maintain their 'women only' status.

Orientation

The colleges and university buildings comprise the centre of the city – like Oxford, Cambridge has no campus. The central area, lying in a wide bend of the River Cam, is easy to get around on foot or by bike. The best known section of the Cam is the Backs, which combines lush river scenery with superb views of six colleges, including King's

Cambridge, aka...

It seems quite ironic that in a city renowned for its academic excellence and the superior quality of its scholarly research, there is still doubt over how exactly Cambridge got its name. One thing, however, is certain: at the heart of the matter are two rivers, the Cam and its tributary the Granta, although until at least AD 1000 it was the latter that was deemed more important. Britain's first historian, the venerable Bede, made reference to the settlement of *Grantacaestir* in around AD 730, while 15 years later Felix of Crowland wrote of *Grontricc*. In 875, the Anglo-Saxon Chronicle mentioned *Grantebrycge*, but from 1107 the town was known variously as *Caumbrigge, Caumbregge, Caumberage* and *Cantabrigia*. The first line of Chaucer's *Reeve's Tale,* written at the end of the 14th century, reads: 'At Trumpington, not fer fro Cantebrigge'. But still the town's name continued to change. In 1478 it became Camebrygge, and only became Cambridge during Elizabethan times.

College Chapel. The other 25 colleges are scattered throughout the city.

The bus station is in the centre on Drummer St, but the train station is a 20-minute walk to the south. Sidney St – which becomes St Andrew's St to the south and Bridge and Magdalene Sts to the north – is the main shopping street.

Information

The university has three eight-week terms: Michaelmas (October to December), Lent (mid-January to mid-March) and Easter (mid-April to mid-June). Exams are held from mid-May to mid-June. There's general mayhem for the 168 hours following exams – the so-called May Week. Most colleges are closed to visitors for the Easter term, and all are closed for exams. Precise details of opening hours vary from college to college and year to year, so contact the TIC for up-to-date information. Five colleges (King's, Queen's, Claire, Trinity and

St John's) charge admission to tourists (£1.20 to £3.50). You may, however, find that admission to tourists is now denied entirely at some of the colleges described below. Each year more colleges decide that the tourist hordes are just too disruptive. For all university-related enquiries, call the university's central office at ☎ 337733.

Tourist Office The TIC (☎ 322640, fax 457588, e tourism@cambridge.gov.uk), Wheeler St, opens 10 am to 6 pm Monday to Friday, to 5 pm on Saturday and 11 am to 4 pm on Sunday, April to October. The rest of the year it opens 10 am to 5.30 pm Monday to Saturday. It organises walking tours (☎ 457574 for information) at 1.30 pm every day, all year, with more during summer. Group sizes are limited, so buy your ticket in advance (£7 including King's College, £6 including St John's College). See also the Web site at www.cambridge.gov.uk.

Post & Communications The main post office (☎ 323325) is at 9–11 St Andrew's St. It opens 9 am to 5.30 pm from Monday to Saturday.

To collect your email, or make cheap in-

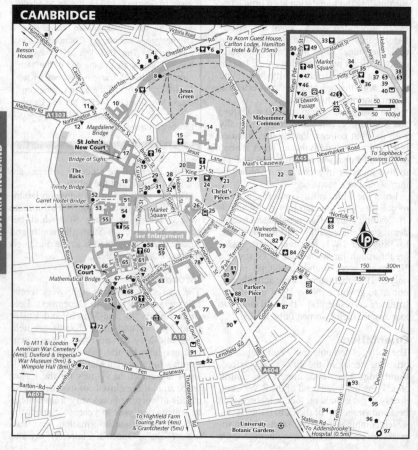

ternational phone calls, go to the International Telecom Centre (☎ 357358) directly opposite the TIC. It opens 9 am to 10 pm daily. CB1 (☎ 576306), 32 Mill Rd, is an Internet cafe with nine terminals and the walls are stacked with second-hand books. They charge £3 per hour. It opens 10 am to 8 pm.

Money There are plenty of banks with ATMs around the city centre. Abbey National (☎ 350495) has a branch at 60 St Andrew's St and HSBC (☎ 314822) is at 75 Regent St. American Express (AmEx; ☎ 345203) is at 25 Sidney St. It opens 9 am to 5.30 pm Monday to Friday (to 5 pm on Saturday). Thomas Cook (☎ 543100) is at 8 St Andrew's St. It opens 9 am to 5.30 pm

Monday to Saturday (from 10 am on Wednesday).

Bookshops As you would expect, Cambridge is chock full of excellent bookshops. The largest of all is Heffers (☎ 568582), 20 Trinity St, almost directly across from Trinity College. Not surprisingly, it specialises in academic books, but it also has a large map department. Heffers Plus (☎ 568596), 31 St Andrew's St, is where you'll find general paperbacks including guidebooks. Heffers Children's Bookshop (☎ 568551) is at 29–30 Trinity St, while Heffers Music (☎ 568562), 19 Trinity St, is renowned throughout England for its excellent selection of classical CDs, particularly of the choral kind.

CAMBRIDGE

PLACES TO STAY

1	Antony's Guest House
2	Belle Vue Guest House
3	Arundel House Hotel
4	Aaron House
68	Garden House (Moat House)
80	University Arms Hotel
82	Warkworth House
87	YMCA
92	Lensfield Hotel
93	Cambridge Youth Hostel; Six Steps Guest House
94	Tenison Towers Guest House
96	Sleeperz

PLACES TO EAT

6	Twenty-two
12	Michel's Brasserie
13	Midsummer House
23	Efe's Restaurant
27	Clowns
32	Tatties
44	No 1 King's Parade; The Eagle Pub
45	Rainbow
46	Nadia's (King's Parade)
62	Fitzbillies
67	Nadia's (Silver St)
73	Choices Café
76	Browns
78	The Dôme
81	Hobb's Pavilion
88	The Depot
90	Shalimar Restaurant

PUBS, BARS & CLUBS

5	Boathouse
9	Rat & Parrot
15	Po Na Na
24	Champion of the Thames
33	Fez
35	Fifth Avenue
49	Bar Ha! Ha!
72	Granta (& Punt Hire)
83	The Man on the Moon

OTHER

7	Laundrette
8	Cambridge River Cruises
10	Magdalene College
11	Kettle's Yard
14	Jesus College
16	Round Church
17	St John's College
18	Trinity College
19	Vantage Pharmacy
20	Westcott
21	All Saints Church
22	Grafton Centre
25	Bus Station (Drummer Street)
26	Christ's College
28	Amex
29	Galloway & Porter
30	Heffers Music
31	Dillons
34	Boots
36	WH Smith
37	Heffers Plus
38	Abbey National (Bank)
39	Thomas Cook
40	Post Office

41	International Telecom Centre
42	Tourist Information Centre
43	Arts Theatre
47	Heffers Bookshop
48	Great St Mary's Church
50	Heffers Children's Bookshop
51	Gonville & Caius College
52	Trinity Punts
53	Trinity Hall College
54	Senate House
55	Clare College
56	King's College Chapel
57	King's College
58	Saxon Tower
59	Corn Exchange
60	St Benet's Church
61	Corpus Christi College
63	Pembroke College
64	Ben Hayward Cycles
65	St Catherine's College
66	Queens' College
69	Scudamore's Punt Hire
70	Little St Mary's Church
71	Peterhouse College
74	Cambridge Recycles
75	Fitzwilliam Museum
77	Downing College
79	Emmanuel College
84	Police Station
85	Mike's Bikes
86	CB1
89	HSBC (Bank)
91	Sub Post Office
95	Geoff's Bike Hire
97	Train Station

EASTERN ENGLAND

There is a branch of Dillons (☎ 351688) at 22 Sidney St and a branch of WH Smith (☎ 311313) at 26 Lion Yard. An excellent second-hand bookshop is Galloway & Porter (☎ 367876) at 30 Sidney St, which does mostly remaindered and damaged stock.

Laundry Cleanomat Dry Cleaners (☎ 464-719) is at 10 Victoria Ave, just north of the bridge and near Chesterton Rd. You can drop off your laundry or do it yourself.

Medical Services The Addenbrooke's Hospital (☎ 245151) is about half a mile south of the train station, just off Hills Rd. There are plenty of pharmacies dotted around the city centre, including two outlets of Boots; one at 28 Petty Cury (☎ 350213), the other in the Grafton Centre (☎ 302576). Both open 8.30 am to 5.30 pm Monday to Friday, 8.45 am to 6 pm on Saturday and 10 am to 5 pm on Sunday. Vantage Pharmacy (☎ 353002), at 66 Bridge St, opens 9 am to 6 pm Monday to Friday and 9 am to 5.30 pm on Saturday.

Emergency The police station (☎ 358966) is on Parkside, just across Parker's Piece from the city centre.

Walking Tour One

This three-hour walk visits King's College Chapel and the most central colleges, and includes a stretch along the river.

From the TIC, walk one block west to King's Parade, turn right and continue north to **Great St Mary's Church** (☎ 741716) on Senate House Hill. This university church, built between 1478 and 1519 in the late-Gothic perpendicular style, has a feeling of space and light inside thanks to its clerestory, wide arch and wood carving. The traditional termly university sermons are preached here. To get your bearings, climb the 123 steps of the tower (£1.75) for a good view of the city. The building across King's Parade, on the right-hand side of the square, is the **Senate House**, designed in 1730 by James Gibbs. It's the most beautiful example of pure classical architecture in the city; graduations are held here.

Gonville & Caius Now walk into Trinity St, head north, and turn left into the first gateway to reach this fascinating old college (☎ 332400). It was founded twice, first by a priest called Gonville, in 1347, and then again by Dr Caius (pronounced keys), a brilliant physician and scholar, in 1557. Of special interest here are the three gates: Virtue, Humility and Honour. They symbolise the progress of the good student, since the third gate (the *Porta Honoris*, a fascinating confection with a quirky dome and sundials) leads to the Senate House and thus graduation. Walk through the gate, turn right, then left, to reach King's College Chapel. See the Web site at www.cai.cam.ac.uk.

King's College Chapel All the college chapels are individually remarkable but King's College Chapel is supreme in its grandeur. It's one of the finest examples of Gothic architecture in England, and would certainly give the cathedral in Chartres a run for its money.

The chapel was conceived as an act of piety by the young Henry VI and was dedicated to the Virgin Mary. Its foundation stone was laid by the king in 1446 and building was completed around 1516. Henry VI's successors, notably Henry VIII, glorified the interior (and themselves in so doing). Services are led by its choir, originally choristers from Eton College, another of Henry VI's foundations. The choir's Festival of the Nine Lessons and Carols on Christmas Eve are heard all over the world.

Enter through the south porch. Despite the original stained-glass windows, the atmosphere inside is light. Cromwell's soldiers destroyed many church windows in East Anglia but it is believed that, having been a Cambridge student, their leader spared King's.

The stunning interior of 12 bays is about 11m wide, 22m high and 80m long. This vast expanse is the largest in the world canopied by fan vaulting. It's the work of John Wastell, and is a miracle of beauty and skill; upon seeing it, Christopher Wren reputedly stated that he could have built it, but only if someone had shown him where to set the first stone.

The elaborate carvings, both in wood and stone, include royal coats of arms, intertwined initials, the royal beasts of heraldry, and flowers that were the emblems of Tudor monarchs and related families. Among the Yorkist roses on the western wall is the figure of a woman within a rose. Some claim she is Elizabeth of York, but it's more likely that she's the Virgin Mary.

The ante-chapel and the choir are divided by the superbly carved **wooden screen**, another gift of Henry VIII. Designed and executed by the king's master carver Peter Stockton, the screen bears Henry's initials entwined with those of Anne Boleyn, who supposedly inspired Henry's act of generosity. Almost concealed by the mythical beasts and symbolic flowers is one angry human face: perhaps it is Stockton's jest for posterity?

Originally constructed between 1686 and 1688, the magnificent **organ** has been rebuilt and developed over the years, and now its pipes top the screen on which they rest.

The **choir stalls** were made by the same craftsman who worked on the screen, but the canopies are Carolingian. Despite the dark wood, the impression is still of lightness as one approaches the **high altar**, which is framed by Rubens' *Adoration of the Magi* and the magnificent east window.

The excellent **Chapel Exhibition** is in the northern side chapels, to the left of the altar. Here, you can see the stages and methods of building set against the historical panorama from inception to completion. On display are costumes, paintings, illuminated manuscripts and books, plans, tools and scale models, including a full-size model showing how the fan vaulting was constructed.

Admission costs £3.50/2.25. The vergers are helpful with information and there are occasional guided tours at the weekend. Weekday tours can be arranged at the TIC.

King's College Chapel (☎ 331100) comes alive when the choir sings; even the most pagan heavy-metal fan will find **Choral Evensong** an extraordinary experience. There are services mid-January to mid-

March, mid-April to mid-June, mid-July to late July, early October to early December and on 24 and 25 December. Evensong is at 5.30 pm, Tuesday to Saturday (men's voices only on Wednesday, a cappella on Friday) and twice on Sunday, at 10.30 am and 3.30 pm. See the Web Site at www.kings.cam.ac.uk.

Trinity College From King's College Chapel, return to King's Parade and follow it north into Trinity St; the entrance to the college (☎ 338400) is opposite Heffers bookshop. Henry VIII founded Trinity in 1546, but it was left to Dr Nevile, Master of Trinity (1593–1615) in Elizabeth's reign, to fulfil his wishes, as Henry died six weeks later.

As you walk through the impressive brick gateway (1535), have a look at the statue of Henry that adorns it. His left hand holds a golden orb, while his right grips a table leg, put there by students who removed the golden sceptre years ago. As you enter the **Great Court** scholastic humour gives way to a gaping sense of awe, for it is the largest of its kind in the world. The place is literally dripping with history: to the right of the entrance is a small tree planted in the 1950s reputed to be a descendant of the apple tree made famous by Trinity alumnus Sir Isaác Newton.

The square is also the scene of the famous run in the film *Chariots of Fire* – 380 yards (347.5m) in 43 seconds (the time it takes the clock to strike 12). Although plenty of students have a go, Harold Abrahams (the hero of the film) never actually attempted it and his fictional run wasn't even filmed here. If you fancy your chances remember that you'll need Olympian speed to even come close to making it in time (we tried and failed miserably!).

The Gothic ante-chapel to the right of the gate is full of huge statues of famous Trinity men such as Tennyson and Newton. The vast hall has a hammerbeam roof and lantern. Beyond the hall are the cloisters of Nevile's Court and the dignified **Wren Library**, complete with 55,000 books printed before 1820 and over 2500 manuscripts, including AA Milne's original *Winnie the*

Pooh. Both he and his son Christopher Robin were graduates. The library opens to visitors noon till 2 pm Monday to Friday and (during term) 10.30 am to 12.30 pm on Saturday. It is certainly worth visiting, though you may have to queue. Admission to the college costs £1.75. See also the Web site at www.trin.cam.ac.uk.

Along the Backs Walk out of the cloisters and turn right to look at St John's New Court on the western bank. It's a 19th-century residence block connected with the rest of **St John's College** by two bridges: Kitchen Bridge and the **Bridge of Sighs** (a replica of the original in Venice built in 1831). Cross Trinity Bridge and turn left, following the footpath until you come to Garret Hostel Bridge. Pause on top to watch the punts below and look upstream to the bridge at **Clare College**. It's ornamented with decorative balls and is the oldest (1639), most interesting bridge on the Backs. Its architect was paid the grand total of 15 pence for his design, which so aggrieved him that he cut a slice out of one of balls adorning the balustrade (the next to last one on the left). In so doing, he ensured that the bridge would never be 'complete' –

or so the story goes. Walk on, then turn right into Trinity Hall.

Trinity Hall College This is a delightfully small college (☎ 332500), wedged among the great and the famous. Despite the name, it has nothing to do with Trinity College. It was founded in 1350 as a refuge for lawyers and clerics escaping the ravages of the Black Death, thus earning it the nickname of the 'Lawyers' College'. You enter through the newest court, which overlooks the river on one side and has a lovely fellows' garden on another. Walking into the next court, you pass the 16th-century library, which has original Jacobean reading desks and books chained to the shelves to prevent their permanent removal – the 16th century's equivalent of electronic bar codes.

Old Schools As you walk out of the first court, you'll see a tall, historic gate that receives little attention. It's the entry to Old Schools, the administrative centre of the university. The lower part dates back to 1441, though the upper section was added in the 1860s. You are now back in the heart of the university.

Walking Tour Two

This walk visits Christ's College, Jesus College, the Round Church and Magdalene College. The walk should take about two hours and you could continue afterwards to see the Kettle's Yard art gallery. Start outside Christ's on the corner of St Andrew's and Hobson Sts. Christ's only opens to visitors 10.30 am to 12.30 pm and 2 to 4 pm, so plan your walk accordingly.

Christ's College Christ's (☎ 334900) was founded in 1505 by that pious and generous benefactress, Lady Margaret Beaufort, who also founded St John's. It has an impressive entrance gate emblazoned with heraldic carving. The figure of the founder stands in a niche, hovering over all like a guiding spirit. Note the stout oak door leading into First Court, which has an unusual circular lawn, magnolias and wisteria creepers. The court is a mixture of original buildings and 18th-century facings and windows. The hall was rebuilt in neo-Gothic style last century, and the chapel's early sections include an oriel window that enabled the founder to join in services from her 1st-floor room.

The Second Court has an interesting fellows' building, dating back to 1643. Its gate leads into a fellows' garden, which contains a mulberry tree under which Milton (who came up to the college in 1628) reputedly wrote *Lycidas*. Continuing through Iris Court, you're confronted by the stark, grey, modern students' block, which seems totally out of place. Look at the little theatre tucked into the right-hand corner, then walk out past New Christ's into Hobson St; turn right, then left and right into Jesus Lane. You'll pass Westcott, another theological college (not part of the university), then All Saints Church – dubbed St Op's (St Opposite) by Jesus students. Charles Darwin studied here.

Jesus College The approach to Jesus (founded 1496; ☎ 339339) via the long 'chimney' is impressive, as is the main gate, which is under a rebus of the founder, Bishop Alcock. A rebus is a heraldic device suggesting the name of its owner: the bishop's consists of several cockerels. The spacious First Court, with its red-brick ranges, is open on the western side – an unusual feature.

The best parts of Jesus are the tiny, intimate cloister court, to your right, and the chapel, which dates back to the St Radegund nunnery. The bishop closed the nunnery, expelled the nuns for misbehaving and founded the new college in its place.

The chapel is inspiring and reflects Jesus' development over the centuries. It has a Norman arched gallery from the nunnery building, a 13th-century chancel and beautiful restoration work and design by Pugin, Morris (ceilings), Burne-Jones (the stained glass) and Madox Brown.

The other buildings in Jesus are rather an anticlimax, but the extensive grounds, which include a cricket pitch, are pleasant to walk through.

Round Church Turn right out of Jesus College, go up Jesus Lane, turn right into Park St and left into Round Church St. At the top of this street is the amazing Round Church, or Church of the Holy Sepulchre (☎ 518219). It was built in 1130 to commemorate its namesake in Jerusalem and is one of only four in England. It is strikingly unusual, with chunky, round Norman pillars that encircle the small nave. The rest of the church was added later in a different style; the conical roof dates from only the 19th century. No longer a parish church, it's now a brass-rubbing centre (☎ 07831 839261). Depending on the size of the brasses, this costs from £4 to £22. It opens 10 am to 6pm daily in summer, 1 to 4 pm daily in winter.

Magdalene College Turn right down Bridge St. It was around Magdalene Bridge, ahead, that the Romans built the bridge that marked the origins of Cambridge. Boats laden with cargo tied up and unloaded where the block of flats now stands on the river bank. Facing you across the river is Magdalene (**mawd**-lin), which you enter from Magdalene St.

Originally a Benedictine hostel, the college (☎ 332100) was refounded in 1542 by

Lord Audley. It has the dubious honour of being the last college to allow women students; when they were finally admitted in 1988, male students wore black armbands and flew the college flag at half-mast.

Its river setting gives it a certain appeal, but its greatest asset is the Pepys Library, housing the magnificent collection of books the famous diarist bequeathed to his old college – he was a student here in 1650–3.

Walking Tour Three

Taking in the colleges just to the south of the city centre, including Corpus Christi, Queen's and Emanuel, this walk takes about 2–2½ hours.

Corpus Christi From King's Parade, turn into Bene't (short for Benedict) St to see the oldest structure in Cambridgeshire – the Saxon tower of the Franciscan parish church (☎ 353903), built in 1025. The rest of the church is newer, but full of interesting features. The round holes above the belfry windows were designed to offer owls nesting privileges; their services were valued as mice-killers. It was here in 1670 that parish clerk Fabian Stedman invented change-ringing (the ringing of bells with different peals in a sequential order). The church also has a bible that belonged to Thomas Hobson, owner of a nearby livery stable who insisted that customers renting a horse take the one nearest the door because that had rested longest – hence the term 'Hobson's choice', meaning no choice at all.

The church served as chapel to Corpus Christi (☎ 338000), next door, until the 16th century when the college built its own. There's an entrance to the college leading into Old Court, which has been retained in its medieval form and still exudes a monastic atmosphere. The door to the chapel is flanked by two statues; on the right is Matthew Parker, who was college Master in 1544 and Archbishop of Canterbury for much of the reign of Elizabeth I. A pretty bright lad, Mr Parker was known for his curiosity, and his endless questioning gave us the term 'nosey parker'. Christopher Marlowe was a Corpus man, as a plaque, next

to a fascinating sundial, bears out. New Court, beyond, is a 19th-century creation.

The college library has the finest collection of Anglo-Saxon manuscripts in the world. Together with other valuable books, they were saved from destruction at the time of the dissolution of the monasteries.

Queens' College One of the Backs' colleges, Queens' (☎ 335511) was the first Cambridge college to charge admission – now £1.20. This was initiated to pay for soundproofing its vulnerable site on this busy street. It takes its name from the two queens who founded it – Margaret of Anjou (wife of Henry VI) and Elizabeth of Woodville (wife of Edward IV), in 1448 and 1465 respectively – yet it was a conscientious rector of St Botolph's Church who was its real creator.

The college's main entrance is off Queens' Lane. The red-brick gate tower and Old Court, which immediately capture your attention, are part of the medieval college. So is Cloister Court, the next court, with its impressive cloister and picturesque, half-timbered President's Lodge (president is the name for the master). The famous Dutch scholar and reformer Erasmus lodged in the tower from 1510 to 1514. He wasn't particularly enamoured of Cambridge: he thought the wine tasted like vinegar, the beer was slop and the place was too expensive, but he did write that the local women were good kissers. The Cam is outside Cloister Court, and is crossed by the wooden Mathematical Bridge that brings you into the 20th-century Cripps Court.

Peterhouse College Founded in 1284 by Hugh de Balsham, later Bishop of Ely, Peterhouse (☎ 338200) is the oldest and smallest of the colleges. It stands to the west of Trumpington St, just beyond the Church of St Mary the Less (better known as Little St Mary's). The church's original name was the odd-sounding St Peter's-without-Trumpington-Gate (because it stood outside, or 'without', the old gate) and it gave the college its name. Inside is a memorial to Godfrey Washington, an alumnus of the college and a great-uncle of George Washington. His family coat of arms was the stars and stripes, the inspiration for the US flag. A walk through Peterhouse gives you a clear picture of the 'community' structure of a Cambridge college, though, unusually, the master's house is opposite the college, not within it. The college's list of notable alumni includes the poet Thomas Grey, who came up in 1742, and Henry Cavendish, the first person to measure the density of water. He also calculated the mass of planet Earth: if you must know, it is six thousand million million tonnes.

First Court, the oldest, is small, neat and bright, with hanging baskets and window boxes. The 17th-century chapel is on the right, built in a mixture of styles that blend well. Inside, the luminous 19th-century stained-glass windows contrast with the older eastern window.

The Burrough range, on the right, is 18th century and the hall, on the left, a restored, late-13th-century gem. Beyond the hall are sweeping grounds extending to the Fitzwilliam Museum. Bearing right, you enter a court with an octagonal lawn, beyond which are the library, theatre and First Court. See also the Web site at www.pet .cam.ac.uk.

Pembroke College Pembroke (☎ 338100) has several courts linked by lovely gardens and lawns. It was founded in 1347 by Marie de St Pol de Valence, the widowed Countess of Pembroke. At 17 she had married the 50-year-old earl, but he was killed in a joust on their wedding day, making her 'maid, wife and widow all in one day'. As usual, the oldest court is at the entrance. It still retains some medieval corner sections. The chapel, on the extreme right, is an early Wren creation (1665) – his uncle Mathew Wren, Bishop of Ely, had spent 18 years imprisoned in the Tower of London courtesy of Oliver Cromwell, and had promised that if he was released he would build a chapel in his old college.

Crossing Old Court diagonally, walk past the handsome Victorian dining hall and into the charming Ivy Court. Walk through the court and round the corner to see a sweep-ing lawn with an impressive statue of Pitt the Younger (prime minister in the 18th century) outside the ornate library clock tower.

Continue through the garden, past the green where students and fellows play croquet after exams in summer, and out, right, onto Pembroke St.

Emmanuel College Founded in 1584, Emmanuel College (☎ 334200), on St Andrew's St, is a medium-sized college comprising a community of some 600 people.

If you stand in Front Court, one of the architectural gems of Cambridge faces you – the Wren chapel, cloister and gallery, completed in 1677. To the left is the hall; inside, the refectory-type tables are set at right angles to the high table.

The next court, New Court, is round the corner. It has a quaint herb garden reminiscent of the old Dominican priory that preceded the college. There are a few remnants of the priory in the *clunch* (chalk) core of the walls of the Old Library. Turn right to re-enter Front Court and go into the chapel. It has interesting windows, a high ceiling and a painting by Jacopo Amigoni. Near the side door is a plaque to a famous scholar, John Harvard (who gained his BA in 1632), who was among 30 Emmanuel men who settled in New England. He left money to found the university that bears his name in the Massachusetts town of Cambridge. His portrait also features in one of the stained-glass windows but, as the artist had no likeness of Harvard from which to work, he used the face of John Milton, a contemporary of Harvard's at the college.

Fitzwilliam Museum

This massive neoclassical edifice with its vast portico takes its name from the seventh Viscount Fitzwilliam, who bequeathed his fabulous art treasures to his old university in 1816. The building in which they are stored was begun by George Basevi in 1837, but he did not live to see its completion in 1848: while working on Ely Cathedral he stepped back to admire his handiwork, slipped and fell to his death. It was one of the first public art museums in

EASTERN ENGLAND

England, and has been called the 'finest small museum in Europe'.

In the lower galleries are ancient Egyptian sarcophagi and Greek and Roman art, as well as Chinese ceramics, English glass and illuminated manuscripts. The upper galleries contain a wide range of paintings, including works by Titian, Rubens, Gainsborough, Stubbs and Constable, right up to the French impressionists, Cézanne and Picasso. It also has fine antique furniture.

The museum (☎ 332900) opens 10 am to 5 pm Tuesday to Saturday and 2.15 to 5 pm on Sunday. There are guided tours of the museum at 2.30 pm on Sunday. Admission is free. Its Web site is at www.fitzmuseum .cam.ac.uk.

Kettle's Yard

On the corner of Northampton and Castle Sts, this museum and gallery (☎ 352124) was the home of HS 'Jim' Ede, a former assistant keeper at Tate Britain in London, and his wife Helen. In 1957 they opened their home to young artists with a view towards creating 'a home and a welcome, a refuge of peace and order, of the visual arts and of music'. Their efforts resulted in a beautiful collection of 20th-century art, furniture, ceramics and glass by such artists as Henry Moore, Henri Gaudier-Brzeska and a host of British others. In 1966 they donated their home and collection to the university, who in turn opened it as a museum but didn't touch the arrangement of the pieces. In the adjoining exhibition gallery (opened in 1970) there are temporary exhibits of contemporary art.

Kettle's Yard museum opens 2 to 4 pm Tuesday to Sunday. The gallery opens 12.30 to 5.30 pm Tuesday to Saturday and 2 to 5.30 pm on Sunday. Admission is free. Take a look at the Web site at www.kettlesyard .co.uk.

Punting

Taking a punt along the Backs is sublime, but it can also be a wet and hectic experience, especially on a busy weekend. Look before you leap. If you do wimp out, the Backs are also perfect for a walk or a picnic.

Rental prices vary considerably. Cheapest, but not always available, are those at Trinity Punts (☎ 338483), behind Trinity College. They charge £6 per hour (plus £25 deposit). Next is the punt hire at the Granta pub, Newnham Rd, for £7 per hour with a £30 deposit. Punts hired by Magdalene Bridge, or outside the nearby Rat & Parrot pub, cost £7 per hour plus £30 deposit.

By Silver St, Scudamore's (☎ 359750) charges £10 per hour plus £50 deposit or a credit card imprint. If you don't feel confident about your abilities in a punt, consider renting one with a chauffeur; it costs £35 per punt, and the trip lasts 45 minutes. Due to traffic on the Cam, between 1 and 6 pm the punts carry a maximum of 12 people; at other times they can carry up to 18.

Punting the 3 miles (5km) up the river to the idyllic village of Grantchester makes a great day out.

Walking & Cycling

The best outing in the area is to Grantchester. If you don't want to punt, you can travel the 3 miles (5km) along the towpath on foot or by bike. For longer walks, the TIC stocks a number of guides, including *Walks in South Cambridgeshire*.

If you're a lazy cyclist, the flat topography makes for ideal cycling country, although the scenery can become a little monotonous. The TIC also stocks *Cycle Routes and the Cambridge Green Belt Area* and the *Cambridge Cycle Route Map*, which are useful guides. For further information on cycling in the area, contact the Cyclists' Touring Club (☎ 563414).

Organised Tours

Guide Friday (☎ 362444) runs hop-on hop-off tour buses round the city, calling at the train station. Tours are daily, year-round; tickets cost £8.50/2.50 for adults/children, and £7 for students.

Cambridge River Cruises (☎ 300100) runs 90-minute cruises from the river near Jesus Green for £7/5. There's at least one departure daily at 1 pm, April to September, with more frequent departures in midseason.

Places to Stay – Budget

Camping About 4 miles (6km) south-west of Cambridge is *Highfield Farm Touring Park* (☎/fax 262308, Long Rd, Comberton). During July and August it costs £8.75 for a two-person tent (£7.25 at other times). It opens April to October only.

Hostels The *Cambridge Youth Hostel* (☎ 354601, fax 312780, 97 Tenison Rd) has small dormitories and a restaurant near the train station. It's very popular so book ahead. Adult/junior rates are £11.90/8.20 for YHA members; nonmembers have to pay an extra £2.

B&Bs & Hotels There are numerous B&Bs to choose from at any time of the year, even more during university holidays from late June to late September. The two B&B areas are on Tenison Rd, which runs south-east of Parker's Piece, and north of the city around Chesterton Rd.

Right outside the train station is *Sleeperz* (☎ 304050, fax 357286, e info@sleeperz .com, Station Rd), an attractively converted railway warehouse with single/twin rooms for £35/45 with shower and breakfast. Rooms with a double bed are larger and

cost £55. It's nonsmoking and there's wheelchair access to some rooms.

The *Tenison Towers Guest House* (☎ 363924, 148 Tenison Rd) is a clean, standard place that charges from £22 to £27 per person. The *Six Steps Guest House* (☎ 353968, fax 356788, 93 Tenison Rd) costs from £25 per person. One reader eulogised about the food here: 'the only good bread I tasted in the UK'.

Just off Tenison Rd, *Warkworth House* (☎ 363682, fax 369655, Warkworth Terrace) is a lovely Victorian terraced house with comfortable singles/doubles from £35/55. The breakfast is delicious, and the owner is extremely friendly. It is popular with students from overseas.

The *YMCA* (☎ 356998, fax 312749, Gonville Place) charges £22.65/37 and is good value for weekly stays (£127.50/224). Breakfast is included.

Antony's Guest House (☎ 357444, 4 Huntingdon Rd) is spacious and comfortable, with four singles, four doubles and three triples at £15 to £22 per person. Similarly priced but a bit farther out, *Benson House* (☎/fax 311594, 24 Huntingdon Rd) has well-equipped doubles with showers – and a friendly cat. It is strictly nonsmoking.

How to Punt

Punting looks pretty straightforward, but believe us, it's not. As soon as we had dried off and hung our clothes on the line, we thought it was a good idea to offer a couple of tips on how to move the boat and stay out of the water.

JANE SMITH

1. Standing at the end of the punt, lift the pole out of the water at the side of the punt.

2. Let the pole slide through your hands to touch the bottom of the river.

3. Tilt the pole forward (ie in the direction of travel of the punt) and push down to propel the punt forward.

4. Twist the pole to free the end from the mud at the bottom of the river, and let it float up and trail behind the punt. You can then use it as a rudder to steer with.

5. If you've not yet fallen in, raise the pole out of the water and into the vertical position to begin the cycle again.

Carlton Lodge (☎ *367792, fax 566877,* e *info@carltonlodge.co.uk, 245 Chesterton Rd)* is run by widely travelled, friendly people. Rooms cost £19/38. Smoking is strictly prohibited.

Places to Stay – Mid-Range

Close to the city centre, the *Belle Vue Guest House* (☎ *351859, 33 Chesterton Rd)* has comfortable doubles for £40.

Aaron House (☎ *314723, 71 Chesterton Rd)* is a small place with singles from £27 to £29 and doubles from £44 to £56. All are en suite.

Farther east, *Acorn Guest House* (☎ *353888, fax 350527, 154 Chesterton Rd)* has well-appointed rooms from £25/40 to £45/58, all with bathrooms. Vegetarians are catered for; smokers are not. The nearby *Hamilton Hotel* (☎ *365664, fax 314866,* e *enquiries@hamiltoncambridge.co.uk, 156 Chesterton Rd)* has 25 rooms from £22/50 to £40/65. Most are en suite.

Places to Stay – Top End

An elegant option is *Arundel House Hotel* (☎ *367701, fax 367721, 53 Chesterton Rd),* a large Victorian building overlooking the Cam. There are 42 single rooms ranging from £53 to £72.50, and 60 doubles from £69 to £96, all with bathrooms.

The *Lensfield Hotel* (☎ *355017, fax 312022,* e *enquiries@lensfieldhotel.co.uk, 53 Lensfield Rd)* is well located near the Fitzwilliam Museum. It has 32 rooms and charges from £55/70 for a single to £80 for a double. Pricey, but the rooms are very well appointed.

The posh *Garden House (Moat House)* (☎ *259988, fax 316605, Granta Place, Mill Lane)* is in the centre, right on the Cam, and has its own private garden. There are 117 luxurious bedrooms with prices to match – £140/245 (not including breakfast). There are serious discounts available on weekend rates.

The *University Arms Hotel* (☎ *351241, fax 461319,* e *devere.uniarms@airtime .co.uk, Regent St),* a huge Victorian mansion overlooking Parker's Piece, is the other top place in town. It charges £110/135.

Places to Eat

Restaurants There's a number of reasonably priced restaurants on Regent St.

The Depot (☎ *566966, 41 Regent St)* is stylish yet good value, offering an interesting international menu based around starters (around £4.50 each). Over the road, *Shalimar Restaurant* (☎ *355378, 84 Regent St)* is an Indian place offering discounts to students.

Across the road from King's College is *Rainbow* (☎ *321551, 9 King's Parade),* a good vegetarian restaurant. Couscous is £6.

No 1 King's Parade (☎ *359506)* is a cellar bar-restaurant opposite King's College. An express two-course lunch costs £6.95. Wild boar and apple sausages cost £8.25.

Efe's Restaurant (☎ *350491, 80 King St)* is a good-value Turkish restaurant where mains cost between £6 and £7. It opens noon to 2.30 pm and 6 to 11 pm Monday to Saturday and noon to 11 pm on Sunday.

Occupying the old cricket pavilion, *Hobb's Pavilion* (☎ *367480, Park Terrace)* specialises in filled pancakes. It's closed on Sunday and Monday.

One of the most pleasant and central dining options is *The Dôme* (☎ *313818, 33–4 St Andrew's St),* a French-style brasserie with friendly staff, a small garden at the back and a fabulous steak sandwich for £9. There are a few vegetarian options too.

Browns (☎ *461655, 23 Trumpington St)* is part of the chain that has branches in several university towns. It's not as expensive as it looks – mains cost around £7.

Michel's Brasserie (☎ *353110, 21 Northampton St)* has set lunches from £7.25 and more expensive a la carte dinners.

It may look like just another house among the hotels and B&Bs on this road, but inside *Twenty-two* (☎ *351880, 22 Chesterton Rd),* near the Boathouse pub, is a gourmet restaurant. A set dinner costs £25.

The city's best cuisine is served overlooking the river on Midsummer Common at *Midsummer House* (☎ *369299).* It's a smart, sophisticated place, said to have one of the most comprehensive wine lists outside Paris. There are set lunch menus at around £27.50 and set dinners at £42. It's open for lunch Tuesday to Friday and on Sunday, and for dinner from Tuesday to Saturday. You may need to book several weeks in advance.

Cafes Cambridge may be a university town, but tourism is an enormous cash cow, a fact reflected in restaurant prices. There are, however, a number of reasonably priced cafes, some of which give student discounts.

Nadia's is a small chain of bakeries that are excellent value (a bacon sandwich and coffee bought before 10.30 am costs 95p). A smoked ham and Emmental cheese baguette is £1.05. There are branches on King's Parade and Silver St.

Tatties (☎ 323399, 11 Sussex St) has long been a budget favourite. It specialises not only in baked potatoes stuffed with a variety of tempting fillings, but also in breakfasts, filled baguettes, salads and cakes. The delicious Breakfast Baguette (hot Cambridge sausages) costs £2.50.

Popular with students, *Clowns (☎ 355711, 54 King St)* serves light meals that are good value.

Choices Café (☎ 360211, Newnham Rd) will make up picnic hampers for punters for about £4 per person.

Fitzbillies (☎ 352500, 52 Trumpington St) is a brilliant bakery/cafe. The Chelsea buns (80p) are an outrageous experience, and so is the chocolate cake beloved by generations of students, but there are many other temptations in addition to the usual sandwiches and pies – stock up before you go punting. Cakes and buns are also available by mail order.

Bar Ha! Ha! (☎ 305089, 17 Trinity St) is a trendy new cafe-bar with a good selection of salads and sandwiches between £3 and £6.

Entertainment

Pubs As punting is such a big part of the Cambridge tourist experience, there are a number of bars that cater to this trade; some even rent out boats.

The *Rat & Parrot (☎ 311701, Thompson's Lane)* is by the river, north of Mag-

---

Walks in Eastern England

One of the prettiest walks in the whole region is the 3-mile (5km) walk to Grantchester from Cambridge along the Cam. More of a gentle stroll than a walk, all you have to do is follow the meander of the river as it winds its way south-west – in fine weather the river is full of punts.

Even if you don't fancy taking the whole of the 50-mile (80km) Suffolk Coast Path, you should consider the lovely walk between Aldeburgh and Snape, 3 miles up the Alde River. The path leads you along the river past some pleasant wooded areas and fields. Just follow the signs for Snape Maltings.

---

dalene Bridge; punts are available from here. The *Granta (☎ 505016, Newnham Rd)* is another pub with punt hire beside it. The *Boathouse (14 Chesterton Rd)* can be visited by punt and even has its own mooring place.

Nobel prize-winning scientists Crick and Watson spent equal time in the laboratory and *The Eagle (☎ 505020, Bene't St)*, so perhaps Greene King, the Suffolk brewers, played a part in the discovery of the structure of DNA. This 16th-century pub was also popular with American airmen in WWII; they left their signatures on the ceiling.

Champion of the Thames (☎ 352043, 68 King St) is a simple place that makes no effort to draw in the punting crowd or cash in on Cambridge's moneyed youth. It's a regulars' ale house: no food, no music, just Greene King beer – it reputedly has the best Abbot Ale in town.

If you're looking for bars with a more contemporary feel, there has been a spate of new openings. *Bar Ha! Ha! (☎ 305089, 17 Trinity St)* is popular with the trendy young things (see also 'Places to Eat' earlier).

The oddly named *Sophbeck Sessions (☎ 569100, 14 Tredgold Lane)* is a Cajun-style bar in the north-east of town that is fast gaining in popularity among students and visitors alike as a good place to have a drink and enjoy some jazz and soul.

Nightclubs With such a large student population, it is hardly surprising that Cambridge has its fair share of busy nightclubs, even though the scene is anything but alternative or underground. The music on offer is pretty straightforward – you'll hear everything from commercial house anthems to sexy R&B.

The most popular club at the time of writing was *Fez (☎ 519224, 15 Market Passage)*. There are queues most nights and the music is loud and thumping. It opens 8 pm to 2 am Monday to Saturday; admission costs between £2 and £7, depending on the night (free before 9 pm on Monday and Wednesday).

Po Na Na (☎ 323880, 7b Jesus Lane) is a terrific new bar and club in the basement of a neo-classical building. The style is Moroccan casbah, and the DJs spin a mix of Latin, house and other funky rhythms. Admission costs £1.50 and it is open until 2 am.

Also popular is *Fifth Avenue (☎ 364222, Heidelburg Gardens, Lion Yard)*; it's a bit of a meat market but can be good fun. With nights called 'Desire', 'Hustle' and 'A Kick up the 90s' it is Cambridge's own version of 'Ibiza Uncovered'. Admission costs around £7. Dress neatly at the weekend.

The Man on the Moon (☎ 474144, 2 Norfolk St) is the only spot where you'll come across anything resembling an underground dance scene in Cambridge – and it closes at 11 pm. Despite the limited opening hours, the place is renowned for its promotion of breakbeats and hard techno. Admission is usually between £1 and £2 and in keeping with its underground status, the dress code is whatever you've got in your wardrobe, folded or otherwise.

Theatre The *Corn Exchange (☎ 357851)*, near the TIC, is the city's main centre for arts and entertainment, with shows as diverse as the English National Ballet and Sesame Street Live! The restored *Arts Theatre (☎ 503333)* is at 6 St Edward's Passage. The King's College Choir is unique to Cambridge – don't miss it (see Walking Tour One earlier for more details).

Getting There & Away

Cambridge can easily be visited as a day trip from London (although it's worth staying at least a night) or en route north. It's well served by rail, but not so well by bus.

Bus For bus information, phone ☎ 317740. National Express (☎ 0870 580 8080) has hourly buses to London (£8, 2½ hours), and four buses a day to/from Bristol (two stop at Bath; £25.75, six hours). Unfortunately, connections to the north aren't straightforward. To get to Lincoln or York you'll have to change at Peterborough or Nottingham, respectively. King's Lynn is also only accessible via Peterborough – it's easier to take a train.

Cambridge Coach Services (☎ 423900) runs the Inter-Varsity Link via Stansted airport to Oxford six times daily (£8/14 for a single/return, three hours). It also runs buses to Heathrow (£15.50) and Gatwick (£18.50) airports.

Train There are trains every half-hour from London's King's Cross and Liverpool St stations (£14.50, 55 minutes). Network railcards are valid. If you catch the train at King's Cross you travel via Hatfield and Stevenage. There are also hourly train connections to Bury St Edmunds (£5.30, 45 minutes), Ely (£2.90, 15 minutes) and King's Lynn (£6.90, 50 minutes). There are connections at Peterborough with the main northbound trains to Lincoln, York and Edinburgh. If you want to head west to Oxford or Bath, you'll have to return to London first.

Getting Around

Most vehicles are now banned from the centre of Cambridge. Using the well signposted Park & Ride car parks (£1.25) is recommended.

Bus There's a free, gas-powered shuttle service, which stops at Emmanuel St in the centre. Cambus (☎ 423554) runs numerous buses (50p) around town from Drummer St, including bus No 1 from the train station to the town centre.

Taxi For a taxi, phone Cabco (☎ 312444). Unless you have a lot of luggage, it's not really worth taking one from the train station to the centre. It costs between £3 and £3.60 and takes about 10 minutes (longer during the rush hour); you can walk it in about 25 minutes.

Bicycle It's easy enough to get around Cambridge on foot, but if you're staying out of the centre, or plan to explore the fens, a bicycle can be useful. You don't need a flash mountain bike because there are few hills; most places rent three-speeds. Ben Hayward Cycles (☎ 35229), 69 Trumpington St, rents out bikes for £10 per day mid-May to mid-October. You can book on-line at www.benhaywardcycles.com. Geoff's Bike Hire (☎ 365629), 65 Devonshire Rd, near the youth hostel, charges £7 per day and around £15 per week, but gives a 10% discount to YHA members. Cambridge Recycles (☎ 506035), 61 Newnham Rd, charges £6 to £10 per day. Mike's Bikes (☎ 312591), Mill Rd, is the cheapest at £5 per day or £8 per week (plus £25 deposit) for a bike with no gears.

AROUND CAMBRIDGE
Grantchester
Three miles (5km) south-west of Cambridge, Grantchester is a delightful village of thatched cottages and flower-filled meadows beside the River Granta (as the Cam was once known and is still known here). Its quintessential Englishness was recognised by the poet Rupert Brooke, who was a student at King's before WWI, in the immortal lines: 'Stands the church clock still at ten to three, And is there honey still for tea?' Grantchester's most famous resident is the novelist Jeffrey Archer, who lives in the Old Vicarage.

There are teashops and some attractive pubs – try the ***Orchard Tea Gardens*** (☎ 845788, 45 Orchard House, Mill Way), where cream teas are served under apple trees. The best of the pubs is the ***Red Lion*** (☎ 840121, 33 High St), near the river, which has a very pleasant garden.

Get here via the towpath or hire a punt in Cambridge (see the boxed text 'Punting' in the earlier Cambridge section for details).

American War Cemetery
Four miles (6km) west of Cambridge at Madingley, is an extremely moving cemetery with neat rows of white-marble crosses stretching down the sloping site to commemorate the 3811 Americans killed in WWII while based in Britain. The latest soldier to be buried here died during the Gulf War in 1991. The cemetery (☎ 01954-210350) opens 8 am to 5.30 pm, April 16 to September 30 (until 5 pm the rest of the year).

You can visit the cemetery as part of a Guide Friday tour (see Organised Tours under Cambridge earlier).

Duxford Imperial War Museum
Military hardware enthusiasts should head for this war museum (☎ 01223-835000), 9 miles (14km) south of Cambridge, right by the motorway. The museum is housed in an airfield that played a significant role in WWII, especially during the Battle of Britain. It was the home of the famous Dambuster squadron of Lancasters, and today is home to the Royal Air Force's Red Arrows squadron, which performs all kinds of celestial trickery at air shows throughout the world.

Here you'll find Europe's biggest collection of historic aircraft, ranging from WWI biplanes to jets, including Concorde. The new **American Air Museum**, also on the site, has the largest collection of US civil and military aircraft outside of America. Air shows are frequently held here and battlefield scenes are displayed in the land warfare hall, where you can check out WWII tanks and artillery. Kids will enjoy the adventure playground and the flight simulator. In 1998 the museum was awarded the Stirling Prize, Britain's most coveted architecture award.

Opening hours are 10 am to 6 pm, July to August (to 4 pm the rest of the year). Admission costs £7.40/3.70. The museum runs courtesy buses – the price of the journey is included in the admission – from

EASTERN ENGLAND

The Fens

The fens were strange marshlands that stretched from Cambridge north to The Wash and beyond into Lincolnshire. They were home to people who led an isolated existence among a maze of waterways; fishing, hunting and farming scraps of arable land. In the 17th century, however, the Duke of Bedford and a group of speculators brought in Dutch engineer Cornelius Vermuyden to drain the fens, and the flat, open plains with their rich, black soil were created. The region is the setting for Graham Swift's excellent novel *Waterland*.

As the world's weather pattern changes and the sea level rises, the fens are beginning to disappear underwater again. It's estimated that by the year 2030 up to 400,000 hectares could be lost.

Cambridge train station every 40 to 50 minutes between 9.40 am and 4.40 pm (until 2.20 pm September to June); they also stop outside the Crowne Plaza Hotel by the Lionyard.

Wimpole Hall

Until recently the home of Rudyard Kipling's daughter, Wimpole Hall is now an NT property. It is a large, gracious, 18th-century mansion set in 140 hectares of beautiful parkland. Wimpole Home Farm, next to it, was established in 1794 as a model farm; today, it's home to a number of rare breeds.

Wimpole Hall (☎ 01223-207257) is 8 miles (13km) south-west of Cambridge on the A603. The farm opens 10.30 am to 4 pm daily except Monday and Friday, March to November; until 5 pm in July and August. The hall opens 1 to 5 pm daily except Monday and Friday; these hours are currently under review. Please call for details. Admission costs £5.90, or £8.50 including the Home Farm (children half-price). There's no charge to just walk in the park.

Whippet service No 175 passes this way from Cambridge. Alternatively, you could try walking the Wimpole Way, a 13-mile

(21km) waymarked trail from Cambridge. A leaflet is available from the TIC.

ELY

☎ 01353 • pop 9000

Ely (ee-lee) is an unspoiled market town with neat Georgian houses, a river port and one of the country's great cathedrals. It stands in the centre of the fens (see 'The Fens' boxed text for more details). Ely used to be an island and derived its name from the eels that frequented the surrounding waters.

Orientation & Information

Ely is an easy day trip from Cambridge and is so small that you'll have no problems getting around. The TIC (☎ 662062, fax 668518) is in Oliver Cromwell's House. It opens 10 am to 5.30 pm daily, April to September; and 10 am to 5 pm Monday to Saturday and 11 am to 4 pm on Sunday the rest of the year.

A joint ticket, the 'passport to Ely', is available for £9 (£7 for students) for the main sights – Ely Cathedral, the stained glass museum, Ely Museum and Oliver Cromwell's House.

The post office (☎ 669946) is at 19 High St, at the back of the building that also houses Lloyd's Chemist (☎ 662226). The Princess of Wales Hospital (☎ 652000) is about a mile north of the town centre, just off the Lynn Rd. The police station (☎ 01223-358966) is on Lynn Rd, though oddly you must call the police in Cambridge, who will then transfer you to the Ely office.

Ely Cathedral

The cathedral's origins stem from a remarkable queen of Northumbria called Etheldreda. She had been married twice, but was determined to pursue her vocation to become a nun. She founded an abbey in 673 and, for her good works, was canonised after her death. The abbey soon became a pilgrimage centre.

It was a Norman bishop, Simeon, who began the task of building the cathedral. It was completed in 1189 and remains a splendid example of the Norman Romanesque style. In 1322 – after the collapse of the central tower – the octagon and lantern, for which the cathedral is famous, were built. They have fan vaulting and intricate detail.

Other features of special interest include the Lady Chapel, the largest of its kind in England, which was added in the 14th century. The niches were rifled by iconoclasts, but the delicate tracery and carving remain intact. There's an amazing view from just inside the west door, right down the nave, through the choir stalls and on to the glorious east window – no clutter, just a sublime sense of space, light and spirituality.

Ely was the first English cathedral to charge admission (now £4) and, with funds gathered since 1986, it has managed to restore the octagon and lantern tower. There are free guided tours and also a tour of the octagon and roof. There's also a stained glass museum (£3.50) in the south triforium. The cathedral (☎ 667735) opens 7 am to 7 pm (5 pm in winter). Choral Sunday service is at 10.30 am and evensong is at 3.45 pm.

Other Attractions

The area around the cathedral is historically and architecturally interesting. There's the Bishop's Palace, now a nursing home, and King's School, which supplies the cathedral with choristers.

Oliver Cromwell's House (☎ 662062) stands to the west, across St Mary's Green. Cromwell lived with his family in this attractive, half-timbered, 14th-century house from 1636–46, when he was the tithe collector of Ely. The TIC, occupying the front room in the house, offers an audiovisual presentation and an interesting tour of the rooms (£3/2.40).

The history of the town is told in **Ely Museum** (☎ 666655), in the Old Gaol House. It opens 10.30 am to 5.30 pm daily (to 4.30 pm November to April); entry costs £2/1.25.

It's worth walking down to the river by following the signs. There is an interesting **antiques centre** near the river. The **Old Maltings** (☎ 662633), on Ship Lane, which stages exhibitions and has a cafe (the Waterfront Brasserie), is nearby. The **River Great Ouse** is a busy thoroughfare – swans and ducks compete with boats for space on the water. The towpath winds up and downstream: for a quiet walk, turn left; for the pub and tea garden, turn right. If you continue along this path you'll see the fens stretching to the horizon.

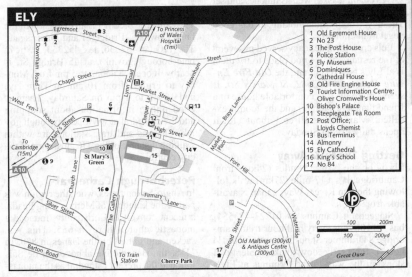

ELY

1	Old Egremont House
2	No 23
3	The Post House
4	Police Station
5	Ely Museum
6	Dominiques
7	Cathedral House
8	Old Fire Engine House
9	Tourist Information Centre; Oliver Cromwell's Houe
10	Bishop's Palace
11	Steeplegate Tea Room
12	Post Office; Lloyds Chemist
13	Bus Terminus
14	Almonry
15	Ely Cathedral
16	King's School
17	No 84

EASTERN ENGLAND

Places to Stay

There are few budget options in Ely.

Several B&Bs are on Egremont St. At No 31, **Old Egremont House** (☎ 663118, fax 666968) offers comfortable singles/doubles for £40/46 in an attractive house with a large garden. At **No 23** (☎ 664557), B&B costs £25/40. **The Post House** (☎ 667184), at 12a, is unmissable with the Union Jack raised outside. Rooms cost £19/38.

On Broad St, **No 84** (☎ 666862) has just one double room for £18/32.

Cathedral House (☎/fax 662124, [e] farn dale@cathedralhouse.co.uk, 17 St Mary's St) offers extremely comfortable B&B for £40/50.

Places to Eat

Steeplegate Tea Room (☎ 664731, 16 High St) is right beside the cathedral. Light lunches and baked potatoes from £2.50 are available.

Close by, virtually in the grounds of the cathedral, is an attractive garden restaurant, the **Almonry** (☎ 666360), to the left of the Lady Chapel. There's a wide range of teas and coffees here.

Dominiques (☎ 665011, St Mary's St) serves cream teas, as well as lunches and set dinners (£18). It's closed on Monday and Tuesday. Totally nonsmoking, it has good vegetarian choices.

Eels are a local delicacy served in several of the restaurants. A good place to try them is at Ely's best restaurant, the **Old Fire Engine House** (☎ 662582, St Mary's St). It seems more like the comfortable house of a friend than a restaurant, and the food is excellent. Main dishes all cost about £12. It opens daily except Sunday.

Getting There & Away

Ely is on the A10, 15 miles (24km) from Cambridge. It's a 17-mile (27km) walk following the Fen Rivers Way; a map is available from TICs.

Stagecoach Cambus (☎ 01223-423554) bus No 106 runs every half hour from Cambridge's Drummer St bus station (£3.10, 1¼ hours). It's pretty slow, making plenty of stops on the way to the terminus at Ely's

Market St. The faster X8 runs hourly and takes only 40 minutes.

Faster (and cheaper) still is to go by train – there are hourly departures from Cambridge (£2.90, 15 minutes).

PETERBOROUGH
☎ 01733 • pop 156,600

Peterborough likes to advertise itself as the capital city of shopping, and while this may do wonders for the retail trade, it does precious little for tourism, especially the kind that is familiar with British malls and high-street chain stores. It is undoubtedly an industrious place, a product of having been part of the 1960s 'New Towns' program – which lead to a substantial urban renewal, including the construction of new residential townships and a number of dual carriageways – but aside from a few central sites of historic importance it is a little grim. Construction continues to this day, with the last of the four planned townships – Hampton – being agreed on the city's south side. Yet Peterborough is home to a wonderful cathedral that is worth making the trip for, but only just. Luckily, it's an easy day trip from Cambridge.

Orientation & Information

The cathedral precinct is an extension of the busy Cowgate, Bridge St and Queensgate. The TIC (☎ 452336, fax 452353, [e] tic@ peterborough.gov.uk), at 45 Bridge St, is nearby. It opens 8.45 am to 5 pm from Monday to Friday (from 10 am on Thursday) and 10 am to 4 pm on Saturday. There is good online information about shopping and the cathedral at www.peterborough.gov.uk. The bus and train stations are within walking distance of the TIC, just west of the city centre.

Peterborough Cathedral

In Anglo-Saxon times, when the region was part of the kingdom of Mercia, King Peada, a recent convert to Christianity, founded a monastic church here in 655. This was sacked and gutted by the Danes in 870. In 1118, the Benedictine abbot John de Sais founded the present cathedral as the monastic church of the Benedictine abbey. It was finally consecrated in 1237.

As you enter the precinct from Cathedral Square you get a breathtaking view of the early-13th-century western front, one of the most impressive of any cathedral in England.

On entering you're struck by the height of the nave and the lightness, which derives not only from the mellow Barnack stone (quarried close by and transported via the River Nene), but also from the clerestory windows. The nave, with its three storeys, is an impressive example of Norman architecture. Its timber ceiling is one of the earliest of its kind in England (possibly in Europe) and its original painted decoration has been preserved.

The Gothic tower replaced the original Norman one, but had to be taken down and carefully reconstructed after it began to crack in the late 19th century.

In the north choir aisle is the tombstone of Henry VIII's first wife, the tragic Catherine of Aragon, buried here in 1536. Her divorce, engineered by the king because she could not produce a male heir, led to the Reformation in England. Her only child (a daughter) was not even allowed to attend the funeral. Directly opposite, in the south aisle, two standards mark what was the grave of Mary Queen of Scots. On the accession of her son, James, to the throne, her body was moved to Westminster Abbey.

The eastern end of the cathedral, known as the New Building, was added in the 15th century. It has superb fan vaulting, probably the work of master mason John Wastell, who worked on King's College Chapel.

The cathedral (☎ 343342) opens 8.30 am to 5.15 pm; admission is free (but a 'donation' of £3 is encouraged). Every 29 January there is a procession in the cathedral to mark the death of Catherine.

Places to Stay & Eat
If for some reason you're stuck in Peterborough for the night, you should have no problem finding a place to stay north of the city centre, especially on Oundle Rd.

The *Graham Hotel* (☎/fax 567824, 296

Oundle Rd) has singles/doubles for £18/35. It is about 400 yards north of the town centre. The *Longueville Guesthouse* (☎/fax 233422, 411 Oundle Rd)* has better quality rooms for £30/40.

Papillon Café (☎ 314659, 9 Queensgate Centre)* is a nice place to get a bite, serving sandwiches and hot dishes for around £4. The *Nip In Café* (☎ 34603835 Hereward Cross)* is another good option with a similarly priced menu.

There's a branch of the cafe *Clown's* (☎ 341124, 5 Midgate)* in the centre of town.

Getting There & Away
Peterborough is 37 miles (60km) north of Cambridge. Stagecoach United Counties (☎ 01604-620077) and National Express (☎ 0870 580 8080) run buses from Cambridge (£7, one hour); some services require a change in Huntingdon. There are hourly trains from Cambridge (£8.60, 55 minutes).

Lincolnshire

Sneering southerners who've never visited tend to think of Lincolnshire as flat and boring. Although far from alpine, the county is made up of several diverse landscapes, from the hilly countryside of the western county to the flat marshlands of the east. It's easy cycling and walking country, but has a number of other attractions that make a visit worthwhile. The unspoiled nature of some of the Lincolnshire towns – cobbled streets, solid stone-built houses with red-tiled roofs – attracts film companies as well as tourists. One of the finest Gothic buildings in the country and in Europe, Lincoln Cathedral, has a wealth of beautiful parish churches, built on the proceeds of the flourishing wool trade.

The Lincolnshire Wolds, to the north and east of Lincoln, are comprised of low rolling hills and small market towns. To the south-east, the flat Lincolnshire Fens are fertile agricultural land reclaimed from the sea. The whole area is criss-crossed by a network of rivers and dikes, while the coastline to the east is marked by wide sandy beaches as well as salt marshes, dunes and pools.

Another plus is the weather. Although hardly tropical, Lincolnshire receives only half the national average of rainfall, hence the county's slogan: 'The drier side of Britain'.

GETTING AROUND

Regional transport is poor but the main routes are well enough served by train or bus. The main East Coast rail line links all of the major towns, and there's a number of private bus operators that fill in the gaps in-between. The Lincolnshire timetable hotline (☎ 01522-553135) has details of bus and rail times for the county; it operates 8 am to 4.45 pm Monday to Friday.

The Viking Way is a 140-mile (225km) waymarked trail that runs from the Humber Bridge, through the Lincolnshire Wolds, to Oakham in Leicestershire.

Renting a bike in Lincoln, or bringing one with you, is an excellent idea. TICs stock sets of *Lincolnshire Cycle Trails.*

LINCOLN
☎ 01522 • pop 81,500

Since it's not on a direct tourist route, many people bypass Lincoln, missing an interesting city with a compact medieval centre of narrow, winding streets and a magnificent 900-year-old cathedral (the third largest in Britain), as well as one of the steepest urban climbs this side of San Francisco. The suburbs are unattractively built-up and depressed but, perhaps because Lincoln escapes the hordes of visitors that places such as York attract, the people are particularly friendly. The presence of a university means that there are plenty of young people around.

History

For the last 2000 years, most of Britain's invaders have recognised the potential of this site and made their mark. Lincoln's hill was of immense strategic importance, giving views for miles across the surrounding plain. Communications were found to be

excellent – below it is the River Witham, navigable to the sea.

The Romans established a garrison and a town they called Lindum. In AD 96 it was given the status of a colonia, or chartered town – Lindum Colonia, hence Lincoln. Gracious public buildings were constructed and it became a popular place for old soldiers past their prime to spend their twilight years.

The Normans began work on the castle in 1068 and the cathedral in 1072. In the 12th century the wool trade developed and wealthy merchants established themselves. The city was famous for the cloth known as Lincoln green, said to have been worn by Robin Hood. Many of the wealthiest merchants were Jews, but following the murder of a nine-year-old boy in 1255 for which one of their number was accused, they were mercilessly persecuted and many were driven out.

During the Civil War the city passed from Royalist to Parliamentarian and back again, but it began to prosper as an agricultural centre in the 18th century. In the following century, after the arrival of the railway, Lincoln's engineering industry was established. Heavy machinery produced here included the world's first tank, which saw action in WWI.

Orientation & Information

The cathedral sits on top of the hill in the centre of the old part of the city, with the castle and most of the other things to see conveniently nearby. Three-quarters of a mile down from the cathedral (a 15-minute walk) lies the new town, and the bus and train stations. These two parts of Lincoln are connected by the appropriately named Steep Hill.

Tourist Office The TIC (☎ 529828, fax 564506) is in the old black-and-white building at 9 Castle Hill. It opens from 9 am to 5.30 pm Monday to Thursday, and until 5 pm on Friday and at the weekend.

Guided walking tours (£3/2) from the TIC take place at 11 am and 2 pm daily in summer, and at the weekend in June, September and October. There are also Guide Friday bus tours (☎ 01789-294466) daily, April to September (£5.50/2).

Post & Communications The post office (☎ 526031) is at 90 Bailgate, next to the TIC. You can check email at Trayer's Bookshop (☎ 511156), 211 High St, down a flight of stairs behind Stokes High Bridge Café (see Places to Eat later in the section). There's only one terminal, but you get a free cup of coffee. It opens 10 am to 5.30 pm Tuesday to Friday, 9 am to 5 pm on Saturday and 11 am to 4 pm on Sunday. Charges are £1 for 15 minutes.

Laundry Abbey Washerteria (☎ 530272) is at 197 Monks Rd. It opens 9 am to 7 pm Monday to Friday, 8.30 am to 5 pm on Saturday and 9 am to 5 pm on Sunday. A small machine costs £5.50, a large machine £6.50, but for an extra £1 you can leave it as a service wash.

Medical Services There are plenty of pharmacies in town, including a branch of Dixons Pharmacy (☎ 524821) at 194 High St. The County Hospital (☎ 573103) is half a mile east of the TIC, just off Greetwell Rd.

Emergency The police station (☎ 882222) is on West Parade.

Lincoln Cathedral

This superb cathedral (☎ 544544) is the county's greatest attraction. Its three great towers dominate the city and can be seen from miles around. The central tower stands 83m high, which makes it the second-highest in the country after Salisbury Cathedral. While this is impressive enough, try imagining it twice as high, which it was until toppled by a storm in 1547.

Lincoln Cathedral was built on the orders of William the Conqueror and construction began in 1072. It took only 20 years to complete the original building,

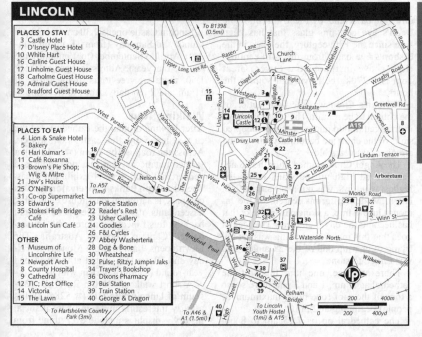

LINCOLN

PLACES TO STAY
3 Castle Hotel
7 D'Isney Place Hotel
10 White Hart
16 Carline Guest House
17 Linholme Guest House
18 Carholme Guest House
19 Admiral Guest House
29 Bradford Guest House

PLACES TO EAT
4 Lion & Snake Hotel
5 Bakery
6 Hari Kumar's
11 Café Roxanna
13 Brown's Pie Shop;
   Wig & Mitre
21 Jew's House
25 O'Neill's
31 Co-op Supermarket
33 Edward's
35 Stokes High Bridge
   Café
38 Lincoln Sun Café

OTHER
1 Museum of
  Lincolnshire Life
2 Newport Arch
8 County Hospital
9 Cathedral
12 TIC; Post Office
14 Victoria
15 The Lawn

20 Police Station
22 Reader's Rest
23 Usher Gallery
24 Goodies
26 F&J Cycles
27 Abbey Washerteria
28 Dog & Bone
30 Wheatsheaf
32 Pulse; Ritzy; Jumpin Jaks
34 Trayer's Bookshop
36 Dixons Pharmacy
37 Bus Station
39 Train Station
40 George & Dragon

EASTERN ENGLAND

which was 99m long with two western towers, but in 1185 an earthquake caused severe damage. Only the west front of the old cathedral survived. Rebuilding began under Bishop Hugh of Avalon (St Hugh) and most of the current building dates from the late-12th to late-13th centuries, in the Early English style.

The entrance is below the famous mid-12th-century frieze on the **west front**. Unfortunately, the frieze is currently hidden behind the scaffolding of a long-term restoration project. Emerging into the **nave,** most people are surprised to find a substantial part of the cathedral empty, but this is actually how it would have looked back in 1250 when it was completed. Medieval cathedrals and churches, like mosques and Hindu temples today, did not have pews. This open area is now used for concerts and plays; services take place in St Hugh's choir. The stained glass in the nave is mostly Victorian, but the **Belgian marble font** dates back to the 11th century.

There are interesting stained-glass windows at each end of the transepts. The **Dean's Eye** contains glass that has been here since the 13th century; the glass in the **Bishop's Eye** dates from the 14th century. High above in the central tower, Great Tom is a 270kg bell that still sounds the hours.

St Hugh's Choir was the first section of the church to be rebuilt. The vaulting above is arranged at odd angles, but the canopied stalls of the choir are beautifully carved and are over 600 years old.

The **Angel Choir**, named after the 28 angels carved high up the walls under the highest windows, was built as a shrine to St Hugh. Modern pilgrims search for the famous **Lincoln Imp**, a stonemason's joke that has become the city's emblem. The legend goes that this malevolent being was caught trying to chat up one of the 28 angels and was turned to stone.

There are free, one-hour tours of the cathedral at 11 am, 1 and 3 pm; there's also a tour of the roof (one hour; maximum 14 people) beginning at 2 pm.

The cathedral opens 7.15 am to 8 pm Monday to Saturday (to 6 pm on Sunday) June to August and 7.15 am to 6 pm Monday to Saturday (to 5 pm on Sunday) the rest of the year. Admission costs £3.50/3. There's evensong daily except Wednesday at 5.15 pm (3.45 pm on Sunday), and sung Eucharist at 9.30 am on Sunday.

Lincoln Castle

Begun in 1068, just four years before the cathedral, the castle (☎ 511068) was built over the original Roman town and incorporates some of the old Roman walls. As well as the usual views from the battlements that one expects from a castle, the old prison is particularly interesting. Public executions used to draw crowds of up to 20,000 people, taking place in front of Cobb Hall, a horseshoe-shaped tower in the north-east corner that served as the city's prison for centuries. The red-brick building on the east side replaced it and was used until 1878.

In the same building as the chapel, Lincoln's copy of the Magna Carta is on display.

Lincoln Castle opens 9.30 am to 5.30 pm Monday to Saturday (from 11 am on Sunday), April to September (to 4 pm daily the rest of the year). Admission costs £2.50/1.50; there are free tours of the castle at 11 am and 2 pm daily, April to September.

Walking Tour

After looking around the cathedral and the castle, leave by the castle's west exit. Across the road is **The Lawn** (☎ 560306), a former lunatic asylum that now houses a concert hall and several exhibition areas. The **Sir Joseph Banks Conservatory**, in this complex, is a tropical glasshouse containing descendants of some of the plants brought back by this Lincoln explorer who accompanied Captain Cook to Australia. The Lawn opens 9 am to 5 pm Monday to Friday and 10 am to 5.30 pm at the weekend year-round (shorter hours in winter).

A short walk up Burton Rd is the **Museum of Lincolnshire Life** (☎ 528448). It's a fairly interesting museum of local social history – displays include everything from an Edwardian nursery to a WWI tank built here. It opens 10 am to 5.30 pm; admission costs £2/60p.

Return to Westgate and continue east to Bailgate. Turn left to see the **Newport Arch**. Built by the Romans, this is the oldest arch in England that still has traffic passing through it. Walk back along Bailgate and continue past the TIC down **Steep Hill**. There are several shops to tempt the tourist, including second-hand bookshops (the Reader's Rest is good) and teashops.

As well as the black-and-white Tudor buildings on Steep Hill, **Jew's House** is of particular interest, being one of the best examples of 12th-century domestic architecture in England. It's now an upmarket restaurant (see Places to Eat later). A few doors down is **Goodies** (☎ 525307), a traditional sweet shop that has 300 varieties in stock – bull's eyes, pear drops, sherbet lemons and humbugs (goodies is Lincolnshire dialect for 'sweets').

Located one block east of Jew's House, on Lindum Rd, is the **Usher Gallery** (☎ 527980), the city's art gallery. It opens 10 am to 5.30 pm Monday to Saturday and 2.30 to 5 pm on Sunday. Admission costs £2/30p.

Places to Stay

Camping About 3 miles (5km) south-west of the train station is *Hartsholme Country Park* (☎ 873577, Skellingthorpe Rd). It charges £4.40 for a tent and two people. It opens 31 March to 31 October. To get there, take the R66 bus from the main bus station in the direction of Birchwood Estate; ask the driver to drop you off (it's about a 20-minute ride).

Hostel Good budget accommodation can be found at the *Lincoln Youth Hostel* (☎ 522076, fax 567424, 77 South Park Ave), from a double for £18 to a five-bed dorm room for £42.50. It opens daily February to October, and on Friday and Saturday in November and December. It's about a mile south of the city centre: cross Pelham Bridge, go through the first set of traffic lights and the hostel is on your right.

B&Bs & Hotels There's a good group of B&Bs on West Parade, west of the modern centre of Lincoln. *Linholme Guest House* (☎ 522930), at No 116, is small with two twins and a double at £18 per person. It's a pleasant place to stay and two rooms have bathrooms.

Parallel to and just south of West Parade is Carholme Rd, also with numerous B&Bs. *Carholme Guest House* (☎ 531059, fax 511590), at No 175, has five rooms – all en suite – and charges from £20 for a single and £38 for a double.

Admiral Guest House (☎/fax 544467, 16–18 Nelson St), a lovely 100-year-old house just off Carholme Rd, charges £22/36 for a single/double.

Bradford Guest House (☎ 523947, 67 Monks Rd) is good value at £20/35. The rooms are neat and tidy, and all have showers.

More upmarket is *Carline Guest House* (☎/fax 530422, 1 Carline Rd). The 12 rooms have been individually furnished and all have private bathrooms. Room rates are £30/42. It's vehemently nonsmoking.

The *D'Isney Place Hotel* (☎ 538881, fax 511321, ⓔ info@disney-place.freespace .co.uk, Eastgate) is small and comfortable, with rooms from £61.50/79 including breakfast in bed.

The *Castle Hotel* (☎ 538801, fax 575547, Westgate), directly across from the TIC, is in a restored 19th-century building with rooms for £62/79. It's fancy and comfortable.

The *White Hart Hotel* (☎ 526222, fax 531798, ⓔ heritagehotels-lincoln.white -hart@forte-hotels.com, Bailgate), by the cathedral, is Lincoln's top hotel. It's a luxurious place with prices to match – doubles go for £114.

Places to Eat

As one might expect in a city of this size, there's a reasonable range of places to eat, some of them particularly good value, even if in most places the food can be a little bland. There's a pretty good *bakery* on the corner of Westgate and Bailgate, and a *Co-op* supermarket on Silver St.

EASTERN ENGLAND

The *Lion & Snake Hotel* (☎ 523770, 79 Bailgate) was founded in 1640, which makes it Lincoln's oldest pub. It's probably better known for its real ale and good-value, home-made bar food.

Hari Kumar's (☎ 537000, 80 Bailgate) is a stylish restaurant serving Indian and English food. Saffron breast of chicken costs £6.95.

Across the road is *Café Roxanna* (☎ 546464) where you can choose between a set meal at £8 or an international 'game fayre platter' of wild boar, alligator, pheasant, pigeon, kangaroo and ostrich for a mere £75.50 (24 hours' notice required).

Highly recommended is *Lincoln Sun Café* (☎ 569292, 7 St Mary's St). Not only is it a popular cafe but it is also a familiar meeting spot for the city's artists and writers who have formed an artists' collective. There are monthly one-person shows of their work. As you would expect, the food is pretty cheap – no dish is more than £5.

Brown's Pie Shop (☎ 527330, 33 Steep Hill) is close to the cathedral and popular with tourists. It's nonetheless worth eating here since pies are a Lincolnshire speciality. Rabbit pie with Dorset scrumpy costs £8.95 but there are cheaper options.

The *Wig & Mitre* (☎ 535190, 29 Steep Hill) is near Brown's Pie Shop. It's a pub with a restaurant, open daily. It serves typical pub grub and hot platters: cottage pie costs £4.95.

A branch of *O'Neill's* (☎ 556011) dominates the north end of the High St, but a cooler place to hang out is *Edward's* (☎ 519144, 238 High St), one block south. At this stylish bar-brasserie you can get everything from a coffee or a beer to a full meal.

Stokes High Bridge Café (☎ 513825, 207 High St) is popular with tourists since it's in a 16th-century timbered building right on the bridge over the River Witham. Consequently, it's a little pricier and you won't get much change out of £10, even for a simple lunch dish. It opens 9 am to 5 pm Monday to Saturday.

Lincoln's top restaurant is the *Jew's House* (☎ 524851, Steep Hill), occupying a 12th-century building that's an attraction in its own right. A three-course set dinner costs £28; set lunches are £13.95.

Entertainment

Pubs Every guided tour makes a stop at (or at least acknowledges) the *Victoria* (☎ 536048, 6 Union Rd), Lincoln's most famous public house. It doesn't disappoint: it's a terrific bar with a huge selection of beers.

The *Dog & Bone* (☎ 522403, 10 John St) is a distinctive bar with a fine selection of ales east of High St, just off Monks Rd.

The *George & Dragon* (☎ 520924, 100 High St) is one of the more popular pubs in town, and what it lacks in original character it more than makes up for in friendly ambience – though it can get very crowded at the weekend.

The *Wheatsheaf* (☎ 525627, 11 Broadgate) is strictly a locals' bar, and all the better for it.

The *Lion & Snake Hotel* (☎ 523770, 79 Bailgate) is a fairly pleasant place to have a drink, even though most of the action takes place south of here, down Steep Hill. See also Places to Eat earlier.

Nightclubs With three clubs in one, *Pulse-Ritzy-Jumpin Jaks* (☎ 522314, Silver St) aims to grab as much of the younger, student crowd as it can, and it does. Pulse (open 10 pm to 2 am Tuesday, Friday and Saturday) is the more hardcore venue, featuring the heavy sound of speed garage. Ritzy (open 10 pm to 2 am daily except Monday and Wednesday) is an uptempo dance club where you'll bop to mostly commercial stuff. Jumpin Jaks (open 8 pm to 2 am Wednesday to Sunday) is more of a bar than a club, but the music is loud and drawn from a mixed bag. Admission to all three varies from £3 to £7, depending on the night, but there are discount fliers handed out in many of the city's bars.

Getting There & Away

Lincoln is 132 miles (213km) from London, 85 miles (137km) from Cambridge and 75 miles (121km) from York.

Bus National Express (☎ 0870 580 8080) operates a daily direct service (at 7.55 am) between Lincoln and London (£19.25, 4½ hours) via Stamford (£8.75, 1½ hours). There are also direct services to Birmingham (£10.75, 2¾ hours) and Glasgow (£32.50, nine hours). For Cambridge (£15.25, three hours) you must change at Peterborough, usually with a lengthy wait.

The main local bus company is Lincolnshire Roadcar (☎ 532424). It runs hourly buses between Lincoln and Grantham (£2.60, 1¼ hours), Monday to Saturday. Stamford is also served by Kimes Coaches (☎ 01529-497251), albeit on Saturday only with a departure at 4 pm (£3 return, 1½ hours). From Lincoln to Boston (£3.15, 1¾ hours) there are nine buses, Monday to Saturday only, run by Brylaine Travel (☎ 01205-364087).

Train To get to and from Lincoln usually involves a change. Hourly trains to Boston (£7.20, 1¼ hours) and Skegness (£9.80, two hours) include a change at Sleaford. For Cambridge (£20.80, 2½ to three hours), you must change at Peterborough (£13.40, 1½ hours), Ely (£19.10, two hours, 20 minutes) and sometimes also at Newark, although there are a handful of trains that include only a stop at Peterborough. There are hourly departures throughout the day. Grantham (£6.40, 40 minutes) is on the main London to Glasgow line, so you'll need to change at Newark; there are about 20 trains a day.

Getting Around

Bus The city bus service is efficient. From the bus and train stations, bus No 51 runs past the youth hostel and Nos 7 and 8 link the cathedral area with the lower town. Fares are 50p.

Bicycle You can rent everything from a three-speed to a mountain bike from F&J Cycles (☎ 545311), 41 Hungate, but 21 speeds are hardly an essential requirement for cycling in this flat county. An 18-speed costs from £6 to £8 per day, and up to £25 per week.

GRANTHAM
☎ 01476 • pop 31,000

This pleasant, red-brick town has an interesting parish church, **St Wulfram's**, with an 85m-high spire, the sixth-highest in England. It dates from the late 13th century. Sir Isaac Newton lived in Grantham and received his early education here; there's a **statue** of him in front of the Guildhall. The town's **museum**, St Peter's Hill, has sections devoted both to him and to former prime minister Lady Margaret Thatcher, who was born in Grantham in 1925. The museum opens 10 am to 5 pm Monday to Saturday; admission is free. Lady Thatcher lived at 2 North Parade, above her father's grocery shop; today it is a chiropractor's clinic.

Three miles (5km) north-east of Grantham on the A607 is **Belton House** (NT; ☎ 566116), one of the finest examples of Restoration country house architecture. Built in 1688 for Sir John Brownlow, the house is known for its ornate plasterwork ceilings and wood carvings attributed to the Dutch carver Grinling Gibbons. Set in a 400-hectare park, it opens 1 to 5 pm Wednesday to Sunday, April to October; admission costs £5.20. Bus Nos 601 and 609 pass this way.

The TIC (☎/fax 406166) is by the Guildhall on Avenue Rd. It opens 9.30 am to 5 pm Monday to Saturday.

Places to Stay & Eat

The *Red House* (☎ 579869, fax 401597, 74 North Parade) is in a listed Georgian building in the town centre. It has three en-suite rooms; singles/doubles cost £21/43.

Just outside Belton House, *The Coach House* (☎/fax 573636, ⓔ coachhousenn@cwcom.net) is a listed building with rooms for £22.50 per person including breakfast. Smokers will have to exercise their lungs in the large garden – indoors it's smoke-free.

The *Beehive* (☎ 404554, Castlegate) is best known for its pub sign – a real beehive full of live South African bees! The bees have been here since 1830, which makes them one of the oldest populations of bees

EASTERN ENGLAND

in the world. Good, cheap lunches are available, and the bees stay away from the customers.

Getting There & Away

Grantham is 25 miles (40km) south of Lincoln. Lincolnshire Roadcar (☎ 01522-532424) runs buses every hour between these two towns, Monday to Saturday, and four on Sunday (£2.60, one hour, 10 minutes). It also runs a service to Stamford (£2.25, 1½ hours, four daily, Monday to Saturday); National Express runs one bus daily, Monday to Saturday.

By train (£6.40, 40 minutes), you'll need to change at Newark to get to Lincoln. There is at least one train per hour throughout the day. Direct trains run from London Kings Cross to Grantham (£18.90, one hour).

STAMFORD
☎ 01780 • pop 16,000

This beautiful town of stone buildings and cobbled streets was made a conservation area in 1967 and is one of the finest stone towns in the country. The TIC (☎/fax 755611) is in the Stamford Arts Centre at 27 St Mary's St. It opens 9.30 am to 5 pm Monday to Saturday (and 10 am to 3 pm on Sunday, April to October).

It's best just to simply wander round the town's winding streets of medieval and Georgian houses, but the **Stamford Museum** (☎ 766317), Broad St, is certainly worth visiting. As well as displays charting the history of the town, there's a clothed model of local heavyweight Daniel Lambert, who tipped the scales at 336kg before his death in 1809. After his death his suits were displayed in a local pub where Charles Stratton, better known as Tom Thumb, would put on a show by fitting into the suit's armholes. Hilarious, apparently. It opens 10 am to 5 pm daily (2 to 5 pm on Sunday, April to September).

Places to Stay & Eat

There's B&B at *St Peter's Rectory* (☎ 753999, fax 766667, 8 St Peter's Hill), which has rooms for £18/36.

St George's B&B (☎ 482099, 16 St George's Square), not to be confused with the George Hotel (see below) is a gorgeous 19th-century house decorated with Victorian fireplaces and antiques. It also has a private garden. Singles/doubles cost £22/35.

Martin's (☎ 752106, fax 482691, 20 St Martin's Rd) is another great B&B just beyond the bridge over the Welland River only a couple of minutes' walk from the centre of town. Rooms cost £30/50.

There are a number of historic pubs that also offer accommodation. The *Bull & Swann Inn* (☎ 763558, High St) does good meals and has rooms with bathrooms for £35/45.

The *George Hotel* (☎ 750750, fax 750701, e georgehotelofstamford@btinternet.com, 71 St Martin's St), across the street, is the top place to stay. It's a wonderful old coaching inn, parts of the building dating back a thousand years. There's excellent upmarket pub fare, a cobbled courtyard and luxurious rooms from £78/100. There's also an excellent restaurant, where you should expect to fork out at least £20.

Getting There & Away

Stamford is 46 miles (74km) from Lincoln and 21 miles (34km) south of Grantham.

National Express (☎ 0870 580 8080) serves Stamford from London (£8.50, 2¾ hours) and from Lincoln (£7.50, 1½ hours). Lincolnshire Roadcar (☎ 01522-532424) operates four buses daily, Monday to Saturday only, between Stamford and Grantham (£2.25, 1½ hours). National Express also runs one bus daily.

There are 16 trains daily to Cambridge (£11.90, 1¼ hours) and Ely (£7.90, 55 minutes). Norwich (£13.50, one hour and 50 minutes) is on the same line, but there are fewer direct trains; you will most likely have to change at Ely.

AROUND STAMFORD
Burghley House

Just a mile south of Stamford, this immensely grand Tudor mansion (pronounced **bur**-lee) is the home of the Cecil family. It was built between 1565 and 1587 by William Cecil, Queen Elizabeth's adviser.

It's an impressive place with 18 magnificent state rooms. The Heaven Room was painted by Antonio Verrio in the 17th century and features floor-to-ceiling gods and goddesses disporting among the columns. There are over 300 paintings, including works by Gainsborough and Brueghel; state bedchambers, including the four-poster Queen Victoria slept in; and cavernous Tudor kitchens.

The house (☎ 01780-52451) opens 11 am to 4.30 pm daily, April to early October. Admission costs £5.85 for an adult and there's no charge for one accompanying child. It's a pleasant 15-minute walk through the park from Stamford train station. The Burghley Horse Trials, which take place here over three days in early September, are of international significance.

BOSTON
☎ 01205 • pop 34,000

A major port in the Middle Ages, Boston lies near the mouth of the River Witham, on the bay known as The Wash. By the end of the 13th century the town was one of the most important wool traders in the country, exporting the fleeces of three million sheep annually. By the end of the 14th century, however, the town was in decline due to the silting up of the port – at one time the second-busiest after London – which more or less killed the wool trade. Boston's other claim to fame came in the 17th century, when it temporarily imprisoned a group of religious separatists looking to settle in the virtually unknown territories of the New World. These later became known as the Pilgrim Fathers, the first white settlers of the US. Word of their success made it back to the English Boston, whereupon a crowd of locals decided to sail across the Atlantic, where they founded a namesake town in the new colony of Massachusetts.

Today the town is but a shadow of its former self, but it has retained much of its medieval appearance, down to the street grid, whereby the two main streets flank both sides of the river and are linked by small foot bridges. It's an easy place to wander about in, and has a number of interesting sites.

The TIC (☎/fax 356656) is under the Assembly Rooms on Market Place. It opens 9 am to 5 pm Monday to Saturday. Market days are Wednesday and Saturday; you can buy pretty much everything from a fish to a bicycle.

Things to See
St Botolph's Church In keeping with its medieval high-flying status as a major wool trader, the town commissioned the construction of an impressive church in 1309, the result of which was this rather imposing structure and its 88-metre tower known as the 'Boston Stump'. The fenland on which it is built was not solid enough to support a thin spire, hence the more solid-looking tower, which is the tallest in the country. You can climb the 365 steps to the top, from where on a clear day you can see Lincoln, 30 miles (48km) away.

Inside there is a splendid 17th-century pulpit from which John Cotton, the fiery vicar of St Botolph's, delivered five-hour catechisms and two-hour sermons during the 1630s. By all accounts, it was he who convinced his parishioners to follow in the footsteps of the Pilgrim Fathers and emigrate.

The church (☎ 362864) opens 9 am to 4.30 pm Monday to Saturday, and also on Sunday between services. Admission to the tower costs £2/1, admission to the church is free.

Guildhall Museum It was from Boston that the Pilgrim Fathers made their first break for the freedom of the New World in 1607. They were imprisoned in the Guildhall, which has now been converted into the town's museum. As well as the cells in which the first pilgrims to America were imprisoned, you can check out a virtual diorama of how the town looked in 1536. Since autumn 2000, a major expansion and refurbishment has been planned with a view towards turning it into a multi-exhibit visitor centre. At the time of writing it was predicted that the work would be complete by summer 2001. The museum (☎ 365954) opens 10 am to 5 pm Monday to Saturday (1.30 to 5 pm on Sunday, summer only). Admission costs £1.25.

Places to Stay & Eat

A five-minute walk from the marketplace, *Park Lea (☎/fax 356309, 85 Norfolk St)* has singles/doubles for £24/36 with bathroom; there's also a double without bathroom for £32.

An old 18th-century farmhouse, *Bramley House (☎/fax 354538 ℯ bramleyhouse@ ic24.net, 267 Sleaford Rd)* is about half a mile west of town along the Sleaford road. It has nine comfortable rooms for £20/37.50.

The *White Hart (☎ 364877, fax 355974, Bridge Foot)* has 21 rooms with bathrooms at £40/65, breakfast included. It also does good pub grub.

Getting There & Away

From Lincoln it's easier to get to Boston by train than by bus, but even that involves a change at Sleaford. Trains run from Lincoln hourly (£7.20, 1¼ hours).

SKEGNESS
☎ 01754 • pop 18,000

'Skeggy' is a classic English seaside resort, the Blackpool of the east coast. There are rows of jolly B&Bs, bingo every evening and donkeys on the 6 miles (10km) of beach. Danny La Rue, Chas 'n' Dave and a host of Abba tribute bands appear throughout the year at the Embassy Centre (☎ 768333; shows usually kick off around 7.30 pm) and the whole place twinkles with 25,000 light bulbs every night from July to October during the Skegness Illuminations. It's the kind of place the English middle and upper classes wouldn't be seen dead in.

The TIC (☎/fax 764821), in the Embassy Centre on Grand Parade, has all the information on B&Bs. They can be cheap, from £15 per person. The opening hours are 9 to 5.30 pm Monday to Saturday (until 6 pm from April to September).

Skegness is pretty easy to get to by either bus or train. From Boston, Lincolnshire Roadcar runs five buses daily, Monday to Saturday (£2.40, 1¼ hours). Brylaine Travel (☎ 01205-364087) runs three buses daily along the same route (tickets are only valid on the service provided by the issuing company). From Lincoln, Lincolnshire Roadcar buses run hourly, Monday to Saturday, and five times on Sunday (£3.35, 1¾ hours).

There are 15 trains daily, Monday to Saturday, and eight on Sunday, between Skegness and Boston (£4.20, 35 minutes). Although there is a train link between Skegness and Lincoln, it involves a change at Sleaford; you're better off getting the bus.

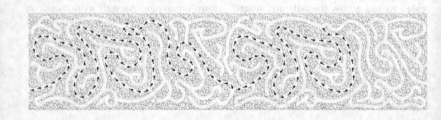

North-Western England

North-Western England is a mixture of densely populated urban centres and rolling hills of quintessential English countryside. The jam-packed, overdeveloped conurbation of Manchester and Liverpool is sandwiched between the historic towns and sparsely populated moorland of Lancashire to the north and prosperous Cheshire to the south.

First-time visitors may not want to linger in the cities, but both Manchester and Liverpool have pockets of great vitality and interesting old buildings and museums. The walled city of Chester is often used as a staging post for getting from the southern Midlands to the Lake District and Scotland, or to northern Wales.

If you want to experience the tacky taste that is a British seaside resort, big, brash Blackpool fits the bill perfectly. Afterwards you can stop off in Lancaster, a manageably small town with an outsize castle and not too much tourist traffic.

Manchester

☎ 0161 • pop 460,000

Probably best known around the world for its football team, the modern city that produced Oasis, Take That, Simply Red and the distinctive 'Manchester sound' is also a monument to England's industrial history. In the 19th century, Friedrich Engels (co-author of the *Communist Manifesto*) used Manchester to illustrate the evils of capitalism and perhaps someone making a similar study today might uncover echoes behind the sometimes-glitzy facade.

The 1990s have seen a gradual transformation of parts of the city centre, a process given added impetus by the IRA bomb blast of 1996 that devastated much of the area around the Arndale Shopping Centre. If every cloud has a silver lining, then the 1996 bombing that ripped the heart out of Manchester has allowed the city to create some wonderful public spaces with stunning modern architecture. More money has been poured into the city's development at it gets set to host the 2002 Commonwealth Games, the biggest multi-sport event to be seen in Britain. There are still areas where empty warehouses and factories rub shoulders with stunning Victorian Gothic buildings, rusting train tracks and motorway overpasses with flashy bars and nightclubs. But things are improving as warehouses are given new life as upmarket apartment blocks.

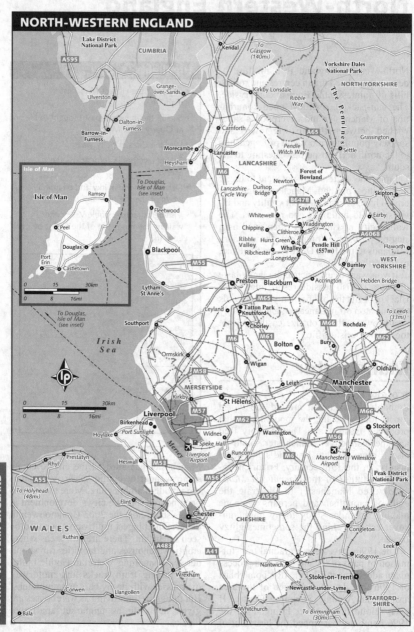

NORTH-WESTERN ENGLAND

Lake District
National Park

CUMBRIA

Kendal

To
Glasgow
(140mi)

A595

Yorkshire Dales
National Park

NORTH YORKSHIRE

Kirkby Lonsdale

Ribble
Way

Grange-
over-Sands

The Pennines

Ulverston

Carnforth

Grassington

A65

Dalton-in-
Furness

Morecambe

Lancaster

Pendle
Witch Way

Settle

Barrow-in-
Furness

Heysham

LANCASHIRE

Forest of
Bowland

M6

Newton

Skipton

Lancashire
Cycle Way

Dunsop
Bridge

B6478

A59

Whitewell

Sawley

Ribble

Earby

Fleetwood

Chipping

Waddington

A6068

Isle of Man

Ramsey

Ribble
Valley

Clitheroe

Haworth

Peel

Hurst Green

Whalley

Pendle Hill
(557m)

WEST
YORKSHIRE

Douglas

Blackpool

Ribchester

Longridge

Burnley

Port
Erin

Castletown

M55

Preston

Blackburn

Accrington

Hebden Bridge

0   15   30km
0   8   16mi

Lytham
St Anne's

M65

Leyland

Tatton Park
Knutsford

M66

Rochdale

A65

M62

To Douglas,
Isle of Man
(see inset)

Southport

Chorley

M6

M61

Bolton

Bury

To Leeds
(33mi)

Irish
Sea

Ormskirk

Wigan

Leigh

Manchester

M58

Oldham

0   15   30km
0   8   16mi

MERSEYSIDE

Kirkby

St Helens

M66

To Douglas,
Isle of Man
(see inset)

Liverpool

M57

M62

Warrington

Stockport

Birkenhead

Port Sunlight

Widnes

Runcorn

M56

Hoylake

Speke Hall
Liverpool
Airport

Manchester
Airport

Wilmslow

Heswall

Mersey

M53

Peak District
National Park

Rhyl

Prestatyn

A55

Northwich

Macclesfield

To Holyhead
(48mi)

Flint

Ellesmere Port

A556

Congleton

WALES

Ruthin

Chester

CHESHIRE

Leek

A483

Crewe

Kidsgrove

Corwen

Llangollen

A41

Nantwich

Stoke-on-Trent

Wrexham

Newcastle-under-Lyme

STAFFORD-
SHIRE

Bala

Whitchurch

To Birmingham
(30mi)

You're unlikely to fall in love with Manchester at first sight, especially if one of your first encounters is with the ugly Piccadilly Gardens (although even it is being given a facelift). The longer you stay, the greater the likelihood that you'll find yourself succumbing to the city's hidden charms. Not many cities in England can rival Manchester for its vibrancy and nightlife, its gay scene and fantastic sports facilities. Coupled with the fact that it has the largest student population in England, which gives it that extra spark, you'd be hard pressed not to have a good time in Manchester.

History

Manchester has been an important area since Roman times. In the 14th century, Flemish weavers (who worked primarily in wool and linen) settled the area. When cotton from the American colonies became available in the 18th century the city – with its weaving tradition, accessible supplies of coal and water and canal links to surrounding towns – became the hub of the new textile industry and, in effect, of the Industrial Revolution.

As the city grew, demands for reform of the parliamentary system and for free trade increased; the artificial protection of corn prices by the Corn Law tariffs was particularly unpopular. In 1819, 60,000 people assembled in St Peter's Field, a site now occupied by the Free Trade Hall. The authorities ordered mounted troops to arrest the speakers. In the ensuing melee 11 people were killed and 400 injured. The affair came to be known as Peterloo – the poor man's Waterloo – and it provided a rallying point in the battle for reform. Two years after Peterloo, the *Manchester Guardian* was founded to foster parliamentary reform and free trade; today's *Guardian* newspaper is a direct descendent.

The late 19th century brought economic depression as textile exports suffered from growing competition from the USA and Europe. Rather than re-equip themselves with modern machines the mill owners exploited the captive markets of the Empire, a

process that continued into the 20th century and led to the industry's final decline.

In an attempt to reduce the loss of its industry to Liverpool and its reliance on cotton, the Ship Canal to the River Mersey was built in 1894. Manchester briefly flourished as Britain's third-largest port until the post-WWII decline.

The city was badly damaged by WWII bombing and then battered by the postwar decline in the manufacturing industries. But the robust northern city has managed to bounce back from both setbacks and today it is one of England's most important commercial and financial centres, with a thriving cultural life. In 1996 central Manchester was badly damaged by an IRA bomb, and work to put right the damage is still going on.

Orientation

Central Manchester is easy to get round on foot or by the excellent Metrolink tramway. The heart of the city, if only because all the buses converge on it, is the hideous, gardenless Piccadilly Gardens. Canal St and Manchester's famous Gay Village (see the boxed text 'Gay & Lesbian Manchester' later in this section) lie a few streets to the southwest of the Gardens, the Castlefield Urban Heritage Park a little farther to the west. The University of Manchester lies south of the city centre (on Oxford St/Rd). Continue south along Wilmslow Rd and you'll reach the cheap Indian restaurants of Rusholme and the student area. West of the university is Moss Side, a ghetto with high unemployment and a thriving drug trade controlled by violent gangs – a place to avoid. Farther west again, near the Bridgewater Canal, is Old Trafford, the home of Manchester United, England's most famous (and currently most successful)football team, and Lancashire County Cricket Club's oval.

Information

Tourist Offices The helpful tourist information centre (TIC; ☎ 234 3157, fax 236 9900), in the town hall extension off St Peter Square, opens 10 am to 5.30 pm Monday to Saturday and 11 am to 4 pm Sunday.

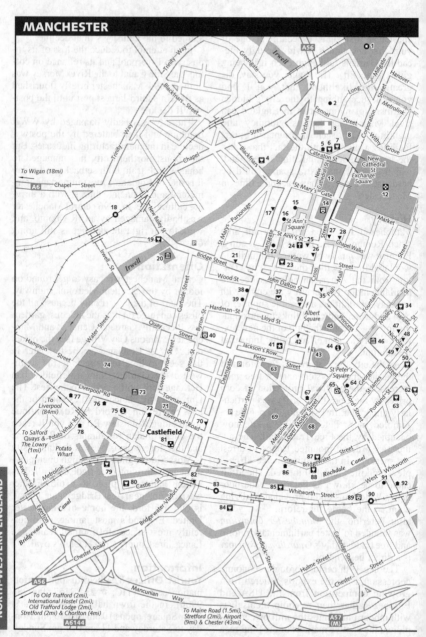

MANCHESTER

To Wigan (18mi)

To Liverpool (84mi)

To Salford
Quays &
The Lowry
(1mi)

Castlefield

Potato
Wharf

To Old Trafford (2mi),
International Hostel (2mi),
Old Trafford Lodge (2mi),
Stretford (2mi) & Chorlton (4mi)

To Maine Road (1.5mi),
Stretford (2mi), Airport
(9mi) & Chester (43mi)

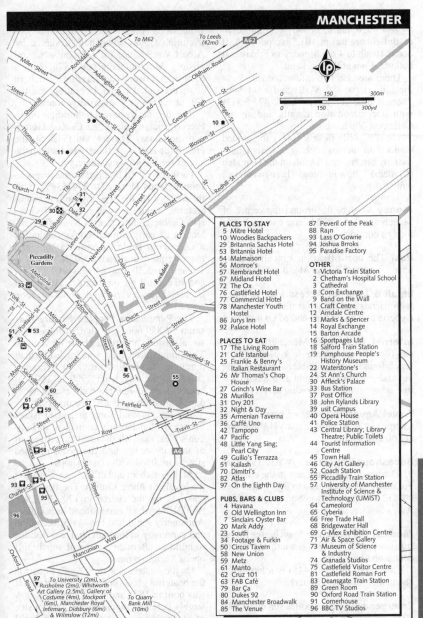

MANCHESTER

PLACES TO STAY
5 Mitre Hotel
10 Woodies Backpackers
29 Britannia Sachas Hotel
53 Britannia Hotel
54 Malmaison
56 Monroe's
57 Rembrandt Hotel
67 Midland Hotel
72 The Ox
76 Castlefield Hotel
77 Commercial Hotel
78 Manchester Youth Hostel
86 Jurys Inn
92 Palace Hotel

PLACES TO EAT
17 The Living Room
21 Café Istanbul
25 Frankie & Benny's Italian Restaurant
26 Mr Thomas's Chop House
27 Grinch's Wine Bar
28 Murillos
31 Dry 201
32 Night & Day
35 Armenian Taverna
36 Caffé Uno
42 Tampopo
47 Pacific
48 Little Yang Sing; Pearl City
49 Guilio's Terrazza
51 Kailash
70 Dimitri's
82 Atlas
97 On the Eighth Day

PUBS, BARS & CLUBS
4 Havana
6 Old Wellington Inn
7 Sinclairs Oyster Bar
20 Mark Addy
34 Footage & Furkin
50 Circus Tavern
58 New Union
59 Metz
61 Manto
62 Cruz 101
79 FAB Café
80 Bar Ça
80 Dukes 92
84 Manchester Broadwalk
85 The Venue

87 Peveril of the Peak
88 Rajn
93 Lass O'Gowrie
94 Joshua Brroks
95 Paradise Factory

OTHER
1 Victoria Train Station
2 Chetham's Hospital School
3 Cathedral
8 Corn Exchange
9 Band on the Wall
11 Craft Centre
12 Arndale Centre
13 Marks & Spencer
14 Royal Exchange
15 Barton Arcade
16 Sportpages Ltd
18 Salford Train Station
19 Pumphouse People's History Museum
22 Waterstone's
24 St Ann's Church
30 Affleck's Palace
33 Bus Station
37 Post Office
38 John Rylands Library
39 usit Campus
40 Opera House
41 Police Station
43 Central Library; Library Theatre; Public Toilets
44 Tourist Information Centre
45 Town Hall
46 City Art Gallery
52 Coach Station
55 Piccadilly Train Station
57 University of Manchester Institute of Science & Technology (UMIST)
64 Cameolord
65 Cyberia
66 Free Trade Hall
68 Bridgewater Hall
69 G-Mex Exhibition Centre
71 Air & Space Gallery
73 Museum of Science & Industry
74 Granada Studios
75 Castlefield Visitor Centre
81 Castlefield Roman Fort
83 Deansgate Train Station
89 Green Room
90 Oxford Road Train Station
91 Cornerhouse
96 BBC TV Studios

NORTH-WESTERN ENGLAND

Castlefield has its own visitor centre (☎ 834 4026, fax 839 8747, ⓔ enquiries@castlefield.org.uk) at 101 Liverpool Rd. It opens 10 am to 4 pm Monday to Friday and noon to 4 pm at the weekend.

There are also two information desks at the airport (☎ 489 6412) and a 24 hour Phone Guide service (☎ 0891 871 5533) with accommodation details and so on. Calls cost 60p a minute.

The TIC sells tickets (£4/3) for guided walks with themes such as 'Canals Under the City Streets' and 'Death on the Doorstep (Cholera)' – how inviting! These run almost daily.

Money Most banks around the centre of Manchester have ATMs and can exchange foreign currency.

Post The post office on Lincoln Square opens 9 am to 5.30 pm Monday to Friday.

Email & Internet Access Keep in touch with friends and family at the Internet cafe Cyberia at the northern end of Oxford St.

Internet Resources Manchester's Web site (www.manchester.gov.uk/24hrcity) offers information on subjects such as eating out and entertainment, and also has an on-line accommodation-booking service.

Travel Agencies There is a branch of usit Campus (☎ 833 2046) in the YHA building at 166 Deansgate.

Bookshops Waterstone's (☎ 832 1992), at 91 Deansgate, is the biggest in the country. For all things sport, head to Sportpages Ltd (☎ 832 8530) on Barton Square, just off St Ann's Square.

Medical Services The Manchester Royal Infirmary (☎ 276 1234) is south of the city centre on Oxford Rd.

Cameolord (☎ 236 1445) is a late-night chemist on St Peters Square.

Emergency There is a police station (☎ 872 5050) on Bootle St, near the town hall.

City Centre

Dominating Albert Square is the enormous Victorian Gothic **town hall**, designed by Albert Waterhouse (of London's Natural History Museum fame) in 1876, with a 85m-high tower. The interior is rich in sculpture and Baroque decoration; ask the TIC about the very informative tours.

The distinctive circular building on St Peter's Square houses the **Central Library** and the **Library Theatre**. On Peter St, the **Free Trade Hall** is the third to be built on the site of the Peterloo massacre.

Farther west on Deansgate, the gorgeous **John Rylands Library** (☎ 834 5343), built in memory of the wealthy cotton manufacturer, is another good example of Victorian Gothic architecture. It has a fine collection of early printed books (including a Gutenberg Bible, several Caxtons and manuscripts dating from 2000 BC). It opens 10 am to 5.30 pm Monday to Friday, and 10 am to 1 pm on Saturday. Admission is free. Tours every Wednesday at noon cost £1.

The **Pumphouse People's History Museum** (☎ 839 6061), Bridge St, focuses on social history and the Labour movement. The pumphouse itself was an Edwardian pumping station that provided hydraulic power to the city from 1909 to 1972. It opens 11 am to 4.30 pm daily except Monday. Admission costs £1 (free on Friday).

The area around King St and St Ann's Square is Manchester's equivalent of London's West End. It's the most attractive part of the city centre and the pedestrianised streets are lined with classy shops.

At the southern end of St Ann's Square is the lovely **St Ann's Church**. The first stone was laid for the church in 1709 by Lady Ann Bland, who commissioned its building. Apparently she'd had enough of the pomp and ceremony in the cathedral and decided to build an alternative place of worship. It opens 8 am to 6 pm.

On the western side of St Ann's Square is the beautiful glass-roofed **Barton Arcade**. It was built in 1871 and unfortunately is now largely bereft of shops. On the eastern side of St Ann's Square is the imposing **Royal**

Exchange, originally at the hub of the city's commerce. Trading boards still show the exact price of raw cotton around the world on the day the building closed. It's now home to shops, a cafe-bar and a theatre.

Opposite, and in stark contrast, stands the hideous monstrosity of the **Arndale Centre**, at 10 hectares one of the largest (and surely ugliest) covered shopping areas in Europe. It, too, is being rebuilt after the bomb blast. Farther up Deansgate, the 15th-century perpendicular **cathedral** was the focal point of medieval Manchester. It was substantially restored after bomb damage in WWII. Across Fennel St from the Cathedral is **Chetham's Hospital**, a medieval manor house that is now a national school for young musicians.

The **City Art Gallery**, on the corner of Princess and Mosley Sts, was designed by Sir Charles Barry (architect for the Houses of Parliament) in 1824. It is currently undergoing a £25 million expansion scheme, which includes the refurbishment of current galleries, the creation of new galleries and an education centre, and the provision of full access for disabled persons. Its impressive collection covers everything from early Italian, Dutch and Flemish painters to Gainsborough, Blake, Constable and the Pre-Raphaelites. It should be open again by late 2001; check with the TIC for daily opening times.

Castlefield Urban Heritage Park

In AD 79, Castlefield was at the heart of Manchester's fortunes when a Roman fort was built here. It starred again from 1761 when the opening of the Bridgewater Canal put it at the centre of a revolutionary transport network. In 1830 the world's first passenger train station opened in Liverpool Rd. The legacy of all this is an extraordinary industrial landscape littered with the enormous weather-stained brick and rusting cast-iron relics of canals, viaducts, bridges, warehouses and market buildings, all in various stages of decay and renovation and tumbled together like giant pieces of Lego.

Unpromising as this may sound, Castlefield has been imaginatively redeveloped with an eye to the tourist pound. Come here for the Granada Studios Tour, the Museum of Science & Industry, the reconstructed fort, footpaths, the youth hostel and several trendy pubs and restaurants.

Granada Studios The Granada Studios (☎ 832 4999), in Water St, have been responsible for many of Britain's best-loved television series, first and foremost *Coronation Street* but also *Brideshead Revisited* and *The Adventures of Sherlock Holmes*. For those who don't know it, *Coronation Street* is the archetypal soap opera, dealing with the lives of the residents of a street in the fictional Lancashire town of Weatherfield. It's been running since 1960 and you can walk around the sets and poke your head in at the famous *Rovers Return* pub.

Elsewhere, the Granada Studios Tour offers a mix of sets, live shows and rides – enough to fill a day. There's even a mockup of the House of Commons where you can take part in what is sure to be a more polite debate than the real thing at Westminster. At the time of writing the studios were closed for refurbishment, but they should have reopened by the time you read this. Call to obtain up-to-date details of prices and opening times.

Museum of Science & Industry This museum (☎ 832 2244) is an impressive monument to the Industrial Revolution, built on the site of the world's first passenger train station in Liverpool Rd. There are working steam engines and locomotives, factory machinery from the mills, an excellent exhibition telling the story of Manchester from the sewers up, and an **Air & Space Gallery** featuring historic aircraft and a planetarium. A £15-million development scheme is currently underway to make better use of the 3-hectare site; it includes the upgrade of existing displays and centres, and the creation of interactive exhibits and galleries. The best sources of information in the museum are the steam engine operators themselves, who can answer most of your questions. The museum will be open throughout the work, which is due to finish in 2002. It opens 10 am to 5 pm daily. Admission is £5/free. Allow at least three hours.

The Lowry

Manchester's new pride and joy, The Lowry (☎ 876 2020), on Pier 8 at Salford Quays, is a sight to behold. The glass and steel construction is a mish-mash of angles reflected in the Manchester Ship Canal on Salford Quay. Whether you think it a monster or a marvel, it's definitely eye-catching, and that's only from the outside. Once inside, the colourful interior is not so much warm but striking. The complex is named after one of England's favourite artists, LS Lowry, who is mostly noted for his industrial landscapes and impressions of northern towns, and contains over 300 of his paintings and drawings. It also encapsulates two theatres, a number of galleries hosting contemporary art exhibitions, shops, restaurants and bars. The theatres host a diverse range of performances, from dance to comedy. To find out what is playing and to book tickets call the box office (☎ 876 2000).

The Lowry opens 9.30 am to midnight daily and guided tours are available that leave from the galleries and cost £2. The galleries themselves open 11 am to 5 pm Monday to Wednesday; to 8 pm Thursday, Saturday and Sunday; and to 10 pm Friday. Admission is free. Take the Metrolink from the centre to either Broadway or Harbour City; a return ticket costs £1.80.

Manchester Museum

The Egyptian exhibition of the Manchester Museum (☎ 275 2634), Manchester University, is alone worth the mile trip from the centre, which isn't surprising considering that the museum has been one of the forerunners in the study of Egyptology since a number of objects from the town sites of Kahun and Gurob were donated in 1890. If Egyptian artefacts are not your thing, there are plenty of other displays to keep you happy, from botany to archery. The museum is currently undergoing a facelift that should be completed by the time you read this and will result in new galleries, a 'Sci-ence for Life' exhibition and a new Discovery centre.

The museum opens 10 am to 5 pm Monday to Saturday. Admission is free. Regular buses run from the centre down Oxford St to the University.

Whitworth Art Gallery

In parkland half a mile south of Manchester University on Oxford Rd, Whitworth Art Gallery (☎ 275 7450) has an important collection of English watercolours (including various Turners and Blakes), contemporary paintings, textiles and wallpapers. It opens 10 am to 5 pm Monday to Saturday and 2 to 5 pm on Sunday. Admission is free. It has an excellent gallery bistro with an outdoor terrace for sunny days.

Gallery of Costume

Farther south on Oxford Rd in Platt Hall is the Gallery of Costume (☎ 224 5217), displaying an array of garments from the 17th and 18th centuries to the present day. It opens 10 am to 5.30 pm daily March to October and to 4 pm the rest of the year. Admission is free.

Special Events

Manchester's most important special events are tied up with the city's gay and lesbian scene; see the boxed text 'Gay & Lesbian Manchester' for details.

Places to Stay

There's a reasonable range of places to stay, but most cheap options are some way from the centre. The big central hotels cater to businesspeople during the week and often offer excellent weekend rates. The TIC charges £2.50 to make bookings so try ringing round yourself first.

Note that beds fill up quickly whenever Manchester United is playing at home.

Places to Stay – Budget

The stunning *Manchester Youth Hostel* (☎ 839 9960, fax 835 2054, ℮ manchester@yha.org.uk, Potato Wharf), near the Museum of Science & Industry in the Castlefield area, has comfortable four-bed dorms for £18/13.50 for adults/under-18s, and Internet access.

From mid-June to mid-September, the University of Manchester lets student rooms to visitors from around £12.25 per person, £8 if you're a student. Contact *St Anselm Hall* (☎ *224 7327, 14 Victoria Park)* or *Woolaton Hall* (☎ *224 7244, Whitworth Lane)*, in Fallowfield, 3 miles (5km) from the city centre.

Stretford, 2 miles (3km) south of the centre, has two private hostels with cooking facilities and TV lounges. The closest Metrolink stop to both is Old Trafford. Tiny *Peppers* (☎ *848 9770, 17 Greatstone Rd)* is a good cheap option with beds from £8 for longer stays. The *International Backpackers' Hostel & Guest House* (☎ *872 3499, 41 Greatstone Rd)* is accommodating and friendly, and has beds from £10.

The newly opened *Woodies Backpackers* (☎ *228 3456,* [e] *backpackers@woodiesuk .freeserve.co.uk, 19 Blossom St)*, 10 minutes' walk north-east of Piccadilly Gardens, is modern and comfortable and offers Internet access; dorm beds are £12 per night.

Places to Stay – Mid-Range
City Centre Liverpool Rd in Castlefield offers up three good accommodation options.

Commercial Hotel (☎ *834 3504, 125 Liverpool Rd)* is a traditional pub close to the Museum of Science & Industry with singles/doubles for £25/40.

Rather pricier is the modern *Castlefield Hotel* (☎ *832 7073, fax 837 3534, 3 Liverpool Rd)* with rooms for £49/59 at the weekend, including use of its own sports facilities.

The Ox (☎ *839 7740, fax 839 7760, 71 Liverpool Rd)* has comfortable and modern rooms from £44.95 for a single.

The warm and welcoming *Mitre Hotel* (☎ *834 4128, fax 839 1646, Cathedral Gates)* is well placed near Victoria station. Rooms without bathroom can cost as little as £20 per person; ask for one with views of the cathedral.

The new *Jurys Inn* (☎ *953 8888, fax 953 9090,* [e] *info@jurys.com, 56 Great Bridge-*

water St) charges a fixed rate of £59 per room, which sleep up to three adults.

Opposite Piccadilly train station, *Monroe's* (☎ *236 0564, 38 London Rd)* is popular with a gay clientele and offers rooms for £25/36. Another popular gay hotel and hangout is *Rembrandt Hotel* (☎ *236 1311, fax 236 4257,* [e] *therembrandthotel@ aol.com, 1 Sackville St)* in the heart of the Gay Village on the corner of Canal St. Rooms with bathrooms cost £35/50.

Suburbs Didsbury is an attractive southern suburb, with good local pubs and frequent buses into the city. Wilmslow and Palatine Rds have many hotels in converted Victorian houses.

The comfortable *Elm Grange Hotel* (☎/*fax 445 3336,* [e] *elmgrange.hotel@tvc .org.uk, 561 Wilmslow Rd)* has singles/ doubles from £31/48.

Fernbank Guest House (☎ *01625-523729, fax 539515, 188 Wilmslow Rd)* is 12 miles (19km) from the centre, but only 10 minutes from the airport. It is comfortable and similarly priced to the Elm Grange.

The *Crescent Gate Hotel* (☎ *224 0672, fax 257 2822, Park Crescent)* is within walking distance of Rusholme's Indian restaurants and well served by buses into the city centre. Most of the comfortable rooms (£38.50/52) have bathrooms.

Cricket fans can stay at the *Old Trafford Lodge* (☎ *874 3333, fax 874 3399,* [e] *sales.lancs@ecb.co.uk, Talbot Rd)*, with modern rooms overlooking the Lancashire cricket ground. Rooms cost £42 at the weekend; book ahead when there's a match on.

Chorlton also has plenty of B&Bs, which are reasonably convenient for Old Trafford to the south-west of the city centre.

Places to Stay – Top End
Britannia Hotel (☎ *228 2288,* [e] *sales@ britannia-man.itsnet.co.uk, Portland St)* is a cotton warehouse that has been converted into a luxury four-star hotel. Singles/ doubles cost from £39.50/65.

Britannia Sachas Hotel (☎ *228 1234,*

fax 236 9202, e *brit-sachas@connectfree .co.uk, Tib St)*, which looks run down but is in fact quite nice inside, has rooms from £45/65 at the weekend.

The sumptuous Edwardian *Midland Hotel* (☎ *236 3333, fax 932 4100,* e *sales@ mhccl.demon.co.uk, Peter St)*, opposite the G-Mex Exhibition Centre, is where Mr Rolls and Mr Royce supposedly met. Weekend rates start at £99.

Across the road from Manchester's Piccadilly station is the luxurious *Malmaison* (☎ *278 1000, fax 278 1002,* e *manchester@ malmaison.com, Joshua Hoyle Bldg, Auburn St)*, with rooms for a flat-rate £110 and a French brasserie.

On Oxford St near the station is the *Palace Hotel* (☎ *288 1111, fax 288 2222)*, converted from an enormous 19th-century insurance-company building. It has rooms, some more interesting than others, from £99 per single at the weekend, but cheaper deals do exist depending on availability.

Places to Eat
The most distinctive restaurant zones are Chinatown in the city centre and the predominately Indian Rusholme in the south. But there are plenty of quality eateries scattered around the centre of the city offering a variety of cuisines. The recommendations listed below represent just the tip of the iceberg.

City Centre Albert Square is gradually filling up with places to eat. Alongside *Caffé Uno* (☎ *834 7763, 2–8 Commercial Union House)*, look out for *Tampopo* (☎ *819 1966)*, a minimalist noodle bar where *mee goreng* costs £6.25.

More unusual is the basement *Armenian Taverna* (☎ *934 9025, 3–5 Princess St)*, which will do you a couscous *bidaoui* for £7.90 or a Tbilisi kebab for £7.95. It closes on Monday.

The name may not be inviting, but the food at *Mr Thomas's Chop House* (☎ *832 2245, 52 Cross St)* is. It's probably the best pub-food in town and they pour great real ale; dishes start at £6.50.

Grinch's Wine Bar (☎ *907 3210, Chapel Walks)* serves chilled crispy duck wrap for £5.25 in arty surroundings.

Murillos (☎ *819 1997, Chapel Walks)*, two doors along from Grinch's, has a wide range of Spanish tapas for around £4.50 and *platos combinados* for around £7.50.

Frankie & Benny's Italian Restaurant (☎ *835 2479, 36 St Ann St)* is good value and does *spaghetti ragu bolognese* for £5.45.

Farther west is the colourful *Café Istanbul* (☎ *833 9942, Bridge St)*, serving up a nice range of dishes, including Istanbul chicken for £8.60.

Guilio's Terrazza (☎ *236 4033, 14 Nicholas St)* dishes up business lunches for £6.50.

Vegetarians could try *On the Eighth Day* (☎ *273 4878, 111 Oxford Rd)* next to Manchester Metropolitan University for a good selection.

Pleasant *Dimitri's* (☎ *839 3319, Campfield Arcade)*, near Castlefield, serves up a mixture of Greek, Italian and Spanish food. A quick lunch will set you back £3.

Cafe bars, as in many other cities, are big in Manchester. The first, *Dry 201* (☎ *236 5920, 28 Oldham St)* is still among the coolest and the best. Next door at No 26, *Night & Day* (☎ *236 4597)* attracts a more alternative crowd. *Atlas* (☎ *834 2124, 376 Deansgate)*, wedged beneath the railway line and a couple of busy streets, is a funky place serving up good Italian food.

Chinatown Bounded by Charlotte, Portland, Oxford and Mosley Sts, Chinatown (not surprisingly) has lots of restaurants. Many but not all of them are Chinese, and most are not particularly cheap.

Highly acclaimed is *Little Yang Sing* (☎ *228 7722, 17 George St)*, which specialises in Cantonese cuisine. During the day there is a set menu for £8.95, but expect to pay twice that in the evening.

Readers rate *Pearl City* (☎ *228 7683, 23 George St)* where the house banquet for two is £19.50 per person.

Pacific (☎ *228 6668, 58 George St)* is a highly rated Thai/Chinese restaurant serving up fantastic food.

The deservedly popular *Kailash (☎ 236 1085, 34 Charlotte St)* serves high-quality Nepalese and Indian dishes – whole four-course lunches cost £5.80.

Rusholme Wilmslow Rd (the extension of Oxford St/Rd) in Rusholme is more commonly known as Curry Mile due to its concentration of Indian/Pakistani restaurants, which is unsurpassed in Europe.

Darbar (☎ 224 4392, 65–67 Wilmslow Rd) is not only cheap (*and* they offer student discounts) but exceptionally good; most main courses are between £6.50 and £6.90. Bring your own booze.

Try *Sanam Sweet House & Restaurant (☎ 224 8824, 145 Wilmslow Rd)*, which does Karachi chicken for £5.50 as well as an array of mouth-watering sweets.

Closer to the centre is *Sangram (☎ 257 3922, 13–15 Wilmslow Rd)*, which is more expensive and serves up all your favourites; vegetarian thali for two costs £19.90.

Entertainment

In keeping with its old Madchester reputation, Manchester comes into its own at night, offering all sorts of high-quality entertainment. *City Life*, an invaluable fortnightly what's-on magazine, has the details.

Pubs & Bars There are plenty of places to go if all you're looking for is a pint. *Lass O'Gowrie (☎ 273 6932, 36 Charles St)*, off Oxford St, is a popular student hang-out with an excellent small brewery on the premises and good-value bar meals.

Footage & Firkin, in the old Portico Library at 137 Grosvenor St, offers up much the same but in a more central location.

Two historic pubs that required a lot of repair after the 1996 bomb are the *Old Wellington Inn (☎ 830 1440, 4 Cathedral Gates)* and *Sinclairs Oyster Bar* at the top of New Cathedral St. Both are great for a quiet pint or for soaking up the sun outdoors.

Peveril of the Peak (☎ 236 6364, 127 Great Bridgewater St) is another unpretentious pub with wonderful Victorian glazed tilework outside.

Opposite the Peveril is *Ra¡n (☎ 235 6500, 80 Great Bridgewater St)*, a relaxed joint with a huge balcony at the back.

If you're feeling agoraphobic head for the popular local *Circus Tavern (Portland St)*, the smallest pub in Manchester.

If you want to catch a glimpse of the Manchester United players, try the ultra-trendy *The Living Room (☎ 832 0083, 80 Deansgate)* on Deansgate.

There are several popular places to drink in Castlefield, including *Bar Ça (☎ 839 7099, Catalan Square)*, which is owned by Mick Hucknall of Simply Red and has outdoor seating for sunny days. *Dukes 92 (☎ 839 8646, 2 Castle St)* is another popular canal-side pub in the Castlefield area.

For more waterside views, try *Joshua Brooks (☎ 274 4059, Charles St)*, with a canalside balcony, or *Mark Addy (☎ 832 4080, Stanley St)*, one of the few places overlooking the River Irwell.

Clubs The clubbing scene in Manchester is London's biggest challenger for England's clubbing crown, and the following is but a small selection of the huge choice. Clubs are forever changing and hosting a mixture of dance nights, so check *City Life* for what's on when you're in town. Many of the cafes mentioned in Places to Eat hold regular club nights, in particular the Dry Bar and Night & Day, as does the pub Joshua Brooks in a downstairs area (see Pubs & Bars).

South (☎ 831 7756, 4A King St) is a popular club, especially on Saturday nights when funk and disco fill the air.

If you're a big fan of the TV series *Thunderbirds* check out *FAB Café (☎ 236 2019, 111 Portland St)*. The music is loud but best of all are the Thunderbirds models and puppets decorating the club. FAB Virgil!

Paradise Factory (☎ 273 5422, 112 Princess St) plays House and Garage into the early hours.

For Latino grooves head to *Havana (☎ 832 8900, 42 Blackfriars St)*, where you can get the occasional free dance lesson early in the evening.

Gay & Lesbian Venues See the boxed text 'Gay & Lesbian Manchester' below for details.

Live Music The famous music scene that spawned The Smiths, Joy Division, New Order, and the 'Manchester Sound' of the Stone Roses, The Charlatans and the Happy Mondays continues, although it's more subdued than at its peak.

One of the best live music venues is *Band on the Wall (☎ 832 6625, Swan St)*, which hosts everything from jazz to blues, folk and pop.

Manchester Board Walk (☎ 228 3555, Little Peter St) and *Venue (☎ 236 0026, Whitworth St West)* are also good venues.

Classical Music & Opera Manchester has two world-famous symphony orchestras, the cash-strapped Hallé and the BBC Philharmonic.

The enormous and impressive *Bridgewater Hall (☎ 907 9000, Lower Mosley St)*, home to the Hallé, was completed in 1996 at a cost of £42 million. The BBC Philharmonic is based at New Broadcasting House, Oxford Rd.

Another large venue is *Opera House (☎ 242 2509)* on Quay St.

Theatre, Cinema & Exhibitions Manchester's premier fringe venue is *Green Room (☎ 236 1677, 54 Whitworth St West)*. It also has a good cafe-bar.

There's nearly always something interesting on at the *Royal Exchange (☎ 833 9833, St Ann's Square)* or the *Library Theatre (☎ 236 7110)*.

The *Cornerhouse (☎ 228 2463, 70 Oxford St)* houses a decent cinema, a gallery and a cafe.

Opposite the Bridgewater Hall, the *G-Mex Exhibition Centre (☎ 834 2700)*, cleverly converted from the derelict Central train station, hosts exhibitions, concerts and indoor sporting events.

Spectator Sports

Manchester United Many regard Manchester United's Old Trafford stadium as holy ground – almost every week support-

---

Gay & Lesbian Manchester

Apart from London, Manchester has the best gay scene in Britain, which was boosted by the *Queer as Folk* series, screened on primetime British television in 1999. Following the lives and loves of three young men in and around the 'Gay Village', it attracted first criticism then acclaim and focused the spotlight on Manchester's gay life.

The TIC stocks the useful *Gay & Lesbian Village Guide* that lists numerous gay bars, clubs, galleries and groups, including the Manchester Gay Centre (☎ 274 3814) on Sydney St. The Lesbian & Gay Switchboard (☎ 274 3999) operates 4 to 10 pm daily. *All Points North* is a good free monthly paper covering the north of England.

The centre of Manchester's vibrant gay nightlife scene is Canal St. There are said to be over 30 bars and clubs in the so-called 'Gay Village'. The ground-breaker was the *Manto Bar (☎ 236 2667, 46 Canal St)*, which has been copied around the world. Across the canal is *Metz (☎ 237 9852)*, another cafe-bar, and currently more fashionable than Manto. There are several more traditional pubs nearby, including the *New Union (☎ 228 1492)*. On Friday there's a women-only night at the upstairs bar at the *Rembrandt Hotel* (see Places to Stay).

The club scene changes so quickly it's difficult to make recommendations, but the *Paradise Factory* (see Pubs & Clubs) is usually popular. *Cruz 101 (☎ 237 1554)*, nearby at 101 Princess St, is the largest gay nightclub in the city.

Britain's biggest gay and lesbian arts festival, It's Queer Up North (IQUP), takes place every two years – next in spring 2002. The Manchester Mardi-Gras kicks off around the end of August each year and attracts around 500,000 people each year.

ers demonstrate this literally by asking to have their ashes scattered on the pitch (and they are – behind the goals, where it doesn't matter if it damages the grass).

There are tours (☎ 868 8631) every 10 minutes from 9.30 am to 4.30 pm daily (except match days). There's also a museum, open 9.30 am to 5 pm daily. Admission to the museum and the tour costs £8/5.50; the museum only costs £5/3.50. Tickets to games are as scarce as hen's teeth, even if Manchester United is playing a friendly against Scunthorpe United. A return metro ticket to Old Trafford from the centre costs £1.80.

Manchester City Manchester's second premiership club (although some would say the first) is enjoying a resurgence in its fortune at present; over the last few years it's tumbled from the premiership to the second division and back again. The club enjoys a fanatical following so tickets will be just as hard to come by at Maine Road (the club ground) as at Old Trafford, but you can try on ☎ 226 2224. There's also a tour of the ground (☎ 226 1782), which is situated in the heart of Moss Side; tickets cost £3. If you plan to talk footy while in town, whatever you do don't mix the teams up!

Lancashire County Cricket Club The Lancashire Club (☎ 282 4000), Warwick Rd, hosts county matches throughout the summer, and international test matches. Admission to county games costs £8 to £10.

Shopping

On Oldham St, to the north of Piccadilly Gardens, **Affleck's Palace** is a restored warehouse full of stalls, shops and cafes selling clubbing gear from young designers, second-hand clothes, crystals, leather gear, records – you name it. A thriving, buzzy place with a great atmosphere, it opens 10 am to 5.30 pm Monday to Saturday. Don't miss it.

The world's largest **Marks & Spencer**, newly built on the spot of the IRA bombing, covers a whopping 23,000 sq metres of shopping heaven. The building itself is a commanding state-of-the-art construction. A handy walkway connects the shop with the Arndale Centre.

One block north in Oak St is Manchester's impressive **Craft Centre** (☎ 832 4274), which is housed in the old fish and poultry market building and opens 10 am to 5.30 pm Monday to Saturday.

All your regular 'high street' names can be found at the northern end of Deansgate.

Getting There & Away

Manchester is about 200 miles (322km; three hours) from London, 250 miles (402km; 3½ hours) from Glasgow, 60 miles (97km; two hours) from York and 35 miles (56km; 30 minutes) from Liverpool by road.

Air Manchester airport (☎ 489 3000) is the largest outside London, serving 35 countries. It's worth considering if you're heading to/from the north or the Lake District. The train to the airport costs £2.70; the coach costs £2. The excellent TIC at the airport can recommend nearby B&Bs, some of which will pick you up and drop you off.

Bus National Express (☎ 0870 580 8080) offers numerous coach links with the rest of the country from Chorlton St coach station in the city centre. There's an almost hourly service from Manchester to Liverpool (£4, one hour) and Leeds (£7, 80 minutes). A coach to London costs £15 (4¾ hours).

Train Piccadilly is the main station for trains to and from the rest of the country, although Victoria station serves Halifax and Bradford. The two stations are linked by Metrolink. A single ticket to Liverpool Lime Street costs £6.95 (one hour), but the train is slower now than it was in Victorian times! Numerous trains service the following; London (£44, three hours), Glasgow (£38.90, three hours) and Newcastle (£32.50, three hours).

Getting Around

Day Saver tickets allow one day's travel throughout the Greater Manchester area and cover a range of transport combinations: bus only (£3), bus and train (£3.50), bus and Metrolink (£4.50) train and Metrolink (£5) and all three (£6.50). For inquiries about local transport, including night buses, phone ☎ 228 7811 from 8 am to 8 pm daily.

Bus Centreline bus No 4 provides a free service around the heart of Manchester every 10 minutes. Stops on its route include Piccadilly station, the coach station, Spring Gardens, Deansgate, Marks & Spencer and Piccadilly Gardens. Most local buses start from Piccadilly Gardens where the downside of bus deregulation is obvious in the crush of multi-coloured vehicles, all touting different fares to move you about the city. The central Travelshop has timetables but no fares, forcing you to consult each bus driver individually.

Train Castlefield is served by Deansgate station with rail links to Piccadilly, Oxford Rd and Salford Crescent stations.

Metrolink The Metrolink trams operate on a mixture of disused rail tracks and tracks laid along the city-centre streets. There are frequent links between Victoria and Piccadilly train stations and G-Mex (for Castlefield). Buy tickets from the machines on the platforms. For information phone ☎ 205 2000, or pick up a Metrolink map from the TICs.

AROUND MANCHESTER
Quarry Bank Mill

In Wilmslow, 10 miles (16km) south of Manchester, you can visit an 18th-century cotton mill in beautiful Styal Country Park. Not only can you see the old waterwheel that used to power the mill and some of the old machinery, but costumed guides in the **Apprentice House** will also give you a depressing insight into the life of some of the mill's younger workers, a life of shared beds, and brimstone and treacle cures. Run by the National Trust (NT), the Mill (☎ 01625-527468) opens 11 am to 6 pm April to September, closing at 5 pm and on Monday the rest of the year. The Apprentice

House opens 2 to 6 pm (to 5 pm in winter) Tuesday to Friday and from 11.30 am at the weekend. Admission costs £6/3.70 for both, £4.80/3.40 for the Mill only and £3.80/2.70 for the Apprentice House only. To get there take a train (except Sunday) to Styal station and walk for half a mile, or catch the free No 200 bus from Manchester airport. The car park costs £2.

Wigan Pier Heritage Centre

Home to the now defunct band The Verve and one of England's top rugby league teams, Wigan is otherwise a dreary town, famous mainly because George Orwell used it as the basis for his book, *The Road to Wigan Pier*. But forget any thought of fortune-telling booths and kiss-me-quick hats – this pier was never more exciting than a contraption used for tipping coal into barges on the Leeds & Liverpool Canal.

Nevertheless, the site has been used to create a fine heritage centre that attempts to bring to life what it was like to work in a mine in the late 19th century. You can also see inside an old textile mill, whose machinery can still be set working for visitors, and visit Opies Museum, a collection of memorabilia from the 1900s to the present day.

The centre (☎ 01942-323666) opens 10 am to 5 pm Monday to Thursday and from 11 am at the weekend. Admission to all the attractions costs £6.95/5.25. There's also a TIC (☎ 01942-825677) in the mill building that provides an accommodation service. To get there, take bus No 32 from Cannon St in Manchester city centre (1¼ hours), or a train to Wigan station from Manchester (£3.20, 40 minutes, every 10 minutes) or Liverpool (£3.55, 30 minutes, every half an hour).

Cheshire

You can investigate the canals at the wonderful Boat Museum at Ellesmere Port (see Around Chester) or visit the quaint villages on the Cheshire Plain, but when it comes right down to it Cheshire is all about Chester.

CHESTER

☎ 01244 • pop 80,000

Despite steady streams of tourists Chester remains a beautiful town, ringed by an almost continuous red sandstone wall that dates back to Roman times. However, appearances can be deceptive – many of the medieval-looking buildings in the centre are actually Victorian.

History

Roman Chester was the fortress city of Deva, a bulwark against the fierce Welsh tribes. It wasn't completely abandoned when the Romans withdrew in the 5th century, but the Welsh border is only a stone's throw west of Chester and the Welsh remained a threat long after the Romans had gone. It was only in the 14th century that the danger subsided and the regulations that banned the Welsh from the town after dark and stipulated that they couldn't bear arms, hold meetings or enter pubs were withdrawn.

Medieval Chester became the largest port in the North-West, but in the Civil War the city took the Royalist side and was besieged for 18 months (1645–6) by Cromwell's forces. It wasn't until the next century that the walls were repaired and took on a new role as a tourist attraction. The first guidebook to Chester was published in 1781!

Orientation

Nestling in a bow formed by the River Dee, the walled centre is now surrounded by suburbs. Most places of interest are inside the walls where the Roman street pattern is relatively intact. From High Cross (the stone pillar that marks the town centre), four roads fan out to the four principal gates. A nasty ring road, which cuts through the city walls, also encircles the centre.

Information

Tourist Offices Chester's TIC (☎ 402111, e tourism@chester.org) is in the town hall opposite the cathedral on Northgate St. It opens 9 am to 5.30 pm Monday to Saturday, and 10 am to 4 pm Sunday; May to October. The rest of the year it opens 10 am to 5 pm Monday to Saturday.

Chester visitor centre (☎ 402111), just east of the city walls in Vicar's Lane, has displays and audiovisuals on the town's architecture, the development of the Rows and the events of the Civil War, plus the usual tourist information and brochures. It opens 10 am to 5.30 pm Monday to Saturday, and 10 am to 4 pm on Sunday, May to October. It closes half an hour earlier on Monday to Saturday the rest of the year.

City walks (£3/2.30) depart daily from Chester visitor centre at 10.30 am and from the town hall at 10.45 am. Ghosthunter Trails, leaving from the TIC, take place at 7.30 pm on Thursday, Friday and Saturday, June to September; and Roman Soldier Wall Patrols leave the visitor centre at 1.45 pm and the TIC at 2 pm on Thursday, Friday and Saturday, June to August; prices are the same as for the regular city walks.

Money There are plenty of banks with ATMs and foreign currency exchange desks inside the city walls.

Post There's a post office at 2 St John St. It opens 9 am to 5.30 pm Monday to Saturday.

Email & Internet Access Internet access is available (£2 for 40 minutes) at *i*-station (☎ 401680) in Rufus Court, in the library next to the TIC.

Medical Services & Emergency The Chester Royal Infirmary (☎ 365000) is on St Martin's Way.

The Cheshire Constabulary (☎ 350000) is close to the castle on Castle Esplanade.

Disabled visitors should head for the very helpful Dial House (☎ 345655), in Hamilton Place, which offers advice and a cafe. It opens 10 am to 4 pm Monday to Friday (closed Wednesday afternoon). The cafe also opens 10 am to 3 pm Saturday.

A Tour of the City Walls

Chester's walls were originally built around AD 70 to protect the Roman fort of Deva. Between AD 90 and 120 the Roman 20th Legion rebuilt them in stone. Over the

CHESTER

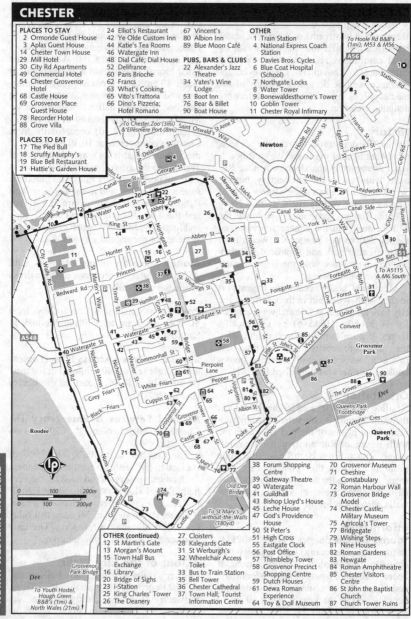

PLACES TO STAY
2 Ormonde Guest House
3 Aplas Guest House
14 Chester Town House
29 Mill Hotel
30 City Rd Apartments
49 Commercial Hotel
54 Chester Grosvenor Hotel
68 Castle House
69 Grosvenor Place Guest House
78 Recorder Hotel
88 Grove Villa

PLACES TO EAT
17 The Pied Bull
18 Scruffy Murphy's
19 Blue Bell Restaurant
21 Hattie's; Garden House
24 Elliot's Restaurant
42 Ye Olde Custom Inn
44 Katie's Tea Rooms
46 Watergate Inn
48 Dial Café; Dial House
52 Delifrance
60 Paris Brioche
62 Francs
63 What's Cooking
65 Vito's Trattoria
66 Dino's Pizzeria; Hotel Romano

67 Vincent's
80 Albion Inn
89 Blue Moon Café

PUBS, BARS & CLUBS
22 Alexander's Jazz Theatre
34 Yates's Wine Lodge
53 Boot Inn
76 Bear & Billet
90 Boat House

OTHER
1 Train Station
4 National Express Coach Station
5 Davies Bros. Cycles
6 Blue Coat Hospital (School)
7 Northgate Locks
8 Water Tower
9 Bonewaldesthorne's Tower
10 Goblin Tower
11 Chester Royal Infirmary

OTHER (continued)
12 St Martin's Gate
13 Morgan's Mount
15 Town Hall Bus Exchange
16 Library
20 Bridge of Sighs
23 i-Station
25 King Charles' Tower
26 The Deanery
27 Cloisters
28 Kaleyards Gate
31 St Werburgh's
32 Wheelchair Access Toilet
33 Bus to Train Station
35 Bell Tower
36 Chester Cathedral
37 Town Hall; Tourist Information Centre

38 Forum Shopping Centre
39 Gateway Theatre
40 Watergate
41 Guildhall
43 Bishop Lloyd's House
45 Leche House
47 God's Providence House
50 St Peter's
51 High Cross
55 Eastgate Clock
56 Post Office
57 Thimbleby Tower
58 Grosvenor Precinct Shopping Centre
59 Dutch Houses
63 Dewa Roman Experience
64 Toy & Doll Museum

70 Grosvenor Museum
71 Cheshire Constabulary
72 Roman Harbour Wall
73 Grosvenor Bridge Model
74 Chester Castle; Military Museum
75 Agricola's Tower
77 Bridgegate
79 Wishing Steps
81 Nine Houses
82 Roman Gardens
83 Newgate
84 Roman Amphitheatre
85 Chester Visitors Centre
86 St John the Baptist Church
87 Church Tower Ruins

To Hoole Rd B&B's (1mi); M53 & M56

To Chester Zoo (3mi) & Ellesmere Port (8mi)

To A5115 & M6 South

To St Mary's without-the-Walls (180yd)

To Youth Hostel, Hough Green B&B's (1mi) & North Wales (21mi)

NORTH-WESTERN ENGLAND

following centuries they were often altered, but their present position was established around 1200. After the Civil War the walls were rebuilt as a fashionable promenade.

Nowadays the 2-mile (3km) circuit of the walls makes an excellent introduction to Chester and should take 1½ to two hours. This suggested circuit proceeds clockwise from **Eastgate** at the prominent **Eastgate Clock**, built for Queen Victoria's Diamond Jubilee in 1897.

The **Thimbleby Tower**, also known as the Wolf Tower, was destroyed during the Civil War and never rebuilt. From here you can look down on the foundations of the south-eastern tower of the old Roman fort. Just beyond is **Newgate**, added in 1938, but in medieval style. From here the original Roman fortress walls ran westward, roughly following the course of the modern ring road to **St Martin's Gate**. From Newgate the partly excavated remains of the **Roman Amphitheatre** can be seen.

Outside the walls, the **Roman Gardens** (open year-round; free) contain a collection of Roman stonework brought here from excavations around Chester. Descend the **wishing steps** at the corner of the wall. They were added in 1785 and local legend claims that your wish will come true if you can run up and down the steps while holding your breath.

Continue past the **Recorder Hotel** (see Places to Stay) to the **Bridgegate** beside the **Old Dee Bridge**. This oft rebuilt bridge dates from 1387, although parts of it are centuries newer. Just inside the gate is the 1664 **Bear & Billet** pub, once a tollgate into the city.

Beyond Bridgegate the walls disappear for a short stretch. Inside the walls, **Agricola's Tower** is virtually all that remains of the medieval castle. Turn the corner beside the castle ruins.

Cross Grosvenor Rd to where the wall runs alongside the **Roodee**, Chester's ancient horse-racing track built on grassland left when the river changed course. The Roodee hosts the country's oldest horse race, which, uniquely, is run counter-clockwise. The city wall stands atop a stretch of **Roman Harbour Wall**. Cross **Watergate** and look left to the **Watergate Inn**, where the river once passed.

Continue to the north-western corner, where a short peninsula of wall leads out to the **Water Tower**. **Bonewaldesthorne's Tower**, actually on the corner, once guarded the river at this point, but when it shifted course in the 14th century the extension to Water Tower had to be built. In subsequent centuries the river has moved even farther west leaving both towers high and dry.

A little farther on, below the walls, you can see the **Northgate Locks**, a short but steep series of locks built in 1779 by Thomas Telford, the pioneering canal engineer. Continue past **Morgan's Mount** where a Captain Morgan defended the city during the Civil War. Across the canal is the **Blue Coat Hospital (School)**, now closed.

From Northgate the walls tower above the **Shropshire Union Canal**, which runs in what was once a moat-like ditch constructed by the Romans outside the walls. From **King Charles' Tower** at the corner, Charles I looked out to see his defeated army straggling back from battle in 1645.

Pass the 1275 **Kaleyards Gate** through which monks would go to work in their vegetable gardens outside the walls; it's still ceremonially locked every night at 9 pm. Traces of the original Roman wall are still visible from outside the walls just south of Kaleyards Gate. Continue past **Chester Cathedral** and the **Bell Tower** and you'll be back at the Eastgate Clock.

Chester Cathedral

A Saxon church dedicated to St Werburgh was built here in the 10th century, but in 1092 it became a Benedictine abbey and a Norman church replaced the earlier construction. The abbey was closed in 1540 with Henry VIII's dissolution of the monasteries and a year later the building became a cathedral. The 12th-century cloister and its surrounding buildings are essentially unaltered and retain much of the early monastic structure.

The present cathedral (☎ 32476) was built between 1250 and 1540, but there were later alterations and a lot of Victorian reconstruction. It opens 7.30 am to 6.30 pm daily. Visitors are asked to donate £2.

The Rows

Chester's eye-catching two-level shopping streets may date back to the post-Roman period. As the Roman walls slowly crumbled into rubble, medieval traders may have built their shops against the rubble banks, while later arrivals built theirs on top of the banks. Whatever their origins, the Rows make a convenient rainproof shopping promenade along the four ancient streets fanning out from the Cross.

Dewa Roman Experience

The Dewa Roman Experience (☎ 343407), Pierpoint Lane (off Bridge St), aims to show what life was like in Roman times. Your tour begins in a reconstructed galley after which you move into a Roman street and watch an entertaining audiovisual presentation. After that you can wander at your own pace past the Roman castle foundations and medieval rubbish pits, and through the interesting museum and finds room. It opens 9 am to 5 pm daily. Admission costs £3.95/2.25.

Museums

In Grosvenor St, the **Grosvenor Museum** (☎ 402008) has the usual hodgepodge of paintings and silver, but the displays on Roman Chester and particularly the Roman tombstones are very good, as is the new Chester Timeline Gallery spelling out the city's past. The Stuart, mid-Georgian and Victorian period rooms are also worth seeing. It opens 10.30 am to 5 pm Monday to Saturday and 2 to 5 pm Sunday. Admission is free.

'All things toys' is the idea behind the **Toy & Doll Museum** (☎ 346297) on Lower Bridge St, which displays an eclectic array of antique toys and dolls and opens 10 am to 5 pm Monday to Saturday and 11 am to 5 pm Sunday; £2/1.

The history of the soldiers of Cheshire is told at the **Cheshire Military Museum** (☎ 327617) in part of **Chester Castle**. Both

are pretty uninspiring unless you're into that sort of thing. The museum opens 10 am to 5 pm daily. Admission costs £1/50p.

St John the Baptist Church

Directly opposite the visitors centre in Vicar's Lane stands **St John's Church**, built on the site of an older Saxon church in 1075. It started out as a cathedral of Mercia, before being rebuilt by the Normans. The foundations mustn't have been too sound as the north-western tower collapsed twice in its history, in 1573 and 1881. The eastern end of the church, abandoned in 1581 when St John's became a parish, now lies in peaceful ruin and includes the remains of a Norman choir and medieval chapels. The church opens 9.15 am to 6 pm daily.

Chester Zoo

Chester is home to England's largest zoo (☎ 380280), noted for its pleasant garden setting. It opens 10 am to 5.30 pm daily, April to October, and to 3.30 pm the rest of the year. Admission costs £9.50/7.

The zoo is on the A41, 3 miles (5km) north of the city centre. Bus Nos 11C and 12C run every 15 minutes (£1.80 return) from the Town Hall Bus Exchange Monday to Saturday and twice-hourly on Sundays.

River Activities

Beyond the city walls, The Groves is a popular riverside promenade leading to Grosvenor Park. There's a stand on the bank, near Handbridge, from where you can hire rowing boats (£4 an hour), pedal boats (£4 per 30 minutes) or motor boats (£4 per 30 minutes), or take a short cruise (£2.50/1.50 per 30 minutes).

Places to Stay

Although Chester has numerous places to stay, unbooked late arrivals may have to do some searching in summer. Most places are outside the city walls but within easy walking distance of the centre. Both the TIC and the visitor centre can arrange accommodation, but charge £3 for the service.

Hostels A mile south-west of the city centre, across Grosvenor Park Bridge, is the *youth hostel* (☎ 680056, fax 681204, ✉ chester@yha.org.uk, 40 Hough Green). The nightly cost for adults/under-18s is £10.85/7.40 and it opens year-round.

If you just want a bed try *City Rd Apartments* (☎ 813125, ✉ cityroad@lineone.net, 18 City Rd). It's close to the city centre with basic beds for £10 a head, sharing a shower.

B&Bs & Hotels – Outside the Walls

Brook St, near the train station, has a couple of good-value B&Bs for a reasonable price.

The friendly and accommodating *Ormonde Guest House* (☎ 328816, 126 Brook St) has rooms starting at £17 per person. *Aplas Guest House* (☎ 312401, 106 Brook St) has adequate rooms for much the same price.

Hoole Rd, the road to or from the M53/M56 and beyond the railway lines, is lined with low to medium-price B&Bs about 10 to 15 minutes' walk north-east of the centre.

Bawn Park Hotel (☎ 324971, fax 310951, 10 Hoole Rd) is cosy, with B&B starting at £17 per person. In the same range and similar quality is the *Glen-Garth Guest House* (☎ 310260, 59 Hoole Rd), farther out of town.

Ba Ba Guest House (☎ 315046, 315047, ✉ reservations@babaguesthouse.freeserve .co.uk, 65 Hoole Rd) is worth the extra few pounds; comfortable rooms start at £20 per person.

Attractive, small *Glann Hotel* (☎ 344800, 2 Stone Place), with a friendly cat, is one minute's walk east off Hoole Rd and charges from £26 per person.

The Victorian *Grove Villa* (☎ 349713, ✉ grove.villa@tesco.net, 18 The Groves), with views of the River Dee, is one of the better B&Bs in town and has beautiful rooms with bathrooms for £20 per person.

Larger *Mill Hotel* (☎ 350035, fax 345635, ✉ reservations@millhotel.com, Milton St), on either side of the canal, boasts a health club, swimming pool, canal cruises and singles/doubles from £49/65.

B&Bs & Hotels – Inside the Walls

Centrally situated, the *Grosvenor Place Guest House* (☎ 324455, fax 400225, 2–4 Grosvenor Place) has singles/doubles at £36/44 with bathroom.

Nearby is *Castle House* (☎ 350354, 23 Castle St), which dates from the 16th century and its comfortable rooms (some with bathrooms) cost from £23 per person.

You can't get more central than the *Commercial Hotel* (☎ 320749, fax 348318, St Peter's Church Yard), hidden away just off Northgate St, offering rooms from £35 per person.

The eager-to-please *Recorder Hotel* (☎ 326580, ✉ ebbs@compuserve.com, 19 City Walls) is just off Lower Bridge St, right on the walls and river. The newly refurbished rooms are lovely and cost from £35 per person.

The *Chester Town House* (☎ 350021, ✉ davidbellis@chestertownhouse.co.uk, 23 King St) resides in a quiet, pleasantly olde-worlde street and dates from 1680. Rooms with bathrooms cost £35/50. Around the corner is *The Pied Bull* (☎ 325829, Northgate St), a beautiful old inn. Take care with the original handmade staircase, it dates from 1533. Rooms for a night cost £45.50.

At *Hotel Romano* (☎ 320841, 51 Lower Bridge), above Dino's pizzeria, rooms cost £45/65.

If you're pushing the boat out, the *Chester Grosvenor Hotel* (☎ 324024, ✉ chesgrove@chestergrosvnor.co.uk, 58 Eastgate St) has an unmatchable location in Eastgate. Expect to pay £130/165 in the low season.

Places to Eat

Restaurants Chester has the usual selection of international fast-food outlets, plus a few centrally located fish and chip places, particularly in Lower Bridge St. *Paris Brioche* (☎ 348708, 39 Bridge St) and *Delifrance* (☎ 322024, 30 Northgate St) both turn out good sandwiches and baguettes to eat in or take away.

Very popular, and deservedly so, *Francs* (☎ 317952, 14 Cuppin St) turns out traditional French food every day. Nearby on the corner of Cuppin St, **What's Cooking** (☎ 346512, 14–16 Grosvenor St) offers burgers and other American-style food.

Vito's Trattoria (☎ 317330, 25 Lower Bridge St) is a standard pizza and pasta specialist. A little farther down is **Dino's Pizzeria** (☎ 325091, 51 Lower Bridge St) serving up similar fare. Colourful **Vincent's** (☎ 310854, 58-60 Lower Bridge St) cooks up Caribbean cuisine; blue marlin costs £12.95.

In Rufus Court, the **Garden House** (☎ 320004) serves English food and has more than the average choice of vegetarian dishes. **Elliot's Restaurant** (☎ 329932, 2 Abbey Green) also serves modern English food. Check the board for the daily specials.

Blue Bell Restaurant (☎ 317758, 65 Northgate St) serves up a high standard of international cuisine in a 13th-century building; escalope of calves livers is £12.95.

The pubs around town are a good option for basic food at reasonable prices.

Scruffy Murphy's (☎ 321750, 59 Northgate St) is a standard pub for a bar meal in an unpretentious atmosphere. Chester's original coaching inn **The Pied Bull** (see Places to Stay) offers much the same as Scruffy Murphy's.

On Watergate St, **Ye Olde Custom Inn** still keeps a semblance of a real ale pub and serves filling food; chicken burger and chips for £3.15. At No 11 **Watergates** (☎ 320515), a moody restaurant/bar set in the superb surroundings of an old crypt, does a great hot lemon chicken salad for £5.95.

If you want to take a step back in time, head to the fine Edwardian **Albion Inn** (☎ 340345, Park St). Reliable English food without chips or fry-ups can be ordered, along with the best real ale in town among the war-memorabilia-covered walls.

Cafes The gorgeous cathedral *refectory* (☎ 313156, Abbey Square) serves soup of the day for £1.95 and is one of the more beautiful places to relax and enjoy lunch.

The stoned walled **Katie's Tea Rooms** (☎ 400322, 34 Watergate St), spread over three floors of a historic building, gives the refectory a run for its money for the best place for a light lunch.

Cheaper is **Hattie's**, (☎ 345173, 5 Rufus Court), a teashop in Rufus Court, near the Northgate, but it's nowhere near as aesthetically appealing.

The 50s-style **Blue Moon Café** is a good spot for a bite to eat if you want river views. **Dial Café** (☎ 345655, Hamilton Place) offers disabled access in a town that isn't easy for wheelchair users.

Entertainment
Pubs The pubs mentioned in the Places to Eat section are all equally good for a pint or two.

Overlooking the river, **Boat House** (☎ 328709, The Groves) is a good spot for a pint while watching the boats go by.

Boot Inn (Eastgate Row) is rich in atmosphere and history; 14 Roundheads were killed in the back room.

Live Music & Comedy If you're looking for live music try **Yates's Wine Lodge** (☎ 344813, 19 Frodsham St), which attracts a noisy, young crowd at night. *Scruffy Murphy's* (see Places to Eat) also supplies live music on a regular basis.

Alexander's Jazz Theatre (☎ 340005, Rufus Court) is a combination of wine bar, coffee bar and tapas bar. Admission is sometimes free before 10 pm; otherwise it costs £2 to £7.50, depending on what's on; it hosts jazz, blues and comedy nights.

Theatre *Gateway Theatre* (☎ 340392, Hamilton Place) is beside the Forum Shopping Centre.

Getting There & Away
Chester is 188 miles (303km) north-west of London, 85 miles (137km) north-west of Birmingham, 40 miles (64km) south-west of Manchester and 18 miles (29km) south of Liverpool. It has excellent transport connections, especially with North Wales.

Bus Just north of the city walls inside the ring road is the National Express (☎ 0870

580 8080) bus station. It has numerous services: one a day to Glasgow (£22.50, six hours); three a day to Manchester (£4.50, 1¼ hours) and Bristol (£17.50, four hours); two a day to Llandudno (£5.50, 1¾ hours); four a day to Liverpool (£5, one hour); and five a day to Birmingham (£8.25, 2½ hours) and London (£15, 5½ hours).

For information on local bus services, ring Cheshire Bus Line (☎ 602666). Local buses leave from Market Square behind the town hall. On Sunday and bank holidays a Sunday Adventurer ticket gives you unlimited travel in Cheshire for £3/2.

Train The train station is a 15-minute walk north-east of the city centre via City Rd or Brook St. City-Rail Link buses are free to people with rail tickets and stops outside the station and on Frodsham St.

There are numerous trains to Shrewsbury (£5.80, one hour); Manchester (£8.50, 1½ hours) and Liverpool (£3, 40 minutes); Holyhead (£16.15, two hours) via the North Wales coast, for Ireland; and London Euston (£44, £19 if booked 14 days in advance, three hours).

Getting Around
Much of the city centre is closed to traffic from 10.30 am to 4.30 pm, so a car is likely to be a handicap. The walled city is easy to walk around and most places of interest are close to the wall walk.

Bus City buses (☎ 602666) depart from the town hall bus exchange. Guide Friday (☎ 347457) offers hop-on top-bus tours of the city; an all-day ticket costs £6.50/2; £8/2.50 if you want a half-hour river cruise included.

Bicycle Davies Bros Cycles (☎ 371341), 5 Delamere St, hires out mountain bikes for £10 per day.

AROUND CHESTER
Ellesmere Port
The superb Boat Museum (☎ 0151-355 5017), 8 miles (13km) north of Chester on the Shropshire Union Canal, has a large collection of canal boats as well as indoor exhibits. It opens 10 am to 5 pm daily, April to October; and 11 am to 4 pm Saturday to Wednesday in winter. Admission costs £5.50/3.70.

The museum is about 15 minutes' drive north from Chester on the M53. Take Bus No 4 from the bus exchange in Chester (45 minutes) or it's a 10-minute walk from Ellesmere Port train station.

Knutsford
☎ 01565 • pop 13,700
The small village of Knutsford, 15 miles (24km) south of Manchester, makes the most of its famous former resident, Elizabeth Gaskell, who spent her childhood here. Gaskell based Cranford on the town, in a novel of the same name. But even without the famous connection, Knutsford makes a pleasant detour from the big cities of the North-West.

King St, the town's main street, has a good selection of shops, restaurants, lovely pubs and quaint cobblestoned courtyards and alleyways. The TIC (☎ 632611) is situated in the Council Offices on Toft Rd and opens 8.45 am to 5 pm Monday to Thursday, to 4.30 pm Friday and 9 am to 1 pm Saturday.

Those wanting more information on Elizabeth Gaskell should head to the **Knutsford Heritage Centre** (☎ 650506), 90a King St, which illustrates her connection to the town. Richard Watt, a self-made millionaire and philanthropist who settled in Knutsford, is also well represented at the centre. It opens 1.30 to 4 pm Monday to Friday, noon to 4 pm Saturdays, and 2 to 4.30 pm Sundays. Admission is free.

Richard Watt's affection for the town can be seen in its buildings: the eye-catching **Gaskell Memorial Tower** and the **King's Coffee House** (meant to lure the men from the pubs) on Kings St and the **Ruskins Rooms** on Drury Lane, built as recreation rooms for the general populace.

Don't be surprised if you arrive on May Day to find the streets covered in colourful messages written in sand. Legend has it that the Danish King Canute, while crossing the marsh between Over and Nether Knutsford, scrawled a message in the sand wishing happiness to a young couple on the way to their wedding. The custom is also practised on weddings and feast days.

The TIC can organise accommodation if required.

Royal George Hotel (☎ *634151, King St*) is well located in the centre of town and has B&B for £65.45/72.40 for a single/double.

You can dine in the lovely surroundings of the King's Coffee House at *La Belle Epoque* (☎ *632661, 60 King St*), well renowned in the area for its food. Set lunch is £6.95, with evening meals a little pricier.

The Treasure Village (☎ *651537, 84 King St*) is an inexpensive restaurant specialising in Peking and Cantonese cuisine and offers a lunch menu for £5.80.

Knutsford is on the Manchester to Chester rail line so there are frequent connections to both; a single to Chester is £6.95 (30 minutes) and to Manchester £3.70 (30 minutes). The train station is on Adams Hill, at the southern end of King St.

Tatton Park

Three and a half miles (6km) north of Knutsford, Tatton Park (☎ 01625-534435; NT) is a huge estate set around 19th-century Wyatt House, with a medieval great hall, 1930s-style working farm and a series of gardens. Wyatt House opens noon to 4 pm daily except Monday, April to October; the park opens 10 am to 7 pm daily. Only the house and gardens are free to NT members. Admission to the mansion costs £3/2, the farm £2.50/1.50 and the old hall £2.50/1.50. Tickets to any two of the Tatton attractions cost £4.50/2.50. Car entry to the park is £3.50.

On Sunday Bus No X2 links Tatton Park with Chester (one hour).

Nantwich

☎ 01270 • pop 12,000

Nantwich made an astounding recovery after being almost totally destroyed by fire in 1583. A big salt producer of the time, the town began to rebuild itself with the help of a £1000 donation from Elizabeth I. Today,

it is a small and bustling place made for strolling around with a fine church and eye-catching black-and-white timbered buildings reminiscent of Chester.

The helpful TIC (☎ 610983, fax 610880, ℮ touristi@netcentral.co.uk) on Church Walk is near the main square and opens 9.30 am to 5 pm Monday to Friday, 10 am to 4 pm on Saturday and 11 am to 3 pm on Sunday.

It's a wonder how some of the striking black-and-white buildings around the town are still standing, especially the **Brookland Bookshop**, on the High St, which looks about to collapse in on itself. Opposite is the **Queen's Aid House**, which proudly displays a plaque commemorating the donation made by Elizabeth I. Farther along the High St is the **Crown Hotel**, built in 1585 on the site of the original inn destroyed in the fire. It's a great place to hang out and soak up the atmosphere.

The 14th-century **Church of St Mary** (☎ 625268) was one of three buildings to survive the fire, built from local red sandstone. It's a fine example of medieval church architecture and the stone pulpit is a bit of a rarity, dating from the 14th century. The church opens 9 am to 5 pm daily and concerts are held inside every Thursday lunchtime from June to August. There's also a small visitor centre inside the main entrance open 10 am to 4.30 pm Monday to Friday, March to December.

Apart from salt, the town grew up around cheese and leather production, and all three are depicted in the **Nantwich Museum** (☎ 627104), Pillory St. It opens 10.30 am to 4.30 pm Monday to Saturday, April to September; and Tuesday to Saturday, October to March. Admission is free.

For comfortable B&B, try *The Limes* (☎/*fax 624081, 5 Park Rd*), where spacious rooms start at £20 per person.

By far the best place to stay is the characterful *Crown Hotel* (☎ *625283, fax 628047, ℮ crownhotel@highstnantwich .freeserve.co.uk, High St*). Of course, it's not the cheapest with rooms for £59/69, but lower rates are available at the weekend.

For a lunchtime filler, the *Pillory House*

& Coffee Shop (☎ 623524, Pillory St) does the trick nicely. Above a rather expensive knick-knack shop, this old-style tearoom serves more than just sandwiches: chicken and mushroom pie costs £2.85.

For an evening meal, pubs are a good option, such as the *White Horse (☎ 624801, Pillory St)*. *Crown Hotel* (see above for details) offers a couple of choices for dining, either in its atmospheric bar or its Italian restaurant, *Casa Italiana*.

Arriva Midlands (☎ 505855) operates an hourly bus service from Nantwich to Chester from the bus station on Beam St, two minutes' walk north of the TIC.

Nantwich is on the Manchester to Cardiff line so there are regular trains to Manchester (£7.70, 1¼ hours). The train station is about five minutes' walk south of the centre.

Liverpool

☎ 0151 • pop 510,000

Of all the cities in northern England, Liverpool has perhaps the strongest sense of its own identity, which is closely tied up, as you'll discover on even the shortest visit, with the totems of the Beatles, the Liverpool and Everton football teams, and the Grand National, run at Aintree since 1839.

The city has a dramatic site, rising on a series of steps above the broad River Mersey estuary with its shifting light, its fogs, its gulls and its mournful emptiness. You're bound to be struck by the contrast between the grandeur and the decay, between the decrepit streets and boarded-up windows and the massive cathedrals and imperious buildings.

Liverpool's economic collapse has been even more dramatic than Manchester's and it gives the whole city a sharp edge you'd do well not to explore. When people party, they seem to do so with a touch of desperation, certainly with plenty of abandonment. At the weekend the city centre vibrates to music from countless pubs and clubs.

It's well worth setting aside time to explore Liverpool properly. The Albert Dock, the Western Approaches Museum, the twin cathedrals and the city streets themselves offer vivid testimony to the city's rugged history and the perverse exhilaration of its present-day decline.

History

Like Bristol, 18th-century Liverpool prospered on the back of the infamous triangular trading of slaves for raw materials. From 1700 ships carried cotton goods and hardware from Liverpool to West Africa, where they were exchanged for slaves. The slaves were, in turn, carried to the West Indies and Virginia where they were exchanged for sugar, rum, tobacco and raw cotton, a story retold in an excellent gallery in the Merseyside Maritime Museum (see Albert Dock later in this chapter).

As a great port, the city attracted thousands of immigrants from Ireland and Scotland and its Celtic influences are still apparent; but between 1830 and 1930 nine million emigrants – mainly English, Scottish and Irish, but also Swedes, Norwegians and Russian Jews – sailed from Liverpool for the New World.

WWII led to a resurgence in Liverpool's importance. Over one million GIs disembarked here before D-Day and the port was, once again, hugely important as the western gateway for transatlantic supplies. The city also accommodated the Combined Headquarters of the Western Approaches, which coordinated the transatlantic convoys and the battle against German U-boats.

Liverpool has a long history of left-wing radicalism. Outrageous excesses of 19th-century capitalism led to bitter and violent confrontations with increasingly well organised labour organisations. More recently, unemployment and housing problems have dragged the city down. In the early 1980s racial tensions led to rioting in Toxteth, a run-down suburb just south of the city centre.

As elsewhere, the previous Conservative government saw tourism as a way out of Liverpool's problems and money was poured into the redevelopment of the Albert

LIVERPOOL

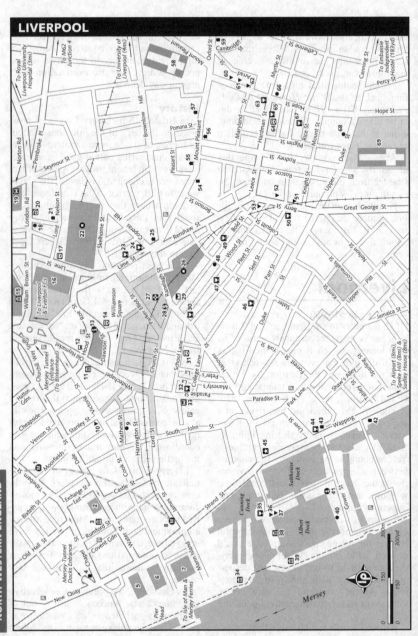

LIVERPOOL

PLACES TO STAY		32	The Escape	17	The Empire
4	Tower Thistle	35	Pump House	18	Mars
21	Lord Nelson Hotel	44	The Baltic Fleet	19	National Express Coach
25	Britannia Adelphi Hotel	46	Cream		Station
42	Campanile Hotel	47	RSVP; Baa Bar	20	Planet Electra
43	Youth Hostel	49	Mardi Gras	22	Lime Street Train Station
54	YMCA	50	Blue Angel	26	Central Train Station
55	Belvedere; Aachen Hotel	63	Philharmonic Dining Room	27	Clayton Square Shopping
56	Selhal	65	Flying Picket		Centre
57	Feathers Hotel	67	Ye Cracke	28	Thomas Cook
59	University of Liverpool			29	Post Office
		OTHER		31	Bluecoat Arts Centre
PLACES TO EAT		1	Moorfields Train Station	33	Bus Station & Parking
10	Casa Bella	2	Town Hall	34	Museum of Liverpool Life
36	Est Est Est	3	Western Approaches Museum	38	Merseyside Maritime
37	Blue Bar & Grill	5	Royal Liver Building		Museum
51	Far East	6	Cunard Building	39	Tate Gallery Liverpool
52	Hub Cafe	7	Port of Liverpool Building	40	The Beatles Story
53	Cafe Tabac	8	James Street Train Station	41	Tourist Information Centre
60	Everyman Bistro & Theatre	9	Cavern Club		(Albert Dock)
61	El Macho	11	Conservation Centre	45	Police Headquaters
62	Becker's Brook	12	Queen Square Bus Stops	48	Waterstones
		13	Tourist Information Centre	58	Metropolitan Cathedral
PUBS, BARS & CLUBS		14	Liverpool Playhouse	64	Unity Theatre
23	American Bar	15	Liverpool Museum;	66	Philharmonic Hall
24	Vines		Walker Art Gallery	68	Institute for Performing Arts
30	Revolution; Krazy House	16	St George's Hall	69	Anglican Cathedral

Dock, with an offshoot of London's Tate galleries, several museums and a range of shops and restaurants.

Orientation

Liverpool stretches north–south along the River Mersey estuary for more than 13 miles (21km). The main visitor attraction is the Albert Dock on the waterfront west of the city centre. The centre, including the two cathedrals to the east, is quite compact and easy to explore on foot.

Lime Street, the main train station, is just to the east of the city centre. The National Express coach station is a few blocks north, on the corner of Norton Rd and Islington St. The bus station is in the centre on Paradise St.

Information

Tourist Offices The main TIC (☎ 709 5111, ℮ askme@visitliverpool.com), in the Queen Square Centre, opens 9 am to 5.30 pm Monday to Saturday and 10.30 am to 4.30 pm Sunday, while the branch in the

Albert Dock (☎ 708 8854) opens 10 am to 5.30 pm daily. Both can book accommodation for you.

Look for the excellent *Liverpool Heritage Walk*, an illustrated guide to the city's landmarks, identified by numbered metal markers set in the footpath.

Both TICs sell tickets for city bus tours. The hop-on hop-off bus tour has 11 stops and costs £6/4.50. There's also a highly recommended 2¼-hour Beatles tour (see the boxed text 'Doing the Beatles to Death' later in this section).

If you're planning on visiting several museums make sure to spend £3/1.50 on an NMGM Eight Pass, covering admission to six city-centre attractions – Liverpool Museum, Walker Art Gallery, Merseyside Maritime Museum, HM Customs & Excise National Museum, Museum of Liverpool Life and the Conservation Centre – as well as to the Lady Lever Art Gallery in Port Sunlight and to Sudley House (☎ 724 3245) in Aigburth. It's valid for 12 months and is on sale at all the museums.

Money Almost all banks in the centre of town have ATM machines.

Post The post office at 1 Bold St opens 9 am to 5.30 pm Monday to Saturday.

Email & Internet Access Planet Electra (☎ 708 0303), 36 London Rd, is a regular cafe with Internet access.

Internet Resources Check out www.visitliverpool.com for online information on Liverpool.

Travel Agencies Thomas Cook Travel (☎ 552 1300) is at 75 Church St.

Bookshops Waterstones (☎ 708 6861), at 14 Bold St, stocks a good range of titles.

Medical Services & Emergencies The closest hospital to Liverpool centre is the Royal Liverpool University Hospital (☎ 706 2000), about 3 miles (5km) east on Prescot St. If you require a late-night pharmacy head to Mars (☎ 709 5271), 68 London Rd.

Merseyside Police Headquarters (☎ 709 6010) is opposite Albert Dock on Canning Place.

Dangers & Annoyances It pays to be a bit careful in Liverpool. Ideally, avoid walking along side streets or along Duke St, the main drag linking the Anglican cathedral with Hanover St, after dark.

City Centre

At the end of Castle St, the **town hall** was designed by John Wood the Elder, of Bath, and completed in 1754. Both the dome and the impressive portico and balcony, where the Beatles were received by the Lord Mayor in 1964, were added later.

The confusing **Clayton Square** is a modern shopping centre opposite Central station. **Bold St**, south of Central station, was once a ropewalk used in the manufacture of ropes for visiting ships.

Once considered one of the world's most luxurious hotels, the **Britannia Adelphi**

Hotel in Lime St was completed in 1912 to serve wealthy passengers staying overnight before or after the Atlantic crossing. Farther north along the same road is the superb Edwardian pub **Vines**, with its luxurious interior (built in 1907) and the welcoming **American Bar**, favoured by the US forces during WWII. In the 19th century, Lime St was famous for prostitution and was immortalised in the song *Maggie May*.

A group of Liverpool's most impressive buildings are clustered together opposite Lime Street station, although traffic funnelling into the city and the entrance of the Queensway Mersey Tunnel makes it difficult to appreciate them. Built as a concert hall in 1854, **St George's Hall** (☎ 707 2391) is considered one of the world's greatest neoclassical buildings; its exterior is Greek, its interior Roman. Admission costs £2 and tours take place daily except Sunday mid-July to August for £1.50.

Liverpool Museum & Walker Art Gallery

Liverpool Museum (☎ 478 4399) is a traditional museum covering everything from archaeology to natural history, but also houses a planetarium and hosts interesting temporary exhibitions. As well as its renowned collection of Pre-Raphaelite art, the Walker Art Gallery (☎ 478 4199) has an important collection of Italian and Flemish paintings and some interesting Impressionists and post-Impressionists, including a Degas, Cézanne and Matisse. There's a pleasant cafe on the ground floor.

The museum and gallery, side by side in William Brown St, open 10 am to 5 pm Monday to Saturday, from noon to 5 pm Sunday. Admission to each costs £3/1.50.

Western Approaches Museum

The Combined Headquarters of the Western Approaches (☎ 227 2008), the secret command centre for the Battle of the Atlantic, was buried under yards of concrete beneath an undistinguished building behind the town hall in Rumford Square. At the end of the war the bunker was abandoned with virtually everything left intact. It opens

10.30 am to 4.30 pm daily Monday to Thursday and Saturday, March to October. Tickets cost £4.75/3.45.

Conservation Centre

The Conservation Centre (☎ 478 4999), in the old Midland Railway Goods Depot in Old Haymarket, is a state-of-the-art exhibition telling the story behind the conservation of the items on display in local museums and art galleries. Hand-held wands allow you to tune into different stories as you walk around and you'll probably be surprised to discover how much fun it all is. Did you know, for example, that a toucan's bill must be repainted after death? The Conservation Centre opens 10 am to 5 pm Monday to Saturday and noon to 5 pm on Sunday. Admission costs £3/1.50.

The Cathedrals

As you walk along Hope St you can see Liverpool's twin cathedrals looming on either side of you vying for dominance, the Roman Catholic version to the north, the Anglican to the south.

Metropolitan Cathedral According to Sir Edwin Lutyens' original plans, Liverpool's Roman Catholic cathedral (☎ 709 9222) would have been larger than St Peter's in Rome. Unfortunately, the war and Liverpool's decline forced the priests to lower their sights. The present church-in-the-round (known locally as 'Paddy's Wigwam') was completed in 1967 and incorporates Lutyens' crypt. The soaring exterior is strikingly successful and the interior space impressive, although opinions on the modern decorations vary. The cathedral opens 8 am to 6 pm daily (5 pm in winter).

Anglican Cathedral Work on the red sandstone, neo-Gothic Anglican Cathedral (☎ 709 6271) started in 1902 and was finally completed in 1978, by which time it was only exceeded in size by St Peter's and the Milan and Seville cathedrals. Almost everything about the place is larger than life, including the central bell, which is the

worlds' third largest. The cathedral was the life work of Sir Giles Gilbert Scott (1880–1960) who worked on it until his death. Scott was also responsible for the design of the old red telephone booth, which explains why one of these is tucked away upstairs.

Even those who don't usually care for neo-Gothic are likely to be awed by this great, austere sea of space. The best views of Liverpool are from the top of the 101m tower. The cathedral opens 7.30 am to 6 pm daily and a donation of £2 is requested. The tower opens 11 am to 3 pm Monday to Saturday (£2.50/1.50), as does the exhibition of ecclesiastical embroidery. The excellent refectory opens 11 am to 4 pm.

Beside the porch steps, look out for a **memorial** to the 96 Liverpool football fans who died in the crush at Hillsborough Stadium in 1989. The imitation Greek temple nearby is the **Oratory**, designed in 1929 and open to visitors from Easter to September.

Albert Dock

Built between 1841 and 1848, the Albert Dock was one of the earliest enclosed docks in the world. Now 2.75 hectares of water are ringed by a colonnade of enormous cast-iron columns and impressive five-storey warehouses.

In the 1980s the warehouses were restored and now house several outstanding museums, numerous shops and restaurants, offices, studios for Granada TV, a branch of the TIC and several tacky tourist attractions. The site could easily absorb four hours, and that's without exploring the impressive buildings north along the waterfront. The Waterfront Pass saves you money on The Beatles Story, Merseyside Maritime Museum and a cruise on a Mersey Ferry; £9.99/6.99.

Merseyside Maritime Museum This museum (☎ 478 4499) has a large range of imaginatively developed exhibits. Major displays focus on Emigrants to a New World, the WWII Battle of the Atlantic, and Builders of Great Ships. The latest addition is the new gallery dedicated to merchant ships and their crew. There is also an absorbing Transatlantic Slave Gallery that describes the shameful trade and its repercussions in the form of modern racism. Anything to Declare? is a gallery devoted to the history of HM Customs & Excise; it sounds pretty dry but gives you the chance to find out whether you could catch a smuggler.

The museum opens 10 am to 5 pm daily. Admission costs £3/1.50.

Museum of Liverpool Life This museum (☎ 478 4080) looks at four main themes: Mersey Culture, especially entertainers; Making a Living, showing regional trades; Demanding a Voice, about the growth of unionism and democracy; and A Healthy Place to Live? a look at Liverpool's record on public health. It opens 10 am to 5 pm daily. Admission costs £3/1.50.

Tate Liverpool It's particularly appropriate that Liverpool should have been chosen as home to this extension of London's Tate galleries since Henry Tate, benefactor of the original gallery, co-founded the famous Tate & Lyle sugar business here. The newly refurbished Albert Dock gallery (☎ 702 7400) hosts high-quality changing exhibitions. It opens 10 am to 6 pm Tuesday to Sunday. Admission is free.

The Beatles Story Despite its promising name this attraction (☎ 709 1963) fails to capitalise on its subject's potential – fanatics won't discover anything they don't already know, and aside from some old TV clips there's little to kindle excitement for later generations. It opens 10 am to 6 pm daily, but it's a high price at £6.95/4.95 for admission. A Beatles Combo ticket of £15 gets you into the exhibition and a seat on the Magical Mystery Tour (see the boxed text 'Doing the Beatles to Death').

North of Albert Dock The area to the north of Albert Dock is known as **Pier Head**, after a stone pier built in the 1760s. This is still the departure point for ferries across the River Mersey (see Getting Around later in

this section), and was, for millions of migrants, their final contact with European soil.

Today it's dominated by a trio of self-important buildings dating from the days when Liverpool's star was still in the ascendant. The southernmost, with the dome mimicking St Paul's Cathedral, is the **Port of Liverpool Building**, completed in 1907. Next to it the **Cunard Building**, in the style of an Italian palazzo, was once HQ to the Cunard Steamship Line. Finally, the **Royal Liver Building** (pronounced **lie**-ver) was opened in 1911 as the head office of the Royal Liver Friendly Society. It's crowned by the famous 5.5m copper Liver Birds, Liverpool's symbol. Tours of the building are free of charge but must be pre-booked (☎ 236 2748). Liverpool's original seal depicted an eagle, but over time artists' representations came to look more like a seagull or cormorant!

Places to Stay

Note that beds can be hard to find when Liverpool or Everton football clubs are playing at home. You'll also be lucky to find anything if you haven't booked ahead for the third week of August when the Beatles annual convention comes to town. The TIC offers a free accommodation service.

Hostels The excellent and welcoming *Embassie Independent Hostel (☎ 707 1089, fax 707 8289, 1 Falkner Square)* is east of the Anglican Cathedral but still within walking distance of the centre. Dormitory beds here cost £11.50, including tea and coffee, and facilities include a laundry and TV lounge.

The new YHA *youth hostel (☎ 709 8888, fax 709 0417, e liverpool@yha.org.uk, 25 Tabley St)* is across the road from Albert Dock, three-quarters of a mile south of James Street station. Beds cost £17.40/13.10 for adults/under-18s, including breakfast.

Spartan *Selhal (☎ 709 7791, 1 Rodney St)* is off Mount Pleasant where the YWCA used to be and charges £12 per night.

The *YMCA (☎ 709 9516, 6 Mount Pleasant)* offers B&B for £14.50 per person.

Doing the Beatles to Death

A Victorian warehouse in Mathew St was once home to a music venue called the Cavern Club. Between March 1961 and August 1963, the Beatles played here a staggering 275 times. Other bands such as Gerry and the Pacemakers who helped define 'beat' music and the 'Mersey sound' were also regulars. Cilla Black was in charge of the cloakroom.

Turn down Mathew St today and you're hardly able to move for businesses cashing in on the Beatles phenomenon. There's an Abbey Rd Oyster Bar, an Abbey Rd Shop, a Lucy in the Sky with Diamonds cafe and a Lennon Bar... and that's before you stumble on Cavern Court and the Cavern Walks shopping mall.

The irony is, of course, that the original Cavern Club, where the Fab Four started their career, was closed in 1973 and the site ruthlessly redeveloped in 1980. A statue of Lennon in his Hamburg period may slouch against the wall of the memorabilia-crammed Cavern Pub (☎ 236 1957), but the present day Cavern Club (☎ 236 1964), at 2 Mathew St, only opened in 1984. You may well find it hosting a disco or closed for a private party.

Serious Beatles fans might prefer to head off in search of other Liverpool sites associated with the mopheads. Both tourist information centres sell tickets to the Magical Mystery Tour (☎ 709 3285), a 2¼-hour bus trip taking in Penny Lane, Strawberry Fields and many other landmarks. It departs daily from opposite the Pump House pub in Albert Dock at 2.20 pm and from the main TIC at 2.30 pm. In July and August there are also Saturday tours at 11.50 am. Tickets cost £10.95. Better value is the Beatles Combo ticket of £15, which covers entry to the **Beatles Story** (☎ 709 1963) and a seat on the Mystery tour.

If you'd rather do it yourself, the TICs also stock the *Discover Lennon's Liverpool* guide and map, and Robin Jones' *Beatles Liverpool*.

The *University of Liverpool* (☎ 794 3298, fax 794 3816, Mulberry Court, Oxford St) has self-catering rooms, near the Metropolitan Cathedral, for £16 a head; it also offers *B&B* (☎ 794 6440, fax 794 6520, Greenbank House, Greenbank Lane) over Easter, mid-April to mid-May and mid-June to mid-September from £15.50.

B&Bs & Hotels – Mid-Range There's a handy group of hotels on Mount Pleasant, between the city centre and the Metropolitan Cathedral.

The cheapest option is the *Belvedere* (☎ 709 2356, 83 Mount Pleasant), with beds from £18.50.

Feathers Hotel (☎ 709 9655, fax 709 3838, ℮ feathershotel@feathers.uk.com, 117–125 Mount Pleasant) is a good mid-range hotel. The 75 rooms boast a variety of facilities. Singles/doubles (some very small) start at £29/44.

The award-winning *Aachen Hotel* (☎ 709 3477, fax 709 1126, 89 Mount Pleasant) has well-equipped rooms, most with showers, for £34/40.

Handy to both Lime Street station and the coach station is *Lord Nelson Hotel (☎ 709 4362, fax 707 1321, Hotham St)*, on the corner of Lord Nelson St. Rooms cost £23/38 without bathroom.

Close to Albert Dock, the modern *Campanile Hotel (☎ 709 8104, fax 709 8725, Chaloner St)* offers flat-rate rooms for £39.50.

Hotels – Top End When it was completed in 1912, the 391-room *Britannia Adelphi Hotel (☎ 709 7200, fax 708 0743, Ranelagh Place)* was considered one of the world's most luxurious hotels. Some readers have commented on poor service but it's in a wonderfully central location and charges £45/60.

The five-star *Tower Thistle (☎ 227 4444, fax 236 3973, Chapel St)* is virtually beside the Royal Liver Building and is a modern multistorey hotel with good views over the River Mersey. Rooms are from £80/90, but there are good-value weekend breaks.

Places to Eat

The area around Slater St and Bold St is worth trying with a reasonable choice of places to eat. Liverpool's Chinatown has declined since its glory days, but there are still several Chinese restaurants around Berry St and it does have the largest Chinese gate in Europe.

Restaurants Underneath the Everyman Theatre, *Everyman Bistro (☎ 708 9545, 5 Hope St)* is highly recommended as a place to tuck into cheap, good food (pizza slices for less than £2 and delicious desserts).

Also on Hope St, *El Macho (☎ 708 6644, 23 Hope St)* has a cheerful atmosphere and enormous servings of spicy Mexican food. Most main dishes are around £9, but the lunch menu is cheaper, for example nachos are £3.

Becker's Brook (☎ 707 0005, 29A Hope St), a few doors south, does classy new British cuisine and is one of the better restaurants in town.

One of the most popular restaurants in Chinatown is *Far East (☎ 709 3141, 27 Berry St)*, above a Chinese supermarket. Set menus start at £15.50, but you could eat for less – there are plenty of dishes for around £8 and on Tuesday and Thursday you can stuff yourself on 11 courses for £12.50.

Casa Bella (☎ 258 1800, 25 Victoria St) is a good, cheap Italian serving pizza and pasta from £6.30.

Albert Dock is also a good place to look for something to eat. *Est Est Est (☎ 708 6969, Edward Pavilion)* is modern, trendy and serves up pizza and pasta for around £6.

Close by, enjoy the comfortable couches and views of the dock at *Blue Bar & Grill (☎ 709 7097, 17 Edward Pavilion)*. Main courses are around £8.

Cafes At the eastern end of Bold St, *Cafe Tabac (☎ 709 3735, 126 Bold St)* is a relaxed cafe that attracts a young crowd; roasts on Sunday cost around £4.25.

Hub Cafe (☎ 707 9495, 9–13 Berry St) is a groovy brick place worthy of chilling out in for the afternoon.

The *refectory (☎ 707 1722, St James Mount)*, at the Anglican Cathedral, serves great value hot lunches for around £4. There are also excellent cafes in the Walker Art Gallery and the Conservation Centre.

Entertainment

To find out what's on where, look out for the free monthly entertainment guide *In Touch*.

Pubs & Clubs Liverpool has a thriving, and changeable, nightlife. Wander around Mathew St and south-east to Bold, Seel and Slater Sts and you'll stumble upon an amazing array of clubs and pubs catering for every imaginable taste.

Blue Angel (☎ 428 1213, 108 Seel St) is a popular haunt with the local student population.

For a bit of indie rock try the *Flying Picket (☎ 708 5318, 24 Hardman St)*. The *Baa Bar (☎ 707 0610, 43 Fleet St)* pulls in the punters with some beers at £1 a bottle.

For all things vodka head to *Revolution (☎ 707 2727, Wood St)*, a bit of a specialist in the area, which plays tunes by the likes of New Order.

RSVP (☎ *707 6470, Wood St*) is a cavernous place on concert square with good outside seating on sunny summer days.

On the corner of Hope and Hardman Sts, the ***Philharmonic Dining Room*** (☎ *709 1163, 36 Hope St*), built in 1900, is one of England's most extraordinary pubs. The interior is resplendent with etched glass, stained glass, wrought iron, mosaics and ceramic tiling – and if you think that's good, just wait until you see inside the toilets.

A little more ordinary but still wonderful is ***The Baltic Fleet*** (☎ *709 3116, 33 Wapping*), next to the YHA Hostel, which pours a superb traditional ale.

Ye Cracke (☎ *709 4171, 13 Rice St*) has long been favoured by students from the nearby College of Art. John Lennon and Cynthia Powell were regular customers.

Best known of the clubs is ***Cream*** (☎ *709 1693, 40 Slater St*), off Parr St, which rings the changes between jazz, samba and techno. Another club worth checking out is the colourful ***Krazy House*** (☎ *708 5016, 16 Wood St*) for 'shaking that booty'.

The Escape (☎ *708 8909, Fifth Ave, Paradise St*) is a popular gay hang-out.

Theatre & Classical Music The *Everyman Theatre* (☎ *709 4776, Hope St*) is one of England's most famous repertory theatres and has featured the works of local playwright Alan Bleasdale, among others.

The ***Liverpool Playhouse*** (☎ *709 8363, Williamson Square*), or ***The Empire*** (☎ *709 1555, Lime St*) could be staging anything from straight plays to musicals.

Bluecoat Arts Centre (☎ *709 5279, School Lane*) and ***Unity Theatre*** (☎ *709 4988, Hope Place*) host innovative, small-scale companies.

The Royal Liverpool Philharmonic Orchestra plays in the ***Philharmonic Hall*** (☎ *709 3789, Hope St*).

Spectator Sports

Everton Fans of Everton Football Club will want to head out to Goodison Park to tour the club grounds and find out more about its history. Tours take place at 11 am and 2 pm Monday, Wednesday, Friday and Sunday except on match days, but you must book in advance (☎ 330 2266). They cost £5/3.30 per person. Tickets to games are hard to come by, and the best bet is probably to turn up on the day and try your luck.

Liverpool Fans of Liverpool FC should make for Anfield Rd where a similar experience is available (☎ 260 6677). To visit the museum and take a tour costs £8.50/5.50; to visit the museum only costs £5/3. It's also a similar experience trying to get hold of tickets to Liverpool home games as it is for Everton games.

Getting There & Away

See the fares tables in the Getting Around chapter. Liverpool is 210 miles (338km) north-east of London, 100 miles (161km) from Birmingham, 75 miles (121km) from Leeds and 35 miles (56km) south-west of Manchester.

Air Liverpool airport (☎ 288 4000), 8 miles (13km) to the south of the city centre, has flights to Belfast, Dublin, the Isle of Man and a number of destinations in Continental Europe. The no-frills airlines easyJet and Ryanair fly here. Bus No 80A/180 departs the Paradise Street station every 20 minutes.

Bus National Express services (☎ 0870 580 8080) link Liverpool to most major towns. To get to the town centre from the coach station, turn right up Seymour St and then right again along London Rd. To get to Chester catch bus No X8 from Queen Square in the city centre.

Train Numerous services run to Lime Street station. A train to Wigan costs £3.55 (50 minutes), Chester £3 (40 minutes), Manchester £6.95 (one hour) and London £44 (three hours).

Boat The Isle of Man Steam Packet Company (☎ 0870 552 3523) operates a service between Douglas and Liverpool (Pier Head) every weekend throughout the year and more frequently during summer. The journey time is 4½ hours by ferry or 2½ hours by catamaran. Foot-passenger fares start at £25 single, but are cheaper at off-peak times. Bicycles are transported free, but a car will cost from £72 each way.

Getting Around

Local public transport is coordinated by Merseytravel (☎ 236 7676). Various zonal tickets are also sold at post offices; an all-zone all-day ticket for bus, train and ferry (except cruises) costs £4.30. The four Merseyrail train stations are connected by an underground service.

Bus Most local buses leave from Queen Square to the east of St George's Hall. Smart Bus Nos 1 and 5 link Albert Dock with the city centre and the university every 20 minutes.

Taxi Mersey Cabs (☎ 298 2222) operates tourist taxi services and has some cabs adapted for disabled visitors.

Ferry The famous ferry across the River Mersey (£1.05/80p), started 800 years ago by Benedictine monks but immortalised by Gerry and the Pacemakers, still offers one of the best views of Liverpool. Boats for Woodside and Seacombe depart from Pier Head Ferry Terminal, next to the Liver Building to the north of Albert Dock. Special one-hour commentary cruises run year-round departing hourly from 10 am to 3 pm on weekdays and until 6 pm at the weekend (£3.50/1.80). Phone ☎ 639 0609 for more information.

AROUND LIVERPOOL
Port Sunlight

South-east of Liverpool, across the River Mersey on the Wirral peninsula, is Port Sunlight, a picturesque 19th-century village created by the philanthropic Lever family to house its soap-factory workers. It's a surprise to find such a peaceful place surrounded by the hustle and bustle of the Merseyside area. The main reason to come here is the wonderful **Lady Lever Art Gallery** (☎ 478 4136) where you can see some of the greatest works of the Pre-Raphaelite Brotherhood, as well as some fine Wedgwood pottery. It opens 10 am to 5 pm Monday to Saturday and from noon on Sunday. Admission costs £3/1.50.

Also in the village is the **Heritage Centre** (☎ 644 6466), 95 Greendale Rd, which tells the story of the creation of Port Sunlight. It opens 10 am to 4 pm daily, 11 am at the weekend in winter. Admission costs 60/30p.

If you need to stay, *The Bridge Inn (☎ 645 8441, Bolton Rd)* has nice, bright rooms from £28.50 per person. Pub food is available at the bar.

Trains run from Lime Street station to Port Sunlight (£1.45, 20 minutes, every 15 minutes).

Speke Hall & 20 Forthlin Rd

Six miles (10km) south of Liverpool is Speke Hall (☎ 427 7231; NT), a marvellous black-and-white half-timbered hall, with several priest's holes where Roman Catholic priests could hide in the years of the 16th century when they were forbidden to hold masses. The hall opens 1 to 5.30 pm daily except Monday, April to October; and 1 to 4.30 pm over winter weekends. Admission costs £4.20/2.10.

Bus No 80/82 from Lime Street station will drop you within a mile of Speke Hall. Visitors to Speke Hall can also go by minibus to 20 Forthlin Rd, Liverpool, once home to Beatle Paul McCartney. It's been restored to its 1950s appearance, although there's little directly linked to the great Macca. Tours leave Speke Hall at 3.10 and 4 pm, Wednesday to Saturday, Easter to October. A combined ticket with Speke Hall costs £5.10/2.60. It's advisable to pre-book; phone ☎ 486 4006. Tours also run from outside The Beatles Story at Albert Dock.

St Helens World of Glass

Ten miles (16km) north-east of Liverpool is the World of Glass (☎ 0870 744 4777), Chalon Way East, near the centre of St Helens. The centre delves into the history of glass and the development of glassmaking, in particular St Helens connection to Victorian glassmaking. And if you haven't seen glass being blown, there are live demonstrations. The World of Glass opens 10 am to 5 pm daily and costs £5/3.60.

The centre is close to St Helens train station, which has good connections to Liverpool (£2.30, 20 minutes, every 15 minutes) and Wigan (£2.35, 20 minutes, every 20 minutes).

Isle of Man

☎ 01624 • pop 70,000

Ask an English person about the Isle of Man and more often than not the answer will be 'weird place, full of inbreeds!' And yet the majority of mainlanders have never set foot on the Isle. It's a pity because the Isle of Man has much to offer. Lush valleys, barren hills and rugged coastlines make for great walks, cycle trails and drives and the Isle's rich history is well told in castles and museums.

But it has to be said, the Isle of Man is a quirky world of its own. The number one industry is tax avoidance – wealthy Brits can shelter their loot here without having to move to Monte Carlo or the Cayman Islands. And the Isle of Man is a motorcyclist's mecca; each year's May to June TT (Tourist Trophy) races add 45,000 to the island's small population. Petrol-heads are likely to start their island circuit with motorcycling's Mountain Circuit. At 50 mph some of the long sweeping bends are a delight; at 150 mph they must be terrifying.

Home to the world's oldest continuous parliament, the Isle of Man enjoys special status in Britain, and its annual parliamentary ceremony honours the 1000-year history of the Tynwald (a Scandinavian word meaning 'meeting field'). The Isle of Man also boasts some unique fauna, including the tail-less Manx cat and the four-horned loghtan sheep. Unfortunately Douglas, the capital, is a run-down relic of Victorian tourism with fading B&Bs.

ORIENTATION

Situated in the Irish Sea, equidistant from Liverpool, Dublin and Belfast, the Isle of Man is about 30 miles (48km) long by 10 miles (16km) wide. Ferries arrive at Douglas, the port and main town on the south-east coast. Flights come in to Ronaldsway airport, 10 miles south of Douglas.

INFORMATION

Most of the island's historic sites are operated by Manx National Heritage, which offers free entrance to NT or EH members. Unless otherwise indicated, Manx Heritage (MH) sites open 10 am to 5 pm daily, Easter to October. The phone number for all inquiries is ☎ 648000.

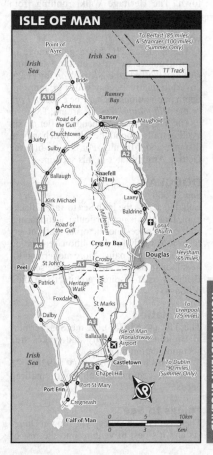

ISLE OF MAN

WALKING & CYCLING

The best way to appreciate the Isle of Man is either on foot or by bicycle. A number of well marked paths criss-cross the Isle and the particularly popular 90-mile (145km) Raad ny Foillan, or Road of the Gull, is a coastal walking path that makes a complete circuit of the island. The Millennium Way, named after the Millennium year of Tynwald, the Parliament of the Island, traverses the island north-east to south-west, following the route of a medieval highway. The path's length is about 28 miles (45km), starting at Ramsey and finishing in Castletown. The Heritage Walk, running from Douglas to Peel, follows a disused railway line for 10 miles (16km) and is a nice flat walk.

The Douglas TIC has a good range of helpful guides to walks on the Isle, from *Holiday Walks in the Isle of Man* for £1.95, covering relatively easy walks to, more in-depth publications such as the *Coastal Path* or the *Millennium Way* for around £8.

The TIC produces a handy leaflet on six cycling trails around the Isle, which vary in distance and difficulty. For bicycle hire see Getting Around later in this section.

DOUGLAS

pop 20,000

Looking across the Irish Sea towards Blackpool, Douglas is not particularly endearing. Half of the once-fine Victorian seafront terraces look ready for demolition, renovation or a good coat of paint. More modern buildings look to have been designed by some of Britain's least inspired architects on their off days.

Information

The TIC (☎ 686766), in the Sea Terminal Building, opens daily and makes free accommodation bookings.

Feegan's Internet Lounge (☎ 679280), 22 Duke St, can handle all your emailing needs.

Things to See

There isn't much to keep you long in Douglas and it's best to venture into the rest of the island. However, call at the **Manx Museum** (☎ 648000; MH) before you leave. It gives a good introduction to everything from the island's prehistoric past to the latest TT race winners. It opens 10 am to 5 pm Monday to Saturday. Admission is free.

Places to Stay

The TIC's camp sites information sheet lists sites all around the island. Everything is booked out for TT week and the weeks each side of it, often years ahead.

The seafront promenade is shoulder-to-shoulder with B&Bs where you should find something for around £20 a head.

In the first section of the seafront promenade is the ***Curnard Hotel*** *(☎/fax 676728, 28–29 Loch Promenade)*, with simple but adequate rooms.

Marginally more expensive is the ***Modwena Hotel*** *(☎ 675728, 39–40 Loch Promenade),* a few doors down along the promenade.

Sefton Hotel *(☎ 645500, Harris Promenade)* is more upmarket, with comfortable rooms at £35 per person.

Castle Mona Hotel *(☎ 624540, Central Promenade)* is also good quality with rooms starting at £33 per person.

Places to Eat

Even the big fast food outlets skip round Douglas, leaving a choice of fish and chip shops, Chinese takeaways and a handful of restaurants.

The ***New Dynasty Chinese Restaurant*** *(☎ 613061, 1 Empress Terrace)*, down by the promenade, is popular on a Monday night with a buffet for £11.50. Otherwise, main courses are around £7.

Scott's Bistro *(☎ 623764, John St)* is pleasant and moderately priced with Manx trout for £9.95. Set in a lovely stone building overlooking the quay, ***Blazer's*** *(☎ 673222)*, on the corner of North Quay and Bridge St, is a wine bar with pub-style food.

Underneath Blazer's is the ***Waterfront*** *(☎ 673222, North Quay)*, a quality restaurant but one of the more pricey places in town.

L'Expérience *(☎ 623103, Summerhill)*, at the bottom of Summerhill, is a smart

French restaurant that serves *queenies* (local scallops).

There are a few good pubs around, including the popular local hang-out *Tramshunter* on the seafront promenade.

The originally named *Rovers Return (☎ 676459, 11 Church St)* specialises in the locally brewed Bushy Ales and is a relatively lively place.

The Outback, decked out as an Australian outback pub, hosts live jazz every Wednesday night. Those Australians do get everywhere!

CASTLETOWN TO PORT ERIN

Inviting beaches and protected harbours break up the windswept coast of the southern end of the Isle of Man, and a scattering of small town's dot its rolling hills.

Things to See

At the southern end of the island is Castletown, a quite harbour town, Isle of Man's original capital. The town is dominated by the impressive 13th-century **Castle Rushen** (MH), the last to surrender during the English Civil War (probably because it was the hardest to get to). It's quite a maze of well refurbished rooms, giving you a good idea of how life passed within its walls. A five-minute film also helps to explain the history of the castle. The flagtower affords fine views of the town and coast. Admission costs £4/2.

There's also a small **Nautical Museum** (MH) displaying, among other things, its pride and joy *Peggy*, a boat built in 1791 and still housed in its original boathouse. Admission costs £2.50/1.50.

A school dating back to 1570 in **St Mary's church** (MH) is located behind the castle. Admission is free.

On the southern tip of the island, the **Cregneash Village Folk Museum** (MH) recalls traditional Manx rural life. Admission is £2.75/1.50.

The **Calf of Man**, the small island just off Cregneash, is a bird sanctuary. Calf Island Cruises (☎ 832339) visits regularly during the summer for £10/5 from Port Erin.

Between Castletown and Cregneash, the Iron-Age hillfort at **Chapel Hill** encloses a Viking ship burial site.

Port Erin, the island's southern Victorian seaside resort, plays host to the small **Railway Museum** depicting the history of steam railway on the island. Admission costs £1/50p.

Places to Stay & Eat

Port Erin has a good range of accommodation, as does Port St Mary.

On the Promenade in Port St Mary, *Aaron House (☎ 835702, ⓔ aaron_house_iom@ yahoo.com)* is a splendid Victorian-style B&B with sea views. Rooms are £25 per person.

Two minutes' walk west from the train station on the waterfront in Port Erin is the *Falcon's Nest Hotel (☎ 834077, fax 835931, Station Rd)*, with adequate accommodation starting at £25 per person.

Balmoral Hotel (☎ 833126, fax 835343, ⓔ balmoralpe@adusys.co.uk, Promenade), with similar accommodation from £25 per person, is literally around the corner.

Port Erin also makes a good stop for a bite to eat. North of the town centre is the *Bradda Glen Cafe Bar (☎ 833166, Bradda Glen)*, offering up fine food and great views of the harbour. Walk off their meal by taking the Coronation footpath to Bradda Head from here, a short distance north along the coast.

In the train station, the *Whistle Stop Coffee Shop (☎ 833802)* offers filling sandwiches (around £2) and lovely home-made cakes.

PEEL

Peel, the largest settlement on the west coast, is a pretty harbour town with a couple of good attractions.

Dating from the 11th century, **Peel Castle** (MH), with its long curtain wall, is stunningly positioned atop St Patrick's Island, joined to Peel by a causeway. Admission costs £3/1.50.

The excellent **House of Manannan** (MH) museum uses interactive displays to explain Manx history and its seafaring traditions.

Admission costs £5/2.50. A combined ticket for both is £7/3.50.

Just before Peel is the **Tynwald Hill** at St John's where the annual parliamentary ceremony takes place on 5 July.

Places to Stay & Eat

Peel has several B&Bs on Marine Parade including the *Fernleigh Hotel (☎ 842435)*, where rooms start at £17 per person.

Opposite the House of Manannan is the *Creek Inn (☎ 842216, fax 843359, East Quay)* offering self-catering rooms from £30. It's also popular for food, serving Manx queenies for £6.95.

Karl's Bistro, *(☎ 844144, East Quay)* next to the Creek Inn, has a nice spot close to the marina and serves the likes of mixed grill for £10.90.

RAMSEY TO DOUGLAS

You can follow the TT course up and over the mountain, or wind around the coast. The mountain route takes you close to the summit of **Snaefell** (621m/2036 feet), the island's highest point. It's an easy walk up to the summit, or you can take the electric tram from Laxey on the coast. The tram stops by the road where **Murray's Motorcycle Museum** displays motorcycles and TT memorabilia.

On the edge of Ramsey is the **Grove Rural Life Museum** (MH) showing life in Victorian times. Admission costs £2.75/1.50.

At the small and isolated village of **Maughold**, the village church is on the site of an ancient monastery; a small shelter houses quite a good selection of stone crosses and ancient inscriptions. Bus No 16 runs from Ramsey to Maughold.

Describing the **Laxey Wheel** (MH) – built in 1854 to pump water from a mine – as a 'great' wheel is hardly an exaggeration; it measures 22m across and can draw 1138L of water per minute from a depth of 540m and is supposedly the largest waterwheel in the world. Admission costs £2.75/1.50.

The wheel-headed cross at **Lonan Old Church** is the island's most impressive early Christian cross.

Places to Stay & Eat

Overlooking Ramsey Bay is the Georgian *Grand Island Hotel (☎ 812445, fax 815291, Bride Rd)*. All rooms have bathrooms and they cost from £42.50 for a single.

The *Narrow Gate Guest House (☎ 861 966, fax 661229, Old Laxey Hill)*, in Old Laxey, is two minutes from the beach and charges £18 per person.

In Ramsey, the *Harbour Bistro* occupies a nice spot overlooking the harbour and serves produce from the sea.

By the station at Laxey is the Mines Tavern with outside seating and food available.

GETTING THERE & AWAY
Air

Manx Airlines (☎ 0845 725 6256) has frequent connections with much of Britain and Ireland, as does Jersey European (☎ 0870 567 6676). There are other smaller operators. Typically, you're looking at around £140 return for a weekend London connection, but it can be as low as £59 from Liverpool.

Boat

The Isle of Man Steam Packet (☎ 0870 552 3523) operates regular car ferries and high-speed SeaCat catamarans to Douglas from Dublin, Belfast, Heysham, Fleetwood, Liverpool and Ardrossan. Foot-passenger fares start at £25 single, but you'll have to pay from £72 to take a car across. At times, though, it can be cheaper to fly and hire a car on arrival. The crossing from Liverpool takes 2½ hours by SeaCat or four hours by ferry. From time to time you can get special fares, so it's worth calling ahead or checking out its Web site at www.steam-packet.com. There are luggage lockers at the terminals.

GETTING AROUND
To/From the Airport

A taxi from the airport into Douglas will cost about £15 compared with £1.50 by bus. Bus Nos 1 and 2 run from Port St Mary to Douglas via the airport.

Bus

The Isle has a comprehensive bus service with frequent buses linking all the major towns; the TIC in Douglas has timetables and fares, or you can phone ☎ 662525 for information.

Train

Several interesting rail services (☎ 663366) operate Easter to September. These include the Douglas–Laxey–Ramsey electric tramway; a steam train operating Douglas–Castletown–Port Erin; the Snaefell Mountain Railway; and the narrow-gauge Groudle Glen Railway. A ticket covering rides on all of these trains for three days in seven costs £19.90.

Car

There are several car-rental operators at the airport and in Douglas, charging from £26 upwards for a day's rental.

Bicycle

In Douglas, bicycles can be hired at Euro-cycles (☎ 624909), 8a Victoria Rd. The charge is £10 for the first day, £9 per day for three-day hire and £8 per day for five-day hire. Bicycles can also be hired at Pedal Power Cycles (☎ 842472), 19 Michael St, Peel, and Ramsey Cycles (☎ 814076), Bowring Rd, Ramsey.

Lancashire

Lancashire is bordered by the River Mersey to the south, the sea to the west, the Pennines to the east and the Lake District to the north. Manchester and Liverpool, the region's great port, are administered separately.

Business and commerce have gravitated towards the industrial towns of Preston (a major transport interchange), Blackburn, Accrington and Burnley in southern Lancashire, once famous for its coal and cotton industries. Unfortunately there's not much to draw you here, unless to use them as a base for exploring the rest of the county.

Of the traditional seaside resorts serving Manchester and Liverpool, Blackpool lives splendidly, if tackily, on, but Morecambe is in sad decline, worth transiting only to see

the Art Deco Midland Hotel crumbling away on the seafront. To the east of the county, the Forest of Bowland is not actually a forest but moorland and the most beautiful area in Lancashire.

LANCASTER

☎ 01524 • pop 46,300

The historic city of Lancaster is certainly worth a visit, with its good combination of old and new. Standing on the banks of the River Lune, it dates back to Roman times but possesses a wealth of fine Georgian architecture.

Information

Tourist Office Lancaster's TIC (☎ 32878, fax 382849, e tourism@lancaster.gov.uk), 28 Castle Hill, stocks a comprehensive free guide to Lancaster and Morecambe. There's also a toilet for the disabled on the premises. It opens 10 am to 5 pm daily (to 6 pm in July) and books accommodation.

Post The main post office, at 85 Market St, opens 9 am to 5.30 pm Monday to Friday and 9 am to 12.30 pm Saturday.

Email & Internet Access Internet access is available in the City Library on Market Square.

Internet Resources The Web site at www.lancaster.gov.uk has listings on what's on, what to see and accommodation in Lancaster and the surrounding area.

Lancaster Castle & Priory

Lancaster's imposing castle (☎ 64998), part of which is still a prison, was originally built in the 11th century, although what you see now is much newer. Regular tours take in the courtroom and Hadrian's Tower with its display of instruments of torture and the dungeons. One famous trial that took place here was of the so-called Pendle Witches in 1612 (see Clitheroe & Around later in this chapter). It opens 10 am to 5 pm daily, mid-March to mid-December. A full tour costs £4/2.50, less at times when court sittings curtail tours.

Immediately beside the castle is the equally fine **priory church** (☎ 65338), founded in 1094 but extensively remodelled in the Middle Ages. It opens 9.30 am to 5 pm. Admission is free.

Other Things to See

The **Maritime Museum** (☎ 64637), in the 18th-century Custom House on St Georges Quay, recalls the days when Lancaster was a flourishing port at the centre of the slave trade. It opens 11 am to 5 pm daily (12.30 to 4 pm November to Easter). Admission costs £2/1.

The **City Museum** (☎ 64637), Market Square, has a mixed bag of local historical and archaeological exhibits. It opens 10 am to 5 pm Monday to Saturday. Admission is free.

The **Judges' Lodgings** (☎ 32808), off China St, is a 17th-century townhouse containing a Museum of Childhood and some fine furnishings. Admission costs £2/1.

The **Cottage Museum** (☎ 64637), 15 Castle Hill, has been furnished to show life in an artisan's house in the early 19th century and opens 2 to 5 pm daily, April to September. Admission costs 75/25p.

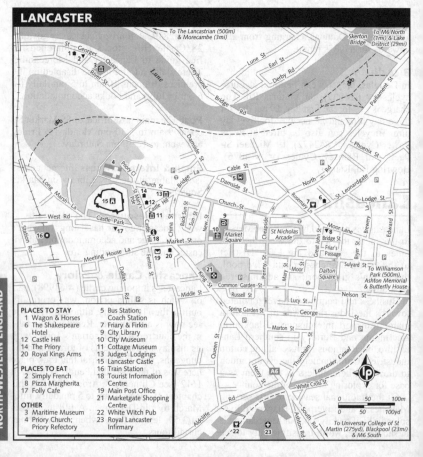

LANCASTER

PLACES TO STAY	5	Bus Station;
1 Wagon & Horses		Coach Station
6 The Shakespeare	7	Friary & Firkin
Hotel	9	City Library
12 Castle Hill	10	City Museum
14 The Priory	11	Cottage Museum
20 Royal Kings Arms	13	Judges' Lodgings
	15	Lancaster Castle
PLACES TO EAT	16	Train Station
2 Simply French	18	Tourist Information
8 Pizza Margherita		Centre
17 Folly Cafe	19	Main Post Office
	21	Marketgate Shopping
OTHER		Centre
3 Maritime Museum	22	White Witch Pub
4 Priory Church;	23	Royal Lancaster
Priory Refectory		Infirmary

For a superb view of Lancaster and the Morecambe Bay area, head for **William-son Park** (☎ 33318), east of the city centre. Here you'll find **Ashton Memorial**, built by Lord Ashton as a tribute to his late wife, and an Edwardian Palm house which now serves as a **Butterfly House**. Memorial and butterfly house both open 10 am to 5 pm daily, April to September; and 11 am to 4 pm, October to February. Admission to both costs £3.25/1.50. The park itself has the same opening hours.

Places to Stay
Lancaster lacks a youth hostel but over Easter and in summer 400 beds are available for B&B at £18.80 a head at the *University College of St Martin* (☎ 384460, fax 384459, e s.fisher@ucsm.ac.uk) accommodation block in Bowerham Rd, less than a mile south of the city centre.

A good choice for a bed is at *The Shakespeare Hotel* (☎ 841041, 96 St Leonardgate), offering B&B from £22.50 per person.

St Mary's Parade on Castle Hill has two good B&Bs in close proximity to the TIC, castle and priory. *Castle Hill* (☎ 849137, 27 St Mary's Parade) is a lovely refurbished Victorian town house charging £25/40 for a single/double. *The Priory* (☎ 845711, 15 St Mary's Parade) is equally beautiful and charges slightly more.

Near the Maritime Museum, the *Wagon & Horses* (☎ 846094, 27 St Georges Quay) is a relaxed pub offering rooms with river views for £25/43.

For something more luxurious, stay at the *Royal Kings Arms* (☎ 32451, 0870 600 3013, fax 841698, e info@menzies -hotels.co.uk, Market St), right in the heart of Lancaster, with rooms for £65/85.

Places to Eat
Pizza Margherita (☎ 36333, 2 Moor Lane) is a relaxed place with great pizzas at a reasonable price – Calzone Mexicana for £5.95.

Next to the Maritime Museum, *Simply French* (☎ 843199, 27A St Georges Quay) serves jugs of Sangria for £5.95 to liven up the place and a filling two-course lunch for £5.

Folly Cafe (☎ 388540, 27 Castle Park), close to the castle, serves dishes such as Morecambe Bay potted shrimps for £4.95 in a building that doubles as a small art gallery.

From Easter to October, teas and lunches are available in the *Priory Refectory* (☎ 65338) in the Priory.

Entertainment
A reasonable student population makes Lancaster a relatively lively place during term.

White Witch Pub (Aldcliffe Rd) has a good spot on the canal for sunny days and cheap pints.

Situated in a renovated church, the *Friary & Firkin* (St Leonardgate) has enough room to accommodate the regular hordes and puts on the occasional live music.

The Lancastrian (Scale Hall Farm, Morecambe Rd), a 15-minute walk from Lancaster on the road to Morecambe, creates a fine atmosphere with great ale and great food.

Getting There & Away
Lancaster is on the main west-coast railway line and on the Cumbrian Coast Line. A train to Kendal costs £5.40 (30 minutes), to Windermere £7.45 (one hour) and £17 (3½ hours) to Carlisle. There are also National Express links with most local towns.

Getting Around
Lancaster is easily accessible on foot. If you need a cab call Lancaster City Cabs (☎ 35666).

THE RIBBLE VALLEY
Hemmed in by Lancaster and Blackpool to the west and urban masses of Preston and Blackpool to the south, the Ribble Valley is the most attractive part of Lancashire. It's basically two areas – the sparsely populated moorland of Forest of Bowland to the north, great for walks, and the River Ribble to the south, with its rolling hills, larger towns and ruins.

NORTH-WESTERN ENGLAND

The Ribble Way, a 70-mile (113km) footpath that follows the River Ribble from its source to the estuary, is one of the more popular walks in the area and passes through Clitheroe.

Clitheroe & Around
☎ 01200

Situated on the banks of the River Ribble, Clitheroe has been a market town since the late 11th century and still holds regular markets on Tuesday, Thursday and Saturday. Its size and location make it a good base for walks in the Ribble Valley. There's a helpful TIC (☎ 425566, fax 426339) at 14 Market Place, open 9 am to 5 pm Monday to Saturday.

Clitheroe's only attractions are the empty 12th-century **Norman Keep**, offering fine views of the township and river, and the **Castle Museum** (☎ 424635). The museum covers local history, archaeology and geology. It opens 11 am to 5 pm daily, May to September, and 11 am to 4.30 pm Saturday to Wednesday, March, April and October to December. Admission costs £1.50/25p. The Keep opens dawn until dusk every day.

A few miles east of Clitheroe is **Pendle Hill**, a target for walkers and, at 557m, has great views of the surrounding area. It's both famous and infamous; in 1652 George Fox had a vision here, which led him to form the Quaker religion. Forty years earlier 10 women were tried and hanged in Lancaster for the alleged practice of witchcraft on the hill. Every Halloween people gather at the summit to sustain the legend of the Pendle Witches.

Pendle Hill Circular Walk

This 9-mile (14.5km) walk takes five to six hours. The trail to Pendle Hill (557m) leaves from Clitheroe and passes through farmland before reaching the summit. The panoramic view from the top takes in Bowland, the Ribble Valley and the Yorkshire Dales. The trail descends and ends in Clitheroe. Clitheroe tourist information centre has detailed information.

West along the river in Ribchester is the **Roman Museum** (☎ 01254-878261), on the site of Roman Fort established in AD 78. Part of the fort has been excavated and there are a number of Roman artefacts on display. It opens 9 am to 5 pm Monday to Friday, and noon to 5 pm at the weekend. Admission costs £1.50/75p.

South of Clitheroe are the picturesque ruins of the 14th-century **Cistercian Abbey** (☎ 01254-822268) and small tea room at Whalley, open 11 am to 5 pm daily. Northeast of Clitheroe is **Sawley Abbey**, but there's not much left to look at.

There is plenty of accommodation in busy Clitheroe, but quiet spots away from the town along the valley can also be found.

In the heart of Clitheroe is the 17th-century *White Lion Hotel* (☎ 426955, 11 Market Place), right opposite the TIC, with rooms starting at £17.50. For a traditional B&B, try the comfortable *Brooklyn Guest House* (☎ 428268, 32 Pimlico Rd), with singles/doubles from £25/40.

In Ribchester, near the Roman museum, the *White Bull* (☎ 01254-878303, Church St) offers comfortable rooms for £25/30.

There are a number of pubs and tea rooms on the main road in Clitheroe serving reasonable food, but for something a bit more upmarket the *Auctioneer Restaurant* (☎ 27153, Eastham House, New Market St), next to the market square, is a treat. South African cuisine is the speciality and a two-course lunch goes for £9.95.

The *Spread Eagle* (☎ 441202), close to the Abbey in Sawley 5 miles (8km) northeast of Clitheroe, provides a country setting and great food.

Buses regularly run from Preston and Blackburn to Clitheroe and there are hourly trains from Manchester (£5.95, 1 hour 10 minutes) and Preston (£4.10, 50 minutes).

Pedal Power (☎ 422066, Waddington Rd) has bicycles for hire.

Forest of Bowland
☎ 01200

Don't come here looking for a forest, because there isn't one. But the moorland that is to be found has been aptly designated an

Area of Outstanding Natural Beauty. It makes for good walking and cycling, including the Pendle Witch Way, a 45-mile (72km) walk from Pendle Hill to Lancaster that cuts right through the area, and the Lancashire Cycleway that runs along the eastern border. The TIC at Clitheroe (see the Clitheroe section earlier in this chapter) can provide leaflets on both, or contact the Bowland visitor centre in Preston on ☎ 01995-640557 (Beacon Fell Country Park) for more information.

For basic, cheap accommodation, camping barns are a good option. Facilities vary between barns, but generally you'd expect to find a shared sleeping area, flush toilet, shower, some type of cooking facility and a place for preparing food. To check the availability or to make a reservation for any of the barns contact the Camping Barns Reservation Office (☎ 420102, fax 420103, e campingbarnsyha@enterprise.net), 6 King St, Clitheroe. The following barns all charge £3.60 per night per person.

Chipping Barn (☎ *01995-61209*) is half a mile west of the village of Chipping and handy for the moors. Breakfast can be booked if required.

Hurst Green Barn (☎ *01254-826304*), 1½ miles (2.5km) west of Hurst Green village, has metered electricity supply and is well placed for walks in the Forest of Bowland.

At the foot of Pendle Hill is ***Downham Barn*** (☎ *441242*), strategically placed near the Pendle, Ribble and Lancashire Ways.

More luxurious accommodation is limited but there are a few villages spattered throughout the area, the largest being Slaidburn, north of Clitheroe on the B6478. Slaidburn ***youth hostel*** (☎ *446656, King's House*), in a former 17th-century village inn, opens mid-April to September. A bed costs £8.10/5.65 for adults/under-18s.

The beautiful ***Hark to Bounty Inn*** (☎ *446246, Townend*) dates back to the 13th century and offers B&B starting from £49.50. Evening meals are also available.

Newton and Dunsop Bridge are both small, attractive villages, as is Whitewell, where you'll find the ***Inn at Whitewell*** (☎ *448222, fax 448298*). It's a deservedly

Chipping Circular Walk

Starting in the pretty village of Chipping, this gentle 3-mile (5km) walk takes you through the lush farmland of the Forest of Bowland and has fine views of the Ribble Valley. It returns to the war memorial in Chipping. The Clitheroe Tourist Information Centre stocks a good leaflet on the walk.

popular place with great food, real ale, a hospitable country feel and characterful singles/doubles starting at £53/75.

Your own wheels are the best way to get around. The Bowland Pathfinder Bus only operates on Sunday and bank holidays but connects Clitheroe and Longridge via Chipping, Dunsop Bridge, Newton, Slaidburn and Waddington. A day ticket for £3/1.50 gives unlimited travel on the service. Contact the TIC in Clitheroe or the Bowland Visitor Centre in Preston for details.

Bike hire is available at Bowland Cycle Hire (☎ 446670) in Slaidburn.

BLACKPOOL
☎ 01253 • pop 147,000

King of the tacky and brazen English seaside resort is Blackpool, with over eight million visitors a year making the journey to let their hair down by the sea. Even though Blackpool is well past its use-by-date, it has to be seen to be believed, so if you're planning on visiting a seaside resort, make sure this is the one.

Blackpool is famous for its tower, its three piers, its Pleasure Beach and its **Illuminations**, a successful ploy to extend the brief summer holiday season. From early September to early November, 5 miles (8km) of the Promenade are illuminated with thousands of electric and neon lights.

Orientation
Blackpool is surprisingly spread out but can still be managed easily without a car because trams run the entire 7-mile (11km) length of the seafront Promenade.

Amusement arcades, with slot machines

and bingo games, stretch all the way along the Golden Mile from South Pier to Central and North piers. South Pier, the least impressive, is alongside Pleasure Beach and The Sandcastle, an enormous indoor pool complex. The town centre and Blackpool Tower lie between Central and North piers.

Information
The helpful TIC (☎ 478222, fax 478210, e tourism@blackpool.gov.uk), at 1 Clifton St, will make free local accommodation bookings. It opens 9 am to 5 pm Monday to Saturday, and 10 am to 3.30 pm on Sunday, Easter to October; and 9 am to 5 pm Monday to Friday, and 9 am to 4.30 pm on Saturday, November to Easter. There are branches in the Pleasure Beach (☎ 403223) and by the North pier (summer only) with the same opening times as the main TIC. For online information check out the Web site at www.blackpooltourism.com.

Blackpool Tower
Europe's second metal tower when built in 1894, Blackpool tower (☎ 622242) is the town's best-known symbol. It's over 150m high and houses a vast entertainment complex, plus a laser show and indoor circus.

The highlight is the magnificent, rococo **ballroom**, with extraordinary sculptured and gilded plasterwork, murals and chandeliers. Couples still glide across the floor to the melodramatic tones of a huge Wurlitzer organ as if time has left them behind; phone ahead for opening times.

The tower opens 10 am to 6 pm daily, Easter to late May; 10 am to 11 pm daily, late May to October; and 10 am to 6 pm at the weekend only, November to Easter. Admission costs £10/5.

Blackpool Pleasure Beach & The Sandcastle
The UK's most visited outdoor attraction, Blackpool Pleasure Beach (☎ 0870 444 5566) is a 16-hectare funfair packed with rides and shows. The most interesting of the rides are the historic wooden roller coasters, particularly the brilliant Grand National and Wild Mouse. But the most

stomach churning is the **Pepsi Max Big One**, the tallest and fastest roller coaster in Europe, and the newest of them all, **Playstation**, with an adrenaline-pumping vertical ascent/descent at 80 mph.

Admission to the park is free. Rides are divided into categories and you can buy tickets for individual categories or for a mixture of them all. An unlimited ticket to all rides costs £25. It opens 10 am until everyone leaves daily, April to early November, and at the weekend the rest of the year.

Across the road is **The Sandcastle** (☎ 343602), an indoor water complex complete with its own rides, open 10 am until at least 5 pm daily, May to October, and at the weekend the rest of the year. Admission costs £4.80, £3.70 after 2 pm.

Sea Life Centre
Close to Tower World in New Bonny St, is the state-of-the-art aquarium (☎ 622445), open 10 am to 8 pm daily. Admission costs £6.99/4.99.

Places to Stay
Reputedly Blackpool has over 2500 hotels, B&Bs and self-catering units, showing just how popular a holiday destination it is. Even with so many places to stay, it's worth booking ahead during the Illuminations. Competition is fierce so you should be able to find somewhere to stay for less than £18 per head, except at the height of summer.

The TIC produces an accommodation guide specifically for gay and lesbian holidaymakers, reflecting Blackpool's popularity as a gay and lesbian holiday destination.

Good places to start looking are Albert Rd and Hornby Rd, 300m back from the sea but close to the tower and the pubs and discos.

Boltonia Hotel (☎ 620248, fax 299064, 124/126 Albert Rd) is an agreeable B&B charging £20 per person. The *Royal Albert Hotel* (☎ 623667, 41–43 Albert Rd) has comfortable rooms for a similar price. Nearby, the pleasant *Hotel Bambi* (☎ 343756, 27 Bright St) charges £17.50 per person.

Quiet Gynn Ave, about half a mile north of North Pier, is lined with B&Bs catering for the mass of visitors.

Possibilities include the **Bramleigh Hotel** (☎ 351568, 15 Gynn Ave) charging from £18 per person. The **Haldene Private Hotel** (☎ 353763, 4 Gynn Ave) also charges around £18 per night for adequate rooms. **The Austen** (☎ 351784, 6 Gynn Ave), next door, is of similar price and quality.

At the base of the North pier, with superb sea views, is the more upmarket **Clifton Hotel** (☎ 621481) charging £35 per person at the weekend and £30 during the week.

Places to Eat

Forget gourmet meals – the Blackpool experience is all about stuffing your face with burgers, hot dogs, doughnuts and fish and chips. Most people eat at their hotels where roast and three vegetables often costs just £3 a head.

There are a few restaurants around Talbot Square (near the TIC) on Queen St, Talbot Rd and Clifton St. The most interesting possibility is the Afro-Caribbean **Lagoonda** (☎ 293837, 37 Queen St), where starters average £4, main meals £9. **Giannini** (☎ 28926, 2 Queen St) does pizza and pasta for around £4.90 to £5.90.

Entertainment

It's quite acceptable to go clubbing at 3 pm on a Friday afternoon, which sets the scene for the weekend entertainment to be had. People are out for a good time, or at least a loud time. There are plenty of clubs and pubs up and down the length of Blackpool so you won't have to search long and hard to find one or the other.

Yates's Wine Lodge (☎ 752443, Talbot Rd), in Talbot Square, is a popular drinking hole, as is its counterpart by the Central Pier.

Bar Me (Clifton St) is colourful and cavernous and, like most places, has gorillas on the door.

For somewhere to go after the pubs close,

head to **Insomnia** (☎ 292923, 30 Topping St), a popular club among the masses. **Heaven and Hell** (☎ 625118, Bank Hey St) is much of the same for late-night clubbing.

Blackpool's thriving gay scene has produced its own form of entertainment in **Funny Girls** (☎ 291144, Queen St), a pub with drag shows.

The dance club **Flamingo's** (☎ 624901, 176 Talbot St) is another creation of the healthy gay scene in Blackpool.

For information on theatre and shows check with the main TIC.

Getting There & Away

Blackpool is about 50 miles (80km) from both Liverpool and Manchester and 250 miles (402km) from London.

Bus One interesting possibility is Primrose Coaches' (☎ 0191-232 5567) daily service No 352 to/from Newcastle-upon-Tyne via Kirkby Stephen, Raby Castle, Barnard Castle and Durham (£16).

National Express has services to most major towns in Britain. The central coach station is on Talbot Rd, near the town centre.

Train To get to Blackpool you often have to change in Preston (£4.85, 30 minutes). The journey from London takes about four hours (£49.50, £25 if booked 14 days in advance).

Getting Around

To get into the swing of things, hop on and off the vintage trams that run up and down the Promenade. The buses are marginally cheaper but nothing like as much fun. A one day travel card covering trams and buses costs £4.50/4.

With more than 14,000 car-parking spaces in Blackpool you'll have no problem finding somewhere to park.

Yorkshire

Yorkshire is a region of contrasts. The tacky seaside towns of its south contrast with the charms of Whitby; the industrial lands of Sheffield and Leeds contrast with the wilds of the national parks; and the tourist mobs of York contrast with the calm of rural towns like Richmond. From the distinctive accents of the locals to its many distinctive beers, Yorkshire is a highly individual part of England.

In the 9th century the Danes made York their capital and ruled the Danelaw – all of England north and east of a line between Chester and London. Later, their Norman cousin William the Conqueror found the people of the north rebellious and difficult, and he responded with brutal thoroughness. After 500 of his knights were massacred at Durham, he burnt York and Durham and devastated the surrounding countryside. Seventeen years later, when the royal commissioners arrived to record the tax capacity of Yorkshire (for the *Domesday Book*), they recorded the simple, but frighteningly eloquent, 'waste' beside many parish names. It took the north generations to recover.

The region again prospered on the medieval wool trade, which sponsored the great cathedral at York and enormous monastic communities, the remains of which can be seen at Rievaulx and Fountains. Centuries later, Leeds, Bradford and Sheffield became powerhouses during the Industrial Revolution.

The countryside is a grand backdrop to this human drama. The Yorkshire Dales is the best known and arguably the most beautiful of England's national parks, but the North York Moors has a great variety of landscapes and includes a superb coastline.

The Danish heritage survives today, especially in the language but also, some would argue, in the independent spirit of the people. Place names ending in *thorp* (village), *kirk* (church) and *by* (town) all have a Danish origin.

Highlights

- Riding the railways of the North Yorkshire Moors
- Walking in the stunning Yorkshire Dales
- Absorbing the history of York Minster
- Munching fresh fish and chips in Whitby
- Walking the windswept coast north of Scarborough
- Sipping an ale in a cosy country pub

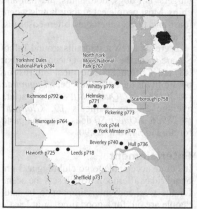

Yorkshire Dales National Park p784

North York Moors National Park p767

Whitby p778

Richmond p792

Helmsley p771

Scarborough p758

Pickering p773

Harrogate p764

York p744
York Minster p747

Beverley p740 Hull p736

Haworth p725 Leeds p718

Sheffield p731

ORIENTATION & INFORMATION

The Pennine hills are the dominant geological feature forming a north-south spine right through the Yorkshire Dales National Park. The major transport routes – the M1/A1 highways and the main London to Edinburgh railway line – basically run east of this spine.

The Yorkshire Tourist Board (☎ 01904-707961, fax 701414, ⓔ info@ytb.org.uk), 312 Tadcaster Rd, York YO24 1GS, has plenty of information. Its Web site, www .ytb.org.uk, has a good accommodation-finding feature.

WALKING

There are many great walks in this region. The most famous is the Pennine Way, which stretches 250 miles (402km) from Edale in the Peak District to Kirk Yetholm near Kelso in Scotland. It cuts a neat path right through the Western Dales. Unfortunately, its popularity means that long sections turn into unpleasant bogs, so it is worth considering other alternatives.

For example, it's possible to walk sections of the difficult 190-mile (306km) Coast to Coast Walk, which crosses eastward from the Lake District, through the Yorkshire Dales and North York Moors.

The Yorkshire Dales and the North York Moors also have numerous walks. See the Activities chapter for information on the beautiful Cleveland Way and the often overlooked Wolds Way. In the Dales, consider the relatively easy, but still interesting, Dales Way, which runs for 81 miles (130km) from Ilkley to Windermere in the Lake District, linking two national parks.

CYCLING
Cycling is a great way to see this part of England; the only disadvantages are the weather, the hills and the fact that, at the weekends, even some of the minor B-roads can be very crowded. On the whole, though, all you need is a good map and some imagination, and you'll have a great time.

The Dales Way (see Yorkshire Dales National Park later in the chapter) is worth considering for cycling as well as walking. It mostly follows the rivers but there are still some steep climbs.

Along the rugged coast between Whitby and Scarborough is a disused railway line that now serves as a bicycle path.

GETTING THERE & AROUND
Bus
Bus transport around the region can be difficult, particularly around the national parks. Fortunately, the national travel information service (☎ 0870 608 2608) now covers all of Yorkshire (and includes trains). National Express (☎ 0870 580 8080) has services to most English cities.

There are a myriad of one-day rover tickets available from the various bus operators in the region. But note that many are only worthwhile if you plan on spending all day on the bus (if this sounds like a good idea, the money might be better spent on mental therapy). It's always worth asking the driver what the best ticketing option is for your intended journey.

Train
The main-line routes from London run north to Edinburgh via York and west to Carlisle through the Dales. Travelling to/from the south, it may be necessary to make connections at Leeds. Scarborough and Hull are well served by trains as are many of the smaller towns such as Beverley and Harrogate. The famous Leeds–Settle–Carlisle Line cuts a scenic swathe north-west through the Yorkshire Dales.

Phone the national enquiry line (☎ 0845 748 4950) for all train inquiries, or see the Web sites at www.railtrack.co.uk and www.thetrainline.com.

Boat
P&O North Sea Ferries (☎ 0148-237 7177) runs nightly ferries from Hull to Rotterdam in the Netherlands and Zeebrugge in Belgium. The journeys take about 13 hours. See the Web site at www.ponsf.com for details.

West Yorkshire

For hundreds of years the prosperity of West Yorkshire depended on wool and cloth manufacturing. The industry flourished through the Middle Ages and was given an added boost by the advent of improved machinery during the Industrial Revolution. A cottage industry that traditionally employed women spinning downstairs while their men wove away upstairs quickly gave way to factories.

By the beginning of the 20th century West Yorkshire, and particularly Leeds and Bradford, dominated the wool industry. Although the industry has almost completely disappeared since WWII, large parts of the landscape are still dominated by reminders of it. Long rows of weavers' cottages (with

YORKSHIRE

Map of Yorkshire showing major towns, roads and National Parks. Labelled locations include:

Durham, Hartlepool, Bishop Auckland, Billingham, Redcar, Saltburn-by-the-Sea, CUMBRIA, DURHAM, Tees, Barnard Castle, Stockton-on-Sea, Middlesbrough, Guisborough, Loftus, Staithes, Appleby, The Pennines, Darlington, Danby, Grosmont, Goathland, Kirkby Stephen, Keld, Reeth, Richmond, Northallerton, North York Moors National Park, Gillamoor, Hutton-le-Hole, Thwaite, Muker, Helmsley, Hawes, Sutton Bank, Pickering, Thirsk, Kilburn, Nunnington Hall, Nunnington, Kirkby Lonsdale, Ingleborough (723m), Pen-y-ghent (694m), Yorkshire Dales National Park, Coxwold, Malton, Norton, Litton, Kettlewell, NORTH YORKSHIRE, Ripon, Cleveland Hills, Castle Howard, Ingleton, Arncliffe, Conistone, Easingwold, Malham Tarn, Grassington, Pateley Bridge, Fountains Abbey, Settle, Malham, Ripley, Knaresborough, York, Forest of Bowland, LANCASHIRE, Skipton, Ilkley, Otley, Harewood, Harrogate, A59, Earby, Colne, Keighley, Bingley, Saltaire, Clitheroe, Haworth, Bradford, Leeds, Selby, Goole, Longridge, Burnley, Heptonstall, Hebden Bridge, Halifax, Castleford, Preston, Blackburn, National Coal Mining Museum, Wakefield, Rochdale, Huddersfield, Bolton, Bury, Barnsley, Earth Centre, Doncaster, Wigan, Oldham, Manchester, Rotherham, Magna, Leigh, Peak District National Park, Sheffield, Gainsborough, Warrington, Stockport, Wilmslow, Worksop, Northwich, CHESHIRE, Macclesfield, DERBYSHIRE, Chesterfield, Congleton, Derwent

YORKSHIRE

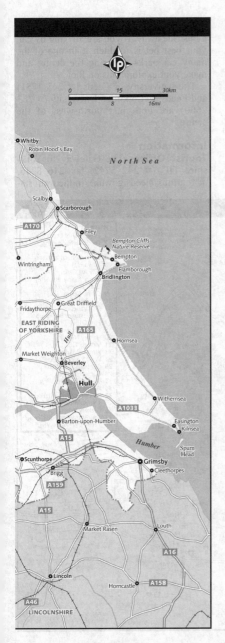

2nd-storey windows to provide light for the loom) and workers' houses built along the ridges overlook multi-storey mills with towering chimneys in the valleys below. These industrial towns and valleys are separated by the wild stretches of moors so vividly described by the Brontë sisters who lived at nearby Haworth.

The Leeds/Bradford conurbation is one of the biggest in the country, virtually running into the industrial towns of Halifax, Huddersfield and Wakefield. It also includes the pretty town of Hebden Bridge and tourist-crammed Haworth.

GETTING AROUND

The Metro public transport network, based in Leeds and Bradford, has won awards for its effective integrated bus and rail services. The area is particularly well served by rail with most towns listed in this section accessible by frequent trains. For extensive travel in West Yorkshire, buy the Metro DayRover tickets (£4.50), good for travel after 9.30 am on weekdays and all day at the weekend. There is also a thicket of additional DayRovers covering just buses and/or trains.

Metroline (☎ 0113-245 7676) answers phone inquiries on all public transport in West Yorkshire from 8 am to 7 pm on weekdays and 9 am to 5.30 pm on Saturday. It also publishes useful maps and timetables, most available in Tourist Information Centres (TICs). Alternatively you could call the national public transit inquiries number (☎ 0870 608 2608).

LEEDS
☎ 0113 • pop 455,000

Leeds is certainly one of the most inviting of England's big cities. Not for nothing has it been dubbed the 'Knightsbridge of the North'; indeed, there are so many shops and shopping centres you could be forgiven for assuming that every single resident of Leeds is in the business of selling fancy frocks and household goods to other Leeds residents. There are over 1000 shops in the compact, pedestrianised centre.

Many of the fine Victorian buildings in

the city centre have already been given a facelift and others are being smartened up as you read this. A large student population ensures a thriving nightlife.

The main tourist attraction in Leeds is the purpose-built Royal Armouries, along the gentrified waterfront. Leeds also makes a good base for excursions to Haworth, Hebden Bridge and Bradford.

Orientation

The city is strung out along the north bank of the River Aire and the Leeds–Liverpool Canal. The train and bus stations are cen-

trally located but most affordable hotels are a bus ride away. If you are arriving by car, your best bet is to ditch it in one of the many car parks that ring the centre and make your explorations on foot.

The University of Leeds (☎ 243 1751) and Leeds Metropolitan University (☎ 283 2600) are both just north-west of the centre.

Information

Tourist Offices The Gateway to Yorkshire TIC (☎ 242 5242, fax 246 8246, e tourinfo@leeds.gov.uk), in the train sta-

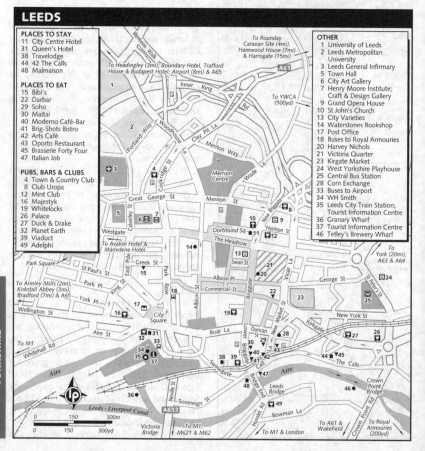

LEEDS

PLACES TO STAY
11 City Centre Hotel
31 Queen's Hotel
38 Travelodge
44 42 The Calls
48 Malmaison

PLACES TO EAT
15 Bibi's
22 Darbar
29 Soho
30 Maitai
40 Moderno Café-Bar
41 Brig-Shots Bistro
42 Arts Café
45 Oporto Restaurant
45 Brasserie Forty Four
47 Italian Job

PUBS, BARS & CLUBS
4 Town & Country Club
8 Club Uropa
12 Mint Club
16 Majestyk
19 Whitelocks
26 Palace
27 Duck & Drake
32 Planet Earth
39 Viaduct
49 Adelphi

OTHER
1 University of Leeds
2 Leeds Metropolitan University
3 Leeds General Infirmary
5 Town Hall
6 City Art Gallery
7 Henry Moore Institute; Craft & Design Gallery
9 Grand Opera House
10 St John's Church
13 City Varieties
14 Waterstones Bookshop
17 Post Office
18 Buses to Royal Armouries
20 Harvey Nichols
21 Victoria Quarter
23 Kirgate Market
24 West Yorkshire Playhouse
25 Central Bus Station
28 Corn Exchange
33 Buses to Airport
34 WH Smith
35 Leeds City Train Station; Tourist Information Centre
36 Granary Wharf
37 Tourist Information Centre
46 Tetley's Brewery Wharf

YORKSHIRE

tion, opens 9.30 am to 6 pm Monday to Saturday and 10 am to 4 pm Sunday.

Post & Communications Leeds' main post office (☎ 237 2849) is right on City Square. It opens 8 am to 5.30 pm Monday to Saturday.

The tiny WH Smith bookshop across from the TIC in the train station has free Internet access. It opens 7 am to 7.30 pm weekdays, 10 am to 6 pm Saturday and 10 am to 4 pm Sunday.

Bookshops All the major chains can be found in Leeds. Waterstone's (☎ 244 4588), 97 Albion St, is one of the larger stores and has a good selection of maps.

Medical Services Leeds General Infirmary (☎ 243 2799) is the huge local hospital. It is west of Calverley St in the city centre.

Royal Armouries

Leeds' pride and joy is the spectacular building created to house the Royal Armouries (☎ 220 1996), on Armouries Dr, on the banks of the Leeds–Liverpool Canal. This grey-and-white edifice looks remarkably like a fortress and finding the way in if you've walked along the canal to get there can seem as tricky as trying to penetrate the defences of a medieval castle. Once inside, however, you'll find four floors of exhibits centred on the themes of war, tournaments, self-defence, hunting and the Orient. The displays are all modern and well done – they deserve credit for showing the realities of war. There are numerous demonstrations throughout the day so be sure to pick up a schedule when you arrive.

Outside you can see displays of jousting and falconry from Easter to October. The Menagerie Court shows off the animals that take part in the displays, while the Craft Court allows you to see gun-makers, armourers and leather-workers in action. Perhaps the most controversial thing about the armouries is that they are in Leeds. When the weapons were on display in the Tower of London, they attracted far more visitors.

The Armouries open 10.30 am to 5 pm daily. Admission costs £4.90/3.90 (a reduction from past years). If you don't want to walk (about 15 minutes from the TIC) you can get there by bus No 95 from Park Row near City Square (towards Clarence Dock).

Tetley's Brewery Wharf

Tetley's (☎ 242 0666) flashy development off Bowman Lane has apparently run dry. It closed in 2000, but it was big and it was flashy so, as they say, watch this space.

Other Things to See & Do

Star attraction of the **City Art Gallery** (☎ 247 8248) on The Headrow is the Henry Moore Collection, to the right inside the front entrance. One of the last century's greatest sculptors, Henry Moore (1898–1986) was a graduate of Leeds School of Art. There is also a notable collection of French post-impressionist art. It opens from 10 am to 5 pm daily, opening at 1 pm on Sunday and closing at 8 pm on Wednesday. Admission is free.

The adjoining **Henry Moore Institute** (☎ 246 7467) stages periodic exhibitions of 20th-century sculpture. Beneath the gallery there's a separate **Craft & Design Gallery**.

Sadly, the **City Museum**, homeless since WWII, has been sent packing – literally – from its temporary location in the library. Call ☎ 214 6526 for details on where the many displays may have found a new home.

Tucked away off northern Briggate is the redundant **St John's Church**, a one-off masterpiece of 17th-century design full of elaborate box-pews and with a wonderful screen resplendent with huge carvings of the coat of arms of James I and of Charles I as Prince of Wales.

Places to Stay

The TIC makes bookings for accommodation and has numerous special offers. Weekend packages aimed at clubbers start from £32 per person per night in fairly swanky hotels.

Camping The most convenient camp site nearby is the *Roundhay Park Caravanning*

& Camping Site (☎ 265 2354, fax 237 0077), 4 miles (6km) north-west in Elmete Lane, Roundhay. From March to November it has pitches for tents for £4.10 per person. Bus Nos 2, 10 and 19 all pass the site.

Hostels There are no youth hostels in Leeds; the nearest are in Haworth and York.

B&Bs There's a group of B&Bs behind the University of Leeds on Woodsley Rd, but you pay for the (relative) convenience. The **Avalon Hotel** (☎ 243 2545, fax 242 0649, 132 Woodsley Rd) has reasonable decor and is well run and comfortable. Most rooms have a bathroom and singles/doubles start at £23/34.

The **Manxdene Hotel** (☎ 243 2586, 154 Woodsley Rd) is similar and charges from £24/36, which includes parking.

There's another batch of B&Bs on Cardigan Rd, Headingley; rates are around £25/35. The **Boundary Hotel** (☎/fax 275 7700, 42 Cardigan Rd) welcomes children and has cable TV in every room.

The unusually named **Trafford House & Budapest Hotel** (☎ 275 2034, fax 274 2422, e trafford@fsbdial.co.uk, 16 Cardigan Rd) is spread over three Victorian homes and has parking.

Hotels The **City Centre Hotel** (☎ 242 9019, 51 New Briggate) has been refurbished. Simple rooms without bathroom cost from £25/40.

The **Travelodge** (☎ 244 5793, fax 246 0076, Blayds Court, Swinegate) is a new and welcome addition to the budget scene. It is close to the train station and has rooms with en suite for £50. Breakfast is extra.

The **Malmaison** (☎ 398 1000, fax 398 1002, e leeds@malmaison.com, Sovereign St) is stylish and chic. The rooms are well equipped and cost from £79/105.

Queen's Hotel (☎ 243 1323, fax 242 5154, City Square) is a huge old railway hotel that has been spruced up. The rooms are aimed at business travellers and cost from £80/105.

In a converted Victorian grain mill overlooking the river is **42 The Calls** (☎ 244 0099, fax 234 4100, 42 The Calls). Rooms start at £98 and boast every luxury.

Places to Eat

The streets between the Corn Exchange and 42 The Calls (see Places to Stay above) harbour all sorts of glitzy bars and restaurants.

In Call Lane you'll find the extremely popular **Oporto Restaurant** (☎ 243 4008, 31–33 Call Lane) where vegetarian meals are under £8; cheaper bites are available in the adjoining bar.

Across the road, **Soho** (☎ 242 9009, 35 Call Lane) has both meaty and vegetarian meals with an artistic bent for under £6.

Nearby, the **Arts Café** (☎ 243 8243, 42 Call Lane) has modern British cuisine in a minimalist setting. Expect to pay from £10 per person.

Brasserie Forty Four (☎ 234 3232), attached to 42 The Calls, is regarded as one of the best restaurants in Leeds. The menu changes by season and you can have a wonderful three-course experience for about £22.

Briggate is also worth exploring. Unflashy **Maitai** (☎ 243 1989, 159 Briggate) serves Thai dishes for around £6.

Moderno Café-Bar (☎ 234 0301, 165 Briggate) has music (from 8 to 11 pm) to go with its sandwiches and pizzas.

Greenery-filled **Brig-Shots Bistro** (☎ 242 5629, 169 Briggate) has a pre-theatre menu for £10.50 until 7 pm. Its modern-European menu is long and interesting.

Despite the modest doorway, **Darbar** (☎ 246 0381, 16 Kirkgate) is a very large, very grand restaurant serving Indian and Tandoori specialities. The food is excellent and most curries cost upwards of £6.50.

The fairly basic **Italian Job** (☎ 242 0185, 9 Bridge End) has an iconic name and offers a good range of Italian food for about £6 per person.

At the much higher end of the price range is the excellent **Bibi's** (☎ 243 0905, 16 Greek St), which has a varied and changing menu of Italian classics and modern renditions. It gets absolutely hopping with pre-clubbers and older folks alike and is a big local favourite. Expect to pay from £10 per person.

Harvey Nichols (☎ 204 8000), 107–11 Briggate, has an *espresso bar* on the ground floor facing into the Victoria Quarter arcade. Upstairs, *The Fourth Floor Café* has innovative casual lunches and formal dinners from £20.

The cheapest snacks can probably be picked up in *Kirkgate Market* but if you're after tea and a bite in more cheerful surroundings, the arcades in the Victoria Quarter (☎ 245 5333) harbour several inviting small places, including *Ruskin's Tea Rooms* and *Café Arcade*. Here, too, you'll find the popular *Indie Joze Coffee Shop* (☎ 245 0569), which stays open until 11 pm for drinks and sandwiches.

Entertainment

The monthly *Leeds Guide* (£1.50) has the lowdown on what's on where. Boar Lane and Call Lane are at the heart of the action, with lots of overdressed people wandering from bar to pub to club.

Pubs Perhaps the most famous Leeds pub is *Whitelocks* (☎ 245 3950, *Turk's Head Yard)*, in a small alley off Briggate. It's a classic Edwardian pub with outside tables and traditional pub food such as Yorkshire pudding (£1.50).

The ornate *Edwardian Adelphi* (☎ 245 6377, 3–5 Hunslet Rd) boasts wood panelling, tiles and engraved glass, and attracts a varied clientele. Considered the home pub for the Carlsberg-Tetley Brewery, it is an attraction itself.

The *Duck & Drake* (☎ 246 5806, 43 Kirkgate) has a good range of real ales and live music several nights a week. In winter it has large fireplaces to bake out the damp.

Possibly the widest choice of ales can be found at the *Palace* (☎ 244 5882, Kirkgate), which has one large room dating from the 1930s. It's popular for its long list of lunch specials and has a good beer garden.

The *Viaduct* (☎ 246 9178, 11 Lower Briggate) is a classic old pub that's had a sensible updating and now includes such amenities as a nonsmoking room and facilities for the disabled. The beer garden is another winner and it's busy at lunchtime.

Clubs Leeds has a tremendous club scene that attracts people from many miles around in addition to the scores of local students. At the weekends you'll see lots of well-dressed young people cavorting in the centre before a night of club-hopping. In winter, lots of people brave the cold wearing next to nothing to avoid cloakroom hassles. Weekend admission charges to the clubs average £5.

The following all have hugely varied line-ups of music and themes. *Club Uropa* (☎ 242 2224, 54 New Briggate) is one of the most popular and attracts top DJs.

Majestyk (☎ 242 4333) and *Planet Earth* (☎ 243 4733) are both on City Square. Most people try to shuttle between both.

The *Town & Country Club* (☎ 280 0100, 55 Cookridge St) is host to gigs and disco nights.

The *Mint Club* (☎ 244 3168, 8 Harrison St) changes constantly. It has very popular women-only nights every week.

Theatre Chaplin and Houdini both performed at *City Varieties* (☎ 243 0808, Swan St), one of England's last old-fashioned music halls.

The *West Yorkshire Playhouse* (☎ 244 2111, Quarry Hill Mount) has a good reputation for live drama. Many local works are performed on its two stages.

At the *Grand Opera House* (☎ 222 6222, 46 New Briggate) tickets for a wide variety of performances (not just opera) cost from £8.

Spectator Sports For many people, Leeds means Headingley and Headingley means cricket. The first cricket match played here was in 1890, and it's still a venue for Test matches and the home ground of the Yorkshire County Cricket Club.

To get to the cricket ground, take bus No 74 or 75 from Park Row or catch a train to Burley Park station, a short walk from the ground. For match bookings (from £18 for a Test match) phone ☎ 278 7394. See the Web site at www.yorkshireccc.org.uk for details.

Shopping

There are scores of places to shop in Leeds. **Granary Wharf** (☎ 244 6570), behind the train station, is reached via the Dark Arches. It's a cobbled area under vaulted arches at the meeting point of the canal and the river, with art and craft shops, free entertainment and markets selling local, hand-made goods on Friday, Saturday and Sunday.

A highlight of any visit is a stroll around the magnificent **Victoria Quarter** (☎ 245 5333) arcades on Briggate, which are roofed with a stained-glass canopy, paved with mosaics and decorated with marble. The shops are suitably upmarket and intimidating, all the more so since **Harvey Nichols** (☎ 204 8000) opened its first store outside London here.

Just as much fun in a more down-to-earth way is the **Kirkgate Market** (☎ 214 5162), once home of Marks, who later joined Spencer. Here, in Europe's largest covered market, arcades of wrought-iron and ceramic tiles surround stalls piled high with fresh produce and cheap baked goods – ideal for stocking up for a picnic. The market is open from Monday to Saturday, closing at 1 pm on Wednesday. The adjoining open-air markets function on Tuesday, Friday and Saturday.

The wonderful circular **Corn Exchange** (☎ 234 0363), built in 1865, is the place to come if you're into one-off clothes shops and specialities such as stencilling. It opens daily.

Getting There & Away

Air Leeds-Bradford airport (☎ 250 9696), 8 miles (13km) north of the city via the A65, offers domestic flights as well as international flights to a few major European cities. The Airlink 757 bus operates hourly between the airport and Leeds' City Square, next to the train station (£1.50, 25 minutes). A taxi will cost around £15.

Bus The Central Bus Station is a 10-minute walk east of the train station, off St Peter's St. National Express has services to most British cities including nine coaches daily to/from London (£12, about four hours 30 minutes) and Manchester (£5, one hour).

Yorkshire Coastliner (☎ 0870 608 2608) has a useful service linking Leeds, York, Castle Howard, Goathland and Whitby (Nos 840 and 842). Many other services link Leeds, York and Scarborough.

Train Leeds City station is large and busy, with hourly services to London King's Cross (£56) that take as little as two hours. It's also the starting point for the famous Leeds–Settle–Carlisle line. There are frequent services to both Sheffield (£4.90, 30 minutes) and York (£6.20, 30 minutes).

Getting Around You can get a Metro bus to most parts of the city and to the suburbs from the Central Bus Station. Most also serve a stop on or near City Square. Ask the TIC or bus drivers about the various Metro DayRover passes that cover trains and/or buses and can be used to get to Bradford, Haworth and Hebden Bridge as well as around the city.

AROUND LEEDS
Armley Mills

Leeds' industrial past is collected and displayed at Armley Mills (☎ 263 7861), a huge old textile mill. The exhibits are a good overview of the Industrial Revolution and cover the 18th and 19th centuries. One area is devoted to Leeds' history as a steam locomotive manufacturer.

Armley Mills is open 10 am to 5 pm (from noon Sunday, closed Monday). It is 2 miles (3km) north of Leeds on Canal Rd off the A65. Bus Nos 14, 66 and 67 stop close by. Admission costs £2/50p.

Kirkstall Abbey

In 1152, Cistercian monks from Fountains Abbey in North Yorkshire began work on a new abbey, which came to be called Kirkstall Abbey (☎ 263 7861). The complex reached its peak in the early 16th century when work on the **crossing tower** was completed. Then Henry VIII made his moves against the church and the roof literally fell in.

The ruins are dark and moody and can make for a very evocative hour-long stroll.

The site is open dawn to dusk daily and there is no admission charge. It's sensibly located on Abbey Rd, which runs off the A65, 3 miles (5 km) north of Leeds. Bus Nos 41, 50 and 50A pass nearby.

Harewood House

Harewood is one of England's most beautiful stately homes but it's also extremely popular at peak periods. The building is great, the interiors are over the top and the surrounding park is glorious, but some may find the perfection and commercialisation rather 'cold'.

Harewood has been home to the Lascelles family since it was built between 1759 and 1772. No expense was spared – Capability Brown was responsible for the grounds, Thomas Chippendale for the furniture, and Italy was raided to create an appropriate art collection (including works by Tintoretto, Titian, Bellini and many others).

In addition to the house, there's the Stables Gallery, the Bird Garden and a children's adventure playground. The stables house a pleasant cafe. Enjoyable walks take you round Harewood Lake and to 15th-century **Harewood Church**, which is no longer in use (the village it originally served was moved when the house was constructed!) but contains some fascinating tombs and monuments.

The house (☎ 0113-218 1010) is 7 miles (11km) north of Leeds on the A61 to Harrogate. Bus Nos 36, 36A, 36C and 781 will get you there from Leeds. It opens 11 am to 4.30 pm daily, April to October. Admission costs £6.95/4.75.

BRADFORD
☎ 01274 • pop 296,000

The centre of Bradford is 9 miles (14km) west of Leeds but the two cities are virtually continuous. Until WWII Bradford was the uncontested capital of the world wool trade. After that, the industry collapsed, leaving the city struggling to find a new role. Since the 1960s over 60,000 Indians and Pakistanis have settled here and helped reinvigorate the city.

Some people come to Bradford for its famous curry houses and others for the National Museum of Photography, Film & Television. However, most are passing through on their way to Saltaire, Haworth or the Dales.

Orientation & Information

Central Bradford is compact. The Bradford Interchange, the combined bus and rail terminal, is right in the centre of town along Bridge St.

Bradford's TIC (☎ 753678, fax 739067, e bradford@ytbtic.co.uk) is in the Central Library on Prince's Way. It opens 9 am to 5.30 pm on weekdays and until 4 pm on Saturday. They have the usual wealth of information on the area including useful accommodation and eating guides.

The library (☎ 753600) has free Internet access. There is parking behind the complex.

Things to See & Do

The **National Museum of Photography, Film & Television** (☎ 202030) is a large and well funded operation right next to the library and TIC on Prince's Way. This is a great place where, as well as learning about the history of photography, you can try out lots of video and graphics technology and play at being a TV newsreader or cameraperson. There is a range of special exhibitions through the year. The museum houses an IMAX cinema and there are other cinemas where off-beat, historical and even mainstream films are shown. The exhibits are open 10 am to 6 pm (closed Monday except for Bank Holidays) and are free. The cinemas are open through the evening and there are varying charges for films.

The **Colour Museum** (☎ 390955), 82 Grattan Rd, home of the Society of Dyers and Colourists, is more interesting than you might expect. It draws on Bradford's woollen past to show how clothes are given their colours. It also has a good section showing how different species sense colour in different ways (what's blue to you isn't blue to Fido). The museum is 10 minutes from the Bradford Interchange. It opens 10 am to 4 pm Tuesday to Saturday. Admission costs £1.50/1.

Bradford Industrial Museum (☎ 631756), Moorside Rd, is in an old spinning mill dating from 1875. Exhibits give an idea of what life was like at the peak of the Industrial Revolution. It opens 10 am to 5 pm (from noon Sunday, closed Monday) and admission is free.

The wonderful **Undercliffe Cemetery** (☎ 642276), between Undercliffe Lane and Otley Rd, has England's best collection of Victorian funerary art. It's open daily during daylight hours and admission is free.

Places to Stay & Eat

The TIC will be very happy to find you accommodation.

The *Castle Hotel* (☎ 393166, 20 Grattan Rd) is near the centre. It has simple singles/doubles that cost from £26/36 without breakfast.

Top choice is the *Quality Victoria Hotel* (☎ 728706, fax 736358, Bridge St), which has been restored its to heyday when it was built in 1875. Rooms are opulent and there's a health club and more. Rooms start at £75 and there are weekend specials.

There's a lot of argument about where England's ubiquitous – and most home-grown – *chicken tikka masala* was first served; it may well have been Bradford. Top among the local curry places is *Kashmir* (☎ 726513, 27 Morley St), which is in the centre and has excellent dishes for around £4. It opens until 2 am.

Bombay Brasserie (☎ 737564, Simes Gate, Westgate) is a high-end (top quality in its price bracket) Indian place with food to match the lovely interior. Here you might pay £6 for a main dish.

Karrotz Cafe Bar (☎ 201787, 1 Petergate) is an organic vegetarian cafe and a bar. It's open for lunch during the week and dinner from Thursday to Saturday. Meals cost under £7 (much less at lunch).

Getting There & Away

Bradford's main station is Bradford Interchange although some trains go from Forster Square on Cheapside, which is a bit less convenient.

There are frequent trains to Bradford from Leeds (£1.80, 20 minutes, every 15 minutes) and York (£7.80, one hour, hourly).

AROUND BRADFORD
Saltaire

Well worth a visit is the **Saltaire** suburb, some 3 miles (5km) north of Bradford. It was built in 1851 by wool-baron Titus Salt, who wanted a company village and factory that contributed to the health of its inhabitants and workers. Care was taken to provide good light, ventilation, heating and other services. If nothing else, Salt created a gem of a village, which is built from the local honey-coloured stone to neo-Italianate designs. **Salt's Mill** (☎ 531163) is the key building and was the largest factory in the world when it was completed. The entire village has been nominated for Unesco World Heritage Site status. One main feature today is the **1853 Gallery** (☎ 531185), dedicated to Bradford-born artist David Hockney.

The TIC (☎ 774993, fax 774464), 2 Victoria Rd, runs guided walks through the year and can book beds in local B&Bs. It opens 10 am to 5 pm. Most sites in Saltaire open 10 am to 6 pm and are free. There are several *cafes* and *tearooms*.

From Bradford, there's a frequent Metro train service from Forster Square Station. From Bradford Interchange, take bus No 679.

At nearby **Bingley** you can see a series of five 18th-century canal locks, which raise the Leeds–Liverpool Canal 18m.

HAWORTH
☎ 01535 • pop 5100

As the village that was home to the Brontë family, Haworth rivals Stratford-upon-Avon as England's most important literary shrine. The surrounding countryside seems to be haunted both by the sisters and their literary creations. Even without this, the old part of the village would still draw tourists; the cobblestoned Main St running steeply down to Bridgehouse Beck (stream) from the parish church provides a quintessential Yorkshire view. In fact one local told us:

'Lots of those people on the coach tours don't even know why they're here. They just want to buy something.' Certainly, retail opportunities abound and you can buy anything imaginable and more bearing the Brontë name or likeness.

Patrick Brontë and his family moved to the Parsonage in 1820. It was not a healthy move. His wife Maria died of cancer at age 38; his daughters Maria and Elizabeth died as children. His son Branwell lasted until he was 31, spending many of his final years in pubs.

Emily, who wrote *Wuthering Heights*, died in 1848 at age 30 after catching a 'chill'. Anne, who penned *Agnes Grey* using the name Acton Bell, died at age 29 in 1849. Of all the siblings, Charlotte held on the longest. She wrote *Jane Eyre* and even married. However, she died shortly afterwards at age 38 in 1855.

Only Patrick survived to old age, dying in the Parsonage at the age of 84. The Parsonage Museum gives a fascinating insight into their lives. Away from the maddening crowds, the West Yorkshire countryside will immediately seem familiar to fans of the sisters' books.

Orientation & Information

Haworth's development parallels that of the textile industry. The old village, with its cottage-based weavers and spinners, grew up along the ridge above the valley. Then in the 19th century the outworkers were replaced by factories.

Haworth's TIC (☎ 642329, fax 647721, ℮ haworth@ytbtic.co.uk), 2–4 West Lane, opens 9 am to 5 pm daily (until 5.30 pm, April to September) and has an excellent supply of information on the Brontë family.

The post office is at 98 Main St and opens 9 am to 5.30 pm weekdays and until 12.30 pm on Saturday.

Venables & Bainbridge, 111 Main St, sells used books, including many vintage Brontë volumes.

Brontë Parsonage Museum

Set in a pretty garden, the Parsonage is a Georgian house overlooking the cemetery. The core of the house is furnished and decorated as it would have been when the Brontës lived there. Some of the furnishings are original and there are many personal possessions on display. The museum section houses lots of material, including the

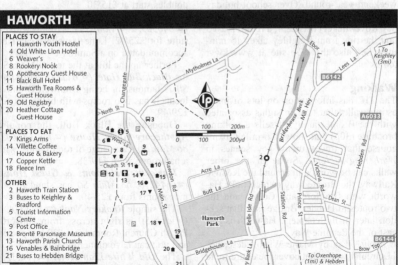

HAWORTH

PLACES TO STAY
1 Haworth Youth Hostel
4 Old White Lion Hotel
6 Weaver's
8 Rookery Nook
10 Apothecary Guest House
11 Black Bull Hotel
15 Haworth Tea Rooms & Guest House
19 Old Registry
20 Heather Cottage Guest House

PLACES TO EAT
7 Kings Arms
14 Villette Coffee House & Bakery
17 Copper Kettle
18 Fleece Inn

OTHER
2 Haworth Train Station
3 Buses to Keighley & Bradford
5 Tourist Information Centre
9 Post Office
12 Brontë Parsonage Museum
13 Haworth Parish Church
16 Venables & Bainbridge
21 Buses to Hebden Bridge

YORKSHIRE

fascinating miniature books the children wrote.

The museum is operated by the Brontë Society, a group that was in the news during 2000 as internal divisions threatened to sink the entire operation. The Parsonage (☎ 642323) opens 10 am to 5.30 pm daily from April to September; from 11 am the rest of the year. Admission costs £4.50/1.40. See the Web site at www.bronte.org.uk for more details.

Keighley & Worth Valley Railway

The K&WV Railway (☎ 645214) is a favourite movie location with film crews, as much for the six restored stations as for the classic steam engines.

Especially on summer weekends, when Haworth can be overflowing with visitors, it's worth parking at Keighley and catching the train to the village. Better yet, you can avoid the drive entirely by taking a regular train to Keighley, which is on the Leeds–Settle–Carlisle line, then changing for the K&WV Railway. The Brontë Parsonage is a 10-minute walk uphill from the station.

Trains operate virtually hourly at the weekend year-round. Over school holiday periods there's a daily service too. A one-day Rover ticket costs £8/4, a return is £6/3 and the ride from Keighley takes 15 minutes. See also the Web site at www.kwvr .co.uk.

Walking

The TIC has information on lots of interesting walks that take in sights associated with the Brontë family. It sells a walking brochure (30p) that shows a 6-mile (10km) course that traces many key scenes in *Wuthering Heights*. Some of the other walks can be worked in around the K&WV Railway, the Brontë Way (which links Haworth with Bradford and Colne) and the two routes to Hebden Bridge (see that section later in the chapter). Haworth is just east of the Pennine Way.

Brontë Way by Marje Wilson describes 11 circular walks that cover the entire route of the Way. Particularly interesting is the fairly strenuous 9-mile (14km) walk from the Parsonage to Colne/Laneshawbridge via Top Withens (Wuthering Heights), Ponden Hall (Thrushcross Grange) and Wycoller Hall (Ferndean Manor). From Laneshawbridge you can catch a bus to Keighley and complete the loop by catching the K&WV Railway back to Haworth.

Places to Stay

Hostels A half-mile walk north-east from the train station is the *Haworth Youth Hostel* (☎ 642234, fax 643023, e haworth@ yha.org.uk, Longlands Dr, Lees Lane). Beds cost £10/6.90 for adults/under-18s. The hostel is closed on Sunday in November and December. You can get any of the buses to/from Keighley to stop at Longlands Dr.

B&Bs & Hotels Although there are lots of places to stay, it's still worth booking ahead in summer. The TIC offers a room-booking service.

Main St, the most atmospheric part of town, has lots of accommodation but might feel a bit oppressive at the height of the tourist season. At *Heather Cottage Guest House* (☎ 644511, 25/27 Main St), singles/doubles start at £15/30.

Across the road, the *Old Registry* (☎ 646503, 2–4 Main St) has rooms with en suite for £25/42. Lone travellers can't be accommodated on a Saturday.

Further up the hill at the top of Main St, the *Black Bull Hotel* (☎ 642249, 119 Main St) is famous for being Branwell Brontë's local. It has two rooms with bathroom for £29/49.

Opposite the Black Bull, the popular *Apothecary Guest House* (☎/fax 643642, 86 Main St) has a range of rooms, most with a bathroom, from £19/38.

Haworth Tea Rooms & Guest House (☎ 644278, 68 Main St) has standard but nice rooms from £25/40.

The simple *Rookery Nook* (☎ 643374, 6 Church St) is right across from Haworth Parish Church. Rooms cost £20 per person and you can have dinner here for £5.

The *Old White Lion Hotel* (☎ 642313, fax 646222, 6 West Lane) is the main hotel in the village. It is almost 300 years old and has a bar and restaurant. Rooms vary in size but average about £44/70.

Also on West Lane, the very comfortable *Weavers (☎/fax 643822, 15 West Lane)* has rooms for £50/75. Some of the rooms are quite romantic.

Places to Eat

Main St and West Lane are lined with tea-rooms and restaurants, many of which are noted above in Places to Stay.

Weavers easily has the best food in town. Its restaurant (closed Sunday and Monday) serves complete meals that feature local specialities and game. Expect to pay at least £20 per person for three courses. The wine list is also good.

The *King's Arms (☎ 643146)* is slightly down Church St, off Main St; turn off at the Black Bull. It has a good beer garden and fine dinners of steaks and the like for about £10.

The *Fleece Inn (☎ 642172, 51 Main St)* has a good range of real ales and fine pub lunches for under £5. The *Black Bull Hotel* wins plaudits for its dinners.

The *Copper Kettle (☎ 642809, 81 Main St)* has meals for under £3.50. You can find the usual array of sandwiches and jacket potatoes here.

The friendly *Villette Coffee House & Bakery (☎ 644967, 115 Main St)* is particularly good value with all-day breakfasts for £2.80 and wonderful Yorkshire curd tarts (very sweet, rich and filling) for 75p. They also have veggie burgers.

Getting There & Away

Keighley & District buses Nos 663, 664, and 665 link Haworth with Keighley at least three times an hour (20 minutes). The same company runs a few buses daily direct to Bradford (one hour). In summer, bus No 500 offers a service four times a day between Todmorden, Hebden Bridge, Haworth and Keighley (Wednesday and Sunday in winter).

The previously mentioned K&WV Railway is a good link from Haworth to Keighley and the national rail network.

The drive to Haworth north from Hebden

Bridge on the A6033 is one of the most scenic in Yorkshire.

ILKLEY

☎ 01943 • pop 19,100

Comfortably nestled against moors and on the border with Wharfdale and the Yorkshire Dales National Park, Ilkley may be about the poshest place you'll visit in England. The streets are lined with exclusive shops and boutiques and the roads are lined with Jaguars, BMWs and ubiquitous Range Rovers. Signs at the town entrance recall Ilkley's triumphant victory in a 1990 floral competition.

Ilkley is a pleasant place to spend a night and with its good transport connections is a good hub for exploring West Yorkshire and the southern reaches of the Dales.

Information

The TIC (☎ 602319, e ilkley@ytbtic.co.uk) is across from the bus and train station on Station Rd. It's open 9.30 am to 5.30 pm weekdays, until 5 pm Saturday and 1 to 4 pm Sunday, May to September. The rest of the year it closes at 4.30 pm and all day Sunday.

Walking

The main thing to do in Ilkley is walk around. Besides the various shopping streets

Ilkley Moor

The posh pavements of Ilkley make for a good wander, but it's the moors immediately south of the centre that are the real treat. The TIC has some good walking maps of the many paths. One simple and good walk starts and ends at the train station. Head towards White Wells, which has a nice pub. Then walk west along the moor to Beck Hole. Depending on the season, you'll see all manner of heather as well as traverse several woods. There are numerous options to this walk, but one well-marked route covers 3½ miles (5.5km). There are some fairly steep climbs, but they reward with fine views back across the valley.

YORKSHIRE

such as Brook St and The Grove, there are some lovely walks along the River Wharfe. In town itself there are the remains of a **Roman fort** near Castle Rd and the river. Further out, you can follow the Wharfe for 7 miles (11km) to Bolton Abbey near Skipton and beyond along the **Dales Way**, the long-distance path that starts in Ilkley. See the Activities chapter for more details.

A number of other walks traverse the nearby moors to the south. See the boxed text 'Ilkley Moor' for more details of one. The TIC sells two useful pamphlets (30p): *Walks from Ilkley* and *Longer Walks from Ilkley*.

Places to Stay & Eat
The TIC will book private rooms and other accommodation from about £20 per person.

The *Riverside Hotel* (☎/fax 607338, Bridge Lane) is right in the centre and close to the Riverside Gardens. It has comfortable rooms for £40/55.

The perfectly located *Crescent Hotel* (☎ 600012, fax 601513, e creschot@ dialstart.net, Brook St) combines a fine place to eat, drink and sleep. The pub serves some fine local ales, cheap pub food and is popular with locals; the restaurant has high-end British fare for about £20 per person and the rooms are decorated with antiques. Rooms cost £57/75; ask about special deals.

The *Box Tree* (☎ 608484, 37 Church St) is a Michelin-starred restaurant with a reputation for exquisite food that extends beyond Yorkshire. Set meals are £40.

Getting There & Away
The tidy combined bus and train station is central, but it has no lockers.

There's a regular bus service to Skipton (Nos X84 and 784; 30 minutes) and Keighley (Nos 762 and 765; 30 minutes).

Ilkley is located at the end of the Wharfdale train line from Bradford (£1.80) and Leeds (£2.40). The service to both cities runs every 30 minutes and takes about 30 minutes. Going to or coming from York (£9.30), change trains in Leeds.

PENNINE YORKSHIRE
Deep beneath the rolling hills of Pennine Yorkshire are the seams of coal that for decades fed the Industrial Revolution. This was the heart of coal-mining country and was one of the areas worst hit when Margaret Thatcher pulled the plug on the national coal mines in the early 1980s.

Museums recall this past, while charming once-industrial towns like Hebden Bridge combine beauty with history.

National Coal Mining Museum
Coal-mining began in Yorkshire in the early 1500s when people dug for deposits near the surface. By the 18th century the demand for coal was booming and mining became more complex. One of the first deep shafts was dug near Wakefield. This pit came to known as the Caphouse Colliery and it was continually expanded until it was closed in 1987. Shortly afterwards it reopened as the National Coal Mining Museum (☎ 0192-484 8806).

This is one of the best museums in Yorkshire and it does a fine job of explaining the hard and dirty lives led by generations of miners and their families. Visitors can explore a vast museum that has excellent displays showing how it was the near-forced labour of women and small children in the mines that led to the passage of the first labour acts. The highlight of the visit is the ride in a 'cage' 134m down to one of the main levels used by miners. Most of the guides are former coal miners who take delight in sharing tales from their working days.

The museum is open 9 am to 5 pm daily but be sure to get there by 1 pm to have a chance to see everything above and below ground. Admission costs £5.75/4.25. It is on the A642 about 7 miles (12km) from both Wakefield to the east and Huddersfield to the west. Bus No 231 connects both towns and runs hourly (every two hours Sunday). Huddersfield has regular trains to/from Leeds, Manchester and Sheffield and Wakefield has frequent service to/from Leeds. See the Web site at www.ncm.co.uk for further details.

Hebden Bridge & Heptonstall
☎ 01422 • pop (both) 3400

Heptonstall, with its hill-top location, was settled before Hebden Bridge down in the valley. However the latter was able to take advantage of its riverside location to build mills and it soon eclipsed its elevated neighbour.

Heptonstall consists of typical grey-stone weavers' cottages. The Cloth Hall in the main street is Yorkshire's oldest and dates back to 1554. When steam power arrived, mills were set up in the valley along the River Calder, and the Rochdale Canal was built to provide transport. The mills have now closed and Hebden Bridge seems to huddle apologetically in a valley now given over to tourism. With its canal passing over the River Calder in a huge stone aqueduct, its photographic charms are obvious. Up the hill, you're more than likely to run into a film or TV crew shooting something in preserved Heptonstall.

The late Ted Hughes grew up near Hebden Bridge and wrote many poems about the area. His wife Sylvia Plath is buried in the Wesleyan chapel graveyard at Heptonstall.

Orientation & Information
It's easy to get around Hebden Bridge on foot but the steep half-mile walk up to Heptonstall is a killer. Better to hang on for a bus unless you're feeling energetic. The 8-mile (13km) drive to/from Haworth on the A6033 is lovely.

The villages' TIC (☎ 843831, fax 845266, e hebdenbridge@ytbtic.co.uk), 1 Bridge Gate, opens 10 am to 5 pm daily.

Things to See & Do
Hebden Bridge's streets are lined with all manner of shops selling the usual items that probably weren't sold before the arrival of tourists: dried flowers, decorative flower pots, pillows in the shape of cats, and so on.

Wandering the streets and hills is the chief attraction here. Follow the Rochdale Canal with its famous bridge in any direction. Numerous paths are marked and the TIC can suggest many more. Some follow Hebden Water, the stream that flows into the Calder.

The **Heptonstall Museum** (☎ 843738), Church Bottom, is set in a 17th-century school building. Its limited hours are 1 to 3 pm at the weekend, April to October. Admission costs £1/50p. Otherwise there's not a lot else to do in Heptonstall – besides trip over camera cables of course.

Run by the National Trust (NT), **Hardcastle Crags** (☎ 844518) is an unspoilt wooded valley complete with waterfalls, a mile north-west of town off the A6033. There are numerous walks around here, some of which link to the Pennine Way. Those odd hills you see are made by the valley's often-studied residents, hairy wood ants.

Perhaps it's the honey exhibition that draws tourists to **Walkley Clogs** (☎ 842061) in a manner not unlike flies to... There's all manner of knick-knackery for sale and you can see clog-making amid a clutter of competing attractions. It's a mile west of Hebden Bridge on Burnley Rd (A646). A ticket covering everything costs £4/2.

At **Calder Valley Cruising** (☎ 845557), The Marina on New Rd offers horse-drawn cruises along the Rochdale Canal. The trips last from 20 minutes to two hours and operate from 10 am to 5 pm daily April to October.

Places to Stay
Camping At High Greenwood House, Heptonstall, *Pennine Camp Site* (☎ 842287) has 50 tent pitches and charges £3 per person.

Hostels In an ancient manor house in a typical Yorkshire village, *Mankinholes Youth Hostel* (☎/fax 01706-812340) is near Todmorden, 4 miles (6km) south-west of Hebden Bridge, south of the A646 to/from Rochdale, and half a mile from the Pennine Way. From mid-April to October it's usually open daily except Sunday and possibly Monday; it is worth calling in advance to check. Beds cost £10/6.90 for adults/under-18s. Trains from Leeds to Manchester stop at Todmorden, 2 miles (3km) from the hostel.

YORKSHIRE

B&Bs & Hotels The friendly *Royd Well* (☎ 845304, 35 Royd Terrace) is a three-minute walk from town; rooms with shared bathroom cost from £14 per person.

Redacre Mill (☎/fax 885563, Mytholmroyd) is in a canalside mill surrounded by gardens. Rooms cost from £39.

Robin Hood Inn (☎ 842593, fax 844938, Keighley Rd), 2 steep miles (3km) out at Pecket Well, has four beautifully decorated rooms with nice views costing from £21 per person.

White Lion Hotel (☎ 842197, fax 846619, Bridge Gate) has 10 rooms in a fine riverside location and dates from 1656. Rooms start at £22.50 per person.

Places to Eat & Drink

In Hebden Bridge, *Theo's Greek Restaurant* (☎ 845337, 12–16 Bridge Gate) is properly whitewashed and is good fun. A Greek feast costs £13.

The Shoulder of Mutton (☎ 842585, Bridge Gate) doesn't have sheep on the menu but it does have cheap pub food, a good selection of beer and a fine location on Hebden Water.

If you have a car, it's worth driving out to the *Robin Hood Inn* on Keighley Rd. The *White Lion Hotel* has a fine pub with good beer and food. See the earlier Places to Stay section for contact details for both places.

Getting There & Away

The buses are slower and less frequent than the trains, but in summer, Keighley & District's bus No 500 offers a handy four-times-a-day service between Todmorden, Hebden Bridge, Haworth and Keighley. Most buses stop on New Rd by the TIC.

Hebden Bridge is within the Leeds Metro area. The rail service runs at least hourly from Leeds (50 minutes) and Bradford Interchange (30 minutes) to Hebden Bridge and then continues to Manchester Victoria (40 minutes). Some services run right through from Scarborough and York to Hebden Bridge and Blackpool. The station is a 10-minute walk along the River Calder west from town. It has no lockers.

South Yorkshire

South Yorkshire was once the industrial heart of Yorkshire. Cities like Sheffield, Rotherham and Doncaster were alive with steel-making and metal-bending. Today, they're trying to come back to life after the collapse of both the metal industries and the coal mines used to power them.

SHEFFIELD
☎ 0114 • pop 475,000

Five hundred years ago Sheffield was already renowned for its cutlery production and the words 'Sheffield steel' still have a familiar ring to them. Nowadays the industry employs far fewer people than in the past but they turn out more knives and forks than ever before.

Victorian Sheffield – with its grim factories and mills – was synonymous with the worst excesses of industrial exploitation. Many buildings were damaged in WWII and postwar rebuilding added little to be admired. Despite this, England's fourth-largest city is a lively place. It has an exuberant student population and a much-trumpeted recent survey of British students showed that Sheffield ranked first in terms of 'good times'. The survey avoided discussing what impact this might have on academic achievement.

Until recently, Sheffield didn't feature on many tourist itineraries, but in 1997 the smash-hit film *The Full Monty*, the tale of a group of unemployed steelworkers who turned to stripping to raise much-needed cash, sparked interest in this old industrial city.

Today's visitors find a city working hard to reinvent itself. Galleries and parks are being spiffed up in the centre and attractions pegged to the industrial past are well worth a visit.

Sheffield makes a good base for exploring West Yorkshire, including the Brontë area. The Peak District brushes up against its western outskirts and Chesterfield, with its twisted spire, is just a train hop away (see The Midlands chapter).

Orientation

If you arrive by bus you'll find yourself at the vast Sheffield Interchange on Pond St, which is ringed with roads and high-rises. The train station is clearly signed, three minutes south of the bus stands.

Sheffield's main street changes its name from Glossop Rd to West St to Church St to High St as it proceeds from west to east. Immediately south of West St is the area known as the Devonshire Quarter (Devonshire St, Division St and Barker's Pool) where there are trendy shops and bars. Just west, the Broomhill area and Ecclesall Rd are lined with shops, cafes and pubs.

The two major universities are the University of Sheffield (☎ 222 2000), west of Upper Hanover St, and Sheffield Hallam University (☎ 225 5555), near the train station.

Information

Tourist Offices The TIC (☎ 221 1900, fax 201 1020, ⓔ info@destinationsheffield

.org.uk), at 1 Tudor Square on Surrey St, is very friendly and opens 9.30 am to 5.15 pm weekdays and 9.30 am to 4.15 pm on Saturday.

Post & Communications There is a post office on Norfolk Row that opens 8 am to 5.30 pm on weekdays and until 12.30 pm on Saturday.

Havana Internet Cafe (☎ 249 5453), 32–34 Division St, charges £1.25 for 15 minutes' access. It opens from at least 10 am to 6 pm daily.

Travel Agencies usit Campus (☎ 275 8366) is right across from the train station on Pond St in the Sheffield Hallam University student union.

Medical Services Northern General Hospital (☎ 243 4343) is 3 miles (5km) north of the centre on the corner of Herries and Barnsley Roads.

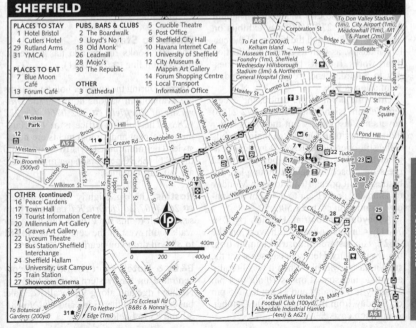

SHEFFIELD

PLACES TO STAY
1 Hotel Bristol
4 Cutlers Hotel
29 Rutland Arms
31 YMCA

PLACES TO EAT
7 Blue Moon Café
13 Forum Café

PUBS, BARS & CLUBS
2 The Boardwalk
9 Lloyd's No 1
18 Old Monk
26 Leadmill
28 Mojo's
30 The Republic

OTHER
3 Cathedral

5 Crucible Theatre
6 Post Office
8 Sheffield City Hall
10 Havana Internet Cafe
11 University of Sheffield
12 City Museum & Mappin Art Gallery
14 Forum Shopping Centre
15 Local Transport Information Office

OTHER (continued)
16 Peace Gardens
17 Town Hall
19 Tourist Information Centre
20 Millennium Art Gallery
21 Graves Art Gallery
22 Lyceum Theatre
23 Bus Station/Sheffield Interchange
24 Sheffield Hallam University; usit Campus
25 Train Station
27 Showroom Cinema

Museums & Art Galleries

By the time you read this the major new **Millennium Art Gallery** should have opened on Surrey St. It will have travelling exhibits from the Victoria & Albert Museum in London and will also be the new home to the city's eclectic **Ruskin Gallery** (☎ 278 2600). The collection was established by the Victorian critic and Gothic-revivalist John Ruskin in 1875 in an attempt to meld art and industry.

The **Peace Gardens** in front of the grand Town Hall are a recent addition to the city centre. Fountains and a range of sculpture enliven what had been a pretty dead spot.

The nearby **Graves Art Gallery** (☎ 278 2600) displays contemporary British and European art atop the City Library on Surrey St. Matisse, Spencer and Nash are some of the artists featured. The space has been refurbished and it is also the site of major touring shows. It opens 10 am to 5 pm Monday to Saturday and admission is free.

A mile west of the centre in pleasant Weston Park, the **City Museum & Mappin Art Gallery** (☎ 278 2600) has exhibits on local archaeology and the history of the cutlery industry, as well as a varied collection of art works. It opens 10 am to 5 pm Tuesday to Saturday and from 11 am Sunday. Admission is free.

One mile north of the centre, the excellent **Kelham Island Museum** (☎ 272 2106) covers not just cutlery but the city's wider industrial heritage. One of the main exhibits is the still-operational River Don Steam Engine, a house-sized, steam-powered metal press once used to make armour plate for battleships. It opens 10 am to 4 pm Monday to Thursday and 11 am to 4.45 pm on Sunday. Admission costs £3.50/2.50.

Abbeydale Industrial Hamlet (☎ 236 7731), 4 miles (6km) south-west on the A621, is a restored industrial hamlet from the 18th century. Here you can see what the steel industry was like when it was literally a cottage industry. It opens 10 am to 4 pm Monday to Thursday and 11 am to 4.45 pm on Sunday from mid-April to late October. Admission costs £3/2.

Other Things to See

In 1914 the 15th-century church of Saints Peter and Paul on West St was upgraded to **cathedral** status. Note, at the western end, the memorial to the crew of the HMS *Sheffield* lost during the Falklands conflict.

Foremost among Sheffield's many parks, the **Botanical Gardens** (☎ 250 0500) on Clarkehouse Rd, a mile south-west of the city-centre, cover 18 acres and contain three restored glasshouses by the Victorian designer Paxton. It opens 7.30 am (from 10 am weekends) to dusk and admission is free.

Climbing

Sheffield's proximity to the Peak District has helped it become a centre for British mountain-climbing training. The **Foundry Climbing Centre** (☎ 279 6331) at 45 Mowbray St is one of several climbing centres in the area. It has over 10,000 sq feet of climbing walls, some of which are 40 feet tall, and there are instructors as well as a climbing shop. It opens 10 am to 10 pm weekdays (until 6 pm weekends) and admission costs £5.30/3.50.

Places to Stay

The TIC books rooms and has a special reservation line (☎ 201 1011).

Dorms During the summer holidays rooms are available in various dorms at the *University of Sheffield* (☎ 222 0260, fax 222 0288). The housing office is at 12 Claremont Crescent and arrangements are hotel-style. The minimum stay is two nights and the cost is £8.90 per person per night. There are laundry facilities.

Hostels The big, slightly Spartan *YMCA* (☎ 268 4807, 20 Victoria Rd) caters for both sexes with rooms for £16/26, but it's a fair walk south-west of the centre. Bus Nos 81 to 88 will drop you nearby.

B&Bs & Hotels Scores of B&Bs are concentrated on the western side of town, in Nether Edge and along Ecclesall Rd. Take bus No 22 to Nether Edge and bus Nos 81, 82 and 83 to Ecclesall Rd.

Gulliver's B&B (☎ 262 0729, 167 Ecclesall Rd) is a simple but comfy place with singles/doubles from £17/32.

Abbey House (☎ 266 7426, 484 Ecclesall Rd) has similar accommodation and charges £20/38.

In Nether Edge, *Lindum Hotel* (☎ 255 2356, fax 249 4746, 91 Montgomery Rd) charges £20/33 for very basic rooms.

More upmarket, the *Nether Edge Hotel* (☎ 255 4363, fax 255 4737, e rec@ nether-edge-hotel.co.uk, 21–23 Montgomery Rd) has rooms with en suite from £30/40.

The *Rutland Arms* (☎ 272 9003, fax 273 1425, 86 Brown St) is a lovely pub near the train station and has numerous rooms from £24/37; many are en suite.

Another good choice in the centre is *Cutlers Hotel* (☎ 273 9939, fax 276 8332, e enquiries@cutlershotel.co.uk, George St). The fairly simple but comfortable rooms all have bathrooms and start at £49/60.

The *Hotel Bristol* (☎ 200 4000, fax 220 3900, e sheffield@bhg.co.uk, Blonk St) is another one of those stylish, modern places happily cropping up throughout England. Rooms cost from £60.

Places to Eat

When it comes to eating you can't go wrong by heading for the Devonshire Quarter. *Forum Café* (☎ 276 6544) in the designer-clothes-filled Forum Shopping Centre (at the junction of Division and Eldon Sts) attracts a young and trendy crowd. Lunch will run to about £5.

The excellent *Blue Moon Café* (☎ 276 3443, Norfolk Row) caters for vegetarians; soup and good bread cost just £1.80. Locals rave about the place but note that it's open for lunch only. The excellent *cafe* at the Showroom Cinema (see Entertainment later) has fresh, reasonably priced food until late.

There are scores of places on Ecclesall Rd. One of the best is *Nonna's* (☎ 268 6166, 539–541 Ecclesall Rd), which is an Italian cafe and bar. The food is fresh and you can have a great meal for £12.

Up in Broomhill, *UK Mama* (☎ 268 7807, 257 Fulwood Rd) is a funky Afro-Caribbean restaurant where, if you're lucky, they'll let you play with the drums. Expect to pay under £8 for dinner.

Across the street, *Balti King* (☎ 266 6655, 216 Fulwood Rd) is an especially fine Indian place that is open most nights until 3 am. Dinner and drinks will cost about £8 per person.

Entertainment

To keep up with Sheffield's vibrant music scene, check out the weekly *Sheffield Telegraph* newspaper (50p), which comes out every Friday.

Pubs In a sad sign of the times, what was once the Division St HQ of the National Union of Mineworkers (when Arthur Scargill ruled the roost in the early 1980s) is now a branch of *Lloyds No 1* (☎ 276 5076). It's at the corner of Division and Holly Sts. There are many more chain bars and pubs nearby.

On Norfolk St, near the TIC, the old TSB Bank is now a particularly grand branch of *Old Monk* (☎ 257 2526).

One of Sheffield's finest pubs is easily the *Fat Cat* (☎ 249 4801, 23 Alma St), near the Kelham Island Museum. Not only do they brew their own beer but they also have a wide range of real ales from all over Yorkshire and a fine collection of Belgian products. The interior is delightfully unreconstructed and there is a fascinating exhibit on local sanitation in the men's toilets (really!).

Clubs & Venues The *Leadmill* (☎ 275 4500, 6–7 Leadmill Rd) has gigs and club nights (see the Web site at www.leadmill .co.uk for more details).

Republic (☎ 276 6777, 112 Arundel St) is known for getting the best DJs.

Planet (☎ 244 9033, 429 Effingham Rd) is a lively gay club 2 miles (3km) north-east of the centre.

Sheffield City Hall (☎ 278 9789) is a grand old performance venue at Division St and Barkers Pool.

The Boardwalk (☎ 279 9090, Snig Hill) is a good place to see top local bands.

At the corner of Paternoster Row and Charles St you'll see a striking stainless-steel building. An unintentional monument to Britain's Millennium excess, it was built to house the National Centre for Popular Music. The centre lasted a mere 16 months before it was closed, having attracted few visitors. The fact that few of the displays were actually connected with pop music seemed to play a big role in its flop. Meanwhile, the ground-floor venue *Mojo's (☎ 249 8885)* has live music on many nights.

Theatre & Cinema The *Crucible* and *Lyceum* theatres face each other across Tudor Square and share the same box office *(☎ 276 9922)*. Both are home to some excellent regional drama.

The *Showroom Cinema (☎ 275 7727, 7 Paternoster Row)* shows off-beat and interesting films. It also has a good bar and cafe.

Spectator Sports Sheffield's two main football teams are:

Sheffield United FC (☎ 221 1889) Bramall Lane, south of the centre
Sheffield Wednesday FC (☎ 221 2400) Hillsborough Stadium, A61, 3 miles (5km) north of the centre

Getting There & Away
Bus Sheffield is 160 miles (257km) from London, just off the M1. National Express services link Sheffield with London (£9.50, four hours) and other major centres in the north. There is a frequent bus service to/from Leeds (£3, one hour). Bus No X18 serves Bakewell and the Peak District to the west.

There are luggage lockers at the Sheffield Interchange bus station.

Train Sheffield's grimy train station is the hub for services throughout the north. There are regular services to Leeds (£4.90, 30 minutes), Manchester Piccadilly (£10.40, one hour), Manchester Airport (£14.05, one hour 10 minutes), York (£11.90, one hour 20 minutes) and Hull (£13.20, one hour).

There are frequent trains from London St Pancras via Leicester and Nottingham or

Derby (£44). Sheffield is also a jumping-off point for the Peak District. The Hope Valley railway line that cuts through the northern Peak District via Edale runs between Sheffield in the east and New Mills and Manchester in the west. The scenery is gorgeous.

Getting Around
Sheffield's privatised buses are a muddle of competing lines and services. Call ☎ 01709-515151 for info on all services in South Yorkshire. There is a useful information centre across from the town hall on Pinstone St. It sells tickets and passes and opens 9 am to 5 pm Monday to Saturday.

First Mainline offers a fare of 20p on its buses within the city centre. Aside from the bus services, Sheffield also boasts a modern Supertram that trundles through the city centre. Fares start at 70p.

The Travelmaster ticket (£4.95) is valid for one day of travel on all of the buses, trams and trains of South Yorkshire.

AROUND SHEFFIELD
Magna
One of Sheffield's many derelict steel mills is set to reopen as a huge new attraction, Magna (☎ 01709-720002), which is being billed a 'science adventure park'. The £37 million scheme has funding from the Millennium Commission, which must cause some fear that it will suffer the same curse of other South Yorkshire commission-funded attractions such as the National Centre for Popular Music in Sheffield (see earlier in the section) and the nearby Earth Centre (see the following section).

Magna will have four themed areas relating to steel production called earth, air, fire and water. It is meant to capture the 'drama and excitement' of steel-making. In Autumn 2000 opening times and admission prices had not been decided. Magna is 2 miles (3km) east of Junction 34 on the M1 motorway on the A6178.

Earth Centre
Ten miles (16km) north-east of Sheffield lies Earth Centre (☎ 01709-513933), a vast

Millennium Commission-funded 'green' exhibition in an abandoned colliery. Originally planned as a sort of theme park for ecologists, Earth Centre combines numerous displays showing how sustainable agriculture and technology can lead to a better future. Unfortunately all the high-minded rhetoric resulted in low visitor numbers. In 2000, the centre partially closed while more Millennium Commission money was shovelled in to make it more 'educational'. If all goes to plan, it should have reopened by the time you read this; the organisers hope to profit from corporate events and from visitors who will snap up locally produced products such as organic cotton and the like.

Call for the latest opening times (if any) and prices. The Earth Centre is off the A6023 near Conisbrough. It's adjacent to the Conisbrough train station, which is on the line linking Sheffield and Dorchester. See also the Web site at www.earthcentre.org.uk.

East Riding of Yorkshire

The word Riding comes from the Danish *treding*, meaning 'third', and dates back to the 9th century when the conquering Danish vikings divided Yorkshire into administrative regions.

The county is mostly flat, although the rolling, attractive Wolds extend northwards in a narrow spine from Lincolnshire. The 79-mile (127km) Wolds Way National Trail runs from near Hull north across the low hills to Filey on the coast where it joins Cleveland Way. See the Activities chapter for details.

The Wolds are the northernmost of the chalk downs that originate in Wiltshire and end at Flamborough Head. The rest of the county was once largely marshland, which has been drained and is now intensively (and rather unattractively) farmed.

Hull, or Kingston-upon-Hull as it is officially known, is a university town and large port, with ferries to Zeebrugge (Belgium) and Rotterdam (Netherlands). Ten miles (16km) north on the edge of the Wolds is the small, unspoilt market town of Beverley, with two superb churches. The coast varies from the tacky (Bridlington) to the remote (Spurn Head).

GETTING AROUND
Hull is easily reached by rail from Leeds and York, and from there a line runs north to Beverley, Filey and Scarborough. Hull is also a hub for regional bus services.

HULL (KINGSTON-UPON-HULL)
☎ 01482 • pop 331,200
Fortunately, only pedants call Hull by its unwieldy official name. Historically, this north-eastern town was a major port, and so it remains today. Hull was hard hit during WWII and today initial impressions are not encouraging. But persevere and you'll be rewarded with a range of diversions. The Old Town retains a feel of Victorian times when Hull and its port were at their peak.

Orientation & Information
The Old Town of Hull is the most interesting part. It is bordered by the Rivers Humber and Hull as well as Ferensway and Freetown Way.

Tourist Offices Hull's TIC (☎ 223559, fax 613959, ℮ hullparagon@ytbtic.co.uk) on Carr Lane is surrounded by the imposing buildings of Register Square. It opens 9 am to 6 pm Monday to Saturday and 11 am to 3 pm on Sunday.

Money Lunn Poly/Amex (☎ 227456), 17 King Edward St, exchanges money. It's open 9 am to 5.30 pm daily except Sunday. It also has a travel agency.

Post The post office, 57 Jameson St, is open 9 am to 5.30 pm daily except Sunday.

Library The Central Library (☎ 210000), Albion St, has Internet access. It's open 9.30 am to 8 pm Monday to Thursday, until 5.30 pm Friday and until 4.30 pm Saturday.

YORKSHIRE

The library is also home to Hull Screen (☎ 616871), which shows off-beat and foreign films on many nights.

Bookshops Waterstones (☎ 580234), 19–21 Jameson St, is probably the best local option.

City Museums

Hull has a remarkable collection of city-run museums (☎ 613902 for all). They open 10 am to 5 pm Monday to Saturday, and 1.30 to 4.30 pm on Sunday. All are free unless otherwise stated.

Queen Victoria Square is the focus of historic Hull. It is flanked by the impressive Ferens Art Gallery and Maritime Museum.

The **Ferens Art Gallery**, built in 1927, has a decent selection of European art and includes a number of classics by old masters including Frans Hals and Henry Moore.

The **Maritime Museum** celebrates Hull's long maritime traditions and dates from 1871. Look for the many nautical figures adorning its decoration. It has displays and models covering all aspects of local history and one of the rooms was once the opulent **Court Room** where hapless ship's captains

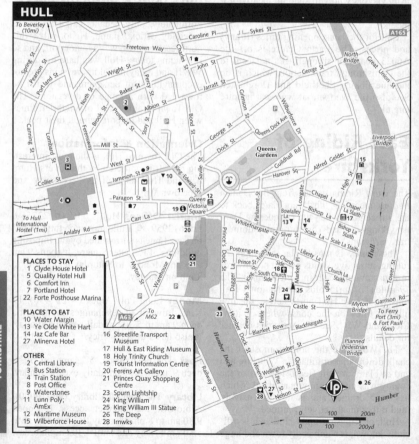

HULL

PLACES TO STAY
1 Clyde House Hotel
4 Quality Hotel Hull
6 Comfort Inn
7 Portland Hotel
22 Forte Posthouse Marina

PLACES TO EAT
10 Water Margin
13 Ye Olde White Hart
14 Jaz Cafe Bar
27 Minerva Hotel

OTHER
2 Central Library
3 Bus Station
4 Train Station
8 Post Office
9 Waterstones
11 Lunn Poly;
    AmEx
12 Maritime Museum
15 Wilberforce House

16 Streetlife Transport
    Museum
17 Hull & East Riding Museum
18 Holy Trinity Church
19 Tourist Information Centre
20 Ferens Art Gallery
21 Princes Quay Shopping
    Centre
23 Spurn Lightship
24 King William
25 King William III Statue
26 The Deep
28 Irnwks

YORKSHIRE

who were accused of causing some calamity were tried.

A few streets east, High St has three more interesting museums. Near Drypool Bridge and the water, **Wilberforce House** was the birthplace in 1759 of the anti-slavery crusader William Wilberforce. It was built in 1639 and the museum, which covers the history of slavery and the campaign against it, overflows into several attractive Georgian houses. Next door is the **Streetlife Transport Museum**, which is just what its name implies and also has a very pleasant garden.

South past Chapel Lane Staith, the **Hull & East Riding Museum** is a fairly entertaining place that traces local history from Roman times to the present. One of the best rooms is entitled Celtic World.

Other Sights

At the heart of the Old Town, a church typifies Hull's importance at early stages of its history. **Holy Trinity Church** (☎ 446757) is a magnificent 15th-century building with a striking central tower. It features huge areas of windows, built not to bring in the light but to keep the weight of the walls down as the soil here is unstable. It opens daily.

Lovely, pedestrianised **Parliament St** suggests that much of 18th-century Hull must have looked like.

The **Spurn Lightship** is now anchored in the marina. Over 100 years old, it once provided guidance for ships navigating the notorious Humber estuary.

On Market Place, the **King William III Statue** was erected in 1734 in honour of William of Orange, who besides being king also has the distinction of being the person to introduce England to gin, which he brought from his native Holland. See the special section on Pubs for the drunken results.

At some point late in 2001, a huge new lottery-funded aquarium called **The Deep** (☎ 615789) is due to open at Sammy's Point, on the east bank of the River Hull at its confluence with the Humber. It will be linked to the centre by a long pedestrian bridge. Check with the TIC for the latest developments.

Midway between the Old Town and ferry docks, **Fort Paull** (☎ 893339) is a lavishly restored fort that for centuries protected the entrance to the Humber. Wax figures recall moments dating back to the time of Cromwell. It opens 10 am to 6 pm, April to October. Admission costs £4.50/3. It's 6 miles (10km) east of the centre along the A1033.

Walking

The TIC sells a brochure called *The Seven Seas Fish Pavement Trail* (40p), which is a highly entertaining self-guiding tour of the Old Town. Fish shapes embedded in the pavement lead visitors on a delightful and historic tour. Kids love it.

Guided walks leave from the TIC at 2 pm daily (except Tuesday and Sunday) from April to October and cost £2.50/1. Customised tours are also offered; call ☎ 878535.

Places to Stay

The TIC has lists of B&Bs, most of which are at least a mile from the centre. Most hotels offer excellent weekend bargains.

Hull International Hostel (☎ 216409, 4 Malm St) has shared rooms and doubles in a small house a mile west of the centre. The cost is £10 per person and you can get a single room for a remarkable £12. From the bus station, bus Nos 2, 39, 60, 64 and 66 pass by Malm St. Get off at the Boulevard stop.

Clyde House Hotel (☎ 214981, 13 John St) is the best budget choice near the Old Town. Its simple rooms start at £24/40.

Comfort Inn (☎ 323299, fax 214730, 11 Anlaby Rd) is charmless and modern. Its rooms cost £55/63.

The *Quality Hotel Royal* (☎ 325087, fax 323172, 170 Ferensway) is part of the train station complex. Fortunately it's cleaner, although it's no great shakes really. Somewhat updated rooms cost £50/70.

Portland Hotel (☎ 326462, fax 213460, Paragon St) is another glumly modern place. The rooms, however, aren't bad and, as they say, it's always better to be inside looking out. Singles/doubles cost £83/93.

YORKSHIRE

Forte Posthouse Marina (☎ *0870 400 9043, fax 213299, Castle St)* is the obvious choice if you want to be right on the water. The well equipped rooms cost £95 midweek and £65 at the weekend.

Places to Eat

There are several lovely old pubs in the Old Town that serve good food. The town centre gets crowded with boisterous youths on weekend nights and pubs respond in two ways; offering lots of lager specials or closing up shop.

Ye Olde White Hart (☎ *326363, 25 Silver St)* dates from the 1700s and has a good range of beer and food (served from noon to 8 pm daily). It is hidden down a small alley and is definitely a throw-back to the 18th century. Definitely have at least one here.

Jaz Cafe Bar (☎ *228063, 41 Lowgate)* has live jazz and an interesting menu with many vegetarian options for around £6. The kitchen opens 11 am to 11 pm daily (from 7 pm Sunday).

Water Margin (☎ *219544, 47 Jameson St)* is one of those Chinese places with a menu that reads like a phone book. Fortunately it's good and is open until midnight daily except Sunday. Most items are £4.

Minerva Hotel (☎ *326909) on Nelson St* doesn't have rooms but it has no end of charm. It has a fine location next to the pier and the decor is maritime; scores of old photos of ships and seamen line the walls. The beer selection is first-rate. Cheap lunches are served daily and dinner on Monday to Thursday.

Entertainment

With live music three nights a week and a beer garden out the back, the *King William* (☎ *227013, 41 Market Place)* is a decent pub that's busy day and night.

Irnwks (☎ *227440, Minerva Terrace)* is a buzzing club with dancing and live music most nights. It's right on the Marina in a low, modern building.

Shopping

Princes Quay Shopping Centre (☎ 586622), an imposing glass building set in a moat facing the modern marina, is filled with chain stores of every kind. It has a commodious parking lot.

Getting There & Away

The bus station is on Ferensway, just north of the train station. National Express has several buses a day to/from London (£17, five hours). There are also several to/from Manchester (£8, four hours) Regional services also leave from here.

The train station is west of Queen Victoria Square, in the centre of town. It is a deplorable place, with few facilities but no shortage of pigeon poop and human piss everywhere. It does have lockers. Hull is on a branch line off the London King's Cross–Edinburgh line and has good rail links north and south, and west to York (£10, one hour, hourly) and Leeds (£11.90, one hour, hourly).

The ferry port is 3 miles (5km) east of the centre at King George Dock. There are shuttle buses between the port and the train station. P&O North Sea Ferries (☎ 377177) has daily ferries to/from Rotterdam (13 hours) and Zeebrugge (13½ hours). The fares on both routes cost £81/136. See the Web site at www.ponsf.com for more details.

Getting Around

Hull's local buses have several operators. The local bus information line (☎ 222222) can tell you where (and how) to go. Most lines start at or pass through the bus station.

HUMBER BRIDGE

Gracefully soaring over the Humber, the 1400m-long Humber Bridge has linked Yorkshire and Lincolnshire since 1981. Near its base on the north side is a small park with nature trails that run from the parking area right down to the river bank. The park can be reached from the bridge access roads.

The park is also home to the Humber Bridge TIC (☎/fax 01482-640852). It handles information requests for all of East Riding of Yorkshire and the Wolds Way. It also has a display documenting the construction of the bridge. It's open 9 am to 5 pm daily (until 3 pm, November to March and to 4 pm, March, April and October).

WOLDS WAY
The 80-miles-long (129km) Wolds Way meanders over the gently rolling Yorkshire Wolds. See the Activities section for more details about the trail.

The northern end of the Wolds Way is at **Filey** (see listing later in the North Yorkshire section), where the trail connects to the popular Cleveland Way. The southern end of the trail is in **Hessle**, a riverside town 4 miles (6km) west of Hull. Bus Nos 1 and 68 run to Hull's centre. Hessle is also a stop for local trains on the line west from Hull to Leeds, Doncaster and Sheffield. The Humber Bridge TIC is a mile farther west and the trail passes very close.

BEVERLEY
☎ 01482 • pop 21,900
At the centre of a rich agricultural region and once the capital of the East Riding, Beverley is a gem of an 18th-century market town hardly marred by modern development. It's dominated by the beautiful Beverley Minster, formerly a monastic church and still the equal of many cathedrals in magnificence.

Orientation & Information
Beverley is compact and easily walked to from either the train or bus stations.

Beverley TIC (☎ 867430, fax 885237, e beverley@ytbtic.co.uk), 34 Butcher Row, opens 9.30 am to 5.30 pm weekdays and until 5 pm on Saturday. It also opens 10 am to 2 pm on Sunday, June to August.

The post office is on Register Square and is open 9 am to 5.30 pm weekdays and until 1 pm Saturday.

The library (☎ 885355) is on Champney Rd and is open 9.30 am to 5 pm weekdays (until 7 pm Tuesday, Thursday and Friday) and 9 am to 1 pm on Saturday. It also has a small art gallery.

The Beverley Bookshop (☎ 868132), 16 Butcher Row, is a good locally owned bookshop.

Beverley Minster
The first church on the site was built in the 7th century when a monastery was established. The present building (☎ 887520) dates from 1220 but construction continued for two centuries, spanning the Early English, Decorated and perpendicular periods. The end product is best known for its magnificent Gothic perpendicular west front (1420) with its twin towers and wonderful sculpture. Overall, the minster is hailed for its uniform Early English facade.

Inside, extraordinary medieval faces and demons peer down from every possible vantage point, while stone angels play a variety of silent instruments. Note particularly a 10th-century Frith Stool (or sanctuary chair); the canopy of the Percy Tomb (to the north of the altar); and the 68 medieval misericords (support ledges for choristers).

There is a good display showing not only the history of the minster but also of Beverley as well. It's worth checking out the rebuilt treadwheel crane, which was where hapless workers ground around like hamsters in a cage in order to lift the huge loads needed to build medieval buildings.

The minster opens 9 am to 5 pm Monday to Saturday and noon to 5 pm Sunday. It sometimes opens later from June to August. Donations of £1 are requested.

St Mary's Church
Stately St Mary's Church (☎ 865709) would attract all the attention if it were anywhere else but Beverley. Here it inevitably plays second fiddle to the minster. Still, if you like medieval churches, this is a particularly fine example, built in stages between 1120 and 1530. In the North Choir Aisle look out for a carving thought to have inspired Lewis Carroll's White Rabbit. The church was built by the rich Beverley musical guilds and this patronage is honoured in the lavish carvings showing musical instruments.

Its hours are similar to the minster. Admission is free.

Museum of Army Transport
All manner of military transport is on display at the Museum of Army Transport

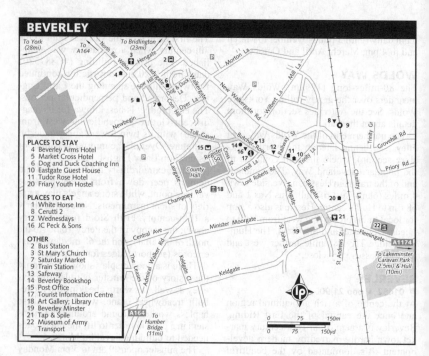

BEVERLEY

To York (28mi)
To A164
To Bridlington (23mi)
North Bar Within
Hengate
Ladygate
Sow Hill Rd
Walkergate
Morton La
New Walkergate Rd
Wilbert La
Mill La
Dog & Duck La
Dyer La
Corn Hill
Newbegin
Toll Gavel
Butcher Row
Railway St
Trinity Gr
Grovehill Rd
Priory Rd
Register Sq
Cross St
Well La
Lord Roberts Rd
Highgate
Eastgate
Trinity La
Chantry La
County Hall
Champney Rd
Minister Moorgate
Central Ave
The Leases
Admiral Walker Rd
Keldgate Cl
Keldgate
St John St
St Andrews St
Flemingate
A1174
To Lakeminster Caravan Park (2.5mi) & Hull (10mi)
A164
To Humber Bridge (11mi)

PLACES TO STAY
4 Beverley Arms Hotel
5 Market Cross Hotel
6 Dog and Duck Coaching Inn
10 Eastgate Guest House
11 Tudor Rose Hotel
20 Friary Youth Hostel

PLACES TO EAT
1 White Horse Inn
8 Cerutti 2
12 Wednesdays
16 JC Peck & Sons

OTHER
2 Bus Station
3 St Mary's Church
7 Saturday Market
9 Train Station
13 Safeway
14 Beverley Bookshop
17 Post Office
18 Tourist Information Centre
19 Beverley Minster
21 Tap & Spile
22 Museum of Army Transport

0   75   150m
0   75   150yd

LP

(☎ 860445). The exhibits are indoors, cover 2 acres and include trains, planes and trucks – lots and lots of trucks. The air is redolent with the rich odours of rubber and oil.

The museum is just east of the minster at Flemingate. It's open 10 am to 5 pm daily and costs £4/2 for adults/children.

Markets
General markets are held on Wednesday (near the minster) and Saturday (on Marketplace, off Lairgate). A 400-year-old cattle and pig market is held to the north of the town centre every Tuesday and Wednesday (Wednesday is the big day; selling starts at 10.30 am and finishes by 1 pm).

Places to Stay
The TIC has a lengthy list of B&Bs.

Camping The *Lakeminster Caravan Park* (☎ 882655) has camping. It is 2½ miles

(4km) east of town on Hull Rd. Tent sites cost £10.

Hostels In a beautifully restored 14th-century Dominican friary, *Friary Youth Hostel* (☎ 881751, fax 880118, Friar's Lane), is open daily except Sunday from mid-April to October. Beds cost £8.50/5.75 for adults/under-18s.

B&Bs & Hotels Most of the cheaper B&Bs are a short walk north of the minster. *Eastgate Guest House* (☎ 868464, fax 871899, 7 Eastgate) has singles/doubles starting at £21/34. It is close to the train station.

Market Cross Hotel (☎ 679029, 12–14 Lairgate) is another central place that charges from £23 per person. It's recently been refurbished.

The *Dog and Duck Coaching Inn* (☎ 886079, fax 862419, 33 Ladygate) is a very pleasant pub, which has rooms for rent that open onto a garden. Rooms are £25/38.

YORKSHIRE

Tudor Rose Hotel (☎ 882028, Wednesday Market) is well located and has comfortable rooms above a good pub and restaurant. It costs about £20 per person.

The *Beverley Arms Hotel (☎ 869241, fax 870907, North Bar Within)* is a dignified old Georgian mansion. It has rooms from £48/85.

Places to Eat
Most of the pubs also serve food. *The Tudor Rose Hotel* (see Places to Stay) has a Polish restaurant where a four-course feast costs £16.

JC Peck & Sons (☎ 862353, 26 Butcher Row) is a sparkling place for fish and chips (£4.30). It has an interesting menu with items like poached salmon salad and is open for take-away until 5 pm. A small cafe area is open for lunch.

Tap & Spile (☎ 881547, 1 Flemingate) claims to be Beverley's oldest pub. It's well located across from the minster and has an excellent beer list.

White Horse Inn (☎ 861973, 22 Hengate) is also called Nellie's. It is lovely, with many rambling rooms, open fires and outside tables. On many nights there is live folk or jazz music.

Cerutti 2 (☎ 866700, Station Square) is the best thing about the train station. It's a stylish Italian restaurant with excellent food; allow for about £20 per person. It's open for lunch and dinner daily except Sunday.

Wednesdays (☎ 869727, 8 Wednesday Market) is much acclaimed. The menu melds Europe with Asia and the wine list is excellent. You can enjoy three courses for about £20. It serves lunch and dinner and is closed Sunday.

Safeway supermarket *(☎ 868885, 25 Butcher Row)* is right across from the TIC.

Getting There & Away
The train station lies just east of the town centre. For such a good day-trip city, it's a scandal that no luggage lockers are provided. The bus station is north on Sow Hill.

Bus East Yorkshire bus No X46 links Beverley with York (£3.15, one hour 10 min-

utes, hourly). Buses Nos 121, 122, 246 and X46 run to/from Hull at least twice an hour (£1.90, 30 minutes).

Train There are regular trains to/from Scarborough via Filey (£7.10, one hour 20 minutes). Trains to/from Hull (£3.10, 15 minutes) run at least hourly.

EAST RIDING OF YORKSHIRE COAST
There are some long stretches of relatively unspoiled coast along this part of the Yorkshire Coast. The major town, Bridlington, is a typical seaside resort. The highlights here are the Bempton Cliffs Nature Reserve in the north and Spurn Head in the South.

Bempton Cliffs Nature Reserve
Run by the Royal Society for the Protection of Birds (☎ 01262-851179), Bempton Cliffs Nature Reserve is a delightful place whether you're a hardcore bird-watcher or not. The imposing chalk cliffs are home to over 200,000 nesting birds every spring and summer. There are many other feathered residents in place the rest of the year as well. Among the species flapping about are the gannet, pied flycatcher, linnet and the ever-popular puffin.

There is a good visitors centre with a small snack bar set back from the cliffs, and numerous marked paths. Binoculars can be rented for £2 and there are usually volunteers on hand to provide guidance. The reserve is open 10 am to 5 pm daily, March to November (weekends only the rest of the year). Admission is free unless you have a car in which case you pay £3 parking.

The reserve is a well marked 1¼ miles (2km) from the village of Bempton and the B1229. By public transport, take one of the hourly trains on the Hull–Scarborough line and then walk.

Flamborough
A small village east of Bempton and Bridlington, Flamborough is notable for two things: the great views from Flamborough Head, 2 miles (3km) east of the village; and its pub.

Seabirds (☎ *01262-850242)* is at the junction of the B1255 and the B1229. It is a classic country pub with several rooms, open fires and a beer garden. The real ale selection is good and the seafood lunches and dinners excellent (£4 to £9).

Bridlington

This is a classic seaside resort with all the good and bad that entails. Its primary charm is the long sandy **beach** that runs from the unfortunately named Sewerby just north of Bridlington all the way south to Spurn Head. The promenade features every sort of traditional English seaside pleasure palace imaginable. From candyfloss to penny games to cheap lager, it's here.

The TIC (☎ 01262-673474), 25 Prince St, is near the beach and has short-term parking at the front. It's open 9.30 am to 5.30 pm daily (closed Sunday, November to March) and can book a vast array of rooms.

Bridlington is on the line from Hull to Scarborough with frequent trains to the former (£6.80, 45 minutes) and hourly trains to the latter (£4.10, 40 minutes).

Spurn Head

Spurn Head is a long sandbank hanging down like an appendix on the north side of the Humber estuary. It has a long military history and is an important nature reserve.

In 1804, gun batteries were built on Spurn Head in case the French came calling. In following decades the fortifications were greatly expanded to meet various threats. By WWII there were guns of all sizes mounted in heavy concrete emplacements. After the war, the odds of some enemy force arriving in assault boats faded and the guns were removed, although remnants of the many concrete emplacements and roadways survive.

A benefit of the years of military use is that Spurn Head was spared commercial development. Today it is made up of large rolling sand dunes covered with various sea grasses. Most of the land is now part of the **Spurn National Nature Reserve**.

There are two TICs. One has a cafe and is at the end of the B1445 in Kilnsea, the last village on the mainland. Called the *Blue Bell Tea Room* (☎ *01964-650139)*, it is open 11 am to 5 pm daily (weekends only, September to May). Close to the beach, it allows free camping on its grassy land. The other TIC is a mile farther south along the Spurn Head access road. This one has a full collection of materials outlining the unusual nature of the sandbank. *Spurn: the moving story* details the shifting nature of the sands and shows how one good storm could wash the entire head a way. It's open 10 am to 5 pm at the weekend.

Entrance to Spurn Head costs £2.50 per car. The single-track road to the point is 2½ miles (4km) long. There are many good walks, and at the tip of the head, you can see the spurting tides of the Humber as well as the busy shuttle boats used by the pilots of the many passing freighters.

Back in Kilnsea, the *Crown and Anchor* (☎ *01964-650276)* is a fine waterfront pub along the B1445 with good meals and rooms for £30/39.

Public transport to Kilnsea and Spurn Head is nonexistent. The town is 28 miles (45km) east of Hull. The roads are good for bikes.

North Yorkshire

North Yorkshire is one of England's largest counties, containing some of the finest monuments, most beautiful countryside and most spectacular coastline in the country. It includes two national parks (the Yorkshire Dales and North York Moors), the medieval city of York, the great monastic ruins of Rievaulx and Fountains abbeys, the classical beauty of Castle Howard and the grim castles of Richmond and Bolton.

Most of North Yorkshire was untouched by the Industrial Revolution and, to a large extent, the accompanying agricultural revolution. The winter climate is harsh and much of the countryside lends itself to sheep grazing, an activity largely unchanged from medieval times. Great fortunes – private and monastic – were founded on wool.

In the west the Pennines, including the peaks of Ingleborough (723m) and Pen-y-ghent (693m), dominate the beautiful dales, whose flanks are defined by snaking stone walls and overlooked by wild, heather-clad plateaus. In the east, stone villages shelter at the foot of bleak and beautiful moors. These stretch to the high cliffs of the east coast, with its fishing villages and the holiday towns of Whitby and Robin Hood's Bay.

GETTING THERE & AROUND

A spider's web of buses and trains connect places in North Yorkshire. Call ☎ 0870 608 2608 for all Yorkshire bus and train information. There are various explorer tickets covering the North Yorkshire Moors. Individual bus and train companies also offer their own schemes, so it's always worth asking for advice on the best deal when you buy your ticket.

YORK

☎ 01904 • pop 123,000

For nearly 2000 years York has been the capital of the north. Its city walls, built during the 13th century, are among the most impressive surviving medieval fortifications in Europe. They encompass a thriving, fascinating centre with medieval streets, grand Georgian town houses, riverside pubs and modern shops. The crowning glory is the minster, England's largest Gothic cathedral, but there's a bewildering array of things to see and do. If you arrive by car on the B1363 from the north, you'll be treated to a sudden view of the minster, across fields, that has been unchanged for centuries. As you take in the view, imagine how it must have affected pilgrims hundreds of years ago.

York attracts millions of visitors, and the July and August crowds can get you down; try to visit out of season if you can.

History

It's thought that the Brigantes had a settlement at the meeting point of the Rivers Foss and Ouse before the Romans arrived to set up a walled garrison called Eboracum in AD 71.

Eboracum was strategically important, hence the visits of several emperors: Hadrian used it as a base in 121; Septimius Severus used it to hold Imperial Court in 211; and in 306 Constantius Chlorus died here. He was succeeded by his son Constantine, the first Christian emperor and founder of Constantinople (Istanbul), who was probably proclaimed emperor on the site of the cathedral.

The Anglo-Saxons founded the cathedral city of Eoforwic on the Roman ruins. Eoforwic was the capital of the independent kingdom of Northumbria, which, like that of the Brigantes, stretched from the Humber to the Firth of Forth.

In 625 Christianity was brought here by Paulinus, a Roman priest who had joined Augustine's Canterbury mission. He succeeded in converting the Saxon king of Northumbria, King Edwin, and his nobles. The first wooden church was built in 627 and became a centre of learning that attracted students from around Europe.

The Danish Vikings captured and burnt the city in 867 but then made it their capital, Jorvik, for nearly 100 years. Under their rule it became an important trading port. Not until 954 did the kings of Wessex succeed in reuniting Danelaw with the south but their control remained tenuous. King Harold was forced to tackle a Norwegian invasion-cum-uprising at Stamford Bridge, east of York, immediately before the Battle of Hastings.

William the Conqueror was also faced with rebellion. After the north's second uprising in 1070, he burnt York and Durham and laid waste to the countryside – the 'harrying of the North'. Afterwards, the Normans rebuilt the walls and erected two castles and a new cathedral. York once again became an important port and the centre of the profitable new trade in wool.

In the 15th century the city declined, losing influence and power to London. During the Civil War, York twice came under siege from the Parliamentarian army. The first siege was lifted after two months by the arrival of an army under the command of King Charles' nephew Prince Rupert. In the

YORKSHIRE

YORK

YORK

PLACES TO STAY
1 Gables Guest House
2 Brontë House
3 Claremont Guest House
4 Hudson's Hotel
5 Elliotts Hotel
6 Alcuin Lodge
7 Martins Guest House
8 Briar Lea Guest House
9 Riverside Walk B&B;
   Abbey Guest House
10 Crook Lodge
11 23 St Mary's
12 Treetops Guest House
13 Coach House Hotel
14 Jorvik Hotel
27 Dean Court Hotel
35 Judges Lodging Hostel
44 Monkbar Hotel
65 Royal York Hotel
75 York Backpackers
81 York Youth Hotel
101 St Denys Hotel
108 Wheatlands House
109 Nunmill House
110 Acorn Guest House
111 Rowntree Park Camping

PLACES TO EAT
20 Café No 8
22 Juice Up
34 Pizza Express
36 Ask; Grand Assembly Rooms
39 Taylor's
42 St William's College
46 La Piazza
47 Lime House
48 Siam House
49 Coffee Espress
52 Scott's of York
53 Oscar's Wine Bar & Bistro
54 Victor J's

57 The Rubicon
59 Betty's
73 Jinnah
74 Blake Head Bookshop &
   Café
89 Fiesta Mexicana
96 Blue Bicycle
100 Loucedes Tapas

PUBS, BARS & CLUBS
38 Ye Olde Starre
51 Old White Swan
62 Maltings
77 Ziggy's
82 King's Arms
85 Lowther Arms
92 Blue Bell
94 Fibbers
102 Spread Eagle

OTHER
15 Gatehall; Hospitium
16 St Mary's Lodge
17 St Olave's Church
18 St Mary's Abbey
19 Kaos
21 Bootham Tower
23 Bootham Bar;
   Steps to city walls
24 Exhibition Square
25 York City Art Gallery
26 Tourist Information Centre
28 York Theatre Royal
29 Yorkshire Museum
30 Observatory
31 Museum Gardens Lodge
32 Multangular Tower
33 Museum Docks
37 AmEx
40 York Minster
41 Treasurer's House
43 Bob Trotter Bike Hire

45 Monk Bar; Richard III
   Museum; Steps to City Walls
50 Holy Trinity, Goodramgate
55 Nevisport
56 Borders
58 Internet Exchange
60 City Screen
61 Post Office
63 Bus Stops (Rougier St);
   National Express Shop
64 Steps to City Walls
66 York Model Railway
67 Train Station
68 Information Office
69 Hertz
70 Station Taxis
71 Europcar
72 York Brewery
76 Wildcat Records;
   Ken Spellman Booksellers
78 All Saints
79 Bus Information Office
80 Practical Car & Van Rental
83 Thomas Cook
84 Grand Opera House
86 York Dungeon
87 Riding Lights Theatre
88 Yorkboat River Trips
90 Jorvik Viking Centre
91 All Saints Pavement
93 Archaeological Resource
   Centre
95 Jack Duncan Books
97 Merchant Adventurers' Hall
98 Fairfax House
99 St Denys Church
103 Walmgate Bar
104 York Barbican Centre
105 York Castle Museum
106 Clifford's Tower
107 Eddie Brown Tours
112 The Washeteria

war's bloodiest battle, Prince Rupert chased the retreating Parliamentarians to Marston Moor where they turned on him and cut his army to pieces, killing 4000 men. The siege was resumed, and the city finally fell in July 1642. Fortunately, the commander of the Parliamentarian forces, Sir Thomas Fairfax, a local man, prevented the troops pillaging the minster.

The coming of the railway in 1839 once again placed York at the hub of the north-east.

Orientation

Though the centre is relatively small, York's streets are a confusing medieval tangle. Remember that, in York, *gate* means street and *bar* means gate. The city is circled by a ring road. There are five major landmarks in the town: the wall enclosing the city centre; the minster at the northern corner; Clifford's Tower, a 13th-century castle and mound at the southern end; the River Ouse that cuts the centre in two; and the enormous train station just outside the western corner.

YORKSHIRE

Information

Tourist Offices The main TIC (☎ 621756, fax 551888, ⓔ tic@york-tourism.co.uk), is in De Grey Rooms, Exhibition Square, north of the river near Bootham Bar. It opens daily from 9 am to 6 pm (10 am to 4 pm on Sunday). There's also a small TIC at the train station. It opens 9 am to 6 pm daily (until 5 pm on Sunday, and until 7 pm from June to August). The TIC sells the use-

---

Minding the Minster

Its grey stone eminence dominating the views from all directions, York Minster looks the very image of permanence. But all is not as it seems as the glorious structure has regularly faced ruin through the centuries and only extraordinary efforts have brought about its resurrection.

Although it seems as if it's all stone, the Minster actually has a substantial part of its structure made from wood and this has fuelled several disastrous fires through the years. In 1829 a deranged man hid in the Minster until after closing and then he set the choir on fire. Only two stalls survived and the flames also took out the organ, parts of the roof and caused additional wide-spread damage. Records allowed most of the wooden detail of the choir to be recreated.

This catastrophe resulted in greater security for the Minster, but this wasn't enough to prevent another blaze just 11 years later. Caused by an unattended candle, the conflagration shot up the south-west tower and spread to the roof over the nave all the way to the central tower. Again, massive reconstruction was needed, although the accuracy of some of the detail is a bit dubious. One of the replaced bosses – the ornamental hubs where the roof vaulting meets – shows a nativity scene with Jesus nursing from a bottle (look for the second boss from the Minster's west end). Having been nearly destroyed by fire twice in only 11 years meant that the Minster was almost broke. The public had been generous with funds for restoration after the first fire but donations after the careless 1840 fire were sparse. It took decades for the Minster to get its books back in order.

As opposed to maniacs or candles, God took the blame for the 1984 fire in the south transept. A lightning bolt started a blaze that destroyed the roof and severely damaged the 16th-century rose window and the surrounding structure. The restoration, which took four years, includes six bosses designed by contest winners of the children's TV show *Blue Peter*; an easy one to spot features a scuba diver with a whale. Restoring the rose window was a challenge as the heat had broken the glass into 40,000 pieces, which had to be epoxied back together by hand.

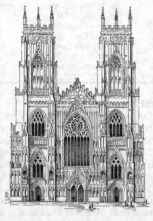

Fire hasn't been the only threat to the Minster – the ground itself has placed the structure in peril. In 1407 the original central tower collapsed thanks to dubious foundations dug into the poor-quality subsoil. From 1420 to 1472 a new central tower – the one you see proudly rising 60m above the horizon today – was built. But the same dodgy subsoil that claimed the first tower began giving way under the 16,000 tonnes of the second. The process was slow and despite occasional warnings over the centuries, nothing of substance was done until 1967 when an inspection revealed that the tower was ready to collapse and would shortly become so unstable that there would be no way to repair it. An emergency appeal brought in £2 million and an entirely new foundation was constructed of concrete set deep into the ground. Work stretched from the choir all the way to the west towers. You can see this massive undertaking by touring the Treasury.

ful *York Map & Guide* (80p). See also the York Tourism Bureau's Web site at www .york-tourism.co.uk.

Money AmEx (☎ 676501), 6 Stonegate, has an exchange service open 9 am to 5.30 pm daily except Sunday.

Post & Communications The post office is at 22 Lendal and opens 9 am to 5.30 pm Monday to Saturday.

The Internet Exchange (☎ 638808), 13 Stonegate, has a minimum charge of £1 and an additional fee of 10p per minute for Web surfing.

Travel Agencies Thomas Cook (☎ 653626), 4 Nessgate, is a travel agent offering a full service.

Bookshops All the usual high-street bookshops can be found in York. The largest is Borders (☎ 653300), 1–5 Davygate, which occupies part of a 19th-century chapel. It opens 8 am to 10 pm (11 am to 5 pm on Sunday). There is a wealth of used and antiquarian bookshops. See the Shopping section later for details.

Laundry The Washeteria (☎ 656145), 148 Bishopthorpe Rd, is about a 10-minute walk south of the centre.

Medical Services York District Hospital (☎ 631313) is a mile north of the centre on Wiggington Rd.

York Minster

York Minster (☎ 624426), or the Cathedral & Metropolitan Church of St Peter, is Europe's largest medieval cathedral and one of the world's most inspiring buildings. The word 'minster' suggests that one of the previous buildings was once connected with a monastery. The minster is the seat of the archbishop of York, who holds the title of Primate of England and is second only in importance to the archbishop of Canterbury, the Primate of *All* England.

The minster, a time capsule incorporating the remains of seven buildings, is most famous for its extensive medieval stained-glass, particularly in the enormous Great East Window (1405–8).

The first church on the site was a wooden chapel built for Paulinus' baptism of King Edwin on Easter Day 627; its site is marked

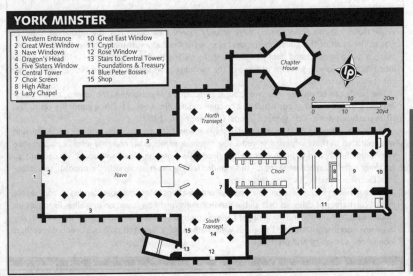

YORK MINSTER

1 Western Entrance
2 Great West Window
3 Nave Windows
4 Dragon's Head
5 Five Sisters Window
6 Central Tower
7 Choir Screen
8 High Altar
9 Lady Chapel
10 Great East Window
11 Crypt
12 Rose Window
13 Stairs to Central Tower; Foundations & Treasury
14 Blue Peter Bosses
15 Shop

Chapter House

North Transept

Nave

Choir

South Transept

in the crypt. This church was built near the site of a Roman basilica, a vast assembly hall at the heart of Roman military headquarters; parts can be seen in the foundations. A stone church was started but fell into disrepair after Edwin's death. St Wilfred built the next church but this was destroyed as part of William's brutal response to a northern rebellion. The first Norman church was built in stages from 1060 to 1080; you can see surviving fragments in the foundations and crypt.

The present building, built mainly from 1220 to 1480, incorporates several architectural styles. The northern transept was built in Early English style between 1241 and 1260; the nave, choir and octagonal chapter house were built in Decorated style between 1260 and 1405; and the central, or lantern, tower was the last addition, built in perpendicular style from 1460 to 1480.

You enter from the western end. The nave is unusually tall and wide. Although the aisles (to the side) are roofed in stone, the central roof is wood painted to look like stone. On both sides of the nave are the shields of nobles who met Edward II at a parliament in York. Also note the **dragon's head** projecting from the gallery – it's a crane believed to have been used to lift a font cover. There are several fine **windows** dating from the early 14th century, but the most dominating is the **Great West Window,** from 1338, with beautiful stone tracery.

The transepts are the oldest part of the building above ground and the **Five Sisters Window**, with five lancets over 15m high, is the minster's oldest complete window; most of it is from around 1260. In 1984 the south transept was destroyed in a fire. Six of the **bosses** in the new roof were designed by children who won a competition sponsored by the popular TV program *Blue Peter*.

Medieval Guilds

In medieval and Tudor times, craftsmen and tradesmen formed themselves into guilds, which were basically a form of trade union or professional association. Crafts and trades were restricted to the members of an appropriate guild except at markets (which were usually weekly) or fairs (which were usually annual).

The guilds checked the quality of the work done, investigated complaints and regulated prices. While those first two activities may have actually served their customers, the regulation of prices was at the heart of the guilds' existence. Prices were fixed at levels that allowed for comfortable margins and a basic fat and happy existence. If there's any doubt about the profits these monopolistic practices allowed, just look at some of the surviving guild halls in England such as York's Merchant Adventurers' Hall.

The guilds can be divided into two groups: merchants and craftsmen. The former, as the name implies, sold and traded goods whether it be commodities like wool or finished goods like cloth. The latter produced items such as metal-goods, furniture or foodstuffs.

Competition among guild members was only allowed in terms of quality and service. Admission was restricted to those who had served a seven-year apprenticeship and paid a fee. An apprentice was completely bound to his master and received little more than food and board. He couldn't do anything without explicit permission – this included having any relations with the opposite sex. Imagine: 'Excuse me master, I've met this wench...'

The guilds also had a valuable role as social organisations. Most members tended to congregate in particular areas of cities, so that all the candlemakers might be found on one alley. Examples include Swinegate in York and Ironmonger Lane in London. Surviving accounts show that as with any large and social organisations, the guilds were hotbeds of gossip and politics as various members lobbied for advantage and prestige.

The **chapter house** is a magnificent example of the Decorated style. Superb stonework decorated with tiny individual stone heads surrounds a wonderful space uninterrupted by a central column.

The heart of the church is dominated by the awesome **central tower**. The 15th-century **choir screen** depicts the 15 kings from William I to Henry VI.

The **lady chapel** behind the **high altar** is dominated by the **Great East Window**, the largest intact stained-glass medieval window in the world. Created between 1405 and 1408, it illustrates the beginning and end of the world as described in Genesis and the Book of Revelations.

Entered from the southern choir aisle, the **crypt** contains fragments from the Norman cathedral. The font shows King Edwin's baptism and marks the site of Paulinus' original wooden chapel.

In the south transept, the **Rose Window** commemorates the union of the royal houses of Lancaster and York, through the marriage of Henry VII and Elizabeth of York, which ended the Wars of the Roses and began the Tudor dynasty.

The entry to the stairs up to the tower and down to the foundations and treasury is also in the south transept. The queues for the tower can be long but the reward for a steep, claustrophobic climb (275 steps) to the top is an excellent view over York and the surrounding countryside.

The **foundations** and **treasury** shouldn't be missed. In 1967 the foundations were excavated when the central tower threatened to collapse; while engineers worked frantically to save the building, archaeologists uncovered Roman and Norman ruins that now illustrate the site's ancient history – one of the most extraordinary finds is a Roman culvert, still carrying water to the River Ouse. The treasury houses artefacts from the 11th century, including relics from the graves of medieval archbishops.

To see everything could easily absorb the best part of a day. The minster opens 7 am to 6 pm daily (from 1 pm Sunday) and has extended hours June to September. Admission is free, but a £2 donation is re-quested. There are charges for access to: the crypt, foundations and treasury (£3/1); the chapter house (£1); and the tower (£3/1). The worthwhile guided tours are free.

Around the Minster

Owned by the minster since the 15th century, **St William's College** (☎ 637134), College St, is an attractive half-timbered Tudor building housing an excellent restaurant (see Places to Eat).

The **Treasurer's House** (☎ 624247; NT), Minster Yard, was home to the minster's medieval treasurers. Substantially rebuilt in the 17th and 18th centuries, it now houses a fine collection of 18th-century furniture and gives a good insight to life at that time. It opens 10.30 am to 5 pm daily except Friday, April to October. Admission costs £3.50/1.75.

City Walls

You can get onto the walls, built in the 13th century, via steps by **Bootham Bar** (on the site of a Roman gate) and follow them clockwise to Monk Bar, a walk offering particularly beautiful views of the minster. There are oodles more access points including off Station Rd and Monkgate.

Monk Bar is the best preserved medieval gate, with a small **Richard III Museum** (☎ 634191) upstairs. The museum sets out the case of the murdered 'Princes in the Tower' and invites visitors to decide whether their uncle, Richard III, killed them (see the Tower of London in the London chapter for more details). It's open daily 9 am to 5 pm (9.30 am to 4 pm November to February) and admission costs £1.50/50p.

Walmgate Bar is England's only city gate with an intact barbican, and was built during the reign of Edward III. A barbican is an extended gateway designed to make life difficult for uninvited guests.

Museum Gardens

The Museum Gardens make a peaceful 10-acre city-centre oasis. Assorted picturesque ruins and buildings include the **Museum**

Gardens Lodge (Victorian Gothic Revival, 1874) and a 19th-century working **observatory**. The **Multangular Tower** was the western tower of the Roman garrison's defensive wall. The small Roman stones at the bottom have been built up with 13th-century additions.

The **Yorkshire Museum** (☎ 629745), in a classical building completed in 1829, has some interesting Roman, Anglo-Saxon, Viking and medieval exhibits and is worth visiting if there's a good temporary exhibition. It opens 10 am to 5 pm daily and admission costs £3.95/2.50.

The **Gatehall** was the main entry to **St Mary's Abbey**, a Benedictine monastery founded in 1080 with a later Early-English-style church. The ruined 15th-century gateway provided access from the abbey to the river. The adjacent **Hospitium** dates from the 14th century, although the timber-framed upper storey is a much-restored survivor from the 15th century; it was used as the abbey guesthouse. **St Mary's Lodge** was built around 1470 to provide VIP accommodation.

St Olave's Church dates from the 15th century, but there has been a church dedicated to the patron saint of Norway on this site since 1050 or earlier.

The gardens open daily until dusk.

Merchant Adventurers' Hall

Built in the mid-14th century, the Merchant Adventurers' Hall (☎ 654818) on Fossgate (access also from Piccadilly) testifies to the power of the medieval guilds (see the boxed text earlier in this section). They controlled all foreign trade into and out of York – a handy little monopoly. The guildhall with its massive oak timbers is outstanding.

The hall opens 9.30 am to 5 pm daily (noon to 4 pm Sunday), April to mid-November; 9.30 am to 3.30 pm daily except Sunday, the rest of the year. Admission costs £2/70p.

Jorvik Viking Centre

From 1976 to 1981 excavations in Coppergate uncovered Jorvik, the 9th-century Viking settlement that preceded modern York. Jorvik Viking Centre (☎ 643211),

Coppergate, is one of York's most popular attractions and you may have to queue for up to 30 minutes to get in. You travel in a 'time car' to a smells-and-all re-creation of what the Viking town probably looked like, complete with fibreglass figures speaking a language derived from modern Icelandic. At the end of the ride there's a chance to inspect finds from the site. It's all less corny than it sounds and is well worth a visit.

The centre opens 9 am to 5.30 pm daily, April to October. There are shorter hours during the rest of the year. Admission costs £5.65/4.25. See also the Web site at www.jorvik-viking-centre.co.uk.

The Jorvik people also run the **Archaeological Resource Centre** (ARC; ☎ 654324) in the old church at St Saviourgate. It has various programs that allow for hands-on exploration of archaeology. Call for details.

Clifford's Tower

After laying waste to the north as punishment for its rebellion, William the Conqueror built two mottes (mounds) crowned with wooden towers. The original one on this site was destroyed by fire during anti-Jewish riots in 1190 when 150 Jews sheltering in the castle took their own lives. It was then rebuilt into the keep for York Castle using the highly unusual figure-eight design. Run by English Heritage (EH) there's actually not much to see inside (☎ 646940) but the views over the city are excellent. It opens 10 am to 6 pm daily, April to October; 9.30 am to 7 pm, July and August; and 10 am to 4 pm, the rest of the year. Admission costs £1.80/90p.

York Castle Museum

One of England's most popular museums, York Castle Museum (☎ 653611) contains displays of everyday life, complete with Victorian and Edwardian streets and fascinating reconstructions of domestic interiors. An extraordinary collection of everyday objects from the past 400 years includes old TVs, radios, washing machines, vacuum cleaners and gadgets guaranteed to bring childhood memories flooding back for any

Brit. Others may find it comparable to an extended stray into the attic of a keen hoarder.

The museum opens 9.30 am to 5 pm daily, April to October (until 4 pm the rest of the year). Admission costs £5.25/3.50.

National Railway Museum

This museum (☎ 621261), east of the train station on Leeman Rd, is one of the world's biggest railway museums. It focuses on the all-too-distant past when Britain was a leader in railway technology. This legacy is traced via an impressive collection of carriages (including Queen Victoria's saloon) and locomotives (including the speed-record-breaking *Mallard*). A vast annexe includes the restoration shops, which you can visit. Allow two hours to do the museum justice. It opens from 10 am to 6 pm daily. Admission costs £6.50 for adults (an enlightened nothing for those aged 16 and under).

Medieval Churches

Of York's 41 pre-16th-century churches, 20 still survive, many with their stained glass intact. The finest is **All Saints, North St** (☎ 728122), which John Betjeman dubbed 'the best reconstruction of a medieval interior'. It has wonderful 14th-century glass including one bit depicting a man wearing glasses. It's easily spotted by the octagon rising above its tower. It's only open, however, from 1.30 to 3.30 pm on Thursday.

Just as atmospheric, if more homely, is **Holy Trinity, Goodramgate** (☎ 613451), tucked away in a churchyard popular with lunching shopworkers. Inside, box pews surround an 18th-century two-tier pulpit and there's not a straight line in view. It opens 9.30 am to 5.30 pm Tuesday to Saturday.

On a busy corner, **All Saints Pavement**, between High Ousegate and Coppergate, has a fine lantern tower and 14th-century stained glass. It opens 9.30 am to 4 pm.

Quiet **St Denys Church** is on Walmgate. It has the oldest glass in York and a Norman porch. It opens 10 am to 4.30 pm, April to October.

Other Things to See & Do

On Castlegate, **Fairfax House** (☎ 655543) is a beautiful Georgian house with a renowned collection of 18th-century furniture and clocks. It's one of many buildings that have been restored by the York Trust, a local preservation group. It opens 11 am to 5 pm Monday to Thursday and Saturday; and 1.30 to 5 pm on Sunday, March to December. Admission costs £4/1.50.

Opposite the TIC, **York City Art Gallery** (☎ 551861), Exhibition Square, has a range of paintings including works by Lely, Hogarth, Reynolds, Nash and Lowry. It opens 10 am to 5 pm daily. Admission costs £2/1.50.

York Brewery (☎ 621162), 12 Toft Green, has tours of its small plant and all-important tastings throughout the day, year-round. The cost is £4.25/3.

York Dungeon (☎ 632599), 12 Clifford St, is what you'd expect – a series of gruesome historical reconstructions, intended to scare those who find the Chamber of Horrors tame. For the especially hardened there's a lovely bit on the plague. It opens 10 am to 5.30 pm daily (until 4.30 pm, October to March) and costs £6.50/4.95.

In the heart of York, the quaintly cobbled **Shambles** hints at what a medieval street might have looked like if it was overrun with people told they have to buy something silly and be back on the tour bus in 15 minutes. It takes its curious name from the Saxon word *shamel*, meaning slaughterhouse.

If modern British train technology has failed you and you have time to kill at the station, you might find the **York Model Railway** (☎ 630169) diverting. It's right next to the station entrance and comprises a huge set-up where, at least in this miniature world, the trains always run on time. It opens 9.30 am to 6 pm daily, March to October (10.30 am to 5 pm the rest of the year). Admission costs £2.95/1.95.

Organised Tours

Bus For a good overall introduction to the city you might consider one of the open-top buses that trundle about town. Tours leave from Exhibition Square outside the main TIC.

First York (☎ 622992) runs guided double-decker bus tours that circle the city calling at the main sites; you can get on and off where you please (buses run every 20 minutes) and tickets are valid all day.

Guide Friday (☎ 640896) operates essentially the same service. Competition between the two is fierce and frequent price wars mean that the usual fare of £7.50/2.50 is often heavily discounted.

Eddie Brown (☎ 640760), 8 Tower St, runs a range of good-value day bus tours into the surrounding countryside. These include Castle Howard for £6.50, North York Moors Railway and Moorland for £15.95, and Yorkshire Dales and Herriot Country for £22.50. Prices don't include admission charges. Children under 14 travel free on most tours.

Boat Yorkboat River Trips (☎ 628324), Lendal Bridge, runs cruises along the River Ouse. One-hour return trips depart from King's Staith (behind the fire station) and Lendal Bridge (next to the Guildhall, under the bridge) from 10.30 am daily. The frequency varies with the season and the cost is £4/2. From April to October, there's the obligatory ghost cruise at 7 pm daily from King's Staith (£5.50/2.75).

Walking Yorkwalk (☎ 622303) offers a series of two-hour themed walks on Roman York, medieval York, the snickelways (alleys) of York, saints and sinners of York and many more, including one on Jewish York. Each walk costs £4.50/1 and walkers get a £1 discount off Guide Friday tours. Walks depart from Museum Gardens Gate.

The Association of Voluntary Guides (☎ 640780) has free walking tours of the city from Exhibition Square in front of York City Art Gallery at 10.15 am daily, year-round. There is also a 2.15 pm tour from April to October and a 7 pm tour from June to August.

The Complete York Tour (☎ 706643) is a detailed and scholarly walk. Call for details.

York has many companies offering ghost walks that are heavy on drama and light on facts. The following are the bare bones: the Original Ghost Walk of York (☎ 01759-373090) leaves the King's Arms at 8 pm daily; the Ghost Hunt of York (☎ 608700) leaves the Shambles at 7.30 pm daily; Mad Alice Ghost Tours (☎ 425071) leaves from Clifford's Tower at 7.30 pm daily; and the Haunted Walk of York (☎ 621003) leaves from the front of York City Art Gallery at 8 pm daily. All cost £3/2; you should phone first to make certain that the guides haven't given up the ghost and taken a day off.

Places to Stay

Despite the existence of hundreds of hotels and B&Bs, it can be difficult to find a bed in midsummer. Prices also jump significantly in the high season. The TIC has an efficient accommodation booking service that charges £4.

Camping There are a dozen camp sites and caravan parks around York but most are at least 4 miles (6km) from the centre. The closest is *Rowntree Park Camping* (☎ 658997) on Terry Ave, a 20-minute walk south-east of the station in a park by the river. There are a few sites for backpackers at £10 for two adults. There's little grass on the sites so, although tents are allowed, you'll need something soft to sleep on.

Hostels Open year-round is *York Youth Hostel* (☎ 653147, fax 651230, e york@ yha.org.uk, Water End, Clifton). Adults/under-18s pay £15.50/11.50, including breakfast. It's a large but very busy YHA hostel so book ahead. The hostel is about a mile north-west of the TIC; turn left into Bootham, which becomes Clifton (the A19), then left into Water End. Alternatively, there's a riverside footpath from Lendal Bridge.

York Youth Hotel (☎ 625904, fax 612494, e info@yorkyouthhotel.demon.co.uk, 11 Bishophill Senior) is equally popular, particularly with school and student parties. There's a range of rooms, from 20-bed dorms (£11) to twin bunk rooms (£15 per person).

York Backpackers (☎ 627720, fax 339350, e *yorkbackpackers@cwcom.net, 88–90 Micklegate)* is a friendly place in a 1752 Georgian building. Beds in the large dorms cost £11; doubles are £30.

The University of York offers accommodation in its halls of residence during holiday times. *Fairfax House (☎ 432095,* e *aeg2@york.ac.uk, 99 Heslington Rd)* is a 20-minute walk south-east of the city. It has singles with washbasins for £20 per person.

B&Bs – North-West There are lots of B&Bs and hotels in the streets north and south of Bootham (the A19 to Thirsk), to the north-west of the city. Running parallel to the railway line, Bootham Terrace, Bootham Crescent and Grosvenor Terrace are virtually lined with B&Bs. Most are fairly average but the position is central. Marygate is a good street to try as it's quiet and the road leads right down to the river. Longfield Terrace is quiet and can be easily reached from the river path.

Martins Guest House (☎ 634551, fax 339063, e *martinsbb@aol.com, 5 Longfield Terrace)* is one of several B&Bs in a long Victorian row. Standard rooms with bathroom cost from £18 per person.

Briar Lea Guest House (☎ 635061, fax 330356, e *briargh8l@aol.com, 8 Longfield Terrace)* has rooms with en suite that cost from £25/36.

Claremont Guest House (☎ 625158, e *claremont.york@dial.pipex.com, 18 Claremont Terrace)* charges from £18 per person for its two double rooms.

Sycamore Place, off Bootham Terrace, has several places. At No 15 there's the *Alcuin Lodge (☎ 632222, fax 626630,* e *alcuinlodg@aol.com)*, which has decent en suite doubles from £35.

Boasting a central position beside the river, the *Abbey Guest House (☎ 627782, fax 671743,* e *abbey@rsummers.cix.co.uk, 14 Earlsborough Terrace)* is a standard B&B with rooms starting at £20 per person.

Nearby, the comfortable *Riverside Walk B&B (☎ 620769, fax 646249,* e *julie@ riversidewalkbb.demon.co.uk, 9 Earlsbor-* ough Terrace) has rooms with bathroom from £24 a head.

The *Gables Guest House (☎ 624381, fax 624381, 50 Bootham Crescent)* is a basic place charging from £20 per person.

Treetops Guest House (☎ 658053, 21 St Mary's) is a basic place that is entirely nonsmoking. Rooms cost from £24 per person.

Behind Treetops, the pleasant *Brontë House (☎ 621066, fax 653434,* e *bronte _guest_house@compuserve.com, 22 Grosvenor Terrace)* has rooms with en suite from £35/46.

Crook Lodge (☎ 655614, fax 655614, 26 St Mary's) has comfortable double rooms starting at £48 and parking for guests.

Opposite, *23 St Mary's (☎ 6226378, fax 628802, 23 St Mary's)* has fully equipped rooms from £32/54. It is surrounded by flowers and has many little touches such as a rocking horse in the drawing room.

B&Bs – South-West There are many B&Bs clustered around Scarcroft Rd, Southlands Rd and Bishopthorpe Rd, the continuation of Bishopgate, which takes off from the southern corner of the wall after Skeldergate Bridge.

Acorn Guest House (☎ 620081, 1 Southlands Rd) is a decent place with rooms with en suite that cost from £18 per person.

Nunmill House (☎ 634047, fax 655879, e *b&b@nunmill.co.uk, 85 Bishopthorpe Rd)* has good rooms with en suite from £25 per person.

A whole row of attractive, listed Victorian villas comprises *Wheatlands Lodge (☎ 654318, fax 654318,* e *wheatlodge@ aol.com, 75 Scarcroft Rd)* Most of the 60 rooms are sunny and rates start at £28/40.

Hotels – North-West At the small *Elliotts Hotel (☎ 623333, fax 654908,* e *elliottsht @aol.com, 2–4 Sycamore Place)*, good rooms with private facilities go for £35/ 52.

The *Coach House Hotel (☎ 652780, fax 679943, 20/22 Marygate)* has 12 rooms in a quiet spot across from the city walls.

The small restaurant has meals for under £10. Rooms cost from £31/56.

Jorvik Hotel (☎ 653511, fax 627009, 50 Marygate) has a walled garden and 23 comfortable rooms with bath. Doubles cost between £50 and £70, and there's one single for £32.

Hudson's Hotel (☎ 621267, fax 654719, 60 Bootham) has 30 well equipped rooms in a modern annexe, and a restaurant and bar in a Georgian town house. Rooms cost from £65/105 for a single.

Hotels – Centre Prices are a bit higher in the centre of York and you don't have the leafy charms of the less-central streets of the places described above.

St Denys Hotel (☎ 622207, fax 624800, e thestdenys@aol.com, St Denys Rd) has a good location opposite the church of the same name. Rooms with en suite cost from £45/55.

Judges Lodging Hotel (☎ 638733, fax 679947, 9 Lendal) is a classy place in a Georgian mansion. Well equipped rooms go for £75/100.

Dean Court Hotel (☎ 625082, fax 620305, e deancourt@btconnect.com, Duncombe Place) has a commanding position across from the minster. The rooms are very comfortable and cost from £80/95.

Monkbar Hotel (☎ 638086, fax 629195, St Maurice's Rd) is a full-service hotel just outside the gate. The rooms have air-con and there is parking and a central garden. Prices start at £74/120.

Royal York Hotel (☎ 653681, fax 623503, Station Rd) is a huge, grand, Victorian railway hotel adjoining the station. There are three acres of gardens and a new health spa. Most of the rooms have been lavishly redone and cost from £90/110.

Places to Eat

There's a huge range of eateries with all styles of food, for all budgets in York. See the listings in the Entertainment section following for pubs that serve food.

Restaurants There's a funky burger joint, *Victor J's (☎ 673788, 1 Finkle St)*, that's open until 7 pm weekdays and later at the weekend. It's very central and it has a bar. The burgers cost £3.50.

Pizza Express (☎ 672904, 17 Museum St) serves the usual range of good pizzas (about £5) in the elegant surroundings of what was once a gentlemen's club overlooking the Ouse.

Fiesta Mexicana (☎ 610243, 14 Clifford St) is popular with students for its cheap burritos (£3) and strong margaritas. It can get delightfully rowdy.

La Piazza (☎ 642641, 51 Goodramgate) has excellent Italian food, including pizzas from £5.30.

Atmospheric *Oscar's Wine Bar & Bistro (☎ 652002, 8 Little Stonegate)* has an outdoor area and a wide range of interesting dishes (including vegetarian meals). Most dishes cost from £5 to £8.

Siam House (☎ 624677, 63a Goodramgate) has fresh Thai food in a lovely upstairs dining room. The menu is endless and most dishes cost £4 to £5.

The Rubicon (☎ 676076, 5 Little Stonegate) is an airy vegetarian restaurant that offers two-course lunches for £5 and three-course meals for £7.

Jinnah (☎ 659999, 105–7 Micklegate) is a fine Indian restaurant that's a few cuts above average. The dishes cost about £7 and are carefully prepared and creatively served. It's open until midnight.

Café No 8 (☎ 653074, 8 Gillygate) serves lunch, tea and dinner. It has a fine Modern British menu. Most items cost under £10. It's closed Sunday.

Loucedes Tapas (☎ 674848, 48 Walmgate) is run by two local women who cook up a good array of Spanish tapas treats that cost about £4 each.

The gorgeous Grand Assembly Rooms on Blake St are home to *Ask (☎ 637254)*, a good Italian place for lunch and dinner (about £11).

Lime House (☎ 632734, 55 Goodramgate) is busy, especially at the weekends (closed Monday and Tuesday). The speciality is steak (£12) and it also offers vegetarian dishes (£8.50).

St William's Restaurant (☎ 634830), off

College St, is a great spot to relax after exploring the minster. It opens from 10 am to 10 pm. Lunch includes soups for £3.25, and two-course dinners are £12.95. There is a beautiful, cobbled courtyard.

Blue Bicycle (☎ 673990, 34 Fossgate) is a popular place with locals who love the romantic, candle-lit atmosphere and tasty, French seafood dishes. Expect to pay at least £15 per person.

Cafes With a range of coffees and free Internet access for its customers, *Coffee Espress (60 Goodramgate)* opens from at least 8 am to 10 pm daily.

Betty's (☎ 659142) is an very popular, extremely elegant bakery and tearoom on St Helen's Square. Depending on your mood, you can choose to relax in the spacious, airy upstairs or the wood-panelled nonsmoking room downstairs. A pot of tea is £2 and sandwiches are about £4. Betty's opens from 9 am to 9 pm; a pianist plays from 6 pm.

There's more tea on offer upstairs in *Taylor's* (☎ 622865, 46 Stonegate), where queues are as likely as at Betty's. A traditional Yorkshire high tea here costs £9 and would set you up for a week.

The best vegetarian eatery in York is the *Blake Head Bookshop & Café* (☎ 623767, 104 Micklegate). The emphasis is on simple but imaginative cooking. It's open daily for lunch; soup costs £2.50, a three-course meal £7.50.

Other There are often lines down the street for *Scott's of York* (☎ 622972, 81 Petergate), a butcher where you can buy pork pies to make the taste buds weep from £1.85.

Juice Up (☎ 677732, 3 Bootham) has a healthy range of fresh juices and sandwiches (under £3). It has a few stools at a counter but is mostly a takeaway.

Entertainment

York Music is a useful monthly flyer that provides a guide to the local music scene. You can find it at the TICs as well as in many pubs.

Pubs & Clubs The *Old White Swan* (☎ 540911, 80 Goodramgate) has a range of live music, from jazz to polka to rock.

Although it's in tourist central, *Ye Olde Starre* (☎ 623063, 40 Stonegate) is a popular place with locals. It has decent ales and lots of tables outside its hidden location.

The *King's Arms* (☎ 659435, King's Staith) does lunch (£5) and has tables overlooking the river on the south-eastern side of the Ouse Bridge (the middle of the three main bridges).

The *Lowther Arms* (☎ 622987, 8 Cumberland St) has bar meals for under £4 but its chief charm seems to be that it's open until midnight.

Maltings (☎ 655387, Tanners Moat), below Lendal Bridge, has a great beer selection, a fine atmosphere and good lunch specials.

Spread Eagle (☎ 635868, 98 Walmgate) is a popular pub with locals who enjoy the good beer selection and decent menu of typical bar chow. There's a garden at the back.

Blue Bell (☎ 654907, 53 Fossgate) first opened in 1798 and seems little changed since. Certainly the characters found in the small front and back bars are timeless.

You should visit *Fibbers* (☎ 625250, 8–12 The Stonebow) after dark so you can't see its hideous building. However, this is a place for the ears, with regular offerings of local music.

Ziggy's (☎ 620602, 53–5 Micklegate) is a relaxed club with theme nights ranging from Goth to disco.

Theatres & Venues Staging well regarded productions of theatre, opera and dance is *York Theatre Royal* (☎ 623568, St Leonard's Place). Despite its name, the *Grand Opera House* (☎ 671818) on Clifford St puts on a wide range of productions. *Riding Lights Theatre* (☎ 0845 961 3000, Lower Friargate) is a good place for serious drama.

For big-name concerts head for *York Barbican Centre* (☎ 656688), in an interesting, partly pyramidal, modern building on Barbican Rd.

Cinema There's a big multiplex, *City Screen* (☎ 541144), off Coney St on the Ouse, which has a big bar overlooking the river.

Shopping

Coney St is the hub of York shopping and stores can be found on all the adjoining streets.

Nevisport (☎ 639567), 8 St Sampson Square, is a large sporting-goods shop with walking and camping gear as well as maps and guides.

Kaos (☎ 611532), 5 Gillygate, has all sorts of trendy and stylish clothes for parties and clubbing. There are many other interesting and unusual shops on this bit of Gillygate.

Wildcat Records (☎ 625456), 76 Micklegate, has an off-beat selection of used and new CDs and LPs.

York has many bookshops selling used and antiquarian books. They are clustered in two main areas, Micklegate and Fossgate. Ken Spellman Booksellers (☎ 624414), 70 Micklegate, stocks rare books covering fine arts and literature. Jack Duncan Books (☎ 641389), 36 Fossgate, sells cheap paperbacks and more unusual books. It also has a rotating exhibition of cartoons.

Getting There & Away

Bus The main bus stops are along Rougier St (off Station Rd, inside the city walls on the western side of Lendal Bridge) but some local and regional buses leave from outside the train station.

There is a very useful Bus Information Office (☎ 551400), 20 George Hudson St, that has complete schedule information. It also sells local, regional and National Express tickets. It opens 8.30 am to 5 pm weekdays and 9 am to 12.30 pm on Saturday.

National Express buses leave from Rougier St. There are at least three services daily to London (£18, five hours), two daily to Birmingham (£17, three hours) and one to Edinburgh (£21.75, six hours).

For information on regional buses (to Castle Howard, Helmsley, Scarborough, Whitby, Leeds and so on), call the National Travel Information Service (☎ 0870 608 2608). Local services are operated by a score of companies, some of which offer their own passes.

Train When York's train station opened in 1877 it was the largest in the world and the city is still well served by rail. The station has numerous food outlets and you can leave luggage at the Europcar office by platform 1.

There are numerous trains from London's King's Cross (£59, two hours) and on to Edinburgh (£47, three hours). North-south trains also connect with Peterborough (£33, one hour 50 minutes) for Cambridge and East Anglia. There are good connections with southern England including Oxford (£49.50, 4¼ hours), via Birmingham (£25.50, 2½ hours).

Local trains to/from Scarborough take 45 minutes (£9.10). For Whitby it's best to get a bus from Scarborough.

Car & Motorcycle By road York is about 200 miles (322km) from London and Edinburgh and 25 miles (40km) from Leeds and Helmsley.

Europcar (☎ 656161) is right by platform 1 in the station. Besides a full range of cars, it rents bicycles and stores luggage. Hertz (☎ 612586) is near platform 3 in the station.

Practical Car & Van Rental (☎ 624848), 10 Fetter Lane, is a five-minute walk from the station and often has good deals.

Getting Around

York is easily walked on foot. You're never really more than 20 minutes from any of the major sights or areas.

Bus The local bus service is provided by First York, which sells a day pass valid on all of its local buses after 9.30 am, for £1.70. The Bus Information Office has service details (see Bus in the Getting There & Away section).

Car & Motorcycle York gets as congested as most British cities in summer and car parking in the centre can be expensive (up to £8 for a day).

Taxi Try Station Taxis (☎ 623332), which has a kiosk outside the train station, ABC Blue Circle (☎ 638787) or Ace Taxis (☎ 638888).

Bicycle You can hire bicycles for £9.50 a day from Bob Trotter (☎ 622868) at 13 Lord Mayor's Walk outside Monk Bar. Europcar in the train station rents bikes for the same price.

The Bus Information Office has a useful free map showing York's bike routes.

If you're energetic you could do an interesting loop out to Castle Howard (15 miles/24km), Helmsley and Rievaulx Abbey (12 miles/19km) and Thirsk (another 12 miles), where you could catch a train back to York. There's also a section of the Trans-Pennine-Trail cycle path from Bishopthorpe in York to Selby (15 miles/24km) along the old railway line. The TICs have maps.

CASTLE HOWARD

There are few buildings in the world that are so perfect that their visual impact is almost a physical blow – Castle Howard (☎ 01653-648333), of *Brideshead Revisited* fame, is one. It has a picturesque setting in the rolling Howardian Hills and is surrounded by superb terraces and landscaped grounds dotted with monumental follies.

Not surprisingly, Castle Howard is a major tourist attraction and draws enormous crowds. Outside weekends, however, it's surprisingly easy to find the space to appreciate this extraordinary marriage of art, architecture, landscaping and natural beauty. Wandering about the grounds, views open up over the hills, the Temple of the Four Winds and the Mausoleum, but the great Baroque house with its magnificent central cupola is an irresistible visual magnet.

The house is full of treasures and the grounds include a superb walled rose garden.

In 1699 the earl of Carlisle made an audacious choice when he picked a successful playwright and army captain, Sir John Vanbrugh, as architect. Vanbrugh in turn chose Nicholas Hawksmoor, who had worked for Christopher Wren, as his clerk of works. This successful collaboration was subsequently repeated at Blenheim Palace.

Castle Howard is 15 miles (24km) northeast of York, 4 miles (6km) off the A64. It opens 10 am (grounds) or 11 am (house) to 4.30 pm daily, mid-March to October. Admission to the house and garden costs £7/4. All in all, it could absorb the best part of a day; there are a couple of rather twee cafes, but it's best to take a picnic.

Visit the Web site at www.castlehoward .co.uk for further details.

Getting There & Away

The castle can be reached by several tours from York. Check with the TIC for up-to-date schedules. Yorkshire Coastliner has a useful bus service that links Leeds, York, Castle Howard, Pickering, and Whitby (Nos 840 and 842). A Freedom ticket good for unlimited rides all day costs £8.60.

NUNNINGTON HALL

This 17th-century manor house is a good example of how one could live when one had plenty of serfs to do the heavy lifting out on the estate. A forest of hardwoods went into the rich panelling of the public spaces. Outside, the walled garden is a perfect refuge from the demands of running the house. The combination of the River Wye and the various water fowl and fruit trees is magical.

Nunnington Hall (☎ 01439-748283; NT) is in the tiny village of Nunningon, which is just off the B1257, 4½ miles (7km) southeast of Helmsley. It's easily combined with a visit to Castle Howard, which is 7 miles (11km) south via Slingsby. The property is open 1.30 to 4.30 pm Wednesday to Sunday, April to October (also open on Tuesday, June to August). Admission is £4/2.

SCARBOROUGH

☎ 01723 • pop 39,300

Scarborough is a large, often kitsch, seaside resort. Unlike Blackpool (and many other places of that ilk), however, it has a long history and, most importantly, a spectacular site. These, combined with the traditional

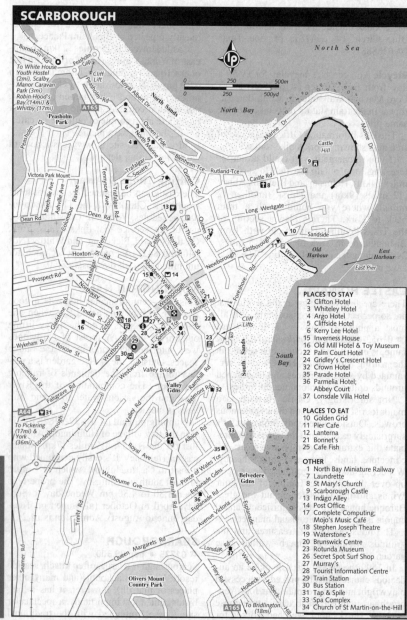

SCARBOROUGH

Burniston Rd
To White House
Youth Hostel
(2mi), Scalby
Manor Caravan
Park (3mi),
Robin Hood's
Bay (14mi) &
Whitby (17mi)

North Sea

North Bay

Castle Hill

North Sands

Royal Albert Dr

Marine Dr

East Harbour

East Pier

South Bay

South Sands

Old Harbour

West Pier

Cliff Lifts

Sandside

Eastborough

Newborough

Foreshore Rd

Castle Rd

Long Westgate

Rutland Tce

Queens Tce

St Thomas St

Aberdeen Walk

Westborough

Vernon Rd

Falsgrave Rd

Valley Bridge

Valley Gdns

Belvedere Gdns

Esplanade Gdns

Esplanade

Avenue Victoria

Lonsdale Rd

Filey Rd

West St

Holbeck Rd

Olivers Mount
Country Park

To Bridlington
(18mi)

To Pickering
(17mi) &
York
(36mi)

Peasholm
Park

Peasholm Dr

Victoria Park Mount

Dean Rd

Prospect Rd

Hoxton Rd

Tindall St

Roscoe St

Wykeham St

Commercial St

Gladstone Rd

Columbus Ravine

Tennyson Ave

Trafalgar Rd

Trafalgar Square

Queen's Pde

North Marine Rd

Blenheim Tce

Queens Tce

North St

Castle Rd

Westwood

Ramshill Rd

Belmont Rd

Albion Rd

Prince of Wales Tce

Westbourne Gve

Valley Rd

Royal Ave

Trinity Rd

Seamer Rd

Queen Margarets Rd

A165

A64

A165

PLACES TO STAY
2   Clifton Hotel
3   Whiteley Hotel
4   Argo Hotel
5   Cliffside Hotel
6   Kerry Lee Hotel
15 Inverness House
16 Old Mill Hotel & Toy Museum
22 Palm Court Hotel
24 Gridley's Crescent Hotel
32 Crown Hotel
35 Parade Hotel
36 Parmelia Hotel;
    Abbey Court
37 Lonsdale Villa Hotel

PLACES TO EAT
10 Golden Grid
11 Pier Cafe
12 Lanterna
21 Bonnet's
25 Cafe Fish

OTHER
1   North Bay Miniature Railway
7   Laundrette
8   St Mary's Church
9   Scarborough Castle
13 Indigo Alley
14 Post Office
17 Complete Computing;
    Mojo's Music Café
18 Stephen Joseph Theatre
19 Waterstone's
20 Brunswick Centre
23 Rotunda Museum
26 Secret Spot Surf Shop
27 Murray's
28 Tourist Information Centre
29 Train Station
30 Bus Station
31 Tap & Spile
33 Spa Complex
34 Church of St Martin-on-the-Hill

trappings of an English seaside holiday resort, make it an appealing, enjoyable place.

Although some parts are a bit rundown, Scarborough has, for the most part, survived the 20th century and the impact of cheap package holidays to the Mediterranean. It remains a classic resort, with two beautiful bays separated by a castle-crowned headland, and is popular with young families and pensioners from all round the north. In 1998 it got a new dose of fame from the delightful movie *Little Voice*, which was shot in Scarborough and starred Michael Caine and Jane Horrocks.

Scarborough markets itself with Whitby, which is listed later in the chapter, as part of the North York Moors National Park.

History
The headland that separates the North and South bays has an impressive defensive position and has been occupied since Celtic times. A fishing village was, according to tradition, established by Vikings in the 9th century around what is now known as the Old Harbour. The Normans built their castle in around 1130 and it survived until 1648 when it was heavily damaged by the Parliamentarians. It was also bombarded by a German battleship in 1914.

The medieval fishing and market town grew up around the Old Harbour. Mineral springs were discovered in 1620 and it was transformed into a fashionable spa town. It became one of the first places in England where sea bathing was popular and since the mid-18th century it has been a successful seaside resort. It therefore has a legacy of fine Georgian, Victorian and Edwardian architecture.

Orientation
Modern suburbs sprawl west of the town centre, which is above the old town and the South Bay. The town is on a plateau above the beaches; three cliff lifts, steep streets and footpaths provide the links. The Victorian development to the south is separated from the town centre by a steep valley, which has been landscaped and is crossed by high bridges.

The main shopping street, Westborough, has a dramatic view of the castle rising in the distance. The North Bay is home to all the tawdry seashore amusements; the South Bay is more genteel. The old town lies between St Mary's Church, the castle and the Old Harbour.

Information
The busy TIC (☎ 373333, fax 363785, e dtls@scarborough.gov.uk) is right at the corner of Westborough and Valley Bridge Rd. It opens 9.30 am to 6 pm, May to September; and 10 am to 4.30 pm, the rest of the year.

Post The post office is at 11–15 Aberdeen Walk. It opens 9 am to 5.30 pm weekdays and until 12.30 pm on Saturday.

Email & Internet Access Complete Computing (☎ 500990), 14 Northway, offers Internet access costing £1.50 for 15 minutes.

Bookshop Waterstone's (☎ 500414) has a good-sized shop at 97–8 Westborough.

Laundry A handy laundrette (☎ 375763) is at 48 North Marine Road.

Things to See
Well it's a beach resort, innit? So there are all the things the English do at beaches, plus some bonuses.

Scarborough Castle (☎ 372451; EH), approached via a 13th-century barbican, survives, as do the curtain walls dating from around 1130 and the shell of a keep built around 1160. There are excellent views. It opens 10 am to 6 pm daily, April to September; and 10 am to 4 pm Wednesday to Sunday, the rest of the year. Admission costs £2.30/1.20, which includes an audio guide.

Below the castle is **St Mary's Church** (☎ 354555) dating from 1180 and rebuilt in the 15th and 17th centuries, with some interesting 14th-century chapels. Anne Brontë is buried in the churchyard. It opens 10 am to 4.30 pm weekdays (2 to 4 pm Sunday), May to September.

The **Church of St Martin-on-the-Hill**
(☎ 360437) is on Albion Rd, south of the
centre. It was built in 1863 to a very high
standard and has some pre-Raphaelite
stained-glass windows. The doors are open
7.30 am to 5.30 pm daily. Nearby along
the shore, the grand old **Spa Complex** hints
at Scarborough's roots as a fashionable resort. It is now a venue for conferences
(☎ 376774).

The **Rotunda Museum** (☎ 374839) on
Vernon Rd traces local history from prehis-
toric times right up to the present. It opens
10 am to 5 pm daily except Monday, at
Easter and from late May to late October.
Admission costs £2/1.

North Bay Miniature Railway (☎ 381344)
is north of the centre across Burniston
Rd from Peasholm Park. It operates daily
from mid-April to October and rides cost
£1.40/80p.

The Old Mill Hotel (see Places to Stay
later) has a small **toy museum** (☎ 372735).
It opens 10 am to 4 pm at the weekend,
April to October (daily except Monday in
July and August).

Activities

See the Whitby section for details about
the 20-mile (32km) Whitby–Scarborough
Coastal Cycle Trail.

There are some decent waves out in the
North Sea and the Secret Spot Surf Shop
(☎ 500467), 19 York Place, is staffed with
friendly folk who can advise on conditions
and offer lessons. The shop rents all manner
of gear. The best time for waves locally is
September to May.

For local diving information, contact the
Scarborough Sub Aqua Club (☎ 372036).

Places to Stay

The TIC will only book accommodation for
you if you go there in person.

Camping Three miles (5km) north of town
is *Scalby Manor Caravan Park* (☎ 366212)
on Burniston Rd. It's a large park with
plenty of pitches for vans and tents, which
cost up to £9 for a site. There are good
views of the moors. Take bus No 12 or 21.

Hostels In a converted water mill, the
White House Youth Hostel (☎ 361176,
fax 500054, **e** scarborough@yha.org.uk)
on Burniston Rd is 2 miles (3km) north of
town along the A166 to Whitby, off a sharp
turn by the bridge. It opens daily from April
to August but its opening times are complex
so ring ahead. Beds cost £10/6.90 for
adults/under-18s. Take bus No 12 or 21
from town.

B&Bs There are literally hundreds of
B&Bs; competition is intense and it's difficult to separate them. Singles are hard to
find because the market largely caters for
family groups. There are many overlooking
North Bay along Queens Parade, Blenheim
Terrace and North Marine Rd, and another
big zone south of Valley Gardens, especially along the Esplanade and West St.

Trafalgar Square is crowded with B&Bs
and one of the best-value places is the nonsmoking *Kerry Lee Hotel* (☎ 363845, 60
Trafalgar Square). The standard rooms start
at £12 per person.

The *Argo Hotel* (☎ 375745, 134 North
Marine Rd) is a pleasant, small B&B
overlooking the cricket ground. Rates are
from £14.

Inverness House (☎ 369770, 22 Aberdeen Walk) has a great position (although
you sacrifice a view). It's a classic but comfortable place that costs from £16.

Cliffside Hotel (☎ 361087, 79–81
Queens Parade) is a well kept, traditional
place with rooms from £19 per person. It
has good views.

Abbey Court (☎ 360659, 19 West St) is
good value with rates from £20. Most
rooms have a bathroom and there are numerous added touches.

The 10-room *Whiteley Hotel* (☎ 373514,
fax 373007, **e** whiteley_hotel@compuserve
.com, 99 Queens Parade) has some rooms
with bathroom from £21 per person. It also
has a few singles and has parking.

Hotels On the southern side of town, but
without views, the stately *Lonsdale Villa
Hotel* (☎ 363383, **e** lonsdale@scarborough
.co.uk) on Lonsdale Rd has nine comfort-

YORKSHIRE

able rooms, most with bathroom but also a single without. Vegetarians are catered for and the daily rate is £19.50.

In a classic Victorian building, the *Parmelia Hotel* (☎ 361914, e parmeliahotel@ btinternet.com, 17 West St) is mostly non-smoking. Rooms with a bathroom cost £19.50 per person.

Parade Hotel (☎ 361285, 29 Esplanade) has great views and 17 well equipped rooms for around £25 per person. It has a full bar and is on a quiet stretch of South Cliff.

Old Mill Hotel (☎ 372735, fax 377190, e windmill@scarborough.co.uk, Mill St) is set in a converted 18th-century windmill in the centre. Singles/doubles start at £33/48 and there's even a small toy museum (see Things to See earlier).

Clifton Hotel (☎ 375691, fax 364203, Queen's Parade) is a substantial Victorian building with great views over North Bay. It has a ballroom with frequent tea dances. Rooms start at £35/50.

Palm Court Hotel (☎ 368161, fax 371547, St Nicholas Cliff) has well equipped rooms and an indoor pool. Rooms cost from £40/60.

Gridley's Crescent Hotel (☎ 360929, fax 354126, The Crescent) has a fine position near the centre and South Bay. It has two restaurants and is located on a small park. Rooms cost from £43/75.

The grand *Crown Hotel* (☎ 373491, fax 362271, Esplanade) has views of the castle and South Bay. Rooms start at £65/85.

Places to Eat

There's a bunch of traditional fish and chip places on Foreshore Rd. In general, though, the possibilities aren't immense so most people either eat at their hotels – many B&Bs do evening meals and some have alcohol licences – or stay in self-catering flats.

Lanterna (☎ 363616, 33 Queen St) is a splendid Italian dinner spot that specialises in fresh local seafood. The salmon-filled ravioli and various risottos are tops. Expect to pay upwards of £25 each. Booking is advised and it's closed on Sunday.

At *Cafe Fish* (☎ 500301, 19 York Place) you select your fresh fish from a case, specify how you would like it prepared and then pay based on its weight (usually £10 to £15 per person).

In the Stephen Joseph Theatre (see Entertainment), the *restaurant* (☎ 368463) has interesting and fresh fare. Lunch is a bargain, with sandwiches under £2, while a three-course dinner from the changing menu costs £14.50.

Golden Grid (☎ 360922, 4 Sandside), on the foreshore, has been selling fish and chips since 1883. It's bright, popular and across from the fishing fleet, so there's a good chance the fish is fresh; cod costs from £4. There's also a vegetarian menu.

Nearby, *Pier Cafe* sells simple, honest fare such as Yorkshire pudding with gravy (£1.50).

Bonnet's (☎ 361033, 38–40 Huntriss Row) is an excellent tearoom with fine cakes and a serene courtyard. It also has an upstairs restaurant open Thursday to Saturday evenings where fresh fish costs around £11. It sells delicious hand-made chocolate too.

Mojo's Music Café (☎ 351983, 18–20 Northway) combines a funky CD shop with a diner. It opens 10 am to 6 pm daily except Sunday and serves fresh soups, salads and sandwiches for less than £4.

Entertainment

Indigo Alley (☎ 375823, North Marine Rd) is a welcome addition to local nightlife. It has a good range of beers, and live jazz and blues.

Murray's (☎ 503170, Westborough) is right next to the TIC. Local rock bands perform several nights a week.

The *Tap & Spile* (☎ 363837, 94 Falsgrave Rd) is a relaxed pub with a good selection of Yorkshire ales. It has folk music on many nights.

The *Stephen Joseph Theatre* (☎ 370541, Westborough) is in an imposing building by the train station. It stages a good range of drama, including original works by local playwright Alan Ayckbourn. It also has a fine restaurant.

Getting There & Away

Scarborough is a good transport hub. It's 230 miles (370km) from London, 70 miles (113km) from Leeds, 16 miles (26km) from Pickering and 20 miles (32km) from Whitby.

The train station is conveniently central with the bus station behind it. However, note that buses may also leave from the east side of Brunswick Centre.

Bus There are reasonably frequent Scarborough & District buses along the A170 to Pickering and Helmsley (No 128, one hour). They leave from Westborough.

There are regular buses, Nos 93 and 93A (via Robin Hood's Bay), to/from Whitby (£2.70, one hour). Yorkshire Coastliner has a frequent service between Leeds and Scarborough (No 843) via York (£8.40).

Train Scarborough is connected by regular trains with Leeds (£15.40, one hour) via York and Harrogate. There's a service to/from York (£9.50, 45 minutes) every 30 minutes. Trains also serve Hull via Beverley. The journey from Leeds shows a good cross section of Yorkshire.

Getting Around

Bus Local buses leave from the western end of Westborough and outside the train station.

Taxi There's a taxi rank outside the train station or contact Station Taxis (☎ 361009 or 366366), a 24-hour service; £3 should get you to most places in town.

FILEY
☎ 01723 • pop 16,400

Think of Filey as Scarborough Lite. In fact it even markets itself with Scarborough and Whitby.

There's less of everything in Filey, so if you're looking for a quieter beach town this might be a good bet; however if you want a good dose of culture as well, then you're better off in Whitby.

Filey is an important walking centre as it's the hub for the Cleveland Way and the Wolds Way. It has a full-range of stores where you can kit yourself out for your rambles. Murray St is lined with shops and links the train and bus stations to the beach.

Filey's TIC (☎ 512204, fax 516893, e filey@ytbtic.co.uk) on John St is well marked. It's open 10 am to 5.30 pm daily, May to September, and until 4.30 pm weekends only at other times. It books local accommodation in all price ranges.

Filey is well served by hourly trains on the line between Hull and Bridlington to the south and Scarborough to the north. The bare-bones station is about a mile west of the beach. The town is 7 miles (11km) south of Scarborough on the A165.

HARROGATE
☎ 01423 • pop 65,800

Harrogate is close to the eastern edge of Yorkshire Dales National Park, but its urbanised feel puts it far from the park in spirit.

After the grimy cities of the Midlands and parts of Yorkshire, Harrogate is reminiscent of the more prosperous south. Primarily built in the 19th century as a fashionable spa town, it has managed to remain affluent, although its original reason for existence – the health-giving effects of the mineral springs – doesn't really hold water anymore.

The town is famous for its spring and summer floral displays but the extensive gardens flanked by stately Victorian terraces are beautiful at any time of year. There are numerous high-quality hotels, B&Bs and restaurants that help to make Harrogate a restorative stop, especially if you've been busy tackling the Dales.

Orientation & Information

Harrogate is actually just south-east of the national park but makes an excellent touring base. The town is almost surrounded by gardens including the 200-acre Stray in the south.

The main shopping streets – Oxford St and Cambridge St – are lined with smart shops and shopping centres and are mostly pedestrianised. The Conference Centre (☎ 500500) is on Kings Rd.

Harrogate's TIC (☎ 537300, fax 537305, e tic@harrogate.gov.uk), in the Royal Baths Assembly Rooms on Crescent Rd, opens 9 am to 6 pm Monday to Saturday and noon to 3 pm on Sunday, April to September (9 am to 5 pm weekdays and until 4 pm on Saturday the rest of the year).

The post office, 11 Cambridge Rd, opens 9 am to 5.30 pm Monday to Saturday.

The Waters
A visit should start at the ornate **Royal Pump Room Museum** (☎ 503340), Crown Place, built in 1842 over the most famous of the sulphur springs. It gives quite a curious insight into the phenomenon. The museum opens 10 am to 5 pm (from 2 pm on Sunday), April to October. The rest of the year it closes daily at 4 pm. Admission costs £2/1.25. There are frequent special exhibitions.

You can experience the waters first-hand at the **Turkish Baths** (☎ 556746) in the Royal Baths Assembly Rooms. The entrance is on Parliament St around the corner from the TIC. The restored facility offers a full range of watery delights and a visit should last at least two hours. Start in the steam room, then plunge into the cold pool, recover your senses in the tepid pool and sympathise with lobsters in the hot pool. You can repeat this process as often as you like before relaxing in the Frigidarium, where you can have a drink and read magazines.

Of course you enjoy the waters naked and, this being England and all, means that there's a complicated schedule of opening hours that are, at turns, men-only and women-only – call for more details. Overall the baths open 9 am to 9 pm daily and admission costs £9.50. There are a range of massages and other therapies for an extra cost that you can pre-book.

Mercer Art Gallery
The Mercer Art Gallery (☎ 556188), Swan Rd, is home to locally produced works of art and visiting shows. It also has a collection of local archaeological finds. It opens 10 am to 5 pm Tuesday to Saturday (from 2 pm on Sunday) and admission is free.

Gardens
The **Valley Gardens** are quite beautiful. Their crown jewel is the **Sun Pavilion** *(☎ 522588)*, a vast and ornate glass-covered shelter that was built in 1933. Recently restored, it is the scene of concerts on Sunday afternoons from June to August.

The **West Park Stray** is another fine garden and park, south of the centre.

Walking
There are free historical walking tours offered daily from late April to October. Times vary; check with the TIC for details.

Special Events
The Harrogate Flower Show is held in April. It is predictably immense.

The Great Yorkshire Show (☎ 541000) is the major annual exhibition staged each July by the Yorkshire Agricultural Society. It's a real treat, with all manner of farm critters competing for prizes and last year's losers served up in a variety of ways at innumerable food stands.

Places to Stay
Camping Sites for tents can be found at *Bilton Park* (☎ 863121, e tony@bilton -park.swinternet.co.uk, Village Farm, Bilton) 2 miles (3km) north of town; they cost £8. It opens late April to October.

B&Bs Standards of accommodation in Harrogate are high and even at the cheapest places you can expect every room to be en suite and have a colour TV.

The *Franklin Hotel (☎ 569028, e flack@ frantel74.freeserve.uk, 25 Franklin Rd)* has simple singles/doubles going for £17/36.

Dragon House (☎ 569888, 6 Dragon Parade) has six basic rooms costing £18/36.

Nearby, *Daryl House Hotel (☎ 502775, fax 502775, 42 Dragon Parade)* has a pretty and quiet location and charges £19/38.

The Alexander (☎ 503348 fax 540230, 88 Franklin Rd) is a fully restored Victorian mansion that is entirely nonsmoking. The comfortable rooms cost £24/46.

Near the Valley Gardens, the *Cavendish*

Hotel (☎ 509637, fax 504434, 3 Valley Dr) has very comfortable rooms and can cater for vegetarians. Rates start at £32/50.

Ashbrooke House (☎/fax 564478, 140 Valley Dr) is close to Valley Gardens and has fine rooms that cost £27/50.

Hotels The *Harrogate Brasserie & Hotel* (☎ 505041, fax 722300, ⓔ harrogate .brasserie@zoom.co.uk, 28–30 Cheltenham Parade) has 14 rooms, each with its own stylish decor, costing from £45/65. It has an excellent restaurant and frequent live jazz.

The Imperial (☎ 565071, fax 500082, Prospect Place) is a grand hotel in the centre of town with good views of the Stray. The ornate rooms start at £95/109.

St George Hotel (☎ 561431, fax 530037, 1 Ripon Rd) has a commanding position across from the TIC. The rooms are posh and there's an indoor pool, health club and more. Rooms start at £95/120. The hotel was recently bought by the Marriott organisation.

Old Swan Hotel (☎ 500055, fax 501154) on Swan Rd is an ivy-clad 18th-century coaching house set in 5 acres of gardens. This is where Agatha Christie chose to hide

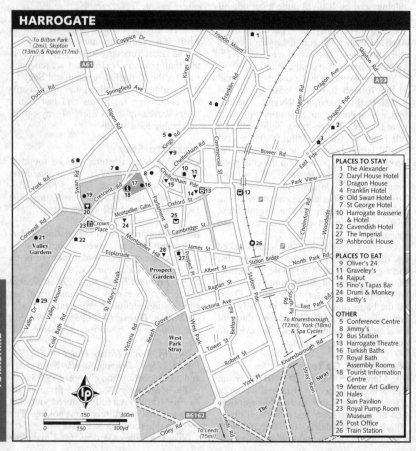

HARROGATE

PLACES TO STAY
1 The Alexander
2 Daryl House Hotel
3 Dragon House
4 Franklin Hotel
6 Old Swan Hotel
7 St George Hotel
10 Harrogate Brasserie & Hotel
22 Cavendish Hotel
27 The Imperial
29 Ashbrook House

PLACES TO EAT
9 Oliver's 24
11 Graveley's
14 Rajput
15 Fino's Tapas Bar
24 Drum & Monkey
28 Betty's

OTHER
5 Conference Centre
8 Jimmy's
12 Bus Station
13 Harrogate Theatre
16 Turkish Baths
17 Royal Bath Assembly Rooms
18 Tourist Information Centre
19 Mercer Art Gallery
20 Hales
21 Sun Pavilion
23 Royal Pump Room Museum
25 Post Office
26 Train Station

from the world when she did a runner in 1926. Rooms cost from £105/120.

Places to Eat
Harrogate Brasserie & Hotel (see Places to Stay) has a French dinner menu with many vegetarian options. There's a good wine list and you can have three courses for £15.

The ***Drum & Monkey*** (☎ 502650, 5 Montpellier Gardens) is a hugely popular, traditional seafood restaurant that fairly reeks of garlic butter. The changing menu always reflects what's fresh. Expect to pay £20 and up per person. It's closed on Sunday.

Fino's Tapas Bar (☎ 565806, 31 Cheltenham Parade) is bright and cheerful, not unlike the food. The long list of small dishes average about £4.

Rajput (☎ 562113, 9–11 Cheltenham Parade) has very good Indian food for £4 to £6. It's open until 11 pm.

Oliver's 24 (☎ 568600, 24 Kings Rd) is a light and airy cafe set in an old Victorian house. Very good Modern British meals cost £10.50/13.95 for two/three courses.

Betty's (☎ 502746, 1 Parliament St) is a classic Yorkshire tearoom dating from 1919. It has a large variety of teas, coffees and teacakes, and reasonably priced soups, sandwiches and main meals (under £7). It opens 9 am to 9 pm. A pianist plays from 6 pm.

Graveley's (☎ 507093, 8–10 Cheltenham Parade) serves tasty fish and chips (£5.50) from its takeaway operation. There are outside tables. The main restaurant has a long and varied menu with many fish items for £5 to £8.

Harrogate Theatre (see the following Entertainment section) has a grand old cafe that's popular at lunch.

Entertainment
Hales (☎ 725571, 1 Crescent Rd) is a traditional pub serving meals. A highlight of the wooden interior is the vintage gas lighting.

There's nothing traditional about ***Jimmy's*** (☎ 544100, 16 Kings Rd), which is a raucous nightclub popular with a young crowd.

Harrogate Theatre (☎ 502116, Oxford St) stages serious drama through the year.

Getting There & Away
Harrogate is roughly between Leeds (15 miles/24km) and York (22 miles/35km) and is best reached by train. It is on the line that runs between Leeds (£4.10, 38 minutes, every 30 minutes) and York (£4.10, 40 minutes, hourly). The modern train station has lockers.

Getting Around
Harrogate is easily walkable (and a healthy stroll is in keeping with local traditions).

Spa Cycles (☎ 887003), 1 Wedderburn Rd, about 10 minutes south-east of the train station, rents bicycles from £10 per day.

THIRSK
☎ 01845 • pop 6800
Thirsk is a small market town that occupies the narrow bit of land in North Yorkshire between the eastern side of the Yorkshire Dales National Park and the western edge of the North York Moors National Park, below the Hambleton Hills in the Vale of Mowbray.

It's the fictional 'Darrowby' of James Herriot's stories of life as a Yorkshire vet. Although it's known locally for its large market square (markets held Monday and Saturday), the opening of the flashy World of James Herriot attraction is drawing the tourist hordes.

Thirsk's TIC (☎ 522755, fax 526230, e thirsk@ytbtic.co.uk), in the World of James Herriot, opens 10 am to 5.30 pm daily.

World of James Herriot
His name was actually Alfred Wight but to millions of fans he's James Herriot, the wry Yorkshire veterinarian whose adventures were recorded in a series of books – *All Creatures Great and Small* and so on – and in a much-loved 1970s TV show. The building at 23 Kirkgate where the real Dr Wight lived, worked and wrote his books has been lavishly turned into the World of James Herriot (☎ 524234). It has been restored to its 1940s appearance, complete with vintage

copies of trade journals such as *Tail-Wagger* lying about.

But there's much more here than just artefacts from Wight's life (he used a pen-name because his professional organisation said that writing of his practice under his real name would be 'marketing'). There's a video documentary on his life and a re-creation of the TV show sets. It's all quite well done and you'll be in the company of true fans, many of whom have that look of pilgrimage on their faces. It opens 10 am to 6 pm daily (to 5 pm from November to February) and admission costs £4/3. Note that although animals are celebrated inside, they're required to stay outside.

Thirsk Museum

Housed in the home where Thomas Lord (of Lord's Cricket Ground fame) was born in 1755, the tiny museum (☎ 527707), 14–16 Kirkgate, has a small collection of items from Neolithic times to the Herriot era. It opens 10 am to 4 pm (closed Thursday and Sunday) and admission costs £1/50p.

Places to Stay & Eat

The TIC books B&Bs. There are several pubs offering accommodation around Market Place. The first, of what may prove to be many, ice cream/fudge shops has also opened.

The *Three Tuns Hotel* (☎ 523124, fax 526126, Market Place) has decent rooms from £35/55. Meals start at £5 and there are vegetarian options.

On Market Place, the *Golden Fleece* (☎ 523108, fax 523996) has quite nice rooms starting at £60/80. The food is also fairly creative and dishes cost from £7.

Getting There & Away

Stephenson's bus No 57 runs twice daily (no service on Sunday) between Thirsk and Helmsley.

Thirsk is well served by trains on the line between York and Middlesbrough. However the train station is a mile west of town and the only way to cover that distance is by foot or cab (☎ 522473).

North York Moors National Park

Only Exmoor and the Lake District rival the North York Moors National Park for natural beauty, but the North York Moors are less crowded than the Lake District and more expansive than Exmoor. The coast is superb, with high cliffs backing onto beautiful countryside. From the ridge-top roads and open moors there are wonderful views, and the dales shelter abbeys, castles and small stone villages.

One of the principal glories of the moors is the vast expanse of heather. From July to early September it flowers in an explosion of purple. Outside the flowering season its browns-tending-to-purple on the hills – in vivid contrast to the green of the dales – give the park its characteristic and moody appearance.

ORIENTATION

The park covers 553 sq miles (1432 sq km). The western boundary is a steep escarpment formed by the Hambleton and Cleveland hills; the moors run east-west to the coast between Scarborough and Staithes. Rainwater escapes from the moors down deep, parallel dales – to the Rye and Derwent Rivers in the south and the Esk in the north.

After the open space of the moors, the dales form a gentler, greener landscape, sometimes wooded, often with a beautiful stone village or two.

The coastline is as impressive as any in England, and considerably less spoilt than most; Whitby is a popular resort and it retains more of its charm than Scarborough to the south. Helmsley (near Rievaulx, pronounced **ree**-voh) is the centre for the western part of the park.

INFORMATION

There are visitors centres at Sutton Bank, Danby, Robin Hood's Bay and Ravenscar. The TICs in Whitby, Pickering and Helmsley are open for most of the year. A very useful tabloid visitors' guide (50p) is widely

available. The park's Web site is at www
.northyorkmoors-npa.gov.uk.

WALKING

There are a huge number of walks in the
park. The Cleveland Way (see the Activities
chapter) covers a good cross-section of the
park and the spectacular coastline.

With a little imagination, it's possible to
put together some interesting itineraries that
make the most of the varied scenery and the
limited, but interesting, railway lines. One
possible itinerary starting in York involves
taking a bus to Castle Howard, a bus to
Pickering, the North York Moors Railway
(NYMR; see later in this chapter) to Grosmont and the Esk Valley line to Whitby,
then walking to Scarborough and taking a
bus to Helmsley, then another back to York.

If you're feeling a bit more energetic,
take a bus to Pickering, the NYMR to Grosmont and the Esk Valley line to Kildale.
From there, walk along the Cleveland Way

north-east to Saltburn-by-the-Sea, then
south to Whitby and Scarborough, from
where you can catch a bus to Helmsley.

PLACES TO STAY

The park is ringed with small villages, all of
which have a good range of accommodation. Most of the rural pubs have a few
rooms. There's a reasonable sprinkling of
youth hostels that provide good walking
bases at Boggle Hole, Robin Hood's Bay,
Helmsley, Lockton (north of Pickering),
Wheeldale (near Goathland) and Whitby.

Another possibility is the network of
camping barns, which are particularly useful for walkers equipped to cope with basic
accommodation. The barns basically provide a roof over your head, a sleeping platform (you bring your own foam pad and
sleeping bag), a toilet and running water.
They cost £3.60 per person. The barns are
administered by the YHA but you don't
have to be a member.

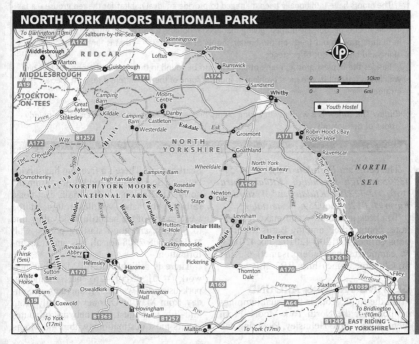

The Unnaturally Natural Lands

The North York Moors and Yorkshire Dales national parks are home to an astonishing range of flora and fauna. As some of the largest tracts of open land in England, the parks provide an excellent environment for scores of species. However, open land should not be confused with unspoiled land. Centuries ago much of Yorkshire was wooded, especially the Dales and the Moors. The land today is heavily managed and is used primarily as grazing land for sheep or is planted with grasses for harvest as hay and silage. The former is left to dry in the fields before it is baled while the latter is cut while young and then covered in plastic, which greatly inhibits decomposition and gives the farm critters their own 'fresh' produce out of season.

The vast pastures are subject to a variety of farming techniques including heavy fertilisation and the sowing of hybrid and foreign species. Government-sponsored programs are encouraging farmers to preserve fields and cultivate a more traditional range of plants.

Meadows and pastures that have been left to develop naturally are marked by a variety of plants with many different colours of flowers. Look for wood cranesbill with its broad pink flowers as well as the mountain pansy, yellow rock rose, white clover and the ever-popular golden buttercup.

Wet, boggy areas also feature cotton grass, sphagnum moss and insect-eating sundew plants. These patches are commonly found in large open areas where water accumulates with no possibility of run-off.

The North York Moors have the largest expanse of heather moorland in England although the Yorkshire Dales also have great swaths. You can see three species: ling, the most widespread, has a pinkish-purple flower and is most spectacular in late summer; bell heather is deep purple; and cross-leaved (or bog) heather prefers wet ground, unlike the first two, and tends to flower earlier.

The moors have traditionally been managed to provide an ideal habitat for the red grouse – a famous game bird. The shooting season lasts from the 'Glorious Twelfth' of August to 10 December. The heather is periodically burned, giving managed moorland a patchwork effect. The grouse nests in mature growth but feeds on the tender shoots of new growth – that is, until someone comes along and blasts it out of existence.

Besides the hapless grouse, many other birds can be found in the dales and moors. In fact birdwatchers shouldn't have a great problem in spotting some of the 150 different resident species. They include:

Curlew The curlew is a wader with a long pointy bill used for nabbing little critters in the muddy bogs of the uplands.

The barns are ***Farndale Barn*** (☎ *01751-433053, High Farndale*), ***Kildale Barn*** (☎ *01642-722135, Kildale*) and ***Westerdale Farm*** (☎ *01287-660259, Westerdale*).

To check availability and make reservations, contact the Camping Barns Reservations Office (☎ 01200-420102, fax 420103, e campbarnsyha@enterprise.net) 6 King St, Clitheroe, Lancashire, BB7 2EP.

GETTING THERE & AROUND

From the south, York is the usual jumping-off point for the North York Moors. From there, buses run to Helmsley, Pickering and Scarborough. There's a frequent bus service between Scarborough and Whitby. From the north, Darlington, on the main east-coast railway line, and Middlesbrough, at the western end of the beautiful Esk Valley line to Whitby, are good starting points. Call ☎ 0870 608 2608 for all bus and train information.

There is a highly useful Moorsbus network (☎ 01845-597426) that is aimed at park-users and walkers. It operates on Sunday from May to October and daily from mid-July to August. The network of routes covers most destinations within the Moors

The Unnaturally Natural Lands

Great-crested grebe This majestic bird with dramatic stripes can be seen swooping across the waters of natural and man-made lakes.

Kestrel This is one of many species – including swallows and starlings – that happily inhabit the many barns and other outbuildings scattered around the countryside; look for its striped tail feathers.

Peregrine falcon Almost wiped out by pesticides, the graceful peregrine can be seen soaring over limestone pastures looking for the odd mouse or unlucky pigeon.

Yellow wagtail This is a small bird with a yellow front that enjoys the flower-filled meadows during summer when it feeds on insects.

You'll have no problem spotting all the sheep and cattle you care to across the large pastures. In fact you might amuse yourself spotting the many breeds of each. Watch too for the classic sheep-dogs busily going about their duties while their owners shout and whistle directions. Look closer, however, and you'll see many wild species as well.

Badger Easily identified for its bold black and white striped head, the badger prefers digging up earthworms in the woods.

Fox Easily spotted, the red fox feeds on small mammals, although farmers no doubt wish it did a better job with the rabbits.

Hedgehog Small and spiny, the slow-moving hedgehog is sadly most often seen by the side of the road having been run over by a car. Not the most energetic of creatures, it hibernates from October to March.

Mink Not native to England, this ferocious feeder is rapidly replacing the native otter along creeks and rivers. Its introduction is primarily due to the misguided antics of 'animal rights' activists who have released minks from fur farms.

Otter Over 1m long, the fish-eating otter is finding it hard to compete against the much smaller and much more aggressive mink.

Rabbit The common rabbit is the most prevalent wild animal in the Dales and Moors. The scourge of farmers, it gobbles up great amounts of pasture grasses while it negates efforts to kill it by breeding like, well, a rabbit. One female can produce 30 offspring a year.

Roe deer Usually found in and around wooded areas, these small deer are growing in numbers. Males have short, stumpy horns.

---

and connects with the regular trains and buses.

The private NYMR cuts across an interesting section of the park from Pickering to Grosmont on the Esk Valley line.

The Moorslink ticket allows unlimited travel on the Esk Valley line as well as the NYMR and the Moorsbus network. It costs £12.50/6.25 and is a good deal if you plan to really make a day of it.

SUTTON BANK

On the A170 between Thirsk and Helmsley, Sutton Bank is the western escarpment of the Hambleton Hills, with magnificent views across the Vale of Mowbray to the Pennines and Yorkshire Dales. From the car park at the top there are walks to Lake Gormire and the Kilburn White Horse, and along the Cleveland Way.

The National Park Visitors Centre (☎ 01845-597426), off the A170 right at Sutton Bank, is an excellent resource centre with exhibitions on the moors and more. Check out the one showing the predictable results of what happens when car meets sheep. It opens 10 am to 5 pm daily, April to October (until 5.30 pm in August). The rest of the year it is open 11 am to 4 pm daily (weekends only in January and February). It also has a nice cafe.

There is also a mountain-bike rental service at the visitors centre. It opens at the weekend from April to October (daily from mid-July to August). The charge is £12 a day, and you should book ahead (☎ 01845-597426).

COXWALD & KILBURN

These two perfect tiny villages are down in the valley from Sutton Bank. From both you can see the White Horse, a huge drawing that was carved into the side of the hills in 1857. There is a good and well-marked 8-mile (13km) circular trail that links the villages and the hill with the drawing.

Fauconberg Arms (☎ 01347-868214) is a good country pub with fine food (most under £10) and lots of real ale. Rooms cost about £30 per person. The staff can give walking advice.

HELMSLEY
☎ 01439 • pop 1540

Helmsley is a classic Yorkshire market town, built around the expansive Market Place that still hosts a busy Friday market. Narrow Etton Gill runs west of Market Place before joining the River Rye in the south and there are some fascinating cottages along its banks, many built traditionally in grey-yellow limestone with red pantile roofs.

Almost all elements of the Moors' history and architecture come together in and around Helmsley: the ruins of a 12th-century Norman castle stand south-west of Market Place; a grand 18th-century country house, Duncombe Park, lies beyond the castle; the superb ruins of the 12th-century Cistercians' Rievaulx Abbey shelter in Ryedale, 3 miles (5km) to the west; a 16th-century manor house, Nunnington Hall, is 4 miles (6km) south-east; and there's the vernacular architecture of the town itself.

Helmsley makes an ideal base for exploring the North York Moors. There are numerous short walks in the surrounding countryside that take in the aforementioned sights and, for the more ambitious, Helms-ley is a starting point for the Cleveland Way (see the Activities chapter for details).

Orientation & Information
Everything radiates out from the central Market Place – the parish church is to the north-west and the castle and Duncombe Park are to the south-west.

The TIC (☎ 770173, e helmsley@ytbtic .co.uk) is on Market Place. It opens 9.30 am to 6 pm daily, April to October; and 10 am to 4 pm Friday to Sunday during the rest of the year.

The post office is on Bridge St and is open 9 am to 5.30 pm weekdays and until 12.30 pm on Saturday.

The Moreland Walker (☎ 771935), 14 Market Place, has outdoor gear and walking information.

Helmsley Castle
The castle (☎ 770442; EH) is most famous for its extensive surrounding earthworks – huge earthen banks and ditches – but parts of the curtain wall, the keep and a 16th-century residential wing survive. Begun in the early 12th century, various additions were made through to the Civil War when, after a three-month siege in 1644, it surrendered.

A retired London banker, Thomas Duncombe, bought the castle in 1689 and later built neighbouring Duncombe Park. Once the castle was no longer used as a residence it fell into disrepair, but it still makes a picturesque sight.

It opens 10 am to 6 pm daily, April to October; and until 4 pm Wednesday to Sunday the rest of the year. Admission costs £2.30/1.20.

Duncombe Park
Duncombe Park dates from 1713 and was built for Thomas Duncombe by William Wakefield, a friend of Vanbrugh. It was restored in the 1980s after 60 years as a girls' school. The building is neoclassical and is beautifully located in 600 acres of landscaped parkland. There are enormous lawns and terraces with views across the moors and surrounding countryside (see Rievaulx Terrace & Temples in the following Around

Helmsley section); the park has a number of walks.

The entrance to the house (☎ 770213) is signposted from the A170 from Thirsk. It opens 10.30 to 6 pm daily, April to October. Tickets for the house and grounds cost £6/3; admission only to the grounds costs £4/2.

All Saints Church
Surrounded by a nice garden, All Saints Church is a classic little English parish church. Although it was largely reconstructed in 1860, the 12th-century Norman doorway survives.

Places to Stay
The TIC books accommodation and has a list of B&Bs.

Two miles (3km) south-east of town and off the A170, *Foxholme Caravan Park* (☎ 770416, Harome) has 60 individual pitches among trees, costing from £7 per day.

The *Helmsley Youth Hostel* (☎ 770433, fax 770433, Carlton Lane) is a purpose-built place a quarter of a mile east of Market Place along Bondgate and Carlton Rd. It opens daily, April to August (closed Sunday and Monday in September and October). Rates are £9.25/6.50 for adults/under-18s.

There are several B&Bs on Ashdale Rd; leave Market Place at the north-eastern corner along Bondgate, and Ashdale Rd is the second street on the right. *Ashberry* (☎ 770488, 41 Ashdale Rd) is a traditional B&B with shared facilities costing from £17 per person.

Several places look onto Market Place. *Royal Oak* (☎ 770450, 15 Market Place) is a friendly pub with homely doubles for £50. *Feathers* (☎ 770275, Market Place) is a soft-spoken pub with nice rooms for £30 per person.

The *Black Swan Hotel* (☎ 770466, fax 770174, Market Place) has upmarket rooms that overlook the lovely back gardens. Prices start at £80/110.

Places to Eat
An ideal place to stock up for a picnic is *Nicholson's* (☎ 770249, Market Place), which has a large deli.

Just south of Market Place, *Gepetto's* (☎ 770479, 8 Bridge St) is a great Italian restaurant with an open kitchen, good smells and pizzas for £6.

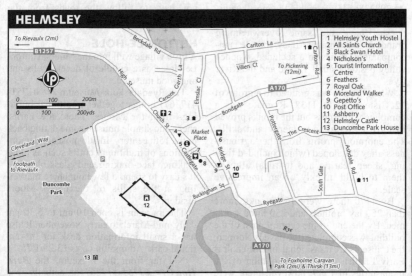

HELMSLEY

To Rievaulx (2mi)
B1257
Beckdale Rd
Carlton La
Villiers Ct
To Pickering (12mi)
Carlton Rd
High St
Garth La
Canons
Elmslac Cl
A170
Bondgate
Church St
Market Place
Castlegate
Bridge St
Pottergate
The Crescent
Cleveland Way
Footpath to Rievaulx
Duncombe Park
Buckingham Sq
South Gate
Ashdale Rd
Ryegate
Rye
A170
To Foxholme Caravan Park (2mi) & Thirsk (13mi)

0   100   200m
0   100   200yds

1 Helmsley Youth Hostel
2 All Saints Church
3 Black Swan Hotel
4 Nicholson's
5 Tourist Information Centre
6 Feathers
7 Royal Oak
8 Moreland Walker
9 Gepetto's
10 Post Office
11 Ashberry
12 Helmsley Castle
13 Duncombe Park House

YORKSHIRE

Of the Places to Stay listed above, the **Royal Oak** has basic food for under £6; **Feathers** is the pub of choice and serves good steaks (from £8); and the **Black Swan Hotel** has a fine restaurant offering lunch, tea and dinner (about £15).

Getting There & Away
Stephenson's bus No 57 runs twice daily between York and Helmsley (one hour) via Thirsk. Scarborough & District bus No 128 has an hourly service between Helmsley and Scarborough (one hour) via Pickering (40 minutes). There are only four buses on Sunday. Buses stop on Market Place.

Getting Around
Ring A&R (☎ 771040) for a taxi. Footloose (☎ 770886), on Borogate just off Market Place, hires bicycles for £7.50 per day. Booking is advisable.

AROUND HELMSLEY
Rievaulx Abbey
An enjoyable 3-mile (5km) uphill walk from Helmsley, following the first section of the Cleveland Way, leads to the remains of the 13th-century Rievaulx Abbey (☎ 798228; EH), arguably the most beautiful monastic ruin in England. Although it doesn't have the same overwhelming grandeur as Fountains Abbey, the site is incomparable. It lies in a secluded, wooded valley beside a small village and the River Rye.

When the site was granted to a group of 12 Cistercians in 1132, Ryedale was a complete wilderness but the monks proved to have extraordinary energy and skills. The enormous profits from the 'agribusiness' they developed (which included fishing, sheep rearing and textiles) allowed them to build quickly on an impressive scale.

By 1170 there were 150 monks, more than 250 lay brothers and 250 hired workmen. By the end of the century most of the building was complete (the nave is Norman, the transepts are transitional and the choir is Early English). By the dissolution of the monasteries in 1539, however, there were only about 20 monks. Many of the surrounding buildings, including much of pretty Rievaulx village, were constructed from stone pillaged from the ruins.

Rievaulx Abbey, off the B1257 to Stokesley, opens 10 am to 6 pm daily, April to September (9.30 am to 7 pm in July and August); and 10 am to 4 pm the rest of the year. Admission costs £3.40/1.70 and includes an audio tour. There is also an excellent small, new museum.

Rievaulx Terrace & Temples
In the 1750s Duncombe Park was landscaped to create a romantic series of views overlooking Rievaulx Abbey, Ryedale and the Hambleton Hills. Rievaulx Terrace & Temples (☎ 798340; NT) consists of a half-mile-long grass-covered terrace with carefully planned openings into the surrounding woods. It's all a bit of a snooze actually, but a worthy stop if you're on a circular walk.

The terrace, which includes a new historic exhibition in the Ionic Temple, opens 10.30 am to 5 pm from April to late October. Admission costs £3/1.50. There's no foot access to the abbey from the terrace – you have to follow the roads from the B1257.

HUTTON-LE-HOLE
A little village well into the Moors, Hutton-Le-Hole has a couple of decent pubs and one good museum.

The **Ryedale Folk Museum** (☎ 01751-417367) brings together traditional buildings from the Moors. There are barns, sheds and simple houses, some dating back to the 15th century. Inside most are demonstrations of traditional crafts such as clog-making, lace-making and glass-blowing. It's easy to spend a few hours here marvelling at the skills of the hardy Moors residents.

The museum is open 10 am to 5.30 pm daily, mid-March to early November. It also has a small information desk for the national park. Admission costs £3.25/1.75.

Not far from the museum, the **Barn Hotel** (☎ 01751-417261) is actually in a

YORKSHIRE

Fresh seafood in Scarborough, North Yorkshire

A sculpture at Helmsey Castle, North Yorkshire

Fleeting impressions: street art in York

Hear ye, hear ye: Manchester's town crier

Whitby, North Yorkshire: a historic shipbuilding centre, and one-time home to Captain James Cook

Nets in Whitby, where fishing is still an important industry

Borrowdale, Cumbria: a beautiful base for climbing some of England's finest mountains

row of stone houses. Doubles cost about £30.

Hutton-Le-Hole is 2 miles (3km) north of Kirbymoorside and the A170, midway between Helmsley and Pickering.

PICKERING
☎ 01751 • pop 5315

Once you get away from the traffic along the A170, Pickering is a surprisingly attractive little town. As the main starting point for trips on the NYMR, it also draws an enormous number of tourists.

Orientation & Information

Most of the town is within a five-minute walk of Market Place, a long narrow rectangle.

The TIC (☎ 473791, fax 473487, e pickering@ytbtic.co.uk) is in The Ropery across from the main car park. It opens 9.30 am to 5.30 pm daily, March to October (until 4.30 pm daily except Sunday the rest of the year).

The post office, 7 Market Place, is in a shop that sells newspapers and snacks.

The library (☎ 472185) is in The Ropery. It has Internet access and is open 9.30 am to 5 pm Monday, Tuesday and Thursday; until 7.30 pm Friday; and until 12.30 pm Saturday.

The Ryedale Rambler (☎ 476966), 14 Birdgate, has outdoor gear and local walking information.

Pickering Castle

The main attraction, Pickering Castle (☎ 474989; EH), was founded by William the Conqueror, but the remaining ruins date from a later period. Some of the curtain walls with towers, and part of the keep on a 40-foot-high motte, survive. It's a beautiful site with good views over the town. It opens 10 am to 6 pm April to September and until 4 pm the rest of the year. Admission costs £2.30/1.20.

Other Things to See

The **Beck Isle Museum** (☎ 47365) is off Bridge St and is like a 200-year-old carboot (garage) sale, containing just a lot of oddball (and a few interesting) items. It's open 10 am to 5 pm, April to October and admission costs £2.50/2.

The **Parish Church of St Peter & St Paul** (☎ 472983) sits on a prominent perch. It has

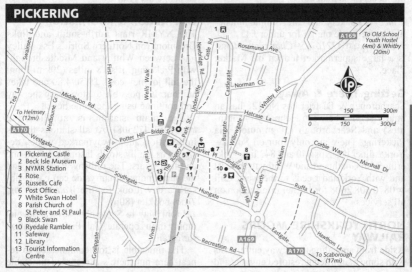

PICKERING

1 Pickering Castle
2 Beck Isle Museum
3 NYMR Station
4 Rose
5 Russells Cafe
6 Post Office
7 White Swan Hotel
8 Parish Church of St Peter and St Paul
9 Black Swan
10 Ryedale Rambler
11 Safeway
12 Library
13 Tourist Information Centre

To Old School Youth Hostel (4mi) & Whitby (20mi)

To Helmsley (12mi)

To Scarborough (17mi)

YORKSHIRE

frescoes that date from the 14th century. It's open during daylight hours year-round.

Places to Stay & Eat

The nearest youth hostel is the *Old School Youth Hostel* (☎ 460376, fax 460376, Lockton) about 4 miles (6km) north on the A169 between Pickering and Whitby. It's about 2 miles (3km) from the NYMR station at Levisham and is served by Yorkshire Coastliner's bus No 840 that travels between Leeds/York and Whitby. The hostel makes a good walking base. It opens daily in July and August, and Monday to Saturday from mid-April to June and in September. Rates are £7.50/5.25 for adults/under-18s.

The *Black Swan* (☎ 472286, fax 472926, 18 Birdgate) is a popular pub. B&B starts at £22.50 per person.

White Swan Hotel (☎ 472288, fax 475554, e welcome@white-swan.co.uk, Market Place) is a highly acclaimed small inn. Rooms cost from £30 to £45 per person. The pub has fine ales and the food is made from local produce. A three-course meal will run to about £20.

The hospitable *Rose* (☎ 475366) pub is near the NYMR station on Bridge St. Bar meals cost less than £5.

Russells Cafe (☎ 472749, 20 Market Place) is a bakery and cafe. Simple lunches like home-made pie go for under £4.

Safeway (☎ 472162, 59 Champleys Mews) is a large supermarket hidden off Market Place.

Getting There & Away

Scarborough & District bus No 128 has an hourly service between Helmsley (40 minutes) and Scarborough (50 minutes) via Pickering. There are only four on Sunday. Yorkastliner bus Nos 840 and 842 link Pickering with Goathland and Whitby to the east and with York and Leeds to the west. Call ☎ 0870 608 2608 for further information on all services.

NORTH YORKSHIRE MOORS RAILWAY

Aside from appealing to railway enthusiasts with some magnificent restored engines and carriages, the NYMR cuts across an interesting section of the moors and opens up some excellent day walks. And it still fulfils its original function of providing a transport link to Whitby.

History

The line from Pickering to Whitby was the third passenger line to open in Yorkshire, coming 10 years after the Stockton–Darlington Railway. For the first 10 years of its life, carriages on the Pickering–Whitby line were pulled by horses, except at Beck Hole, where the 1:15 incline was conquered by a balancing system of water-filled tanks, and on downhill stretches where the horses were put in a carriage and the train freewheeled! The first steam locomotive was used in 1847.

In the 1950s government policy went against common sense and the railways; after 1965 only the Esk Valley line remained in operation. Thousands of locals opposed the 'rationalisation' however, and in 1967 a volunteer preservation society was formed to restore and operate the Grosmont–Pickering line, which dates from 1835. Today the NYMR carries 310,000 passengers a year.

Orientation & Information

The NYMR runs north-south and links Grosmont (on Northern Spirit's Esk Valley line between Whitby and Middlesbrough) with Pickering. It's 18 miles (29km) long; the full journey costs £9.50/4.80 and takes an hour. It's possible to stop along the way and continue using the same ticket.

The main station is at Pickering (☎ 01751-472508). At all stations there's information about waymarked walks, designed as family strolls lasting between one and four hours. The railway, Pickering and the surrounding countryside can easily absorb a day. Look for the *Walks from the Train* booklet (80p).

From May to September several special dining trains operate. Call Pickering Station for details.

The timetable is too complicated to repeat here but there's a recorded timetable

(☎ 01751-473535). Roughly speaking, there are five to eight trains daily between April and early November.

The Journey
From Pickering the line follows Pickering Beck. The first stop is **Levisham station**, a mile west of beautiful **Levisham** village, which faces **Lockton** across a steep valley. Lockton, off the A169 between Whitby and Pickering, has the *Old School Youth Hostel* (see the Pickering section for details).

Goathland is a picturesque village 152m above sea level among the heather-clad moors. Most passengers get off here to view the village because it's used in the British TV series *Heartbeat*. Even more people will be getting off to see the station that was used in the *Harry Potter* film. You can camp at *Abbott's House Farm* (☎ 01947-896270) for £6 and at *Brow House Farm* (☎ 01947-896274) for £5. *Heatherdene Hotel* (☎/fax 01947-896334) is in the Old Vicarage. It's a licensed place with good meals (under £7) and rooms from £29 per person. There are many more B&Bs.

The sleepy, little village of **Grosmont** (**grow**-mont) has accommodation at *Hazelwood House* (☎ 01947-895292), which charges upwards of £19 per person. There's also one pub, the *Station Tavern* (☎ 01947-895060), and several shops selling sundries.

Walking
There are good walks at virtually every stop on the NYMR. One good one runs for 3½ miles (6km) from Goathland to Grosmont. The trail follows the route of the original railway, built in 1836, along the river. Be sure to pick up the trail handbook (£1.10), which explains a myriad of features along the route. Its available at Goathland station and at any park office.

Another local booklet worth buying is *Walks from the Train* (80p).

Getting There & Away
Most passengers begin their journey at Pickering. A good day would feature a triangular tour combining the NYMR, the Esk Valley line to Whitby and the Yorkshire Coastliner bus to Pickering. Check the schedules carefully in advance and you should be able to complete the triangle and have several stops along the way.

There are usually five trains daily on the Esk Valley line between Middlesborough and Whitby that stop at Grosmont.

DANBY
☎ 01287 • pop 400
Danby (sometimes referred to as Danby-in-Cleveland) is at the head of Eskdale, and the surrounding countryside is particularly beautiful. Fourteenth-century Danby Castle can be seen from the road; Danby Beacon, 2 miles (3km) to the north-east, has great views; and Duck Bridge, downstream from the village, is a 14th-century packhorse bridge.

The Moors Centre (☎ 660654), the main headquarters for the national park, is in Danby, half a mile from the village proper. There are displays, information, an accommodation-booking service and tearooms in an 18th-century manor house. The centre opens 10 am to 5 pm daily, April to October; 11 am to 4 pm daily, the rest of the year (weekends only in January and February). There are several short circular walks from the centre.

Places to Stay & Eat
Some local farms offer good-value B&B, costing around £18 per person. One example is *Crag Farm* (☎ 660279).

The *Fox & Hounds* pub (☎ 660218, fax 660030, e ajbfox@globalnet.co.uk) near the train station has good views and rooms from £27 per person. It also has a good restaurant.

Getting There & Away
There are five trains daily on the Esk Valley line. Whitby is 20 minutes east (£2.50); Middlesbrough is one hour west (£4.50).

STAITHES
☎ 01947 • pop 1000
Tucked beneath high cliffs and running back along the steep banks of a small river, the old fishing village of Staithes is one of

the most picturesque on the English coast. The idyll is somewhat spoiled, though, by the large potash mine in the hills behind.

In some ways, the village seems untouched by the 20th century, focusing still on its centuries-old battle with the sea. James Cook served as an apprentice grocer in a shop that has since been reclaimed by the sea; the shop and the street have been recreated in the **Capt Cook & Staithes Heritage Centre** (☎ 841454). Legend says that fishermen's tales of the high seas and bad treatment by his master led him to steal a shilling from the till and run away to Whitby and the sea. The centre opens 10 am to 5.30 pm daily. Admission costs £2.25/1.

The TIC in Whitby handles bookings and information for Staithes. There's accommodation in the two pubs and in a couple of guesthouses. *Springfields (☎ 841011, 42 Staithes Lane)* is a Victorian house with good views, which charges £15 per person.

WHITBY
☎ 01947 • pop 15,200

Somehow Whitby transcends the amusement arcades, fish and chip shops, and coaches – the imposing ruins of an abbey loom over red-brick houses that spill down a headland to a beautiful estuary harbour. This small town has had a disproportionate impact on world history, both as the site for the Synod of Whitby (which determined the nature of the medieval English church) and as the starting point for the maritime career of one of the world's greatest explorers, Captain James Cook.

Whitby is one of the most interesting and attractive towns on the English coast and is among the highlights of a trip to the north. It's the perfect base from which to explore the nearby cliffs, coves, fishing villages and beaches, which are among the most spectacular on this island. Watch for the salmon, which come up the River Esk in the spawning season and the seals that follow and feed on them.

The town itself combines the colour of a working harbour (on the estuary of the Esk), a muddle of medieval streets with a range of restaurants and pubs, the silhouette of the abbey, which seems to float over the town, and the paraphernalia of a seaside resort. It attracts a diverse group of people – not just retirees and young families.

The past is powerfully evoked, particularly when mists roll up the Esk Valley but also when Whitby is at its sunniest and loveliest. And you'll never have any doubt that you're close to the water, thanks to the shrieks of seagulls and the smells from the sea.

History

The Romans had a signal station on the high cliffs east of town. Over 200 years after their departure, Celtic Christianity was firmly established in the kingdom of Northumbria by St Aidan. In 635 he founded the great Lindisfarne monastery (see Holy Island in the North-Eastern England chapter). In 657 St Hilda, a Northumbrian princess, established a monastery at Streoneshalh (as Whitby was known before the Danish Viking invasions). In 664 the Celtic and Roman churches met at the abbey to resolve their differences. Eventually, the grand bishops, monks and nuns of the Synod (or Council) of Whitby on their windy headland decided the future of the English church in favour of Rome and its organisation based at Canterbury. See the boxed text 'Christianity & the Synod of Whitby' on the next page for more details.

The Danes destroyed the abbey in 867 but they recognised Whitby's potential as a port. The abbey was refounded by Benedictines in 1078 and flourished until the dissolution in 1539 – the Benedictine ruins survive today.

From the Middle Ages, the importance of Whitby as a maritime centre increased; Whitby-built and Whitby-crewed ships were to serve generations of traders, whalers, fishermen and explorers. In 1746, the 18-year-old James Cook arrived in the town as an apprentice to a local shipowner. For nine years Cook worked on Whitby cats – unique local-built colliers that carried coal from the Durham coalfields to London. These sturdy flat-bottomed vessels were specially designed to allow them to be beached for loading and off-loading.

In 1755 Cook joined the navy, and in

Christianity & the Synod of Whitby

When the Romans withdrew from Britain at the beginning of the 5th century, they left behind the Christian faith. Although the Angles and Saxons who arrived next weren't Christians, the Celts kept the religion alive, especially in Cornwall, Wales and Ireland.

Pope Gregory's missions to the Angles, led by Augustine in Kent (AD 597) and Paulinus in Northumberland (AD 627), gained tenuous footholds but lasted only six years in the case of Paulinus. His Northumbrian patron, King Edwin, was defeated and killed by Welsh and Mercian invaders. However, Edwin's heir, Oswald, was exiled on the island of Iona, a Celtic Christian outpost. When he won back power in 635 he appealed to the Iona monks to help him restore Christianity.

The saintly Aidan met this request and succeeded in planting Christianity so deeply in the north that it was never again challenged. The conversion of the Mercian kingdoms of the Midlands began and the forgotten arts of writing and keeping records were re-established. A great monastery was founded on Lindisfarne while St Hilda, a Northumbrian princess, established a monastery at Streoneshalh (Whitby's name before the Danish Viking invasions) in 657.

In 664, the Celtic and Roman churches gathered at Streoneshalh to resolve their differences at an ecclesiastical meeting (synod). Most importantly, the Roman church, under the leadership of the pope, was intent on establishing a centralised organisation transcending the tribal distinctions that had left much of Europe in an almost continuous state of war since the collapse of the Roman Empire. Matters of ritual also differed – the churches celebrated Easter on different days, for instance – and Celtic priests and monks preferred a system that allowed them to follow their individual consciences rather than an autocratic rule.

Eventually, the synod decided in favour of the Roman church's rites and organisation, although the decision wasn't entirely unanimous. The Roman archbishop of Canterbury, Theodore, allowed a number of Celtic practices to continue, including divorce and remarriage in certain cases and the private confession of sins rather than confession in front of a congregation.

1768 he began the first of three voyages of discovery. On all three voyages the ships he chose to use, including the *Endeavour*, were Whitby cats.

Orientation

Old Whitby grew up along the steep sides of the Esk estuary. Until the 18th century the eastern bank was the most important, but in the 19th century a new town with terraced crescents grew up on the western side, catering for the new tourist industry. This is also where most 20th-century development has occurred.

To confuse matters, some streets have two names: for example, the southern side of one street is Hudson St, while the northern side is Abbey Terrace.

Information

The TIC (☎ 602674, fax 606137), Langborne Rd, near the train station, opens from 9.30 am to 6 pm daily, May to September, and 10 am to 4.30 pm daily, October to April. It has a wealth of information on this part of the moors and the coast.

The post office is across from the TIC on Endeavour Wharf inside the Co-op Supermarket. It opens 8.30 am to 5.30 pm Monday to Saturday.

There's a laundrette at 72 Church St.

Whitby Abbey & St Mary's Church

Nothing survives of the Saxon abbey founded by St Hilda; it lay a little to the north of the existing ruins. A Benedictine abbey was re-established on the site in 1078 and the remains visible today are of the Benedictine church built in the 13th and 14th centuries (mainly in the Early English style).

The abbey (☎ 603568; EH) opens 10 am to 6 pm daily, April to September, and until

YORKSHIRE

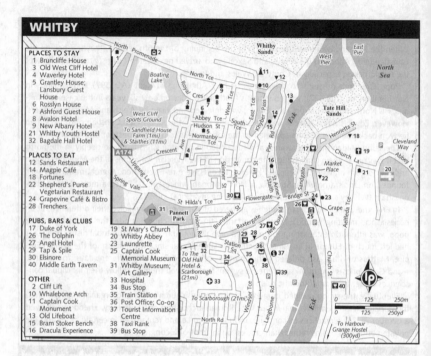

WHITBY

PLACES TO STAY
1 Bruncliffe House
3 Old West Cliff Hotel
4 Waverley Hotel
5 Grantley House;
  Lansbury Guest
  House
6 Rosslyn House
7 Ashford Guest House
8 Avalon Hotel
9 New Albany Hotel
21 Whitby Youth Hostel
32 Bagdale Hall Hotel

PLACES TO EAT
12 Sands Restaurant
14 Magpie Café
18 Fortunes
22 Shepherd's Purse
   Vegetarian Restaurant
24 Grapevine Café & Bistro
28 Trenchers

PUBS, BARS & CLUBS
17 Duke of York
26 The Dolphin
27 Angel Hotel
29 Tap & Spile
30 Elsinore
40 Middle Earth Tavern

OTHER
2 Cliff Lift
10 Whalebone Arch
11 Captain Cook
   Monument
13 Old Lifeboat
15 Bram Stoker Bench
16 Dracula Experience
19 St Mary's Church
20 Whitby Abbey
23 Laundrette
25 Captain Cook
   Memorial Museum
31 Whitby Museum;
   Art Gallery
33 Hospital
34 Bus Stop
35 Train Station
36 Post Office; Co-op
37 Tourist Information
   Centre
38 Taxi Rank
39 Bus Stop

4 pm the rest of the year. Admission costs £1.70/90.

In many ways, the nearby St Mary's Church is more interesting than the abbey ruins. It's a lovely medieval church with a low Norman tower and an atmospheric, extraordinary interior full of skewwhiff Georgian galleries and box pews. The nautical term 'crow's nest' may have come from the name given to the high pulpit from which the priest, dressed in black, gave his sermon. The climb of 199 steps up the side of the cliff is worth it just for the view.

The church (☎ 603421) opens 10 am to 5 pm daily (until 4 pm November to March) and admission is free. Parking costs £1.50.

Captain Cook Memorial Museum

The museum is in the harbourside house, below the abbey. It was once owned by John Walker, the Quaker captain to whom Cook was apprenticed. Cook sometimes lodged in the attic. It's well worth a visit for the house itself and for the interesting displays on Cook's life and voyages.

The museum (☎ 601900) opens 9.45 am to 5 pm daily, April to October. In March it opens 11 am to 3 pm at the weekend only. Admission costs £2.80/2.

Whitby Museum

Whitby Museum (☎ 602908), in Pannett Park, was founded in 1823 and is a traditional place full of dusty glass cabinets displaying fascinating stuff. It has a good collection of fossils including ones of a crocodile and a dinosaur, both found locally. There is also a fine collection of ship models. It's surrounded by a beautiful, steep garden with views (partly marred by an ugly block of modern flats) that give you another perspective on the town.

The museum opens 9.30 am to 5.30 pm on weekdays and 2 to 5 pm Sunday, May to

Dracula

Bram Stoker wrote the story of Dracula in 1897 while staying at a B&B in Whitby. And indeed the seashore resort plays a crucial role in three chapters. If you are familiar with the book – as opposed to the lurid Hollywood versions that spend much of their time in deepest, darkest Transylvania – then you will recognise some of the following sites.

The car park in front of Whitby train station was once sidings for freight cars. It's here that Dracula left Whitby for London in one of his boxes of dirt. Over at the Lower Harbour, look for the stone jetty out into the water. This is where the Russian boat chartered by Dracula was wrecked as it flew into the harbour ahead of a huge storm. Onlookers found the ship deserted except for a huge and ill-tempered black dog who jumped off and took flight. This scene from the book has its basis in the wreck of an actual Russian boat in 1885, although this one had a crew and not a dog with unusual tastes.

You can climb the same 199 stone steps that the heroine Mina ran up when trying to save her friend Lucy, who met a fellow not unrelated to the big black dog... The steps lead to St Mary's Church, the moody, medieval house of worship where Mina first saw Lucy sitting on a bench with a suspicious black being next to her. By that time, of course, it was too late.

There are many other important Dracula sites in Whitby. To get a good overview, have a seat on the Bram Stoker Bench, an otherwise ordinary looking bench that has the distinction of being placed on the spot where Stoker conceived most of the local scenes for *Dracula*. The bench is on the ridge that is immediately east of Khyber Pass; of the various motley benches up there, the Stoker one is furthest to the right when facing the harbour. From here you can see the location of most of the Whitby scenes portrayed in the book. For more information, the TIC sells an excellent walking tour leaflet for 30p.

September; 10 am to 1 pm Tuesday, 10 am to 4 pm Wednesday to Saturday and 2 to 4 pm Sunday, October to April. Admission costs £2/1. There's also a small art gallery open the same hours, which is free.

Dracula Experience
Always looking for a way to sink their teeth into tourists, local promoters have scored big with the Dracula Experience (☎ 601923) at 9 Marine Parade. With lots of lights and mirrors, it puts on a show loosely based on the Bram Stoker novel, parts of which are set in Whitby (see the boxed text 'Dracula' for details). It opens 10 am to 10 pm daily, May to September, before retiring to the modest hours of noon to 5 pm, weekends only, the rest of the year. Admission costs £1.95/1.50.

Monuments
At the top of the cliff near East Terrace, there is a **Captain Cook Monument** that shows him looking out to sea. Not far away, the **Whalebone Arch** is just that. It's made from the huge jawbones of whales once caught by Whitby's long-defunct whaling industry.

Tours

Several companies along the eastern bank of the estuary offer boat and fishing trips; a full list of operators is available from the TIC. You can also haggle for rides with the operators of the old lifeboat (☎ 821553) docked along Pier Rd.

The wonderfully named Heritage Harry (☎ 821734) offers walking tours of the town that depart from the TIC at 11.30 am on Tuesday and Thursday from July to September. The cost is £3/1. Harry also offers tours at other times as well as Dracula and ghost tours.

The Whitby Tour (☎ 0191-521 0202) uses an open-top bus that prowls the city daily from the Co-op Supermarket. The fare is £4.50/3.

Walking

The cliff-top walk from the evocative Whitby Abbey south to Robin Hood's Bay is a real treat. Although the path – part of the Cleveland Way – traverses a variety of terrain, it's fairly mild over its 7-mile (11km) length. There are good views far out to sea and you can view scores of birds. In Robin Hood's Bay, you can plunge into its touristy quaintness or imbibe a restorative pint in one of the many pubs. To round off the trip, take one of the fairly frequent buses that travel back to Whitby.

Alternatively, there are also some beautiful, small fishing villages, such as Staithes, to the north, also on the Cleveland Way.

Cycling

The **Whitby–Scarborough Coastal Cycle Trail** follows the 20-mile (32km) route of the old railway line and is an excellent trip. Trailways (☎ 820207) is a bicycle-rental firm based in the Old Railway Station in Hawsker, 2 miles (3km) south of Whitby towards Robin Hood's Bay. Rental prices start at £5 per day and the company will pick you up at Whitby train station or deliver your bike to you there.

Places to Stay

There are plenty of places to stay, but beware the Easter weekend, Whitby Festival (mid-June) and Whitby Regatta (August), when the place can be booked out.

Camping From £7 per night, *Sandfield House Farm* (☎ 602660, fax 606274), on Sandsend Rd (the A174), has five tent sites and 50 touring pitches. Take the No X56 bus a mile north-west towards Middlesbrough.

Hostels Beside the abbey, *Whitby Youth Hostel* (☎ 602878, fax 825146, East Cliff), at the top of the 199 steps, has great views over the town. It opens daily from late May to early September but closes during the day until 5 pm. Call for the complex hours for the rest of the year. Beds cost £10/6.90 for adults/under-18s.

The alternative is the well-designed and well-positioned *Harbour Grange Hostel* (☎ 600817, e backpackers@harbourgrange .onyxnet.co.uk, Spital Bridge) on the eastern side, a 10-minute walk from the TIC. It opens all day, year-round. There are family rooms, parking, and beds costing £8 (£1 for linen).

B&Bs A number of places in the centre of the medieval town (on the eastern side of the river) offer B&B. There is accommodation above the *Shepherd's Purse Vegetarian Restaurant* (☎ 820228, 95 Church St) with pleasant rooms, including a vegetarian breakfast, from £17 per person.

Most accommodation, however, is on the western side, the part of town that developed in Victorian times. A walk along Royal Crescent, Crescent Ave, Hudson St/Abbey Terrace and East Terrace will turn up many decent possibilities.

The *Ashford Guest House* (☎ 602138, fax 821734, e fcoll@globalnet.co.uk, 8 Royal Crescent) is an unspoilt place with sea views and a range of rooms from £20 per person, all nonsmoking.

Waverley Hotel (☎/fax 604389, 17 Crescent Ave) has doubles from £20 per person. It also has a small bar in the basement.

Bruncliffe House (☎ 602428, 9 North Promenade) is a bit west by the cricket field, where its quiet. Simple rooms cost £23 per person.

In a nice old Victorian building, the *Old West Cliff Hotel* (☎ 603292, fax 821180, 42 Crescent Ave) has six rooms with bathroom from £25 per person.

The *New Albany Hotel* (☎ 603711, 3 Royal Crescent) has decent rooms with sea views from £25 per person.

Possibilities on Hudson St/Abbey Terrace include *Rosslyn House* (☎/fax 604086, 11 Abbey Terrace), which has eight rooms, each with TV, that cost from £16 per person. *Lansbury Guest House* (☎/fax 604821, 29 Hudson St) has comfortable singles and doubles from £20 per person, and *Grantley House* (☎ 600895, 26 Hudson St) has rooms with numerous amenities that cost from £20 per person.

Hotels In a Jacobean house built in 1603, overlooking the Esk Valley, is *The Old Hall Hotel* (☎/fax 602801) on High St, Ruswarp. There's quite a range of rooms, some with bathroom, from £22 to £33 per person.

Avalon Hotel (☎ 820313, fax 602349, e avalon@avalonhotel.freeserve.co.uk, 13–14 Royal Crescent) has good singles/doubles with great views from £30/40.

The *Bagdale Hall Hotel* (☎ 602958, fax 820714, 1 Bagdale) has very comfortable rooms and good service. It costs from £39 per person, and there are also simple lodge rooms in a nearby building available for £39 a night that sleep up to five.

Places to Eat

There are plenty of reasonable eating places in Whitby, with a predictable emphasis on seafood.

Restaurants On the eastern side of the river, the *Shepherd's Purse Vegetarian Restaurant* (see Places to Stay earlier) is at the back of the wholefood shop opposite Market Place. High-fibre main courses are under £7. Takeaways are available and it also has an outside courtyard.

A delightful addition nearby is the *Grapevine Café & Bistro* (☎ 820275, 2 Grape Lane). Lunch baguettes with interesting fillings cost £3.25. At dinner, Mediterranean tapas dishes are around £5

each. The food is excellent and you'd best book for dinner.

Pubs At the end of Church St and overlooking the harbour, the *Duke of York* (☎ 600324, Church St) has good seafood meals for under £8 and a decent beer selection.

The *Dolphin* (☎ 602197, Bridge St) has comfortable tables inside or picnic tables outside. The cod and chips is succulent (£5.95) and there are more complex seafood dishes as well.

Fish & Chips It's claimed that the *Magpie Café* (☎ 602058, 14 Pier Rd) does the best fish and chips in the world, but unfortunately most of the world knows, so there are often long queues. Staff will fry, grill or poach the fish of your choice (from £6 to £10); there are also some vegetarian meals. It's open from 11.30 am to 9 pm.

Trenchers (☎ 603212, New Quay Rd), near the train station, is also highly regarded for its fish – it can get busy. A recent expansion means that it's better equipped for the mobs.

There are numerous other fish and chips places in town, costing a little less – just take your pick.

Overlooking the sea, *Sands Restaurant* (☎ 603500, Khyber Pass) is on the cutting that links the western cliffs and the old town. The views are the priority here; basic fish and chips costs £6.

Although you can't eat here, one of the most famous contributors to English cuisine is *Fortunes* (☎ 601659, 20 Henrietta St), a small family company that has produced and sold kippers since 1872. Kippers are fish (traditionally herring) that have been salted and smoked.

Entertainment

There are several quite lively pubs that are good for music. Check the *Whitby Gazette*, which comes out on Tuesday and Friday, to see what's on.

The *Angel Hotel* (☎ 602943) on New Quay Rd has live music attracting a young and boisterous crowd. The *Tap & Spile*

(☎ 603937), also on New Quay Rd, opposite the train station, is similar.

For a quieter pint away from the crowds try *Middle Earth Tavern* (☎ 606014, 26 Church St). It often has folk music.

Dracula fans and Goths congregate at the *Elsinore* (☎ 603975, Flowergate), an otherwise unremarkable pub except for its clientele.

Shopping

Jet (black fossilised wood) is found around Whitby. In Victorian times over 200 workshops produced jet jewellery; only a few still do so today. Some shops around town sell it.

Getting There & Away

Whitby is 20 miles (32km) from Scarborough, 45 miles (72km) from York and 230 miles (370km) from London.

Bus North East has a number of services in the Whitby area. There are regular buses, Nos 93 and 93A (via Robin Hood's Bay), to/from Scarborough (£2.70, one hour). Yorkshire Coastliner has useful services (bus Nos 840 and 842) between Whitby and Leeds (£8.10) via Goathland, Pickering and York. Note that, in another privatisation nightmare, the various bus companies have stopped using the coach station and now stop near the old station or out past the TIC on Langborne Rd.

Train Although it's not, in some ways, particularly efficient, you can get to Whitby by train. The Esk Valley line from Middlesbrough (£6.60) is one of the most attractive in the country – even more interesting scenically than the much-promoted NYMR (see the NYMR section earlier in this chapter).

En route, it's possible to connect with the northern terminal of the NYMR at Grosmont (to visit Danby) and Kildale (a possible starting or finishing point for the Cleveland Way). However, the Esk Valley line is only really efficient if you are coming from the north. There are only four trains a day and you have to change at Middlesbrough. If you are travelling from the south and London, it is much quicker to get

a train to Scarborough from York, then a bus from Scarborough.

Getting Around

Whitby is a compact place but there are those 199 steps to help you burn off the fish and chips. The cliff lift to/from Whitby Sands operates May to September.

Taxi The main taxi rank is beside the TIC, opposite the train and bus station. Harrison Taxis (☎ 600606) is one of the main operators. The minimum fare is £1.50 and you can get to most places around Whitby for less than £3.

COOK COUNTRY WALK

Explorer and navigator Captain James Cook was born and raised in the north of this area, and there are a number of museums and monuments commemorating his life. The Cook Country Walk, a 40-mile (64km) hike, links the most important sites of Cook's early years. The first half basically follows the northern flanks of the Cleveland Hills east from Marton (near Middlesbrough), then the superb coast south from Staithes to Whitby. It's designed to be broken into three easy days. The TICs in the region all have maps and leaflets.

ROBIN HOOD'S BAY
☎ 01947 • pop 1200

Bay or Baytown, as the locals call it, probably has a lot more to do with smugglers than with the Sherwood Forest hero, but it's a picturesque haven. A steep road drops from the coastal plateau down to the sea. There's compulsory parking at the top – don't even think about cheating and driving down, because there's hardly even room to turn at the bottom.

The village is a honeycomb of cobbled alleys and impossibly small houses that seem to hide in secret passages. There are a few gift shops and a trail of pubs (start from the bottom and work your way up) but really this is a place to just sit and watch the world go by, preferably out of season.

The National Trust has recently opened a major new visitors centre in the village in conjunction with the North York Moors National Park Authority. Housed in the restored 19th-century Old Coastguard Station next to the slipway on the bay, exhibits look at the life and ecology of the moors and coast. The former station also provides a superb vantage point across the bay. The centre opens 10 am to 5 pm daily, June to September, 10 am to 5 pm at the weekend in April and May, and 11 am to 4 pm at the weekend, November to March.

Unless you book, don't plan on staying. You could walk a mile (along the beach at low tide or the cliff at high tide) to the popular *Boggle Hole Youth Hostel* (☎ 880352, fax 880987, e bogglehole@yha.org.uk, Mill Beck, Fylingthorpe). Beds cost £10/6.90 for adults/under-18s.

Victoria Hotel (☎ 880205, fax 881170, Station Rd), across from the car park at the entrance to the village, has a commanding view. Singles/doubles with bathrooms cost from £40/58.

The Olde Dolphin (☎ 880337), accessed from King St, has huge bar meals (from £5), which feature seafood and vegetarian choices.

North East bus Nos 93 and 93A offer an hourly service between Whitby and Scarborough via the Bay.

RAVENSCAR

Billed as 'The Town That Never Was', Ravenscar is so tiny it's barely there. In the late 19th century developers laid out streets for a grand new seaside resort a la Scarborough, but Ravenscar proved to a be one resort too many and the scheme went bust.

Today we can thank the misfortune of old as the Ravenscar area has some fine walks. The National Trust operates a visitors centre (☎ 01723-870423) for the park and coast in Ravenscar. It has some simple displays and piles of maps and walking guides. It's open 10.30 am to 5 pm daily April to October.

There is a 3-mile (5km) interpretive trail behind the centre that takes in some of the area's unique geography including an old alum quarry. The Cleveland Way passes through the site. It's 3½ miles (6km) north

to Robin Hood's Bay and 11 miles (17km) south to Scarborough. There are two buses a day to/from Scarborough.

Yorkshire Dales National Park

Austere stone villages with simple, functional architecture; streams and rivers cutting through the hills; wide, empty moors and endless stone walls snaking over the slopes – this is the region made famous by James Herriot and the TV series *All Creatures Great and Small* (even if he lived in Thirsk outside the park to the east; see earlier in this chapter).

The landscape is completely different from that of the Lake District – the overwhelming impression is of space and openness. The high tops of the limestone hills are exposed moorland, and the sheltered dales between them range from Swaledale, which is narrow and sinuous, and Wensleydale and Wharfedale, which are broad and open, to Littondale and Ribblesdale, which are more rugged.

The Yorkshire Dales are very beautiful but in summer, as with the Lake District, they are extremely crowded. Avoid weekends and the peak summer period, or try to get off the beaten track. The famous Pennine Way runs through the area and can be unbelievably busy while other local footpaths are deserted.

ORIENTATION

The 683 sq miles (1769 sq km) of the Yorkshire Dales can be broken into northern and southern halves. In the north, the two main dales run parallel and east-west. Swaledale, the northernmost, is particularly beautiful. If you have your own transport, the B6270 from Kirkby Stephen to Richmond is highly recommended. Parallel and to the south is broad Wensleydale.

In the south, Ribblesdale runs north–south and is the route taken by the Leeds–Settle–Carlisle railway line, which provides access to a series of attractive towns.

YORKSHIRE DALES NATIONAL PARK

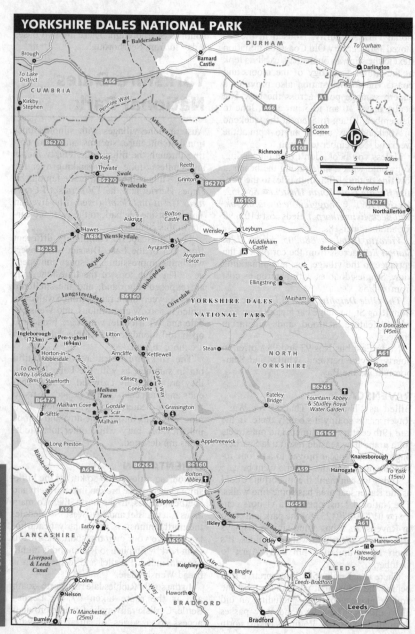

Wharfedale is roughly parallel and to the east.

Skipton is the most important transport hub for the region but apart from its castle it isn't very interesting. Richmond, handy for the north, is a beautiful town. For visitors without their own transport, the best bet will be those places accessible on the Leeds–Settle–Carlisle line: Kirkby Stephen, Dent and Settle.

INFORMATION
The main National Park Visitors Centre (☎/fax 01756-752774) is in Grassington, 6 miles (10km) north of Skipton. It opens 9.30 am to 5 pm daily from April to October, but much less often at other times; call for details. It has a huge and pretty grass parking area that's good for picnics.

Among the other visitors centres is a useful one in Malham (see Malham later in the chapter).

The centres have stacks of the useful *Visitor* newspaper, which, among other things, has a good listing of the myriad of events occurring within the confines of the park. They also have a huge range of publications, including an excellent series about the park's flora, fauna and history. See also the Web site at www.yorkshiredales.org.uk for details.

WALKING
There's a huge range of walks from easy strolls to extremely challenging hikes; the TICs are good places to get information on day walks.

The Pennine Way crosses the park; it's a demanding and deservedly popular walk through the rugged western half. Another possibility is the Dales Way, which begins in Ilkley, follows the Rivers Wharfe and Dee to the heart of the Dales, and finishes at Bowness-on-Windermere in the Lake District. If you started at Grassington, it would be an easy five-day, 60-mile (97km) walk. See the Activities chapter for details of both of these walks.

The Yorkshire Dales Walking Company (☎ 01969-624699) runs a huge range of guided walks, from 5 to 11 miles (8km to 18km) in length, throughout the year. Fees start at £4 depending on the walk. Visit its Web site at www.ydwc.co.uk for details.

CYCLING
Outside busy summer weekends, the Dales provide ideal cycling country. Most roads follow the rivers along the bottom of the dales so, although there are still some steep climbs, there's also plenty on the flat.

The Cyclists' Touring Club (CTC; see the Activities chapter) and the National Park Visitors Centre at Grassington have information about the 131-mile (210km) Yorkshire Dales Cycle Way that loops through some of the lesser known dales, following small B-roads.

ACCOMMODATION
There are many small villages in and around the park, all of which have a good range of accommodation. Most of the rural pubs have a few rooms. There's a reasonable sprinkling of youth hostels that provide good walking bases in or near Settle, Dent, Kirkby Stephen, Grassington and Richmond.

Another possibility is the network of camping barns; see Places to Stay in the North Yorkshire Moors National Park section for details. In the Dales, the *Low Row Barn* (☎ 01748-884430) is on Low Whita Farm in Swaledale, a mile off the Coast to Coast Walk (see the earlier Activities chapter for details).

GETTING THERE & AROUND
For public-transport users from the south, the Dales are best accessed from Leeds using the Leeds–Settle-Carlisle line to Skipton, which also gives good access to the west. This line also has Carlisle as a jumping-off point in the north-west. Life is more difficult in the north-east and east, although buses run to Richmond, Harrogate and Ripon.

As a rule, however, public transport is grim. There is a free timetable for bus and train services within the Dales available from the visitor centres and TICs. Your best source of information will be to call one of these centres to get local advice.

LEEDS–SETTLE–CARLISLE LINE

The Leeds–Settle–Carlisle line was one of the greatest engineering achievements of the Victorian era, and it takes passengers across some of the best countryside in England. It serves a number of attractive market towns and gives excellent access to the western dales.

Orientation & Information

The LSC line runs between Leeds and Carlisle, along the Aire Valley then through Ribblesdale, Dentdale and the western edge of the Dales. There are good walks from some of the small stations along the way.

There are trains roughly every two hours Monday to Saturday year-round, and five on Sunday. The entire journey takes two hours 40 minutes and costs £17.90 one way. There is a Freedom of the Line ticket for £30 valid for three days of unlimited travel.

The line is part of the national rail network, and schedule and fare information is available by calling ☎ 0845 748 4950. Various special trains operate through the year; call ☎ 0906 566 0607 for details.

The Journey

The first section of the journey is along the Aire Valley from Leeds.

The first stop is **Keighley,** the starting point for the Keighley & Worth Valley Railway to Haworth (of Brontë fame). See the Haworth section earlier in this chapter for details.

Skipton is considered the gateway to the southern dales. After Skipton the railway crosses the moors to Ribblesdale and the attractive market town of **Settle**. Both of these towns are covered later in this chapter.

Next is the spectacular Ribbleshead Viaduct and Blea Moor Tunnel, linking Ribblesdale with Dentdale. The line crosses into Cumbria, where there's the attractive and popular village of **Dent**, 4 miles (6km) west of the station.

Dentdale Youth Hostel (☎ 01539-625251, fax 625068) is 2 miles (3km) south of Dent station. Call for the hostel's odd opening times. Beds cost £9.25/6.50 for adults/under-18s. The *Sun (☎ 01539-625208)* is an excellent pub with beers from the nearby Dent Brewery and rooms from £19 per person.

After **Garsdale**, the train reaches its highest point (356m) at Ais Gill. Before **Kirkby Stephen** (see later in this chapter) are the ruins of Pendragon Castle, built in the 12th century and reputed to be the home of King Arthur's father.

Appleby is home to the famous Gipsy Horse Fair, held on the second Wednesday of June. After Appleby and to the east is Cross Fell, at 893m, the highest point on the Pennines. **Langwathby** is just north-west of Penrith, a jumping-off point for the Lakes. Armathwaite Viaduct is above the village and castle of **Combe Eden**, after which you reach **Carlisle** (see the Cumbria chapter).

Getting There & Away

For information about connecting services, see Leeds earlier in this chapter and Carlisle in the Cumbria chapter.

SKIPTON

☎ 01756 • pop 13,000

Skipton is a popular gateway to the Dales and a market town, so it can get very busy on summer weekends. Market days are Monday, Wednesday, Friday and Saturday.

Information

The busy TIC (☎ 792809, fax 797528, e skipton@ytbtic.org.uk), 9 Sheep St, opens 10 am to 5 pm weekdays and from 9 am on Saturday.

Skipton is a good town for provisions before you tackle the Dales. There are several supermarkets. George Fisher (☎ 794305) is a large outdoor gear store near the canal off Canal St.

Things to See & Do

At the top of High St, **Skipton Castle** (☎ 792442) is considered to be one of the best-preserved medieval castles in England. You can tour from the dungeon to the lookout points. It opens 10 am to 6 pm daily (from noon on Sunday). Admission costs £4/2.

The 200-year-old Leeds & Liverpool Canal passes through Skipton and you can use it for **boat rides**. Pennine Boat Trips (☎ 701212) offers daily 75-minute trips April to August. The fare costs £3.50/1.50. Pennine Cruisers (☎ 795478) rents traditional narrowboats for a day or more beginning at £60. Both firms are located off Coach St by the canal.

Places to Stay & Eat

Most accommodation is on Keighley Rd, which is convenient for the train station. *Craven House (☎/fax 794657, 56 Keighley Rd)* has rooms with shared bathroom for £19 per person.

Highfield Hotel (☎/fax 793182, 58 Keighley Rd) has rooms for £19 per person, all with bathroom.

A lovely old 18th-century farmhouse near the centre of Skipton is the home of *Napier's Restaurant (☎ 799688, fax 798111, Chapel Hill)*. The rooms cost from £33.50 per person and, as the name implies, it's also a restaurant, and a good one at that. Expect to pay around £20 per head.

Bizzie Lizzies (☎ 793189, 36 Swadford St), beside the canal, is a modern, large restaurant and takeaway, locally celebrated for the quality of its fish and chips (£4.50).

Royal Shepherd (☎ 793178) is a nice little pub right by the canal off Canal St. It has a lunch menu for under £4 and outdoor tables.

Getting There & Away

The train station is about half a mile out of town on Swadford Rd (A59). It doesn't have lockers, but most buses stop both here and in the centre.

Skipton is on the Leeds–Settle–Carlisle line only three stops north of Keighley; change there for the Keighley & Worth Valley Railway (☎ 01535-645214) to Haworth. It is also the last stop on the Metro network out of Leeds and trains are frequent.

WHARFEDALE

One of the main dales, the main portion of Wharfedale extends north from Ilkley through Grassington to Buckden. It's a remarkably beautiful area. Bus service is patchy but serviceable. Call ☎ 0113-245 7676 to check times in advance.

Grassington

☎ 01756 • pop 1200

Grassington is an attractive village that makes a good base for exploring the Dales, especially Upper Wharfedale. The B6265 from Skipton is a good drive.

The main National Park Visitors Centre (☎/fax 752774) is here. The centre can book accommodation. It is open from 9.30 am to 5 pm daily from April to October, but much less often at other times.

The *Linton Youth Hostel (☎ 752400, fax 753159, Linton)* is three-quarters of a mile (about 1km) south of Grassington, in the adjoining hamlet of Linton. It opens Monday to Saturday from April to September, and daily from June to August; telephone for its complicated opening schedule the rest of the year. Rates are £10/6.90 for adults/under-18s.

Raines Close (☎ 752678, e rainesclose@ yorks.net, 13 Station Rd) has comfortable doubles and twins from £21 per person.

The *Black Horse Hotel (☎ 752770, fax 753425, Garrs Lane)* is a good pub that was once a coaching inn. Rooms start at £30 per person.

Grassington is linked to Skipton by hourly buses except on winter Sundays when the service is greatly reduced.

North of Grassington

The villages get prettier and the scenery more intense as you head north from Grassington on the B6160 or along any of the many trails criss-crossing the hills.

Tiny **Conistone** is home to the Kilnsey Trekking Centre (☎ 01756-752861), which offers tours on both horses and ponies through Wharfedale. A half-day ride costs £14. Call for additional details.

One mile west, **Kilnsey Park** (☎ 01756-752150) is a private park that includes a trout farm and a nature trail up the side of the hill to an old reservoir. It has a good exhibit showing how dry stone walls are constructed. The cafe is good and the smoked trout (£4) is divine.

YORKSHIRE

Rock Piles

The webs of dry-stone walls snaking across the hills are a major part of the Yorkshire Dales landscape. Sometimes straight but more often curved and jagged, the oldest of the walls date from the 16th century or earlier.

The walls make good use of one of the Dales most ubiquitous features – stones. Their construction may seem rudimentary but like so many classic designs the walls are the result of some elegant engineering. No grout or cement is used in their construction, rather the stones are fitted together in a complex jigsaw that has proved remarkably resilient to the tough Yorkshire weather.

Builders have never been able to do much to alter the shape and size of the stones, so a role has been found for the various shapes and sizes. The largest stones form the foundation along the ground. Above this two parallel walls are built with medium-sized stones that slightly tilt towards the other. To prevent a total collapse inwards, small stones are used as filler. Large flat stones are used every few layers as throughstones to link the two sides. Large rounded coping stones cap the wall.

Early in the 19th century, an experienced builder – or waller – could complete about six to seven metres of wall a day. Given the absence of any mechanical aid, this meant lifting about 12 tonnes of stone.

The same techniques were used in the construction of another favourite part of the Dales landscape, the stone barns. They were common throughout the Dales and one farmer might have several scattered across his land to house cattle and protect hay from the elements.

It's easy to spot the key details of the surviving barns – the throughstones tying the walls together often protrude from the sides. The rectangular openings high up the walls were used for forking in hay while the low openings at ground level were used for shovelling out the resulting by-product – manure.

In recent decades, both the walls and the barns have been threatened by changing farming methods. The wide use of tractors means that it's easier to store hay and house cattle in large central – and often ugly – metal buildings. Similarly, cheap wire fencing can be erected in a fraction of the time and at a fraction of the cost of dry-stone walls. Some grants are now available from both the government and the central park committee for the preservation and restoration of these vital elements of the classic Dales landscape.

Kettlewell is a charming village that's at the crossroads of the B6160 and several rugged, rural roads. Over & Under (☎ 01756-760871), Low Hall, is an outdoor-gear shop that is happy to provide oodles of local walking advice. The *Blue Bell Inn* (*☎/fax 01756-760230*) is one of several pubs with rooms in town. It dates from the 1600s and has rooms from £25 per person. There's a daily bus service to/from Skipton.

MALHAMDALE

Amid the stark surrounding hills are three of the dale's top natural attractions: Malham Cove, Malham Tarn and Gordale Scar. All are easily reached by day-tripping walkers from Malham so expect crowds in summer.

But walk a little further or come out of season and you'll enjoy much more contemplative solitude.

Malham
☎ 01729 • 350

This pretty little village is a great 6-mile (10km) walk over the hills east of Settle. It gets crowded, not only for its charm but also for the natural wonders that are nearby. The 4-mile-long (6km) **Malham Landscape Trail** circles Malham Cove, a huge natural amphitheatre. It also covers Gordale Scar, a deep limestone canyon with waterfalls and the remains of an Iron Age settlement. The walking possibilities are many; the Pennine Way passes right through town and you can follow an 11-mile (18km) path east to Grassington.

There's a National Park Visitors Centre (☎/fax 830363), which opens 10 am to 4 pm daily, April to October, but weekends only at other times. It has the usual wealth of information and maps and can also book accommodation.

The *Malham Youth Hostel* (☎ 830321, fax 830551, e malham@yha.org.uk) is right in the village centre. It opens daily and charges £11/7.75 for adults/under-18s.

The *Lister Arms Hotel* (☎ 830330, fax 830323) is a 17th-century coaching inn that has an excellent pub, restaurant and gardens. Rooms cost from £22 per person.

If you don't want to walk, you'll probably have to drive as public transport here is woeful. The surrounding villages are lovely; one was the home of American writer Bill Bryson for many years.

Around Malham

Malham Tarn, a glacial lake, and **Gordale Scar**, a deep valley formed when a limestone cavern collapsed, are worth seeing, unless the crowds are too thick. A well marked circular 8-mile (13km) path covers the Malham Trinity (these two plus Malham Cove). There are numerous good interpretive booklets available at the visitors centre.

Another scenic walk is to follow the River Aire 3 miles (5km) downstream to **Airton** and beyond. You can walk on both sides of the river and construct some fairly complex circular itineraries.

RIBBLESDALE

The dale opens out a bit around Ribblesdale and by walking up any of the hills you can enjoy a sweeping view.

Settle

☎ 01729 • pop 2500

Settle is a pleasant market town in Ribblesdale, on the edge of the geological fault that delineates the limestone to the north and the gritstone to the south. A wander round the village makes a good stroll but you really want to head up into the hills for the scenery and the views. Market day is Tuesday.

The TIC (☎ 825192, fax 824381, e settle @ytbtic.co.uk) in the town hall opens 10 am to 5 pm daily, April to September, and closes at 4 pm during the rest of the year.

Places to Stay & Eat About 3 miles (5km) from Settle, *Knight Stainforth Hall* (☎ 822200, Stackhouse Lane) is opposite the high school. Tent sites start at £8.75.

The *Stainforth Youth Hostel* (☎ 823577, fax 825404, e stainforth@yha.org.uk, Stainforth) is 2 miles (3km) north of Settle on the B6479 to Horton-in-Ribblesdale. It opens every Friday and Saturday night. The rest of the year, the openings are pegged to school holidays; call for details. Beds cost £11/7.75 for adults/under-18s.

The *Golden Lion Hotel* (☎ 822203, fax 824103, Duke St) is central and has nice rooms from £24.50 per person. It also has a deservedly popular pub.

The *Royal Oak* (☎ 822561, fax 823102, Market Place) is a good pub with bar meals starting at around £5, including plenty of vegetarian dishes and salads; it also offers B&B from £28.50 per person.

Getting There & Away Settle supplies the S in the LSC line (see the Leeds–Settle–Carlisle Line section earlier). The train station is close to the centre.

The Three Peaks

The countryside to the north of Ribblesdale is dominated by the well known Three Peaks, which are part of a challenging 25-mile (42km) circuit involving 1500m (5000 feet) of ascent, and which is supposed to be completed in under 12 hours. Beginning at Horton-in-Ribblesdale, you follow the Pennine Way to **Pen-y-ghent** (693m/2273 feet), with a distinctive sphinx-like shape.

Next is **Whernside** (736m/2414 feet), the northernmost peak, then finally **Ingleborough** (723m/2373 feet), which has a distinctive flat top of gritstone and was the site of a Celtic settlement – hut circles and parts of a defensive wall can still be seen.

YORKSHIRE

Horton-in-Ribblesdale

☎ 01729 • pop 320

Strung out along the B6479, Horton-in-Ribblesdale is a good jumping off point for the Three Peaks.

Your first stop locally should be the *Pen-y-ghent Cafe (☎ 860333)*. This cafe-cum-shop functions as the local TIC, sells outdoor gear and maps, brews good coffee and is font of all local knowledge. It's open 9 am to 5.30 pm (closed Tuesday). Among their many other services, the good folks here operate a safety service for walkers. You tell them when you expect to be back and if you're not, they sound the alarm. They also have a long list of local accommodation, from cabins to barns.

The *Golden Lion Hotel (☎/fax 860206, ⓔ the.golden.lion@kencomp.net)* has a pub and serves meals. It has comfortable rooms for £18 per person.

WENSLEYDALE

Wensleydale runs east to west across the northern Dales. Its gently rolling hills are familiar to viewers of the James Herriot TV series and one of its main products, cheese, is familiar to fans of Wallace and Gromit, who sing its praises in marketing campaigns around the dale.

Hawes is the main town of Wensleydale and has a day's worth of diversions alone. The walking routes from here to the west are gentle yet have grandeur brought on by the open spaces. The route via the A684 and B6259 to Kirby Stephen, just across the border in Cumbria, will have you constantly pulling over to soak up the views.

Hawes

☎ 01969 • pop 3100

Hawes is a classic Yorkshire market town (the market is held on Tuesday) and has a large square surrounded by the kind of sturdy stone buildings that are characteristic of the area.

Hawes has many attractions. The **Dales Countryside Museum** (☎ 667450), Station Yard, is a modern and impressive facility that does just what its name implies. Here's the full story on Dales shearing, stacking

and milking. Possibly the best area shows how the once-fully-forested Dales have been brought to their present bald appearance by human actions. The museum is open 10 am to 5 pm daily Easter to October; call for hours other times. Admission is £3/2. The museum is also home to the local TIC.

You can see the cutting of the cheese (and just about anything else cheese-related) at **Wensleydale Creamery** (☎ 667664) on Gayle Lane. Tours show how milk turns into cheese and include the requisite tastings. It's open 9.30 am to 5 pm daily and admission costs £2/1.50 (not the best of deals given that you're herded through a large shop).

The *Hawes Youth Hostel (☎ 667368, fax 667723)* is about 2 miles (3km) west of the centre near the junction of the B6255 and the A684. It's generally open daily although there's the odd closure during winter, call to confirm hours. Rates are £9.80/6.75 per adult/child.

White Hart Inn (☎ 667259) on Main St is right in the centre and has a good pub as well as tasty meals for under £8. The rooms are comfortable and cost from £22 per person.

There several daily buses (Nos 156 and 157) between Hawes and the main-line railway station in Northallerton (two hours). Some of these buses also link Hawes to Richmond daily except Sunday.

RICHMOND

☎ 01748 • pop 8000

Richmond is one of the most beautiful towns in England – and surprisingly few people know. A ruined castle perches high on a rocky outcrop overlooking a rushing stream, and looms over the steeply sloping Market Square, which is surrounded by Georgian buildings. Cobbled streets, closely lined with stone cottages, radiate from the square and run down to the river, providing exhilarating glimpses of the surrounding hills and moors.

The town is just north of Catterick Garrison, one of the most important British Army bases.

Orientation & Information

Richmond is slightly to the east of the national park but it makes an excellent touring base for the park and is definitely in the Yorkshire Dales. Market day on the square is Saturday.

Richmond's TIC (☎ 850252, fax 825994, ⓔ richmond@ytbtic.co.uk), Friary Gardens, Victoria Rd, opens 9.30 am to 5.30 pm daily, April to October, and 9.30 am to 4.30 pm Monday to Saturday, the rest of the year. It has good brochures (from 40p to 90p) showing walks around the town and surrounding countryside, including one to Easby Abbey.

Free walking tours leave from the TIC at 2.15 pm every Sunday from May to September. The self-guiding *Richmond Town Trail* (£1) is an excellent historical booklet sold by the TIC.

The post office, 6 Queen's Rd, opens from 9 am to 5.30 pm weekdays and until 12.30 pm on Saturday.

Richmond Castle

Begun in 1071, Richmond Castle (☎ 822493; EH) was built by William the Conqueror to help subdue the rebellious people of the north. It was one of the first in England to be built of stone and was so stout that it was never successfully besieged. It has had a myriad of uses through the years, including a stint as a prison for conscientious objectors during WWI.

The castle boasts surviving 11th-century curtain walls, a gatehouse, a chapel and what is believed to be the oldest surviving Norman great hall (Scollard's Hall). The impressive 30m-high keep (1171), beside the gatehouse, is in remarkably good condition. It has been refloored and reroofed to give an idea of what it was like in medieval times.

It's a dramatic ruin so it's not surprising that legends (however unlikely) cling to it like moss; some say an underground tunnel links it to Easby Abbey, and that King Arthur and his knights are in a magical sleep here and will wake when the country needs them.

It opens 10 am to 6 pm daily, April to September; and 10 am to 4 pm the rest of the year. Admission costs £2.60/1.30.

Museums

Small **Richmondshire Museum** (☎ 825611), Ryder's Wynd, is an interesting local history museum. It has displays on the lead-mining industry, which forever altered the surrounding landscape. It opens 11 am to 5 pm daily, Good Friday to late October. Admission costs £1.50/1.

Green Howards Museum (☎ 822133), Market Place, shows the history of the Green Howards, a famous Yorkshire regiment that fought battles from the Crimean War to WWII. It opens 9.30 am to 4.30 pm weekdays and from 2 pm on Sunday, April to October; and 10 am to 4.30 pm Monday to Friday in February, March and November. Admission costs £3/2.

Georgian Theatre Royal

Built in 1788, the Georgian Theatre Royal (☎ 823021) on Victoria Rd is the oldest theatre in the UK surviving in its original form. It opens for guided tours 10.30 am to 3.45 pm Monday to Saturday (11 am to 1.15 pm on Sunday), April to October. Admission costs £1.50/1. There are local dramatic productions staged at various times through the year.

Market Place

Staid **Trinity Chapel** dominates Market Place, a classic market square that dates back at least 900 years. It was once the outer bailey of the castle, which accounts for its horseshoe shape. Bits of the chapel once formed the castle's church and in the intervening years it has had a number of uses, including as prison, warehouse and school.

The **Town Hall** is classically Georgian and dates from 1756. The **Market Hall** has a similar pedigree.

Cycling

Cycling on the narrow Dales roads isn't fun on a busy summer weekend; that point aside, this is great cycling country.

One cycle route to consider is a 20-mile (32km) trip to Barnard Castle along the

YORKSHIRE

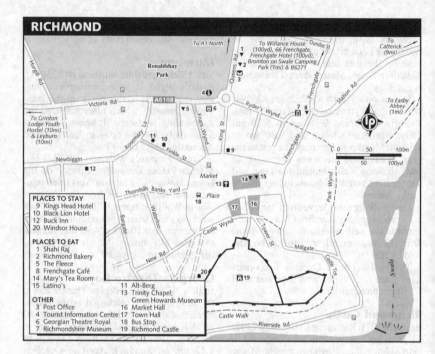

RICHMOND

PLACES TO STAY
9 Kings Head Hotel
10 Black Lion Hotel
12 Buck Inn
20 Windsor House

PLACES TO EAT
1 Shahi Raj
2 Richmond Bakery
5 The Fleece
8 Frenchgate Café
14 Mary's Tea Room
15 Latino's

OTHER
3 Post Office
4 Tourist Information Centre
6 Georgian Theatre Royal
7 Richmondshire Museum

11 Alt-Berg
13 Trinity Chapel;
     Green Howards Museum
16 Market Hall
17 Town Hall
18 Bus Stop
19 Richmond Castle

edge of the Cleveland Plain. Take the
B6271 to Gilling West, then the B-roads
south of the A66 through Whashton, Kirby
Hill, Gayles, Dalton, Newsham, Barning-
ham and Greta Bridge. Turn right onto the
A66 for a short section, then left for
Barnard Castle (a steep climb).

Another possibility is the 33-mile (53km)
trip to Kirkby Stephen along beautiful
Swaledale.

Places to Stay
Camping Offering tent sites (from £3.60)
a mile along the River Swale is *Brompton
on Swale Camping Park* (☎ 824629,
fax 826383). There's a riverside path all the
way to Richmond. To reach the camp by
road, take the B6271 east from where it
branches off from the A6108 just north of
Richmond.

Hostels The nearest is *Grinton Lodge
Youth Hostel* (☎ 884206, *fax 884876*,

ⓔ *grinton@yha.org.uk, Grinton*), 10 miles
(16km) to the west, and south of the B6270
between Richmond and Reeth. Built as a
shooting lodge, the hostel is high on the
moors. It opens daily, April to October;
Monday to Saturday, mid-February to
March; and weekends only in November.
Beds cost £10/6.90 for adults/under-18s.

B&Bs & Hotels With a great position near
Market Place is *Windsor House B&B*
(☎ 823285, 9 Castle Hill); the charge is a
reasonable £18.

The large and rambling *Black Lion Hotel*
(☎ 823121, 12 Finkle St) has decent sin-
gles/doubles from £20/35. The *Buck Inn*
(☎ 822259, 27 Newbiggin) is a nice old pub
charging from £22 to £26 per person.

There's a batch of pleasant places in the
17th- and 18th-century town houses in
cobbled Frenchgate. One of these, *66
Frenchgate* (☎ 823421, ⓔ *paul@66french
.freeserve.co.uk, 66 Frenchgate*), has good

views and is about a 10-minute walk from town. Rooms start at £18 per person.

Willance House *(☎ 824467, fax 824467, 24 Frenchgate)* has doubles with TV and bathroom from £40.

More upmarket, the ***Frenchgate Hotel*** *(☎ 822087, fax 823596, 59–61 Frenchgate)* has comfortable rooms costing between £60 to £78. It has a bar, gardens and parking.

Kings Head Hotel *(☎ 850220, fax 850635,* e *res@khead.demon.co.uk, Market Place)* overlooks the central square and has comfortable rooms and a range of services. There are some nice touches, such as the school photos of the owners' kids scattered about. Rooms cost from £50/70.

Places to Eat
Restaurants & Cafes The ***Shahi Raj*** *(☎ 826070, 8 Queens Rd)* has a classic Indian curry house menu with most items from £5 to £8.

Frenchgate Café *(☎ 824949, 29 Frenchgate)* is open late for coffees. It has good sandwiches at lunch for less than £3. Dinner is served until 9 pm and you can have a two-course Modern British treat for less than £12.

Latino's *(☎ 825008, 2 Trinity Church Square)* is up a flight of stairs and serves an extensive range of fresh pastas and other main courses costing £8 to £15. It has an excellent wine list.

Mary's Tea Room *(☎ 824052, 5 Trinity Church Square)* offers delicious baked goods, including Yorkshire curd tarts and game pies. There's an upstairs cafe serving afternoon tea (£3.95) and hot lunches like shepherd's pie for less than £4. It has a grocery section selling items such as local cheese.

There are cheap, and unremarkable, fish and chips places on almost every block. A better bet for a quick snack or lunch is the excellent ***Richmond Bakery*** *(☎ 850625, 10 Queen's Rd)*.

Pubs These pubs both have the usual bar meals. ***The Fleece*** *(☎ 825733)* on Victoria Rd, near the TIC, is a pretty standard place that gets crowded at the weekend.

The ***Black Lion Hotel*** (see Places to Stay) is friendly and has a good range of beers. It has several different bars scattered about its historic interior.

Shopping
Finkle St, off Market Square, has some interesting shops. Alt-Berg *(☎ 850615)* at No 14 sells a wide range of outdoor gear. They have their own line of boots, rent all manner of walking gear and sell maps.

Getting There & Away
North East bus company runs numerous regular services (bus Nos 27, X27 and 28) to/from Darlington (30 to 50 minutes), which has a major train station at the junction of several lines (including the main east-coast line from London's King's Cross to Edinburgh). There are buses (Nos 156 and 157) Monday to Saturday to/from Hawes (80 minutes). Buses stop on Market Place.

FOUNTAINS ABBEY & STUDLEY ROYAL WATER GARDEN
Sheltered in a secluded valley, with a number of monumental buildings surrounded by extensive parkland and gardens, this complex in the narrow valley of the River Skell is the only World Heritage Site in Yorkshire.

It includes the magnificent ruins of Fountains Abbey, a 12th-century Cistercian abbey; Fountains Hall (1610), a five-storey Jacobean mansion; St Mary's Church, a sumptuous Victorian church built in the 1870s; and a number of 18th-century follies. These are all set within a beautiful, 18th-century, 800-acre, landscaped park built around a series of artificial lakes and designed to feature the abbey ruins.

History
Fountains Abbey began as a small breakaway group of 13 monks from the Benedictine abbey of St Mary's in York. In 1132 the Archbishop of York granted them land in what was virtual wilderness. Lacking assistance from any established abbey or order, they turned to the Cistercian order for help. The Cistercians were often called the

White Monks because they wore a habit of undyed wool, reflecting the austerity and simplicity of their order. They were committed to long periods of silence and eight daily services. Clearly, this didn't leave much time for practical matters. So the Cistercians ordained lay brothers who lived within the monastery but pursued the abbey's ever-growing business interests – wool, lead mining, quarrying, animal breeding and so on.

Sadly, the idealism and purity didn't last long. After economic collapse in the 14th century, the monks rented their lands to tenant farmers and replaced lay brothers with servants. By the beginning of the 16th century the vast abbey had a population of only 30 monks.

After the dissolution the estate was sold into private hands and between 1598 and 1611 Fountains Hall was built with stone from the abbey ruins. The hall passed through several families until it and the ruins were united with the Studley Royal Estate in 1768.

The main house of Studley Royal burnt down in 1946 but the superb landscaping survives virtually unchanged from the 18th century. Studley Royal was owned by John Aislabie, who spent 20 years creating an extensive park. Major engineering works were required to create the lakes and to control the flow of the river.

Orientation & Information

Fountains Abbey lies 4 miles (6km) west of Ripon off the B6265. There are two entrances, one leaving the B road 1 mile from Ripon, for the Canal Gates entrance, and one 3 miles (5km) from Ripon, for the impressive visitor centre (☎ 01765-608888; NT).

The abbey, hall, water garden and visitor centre are open 10 am to 7 pm daily, April to September, and until 5 pm the rest of the year. The deer park opens during daylight hours. St Mary's Church was undergoing restoration in 2000; call for its reopening date.

Admission to the abbey, hall and garden costs £4.30/2.10; the deer park is free.

There are free one-hour guided tours at 2.30 pm daily, April to October; and at 11 am and 3.30 pm, May to September.

There's almost no public transport; call the abbey for details of any buses that might be running.

Cumbria

Much of Cumbria is a scenic feast, with the Lake District National Park at its heart. The mountains, valleys and lakes are beautiful, although ever since they were popularised by the early-19th-century Romantics they've been the centre of a major tourism industry. Nonetheless, if you avoid summer weekends and the main roads, and do some walking, it's still possible, like Wordsworth, to wander 'lonely as a cloud'.

The M6 and west-coast railway cut the county into an eastern third, which runs into the Yorkshire Dales and Pennines, and a western two-thirds that includes the Lake District National Park and England's highest mountains. Not surprisingly, the western two-thirds draws the largest crowds, although bits of the east, particularly the Eden Valley, are also very beautiful.

WALKING
Cumbria offers some of the best walks in England. See the Activities chapter for information on walking the Cumbria Way, and also see the Lake District National Park section later in the chapter for information on walks in the park. For more detailed coverage, see Lonely Planet's *Walking in Britain*.

CYCLING
This is also a good area for cycling. Keen cyclists should consider the waymarked 259-mile (417km) circular Cumbria Cycle Way. It can be completed in five days, but a full week is better. For more details look for *The Cumbria Cycle Way* by Roy Walker and Ron Jarvis. Carlisle tourist information centre (TIC) also stocks plenty of information.

Another possibility is the 140-mile (225km) Sea To Sea (C2C) route from Whitehaven or Workington to Newcastle-upon-Tyne or Sunderland. Most people will need five days to complete this cross-country route. *The Official Guide to the National Cycle Network* gives all the details.

If you're planning to cycle alongside

Highlights

- Walking and cycling through the mountains and valleys of the Lake District
- Taking a cruise on Windermere, Derwent Water, Ullswater and Coniston Water
- Staying at the picture-postcard village of Grasmere in the low season
- Making the pilgrimage to the artistic shrines of poets and writers, scattered throughout the Lakes
- Visiting the beautiful valleys of Borrowdale and Buttermere
- Catching the scenic railways from Carlisle to Windermere or around the coast
- Visiting quaint Alston in the heart of the northern Pennines

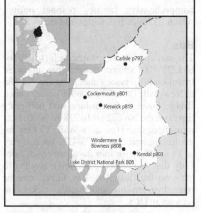

Hadrian's Wall, TICs sell the *Hadrian's Wall Country Cycle Map* (£2.50).

GETTING AROUND
Cumbria Journey Planner (☎ 0870 608 2608) is linked to a nationwide travel line and provides information on all local bus, boat and train services. It opens 9 am to 5 pm weekdays, and 9 am to noon Saturday. The Web site www.cumbria.gov.uk has a

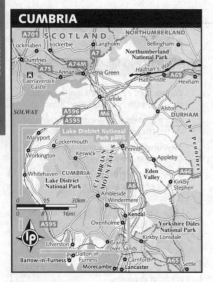

CUMBRIA

comprehensive journey planner online, which includes timetables and maps.

Bus

The main operator is Stagecoach (☎ 01946-63222). Its Explorer tickets give unlimited travel on all services, including the No 685 to Newcastle (☎ 01228-606000), Stagecoach Ribble buses in Lancashire, and half-price travel on the No 682 (☎ 01228-606000) running alongside Hadrian's Wall. Tickets for adults/children cost £5.75/4.25 for one day or £13.60/9.50 for four days, but check carefully that you're doing enough travelling to save on the deal. One-day tickets can be bought on any bus and four-day tickets are on sale at TICs.

Train

Three of England's most scenic train journeys cross Cumbria. The Cumbrian Coast Line runs right around the west coast from Carlisle to Ulverston and Lancaster (see Cumbrian Coast later in the chapter). A branch line runs from Oxenholme to Windermere. Finally, the Leeds-Settle-Carlisle (LSC) line (see the Yorkshire chapter for details), which starts in Yorkshire, enters

Cumbria south of Kirkby Stephen on its way to Carlisle.

Tours

Mountain Goat offers half-day (for around £14) and full-day escorted tours (around £24) of Cumbria and the Lake District in minivans. If you don't have your own transport this offers a good way of getting to some of the more remote areas, especially out of season. Mountain Goat is at Victoria St, Windermere (☎ 015394-45161, e moun tain-goat@lakes-pages.co.uk) and Central Car Park Rd, Keswick (☎ 017687-73962), but has lots of other pick-up points and can collect from hotels.

CARLISLE
☎ 01228 • pop 72,000
Modern Carlisle may be sleepy and small but its location as a border town made peace here impossible for 1600 years as it defended the north of England or the south of Scotland, depending on who was winning at the time. Although its character was spoilt to some extent by 19th-century industrialisation, it's an interesting town and its strategic location can be exploited by visitors to Northumberland, Hadrian's Wall, Dumfries and Galloway, the beautiful Scottish Borders, as well as the Lake District. It's also a hub for five excellent rail journeys (see Getting There & Away under this section for details).

History

Carlisle's history has been dominated by warfare and it seems miraculous that it could be peaceful today. The Romans under Agricola built a military station here, probably on the site of a Celtic camp or *caer* (preserved in the modern name of Carlisle).

Later, Hadrian's Wall was built a little to the north, and Carlisle became the Roman administrative centre for the north-west. But even the mighty Roman Empire was hard-pressed to maintain control and the Picts sacked the town in AD 181 and 367.

Carlisle survived into Saxon times but was under constant pressure from the Scots and was sacked by Danish Vikings in 875.

The Normans seized it from the Scots in 1092 and William Rufus began construction of the castle and town walls, but the Scots gained control again between 1136 and 1157. Forty years later the city withstood a siege by the Scottish king William. A further 60 years on it managed to repulse William Wallace during the Scottish War of Independence.

The Scottish Borders, or the Debateable Lands as they were known, were virtually ungovernable from the late 13th century to the mid-16th century. The great families with their complex blood feuds fought and robbed the English, the Scots and each other. The city's walls, citadels (two rotund structures to the south of the centre) and the great gates that slammed shut every night served a very real purpose.

During the Civil War, Carlisle was Royalist and was eventually taken by the Scottish army after a nine-month siege in 1644–5. In 1745 it also surrendered to Bonnie Prince Charlie, who proclaimed his father king at the market cross.

After the Restoration, peace came at last to Carlisle. So, eventually, did industry, cotton mills and railways.

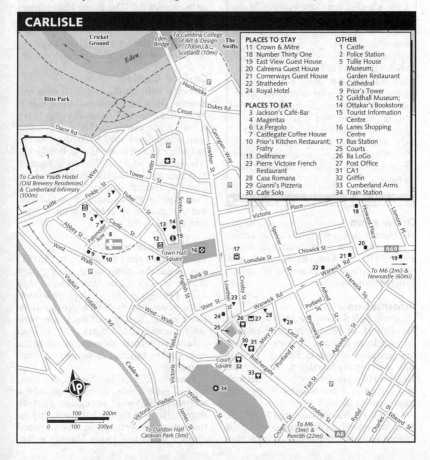

CARLISLE

PLACES TO STAY
11 Crown & Mitre
18 Number Thirty One
19 East View Guest House
20 Calreena Guest House
21 Cornerways Guest House
22 Stratheden
24 Royal Hotel

PLACES TO EAT
3 Jackson's Café-Bar
4 Magentas
6 La Pergolo
7 Castlegate Coffee House
10 Prior's Kitchen Restaurant; Fratry
13 Delifrance
23 Pierre Victoire French Restaurant
28 Casa Romana
29 Gianni's Pizzeria
30 Cafe Solo

OTHER
1 Castle
2 Police Station
5 Tullie House Museum; Garden Restaurant
8 Cathedral
9 Prior's Tower
12 Guildhall Museum;
14 Ottakar's Bookstore
15 Tourist Information Centre
16 Lanes Shopping Centre
17 Bus Station
25 Courts
26 Ba LoGo
27 Post Office
31 CA1
32 Griffin
33 Cumberland Arms
34 Train Station

The Border Reivers

People who fret about the modern-day crime wave should thank their lucky stars they didn't live in the Border Lands during the 400 years when the rapacious Reivers were in control.

The Reivers were brigands whose backgrounds differed but who had in common a complete disregard for the governments of England and Scotland. For the Reivers, sheep rustling and burning the homes of their enemies were a way of life. As a result, northern Cumbria and Northumberland, the southern Scottish Borders, and Dumfries and Galloway are littered with minor castles and tower-houses, as people struggled to protect themselves.

It wasn't until James VI of Scotland succeeded Elizabeth I of England and united the two countries that order was finally reasserted. The Reivers are credited with giving the words 'blackmail' and 'bereaved' to the English language. And if your surname is Armstrong, Carruthers, Dixon, Elliot, Henderson, Johnstone, Maxwell, Nixon, Scott, Taylor, Wilson or Young, genealogists would have us believe you could be descended from a Reiver.

Orientation

The train station is south of the city centre, a 10-minute walk from Town Hall Square and the TIC. The bus station is on the corner of Lowther and Lonsdale Sts, about 250m east of the square.

Information

On Town Hall Square, the TIC (☎ 625600, fax 625604, e tourism@carlisle-city.gov .uk) stocks an enormous quantity of literature; it opens 9.30 am to 5 pm (to 6 pm in July and August) Monday to Saturday and 10.30 am to 4 pm Sunday, May to September; 10 am to 4 pm Monday to Saturday from October to April.

Open Book Visitor Guiding (☎ 515120, e carol.donnelly@dial.pipex.com) offers various tours of Carlisle and its attractions over the summer months. Prices range from £1.50/80p to £3/2. They also provide on-board guides four times daily at the weekend May to September on the Hadrian's Wall bus for no extra charge (see Getting There & Around under Hadrian's Wall in the North-Eastern England chapter for details).

Most of the banks in the town centre have ATMs and there's a post office at 34 Warwick Rd, close to the train station. Ottakar's Bookstore (☎ 542300), 66 Scotch St, covers a good selection of topics.

In an emergency, the Cumberland Infirmary (☎ 523444) is west of the city centre on Newtown Rd. The police headquarters are north of Town Hall Square off Scotch St.

The Web site www.historic-carlisle.org .uk is a good source of online information.

Carlisle Castle

Probably built on the site of British and Roman fortresses, brooding Carlisle Castle (☎ 591922), run by English Heritage (EH), is well worth exploring. The fine Norman keep was built in 1092 by William Rufus, and Mary Queen of Scots was briefly imprisoned here in 1568. There's a maze of passages and chambers and great views from the ramparts. It opens 9.30 am to 6 pm daily, April to September; to 5 pm October, and to 4 pm November to March. Admission costs £3/1.50.

Carlisle Cathedral

The red sandstone cathedral (☎ 548151) was originally constructed as a priory church in 1123 but became a cathedral in 1133. During the 1644–5 siege, two-thirds of the nave was torn down to provide stone for repairing the city wall and castle. Serious restoration didn't begin until 1853 but a surprising amount survives, including the east window and part of the original Norman nave.

Features to look out for are the 15th-century misericords, including one with a mermaid; the lovely Brougham Triptych from Antwerp in the north transept; and the treasury at the western end. The cathedral opens 7.30 am to 6.15 pm Monday to Saturday and 7.30 am to 5 pm Sunday year-round. Visitors are asked to donate £2.

Surrounding the cathedral are other relics of the priory, including the 16th-century **Fratry** (housing the Prior's Kitchen Restaurant; see Places to Eat later) and the **Prior's Tower**.

Tullie House Museum

The excellent Tullie House Museum is particularly strong on Roman Carlisle, with lots of information on Hadrian's Wall. A lively section is devoted to the Border Reivers (see the boxed text 'The Border Reivers' earlier in the chapter). The museum (☎ 534781) opens 10 am to 5 pm Monday to Saturday and noon to 5 pm on Sunday year-round. Admission costs £3.75/2.50. The separate Georgian house outside has a gallery of childhood.

It opens from noon to 4 pm and admission is free. It's worth dropping into the restaurant and the small art gallery afterwards.

Guildhall Museum

The small Guildhall Museum (☎ 532781) was built as a town house in the 15th century but was later occupied by Carlisle's trade guilds. It opens as a local history museum noon to 4.30 pm Thursday to Sunday, Easter to October. Admission is free.

Places to Stay

Camping The *Dalston Hall Caravan Park* (☎ 710165), just off the B5299 to the south of the city, has van and tent sites from £6.

Hostels The Old Brewery Residences (university halls) double as the *Carlisle Youth Hostel* (☎ 597352, e dee .carruthers@unn.ac.uk, Bridge Lane) from early July to early September. A dorm bed costs £12.50/8.75 for adults/juniors.

B&Bs & Hotels With plenty of comfortable B&Bs within walking distance of the centre, you shouldn't have to pay more than £16; Warwick Rd, running east from the city centre, is a good place to start.

The small and friendly *Stratheden*

(☎ 520192, 93 Warwick Rd) has pleasingly decorated rooms for £16 to £20 per person. *Cornerways Guest House* (☎ 521733, 107 Warwick Rd) is larger but as friendly with singles from £16.

East View Guest House (☎/fax 522112, 110 Warwick Rd) has singles/doubles with bath from £20/34. There's a private car park. *Calreena Guest House* (☎ 525020, 123 Warwick Rd) charges from £15 to £16 for adequate rooms.

Just off Warwick Rd is *Number Thirty One* (☎/fax 597080, e bestpep@aol.com, 31 Howard Place), justifiably voted England's best B&B in 1999. Each room is spacious and comfortable, but of course it's a tad more expensive with rooms starting at £45/68.

Closer to the centre and two minutes' walk from the train station, the *Royal Hotel* (☎ 522103, fax 523904, 9 Lowther St) has a range of rooms from £17.50/42.

Moving upmarket, the Edwardian *Crown & Mitre* (☎ 525491, fax 514553) on English St, overlooking Town Hall Square, has been refurbished to provide modern rooms (from £54.50) and has car-parking facilities.

Places to Eat

The *Prior's Kitchen Restaurant* (☎ 543 251) in the old Fratry beside the cathedral provides an atmospheric vaulted room in which to eat light lunches.

Nearby *Castlegate Coffee House*, (☎ 592 353), Castle Court, Castle St, offers an old-fashioned ambience in which to take tea.

There's a branch of *Delifrance* (☎ 591 323, 35 Fisher St) behind the TIC offering great sandwiches.

If you like Italian food, you'll do well in Carlisle where many places have happy hours from 5.30 to 7 pm with meals for around £3.50. *La Pergola* (☎ 534084, 28 Castle St) is a popular place to tuck into pizza and pasta.

Two other restaurants serving the usual Italian fare in distinctly authentic surroundings are *Casa Romana* (☎ 591969, 44 Warwick Rd), on a busy road, and *Gianni's Pizzeria* (☎ 521093, 3 Cecil St), which is in a quieter spot.

If Italian is not your thing, *Cafe Solo* (☎ *631600, 1 Botchergate)*, near the train station, is welcoming and serves international-style food such as nachos grande (£3.95).

Pierre Victoire French Restaurant (☎ *51 5111, 6a Lowther St)* is also good; fillet of salmon costs £8.30.

It's worth dropping into the *Garden Restaurant* at the Tullie House Museum.

For something a bit more upmarket serving modern food, try *Magentas* (☎ *546363, 18 Fisher St)*, where a set menu costs £18 per person.

Jackson's Café-Bar (☎ *596868, 4 Fisher St)* stays open until 2 am and doubles as a club at the weekend.

Entertainment

Bar hopping and 'getting lashed' (which is not being whipped into submission but drinking yourself into oblivion) are common practices in much of northern England, and Carlisle is no exception to the rule. It's hard to find a pub not jam-packed and blaring out music on a Saturday night. Much of the action is centred just south of the centre near the train station.

Ba Lo Go (☎ *526160, 1 The Crescent)* is the flavour of the month for the young and trendy and is good for a loud, brash night out.

CA1 (☎ *530460, 17 Botchergate)* is another popular haunt, with a modern interior, pumping out the latest club favourites.

You'd be hard pressed to find a more buzzing place than the cavernous *Griffin (Botchergate)*, which pulls in the punters by the bus-load.

Like most Carlisle pubs, the *Cumberland Arms* (☎ *536900, 32 Botchergate)* blares out piped-in music but not at ear drum-splitting level.

Getting There & Away

Carlisle is about 58 miles (93km) from Newcastle-upon-Tyne, 95 miles (153km) from Glasgow, 98 miles (158km) from Edinburgh, 115 miles (185km) from both York and Manchester and 295 miles (475km) from London.

Bus Numerous National Express connections can be booked at the TIC. There are five buses to/from London (£22, 6½ hours) and many to Glasgow (£12.75, two hours). Six buses run daily to Manchester (£16, three hours) and three to Bristol (£38.50, seven hours).

Stagecoach (☎ 01946-63222) Lakeslink No 555 passes through Keswick, Grasmere, Ambleside, Windermere and Kendal on its way to Lancaster. Its No 104 service connects Carlisle with Penrith where the No X4/X5 connects with Keswick, Cockermouth and Workington.

A Rail Link (☎ 01387-256533) coach service runs from the train station to Hawick, Selkirk and Galashiels in the Scottish Borders.

Hadrian's Wall bus (No 682) and bus No 685 connect Carlisle with Haltwhistle, Hexham and Newcastle.

Train Fifteen trains daily link Carlisle with London Euston station (from £26, four hours).

Carlisle is the terminus for five famous scenic railways; phone ☎ 0845 748 4950 for information on day Ranger tickets offering unlimited travel and timetable details.

Leeds-Settle-Carlisle (LSC) Line cuts southeast across the Yorkshire Dales through beautiful, unspoiled countryside (£17.90, two hours 40 minutes; see the Yorkshire chapter for more details).

Lakes Line branches off the main north-south Preston and Carlisle line at Oxenholme, just outside Kendal, for Windermere; there are plenty of trains daily (£2.95, 20 minutes).

Tyne Valley Line follows Hadrian's Wall to/from Newcastle-upon-Tyne and is useful for visitors to the wall (£9.10, 1½ hours; see Newcastle-upon-Tyne and Hadrian's Wall in the North-Eastern England chapter).

Cumbrian Coast Line (see Cumbrian Coast later in the chapter) follows the coast in a great arc around to Lancaster, with views over the Irish Sea, and back to the Lake District (£17, one hour).

Glasgow-Carlisle Line is the main route north to Glasgow and gives you a taste of the spectacular Scottish landscape. Most trains make few stops (from £10.80, 1½ hours).

COCKERMOUTH
☎ 01900 • pop 7000

Lying outside the Lake District National Park, Cockermouth is an attractive small town, well placed for exploring the less populous north-west (especially beautiful Crummock Water and Buttermere). In fact, being outside the park has saved it from the worst excesses of the Lakes' tourism. It may have been discovered but so far it hasn't been spoiled.

Information
The TIC (☎ 822634, fax 822603), in the town hall, opens 9.30 am to 4.30 pm Monday to Saturday and to 5 pm July to September.

The main post office is located in Lowther Went shopping centre and opens 8 am to 6 pm Monday to Saturday.

Fellside Sports (☎ 823071) on Main St stocks outdoor gear.

Wordsworth House
This Georgian country house (☎ 824805) on Main St, built in 1745 and run by the National Trust (NT), was the birthplace and childhood home of William Wordsworth and his sister Dorothy. It's furnished in 18th-century style and contains some Wordsworth memorabilia. It opens 10.30 am to 4.30 pm weekdays, late March to October; and on summer Saturdays. Admission costs £3/1.50.

Jenning's Brewery
If you appreciate decent beer, you'll very quickly find yourself enjoying Mr Jenning's traditionally brewed products, particularly the Dark Mild and Bitter, brewed here for over 170 years. The brewery (☎ 821011) alongside the River Cocker offers 1½-hour tours (£3/1.50) at 11 am and 2 pm weekdays, mid-February to October (with extra tours at 12.30 pm in July and August); and at 11 am and 2 pm weekends, April to September. Children aged under 12 are not admitted.

Museums & Galleries
Close to Wordsworth House in the Printing House is the **Museum of Printing** (☎ 824 984), displaying a range of presses and equipment. The oldest, a Cogger Press, dates from 1820. The museum opens 10 am to 4 pm Monday to Saturday and admission costs £2.50.

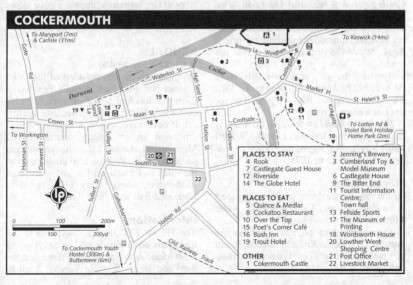

COCKERMOUTH

PLACES TO STAY
4 Rook
7 Castlegate Guest House
12 Riverside
14 The Globe Hotel

PLACES TO EAT
5 Quince & Medlar
8 Cockatoo Restaurant
10 Over the Top
15 Poet's Corner Café
16 Bush Inn
19 Trout Hotel

OTHER
1 Cokermouth Castle
2 Jenning's Brewery
3 Cumberland Toy & Model Museum
6 Castlegate House
9 The Bitter End
11 Tourist Information Centre; Town hall
13 Fellside Sports
17 The Museum of Printing
18 Wordsworth House
20 Lowther Went Shopping Centre
21 Post Office
22 Livestock Market

Depending on your taste, you could also check out the displays at the **Cumberland Toy & Model Museum** (☎ 827606), Banks Court, open 10 am to 5 pm daily, February to November. Admission costs £2.

The listed Georgian **Castlegate House** (☎ 822149), opposite Cockermouth Castle (which is closed to the public), shows works from local artists. It opens 10.30 am to 5 pm Monday to Saturday except Thursday. Admission is free.

Places to Stay

The nearest camp site is *Violet Bank Holiday Home Park* (☎ 822169, Simonscales Lane), off Lorton Rd. Tent pitches cost from £5.

Cockermouth Youth Hostel (☎/fax 822561, e reservations@yha.org.uk, Double Mills) is in a 17th-century water mill on the southern edge of town. From Main St follow Station St, then Station Rd. Keep left after the war memorial, then turn left into Fern Bank Rd. Take the track at the end of Fern Bank. The hostel opens daily, mid-April to October. Beds cost £8.10/5.65 for adults/juniors.

Castlegate Guest House (☎ 826749, 6 Castlegate) is a beautiful Georgian town house with B&B from £17.50 to £20 per person and packed lunches for £3.50. Readers have recommended the similarly priced *Rook* (☎ 828496, 9 Castlegate) across the road.

By the time you read this, *Riverside* (☎ 827504, 12 Market St), next to the TIC, should have opened. It's well placed on the river in a quiet corner.

The Globe Hotel (☎ 822126) on Main St has singles/doubles for £25/48. Robert Louis Stephenson stayed here when he visited Cockermouth in 1871.

Places to Eat

Of the various teashops, perhaps the nicest is the *Poet's Corner Café* (☎ 828676, 1 Old Kings Arms Lane) off Main St.

The tiny but very popular cafe *Over the Top* (☎ 827016, 36 Kirkgate) opens 10 am to 4 pm and 7.30 to 9 pm Wednesday to Saturday.

The *Quince & Medlar* (☎ 823579, 12 Castlegate) is one of the country's best vegetarian restaurants and booking is advisable. The menu features main dishes such as celery and Stilton strudel (£8.45) and starters, which cost around £4.50. It opens evenings Tuesday to Saturday.

The exuberant *Cockatoo Restaurant* (☎ 826205, 16 Market Place) also does vegetarian and vegan food, such as Chinese mushrooms (£9.99). It opens daily except Tuesday.

The *Trout Hotel* (☎ 823591) on Crown St, opposite Wordsworth House, offers good-value traditional bar meals for under £5. *Bush Inn* (☎ 822064) on Main St has similar fare and prices to the Trout.

The Bitter End (☎ 828993, Kirkgate) is Cumbria's smallest brewery and a great pub to boot. Sample Skinners Old Strong or Cockersnoot alongside decent pub grub.

Getting There & Away

Stagecoach (☎ 01946-63222) bus No 600 has two or three services a day, Monday to Saturday, to/from Carlisle (one hour). The more frequent No X5 service between Workington, Keswick and Penrith also stops at Cockermouth; there are three buses on Sunday between Cockermouth and Keswick.

KENDAL
☎ 01539 • pop 23,400

On the south-eastern outskirts of the Lake District National Park, Kendal is a lively town that has had a market since the 12th century. While it's not particularly beautiful, it does have several interesting museums and an art gallery, including the Museum of Lakeland Life, which more than justifies a visit. You can also clamber up to the ruins of Kendal Castle, just to the east of the river, where Henry VIII's last wife Katherine Parr may have lived.

Information

The TIC (☎ 725758, fax 734457) is in the town hall on Highgate and opens 9 am to 5 pm Monday to Saturday (to 6 pm in summer) and 10 am to 4 pm Sunday, April to

October. There's a post office on the main street, Stricklandgate.

Museums & Galleries

To the south of town, on the banks of the River Kent, you'll find the **Museum of Lakeland Life** and the **Abbot Hall Art Gallery** (☎ 722464).

The museum is a delight, with reconstructed period shops and rooms, a model of a local mine and lots of information on lost local industries such as bobbin-making. One room is devoted to local author Arthur Ransome, who wrote the *Swallows & Amazons* books, and another to John Cunliffe, the more-recent creator of Postman Pat who delivers the mail in Greendale (aka Longsleddale).

The gallery also makes much of local man, artist George Romney (1734–1802), many of whose portraits and drawings are on display. The temporary exhibitions on the 1st floor can be particularly worthwhile.

The **Kendal Museum** (☎ 721374) on Station Rd has collections of natural history and archaeology.

All three museums open from 10.30 am to 5 pm daily, mid-February to Christmas; and to 4 pm February, March, November and December. Admission to each costs £3/1.50, although once you've visited one you can see the others for £1.

Places to Stay

Kendal Youth Hostel (☎ 724066, fax 724906, e kendal@yha.org.uk, 118 Highgate) opens daily, mid-April to August; Tuesday to Saturday, September to October and mid-February to mid-April; and Friday and Saturday, November to mid-February. Beds cost £12.80/9.65.

The new backpackers hostel **Fortywinx** (☎ 720576, e fortywinxkendal@hotmail .com, 22 Gillinggate) is a good alternative, with dorm beds starting at £10, breakfast included.

Martindales (☎ 724028, 9/11 Sandes Ave), an adequate B&B, is about five minutes' walk from the train station and charges £28/44 for singles/doubles with bathroom.

The listed **Highgate Hotel** (☎/fax 724 229, e highgatehotel@kendal-hotels.co .uk, 128 Highgate) is central with comfortable rooms (starting at £29 per person) and a friendly welcome.

Places to Eat

Next door to the Highgate Hotel on Highgate is the **Brewery**, one of those wonderful arts complexes that manages to be all things to all people, with a theatre and cinema (☎ 725133) and an excellent bar-bistro. The menu changes fortnightly and prices are reasonable with soup of the day at £2.95 and dishes such as seared tuna with salsa verde for £8.25.

Other possibilities for light meals include **Castle Dairy** (☎ 730334, 26 Wildman St), a lovely 14th-century house, and the **coffee shop** attached to the Abbot Hall Art Gallery.

For fine takeaway fish and chips at £3.40 head to **The Lobster Pot** (☎ 729696, 167 Highgate) opposite Highgate Hotel.

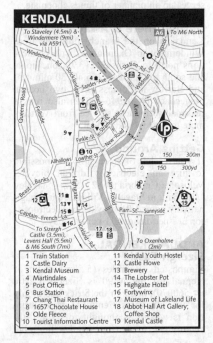

KENDAL

1 Train Station
2 Castle Dairy
3 Kendal Museum
4 Martindales
5 Post Office
6 Bus Station
7 Chang Thai Restaurant
8 1657 Chocolate House
9 Olde Fleece
10 Tourist Information Centre
11 Kendal Youth Hostel
12 Castle Howe
13 Brewery
14 The Lobster Pot
15 Highgate Hotel
16 Fortywinx
17 Museum of Lakeland Life
18 Abbot Hall Art Gallery; Coffee Shop
19 Kendal Castle

The Climbers' Friend

Kendal will be best known to many climbers as home of the mint cake, the high nutrition snack that sustained Sir Edmund Hillary and Sirdar Tenzing on their successful attempt on the summit of Everest in 1953.

These days there's barely a local sweet shop that would see its shelves as properly equipped if they weren't piled high with the brown, white or even chocolate-coated bars.

The *Chang Thai Restaurant (Stramongate)* has a varied vegetarian menu for £5.95 between 5.30 and 6.30 pm.

The *Olde Fleece (Highgate)* is a well refurbished pub serving up fine food and good ale.

Those with a sweet tooth should head for the *1657 Chocolate House (☎ 740702, 54 Branthwaite Brow)* off Stramongate, which serves up all manner of things chocolate.

Getting There & Away

Kendal is on the branch train line from Windermere to Oxenholme, with connections north to Carlisle (£13.20, one hour) and south to Lancaster (£5.40, 30 minutes) and Barrow-in-Furness (£11, two hours). Stagecoach (☎ 01946-63222) also runs a reasonably frequent service from Windermere to Barrow via Kendal.

Getting Around

If you're sick of steep hills it's possible to hire an electrically driven bicycle. Velosolex Cumbria (☎ 822452), 4 Staveley Mill Yard, in Staveley Village, rents imaginatively named Powabykes or Electropeds for £17 per day or £11 per half-day.

AROUND KENDAL
Sizergh Castle

Signposted 3½ miles (5.5km) south of Kendal off the A590 is Sizergh Castle (☎ 560070), home of the Strickland family for over 700 years. Central to its construction is what was thought to be a 14th-century *pele* tower (fortified dwelling), but may in fact be a solar tower with foundations dating back even earlier. Much of the interior is Elizabethan, with some stunning carved wooden chimney-pieces, but the pride and joy of the castle is the newly fitted Elizabethan inlaid chamber panelling, returned by London's Victoria & Albert Museum after 100 years.

The castle opens 1.30 to 5.30 pm Sunday to Thursday, Easter to October and the garden opens one hour earlier. Admission costs £4.60/2.30, £2.30/1.20 to the garden only. Bus No 555 from Kendal runs close to the castle.

Levens Hall

Another 2 miles (3km) south of Sizergh castle is Levens Hall (☎ 60321), an Elizabethan mansion built around a 13th-century pele tower. The house is beautifully kept and contains some wonderful 17th- and 18th-century furniture and a good collection of paintings. The topiary garden is worth the stop alone and dates from the 1690s. The house opens noon to 5 pm and the gardens from 10 am, Sunday to Thursday, April to early October. Admission to the house and gardens costs £5.50/2.80, gardens only £4/2.10. It's best to catch bus No 555 or 556 bus from Kendal or Lancaster, both of which stop outside Levens Hall once per hour.

Lake District National Park

'I wandered lonely as a cloud
That floats on high o'er dales and hills
When all at once I saw a crowd...'

William Wordsworth

The Lake District is one of England's most beautiful corners, a magical mix of dainty green dales, stark and rocky mountains, and the eponymous lakes. It manages to look beautiful even on the murkiest days – which is just as well since few visitors to the Lakes escape without a soaking! The Cumbrian Mountains are not particularly high – none

Warkworth Castle, Northumberland: a dramatic backdrop for a spot of cricket

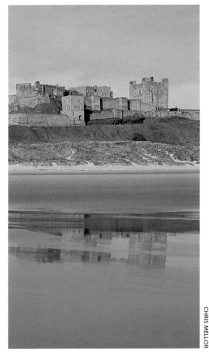

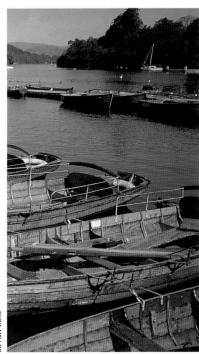

Mighty Bamburgh Castle, Northumberland

Boats for hire, Lake Windermere, Cumbria

A glorious view over Ullswater, Cumbria

Puffins are just some of the sea birds you can see on the Farne Islands, off the Northumberland coast.

A storm brewing over Craster's tiny harbour, Northumberland

reach 1000m (3280 feet) – but they're much more dramatic than their height would suggest.

Unfortunately, an estimated 14 million people pour into the Lake District every year. It's the second-most-visited part of England after London. The crowds can be so dense and the traffic jams so long that it's debateable whether it's worth visiting at any weekend between May and October, or any time at all from mid-July to the end of August. Stick with weekdays in May and June, or in September to October to make the most of the scenery without having to queue. For-

tunately, the National Trust (NT) owns a quarter of the total area, partly thanks to Beatrix Potter who sold them half of her large estate at cost and bequeathed the rest.

ORIENTATION

The two main bases for the Lakes are Keswick in the north (particularly for walkers) and Windermere and Bowness-on-Windermere in the south (two contiguous tourist traps). Coniston is a less hectic alternative and also good for walkers. All these towns have youth hostels, plus numerous B&Bs and places to eat.

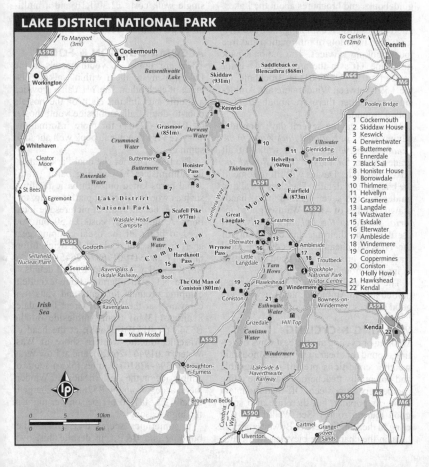

LAKE DISTRICT NATIONAL PARK

1 Cockermouth
2 Skiddaw House
3 Keswick
4 Derwentwater
5 Buttermere
6 Ennerdale
7 Black Sail
8 Honister House
9 Borrowdale
10 Thirlmere
11 Helvellyn
12 Grasmere
13 Langdale
14 Wastwater
15 Eskdale
16 Elterwater
17 Ambleside
18 Windermere
19 Coniston Coppermines
20 Coniston (Holly How)
21 Hawkshead
22 Kendal

Ullswater, Grasmere, Windermere, Coniston Water and Derwent Water are often considered to be the most beautiful lakes, but they also teem with boats. Wast Water (one of the remotest; see Cumbrian Coast later in the chapter for details), Crummock Water and Buttermere are equally spectacular but much less crowded.

In general, the mob stays on the A-roads, and the crowds are much thinner west of a line drawn from Keswick to Coniston.

INFORMATION

The TICs stock a frightening number of guidebooks and brochures about the Lakes. The Windermere and Keswick TICs are good places to start exploring the Lake District; both have lots of information and free local booking services. The national park runs nine TICs in the area, plus a visitor centre (☎ 015394-46601) at Brockhole, on the A591 between Windermere and Ambleside. Altogether there are about 30 TICs dotted around.

If you're staying several days, consider buying a copy of *National Park Walks in the Countryside*, which has 40 walks of all grades, even for kids. *A Walk Round the Lakes* by Hunter Davies will fill in some of the background details. The classic walking guides are the seven hand-written, hand-drawn volumes of Alfred Wainwright's *Pictorial Guide to the Lakeland Fells*, still useful despite their age and cost. Many of the TICs sell cheap leaflets covering local walks of the area and are a good alternative to lugging around a book.

The numerous walking/climbing shops, particularly in Ambleside and Keswick, are good sources for local information.

WALKING & CYCLING

Walking or cycling are the best ways of getting around, but bear in mind that mountain weather conditions prevail – changeable and potentially treacherous – and the going can be very, very steep. Off-road mountain biking is popular, but there are also some good touring routes. See Walking & Cycling in the Windermere & Bowness section later in the chapter for bicycle-hire details.

Several outdoor shops and centres hire boots, tents and hiking equipment. Phone the Weatherline on ☎ 017687-75757 before setting out on ambitious excursions. TICs stock free leaflets with basic information on safety in the fells and on the water.

See the Activities chapter for details on walking the Cumbria Way and see Cycling at the beginning of the chapter for information on the Cumbrian and Sea To Sea Cycle Ways.

Guided walks of a number of towns in South Lakeland are organised from June to August, mainly leaving from the TICs. A single walk costs £2.30/1.10 and a multi-ticket – five walks – costs £7/3. Pick up a brochure from the TICs.

ACCOMMODATION & FOOD

There are almost 30 youth hostels in the Lakes, many of them within walking distance of each other. The YHA also provides a shuttle bus linking eight of the hostels door-to-door. Call Ambleside youth hostel (☎ 015394-32304) for more information. They're very popular so book well ahead in summer.

The Lake District National Park Authority administers 12 camping barns (traditional barns kitted out with basic facilities such as wooden sleeping platform, tap, toilet, table, benches) all in picturesque locations. A night's stay costs £3.50 but you need to bring all the usual camping gear apart from a tent. Contact Keswick Information Centre (☎ 017687-72645), 31 Lake Rd, Keswick CA12 5DQ, for full details.

The NT also operates three excellent camping grounds for tents and vans (not caravans): at the head of Great Langdale, 8 miles (13km) from Ambleside on the B5343 (☎ 015394-37668); at the head of Wasdale, on the western shore of Wast Water (☎ 019467-26620); and at Low Wray (☎ 015394-32810) 3 miles (5km) south of Ambleside on the western shore of Windermere, access from the B5286. The charge is usually £3.50/1.50 per person per night in the high season.

It sometimes seems that every other building is a B&B, but despite this, over summer weekends, you're advised to book and be prepared for high prices. At peak times prices jump by up to 50%.

In general, food is reasonably priced and good. Prices are keenest in the pubs, where servings are hearty and the menus often surprisingly imaginative (even for vegetarians).

GETTING THERE & AWAY
There's a direct rail link from Manchester airport to Barrow-in-Furness (2½ hours) and Windermere (2¼ hours). Carlisle has several bus services to Keswick, the heart of the northern lakes.

Windermere has a train station and good road links, and is the main centre for the southern lakes. To both Windermere and Carlisle, coaches from London take about 6½ hours, trains 3½ hours.

GETTING AROUND
Given the congestion in the Lakes, it's best to avoid bringing a car. If you do bring one, put it in one of the main car parks and use the buses to get around. Theft from cars is quite common so don't leave valuables behind. Since the distance between most points is quite small (for example, Ambleside is 5 miles (8km) from Windermere), you could consider getting around by taxi; expect to pay around £1.50 per mile, with a minimum charge of £2.

Bus
Stagecoach (☎ 01946-63222) has some excellent local bus services, including the No 555 Lakeslink between the main towns and Carlisle; the Nos 505 and 506 Coniston Rambler minibuses on the Beatrix Potter Trail, which link Bowness, Windermere, Ambleside, Hilltop, Hawkshead and Coniston hourly; and the No 517 Kirkstone Rambler over Kirkstone Pass. The free brochure *Explorer* has full details.

Train
Aside from British Rail's Cumbrian Coast Line (see Cumbrian Coast later in the chapter) and the branch line from Oxenholme to Windermere, there are a number of steam railways. The TICs have all the details.

Boat
Windermere, Coniston Water, Ullswater and Derwent Water are all plied by ferries, often providing time-saving links for walkers. See the Windermere & Bowness, Coniston, Keswick and Ullswater sections later in the chapter for details.

WINDERMERE & BOWNESS
☎ 015394 • pop 8300
Windermere was originally the name of England's largest lake. The town of the same name is a reasonably modern development that followed on the heels of the railway in 1847. The Windermere and Bowness conglomerate quickly grew to become the Lake District's largest tourist centre. At times it feels like a seaside resort, thanks to the crowds and the tat, and gives Oxford St in London a run for its money for the build up of exhaust fumes.

Orientation
It's 1½ miles (2.5km) downhill along Main Rd, New Rd, Lake Rd, Crag Brow and Promenade from Windermere station to Bowness Pier; a taxi will run you there for around £2.50. All the way along you'll see B&Bs and hotels. Buses and coaches all leave from outside the train station. Most of the places to eat are concentrated in Bowness, which is the livelier place to be in the evening.

Information
Windermere TIC (☎ 46499) in Victoria St is excellent and visitors can even send and receive faxes at reasonable cost. It also provides an accommodation booking service free of charge covering most of the Lake District. It opens from 9 am to 6 pm daily; to 7.30 pm in summer and 5 pm in winter.

The Brockhole National Park Visitor Centre (☎ 46601), 3 miles (5km) north of Windermere on the A591, opens 10 am to 5 pm daily, April to October.

The small Bowness Bay Information Centre (☎ 42895), in Glebe Rd south of Promenade, opens 9.30 am to 5.30 pm daily, Easter to October.

The post office at 21 Crescent Rd opens

9 am to 5.30 pm weekdays and to 12.30 pm Saturday.

Things to See

The **Windermere Steamboat Museum** (☎ 45565) on Rayrigg Rd, to the north of Bowness on the lakeside, houses a collection of steam and motor boats, including the world's oldest mechanically powered boat. It also offers trips on a small steam launch, the SL *Osprey*. It opens 10 am to 5 pm daily, mid-March to October. Admission to the museum costs £3.25/2 and the steamboat cruises cost £5/4.

The World of Beatrix Potter (☎ 88444), in the Old Laundry in Bowness, cashes in on Pottermania but should keep the kids amused on a wet day with lots of interactive displays. It opens 10 am to 5.30 pm daily, April to September; and to 4.30 pm in winter. Admission costs £3.50/2.

At the southern end of the lake is the **Aquarium of the Lakes** (☎ 015395-30153), a freshwater aquarium centred on fish and animals of the area. The highlights are the playful otters and an underwater tunnel. It opens 9 am to 6 pm daily (to 5 pm in winter); and costs £5.25/3.95. The best way to

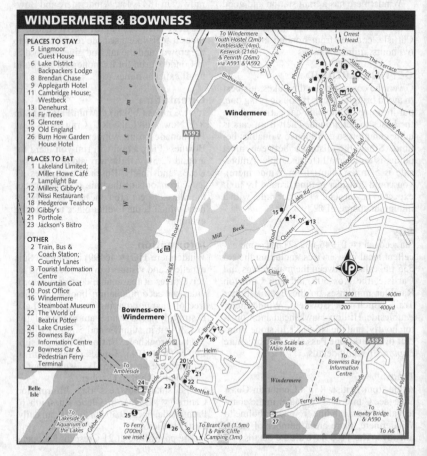

WINDERMERE & BOWNESS

PLACES TO STAY
5 Lingmoor
   Guest House
6 Lake District
   Backpackers Lodge
8 Brendan Chase
9 Applegarth Hotel
11 Cambridge House;
   Westbeck
13 Denehurst
14 Fir Trees
15 Glencree
19 Old England
26 Burn How Garden
   House Hotel

PLACES TO EAT
1 Lakeland Limited;
   Miller Howe Café
7 Lamplight Bar
12 Millers; Gibby's
17 Nissi Restaurant
18 Hedgerow Teashop
20 Gibby's
21 Porthole
23 Jackson's Bistro

OTHER
2 Train, Bus &
   Coach Station;
   Country Lanes
3 Tourist Information
   Centre
4 Mountain Goat
10 Post Office
16 Windermere
   Steamboat Museum
22 The World of
   Beatrix Potter
24 Lake Crusies
25 Bowness Bay
   Information Centre
27 Bowness Car &
   Pedestrian Ferry
   Terminal

get there is to take a cruise from Bowness or Ambleside to Lakeside (see the Other Activities section later for combined cruise/aquarium ticket prices).

Walking & Cycling

Across the main road from the station, Orrest Head, offering one of the classic Lakeland views is just 1½ miles (2.5km) away, although it's a steep climb to get there. Another good viewpoint is Brant Fell, 2 miles (3km) from the Bowness ferry terminal. It's another steep climb but the views of Bowness and Lake Windermere are worth the effort.

Beatrix Potter's cottage at Hill Top and the village of Hawkshead are easily accessible to walkers. Catch the ferry across Windermere (see Boat under Getting There & Away later in the section); it's a 2-mile (3km) walk to Hill Top and another 2 miles to Hawkshead (see Hill Top and Hawkshead later in the chapter).

Country Lanes (☎ 44544), in the train station, organises guided cycle rides to Hawkshead and Hill Top every Wednesday during summer. It's a 17½-mile (28km) ride and costs £17 per person or £5 if you use your own bike. Country Lanes also rent out bikes for £14 per day.

Other Activities

Several companies run cruises around Lake Windermere from Bowness Promenade. Their prices are competitive and their routes very similar, so the most important variables are their timetables and the aesthetic appeal of the boats. Most operators ply Windermere from Ambleside in the north to Lakeside in the south, via Bowness. Cruises to Ambleside take about half an hour and to Lakeside about 40 minutes.

The Windermere Iron Steamboat Company (☎ 015395-31188) has three beautiful old cruisers. Adult single/return tickets from Bowness to Ambleside cost £4/5.80; to Lakeside £4/6. A 45-minute nonstop cruise costs £4.50. A Freedom of the Lake ticket allows unlimited cruises for a 24-hour period from any pier on the Lake. Tickets cost £10/5.

Combined tickets also tie in with the Ambleside/Bowness to Haverthwaite Steam Railway (☎ 015395-31594), which operates from Easter to November and returns cost £9.20 from Bowness and £12.40 from Ambleside. A ticket for the railway alone costs £2.20/1.45. It's also possible to purchase a combined ticket for a cruise and entry to the Aquarium of the Lakes; return from Bowness £10, return from Ambleside £13.20. Rowing boats can be hired at the lake.

Mountain Goat (☎ 45161, e mountain-goat@lakes-pages.co.uk), on Victoria St offers half- and full-day escorted tours of Cumbria and the Lake District in minivans.

Places to Stay

Camping If you're after a camp site with great views, *Park Cliffe (☎ 31344, fax 31971, e parkcliffe@btinternet.com)* on Birks Rd has all mod cons and 180 pitches on grass. It costs £9.60 per two-person tent.

Hostels Within spitting distance of the train station on High St, is the *Lake District Backpackers Lodge (☎ 46374)*, which offers beds in small dorms (£11) and breakfast (£3.50). Guests have access to a kitchen, lounge and washing machine.

Windermere Youth Hostel (☎ 43543, e windermere@yha.org.uk, High Cross, Bridge Lane, Troutbeck) may be larger but is 2 miles (3km) from the station. Leave Windermere on the A591 to Ambleside and turn right up Bridge Lane at Troutbeck Bridge, a mile north of Windermere. Numerous buses run past Troutbeck Bridge and in summer the hostel sends a minibus to meet trains. It opens daily, mid-February to early October; and Friday and Saturday, the rest of the year. Beds cost £10.85/7.40.

B&Bs & Hotels – Budget & Mid-Range

The lovely slate-stone *Brendan Chase (☎ 45638, fax 45638, 1 and 3 College Rd)* has eight rooms ranging from £12.50 to £25 per person.

Farther along College Rd, *Applegarth Hotel (☎ 43206, fax 46636)* is a 19th-century mansion house with 18 modern rooms ranging from £20 to £45 per person.

CUMBRIA

Readers have enjoyed staying at **Denehurst** (☎ 44710, 40 Queens Drive) where beds cost from £19 to £25. It's in a quiet spot and a transfer to and from the bus or train station can be arranged.

Family-run **Lingmoor Guest House** (☎ 44947, e lindsfarne@clara.net, 7 High St) has seven rooms, with beds from £16 to £24; it's nonsmoking.

Those staying at **Cambridge House** (☎ 43846, e mbdfear@aol.com, 9 Oak St) rise to vegetarian breakfasts; it charges £16 to £20 per person. Also on Oak St is **Westbeck** (☎ 44763, 11 Oak St), which charges a similar price to Cambridge House.

Lake Rd, which runs down to Bowness, is solid with hotels. Most have rooms costing around £20 a night, but many show prices and vacancies at the front. Cheaper places sometimes lurk down side streets.

Heading down to Bowness, **Fir Trees** (☎/fax 42272) on Lake Rd is a lovely Victorian hotel with eight rooms with bathroom at £22 to £32 per head. Across the road, **Glencree** (☎/fax 45822, e h.butterworth@ btinternet.com) overlooks woodland and has beds from £20 to £30.

B&Bs & Hotels – Top End Two minutes' walk from the lake, with a mixture of motel-style chalets and rooms and a restaurant in a large Victorian house, **Burn How Garden House Hotel** (☎ 46226, fax 47000, e burnhowhotel@btinternet.com) on Back Belsfield Rd has rooms starting at £38 per person.

In the heart of Bowness overlooking the lake, the elegant **Old England** (☎ 0870 400 8130), Church St, is a Georgian country mansion with an open-air heated pool. At the weekend rooms cost £75 per person but enquire about short-break deals.

Holbeck Ghyll Country House Hotel (☎ 32375, fax 34743, e accommodation@ holbeck-ghyll.co.uk, Holbeck Lane) is in a 19th-century hunting lodge overlooking the lake. Prices are from £65 to £120 per person.

Places to Eat

At first sight neither Bowness nor Windermere offer much in the way of gourmet cuisine, although the restaurants at the Burn How and Holbeck Ghyll hotels serve top-class, expensive cuisine.

Few of the teashops are particularly inspiring, but you could drop into the **Old England** (see Places to Stay – Top End) for a cuppa with a lake view.

Alternatively try the **Hedgerow Teashop** (☎ 45002), above a bookshop on Crag Brow, serving light lunches for around £4.

In Windermere surprisingly nice cakes can be had in the **Miller Howe Café** (☎ 46732, Station Precinct) in the unlikely surrounds of the Lakeland Limited factory shop behind the station.

Millers (☎ 43877, 31 Crescent Rd) offers a standard, cheapish tourist menu. During the day **Gibby's** (☎ 43267, 43 Crescent Rd), a few doors down, serves cheap and filling food such as home-made chicken and mushroom pie (£4.60).

The **Lamplight Bar** (☎ 43547) at the Oakthorpe Hotel on High St is popular with the locals and occasionally has live folk music. The menu ranges from Mexican chilli (£7.50) to whole grilled plaice (£9.75).

In the evening, Bowness is more promising. A good place to start looking is pedestrianised Ash St, which has Italian and Indian restaurants. Here you'll also find the **Porthole** (☎ 42793, 3 Ash St), a wine buff's paradise with relatively pricey Italian and modern British dishes from £6 to £16. Book ahead. Immediately across the street is another branch of **Gibby's** (☎ 43060, Royal Square), open in the evening and serving a set three-course menu for £7.15.

Just up the road on Crag Brow, the **Nissi Restaurant** (☎ 45055) is a Greek place selling lobster soup (£3.25), kebabs (£7.50) and vegetarian dishes (£6.95).

Jackson's Bistro (☎ 46264, West End) is pleasant and reasonable with a three-course dinner for £11.95.

Getting There & Away

Windermere is 265 miles (427km) from London, 55 miles (89km) from Blackpool, 45 miles (73km) from Carlisle and 5 miles (8km) from Ambleside.

Bus There are two National Express buses a day from Manchester via Preston (£14, three hours) and on to Keswick (£17, 4½ hours). There's also a service from London (£24, 7½ hours) and on to Keswick (£24, 8½ hours).

Stagecoach (☎ 01946-63222) has several useful services, including the No 555 Lakeslink, which links Lancaster with Keswick, via Kendal, Windermere (train station, Troutbeck Bridge and Brockhole), Ambleside, Grasmere and Carlisle. The No 618 runs between Ambleside and Barrow-in-Furness, passing through Windermere, Newby Bridge, Haverthwaite and Ulverston. No 505/506, links Kendal to Coniston via the Steamboat Museum, Brockhole and Ambleside. The No 599 service runs between Grasmere, Ambleside, Brockhole, Bowness, Windermere train station and Kendal. A Round Robin Ticket allows five breaks of journey between Bowness and Grasmere for £5.

Train Windermere is at the end of a spur line from Oxenholme, which connects with the main line from London Euston to Glasgow every hour. There are 10 trains a day from London Euston station (£60.70, £26 if booked 14 days in advance, 3½ hours).

Boat See Other Activities earlier in this section for details on cruises. The Windermere ferry plies across the lake from Bowness to Far Sawrey every 20 minutes from around 7 am to 10 pm. A single ticket costs 40p.

AMBLESIDE
☎ 015394 • pop 2900

The pretty little town of Ambleside is a major centre for climbers and walkers and makes a good base for the southern lakes. But although it has an attractive position half a mile north of the lake, its narrow streets can barely cope with the numbers of walkers in fluorescent outdoor gear who regularly descend on it. Inevitably it's choked with B&Bs, teashops and outdoor equipment shops.

Information
If you need advice on where to go, the TIC (☎ 32582, e ambleside-tic@telinco.co.uk), on the corner of Market Cross and Rydal Rd, is open from 9 am to 5.30 pm daily.

Compston Rd is particularly full of equipment shops, with branches of Rohan (☎ 32946), Hawkshead (☎ 35255) and the YHA Adventure Shop (☎ 34284). The vast Climber's Shop (☎ 32297) also hires out camping gear, boots and waterproofs.

Things to See & Do
The one specific attraction is **The Armitt** (☎ 31212) on Rydal Rd, a lavish, if rather specialist exhibition about Lakeland's less famous literary characters. It opens 10 am to 5 pm daily. Admission costs £2.50/1.80.

Walks head off in every direction. The TIC provides plenty of information on walks in the area and whether you can complete them or not! The Loughrigg circuit, which is 7 miles (11km) long, running from the Rydal Rd car park to Grasmere Lake and back, is a good combination of woods, farmland, steep hills and great views. For a shorter walk of 2 miles (3km) but still taking in the views, head for Stockghyll Force, east of Ambleside. You can either head back to Ambleside through farmland or push on to the village of Troutbeck, returning via Jenkyn's Crag, a rocky outcrop offering superb views of Lake Windermere. The 7-mile (11km) circuit requires good boots.

Places to Stay
A NT camp site, **Low Wray** (☎ 32810), is 3 miles (5km) south of Ambleside on the western shore of Windermere (access from the B5286). It opens Easter to October and charges £3.50 per person per night plus £2 for a car.

One mile south of the village on Lake Windermere, **Ambleside Youth Hostel** (☎ 32304, e ambleside@yha.org.uk), Windermere Rd (A591), has Internet access and is open all year; beds cost £12.95/9. The free YHA shuttle bus meets trains at Windermere station from spring to autumn.

The B&Bs mentioned here are just the tip of the accommodation iceberg. But even in

Ambleside during the popular holiday months of summer the whole place can be booked out, so ring ahead or check with the TIC before you arrive.

Church St and Compston Rd are good places to start the search. On Church St, *3 Cambridge Villas (☎ 32307)* is a classic B&B with rooms from £16 to £20 per person.

The welcoming and accommodating *Melrose Hotel (☎ 32500)*, also on Church St, charges £14 to £25 per person and serves filling breakfasts.

On Compston Rd, The *Compston House Hotel (☎ 32305, e compston@globalnet .co.uk)* has views and comfortable rooms with bathroom from £25 to £29 per person.

Mill Cottage (☎ 34830), Rydal Rd, above a centrally positioned teashop, has beds for £21 to £30.

Places to Eat

For a solid morning start, *Pippins (☎ 31 338, 10 Lake Rd)* is a long-lived cafe doing English breakfasts (£4.95) and burgers (from £3).

There are a couple of great eateries on Church St. *Lynchristies (☎ 33332)* in the Kelsick Old Hall, serves international food with a Cumbrian twist; Winnsboro bean rarebit costs £3.95. The lively and very popular *Lucy's on a Plate (☎ 31191)*, Church St, offers more European-style food and a thought for the day on the blackboard outside; Greek salad costs £3.95.

At *Zeffirelli's Wholefood Pizzeria (☎ 33 845)* on Compston Rd you can tuck into pizza before adjourning to the cinema attached; the £15.50 'double feature' menu covers a three-course dinner and cinema ticket.

Another stylish addition to the eating scene is *The Glass House (☎ 32137)*, attached to the glass-blowing studio in Rydal Rd. It opens for teas, lunches and evening meals serving a mix of Mediterranean and British food.

Popular with walkers is the *Golden Rule (☎ 32257, Smithy Brow)*, a welcoming pub away from the buzz of tourists; it pours a fine pint of ale. For a younger crowd and rowdier atmosphere, head for the *Royal Oak* pub *(☎ 33382, Market Place)* at the top of Church Rd.

Getting There & Around

The bus stop is 150m south of Church St. Bus No 555/599 connects to Windermere, Grasmere and Keswick and No 505 runs to Coniston.

Bike Treks (☎ 31505), Compston Rd, hires out bicycles for £14 per day.

GRASMERE & WORDSWORTH COUNTRY
☎ 015394

Grasmere is a picture-postcard village and a lovely place to stay out of season. In summer, its good looks together with its associations with the poet Wordsworth ensure that it's overrun with tourists. Most of the buildings date from the 19th and 20th centuries, but the village is actually ancient. St Oswald's Church, with its complicated raftered roof, dates from the 13th century. Wordsworth is buried in the churchyard with his wife Mary and sister Dorothy.

Information

The TIC (☎ 35245), Red Bank Rd, has a helpful visual display on walks around Grasmere, and opens 9.30 am to 5.30 pm daily.

Dove Cottage & Wordsworth Museum

Dove Cottage, just off the A591 on the outskirts of Grasmere, is the main Wordsworth shrine where he wrote his greatest poems. Once a public house, it has flagstone floors, panelled walls and fine lake views but is far too small for the crush of people who want to see it – do yourself a favour and visit out of season. The half-hour guided tours are particularly worthwhile. Bus No 555 runs past here.

The Wordsworth Museum houses manuscripts and paintings along with personal possessions. The complex (☎ 35544) opens 9.30 am to 5.30 pm daily, except early January to early February. Keep your ticket if you plan to visit Rydal Mount, as you'll receive a 15% discount.

Rydal Mount

Following his marriage, Wordsworth lived at Rydal Mount from 1813 to 1850. Even then, as many as 100 fans a day would visit in the hope of catching a glimpse of the only poet laureate who never wrote a line of official verse. Rydal Mount is a 16th-century farmhouse with 18th-century additions set in 1¾ hectares of gardens (they were originally landscaped by Wordsworth). It contains some of his furniture as well as manuscripts and possessions. The house (☎ 33002) is still owned by one of Wordsworth's descendants.

It opens 9.30 am to 5 pm daily, March to October; and 10 am to 4 pm in winter except Tuesday and most of January. Admission costs £3.75/3, although you can visit the grounds only for £1.75/1.25.

In spring it's worth diverting through the churchyard below the Mount to see **Dora's Field**, planted with daffodils in memory of Wordsworth's daughter.

Places to Stay

Hostels Grasmere has two youth hostels, one close to the village, the other a mile away in an old farmhouse.

Butterlip How Youth Hostel (☎ 35316, fax 35798, e grasmere@yha.org.uk) is just north of the village; follow the road to Easedale for 140 metres, then turn right. It opens daily, mid-February to October; Friday and Saturday, November to mid-December; and Thursday to Monday, the rest of the year. Overnight charges are £11.90/8.20.

Thorney How Youth Hostel (same contact details as the Butterlip How), farther out on Easedale Rd, opens April to October and is a little cheaper at £9.80/6.75.

B&Bs & Hotels About a 10-minute walk west of the town centre on Easedale Rd is the friendly *Glenthorne Quaker Guest House* (☎/fax 35389, e gthorn@global net.co.uk), part of which used to be a coffin makers. It's well set up for walkers on the Cumbria Way, with good drying facilities and offering dinner. B&B is £19 per person, and full board £39 per person.

The Wordsworth Trust owns *How Foot Lodge* (☎ 35366), in a quiet spot literally yards from Dove Cottage, where rooms start at £23 per person.

The Travellers Rest Inn (☎ 35604, e travellers@lakelandsheart.demon.co.uk) has it all – comfortable rooms, excellent pub food, and a warm, welcoming bar – but it also has the A591 running past its door. Rooms start at £29 per person, but are more at weekends. It's just north of Grasmere and bus No 555 stops outside.

Places to Eat

At Dove Cottage the *Dove Cottage Tea Rooms & Restaurant* (☎ 35268) is an impressive modern vegetarian enterprise offering pasties and pies from £3.30, as well as a range of cakes and sandwiches. The restaurant opens evenings Tuesday to Saturday and the tearooms open 10 am to 5 pm daily.

In the village itself, *Baldry's Tea Room* (☎ 35301, Red Lion Square) is a wholefood place serving hot lunches for around £5.50 and mouth-watering home-made bread-and-butter pudding for £2.95.

As you leave the churchyard follow your nose to find *Sarah Nelson's Gingerbread Shop* (☎ 35428, Church Stile), which has been trading on the same spot for more than 130 years.

Getting There & Away

Stagecoach (☎ 01946-63222) bus No 555 runs from Ambleside to Grasmere, stopping at Rydal church and outside Dove Cottage. A 2½-mile (4km) walk links Grasmere and the two Wordsworth shrines.

LANGDALE

☎ 015394

The turning at Skelwith Bridge on the A593, 2½ miles (4km) west of Ambleside, leads up into Great Langdale, a valley dwarfed by a range of five fells commonly known as the Langdale Pikes. The road passes the pretty little hamlet of Elterwater (see following), a mile north-west of the turn-off, before continuing on to the base of the pikes.

Another mile on from Skelwith Bridge is a second turning, this time leading to Little Langdale. At the head of the valley you can either turn right onto the connecting road to Great Langdale or continue on over Wrynose and Hardknott Passes to the coast. But be warned, the road is not for the faint-hearted.

Elterwater

Elterwater is superbly located at the end of a small lake, tucked in under the Langdales. It's on the Cumbria Way with good walks around and about. There's a wonderful view from Loughrigg Terrace at the southern end of Grasmere, looking north over the lake and the village. Follow the road to High Close Youth Hostel and continue to the east, taking a footpath to the right off the road. It's approximately 3 miles (5km) return to Elterwater. The Maple Tree Corner Store, on the central green, can handle most of your consumer needs.

Elterwater Youth Hostel (☎ 37245, fax 37120, e *elterwater@yha.org.uk*) is a nice slate hostel in town, over the bridge, which opens daily April to September; Friday and Saturday only, January; and weekdays, the rest of the year. Beds cost £9/6.20.

On the hills to the east, a mile from the village, *Langdale High Close Youth Hostel* (☎ 37313, e *Keswick@yha.org.uk*) is a rambling Victorian mansion in extensive gardens with great views. Generally it opens daily, April to October but closes at irregular times; phone ahead to be sure it's open. Beds cost £9.80/6.75.

Barnhowe (☎ 37346), 90m from the village centre, is a cosy B&B with two doubles and a single from £17 per person.

The friendly *Britannia Inn* (☎ 37210, fax 37311, e *info@britinn.co.uk*) has a pleasant patio overlooking the 'main' street and good-value food and guest ales; the home-grown local speciality, Herdwick Lamb, costs around £7. The inn also has comfortable rooms from £27 to £35 per person.

Elterwater is 3½ miles (5.5km) from Ambleside (take bus No 516) and 5 miles (8km) from Coniston.

Elterwater to Old Dungeon Ghyll

The valley continues for another 3½ miles (5.5km) past Elterwater to the base of the Langdale Pikes. It's an extremely popular area for walks to the fells and up to Harrison Stickle (724m) and Pike o' Stickle (697m) and has a range of good accommodation facilities.

Two and a half miles (4km) on from Elterwater is *Sticklebarn Tavern* (☎ 37356, *Great Langdale*), offering bunk barn accommodation in a traditional stone barn and stable for £10 per person. Meals are available at the tavern and you're expected to provide your own sleeping bag.

For comforts sake, stay at *The New Dungeon Ghyll Hotel* (☎ 37213, fax 37666, e *enquiries@dungeon-ghyll.com*), next to the Sticklebarn. Its more modern than the Old Dungeon (see later in the section) but lacks the charm; B&B in the height of summer costs £39 per person and £59 with dinner.

About a mile back farther up the valley is the *Great Langdale Campsite* (☎ 37668). It occupies a quiet spot and provides the usual amenities and a weekly weather report at the shop. Tent sites cost £3.25/1.50, slightly more in July and August.

Opposite the camp site at the foot of the Langdale Pikes is *The Old Dungeon Ghyll Hotel* (☎ 37272). Its superb location, welcoming hosts, warm bar and hearty menu have made the hotel a favourite of many a famous climber and not-so-famous tourist. Comfortable rooms start at £32, and local fare, such as Herdwick Lamb for £6.95, is available on the premises.

Bus No 516 runs from Ambleside to the Old Dungeon Ghyll Hotel at least five times daily, Easter to October.

Little Langdale

Separated by Lingmoor Fell (459m) from Great Langdale, Little Langdale is a quiet village on the road running up to Wrynose Pass. The surrounding area doesn't offer the grand choice of walks the Langdale Pikes do but there is plenty to exercise the legs in one of the more peaceful areas of the Lakes. At the head of the valley is the **Three Shire Stone** marking the traditional meeting point of Cumberland, Westmoreland and Lancashire. Be prepared for a hair-raising drive up over Wrynose Pass – the grade gets as steep as 1 in 4 on the single-lane road – and it's not uncommon to find some poor sod on the hard shoulder with a burnt-out clutch. The road carries on to Eskdale and the Cumbrian coast (see Ravenglass to Whitehaven later in the chapter) over Hardknott Pass, possibly more alarming than Wrynose Pass.

Unfortunately accommodation is scarce, but quality is definitely better than quantity in these parts. The *Three Shires Inn* (☎ *37215,* e *enquiry@threeshiresinn.co .uk*) in the village of Little Langdale is one of the better hotels in the Lake District. This inviting 19th-century inn is well set up for walkers and cyclists and offers a warm welcome to all. Comfortable rooms start at £33 per person, cheaper the longer you stay. The attractive bar, with its ceiling of wooden beams, serves great real ale and food with the likes of local lamb for £10.25.

Bus No 506 from Ambleside or Coniston drops you at the junction of the A593 and the road heading to Little Langdale. It's still a 2 mile (3km) hike up to the village from the bus stop, so your own transport is a huge advantage. The Three Shires Inn can arrange for a taxi to collect you if required.

CONISTON
☎ 015394 • pop 1800

John Ruskin, the famous Victorian art critic, thought Coniston Water 'more beautiful than anything I had ever seen to my remembrance in gladness and infinitude of light'. And you'd be hard pressed not to agree. Coniston itself has the manicured look of a classic Lake District tourist town, but magnificent craggy hills glower over it and there are refreshingly few tourist shops. Needless to say, there are a number of superb walks in the neighbouring countryside (see Walking later in the section).

Information
The TIC (☎ 41533, e conistontic@lake -district.gov.uk), on the road to Hawkshead, is well equipped and displays a useful topographical map of the surrounding area. It opens 9.30 am to 5.30 pm daily, Easter to October, and 10 am to 3.30 pm at the weekend in winter.

Summitreks (☎ 41212, e info@summi treks.co.uk), 14 Yewdale Rd, offers a range of adventure activities and hires out walking and climbing gear.

Ruskin Museum
The recently renovated and expanded Ruskin Museum (☎ 41164) not only delves into the life and times of John Ruskin but also covers the story of Coniston itself. Interactive screens provide a good introduction to Ruskin and his work and there are a few of his watercolours and drawings on display.

The rest of the museum is a mixed bag of local industry, and there's also a shrine to the late great speed demon Donald Campbell, the only person in the world to hold both water and land speed records in the same year. Tragically, he died in 1967 in his *Bluebird K7* boat on Coniston Water while breaking the 300mph barrier. The museum opens 10 am to 5.30 pm daily, April to early November, and admission costs £3/1.75.

Brantwood
Brantwood, the house created by John Ruskin, has a beautiful site overlooking Coniston Water with The Old Man of Coniston behind.

It opens 11 am to 5.30 pm daily, mid-March to mid-November; 11 am to 4 pm Wednesday to Sunday in winter. The best way to get there is by boat (see Boat trips following). Admission costs £4/1 and there's a good teashop.

Boat Trips
Now owned by the NT, the unique and beautiful steam yacht *Gondola*, with its luxurious saloons, was launched on Coniston Water in 1859. The *Illustrated London News* described it as 'a perfect combination of the Venetian gondola and the English steam yacht'.

The *Gondola* (☎/fax 63856) sails daily, April to October and services Brantwood and Park-a-Mor on the eastern side of Coniston. A round trip costs £4.70/2.80, although you can also take shorter hops.

The motorised *Coniston Launch* (☎/fax 36216) is another option to cruise the lake and visit Brantwood. The North Lake sailing calls at four jetties, including Brantwood, for £3.60 return (£7.10/2.80 including entry to Brantwood House). The South Lake cruise sails as far as Lake Bank at the southern end of the lake, and also calls at Brantwood. Tickets are £5.80 return. It's possible to break your journey and catch the later ferry, or walk to the next jetty.

For a bit more fun hire a boat at the Coniston Boating Centre on Coniston jetty (☎ 41366). Motor boats cost £10 per hour, and the more exhausting canoes cost £18 per day.

Walking

One of the more popular walks in the Lakes is the assent of The Old Man of Coniston (801m). The walk starts at St Andrew's Church in Coniston and winds its way to the summit and back again. On a clear day the breathtaking view from the top takes in the Cumbrian coast and across to Lake Windermere. The walk is 7½ miles (12km) and will take approximately 4½ hours.

Another popular walk heading north from St Andrew's Church takes in the Yewdale Valley and Tarn Hows. It's a relaxing walk through picturesque woods and farmland before a steep climb next to a waterfall, to Tarn Hows, an artificial body of water surrounded by woods with views of the immediate mountains. Allow 2½ to three hours for the round trip. The TIC has useful leaflets on both walks. Tarn Hows is one of the few upland tarns accessible by road. A free bus service runs on Sundays, from Easter to the end of October between Coniston and Hawkshead giving you a full day to explore the area.

Places to Stay

Camping Beside the lake, *Coniston Hall Camp Site* (☎ 41223) has plenty of tent sites (£3.50 per person, £8.50 for a car and two persons). To get there, turn left opposite

the Catholic church and keep left down to the lake.

Hostels A few minutes' walk from the town centre, just off Ambleside Rd (the A593) is **Holly How Youth Hostel** (☎ 41323, fax 41803, e conistonhh@yha .org.uk, Far End). It opens daily over Easter and from late June to late September, and weekends at other times; beds cost £9.80/ 6.75.

Coppermines Youth Hostel (☎/fax 41261) has a spectacular mountain setting but is only just over a mile from Coniston; take the minor road between the Black Bull and the Co-op. Don't try to drive there, the road is quite bad. It opens daily, late May to August and Tuesday to Saturday, April to late May, September and October. Beds cost £9/6.20.

B&Bs & Hotels Both Tilberthwaite Ave and Yewdale Rd are good places to look for accommodation.

The **Beech Tree Guest House** (☎ 41717), formerly the Old Vicarage, Yewdale Rd, offers vegetarian cooking and eight rooms, some with bathroom, from £18 to £25 per person.

Oaklands (☎ 41245, fax 41234) on Yewdale Rd is a small, nonsmoking place with rates from £18 to £20. Close by, also on Yewdale Rd, is **Orchard Cottage** (☎ 41 373), with rooms with bathroom from £19 to £22.

Just east of town on Tilberthwaite Ave, **Lakeland House** (☎ 41303) is a friendly B&B with nine rooms with beds from £16 to £40 per person. On the same street, **Shepherds Villa** (☎ 41337) has rooms with bathroom from £18 to £24 per person.

The highly rated **Coniston Lodge Hotel** (☎/fax 41201), Station Rd, is superb so try and book ahead. Its six rooms all have a bathroom and range in price from £29.50 to £45.50 per person.

Places to Eat

The **Sun Hotel** (☎ 41248, fax 41219) is worth the effort of finding it; walk out of town towards Ulverston, cross the bridge and turn right up the hill. Specials include dishes such as vegetable peanut roast and home-made pies. It also has rooms with views from £30 per person.

The **Blue Cafe** (☎ *41649*) on Lake Rd, down by the ferry landings on Coniston Lake, meets the boats coming in with filling jacket potatoes for £3.

For a local pint, head to the **Black Bull** (☎ *41335*) on Yewdale Rd, which brews its own Bluebird beer.

Getting There & Around

Stagecoach's (☎ 01946-63222) No 505/506 Coniston Rambler service runs from Bowness Pier to Brockhole, Ambleside and Coniston. In summer there are half a dozen services daily and three on Sunday; and in winter only two services on Saturday and none on Sunday.

Coniston Mountain Bikes, in Summitreks, rents bicycles for £13 per day.

HAWKSHEAD

☎ 015394

With lovely cobblestoned streets, quaint houses and scenic countryside, it's easy to see why Hawkshead is popular with tourists. But at least the local council has had the sense to provide parking on the outskirts of the village, thus making Hawkshead a relatively traffic and carbon monoxide-free place.

Wool was the big money-spinner for Hawkshead in medieval times, and the town still carries on the tradition in the Hawkshead clothing company, a popular outdoor clothing maker. Wool was so important to the British economy at one time that the government passed a law stating that people had to be buried wrapped in wool blankets, just to increase the use of the material!

The TIC (☎ 36525, fax 36349), next to the main car park to the south of the town centre, has a good supply of information about the surrounding area. It opens from 9.30 am to 5.30 pm daily, April to October; to 6 pm July and August; and 9.30 am to 5.30 pm weekends, November to March.

Hawkshead's two attractions are at either end of the town.

The **Hawkshead Grammar School**, across Main Street from the TIC, was founded in 1558 by the Archbishop of York. It makes a big fuss of its most famous pupil, William Wordsworth, who attended the school from 1779 to 1798 and vandalised a desk, which is on display, by carving his name on it. The school opens 10 am to 5 pm daily, Easter to October and admission costs £2.50/2.

Right on Red Lion Square is the **Beatrix Potter Gallery** (☎ 36355; NT), in what was once the office of her husband, William Heelis. The gallery houses original illustrations from her children's books, which are changed each year. It opens 10.30 am to 4.30 pm Sunday to Thursday, April to October. Admission costs £3/1.50 and is timed, so don't expect to linger too long over the displays.

Places to Stay and Eat

The TIC can arrange accommodation if required. There are a couple of camping options near to Hawkshead, the closest being **Croft Camping & Caravanning** (☎ *36374, fax 36544*) on North Lonsdale Rd, just east of the town centre. It opens mid-March to mid-November and charges between £9.50 and £10 for two persons and a car per night.

The **Hawkshead Youth Hostel** (☎ *36293, fax 36720,* e *hawkshead@yha.org.uk*) is about a mile south on the road to Newby Bridge, bus No 505/506 passes by. Beds cost £10.85/7.40.

The lovely **Anne Tyson's Cottage** (☎ *36405*) is just off the main square on Wordsworth St and has comfy rooms from £21.

Around the corner on Main St is the welcoming well equipped **Ivy House Hotel** (☎ *36204,* e *ivyhousehotel@btinternet.com*) offering B&B from £30.

South of the centre is the **Old School House** (☎ *36403*), set back from Main St making it a quiet stopover. Rooms are pleasant and start at £19 per person.

All four pubs offer accommodation if a pub stay is preferred.

Hawkshead has a good selection of eating options in pubs and tearooms. Family-run **Grandy Nook** (☎ *36404, Vicarage*

Lane) has a quiet spot around the corner from Anne Tyson's Cottage and serves sandwiches that cost from £2.25.

The 15th-century *Minstrels Gallery* (☎ *36423, The Square)* is a beautiful place for a bite to eat with home-made soup for £2.20.

For pub food try the *Queens Head* (☎ *36271)* on Main St; it has filling meals and a good vegetarian selection. The *Kings Arms* (☎ *36372, The Square)* is pleasant and accommodating and serves trout fillet for £7.95. Both pubs are central and offer bar meals and restaurant seating.

Getting There & Away

Hawkshead is frequently linked with Bowness, Ambleside and Coniston by bus No 505/506, which continues on to Hill Top (see later in the section).

AROUND HAWKSHEAD
Grizedale Forest

Taking up most of the space between Coniston Water and Esthwaite Water 3 miles (5km) south of Hawkshead is Grizedale Forest, a cross between an outdoor pursuits area and an open-air contemporary art exhibition. Artists have been coming here since 1977 to create sculptures in the forest, and some can be surprising when stumbled upon (you don't exactly expect to find an elephant in the middle of England). Over 90 sculptures are scattered throughout the forest, mainly made out of natural materials, but some of the most recent are of manmade products, perhaps reflecting what the artists now find in the forest.

The Grizedale Visitors Centre (☎ 01229-860010, fax 860273), in the heart of the forest, provides information on trails and activities and opens 10 am to 5 pm May to September; 11 am to 4 pm January to March; and 10 am to 4 pm the rest of the year. There's also a cafe on site in which to refuel.

Even without the novel sculptures, Grizedale Forest is good for a bit of walking and cycling. Bicycles can be hired from Grizedale Mountain Bike Hire (☎ 01229-860369) at the Park Centre, for £14 for a full day or £9 a half-day, to tackle the 40 miles (65km) of marked cycle trails. Hourly hire for £3 is also available.

On the southern side of the visitor centre is the *Grizedale Campsite* (☎ *01229-860257)* with tent sites for £3.20 per person.

B&B accommodation is available at *Grizedale Lodge* (☎ *015394-36532,* e *enquiries@grizedale-lodge.com)*, half a mile north of the visitor centre on the road to Hawkshead. Comfortable rooms with bathroom start at £30 per person.

Grizedale Forest is not well connected by public transport. Postbus No 522 runs from Ulverston to Hawkshead via Grizedale twice daily and Byways (☎ 01524-850349) bus No 525 meets the Windermere ferry at Ash Landing before returning to Grizedale six times daily in August and weekends, Easter to October.

Hill Top

Beatrix Potter wrote many of her famous children's stories in the 17th-century farmhouse at Near Sawrey (☎ 36269; NT), 2 miles (3km) south of Hawkshead, and it is packed with visitors in summer. The place is a shoebox so you may have to wait to get inside during school holidays. It opens 10.30 am to 5 pm June to August; 11 am to 4.30 pm March to May; and Saturday to Wednesday, September and October. Admission costs £4/2. See Walking & Cycling under Windermere & Bowness earlier in the chapter for details of how to get there; or catch bus No 505 from Ambleside or Coniston.

KESWICK
☎ 017687 • pop 5000

As the northern centre for the Lakes, Keswick has been on the tourist map for over 100 years and is very busy indeed. An important walking base on the Cumbria Way, it lies between the great rounded peak of Skiddaw and Derwent Water, although the town is cut off from the lake shore by a busy main road. Controversy rages over whether Derwent Water, Ullswater or Crummock Water is the most beautiful lake, but Derwent Water is certainly the most accessible for those without private transport. An old market town, Keswick became the centre of a mining industry in the 16th century. These days you can't move for tearooms, B&Bs and outdoor equipment shops.

Information

The busy but helpful TIC (☎ 72645, fax 75043, e keswicktic@lake-district.gov.uk), Moot Hall, Market Place, opens 9.30 am to 4.30 pm daily year-round; for most of summer it opens 9.30 am to 5.30 pm. A free accommodation booking service is provided and the TIC staff are a great source of information on local walks.

The main post office is at 48 Main St and above it you can log onto the Internet at U-Compute (☎ 75127). George Fisher (☎ 72178), 2 Borrowdale Rd, is an enormous outdoor equipment shop with gear for hire.

Boat Trips

Derwent Water has an excellent lake transport service. From mid-March to November (and less frequently the rest of the year) a regular service calls at seven landing stages

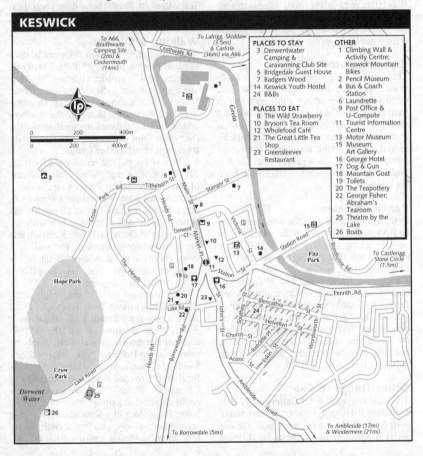

KESWICK

PLACES TO STAY
3 Derwentwater Camping & Caravanning Club Site
5 Bridgedale Guest House
7 Badgers Wood
14 Keswick Youth Hostel
24 B&Bs

PLACES TO EAT
8 The Wild Strawberry
10 Bryson's Tea Room
12 Wholefood Café
21 The Great Little Tea Shop
23 Greensleeves Restaurant

OTHER
1 Climbing Wall & Activity Centre; Keswick Mountain Bikes
2 Pencil Museum
4 Bus & Coach Station
6 Laundrette
9 Post Office & U-Compute
11 Tourist Information Centre
13 Motor Museum
15 Museum; Art Gallery
16 George Hotel
17 Dog & Gun
18 Mountain Goat
19 Toilets
20 The Teapottery
22 George Fisher; Abraham's Tearoom
25 Theatre by the Lake
26 Boats

around the lake: Ashness Gate, Lodore Falls, High Brandlehow, Low Brandlehow, Hawse End, Nichol End and back to Keswick.

Boats of the Keswick Launch Company (☎ 72263) leave every half-hour, one going clockwise, the next going anticlockwise; the round trip takes 50 minutes (£5/2); each stage is about 10 minutes (75p/30p). Discounted tickets can be bought at the TIC. Rowing boats and motor boats are also for hire.

The launches give access to some excellent walks and provide an exhaustion-saving option for those walking the Cumbria Way (the long walk from Elterwater or Dungeon Ghyll). The walk around the western side of the lake isn't particularly interesting, but Borrowdale is beautiful.

Castlerigg Stone Circle
This beautiful egg-shaped stone circle of 48 stones, believed to be between 3000 and 4000 years old, is set on a hilltop between Skiddaw and Helvellyn, and offers brilliant views. It's a Neolithic and Bronze Age sacred meeting place, with none of the tacky tourist infrastructure associated with other circles. The TIC has a good leaflet for 40p outlining a 4-mile (6km) circular walk from the centre of Keswick.

Pencil Museum
In the 16th century graphite was discovered in Borrowdale, leading to the creation of a pencil-making industry that is still going strong, even though the components are now imported from as far afield as Sri Lanka and California. The museum attached to the Derwent Watercolour pencil factory tells the whole story with the help of a video. You get to see the world's largest pencil too. The museum and pencil shop (☎ 73626) are open 9.30 am to 4 pm daily, but this may be extended at peak times. Admission costs £2.50/1.25.

Other Things to See
The local **Museum & Art Gallery** (☎ 73263) in Station Rd displays some original manuscripts from the Lake poets and various archaeological finds of the area. It opens

10 am to 4 pm daily, April to October and admission costs £1/50p.

For a bit of fun head for the **Cars of the Stars Motor Museum** (☎ 73757) on Standish St. Pick your favourite from an array of cars, including Chitty Chitty Bang Bang, the Aston Martin from *Goldfinger* and Lady Penelope's Rolls Royce to name a few. The museum opens 10 am to 5 pm daily, a week before Easter to November; for two weeks in mid-February; and weekends only in December. Admission costs £3.50/2.50.

People interested in seeing how novelty teapots are made should drop in to **The Teapottery** (☎ 73983) behind the central car park. It opens 9 am to 5 pm daily.

Walking & Cycling
Many interesting walks or rides can be constructed around the youth hostel network. Walkers could consider climbing Skiddaw and continuing on to Skiddaw House Youth Hostel and Caldbeck along the Cumbria Way, or catching the launch to the southern end of the lake and walking up Borrowdale. (See Boat Trips earlier in the section for information about the launches).

There is a popular circular walk from the TIC in Keswick that follows the shoreline of Derwent Water to Friars Crag, a rocky outcrop once used by monks as a ferry landing. It then turns back towards Keswick and climbs Castlehead (159m), a hill with superb views of Derwent Water, Keswick and the surrounding mountains. The trail is 3 miles (5km), and takes approximately 1½ hours to complete. The TIC supplies a handy leaflet covering the walk.

Cyclists could make a challenging 30-mile (48km) circuit from Keswick. Head south along the western bank of Derwent Water, along Borrowdale Rd (the B5289) and past Borrowdale hostel. Then climb the brutally steep Honister Pass, passing Black Sail hostel, before running down to beautiful Buttermere (and Buttermere hostel) and Crummock Water. From Buttermere you could finish the loop by returning below Knott Rigg along the Keskadale Beck past Stair. Alternatively, you could continue on to Cockermouth and return via the B5292.

Other Activities

Various outdoor activities and courses, such as canoeing, abseiling and cycling, are organised by the knowledgeable and friendly Climbing Wall & Activity Centre (☎ 72 000), behind the Pencil Museum.

Mountain Goat (☎ 73962) on Central Car Park Rd offers half- and full-day escorted tours of Cumbria and the Lake District in minivans.

Places to Stay

Camping There are tent pitches at *Braithwaite Camping Site (☎ 78343)*, just off the A66 on the B5292, from £3.10 per person. The *Derwentwater Camping & Caravanning Club Site (☎ 72392)*, close to the lakeshore a few minutes walk from town, has van sites and tent pitches from £3 per person.

Hostels A short walk down Station St from the TIC (turn left on the walkway by the river) is the *Keswick Youth Hostel (☎ 72484, fax 74129, e Keswick@yha .org.uk)* on Station Rd. It opens daily, mid-February to December; beds cost £10.85/ 7.40, B&B £14.05/10.60.

Five miles (8km) from Keswick at the head of Thirlmere on the A591 to Ambleside is *Thirlmere Youth Hostel (☎/fax 73224, Old School, Stanah Cross)*, with basic accommodation facilities for £6.65/ 4.65. Bus No 555 to Ambleside passes by the hostel.

Skiddaw House Youth Hostel (Bassenthwaite, Keswick CA12 4QZ; book by post, or call Carrock Fell Hostel ☎ 016974-78325), on the Cumbria Way, is in a remote location behind Skiddaw, 6 miles (10km) from Keswick, and can only be reached on foot. A bed for the night costs £7.35/5.15.

B&Bs & Hotels One of the best value B&Bs in the Lake District, the *Bridgedale Guest House (☎ 73914, 101 Main St)* has a range of rooms, some with private showers, for just £16 per person. Without breakfast this drops to £12, which is only slightly more than the youth hostel. You can leave

your bags here for £2 if you're just passing through by bus.

Badgers Wood (☎ 72621, 30 Stanger St), close to the centre, is friendly and welcoming, with comfortable rooms starting at £17.50 without bathroom.

To the east of the town centre along Southey, Blencathra, Helvellyn and Eskin Sts, virtually every house is a B&B. Prices are competitive and standards high. Unless otherwise stated, rooms have bathroom and the price is per person per night.

In Eskin St, the nonsmoking *Allerdale House (☎ 73891, fax 74068, 1 Eskin St)* has excellent rooms from £24 per person. *Charnwood (☎ 74111, 6 Eskin St)*, a listed Victorian house, has comfortable beds from £19 to £26.

Another nonsmoking B&B is *Clarence House (☎ 73186, fax 72317, e clarenceho@ aol.com, 14 Eskin St)* charging from £21 for a room. *Braemar (☎ 73743, e braemar@ kencomp.net, 21 Eskin St)*, a few doors along, is slightly cheaper with rooms staring at £17.

Moving onto Southey St, *Bluestones (☎/fax 74237, e bluestones-keswick@cw com.net, 7 Southey St)* has adequate rooms from £15 to £19. *Glendene (☎ 73548, 8 Southey St)* has private parking and can also serve dinner. Singles/doubles start at £15/ 24.

Slightly better in quality is the *Avondale Guest House (☎ 72735, fax 75431, 20 Southey St)*, but the price is also a little higher: B&B costs from £19.75. The *Edwardene Hotel (☎ 73586, fax 73824, 26 Southey St)* is more than comfortable and accommodating with rooms for £25/38.

In Blencathra St, *The Derwentdale (☎/fax 74187, 8 Blencathra St)* has a good range of rooms with beds from £17.50 to £20.50. The small *Blencathra (☎ 71435, 48 Blencathra St)* has two family rooms for £16.50 per person but only opens from March to September.

Places to Eat

For teas and light lunches *Bryson's Tea Room (☎ 72257, 42 Main St)* is an excellent bakery, exporting its cakes as far afield as the USA. It also serves meals during the day.

Abraham's Tearoom (☎ 72178, 2 Borrowdale Rd) tucked into the rafters of the enormous George Fisher outdoor equipment shop, offers great views and light meals such as Cumberland rarebit for £3.95.

There's also the inviting *Wholefood Café (☎ 74492)* in Hendersons Yard, off Market Place. *The Wild Strawberry (☎ 74399, 54 Main St)* makes for a good stop for a quick bite to eat.

In the evening, pubs are a good bet. The *Dog & Gun (☎ 73463, 2 Lake Rd)* is good value with home-made lamb curry for £5.75. The *George Hotel (☎ 72076, 3 St John's St)* is another fine establishment serving up pub food.

Greensleeves Restaurant (☎ 72932, 26 St John's St) is a large 'tourist' restaurant, but it has a good-value menu with pasta from around £5.30 and dishes such as supreme of salmon for £8.50.

Serving a good range of evening meals, and a separate vegetarian menu, is *The Great Little Tea Shop (☎ 73545, 26 Lake Road)*. Mains start at £6.95, including vegetable Thai curry.

Getting There & Away

Keswick is 285 miles (459km) from London, 31 miles (50km) from Carlisle and 15 miles (24km) from Penrith.

Bus See Windermere & Bowness earlier in the chapter for information on National Express and Stagecoach buses and connections to Keswick.

In summer, Keswick is also accessible from Penrith train station with Wright Brothers' (☎ 01434-381200) No 888 service (one or two services Monday to Saturday, one on Sunday). This service continues across country from Penrith to Langwathby, on the LSC line, to Hexham and Corbridge, on Hadrian's Wall, and finally to Newcastle upon Tyne.

Stagecoach's (☎ 01946-63222) Lakeslink (No 555) runs from Carlisle to Lancaster via Keswick, Ambleside, Windermere and Kendal. There are frequent services between Keswick and Kendal. Three a day go on to Carlisle from Monday to Saturday.

Getting Around

Behind the pencil museum, two places hire out bicycles. Keswick Mountain Bikes (☎ 75202, fax 74407), 1 Daleston Court, has bikes for hire from £13/10 per day/half-day. The Keswick Climbing Wall & Activity Centre (☎ 72000, fax 75872), Southey Hill Trading Estate Greta Side, rents bikes for £14/8.50.

BORROWDALE & BUTTERMERE
☎ 017687

The B5289 road running south of Keswick takes you into some of the most beautiful valleys of the Lakes. Borrowdale, stretching for 6 miles (10km) from the northern end of Derwent Water to Honister Pass, is lush and green with great accommodation and walking options. The Buttermere valley, running north-west from Honister Pass along the shores of Buttermere and Crummock Water towards Cockermouth, is more barren but just as stunning.

Borrowdale & Around

Borrowdale's access to Derwent Water and the high peaks of Scafell, Scafell Pike and Great Gable make it a popular destination for walkers. In the height of summer it can be as busy as some of the Lakes' main towns.

About 100m past the turn-off to Watendlath, a small hamlet set by a small tarn, is *Derwentwater Youth Hostel (☎ 77246, fax 77396, **e** derwentwater@yha.org.uk, Barrow House)*, 2 miles (3km) from Keswick. It opens daily, mid-February to early November; Friday and Saturday, much of the rest of the year. A night costs £10.85/7.40. In its grounds are **Lodore Falls**, descending over 30m, but they are only worth a visit after a heavy downpour.

Continuing on the B5289, *The Borrowdale Hotel (☎ 77224, fax 77338, **e** the borrowdalehotel@yahoo.com)* is 3 miles (5km) from Keswick and is welcoming. Rooms are spacious and equipped with everything you need and singles/doubles start at £38/48. The restaurant on the premises is well renowned in the area.

Grange, a small village near the southern end of Derwent Water, is a popular base for walks. *Hollows Farm (☎ 77298)* is a short amble from the village and has adequate accommodation from £17 a night.

The next small hamlet south is **Roswaithe**, where a 1½ mile (2.5km) public bridleway winds its way to Watendlath. Accommodation possibilities are above average here, starting with *Scafell Hotel (☎ 77208)*. Comfy rooms cost £40 per person for B&B, or £61 with dinner included at the hotel's Riverside Bar. *Yew Craggs (☎ 77260,* [e] *yewcraggs@aol.com)* has cheaper accommodation with rooms from £17.

The *Borrowdale Youth Hostel (☎ 77257, fax 77393,* [e] *borrowdale@yha.org.uk, Longthwaite, Borrowdale)* is a mile on from Roswaithe at the head of beautiful Borrowdale and charges £10.85/7.40.

Seatoller, the last stop before Honister Pass, is another village offering accommodation and the Seatoller Barn Information Centre (☎ 77294) opens 10 am to 5 pm daily, Easter to November. *Seatoller House (☎ 77218)* is accommodating and charges £30.50/57. A four-course evening meal is available for an extra £11. Next door is the *Yew Tree Restaurant (☎ 77634)*, where you can sample the local food and get clothed in outdoor gear.

Getting There & Away Stagecoach (☎ 01946-63222) bus No 79 provides a regular service for the valley from Keswick bus station to Seatoller. From Easter to October bus No 77/77A makes the round trip from Keswick to Buttermere via Borrowdale and the Honister Pass.

On Sundays in summer the National Trust operates a minibus every few hours from Keswick to Watendlath. The minibus stops at Ashness Bridge and Surprise View, both with impressive views of Derwent Water.

Buttermere & Around

From Seatoller, it's possible to enter the Buttermere valley over the steep Honister Pass, which can reach gradients of 1 in 4 in places. Apart from the steep gradient, the only other problem you'll encounter if you're driving is wandering sheep, who have the freedom of the valley.

At the summit of the pass is *Honister Hause Youth Hostel (☎/fax 77267, Seatoller)*, 4 miles (6km) from Buttermere. A bed for the night costs £9/6.20. A track to Great Gable starts here. The views from the top of the pass down into Buttermere valley are quite stunning.

Black Sail Youth Hostel (☎ 0411-108450, fax 159472, Black Sail Hut, Ennerdale, Cleator) is in a quiet wooded valley 2½ miles (4km) west of Honister Pass and only accessible by foot. The price for a night is £8.10/5.65.

Farther away from Buttermere is *Ennerdale Youth Hostel (☎ 01946-861237, Cat Crag, Ennerdale, Cleator)* in a remote location at the head of Ennerdale, 5 miles (8km) from Ennerdale Bridge and 2½ miles (4km) from Bowness Knott car park. From Black Sail youth hostel it's a flat 4-mile (6km) walk west. Accommodation is £8.10/5.65.

The twisting road finally reaches the bottom of the pass and skirts around the edge of Buttermere to **Buttermere village**, 4 miles (6km) from Honister and 9 miles (14km) from Keswick. *Buttermere Youth Hostel (☎ 70245, fax 70231,* [e] *buttermere@yha .org.uk, Buttermere)* overlooks Buttermere and is about the only sheep-free place around! A night's accommodation costs £10.85/7.40.

The *Dalegarth Guest House (☎ 70233, Buttermere)* provides traditional B&B accommodation from £22/34 for singles/doubles and camping facilities at £4 to pitch a tent.

For a more luxurious stay, *Bridge Hotel (☎ 70252, fax 70215, Buttermere)* is a good bet. Spacious and comfortable rooms are priced from £39/56.

From Buttermere, the B5289 cuts north along the eastern shore of picturesque Crummock Water. At its southern end is the superbly located *Woodhouse Guest House (☎ 70208)*, with views of the lake. The peaceful surroundings make for a relaxing stay and rooms are £43/70.

From Woodhouse, it's another 6 miles (10km) north to the junction of the B5292 road, which heads north-west to Cockermouth or east to Keswick.

Getting There & Away Bus No 77/77A services the Buttermere valley four times daily, Easter to October from Keswick, traversing the steep Honister Pass.

ULLSWATER & AROUND
☎ 017684

Ullswater, the most north-eastern of the lakes, is closer to Penrith than the Lake District towns. Many visitors never make it to the Lake District's second-largest lake, but even in the height of summer it can still be bumper to bumper on the A592 road running along its northern edge. The main hamlets near the lake are Pooley Bridge to the north and Glenridding and Patterdale to the south.

There are plenty of accommodation possibilities on the northern edge of Ullswater – so much so that it seems that every few yards another B&B or hotel sign pops up.

Boat Trips
A good way to see the lake is from the **Ullswater 'Steamers'** (☎ 017684-82229), which run from Pooley Bridge to Glenridding. Steamboats started plying the lake in 1859 but the current vessels, *Lady* (in operation since 1887) and *Raven* (in operation since 1889) have now been converted to conventional power. A return trip from either end of the lake takes two hours and costs £4.40/2.20 for a single or £6.60/3.30 for a return. From mid-April to September the steamers sail every two hours and from mid-March to mid-April and October there is a limited service.

Pooley Bridge
The quiet town of Pooley Bridge, 5 miles (8km) south-west of Penrith, occupies a pretty spot at the northern end of Ullswater looking back over the western mountains.

In Finkle St, the TIC (☎/fax 86530, e pooleybridgetic@lake-district.gov.uk) opens 10 am to 5 pm daily, April to November. In an effort to cut down on congestion and pollution in the Lakes the TIC has arranged a good display on day trips in Cumbria using the buses rather than taking your own car.

For control of your own destiny on the lake, boats can be hired at the Lakeland Boat Hire (☎ 07773-671399), Lakeside. Motor boats cost £7 per person for an hour and rowing boats £5.

Park Foot Camping (☎ 86309, 86041, e *holidays@parkfootullswater.co.uk*) on Howtown Rd has a nice spot by Ullswater a mile south of Pooley Bridge on the road to Howtown. Tent sites for two people and a car cost £9.

Elm House (☎ 86334) on High St, two minutes' walk from the lake, is comfortable and pleasant, and has rooms for £21 per person.

Opposite the TIC is *The Pooley Bridge Inn* (☎ 86215, fax 86776), which would look just as well placed in the Austrian Lake District. Standard double rooms cost £65, but are cheaper the longer you stay. There's a courtyard restaurant on site for evening meals.

The *Heughscar Tea Rooms* has outdoor seating by the river, near the lake. Sandwiches cost around £2 and fresh apple pie is £1.95.

Glenridding
Seven miles (11km) from Pooley Bridge at the southern end of the lake is Glenridding. The small village is overshadowed by Helvellyn (949m), one of the highest peaks in the Lakes, and makes a great base for walks to its summit. The Ullswater steamer stops here, so it's also a good base for exploring the lake.

The Ullswater Information Centre (☎/fax 82414, e glenridding@lakedistrict .gov.uk), main car park, is set back off the main road and opens 9 am to 6 pm daily, April to October and Friday to Sunday, November to March.

Helvellyn Youth Hostel (☎ 82269, fax

82009, ⓔ *helvellyn@yha.org.uk, Green-side)* is 1½ miles (2.5km) from Glenridding and is a good early-morning starting point for an attempt on Helvellyn. It's possible to drive up, but care should be taken. The hostel opens Monday to Saturday, mid-April to June; daily, July and August; Friday and Saturday, November; and Tuesday to Saturday, the rest of the year. A night's stay costs £9.80/6.75.

Back in Glenridding, the *Fairlight* (☎ *82397, fax 82168)*, next to the information centre car park, has adequate rooms with bathroom for £22 and without for £18, and serves food such as haddock and peas, and fish and chips for around £5.

Moss Crag Guest House (☎/fax 82500) has a quiet spot off the main road close to the information centre. Singles/doubles cost from £19.50/34.50. Afternoon teas and light lunches are also available.

The plush accommodation in town is the *Glenridding Hotel (☎ 82228, fax 82500)*, complete with indoor swimming pool, reputable restaurant and Internet cafe (open 10 am to 5 pm). Rooms start at £49/67.

Patterdale

Less than a mile south of Glenridding and 12 miles (19km) from Penrith is Patterdale, a small accommodation hub.

At the southern end of the village is the *Patterdale Youth Hostel (☎ 82394, fax 82034, ⓔ patterdale@yha.org.uk, Patterdale)*, a 20-minute walk from Glenridding. It opens daily, April to October; Friday and Saturday, November to mid-February (daily over Christmas); and Thursday to Monday, mid-February to March. Beds for the night cost £10.85/7.40 for adults/juniors.

Two lovely B&Bs are almost opposite each other on the main road, just before you reach the youth hostel. The slate-stone *Ullswater View (☎ 82175, fax 82121, ⓔ ext@btinternet.com)* is close to the lake and has comfortable rooms from £18 per person. *Barco House (☎ 82474)* is a little more expensive at £23 per person, but if you're planning on being around for a while, the rates get cheaper the longer you stay.

Getting There & Around

Stagecoach (☎ 01946-63222) bus No 108 runs from Penrith to Patterdale, calling in at Pooley Bridge and Glenridding. In the height of summer buses basically run every hour Monday to Saturday but there are only three on Sunday. Bus No 517 runs from Bowness Pier to Glenridding three times daily, late July to early September and weekends, mid-April to late July.

East Cumbria

It's easy to forget there is anything outside the Lake District in Cumbria, but the Eden Valley and western fringe of the northern Pennines that make up East Cumbria should not be overlooked. The Eden Valley runs from Kirkby Stephen in the south to the bustling town of Penrith in the north; its largest urban centre with good transport links to Carlisle and Lancaster. North-east of Penrith is the quaint town of Alston in the heart of the northern Pennines, well located for walks on the moors and trips to Hadrian's Wall. Kirkby Lonsdale and Kirkby Stephen are just across the boundary of the Yorkshire Dales National Park and make good bases for your explorations.

PENRITH
☎ 01768

The look and feel of Penrith pays closer resemblance to Carlisle than to the pretty towns scattered around the Lake District. It's well placed for trips into the eastern lakes to the west, the picturesque Eden Valley to the south and the northern Pennines to the east. The town comes alive on Tuesdays, market day.

Information

The TIC (☎ 867466, fax 891754, ⓔ pen.tic@eden.gov.uk), Robinson's School, Middlegate, has plenty of information about the Eden Valley and the Lakes. It opens 9.30 am to 6 pm Monday to Saturday and 1 to 5.45 pm Sunday, mid-July to August; and 9.30 am to 5 pm Monday to Saturday, the rest of the year.

Internet access is available in the Public Library (☎ 242100), St Andrew's Church-yard, which opens Monday to Saturday.

Things to See

Penrith was once the capital of Cumbria but there isn't much left to show for it, except the empty ruins of **Penrith Castle** and the red sandstone **St Andrew's Church**. The castle was built in the late 14th century by William Strickland (who climbed the career ladder to Bishop of Carlisle and later Arch-bishop of Canterbury) because of repeated Scottish raids, one of which razed the town in 1345. It was then passed on to the future Richard III who expanded the castle but it fell into disrepair in the 16th century. You're free to wander around what's left of the castle 7.30 am to 9 pm daily, Easter to October and 7.30 am to 4.30 pm October to Easter.

The small **Penrith Museum** (☎ 212228), which shares the same building as the TIC, delves into the history of the town. It opens 10 am to 5 pm Monday to Saturday year-round, and 1 to 5 pm on Sunday, April to October.

Places to Stay & Eat

There's plenty of accommodation available, particularly on Portland Place to the north of the town centre and Victoria Rd to the south. The TIC can book accommodation for you.

The *Glendale Guest House* (☎ 862579, fax 895080, e glendale@lineone.net, 4 Portland Place) is a pleasant family-run B&B with rooms starting at £15.

Behind St Andrew's Church is the listed *Friarage* (☎/fax 863635, Friargate) with comfortable rooms also starting at £15.

More upmarket and central is the *George Hotel* (☎ 862696, fax 868223) on Devonshire St, a 300-year-old coaching inn. Rooms start at £33 per person.

Penrith has a small but varied selection of places to eat. The *George Hotel* serves international food in relaxed surroundings, with a two-course lunch menu for as little as £7.50.

For something a bit more lively, head to *"Costas" Tapas Bar & Restaurant* (☎ 895550, 9 Queen St) on a Thursday night for typical Spanish food and a flamenco show thrown in. Who could ask for more! Mains are around £12 and it's open daily except Monday.

Try *Dolce Vita* (☎ 891998, Bishop Yards) for filling Italian food with pizza and pasta around the £5 mark.

Getting There & Away

Bus Stagecoach (☎ 01946-63222) bus No 104 frequently runs between Penrith and Carlisle. Bus No X4/X5 connects Penrith to the Lakes and the Cumbrian coast hourly Monday to Saturday and three times on Sunday, calling at Keswick and Cockermouth before terminating at Workington.

Train Penrith has frequent connections to Carlisle (£5.40, 19 minutes) and Lancaster (£13.20, 40 minutes).

AROUND PENRITH
Rheged Discovery Centre

The largest underground building in England, which houses the Rheged Discovery Centre (☎ 01768-686000), Redhills, about two miles (3km) west of Penrith just before the turn-off to Ullswater on the A66, is hard to spot. But that's the plan. The centre, built on a former quarry and rubbish site, has been designed to blend in with its environment and it certainly succeeds.

Inside you'll find a complex devoted to Cumbria, including restaurants using locally produced ingredients, shops selling pieces by local artists and manufacturers, and even a local potter in action. Supposedly the highlight of the centre is a film capturing the mysteries of Cumbria shown on a huge screen. The scenery shots are fantastic but the actual film is a letdown and looks more like a bad made-for-TV movie than anything else. It follows the dramatised story of a young American tracing his roots to Cumbria and delves into a few of the mysteries of the region, in particular about the Saxon King Rheged.

The short film shown before you enter the main cinema is much better, giving you a brief glimpse into the way of life of Cumbrians.

The centre opens 10 am to 6 pm daily year-round and the films are shown from 10 am to 4 pm on the hour with the last screening at 4.45 pm. Admission to the film complex costs £4.95/3.50.

The frequent No X4/X5 bus, which runs between Penrith and Workington, stops at the centre.

Long Meg and Her Daughters

The myths and legends of the Eden valley are full of giants, witches and ghosts, and Meg and her Daughters are no exception. The prehistoric stone circle, 6 miles (10km) north-east of Penrith off the A686 to Alston, is said to be a coven of witches turned to stone by a wizard and is supposedly uncountable. You'll need your own transport to visit the stones.

ALSTON & AROUND
☎ 01434

Alston is one of the forgotten gems of Cumbria. The cobblestone streets and alleys of the small village in the heart of the northern Pennines are so reminiscent of a bygone era that it was used as a backdrop to the latest TV adaptation of Charles Dickens' *Oliver Twist*. It claims to be the highest market town in England at 290m (950 feet), even though the market no longer takes place.

South of the town square is the TIC (☎ 382244, fax 382255), in the Town Hall, open 10 am to 5.30 pm Monday to Saturday and to 4 pm Sunday, April to October.

The narrow-gauge **South Tynedale Railway** (☎ 381696, ☎ 382828 for a talking timetable) runs from Alston to Kirkhaugh following the River Tyne north through the pretty Tyne valley. The round trip takes 60 minutes, but it's a good idea to spend some time at Kirkhaugh and catch the next train back. A return trip costs £3.50/2.

It's possible to purchase a joint ticket for the railway and Killhope Lead Mining Centre for £5.70/2.35 (see Weardale in the North-Eastern chapter) or Nenthead Mines for £5.45/2.35 (see following).

Nenthead

About 5 miles (8km) east of Alston on the road over the northern Pennines to Durham is Nenthead, a small village on the C2C cycle route and home to the **Nenthead Mines** (☎ 382037).

The big attraction of the mines is a trip down the disused lead mine. Only a small section of the 40 miles (64km) of tunnel are used for the guided tour, which takes about 1¼ hours. The day-to-day grind the miners put up with and the methods they used to extract the lead are well explained. Sturdy shoes and something warm is required; it's a constant 10°C in the mine year-round and you may get slightly dirty. Admission plus the mine trip costs £4.75/2.25, without the mine trip £2.75/1.50. It's possible to purchase a combined ticket for the mine and the South Tynedale Railway (see Alston earlier).

If you are looking for a place to stay there are a couple of bunkhouses in the village. The family-run *Mill Cottage Bunkhouse* (☎ 382771) is on the mine premises and provides clean, centrally heated bunk-bed accommodation for £8. Cooking facilities are available for use, or you can arrange B&B for £12.

Places to Stay & Eat

Accommodation options are good in Alston, with a youth hostel, a few B&Bs and a number of inns scattered around the small town.

The *Alston Youth Hostel* (☎ 381509, fax 382401, The Firs) lies five minutes' walk south of the town centre and is popular with walkers on the Pennine Way and cyclists on the C2C route. It opens daily, mid-April to August and Tuesday to Saturday, September to October. A bed for the night costs £9/6.20.

On a quiet cobblestoned street off the town square with the northern Pennines as a backdrop is the lovely *Chapel House* (☎ 381112, Overburn) with B&B starting at £15.

Cheap pub accommodation is available at the *Angel Inn* (☎ 381363) on Front St, opposite the TIC. The simple but adequate rooms cost £15 per person. The small bar serves filling pub food as well.

Blueberry's Teashop (☎ 381928, *Market Place*) is a great place for tea and scones, light lunch or a hefty snack. It's warm and cosy and the personal touches such as colourful hand-knitted tea cosies make you feel very welcome. Hot and cold sandwiches cost around £2 and large meals between £4 and £5. B&B accommodation is also available at £19.50/34 for singles/doubles.

Getting There & Away

Wright Brothers' (☎ 01434-381200) bus No 888 runs between Newcastle and Keswick via Alston and Penrith once daily. No 680 runs from Nenthead to Carlisle via Alston up to three times a day, Monday to Saturday and No 681 runs from Nenthead to Haltwhistle via Alston twice a day, Monday to Saturday. Arriva (☎ 0191-212 3000) bus No X85 connects Durham and Kendal via Alston and Nenthead once a day on Saturdays, late May to September.

KIRKBY LONSDALE
☎ 01524 • pop 1200

Kirkby Lonsdale is just outside the western boundary of the Yorkshire Dales National Park (see Yorkshire Dales National Park in the Yorkshire chapter) but it's essentially a Dales town, both in appearance and as a useful touring centre if you have your own transport. It has all the usual stores. The town itself is good for an hour's stroll and there are many walks into the countryside.

The TIC (☎/fax 271437), 24 Main St, opens 9.30 am to 5 pm Monday to Saturday, 10.30 am to 4.30 pm Sunday, April to October; and 10.30 am to 4.30 pm Thursday to Sunday, the rest of the year. It can find accommodation in the area, a useful service when towns inside the Dales are fully booked.

Royal Hotel (☎ 271217, *fax 272228, Market Place*) is a rambling old place with good-value rooms at £30/45 for singles/doubles, a good pub and fine food (under £10 a person). There are several decent pubs with accommodation as well.

Kirkby Lonsdale is 17 miles (27km) from

Settle and 15 miles (24km) from Windermere; the nearest railway connection is at Oxenholme (12 miles/19km). Bus connections are not good at all.

KIRKBY STEPHEN
☎ 017683 • pop 1800

Kirkby Stephen is a classic market town with stone Georgian-style houses flanking an attractive High St. There's nothing very remarkable about the place but as it's only 4 miles (6km) from the north-west corner of the Dales, it's a very useful base. The market day is Monday.

The TIC (☎ 71199, fax 72728), Market St, opens 9.30 am to 5.30 pm Monday to Saturday, 10 am to 4 pm Sunday, April to October; 10 am to noon and 2 to 4 pm Monday to Saturday, the rest of the year. It can find accommodation.

Kirkby Stephen is the central point on the **Coast-to-Coast Walk**, which runs from St Bees Head on the west coast to Robin Hood's Bay on the east (see the Activities chapter for details).

Kirkby Stephen Youth Hostel (☎/fax 717930) on Market St is in a converted chapel in the centre of town, south of Market Square. It opens Thursday to Monday, April to June; daily in July and August; and Wednesday to Monday in September and October. Beds cost £10/6.90.

The *Old Court House* (☎/fax 71061, e hilary-claxton@hotmail.com) on High St has excellent accommodation and, yes, it's in the Old Court House. Rooms cost £17.50 per person.

Kirkby Stephen is on the LSC line, the station is a 1½ mile (2.5km) walk from town. Avoid the road and use the marked footpath.

Cumbrian Coast

The Cumbrian Coast Line, the railway line serving the industrial towns and ports of the Cumbrian coast, loops 120 miles (193km) from Carlisle to Lancaster (both cities are on the main line between London Euston and Glasgow). For most of the way it skirts the coast and although parts are beautiful –

especially between Ravenglass and Barrow-in-Furness – it also passes some depressing industrial towns in terminal decline and the eyesore of Sellafield Nuclear Power Plant.

Most of it lies outside the Lake District National Park boundary, but the line provides useful access points for the western lakes. It's also a potential return link for walkers on the Cumbria Way who've left their vehicles at Carlisle, and walkers on the Coast-to-Coast Walk (see the Activities chapter) who've left their vehicles at St Bees.

There are about two trains an hour Monday to Saturday, and one train an hour on Sunday, running between Lancaster and Carlisle. A one-way ticket booked a week ahead is £15. Phone ☎ 0845 748 4950 for full details.

Note that Carnforth station was the one immortalised in the Trevor Howard/Celia Johnson classic film *Brief Encounter*, although these days it looks more like an air-raid shelter.

GRANGE-OVER-SANDS
☎ 015395
Originally, the quickest access to the Lake District was via Grange-over-Sands across the sands of Morecambe Bay at low tide, with Cartmel monks moonlighting as guides for travellers, and later coaches using the trail as a short cut. The Victorian resort town of Grange grew up around the flow of travellers but today there's not much left to keep you here. It's still possible to cross the bay on guided walks but only with the official Queen's Guide to the Sands.

The TIC (☎ 34026, fax 34331), Victoria Hall, Main St, has information on times and starting and finishing points. It opens 10 am to 5 pm daily Easter to October.

Arnside Youth Hostel (☎ 01524-761781, fax 762589, @ arnside@yha.org.uk) on Redhills Rd, Arnside, is a 10-minute train ride from Grange. It costs £9.80/6.75 and opens year-round.

If you need to stay in town, Kents Bank Rd, running south of the town centre, is full of places to stay, such as *Somerset House*

(☎ 32631) offering accommodating singles/doubles for £21/40.

More upmarket is the *Grange Hotel* (☎ 33666, @ fp@grange-hotel.co.uk, Station Square), right across from the train station. It has good views of the town and bay and charges from £49 per person.

Eating is pretty limited in Grange, but you could do worse than join the queue at *Higginsons* (☎ 34367, Keswick House) on Main St, one of England's best butchers, which serves up the finest pies and pasties for miles around. Also on Main St, *The Coffee Pot* (☎ 33269), across from the TIC, has light meals and sandwiches for around £3 and views of Morecambe Bay.

Getting There & Away
Both the train station and bus stop are a short walk north of the TIC. National Express buses to Kendal cost £2 (15 minutes) but its more fun and scenic to take the train to Grange, which is on the Cumbrian Coast Line with frequent connections to Lancaster (£3.35, 20 minutes) and Carlisle (£18.25, three hours).

CARTMEL
☎ 015395
In the medieval town of Cartmel, a mile west of Grange-over-Sands, stands the magnificent 12th-century **Cartmel Priory** (☎ 36261). Fortunately the church was not demolished during the dissolution of the monasteries in the 16th century and survives as one of the finest in the north-west. Everything else in the town pales in comparison. The 45-foot-high east window is quite stunning, as are the intricately carved choir stalls dating from 1440. It opens 9 am to 5.30 pm daily (to 3.30 pm in winter), with guided tours at 11 am and 2 pm on summer Wednesdays.

The town is centred on the small market square where you'll find the **Cartmel Heritage Centre** (☎ 36499), which offers a brief glimpse into the local history and tours of the village. It opens Wednesday to Sunday. Apart from the priory, Cartmel is famous for its racecourse and sticky-toffee pudding. Set by the River Eea, the charming racecourse comes alive on race days (last weekend in May and August) and the town is packed to the gunnels. Mouth-watering sticky-toffee pudding can be found at the Cartmel Village Shop (☎ 36201) on the square.

The *Cartmel Caravan & Camping Park* (☎ 36270) at Wells House Farm occupies a tranquil site only two minutes' walk from the village square. Tent sites for two people and a car are £9.

A quiet B&B just off Market Square is the *Bank Court Cottage* (☎ 36593) with rooms for £18.50 per person.

The *Bluebell House* (☎ 36658, Devonshire Square) is a former coaching inn built around 1660 with views of the priory. It's welcoming and comfortable with rooms starting at £25.

Remember it's almost impossible to find accommodation on race weeks.

The pubs are the best place for a bite to eat. Just off the square past the gatehouse on Cavendish St, the *Cavendish Arms* (☎ 36240, e thecavendish@compuserve .com) is a beautifully refurbished 16th-century inn with great food and its own excellent beer. It's also possible to stay the night; B&B starts at £30.

Getting There & Away

On a regular basis bus No 532 runs from Grange to Cartmel via Cark, which is 2 miles (3km) to the south-west, the nearest train link.

ULVERSTON
☎ 01229

Time seems to have passed Ulverston by – if you're looking for an antidote to the tourist tat of the Lake District towns, this could fit the bill nicely. It's also the starting point for the Cumbria Way.

The helpful TIC (☎ 587120, fax 582626, e ulvtic@telinco.co.uk), in Coronation Hall, County Square, can help with booking accommodation along the Cumbria Way. It opens 9 am to 5 pm Monday to Saturday.

Things to See

Comedian Stan Laurel was born at 3 Argyle St and fans of Laurel and Hardy will want to make the pilgrimage to 4c Upper Brook St. The **Laurel & Hardy Museum** (☎ 582 292) is floor to ceiling with memorabilia. Admission costs £2/1, which lets you sit in on some of the old movies too. It opens from 10 am to 4.30 pm daily except in January.

The small **Heritage Centre** (☎ 580820) in Lower Brook St tells the story of the days before rail and road when getting to Ulverston from Lancaster involved a treacherous journey across the Leven or Kent Sands. It opens 9.30 am to 4.30 pm Monday to Saturday (closed Wednesdays January to April) and admission costs £2/1.

Coming into town by train you'll see a tower on top of Hoad Hill. This commemorates Sir John Barrow (1764–1848), a local explorer.

If you arrive in Ulverston and wonder why a high proportion of the population is wandering around in purple sheets, it's because of **Conishead Priory**. A 19th-century Gothic mansion 2 miles (3km) south of Ulverston on the A5087 coast road, the priory (☎ 584029) has been home to a Manjushri Buddhist Centre since 1977. It has been beautifully restored to its former glory and a Buddhist temple has been added to the grounds, housing some of the largest Buddhist statues in Europe. The priory opens to the public 2 to 5 pm weekends, Easter to October but closes late May to early June and late July to late August. Tours of the mansion and temple (£2/75p) leave at 2.30 and 3.45 pm and weekend meditation retreats are available throughout the year. Bus No 11 makes regular trips from Ulverston to Barrow-in-Furness via the priory.

Places to Stay

The friendly and welcoming *Walkers Hostel* (☎/fax 585588, e povey@walkers hostel.freeserve.co.uk, Oubas Hill) is a 10-minute walk from the centre on the A590 to Kendal. B&B in dorm rooms costs £10 (£16 with evening meals).

Right in the centre of town, *Church Walk House* (☎ 582211, Church Walk) is opposite Stables furniture shop and has rooms with bath from £20 per person. *Rock House*

(☎ 586879, 1 Alexander Rd) has three large family rooms and a single for £20 per head.

The *Trinity House Hotel* (☎ 587639) on Princes St has six rooms for £22.50 to £37.50 per person. Best of all is the Elizabethan *The Whitehouse* (☎ 583340), Market St, a superbly renovated 300-year-old cottage on Market St at a bargain £25/40.

Places to Eat

For a lunchtime snack, the *Hot Mango Cafe* (☎ 584866, 27 King St) makes great cold sandwiches for £4, or hot for £5. The *Rose & Crown* (☎ 583094), also on King St in the town centre is a classic pub with excellent food, enormous servings and reasonable prices.

The *Farmers Arms*, (☎ 861277, Lowick Garden), overlooking Market Place, has a few outdoor tables for sunny days. The recommended *Ugly Duckling Restaurant* (☎ 581573, 1 Buxton Place), in the Buxton Place car park, serves tasty international cuisine evenings only Tuesday to Saturday. Mains are around £12.

Getting There & Away

The Cumbrian Coast Line train from Lancaster (£5.20, 30 minutes) stops at Ulverston station, five minutes' walk south of the centre. Alternatively Stagecoach (☎ 01946-63222) has services linking Ulverston to Barrow-in-Furness and to Ambleside, via Windermere (except Sunday). Monday to Friday you can also get to Cartmel from Ulverston by bus (30 minutes).

BARROW-IN-FURNESS & AROUND
☎ 01229

Ten miles (16km) south-west of Ulverston is Barrow-in-Furness, a town originally developed to supply the railway with iron and steel. It soon became a busy port and a lot of industry is still based in the area. Barrow is by no means a pretty town and has an almost 1960s feel with its wide streets and square buildings.

The TIC (☎ 894784), Forum 28, Duke St, is opposite the town hall and opens 9.30 am to 5 pm weekdays (from 10.30 am on

Thursday) year-round; and 10 am to 4 pm on Saturday, April to October and 10 am to 2 pm on Saturday, November to March.

The big attraction of Barrow is the **Dock Museum** (☎ 89444), half a mile from the city centre and well signposted. Housed in a thoroughly modern building built over an old Victorian graving dock, the museum tells the tale of Barrow's fortunes, of how it grew from a tiny village into a huge shipbuilding port. It opens 10 am to 5 pm Tuesday to Friday and 11 am to 5 pm weekends, Easter to October and 10.30 am to 4 pm Wednesday to Friday and noon to 4 pm weekends, November to Easter. Admission is free.

There is no real need to stay in Barrow but if you do, the TIC has an accommodation booking service.

Barrow is on the Cumbrian Coast Line so there are frequent connections to Carlisle (£11.15, 2½ hours) and Lancaster (£8.10, one hour). There is also a direct rail link from Manchester airport to Barrow. Stagecoach (☎ 01946-63222) bus No 618 runs from Barrow to Ambleside via Ulverston and Windermere at least three times daily.

Furness Abbey

Founded by King Stephen in the early 12th century, Furness Abbey (☎ 823420; EH) is hidden away in the tranquil setting of the 'Vale of Deadly Nightshade', 1½ miles (2.5km) north of Barrow-in-Furness. In its heyday, the red sandstone abbey was among the most powerful in the north and its wealth attracted both welcome and unwelcome visitors, including the Scots who raided it twice. It survived until 1537 at which time Henry VIII dissolved the monasteries for his own benefit.

Today's romantic ruins are some of the most impressive in the north-west and include two 13th-century effigies of knights in armour in the infirmary chapel, which could be among the oldest in England. A small museum on site relates the story of the abbey and contains a superb collection of stone carvings. The abbey opens 10 am to 6 pm daily, April to October and 10 am to 4 pm Wednesday to Sunday, November to March; admission costs £2.60/1.30.

Replenish the weary body with food and drink at the *Abbey Inn* (☎ *825359, Abbey Approach*), right outside the abbey entrance.

You can pick up Stagecoach (☎ 01946-63222) bus No X35 from outside the Barrow town hall, which passes by the abbey on a regular basis.

Piel Castle

Originally built by the monks of Furness Abbey as a defensive outpost against raids on Piel Island, Piel Castle went on to double as a warehouse for trading and smuggling goods to Ireland. The windswept island and castle, 5 miles (8km) south-east of Barrow, are *normally* accessible by ferry from Roa Island (which is attached to the mainland), weather permitting. The ferry (☎ 835809) runs 11 am to 5 pm Monday to Saturday and 11 am to 6 pm Sunday, Easter to September; the cost is £1.50/75p each way. The channel is a windsurfers' haven (one of the best spots in the north-west) as even with the tide out it holds enough water to zip around on and there is usually a prevalent wind.

You can grab a bite to eat at *Bosun's Locker Cafe* next to the ferry landing on the mainland.

Bus No 11 runs to Ulverston from Barrow-in-Furness via Roa Island regularly.

South Lakes Wild Animal Park

Even if you detest zoos, make an effort to visit the South Lakes Animal Park (☎ 466 086), 5 miles (8km) north of Barrow near Dalton-in-Furness. The park has been designed with the animals, rather than the visitors, in mind. Trenches and ditches replace a lot of cages and it's possible to get up close to a number of animals. The showpiece of the park has to be the tiger feeding at 2.30 pm daily. Unique to Europe, enrichment feeding (making the tigers climb and 'hunt' for their food) is quite a sight and shows just how agile and strong these big cats are.

It opens 10 am to 6 pm daily, and till dusk November to Easter; admission costs £6.50/ 3.25. Using your own transport is your best bet but from Easter to September a bus links the zoo to both the Dalton and Askam rail stations.

RAVENGLASS TO WHITEHAVEN

The Cumbrian coast road skirts the western edge of the Lake District National Park and provides access to small port towns and Wast Water and Eskdale, some of the more remote parts of the Lake District.

Ravenglass & Eskdale

Your first point of call on the trip north along the Cumbrian coast is Ravenglass, 27 miles (44km) north of Barrow, used by the Romans because of its sheltered harbour. The remains of a 4th-century **Roman fort**, signposted 'Roman Bath House', are close to the train station. Here you can swap from the normal train line to the private narrow-gauge **Ravenglass to Eskdale** railway, originally built in 1875 to carry iron ore. The beautiful 7-mile (11km) journey runs up into the foothills of the Lake District mountains and costs £6.80/3.40 return. Phone ☎ 01229-717171 or email ⓔ rer@ netcomuk.co.uk for timetable details.

Alighting at Eskdale (the station is called Dalegarth), it's another few hundred metres to **Boot**, a pretty little village in the shadow of Scafell Pike (977m), England's highest mountain. It makes a good base for walks, or escaping the Lake District crowds.

Three miles (5km) farther on from Boot is **Hardknott Roman Fort** with stunning views back down the valley. If you've arrived by car you can follow the road up and over the Hardknott Pass and Wrynose Pass down into Little Langdale (see earlier in the chapter). But be warned; the road seems to have a mind of its own and takes sharp bends without warning. The grade is 1 in 4 in places and single lane so make sure those brakes are in perfect working order.

The *Eskdale Youth Hostel* (☎ 019467-23219, fax 23163, ⓔ *eskdale@yha.org.uk, Boot*), 1½ miles (2.5km) east of Dalegarth station towards Hardknott Pass, is well set up for families and charges £9.80/6.75. It opens Tuesday to Sunday, March to Easter and September to October; Monday to Sat-

World Champions with a Difference

Every year in November the Bridge Inn at Stanton Bridge (see the Wast Water section) holds the World's Biggest Liar Competition. The competition is in honour of Will Ritson, a legendary liar in the 19th century, who opened the first pub in the area at the head of Wast Water. Members of the legal profession and politicians are not allowed to enter for obvious reasons. Contact Copeland Council (☎ 01946-67575) for tickets.

If you're more of a visual person make sure you arrive in Egremont for its annual Crab Fair in mid-September for the World Gurning Competition. Gurning is the art of contorting the face into something incredibly ugly, and supposedly dates back to the 12th century when the lord of the manor would hand out incredibly sour crab apples to his workers. Contact Crab Fair & Sports (☎ 01946-821554) for more details.

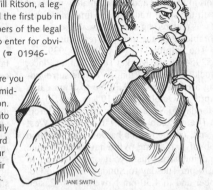

JANE SMITH

urday, Easter to June; and daily, July and August.

The closest accommodation to Dalegarth station is the family-run **Brook House Inn** (*☎ 019467-23288, fax 23160, Boot*). B&B starts at £29 per person but gets cheaper the longer you stay, and good evening meals are available.

Half a mile before the youth hostel is the popular **Woolpack Inn** (*☎ 019467-23230, Boot*) with comfortable rooms from £19.50 and filling food and real ale in the bar.

Ravenglass is on the Cumbrian Coast Line so there are frequent links north and south along the coast. Transport to Eskdale is either the private railway or your own wheels.

Wast Water

To escape the vast crowds in summer head to remote Wast Water, 5 miles (8km) east of Gosforth. Hemmed in by some of the highest peaks in England (Scafell Pike and Great Gable are close at hand), it's definitely in contention for being one of the most beautiful of the Lake District's many lakes.

Accommodation is scarce but good. At the southern end of the lake is the **Wastwater Youth Hostel** (*☎ 019467-26222, fax 26056, e wastwater@yha.org.uk, Wasdale Hall*), open Thursday to Monday, January to Easter, September and October; daily, Easter to August; and Sunday to Thursday, November to January. Beds cost £9.80/6.75.

Four miles (6km) north-east of the youth hostel in Wasdale Head is **Wasdale Head Inn** (*☎ 019467-26229, fax 26333, e wasdale headinn@msn.com*). It's a peaceful retreat in a relaxing atmosphere with rooms from £35 per person and good food.

There's also the NT-run **Wasdale Head Campsite** (*☎ 019467-26220*) nearby, charging £3.50 per person and £2 for a vehicle.

Two and a half miles (4km) south-west of Wast Water is **The Bridge Inn** (*☎ 019467-26221, fax 26026*) in the tiny hamlet of Stanton Bridge. Apart from serving excellent food and providing comfy rooms it hosts the Worlds Biggest Liar Competition in September (see the boxed text 'World Champions with a Difference' above). Rooms cost £45/55.

Public transport is rare indeed. Postbus No 13 leaves Seascale for Wasdale Head via the youth hostel at 8.25 am and 3.20 pm weekdays and mornings only Saturday. You need your own transport to get to Stanton Bridge.

CUMBRIA

Whitehaven & Around

Thirteen miles (21km) south-west of Cockermouth is the harbour town of Whitehaven. Its harbour was at one time the third-largest port in England and was intimately involved with the slave trade. At the time of writing it was undergoing a facelift, which should be completed by the time you read this.

The helpful TIC (☎ 01946-852939, fax 852954) in the Market Hall, Market Place, stocks lots of information on the surrounding area and opens 9.30 am to 5 pm daily, April to October; and 10 am to 4.30 pm Monday to Saturday, November to March.

The Beacon (☎ 01946-592302), West Stand, on the town's harbour, does a good job of explaining Whitehaven's maritime and industrial history. It opens 10 am to 5.30 pm Tuesday to Sunday, Easter to October and to 4.30 pm November to Easter. Admission costs £4/2.65.

Whitehaven's new attraction is **The Rum Story** (☎ 01946-592933), on Lowther St. It's set in an original rum warehouse and delves into the history of rum, such as its boozy connection to the Royal Navy and the Slave Trade. It opens 10 am to 6 pm daily, Easter to September and to 4 pm Wednesday to Sunday, October to Easter. Admission costs £4.50/3.50.

St Bees, 5 miles (8km) south of Whitehaven, is the starting point of the Coast-to-Coast Walk, which ends in Robin Hood's Bay.

Five miles (8km) farther south is the **Sellafield Nuclear Power Plant** and its visitor centre (☎ 019467-27027). The centre tries to improve the image of nuclear power with interactive displays. It opens 10 am to 6 pm daily, April to October and to 4 pm November to March. Admission is free.

If you need to stay in Whitehaven try the inviting Georgian *Corkickle Guest House* (*☎ 01946-692073, 1 Corkickle*), 300 metres north-east of Corkickle train station. Rooms start at £22.50 per person.

A pleasant place to eat in Whitehaven is *Efes Restaurant* (*☎ 01946-695141*) at the Globe Hotel in Duke St, which serves Turkish food for around £7 for mains.

Whitehaven is on the Cumbrian Coast Line.

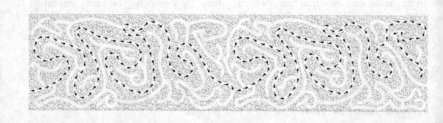

North-Eastern England

North-Eastern England is quite different from the rest of the country, although it's misleading to think of it as a single entity. Collectively known as Northumbria, the major sections are Durham in the south and Northumberland in the north, with the latter area bordering Scotland. The urban metropolis of Newcastle-upon-Tyne is squeezed between the two.

As a rule, the countryside here is harder and more rugged than in the south, and it's as if history reflects this, because every inch has been fought over. The central conflict was the long struggle between north and south, with the battle lines shifting over the centuries.

In the years before the Roman invasion, the area from the River Humber to the Firth of Forth was ruled by a confederation of Celtic tribes known as the Brigantes. The Romans were the first to attempt to delineate a border: Hadrian's Wall, stretching 73 miles (117km) from Newcastle to Bowness-on-Solway near Carlisle, was the northern frontier of the Empire for almost 300 years. It was abandoned around AD 410, but enough remains to bring the past dramatically alive.

The struggle for the dominance of the area didn't end until the 18th century. Saxon rule, Viking raids and the uncontrollable Reivers kept the local populace in constant fear; the plethora of *pele* towers (fortified buildings) and castles testify to the war-like times. The Norman kings attempted to bring peace to the land and left a legacy of spectacular fortresses and the marvellous Durham Cathedral.

County Durham is rich in the history of the prince bishops who, due to the fierce nature of the area, ruled the area almost as a separate kingdom. Picturesque valleys lie to the west, while unsightly industrial towns spread east to the coast.

Newcastle is the natural hub of the northeast. Situated near the mouth of the River Tyne, it was only natural that it became rich and prosperous on the back of coal export-

Highlights

- Being awestruck by Durham Cathedral
- Getting off the beaten track in the dales of Durham County
- Partying with the Geordies in Newcastle
- Exploring the coastal castles – especially Alnwick and Bamburgh
- Walking the robust city walls of Berwick-upon-Tweed
- Hiking the windswept Hadrian's Wall
- Visiting Victorian Cragside, first in the world to be lit by hydroelectric power
- Getting away from it all at Kielder Water and the Northumberland National Park

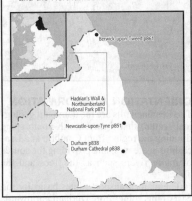

Berwick-upon-Tweed p861

Hadrian's Wall & Northumberland National Park p871

Newcastle-upon-Tyne p851

Durham p838
Durham Cathedral p838

ing and shipbuilding. Economic depression hit hard after the decline of industry in the area, but today Newcastle is very much alive and kicking and well worth exploring.

Visitors seeking seclusion should opt for the Northumberland National Park, which lies north of Hadrian's Wall, incorporating the open, sparsely populated Cheviot Hills. The walks cross some of the loneliest parts of England and can be challenging. The most interesting part of Hadrian's Wall is also included (along the southern boundary) – see the Hadrian's Wall section later.

NORTH-EASTERN ENGLAND

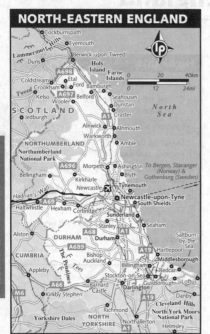

ORIENTATION & INFORMATION

The Pennine Hills are the dominant geological feature that form a north–south spine dividing the region from Cumbria and Lancashire in the west and providing the source of major rivers such as the Tees and the Tyne.

The major transport routes basically run east of this spine: from Durham northwards to Newcastle and Edinburgh. Newcastle is an important ferry port for Scandinavia.

There is a YHA hostel at Newcastle and, more importantly, others scattered throughout the more remote countryside in the west. Make sure you book in summer.

WALKING

There are many great hikes in this region. The most famous is the Pennine Way, which stretches 250 miles (404km) from Edale in the Peak District to end at Kirk Yetholm near Kelso in Scotland. Unfortunately, its popularity means that long sections turn

into unpleasant bogs, so it is worth considering quieter alternatives. For example, it's possible to walk sections of Hadrian's Wall, or to hike in the remote Cheviot Hills of the Northumberland National Park.

CYCLING

Cycling is a great way to see this part of England; the only disadvantages are the weather, the hills and the fact that, at the weekend, even some of the minor B-roads can be very crowded. On the whole, however, all you need is a good map and some imagination, and you'll have a great time.

There's an 88-mile (142km) Sea to Sea (C2C) cycle route from Whitehaven on the west coast to Sunderland or Newcastle on the east coast cutting through the Lake District and Northumberland National Park. Also worth considering is the Coastal Route, which takes in much of the Northumberland coast. A good map and accommodation guide costing £5.99 is available from Sustrans (☎ 0117-926 8893), 35 King St, Bristol BS1 4DZ.

If you are planning to cycle along Hadrian's Wall, tourist information centres sell the *Hadrian's Wall Country Cycle Map*.

GETTING THERE & AROUND
Air

Teesside International Airport (☎ 01325-332811) is an option if you are flying from Continental Europe or Dublin to the north (see Getting There & Away under Darlington later in the chapter).

Newcastle International Airport (☎ 0191-286 0966) has direct services to Aberdeen, London, Cardiff, Dublin, Belfast, Oslo, Amsterdam, Paris and Brussels.

Bus

Bus transport around the region can be difficult, particularly around the remoter parts of Northumbria in the west. For all your transport needs in the north-east call ☎ 0870 608 2608 for information on connections, timetables and prices.

Several one-day Explorer tickets are available; always ask if one might be appropriate. The Explorer North East is particularly interesting. It covers a vast area north of York to the Scottish Borders and west to Hawes (in the Yorkshire Dales) and Carlisle. The major operator in the scheme is Arriva (☎ 0191-212 3000), which can help plan an itinerary. Unlimited travel for one day costs £5.25/£4.25 for adults/juniors, and there are also numerous admission discounts for holders of Explorer tickets (available on buses).

Train

The main-line routes run north to Edinburgh via Durham, Newcastle-upon-Tyne and Berwick-upon-Tweed; and west to Carlisle roughly following Hadrian's Wall. Travelling to/from the south, it may be necessary to make connections at Leeds. Phone ☎ 0845 748 4950 for all train enquiries.

There are numerous Rover tickets, for single-day travel and longer periods, so ask if one might be appropriate. For example, the North Country Flexi Rover allows unlimited travel throughout the north (but not including Northumberland) for any four days out of eight for £55.

Boat

Norway's Fjord Line (☎ 0191-296 1313) operates two ferries a week from Newcastle to Stavanger, Haugesund and Bergen in Norway. DFDS Seaways (☎ 0870 533 3000) operates ferries from Newcastle to Kristiansand (Norway), Gothenburg (Sweden) and Amsterdam (the Netherlands). See the introductory Getting There & Away chapter.

County Durham

The Durham area includes some of the most beautiful parts of the northern Pennines, one of the greatest Christian buildings in the world, and an ancient mining heritage that has left a legacy of uninspiring half-towns.

Although its history isn't as turbulent as that of neighbouring Northumberland (which actually formed Durham's defensive buffer), Durham has known its fair share of bloodshed. In the Middle Ages it was still wild enough to warrant the prince bishops

of Durham having virtually limitless power. They combined lay and religious responsibilities as the rulers of a palatinate (a kingdom within a kingdom). The prince bishop (aka the count palatine) had the right to have his own army, nobility, coinage and courts. His great cathedral and castle were once described by Sir Walter Scott as 'Half church of God, half castle 'gainst the Scot'.

The prince bishops did bring peace to Durham, allowing the county to develop long before Northumberland, a fact reflected in the higher population density and the neat hedges and stone-walled fields. The western half of the county is dominated by the heather-covered hills of the northern Pennines, while the eastern half was, from the 18th century, the centre for a major coal-mining industry that has now largely disappeared.

GETTING AROUND

The Durham County Council transport enquiry line (☎ 0191-383 4138) opens from 8.30 am to 5 pm weekdays (to 4.30 pm Friday). The Explorer North East ticket (see the earlier North-Eastern England Getting There & Around section) is valid on many services in the county.

DURHAM
☎ 0191 • pop 83,000

Durham is the most dramatic cathedral city in England, with a massive Norman cathedral dominating a wooded promontory high above a bend in the River Wear. Other cathedrals are more refined but none have more impact – it's an extraordinary structure built to survive, with utter confidence in the enduring qualities of faith and stone. It is impressive from a distance and simply astounding up close.

The story of Durham begins with the monks of Holy Island (Lindisfarne) fleeing from Viking raiders with their most precious treasures, St Cuthbert's body and the illuminated Lindisfarne Gospels. The Lindisfarne monastery had thrived for 240 years, but in 875 the monks began a search for a safer site. Finally, in 995, they found a perfect, easily defended position above

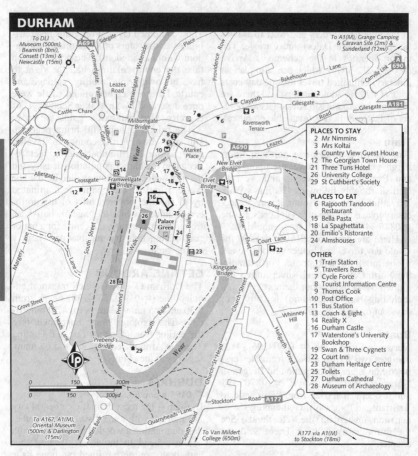

DURHAM

To DLI
Museum (500m),
Beamish (8mi),
Consett (13mi) &
Newcastle (15mi)

To A1(M), Grange Camping
& Caravan Site (2mi) &
Sunderland (12mi)

NORTH-EASTERN ENGLAND

PLACES TO STAY
2 Mr Nimmins
3 Mrs Koltai
4 Country View Guest House
12 The Georgian Town House
21 Three Tuns Hotel
26 University College
29 St Cuthbert's Society

PLACES TO EAT
6 Rajpooth Tandoori
   Restaurant
15 Bella Pasta
18 La Spaghettata
20 Emilio's Ristorante
24 Almshouses

OTHER
1 Train Station
5 Travellers Rest
7 Cycle Force
8 Tourist Information Centre
9 Thomas Cook
10 Post Office
11 Bus Station
13 Coach & Eight
14 Reality X
16 Durham Castle
17 Waterstone's University
   Bookshop
19 Swan & Three Cygnets
22 Court Inn
23 Durham Heritage Centre
25 Toilets
27 Durham Cathedral
28 Museum of Archaeology

To A167, A1(M),
Oriental Museum
(500m) & Darlington
(15mi)

To Van Mildert
College (650m)

A177 via A1(M)
to Stockton (18mi)

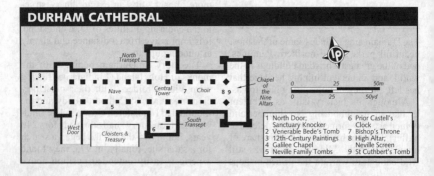

DURHAM CATHEDRAL

North
Transept

Nave

Central
Tower

Choir

Chapel
of
the
Nine
Altars

West
Door

Cloisters &
Treasury

South
Transept

1 North Door;
   Sanctuary Knocker
2 Venerable Bede's Tomb
3 12th-Century Paintings
4 Galilee Chapel
5 Neville Family Tombs

6 Prior Castell's
   Clock
7 Bishop's Throne
8 High Altar;
   Neville Screen
9 St Cuthbert's Tomb

the River Wear. The current cathedral is the third church to be built on the site; its foundation stone was laid on 12 August 1093.

The prince bishops reached the peak of their power in the 14th century, and although they survived with great pomp and ceremony into the 19th century, their real influence ebbed away. In 1836 the last privileges were returned to the Crown and the last count palatine gave the castle to the newly founded Durham University (1832), the third-oldest university in England. Durham is still the centre for local government in the county.

Orientation

Durham is surprisingly small. The centre of town is limited by the space available on the teardrop-shaped peninsula, and although the city, especially the university, has now overflowed to some extent, everything is within easy walking distance.

Market Place (and the TIC), the castle and cathedral are all on the peninsula surrounded by the River Wear. The train station is north-west of the cathedral on the other side of the river. The bus station is also on the western side. Using the cathedral as your landmark, you can't really go wrong.

Information

The TIC (☎ 384 3720, e tic@durhamtic .demon.co.uk), Market Place, a short walk north of the castle and cathedral, opens from 10 am to 5 pm Monday to Saturday. For foreign currency exchange there's a Thomas Cook office (☎ 382 6600) at 24–25 Market Place, near the TIC. The Silver St post office opens 9 am to 5.30 pm Monday to Saturday and Internet access is available at Reality X (☎ 384 5700), 2nd Floor, 1 Framwellgate Bridge, west of Market Place. It's on the right on your way to the bus station. Waterstone's University Bookshop (☎ 384 2095), 55 Saddler St, has a good selection of titles.

Durham Cathedral

Built as the shrine for St Cuthbert, Durham Cathedral dates almost entirely from the 12th century and is the most complete and

spectacular example of Norman architecture. The Romanesque style as developed by the Normans had a monumental simplicity, characterised by great scale, round arches, enormous columns and zigzag chevron ornament – all shown at their best in Durham. The cathedral's vast interior is like a cave that is only partly artificial; its exterior is like time-worn cliffs.

A number of walks give good views of the exterior; perhaps the two most famous are from Framwellgate Bridge and Prebend's Bridge, although the approach across Palace Green is also impressive.

History The choir, transepts and nave of the cathedral were built between 1093 and 1133 and still survive in uncompromised Romanesque form. There have been four major additions, all successful: the beautiful Galilee Chapel, with its slim pillars of Purbeck marble at the western end, built between 1170 and 1175; the western towers, built from 1217 to 1226; the Chapel of Nine Altars, with the pointed arches and carved capitals of the Early English style, built between 1242 and 1280; and the central tower, which was rebuilt between 1465 and 1490.

Information The cathedral (☎ 386 4266) opens 9.30 am to 8 pm Monday to Saturday and 12.30 to 8 pm Sunday, late May to September; and 9.30 am to 6 pm Monday to Saturday and 12.30 to 5 pm Sunday, October to early May; a donation is requested. It is only open for private prayer from 7.30 to 9.30 am Monday to Saturday and 7.45 am to 12.30 pm on Sunday, year round. The guided tours (£3/free for under-16s) start at 10.30 am and 2 pm Monday to Saturday from late May to September, and also at 11.30 am in August. Evensong is at 5.15 pm Tuesday to Saturday (Evening Prayer on Monday) and at 3.30 pm Sunday.

Inside the Cathedral The main entry is through the **north door**. Note the great bronze knocker. This was a sanctuary knocker and was used by people escaping the rough justice of the Middle Ages and seeking the protection of the church. They would bang the knocker to attract the attention of two watchmen who slept in a room above the door; they were then allowed to choose between trial and voluntary exile.

The nave is dominated by massive carved piers; every second one is round and carved in geometric designs. The round piers have an equal height and circumference of 6.6m (22 feet). Durham was the first European cathedral to be roofed with stone-ribbed vaulting and has the earliest pointed transverse arches in England.

The **Galilee Chapel** is one of the most beautiful parts of the cathedral. The **paintings** on the northern side are among the few surviving examples of 12th-century wall painting and probably feature St Cuthbert and St Oswald. The chapel also contains the **tomb of the Venerable Bede**, the author of the *Ecclesiastical History of the English People*. Bede was an 8th-century Northumbrian monk, a great historian and polymath whose work held a pre-eminent role in Latin literature for four centuries and is still the prime source of information on the development of early Christian society and institutions in Britain. Among other things, dating years from the birth of Jesus was a practice that he introduced.

The lords of Raby, the great Neville family (see the boxed text 'The Rising of the North' later in the chapter), were the first lay people to be buried in the cathedral (in the late 14th century), but their **tombs** and a later chantry were badly damaged by Scottish prisoners taking revenge on their traditional enemy.

The only wooden item in the cathedral to survive the anger of the Scots was **Prior Castell's Clock**, a much-restored clock dating from the late 15th century – it possibly survived because of the Scots thistle towards the top of the case. The clock was recently given a clean (as was the whole interior of the cathedral), possibly its first in 490 years.

The **Bishop's throne**, built over the tomb of Bishop Thomas Hatfield, dates from the mid-14th century, and Hatfield's effigy is the only one to have survived. The **high altar** is separated from **St Cuthbert's tomb** by the beautiful stone **Neville Screen**, made around 1375.

St Cuthbert was originally a shepherd but he became an inspirational leader of the northern church and he was also widely loved by the northern peasants. At times he would meditate for days without food and it is said that eider ducks would nestle in his clothing. He died in 687 and, when the Viking raids made Lindisfarne untenable, the monks carried his miraculously preserved body with them. His reputation attracted many pilgrims to Durham.

The Chapel of the Nine Altars actually did once have nine altars – in order to facilitate giving Mass to all the monks!

Cloisters The monastic buildings are centred on the cloisters. They were heavily rebuilt in 1828. The west door to the cloisters is particularly famous for its 12th-century ironwork. On the western side is a monastic dormitory, now a library, and an undercroft that now houses the Treasury and restaurant.

Treasury Museum The recently refurbished Treasury Museum is definitely worth visiting as it includes relics of St Cuthbert from the 7th century and an interesting collection of illuminated manuscripts and cathedral 'paraphernalia'. It opens 10 am to 4.30 pm from Monday to Saturday; and 2 to 4.30 pm on Sunday. Admission costs £2/1.50 for adults/juniors.

Durham Castle

Building of the castle was begun in 1072 and it served as the home for Durham's prince bishops. It has been substantially rebuilt over the years, but still preserves the fundamental layout of a Norman motte-and-bailey castle. It is now a residential college for the university, and it is possible to stay here during summer holidays (see Places to Stay later). There are guided tours 10 am to 12.30 pm and 2 to 4 pm Monday to Saturday, late March to early October; 10 am to noon and 2 to 4 pm Sunday, and 2 to 4 pm on Monday, Wednesday, Saturday and Sunday, the rest of the year. Admission costs £3/2 and tours are included in the price.

Museum of Archaeology

In an old fulling mill on the banks of the Wear between Framwellgate and Prebend's Bridges, the Museum of Archaeology (☎ 374 3623) has a collection illustrating the history of the city. It opens 11 am to 4 pm daily, April to October; and 11.30 am to 3.30 pm Friday to Monday, November to March. Admission costs £1/50p.

Other Museums

Three noteworthy museums are dotted around Durham.

Near the cathedral in what was the St Mary le Bow Church you'll find the **Durham Heritage Centre** (☎ 386 8719), St Mary le Bow, North Bailey, with displays on the history of the County of Durham. It opens 11 am to 4.30 pm daily, July and August; 2 to 4.30 pm daily, June and September; and 2 to 4.30 pm weekends, April and May. Admission costs £1/30p.

Half a mile north-west of Durham city is the **Durham Light Infantry (DLI) Museum** (☎ 384 2214), Aykley Heads, covering the history of Durham's County Regiment and its part in various wars. It opens 10 am to 4 pm daily and costs £2.50/1.25.

The **Oriental Museum** (☎ 374 7911), Elvet Hill, a few miles south of the city centre in the university, is totally devoted to Oriental art and has a good collection spanning the whole Asian continent. It opens 10 am to 5 pm Monday to Friday and noon to 5 pm weekends. Admission costs £1.50/75p. Take bus No 5 or 6 heading to Bishop Auckland.

Walking

There are superb views back to the cathedral and castle from the outer bank of the river; walk around the bend between Elvet and Framwellgate Bridges, or hire a boat at Elvet Bridge.

Blue Badge 1½-hour guided walks of the city (£3/free) leave from outside the TIC at 2 pm on Wednesday and at the weekend, June to September.

Cruises

The Prince Bishop River Cruiser (☎ 386 9525), Elvet Bridge, offers one-hour cruises along the river. Trips run at 2 and 3 pm June to September and cost £3.50/1.50.

Rowing boats can be hired for £2.50 per person per hour from Browns Boathouse (☎ 386 3779) below Elvet Bridge.

Places to Stay

The TIC makes local bookings free of charge, which is useful since convenient B&Bs aren't numerous; the situation is particularly grim during graduation week in late June.

Camping Two miles (3km) north-east of the city centre is **Grange Camping & Caravan Site** (☎ 384 4778, Meadow Lane). A site for car, two people and a tent costs from £8.40.

B&Bs & Hotels Several colleges rent their rooms during the university holidays (particularly July to September). The Web site www.dur.ac.uk/conference_tourism/colleges .htm provides information and links to all the university accommodation available. The most exciting possibility is **University College** (☎ 374 3863, e Durham.castle@ durham.ac.uk), in the old Durham Castle grounds, which has B&B singles/doubles for £20.50 per person. The cheapest university accommodation is at **St Cuthbert's Society** (☎ 374 3364, 12 South Bailey), south of the cathedral, which charges £19 per person.

There are a few unpretentious B&Bs starting around £16 per person on Claypath, which turns into Gilesgate.

Leave Market Place from its northern end and cross over the A690 onto Claypath, where you'll find **Country View Guest House** (☎ 386 1436, 40 Claypath) with rooms for £20/34. **Mrs Koltai** (☎ 386 2026, 10 Gilesgate) has three reasonable rooms at £16 per person. A few doors along is **Mr Nimmins** (☎ 384 6485, e bb@nimmins.co .uk, 14 Gilesgate) with adequate accommodation from £17.

More upmarket and comfortable is **The Georgian Town House** (☎/fax 386 8070, 10 Crossgate) where breakfast is served in the garden, weather permitting. Rooms start at

£45.50/60, some with cathedral views. In the town centre, the *Three Tuns Hotel* (☎ *386 4326, New Elvet)* is a historic hotel with luxury facilities from £65/75.

Places to Eat

Most of the eating possibilities are within a short walk of the market square. *Emilio's Ristorante (☎ 384 0096, 96 Elvet Bridge)*, just over Elvet Bridge, is good value and reputable with pizzas and pastas from £5.45.

On the other side of the peninsula, *Bella Pasta (☎ 386 1060, 20–21 Silver St)*, on the eastern side of Framwellgate Bridge, has good views over the river; between 5 and 7 pm two courses go for £5.95.

The *Almshouses (☎ 386 1054, Palace Green)* serves up an imaginative and satisfying selection in a 17th-century house. It opens 9 am to 5 pm (to 8 pm from April to September). Choices include spinach pie (£4.60) and celery soup with roll (£2.75).

Rajpooth Tandoori Restaurant (☎ 386 1496, 80 Claypath) has a good reputation for Indian food; mains start at £5.95. The Italian *La Spaghettata (☎ 383 9290, 66 Saddler St)* has a good selection of tasty pizzas and pastas.

Entertainment

If you want to check out what's going on, a half-hour walk will give you an idea. The TIC has a *What's On* guide.

There are a couple of pubs on Claypath, including the pleasant *Travellers Rest*. A rowdy possibility on the western side of Framwellgate is the *Coach & Eight (☎ 386 5341, Bridge House, Framwellgate Bridge)*. The *Swan & Three Cygnets (☎ 384 0242, Elvet Bridge)* is a bright riverside pub with tables overlooking the river and good bar food.

The *Court Inn (☎ 384 7350, Court Lane)* is a popular local haunt with a good mix of students and professionals.

Getting There & Away

Durham is 260 miles (419km) from London, 75 miles (121km) from Leeds and 15 miles (24km) from Newcastle.

Bus There are six National Express buses a day to London (£20, 6½ hours), one to Edinburgh (£17.50, 4½ hours), and numerous buses to/from Birmingham (£26.50, 6¾ hours) and Newcastle (£2.75, 30 minutes). There's one bus a day (No 383) between Durham and Edinburgh via Jedburgh and Melrose in the Scottish Borders.

Primrose Coaches (☎ 232 5567) has a daily service between Newcastle and Blackpool via Durham, Barnard Castle, Raby Castle and Kirkby Stephen (No 352). It leaves Durham from the main bus station.

Train There are numerous trains to York (£13.90, one hour), many of which continue to London (£76, £23 if booked seven days in advance, three hours) via Peterborough (for Cambridge). Newcastle is only 15 minutes away (£3.10) and frequent trains from London continue through to Edinburgh (£32.50, two hours).

Getting Around

Pratt's Taxis (☎ 386 0700) charges a minimum of about £1.80.

Cycle Force (☎ 384 0319) at 29 Claypath charges £15 per day for hiring out mountain bikes.

BISHOP AUCKLAND
☎ 01388 • pop 32,600

The big reason to visit the town of Bishop Auckland, 11 miles (18km) south-west of Durham, is Auckland Castle, the country residence of the bishops of Durham since the 12th century.

The TIC (☎ 604922, fax 604960) is located in the town hall on Market Place and opens 10 am to 5 pm Monday to Friday, and 9 am to 4 pm Saturday, year round; and 1 to 4 pm Sunday, April to September.

The challenging gates of **Auckland Castle** (☎ 601627), just off Market Place behind the town hall, are hard to miss. Originally built as a banqueting hall in the 12th century and now the official home of the bishop of Durham, the castle, which is more of a palace, was extended every 200 years to the whims of the prince bishops. The outstanding attraction of the castle is the 17th-century chapel built on the ruins of the banqueting hall. The grounds double as a deer park and contain an 18th-century deer shelter. The castle opens 2 to 5 pm Sunday to Friday, mid-July to August; and Friday and Sunday, May to mid-July and September. Admission is £3/free. The deer park opens dawn to dusk and admission is free.

One and a half miles (2.5km) north of Bishop Auckland is another remnant of the Romans' achievements in northern England, **Binchester Roman Fort** (☎ 663089), or Vinovia as it was originally called. The fort, first built in wood around AD 80 and rebuilt in stone early in the 2nd century, covers 10 acres but only a small part of it has been excavated. The most important features on show are the remains of Dere Street, a fortified supply route running from York to Hadrian's Wall, and a system to heat the commandants' private bath suite, built in the late 4th century. The excavations open 11 am to 5 pm daily, Easter to September. Admission costs £1.50/75p. Last admission to the site is 4.30 pm.

Ever practical, the local people of the area began to use stones of the abandoned Binchester Fort for other constructions, including **Escomb Church** (☎ 602861). The quaint Saxon church dates from the 7th century making it one of the oldest in England. Escomb is 3 miles (5km) west of Bishop Auckland and the church opens 9 am to 8 pm in summer and 9 am to 4 pm in winter. Admission is free. Take bus No 86 to Escomb.

If you plan on staying in Bishop Auckland the *Albion Cottage Guest House* (☎ 602217, Albion Terrace) is, like the resident dog, welcoming and friendly. It charges £18/34 for singles/doubles without bathroom. For more central accommodation the *Queens Head Hotel* (☎ 603477, 38 Market Place), right next to the TIC, is pleasant and has rooms from £30/50.

There are a number of tearooms in and around Market Place but for a fuller meal try the *Fortune Court* (☎ 602888, 23–25 Market Place). The special lunch menu consisting of three Chinese courses for £6 is served 11 am to 2 pm Monday to Saturday. Evening mains are pricier.

Bus No 352 running from Newcastle to Blackpool passes through Bishop Auckland daily, March to November, while bus No X85 from Durham to Kendal stops once on Saturday, late May to September.

You need to change at Darlington for regular trains to Bishop Auckland (£2.50, 24 minutes, every two hours).

BEAMISH OPEN-AIR MUSEUM

Beamish (☎ 01207-231811) was founded on the ruins of Durham's coal industry; overheard from a grizzled ex-miner sitting in the sun at the entrance waiting for his grandchildren to return: 'Spent half my life down a pit. No way am I going to pay seven quid to go down one again!'

Visitors can go underground, and explore mine heads, a working farm, cottages, a school, a pub and shops.

Beamish opens 10 am to 5 pm daily, April to October; and until 4 pm the rest of the year. Allow a minimum of two hours to do the place justice. Ticket prices range from £3 in winter to £10/7 in summer.

Beamish is about 8 miles (13km) north-west of Durham; it's signposted from the A1(M) – take the A691 west at junction 63. Bus Nos 709 from Newcastle, 720 from Durham and 775 and 778 from Sunderland and Chester-Le-Street run to the museum.

BARNARD CASTLE
☎ 01833 • pop 6070

Barnard Castle isn't as self-contained or picturesque as Richmond (see the Yorkshire chapter), but it's still an attractive market town, and makes a good base for exploring Teesdale and the northern Pennines.

The TIC (☎ 630272, 690909, **e** tourism@ teesdale.co.uk), Flats Rd, opens 10 am to 6 pm daily, April to October and 11 am to 4 pm daily, November to March.

Run by English Heritage (EH), the ruins of Barnard Castle (☎ 638212), on the banks of the Tees, cover almost six acres and testify to its importance; it was founded by Guy de Bailleul and rebuilt by his nephew

The Rising of the North

Barnard Castle played its most important role in 1569 during the reign of Elizabeth I. The Percys (earls of Northumberland) and the Nevilles (earls of Westmoreland) plotted at nearby Raby Castle to release Mary Queen of Scots from Bolton Castle in Wensleydale, where she was imprisoned, place her on the throne and restore Roman Catholicism.

Sir George Bowes remained loyal to Elizabeth, however, and he and other loyalists held Barnard Castle. On 2 December, 5000 rebels besieged Barnard. On 8 December, the walls were breached and Bowes retreated to the Inner Ward. On 12 December, Bowes was finally forced to surrender, but the delay had allowed the earl of Sussex to assemble his forces at York and the rebels were defeated.

around 1150. It opens 10 am to 6 pm daily, April to September; to 5 pm daily, October; and 10 am to 1 pm and 2 to 4 pm Wednesday to Sunday, November to March. Admission costs £2.30/1.70.

The completely out-of-place but impressive 19th-century French chateau built 1½ miles (2.5km) west of town houses the **Bowes Museum** (☎ 690606). The chateau was purposely built by local businessman John Bowes and his French wife to exhibit their art collection, which includes paintings by El Greco and Goya. A prime exhibit is the 18th-century mechanical silver swan in the hall; ask when you can see it in operation. The museum opens 11 am to 5 pm daily. Admission costs £3.90/2.90.

Accommodation can be hard to find in summer so the TIC's accommodation booking service can be particularly useful. Galgate, which heads north-east from the castle, is a good place to start the search for accommodation.

Marwood House (☎ 637493, ℮ john@ kilgarriff.demon.co.uk, 98 Galgate) is good value at £20 per person and serves evening meals. Across the road *Greta House* (☎ 631193, 89 Galgate) is really lovely but charges a little more at £25 per person.

The *Old Well* pub (☎ 690130, 21 The Bank), downhill from Market Cross, has good, filling pub food, and comfortable doubles with bathroom for £60. There are not a lot of options for a bite to eat but the *Hayloft* off Horsemarket is nicely tucked away from the busy main street and serves sandwiches and light meals.

Primrose Coaches (☎ 0191-232 5567) has a daily service between Newcastle and Blackpool via Durham, Barnard Castle, Raby Castle and Kirkby Stephen (No 352). Arriva (☎ 0191-212 3000) bus No 75 frequently runs between Durham and Barnard Castle as does No 76 from Darlington.

AROUND BARNARD CASTLE

If you're looking to stretch the legs a little, the ruins of **Egglestone Abbey**, open dawn till dusk, are on a lovely bend of the Tees, a pleasant mile walk south of Barnard Castle. Otherwise it's a five-minute drive. **Raby Castle** (☎ 660202) is a romantic-looking 14th-century castle, a stronghold of the Neville family until the Rising of the North (see the boxed text). Most of the interior has been substantially altered, but the exterior remains true to the original design, built around a courtyard and surrounded by a moat. The castle and its beautiful grounds open 1 to 5 pm Wednesday and Sunday, May and September; and Sunday to Friday, June to August. Admission costs £5/2. Bus No 8 travels the 6 miles (10km) north-east of Barnard Castle off the A688.

THE DURHAM DALES

The relatively unspoilt dales of Durham make up the western half of the county bordering the northern Pennines. Two rivers cut through the dales – the Rivers Tees and Wear – creating the valleys of Teesdale to the south and Weardale to the north.

Teesdale
☎ 01833

Starting at the meeting point of the Rivers Greta and Tees and continuing on to Caldron Snout at the source of the Tees, Teesdale is a valley of small villages and rolling hills. The Pennine Way snakes along most of the valley before leaving in search of better pastures.

Middleton-in-Teesdale A pretty village of white houses mixed in with stone constructions, Middleton-in-Teesdale is 10 miles (16km) north-west of Barnard Castle. It was once completely owned by the Quaker London Lead Company, so can't have been a huge party town at the time. It's a pleasant place to stay overnight but there is nothing of specific interest to look at.

Bluebell House (☎ 640584, *Market Place*), in the heart of the village, is accommodating and welcoming with rooms starting at £17 per person. Somewhat more plush is *Brunswick House* (☎/fax 640393, **e** *brunswick@teesdaleonline.co.uk, 55 Market Place*), an 18th-century stone house. Rooms cost from £22.50/38.

For a bite to eat, the *King's Head* (☎ 640647, *53 Market Place*), across the road from Bluebell House, has haddock and corn chowder for £6.95.

Bowlees Visitor Centre (☎/fax 622292), a few miles up the valley from Middleton, has information on the surrounding area and a small display on the local wildlife. There are a couple of reasonably gentle walks from the visitor centre, taking in the adjacent wooded picnic area, nearby Newbiggin, and High Force. A brochure covering the walks is available at the centre for a whopping 30p. The centre opens 10.30 am to 5 pm daily, March to October; and 10.30 to 4 pm Saturday and Sunday, November to February. It costs £1 to view the wildlife display.

Four and a half miles (7km) from Middleton is the celebrated **High Force** waterfall, where the River Tees jumps 15m, considered one of the best in Britain. It's a surprise to have to pay £1 to have the privilege of seeing it, when walkers of the Pennine Way on the left-hand bank view for free. The car park is an additional £1.50. The **Low Force** waterfall, near the Bowlees Visitor Centre, is less impressive.

Next to the High Force car park is the excellent *High Force Hotel & Brewery* (☎ 622222, *Forest-in-Teesdale*). The walls of the bar are adorned with photographs of High Force in spectacular flood, and the ales brewed on the premises have won a number of awards. Beware the Cauldron Snout: it's got a kick like a mule. If you've had one too many the hotel serves both lunch and evening meals and provides B&B from £25 per person.

The B6277 leaves the River Tees at High Force and continues up to Langdon Beck, where the scenery quickly turns from rolling hills to the rugged landscape of the northern Pennines. You can either continue on the B6277 over the northern Pennines to Alston and Cumbria (see the Cumbria chapter for details) or turn right and take a minor road over the moors to St John's Chapel in Weardale (see Weardale later in the chapter).

A mile before Langdon Beck is the *Langdon Beck Youth Hostel* (☎ 622228, *fax 622372,* **e** *langdonbeck@yha.org.uk, Forest-in-Teesdale*), which serves as a stopping point for walkers on the Pennine Way. It's also a good base for short walks into the dales and the Pennines, in particular to Cow Green Reservoir, the source of the River Tees. The hostel opens Monday to Saturday, mid-April to mid-July, daily, mid-July to August; Friday and Saturday, November; and Tuesday to Saturday, September to October and February to mid-April. It costs £9.80/6.75.

Hodgson's (☎ 630730) bus No 73 connects Middleton and Langdon Beck at least once a day Tuesday, Wednesday, Friday and Saturday. Arriva (☎ 0191-212 3000) bus Nos 95 and 96 frequently serve Middleton from Barnard Castle daily.

Weardale
☎ 01388

The Wear valley's history is entwined with mining and quarrying. Fosterley and Stanhope, at the head of the valley, were sites of limestone quarries and Killhope, at the top, is the site of a well-preserved lead mine. The valley also offers plenty of opportunities for walks into the surrounding countryside.

About 15 miles (24km) north-west of Bishop Auckland is the quiet town of

Fosterley at the start of the valley, renowned for its 'marble' (in fact fossil-rich black limestone). There are some good cycle tracks in nearby **Hamsterley Forest** and you can hire a bike at Weardale Mountain Bikes (☎/fax 528129), Front St, for £13 per day. It opens daily except Tuesday and winter Sundays. Unfortunately there is no public transport to the forest.

The ***Black Bull Inn (☎ 527784, Bridge End)*** has a nice spot at the western end of Fosterley, 100m from the main road on the way to White Krikley. Comfy en suite rooms are £25/38 and meals are served every evening except Tuesday.

Two miles (3km) farther up the valley is **Stanhope**, in the heart of limestone quarries. It's another peaceful town full of stone houses and makes a good base for walks across the moors. The Durham Dales Centre (at the western end of Stanhope, opposite Stanhope Castle) is the site of a TIC and small tearoom. The TIC (☎ 527650, fax 527461) offers an accommodation booking service for the dales and opens 10 am to 5 pm daily, April to October; to 4 pm Monday to Friday and from 11 am weekends, November to March.

Opposite the Dales Centre is the friendly and homely ***Redlodge Guest House (☎ 527 851, 2 Redlodge Cottages, Market Place)***, which has rooms from £20 per person. Ring ahead to check availability as Stanhope is the last stop on the C2C route before cyclists push on to Sunderland.

The **Weardale Museum** (☎ 537417), 8 miles (13km) on from Stanhope in Ireshopeburn, provides a brief glimpse into local history and how life was led by lead-miners and farming families 100 years ago. It opens 2 to 5 pm Wednesday to Sunday, May to September and daily in August. Admission costs £1/30p.

At the top of the valley 13 miles (21km) from Stanhope is the **Killhope Lead Mining Centre** (☎ 537505). The site is aptly named when you realise how the men who worked the mine actually lived. A small exhibition at the centre explains what life was really like for the miners: poor pay, even poorer living conditions and the constant threat of

illness forced many of the workers into an early grave in their 20s and 30s. The mine closed in 1910 but you can still visit its underground network on an hour-long guided tour, but bring warm clothes. The site is dominated by the 10m-high working water wheel, originally built to work a crushing mechanism. The centre opens 10.30 am to 5 pm daily April to October and 10.30 am to 4 pm Sunday in November, and admission costs £5/2.50 including a mine trip, £3.40/1.70 without. It's possible to purchase a combined ticket for the mine and the South Tynedale Railway (see the Alston section in the Cumbria chapter). From the mining centre it's another 7 miles (11km) up over the highest main road in England (617m) and the northern Pennines and down into Alston (see the Cumbria chapter for details).

Weardale Motor Services (☎ 528235) bus No 101 makes the regular journey up the valley from Bishop Auckland to Cowshill (a few miles south of Killhope) daily, but it's possible to arrange for the driver to drop you off at the Killhope Mining Centre. Bus No X21 runs from Newcastle to Stanhope Wednesday and Saturday only and offers a day return to the Killhope Mining Centre for £4 in the mornings. Arriva (☎ 0191-212 3000) bus No X85 journeys from Durham to Kendal in Cumbria via Weardale once a day on Saturday, late May to September.

NORTH TO HADRIAN'S WALL

The wilds of the northern Pennines finally putter out just before Hadrian's Wall, and are home to just two picturesque valleys north of Weardale.

Blanchland & Around

The tiny village of Blanchland, a picturesque grouping of squat stone buildings surrounded by trees, is both an unexpected and pleasant surprise. It's 12 miles (19km) north of Stanhope and 10 miles (16km) south of Hexham on the B6306. The village was originally the site of a 12th-century Premonstratensian Abbey. Around 1750 the prince bishop of the time, Lord Crewe, seeing the village and abbey falling into disrepair, bequeathed the buildings to trustees on the condition that they were protected and looked after.

Unfortunately there's only one place to stay and eat but the *Lord Crewe Arms Hotel* (☎ *01434-675251*) is a gem. It was originally the abbot's lodge and the interior shows this, with warming fireplaces, hidden corners and a wholly rich feel. It's a beautiful place to stay but is quite pricey at £80/110 for singles/doubles.

Four miles (6km) east of Blanchland on the B6306 along the southern edge of **Derwent Reservoir** is another inviting village, **Edmundbyers**. It's a quiet spot, and it's possible to stay here at the *Edmundbyers Youth Hostel* (☎*/fax 01207-255651, Low House)*. The hostel helps to serve walkers in the area and cyclists on the C2C route. Beds cost £8.10/5.65. It opens from mid-April to October.

Bus No 773 runs from Consett to Blanchland via Edmundbyers at least four times a day, Monday to Saturday.

Allen Valley
Because **Allendale Town** is smack-bang in the middle of the moors of the northern Pennines, it's a great base for walking. It's quite a small place, 7 miles (11km) from Hexham on the B6295, but it has everything you need for a few nights' stay. The rural town lets its hair down come New Year's Eve when the 'Tar Barrels' ceremony is performed. It involves a few of the locals walking around with lit tar barrels on their heads before dumping them in a raging bonfire in the centre of town, trying not to set themselves alight.

Allentown offers up a couple of good places to stay. Right by the bus stop is the *Allendale Tea Rooms* (☎ *683575, Market Place)*, which doubles as a B&B and has rooms from £20 per person. *Kings Head Hotel* (☎ *683681, Market Square)* is the town's best pub accommodation with rooms starting at £22.50 per person. Food is also available at the bar.

Four miles (6km) farther south towards the Wear Valley is **Allenheads**, nestled at

the head of Allen Valley. It's another tranquil place that makes for a relaxing stay.

Allenheads has two attractions, the **Heritage Centre** and the **Allenheads Inn** (☎ 685200). The centre delves into the history of the village and surrounding area and includes a small nature walk. It opens 9 am to 5 pm daily, April to October. Admission costs £1/50p.

Allenheads Inn, run by a wonderfully eccentric Englishman, holds an amazing 5000 assorted objects. It's possible to stay here among the bizarre collection for £21/42, and the food is quite good at the bar.

The *Hemmel Coffee Shop* (☎ 685395) is part of the heritage centre, set in a converted barn, and is a comfortable and relaxing place to grab a bite to eat. It opens year round.

Bus No 688 runs up and down the Allen Valley from Hexham to Allenheads (stopping at Allendale Town) on a regular basis Monday to Saturday but only completes four circuits on Sunday.

The Tees Valley

The Tees Valley is very much a forgotten corner of northern England, and at first glance it's easy to understand why. The area's history is entwined with the industrial age and a great deal of it still reflects this heritage, with smoke stacks and factory pipes clogging up the land around the River Tees outlet to the sea. But a few places have attempted to redevelop themselves to attract the tourist pound, such as Darlington, with its rich railway past, and the coastal towns of Saltburn-by-the-Sea and Hartlepool with their maritime history and occasionally sun-drenched sandy beaches.

DARLINGTON
☎ 01670 • pop 99,700
In 1825 Darlington hit the headlines the world over as the first railway line to carry passengers was opened between Stockton and Darlington. *No 1 Locomotion* chugged along at the breakneck speed of 10–13mph

to the delight of the passengers, and the form of transport soon caught the imagination of people worldwide.

The Darlington of today grew up around the railway industry that followed all the excitement, which soon eclipsed much of what was then a traditional market town. Not much of the quaintness of a market town is left but habits die hard: Monday to Saturday there's a covered market in the centre of town (one of the largest in England) and on Monday and Saturday an open-air market takes centre stage on Market Place.

Darlington's TIC (☎ 388666, e infodarl @darlingtoneru.demon.co.uk) is located on Market Place at 13 Horsemarket and opens from 9 am to 5 pm Monday to Friday (9.30 am on Wednesday) and 10 am to 4 pm Saturday.

Internet access is available at the Darlington Library and Art Gallery (☎ 462034) on Crown St.

Things to See & Do

The **Railway Centre & Museum** (☎ 460532), a mile north of the town market, makes good use of Darlington's place in railway history chronicles. Its pride and joy is the original steam engine *Locomotion*, but it also houses a number of other locomotives, including the *Derwent*, the earliest surviving Darlington-built engine. There are plenty of signs pointing you in the direction of the museum from the town centre, otherwise take a bus from High Row. The Darlington–Bishop Auckland train stops at North Road Station, built in 1842, which houses the museum. The museum opens 10 am to 5 pm daily and charges £2.10/1.05.

St Cuthbert's Church, founded in 1183, is a fine example of Early English design and is topped by a 14th-century spire, just east of Market Place. It opens 11 am to 2 pm daily Easter to September, and weekends only in winter.

Places to Stay & Eat

Accommodation is fairly uninspiring in Darlington but the ***Balmoral Guest House*** (☎ 461908, 63 Woodland Rd) is a lovely Victorian house with nine rooms starting at

£21 per person. Right next to the train station is the ***Coachman Hotel*** (☎ 286116, fax 382796, Victoria Rd), a good option if you're too tired to walk another step after getting off the train. Singles/doubles with bathroom cost £48/58.

The excellent ***Quaker Coffee House*** (☎ 468364, Mechanics Yard), between Skinnergate and High Row, is two places in one: tasty and filling food is served in the upstairs restaurant and the best traditional ales in town are poured in the relaxed bar underneath. A close second for atmosphere and good real ale is ***Number 22*** (☎ 354590, 22 Coniscliffe Rd).

Getting There & Away

Air Teesside International Airport (☎ 01325-332811) is approximately 8 miles (13km) from Darlington on the A67. Bus No 74 runs between Darlington and the airport every 30 minutes.

Bus There are frequent buses between Darlington and Durham (£2.50, 35 minutes). Stagecoach (☎ 01325-384573) bus No X90 runs almost hourly from Darlington to Newcastle (£3, 1¼ hours).

Train Darlington is on the York (£10.20, 30 minutes) to Newcastle (£4.90, 40 minutes) line so there are frequent connections to both.

AROUND DARLINGTON
Piercebridge

It's hard to imagine the sleepy village of Piercebridge, 5 miles (8km) west of Darlington on the A67, as a bustling Roman town, but its strategic position on the River Tees gives it away. The Romans probably settled the area in the late 1st century because of its important river crossing. The east gate and defences of a second fort, built around 270, have been excavated east of the village green and information plaques are scattered throughout the excavations providing helpful descriptions. Admission is free.

If for some reason you are stuck in Piercebridge overnight, the ***Bridge House***

(☎ 374727) has comfortable rooms and an adjoining riverside garden. B&B starts at £20 per person.

Hourly buses from Darlington to Barnard Castle stop at Piercebridge.

HARTLEPOOL
☎ 01429 • pop 94,400
On the northern side of Tees Bay, 19 miles (31km) from Durham, is Hartlepool, the third-largest port in England in the 19th century and a major shipbuilding centre until economic decline hit. Nowadays it focuses on its connection to the sea and tries hard to pull in the tourists by drawing on its maritime history. Its most famous story is of the hanging of a monkey (see the boxed text 'Don't Spank the Monkey, Hang It!').

The TIC (☎ 869706, e hpool@hartle pool.gov.uk), Church Square, shares the refurbished Christ Church with the **Hartlepool Art Gallery** and opens from 10 am to 5.30 pm Tuesday to Saturday and 2 to 5 pm Sunday.

The main attraction in town is the **Hartlepool Historic Quay and Museum** (☎ 860006), Jackson Dock, Maritime Ave,

overlooking the harbour. The quay has been successfully re-created into an 18th-century port with lots of hands-on activities and displays. It opens 10 am to 5 pm daily and costs £4.95/2.50.

Once inside, you can also visit the **HMS Trincomalee** (☎ 223193), Britain's oldest warship still afloat, built in 1817. The ship opens 10.30 am to 3.30 pm Monday to Friday and 10.30 am to 4.30 pm at the weekend. The admission fee for the Historic Quay doesn't cover entry to the ship, which is another £2.50.

Hillcarter Hotel (☎ 855800, fax 855829, e *hillcarter@btinternet.com, 31–32 Church St*) is right opposite the train station with spacious singles/doubles, all en suite, for £55/60. The hotel also has a rooftop restaurant with international cuisine and superb views of the harbour.

Trains leave every half hour for Newcastle (£4.50, 50 minutes).

SALTBURN-BY-THE-SEA
☎ 01287 • pop 20,000
Even though its days as a popular Victorian seaside resort have long gone, Saltburn, 11

NORTH-EASTERN ENGLAND

Don't Spank the Monkey, Hang It!

The legend of the hanging of a monkey, well known throughout England, is arguably what Hartlepool is most famous (or infamous) for – and the legend is still debated to this day.

The story goes like this: one December day at the beginning of the 1800s a particularly strong storm hit the north-east coast. At the time England was engaged in the Napoleonic wars with France. A French ship, the *Chasse Maree*, was spotted in trouble off the coast of Hartlepool, so the local fishermen were on guard, expecting an invasion. The vessel was no match for the storm and sunk, but much of the wreckage was washed ashore, including the sole survivor, a monkey dressed in a military uniform. The fishermen, supposedly never having seen either a monkey or a Frenchman before, took them for one and the same and came to the conclusion that the waterlogged fellow had to be a spy! The monkey was then questioned and, since no one could speak French or simian, he (or she) was found guilty and promptly hung.

Another version of the legend is even weirder. The French vessel was in fact a craft from outer space and the shipwrecked monkey was an alien. To cover it all up, the local authorities removed the alien and told the fishermen to spread a story about a monkey being found; they then adapted the technology from the craft to kick start the Industrial Revolution! The spacecraft is supposedly buried under the site of a nuclear power plant south of Hartlepool.

Even though Hartlepudlians are commonly referred to as 'monkey hangers' it may not be a very wise move to greet them as such. Many are, to say the least, still a little sensitive about the subject!

miles (18km) from Middlesbrough, still can play the part. Come mid-August the whole town dresses up in Victorian garb for a week to blend in better with the surroundings.

The TIC (☎ 622422, fax 625074), 3 Station Buildings, can arrange accommodation if required. It opens 9 am to 5 pm Monday to Saturday, May to October; and Monday, Tuesday and Thursday to Saturday, the rest of the year.

A big reminder of the town's Victorian popularity is its **inclined tramway** (☎ 622 528). Built in 1884, this water balanced lift drops 36m (120 feet) from the town to the sandy beach and pier. The pier is currently closed, awaiting refurbishment. You can ride the tram 10 am to 5 pm at the weekend, April to May; daily mid-September to October; and to 7 pm daily from May to mid-September. It costs 55p.

The **Smugglers Heritage Centre** (☎ 625 252), 200m east of the pier, spells out the popular pastime of smuggling in the late 18th century. It opens 10 am to 6 pm daily, April to September. Admission costs £1.80/1.30.

While you're here you might as well check out **Redcar**, 5 miles (8km) north-west of Saltburn, the north-east coast's answer to Blackpool. Remember to book well in advance if you plan to visit during the Victorian Celebrations.

Brydene (☎ *622653, 23 Ruby St*) has simple but adequate rooms and charges £14 per person. For fine views over the bay and comfortable rooms head to the ***Spa Hotel*** (☎ *622544, fax 625870,* **e** *spahotels@ aol.com, Saltburn Bank*) with B&B for £35/50. You can also enjoy the view even if you're not staying there by dining at the ***Conservatory Restaurant***, which is part of the hotel.

The ***Ship Inn*** (☎ *622361)*, next to the Smugglers Heritage Centre, is a superb pub offering good bar food, great views and a well drawn pint.

Saltburn has frequent train connections to Darlington via Redcar (£4.50, 50 minutes). Bus No 71 runs to Middlesbrough and stops outside the train station.

Newcastle-upon-Tyne

☎ 0191 • pop 210,000

Newcastle is the largest city in the northeast. It grew famous as a coal-exporting port, and in the 19th century became an important steel, shipbuilding and engineering centre – all industries that went into serious decline after WWII. It had a dour struggle to survive, but retains some 19th-century grandeur, and the famous six bridges across the Tyne are an arresting sight.

Newcastle is currently undergoing a substantial face-lift to boost its image as a major city in Britain. Geordies, as the locals are known, are fiercely proud of their city and their independence, and would say Newcastle already is without equal. Money is being poured into the city and is especially apparent around the Quayside area. The brand new International Centre for Life and the revamping of the Baltic Flour Mill, on the southern side of the quays, as a contemporary visual arts centre (due to open in late 2001) testifies to the headway Newcastle is making.

Plan to stay at least one night; the exuberance with which Geordies let their hair down is well worth getting involved in.

Orientation

Although Newcastle is dauntingly large, the city centre is easy to get around on foot, and the Metro (convenient for hostels and B&Bs) is cheap, efficient and pleasant to use.

The Central Station (train) is just to the south of the city centre. The coach station is on Gallowgate. Local buses, and buses for Beamish, leave from Eldon Square and buses for the north leave from Haymarket.

Maps The Newcastle Map Centre (☎ 261 5622), 55 Grey St, has a good supply of maps and guides.

Information

The convenient train station TIC (☎ 277 8000) opens 10 am to 5 pm Monday to

NEWCASTLE-UPON-TYNE

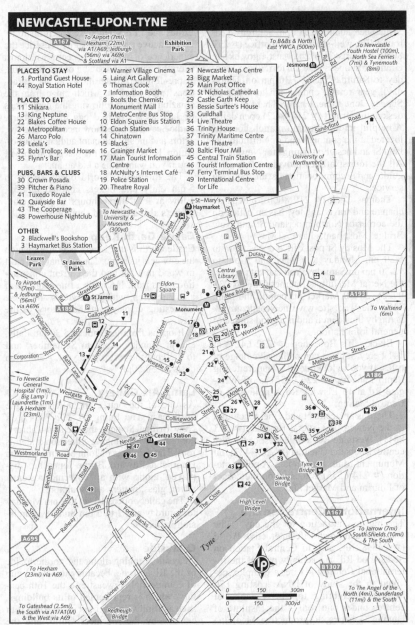

PLACES TO STAY
1 Portland Guest House
44 Royal Station Hotel

PLACES TO EAT
11 Shikara
13 King Neptune
22 Blakes Coffee House
24 Metropolitan
26 Marco Polo
28 Leela's
32 Bob Trollop; Red House
35 Flynn's Bar

PUBS, BARS & CLUBS
30 Crown Posada
39 Pitcher & Piano
41 Tuxedo Royale
42 Quayside Bar
43 The Cooperage
48 Powerhouse Nightclub

OTHER
2 Blackwell's Bookshop
3 Haymarket Bus Station

4 Warner Village Cinema
5 Laing Art Gallery
6 Thomas Cook
7 Information Booth
8 Boots the Chemist;
   Monument Mall
9 MetroCentre Bus Stop
10 Eldon Square Bus Station
12 Coach Station
14 Chinatown
15 Blacks
16 Grainger Market
17 Main Tourist Information
   Centre
18 McNulty's Internet Café
19 Police Station
20 Theatre Royal

21 Newcastle Map Centre
23 Bigg Market
25 Main Post Office
27 St Nicholas Cathedral
29 Castle Garth Keep
31 Bessie Surtee's House
33 Guildhall
34 Live Theatre
36 Trinity House
37 Trinity Maritime Centre
38 Live Theatre
40 Baltic Flour Mill
45 Central Train Station
46 Tourist Information Centre
47 Ferry Terminal Bus Stop
49 International Centre
   for Life

NORTH-EASTERN ENGLAND

Friday, October to May; to 8 pm June to September; and 9 am to 5 pm Saturday, year round. The well-stocked main office (☎ 277 8000, e tourist.info@newcastle.gov.uk) on Grainger St opens 9.30 am to 5.30 pm Monday to Saturday (until 7.30 pm on Thursday), year round; and 10 am to 4 pm on Sunday, June to September. There is also a desk at the airport (☎ 214 4422) open daily. A helpful interactive information booth is located at the southern end of Northumberland St and has good listings for Newcastle. All the tourist offices provide a free map, guide, and accommodation list and booking service.

Thomas Cook (☎ 219 8000), bureau de change and travel agency, has an office on the corner of Northumberland St and New Bridge. Most banks have ATMs.

The Mosley St post office opens 9 am to 5.30 pm Monday to Friday and 9 am to 12.30 pm on Saturday. You can eat and surf the Net at McNulty's Internet Café (☎ 232 0922), 26–30 Market St, behind the main TIC. The Web site www.newcastle.gov.uk is run by the council and is a good source of general information.

Blackwell's Bookshop (☎ 232 6421) at 141 Percy St has a comprehensive range of titles. If you're looking for a laundrette Big Lamp Laundry (☎ 226 0536) is off Westgate Rd at 13 Elswick Rd, a mile west of Central Station.

There is an accident and emergency unit at the Newcastle General Hospital (☎ 273 8811), Westgate Rd, a mile west of the city centre. Boots the Chemist (☎ 232 4423), on Monument Mall, is open late. A police station (☎ 214 6555) is located on the corner of Pilgrim and Market Sts.

International Centre for Life

The big new attraction for the city is the colourful and brash Life Interactive World (☎ 243 8210), next to Central Station on Scotswood Rd. It's actually part of the International Centre for Life, a complex devoted to the study of DNA, costing £70 million, which brings together a number of centres under one roof – the Institute of Human Genetics, Reproductive Medicine

Centre, Bioscience Centre, and the Policy, Ethics and Life Science Research Institute.

Interactive is the right word to describe the experience of visiting the centre as almost everything is set up for a bit of hands-on fun. A pre-designed route allows all the attractions to be taken in, which range from the amazing 3-D film following the beginnings of Jack as a fertilised egg to a newborn, to the Secret of Life show incorporating live actors and mostly reluctant audience participation. Kids will love the place, and so will you if you want to be a kid again.

The Interactive World opens 10 am to 5 pm daily and tickets cost £6.95/4.50; allow at least three hours to get round. There's also a cafe and shop on site.

Castle Garth Keep

Castle Garth is the 'new' castle from which the city gets its name. The original was built in wood in 1080 and the current construction dates from 1168. It's a fine example of a square keep, with good views and some interesting displays on the history of the city.

It opens from 9.30 am to 5.30 pm daily, except Monday, April to September; and to 4.30 pm the rest of the year. Admission costs £1.50/50p.

Laing Art Gallery

As one of the better art galleries in the north-east, The Laing (☎ 232 7734), on New Bridge St near the Central Library, contains a wide-ranging collection under its roof. The paintings of John Martin, William Hunt and Edward Burne-Jones are displayed, along with art covering costume, silver, glass, pottery and sculpture.

The gallery opens 10 am to 5 pm Monday to Saturday and 2 to 5 pm Sunday. Admission is free.

Quayside

Quayside, running along the northern side of the River Tyne, became the natural hub of commercial Newcastle in the 16th century, which is represented in its buildings, such as Trinity House, built in the early 16th century by the Mariners Guild, and the rounded **Guildhall**, built in 1658. Recently Quayside has enjoyed a resurgence and is bursting with bars and restaurants. **Bessie Surtees' House** (☎ 261 1585; EH) is a lovely combination of two 16th- and 17th-century merchant houses on Sandhill. Bessie Surtees was the daughter of a wealthy banker; she, God forbid, fell in love with John Scott, a pauper. They eloped to Scotland, but all ended well when he went on to become the lord chancellor of England. The house opens 10 am to 4 pm Monday to Friday. Admission is free.

The **Trinity Maritime Centre** (☎ 261 4691), 29 Broad Chare, next to Trinity House, covers Newcastle's seafaring history and the history of Quayside itself. It opens 11 am to 4 pm Monday to Friday, April to October. Admission costs £1.50/80p.

Tyne Bridges & Sightseeing Cruises

The most famous view in Newcastle is of the six bridges over the Tyne, and the most famous of the bridges is the **Tyne Bridge**, built between 1925 and 1928 at about the same time as Australia's Sydney Harbour Bridge (of which it is very reminiscent). Perhaps the most interesting is the **Swing Bridge**, which pivots in the middle. The **High Level Bridge**, designed by Robert Stephenson, was the world's first road and railway bridge and was opened in 1849.

Sightseeing cruises are run by River Tyne Cruises (☎ 251 5920) from Quayside pier (a quarter of a mile downriver from the Tyne Bridge) at 2 pm Sunday, May to early September. They last three hours and cost £7/5.

The University Museums

To the north of the city centre is Newcastle University, which is the location for an array of museums and galleries. **Hancock Museum** (☎ 222 6865), Barras Bridge, across Claremont Rd from the university grounds, is a classic natural history museum open 10 am to 5 pm Monday to Saturday and 2 to 5 pm Sunday. Admission costs £2.25/1.50.

On the main university courtyard is the **Museum of Antiquities** (☎ 222 7849), The Quadrangle, which has an impressive collection of Roman artefacts from Hadrian's Wall along with other finds dating from 6000 BC to AD 1600. It opens 10 am to 5 pm Monday to Saturday and admission is free. **Shefton Museum of Greek Art & Archaeology** (☎ 222 7966), Armstrong Building, is small but well stocked and opens 9.30 am to 12.30 pm and 2 to 4.30 pm Monday to Friday. Admission is free.

There's also **Hatton Gallery** (☎ 222 6057), The Quadrangle, with a permanent collection of West African art, open 10 am to 5 pm Monday to Saturday, and the **University Gallery** (☎ 227 4424), Library Building, focusing on work from the 20th century and local artists, it opens 10 am to 5 pm Monday to Thursday and to 4 pm Friday and Saturday. Both are free.

Markets

When it opened in 1835 **Grainger Market**, in a magnificent building on Grainger St, was Europe's largest undercover shopping centre. It mainly sells fruit and vegetables, but there are other interesting stalls, including the Marks & Spencer Original Penny Bazaar where unfortunately the original motto of 'Don't ask the price – it's a penny!' doesn't count these days. **Quayside Market**, a popular flea market, is held beneath the Tyne Bridge 9 am to 2.30 pm on Sunday. **Bigg Market** is held in the street of the same name on Tuesday, Thursday and Saturday.

Jarrow

The eastern suburb of Jarrow is embedded in labour history for the 'Jarrow Crusade' in 1936, when 200 men set out to walk all the way to London to protest against the appalling conditions brought about by unemployment.

Today's visitors to this grim district might think little has changed. However, Jarrow is also famous as the home of the Venerable Bede (author of the *Ecclesiastical History of the English People*), and parts of St Paul's Church date back to the

7th century. Together with a museum and Jarrow Hall, it forms part of **Bede's World** (☎ 489 2106), a park with many reconstructed medieval buildings. It opens 10 am to 5.30 pm Tuesday to Saturday, noon to 5.30 pm Sunday, April to October; and 11 am to 4.30 pm Tuesday to Saturday, and 2.30 to 5.30 pm Sunday, November to March. Admission costs £3/1.50. Jarrow and Bede's World are accessible via the Metro.

Segedunum

Four miles (6km) east of Newcastle at Wallsend is the site of Segedunum (☎ 295 5757), the last outpost of Hadrian's Wall. A lot of work has been put in to bringing the wall to life again, including ongoing excavations of fort ruins, a reconstructed Roman bathhouse (the only one in Britain) and a 35m tower with views of the whole site. Good interactive displays also do the trick. The site opens 10 am to 5 pm daily, April to August, and to 3.30 pm September to March. Admission costs £2.95/1.95. From Newcastle centre catch the Metro to Wallsend.

The *Angel of the North*

Made from 200 tonnes of steel, The *Angel of the North* (a human frame with wings), created by sculptor Antony Gormley, is the largest sculpture in Britain at 20m high and with a wingspan wider than a Boeing 767. It towers over the A1(M) 5 miles (8km)

JANE SMITH

south of Newcastle, and is hard to miss heading north or south. It's best to make your own mind up over the mass of steel – controversy rages over whether it's a total waste of money or a spectacular creation attracting attention to the north.

Places to Stay

Camping The nearest sites are in South Shields. *Sandhaven* (☎ 454 5594, Bents Park Rd) has sites for £9.50 for two people and a car. The nearby *Lizard Lane* (☎ 454 4982, Marsden) has sites at £7.20 for a two-person tent and car.

Hostels The *Newcastle Youth Hostel* (☎ 281 2570, ℮ Newcastle@yha.org.uk, 107 Jesmond Rd), north of the city centre, opens February to November (Friday to Sunday only, the rest of the year). A bed costs £10.85/7.40. Call in advance, as it can be busy. Jesmond is the closest station on the Metro.

North East YWCA (☎ 281 1233, Jesmond House, Clayton Rd) accepts male and female guests for £16 per person. Turn left onto Osborne Rd from Jesmond station and take the second street on the right.

B&Bs & Hotels For its size, Newcastle is a little sparse on cheap accommodation in the centre of town. Most of it is concentrated in the suburb of Jesmond, north-east of the city. There are quite a number of B&Bs along Osborne Rd and the best way to get there from central town is to catch the Metro to West Jesmond Station, or catch bus No 33 from Central Station, Grainger St or the corner of New Bridge and Pilgrim St.

The *Portland Guest House* (☎ 232 7868, 134 Sandyford Rd) is about the closest reasonably priced B&B to the centre of town as you're going to get. Singles/doubles without bathrooms start at £18/36.

Anyone hunting on Osborne Rd should consider the *Gresham Hotel* (☎ 281 4341, 92 Osborne Rd), a medium-sized, comfortable hotel from £29/39, although at that price in Newcastle you still share a bathroom. The *Minerva Hotel* (☎ 281 0190, 105

Osborne Rd) is a small place with decent prices. Rooms cost £22.50/35.

The friendly *George Hotel (☎ 281 4442,* **e** *georgehotel@dial.pipex.com, 88 Osborne Rd)* has clean and comfortable rooms for £35/46.

At the top end, the *Cairn Hotel (☎ 281 1358, 97 Osborne Rd)* is a large four-star hotel with rooms from £42/60.

The *Adelphi Hotel (☎ 281 3109, 63 Fern Ave)* is an attractive terraced house with rooms for £29.50/49.50. Fern Ave is the fifth street on the right if you head down Osborne Rd from Jesmond station.

Westland Hotel (☎ 281 0412, 27 Osborne Ave, off Osborne Rd) has 15 rooms from £22/40.

Beside Central Station, the impressive *Royal Station Hotel (☎ 232 0781, Neville St)* has rooms from £60/72.50, as well as cheaper weekend deals.

Places to Eat

Newcastle has a most un-English attitude to food. Geordies believe in going out to eat and they believe the food should be cheap. As a result, Newcastle has plenty of restaurants to choose from. It's best to eat early in the evening, as many places have 'happy hours' when you can get cheap specials.

Restaurants are widely scattered. There are some at the northern end of town (handy for the university, the youth hostels and the B&Bs on Osborne Rd), and Chinatown is on Stowell St to the west of Eldon Square. Perhaps the most interesting zone to explore, however, is south of the city centre. Walk south down Grey St (lined with beautiful Georgian and Victorian offices), which becomes Dean St, then The Side and takes you down to the River Tyne and Quayside.

On Grey St itself, *Blakes Coffee House (☎ 261 1235, 53 Grey St)* is good for a coffee and a bite to eat. For a fuller meal try *Metropolitan (☎ 230 2306, 35 Grey St)*, which is a local favourite serving up sandwiches and English-style food.

Dean St offers up a number of restaurants, the best being *Leela's (☎ 230 1261, 20 Dean St)*. Exceptionally good southern Indian dishes can be had for around £10. If you're looking for a cheap meal, *Marco Polo (☎ 232 5533, 33 Dean St)* has pizzas and pasta for as little as £2.95.

There are a number of interesting foodie pubs at the bottom of the hill. *Flynn's Bar (☎ 232 7218, 63 Quayside)* has a beer garden and cheap food and drink. Close by is the *Bob Trollop* (voted best veggie pub 2000) and *Red House*, which have pub meals for about £3.

One of the most acclaimed restaurants in town is *Shikara (☎ 233 0005, 52 St Andrew's St)*, serving excellent Indian food; it's cheap for lunch, most mains in the evening cost £6 to £10. *King Neptune (☎ 261 6657, 34 Stowell St)* is one of the better Chinese restaurants and specialises in seafood and Peking dishes. Set menus start at £14.80 per person.

If you like train rides and fancy a slightly different dining experience you might want to try *The Valley Restaurant* (see Places to Stay & Eat under Corbridge later in the chapter).

Entertainment

Newcastle caters to most tastes, with high culture and low. At the weekend young people come from other parts of the country to enjoy Newcastle's nightlife. There are a number of guides to what's on: *Paint it Red* and *the crack* (free), and the *Evening Chronicle* on Wednesday.

Geordies take going out, drinking beer and dancing seriously (though not necessarily in that order). The Bigg Market area is notorious for the crowds of young people it attracts – especially on Friday nights when groups of scantily clad young women and increasingly drunken young men circulate the streets ogling each other. If it all looks like something out of *Viz* magazine, it probably is – Newcastle is where it's based.

Be prepared for queues, thick-necked bouncers and infuriating dress codes in some bars and clubs – trainers will be out, and some places insist on a collar and tie. Otherwise the following standard applies – shirts are in, jackets are out, even on the coldest of nights!

The pubs and clubs around Quayside are

more relaxed. If real ale and unspoilt pubs are your thing, head for the **Crown Posada** (☎ 232 1269, 31 The Side). Long and narrow, it's a wonderful place full of character, and serves one of the best pints in town. The **Quayside Bar** (35 The Close, Quayside) is a well-restored warehouse with a great spot right on the river and a quiet courtyard.

The **Cooperage** (☎ 232 8286, 32 The Close, Quayside) is a popular pub with a wide-ranging clientele, and doubles as a club after 9 pm Friday and Saturday. Its timbers are supposedly from ships sunk in the Tyne.

Although it's part of a bar chain, the **Pitcher & Piano** (☎ 232 4100, 108 Quayside) is actually worth going to! It's a fine modern construction, with huge plate-glass walls and a prime spot overlooking the Tyne across to the Baltic Flour Mill.

One of the more unusually located and popular clubs is **Tuxedo Royale** (☎ 477 8899, Hillgate Quay), on the Tuxedo Princess ship under the Tyne Bridge. Tuesday is a big student night.

On Waterloo St, **Powerhouse Nightclub** (☎ 261 4507) is a gay and lesbian venue.

The Royal Shakespeare Company is a regular visitor to the superb **Theatre Royal** (☎ 232 0997, 100 Grey St) but there are also fringe companies such as the **Live Theatre** (☎ 232 1232, 27 Broad Chare, Quayside).

Warner Village Cinema (☎ 221 0222, Manors) is one of the better cinemas in town.

Spectator Sports

St James' Park (☎ 201 8400), on Strawberry Place west of Eldon Square, is holy ground to Geordies who follow the local football team, **Newcastle United**. Tours of the ground are available but it's advisable to book in advance. They cost £5/3. And like all teams that play in the most popular football league in the world, it's almost impossible to get a ticket to a game, but you can try on ☎ 261 1571.

Shopping

Shopaholics might be tempted by the MetroCentre at Gateshead, an enormous shopping centre – one of the largest in Europe – with 360 shops, 50 places to eat (mostly fast food) and fairground rides. A free bus runs to the centre from the Metro-Centre bus stop in town.

Eldon Square in the heart of Newcastle is Britain's largest city centre shopping complex and is another enormous modern shrine to consumerism. Needless to say, the markets like old Grainger Market have *much* more character.

Blacks (☎ 261 8613), the outdoor equipment chain, has a shop in the heart of the city at 81–83 Grainger St.

Getting There & Away

Newcastle is 275 miles (443km) from London (about five hours by car), 105 miles (169km) from Edinburgh (about 2½ hours), 57 miles (92km) from Carlisle, 35 miles (56km) from Alnwick and 15 miles (24km) from Durham. It's a major transport hub, so travellers have many options, including air and sea links.

Air Newcastle International Airport (☎ 286 0966) is 7 miles (11km) north of the city. It's linked by the Metro and is 20 minutes by car off the A696. There are direct scheduled services to Aberdeen, London, Cardiff, Dublin, Belfast, Oslo, Amsterdam, Paris and Brussels.

Bus There are numerous National Express connections with virtually every major city in the country. There are buses every two hours to London (£15, 5¼ hours) and Edinburgh (£7.50, 3¼ hours), and a number of buses each day from York (£12, 2¼ hours).

For local buses around the north-east, don't forget the excellent-value Explorer North East ticket, valid on most services for £5.25. Arriva (☎ 212 3000) has details on services to Berwick-upon-Tweed (No 505) and along Hadrian's Wall (No 685); see the appropriate sections in this chapter for details.

April to September, Keswick can be reached with Wright Brothers' (☎ 01434-381200) daily No 888 service.

Train Newcastle is on the main London–Edinburgh line so there are numerous trains: Edinburgh (£31.50, 1¾ hours), London's King's Cross (£74, £23 if booked seven days in advance, three hours), York (£11.30, one hour). Berwick-upon-Tweed (£10.30, 1¾ hours) and Alnmouth (£5.70, 30 minutes), for connections to Alnwick, are north on this line.

There's also the interesting, scenic Tyne Valley Line west to Carlisle. See Getting There & Around under Hadrian's Wall for details.

It's possible to leave your luggage at Central Station between 8 am and 6 pm daily. Prices range from £2 to £4 for 24 hours.

Boat See the Getting There & Away chapter for details of ferry links to Stavanger, Haugesund, Bergen and Kristiansand in Norway; IJmuiden (the Netherlands); and Gothenburg (Sweden).

Getting Around

To/From the Airport The airport is linked to town by the excellent Metro system. There are frequent services daily, and the fare is £1.70.

To/From the Ferry Terminal Bus No 327 links the ferry (at Tyne Commission Quay), Central Station and Jesmond Rd (for the youth hostel and B&Bs). It leaves the train station 2½ and 1¼ hours before each sailing; the fare is £3.

There's a taxi rank at the terminal; it costs £12 to the city centre.

Bus, Metro & Car There's a large bus network but the best means of getting around is the excellent, cheap, underground railway known as the Metro, with fares from 55p. A DaySaver ticket costs £3 or you can get a day Network Travel Ticket, covering all modes of transport in the Tyne & Wear county, for £3.50. For advice and information ring the travel line (☎ 232 5325). The TIC can supply you with route plans for the bus and Metro networks.

Driving in and around Newcastle isn't fun thanks to the web of roads and motorways, the bridges and the one-way streets in the centre – avoid peak hours. Saying that, there are plenty of car parks.

Taxi On weekend nights taxis can be hard to come by; try Noda Taxis (☎ 222 1888), which has a kiosk outside the entrance to Central Station.

Northumberland Coast

Taking its name from the Anglo-Saxon kingdom of Northumbria (north of the River Humber), Northumberland is one of the wildest and least spoilt of England's counties. There are probably more castles and battlefield sites here than anywhere else in England, testifying to the long, bloody struggle with the Scots.

After the arrival of the Normans in the 11th century, large numbers of castles and fortified buildings, or *peles*, were built. Many changed hands several times as the Scottish border was pushed back and forth for the next 700 years. Most have now lapsed into peaceful ruin, but others, such as Bamburgh and Alnwick, were converted into great houses, which can be visited today. Understandably, many have been used as backdrops for a number of films, such as the recent *Elizabeth* and Mel Gibson's *Hamlet*. The scenic Coastal Route drive is well signposted but should be re-named the Castle Route considering the amount of castles and ruins it passes.

Some of the more remote beaches can be found along this stretch of English coastline and make for great walks. Swimming, on the other hand, is a cold affair – only for the extremely warm-blooded or the insane.

GETTING AROUND

The excellent *Northumberland Public Transport Guide* is available from local TICs or from the Section Manager Public Transport (☎ 01670-533128), Northumberland County Council, County Hall, Morpeth

NE61 2EF. Transport options are good, with a train line running along the coast from Newcastle to Berwick-upon-Tweed and on to Edinburgh. The principal bus operator is Arriva (☎ 0191-212 3000) but there are many other smaller operators.

WARKWORTH
☎ 01665 • pop 1600

Warkworth is a small, quaint village beneath the formidable remains of a 14th-century castle and set in a loop of the River Cocquet. Of interest are the impressive ruins of **Warkworth Castle** (☎ 711423; EH), immortalised in Shakespeare's *Henry IV*, and the tiny **Warkworth Hermitage**, a short boat trip up river from the castle. The castle opens 10 am to 6 pm daily, April to September; to 5 pm October; and to 4 pm November to March. Admission costs £2.40/1.20. The hermitage only opens from 11 am to 5 pm Wednesday and Sunday, April to September. Admission costs £1.60/80p.

The village has a number of B&Bs, including *Bide a While* (☎ 711753, 4 Beal Croft), with rooms from £16 per person. The *Roxbro House* (☎ 711416, 5 Castle Terrace), across from the castle, charges £35 per person for comfortable rooms. More upmarket is the *Sun Hotel* (☎ 711259, fax 711833, 6 Castle Terrace), which has views of both the castle and the river and rooms starting at £49/75. *The Green House* (☎ 712322, 22 Dial Place) in the centre of the village makes great coffee and snacks.

Warkworth is served by Arriva (☎ 0191-212 3000) bus No X18 linking Newcastle, Warkworth, Alnmouth and Alnwick. There's a train station on the main east-coast line, about 1½ miles (2.5km) west of town.

ALNWICK
☎ 01665 • pop 7000

Alnwick (pronounced annick) is a charming market town that has grown up in the shadow of magnificent Alnwick Castle. The attractive old town still has a medieval feel with narrow, cobbled streets and a market square.

The castle is on the northern side of town and overlooks the River Aln. The TIC (☎ 510665, e alnwick@northumberland .gov.uk), at The Shambles, the traditional location for butchers' stalls, adjacent to the market, opens 9 am to 5 pm Monday to Saturday, and 10 am to 4 pm Sunday.

Internet access is available at Barter Books (☎ 604888), Alnwick Station, a five-minute walk north-west along the road heading towards Newcastle. It's one of the largest second-hand bookshops in Britain and is situated in a lovely Victorian railway station. It opens 9 am to 7 pm daily.

Alnwick Castle

Outwardly the castle hasn't changed much since the 14th century, but the interior has been substantially altered, most recently in the 19th century. If you enjoy castles, don't miss this one.

The six rooms open to the public – state rooms, dining room, guard chamber and library – have an incredible display of Italian paintings, including 11 Canalettos and Titian's *Ecce Homo*. There are also some fascinating curiosities, including Oliver Cromwell's camp pillow and night cap, and a hairnet used by Mary Queen of Scots that is actually made from her hair!

The castle (☎ 510777) opens 11 am to 5 pm daily, Easter to October and admission costs £6.25/3.50. For a great view back to the castle, looking up the River Aln, take the B1340 towards the coast.

Places to Stay & Eat

Aln House (☎ 602265, e alyn@alnhouse .freeserve.co.uk, South Rd, the A1 Newcastle road), near the roundabout, is an Edwardian house with rooms for £20 per person.

Bondgate Without, just outside the town's medieval gateway, has several accommodation possibilities. The small *Lindisfarne Guest House* (☎ 603430, 6 Bondgate Without) has rooms for £16 with a vegetarian breakfast option.

The original panelling, ceiling and stained-glass windows from the dining room of the *Olympic*, sister ship to the *Titanic*, have been set up in the *White Swan Hotel*

(☎ 602109, fax 510400, Bondgate Within).
Stop in for a look. Rooms at the hotel start at £30/42.

Half wine shop, half cafe, the *Wine Cellar Café Bar (☎ 605264, Bondgate Within)* is pleasant and relaxed, with a fine selection of bloomers (sandwiches) and baguettes for £2.95.

The pubs also present good options for a meal; wander around town before making a choice. *Market Tavern (☎ 602759, 7 Fenkle St)*, near the market square, is friendly and the food is good and generous; a giant beef stottie costs £4.50.

Ye Old Cross (☎ 602735, Narrowgate), a pub locally known as 'Bottles', is worth noting for the pure fact that the bottles in the front window haven't been moved for 150 years. Supposedly the owner collapsed and died while trying to move the bottles and superstition has prevented anyone from touching them since.

Getting There & Away
Alnwick has reasonable transport links since it's on the A1 between Newcastle and Edinburgh. Arriva (☎ 0191-212 3000) has a number of services linking Newcastle and Berwick-upon-Tweed. Bus No X18 has services to the attractive towns of Warkworth and Alnmouth (also stopping at the train station there, which is the nearest to Alnwick).

DUNSTANBURGH CASTLE
In its heyday, barren and windswept Dunstanburgh Castle (☎ 01665-576231) was one of the largest border castles, but not much is left of the defensive structure started in 1314. It was strengthened during the War of the Roses, after which it was left to lie in ruin. The striking ruins are built on a high rocky outcrop and only parts of the original wall and gatehouse keep are still standing. It opens 10 am to 6 pm daily, April to October; and 10 am to 4 pm Wednesday to Sunday, November to March. Admission costs £1.80/90p.

There are no roads to the castle, but it's a pleasant 30-minute walk along the coast from **Craster**, a tiny fishing village about

6 miles (10km) north-east of Alnwick and 1 mile south of the ruins. There's a TIC (☎/fax 01665-576007) by the town's car park. It opens 9.30 am to 4.30 pm daily, April to June, September and October; weekends, November to March; 9.30 am to 5 pm daily in July and August.

Craster is famous for its kippers; a great place to sample the day's catch and take in the fine sea views is the *Jolly Fisherman (☎ 01665-576218)*.

Bus No 501/401 runs from Alnwick to Belford via Craster. A pay-and-display car park is the only place in Craster where it's possible to park your car.

FARNE ISLANDS
Owned and managed by the National Trust (NT), the Farne Islands lie 3 to 4 miles (5km to 6km) offshore from Seahouses. Despite being basically bare rock, they provide a home for 18 species of nesting sea birds, including puffins, kittiwakes, Arctic terns, eider ducks, cormorants and gulls. There are also colonies of grey seals. There are few places in the world where you can get so close to nesting sea birds. It's an extraordinary experience.

St Cuthbert, of Lindisfarne fame, died on the islands in 687, and there's a tiny chapel to him on Inner Farne, where it's possible to land. The best time to go is in the breeding season (roughly May to July), when you can see chicks being fed by their parents.

Crossings can be rough – and may not be possible at all in bad weather. Tours take between two and three hours; inexplicably, they use open boats with no proper cabin, so make sure you've got warm, waterproof clothing if there's a chance of rain.

There are various tours and tour operators. There's really nothing to separate the operators, but it's definitely worth landing on one of the islands – preferably Inner Farne. Tours start at 10 am April to September. A three-hour tour around the islands and a landing on Inner Farne costs £7/5; there's an additional £4/2 fee payable to the NT (if you're not a member) for landing. The TIC (☎ 01655-721099), close to the pier, can provide more information.

NORTH-EASTERN ENGLAND

Tickets are available from booths beside the pier in Seahouses, a couple of miles along the coast from Bamburgh. Operators include Billy Shiel (☎ 01665-720308) and Hanvey & Sons (☎ 01665-720388). There's a TIC (☎ 01655-720884, fax 721436) in the Seafield Rd car park near the harbour. It opens 10 am to 4 pm daily, April and October; and 10 am to 6 pm daily, May to September.

There isn't much to Seahouses but if you need a place to stay the *Olde Ship Hotel* (☎ *01665-720200,* e *theoldeship@ seahouses.co.uk, Main St)* covers all you need: fine food, good ale and comfortable rooms starting at £33.

BAMBURGH
☎ 01668 • pop 440
Bamburgh is an unspoilt hamlet just inland from miles of magnificent sandy beaches, and dominated by the romantic profile of a stunning castle.

Bamburgh Castle
This fortress, impressive-looking by day but even more so by night, sits on a basalt crag rising from the sea and dominates the coast for miles. The site has been occupied since prehistoric times, but the current castle is largely a 19th-century construction, the passion of the first Lord Armstrong, and is still the home of the Armstrong family. The castle (☎ 214515) opens 11 am to 5 pm daily, April to October. Admission costs £4/1.50.

Places to Stay
Bradford Cairns Caravan Park (☎ *214366)* has grass pitches and all mod cons, including showers and laundrette. The price of a pitch varies from £7 to £8 according to the season. The caravan park is north of Bamburgh on the B1341 towards Lucker.

Greengates (☎ *214535, 34 Front St)* is open year round and offers B&B for £19.

Getting There & Away
Arriva (☎ 0191-212 3000) bus No 501 runs from Alnwick to Berwick-upon-Tweed via Seahouses and Bamburgh; there are services every one to two hours, Monday to Saturday. Bus No 401 from Alnwick stops in Seahouses and Bamburgh.

HOLY ISLAND (LINDISFARNE)
The most exciting part of Holy Island (or Lindisfarne as it was once known) is the drive from the mainland over a causeway that crosses 3 miles (5km) of fascinating muddy flats. And there's always a chance of getting caught midway by the incoming tide, an occurrence that happens all too frequently despite the warnings. Even in the off-season, the windswept, 2-mile-square island is full of tourists, but seems to have few facilities for them.

St Aidan founded a monastery here in 635, and it became a major centre of Christianity and learning. The exquisitely illustrated *Lindisfarne Gospels*, which originated here, can be seen in the British Library in London. St Cuthbert lived on Lindisfarne for a while, but even he didn't like it and went to the Farne Islands after a couple of years.

Lindisfarne Priory (☎ 01289-389200; EH) consists of the remains of the priory's church and the later 13th-century St Mary the Virgin Church. The museum next to these shows the remains of the first monastery and how monks used to live. It opens 10 am to 6 pm daily from April to September; to 5 pm in October; and 4 pm from November to March. Admission costs £2.80/1.40.

Lindisfarne Castle (☎ 01289-389244; NT) was built in 1550, and restored and converted by Sir Edward Lutyens in 1903. Note that it is half a mile from the village, and there's no toilet. It always opens from noon to 3 pm (but this may be extended depending on the tide) daily, April to October; £4.

It's possible to stay on the island, but try to book. Probably the best bet is *The Ship* (☎ *01289-389311, fax 389316, Marygate),* with three comfortable rooms staring at £22 per person and serving up good local seafood in the bar. *Britannia House* (☎ *01289-389218, near the town green),* a traditional B&B, has rooms from £20 per person.

Holy Island can be reached by bus No 477 from Berwick-upon-Tweed and is 14 miles (23km) from Berwick-upon-Tweed train station. People taking cars across are requested to park just outside the village and to walk into town; it costs £2 per day for the privilege. The sea covers the causeway and cuts the island off from the mainland for about five hours each day. Tide times are printed in local papers and at each side of the crossing.

BERWICK-UPON-TWEED
☎ 01289 • pop 13,000

The stone-built town of Berwick, the northernmost town in England, has a dramatic site flanking the estuary of the River Tweed. The river, often graced with flotillas of swans, is crossed by a low stone bridge (built in 1634), the soaring arches of the railway bridge (1850) and a concrete span for road traffic (1928).

From the 12th to the 15th centuries, Berwick changed hands between the Scots and the English no less than 13 times. This merry-go-round ceased prior to the construction of massive Elizabethan ramparts that still enclose the town centre – although, reflecting geographical realities, the football team still plays in the Scottish League!

Berwick is a great place to explore on foot. There are several small museums, but there's nothing, apart from the walls, that has to be seen.

Orientation

The fortified town of Berwick proper is on the northern side of the Tweed; the three bridges link with the suburbs of Tweedmouth, Spittal and Eastcliffe. The town centre is compact and easy to walk around, but some B&Bs are quite far-flung.

Information

The TIC (☎ 330733, fax 330448, ℮ tourism @berwick-upon-tweed.gov.uk), 106 Marygate, opens 10 am to 7 pm daily, July to September; to 6 pm Easter to June; and to 4 pm Monday to Saturday, the rest of the year.

The main post office at 77 Castlegate opens 9 am to 5.30 pm Monday to Friday and 9 am to 12.30 pm Saturday. Internet access is available at Business Link (☎ 331 084), Anderson Court, off Hide Hill, which opens 8.30 am to 5 pm Monday to Friday.

The Walls

Berwick has had two sets of walls: little remains of the first, which were built during the reign of Edward II; the current ones were begun in 1558 and are still intact. They represented the most advanced military technology of the day and were

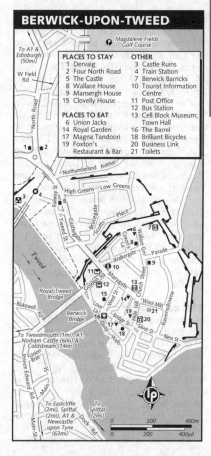

BERWICK-UPON-TWEED

PLACES TO STAY
1 Dervaig
2 Four North Road
5 The Castle
8 Wallace House
9 Mansergh House
15 Clovelly House

PLACES TO EAT
6 Union Jacks
14 Royal Garden
17 Magna Tandoori
19 Foxton's Restaurant & Bar

OTHER
3 Castle Ruins
4 Train Station
7 Berwick Barracks
10 Tourist Information Centre
11 Post Office
12 Bus Station
13 Cell Block Museum; Town Hall
16 The Barrel
18 Brilliant Bicycles
20 Business Link
21 Toilets

designed both to house the increasingly effective artillery (in arrow-head-shaped bastions) and to withstand it (the walls are low and massively thick, but it's still a long way to fall).

It's possible to walk virtually the entire length of the walls, and this is a must for visitors. There are some wonderful views and the entire circuit takes about 1½ hours on foot. The TIC has a brochure describing the main sights. There are recommended guided tours, at 11.15 am Monday to Saturday, and 2.30 pm Sunday, Easter to October. A tour is £2.50/free.

Other Things to See & Do

The original jail cells in the upper floor of the town hall have been preserved to house the **Cell Block Museum** (☎ 330900), devoted to crime and punishment. Tours are at 10.30 am and 2 pm Monday to Friday, Easter to October; and cost £1.50/50p.

The oldest purpose-built barracks in Britain have been turned into an eclectic collection of museums under the name of **Berwick Barracks** (☎ 304493; EH), The Parade. There's a couple of regular military museums, By the Beat of Drum and the Regiment Museum, covering the life and times of soldiers in the border country, and the Borough Museum and Art Gallery, displaying a wide range of art pieces from Venetian glassware to Japanese imari pottery. The Barracks open 10 am to 6 pm daily, April to September; to 4 pm in October; and 10 am to 4 pm Wednesday to Sunday, November to March. Admission costs £2.60/2.

Places to Stay

If you have no luck finding accommodation around the centre of town, there are plenty of cheap B&Bs south of the river in Tweedmouth, Spittal and Eastcliffe; fortunately there are frequent buses. Bus No B1 runs from the main bus station on Golden Square (Bridge St) across the bridge to Tweedmouth, before turning off and heading to Spittal. The TIC provides an accommodation booking service.

There are several good accommodation choices north of the centre of Berwick on North Rd. *Dervaig* (☎ 307378, e dervaig@ btinternet.com, 1 North Rd)* is two minutes from the train station and has two double rooms with bathroom from £20 per person. The friendly, nonsmoking *Four North Road* (☎ 306146, e sandra@thorntonfour .freeserve.co.uk), surprisingly at 4 North Rd, has clean rooms from £16 per person, including large breakfasts.

It's preferable to stay in the centre of town, but it can be hard to find a room. *Mansergh House* (☎/fax 302297, 86 Church St) is clean and comfortable with rooms from £18 per person. Similarly priced is the adequate *Wallace House* (☎/fax 306539, 1 Wallace Green).

Clovelly House (☎/fax302052, e vivroc @clovelly53.freeserve.co.uk, 58 West St)* has to be one of the best B&Bs in town with great breakfasts and comfy, warm rooms from £17.50 per person.

If a pub stay is preferable, *The Castle* (☎/fax 307900, 103 Castlegate) is good value at £20 per person.

Places to Eat

Union Jacks (☎ 306673, 3 Wallace Green) has a large variety of meals, some with a military name, for around £5.50; the dish called Officers Messroom is chicken in breadcrumbs.

Magna Tandoori (☎ 302736, 39 Bridge St) is probably the best Indian restaurant in town; most mains cost £5.50 to £10, and are good quality. For Chinese, head to *Royal Garden* (☎ 303939, 35 Marygate), with a filling three-course lunch for £4.90.

Foxton's Restaurant & Bar (☎ 303939, 26 Hide Hill) is a great place for both a drink and a meal. The Mediterranean veggie quiche for £5.20 is a good choice. For real ale you can't go past *The Barrel* (☎ 308013, 56 Bridge St), a welcoming place with occasional live music.

Getting There & Away

Berwick is quite a transport hub; it's on the main east-coast railway line and road, and also has good links into the Scottish Borders.

Bus Arriva (☎ 0191-212 3000) has several services linking Newcastle and Berwick (No 505). Bus No 501 runs to Alnwick via Seahouses and Bamburgh.

Berwick is a good starting point to explore the Scottish Borders. There are buses to Edinburgh, around the coast via Dunbar and west to Coldstream, Kelso and Galashiels. For information on buses in the Scottish Borders phone ☎ 01835-824000.

Train Berwick is on the main east-coast London–Edinburgh line, and there are numerous trains south to Newcastle (£10.30) and north to Edinburgh (£12 day return).

Getting Around
Taxi Try Blue Star (☎ 305660).

Bicycle Brilliant Bicycles (☎ 331476, ⓔ comments@brilliantbicycles.co.uk), 17 Bridge St, hires out mountain bikes for £15 a day.

AROUND BERWICK-UPON-TWEED
Norham Castle
Six and a half miles (10km) south-west of Berwick on a minor road off the A698 are the ruins of Norham Castle (☎ 01289-382329) occupying a picturesque spot overlooking the River Tweed. It was originally built by the prince bishops of Durham in 1160 to guard a crossing on the river. The castle opens 10 am to 6 pm daily, April to September; and to 4 pm in October. Admission costs £1.80/90p.

Arriva (☎ 0191-212 3000) bus No 23 regularly passes Norham Castle from Berwick train station on its way to Kelso in Scotland.

Etal
The pretty little village of Etal sits at the northern end of a 6000-hectare working rural estate, 12 miles (19km) south of Berwick-upon-Tweed on the B6354.

Etal Castle (☎ 01890-820332; EH), a 14th-century construction on the banks of the River Till, has yet more displays and information on the Border Wars that once

ravaged the surrounding area. It opens from 10 am to 6 pm daily, April to September; to 5 pm October. Admission costs £2.60/1.30.

The black and white *Black Bull* (☎ *01890-820200*) is unique to the area; it's the only thatched pub in Northumberland. Its serves great pub food and pours a variety of well-kept ales. For a lighter bite to eat the *Village Post Office* (☎ *01890-820220*) doubles as a tearoom and plans to open as a B&B in the near future.

Ford
One and a half miles (2.5km) south-east of Etal, Ford is another picturesque village located on the rural estate. There's not a lot to see but the Lady Waterford Hall (☎ 01890-820524) is well worth a stop. In 1860 Louisa Anne, marchioness of Waterford, commissioned the building of the hall to serve as a school for the village. For the next 21 years she decorated the walls with beautiful murals depicting stories from the Bible, using local people, flora and fauna as models. The hall opens 10.30 am to 5.30 pm daily, April to October; other times by appointment. Admission costs £1.50/50p. Unfortunately the proud 14th-century Ford Castle is not open to the public.

There are a couple of peaceful B&Bs in the village. *The Old Post Office* (☎ *01890-820286, 2 Old Post Office Cottages*), farther into the village from Lady Waterford Hall, which even has shoe cleaning and sewing kits, charges £20 per person. Situated in the castle grounds near Waterford Hall, *The Estate House* (☎ *01890-820668*, ⓔ *theestatehouse@supanet.com*) offers great hospitality, a guest living room and a plethora of local information. Rooms start at £23 per person without bathroom.

Heatherslaw
Halfway between Ford and Etal can be found the Heatherslaw Corn Mill and the Heatherslaw Light Railway. The restored 19th-century mill (☎ 01890-820338), on the banks of the River Till, is still in working order and locally grown wheat is used to produce delicious cakes and bread. It opens 10 am to 6 pm daily, April to September;

and to 5 pm in October. At other times, it only opens Monday and when milling. The Light Railway (☎ 01890-820244), which chugs from the mill to Etal Castle, is more for kids. The 3½-mile (5.5km) return journey follows the river through pretty countryside and costs £3.70/2.20. There's an hourly service 10.30 am to 3.30 pm daily, April to October; and to 4.30 pm mid-July and August.

Crookham

One and a half miles (2.5km) west of Crookham on a minor road off the A697 is the site of the **Battle of Flodden**, where the English defeated the Scots in 1513. Crookham itself is 3 miles (5km) west of Ford. A monument 'to the brave of both nations' on top of a hill overlooking the battlefield is the only memorial to the thousands used as arrow fodder. An information board next to the monument gives a brief account of how the English outflanked the Scots.

The Coach House (☎ 01890-820293), also in Crookham, serves exceptionally good food and also provides a place to stay with rooms from £23 to £39 per night.

Hadrian's Wall

Hadrian's Wall was the most monumental attempt in the island's history to divide the north from the south. It cuts 73 miles (118km) across the narrow neck of the country, from Solway Firth in the west, virtually to the mouth of the Tyne in the east, through beautiful, varied countryside. It is a World Heritage Site, and although mainly foundations survive, the ruins and their beautiful locations are extraordinarily evocative.

The wall was the greatest single engineering project undertaken by the Roman Empire – it involved moving two million cubic yards of soil and took over six years (from 122) to build.

The section from Newcastle to the River Irthing was built of stone, and turf blocks were used on the section to Solway – roughly 10 feet (3m) thick and 15 feet (4.5m) high. A 10-foot-deep, 30-foot-wide

ditch and mound were excavated immediately in front (except where there were natural defences). Every Roman mile (1620 yards) there was a gateway guarded by a small fort (milecastle) and between each milecastle were two observation turrets. Milecastles are numbered right across the country, starting with Milecastle 0 at Wallsend and ending with Milecastle 80 at Bowness-on-Solway. The intermediate turrets are tagged A and B, so Milecastle 37 (quite a good one) will be followed by Turret 37A, Turret 37B and then Milecastle 38. A second ditch (the vallum) and a military road were built between 200 and 500 feet (60m and 150m) to the south.

A series of forts were developed as bases some distance south (and may actually predate the wall), and 16 actually lay astride it. The prime remaining forts on the wall are Cilurnum (Chesters), Vercovicium (Housesteads) and Banna (Birdoswald). The best forts behind the wall are Corstopitum, at Corbridge, and Vindolanda, north of Bardon Mill.

Today it's possible to visit a number of picturesque surviving sections of the wall, milecastles, forts and turrets, and some excellent museums. Several attractive small towns make good touring bases.

HISTORY

By building the wall, Emperor Hadrian intended simultaneously to establish control over a clearly delineated frontier and reduce the demand on manpower. He came to Britain in 122 to see it started, and the actual building was undertaken by Roman legions. The wall was primarily a means of controlling the movement of people across the frontier – it could easily have been breached by a determined attack at any single point – and of preventing low-level border raiding.

No one knows when the troops finally abandoned their posts; it's most likely that around AD 400 Britain was set adrift as the Roman Empire fragmented. When pay stopped arriving the soldiers remaining on the wall would simply have left for greener pastures.

ORIENTATION
Hadrian's Wall crosses beautiful, varied country. Starting in the lowlands of the Solway coast, it crosses the lush hills east of Carlisle to the ridge of basalt rock known as Whin Sill (which is bleak and windy, still) overlooking Northumberland National Park, and ends in the urban sprawl of Newcastle. The most spectacular section is between Brampton and Corbridge.

Carlisle, in the west, and Newcastle, in the east, are good starting points, but Brampton, Haltwhistle, Hexham and Corbridge all make good bases.

The B6318 basically follows the course of the wall from the outskirts of Newcastle to Birdoswald; from Birdoswald to Carlisle it pays to have a detailed map. The main A69 road and the railway line follow 3 or 4 miles (6km) to the south.

INFORMATION
Carlisle and Newcastle TICs are good places to start gathering information, but there are also TICs in Hexham and Haltwhistle (open year round), and in Corbridge and Brampton (open seasonally). The extremely helpful Northumberland National Park Visitor Centre (☎ 01434-344396) off the B6318 at Once Brewed, opens 9.30 am to 5 pm daily, March to October.

See the Activities chapter for information on walking Hadrian's Wall. If you're planning to cycle along Hadrian's Wall, TICs sell the *Hadrian's Wall Country Cycle Map*.

PLACES TO STAY & EAT
For nearby options see the Newcastle-upon-Tyne section earlier in this chapter, and the Carlisle section in the Cumbria chapter. Brampton and Corbridge are the most attractive small towns close to the wall, but Haltwhistle is also convenient and bustling Hexham is another good possibility. All have a plentiful supply of B&Bs. There are also a few well-placed lodgings along the wall itself and three usefully located youth hostels (book ahead in the summer): Greenhead, Once Brewed and Acomb.

GETTING THERE & AROUND
Bus
West of Hexham the wall runs parallel to the A69, between Carlisle and Newcastle. Bus No 685, operated jointly by Arriva (☎ 0191-212 3000) and Stagecoach Cumberland (☎ 01946-63222), runs between those cities on the A69 hourly. It passes relatively near the youth hostels and 2 to 3 miles (5km) south of the main sites.

Late May to September the special hail-and-ride Hadrian's Wall bus (No 682) runs between Hexham and Carlisle via Haltwhistle train station, connecting with trains. It follows the B6318, which runs close to the wall, calling at the main sites, the Northumberland National Park Visitor Centre and the youth hostel at Once Brewed. This puts the youth hostels at Acomb and Greenhead within easy reach. A Day Rover ticket costs £5/3 and is half-price to holders of Explorer North East bus tickets or Stagecoach Cumberland Explorer tickets. It's also possible to purchase a Rover ticket that allows you two days travel in a three-day period. On-board guides are provided for no extra charge four times daily at the weekend, May to September (see the Information section of Carlisle in the Cumbria chapter for more details). For further information contact Hexham TIC (☎ 01434-605225), or pick up a timetable at any of the Hadrian's Wall TICs.

Train
The railway line between Newcastle and Carlisle (Tyne Valley Line) has stations at Corbridge, Hexham, Haydon Bridge, Bardon Mill, Haltwhistle and Brampton. This service runs daily, but not all trains stop at all stations.

Taxi
Sproul's (☎ 01434-321064) and Turnbull's (☎ 01434-320105) in Haltwhistle charge around £15 to Hexham.

CORBRIDGE
☎ 01434 • pop 3500
Quaint and picturesque Corbridge is one of the more attractive towns near the wall. It's

on the banks of a beautiful stretch of the River Tyne, 17 miles (27km) west of Newcastle, and has attractive stone houses (some very old) lining tree-shaded cobbled streets. It has an ancient history beginning with the Romans. An Anglo-Saxon monastery followed and the town thrived despite being burned three times in border clashes.

St Andrew's Church, mostly rebuilt in the 13th century but with some Anglo-Saxon features, also has a fascinating 14th-century pele tower (a fortified vicarage) in its grounds. The TIC (☎ 632815), Hill St, opens 10 am to 1 pm and 2 to 6 pm, Monday to Saturday; and 1 to 5 pm on Sunday, April to October.

Corbridge Roman Site & Museum

Corbridge (or Corstopitum to the Romans) was a garrison town. There were a succession of forts and supply depots, and a surrounding civil settlement. It lies south of the wall on what was the main road from York to Scotland.

The site (☎ 632349; EH) is half a mile west of Corbridge off Trinity Terrace (just over a mile from Corbridge train station). It opens 10 am to 6 pm daily, April to September; to 5 pm daily October; and 10 am to 1 pm and 2 to 4 pm Wednesday to Sunday, November to March. Admission costs £2.80/1.40.

Places to Stay

There are several attractive places to stay, most of which serve bar meals.

The 17th-century *Angel Inn* (☎ 632119, *Main St)* has comfortable rooms with bathroom for £42 per person.

Opposite the Angel Inn is the *Riverside Guest House* (☎ 632942, fax 633883, *e riverside@ukonline.co.uk, Main St)*, a traditional B&B with rooms starting at £22 per person.

Town Barns (☎ 633345), off Trinity Terrace, offers a single, a double and a family room for £24 per person. *Holmlea* (☎ 632 486, Station Rd), near the station, is a terraced house with a comfortable double and family room from £20 per person.

Places to Eat

The pubs are probably your best bet for food. The *Angel Inn* (see Places to Stay earlier) serves good and quite adventurous food for a pub. The *Golden Lion* (☎ 632 216, Hill St) is cheaper with filling meals for under £4.

For something other than pub grub you could try *Corbridge Tandoori* (☎ 633676, 8 Market Place), on the central square, where mains cost £5.75 to £14.95.

Above the railway station *The Valley Restaurant* (☎ 633434, Station Rd) supplies a unique service as well as delicious Indian food. A group of 10 or more diners from Newcastle can catch the train to Corbridge accompanied by a waiter, who will supply snacks and phone ahead to have the meal ready when the trains arrives. Talk about takeaway service!

Getting There & Away

Bus No 685 between Newcastle and Carlisle comes through Corbridge, as does bus No 602 from Newcastle's Eldon Square to Hexham. The town is also on the Newcastle–Carlisle railway line.

HEXHAM
☎ 01434 • pop 11,300

Hexham is quite an interesting town, with a couple of attractive cobble-stoned alleyways and eye-catching stone buildings around the centre, but it's rather marred by being a busy shopping mecca.

The TIC (☎ 605225, e zu89@dial.pipex .com), in Safeway's car park north-east of the town centre, opens 9 am to 6 pm Monday to Saturday, and 10 am to 5 pm Sunday, Easter to September; and 9 am to 5 pm daily, the rest of the year.

Hexham Abbey (☎ 602031), surrounded by a park, is considered a fine example of Early English architecture. The crypt survives from St Wilfrid's Church, which was built in 674, and inscribed stones from Corstopitum can be seen in its walls. At night it looks quite stunning. Opening hours are 9 am to 7 pm daily, May to September; and 9 am to 5 pm daily, October to April.

The Old Gaol (☎ 652349), completed in

1333 as England's first purpose-built prison, is the setting for the **Border History Museum**. The history of the Border Reivers (see the boxed text 'The Border Reivers' in the Cumbria chapter) is retold along with the punishments handed out in the prison. The museum opens 10 am to 4.30 pm daily, April to October; and Monday, Tuesday and Saturday, February, March and November. Admission costs £2/1.

Hexham's size means it's the best place near the wall for accommodation and places to eat. The TIC can book accommodation for you.

West Close House (☎ *603307, Hextol Terrace*), off Allendale Rd (the B6305), is great value and has a range of comfortable rooms from £18 per person. To the west of the town centre near the police station, the eclectically cluttered *Burncrest Guest House* (☎/fax *605163, Burnland Terrace*) has comfortable rooms starting at £20 per person. It's also nonsmoking. The *Beaumont Hotel* (☎ *602331, fax 606184,* e *beaumont.hotel@btinternet.com, Beaumont St*) occupies a good spot overlooking the abbey and offers high-quality accommodation from £45 per person.

There are several bakeries on Fore St and, if you turn left into the quaintly named Priestpopple near the bus station, you'll find some decent restaurants.

One of the cheaper and more popular options is *Restaurant Fortini* (☎ *603350, 36–38 Priestpopple*), with pizza and pasta for around £5 to £6. Next door, the *Coach & Horses* (☎ *600492*) is a pleasant pub with a beer garden and decent bar meals. Across the road, *Diwan-E-Am Tandoori* (☎ *606575, 23 Priestpopple*) serves all the traditional Indian dishes in an upmarket setting.

Bus No 685 between Newcastle and Carlisle comes through Hexham, and the town is also on the Newcastle–Carlisle railway line.

HEXHAM TO HALTWHISTLE
Chesters Roman Fort & Museum

Chesters (☎ 01434-681379; EH) is even more extensive and well preserved than Housesteads, but although the surroundings are attractive, they're not as dramatic as the latter's. The remains are of a Roman cavalry fort and include part of a bridge across the River North Tyne (very complex and beautifully constructed), an extraordinary bath-house and a well-preserved underfloor heating system. The museum has an extensive collection of Roman sculpture and stone inscriptions. They open 10 am to 6 pm daily, April to September; to 5 pm in October; and to 4 pm November to March. Admission costs £2.80/2.10.

Brunton Water Mill (☎ *01434-681002,* e *pesarra@bruntonmill.freeserve.co.uk, Chollerford*) is just a stone's throw from Chollerford bridge and B&B costs from £20 per person. At the much pricier but pleasant *George Hotel* (☎ *01434-681611*), beside the bridge, B&B costs from £85.

The Chesters fort site has an excellent small cafe, *Lucullus Larder*, and the George Hotel has a reputable restaurant.

Chesters is half a mile west of Chollerford on the B6318 and 5½ miles (9km) from Hexham and is on the No 682 bus route.

Housesteads Roman Fort & Museum

Perched high on a ridge overlooking the moors of Northumberland National Park, Housesteads (☎ 01434-344363; EH) is one of the best known, best preserved and most dramatic of the sites on the wall. The fort covers five acres, and the remains of many buildings, including granaries, barracks, latrines and a hospital, can be seen. This is the starting point for some excellent walks and the one to Steel Rigg is considered the most spectacular section of the entire wall.

Housesteads is 2½ miles (4km) north of Bardon Mill on the B6318, and about 3 miles (5km) from Once Brewed. It's popular, so try to visit outside summer weekends. Opening times are the same as the Chesters Roman Fort & Museum and admission costs £2.80/2.10.

Vindolanda Roman Fort & Museum

Vindolanda (☎ 01434-344277), 1½ miles (2.5km) north of Bardon Mill between the

NORTH-EASTERN ENGLAND

Hadrian's Wall Circular Walk

Starting at Once Brewed National Park Centre, this walk takes in the most complete stretch of Hadrian's Wall. The walk is 7½ miles (12km) and takes approximately 4½ hours. The wall follows the natural barrier created by crags (steep cliffs) and the views north are quite stunning. Some parts of the wall are so well preserved that they have featured in films. You'll recognise Milecastle 39, which outshone Kevin Costner in one scene of the film *Robin Hood – Prince of Thieves*. The trail returns to the youth hostel across rolling farmland. The centre has a good map.

A69 and B6318 and a mile from Once Brewed, is an extensively excavated fort (excavations are still continuing) with accompanying civil buildings. There are reconstructions of the stone wall with a turret, a length of turf wall and a timber milecastle gate. The museum has some extraordinary relics, including a leather shoe and a fragment of a letter on a wooden writing tablet that talks of socks and underclothes being sent to a soldier on the wall. Nothing has changed: in this climate you can never have too many.

It's managed by the Vindolanda Trust and opens 10 am daily from mid-February to mid-November but closes at different times during the year: 4 pm in February and November, 5 pm in March and October, 6 pm in May and June and 6.30 pm in July and August. Admission costs £3.80/2.80 or £5.60/4.10 with a joint ticket for the Roman Army Museum (see Haltwhistle to Brampton later).

Hostels

Once Brewed Youth Hostel (☎ 01434-344360, e oncebrewed@yha.org.uk, Military Rd, Bardon Mill) is a modern and well-equipped hostel central for visiting both Housesteads Fort (3 miles/5km) and Vindolanda (1 mile). Bus No 685 (which you can catch at Hexham or Haltwhistle train stations) will drop you at Henshaw,

2 miles (3km) south, or you could leave the train at Bardon Mill 2½ miles (4km) south-east. Hadrian's Wall bus drops you at the door late May to September. It opens daily, late March to October; Monday to Saturday, February and March; and Friday and Saturday only in November. Beds cost £10.85/7.40.

Acomb Youth Hostel (☎ 01434-602864, Main St) is on the edge of Acomb village about 2½ miles (4km) north of Hexham and 2 miles (3km) south of the wall. Hexham can be reached by bus or train. It opens Friday and Saturday, January to March; Wednesday to Sunday, April, May, September and October; Tuesday to Sunday, June; and daily, mid-July to August. A bed costs £6.65/4.65.

Set in 18 acres of countryside, **Hadrian's Wall Backpackers** (☎ 01434-688688, North Rd, Haydon Bridge) is just north of the A69, and is accessible by bus or train. Dorm beds cost £8, or £12.50 with breakfast. It opens daily April to October.

HALTWHISTLE
☎ 01434 • pop 3750

Haltwhistle, just north of the A69, is a small market town that straggles some distance along Main St. It's a pleasant-enough place, but doesn't have quite the charm of either Brampton or Corbridge.

The TIC (☎ 322002), in the train station, opens 10 am to 1 pm and 2 to 6 pm Monday to Saturday, and 1 to 5 pm Sunday, Easter to October; and 10 am to 12.30 pm and 1 to 3.30pm Thursday to Tuesday, the rest of the year.

Ashcroft (☎/fax 320213, Lanty's Lonnen) is an attractive B&B with rooms from £22.50 to £30 per person. **Manor House Hotel** (☎ 322588, Main St) is central, very friendly and has good pub food; B&B starts at £16.50 per person and goes up to £25 per person.

Bus No 685 between Newcastle and Carlisle comes through Haltwhistle, as does Hadrian's Wall bus No 682. Bus No 681 heads south to Alston. The town is also handily located on the Newcastle–Carlisle railway line.

HALTWHISTLE TO BRAMPTON
Roman Army Museum
One mile north-west of Greenhead near Walltown, this museum (☎ 016977-47485) has models and reconstructions featuring the Roman army and the troops that garrisoned the wall. Children will especially enjoy it.

The museum has the same opening hours as the Vindolanda Roman Fort & Museum (see the earlier Hexham to Haltwhistle section). Admission costs £3/2.10, or £5.60/4.10 if you have a joint ticket also valid for Vindolanda.

Birdoswald Roman Fort
Birdoswald (☎ 016977-47602; EH) is one of the most interesting of the ruins along the wall, with a well-preserved fort on an escarpment overlooking the beautiful Irthing Gorge. The Willowford Bridge abutment, across the river, is well worth seeing. There's also a good stretch of wall and the exhibition centre features displays on how life must have been for the Roman soldiers and local people.

The fort is on a minor road off the B6318 about 3 miles (5km) west of Greenhead. It opens 10 am to 5.30 pm daily from late March to November. Admission costs £2.50/1.50.

Lanercost Priory
Three miles (5km) north-east of Brampton are the peaceful ruins of Lanercost Priory (☎ 016977-3030; EH), originally founded in 1166 by Augustinian canons. Most of it lies in decay but the Early English nave is now used as the local priory church. It opens 10 am to 6 pm daily, April to September; and 10 am to 5 pm October. Admission costs £2/1. Hadrian's Wall bus can drop you at the gate.

Places to Stay
The cheapest accommodation around is very close to Banks East Turret (4 miles east of Brampton, 2 miles west of Birdoswald) at *Bankshead Camping Barn* (☎ 01200-420102, e campbarnsyha@ enterprise.net). It's basic but adequate, with shower and cooking facilities provided and a dry space for 10 people to sleep. A night will only put you back £3.60 and Hadrian's Wall bus drops you outside.

Greenhead and nearby Gilsland have pubs and B&Bs. *Greenhead Youth Hostel* (☎ 016977-47401) is in a converted Methodist chapel 3 miles (5km) west of Haltwhistle train station. It's also served by bus No 685 (see Getting There & Around under Hadrian's Wall earlier). It opens Monday to Saturday, April to June; daily July and August; Friday to Monday, September to October. Beds cost £8.10/5.65.

For your own bedroom in a lovely old farmhouse, try the *Holmhead Guest House* (☎ 016977-47402, e holmhead@hadrians wall.freeserve.co.uk), up behind the youth hostel. Rooms start at £26 per person.

BRAMPTON
☎ 016977 • pop 5000
Brampton is a charming market town built in red Cumbrian sandstone and surrounded by beautiful countryside. The town is particularly interesting on market day (Wednesday). It makes a great base for exploring Hadrian's Wall, and it's on the Cumbrian Cycle Way (see the Activities chapter).

The TIC (☎ 3433) opens from 10 am to 5 pm, Monday to Saturday, from Easter to October.

Cobblelane Cottage (☎ 3676, e kate@ footlights.demon.co.uk, Church Lane), behind St Mary's Church, is lovely and charges £25 per person, but only opens May to October.

The 17th-century *White Lion Hotel* (☎ 2338, High Cross St) is one of several pubs serving good bar meals from around £5; gammon steak here costs £5.95. It also has comfortable rooms with bathroom from £17.50 to £31.50 per person. The *Capon Tree Cafe* (☎ 3649, 27 Front St) is small and cosy and serves a good selection of snacks.

Bus No 685 between Newcastle and Carlisle comes through Brampton, and the town is also on the Newcastle–Carlisle railway line.

Northumberland National Park

Northumberland National Park covers 398 square miles of some of the emptiest country in the British Isles. The landscape is characterised by windswept grassy hills cut by streams, and is almost empty of human habitation.

After the Romans left, the region remained a contested zone between Scotland and England, and home to warring clans and families. Few buildings constructed prior to the 18th century survive, partly because few were built. The cattle-farming families lived in simple structures of turf that could be built quickly and cheaply, and be equally quickly abandoned. Peace came in the 18th century, but coincided with new farming practices so the tenant farmers were dispossessed, leaving large estates. Unlike the rest of England, this area has no scattering of villages, few stone walls and few small farms. Scenically, it has a bleak grandeur, with wide horizons and vast skies.

ORIENTATION & INFORMATION

The park runs from Hadrian's Wall in the south, takes in the Simonside Hills in the east and runs into the Cheviot Hills along the Scottish border. There are few roads.

For further information, contact the Information Officer (☎ 01434-605555), Eastburn, South Park, Hexham, Northumberland NE46 1BS.

There are several visitor centres: Ingram (☎ 01665-578248) for the Cheviots, opens daily, April to September and weekends, October; Rothbury (see the Rothbury section later); and Once Brewed (see Information under Hadrian's Wall earlier) for the Hadrian's Wall area. There's also a centre (☎ 01434-344525), in partnership with the NT, at Housesteads on Hadrian's Wall (see Housesteads Roman Fort & Museum earlier); it opens daily, April to October and weekends, November to March. All handle accommodation bookings.

WALKING & CYCLING

Walkers are attracted to the **Pennine Way**, which enters the park at its south-eastern corner on Hadrian's Wall, continues to Bellingham, crosses The Cheviot (814m high), and leaves the park near Kirk Yetholm. This is a demanding walk and should be undertaken only if you're properly equipped to deal with tough conditions.

In preparation for opening in 2002 is the 81-mile (130km) **Hadrian's Wall Path** from Bowness-on-Solway in Cumbria to Wallsend in Newcastle, which will pass through the south of the park.

Though at times strenuous, cycling in the park is a pleasure; the roads are good and the traffic is light. There's off-road cycling in Border Forest Park.

PLACES TO STAY

There's plenty of accommodation in the south around Hadrian's Wall, but the possibilities farther north are extremely limited. There are a few B&Bs in Bellingham and Otterburn, and hostels in Bellingham and Byrness (on the Pennine Way). **Byrness Youth Hostel** (☎ 01830-520425) opens daily, April to September. Beds cost £7.35/5.15.

GETTING THERE & AROUND

Public transport options are limited, aside from buses on the A69. Bus No 808 operates two to three times a day Monday to Saturday between Otterburn and Newcastle. Postbus No 815, operated by the Royal Mail (☎ 01325-38112, Darlington), runs twice daily weekdays between Hexham and Bellingham; bus No 880 runs more frequently.

National Express has two services a day between Newcastle and Edinburgh via Otterburn, Byrness, Jedburgh, Melrose and Galashiels. See the earlier Hadrian's Wall section for access to the south.

BELLINGHAM
☎ 01434 • pop 900

There is not much in Bellingham but it's surrounded by beautiful countryside, particularly south towards Hadrian's Wall, and

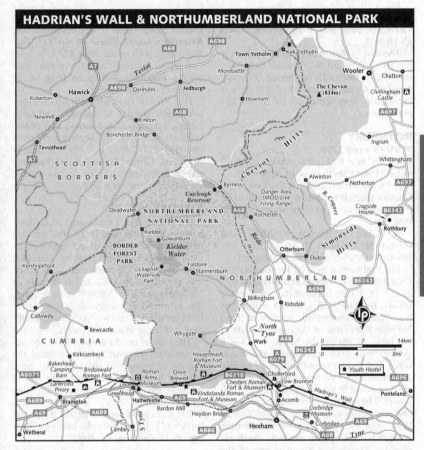

HADRIAN'S WALL & NORTHUMBERLAND NATIONAL PARK

makes a good base for day trips in the national park.

The TIC (☎ 220616), Main St, opens from 10 am to 1 pm and 2 to 6 pm, Monday to Saturday, and 1 to 5 pm Sunday, Easter to October; and 2 to 5 pm Monday to Friday, November to March.

The 12th-century **St Cuthbert's Church** is unique to the area because it still retains its original stone roof. During the time of the Reivers and Border Wars most buildings in the area were destroyed, mainly by fire. St Cuthbert's survived due to its nonflammable roof, and became a place of refuge for the local population. **Cuddy's Well**, close by, is supposedly consecrated by St Cuthbert and alleged to have healing powers. The **Hareshaw Linn Walk** is a pleasant way to spend two hours, leading to a 9m-high waterfall 2½ miles (4km) north of Bellingham (*linn* is an Old English name for waterfall).

Bellingham is on the Pennine Way so it's advisable to book ahead for accommodation in summer.

Bellingham Youth Hostel (☎/fax 220 313, Woodburn Rd) is fairly spartan but cosy and opens from Monday to Saturday mid-April to June, September and October; and daily, July and August. A bed costs £8.10/5.65.

The lovely *Westfield House* (☎ 220340) has five rooms, all with private bathroom, which cost from £25 per person. Friendly *Lyndale Guest House* (☎ 220361) is a home away from home with B&B from £20 per person.

ROTHBURY
☎ 01669 • pop 1700

Rothbury is a traditional market town 12 miles (19km) south-west of Alnwick situated on the River Coquet at the foot of the Cheviot Hills. It's a quaint place centred on the parallel Front and High Sts and Market Place.

A TIC and visitor centre (☎ 620887) is on Church St; it's open 10 am to 5 pm late March to October (to 6 pm in summer).

The real reason to head for Rothbury is **Cragside House, Garden and Estate** (☎ 620 333; NT), 1 mile north of the town on the B6341. Built by the first Lord Armstrong as his Victorian countryside retreat, he hired Norman Shaw, one of the top architects of the time, to design the house. In 1878 a system was developed using man-made lakes and underground piping to supply the house with hydroelectricity, making it the first house in the world to be lit by such power. The restored hydroelectric machinery can be viewed on the Power Circuit Walk. The Victorian mansion and gardens are quite stunning and are well worth exploring. Around the house is one of the world's largest rock gardens and a 19th-century clock tower, still chiming out the passing hours. There's also a visitor centre, restaurant and shop in the grounds.

Cragside House opens 1 to 5.30 pm daily, except Monday, April to October, while the estate and gardens open 10.30 am to 7 pm. Admission to all three costs £6.50/3.25, for just the estate and gardens £4/2. There is no public transport to the front gates from Rothbury; try Rothbury Motors (☎ 620516) for a taxi.

High St is a good place to look for accommodation. *Alexander House* (☎ 621 463) offers B&B from £19 per person. Farther along High St is the comfortable *Katerina's Guest House* (☎ 602334, Sun Buildings), with rooms from £23.

A few of the pubs do meals, or you could try the *Rothbury Bakery* on High St for fresh pies and sandwiches.

Bus No 416 from Morpeth leaves every two hours Monday to Saturday and three times on Sunday. On Sundays and public holidays late May to September Arriva (☎ 0191-212 3000) bus No 508 leaves Newcastle Central Station at 10.30 am and arrives in Rothbury at noon, before making the return journey at 4.35 pm.

KIELDER WATER

Eight miles (13km) north-west of Bellingham on the C200 road is the southern end of Kielder Water, one of the largest manmade lakes in northern Europe. The lake, built to supply the north-east with water, was completed in 1982 and is capable of holding a massive 200,000 million litres. The surrounding countryside is some of the most remote and sparsely populated in England and home to Kielder Forest.

The lack of good transport links and accommodation seems to have stunted the growth of tourism in the area, plus from May to September there are millions of midges (small flying insects that bite); bring good repellent.

But it is a good place to get off the beaten track and enjoy some of the best local hospitality England has to offer.

Information
The Tower Knowe Visitor Centre (☎ 01434-240398), near the southern end of the lake, has plenty of information on the area. There's a cafe on site and a small exhibition on the history of the valley and lake. Admission is £1/free. It opens 10 am to 5 pm daily, Easter to May and August to October; to 6 pm daily, May to August and to 4 pm daily, November to Easter.

Things to See & Do
A few miles farther north along the lake is the **Leaplish Waterside Park** (☎ 01434-

250312) where most of the water activities on the lake take place. This purpose-built complex has a number of accommodation possibilities (see Places to Stay & Eat later), a restaurant and coffee shop, fishing, cycle hire and even a heated indoor swimming pool. Also at the park is the **Kielder Bird of Prey Centre** (01434-250400), with a good collection of owls; the birds are flown twice a day in summer. It opens 10.30 am to 5 pm daily. Admission costs £3/2.

For a closer look at the lake, the **Osprey ferry** (☎ 01434-240398) cruises between Leaplish and Tower Knowe four times a day April to October, with evening cruises Sunday, July and August. A round trip costs £4.20/2.50.

At the northern end of the lake, another 6 miles (10km) on from Leaplish and 3 miles (5km) from the Scottish border, is the sleepy village of **Kielder**. The only attraction, **Kielder Castle** (☎ 01434-250209), was actually built in 1775 as a hunting lodge by the Duke of Northumberland and now houses an information and exhibition centre run by the Forest Enterprise. The castle opens 10 am to 5 pm daily, March to October; to 6 pm August; and 11 am to 4 pm weekends, November to December. Admission is free.

If you're planning on a bit of walking or cycling in the area it's a good idea to pick up the helpful *Cycling at Kielder* and *Walking at Kielder* leaflets from Tower Knowe Visitor Centre (£2 each). They give you a good idea of the trails in and around the forest and, more importantly, how long it's going to take and how draining they are.

Places to Stay & Eat

Accommodation is pretty limited so call ahead to make sure something is available.

Leaplish Campsite (☎ 01434-250312) at the waterside park charges £8 for a two-person tent and £1 for showers.

Kielder Camping and Caravan Site (☎ 01434-250291), about two minutes' walk north of Kielder village on the edge of the forest, is only open late March to late September and charges from £6.80 for a tent pitch.

For budget accommodation head for *The Reiver's Rest* (☎ 01434-250312) at Leaplish; it has adequate facilities for £11 per person in dorm rooms. Separate rooms are also available.

One of the best B&Bs in England has to be *Mrs JA Scott* (☎ 01434-250254). Situated on the eastern side of the lake at Gowanburn, the only road leading to the B&B is from Kielder and the only public transport available is the school bus or postbus, which seldom run. Its remoteness is one of the bonuses of staying here, with the lake basically on the doorstep and walks leading off from the house in all directions. More of a home away from home, the welcome is warm and the breakfast's fantastic. It opens Easter to October and charges £17 per person – ring ahead to check availability. Some people have been coming here for over 20 years!

Braefoot (☎ 01434-240238), above the local store in Falstone, is very relaxed and hospitable; single rooms without bathroom cost £20 per person and doubles with bathroom £45.

The *Falstone Tea Room* (☎ 240459, *Old School House, Falstone*) has filling all-day breakfasts for £3.50.

Getting There & Around

Snaiths Travel (☎ 01830-520609) operates a limited bus service No 814 from Otterburn to Kielder Village calling at Bellingham, Stannersburn, Falstone, Tower Knowe Information Centre and Leaplish. Postbus No 815 runs between Hexham (calling at the railway station) and Kielder on a similar route along the lake and makes a detour to Gowanburn and Deadwater in the morning. Neither service operates on Sunday. On Sunday from late May to September and Wednesday in late July and August Arriva (☎ 0191-212 3000) bus No 714 makes the journey from Newcastle to Kielder in the morning and returns late in the afternoon giving you about five hours in Kielder.

For the energetic out there, Kielder Bikes (☎ 01434-250392), opposite Kielder Castle, Kielder Village, rents out bikes for £14 per day and opens 10 am to 6 pm year round,

Humbleton Hill Circular Walk

A popular walk from Wooler bus station takes in **Humbleton Hill**. It's the site of an Iron Age hillfort and the views from the hill of the wild Cheviot Hills to the south and plains to the north are far-reaching.

The hill is the site of yet another battle between the Scots and the English, this time in 1402. The battle has been immortalised in Shakespeare's *Henry IV* and the *Ballad of Chevy Chase* (not the actor!).

The trail is 4 miles (6km), well signposted and returns to Wooler. It takes approximately two hours.

closing Friday off-peak. Another office can be found at Hawkhope Centre on the northern side of Kielder Dam but it only opens 10 am to 5 pm weekends, Easter to October.

WOOLER & AROUND

Wooler, on the A697, is a small town on the edge of the Northumberland National Park 20 miles (32km) north of Rothbury and the same distance south of Berwick. There's nothing really to attract you to the town itself, unless you're mad on grey-stone buildings, but it does make a great base for walks into the remote Cheviot Hills. Wooler is also the midway point for the 65-mile (105km) St Cuthbert's Way running from the picturesque Scottish town of Melrose to Holy Island on the coast.

The TIC (☎ 01668-282123), on Market Place, is a good source of information for walks in the hills and can book accommodation. It opens 10 am to 4 pm Monday to Saturday and to 2 pm Sunday, April to October.

The Cheviot (814m), 6 miles (10km) south-east and the highest in the group of hills, is barren and wild; it takes around four hours to reach the top from Wooler. Check with the TIC for information before setting out.

A more sedate walk takes in Humbleton Hill (see the boxed text 'Humbleton Hill Circular Walk' above).

Highburn House (☎ *01668-281344, fax 281839*), a camp site just north of the town on Burnhouse Rd, has tent sites from £7 per night. The *Wooler Youth Hostel* (☎ *01668-281365, fax 282368, 30 Cheviot St*) is a medium-sized hostel with all the normal amenities. A night's stay costs £9/6.20. The High St has a couple of good B&Bs, in particular *Southgate* (☎ *01668-282004, 20 High St*), with rooms from £16 per person. Most of the pubs also offer accommodation.

The food options are not overwhelming but you could do worse than the filling bar meals at the *Black Bull* (☎ *281309, 2 High St*) pub. For a lunchtime bite to eat, the *delicatessen* opposite the Black Bull has delectable sandwiches and pies.

Wooler has good bus connections to the major towns in Northumberland. Arriva (☎ 0191-212 3000) operates buses from Berwick (No 464) and Alnwick (Bus No 470/473) on a regular basis, which stop behind High St.

Cycle hire is available at Haugh Head Garage (☎ 01668-281316) in Haugh Head, 1 mile south of Wooler on the A697.

Chillingham Castle

Six miles (10km) south-east of Wooler is Chillingham Castle (☎ 01668-215359). The castle, first built in 1150, was fully fortified in the 14th century and has remained in the Grey family since 1245. It's possible to visit a number of stately rooms, dungeons and a torture chamber and the castle houses a museum displaying an eclectic collection of odds and ends from all over the world. Sir Jeffrey Wyatville, landscaper for Windsor Castle, designed the gardens and grounds.

The castle opens noon to 5 pm daily July and August; Wednesday to Monday, May, June and September; and Easter weekend. Admission is £4.50/free.

In the 13th century the borderlands were so wild and unruly that, to protect the wild cattle that were the source of food and hunting for the castle, 365 acres of land were enclosed by a high fence to keep out intruders. Thus, the **Chillingham Wild Cattle**

(☎ 01668-215250) were cut off from mixing with other breeds and today are the only cattle in the world to have remained pure. A maximum number of 60 make up the total population of these wild white cattle, the last of the herds that once grazed Britain. The park opens 10 am to noon and 2 to 5 pm Wednesday to Sunday (afternoons only on Sunday), April to October. Admission costs £3/1.

It's possible to stay at the medieval fortress in the seven apartments designed for guests, where the likes of Henry III and Edward I once stayed. Prices vary depending on the luxury of the apartment; the Grey Apartment is the most expensive at £46 per person in the high season, while the Guard Room, separated from the castle, costs £35 per person. Free entry and a personal tour of the castle are thrown in with the price of accommodation. All of the apartments are self-catering.

Arriva (☎ 0191-212 3000) bus No 470 running between Alnwick and Wooler stops at Chillingham four to five times a day Monday to Saturday.

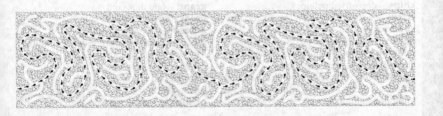

Glossary

agister – someone paid to care for stock
aka – also known as
almshouse – accommodation offered to the aged or needy
AONB – Area of Outstanding Natural Beauty

BABA – Book-A-Bed-Ahead scheme
bailey – outermost wall of a castle
bairn – baby (Newcastle-upon-Tyne)
banger – old, cheap car
bangers – sausages
bap – bun
bar – gate (York)
bent – not altogether legal
bevvied – drunk
bevvy – a drink
bevvying – drinking
billion – a million million
bitter – a type of beer
black pudding – a type of sausage made from dried blood and other ingredients
blatherskite – boastful or talkative person (northern England)
bloke – man
bloody (adj) – damn
bodge job – poor-quality repairs
bridleway – path that can be used by walkers, horse riders and cyclists
Brummie – a native of Birmingham
BTA – British Tourist Authority
bus – local bus; *see also* coach
BYO – bring your own

caff – cheap cafe
canny – good, great (Newcastle-upon-Tyne)
cheers – a drinking toast; thanks
chemist – pharmacist
chine – valley-like fissure leading to the sea
chips – deep-fried potatoes
circus – a junction of several streets, usually circular
coach – long-distance bus; *see also* bus
coaching inn – inn along a coaching route at which horses were changed
coasteering – steering your way around the coastline by climbing, jumping, swimming or scrambling

Corbett – mountain of between 762m and 914m
couchette – sleeping berth in a train or ferry
courts – courtyards
crack – good conversation (originally from Ireland)
crannogh – artificial island settlement
crisps – potato chips
croft – plot of land with adjoining house worked by the occupiers

dear – expensive
DIY – do-it-yourself
dolmen – chartered tomb
dosh – money
dough – money
downs – rolling upland, characterised by a lack of trees
duvet – continental quilt

EH – English Heritage
EU – European Union
evensong – daily evening service (Church of England)

fag – cigarette; a boring task
fagged – exhausted
fanny – female genitals
fen – drained or marshy low-lying flat land
fiver – £5 note
flat – apartment
flip-flops – thongs
fussock – irritating woman (Yorkshire)

gaffer – boss or foreman
gate – street (York)
ginnel – alleyway (Yorkshire)
gobslutch – slovenly person (northern England)
grand – one thousand
greasy spoon – cheap cafe
gutted – very disappointed
guv, guv'nor – governor, term of address for owner or boss, can be used ironically

hammered – drunk
hire – rent
hosepipe – garden hose

hotel – accommodation with food and bar, not always open to passing trade
Huguenots – French Protestants

inn – pub with accommodation

jumper – sweater

kyle – narrow strait

lager lout – drunken hooligan
lass – young woman (northern England)
ley – clearing
lock – part of a canal or river that can be closed off and the water levels changed to raise or lower boats
lolly – money; a sweet on a stick (possibly frozen)
lorry – truck
love – term of address, not necessarily to someone likeable

machair – grass- and wildflower-covered sand dunes
manky – low quality (southern England)
Martello tower – small, circular tower formerly used for coastal defence
mate – a friend; term of address
midge – a mosquito-like insect
motte – mound on which a castle was built

naff – inferior; in poor taste
NT – National Trust

oast house – building containing a kiln for drying hops
off-licence (offie) – shop selling alcoholic drinks
OS – Ordnance Survey
owlers – smugglers

pee – pence
pele – fortified houses
pissed – drunk
pissed off – angry
pitch – playing field
ponce – ostentatious or effeminate male
pop – fizzy drink
postbuses – minibuses that follow postal delivery routes in rural areas
punter – customer

pub – short for public house, an establishment with a bar, usually serving food, rarely with accommodation

queue – a line of people waiting for something
quid – pound

ramble – to go for a short walk
reiver – warrior (northern England)
return ticket – a ticket for a journey to a destination and back again
roll-up – roll-your-own cigarette
rood – alternative word for cross
RSPB – Royal Society for the Protection of Birds
rubber – eraser; condom
rugger – rugby

sacked – fired
sarnie – sandwich
shag – have sex with
shout – (to buy) a round of drinks, as in 'It's my shout'
shut – partially covered passage
single ticket – one-way ticket
snicket – alleyway (York)
snogging – kissing and cuddling
spondulicks – money
SSSI – Site of Special Scientific Interest
steaming – drunk
stone – unit of mass equal to 14lb or 6.35kg
subway – underpass
sweets – confectionery

ta – thanks
thwaite – clearing in a forest
TIC – Tourist Information Centre
ton – one hundred
tor – Celtic word describing a hill shaped like a triangular wedge of cheese
torch – flashlight
towpath – a path running beside a river or canal
trainers – tennis shoes/sneakers/runners
traveller – nomadic hippy
tron – public weighbridge
twitchers – birdwatchers
twitten – passage, small lane
tube – London's underground railway

Underground – *see* tube

VAT – value-added tax, levied on most goods and services, currently 17.5%
verderer – officer upholding law and order in the royal forests

way – a long-distance trail
wellied – drunk

wellies – Wellington boots, rubber boots
wide boy – ostentatious go-getter, usually on the make
wold – open, rolling country

yob – hooligan

ziggurat – a kind of rectangular temple tower or tiered mound

Glossary of Religious Architecture

abbey
A monastery of monks or nuns or the buildings they used. When Henry VIII dissolved the monasteries between 1536 and 1540, many English and Irish abbeys were destroyed or converted into private homes, though some survived as churches. Thus an abbey today may be a church or a home.

aisle
Passageway or open space along either side of the church's nave and/or down the centre

alignment
Even if this doesn't conform with geography, churches are always assumed to be aligned east–west, with the altar, chancel and choir towards the eastern end and the nave towards the western end.

ambulatory
Processional aisle at the eastern end of a cathedral, behind the altar

apse
Semicircular or rectangular area for clergy, at eastern end of church in traditional design

baptistry
Separate area of a church used for baptisms

barrel vault
Semicircular arched roof

boss
Covering for the meeting point of the ribs in a vaulted roof (often colourfully decorated, so bring binoculars)

brass
Type of memorial common in medieval churches consisting of a brass plate set into the floor or a tomb, usually with a depiction of the deceased but sometimes simply with text

buttress
Vertical support for a wall; *see* Flying Buttress

campanile
Free-standing belfry or bell tower; Chester and Westminster Cathedrals have modern ones.

chancel
Eastern end of the church, usually reserved for choir and clergy. The name comes from the Latin word for lattice because of the screen that once separated the two parts of the church.

chantry
Chapel established by a donor for use in his or her name after death

chapel
Small, more private shrine or area of worship off the main body of the church. In a number of English cathedrals, chapels were established by different crafts guilds.

chapel of ease
Chapel built for those who lived too far away from the parish church

chapterhouse
Building in a cathedral close where the dean meets with the chapter, the clergy who run the cathedral

chevet
Chapels radiating out in a semicircular sweep, common in France but also found at Westminster and Canterbury

choir
Area in the church where the choir is seated, usually to the east of the transepts and nave; sometimes used interchangeably with chancel or presbytery

clerestory
Also clearstory; wall of windows above the triforium

cloister
Covered walkway linking the church with adjacent monastic buildings

close
Buildings grouped around a cathedral, also known as the precincts

collegiate
Church with a chapter of canons and prebendaries, but not a cathedral

corbel
Stone or wooden projection from a wall supporting a beam or arch

crossing
Intersection of the nave and transepts

flying buttress
Supporting buttress in the form of one side of an open arch

font
Basin used for baptisms, usually towards the western end of the building, often in a separate baptistry

frater
Common room or dining area in a medieval monastery

lady chapel
Chapel, usually at the eastern end of a cathedral, dedicated to the Virgin Mary

lancet
Pointed window in Early English style

minster
A church connected to a monastery

misericord
Hinged choir seat with a bracket (often elaborately carved) that can be leant against

nave
Main body of the church at the western end, where the congregation gather

piscina
Basin in which priests wash their hands.

presbytery
Eastern area of the chancel beyond the choir, where the clergy operate

priory
Religious house governed by a prior, inferior to an abbey

pulpit
Raised box where priest gives sermon

quire
Medieval term for choir

refectory
Monastic dining room

reredos
Literally 'behind the back'; backdrop to an altar

rood screen
A screen carrying a rood or crucifix that separates the nave from the chancel

squint
Angled opening in a wall or pillar to allow a view of the altar

transepts
North–south projections from the nave, often added at a later date and giving the whole church a cruciform cross-shaped plan. Some medieval English cathedrals (eg Canterbury, Lincoln and Salisbury) feature smaller second transepts.

triforium
Internal wall passage above the arcade and below the clerestory; behind it is the 'blind' space above the side aisle

undercroft
Vaulted underground room or cellar

vault
Roof with arched ribs, usually in a decorative pattern

vestry
Robing room, where the parson's clerical robes are kept and put on

LONELY PLANET

You already know that Lonely Planet produces more than this one guidebook, but you might not be aware of the other products we have on this region. Here is a selection of titles that you may want to check out as well:

Britain
ISBN 1 86450 147 2
US$27.99 • UK£15.99

Cycling Britain
ISBN 1 86450 037 9
US$19.99 • UK£12.99

Walking in Britain
ISBN 1 86450 280 0
US$21.99 • UK£13.99

British Phrasebook
ISBN 0 86442 484 1
US$5.95 • UK£3.99

London
ISBN 0 86442 793 X
US$15.95 • UK£9.99

London Condensed
ISBN 1 86450 043 3
US$9.95 • UK£5.99

Out to Eat London
ISBN 1 86450 083 2
US$14.99 • UK£7.99

London City Map
ISBN 1 86450 008 5
US$5.95 • UK£3.99

Wales
ISBN 1 86450 126 X
US$15.99 • UK£9.99

Scotland
ISBN 0 86442 592 9
US$15.95 • UK£9.99

Europe on a shoestring
ISBN 1 86450 150 2
US$24.99 • UK£14.99

Western Europe
ISBN 1 86450 163 4
US$27.99 • UK£15.99

Available wherever books are sold

LONELY PLANET

ON THE ROAD

Travel Guides explore cities, regions and countries, and supply information on transport, restaurants and accommodation, covering all budgets. They come with reliable, easy-to-use maps, practical advice, cultural and historical facts and a rundown on attractions both on and off the beaten track. There are over 200 titles in this classic series, covering nearly every country in the world.

 Lonely Planet Upgrades extend the shelf life of existing travel guides by detailing any changes that may affect travel in a region since a book has been published. Upgrades can be downloaded for free from **www.lonelyplanet.com/upgrades**

For travellers with more time than money, **Shoestring** guides offer dependable, first-hand information with hundreds of detailed maps, plus insider tips for stretching money as far as possible. Covering entire continents in most cases, the six-volume shoestring guides are known around the world as 'backpackers bibles'.

For the discerning short-term visitor, **Condensed** guides highlight the best a destination has to offer in a full-colour, pocket-sized format designed for quick access. They include everything from top sights and walking tours to opinionated reviews of where to eat, stay, shop and have fun.

CitySync lets travellers use their Palm™ or Visor™ hand-held computers to guide them through a city with handy tips on transport, history, cultural life, major sights, and shopping and entertainment options. It can also quickly search and sort hundreds of reviews of hotels, restaurants and attractions, and pinpoint their location on scrollable street maps. CitySync can be downloaded from **www.citysync.com**

MAPS & ATLASES

Lonely Planet's **City Maps** feature downtown and metropolitan maps, as well as transit routes and walking tours. The maps come complete with an index of streets, a listing of sights and a plastic coat for extra durability.

Road Atlases are an essential navigation tool for serious travellers. Cross-referenced with the guidebooks, they also feature distance and climate charts and a complete site index.

LONELY PLANET

ESSENTIALS

Read This First books help new travellers to hit the road with confidence. These invaluable predeparture guides give step-by-step advice on preparing for a trip, budgeting, arranging a visa, planning an itinerary and staying safe while still getting off the beaten track.

Healthy Travel pocket guides offer a regional rundown on disease hot spots and practical advice on predeparture health measures, staying well on the road and what to do in emergencies. The guides come with a user-friendly design and helpful diagrams and tables.

Lonely Planet's **Phrasebooks** cover the essential words and phrases travellers need when they're strangers in a strange land. They come in a pocket-sized format with colour tabs for quick reference, extensive vocabulary lists, easy-to-follow pronunciation keys and two-way dictionaries.

Miffed by blurry photos of the Taj Mahal? Tired of the classic 'top of the head cut off' shot? **Travel Photography: A Guide to Taking Better Pictures** will help you turn ordinary holiday snaps into striking images and give you the know-how to capture every scene, from frenetic festivals to peaceful beach sunrises.

Lonely Planet's **Travel Journal** is a lightweight but sturdy travel diary for jotting down all those on-the-road observations and significant travel moments. It comes with a handy time-zone wheel, a world map and useful travel information.

Lonely Planet's eKno is an all-in-one communication service developed especially for travellers. It offers low-cost international calls and free email and voicemail so that you can keep in touch while on the road. Check it out on **www.ekno.lonelyplanet.com**

FOOD & RESTAURANT GUIDES

Lonely Planet's **Out to Eat** guides recommend the brightest and best places to eat and drink in top international cities. These gourmet companions are arranged by neighbourhood, packed with dependable maps, garnished with scene-setting photos and served with quirky features.

For people who live to eat, drink and travel, **World Food** guides explore the culinary culture of each country. Entertaining and adventurous, each guide is packed with detail on staples and specialities, regional cuisine and local markets, as well as sumptuous recipes, comprehensive culinary dictionaries and lavish photos good enough to eat.

LONELY PLANET

OUTDOOR GUIDES

For those who believe the best way to see the world is on foot, Lonely Planet's **Walking Guides** detail everything from family strolls to difficult treks, with 'when to go and how to do it' advice supplemented by reliable maps and essential travel information.

Cycling Guides map a destination's best bike tours, long and short, in day-by-day detail. They contain all the information a cyclist needs, including advice on bike maintenance, places to eat and stay, innovative maps with detailed cues to the rides, and elevation charts.

The **Watching Wildlife** series is perfect for travellers who want authoritative information but don't want to tote a heavy field guide. Packed with advice on where, when and how to view a region's wildlife, each title features photos of over 300 species and contains engaging comments on the local flora and fauna.

With underwater colour photos throughout, **Pisces Books** explore the world's best diving and snorkelling areas. Each book contains listings of diving services and dive resorts, detailed information on depth, visibility and difficulty of dives, and a roundup of the marine life you're likely to see through your mask.

LONELY PLANET

OFF THE ROAD

Journeys, the travel literature series written by renowned travel authors, capture the spirit of a place or illuminate a culture with a journalist's attention to detail and a novelist's flair for words. These are tales to soak up while you're actually on the road or dip into as an at-home armchair indulgence.

The range of lavishly illustrated **Pictorial** books is just the ticket for both travellers and dreamers. Off-beat tales and vivid photographs bring the adventure of travel to your doorstep long before the journey begins and long after it is over.

Lonely Planet **Videos** encourage the same independent, tough-minded approach as the guidebooks. Currently airing throughout the world, this award-winning series features innovative footage and an original soundtrack.

Yes, we know, work is tough, so do a little bit of deskside dreaming with the spiral-bound Lonely Planet **Diary** or a Lonely Planet **Wall Calendar**, filled with great photos from around the world.

TRAVELLERS NETWORK

Lonely Planet Online. Lonely Planet's award-winning Web site has insider information on hundreds of destinations, from Amsterdam to Zimbabwe, complete with interactive maps and relevant links. The site also offers the latest travel news, recent reports from travellers on the road, guidebook upgrades, a travel links site, an online book-buying option and a lively traveller's bulletin board. It can be viewed at **www.lonelyplanet.com** or AOL keyword: lp.

Planet Talk is a quarterly print newsletter, full of gossip, advice, anecdotes and author articles. It provides an antidote to the being-at-home blues and lets you plan and dream for the next trip. Contact the nearest Lonely Planet office for your free copy.

Comet, the free Lonely Planet newsletter, comes via email once a month. It's loaded with travel news, advice, dispatches from authors, travel competitions and letters from readers. To subscribe, click on the Comet subscription link on the front page of the Web site.

LONELY PLANET

Guides by Region

L onely Planet is known worldwide for publishing practical, reliable and no-nonsense travel information in our guides and on our Web site. The Lonely Planet list covers just about every accessible part of the world. Currently there are 16 series: Travel guides, Shoestring guides, Condensed guides, Phrasebooks, Read This First, Healthy Travel, Walking guides, Cycling guides, Watching Wildlife guides, Pisces Diving & Snorkeling guides, City Maps, Road Atlases, Out to Eat, World Food, Journeys travel literature and Pictorials.

AFRICA Africa on a shoestring • Cairo • Cairo City Map • Cape Town • Cape Town City Map • East Africa • Egypt • Egyptian Arabic phrasebook • Ethiopia, Eritrea & Djibouti • Ethiopian Amharic phrasebook • The Gambia & Senegal • Healthy Travel Africa • Kenya • Malawi • Morocco • Moroccan Arabic phrasebook • Mozambique • Read This First: Africa • South Africa, Lesotho & Swaziland • Southern Africa • Southern Africa Road Atlas • Swahili phrasebook • Tanzania, Zanzibar & Pemba • Trekking in East Africa • Tunisia • Watching Wildlife East Africa • Watching Wildlife Southern Africa • West Africa • World Food Morocco • Zimbabwe, Botswana & Namibia
Travel Literature: Mali Blues: Traveling to an African Beat • The Rainbird: A Central African Journey • Songs to an African Sunset: A Zimbabwean Story

AUSTRALIA & THE PACIFIC Auckland • Australia • Australian phrasebook • Australia Road Atlas • Cycling Australia • Cycling New Zealand • Fiji • Fijian phrasebook • Healthy Travel Australia, NZ & the Pacific • Islands of Australia's Great Barrier Reef • Melbourne • Melbourne City Map • Micronesia • New Caledonia • New South Wales • New Zealand • Northern Territory • Outback Australia • Out to Eat – Melbourne • Out to Eat – Sydney • Papua New Guinea • Pidgin phrasebook • Queensland • Rarotonga & the Cook Islands • Samoa • Solomon Islands • South Australia • South Pacific • South Pacific phrasebook • Sydney • Sydney City Map • Sydney Condensed • Tahiti & French Polynesia • Tasmania • Tonga • Tramping in New Zealand • Vanuatu • Victoria • Walking in Australia • Watching Wildlife Australia • Western Australia
Travel Literature: Islands in the Clouds: Travels in the Highlands of New Guinea • Kiwi Tracks: A New Zealand Journey • Sean & David's Long Drive

CENTRAL AMERICA & THE CARIBBEAN Bahamas, Turks & Caicos • Baja California • Belize, Guatemala & Yucatán • Bermuda • Central America on a shoestring • Costa Rica • Costa Rica Spanish phrasebook • Cuba • Dominican Republic & Haiti • Eastern Caribbean • Guatemala • Havana • Healthy Travel Central & South America • Jamaica • Mexico • Mexico City • Panama • Puerto Rico • Read This First: Central & South America • World Food Mexico • Yucatán
Travel Literature: Green Dreams: Travels in Central America

EUROPE Amsterdam • Amsterdam City Map • Amsterdam Condensed • Andalucía • Austria • Baltic States phrasebook • Barcelona • Barcelona City Map • Belgium & Luxembourg • Berlin • Berlin City Map • Britain • British phrasebook • Brussels, Bruges & Antwerp • Brussels City Map • Budapest • Budapest City Map • Canary Islands • Central Europe • Central Europe phrasebook • Copenhagen • Corfu & the Ionians • Corsica • Crete • Crete Condensed • Croatia • Cycling Britain • Cycling France • Cyprus • Czech & Slovak Republics • Denmark • Dublin • Dublin City Map • Eastern Europe • Eastern Europe phrasebook • Edinburgh • England • Estonia, Latvia & Lithuania • Europe on a shoestring • Europe phrasebook • Finland • Florence • France • Frankfurt Condensed • French phrasebook • Georgia, Armenia & Azerbaijan • Germany • German phrasebook • Greece • Greek Islands • Greek phrasebook • Hungary • Iceland, Greenland & the Faroe Islands • Ireland • Italian phrasebook • Italy • Krakow • Lisbon • The Loire • London • London City Map • London Condensed • Madrid • Malta • Mediterranean Europe • Mediterranean Europe phrasebook • Moscow • Munich • Netherlands • Normandy • Norway • Out to Eat – London • Out to Eat – Paris • Paris • Paris City Map • Paris Condensed • Poland • Polish phrasebook • Portugal • Portuguese phrasebook • Prague • Prague City Map • Provence & the Côte d'Azur • Read This First: Europe • Rhodes & the Dodecanese • Romania & Moldova • Rome • Rome City Map • Russia, Ukraine & Belarus • Russian phrasebook • Scandinavian & Baltic Europe • Scandinavian phrasebook • Scotland • Sicily • Slovenia • South-West France • Spain • Spanish phrasebook • St Petersburg • St Petersburg City Map • Sweden • Switzerland • Tuscany • Ukrainian phrasebook • Venice • Vienna • Walking in Britain • Walking in France • Walking in Ireland • Walking in Italy • Walking in Spain • Walking in Switzerland • Western Europe • World Food France • World Food Ireland • World Food Italy • World Food Spain
Travel Literature: After Yugoslavia • Love and War in the Apennines • The Olive Grove: Travels in Greece • On the Shores of the Mediterranean • Round Ireland in Low Gear • A Small Place in Italy

LONELY PLANET

Mail Order

Lonely Planet products are distributed worldwide. They are also available by mail order from Lonely Planet, so if you have difficulty finding a title please write to us. North and South American residents should write to 150 Linden St, Oakland, CA 94607, USA; European and African residents should write to 10a Spring Place, London NW5 3BH, UK; and residents of other countries to Locked Bag 1, Footscray, Victoria 3011, Australia.

INDIAN SUBCONTINENT & THE INDIAN OCEAN Bangladesh • Bengali phrasebook • Bhutan • Delhi • Goa • Healthy Travel Asia & India • Hindi & Urdu phrasebook • India • Indian Himalaya • Karakoram Highway • Kerala • Madagascar • Maldives • Mauritius, Réunion & Seychelles • Mumbai (Bombay) • Nepal • Nepali phrasebook • Pakistan • Rajasthan • Read This First: Asia & India • South India • Sri Lanka • Sri Lanka phrasebook • Tibet • Tibetan phrasebook • Trekking in the Indian Himalaya • Trekking in the Karakoram & Hindukush • Trekking in the Nepal Himalaya
Travel Literature: The Age of Kali: Indian Travels and Encounters • Hello Goodnight: A Life of Goa • In Rajasthan • Maverick in Madagascar • A Season in Heaven: True Tales from the Road to Kathmandu • Shopping for Buddhas • A Short Walk in the Hindu Kush • Slowly Down the Ganges

MIDDLE EAST & CENTRAL ASIA Bahrain, Kuwait & Qatar • Central Asia • Central Asia phrasebook • Dubai • Farsi (Persian) phrasebook • Hebrew phrasebook • Iran • Israel & the Palestinian Territories • Istanbul • Istanbul City Map • Istanbul to Cairo • Istanbul to Kathmandu • Jerusalem • Jerusalem City Map • Jordan • Lebanon • Middle East • Oman & the United Arab Emirates • Syria • Turkey • Turkish phrasebook • World Food Turkey • Yemen
Travel Literature: Black on Black: Iran Revisited • The Gates of Damascus • Kingdom of the Film Stars: Journey into Jordan

NORTH AMERICA Alaska • Boston • Boston City Map • Boston Condensed • British Columbia • California & Nevada • California Condensed • Canada • Chicago • Chicago City Map • Florida • Great Lakes • Hawaii • Hiking in Alaska • Hiking in the USA • Las Vegas • Los Angeles • Los Angeles City Map • Louisiana & the Deep South • Miami • Miami City Map • Montreal • New England • New Orleans • New York City • New York City City Map • New York City Condensed • New York, New Jersey & Pennsylvania • Oahu • Out to Eat – San Francisco • Pacific Northwest • Rocky Mountains • San Francisco • San Francisco City Map • Seattle • Southwest • Texas • Toronto • USA • USA phrasebook • Vancouver • Virginia & the Capital Region • Washington, DC • Washington, DC City Map • World Food New Orleans
Travel Literature: Caught Inside: A Surfer's Year on the California Coast • Drive Thru America

NORTH-EAST ASIA Beijing • Beijing City Map • Cantonese phrasebook • China • Hiking in Japan • Hong Kong • Hong Kong City Map • Hong Kong Condensed • Hong Kong, Macau & Guangzhou • Japan • Japanese phrasebook • Korea • Korean phrasebook • Kyoto • Mandarin phrasebook • Mongolia • Mongolian phrasebook • Seoul • Shanghai • South-West China • Taiwan • Tokyo • World Food Hong Kong
Travel Literature: In Xanadu: A Quest • Lost Japan

SOUTH AMERICA Argentina, Uruguay & Paraguay • Bolivia • Brazil • Brazilian phrasebook • Buenos Aires • Chile & Easter Island • Colombia • Ecuador & the Galapagos Islands • Healthy Travel Central & South America • Latin American Spanish phrasebook • Peru • Quechua phrasebook • Read This First: Central & South America • Rio de Janeiro • Rio de Janeiro City Map • Santiago de Chile • South America on a shoestring • Trekking in the Patagonian Andes • Venezuela
Travel Literature: Full Circle: A South American Journey

SOUTH-EAST ASIA Bali & Lombok • Bangkok • Bangkok City Map • Burmese phrasebook • Cambodia • Hanoi • Healthy Travel Asia & India • Hill Tribes phrasebook • Ho Chi Minh City • Indonesia • Indonesian phrasebook • Indonesia's Eastern Islands • Java • Lao phrasebook • Laos • Malay phrasebook • Malaysia, Singapore & Brunei • Myanmar (Burma) • Philippines • Pilipino (Tagalog) phrasebook • Read This First: Asia & India • Singapore • Singapore City Map • South-East Asia on a shoestring • South-East Asia phrasebook • Thailand • Thailand's Islands & Beaches • Thailand, Vietnam, Laos & Cambodia Road Atlas • Thai phrasebook • Vietnam • Vietnamese phrasebook • World Food Thailand • World Food Vietnam

ALSO AVAILABLE: Antarctica • The Arctic • The Blue Man: Tales of Travel, Love and Coffee • Brief Encounters: Stories of Love, Sex & Travel • Chasing Rickshaws • The Last Grain Race • Lonely Planet ... On the Edge: Adventurous Escapades from Around the World • Lonely Planet Unpacked • Not the Only Planet: Science Fiction Travel Stories • Sacred India • Travel Photography: A Guide to Taking Better Pictures • Travel with Children

Index

Text

A

A la Ronde 428
Abbotsbury 393-4
Abingdon 485
accommodation 92-5
activities 102-20
admission prices 72
AIDS 83-4
air travel 131-8, 143
 Africa 137-8
 airlines 131-2
 airports 131, 242-3
 Asia 137
 Australia 136
 Canada 136
 continental Europe 135
 India 137
 Ireland 135
 New Zealand 136
 Scotland 134
 South America 138
 UK 143
 USA 135-6
Airton 789
Alban Way 336
Aldeburgh 628
Alfred the Great 23
All Saints, Brixworth 560
All Saints, Earls Barton 560-1
Allen Valley 847
Allendale Town 847
Allenheads 847
Alnwick 858-9
Alston 827-8
Althorp 560
Alton Towers 591
Alum Bay 326
Ambleside 811-12
American Air Museum 657-8
American Museum 361
American War Cemetery 657
ancestry 87
Angel of the North 854
Anglo-Saxons 22-3
Appleby 786
Appledore 438
architecture 47-55
Armley Mills 722
Arts and Crafts movement 538
Arundel 304-5
Ashby-de-la-Zouch 569
Athelhampton House 384-5

Attingham Park 576
Audley End House 334
Avebury 413-15, **414**
Axbridge 366
Aylesbury 339

B

Baddesley Clinton 551
Bakewell 598-600, **599**
Bakewell pudding 598
Bamburgh 860
Barnard Castle 843-4
Barnstaple 437
Barrow-in-Furness 831-2
Bath 352-61, **353**
Battle 290-1
Battle of Britain 29
Battle of Flodden 864
Battle of Hastings 23, 291
Beachy Head 294
Beale Park 259
Beamish Open Air Museum 843
Beatles, the 699
Beaulieu 322-3
Becket, Thomas à 23, 268
bed & breakfast 94
Bedford 561-3
Bedfordshire 561-3
Bedruthan Steps 466
beer 98, 122
Bellingham 870-2
Belton House 667
Belvoir Castle 569
Bembridge 325
Bempton Cliffs Nature Reserve 741
Beresford Dale 607
Berkeley 507
Berkshire 251-9
Berwick-upon-Tweed 861-3, **861**
Beverley 739-41, **740**
Bibury 492-3
bicycle travel, see cycling
Biddulph Grange Gardens 590
Bideford 438
Bignor Roman Villa 305
Binchester Roman Fort 843
Bingley 724
Birdoswald Roman Fort 869
birds 37-8

Birmingham 534-43, **536**
Bishop Auckland 842-3
Bishop's Castle 582
Black Country, the 542-3
Black Death 24
black-and-white villages (Herefordshire) 519
Blackpool 711-13
Blair, Tony 32
Blanchland 846-7
Blenheim Palace 485
Blickling Hall 635
Bloody Assizes 387
Blue Pool, Dorset 386
Boadicea 22
boat travel 139-42
 continental Europe 140-1
 Ireland 141-2
boating
 Lake District 809, 815-16, 819-20, 824
 Norfolk Broads 636
Bodiam Castle 291-2
Bodmin 468
Bodmin Moor 4689
Bolventor 468
books 76-77, see also literature
Boot 832
Borrowdale 822-4
Boscastle 468
Boscobel House 542
Boston 669-70
Bosworth Battlefield 569
Bournemouth 380-2
Bournville Village 541-2
Bourton-on-the-Water 493
Bovington Camp Tank Museum 385
Bowness 807-11, **808**
Bowood House 411
Box Hill 265
Bradford 723-4
Bradford-on-Avon 409-11, **409**
Brading 325
Brampton 869
Bredon Hill 532
Bridge Cottage 333
Bridgnorth 580-1
Bridlington 742
Brighstone 326
Brighton 298-304, **299**
Bristol 343-51, **344**

British Empire 26-30
Brixham 430
Broadstairs 276-7
Broadway 495-6
Bromsgrove 529
Brontë family 725
Brontë Way 726
Brownsea Island 382
Bryher 470
Buckfast Abbey 445
Buckfastleigh 444-5
Buckinghamshire 338-9
Buckland Abbey 436
Bude 469
Bunyan, John 562
Burford 491
Burghley House 668-9
Burton-upon-Trent 590-1
Bury St Edmunds 624-7
bus travel 138, 143-6
    continental Europe 138
    UK 143-6
Buscot Park 500
business hours 89
Buttermere 822-4
Buxton 604-7, **605**

C

Cadbury World 541-2
Cadgwith 455
Caer Caradoc 581
Calf of Man 705
Calke Abbey 593
Cambridge 642-57, **644**
Cambridgeshire 641-61
Campaign for Real Ale 122
camper vans 154
canal travel 115-20
canals 115-19
Canterbury 267-75, **269**
car travel 139, 152-5
    continental Europe 139
    driving licence 66
    itineraries 154-5
    motoring organisations 155
    parking 153
    rental 153
    road rules 153
    UK 152-5
Carding Mill Valley 581
Carlisle 786, 796-800, **797**
Carnforth station 829
Cartmel 829-30

Bold indicates maps.

Castle Combe 411
Castle Drogo 447
Castle Howard 757
Castle Rising Castle 640-1
Castle Rushen 705
Castlefield Urban Heritage Park
    677-8
Castlerigg Stone Circle 820
castles
    Alnwick 858
    Arundel 304
    Ashby-de-la-Zouch 569
    Auckland 842-3
    Bamburgh 860
    Barnard 843-4
    Belvoir 569
    Berkeley 507
    Bodiam 291-2
    Carlisle 798
    Castle Drogo 447
    Castle Rising 640-1
    Castle Rushen 705
    Chillingham 874-5
    Clitheroe 710
    Colchester 331
    Corfe 385-6
    Croft 519
    Dartmouth 430-1
    Dover 280
    Dunstanburgh 859
    Dunster 377
    Durham 840
    Eastnor 523-4
    Etal 863
    Farnham 263
    Goodrich 523
    Helmsley 770
    Hever 285
    Kenilworth 548
    Lancaster 707-8
    Launceston 468
    Leeds (Kent) 286
    Lewes 295
    Lincoln 664
    Lindisfarne 860
    Ludlow 584
    Lulworth 386
    Maiden 388-9
    Newark-upon-Trent 615
    Norham 863
    Norwich 630-1
    Okehampton 447
    Old Wardour 405
    Orford 629
    Peel 705
    Pendennis 454
    Penrith 826

Pevensey 291
Peveril 602
Pickering 773
Piel 832
Portland 393
Powderham 428
Raby 844
Richborough 278-9
Richmond 791
St Mawes 454
Scarborough 759
Sherborne 396-7
Shrewsbury 572
Sizergh 804
Skipton 786
Southsea 318
Stafford 588
Sudeley 497
Taunton 372
Tintagel 467-8
Totnes 431
Tower of London 199-200
Warkworth 858
Warwick 548-9
Windsor 254-7
Wolvesey 313
Yarmouth 326
Castleton 601-4, **603**
Castletown 705
cathedrals, see also churches
    Arundel 304
    Birmingham 537
    Bristol 347
    Canterbury 268-71, **270**
    Carlisle 798-9
    Chester 687-8
    Chichester 306-7
    Christ Church, Oxford 477
    Coventry 544-5
    Derby 592
    Durham 839-40, **838**
    Ely 658-9
    Exeter 424
    Gloucester 503-4
    Guildford 261
    Hereford 516-17
    Lichfield 586
    Lincoln 663-4
    Liverpool 697
    Manchester 677
    Norwich 631-2
    Peterborough 660-1
    St Albans 335-6, **336**
    St Edmundsbury, Bury St
        Edmunds 625-6
    St Paul's 197-8
    Salisbury 399-401

Sheffield 732
Southwark 201
Wells 363
Westminster 190
Winchester 309-12, **311**
Worcester 524-5
Caudwell's Mill 608
Celts 21
Cerne Abbas 389
Cerne Giant 389
Chagford 447
chain pubs 126-9
chain restaurants 97
chalk figures 398, 486
Chamberlain, Neville 28
Chapel Hill, Isle of Man 705
Charlecote Park 558
Charles I 25-6
Charles II 542
Charleston Farmhouse 294-5
Charlestown 453
Chartwell 285
Chatsworth 600
Chaucer, Geoffrey 24
Cheddar cheese 365
Cheddar Gorge 365-6
Cheddar village 366
Chedworth Roman Villa 492
Cheltenham 507-12, **509**
chemists 84
Cheshire 684-93
Chesil Beach 393
Chester 685-91, **686**
Chesterfield 593
Chesters Roman Fort &
    Museum 867
Chewton Mendip 366
Chichester 305-8, **306**
children, travel with 86-7
Chilham 276
Chillingham Castle 874-5
Chippenham 411
Chipping 711
Chipping Campden 495
Chipping Norton 491-2
Christchurch 382-3
Christianity 777
Church Stretton 581-2
churches, see also cathedrals
    All Saints, Brixworth 560
    All Saints, Earls Barton
        560-1
    Bath Abbey 356
    Beverley Minster 739
    Glastonbury Abbey 368-9
    King's College Chapel,
        Cambridge 646-7

Malmesbury Abbey 417-18
    St John the Baptist,
        Cirencester 501
    St Martin-in-the-Fields,
        London 186
    St Thomas's, Salisbury 402
    Sherborne Abbey 396
    Shrewsbury Abbey 573
    Southwell Minster 615
    Tewkesbury Abbey 512-13
    Westminster Abbey 187-9
    Wimborne Minster 383
    York Minster 746, 747-9,
        747
Churchill, Winston 28
cinema 44-5
Cinque Ports 265
Cirencester 500-2
Civil War 25, 542
classical music 45
Claydon House 339
Clearwell Caves 514
Cleveland Way 105, 780
Cley Marshes 637
climate 33-4, see also weather
Clitheroe 710
Clouds Hill 385
Clovelly 438-9
Clun 582-3
Coast-to-Coast Walk 108-9
Cockermouth 801-2, **801**
Colchester 331-2
Combe Eden 786
Commonwealth, the 26
Compton Martin 366
Conishead Priory 830
Coniston 815-17
Conistone 787
Constantine Bay 466
consulates 67-8
Cook Country Walk 782
Corbridge 865-6
Corfe Castle 385-6
Cornish (language) 450
Cornwall 449-71, **420**, **459**
    cycling 421
    surfing 421
    walking 419-21
Corsham Court 411
Cotehele 451
Cotswold Way 105, 488-9
Cotswolds, the 488-515, **489**
    cycling 488-9
    walking 488-9
country houses, see stately
    homes
County Durham 837-47

courses 90-1
Coventry 543-7, **544**
Cowes 325
Coxwald 770
Cragside House 872
Craster 859
Cregneash Village Folk
    Museum 705
cricket 100
crime 88
Croft Castle 519
Cromer 637
Cromwell, Oliver 26
Crookham 864
crop circles 416
Crowcombe 372
Crummock Water 823
C2C cycle route, see Sea to
    Sea cycle route
cultural considerations 55-6
Cumbria 795-834, **796**
    cycling 112, 795
    walking 795
Cumbria Cycle Way 112, 795
Cumbria Way 106
Cumbrian Coast Line (railway)
    800, 828-9
customs regulations 68-9
cycling 109-13
    Cornwall 421
    Cotswolds, the 488-9
    Cumbria 795
    Cumbria Cycle Way 112,
        795
    Dartmoor Way 442
    Devon 421, 442
    eastern England 111, 113,
        618
    Exmoor 375
    High Peak Trail 596
    Isle of Man 704
    Lake District 806, 809, 820
    Midlands, the 111
    Norfolk 629
    north-eastern England 836
    northern England 111-12,
        113
    Oxfordshire 473
    Peak District 596-7
    Plym Valley Cycle Way 442
    Sea to Sea cycle route 795
    Shropshire 570
    Somerset 362
    south-eastern England
        110-11
    south-western England 111,
        112-13

Tissington Trail 596
tours 110
Wessex 341-2
Whitby-Scarborough
    Coastal Cycle Trail 780
Wiltshire Cycleway 398
Worcestershire 524
Wye Valley 112
Yorkshire 715
Yorkshire Dales 112, 785,
    791-2

D

Dales Way 108, 715, 785
Danby 775
Danelaw 23
Darlington 847-8
Dartmoor National Park
    439-49, **440**
Dartmoor Way 441, 442
Dartmouth 430-1
Darwin, Charles 572
D-Day 29
Deal 279
Dedham Vale 332-3
Dent 786
Derby 591-3
Derbyshire 591-4
Derwent Valley 608
Devizes 412-13
Devon 421-39, **420**
    cycling 421, 442
    walking 419-21, 441-2
DH Lawrence Birthplace
    Museum 615
Diana, Princess of Wales 30
Didcot Railway Centre 485-6
disabled travellers 85-6
documents 64-7
Donington Park 569
Dorchester 387-8
Dorchester-on-Thames 486
Dorset 380-98
Douglas 704-5
Dovedale 607
Dover 279-83, **279**
Down House 211
Downside Abbey 366
Dozmary Pool 468
Dracula 779
Drayton Manor Park 591
drink-driving 89
drinks 98-9

Bold indicates maps.

driving licence 66
Droitwich Spa 528-9
drugs 89
dry-stone walls 788
Du Maurier, Daphne 468
Dudmaston 580-1
Dulverton 376
Duncombe Park 770-1
Dungeness 283
Dunstanburgh Castle 859
Dunster 376-7
Durham 837-42, **838**
Durham Dales 844-6
Duxford Imperial War Museum
    657-8
Dyrham Park 361-2

E

Eardisland 519
Earth Centre 734-5
East Harptree 366
East Looe 451-2
East Riding of Yorkshire 735-42
East Sussex 287-304
Eastbourne 292-4, **293**
eastern England 616-70, **617**
    cycling 618
    walking 618, 655
Eastnor Castle 523-4
ecology 34-5
economy 39
Edale 604, **603**
Eden Project 451
Edmundbyers 847
education 40
Edward VII 27
Edward VIII 27
Edwardian England 27
Egglestone Abbey 844
electricity 81
Elgar, Edward 530
Elgar's Birthplace Museum
    528
Elizabeth I 25
Elizabeth II 30, 31
Ellesmere Port 691
Elterwater 814
Ely 658-60, **659**
email 74-5
embassies 67-8
emergencies 89
English Heritage 87
entertainment 99
environmental considerations
    34-5, 63
Escomb 843

Eskdale 832-3
Essex 327-34
Etal 863
Eton 254-9, **255**
Eurostar 138-9
Eurotunnel 139
Evesham 531
Exeter 422-8, **423**
Exford 378
Exmoor National Park 373-80,
    374
    cycling 375
    walking 374
Eyam 601

F

Fairford 500
Falmouth 454-5
Farne Islands 859-60
Farnham 263-4
fauna 36-7, 768-9
Fawkes, Guy 25
fax services 74
Felbrigg Hall 637
Fens, the 658
ferry companies 140
Filey 739, 762
films 77-8, see also cinema
Fishbourne Roman Palace &
    Museum 308-9
fishing 114-15
Flamborough 741-2
Flatford Mill 332
flora 35-6
food 95-8
    pubs 129-30
football 99-100
Ford 863
Forde Abbey 396
Foreland Point 379
Forest of Bowland 710-11
Forest of Dean 513-15
Foster, Norman 54
Fosterley 846
Fotheringhay 561
Fountains Abbey 793-4
Fowey 452-3
fox-hunting 56
Frome 367
Furness Abbey 831-2

G

Gainsborough, Thomas 622
gardens
    Biddulph Grange Gardens
    590

Botanic Gardens, Oxford 478
Eden Project 451
Heligan 451
Hidcote Manor Gardens 495
Kew Gardens 212-13
Painswick Rococo Garden 498
Sissinghurst Castle Gardens 283
Stowe Landscape Gardens 339
Studley Royal Water Garden 793-4
Trebah Garden 455
Trelissick Garden 451
Tresco Abbey Gardens 470
Garsdale 786
gay & lesbian travellers 85
genealogy 87
geography 33
Glasgow-Carlisle Line 800
Glastonbury 367-70, **368**
Glen Lyn Gorge 379
Glenridding 824-5
Gloucester 502-7, **503**
Gloucestershire Warwickshire Railway 497
Glyndebourne 297
Goathland 775
Golden Valley 519
golf 101, 113
Goodrich 523
Gordale Scar 789
government 38-9
Grange 823
Grange-over-Sands 829
Grantchester 657
Grantham 667-8
Grasmere 812-13
Grassington 787
Great Central Railway 566
Great Malvern 529-31
Great Yarmouth 636-7
Grizedale Forest 818
Grosmont 775
Guildford 259-63, **260**
guilds 748
Guiting Power 497-8
gurning 833

H
Haddon Hall 600
Hadleigh 624
Hadrian 22

Hadrian's Wall 22, 106, 864-9, 871
Hadrian's Wall Path 870
Hailes Abbey 497
Haltwhistle 868
Hampshire 309-24
Hamsterley Forest 846
Hardcastle Crags 729
Hardknott Roman Fort 832
Hardwick Hall 594
Hardy Way 342
Hardy's Cottage 389
Harewood House 723
Harrogate 762-5, **764**
Hartland Abbey 439
Hartlepool 849
Harwich 332
Hastings 289-90
Hatfield House 338
Hawes 790
Hawkshead 817-18
Hawkstone Historic Park 576
Haworth 724-7, **725**
Hayfield 604
Haynes Motor Museum 373
Hay-on-Wye 519-22, **520**
health 81-4
    AIDS 83-4
health insurance, see insurance
Heatherslaw 863-4
Hebden Bridge 729
Helford 455
Heligan 451
Helmsley 770-2, **771**
Helston 455
Henley-on-Thames 486-8
Henry VIII 25
Heptonstall 729
Hereford 516-19, **516**
Herefordshire 515-24, **473**
    black-and-white villages 519
    walking 515
Hertfordshire 334-8
Hessle 739
Hever Castle 285
Hexham 866-7
Hidcote Manor Gardens 495
High Force 845
High Peak Trail 596-7
Higham Park 275
Hill Top 818
history 21-33
hitching 155-6
Holford 371
Holkham Hall 637
Holy Island 860-1
Hope Colliery Museum 514

horse racing 101
horse riding 115
Horton-in-Ribblesdale 790
Houghton Hall 641
House of Hanover 26-7
House of Lancaster 24-5
House of York 25
Housesteads Roman Fort & Museum 867
Howlett's Animal Park 275-6
Hull 735-8, **736**
Humber Bridge 738-9
Humbleton Hill 874
Hundred Years' War 24
hunting 56
Hutton-le-Hole 772-3
Hythe 283

I
Ickham 276
Ickworth House 627
Ightham Mote 286
Ilfracombe 437
Ilkley 727-8
Ilkley Moor 727
immigration 40
Industrial Revolution 26, 118
Ingleborough 789
insurance 66
Internet
    access 74-5
    resources 75-6
Ipswich 619-20
Ironbridge Gorge 576-9, **577**
Isle of Man 703-7, **703**
    cycling 704
    walking 704
Isle of Wight 324-7, **324**
Isles of Scilly 469-71, **469**
itineraries 61
    driving 154-5
    train 151

J
Jarrow 853-4

K
Kedleston Hall 593
Keighley 786
Keighley & Worth Valley Railway 726
Kelmscott Manor 500
Kendal 802-4, **803**
Kendal mint cake 804
Kenilworth 547-8

Kennet & Avon Canal 398
Kent 265-86
Kentwell Hall 621
Kersey 624
Keswick 818-22, **819**
Kettlewell 788
Kidderminster 528
Kielder 873
Kielder Water 872-4
Kilburn 770
Killhope Lead Mining Centre 846
Kilnsey Park 787
King's College Chapel, Cambridge 646-7
kings 30-1
King's Lynn 637-40, **639**
Kingston Lacy 383
Kingston-upon-Hull, see Hull
Kirkby Lonsdale 828
Kirkby Stephen 786, 828
Kirkstall Abbey 722-3
Knole House 284
Knutsford 691-2

L

Lacock 412
Lady Godiva 545
Lake District National Park 804-25, **805**
  boating 809, 815-16, 819-20, 824
  cycling 806, 809, 820
  walking 806, 809, 811, 816, 820
Lakes Line (railway) 800
Lambert, Daniel 564
Lancashire 707-13
Lancaster 707-9, **708**
Land's End 459-60
Lanercost Priory 869
Langdale 813-15
language 56-7
language courses 90-1
Langwathby 786
Lanhydrock House 453
Launceston 468
laundry 81
Lavenham 623
Lawrence of Arabia 384
Laxey Wheel, Isle of Man 706
Leamington Spa 551
Lechlade-upon-Thames 500

Ledbury 523
Leeds 717-22, **718**
Leeds & Liverpool Canal 786-7
Leeds Castle (Kent) 286
Leeds-Settle-Carlisle Line 786, 800
Leek 591
Leicester 564-8, **565**
Leicestershire 564-70
letterboxing 446
Levens Hall 804
Levisham 775
Lewes 295-7, **296**
Lichfield 586-7
Limestone Way 596
Lincoln 662-7, **663**
Lincolnshire 661-70
Lindisfarne, see Holy Island
listed buildings 53
literature 40-3
Little Langdale 814-15
Little Moreton Hall 590
Little Walsingham 637
Liverpool 693-703, **694**
Lizard Point 455
Lizard, the 455-6
local transport 156
locks (canal) 116-17
Lockton 775
Lodore Falls 822
Lonan Old Church 706
London 158-249, **161-80**
  airports 242-3
  BA London Eye 203
  Bermondsey 200
  Bloomsbury 194-6
  British Library 207
  British Museum 194-6
  Brixton 211
  Buckingham Palace 191
  Camden 207
  Chelsea 203-5
  Chiswick 211-12
  City, the 197-200
  Clerkenwell 196-7
  Docklands 208-9
  Dulwich 210-11
  Earl's Court 203-5
  East End 208
  entertainment 232-40
  Euston 207
  getting around 244-9
  getting there & away 242-4
  Globe Theatre 201-2
  Greenwich 209-10
  Hampstead 207-8
  Hampton Court Palace 213

history 158-9
Holborn 196-7
Holland Park 205
Houses of Parliament 189
Hyde Park 205-6
Imperial War Museum 203
information 160-84
Kensington 205
Kew Gardens 212-13
King's Cross 207
Knightsbridge 205
Lambeth 203
Marylebone 206-7
Mayfair 190-1
Millennium Bridge 202
Millennium Dome 210
National Gallery 185
National Maritime Museum 209-10
National Portrait Gallery 185-6
Natural History Museum 204
Notting Hill 205-6
orientation 159-60
Osterley 213
Pimlico 186-90
places to eat 222-32
places to stay 214-22
Regent's Park 206-7
River Thames 159
St James's 190-1
St Paul's Cathedral 197-8
Science Museum 204
shopping 240-2
South Bank 202-3
South Kensington 203-5
Southwark 200-2
Tate Britain 190
Tate Modern 202
10 Downing St 186
tours 213-14
Tower Bridge 200
Tower of London 199-200
Trafalgar Square 184-6
Victoria & Albert Museum 203-4
Wallace Collection 206
West End 191-4
Westminster 186-90
Whitehall 186-7
Wimbledon 211
Long Man of Wilmington 295
Long Meg and Her Daughters 827
Long Melford 620-1
Long Mynd 581-2

Bold indicates maps.

Longleat 408-9
Looe 451-2
Ludlow 583-5, **583**
Lulworth Cove 386-7
Lundy Island 437-8
Lydford 448-9
Lyme Park 607
Lyme Regis 394-5, **394**
Lymington 324
Lynmouth 379-80
Lynton 379-80

M

magazines 79
Magna 734
Magna Carta 23
Maiden Castle 388-9
Malham 788-9
Malham Tarn 789
Malhamdale 788-9
Malmesbury 417-18
Malvern Hills 530
Manchester 671-84, **674-5**
maps 62-3, 104
Margate 276
Marlborough 417
Matlock 607-8
Matlock Bath 607-8
Maughold 706
McCartney, Paul 702
medical services 84
Melton Mowbray 569
Mendip Hills 366-7
Mercia 22
metric system 81
Middleton-in-Teesdale 845
Midlands, the 533-615, **534-5**
Minack Theatre 458-9
Minehead 377-8
Minster Lovell 491
monarchy 30-1
monasteries, dissolution of the 25
money 27, 69-73
   ATMs 70
   costs 72
   credit cards 70
   taxes 72-3, 92
   tipping 72
   travellers cheques 70
Monkey World, Dorset 385
Monsal Trail 597
Montacute House 372-3
Moretonhampstead 445-7
Moreton-in-Marsh 494-5

Morris, William 538
Moseley Old Hall 542
motorcycle travel 139, 152-5
   continental Europe 139
   itineraries 154-5
   motoring organisations 155
   parking 153
   rental 153
   road rules 153
   touring 154-5
   UK 152-5
Mount Edgcumbe 436
Mousehole 458
Much Wenlock 580
Murray's Motorcycle Museum, Isle of Man 706
museums & galleries
   admission prices 72
   Ashmolean Museum 476
   British Museum 194-6
   Dulwich Picture Gallery 210-11
   Duxford Imperial War Museum 657-8
   Earth Centre 734-5
   Fitzwilliam Museum 651-2
   Haynes Motor Museum 373
   Imperial War Museum 203
   Magna 734
   National Coal Mining Museum 728
   National Gallery 185
   National Maritime Museum 209-10
   National Motor Museum 322-3
   National Portrait Gallery 185-6
   National Railway Museum 751
   Natural History Museum 204
   Royal Armouries 719
   Royal Naval Museum 317
   Science Museum 204
   Tate Britain 190
   Tate Modern 202
   Tate St Ives 461
   Victoria & Albert Museum 203-4
   Wallace Collection 206
music
   classical 45
   opera 45
   popular 45-6

N

Nantwich 692-3
National Coal Mining Museum 728
National Cycle Network 109
national lottery 184
National Motor Museum 322-3
national parks 38, see also Norfolk Broads
   Dartmoor 439-49
   Exmoor 373-80
   Lake District 804-25
   North York Moors 766-83
   Northumberland 870-5
   Peak District 594-608
   Yorkshire Dales 783-94
National Railway Museum 751
National Seal Sanctuary 455
National Space Science Centre 566
National Tramway Museum 608
National Trust 87
Needles Old Battery 326
Needles, the 326
Nenthead 827
Nether Stowey 371
New Forest 321-4, **323**
Newark-upon-Trent 615
Newcastle-upon-Tyne 850-7, **851**
Newent 515
Newland 514
Newquay 464-6, **465**
newspapers 78-9
Newstead Abbey 614-15
Norfolk 629-41
   cycling 629
   walking 629
Norfolk Broads 635-6
   boating 636
Norfolk Coast Path 106-7
Norham Castle 863
Normans 23
North Downs Way 267
North York Moors National Park 766-83, **767**
   walking 767
North Yorkshire 742-66
North Yorkshire Moors Railway 774-5
Northampton 559-60
Northamptonshire 558-61
north-eastern England 835-75, **836**
   cycling 836
   walking 836

Northleach 492
Northumberland 857-75
Northumberland National Park
  870-5, **871**
  walking 870
Northumbria 22
north-western England
  671-713, **672**
Norwich 630-5, **631**
Nottingham 609-14, **610**
Nottinghamshire 608-15
Nunnington Hall 757

O
Oakham 570
oast houses 266
Offa's Dyke 22
Okehampton 447-8
Old Dungeon Ghyll 814
Old Sarum 404-5
Old Wardour Castle 405
opening hours (pubs) 125-6
opera 45
Orford 629
Osborne House 325
Oundle 561
Owlpen Manor 499
Oxford 474-84, **475**
Oxford Bus Museum 485
Oxfordshire 472-88, **473**
  cycling 473
  walking 473
Oxfordshire Way 473

P
Padstow 466-7
Paignton 429-30
Painswick 498
painting 46-7
Pakenham Water Mill 627
palaces
  Blenheim 485
  Buckingham 191
  Hampton Court 213
  Kensington 205
  St James's 190-1
  Wolvesey 313
Parnham 395-6
Patterdale 825
Peak District 594-608, **595**
  cycling 596-7
  walking 596-7
Peak Railway 608

Peddars Way 106-7
Peel 705-6
Pembridge 519
Pendennis Castle 454
Pendle Hill 710
Pennine Way 107, 870
Penrith 825-6
Penshurst Place 285-6
Pen-y-ghent 789
Penzance 456-8, **456**
people 39-40
Pershore 531-2
Peterborough 660-1
Petworth House 309
Pevensey Castle 291
Peveril Castle 602
pharmacies 84
photography &
  video 80
Pickering 773-4, **773**
Piercebridge 848-9
Pilgrim's Progress 562
Plantagenets 23
Plym Valley Cycle
  Way 442
Plymouth 432-6, **433**
politics 38-9
pollution 35
Polperro 452
pony trekking 115
Poole 382
Pooley Bridge 824
pop music 45
population 39-40
Porlock 378-9
Port Erin 705
Port Sunlight 702
Portland 393
Portloe 454
Portsmouth 315-20, **316**
postal services 73
Postbridge 444
Potter, Beatrix 505
Poundbury 389
Powderham Castle 428
Pre-Raphaelite Brotherhood
  538
Priddy 366
Prideaux Place 467
Prince Charles 30
Prince William 30
Princetown 443-4
Prior Park 361
public holidays 89-90
pubs 98, 121-30
puffins 438
punting 653

Q
Quantock Hills 371-2
Quarr Abbey 325
Quarry Bank Mill 684
queens 30-1

R
Raby Castle 844
racism 88-9
radio 79-80
Ragley Hall 558
railways 29
  Cumbrian Coast Line 800,
    828-9
  Glasgow-Carlisle Line 800
  Gloucestershire Warwick-
    shire Railway 497
  Great Central Railway 566
  Heatherslaw Light Railway
    863-4
  Keighley & Worth Valley
    Railway 726
  Lakes Line 800
  Leeds-Settle-Carlisle Line
    786, 800
  North Yorkshire Moors
    Railway 774-5
  Peak Railway 608
  Ravenglass to Eskdale 832
  Romney, Hythe &
    Dymchurch Railway 283
  Severn Valley Railway 528,
    580
  South Tynedale Railway
    827
  steam 120
  Tyne Valley Line 800
  West Somerset Railway 372
Ramsey 706
Ravenglass 832-3
Ravenglass to Eskdale railway
  832
Ravenscar 783
Red House Stables Working
  Carriage Museum 608
Redcar 850
Redditch 529
Reivers, the 798
religion 56
Restoration 26
Reynolds, Joshua 622
Rheged Discovery Centre
  826-7
Ribble Valley 709-11
Ribble Way 710
Ribblesdale 789-90

Bold indicates maps.

Richard I (the Lion-Heart) 23
Richborough Castle 278-9
Richmond 790-3, **792**
Ridgeway, the 107, 342
Rievaulx Abbey 772
Rievaulx Terrace & Temples
    772
rivers 159
    Aire 789
    Dove 607
    Great Ouse 659
    Helford 455
    Ribble 709-11
    Severn 506
    Stour 620
    Thames 159
    Wye 522
Robin Hood 611
Robin Hood's Bay 782-3
Rogers, Richard 54
Roman Army Museum 869
Romans 21-2
Romney Marsh 283
Romney, Hythe & Dymchurch
    Railway 283
Roseland Peninsula 454
Ross-on-Wye 522-3
Roswaithe 823
Rothbury 872
rugby 100-1
Rushton Triangular Lodge 561
Rutland 564, 569-70
Rutland Water 570
Ryde 325
Rye 287-9, **287**

S
safety 88-9
Saffron Walden 333-4
St Agnes (Isles of Scilly) 471
St Albans 334-8, **335**
St Bees 834
St Catherine's Lighthouse 326
St Catherine's Oratory 326
St Helens World of Glass 702-3
St Ives 461-4, **462**
St Just-in-Penwith 460-1
St Just-in-Roseland 454
St Martin's (Isles of Scilly) 471
St Mary's (Isles of Scilly) 470
St Mawes 454
St Michael's Mount 456
Saints' Way 450
Salisbury 398-404, **399**
Saltaire 724
Saltburn-by-the-Sea 849-50

Sandringham House 641
Sandwich 277-8
Scafell Pike 832
Scarborough 757-62, **758**
sculpture 46-7
Sea to Sea cycle route 795
Seatoller 823
Segedunum 854
Sellafield 35, 834
Selly Manor 542
Selworthy 378
senior travellers 86
    seniors cards 67
Settle 786, 789
Sevenoaks 283-4
Severn Bore 506
Severn Valley Railway 528, 580
Severn Way 524
Sezincote House 494
Shaftesbury 397-8
Shakespeare, William 41, 555
Sheffield 730-4, **731**
Shepton Mallet 367
Sherborne 396-7
Sherwood Forest 615
shopping 101
Shrewsbury 570-6, **571**
Shropshire 570-86
    cycling 570
Shugborough 590
Sidmouth 428-9
Silbury Hill 416
Silverstone 560
Sissinghurst Castle Gardens
    283
Sizergh Castle 804
Sizewell 628-9
Skegness 670
Skipton 786-7
Slaughters, the 493
Slimbridge 507
Snaefell 706
Snowshill 496
Somerset 362-73
    cycling 362
    walking 362
South Downs Way 108
South Lakes Wild Animal Park
    832
South Tynedale Railway 827
South West Coast Path 104-5,
    341, 419-21
South Yorkshire 730-5
Southampton 320-1
south-eastern England
    250-339, **252-3**
Southend-on-Sea 327-31, **328**

Southsea 315-20, **316**
Southwell Minster 615
special events 90
spectator sports 99-101
Speke Hall 702
sport 99-101
Spurn Head 742
Stafford 587-8
Staffordshire 586-91
Staithes 775-6
Stamford 668
Stanhope 846
Stanton 496
Stanway 496
stately homes 52
    Althorp 560
    Attingham Park 576
    Audley End House 334
    Belton House 667
    Belvoir Castle 569
    Blickling Hall 635
    Bowood House 411
    Buckland Abbey 436
    Burghley House 668-9
    Buscot Park 500
    Calke Abbey 593
    Castle Howard 757
    Charlecote Park 558
    Chatsworth 600
    Chiswick House 211-12
    Claydon House 339
    Corsham Court 411
    Cotehele 451
    Cragside House 872
    Duncombe Park 770-1
    Dyrham Park 361-2
    Felbrigg Hall 637
    Haddon Hall 600
    Hardwick Hall 594
    Harewood House 723
    Hartland Abbey 439
    Hatfield House 338
    Higham Park 275
    Holkham Hall 637
    Houghton Hall 641
    Ickworth House 627
    Kedleston Hall 593
    Kentwell Hall 621
    Kenwood House 207-8
    Knole House 284
    Lanhydrock House 453
    Leeds Castle (Kent) 286
    Levens Hall 804
    Longleat 408-9
    Lyme Park 607
    Montacute House 372-3
    Mount Edgcumbe 436

Osborne House 325
Osterley House 213
Penshurst Place 285-6
Petworth House 309
Prideaux Place 467
Ragley Hall 558
Sandringham House 641
Sezincote House 494
Shugborough 590
Speke Hall 702
Stokesay Castle 585-6
Stonor Park 488
Stourhead 408
Sulgrave Manor 561
Tatton Park 692
Trerice 466
Waddesdon Manor 339
Wightwick Manor 542-3
Wilton House 405
Wimpole Hall 658
Woburn Abbey 563
steam railways 120
Stoke Bruerne Canal Museum 560
Stoke-on-Trent 588-90
Stoker, Bram 779
Stokesay Castle 585-6
Stonehenge 405-8, **406**
Stonor Park 488
Stour Valley 620-3
Stourhead 408
Stowe Landscape Gardens 339
Stow-on-the-Wold 493-4
Stratford-upon-Avon 552-8, **552**
Street 371
Stroud 498-9
Stuarts 25-6
Studley Royal Water Garden 793-4
Sudbury 621-3
Suffolk 619-29
Suffolk Coast Path 618
Sulgrave Manor 561
surfing 113-14
   Cornwall 421
   Severn Bore 506
Surrey 259-65
Sustrans 109
Sutton Bank 769-70
Sutton Scarsdale Hall 593
Swanage 386
swimming 113-14
Swindon 418

Symonds Yat 523
Synod of Whitby 777

T
Tailor of Gloucester 505
Tarka Trail 374
Tatton Park 692
Taunton 372
Tavistock 449
taxes 72-3, 92
taxis 156
Tees Valley 847-50
Teesdale 844-5
telephone services 73-4
Templer Way 441
1066 Country Walk 288
Tennyson Trail 326
Tetbury 499-500
Tewkesbury 512-13
Thames Path 107-8, 473
Thatcher, Margaret 32
theatre 43-4
Thirsk 765-6
Three Peaks, the 789
Three Shire Stone 815
Tideswell 600-1
time 80-1
Tintagel 467-8
Tissington Trail 596-7
toilets 81
Tolpuddle 384
Torbay 429-30
Torquay 429
Totnes 431-2
tourist offices 63-4
tours 156-7
   cycling 110
   nature 157
   walking 109
train travel 138-9, 146-52, **148**
   continental Europe 138-9
   Eurostar 138-9
   Eurotunnel 139
   itineraries 151
   passes 150-2
   railcards 150
   UK 146-52
travel insurance 66
Trebah Garden 455
Trelissick Garden 451
Trerice 466
Tresco 470
Truro 453-4
Tudors 25
TV 80

20 Forthlin Rd, Liverpool 702
Two Moors Way 342, 374, 441
Tyne Valley Line 800
Tynwald Hill 706

U
Uffington 486
Ullswater 824-5
Ulverston 830-1
Uppingham 570
Upton-upon-Severn 532

V
Vale of Evesham 531-2
Valley of the Rocks 379
Ventnor 326
Veryan 454
Victoria 26
video, see photography & video
video systems 80
Vikings 22-3
Vindolanda Roman Fort & Museum 867-8
visas 65-6

W
Waddesdon Manor 339
walking 102-9
   Alban Way 336
   Brontë Way 726
   Cleveland Way 105
   Coast-to-Coast Walk 108-9
   Cook Country Walk 782
   Cornwall 419-21
   Cotswold Way 105, 488-9
   Cotswolds, the 488-9
   Cumbria 795
   Cumbria Way 106
   Dales Way 108, 715, 785
   Dartmoor Way 441
   Devon 419-21, 441-2
   eastern England 618, 655
   Exmoor 374
   Hadrian's Wall 106
   Hadrian's Wall Path 870
   Hardy Way 342
   Herefordshire 515
   High Peak Trail 596
   Isle of Man 704
   Lake District 806, 809, 811, 816, 820
   Limestone Way 596
   Malvern Hills 530
   Monsal Trail 597

Bold indicates maps.

Norfolk 629
Norfolk Coast Path 106-7
North Downs Way 267
North York Moors 767
north-eastern England 836
Northumberland National
    Park 870
Oxfordshire 473
Peak District 596-7
Peddars Way 106-7
Pennine Way 107, 870
Ribble Way 710
Ridgeway, the 107, 342
Saints' Way 450
Severn Way 524
Somerset 362
South Downs Way 108
South West Coast Path
    104-5, 341, 419-21
Suffolk Coast Path 618
Tarka Trail 374
Templer Way 441
1066 Country Walk 288
Thames Path 107-8, 473
Tissington Trail 596
tours 109
Two Moors Way 342, 374,
    441
Wessex 341-2
West Devon Way 441
Wolds Way 105-6, 739
Worcestershire 524
Yorkshire 714-15
Yorkshire Dales 785
Walsall 542
Wantage 486
Wardour Castle, see Old
    Wardour Castle
Wareham 385
Warkworth 858
Wars of the Roses 24
Warwick 548-51, **549**
Warwickshire 543-58
Wast Water 833
Watermeet 379
waterway travel 115-20
Waverley Abbey 264-5
Weardale 845-6
weather 62, 89, see also

climate
Wedgwood, Josiah 588
weights & measures 81
well dressing 596
Wells 362-5, **363**
Wells-next-the-Sea 637
Wendover Woods 338
Wenlock Edge 579-80
Wensleydale 790
Wessex 22, 340-418, **341**
    cycling 341-2
    walking 341-2
West Devon Way 441
West Harptree 366
West Kennet Long Barrow
    416-17
West Looe 451-2
West Somerset Railway 372
West Sussex 304-9
West Yorkshire 715-30
Westonbirt Arboretum 499
Weymouth 389-93, **390**
Wharfedale 787-8
Whernside 789
Whipsnade 563-4
Whitby 776-82, **778**
Whitby-Scarborough Coastal
    Cycle Trail 780
White Horse, the 486
Whitehaven 834
Widecombe-in-the-Moor 445
Widgery Cross 448
Wigan Pier Heritage Centre
    684
Wight, Alfred 765-6
Wildfowl & Wetlands Centre,
    Slimbridge 507
William the Conqueror 23
Wilmington 295
Wilton House 405
Wiltshire 398-418
Wiltshire Cycleway 398
Wimborne 383
Wimpole Hall 658
Winchcombe 496-7
Winchester 309-15, **310**
Windermere 807-11, **808**
Windmill Hill, Wiltshire 415
Windsor 254-9, **255**

Witley Court 528
Witney 490-1
Woburn Abbey & Safari Park
    563
Wolds Way 105-6, 739
Wolverhampton 542-3
Wolvesey Castle & Palace 313
women travellers 84, 85
Woodchester Mansion 499
Woodhenge 408
Woodstock 484
Wookey Hole 365
Wooler 874-5
Worcester 524-8, **525**
Worcestershire 524-32, **473**
    cycling 524
    walking 524
work 91-2
    permits 65-6
World Gurning Competition
    833
World's Biggest Liar
    Competition 833
Wroxeter Roman City 576
WWI 27
WWII 28-30
Wye Valley 522
    cycling 112

Y
Yarmouth Castle 326
York 743-57, **744**
Yorkshire 714-94, **716-17**
    cycling 715
    walking 714-15
Yorkshire Dales National Park
    783-94, **784**
    cycling 112, 785, 791-2
    walking 785

Z
Zennor 461
Admission Prices 72
Air Travel Glossary 133
Alban Way, The 336
Battle, The 291
Battle for Stonehenge, The 407

Boxed Text

Bloody Assizes, The 387
Border Reivers, The 798
British Museum Highlights 195
Bus Fares from London 145
Buying Theatre Tickets 239
Cambridge, aka... 643
Celebrity Duel: Thomas Gains-borough vs Sir Joshua Reynolds 622
Chain Gangs, The 97
Chalk Figures 398
Charlieville 389
Cheddar Cheese 365
Chipping Circular Walk 711
Choosing a Good Beer 122
Choosing a Good Pub 127
Christianity & the Synod of Whitby 777
Cinque Ports 265
Climbers' Friend, The 804
Daphne Du Maurier Trail, The 468
Doing the Beatles to Death 699
Don't Spank the Monkey, Hang It! 849
Dover's Heights 280
Dracula 779
End-to-End Records 460
English Interior Design 94
Fens, The 658
Ferry Companies 140
406 rms w/vu 52
Garden of Eden, The 451
Gay & Lesbian Manchester 682
Going Round in Circles 416
Hadrian's Wall Circular Walk 868
Hey! We Want Our Marbles Back! 196
How to Punt 653
Humbleton Hill Circular Walk 874
Ilkley Moor 727

John Bunyan & The Pilgrim's Progress 562
Josiah Wedgwood 588
Key to the Locks, The 116-17
Kings & Queens 30-1
Lawrence of Arabia 384
Legend of Robin Hood, The 611
Leicester's Weightiest Citizen 564
Letterboxing 446
Listed Buildings 53
London's Bewildering Post-codes 160
Lottery Bonanza 184
Medieval Guilds 748
Minding the Minster 746
Miners of the Forest of Dean 514
Murder of Becket, The 268
National Gallery Highlights 185
New Forest Ponies 322
No Kilos Please, We're English 81
Norman & Richard Show, The 54
North Downs Way, The 267
Not-So-Dirty Old Man River 159
Oast Houses 266
Of Rakes & Harlots: Hogarth's World 212
Old Bard, William Shakespeare, The 555
On the Elgar Trail 530
Origin of the Broads, The 636
Pendle Hill Circular Walk 710
Penshurst Place Walks 285
Pre-Raphaelites & the Arts and Crafts Movement, The 538
Puffin Pence 438
Rail Fares from London 149
Rising of the North, The 844
Rock Piles 788
Running from the Republicans 542

St Albans Beer Festival 337
Say You Want a Revolution 28-9
Stripping Away the Myth 545
Suggested Driving Itinerary, A 154-5
Suggested Rail Itinerary, A 151
Surfing the Severn Bore 506
Sustrans & the National Cycle Network 109
Tailor of Gloucester, The 505
Tea for Two or More 223
Ten English Films 78
1066 Country Walk, The 288
That'll Be Two Bob 27
Tracing Your Ancestors 87
Tube: Fun Facts to Know & Tell, The 247
Unnaturally Natural Lands, The 768-9
V&A Museum Highlights 204
Walks in Eastern England 655
Wars – a Hundred Years' & the Roses 24
Well-Dressed Derbyshire 596
Wells Cathedral Clock 362
Wendover Woods 338
What's in a Name? 59
What's in a Pub Name? 125
When Did Cornish Die? 450
When I Was a Student... 648
Where to Drink in London 234-5
Which Bakewell Pudding? 598
World Champions with a Difference 833

Bold indicates maps.

MAP LEGEND

BOUNDARIES

International
Regional
Suburb

HYDROGRAPHY

Coastline
River, Stream
Lake
Canal

Park, Gardens
Urban Area, Building

LONDON .... Capital City
Bristol .... City or Large Town
Cambridge .... Town
Bideford .... Village
.... Point of Interest
.... Place to Stay
.... Camp Site
.... Caravan Park
.... Place to Eat
.... Pub or Bar
.... Airport, Airfield
.... Ancient or City Wall
.... Bank
.... Beach
.... Bird Sanctuary
.... Bus Stop, Station
.... Castle or Fort

ROUTES & TRANSPORT

Motorway
Primary Road
Secondary Road
Tertiary Road
Unsealed Road
City Motorway
City Primary Road
City Road
City Street, Lane

Pedestrian Area
Tunnel
Railway & Station
Metro & Station
Tramway
Cable Car or Chairlift
Walking Track
Walking Tour
Ferry Route & Terminal

AREA FEATURES

Forest
Market

Beach
Cemetery

MAP SYMBOLS

.... Cathedral or Church
.... Cave
.... Cinema, Theatre
.... Cliff or Escarpment
.... Embassy
.... Fountain
.... Golf Course
.... Hospital
.... Internet Cafe
.... Lighthouse
.... Lookout
.... Monument
.... Mountain, Range
.... Museum
.... One Way Street

Parking
Pass
Police Station
Post Office
Ruins
Shopping Centre
Ski Field
Stately Home or Palace
Swimming Pool
Telephone
Toilet
Tomb
Tourist Information
Transport
Vineyard
Waterfall
Zoo

Note: not all symbols displayed above appear in this book

LONELY PLANET OFFICES

Australia
Locked Bag 1, Footscray, Victoria 3011
☎ 03 8379 8000 fax 03 8379 8111
email: talk2us@lonelyplanet.com.au

USA
150 Linden St, Oakland, CA 94607
☎ 510 893 8555 TOLL FREE: 800 275 8555
fax 510 893 8572
email: info@lonelyplanet.com

UK
10a Spring Place, London NW5 3BH
☎ 020 7428 4800 fax 020 7428 4828
email: go@lonelyplanet.co.uk

France
1 rue du Dahomey, 75011 Paris
☎ 01 55 25 33 00 fax 01 55 25 33 01
email: bip@lonelyplanet.fr
www.lonelyplanet.fr

World Wide Web: www.lonelyplanet.com or AOL keyword: lp
Lonely Planet Images: lpi@lonelyplanet.com.au